South Africa

written and researched by

Tony Pinchuck, Barbara McCrea, Donald Reid and Greg Mthembu-Salter

with additional research by

Jens Finke, Stefan Gilbert, Jacqueline Kadey, Sam Black, Bianca Coleman, Bronwen Kaplan and Rob Allingham

ROUGH GUIDES

NEW YORK • LONDON • DELHI

www.roughguides.com

Contents

Front section   1–32

Introduction 6
Where to go 8
When to go 11
Things not to miss 12
Wildlife...................................... 19

Basics   33–89

Getting there 35
Visas and red tape 41
Information, websites and
    maps.................................... 42
Insurance.................................. 45
Health 46
Costs, money and banks 50
Getting around......................... 52
Accommodation 58
Eating and drinking.................. 63
Communications...................... 66
The media................................ 68
Opening hours and public
    holidays 70
Parks, reserves and
    wilderness areas 71
Activities and outdoor
    pursuits............................... 77
Spectator sports 79
Crime and personal safety 81
Travellers with disabilities 83
Gay and lesbian travellers........ 85
Travelling with children 86
The environment and ethical
    tourism................................ 88
Directory 88

Guide   91–839

❶ Cape Town 93
❷ The Western Cape 187
❸ The Northern Cape.......... 307
❹ The Eastern Cape........... 363
❺ KwaZulu-Natal................ 457
❻ Free State 567
❼ Gauteng 589
❽ North West Province 651
❾ Mpumalanga.................... 683
❿ Limpopo........................... 727
⓫ Lesotho 759
⓬ Swaziland 809

Contexts   841–928

History 843
Wildlife.................................... 867
Music...................................... 883
Literature 898
Books 918

Language   929–941

English.................................... 931
Afrikaans................................. 932
The Nguni group 933
The Sotho group 933
Pronouncing place names 934
Glossary 937
Food and drink 939

Advertiser   943–958

Small print & Index 959–976

WINDHOEK

NAMIBIA

BOTSWANA

N

KGALAGADI
TRANSFRONTIER
PARK

Nossob River

Molopo River

NORTH WEST

Askam

Kalahari

Kuruman

RICHTERSVELD
TRANSFRONTIER
PARK

Karasburg

Upington

N14

Orange River

Kakamas

Port
Nolloth

Pofadder

N14

Namaqualand

Springbok

N7

NORTHERN CAPE

N8

Orange River

Kimberley

Hopetown

Prieska

N10

Bristown

De Aar

Carnarvon

N12

Victoria
West

N1

ATLANTIC

OCEAN

Calvinia

Williston

Vanrhynsdorp

Great Karoo

TANKWA-KAROO
NATIONAL PARK

Sutherland

KAROO
NATIONAL
PARK

Beaufort
West

Graaff-
Reinet

Vredenburg

Saldanha

WEST COAST
NATIONAL
PARK

N7

Malmesbury

Atlantis

Paarl

CAPE TOWN

Stellenbosch

N2

Franschhoek

Worcester

Robertson

Swellendam

N1

Little Karoo

George

Oudtshoorn

WESTERN CAPE

N9

Willowmore

TSITSIKAMMA
NATIONAL
PARK

GARDEN ROUTE

Knysna

Mossel
Bay

WILDERNESS
NATIONAL
PARK

Plettenberg
Bay

Hermanus

Arniston

DE HOOP
NATURE
RESERVE

*Cape
Agulhas*

4

0   100 km

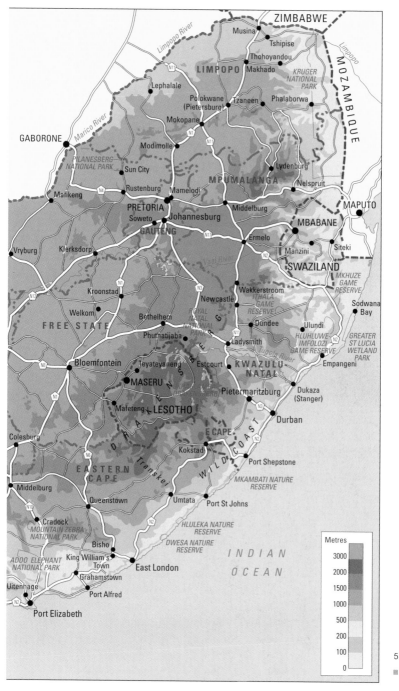

ZIMBABWE

Musina
Tshipise
Thohoyandou
Makhado

LIMPOPO

KRUGER
NATIONAL
PARK

Lephalale

Polokwane
(Pietersburg)   Tzaneen   Phalaborwa

Mokopane

MOZAMBIQUE

Limpopo River

Limpopo River

Marico River

GABORONE

Modimolle

PILANESBERG
NATIONAL PARK   Sun City

Rustenburg   Mamelodi

MPUMALANGA

Lydenburg

Nelspruit

MAPUTO

Mafikeng

PRETORIA

Soweto   Johannesburg

GAUTENG

Middelburg

MBABANE

Ermelo

Manzini   Siteki

Vryburg

Klerksdorp

Vaal River

SWAZILAND

MKHUZE
GAME
RESERVE

Kroonstad

Welkom

FREE STATE

Bethlehem

Newcastle

Wakkerstroom

ITHALA
GAME
RESERVE

Sodwana
Bay

ROYAL
NATAL
NATIONAL
PARK

Dundee

Ulundi

HLUHLUWE-
IMFOLOZI
GAME RESERVE

GREATER
ST LUCIA
WETLAND
PARK

Phuthatijaba

Ladysmith

Tugela River

Bloemfontein

Teyateyaneng   Estcourt

KWAZULU-
NATAL

Empangeni

MASERU

Pietermaritzburg

Dukaza
(Stanger)

Mafeteng   LESOTHO

E CAPE

WILD COAST

Durban

Colesburg

EASTERN
CAPE

Kokstad

Port Shepstone

MKAMBATI NATURE
RESERVE

Middelburg

Queenstown

Transkei

Umtata   Port St Johns

Cradock

MOUNTAIN ZEBRA
NATIONAL PARK

HLULEKA NATURE
RESERVE

DWESA NATURE
RESERVE

INDIAN

OCEAN

Bisho

ADDO ELEPHANT
NATIONAL PARK

King William's
Town   East London

Uitenhage

Grahamstown

Port Alfred

Port Elizabeth

DRAKENSBERG

Metres	
3000	
2000	
1500	
1000	
500	
200	
100	
0	

Introduction to

South Africa

South Africa is a large, diverse and incredibly beautiful country. The size of France and Spain combined, and roughly twice the size of Texas, it varies from the picturesque Garden Route towns of the Western Cape to the raw subtropical coast of northern KwaZulu-Natal, with the vast Karoo semi-desert across its heart and one of Africa's premier safari destinations, Kruger National Park, in the northeast. It's also one of the great cultural meeting points of the African continent, a fact obscured by years of enforced racial segregation, but now manifest in the big cities.

Many visitors are pleasantly surprised by South Africa's excellent infrastructure, which draws favourable comparison with countries such as Australia or the United States. Good air links and bus networks, excellent roads and a growing number of first-class B&Bs and guesthouses make South Africa a perfect touring country. For those on a budget, mushrooming backpacker hostels and backpacker buses provide cost-efficient means of exploring.

Yet despite all these facilities, South Africa is also something of an enigma; after so long as an international pariah, the "rainbow nation" is still struggling to find its identity. The country was organized for the benefit of whites, so it's easy to get a very white-oriented experience of Africa. Most of the tourist industry is still white-run and, as a visitor, you'll have to make an effort to meet members of the country's African majority on equal terms. Apartheid may be dead, but its heritage continues to shape South Africa in a very physical way. Nowhere is this more in evidence than in the layout of towns and cities, the African areas – often desperately poor – usually tucked out of sight.

South Africa's **population** doesn't reduce simply to black and white. The majority are **Africans** (77 percent of the population); **whites** make up 11 percent, followed by **coloureds** (9 percent) – the descendants of white settlers, slaves and Africans, who speak English and Afrikaans and comprise the majority in the Western Cape. The remainder (3 percent)

6

is comprised of **Indians**, who came to South Africa at the beginning of the twentieth century as indentured labourers; most of the Indian community live in KwaZulu-Natal.

Even these statistics don't tell the whole story. A better indication of South Africa's diversity is the plethora of official languages, most of which represent a distinct culture with rural roots in different parts of the country. In each region you'll see distinct styles of architecture, craftwork and sometimes dress. Perhaps more exciting still are the cities, where the whole country comes together in an alchemical blend of rural and urban, traditional and thoroughly modern.

Crime isn't the indiscriminate phenomenon that press reports suggest, but it is an issue. Really, it's a question of perspective – taking care but not becoming paranoid. Statistically, the odds of becoming a victim are highest in downtown Johannesburg, where violent crime is a daily reality. Other cities present a reduced risk – similar to, say, some parts of the United States.

Fact file

• Covering 1,219,090 square kilometres, South Africa has a **population** of 44 million and eleven official **languages**: Zulu, Xhosa, Afrikaans, Pedi, English, Ndebele, Sotho, Setswana, siSwati, Venda and Tsonga. The country's **religions** comprise Christianity (68 percent), Islam (2 percent), Hinduism (1.5 percent) and indigenous beliefs (28.5 percent).

• South Africa is a **multiparty democracy**, the head of state being President Thabo Mbeki. Parliament sits in Cape Town, the **legislative capital**, while Pretoria is the **executive capital**, from where the President and his cabinet run the country. The **judicial capital** is Bloemfontein, where the Supreme Court of Appeal sits, though the Constitutional Court is in Johannesburg. Each of the nine provinces has its own government.

• South Africa has the most advanced **economy** in Africa, with well-developed mining, manufacturing, agricultural and financial sectors. The country also has one of the greatest disparities of wealth in the world.

• **Lesotho** covers 30,355 square kilometres and has a population of 2 million. It is a constitutional monarchy, with King Letsie III as its head. The official languages are Sesotho and English.

• The kingdom of **Swaziland**, ruled by King Mswati III, has an area of 17,363 square kilometres and a population of 1 million. The official languages are siSwati and English.

► Xhosa initiates, Eastern Cape

Sun, sea and sweat

There are few countries in the world where the great outdoors is quite as great as in South Africa. You can, for example, catch the surf at Jeffrey's Bay or dive with great white sharks, go scooting on a sailboard across Table Bay or kayaking up the Wild Coast. You can go rafting on the frothing Great Usutu River in Swaziland, or spend leisurely days drifting down the Orange. If you'd rather do something completely new, try kloofing – basically jumping into a canyon – in the river gorges of the Western Cape. On land, there's always walking (with or without rhinos), or pony-trekking into Lesotho's Highlands, or mountain biking in Hell (Die Hel, to be precise – a pass noted for its impossibly sharp switchbacks). Then again, you can paraglide in the Northern Cape or balloon over baboons in Pilanesberg. If hair-raising descents are more your thing, there's abseiling off Table Mountain, bungee jumping at Bloukrans, even skiing at Tiffendell – enough to leave you breathless.

Where to go

While you could circuit the whole of South Africa in a matter of weeks, a more satisfying approach is to focus your attention on one section of the country. Every one of the nine provinces (plus Lesotho and Swaziland) holds at least a couple of compelling reasons to visit, although, depending on the time of year and your interests, you'd be wise to concentrate on either the **west** or the **east**.

The **west**, best visited in the warmer months (Nov–April), has the outstanding attraction of **Cape Town**, worth experiencing for its matchless setting beneath Table Mountain, at the foot of the continent. Half a day's drive from here can take you to any other destination in the **Western Cape**, a province which owes its distinctive character to the fact that it has the longest-established colonial heritage in the country. You'll find gabled Cape Dutch architecture, historic towns and vineyard-covered mountains in the **Winelands**; forested coast along the **Garden Route**; and a dry interior punctuated by Afrikaner dorps in the **Little Karoo**.

If the west sounds a bit too pretty and you're after a more "African" experience, head for the **eastern** flank of the country, best visited in the cooler months (May–Oct). **Johannesburg** is likely to be your point of entry to this area: its frenetic street life, soaring office blocks and lively mix of people make it quite unlike anywhere else in the country. Half a day away by car lie **Limpopo** and **Mpumalanga** provinces, which share the mighty **Kruger National Park**. Of South Africa's roughly two dozen major parks, the Kruger attracts the largest number of first-time visitors, and is unrivalled on the continent for its cross section of mammal species.

A visit to Kruger combines perfectly with KwaZulu-Natal to the south, and an excellent short cut is to drive through tiny, landlocked **Swaziland**, which has attractions all of its own: a unique Swazi culture and a number of well-managed game parks. **KwaZulu-Natal** itself offers superb game and birdlife; **Hluhluwe-Imfolozi Park** is the best place in the world to see endangered rhinos and there are several

> **Kruger National Park is unrivalled on the continent for its cross section of mammal species**

other outstanding small game reserves nearby, such as Ithala, Mkhuze and Ndumo. For hiking and nature, nothing rivals the soaring **Drakensberg** range. After Cape Town, **Durban** remains the only city in South Africa worth visiting in its own right: a busy cultural melting pot with a bustling Indian district and lively beachfront. The long stretch of **beaches** north and south of Durban is the most developed in the country, but north towards the Mozambique border lies the wildest stretch of coast in South Africa.

Long sandy **beaches**, developed only in pockets, are characteristic of much of the 2500km of shoreline that curves from the cool Atlantic along the Northern Cape round to the subtropical Indian Ocean that foams onto KwaZulu-Natal's shores. **Jeffrey's Bay** on the **Eastern Cape** coast is reputed to be one of the world's top **surfing** spots. Much of the Eastern Cape coast is equally appealing, whether you just want to stroll, sunbathe or take in backdrops of mountains and hulking sand dunes. **Scuba diving**, especially in KwaZulu-Natal, opens up a world of coral reefs rich with colourful fish, and south of the Western Cape winelands, along the **Whale Coast**, is one of South Africa's unsung attractions – some of the best shore-based **whale-watching** in the world.

With time in hand, you might want to drive through the sparse but exhilarating **interior**, with its open horizons, switchback mountain passes, rocks, scrubby vegetation and isolated dorps. The **Northern Cape** and **North West Province** can reveal surprises. Visit the western section of the

▲ Balito beach, near Durban

Northern Cape in August or September, and you'll be treated to a riot of colourful **wild flowers**. From the staunchly Afrikaner heartland of **Free State**, you're well poised to visit the undeveloped kingdom of **Lesotho**, set in the mountains between the Free State and KwaZulu-Natal. Lesotho has few vestiges of royalty left today, but it does offer plenty of spectacular highland scenery, best explored on a sturdy, sure-footed Basotho pony.

When to go

South Africa is a predominantly sunny country, but when it does get cold you really feel it – indoor heating is limited, and everything is geared to fine weather. You'll need to pack with the weather in mind, especially in winter. Southern hemisphere seasons are the reverse of those in the north, with **midwinter** occurring in June and July and **midsummer** over December and January, when the country shuts down for its annual holiday.

South Africa has distinct climatic zones. **Cape Town** and the **Garden Route** coastal belt have a so-called Mediterranean climate, moderated by winds blowing in from the South Atlantic. Summers tend to be warm, mild and unpredictable; rain can fall at any time of the year and winter days can be cold and wet. Many Capetonians regard March to May as the perfect season, when the nagging winds drop, it's beautifully mild and the tourists have all gone home. Subtropical **KwaZulu-Natal** has warm, sunny winters, coral reefs and tepid seas; the province's Drakensberg range

House of the spirits

For thousands of years, San Bushman shamans in South Africa decorated rock faces with powerful religious images. These finely realized paintings, found in mountainous areas across South Africa, include animals, people, and humans changing into animals. Archeologists now regard the images as metaphors for religious experiences, one of the most significant of which is the healing trance dance, still practised by the few surviving Bushman communities. Rockfaces can be seen as portals between the human and spiritual world: when we gaze at Bushman rock art, we are looking into the house of the spirits.

sees misty days in summer and mountain snow in winter. **Johannesburg** and **Pretoria** lie on the highveld plateau and have a near-perfect climate; summer days are hot, with none of the humidity of the KwaZulu-Natal coast, while the winters are dry with chilly nights. East of Johannesburg, the **lowveld**, the low-lying wedge along the Mozambique border that includes the **Kruger National Park**, is subject to similar summer and winter rainfall patterns to the highveld, but experiences far greater extremes of temperature because of its considerably lower altitude.

Average daily maximum temperatures

	Jan	Feb	Mar	Apr	May	June	July	Aug	Sept	Oct	Nov	Dec
Cape Town												
°C	27	27	26	23	20	19	17	18	19	22	24	26
°F	81	81	79	73	68	66	63	64	66	72	75	79
Durban												
°C	27	28	27	26	24	23	22	22	23	24	25	26
°F	81	82	81	79	75	73	72	72	73	75	77	79
Johannesburg												
°C	26	26	24	22	19	16	16	20	23	25	25	26
°F	79	79	75	72	66	61	61	68	73	77	77	79
Kimberley												
°C	33	31	28	25	21	19	19	22	25	28	30	32
°F	91	88	82	77	70	66	66	72	77	82	86	90
Port Elizabeth												
°C	25	26	25	23	22	20	20	20	20	21	22	24
°F	77	79	77	73	72	68	68	68	68	70	72	75
Skukuza (Kruger National Park)												
°C	31	31	30	29	27	25	25	26	29	29	30	30
°F	88	88	86	84	81	77	77	79	84	84	86	86
Maseru (Lesotho)												
°C	20	17	14	11	9	7	7	9	11	14	17	20
°F	68	63	57	52	48	45	45	48	52	57	63	68
Mbabane (Swaziland)												
°C	25	25	24	23	21	19	19	21	23	24	24	25
°F	77	77	75	73	70	66	66	70	73	75	75	77

28

things not to miss

It's not possible to see everything that South Africa has to offer in one trip – and we don't suggest you try. What follows is a selective and subjective taste of the country's highlights, including outstanding national parks, spectacular wildlife, adventure sports and beautiful architecture. They're arranged in five colour-coded categories to help you find the very best things to see, do and experience. All entries have a page reference to take you straight into the guide, where you can find out more.

01 The Wild Coast Page **431** • This part of the Eastern Cape offers peace and seclusion along a remote and spectacular subtropical coastline.

03 Canopy tours at Storms River
Page **288** • Swing from steel cables among the upper branches of arboreal giants, in South Africa's most impressive indigenous forest.

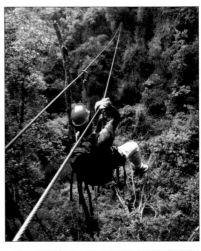

02 The Bo-Kaap
Page **130** • The streets of Cape Town's oldest residential area are filled with colourful Cape Dutch and Georgian architecture.

04 Madikwe Game Reserve
Page **668** • This massive game park sees remarkably few visitors, yet boasts excellent lodges and superb wildlife-spotting opportunities, from wild dogs to lions and elephants.

05 Rafting
Page **836** • Swaziland's Great Usutu River offers some of the most exciting whitewater rafting in southern Africa.

07 The Drakensberg Page **512** • Hike in the mysterious "dragon mountains", which harbour South Africa's highest peaks, plus waterfalls, gorges, Bushman rock art and awesome panoramas.

06 The Cradle of Humankind Page **630** • One of the world's major paleontological sites, the Sterkfontein Caves are home to "Mrs Ples", a female skull some 2.6 million years old.

08 Game trails Page **721** • Combine adventure with wildlife-spotting on a guided hike in the mighty Kruger National Park.

09 Kgalagadi Transfrontier Park Page **336** • View gemsbok and other desert dwellers amid the harsh beauty of the Kalahari.

10 Wine routes Page **192** • The Western Cape's wine estates combine stunning scenery, Cape Dutch architecture and some fine and affordable vintages.

11 **Swartberg Pass** Page **212** • One of the spectacular passes of the Little Karoo, providing exciting drives and mountain biking.

12 **Kruger National Park** Page **710** • Get spine-tinglingly close to big game at Southern Africa's ultimate wildlife destination.

13 **Robben Island** Page **137** • Just half an hour from Cape Town is the notorious offshore jail where political prisoners, including Nelson Mandela, were incarcerated.

14 **The Bulungula Lodge** Page **441** • At a beautiful river mouth on the Wild Coast, this backpackers' lodge offers an all-too-rare opportunity to experience rural African life.

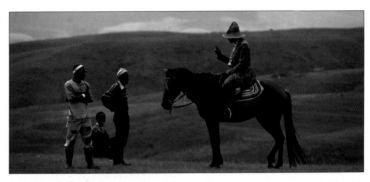

15 Pony-trekking Page **770** • The perfect way to experience the ruggedly beautiful "mountain kingdom" of Lesotho.

16 Storms River Mouth Page **228** • The Garden Route's most dramatic coastline, where the Storms River emerges from a gorge to meet the crashing surf.

17 The Sani Pass Page **797** • The most precipitous pass in southern Africa, connecting Lesotho to neighbouring KwaZulu-Natal, is also the most thrilling to drive down.

18 Live music Page **625** • Johannesburg offers the best nightlife in South Africa, attracting top musical performers from around the country and abroad.

19 Wild flowers Page **344** • Following the winter rains, Namaqualand's normally bleak landscape explodes with colour in one of nature's most brilliant floral displays.

21 **Table Mountain cableway** Page **149** • The most spectacular way to ascend Cape Town's famous landmark is also the easiest – the revolving cable car.

20 **Richtersveld Transfrontier Park** Page **359** • Fierce, rugged and hot, the Richtersveld offers some of the most dramatic mountainscape in the country and comes magnificently alive in the intense light of dawn and dusk.

22 **Whale-watching** Page **241** • Regularly visiting the southern Cape Coast, whales often approach surprisingly close to the shore.

23 **Traditional arts and crafts** Page **756** • Many traditional handicrafts provide useful and beautiful souvenirs in rural and urban areas alike, such as the Venda region of Limpopo.

17

24 Indian culture Page **469** • Durban, Africa's busiest port, boasts a large Indian population.

25 Hluhluwe-Imfolozi Park Page **529** • KwaZulu-Natal's finest game reserve offers an unsurpassed variety of wildlife-spotting activities, from night drives to self-guided walks and even donkey trails.

27 Cape Point Page **161** • The rocky promontory south of Cape Town, angry seas crashing on either side, is one of the most dramatic coastal locations on the continent.

26 Soweto Page **618** • A tour around the vast, sprawling township – South Africa's largest – provides a graphic idea of how the majority of black South Africans live.

28 Vernacular architecture Page **580** • Beautifully decorative Basotho huts are characteristic of the eastern Free State's Highlands Route.

The wildlife of Southern Africa

This field guide provides a quick reference to help you identify the mammals likely to be encountered in Southern Africa. It includes most species that are found throughout these regions, as well as a number whose range is more restricted. The photos show easily identified markings and features. The notes give clear pointers about the kinds of habitat in which you are most likely to see each mammal; its daily rhythm (usually either nocturnal or diurnal); the kind of social groups it usually forms; and general tips concerning its distribution, sighting it on safari and its relations with humans. For further details and background, see p.867.

🌸 HABITAT   ◑ DAILY RHYTHM   🌿 SOCIAL LIFE   ✓ SIGHTING TIPS

Baboon *Papio cynocephalus*

 open country with trees and cliffs; adaptable, but always near water

 diurnal

troops led by a dominant male

✓ common (found across the whole of South Africa and can be seen in most reserves); easily becomes used to humans, frequently a nuisance and occasionally dangerous; very good chance of sightings in the Cape of Good Hope section of Table Mountain National Park

Vervet monkey
Cercopithecus aethiops

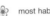 most habitats except rainforest and arid lands; arboreal and terrestrial

 diurnal

troops

✓ found in virtually every game reserve in North West, Limpopo, Mpumalanga and KwaZulu-Natal provinces, as well as along the coast as far west as Mossel Bay; occasionally a nuisance where used to humans

Samango monkey *Cercopithecus mitis*

 forests; arboreal and occasionally terrestrial

 diurnal

families or small troops

✓ found in isolated pockets of forest in Eastern Cape, KwaZulu-Natal and Mpumalanga; shyer and less easily habituated to humans than the vervet

Lesser bushbaby *Galago moholi*

 woodland savanna and riverine woodland

 nocturnal

small family groups

✓ found in Limpopo, Mpumalanga and the eastern part of North West province; generally forage in trees jumping large distances from branch to branch; at 30–40cm from head to tail, it's about half the length of the thick-tailed bushbaby (*Otolemur crassicaudatus*), found in Mpumalanga

✿ HABITAT ◐ DAILY RHYTHM ✿ SOCIAL LIFE ✓ SIGHTING TIPS

Aardvark *Orycteropus afer*

🌸 open or wooded termite country; softer soil preferred

🌓 nocturnal

✌ solitary

✓ found throughout South Africa, though rarely seen; the size of a small pig; old burrows are common and often used by warthogs

Spring hare *Pedetes capensis*

🌸 savanna; softer soil areas preferred

🌓 nocturnal

✌ burrows, usually with a pair and their young; often linked into a network, almost like a colony

✓ rabbit-sized rodent, found in Northern Cape, Eastern Cape, Free State, North West and Limpopo provinces; impressive and unmistakable kangaroo-like leaper

Porcupine *Hystrix africae-australis*

🌸 adaptable to a wide range of habitats

🌓 nocturnal and sometimes active at dusk

✌ family groups

✓ large rodent (up to 90cm in length), rarely seen, but common away from croplands, where it's hunted as a pest; found in South Africa, Lesotho and Swaziland

Bat-eared fox *Otocyon megalotis*

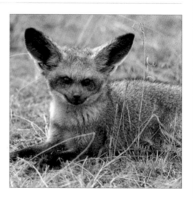

🌸 open country

🌓 mainly nocturnal; diurnal activity increases in cooler months

✌ monogamous pairs

✓ found in the western half of South Africa up to (but excluding) Lesotho, and in the areas bordering the Zimbabwe and Botswana borders; distribution coincides with termites, their favoured diet; they spend many hours foraging using sensitive hearing to pinpoint their underground prey

🌸 HABITAT   🌓 DAILY RHYTHM   ✌ SOCIAL LIFE   ✓ SIGHTING TIPS

Blackbacked jackal *Canis mesomelas*

 broad range from moist mountain regions to desert, but drier areas preferred

normally nocturnal, but diurnal in the safety of game reserves

mostly monogamous pairs; sometimes family groups

✓ common throughout Southern Africa; a bold scavenger, the size of a small dog, that steals even from lions; black saddle distinguishes it from the shyer side-striped jackal

Wild dog *Lycaon pictus*

open savanna in the vicinity of grazing herds

diurnal

nomadic packs

✓ one of the most endangered large predators in South Africa, with just a few packs surviving in the wild; found in Kruger, Hluhluwe-Imfolozi, Madikwe and Pilanesberg reserves; rarely seen, but widely noted when in the area; the size of a large dog, with distinctively rounded ears

Honey badger *Mellivora capensis*

very broad range of habitats

mainly nocturnal

usually solitary, but also found in pairs

✓ widespread (though nowhere common) throughout the region except in Free State and Lesotho; omnivorous, badger-sized animal; extremely aggressive

Civet *Civettictis civetta*

prefers woodland and dense vegetation

mainly nocturnal

solitary

✓ omnivorous, medium-dog-sized, short-legged prowler; found in Limpopo, Mpumalanga and eastern North West province; not to be confused with the smaller genet

🌼 HABITAT ◑ DAILY RHYTHM 🦋 SOCIAL LIFE ✓ SIGHTING TIPS

Small-spotted genet *Genetta genetta*

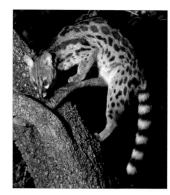

🌸 light bush country, even arid areas; partly arboreal

🌓 nocturnal, but becomes active at dusk

🎏 solitary

✓ quite common, slender, cat-sized omnivore found throughout South Africa except KwaZulu-Natal; often seen at game lodges, where it easily becomes habituated to humans; has a white tail tip, in contrast to the otherwise similar, less widely distributed large-spotted genet (*G. tigrina*), which has a black tail tip

Banded mongoose *Mungos mungo*

🌸 thick bush and dry forest

🌓 diurnal

🎏 lives in burrow colonies of up to thirty animals

✓ over a dozen mongoose species in the region, between them ranging across all of South Africa, Limpopo and Swaziland; the size of a small cat; often seen in a group, hurriedly foraging through the undergrowth

Spotted hyena *Crocuta crocuta*

🌸 tolerates a wide variety of habitat, with the exception of dense forest

🌓 nocturnal but also active at dusk; also diurnal in many parks

🎏 highly social, usually living in extended family groups

✓ the size of a large dog with a distinctive loping gait, quite common in Kruger, Hluhluwe-Imfolozi, Kgalakgadi and Addo; carnivorous scavenger and cooperative hunter; dangerous

Caracal *Caracal caracal*

🌸 open bush and plains; occasionally arboreal

🌓 mostly nocturnal

🎏 solitary

✓ lynx-like wild cat; rarely seen, though it is found throughout the region except in KwaZulu-Natal; most likely to be seen in the Cape of Good Hope section of Table Mountain National Park, and in Mountain Zebra, Kruger and Kgalagadi parks

---

🌸 HABITAT   🌓 DAILY RHYTHM   🎏 SOCIAL LIFE   ✓ SIGHTING TIPS   23

Cheetah *Acionyx jubatus*

 savanna, in the vicinity of plains grazers

 diurnal

solitary or temporary nuclear family groups

✓ found in Kruger, Hluhluwe-Imfolozi and Kgalagadi reserves; much slighter build than the leopard, and distinguished from it by a small head, square snout and dark "tear mark" running from eye to jowl

Leopard *Panthera pardus*

highly adaptable; frequently arboreal

nocturnal; also cooler daylight hours

solitary

✓ the size of a very large dog; not uncommon, but shy and usually infrequently seen; found in Limpopo, North West and Mpumalanga provinces (it's often seen in the Sabi Sands reserve adjoining Kruger) as well as in mountainous regions from KwaZulu-Natal to the Western Cape; rests in thick undergrowth or up trees; very dangerous

Lion *Panthera leo*

 all habitats except desert and thick forest

 nocturnal and diurnal

 prides of three to forty; more usually six to twelve

✓ found in major game reserves including Kruger, Kgalagadi, Hluhluwe-Imfolozi and Addo; commonly seen resting in shade; dangerous

Serval *Felis serval*

 reed beds or tall grassland near water

 normally nocturnal but more diurnal than most cats

 usually solitary

✓ found in KwaZulu-Natal, Limpopo, Mpumalanga and North West provinces; some resemblance to, but far smaller than, the cheetah; most likely to be seen on roadsides or water margins at dawn or dusk

 HABITAT   DAILY RHYTHM   SOCIAL LIFE ✓ SIGHTING TIPS

Dassie or rock hyrax *Procavia capensis*

 rocky areas, from mountains to isolated outcrops

 diurnal

 colonies consisting of a territorial male with as many as thirty related females

✓ found throughout the region, except in Northern Cape and the KwaZulu-Natal coastal belt; very likely to be spotted on Table Mountain and in the Tsitsikamma National Park; rabbit-sized; often seen sunning themselves in the early morning on rocks

African elephant *Loxodonta africana*

 wide range of habitats, wherever there are trees and water

 nocturnal and diurnal; sleeps as little as four hours a day

 almost human in its complexity; cows and offspring in herds headed by a matriarch; bulls solitary or in bachelor herds

✓ found in Kruger, Pilanesberg, Hluhluwe-Imfolozi and Addo reserves; look out for fresh dung (football-sized) and recently damaged trees; frequently seen at water holes from late afternoon

Black rhinoceros *Diceros bicornis*

 usually thick bush, altitudes up to 3500m

 active day and night, resting between periods of activity

 solitary

✓ found in Kruger, Addo, Hluhluwe-Imfolozi, Ithala and Mkhuze reserves, though extremely rare and in critical danger of extinction; largely confined to parks where most individuals are known to rangers; distinctive hooked lip for browsing; small head usually held high; bad eyesight; very dangerous

 HABITAT   DAILY RHYTHM   SOCIAL LIFE ✓ SIGHTING TIPS

A ROUGH GUIDE TO THE WILDLIFE OF SOUTHERN AFRICA

White rhinoceros *Ceratotherium simum*

 savanna

 active day and night, resting between periods of activity

mother/s and calves, or small, same-sex herds of immature animals; old males solitary

✓ rare, restricted to Kruger, Hluhluwe-Imfolozi, Ithala and Mkhuze reserves; distinctive wide mouth (hence "white" from Dutch *wijd*) for grazing; large head usually lowered; docile

Burchell's zebra *Equus burchelli*

savanna, with or without trees, up to 4500m

active day and night, resting intermittently

harems of several mares and foals led by a dominant stallion are usually grouped together, in herds of up to several thousand

✓ found in the major reserves of Mpumalanga and KwaZulu-Natal, and has been reintroduced into reserves and on farms throughout South Africa; distinguished from the far rarer Cape mountain zebra (*E. zebra zebra*) by the presence of shadow stripes in Burchell's

Warthog *Phacochoerus aethiopicus*

savanna, up to an altitude of over 2000m

diurnal

family groups, usually of a female and her litter

✓ found in the northeast along the border with Botswana and in northern KwaZulu-Natal; boars are distinguishable from sows by their prominent face "warts"

Hippopotamus *Hippopotamus amphibius*

slow-flowing rivers, dams and lakes

principally nocturnal, leaving the water to graze

bulls are solitary, but other animals live in family groups headed by a matriarch

✓ found in Kruger National Park, northern KwaZulu-Natal and in odd pockets throughout the country; usually seen by day in water, with top of head and ears breaking the surface; frequently aggressive and very dangerous when threatened or when retreat to water is blocked

Giraffe *Giraffa camelopardalis*

 wooded savanna and thorn country

 diurnal

 loose, non-territorial, leaderless herds

✓ found in the northeast of South Africa, with Kruger National Park the best place to see them

Buffalo *Syncerus caffer*

 wide range of habitats, always near water, up to altitudes of 4000m

 nocturnal and diurnal, but inactive during the heat of the day

 found in Kruger, Hluhluwe-Imfolozi, Addo and Mountain Zebra reserves, and many conservation areas throughout the country; gregarious, with cows and calves in huge herds; young bulls often form small bachelor herds; old bulls are usually solitary

✓ very common; scent much more acute than other senses; very dangerous, old bulls especially so

Hartebeest *Alcelaphus buselaphus*

 wide range of grassy habitats

 diurnal

 females and calves in small, wandering herds; territorial males solitary

✓ restricted to pockets of Mpumalanga and the Northern Cape; hard to confuse with any other antelope except the tsessebe

Blue wildebeest *Connochaetes taurinus*

 grasslands

diurnal, occasionally also nocturnal

intensely gregarious in a wide variety of associations from small groups to sizeable herds

✓ found in Kruger National Park, KwaZulu-Natal province and in conservation areas throughout South Africa; unmistakable, nomadic grazer; long tail, mane and beard; often seen in association with zebras

---

 HABITAT   DAILY RHYTHM   SOCIAL LIFE   ✓ SIGHTING TIPS

Bontebok *Damaliscus dorcas dorcas*

 coastal plain where Cape *fynbos* occurs

 diurnal

 rams hold territories; ewes and lamb herds numbering up to ten wander freely between territories

✓ found in two national parks, namely Bontebok and the Cape of Good Hope section of Table Mountain, and also in the De Hoop Nature Reserve (largest single population); bears resemblance to tsessebe and hartebeest, but is distinguished by its chocolate brown colouring and white facial and rump markings

Tsessebe *Damaliscus lunatus*

 grasslands, showing a marked preference for moist savanna, near water

 diurnal

 females and young form herds with an old male

✓ restricted to northern parts of South Africa bordering Botswana and Mozambique; very fast runners; male often stands sentry on an abandoned termite hill, actually marking the territory against rivals, rather than defending against predators

Springbok *Antidorcas marsupalis*

 arid plains

 seasonally variable, but usually cooler times of day

 highly gregarious, sometimes in thousands; various herding combinations of males, females and young

✓ wild in the Northern Cape, but farmed all over South Africa; medium-sized, delicately built gazelle; dark line through eye to mouth and lyre-shaped pair of horns in both sexes

Impala *Aepyceros melampus*

 open savanna near light woodland cover

 diurnal

 large herds of females overlap with several male territories; males highly territorial during the rut when they separate out breeding harems of up to twenty females

✓ common, medium-sized, no close relatives; distinctive high leaps when fleeing; the only antelope with a black tuft above the hooves; males have long, lyre-shaped horns

 HABITAT DAILY RHYTHM SOCIAL LIFE ✓ SIGHTING TIPS

Reedbuck *Redunca arundinum*

 reedbeds and tall grass near water

 nocturnal and diurnal

 monogamous pairs or family groups in territory defended by the male

✓ medium-sized antelope, with a plant diet unpalatable to other herbivores; only males have horns

Waterbuck *Kobus ellipsiprymnus*

 open woodland and savanna, near water

 nocturnal and diurnal

 territorial herds of females and young, led by dominant male, or territorial males visited by wandering female herds

✓ common, rather tame, large antelope found in Kruger National Park, the Greater St Lucia Wetland Park and along the Limpopo river; their plant diet is unpalatable to other herbivores; shaggy coat; only males have horns

Common duiker *Sylvicapra grimmia*

 adaptable; prefers scrub and bush

 nocturnal and diurnal

most commonly solitary; sometimes in pairs; occasionally monogamous

✓ widespread and common small antelope with a rounded back; seen close to cover; rams have short, straight horns

Nyala *Tragelaphus angasi*

dense woodland near water

primarily nocturnal with some diurnal activity

flexible and non-territorial; the basic unit is a female and two offspring

✓ Kruger National Park and northeastern KwaZulu-Natal province; midway in size between the lesser kudu and bushbuck, and easily mistaken for the latter; orange legs distinguish it; only males have horns

Bushbuck *Tragelaphus scriptus*

🌸 thick bush and woodland close to water

◑ principally nocturnal, but also active during the day when cool

🦌 solitary, but casually sociable; sometimes grazes in small groups

✓ found in KwaZulu-Natal, Limpopo, North West, Mpumalanga provinces, and also on the southern coast of South Africa; medium-sized antelope with white stripes and spots; often seen in thickets, or heard crashing through them; not to be confused with the larger nyala; the male has shortish straight horns

Eland *Taurotragus oryx*

🌸 highly adaptable; semi-desert to mountains, but prefers scrubby plains

◑ nocturnal and diurnal

🦌 non-territorial herds of up to sixty with temporary gatherings of as many as a thousand

✓ found in the Ukhahlamba Drakensberg, Kgalagadi Transfrontier and Kruger parks; common but shy; the largest and most powerful African antelope; both sexes have straight horns with a slight spiral

Kudu *Tragelaphus strepsiceros*

🌸 semi-arid, hilly or undulating bush country; tolerant of drought

◑ diurnal when secure; otherwise nocturnal

🦌 territorial; males usually solitary; females in small troops with young

✓ found in northern Limpopo and North West provinces, and in Mpumalanga, eastern Swaziland and northeastern Kwazulu-Natal, with isolated pockets in the Eastern and Western Cape; impressively big antelope (up to 1.5m at shoulder) with very long, spiral horns in the male; shy and not often seen

Gemsbok *Oryx gazella gazella*

🌸 open grasslands; also waterless wastelands; tolerant of prolonged drought

◑ nocturnal and diurnal

🦌 highly hierarchical mixed herds of up to fifteen, led by a dominant bull

✓ large antelope found in Kgalagadi Transfrontier Park, with unmistakable horns in both sexes; subspecies gazella is one of several similar forms, sometimes considered separate species

🌸 HABITAT   ◑ DAILY RHYTHM   🦌 SOCIAL LIFE   ✓ SIGHTING TIPS

Roan antelope *Hippotragus equinus*

 tall grassland near water

 nocturnal and diurnal; peak afternoon feeding

 small herds led by a dominant bull; herds of immature males; sometimes pairs in season

✓ large antelope found in Kruger National Park; distinguished from the sable by lighter, greyish colour, shorter horns (both sexes) and narrow, tufted ears

Sable antelope *Hippotragus niger*

 open woodland with medium to tall grassland near water

 nocturnal and diurnal

 territorial; bulls divide into sub-territories, through which cows and young roam; herds of immature males; sometimes pairs in season

✓ large antelope found in Kruger National Park; upper body dark brown to black; mask-like markings on the face; both sexes have huge curved horns

Cape grysbok *Raphicerus melanotis*

 thicket adjacent to open grassland

 nocturnal

 rams territorial; loose pairings

✓ small, rarely seen antelope, found in the southwestern and southern coastal belt of Western and Eastern Cape provinces; distinguished from more slender steenbok by light underparts; rams have short horns

Oribi *Ourebia ourebi*

 open grassland

diurnal

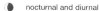 territorial harems consisting of male and one to four females

✓ small antelope localized to small pockets of KwaZulu-Natal, though not hard to see where found; only males have horns; the oribi is distinguished from the smaller grysbok and steenbok by a black tail and dark skin patch below the eye

 HABITAT DAILY RHYTHM SOCIAL LIFE ✓ SIGHTING TIPS

Steenbok *Raphicerus campestris*

 dry savanna

 nocturnal and diurnal

 solitary or (less often) in pairs

✓ widespread small antelope, but shy; only males have horns

Klipspringer *Oreotragus oreotragus*

 rocky country; cliffs and kopjes

 diurnal

 territorial ram with mate or small family group; often restricted to small long-term territories

✓ small antelope inhabiting mountainous areas throughout the region; horns normally only on male; extremely agile on rocky terrain; unusually high hooves, giving the impression of walking on tiptoe

✿ HABITAT ◖ DAILY RHYTHM �֎ SOCIAL LIFE ✓ SIGHTING TIPS

Basics

Basics

Getting there 35

Visas and red tape 41

Information, websites and maps... 42

Insurance 45

Health... 46

Costs, money and banks.. 50

Getting around 52

Accommodation 58

Eating and drinking... 63

Communications.. 66

The media 68

Opening hours and public holidays 70

Parks, reserves and wilderness areas 71

Activities and outdoor pursuits.. 77

Spectator sports 79

Crime and personal safety.. 81

Travellers with disabilities 83

Gay and lesbian travellers.. 85

Travelling with children.. 86

The environment and ethical tourism....................................... 88

Directory 88

Getting there

Most people travel to South Africa by air, and prices are kept competitive by the large number of scheduled flights. A direct flight from the UK or North America makes the twelve-hour-plus journey a little more bearable, but there are cheaper flights via mainland Europe or Africa that involve a change of plane.

Virtually all international flights operate into **Johannesburg** or **Cape Town**, with a few services to **Durban**. Johannesburg actually receives more international flights than any other airport in sub-Saharan Africa, and has the best onward connections in the country to the major centres in South Africa and the rest of the continent. Indeed if you want to fly into **Lesotho** or **Swaziland**, you'll have to pick up a connection in Johannesburg.

Airfares depend on the **season**, with the highest prices and greatest demand occurring in the ten days before Christmas. Prices remain high in the summer holiday season through January, February and March, dropping during the "shoulder" season from April to mid-July, and picking up again between late July and October. You get the best prices during the low season in November and early December.

You can often cut costs by going through a **specialist flight agent** – either a consolidator, who buys up blocks of tickets from the airlines and sells them at a discount, or a **discount agent**, who may also offer special student and youth fares and a range of other travel-related services such as travel insurance, rail passes, car rentals and tours. Some agents specialize in **charter flights**, which may be cheaper than scheduled flights, but departure dates are fixed and cancellation penalties are high. **Package tours** can be a good idea – there are plenty of conducted tours and self-drive deals involving a mix of wildlife spotting and beach activities.

If South Africa is only one stop on a longer journey, it's worth considering a **round-the-world (RTW)** ticket. Some travel agents can sell you an "off-the-shelf" RTW ticket that will have you touching down in about half a dozen cities (Johannesburg is on many itineraries); others will have to assemble one for you, which can be tailored to your needs but is likely to be more expensive. Expect to pay from around £1600/$2200 for a RTW ticket including South Africa.

Those not flying into South Africa usually arrive at the end of an **overland** trip, often in a converted truck and often having started from East Africa. It's possible to book a trans-Africa overland package starting in Britain, Europe or Nairobi and working down to Cape Town. The most popular option is from Nairobi to Cape Town via Mount Kilimanjaro, Victoria Falls and Namibia – for which you can expect to pay around £1500 for a six-week trip (plus about £400 towards the trip kitty), though shorter trips are available, some starting in Harare and taking in Zimbabwe, Botswana and Namibia before reaching South Africa.

Finally, it is possible – though it's not an inexpensive option – to find berths on **cargo ships** sailing between Europe or Australia and South Africa. For details of agents for these trips, see p.38.

Booking online

Many airlines and discount travel websites offer you the opportunity to book your tickets online, cutting out the costs of agents and middlemen.

Online booking agents

ⓦ**www.cheapflights.co.uk** (UK & Ireland),
ⓦ**www.cheapflights.com** (US),
ⓦ**www.cheapflights.ca** (Canada),
ⓦ**www.cheapflights.com.au** (Australia). Flight deals from various travel agents.
ⓦ**www.cheaptickets.com** Discount flight specialists (US only).

ⓦ **www.ebookers.com** (UK),
ⓦ **www.ebookers.ie** (Republic of Ireland). Easy to use flight finder, with competitive fares.

ⓦ **www.expedia.co.uk** (UK),
ⓦ **www.expedia.com** (US),
ⓦ **www.expedia.ca** (Canada). Discount airfares, all-airline search engine and daily deals.

ⓦ **www.flyaow.com** "Airlines of the Web" – online air travel info and reservations.

ⓦ**www.hotwire.com** Bookings from the US only. Last-minute savings of up to forty percent on regular published fares. Travellers must be at least 18 and there are no refunds, transfers or changes allowed.

ⓦ **www.lastminute.com** (UK),
ⓦ **www.lastminute.com.au** (Australia),
ⓦ **www.lastminute.co.nz** (New Zealand). Good last-minute holiday package and flight-only deals.

ⓦ **www.opodo.co.uk** Popular and reliable source of low UK airfares.

ⓦ **www.orbitz.com** US site offering flight, car hire and hotel deals.

ⓦ **www.priceline.co.uk** (UK),
ⓦ **www.priceline.com** (US). Name-your-own-price website that has deals at around forty percent off standard fares.

ⓦ **www.skyauction.com** Bookings from the US only. Auctions tickets and travel packages to destinations worldwide.

ⓦ **www.travel.com.au** (Australia),
ⓦ**www.travel.co.nz** (New Zealand) Comprehensive range of discount fares.

ⓦ **www.travelocity.co.uk** (UK),
ⓦ **www.travelocity.com** (US),
ⓦ **www.travelocity.ca** (Canada),

ⓦ **www.travelshop.com.au** Australian site offering discounted flights, packages, insurance and online bookings.

ⓦ **www.zuji.com.au** (Australia). Hot fares and deals on car rental and accommodation.

From the UK and Ireland

From London there are flights with British Airways and South African Airways to Johannesburg and Cape Town, with prices starting at around £550 for a return trip in low season. Cheaper fares, sometimes as low as £350 return, are available on charter flights and on mainland European and other African carriers, invariably involving at least one change of plane.

From the Republic of Ireland a number of European carriers fly to South Africa via their hub airports, while in high season

there are direct charter flights to Cape Town operated by Slattery's Sun (see the listing under "Tour operators" on p.38).

Airlines

Air France UK ☎0845/359 1000, Republic of Ireland ☎01/605 0383, ⓦwww.airfrance.com. Flights from UK and Irish airports to Paris Charles de Gaulle, from where there's a daily overnight flight to Johannesburg.

Air Mauritius UK ☎ 020/7434 4375, ⓦ www .airmauritius.com. London Heathrow to Mauritius, which has daily links to Johannesburg and less frequent flights to Cape Town and Durban.

Air Namibia UK c/o Aviareps ☎01293/596 654; ⓦwww.airnamibia.com.na. Flights from Frankfurt to Jo'burg and Cape Town, via Windhoek.

British Airways UK ☎0870/850 9850, Republic of Ireland ☎1800/626 747, ⓦwww.ba.com. London Heathrow nonstop to Cape Town and Johannesburg, with onward connections to a few other South African cities.

Iberia UK ☎0845/601 2854, Republic of Ireland ☎01/407 3017, ⓦwww.iberiaairlines.co.uk. From half a dozen UK airports, and Dublin, to Jo'burg via Barcelona or Madrid.

Kenya Airways UK ☎01784/888 222, ⓦwww .kenya-airways.com. Serves Nairobi from London Heathrow, via Nairobi.

KLM (Royal Dutch Airlines) UK ☎0870/507 4074, ⓦwww.klm.com.Flights from UK and Irish airports to Jo'burg and Cape Town, via Amsterdam.

Lufthansa UK ☎0845/773 7747, Republic of Ireland ☎01/844 5544, ⓦwww.lufthansa.com. Flights from UK and Irish airports to Jo'burg and Cape Town, via Frankfurt.

Nationwide Airlines UK ☎020/8897 9995, ⓦwww.flynationwide.co.za. This South African carrier focuses mainly on domestic flights, but also operates a service between London Gatwick and Johannesburg.

Olympic Airways UK ☎0870/606 0460, Republic of Ireland ☎01/608 0090, ⓦwww.olympicairlines .com. From London and Manchester to Athens, from where they have flights to Jo'burg.

South African Airways (SAA) UK ☎0870/747 1111, ⓦwww.flysaa.com. London Heathrow nonstop to Cape Town and Johannesburg, with onward domestic connections available.

Swiss UK ☎0845/601 0956, Republic of Ireland ☎1890/200 515, ⓦwww.swiss.com. Flights from London Heathrow, London City, Birmingham, Manchester and Dublin to Jo'burg, via Zürich.

Virgin Atlantic UK ☎01293/450 150, ⓦwww .virgin-atlantic.com. Nonstop from London Heathrow to Cape Town and Jo'burg.

Flight and travel agents

UK

Bridge the World ☎0870/443 2399, ⊛www
.bridgetheworld.com. Specialists in long-haul
independent travel: flight deals, RTW tickets and
tailor-made packages.

Co-op Travel Care ☎0870/112 0085, ⊛www
.travelcareonline.com. Flights, holidays and informed
advice.

Flightcentre ☎0870/890 8099, ⊛www
.flightcentre.co.uk. Rock-bottom fares worldwide.

Flynow ☎0870/444 0045, ⊛www.flynow.com.
Large range of discounted tickets; official South
African Airways agent.

North South Travel ☎01245/608 291, ⊛www
.northsouthtravel.co.uk. Discounted fares worldwide;
profits are used to support projects in the developing
world.

STA Travel ☎0870/160 0599, ⊛www.statravel
.co.uk. Worldwide specialists in low-cost flights,
overland and holiday deals. Good discounts for
students and under-26s.

Trailfinders ☎020/7938 3939, ⊛www
.trailfinders.com. One of the best-informed and most
efficient agents for independent travellers.

Travel Bag ☎0870/890 1456, ⊛www.travelbag
.co.uk. Discount deals worldwide.

Republic of Ireland

Aran Travel First Choice ☎091/562 595, ⊛www
.firstchoicetravel.ie. Good-value flights worldwide.

Joe Walsh Tours ☎01/676 0991, ⊛www
.joewalshtours.ie. Long-established general budget
fares and holidays agent.

Lee Travel ☎021/427 7111, ⊛www.leetravel.ie.
Flights and holidays worldwide.

McCarthys Travel ☎021/427 0127, ⊛www
.mccarthystravel.ie. Long-established travel agent.

Trailfinders ☎01/677 7888, ⊛www.trailfinders.ie.
Travel agent geared to serving independent travellers.

USIT ☎0818/200 020, ⊛www.usit.ie. Specialists
in student, youth and independent travel, offering
flights and online hostel room bookings in a number
of towns in South Africa.

World Travel Centre ☎01/416 7007, ⊛www
.worldtravel.ie. Competitive fares to South Africa.

Tour operators

UK

Abercrombie & Kent ☎020/7730 9600, ⊛www
.abercrombiekent.co.uk. Upmarket tours, including
packages to southern Africa.

Absolute Africa ☎020/8742 0226, ⊛www
.absoluteafrica.com. Adventure camping overland
trips including ten-week epics from Nairobi to Cape
Town.

Acacia Expeditions ☎020/7706 4700, ⊛www
.acacia-africa.com. Camping-based trips along
classic South African routes, with some trips including
Swaziland, Mozambique and Namibia.

Africa Travel Centre ☎020/7387 1211, ⊛www
.africatravel.co.uk. Experienced Africa specialists
with a variety of tailor-made itineraries; they act
as agents for many South Africa-based overland
operators.

Bales Worldwide ☎0870/241 3208, ⊛www
.balesworldwide.com. High-quality escorted tours
that include Africa.

Dragoman ☎01728/861 133, ⊛www.dragoman
.co.uk. Extended overland journeys in purpose-built
vehicles, plus shorter camping and hotel-based
safaris.

Exodus ☎020/8675 5550, ⊛www.exodus.co.uk.
Small-group adventure tour operator with plenty of
South Africa offerings, include trips in and around Cape
Town and excursions to the country's wildlife reserves.

Explore Worldwide ☎01252/760 000, ⊛www
.explore.co.uk. Good range of small-group South
Africa tours, treks, expeditions and safaris, staying
mostly in small local hotels.

Guerba Expeditions ☎01373/858 956, ⊛www
.guerba.co.uk. Trans-African overland travel, plus a
number of shorter packages exploring different parts
of South Africa.

Kumuka Expeditions ☎0800/068 8855,
⊛www.kumuka.co.uk. Five-week journeys from
Nairobi to Cape Town, and three-week trips from
Victoria Falls in Zimbabwe to Cape Town, plus short
tours around South Africa using local operators.

Kuoni Travel ☎01306/747 002, ⊛www.kuoni
.co.uk. Award-winning major tour operator running
flexible package holidays to South Africa including
safaris, escorted tours and golfing packages.
Especially good deals for families.

Oasis Overland ☎01258/471 155, ⊛www
.oasisoverland.co.uk. One of the smaller overland
companies, often running budget trips through Africa
for under £1000.

Okavango Tours and Safaris ☎020/8343 3283,
⊛www.okavango.com. Old hands with on-the-
ground knowledge of sub-Saharan Africa, offering
fully flexible and individual tours across South Africa.

Phoenix Expeditions ☎01509/881 818, ⊛www
.phoenixexpeditions.co.uk. Africa overland trips with
excursions from Nairobi, Victoria Falls or Harare to
Cape Town.

Rainbow Tours ☎020/7226 1004, ⊛www
.rainbowtours.co.uk. Knowledgeable and sensitive

South Africa specialists whose trips emphasize eco-friendly and community-based tourism, with accommodation in good-value guesthouses, game lodges and independent hotels.

Safari Consultants ☎01787/228 494, ⓦwww .safari-consultants.co.uk. Individually tailored and fairly upmarket holidays across southern Africa, with particular expertise in activity-based holidays, including walking safaris.

Sunvil UK ☎020/8568 4499, ⓦwww.sunvil.co.uk. Small-group tours for independent travellers, as well as tailor-made trips. Specialists in good-quality accommodation/flight deals, and particularly strong on southern Africa.

Tribes ☎01728/685 971, ⓦ www.tribes.co.uk. Unusual and off-the-beaten track safaris and cultural tours in South Africa and Lesotho.

Truck Africa ☎020/7731 6142, ⓦwww.truckafrica .com. Specialist in huge Pan-African overland expeditions, lasting as long as seven months.

Wildlife Encounters ☎01737/218 802, ⓦwww .wildlife-encounters.co.uk. Two rail-based wildlife safaris, one from Cape Town up into Namibia, the other from Jo'burg to KwaZulu-Natal, taking in Kruger and Swaziland.

Wildlife Worldwide ☎020/8667 9158, ⓦwww .wildlifeworldwide.com. Tailor-made trips for wildlife and wilderness enthusiasts, including a Garden Route self-drive package and excursions taking in national parks and the winelands.

Republic of Ireland

CIE Tours International ☎01/703 1888, ⓦ www.cietours.ie. A selection of South Africa tours lasting from five days to nearly three weeks.

Destinations ☎01/855 6641, ⓦwww.destinations .ie. Specialists in long-haul destinations, including South Africa.

Slattery's Sun ☎066/718 6280, ⓦwww .slatterys com. Charter flights, starting at €475, from Dublin to Cape Town, and a number of South African itineraries that take in Cape Town, Kruger National Park and Zululand.

Twohigs ☎01/677 2666. Long-haul specialists.

Worldwide Adventures ☎01/679 5700. Agents for Exodus (see p.37).

Freighter cruises

The Cruise People UK ☎020/7723 2450, ⓦwww.cruisepeople.co.uk. Well informed about cruising berths available on freighters and banana boats, many of which stop in South Africa.

Royal Mail Ship St Helena UK ☎01326/211 466, ⓦ www.rms-st-helena.com. Comfortable cruises on the British merchant navy's last remaining Royal Mail ship, which plies a regular route between Britain, the Azores, St Helena and Cape Town.

From the USA and Canada

From the USA there are a handful of non-stop flights out of **New York** and **Atlanta** to **Johannesburg**, with **Cape Town** flights possible from Atlanta. All these are operated by South African Airways (SAA) together with code-sharing partner airlines, and take around fifteen hours. Most other flights stop off in Europe and involve a change of plane. From Canada you don't have much of a choice, with daily services from **Toronto** and **Vancouver** to **Johannesburg** operated by British Airways and by Northwest/KLM.

On the nonstop flights from the USA to Jo'burg, expect the **fare** to be anything from $1350 to $2000 for a round trip, depending on season; you might save $100–200 if you fly via Europe. Fares from Vancouver to Jo'burg start at Can$2500.

Airlines

Air France US ☎1-800/237-2747, Canada ☎1-800/667-2747, ⓦwww.airfrance.com. From North America to Jo'burg via Paris.

British Airways ☎1-800/AIRWAYS, ⓦwww.ba.com. Flights from several North American cities to London Heathrow, from where they fly nonstop to Jo'burg and Cape Town. Their South African domestic partner Comair provides onward connections (see p.55).

Iberia ☎ 1-800/772-4642, ⓦ www.iberia.com. Flights from Chicago to Jo'burg via Madrid.

Lufthansa US ☎1-800/645-3880, Canada ☎1-800/563-5954, ⓦwww.lufthansa.com. To Jo'burg or Cape Town from US cities, via Frankfurt.

Northwest/KLM ☎1-800/447-4747, ⓦwww .nwa.com, ⓦ www.klm.com. Cape Town or Jo'burg flights from Amsterdam, with connections from North American cities.

South African Airways US ☎1-800/722-9675, Canada ☎ 1-800/387-4629, ⓦ www.flysaa.com. Nonstop services from Atlanta to Cape Town and Jo'burg, and from New York to Jo'burg.

United Airlines Domestic ☎1-800/241-6522, International ☎1-800/538-2929, ⓦwww.united.com.

Virgin Atlantic ☎1-800/862-8621, ⓦwww .virgin-atlantic.com. Flights from several US cities to London, with onward Virgin Air flights to Cape Town or Jo'burg.

Discount travel companies

Air Brokers International ☎ 1-800/883-3273, ⊛ www.airbrokers.com. Consolidator and specialist in RTW tickets.

Airtech ☎ 212/219-7000, ⊛ www.airtech.com. Standby seat broker; also deals in consolidator fares.

Airtreks ☎ 1-877/AIRTREKS, ⊛ www.airtreks.com. RTW specialists; the website features an interactive database that lets you build and price your own itinerary.

Educational Travel Center ☎ 1-800/747-5551 or 608/256-5551, ⊛ www.edtrav.com. Low fares worldwide, student/youth discount offers, car rental and tours.

Flightcentre US ☎ 1-866/WORLD-51, ⊛ www .flightcentre.us, Canada ☎ 1-888/WORLD-55, ⊛ www.flightcentre.ca. Rock-bottom fares worldwide.

STA Travel US ☎ 1-800/329-9537, Canada ☎ 1-888/427-5639, ⊛ www.statravel.com. Worldwide specialists in independent travel.

Student Flights ☎ 1-800/255-8000 or 480/951-1177, ⊛ www.isecard.com/studentflights. Student/youth fares, plus student IDs.

TFI Tours ☎ 1-800/745-8000 or 212/736-1140, ⊛ www.lowestairprice.com. Established consolidator with a variety of global fares.

Travel Avenue ☎ 1-800/333-3335, ⊛ www .travelavenue.com. Full-service travel agent that offers discounts in the form of rebates.

Travel Cuts US ☎ 1-800/592-CUTS, Canada ☎ 1-888/246-9762, ⊛ www.travelcuts.com. Popular, long-established student-travel organization, with worldwide offers.

Travelers Advantage ☎ 1-877/259-2691, ⊛ www.travelersadvantage.com. Discount travel club, with cash-back deals and discounted car rental. Membership required ($1 for 3 months' trial).

Travelosophy US ☎ 1-800/332-2687, ⊛ www .itravelosophy.com. Good range of discounted and student fares worldwide.

Worldtek Travel ☎ 1-800/243-1723, ⊛ www .worldtek.com. Discount travel agency.

Tour operators

Absolute Africa ☎ 1-888/443-2378, ⊛ www .absoluteafrica.net. A range of packages, including South Africa highlights such as the Garden Route and Kruger National Park. Tours combining these with excursions into neighbouring countries are also available.

Adventure Center ☎ 1-800/228-8747 or 510/654-1879, ⊛ www.adventurecenter.com. Wide variety of affordable South African packages including "soft adventure" options.

Adventures Abroad ☎ 1-800/665-3998, ⊛ www .adventures-abroad.com. Small-group and activity tours to South Africa and neighbouring regions, including family-friendly trips.

Cox & Kings ☎ 1-800/999-1758, ⊛ www .coxandkingsusa.com. Stylish operator with classic luxury journeys, including a twelve-day Cape Town to Johannesburg excursion.

Geographic Expeditions ☎ 1-800/777-8183 or 415/922-0448, ⊛ www.geoex.com. Adventure travel and cultural tours, including a two-week South Africa package.

Global Exchange US ☎ 415/255-7296, ⊛ www .globalexchange.org. Human rights organization offering "Reality Tours" involving educational trips to non-touristy South Africa.

Goway Travel Experiences ☎ 1-800/387-8850 or 416/322-1034, ⊛ www.goway.com. Wide range of SA packages covering all corners of the country, including rail journeys and game-viewing holidays featuring the Kruger National Park.

Journeys International ☎ 1-800/255-8735 or 734/665-4407, ⊛ www.journeys-intl.com. Small-group trips with a range of safaris in Southern Africa.

Maupintour ☎ 1-800/255-4266, ⊛ www .maupintour.com. A one-week Cape Town and winelands package, plus a ten-day package involving luxury travel on the Rovos train and visits to Kruger and the Victoria falls in Zimbabwe.

Nature Expeditions International ☎ 1-800/869-0639, ⊛ www.naturexp.com. Compact, upmarket tours of South Africa and her neighbours.

Real Traveller ☎ 1-866/REAL-TVL, ⊛ www .realtraveller.com. Canadian agent for a multitude of adventure companies all over the world, taking small groups on specialist programmes that include a 32-day safari travelling from Nairobi to Johannesburg.

Travel Bound ☎ 1-800/456-8656, ⊛ www .booktravelbound.com. Large range of safari packages in South Africa.

Wilderness Travel ☎ 1-800/368-2794, ⊛ www .wildernesstravel.com. Hiking, cultural and wildlife adventures. South Africa offerings include a sixteen-day package taking in Cape Town, the Garden Route and Kruger.

From Australia and New Zealand

Southern Africa is not a cheap destination for travellers from Australia and New Zealand. **Fares** start at around Aus\$2300 for a return flight from Sydney to Johannesburg, and a flight to Europe with a stopover in

South Africa, or even a RTW ticket, may represent better value than a straightforward return.

There are flights from Australia to Johannesburg with connections to Cape Town; New Zealanders have to fly via Sydney. South African Airways (SAA) and Qantas both serve South Africa from Australia. Some Asian, African and Middle Eastern airlines fly to South Africa via their hub cities, and tend to be less expensive, but their routings often entail more stopovers.

Airlines

Air Mauritius Australia ℡02/9262 2477, ⊛www .airmauritius.com. From Melbourne, Perth and Sydney to Cape Town, Durban and Jo'burg, via Mauritius.

British Airways Australia ℡1300/767 177, New Zealand ℡0800/274 847 or 09/356 8690, ⊛www .britishairways.com. From Australia and New Zealand to Cape Town and Jo'burg, via London.

Emirates Australia ℡1300/303 777 or 02/9290 9700, New Zealand ℡09/377 6004, ⊛www .emirates.com. Jo'burg flights from Dubai, with connections from both Australia and New Zealand.

Qantas Australia ℡13 13 13, New Zealand ℡0800/808 767 or 09/357 8900, ⊛www.qantas .com. From Sydney and Perth to Jo'burg.

Singapore Airlines Australia ℡13 10 11, New Zealand ℡0800/808 909, ⊛www.singaporeair .com. To Cape Town and Jo'burg from Singapore, with connections from Australia and New Zealand.

South African Airways Australia ℡1800/221 699, New Zealand ℡09/977 2237, ⊛www.flysaa .com. Sydney to Jo'burg, with a stopover in Perth.

Travel agents

Flight Centre Australia ℡13 31 33, ⊛www .flightcentre.com.au, New Zealand ℡0800 243 544, ⊛www.flightcentre.co.nz. Rock-bottom fares worldwide.

Holiday Shoppe New Zealand ℡0800/808 480, ⊛www.holidayshoppe.co.nz. Great deals on flights, hotels and holidays.

OTC Australia ℡1300/855 118, ⊛www.otctravel .com.au. Deals on flights, hotels and holidays.

STA Travel Australia ℡1300/733 035, New Zealand ℡0508/782 872, ⊛www.statravel.com. Worldwide specialists in low-cost flights, overlands and holiday deals. Good discounts for students and under-26s.

Trailfinders Australia ℡02/9247 7666, ⊛www .trailfinders.com.au. Well-informed, efficient agents for independent travellers.

Specialist agents and tour operators

Abercrombie & Kent Australia ℡1300/851 800, New Zealand ℡0800/441 638, ⊛www .abercrombiekent.com.au. Classy operator whose packages feature Cape Town, Johannesburg, Kruger and the luxury Rovos rail service.

Africa Travel Centre Australia ℡02/9249 5444 or 1800/000 447, New Zealand ℡09/520 2000. Safaris, flights, transport and accommodation in Africa.

Classic Safari Company Australia ℡1300/130 218 or 02/9327 0666, ⊛www.classicsafaricompany .com.au. Luxury tailor-made safaris to southern and eastern Africa.

ecruising Australia ℡1300/369 848 or 02/9249 6060, ⊛www.ecruising.com.au. Searchable fare database of Cape Town–Australia cruises, useful if you fancy heading out by air and back by sea.

Journeys Worldwide Australia ℡1300/734 788 or 07/3221 4788, ⊛www.journeysworldwide.com.au. Escorted tours of South Africa and neighbouring countries.

Kumuka Expeditions Australia ℡1800/804 277 or 02/9279 0491, ⊛www.kumuka.com.au. Overland expeditions through South Africa and neighbouring countries.

Peregrine Adventures Australia ℡03/9663 8611, ⊛www.peregrine.net.au, New Zealand c/o Adventure Travel Company ℡09/379 9755, ℮advakl@hot.co.nz. Specialist small-group programmes that include a variety of wildlife packages, one of which involves tracking and monitoring animals in a private reserve in KwaZulu-Natal.

Visas and red tape

Nationals of the EU, the USA, Canada, Australia and New Zealand don't require a visa to enter South Africa. As long as you carry a valid passport you will be granted a temporary visitor's permit, which allows you to stay in South Africa for up to three months. All visitors should have a valid return ticket; without one, you may be required to pay the authorities the equivalent of your fare home (the money will be refunded after you have left the country). Visitors may also need to prove that they have sufficient funds to cover their stay.

Citizens of some African and former Eastern Bloc countries do require a visa to enter South Africa, and this must be purchased in advance. If you come under this category and plan to travel to Lesotho and Swaziland during your trip, you'll need a **multi-entry visa** to get back into South Africa. If you don't have one, it will be issued free of charge on your return from Lesotho or Swaziland, although this can be time-consuming.

Applications for **visa extensions** must be made at one of the main offices of the Department of Home Affairs, where you will be quizzed about your intentions and your funds. In Cape Town, go to 56 Barrack Street (☎021 462 4970); in Johannesburg, the office is at the corner of Plein and Harrison streets (☎011 836 3228). They also have offices in a number of towns – check in the telephone directory or on their website (ⓦwww.home-affairs.gov.za/regions.asp), and make sure that the office you're intending to visit is able to grant extensions.

Very few citizens need a **visa** to enter **Swaziland** – and those who do will be issued with one free of charge at the border. Visa requirements for **Lesotho** change from time to time, but the citizens of Commonwealth countries, most EU nations, the USA and Canada are very unlikely to need a visa and should have no problem entering. For stays beyond the standard fourteen days granted at the border, contact the Department of Immigration and Passport Services, Kingsway, Maseru (☎31 7339) or the Lesotho High Commission in Pretoria (see p.42). Note that a brief visit to either Swaziland or Lesotho is not a reliable way of obtaining a new three-month temporary residence permit in South Africa – immigration officials will often only grant a limited stay on re-entry.

South African diplomatic missions

Australia Rhodes Pl, Yarralumla, Canberra, ACT 2600 ☎02/6273 2424, ⓦwww.rsa.emb.gov.au.
Botswana Plot 5131, Kopanyo House, Nelson Mandela Drive, Gaborone ☎390 4800, ⓔsahcgabs.botsnet.bw.
Canada 15 Sussex Dr, Ottawa, Ontario K1M 1M8 ☎613/744-0330, ⓦwww.southafrica-canada.ca.
Ireland 2nd floor, Alexandra House, Earlssort Terrace, Dublin 2 ☎01/661 5553.
Lesotho See p.777.
Malawi 3rd floor, Kang'Ombe House, Robert Mugabe Crescent, Lilongwe 3 ☎01/773 722.
Mozambique Avenue Eduardo Mondlane 41, Maputo ☎01/491 614, ⓔconsular@tropical.co.mz.
Namibia RSA House, corner of Jan Jonker and Nelson Mandela avenues, Windhoek ☎061/205 7111.
Netherlands Wassenaarseweg 40, 2596 CJ, The Hague ☎070/392 4501, ⓔinfo@zuidafrika.nl.
New Zealand c/o the high commission in Australia.
UK Consular Section, 15 Whitehall, London SW1A 2DD ☎020/7925 8900, ⓦwww.southafricahouse.com.
USA 3051 Massachusetts Ave NW, Washington, DC 20008 ☎202/232-4400, ⓦwwww.saembassy.org. Consulates: 333 E 38th St, 9th floor, New York, NY 10016 ☎212/213-4880, ⓦwww.southafrica-newyork.net; 6300 Wilshire Boulevard, Suite 600, Los Angeles, CA 90048 ☎323/651-0902.

Zimbabwe 7 Elcombe St, Belgravia, Harare
ⓣ04/753 147, ⓔsahcomm@ecoweb.co.za.

USA 2511 Massachusetts Ave NW, Washington, DC
20008 ⓣ202/797-5533.

Lesotho diplomatic missions

South Africa 391 Anderson St, Menlo Park, Pretoria
ⓣ012 460 7648, ⓔlesothoh@global.co.za.
UK 7 Chesham Place, Belgravia, London SW1
8HN ⓣ020/7235 5686, ⓦwww.lesotholondon
.org.uk.

Swaziland diplomatic missions

South Africa 715 Government Ave, Arcadia,
Pretoria ⓣ012 344 1910.
UK 20 Buckingham Gate, London SW1E 6LB
ⓣ020/7630 6611, ⓦwww.swaziland.org.uk.
USA 3400 International Drive, Washington, DC
20008 ⓣ202/362-6683.

Information, websites and maps

South Africa is experiencing a boom in tourism, and you should have no difficulty finding maps, books and brochures before you leave. South African Tourism, the official organization promoting the country, is reasonably efficient: if there's an office near you, it's worth visiting for its free map and information on hotels and organized tours. Alternatively, you can check out their website ⓦwww.southafrica.net, which includes content specific to users in South Africa, the UK, the USA, Canada, Germany and France.

In South Africa itself, nearly every town, even down to the sleepiest *dorp*, has some sort of **tourist office** – sometimes connected to the museum, municipal offices or library – where you can pick up local maps, lists of B&Bs and travel advice. In larger cities such as Cape Town and Durban, you'll find several branches offering everything from hotel bookings to organized safari trips. We've given precise **opening hours** of tourist offices in most cases; they generally adhere to a standard schedule of Monday to Friday 8.30am to 5pm, with many offices also open on Saturdays and Sundays. In smaller towns some close between 1pm and 2pm, while in the bigger centres some have extended hours.

In this fast-changing country the best way of finding out what's happening is often by word of mouth, and for this **backpacker hostels** are invaluable. If you're seeing South Africa on a budget, the useful notice boards, constant traveller traffic and largely helpful and friendly staff in the hostels will greatly smooth your travels.

South African Tourism offices

Head office Bojanala House, 90 Protea Road,
Chislehurston, Johannesburg ⓣ011 895 3000,
ⓦwww.southafrica.net.
Australia Level 1, 117 York St, Sydney, NSW 2000
ⓣ02/9261 5000.
Ireland 2nd Floor, Alexandra House, Earlsfort
Terrace, Dublin 2 ⓣ01/676 8022.
UK 5–6 Alt Grove, Wimbledon SW19 4XZ
ⓣ020/8971 9364.
USA 500 Fifth Ave, Suite 2040, New York, NY
10110 ⓣ0212/730-2929.

Regional South Africa tourism authorities

Eastern Cape ⓦwww.ectourism.co.za
Gauteng ⓦwww.gauteng.net
KwaZulu-Natal ⓦwww.tourism-kzn.org.za
Limpopo ⓦwww.limpopotourism.org.za
Mpumalanga ⓦwww.mpumalanga.com
North West ⓦwww.tourismnorthwest.co.za
Northern Cape ⓦwww.northerncape.org.za
Western Cape ⓦwww.tourismcapetown.com

Lesotho and Swaziland tourism authorities

Lesotho ⓦ www.lesotho.gov.ls/lstourism.htm
Swaziland ⓦ www.mintour.gov.sz

Online resources

The tourism industry is one of the most vibrant adopters of online technology, from individuals posting details of their B&Bs to byzantine sites with vast numbers of links. Most of the sites listed here provide political and cultural background information or focus on practicalities, while others, such as the Ananzi and *Mail & Guardian* sites, are excellent lead-ins to other South African topics. For online accommodation booking services see box on p.60; for websites for gay travellers see p.85; and you'll find websites relating to events and other information specific to a particular city or region listed in the relevant place in the Guide.

Governmental travel advisories

Australian Department of Foreign Affairs ⓦ www.dfat.gov.au.
British Foreign & Commonwealth Office ⓦ www.fco.gov.uk/travel.
Canadian Department of Foreign Affairs ⓦ www.dfait-maeci.gc.ca.
Irish Department of Foreign Affairs ⓦ www.irlgov.ie/iveagh.
New Zealand Ministry of Foreign Affairs ⓦ www.mft.govt.nz.
US State Department ⓦ travel.state.gov.

Portals and search engines

Ananzi ⓦ www.ananzi.co.za. South Africa's premier search engine also has an easy-to-use directory organized by topic.
MWEB ⓦ www.mweb.co.za. The site of one of South Africa's biggest Internet service providers offers news and information on a variety of topics including travel.

News and current affairs

Daily Mail & Guardian ⓦ www.mg.co.za. The online presence of the intellectual heavyweight of South Africa's press, the *Mail & Guardian*, with links from its JumpStart page to a vast variety of sites covering local issues.

IOL ⓦ www.iol.co.za. Probably the best web-based South Africa news service.
News 24 wnews24.co.za. Another good source of local and international news.
The Sunday Times ⓦ www.sundaytimes.co.za. Internet version of South Africa's best-selling newspaper, which strives to be a downmarket tabloid and serious investigative broadsheet at the same time.

Arts and culture

Artslink ⓦ www.artslink.co.za. South African arts, culture and entertainment hub offers comprehensive coverage of what's happening in the arts, reviews and a searchable database of what's on.
Computicket ⓦ www.computicket.com. Online booking site for cinema, live events, sport, festivals and bus tickets.
Museums online ⓦ www.museums.org.za. Portal for all South Africa's major museums.
Rage ⓦ www.rage.co.za. An ezine devoted to South African street culture, with coverage of nightlife and *kwaito* and information about what's on in Cape Town, Durban and Gauteng.
Thunda ⓦ www.thunda.com. Club culture site aimed at 18–24s, with coverage of Johannesburg, Pretoria, Durban, Cape Town, Stellenbosch, Port Elizabeth and Plettenberg Bay.
ZA@Play ⓦ www.chico.mweb.co.za/art. Reviews and listings from the *Mail & Guardian* of what's on in Cape Town, Johannesburg, Durban and Pietermaritzburg.

General travel resources

Coast to Coast ⓦ www.coastingafrica.com. Website of *Coast to Coast*, the regularly updated backpackers' and budget travellers' guide to southern Africa.
Getaway ⓦ www.getawaytoafrica.com. Website of South Africa's biggest travel magazine, with a searchable database of domestic destinations and accommodation.
iAfrica ⓦ www.iafrica.com. One of the biggest South African portals, it has a comprehensive travel section with city and regional guides, as well as specialist sections on topics such as surfing, safaris and budget travel.
Lonely Planet Thorn Tree ⓦ thorntree.lonelyplanet.com. Popular travellers' forums, divided by region and by subject.
Rough Guides ⓦ www.roughguides.com. Besides the online forum, called Travel Talk, there are travel tips and features, plus online travel guides.
South African Weather Bureau ⓦwww.weathersa.co.za. Weather forecasts for the whole of South Africa.

Wildlife and safaris

Wildnet Africa ⓦwww.wildnetafrica.com. A commercial website covering wildlife and safaris in Southern Africa, with the facility to find out more about specific destinations, accommodation and safari lodges.

Maps

Many place names in South Africa were changed after the 1994 elections – and changes are still being made – so if you buy a **map** before leaving home, make sure that it's up to date. Bartholomew produces an excellent map of **South Africa**, including Lesotho and Swaziland (1:2,000,000), as part of their World Travel Map series. Also worth investing in are MapStudio's "Miniplan" maps of major cities such as Cape Town, Durban and Pretoria: these are a convenient size and have useful details, such as hotels, cinemas, post offices and hospitals. MapStudio also produces good regional maps, featuring scenic routes and street maps of major towns, and a fine Natal Drakensberg map which shows hiking trails, picnic spots, campsites and places of interest.

South Africa's motoring organization, the Automobile Association (AA; see p.56), offers a wide selection of maps, free to members, which you can pick up from their offices.

Specialist book and map outlets

UK and Republic of Ireland

Blackwell's Map Centre 50 Broad St, Oxford OX1 3BQ ☎01865/793 550, ⓦmaps.blackwell.co.uk. Branches in Bristol, Cambridge, Cardiff, Leeds, Liverpool, Newcastle, Reading and Sheffield.
The Map Shop 30a Belvoir St, Leicester LE1 6QH ☎0116/247 1400, ⓦwww.mapshopleicester.co.uk.
National Map Centre 22–24 Caxton St, London SW1H 0QU ☎020/7222 2466, ⓦwww.mapstore.co.uk.
National Map Centre Ireland 34 Aungier St, Dublin ☎01/476 0471, ⓦwww.mapcentre.ie.

Stanfords 12–14 Long Acre, London WC2E 9LP ☎020/7836 1321; 39 Spring Gardens, Manchester ☎0161/831 0250; 29 Corn St, Bristol ☎0117/929 9966; ⓦwww.stanfords.co.uk.
The Travel Bookshop 13–15 Blenheim Crescent, London W11 2EE ☎020/7229 5260, ⓦwww.thetravelbookshop.co.uk.
Traveller 55 Grey St, Newcastle-upon-Tyne NE1 6EF ☎0191/261 5622, ⓦwww.newtraveller.com.

US and Canada

110 North Latitude US ☎336/369-4171, ⓦwww.110nlatitude.com.
Book Passage 51 Tamal Vista Blvd, Corte Madera, CA 94925 and in the San Francisco Ferry Building ☎1-800/999-7909 or ☎415/927-0960, ⓦwww.bookpassage.com.
Distant Lands 56 S Raymond Ave, Pasadena, CA 91105 ☎1-800/310-3220, ⓦwww.distantlands.com.
Globe Corner Bookstore 28 Church St, Cambridge, MA 02138 ☎1-800/358-6013, ⓦwww.globecorner.com.
Longitude Books 115 W 30th St #1206, New York, NY 10001 ☎1-800/342-2164, ⓦwww.longitudebooks.com.
Map Town 100–400 5 Ave SW, Calgary, AB T2P 0L6 ☎1-877/921-6277 or ☎403/266-2241, ⓦwww.maptown.com.
Travel Bug Bookstore 3065 W Broadway, Vancouver, BC V6K 2G9 ☎604/737-1122, ⓦwww.travelbugbooks.ca.
World of Maps 1235 Wellington St, Ottawa, ON K1Y 3A3 ☎1-800/214-8524 or ☎613/724-6776, ⓦwww.worldofmaps.com.

Australia and New Zealand

Map Centre ⓦwww.mapcentre.co.nz.
Map Shop 6–10 Peel St, Adelaide ☎08/8231 2033, ⓦwww.mapshop.net.au.
Map World (Australia) 280 Pitt St, Sydney ☎02/9261 3601, ⓦwww.mapworld.net.au. Also at 900 Hay St, Perth ☎08/9322 5733, Jolimont Centre, Canberra ☎02/6230 4097, and 1981 Logan Road, Brisbane ☎07/3349 6633.
Mapland 372 Little Bourke St, Melbourne ☎03/9670 4383, ⓦwww.mapland.com.au.
MapWorld (New Zealand) 173 Gloucester St, Christchurch ☎0800/627 967, ⓦwww.mapworld.co.nz.

Insurance

It's wise to take out an insurance policy to cover against theft, loss and illness or injury prior to visiting South Africa. Before paying for a new policy, however, it's worth checking whether you are already covered: some all-risks home insurance policies may cover your possessions when overseas, and many private medical schemes include cover when abroad. In Canada, provincial health plans usually provide partial cover for medical mishaps overseas, while holders of official student, teacher or youth cards in Canada and the US are entitled to (meagre) accident coverage and hospital in-patient benefits. Students will often find that their student health coverage extends during the vacations and for one term beyond the date of last enrollment.

After checking out the possibilities above, you might want to contact a specialist travel insurance company, or consider the travel insurance deal we offer (see box). A typical travel insurance policy usually provides cover for the loss of baggage, tickets and – up to a certain limit – cash or cheques, as well as cancellation or curtailment of your journey. Most of them exclude so-called dangerous sports unless an extra premium is paid: in South Africa this can mean scuba diving, whitewater rafting, windsurfing, horse-riding, bungee jumping and paragliding. In addition to these it's well worth checking whether you are covered by your policy if you're hiking, kayaking, pony trekking or game viewing on safari, all activities people commonly take part in when visiting South Africa. Many policies can be chopped and changed to exclude coverage you don't need – for example, sickness and accident benefits can often be excluded or included at will. If you do take medical coverage, ascertain whether benefits will be paid as treatment proceeds or only after you return home, and if there is a 24-hour medical emergency number. When securing baggage cover, make sure that the per-article limit – typically under £500/$750 and sometimes as little as £250/$400 – will cover your most valuable possession. If you need to make a claim, you should keep receipts for medicines and medical treatment, and in the event you have anything stolen, you must obtain an official statement from the police.

Rough Guides Travel Insurance

Rough Guides has teamed up with Columbus Direct to offer you travel insurance that can be tailored to suit your needs.

Readers can choose from many different travel insurance products, including a low-cost backpacker option for long stays; a short break option for city getaways; a typical holiday package option; and many others. There are also annual multi-trip policies for those who travel regularly, with variable levels of cover available. Different sports and activities (trekking, skiing, etc) can be covered if required on most policies.

Rough Guides travel insurance is available to the residents of 36 different countries, with different language options to choose from, via our website – ⓦ www.roughguidesinsurance.com – where you can also purchase the insurance. Alternatively, UK residents should call ☏0800 083 9507; US citizens should call ☏1-800 749-4922; Australians should call ☏1 300 669 999. All other nationalities should call ☏+44 870 890 2843.

Health

You can put aside most of the health fears that may be justified in some parts of Africa; run-down hospitals and bizarre tropical diseases aren't typical of South Africa. All tourist areas boast generally high standards of hygiene and safe drinking water. The only hazard you're likely to encounter, and the one the majority of visitors are most blasé about, is the sun. In some parts of the country there is a risk of malaria, and you will need to take precautions.

Public **hospitals** in South Africa are fairly well equipped, but they are facing huge pressures under which their attempts to maintain standards are unfortunately buckling. Expect long waits and frequently indifferent treatment. Private hospitals or clinics, which are well up to British or North American standards, are usually a better option for travellers. You're likely to get more personal treatment and the costs are nowhere near as high as in the US – besides which, the expense shouldn't pose a problem if you're adequately insured. Private hospitals are listed in the town and city listings throughout the Guide.

Dental care in South Africa is well up to British and North American standards, and is generally no more expensive. You'll find **dentists** in all the cities and most smaller towns, listed after doctors at the beginning of each town in the telephone directory.

Inoculations

Although no specific **inoculations** are compulsory if you arrive from the West, it's wise to ensure that your **polio** and **tetanus** vaccinations are up to date. A **yellow fever** vaccination certificate is necessary if you've come from a country where the disease is endemic, such as Kenya, Tanzania or tropical South America.

In addition to these, the Hospital for Tropical Diseases in London recommends a course of shots against **typhoid** and an injection against **hepatitis A**, both of which can be caught from contaminated food or water. This is a worst-case scenario, as you probably won't be travelling in areas where these illnesses pose a serious threat. In any case, typhoid is eminently curable and few visitors to South Africa ever catch it.

Vaccination against **hepatitis B** is essential only for people involved in health work; the disease is spread by the transfer of blood products, usually dirty needles.

If you decide to have an armful of jabs, start organizing them **six weeks** before departure. If you're going to another African country first and need the yellow fever jab, note that a yellow fever certificate only becomes valid ten days after you've had the shot.

Medical resources for travellers

Online

ⓦ **health.yahoo.com** Information on specific diseases and conditions, drugs and herbal remedies, as well as advice from health experts.
ⓦ **www.cdc.gov** The website of the US government's Centers for Disease Control has a comprehensive section on travel health.
ⓦ **www.fitfortravel.scot.nhs.uk** Scottish NHS website carrying information about travel-related diseases and how to avoid them.
ⓦ **www.istm.org** The website of the International Society for Travel Medicine, with a full list of clinics specializing in travel health. Publishes outbreak warnings, suggested inoculations, precautions and other background information for travellers.
ⓦ **www.tripprep.com** Database of necessary vaccinations for most countries, as well as information on health and medical service providers, organized by country.

UK

British Airways Travel Clinics 213 Piccadilly, London W1J 9HQ (Mon–Fri 9.30am–5.30pm, Sat 10am–4pm); 101 Cheapside, London EC2 (Mon–Fri 9am–4.30pm; appointments on ☎0845/600 2236); ⓦwww.britishairways.com/travel/healthclinintro. Vaccinations, tailored advice from an online database and a complete range of travel healthcare products.

Hospital for Tropical Diseases Travel Clinic 2nd floor, Mortimer Market Centre, off Capper St, London WC1E 6AU (Mon–Fri 9am–5pm by appointment only; ☎020/7388 9600). A consultation costs £15, which is waived if you have your injections here. The recorded Health Line (☎0906/133 7733; 50p/min) gives hints on hygiene and illness prevention as well as listing appropriate immunizations.

Liverpool School of Tropical Medicine Pembroke Place, Liverpool L3 5QA ☎0151/708 9393, ⓦwww .liv.ac.uk/lstm/lstm. Walk-in clinic Mon–Fri 1–4pm; no appointment required for most jabs.

MASTA (Medical Advisory Service for Travellers Abroad) Forty regional clinics (call ☎0870/606 2782 or see ⓦwww.masta.org for the nearest). Also operates a pre-recorded 24hr Travellers' Health Line (UK ☎0906/822 4100; 60p per min), giving written information tailored to your journey by return of post.

Nomad Pharmacy 40 Bernard St, London WC1N 1LE (Mon–Fri 9.30am–6pm, ☎020/7833 4114 to book vaccination appointment). They can provide advice tailored to your travel needs – free if you go in person, or via their telephone helpline on ☎0906/863 3414 (60p/min).

Travel Medicine Services PO Box 254, 16 College St, Belfast BT1 6BT ☎028/9031 5220. Medical advice before a trip and help afterwards in the event of a tropical disease.

Republic of Ireland

Dun Laoghaire Medical Centre 5 North-umberland Ave, Dun Laoghaire, County Dublin ☎01/280 4996. Advice on medical matters abroad.

Travel Health Centre Department of International Health and Tropical Medicine, Royal College of Surgeons in Ireland, Mercers Medical Centre, Stephen's St Lower, Dublin 2 ☎01/402 2337. Expert pre-trip advice and inoculations.

Tropical Medical Bureau Grafton Buildings, 34 Grafton St, Dublin 2, ☎1850/487 674, ⓦwww .tmb.ie. Vaccinations and health advice.

USA and Canada

Canadian Society for International Health 1 Nicholas St, Suite 1105, Ottawa, ON K1N 7B7 ☎613/241-5785, ⓦwww.csih.org. Distributes a free pamphlet, "Health Information for Canadian Travellers", containing an extensive list of travel health centres in Canada.

International Association for Medical Assistance to Travellers (IAMAT) 417 Center St, Lewiston, NY 14092 ☎716/754-4883; and 1287 St. Clair Avenue West, Suite #1, Toronto, Ontario M6E 1B8 ☎416/652-0137; ⓦwww .iamat.org. A non-profit organization, it provides

a list of English-speaking doctors in South Africa, climate charts and leaflets on various diseases and inoculations.

International SOS Assistance Eight Neshaminy Interplex Suite 207, Trevose, PA 19053-6956 ☎1-800/523-8930, ⓦwww.intsos.com. Members receive pre-trip medical referral info, as well as overseas emergency services designed to complement travel insurance coverage.

MEDJET Assistance ☎1-800/963-3538 or 205/595-6658, ⓦwww.medjetassistance.com. In the event of illness or injury, it flies members of the scheme home or to the hospital of their choice in a medically equipped jet.

Travel Medicine ☎1-800/872-8633, ⓦwww .travmed.com. Sells first-aid kits, mosquito netting, water filters, reference books and other health-related travel products.

Australia and New Zealand

Travellers' Medical and Vaccination Centres ⓦwww.tmvc.com.au. Australian clinics include: 27–29 Gilbert Place, Adelaide ☎08/8212 7522; 5/247 Adelaide St, Brisbane ☎07/3221 9066; 5/8–10 Hobart Place, Canberra ☎02/6257 7156; HSA Level 1 Cavanagh Centre, Cavanagh Street, Darwin ☎08/8981 7492; 2/393 Little Bourke St, Melbourne ☎03/9602 5788; Level 7, Dymocks Bldg, 428 George St, Sydney ☎02/9221 7133. New Zealand clinics include: 1/170 Queen St, Auckland ☎09/373 3531; Shop 15, Grand Arcade, 14–16 Willis St, Wellington ☎04/473 0991. See the website for additional locations as well as health factsheets.

Stomach upsets

Stomach upsets from food are rare. Salad and ice – the danger items in many other Third World countries – are both perfectly safe. As anywhere, though, don't keep food for too long, and be sure to wash fruit and vegetables as thoroughly as possible.

If you do get a **stomach bug**, the best cure is lots of water and rest. Papayas – the flesh as well as the pips – are a good tonic to offset the runs. Otherwise, most chemists should have name-brand anti-diarrhoea remedies, such as Lomotil.

Avoid jumping for **antibiotics** at the first sign of illness. Instead keep them as a last resort – they don't work on viruses and annihilate your "gut flora" (most of which you want to keep), making you more susceptible next time round. Most tummy upsets will resolve themselves if you adopt a sensible fat-free diet for a couple of days, but if they do persist without improvement (or are accompanied by other unusual symptoms), then see a doctor as soon as possible.

The sun

The **sun** is likely to be the worst hazard you'll encounter in Southern Africa, particularly if you're fair-skinned. The dangers of overexposure to the sun, including the risk of skin cancer, is something white South Africans haven't yet caught onto, and locals still regard their tans as more important than their health.

Short-term effects of **overexposure** to the sun include burning, nausea and headaches. This usually comes from overeager tanning, which can leave you looking like a lobster. The fairer your skin, the slower you should take tanning. Start with short periods of exposure and **high protection sunscreen** (at least SPF 15), gradually increasing your time in the sun and decreasing the factor of your screen. Many people with fair skins, especially those who freckle easily, should take extra care, starting with a very high factor screen (SPF 25–30) and continue using at least SPF 15 for the rest of their stay. There's no shame in smearing sensitive areas of your face with total block cream.

Overexposure to the sun can cause sunburn to the surface of the eye, inflammation of the cornea and can result in serious short- and long-term damage. Good **sunglasses** can reduce ultraviolet (UV) light exposure to the eye by fifty percent. A **broad-brimmed hat** is also recommended.

These last measures are especially necessary for children, who should ideally be kept well covered at the seaside. Don't be lulled into complacency on cloudy days, when UV levels can still be high. UV-protective clothing is available locally, but it's best to buy before you arrive; some excellent ranges are made in Australia. If you don't come with this gear, make sure children wear T-shirts at the beach, and use SPF 30 sunscreen liberally and often.

Bilharzia

One ailment that you need to take seriously throughout sub-Saharan Africa is **bilharzia** (schistosomiasis), carried in most freshwater lakes and rivers in South Africa except in the mountains. Bilharzia is spread by tiny, parasitic worm-like flukes which leave their water-snail hosts and burrow into human skin to multiply in the bloodstream; they then work their way to the walls of the intestine or bladder, where they begin to lay eggs.

The chances are you'll avoid bilharzia even if you swim in a suspect river, but it's best to avoid swimming in dams and rivers where possible. If you go canoeing or can't avoid the water, have a test for bilharzia when you return home. Whitewater is no guarantee of safety: although the snails favour sheltered areas, the flukes can be swept downstream.

Symptoms may be no more than a feeling of lassitude and ill health. Once the infection is established, abdominal pain and blood in the urine and stools are common. Fortunately, bilharzia is easily and effectively treated with praziquantel, although the drug can make you feel ill for a few days. No vaccine is available.

Malaria

Most of South Africa is free of **malaria**, a potentially lethal disease that is widespread in tropical and sub-tropical Africa, where it's a major killer. However, protection against malaria is essential if you're planning to travel to any of these areas: northern and northeastern Mpumalanga, notably the Kruger National Park; northern KwaZulu-Natal; the border regions of North West and Limpopo provinces; and low-lying areas of Swaziland. The **highest risk** is during the hot, rainy months from **November to April**. The risk is reduced during the cooler, dry months from May to October, when some people decide not to take prophylactic medication.

Malaria is caused by a parasite carried in the saliva of the female anopheles mosquito. It has a variable incubation period of a few days to several weeks, so you can become ill long after being bitten. The first **symptoms** of malaria can be mistaken for flu, starting off relatively mildly with a variable combination that includes fever, aching limbs and shivering, which come in waves, usually beginning in the early evening. Deterioration can be rapid as the parasites in the bloodstream proliferate.

Malaria is not infectious, but can be fatal if not treated quickly: get **medical help** without delay if you go down with flu-like symptoms within a week of entering or three months of leaving a malarial area.

Protection against malaria

Doctors can advise on which kind of **anti-malarial tablets** to take. It's important to keep to the prescribed dose, which covers the period before and after your trip. The reliable SAA Netcare Travel Clinics (@www .travelclinic.co.za) recommends mefloquine (marketed as Mefliam and Larium as well as under other trade names), doxycycline or atovaquone-proguanil as providing the most effective protection against malaria. Mefloquine isn't recommended for anyone with a history of psychiatric problems or epilepsy; side effects such as paranoia and psychosis have been reported. Doxycycline should be avoided in pregnancy and by children. A combination of proguanil and chloroquine can also be taken and doesn't require a prescription, but it's more complicated and isn't believed to be as effective as the three drugs mentioned above. Consult your doctor several weeks **before you travel**, as you should start taking medication a week or two before entering the affected region – depending on the particular drug you're using.

Whatever you decide to take, be aware that no antimalarial drug is totally effective – your only sure-fire protection is to **avoid getting bitten**. Malaria-carrying mosquitoes are active between dusk and dawn, so try to avoid being out at this time, or at least cover yourself well. Sleep under a **mosquito net** when possible, making sure to tuck it under the mattress, and burn **mosquito coils** (which you can buy everywhere) for a peaceful, if noxious, night. Electric mosquito-destroyers which you fit with a pad every night are less pungent than mosquito coils, though note that you may not have access to a power supply at some safari lodges, or if you're camping. Mosquito "buzzers" are useless. Whenever the mosquitoes are particularly bad – and that's not often – cover your exposed parts with **insect repellent**; those containing diethyltoluamide (DEET) work well. Other locally produced repellents such as Peaceful Sleep are widely available.

Bites and stings

Bites, stings and rashes in South Africa are comparatively rare. **Snakes** are present, but hardly ever seen as they move out of the way quickly. The sluggish puff and berg adders are the most dangerous, because they often lie in paths and don't move when humans approach. The best advice if you get bitten is to note what the snake looked like and get yourself to a clinic or hospital.

Medical kit

Most medicines and medical gear can be bought in pharmacies all over South Africa; only in deeply rural areas where few visitors ever go are you likely to be caught short. If you need specialized drugs, bring your own supply. A very basic medical kit should include:

Antibiotics Potentially useful if you're heading off the beaten track; a broad-spectrum variety is best.

Antiseptic cream Bacitracin is a reliable brand, while Nelson's natural calendula ointment is invaluable for stings, rashes, cuts, sores or cracked skin.

Bandages One wide and one narrow.

Eyedrops Wonderfully soothing if you're travelling on dusty roads.

Fine tweezers Useful for removing thorns or glass.

Insect repellent Essential in malarial areas.

Lip salve/chapstick

Paracetamol For pain and fever relief.

Sticking plasters

Most bites are not fatal and the worst thing you can do is to panic: desperate measures with razor blades and tourniquets risk doing more harm than good.

Tick-bite fever is occasionally contracted from walking in the bush, particularly in long wet grass. The offending ticks can be minute and you may not spot them. Symptoms appear a week later – swollen glands and severe aching of the bones, backache and fever. The disease will run its course in three or four days. Ticks you may find on yourself are not dangerous, just repulsive at first. Make sure you pull out the head as well as the body (it's not painful). A good way of removing small ones is to smear Vaseline or grease over them, making them release their hold.

Scorpion stings and **spider bites** are painful but almost never fatal, contrary to popular myth. Scorpions and spiders abound, but they're hardly ever seen unless you turn over logs and stones. If you're collecting wood for a campfire, knock or shake it before picking it up. Another simple precaution when camping is to shake out your shoes and clothes in the morning before you get dressed.

Rabies is present throughout southern Africa. Be wary of animals and go immediately to a clinic if bitten. Rabies can be treated effectively with a course of injections.

Sexually transmitted diseases

HIV/AIDS and venereal diseases are widespread in southern Africa among both men and women, and the danger of catching the virus through sexual contact is very real. Follow the usual precautions regarding safer sex. There's no special risk from medical treatment in the country, but if you're travelling overland and you want to play it safe, take your own needle and transfusion kit.

Costs, money and banks

Visitors from Europe, North America or Australasia will find South Africa relatively inexpensive, but just how cheap you find South Africa will depend on exchange rates at the time of your visit. At the end of 2001 the *Economist* magazine ranked the rand as the most undervalued currency in the world. Everyone expected the currency to continue its slide against sterling and the dollar, but the rand has rallied vigorously and at the time of writing South Africa had the best-performing currency of any developing country, which means you get less bang for your buck. For a discussion of costs in Lesotho and Swaziland, see the relevant chapters in the Guide.

If you're prepared to stay in backpacker lodges, travel on public transport and eat cheaply or self-cater, you can get by on under **£18/US$30** a day – less if you're camping. If you stay in B&Bs and guesthouses, and eat out regularly, you should budget for at least double that a day. In luxury hotels and game lodges, expect to pay upwards of **£90/US$150** per day. Extras such as car rental, scuba-diving, horse-riding and safaris will add to these figures substantially. While most **museums** and **art galleries** charge an entry fee, it's usually quite low: only the most sophisticated attractions charge more than £1/$1.80.

Currency and exchange

South Africa's currency is the **rand** (R), often called the "buck", divided into 100 **cents**. Notes come in R10, R20, R50, R100 and

R200 denominations and there are coins of 1, 2, 5, 10, 20 and 50 cents, as well as R1, R2 and R5. At the time of writing, the **exchange rate** was hovering at just above R11 to the pound sterling, R6 to the US dollar, 8 to the euro and R4.50 to the Australian dollar.

All but the tiniest settlement will have a **bank** where you can **change money** swiftly and easily. **Banking hours** are Monday to Friday 9am to 3.30pm, and Saturday 9am to 11am; the banks in smaller towns usually close for lunch. In major cities, some banks operate bureaux de change that stay open until 7pm. Outside banking hours, some hotels will change money, although this entails a fairly hefty commission. You can also change money at branches of American Express and Rennies Travel.

Carrying your money

Credit and debit cards are the most convenient way to access your funds in South Africa. Most international cards can be used to withdraw money at **automatic teller machines** (ATMs), open 24 hours a day in the cities and elsewhere. Ask your bank which option you should choose for your card when the machine asks for the account type (cheque, savings, transmission or credit). Remember that all cash advances on credit cards are treated as loans, with interest accruing daily from the date of withdrawal; there may be a transaction fee on top of this. ATM withdrawals made with debit cards aren't liable to interest payments, and the flat transaction fee is usually quite small – your bank will be able to advise on this. Make sure you have a personal identification number (PIN) that's designed to work overseas.

Plastic can come in very handy for hotel bookings and for paying for more mainstream and upmarket tourist facilities, and is essential for car rental. Visa and Mastercard are the cards most widely accepted in major cities.

Traveller's cheques make a useful backup as they can be replaced if lost or stolen. American Express, Visa and Thomas Cook are all widely recognized brands; both US dollar and sterling cheques are accepted in South Africa. The usual fee for traveller's cheque sales is one or two percent, though this fee may be waived if you buy the cheques through a bank where you have an account. It pays to get a selection of denominations. Make sure you keep the purchase agreement and a record of cheque serial numbers safe and separate from the cheques themselves. In the event that cheques are lost or stolen, the issuing company will expect you to report the loss forthwith to their office in South Africa; most companies claim to replace lost or stolen cheques within 24 hours.

Traveller's cheques and plastic are useless if you're heading into remote areas, where you'll need to carry **cash**, preferably in a very safe place, such as a leather pouch or waist-level money belt you can keep under your clothes.

Wiring money

Getting money wired from home using one of the companies listed below is never convenient or cheap, and should be considered a last resort. It's also possible to have money wired directly from a bank in your home country to a bank in South Africa, although this is somewhat less reliable because it involves two separate institutions. If you go this route, your home bank will need the address of the branch bank where you want to pick up the money and the address and telex number of the head office, which acts as the clearing house. Money wired this way normally takes two working days to arrive, and costs around £25/$40 per transaction.

Money-wiring companies

Travelers Express/MoneyGram UK, Ireland, Australia and New Zealand ☎ +800/666 3947, US ☎ 1-800/666-3947, Canada ☎ 1-800/933-3278, ⓦ www.moneygram.com.
Western Union UK ☎0800/833 833, Republic of Ireland ☎66/947 5603, US and Canada ☎1-800/CALL-CASH, Australia ☎1800/501 500, New Zealand ☎0800/005 253, ⓦwww .westernunion.com (customers with US or Canadian credit and debit cards can send money online).

Getting around

Despite the large distances, travelling around most of South Africa is fairly straightforward, with a well-organized network of public transport, a good range of car rental companies, the best road system in Africa, and the continent's most comprehensive network of internal flights. The only weak point is public transport in urban areas, which is almost universally poor and often dangerous. Urban South Africans who can afford to do so tend to use private transport, and if you plan to spend any time in any one town you'd be well advised to do the same. It's virtually impossible to get to the national parks and places off the beaten track by public transport; even if you do manage, you'll most likely need a car once you're there. For information on transport in Lesotho and Swaziland, see the relevant chapters in the Guide.

Buses

South Africa's three established intercity bus companies are **Greyhound**, **Intercape** and **Translux**; between them, they reach most towns in the country. Travel on these buses (commonly called **coaches**) is safe, good value and very comfortable, the vehices invariably equipped with air conditioning and toilets. Fares vary according to distances covered and the time of year, with peak fares corresponding approximately to school holidays; at other times you can expect about thirty percent off. As a rough indication you can expect to pay the following fares from Cape Town: to Paarl, R100 (50km); Mossel Bay, R120 (389km); Port Elizabeth, R250 (738km); East London, R350 (1034km); Umtata, R400 (1214km); and to Durban, R475 (1532km).

If you plan to make several long journeys, it's worth investing in a **Greyhound Travel Pass**, for which you'll have to fill in a form at one of Greyhound's offices. The pass offers seven days' unlimited travel on Greyhound services over a thirty-day period (at a cost of around R1400); fifteen days over thirty days (R2700); or thirty days over sixty days (R4500). Each journey you make with the pass earns you points that can eventually buy you a free bus journey. At the time of writing Translux was planning a similar system of passes.

Baz Bus operates an extremely useful hop-on/hop-off system aimed at backpackers and budget travellers, with intercity buses stopping off at backpacker accommodation en route. Its services run up and down the coast in both directions between Cape Town and Port Elizabeth (1 daily), and between Port Elizabeth and Durban (5 weekly). Inland, it runs buses between Durban and Johannesburg plus Pretoria, operating either via an overnight stop at Manzini in Swaziland (3 weekly), or via the Drakensberg (3 weekly). The only drawback of using the Baz buses, apart from occasionally erratic timing, is that the people you'll meet on them will almost exclusively be other backpackers, rather than locals.

English/Afrikaans street names

Many towns have **bilingual street names** with English and Afrikaans alternatives sometimes appearing along the same road. This applies particularly in Afrikaans areas away from the large cities, where direct translations are sometimes used. Often the Afrikaans name will bear little resemblance to the English one, something it's worth being aware of when trying to map read. Some terms you may encounter on Afrikaans signage are listed in "Language" (see p.932).

MAIN INTERCITY BUS ROUTES

As well as the major bus companies, there is a national network of inexpensive buses, some of which are operated by Translux's sister company Transcity (sometimes called Transtate), others by a host of small private companies. Though Translux offers some information about the Transcity service, it's difficult to get much information about the rest of these bus services from travel agents and tourist offices; your best bet is to enquire at the bus station the day before you travel. Apart from saving money, travelling on these buses enables you to meet black South African travellers, who are distinctly thin on the ground on the luxury coaches.

Intercity bus companies

Baz Bus ☎021 439 2323, ⊛www.bazbus.com. Bookings can also be made through hostels or the Baz offices at the central tourist offices in Cape Town or Durban.

Greyhound ⊛www.greyhound.co.za.
Bloemfontein ☎051 447 1558; Cape Town ☎083 915 9000; Durban ☎031 334 9700;

Johannesburg ☎011 276 8500; Port Elizabeth ☎041 363 4555.

Intercape ☎0861 287 287, ⊛www.intercape.co.za.

Translux Central reservations Johannesburg ☎011 774 3333, ⊛www.translux.co.za; also Cape Town ☎021 449 3333; Durban ☎031 308 8111; East London ☎043 700 1999; Port Elizabeth ☎041 392 1333.

Minibus taxis

Minibus taxis travel absolutely everywhere in South Africa, covering relatively short hops from town to town, commuter trips from township to town and back, and routes within larger towns and cities. However, the problems associated with them – unroadworthy vehicles, dangerous drivers and violent feuds between the different taxi associations competing for custom – mean that you should take local advice before using them. This is particularly true in cities, where minibus taxi ranks tend to be a magnet for petty criminals. The other problem with minibus taxis is that there is rarely much room to put luggage.

However, despite the drawbacks, don't rule out using this form of transport altogether. The government is in the process of regulating the industry, which should help things somewhat in future. And short of renting a car, minibus taxis will often be your only option for getting around in remote areas, where you're unlikely to encounter trouble. You should, however, be prepared for some long waits.

Fares are very low and comparable to what you might pay on the inexpensive intercity buses. Try to have the exact change (on shorter journeys particularly), and pass your fare to the row of passengers in front of you; eventually all the fares end up with the conductor, who dishes out any change. No passes for minibus taxis are available.

Trains

Travelling by train is just about the slowest way of getting around South Africa: the journey from Johannesburg to Cape Town, for example, takes 29 hours – compared with 19 hours by bus. Overnighting on the train does at least save you the cost of accommodation elsewhere, and if you want to you use your own car in both cities but can't face the long drive between them, note that you can actually transport your car on the train. Families with children get their own private compartment on the train, and under-5s travel free. Even with these perks, you'd really need to be a bit of a stalwart for the 36-hour journey between Cape Town and Durban.

Spoornet (℡086 000 8888, ⊛www .spoornet.co.za) runs most of the intercity rail services. Their standard service, Shosholoza Meyl, offers **Sleeper Four** (first-class) and **Sleeper Six** (second-class) travel, in compartments equipped with washbasins. The principal distinction between the two classes is that, as their names suggest, one accommodates up to six people, while the other sleeps a maximum of four and tends to be quieter. **Coupés**, which take two people in Sleeper Four, are ideal if you're travelling as a couple. **Sitter** (third class) travel is pretty crammed and uncomfortable.

The seats in the sleeper classes are comfortable and convert into bunks which offer the real possibility of getting a good night's sleep at night. If you don't have a sleeping bag, you can rent fresh cotton sheets and blankets for the night, which are brought around by a bedding attendant who'll make up your bed in the evening. It's best to buy your bedding voucher when you book your train ticket.

Fares in Sleeper Four are just under R500 from Johannesburg to Cape Town, with Sleeper Four tickets costing just under R350. Tickets must be booked in advance at train stations or at Spoornet offices in the large cities.

A word of warning about **security** on trains: as thieves work the stations, especially around Gauteng, don't leave your valuables unattended in your compartment unless you have some way of locking it and, even so, make sure you close the window if leaving the carriage for a while. This may mean you won't want to eat in the dining car, so it can be worth bringing your own food and drink, although someone usually comes round selling tea or coffee once or twice during the journey.

South Africa offers a handful of **luxury trains**, worth considering if you want to travel in plush surroundings – often through wonderful scenery – and don't mind paying through the nose for the privilege. Spoornet's celebrated **Blue Train** runs between Cape Town and Pretoria, and between Cape Town and Port Elizabeth, the latter being the only passenger rail service on this route. The full Pretoria–Cape Town fare is a tad under R10,000 per person sharing a double berth for the 29-hour journey. Passengers must be dressed in "smart casual" clothes during the day, and appear in formal wear for the evening meal. You can reserve a seat on this popular train by booking through Blue Train's central reservations in Pretoria (℡012 334 8459, www.bluetrain .co.za) or the Cape Town reservations office (℡021 449 2672).

Another luxury rail option is offered by **Rovos Rail** (Cape Town ℡021 421 4020, Pretoria ℡012 315 8242, ⊛www.rovos .co.za), which runs trips on four routes: from Cape Town to Pretoria (R22,000 for two) and George (R15,000); from Pretoria to Durban (R25,000) and from Pretoria to Victoria Falls in Zimbabwe (R24,500).

Domestic flights

Flying between destinations in South Africa is an attractive option if time is short. While it's not particularly cheap, it compares favourably with the money you'll spend covering long distances in a rental car, stopping over at places en route.

By far the biggest airline offering domestic flights is **South African Airways** (SAA), with its two associates **SA Airlink** and **SA Express** (reservations for the three go through SAA). There are a number of smaller airlines, of which the most significant are **British Airways Comair** and its budget subsidiary **Kulula.com**. Other budget airlines include **Nationwide**, which has a fairly extensive network, and **1Time**, which only flies from Johannesburg to Cape Town and Durban.

On SAA and its associates, expect to pay just under R1500 for a one-way tourist-class **fare** from Johannesburg to Cape Town, or from Cape Town to Durban. The Johannesburg–Cape Town route has become particularly cheap since the arrival of kulula.com, which offers one-way fares as low as R500, with new airline-on-the-block 1Time trying to undercut the rest.

None of the airlines offers **discounts** for students or pensioners though, subject to availability, hefty discounts can be expected for booking two weeks ahead on SAA or BA Comair. Booking through travel agents can be a good idea, as they should be able to fish around for the best deals overall.

South African domestic airlines

1Time ☎0861 345 345, ⊛www.1time.co.za. Budget flights from Johannesburg to Cape Town, East London and Durban.
British Airways Comair Cape Town ☎021 936 9000, Durban ☎031 450 7000, Johannesburg ☎011 921 0222, Port Elizabeth ☎041 508 8000. ⊛www.ba.com/travel/home/public/en_za. Flights from Johannesburg to Cape Town, Port Elizabeth and Durban; and from Cape Town to Durban.
kulula.com ☎0861 585 852, ⊛www.kulula.com. Budget flights from Johannesburg to Cape Town, Durban, Port Elizabeth and George; and between Cape Town and Durban.
Nationwide ☎0861 737 737, ⊛www .flynationwide.co.za. Budget flights from Johannesburg to Cape Town, Nelspruit (for Kruger

National Park), Durban, Port Elizabeth and George; Cape Town to Port Elizabeth and Durban; and between Port Elizabeth and Durban.
South African Airways. Central reservations ☎0861 359 722 (daily 5am–11pm), ⊛www .flysaa.com. Together with SA Airlink and SA Express, they serve the major hubs of Johannesburg, Cape Town and Durban. Among other destinations served are Bloemfontein, East London, George, Hoedspruit Kimberley, Margate, Mmabatho, Nelspruit (for Kruger), Phalaborwa, Pietermaritzburg, Plettenberg Bay, Polokwane (Pietersburg), Sun City, Ulundi, Umtata and Upington.

Driving

Short of joining a tour, the only way to get to national parks and remoter coastal areas is by car. Likewise, some of the most interesting places off the beaten track are only accessible in your own vehicle, as buses tend to ply just the major routes.

South Africa is ideal for driving, with a generally well-maintained network of highways and a high proportion of secondary and tertiary roads which are tarred and can be driven at speed. **Renting a vehicle** is not prohibitively expensive and, for a small group, it can work out a cheap option.

Virtually every rental car will take cheaper **unleaded petrol**, which with leaded petrol is available countrywide. **Filling stations** are frequent on the major routes of the country, and usually open 24 hours a day. Off the major routes, though, stations are less frequent, so fill up whenever you get the chance. Stations are rarely self-service; instead, poorly paid attendants fill up your car, check oil, water and tyre pressure if you ask them to, and often clean your windscreen even if you don't. A tip of R3–5 is always appreciated.

Regulations and driving tips

Foreign **driving licences** are valid in South Africa for up to six months provided they are printed in English. If you don't have such a licence, you'll need to get an International Driving Permit (available from national motoring organizations) before arriving in South Africa. When driving, make sure you have your driving licence and passport on you at all times.

You drive on the **left-hand side**; **speed limits** range from 60kph in built-up areas to 100kph on rural roads and 120kph on highways and major arteries. In addition to roundabouts, which follow the British rule of giving way to the right, there are **four-way stops**, where the rule is that the person who got there first leaves first, and you are not expected to give way to the right. Note that traffic lights are called **robots** in South Africa.

The only real challenge you'll face on the roads is **other drivers**. South Africa has among the world's worst road accident statistics – the result of reckless driving, drunken drivers (see p.81) or defective, overloaded vehicles. Keep your distance from cars in front, as domino-style pile-ups are common. Watch out also for overtaking traffic coming towards you. Overtakers often assume that you will head for the hard shoulder to avoid an accident (it is legal to drive on the hard shoulder, but be careful as poor South Africans frequently walk on the hard shoulder). If you do pull into the hard shoulder to let a car overtake, the other driver will probably thank you by flashing the hazard lights. If oncoming cars flash their headlights at you, it probably means that there is a speed trap up ahead.

Other potential **hazards** include animals on the road in rural areas. The problem can be especially dangerous at night, so drive slowly at that time. Finally, the large **distances** between major towns means that falling asleep at the wheel, especially when travelling through long stretches of flat landscape in the Karoo or the Free State, is a real danger. Plan your car journeys carefully to include plenty of breaks and stopovers. Driving in Johannesburg, you risk the danger of being **car-jacked**; see p.598 for safety hints.

Motoring organizations

South Africa

Automobile Association (AA) ☎0800 01 01 01, ⓦwww.aasa.co.za.

UK and Ireland

AA ☎0800/444 500, ⓦwww.theaa.com.
AA Travel Dublin ☎01/617 9988, ⓦwww .aaireland.ie.
RAC ☎0800/550 055, ⓦwww.rac.co.uk.

US and Canada

American Automobile Association (AAA) ☎1-800/222-4357, ⓦwww.aaa.com. Each state has its own club – check the phone book for local details.
Canadian Automobile Association (CAA) ☎613/247-0117, ⓦwww.caa.com. Each region has its own club – check the phone book for local details.

Australia and New Zealand

AAA Australia ☎02/6247 7311, ⓦwww.aaa.asn.au.
New Zealand AA New Zealand ☎0800/500 444, ⓦwww.nzaa.co.nz.

Car rental

Prebooking your rental car with a travel agent before flying out is the cheapest option, and will provide more favourable terms and conditions (such as unlimited mileage and lower insurance excesses). Don't rely on being able to just arrive at the airport and pick up a vehicle without reserving in advance, as the rental firms do run out of cars, especially during the week.

As a rough guideline, for a one-week rental you can expect to **pay** upwards of R1800 (£150/US$280) including ninety percent collision damage and theft waivers, as well as about 1400 free kilometres. Most companies stipulate that drivers must be a **minimum age** of 23 and must have been driving for two years at least. Note that to collect your vehicle, you will need to produce a credit (not debit) card.

The advantage of renting through major companies is that you don't have to return the car to where you hired it, but can deposit it in some other major centre instead – though rental companies usually levy a charge for this. If you're planning to drive into **Lesotho** and **Swaziland**, check that the company allows it – some don't. Insurance often doesn't cover you if you drive off the road surface, so check for this too. Local firms are almost always cheaper than chains, but usually have restrictions on how far you can take the vehicle.

Camper vans and **4WD vehicles** equipped with rooftop tents can be a good idea for getting to remote places where accommodation is scarce. Expect to pay around R1300 (£115/US$210) per day for a vehicle that sleeps two. Some companies offer standby rates that knock fifteen to twenty percent off the price if you book at short notice (one week or less ahead). Vans come fully equipped with crockery, cutlery and linen and usually a toilet. The downside of camper vans and 4WDs is that they struggle up hills and guzzle a lot of fuel (15 litres per 100km in the smaller vans), which could partly offset any savings on accommodation.

Rental agencies

South Africa

Avis ☎0861 021 111, ⓦwww.avis.co.za.
Britz Africa Johannesburg ☎011 396 1860; with branches in Cape Town (☎021 982 5107) and Durban (☎031 702 9326); ⓦwww.britz.co.za. One of the biggest rental outlets for camper vans and 4WDs, they will pick you up from the airport and return you for about R100 each way.
Budget ☎0861 016 622, ⓦwww.budget.co.za.
Drive Africa Cape Town ☎021 447 1144, ⓦwww.driveafrica.co.za. Competitive motorhome deals. If you're planning to be on the road for three months or longer, consider their rental–purchase agreement, under which you buy a car and they guarantee to buy it back for an agreed price.
Europcar ☎0800 011 344, ⓦwww.europcar.co.za.
Hertz ☎0861 600 136, ⓦwww.hertz.co.za.
Imperial ☎0861 131 000, ⓦwww .imperialcarrental.co.za.
National ☎0800 011 323, ⓦwww.nationalcar.co.za.
Tempest ☎0860 031 666, ⓦwww .tempestcarhire.co.za.

UK

Avis ☎0870/606 0100, ⓦwww.avisworld.com.
Budget ☎01442/276 266, ⓦwww.go-budget.co.uk.
Europcar ☎0870/607 5000, ⓦwww.europcar.co.uk.
Hertz ☎0870/844 8844, ⓦwww.hertz.co.uk.
Holiday Autos ☎0870/400 0099, ⓦwww .holidayautos.co.uk.
National ☎0870/536 5365, ⓦwww.nationalcar .co.uk.

Republic of Ireland

Avis ☎021/428 1111, ⓦwww.avis.ie.
Budget ☎09/0662 7711, ⓦwww.budget.ie.
Europcar ☎01/614 2888, ⓦwww.europcar.ie.
Hertz ☎01/676 7476, ⓦwww.hertz.ie.
Holiday Autos ☎01/872 9366, ⓦwww .holidayautos.ie.

US and Canada

Avis US ☎1-800/230-4898, Canada ☎1-800/272-5871, ⓦwww.avis.com.

Budget US ☎1-800/527-0700, Canada ☎1-800/472-3325, ⓦwww.budget.com.
Hertz US ☎1-800/654-3131, Canada ☎1-800/263-0600, ⓦwww.hertz.com.
National ☎1-800/962-7070, ⓦwww.nationalcar .com.

Australia

Avis ☎13 63 33 or 02/9353 9000, ⓦwww.avis .com.au.
Budget ☎1300/362 848, ⓦwww.budget.com.
Hertz ☎13 30 39 or 03/9698 2555, ⓦwww.hertz .com.au.
National ☎13 10 45, ⓦwww.nationalcar.com.au.

New Zealand

Avis ☎09/526 2847 or 0800/655 111, ⓦwww .avis.co.nz.
Budget ☎09/976 2222 or 0800/652-227, ⓦwww.budget.co.nz.
Hertz ☎0800/654 321, ⓦwww.hertz.co.nz.
National ☎0800/800 115 or 03/366-5574, ⓦwww.nationalcar.co.nz.

Cycling

It's easy to see why **cycling** is popular in South Africa: you can get to stunning destinations on good roads unclogged by traffic, many towns have decent cycle shops for spares and equipment, and an increasing number of backpacker hostels rent out mountain bikes for reasonable rates, making it easy to do plenty of cycling without having to transport your bike into the country. You'll need to be fit though, as South Africa is a hilly place, and many roads have punishing gradients. The weather can make life difficult, too: if it isn't raining, there is a good chance of it being very hot, so carry plenty of liquids. Cycling on the main roads is not recommended.

Hitching

Generally speaking, **hitching** in most areas of South Africa is not a good idea, particularly in large towns and cities. Even in rural areas it's risky and, while you might encounter wonderful hospitality and interesting companions, it's generally advisable not to hitch at all.

If you must hitchhike, avoid hitching alone and being dropped off in isolated areas between *dorps*. Ask drivers where they are going before you say where you want to go, and keep your bags with you: having them locked in the boot makes a hasty escape more difficult. Check the notice boards in backpacker lodges for people offering or looking to share lifts – that way, you can meet the driver in advance.

Accommodation

Relative to what's on offer in other developing countries, accommodation in South Africa may seem expensive, but standards are generally extremely high and you get exceptional bang for your buck. Even the most modest backpacker lodge will provide a minimum of fresh sheets and clean rooms. Other than in the very cheapest rooms, a private bath or shower are almost always provided, and you'll often have the use of a garden or swimming pool. You're in luck if you're looking for something special as South Africa has some outstanding boutique hotels, luxury guesthouses and country retreats – invariably in beautiful settings – at fairly reasonable prices by First World standards. The country's national parks and reserves themselves feature a range of accommodation, from fairly basic restcamps to incredibly slick game lodges; for more on these, see p.71. There's information on Lesotho and Swaziland accommodation in the relevant Guide chapters.

The continuing growth in **backpacker accommodation** means that you'll find a hostel in most areas, and many offer excellent facilities. For **camping and self-catering**, you'll be spoilt for choice. This is the preferred form of holiday accommodation of South Africans themselves, and the country is well supplied with camping resorts and self-catering apartments and cottages, as well as caravan parks.

Advance booking is vital if you plan to stay in a national park or in popular areas such as Cape Town or the Garden Route, or if you're travelling in the high season. South Africa's peak season is during the midsummer **Christmas school holiday** period, which coincides with many foreign tourists piling in to catch their winter tan. The **Easter school holiday** is a less intense period, when South African families migrate to the coast and inland resorts. At both Christmas and Easter, prices for budget and mid-priced accommodation (but not backpacker lodges or camping) can double, and most places get booked up months ahead. For more on the school holidays, see p.70.

There's a lull in the midwinter **low season** (June–Aug), during which time you should have no problem finding plenty of good-value places to stay, often with hefty discounts. This is the best time to go on safari in the Kruger National Park or KwaZulu-Natal, with prices at their lowest and with malarial mosquitoes dormant, temperatures moderate and the game viewing at its finest.

There are a couple of useful printed resources for finding accommodation in South Africa. Roger and Kay's Travel Selection (℡021 715 7130, ⊛www.travelselection.co.za) produces a South African accommodation guide listing a fair number of properties in Cape Town (rooms R125–300 per person per night) – choose your place and book directly with the host. The booklet is available online or free from South African Tourism offices worldwide. Also available free at tourist offices are Portfolio Online Reservations' (℡021 689 4020, ⊛www.portfoliocollection.com) useful series of booklets, including Portfolio B&B Collection, in which entries are essentially adverts paid for by the establishments

Accommodation price codes

All the accommodation listed in the Guide has been categorized into one of nine price bands, as set out below. These represent what you can expect to pay for much of the summer **per person**, and are usually based on the rate for **two sharing** a room, apartment or cottage. We've also used a price code in place of giving the rand price of **dorm beds**.

Expect rates in some areas to be significantly higher in peak season (Dec–Jan and Easter), and look out for discounts during the winter.

❶ **Up to R100** Doubles at backpackers' lodges, with shared washing and cooking facilities.

❷ **R100–200** Self-catering accommodation on farms, at resorts and in towns, and the simpler B&Bs in less touristy areas; also covers the most basic national park accommodation in *rondavels* or safari tents with shared washing and cooking facilities.

❸ **R200–300** Good B&Bs across the country, including some in popular areas; most township homestays; en-suite self-catering national park cottages for couples or families.

❹ **R300–400** Better than average guesthouses – and the odd hotel – featuring spacious rooms, gardens with swimming pools, the occasional Jacuzzi, first-class service and above-average food.

❺ **R400–500** Luxury accommodation in country retreats in beautiful settings, or in exceptional guesthouses; also covers the starting prices at the better chain hotels.

❻ **R500–750** Even greater luxury in the form of larger suites, exceptional locations, great style and details such as underfloor heating.

❼ **R750–1000** The final frontier of luxury in guesthouses; also some topnotch boutique hotels, as well as safari lodges and bush camps on game farms or on small private reserves.

❽ **R1000–2000** Standard rooms at South Africa's top hotels, plus mid-range (but pretty luxurious) safari lodges in the sought-after private reserves in Big Five country (such as the Kruger National Park), including full board and game-viewing activities.

❾ **Over R2000** Luxury suites at the top hotels, and accommodation at the most expensive private Big Five game lodges.

listed. Stringent selection criteria make the listings pretty reliable. For websites offering online bookings, see box on p.60.

Hotels

Most of South Africa's cheaper **hotels** are throwbacks to the 1950s and 1960s. Many have degenerated into watering holes, earning most of their keep from the bar, and are being left behind by the growing profusion of guesthouses and B&Bs. Hotels are really only worth considering at the middle to the top end of the scale, and then only if you want plenty of facilities and luxurious accommodation.

At the **bottom end** you can expect unremarkable en-suite rooms from around R120 per person. In smaller places off the tourist routes, you'll often have a choice of one or two hotels of this type, rarely good value. There are exceptions of course – hotels with real charm in *dorps* where you'd least expect them – and we've included many of these in this guide.

Mid-range hotels usually charge R250–500 per person, and you can expect decent – frequently excellent – standards, often in old and characterful refurbished buildings. Along the coastal holiday strips such as the Garden Route and southern KwaZulu-Natal and all the major seaside towns in between, these hotels are ubiquitous and frequently offer rooms right on the beachfront. Many hotels in this category are comparable to similarly priced guesthouses, but they offer an acceptable alternative if you prefer hotel anonymity and facilities such as room service and a private telephone. Many of the mid-priced hotels – especially those on main routes in the interior – are fully booked during the week by travelling salesmen, but over the weekend, when they're often empty, you can usually negotiate reasonable discounts.

Prices at **upmarket** hotels start at R600. The main upmarket hotel **chains** include Holiday Inn and Southern Sun (both Ⓦwww .southernsun.com), Protea (Ⓦwww .protea-hotels.co.za) and Three Cities (Ⓦwww.threecities.co.za), all of which offer reliable but rather soulless accommodation. For the same money, you may be better off at one of the many pleasant country hotels with beautiful gardens tucked away in scenic parts of the country, such as the Garden Route and the KwaZulu-Natal Midlands.

It's worth noting the idiosyncratic demand of many of South Africa's posher hotels for **"smart casual"** wear after 6pm. The directive applies mainly to men, and in practice means you'll need a pair of slacks, a decent shirt with a collar and closed shoes.

B&Bs, guesthouses and farmstays

More and more South Africans are opening their homes to visitors, and in some places you'll be spoilt for choice. The most basic **B&B** consists of just one or two rooms inside a house, where you share washing facilities with the owners and pay around R150 per person. Far more common are B&Bs with en-suite rooms, often in garden cottages or annexes to the main house, and frequently with tea-making facilities and the use of a garden; for these you can expect to pay around R200–500.

For decades the homes of black South Africans were deliberately kept hidden from tourist trails, a situation that has changed dramatically with the proliferation of township tours. Since the late 1990s, township dwellers have begun offering accommodation, opening up new possibilities for experiencing South Africa. **Township B&Bs** are still few in number, but we've tried to cover as many as possible in the Guide; expect to pay R200 per person per night for this type of accommodation. There is no precise dividing line between a B&B and a **guesthouse** and the two terms tend to be used interchangeably.

Along many roads in the countryside you will see signs for "Bed en Ontbyt" (Afrikaans for "bed and breakfast"), signalling **farmstay** accommodation. These offer rooms in the main homestead or in a cottage in its garden, and you can usually expect a hearty Afrikaner breakfast and prices a

---

Booking accommodation online

There's no single website that dominates the online booking of South African accommodation. The websites listed below cover distinct (sometimes overlapping) niches. Many of the larger operators allow online booking through their websites, listed in the Guide.

Capestay Ⓦwww.capestay.co.za. One of the best online resources for all types of accommodation in the Western Cape.

Portfolio online Ⓦwww.portfoliocollection.co.za. The industry leader in select accommodation, with B&Bs, country places and retreats.

SA Venues Ⓦwww.sa-venues.com. Accommodation throughout South Africa as well as Botswana and Namibia.

South African Hotels Ⓦwww.yaysouthafrica.com. Mainly hotels, but also some B&Bs and self-catering accommodation, searchable by region.

Southern Africa Places Ⓦwww.places.co.za. B&Bs, guesthouses and hotels throughout South Africa.

Where to Stay Ⓦwww.wheretostay.co.za. One of the most substantial directories of accommodation in all categories.

little below those of urban B&Bs. Some offer hiking, horse-riding, and other activities and excursions – there are some real gems dotted about, which we've listed in this Guide. Tourist offices almost always have lists of farms in the area that rent out rooms or cottages.

Caravan parks, resorts and camping

Caravanning was once the favourite way of enjoying a cheap family holiday in South Africa, and this accounts for the very large number of **caravan parks** dotted across the length and breadth of the country. However, their popularity has declined and with it the standard of many of the country's **municipal** caravan parks and campsites. Today, municipal campsites are generally pretty scruffy places, though you may find the odd pleasant one in rural areas, or near small *dorps*. Staying in a municipal campsite adjoining a city or large town is often more grief than it's worth; not only will facilities generally be run-down, but theft is a big risk. Most municipal sites charge roughly £5/US$8 per tent.

All in all, you're best off heading for the **privately owned resorts**, where for roughly the same price you get greater comfort. Although private resorts sometimes give off a holiday-camp vibe, they usually provide good washing and cooking facilities, self-catering chalets, shops selling basic goods, braai stands and swimming pools.

Virtually all **national parks** in the country – and many provincial reserves – have campsites and in some of the really remote places, such as parts of KwaZulu-Natal, camping may be your only option. Use of a campsite is unlikely to cost more than £10/US$15. At national parks you can expect well-maintained washing facilities and there are often communal kitchen areas or at the very least a braai stand and running water, as well as decent communal shower, toilet and washing facilities (known locally as "ablutions").

Camping rough is not recommended anywhere in the country; with so many official campsites, even in very remote areas, it's very unlikely you'll have to pitch a tent anywhere else.

Backpacker lodges and youth hostels

Backpacker lodges comprise the fastest-growing category of accommodation in South Africa, and their quality is improving all the time. Most offer basic hostel accommodation in a dormitory for under £7/US$12 per person, and many have some double rooms, which cost a little more. They usually have communal kitchens, an on-site restaurant or café, TV, Internet access and bike rental.

The lodges are invariably good meeting points, with a constant stream of travellers passing through, and useful notice boards filled with advertisements for hostels and backpacker facilities throughout the country. Many lodges operate reasonably priced excursions into the surrounding areas, and will pick you up from train stations or bus stops (especially Baz Bus stops) if you phone in advance. The only drawback with this kind of accommodation is that you tend to meet the same people over and over again as you travel around.

South Africa's **youth hostel** scene is on the small side, with around thirty backpackers' lodges affiliated to Hostelling International South Africa (HISA), part of the Hostelling International (HI) network. These are located in all the major tourist centres, and accommodation at some of the hostels can be booked and paid for through HI offices in your country or on the Internet. HI membership provides ten percent discounts at member hostels (which are vetted annually to maintain standards), as well as reductions on car rental, buses and a number of other facilities, which are detailed on HISA's website.

Youth hostel associations

South Africa

Hostelling International South Africa (HISA)
73 St George's Mall, Third floor, St George's House, Cape Town ☏ 021 424 2511, ⦿ www.hisa.org .za. Annual membership R60 (no age limit) can be taken out through the head office, any member hostel or via the website, and is valid throughout the world. Life membership, which is restricted to South Africans, costs R300.

England and Wales

Youth Hostel Association (YHA) ☎0870/770 8868, ⓦwww.yha.org.uk. Annual membership £13.50; under-18s £6.70; lifetime £195 (or five annual payments of £41).

Scotland

Scottish Youth Hostel Association ☎0870/155 3255, ⓦwww.syha.org.uk. Annual membership £6, for under-18s £2.50.

Ireland

Irish Youth Hostel Association ☎01/830 4555, ⓦwww.irelandyha.org. Annual membership €25; under-18s €10.50; family €50; lifetime €75.
Hostelling International Northern Ireland ☎028/9032 4733, ⓦwww.hini.org.uk. Adult membership £13; under-18s £6; family £25; life £75.

USA

Hostelling International-American Youth Hostels ☎301/495-1240, ⓦwww.hiayh.org. Annual membership for adults (18–55) is $28, for seniors (55 or over) is $18, and for under-18s and groups of ten or more, is free. Life memberships are $250.

Canada

Hostelling International Canada ☎1-800/663 5777 or 613/237 7884, ⓦwww.hihostels.ca. Membership is free for under-18s and you can become a lifetime member for Can$175; otherwise an individual membership is Can$35.

Australia

Australia Youth Hostels Association ☎02/9261 1111, ⓦwww.yha.com.au. Adult membership rate Aus$52 for the first twelve months (under-18s Aus$19) and then Aus$37 each year after.

New Zealand

Youth Hostelling Association New Zealand ☎0800/278 299 or 03/379 9970, ⓦwww.yha.co.nz. Adult membership NZ$40 for one year, NZ$60 for two and NZ$80 for three; under-18s free; lifetime NZ$300.

Self-catering cottages and apartments

Away from the resorts and caravan parks, **self-catering accommodation** in cottages, apartments and small complexes provides the cheapest option apart from staying in a backpackers' lodge. One of the best things about self-catering is the wide choice of location: there are self-catering places on farms, near beaches, in forests and in wilderness areas, as well as in practically every town and city.

Self-catering accommodation starts at about R120 per person per night for two people sharing. Apartments often sleep up to six, and because rates are mostly quoted for entire units, this can be very economical if you're travelling as a family or in a group. You can save a lot of money by cooking for yourself (breakfast is sometimes available for a small extra charge), and you'll get a sense of freedom and privacy missing from the nicest guesthouse or B&B. Standards are fairly high: cottages or apartments generally come fully equipped with crockery and cutlery, and even microwaves and TVs in the more modern places. Linen and towels are often provided; check before you book in.

Eating and drinking

South Africa doesn't really have a coherent indigenous cuisine, although attempts have been made to elevate Cape Cuisine to this status. The one element which seems to unite the country is a love of meat, and as a visitor you might struggle to keep in check the locals' assumption that meat and lots of it is the ideal choice for your meals. Having said that, South Africa is an ideal place to try out all kinds of interesting types of meat, from ostrich to giraffe, and good-quality steaks are inexpensive and freely available. Alternatively, it's well worth paying attention to South Africa's vast array of seafood, which includes a wide variety of fish, lobster (crayfish), oysters and mussels. Locally grown fruit and vegetables are generally of a high standard, and often available from markets and farm stalls in areas such as the Western Cape. Drinking is dominated by South Africa's often superb wines and by a handful of unmemorable lager beers. In the cities, and to a far less extent beyond them, there are numerous excellent restaurants where you can taste a spectrum of international styles.

Styles of cooking

Traditional African food tends to focus around stiff grain porridge called **mielie pap** or pap, made of maizemeal and accompanied by meat or vegetable-based sauces. Among white South Africans, Afrikaners have evolved a style of cooking known as **boerekos**, which can be heavy-going if you're not used to it. People of British extraction favour the traditional English meat and overcooked vegetables.

Some of the best-known South African foods are mentioned below, while there's a list of South African culinary terms, including other local foods, in the Language section on p.939.

Braais

Braai (which rhymes with "dry") is an abbreviation of *braaivleis*, an Afrikaans word translated as "meat grill". More than simply the process of cooking over an outdoor fire, however, a braai is a cultural event arguably even more central to the South African identity than barbecues are to Australians. Despite its identification as part of quintessential white South Africa, braais are now popular across the races, and at any national park, nature reserve or resort you'll never be far from the distinctive odour of gently sizzling meat. A braai is an intensely social event, usually among family and friends and accompanied by gallons of beer. It's also probably the only occasion you'll catch an unreconstructed white South African man cooking.

You can braai anything, but a traditional barbecue meal consists of huge slabs of steak, lamb cutlets and **boerewors** ("farmer's sausage"), a deliciously spicy South African speciality. The real skill comes in knowing when the coals are hot enough to cook the meat and in concocting the marinades and sauces – in fact, discussion on the topic vies with rugby as the subject of the most intense conversation around a braai. The usual accompaniment comprises potatoes and onions wrapped in aluminium foil and placed in the embers.

Potjiekos and boerekos

A variant on the braai is **potjiekos** – pronounced "poy-key-kos"– (pot food), in which the food is cooked, preferably outdoor over an open fire, in a three-legged cast-iron cauldron (the *potjie*). In a similar vein but cooked indoors is **boerekos**, (literally "farmer's food"), a style of cooking enjoyed mainly by Afrikaners. Much of it is similar to English food, but taken to cholesterol-rich extremes, with even the vegetables prepared with butter and

63

sugar. Should you spend the night on an Afrikaans farm, you could well find yourself waking up to a breakfast of several eggs, steak, piles of bacon and *boerewors*. *Boerekos* comes into its own in its variety of over-the-top desserts, including *koeksisters* (plaited doughnuts saturated with syrup) and *melktert* ("milk tart"), a solid rich custard in a flan case.

Cape Cuisine

Styles of cooking brought by Asian and Madagascan slaves have evolved into **Cape Cuisine** (sometimes known as Cape Malay food – a misnomer given that few slaves came from Malaysia). Characterized by mild, semi-sweet curries with strong Indonesian influences, Cape Cuisine is worth sampling at least once, especially in Cape Town, where it developed and is associated with the Muslim community. Dishes include *bredie* (stew), of which *waterblommetjiebredie*, made using water hyacinths, is a speciality; *bobotie*, a spicy minced dish served under a savoury custard; and *sosaties*, a local version of kebab using minced meat. For dessert, dates stuffed with almonds make a light and delicious end to a meal, while *malva* pudding is a rich combination of milk, sugar, cream and apricot jam.

Although Cape Cuisine can be delicious, there isn't that much variety and few restaurants specialize in it. Despite this, most of the dishes considered as Cape Cuisine have actually crept into the South African diet, many becoming part of the Afrikaner culinary vocabulary.

Other ethnic and regional influences

Although South Africa doesn't really have distinct regional cuisines, you will find changes of emphasis and local specialities in different parts of the country. **KwaZulu-Natal**, for instance, particularly around Durban and Pietermaritzburg, is especially good for Indian food. The South African contribution to this great multifaceted tradition is the humble **bunny chow**, a cheap takeaway consisting of a hollowed out half-loaf of white bread originally filled with curried beans, but nowadays with anything from curried chicken to sardines.

Vegetarian food

While not quite a **vegetarian** paradise, South Africa is nevertheless vegetarian-savvy and you'll find at least one concession to meatless food on most menus. Even steakhouses will have something palatable on offer and generally offer the best salad bars around – especially at the *Spur* chain, where you can fill up on greens for not much more than US$3/£1.50. If you're self-catering in the larger cities, delicious dips and breads can be found at delis and Woolworths and Pick 'n Pay supermarkets.

Portuguese food made early inroads into the country because of South Africa's proximity to Mozambique. The Portuguese influence is predominantly in the use of hot and spicy *peri-peri* seasoning, which goes extremely well with braais. The best-known example of this is delicious **peri-peri chicken**, which you will find all over. **Italian food** has also been around for a while, brought over with POWs from the North Africa campaign who were incarcerated in South Africa and stayed on after World War II. You'll find some excellent Italian restaurants in the cities, from small pizzerias to smarter restaurants going the whole hog. Eastern European **Jewish food** arrived with refugees at the turn of the last century and you'll find bagels, chopped liver and chopped herring at delis and some supermarkets.

Eating out

Restaurants in South Africa offer good value compared with Britain or North America. In every city you'll find places where you can eat a decent main course for under R60, while for R150 you can splurge on the best. All the cities and larger towns can boast some restaurants with imaginative menus. **Franschhoek**, a small town in the Winelands, has established itself as a culinary centre for the country, where you'll find some fine eating places in extremely close proximity. As a rule, restaurants are licensed, but Muslim establishments serving Cape Cuisine don't allow alcohol at all.

An attractive phenomenon in the big cities, especially Cape Town, has been the rise of continental-style **cafés** – easy-going places where you can eat just as well as you would in a regular restaurant, but also drink coffee all night without feeling obliged to order food. Service tends to be slick and friendly, and a reasonable meal in one of these cafés is unlikely to set you back more than R45. Don't confuse this new breed of café with traditional South African cafés, found in even the tiniest country town. The equivalent of corner stores elsewhere, they commonly sell a few magazines, soft drinks, sweets, crisps and an odd collection of tins and dry goods, though no sit-down meals. Their only concession to ready-to-eat food is normally a meat pie heated in a microwave, or a leg of chicken that spent a little too long incubating in the warmer.

If popularity is the yardstick, then South Africa's real national cuisine is to be found in its **franchise restaurants**, which you'll find in every town of any size. The usual international names like *KFC* and *Wimpy* are omnipresent, but these are no match for South Africa's own American-style steakhouses, such as *Spur*, which projects a wholesome Wild West image and remains popular with South African families. South Africa's great contribution to the world of fast food is the *Nando's Chickenland* chain, which grills excellent Portuguese-style chicken, served under a variety of spicy sauces. Expect to pay around R30 for a filling burger and chips or chicken meal at any of these places and around R45 for a good-sized steak.

Note that quite a few restaurants don't have well-defined hours of business, in which case we have stated in the Guide which meals they tend to open for. Phone numbers are given where booking a table might be a good idea.

Drinking

White South Africans tend to do their drinking at home, so for them pubs and bars are not the centres of social activity they are in the US or the UK, though in the African townships **shebeens** (informal bars) do occupy this role. Those **bars** that do exist in city centres have traditionally been rough,

men-only places, women being corralled into stiff lounges or ladies' bars attached to hotels. The **Irish/British-style pub** is beginning to make an appearance under the invasion of a series of franchised names, but has no deep roots in South African culture.

Beer, wines and spirits can be bought at supermarkets and bottle stores (the equivalent of the British off-licence), which generally keep normal shopping hours, although some stay open until 6.30pm. Don't expect be able to buy liquor at night or on Sundays.

There are no surprises when it comes to **soft drinks**, with all the usual names available. What does stand out is South African **fruit juice**, the range amounting to one of the most extensive selections of unsweetened juices in the world. One unusual drink you might well encounter in the country's tea rooms is locally produced **rooibos** tea, made from the leaves of an indigenous plant (see box on p.303).

Beer

Although South Africa yearns to be a major wine-producing country, **beer** is indisputably the national drink. Beer is as much an emblem of South African manhood as the braai – and, unlike the braai, it cuts across all racial and class divisions. South Africans tend to be fiercely loyal to their brand of beer, though they all taste pretty much the same, given that virtually all beer in the country is produced by the huge South African Breweries monopoly, one of the world's largest beer makers. It's given a good run for its money by Namibian Breweries, whose Windhoek Lager is rated by cognoscenti as better than SAB's offerings. **Lager** is the predominant style, likely to taste a bit thin and bland to a British palate, though it can be wonderfully refreshing drunk ice-cold on a sweltering day.

One or two **microbreweries** have sprung up, best known of which are Mitchell's in Knysna, which produces some distinctive ales, and Birkenhead in Stanford. These can be found at some bottle stores and bars between Cape Town and Port Elizabeth. **Imported beers** are expensive compared with the local product, with the exception of the great Czech Pilsner Urquell, which has been bought by SAB as part of its global expansion.

Wine

South Africa's **wine industry** has emerged out of years of sanction-enforced doldrums, casting aside a 350-year-old tradition of trying to make French wine, and nailed its colours to the fresh, fruity style of New World wines. Production is rising all the time to meet the demands of the ever-growing export market, and a number of South African winemakers are achieving international recognition with some excellent wines at prices few visitors from overseas are likely to grumble about.

In general, South Africa's **white** wines such as Sauvingon Blanc and Riesling are a slightly better quality overall than its red wines. Among the **reds** you should look out for wines made from the **Pinotage** grape, unique to South Africa. **Port** is also made, though connoisseurs of the Portuguese equivalent will struggle to recognize the over-sweet, over-sticky South African style. On the other hand, a handful of excellent **sparkling wines** are produced.

Wine is available throughout the country, although prices rise as you move out of the Western Cape. **Prices** for quaffable bottles start at R30 or below, and the vast bulk of wines cost less than R100 (anything over R85 is considered outrageously expensive by locals). All this means that anyone with an adventurous streak can indulge in a bacchanalia of sampling without breaking the bank.

The best way to sample wines is by visiting **wineries**, some of which charge a small tasting fee to discourage freeloading. The oldest and most rewarding wine-producing regions are the **Constantia estates** in Cape Town (see p.146) and the region known as the **Winelands** around the towns of Stellenbosch (see p.194), Paarl (see p.201) and Franschhoek (see p.207), which all have institutionalized wine routes. Other wine-producing areas include Robertson, the Orange River (see p.331) and Walker Bay (see p.247).

Communications

The deceptively familiar feel of South African post offices can lull you into expecting an efficient British- or US-style service. In fact, post within the country is slow and unreliable, and money and valuables frequently disappear en route.

Expect domestic delivery times from one city to another of about a week – longer if a rural town is involved at either end. **International airmail** deliveries are often quicker, especially if you're sending or receiving at Johannesburg, Cape Town or Durban – the cities with direct flights to London. A letter or package sent by surface mail can take anything up to six weeks to get from South Africa to London.

Most towns of any size have a **post office**, generally open Monday to Friday 8.30am to 4.30pm and Saturday 8am to 11.30am (closing earlier in some places). **Stamps** are available not only at post offices but also from newsagents, such as the CNA

chain, and postage is relatively inexpensive compared with Britain or North America. You'll find **poste restante** facilities at the main post office in most larger centres, and in many backpackers' hostels.

To send or receive important items, it makes sense to use one of the private **courier services** such as Federal Express, which are more expensive and available only in the larger towns, but far more reliable than the mail.

Phones

South Africa's telephone system, operated by the state monopoly, **Telkom**, generally works well. Public phone booths are found in every city and town, and many more are being installed in rural areas – a tangible result of the ANC government's policy of taking services to the people.

Telkom public phones are either coin-operated or card-operated. While international calls can be made from virtually any phone, it helps to have a phone card, as you'll be lucky to stay on the line for more than a minute or two for R20. Phone cards come in R15, R20, R50, R100 and R200 denominations, available at Telkom offices, post offices and newsagents.

The cheapest time to make **international calls** using Telkom is Monday to Friday 8pm to 8am and during the weekends. Collect or **reverse-charge calls** can be made from any phone through the International Operator Service (☎0900).

If you need to use the phone while staying at a **hotel**, be sure to ask what their rate is – the surcharge is often extortionate. In cities, you'll find **private phone bureaus**, where you can make your call on a normal phone and pay afterwards, but these cost considerably more than a Telkom phone booth. Some of these bureaus will also send and receive **faxes** for you. Many newsagents also offer fax services, advertised in their windows.

Mobile phones

South African cell phones operate on the GSM digital system. They're extremely well established in South Africa, with more mobile than land-line handsets now in use in the

Domestic phone numbers

Officially, any South African land line has a ten-digit number incorporating the old three-digit area code at the start. Since 2001, when this numbering system was introduced, Telkom has claimed that calling a land line requires you to dial all ten digits. However, at the time of writing in 2005, you could still omit the old area code if you were dialling a number with the same first three digits as the number you were calling from.

country. It's easy to spot a local cell-phone number: the first three digits are in the ☎072–074 or 082–084 ranges. The three competing networks, Vodacom, MTN and Cell C, cover all the main areas and the national roads connecting them. Cell-phone **rental** can be arranged at the airports in the main cities as well as through other providers in town.

You can use a GSM/tri-band phone from outside the country in South Africa, but you will need to arrange a **roaming agreement** with your provider at home; be warned this is likely to be expensive. A far cheaper alternative is to buy a **local SIM card** which replaces your home SIM card while you're in South Africa. (For this to work, you'll need to check that your phone hasn't been locked to your home network.) The local SIM card contains your South African phone number, and you pay for airtime with **prepaid cards**. Very inexpensive starter packs (R150 or less) containing a SIM card and some airtime can be bought from the ubiquitous mobile phone shops and a number of other outlets, including supermarkets and the CNA chain of newsagents and supermarkets.

Charge cards

One of the most convenient ways of phoning home from abroad is via a **telephone charge card**, which your home phone provider may supply. Using access codes for the particular country you are in and a PIN, you can make calls from most phones and charge the cost to your home account. Rates aren't necessarily cheaper than calling from a South African public phone, but since most major charge cards are free to obtain, it's certainly worth getting one at least for emergencies; enquire first though whether South Africa is covered.

Internet access

One of the best ways to keep in touch while travelling is by email. Internet access in South Africa is widespread: cybercafés are found even in relatively small towns, and most **backpacker hostels** have Internet and email facilities. On the downside, connecting with sites abroad can be slow.

Before leaving home, you should check whether your existing **email account** offers

Directory enquiries and international codes

Telkom operates an extremely useful **directory enquiry service** (☎1023). However, English is not the first language of many of the operators and, with standards of literacy quite a lot lower than in Europe or North America, be prepared to be patient and to help the operator with spelling. Also remember that the English accents people are accustomed to here may be very different to your own – so talk slowly and clearly.

International calls

To call Southern Africa **from overseas**, dial the international access code (☎00 from the UK and New Zealand; ☎011 from the USA and Canada; ☎0011 from Australia;) followed by one of the country codes below, then the number, remembering to leave out any initial zero.

South Africa ☎27　　　Lesotho ☎266　　　　　Swaziland ☎268

To dial **out of South Africa**, the international access code is ☎09. To dial **out of Lesotho and Swaziland**, the code is ☎00. Remember to omit any initial zero in the number of the place you're phoning.

Australia ☎61　　　　　Republic of Ireland ☎353　New Zealand ☎64

UK ☎44　　　　　　　　USA and Canada ☎1

a Web-based service that enables you to pick up your email from any computer online. Failing this, you can set up a **free** email address with, for example, Yahoo! (🌐www.yahoo.com) or Hotmail (🌐www .hotmail.com).

The media

South Africa's press is rather parochial, with one or two notable exceptions. Unlike Britain, the country lacks a strong tradition of national papers and instead has many regional papers of varying quality. Television delivers a mix of imported programmes and home-grown soaps heavily modelled on US fare, as well as the odd homegrown reality TV show and one or two watchable documentary slots.

Radio is where South Africa is finding it easiest to meet the needs of a diverse and scattered audience. Deregulation of the airwaves has brought to life scores of small new stations.

Newspapers

Of the roughly twenty **newspapers**, most of which are published in English or Afrikaans, the only ones that qualify as nationals are *Business Day* and *ThisDay* (both dailies) and the *Mail & Guardian*, the *Sunday Times* and the *Sunday Independent* (all weeklies). The

Mail & Guardian benefits enormously from its association with the London *Guardian* (from which it draws most of its international coverage); it's unquestionably the country's intellectual heavyweight, although its reporting can be a bit stodgy.

The *Sunday Times* can attribute the fact that it has the biggest circulation in the country – roughly half a million copies – to its well-calculated mix of solid investigative reporting, gossipy stories, material from the Britain's *Telegraph* newspapers and rewrites of salacious tales lifted from foreign tabloids. The *Sunday Independent* is part of the same stable as Britain's *Independent* newspapers and their Irish counterparts; it projects a more thoughtful image than the *Sunday Times*, but is beginning to look a bit thin, with almost all its foreign news lifted from its sister papers.

Of the English dailies, the *Star* in Johannesburg offers less than one might hope for from the mouthpiece of the country's economic hub. *Business Day*, with its solid coverage of local and international news as well as commerce, is South Africa's equivalent of the *Financial Times* or the *Wall Street Journal*. In a similar vein, *This Day* delivers serious national and international news.

The *Sowetan*, targeted at a mainly black Jo'burg audience, is widely available across the country and provides a less exclusively white perspective on South African issues.

Local papers are useful for event listings. In Cape Town you'll find the *Cape Times*, and the *Cape Argus*, sister paper to the *Star*, which identifies itself with issues local to the mother city. Durban brings out the *Daily News* and the *Natal Mercury* in the morning and evening, while Port Elizabeth offers the *Eastern Province Herald* – a tacky broadsheet with the heart of a tabloid. Finally, East London has the *Daily Dispatch*, an Eastern Cape paper packed with local news, which earned some fame in the 1970s for its sympathetic coverage of the black consciousness leader, Steve Biko.

The easiest places to buy newspapers are corner stores and newsagents, especially the CNA chain. These outlets also sell international publications such as *Time*, *Newsweek*, *The Economist* and the weekly overseas editions of the British *Daily Mail*, the *Telegraph* and the *Express*.

Television

The South Africa Broadcasting Corporation's three TV channels churn out a mixed bag of domestic dramas, game shows, soaps and documentaries, filled out with lashings of familiar imports. **SABC 1**, **2** and **3** share the unenviable task of trying to deliver an integrated service, while having to split their time between the eleven official languages.

English turns out to be most widely used, with SABC 3 broadcasting almost exclusively in the language, while SABC 2 and SABC 1 spread themselves thinly across all the remaining ten languages with a fair amount of English creeping in even here.

A selection of sports, movies, news and specialist channels are available to subscribers to the **M-Net** satellite service, which is piped into many hotels. South Africa's first and only free-to-air independent commercial channel **e.tv** won its franchise in 1998 on the promise of providing a showcase for local productions, a pledge it has signally failed to meet – its output has consisted substantially of uninspired and uninspiring imports.

Radio

Given South Africa's low literacy rate and widespread poverty, it's no surprise that **radio** is its most popular medium. The SABC operates a national radio station for each of the eleven official language groups. The English-language service, **SAfm**, is of a generally high standard; its best offerings are the polished evening and morning news programmes.

The SABC also runs **5FM Stereo**, a national pop station broadcasting Top 40 tracks, while their **Radio Metro** is targeted at black urban listeners. Apart from these, there are scores of regional, commercial and community stations, broadcasting a range of material, which makes surfing the airwaves an enjoyable experience, wherever you are in the country.

Foreign broadcasters

On shortwave, the **BBC World Service** (www.bbc.co.uk/worldservice for schedules and frequencies) gives wider coverage than local South African stations, and broadcasts some excellent programmes on its **Africa Service**. Reception can vary considerably; as a rule of thumb, the lower frequencies (below 7000kHz) tend to provide better reception from late afternoon and throughout the evening, while the higher ones are usually better during the day. Also audible are the broadcasts of **Radio Canada** (www.rcinet.ca), and the **Voice of America** (www.voa.gov).

Opening hours and public holidays

The working day starts and finishes early in South Africa: shops and businesses generally open on weekdays at 8.30am or 9am and close at 4.30pm or 5pm. In small towns, many places close for an hour over lunch. Many shops and businesses close around noon on Saturdays, and most shops are closed on Sundays. However, in every neighbourhood, you'll find small shops and supermarkets where you can buy groceries and essentials after hours.

Banking hours are generally Monday to Friday 8.30am to 3.30pm, Saturday 8am to 11am, but you'll find **bureaux de change** in the major cities open until at least 5pm (see "Listings" for each city for late openings) and open at the international airports to meet flights. Government departments are open 8am to 4pm weekdays.

Some establishments have summer and winter opening times. In such situations, you can take winter to mean April to August or September, while summer constitutes the rest of the year.

Holidays

School holidays in South Africa can disrupt your plans, especially if you want to camp, or stay in the national parks and the cheaper end of accommodation (self-catering, cheaper B&Bs, etc), all of which are likely to be booked solid during those periods. If you do travel to South Africa over the school holidays, book your accommodation well in advance, especially for the national parks.

The longest and busiest holiday period is **Christmas (summer)**, which for schools stretches from around December 4 to January 21. Flights and train berths can be hard to get from December 16 to January 2, when many businesses and offices close for their annual break. You should book your flights – long-haul and domestic – as early as six months in advance for the Christmas period. The inland and coastal provinces stagger their school holidays, but as a general rule the remaining school holidays cover the following periods: **Easter**, March 20 to April 15; **winter**, June 20 to July 21; and **spring**, September 19 to October 7.

South African public holidays

For public holidays in Lesotho and Swaziland, see p.769 and p.817.

New Year's Day January 1
Human Rights Day March 21
Good Friday, Easter Sunday, Easter Monday Variable
Freedom Day April 27
Workers' Day May 1
Youth Day June 16
National Women's Day August 9
Heritage Day September 24
Day of Reconciliation December 16
Christmas Day December 25
Day of Goodwill December 26

Parks, reserves and wilderness areas

No other African country has as rich a variety of parks, reserves and wilderness areas as South Africa. Literally hundreds of game reserves and state forests pepper the terrain, creating a bewildering but enticing breadth of choice. While there are dozens of unsung treasures among these, the big destinations amount to some two dozen parks geared to protecting the country's wildlife and wilderness areas.

With a few exceptions these fall under **Kwa-Zulu-Natal Wildlife** (PO Box 13069, Cascades, Pietermaritzburg 3202; ☎033 845 1000, ⓦwww.kznwildlife.com), which controls most of the public reserves in KwaZulu-Natal, and **South African National Parks** (SAN Parks; PO Box 787, Pretoria 0001; street address 643 Leyds St, Muckleneuk, Pretoria; ☎012 428 9111, ⓦwww.parks-sa.co.za), which covers the rest of the country. In addition to the state-run parks there are private reserves, frequently abutting onto them and sharing the same wildlife population.

It's important to realize that only some national parks are game reserves; the chart on p.72 details what to expect from the major parks. While most people come for South Africa's superb **wildlife**, don't let the **Big Five** (buffalo, elephant, leopard, lion and rhino) blinker you into missing out on the marvellous **wilderness areas** that take in dramatic landscapes and less-publicized animal life. There are parks protecting marine and coastal areas, wetlands, endangered species, forests, deserts and mountains, usually with the added attraction of assorted animals, birds, insects, reptiles or marine mammals – South Africa is one of the top destinations in the world for land-based whale watching.

Park fees, reservations and enquiries

Fees given in our park accounts are generally **conservation fees**, payable **daily**. The most expensive places are the Kruger National Park and Kgalagadi Transfrontier Park, for which foreign visitors pay a conservation fee of R120 per person. Elsewhere the conservation fee is generally R60 or R80. As a rule of thumb, foreign visitors aged 12 and under pay half the adult rate; South African citizens pay a quarter of the foreign adult fee, while citizens of the Southern Africa Development Community, to which many countries in the region belong, pay half the foreign adult fee.

If you're planning to visit several parks, you may well find it worthwhile to invest in the **Wild Card**, which provides unlimited access to SANParks-run parks for a period of a year. For foreign visitors, the pass costs R800 for an individual or R1400 for two people; there's also a family version covering two adults plus children up to the age of 18, priced at R1800. South Africans pay roughly two-thirds less for the corresponding passes, and have the additional option of buying passes specific to certain groups of parks. The pass is on sale at SANParks-run parks; for more details of the scheme, and to buy the pass online, check ⓦwww.wildinafrica.com.

Accommodation at most of South Africa's major national parks can be **booked** in advance (to stay in high season, do so several months in advance) through South African National Parks, except at Pilanesberg, for details of which see p.665, and the KwaZulu-Natal reserves, for which you book through KZN Wildlife. Note that if you try booking for South African National Parks over the phone you could well be in for a long wait; contacting them online is recommended. For more on national parks accommodation, see p.61.

Major parks and wildlife areas

KEY PARK	PRINCIPAL FOCUS	DESCRIPTION AND HIGHLIGHTS	DETAILS
Western Cape			
1 Agulhas NP	Marine and coastal	Rugged southernmost tip of Africa with rich plant biodiversity and significant archeological sites	p.251
2 Bontebok NP	Endangered species	At the foot of rugged mountains, it provides refuge to bontebok and Cape mountain zebra	p.239
3 Table Mountain NP (formerly Cape Peninsula NP)	The natural areas of the peninsula	Boasts extraordinarily rich and diverse flora and fauna that lives in the wild areas forming a large part of Cape Town, including Table Mountain, the Boulders Beach penguin colony and the Cape of Good Hope	p.148, p.159 & p.161
4 Karoo NP	Desert reserve	Arid mountainous landscape with ancient fossils, herbivores and wild flowers in spring	p.231
5 Knysna National Lake Area	Marine and coastal/ endangered species	Focused on the Knysna Lagoon and its dramatic Heads that open to the sea, the lake area protects the endangered Knysna seahorse	p.268
6 Tsitsikamma NP	Marine and coastal	Cliffs, tidal pools, deep gorges and evergreen forests; offers snorkelling, scuba and forest trails	p.286
7 West Coast NP	Marine and coastal	Wetland wilderness with birding and watersports	p.295
8 Wilderness NP	Marine and coastal	Lakes, rivers, lagoons, forest, fynbos, beaches and the sea	p.266
Eastern Cape			
9 Addo Elephant NP	Endangered species	The only Big Five national park in the southern half of the country, known for its 300-strong elephant herd	p.377
10 Mountain Zebra NP	Endangered species	Dramatic hilly landscape in flat country with rare mountain zebras and other herbivores	p.403
Northern Cape			
11 Augrabies Falls NP	Desert reserve	Notable for the dramatic landmark from which the park takes its name, where the Orange River plummets down a deep ravine; also great for desert scenery, antelopes and prolific birdlife	p.333
12 Kgalagadi Transfrontier Park	Desert/game reserve	Remote desert with rust-red dunes, desert lions, shy leopards and thousands of antelopes	p.336

KEY PARK	PRINCIPAL FOCUS	DESCRIPTION AND HIGHLIGHTS	DETAILS
Northern Cape			
13 Namaqua NP	Marine and coastal/ wildflowers	Mountainous and coastal region renowned for its display of an estimated 3500 varieties of spring	p.352
14 Ai-Ais Richtersveld Transfrontier Park	Mountain and desert reserve	Craggy *kloofs*, high mountains and dramatic landscapes, sweeping inland from the Orange River, which sustain a remarkable range of reptiles, birds, mammals and plant life	p.359
Free State			
15 Golden Gate Highlands NP	Mountain enclave	Resort at the foot of rich sandstone formations in the heart of the Maluti Mountains; trails	p.583
North West			
16 Pilanesberg NP	Game reserve	Mountain-encircled grassland trampled by the Big Five, accessible from Johannesburg	p.663
Limpopo province/Mpumalanga			
17 Kruger NP	Game reserve	The largest, best-stocked and most popular game reserve in the subcontinent	p.710
18 Marakele NP	Game reserve	Striking landscape of peaks, plateaus and cliffs stocked with lions, elephants, rhinos and a variety of other mammals	p.746
Kwazulu-Natal			
19 Greater St Lucia	Coastal wetland	Vast patchwork of wetlands, wilderness, coast and game reserves	p.532
20 Hluhluwe-Imfolozi GR	Game reserve	KwaZulu-Natal's hillier, smaller answer to Kruger is among the top African spots for rhinos	p.529
21 Ithala GR	Game reserve	Lesser-known small gem of a game reserve in mountainous country	p.549
22 Mkhuze GR	Game/bird reserve	Top birding venue, excellent for rhinos and other herbivores; walks in wild fig forest	p.539
22 Ukhahlamba Drakensberg Park	Mountain reserve	A series of parks covering the highest, most stirring and most dramatic peaks in South Africa	p.512

MAJOR PARKS AND
WILDERNESS AREAS

If you had to choose just one of the country's top three parks, **Kruger**, stretching up the east flank of Mpumalanga and Limpopo province, would lead the pack for its sheer size (it's larger than Wales and roughly the size the Massachusetts), its range of animals, its varied lowveld habitats and unbeatable game-viewing opportunities. After Kruger, the **Tsitsikamma** in the Western Cape attracts large numbers of visitors for its ancient forests, cliff-faced oceans, the dramatic Storms River Mouth as well as its Otter Trail, South Africa's most popular **hike**. For epic mountain landscapes, nowhere in the country can touch the **Ukhahlamba Drakensberg Park**, which takes in a series of reserves on the KwaZulu-Natal border with Lesotho and offers gentle hikes along watercourses as well as ambitious mountaineering for serious climbers.

The unchallenged status of Kruger as the place for packing in elephants, lions and casts of thousands of animals tends to put the **KwaZulu-Natal parks** in the shade, quite undeservedly. As well as offering the

best places in the world for seeing **rhino**, these parks feel less developed than Kruger, often provide superior accommodation at comparable prices. Both Kruger and KwaZulu-Natal parks offer guided **wildlife trails** and **night drives**, a popular way to catch sight of the elusive denizens that creep around after dark.

Also worth a mention is the **Addo Elephant National Park** in the Eastern Cape, which is presently being expanded and has become Big Five country – the only such major game reserve in the southern half of the country. Addo has a lot more in its favour as well: it has the most diverse landscape of any reserve in the country; it is an easy day's drive from Cape Town; and it is the only major game reserve in the country that is malaria-free.

Park accommodation

Accommodation at national parks includes **campsites** (expect to pay about R100 per tent); one-room **rondavels** with shared washing and cooking facilities (R140 per person); **safari tents** at some of the Kruger and KwaZulu-Natal rest camps (from R140 per person); and self-contained **chalets** with private bath or shower and cooking facilities (from R200 per person). For groups of four there are self-contained **family cottages** with private bath and kitchen, where the price of the whole unit is around R800. In national parks accommodation (excluding campsites) you're supplied with bedding, towels, a fridge and basic cooking utensils. In several of the KwaZulu-Natal parks restcamps, however, you aren't allowed to use the kitchen, but give your food to the camp chef and attendants who prepare and serve the meal and wash up, at no extra cost. Some restcamps have a **shop** selling supplies for picnics or braais, as well as a **restaurant**.

The ultimate wildlife accommodation is in the **private game reserves**, most of which are around the Kruger National Park. Here you pay big bucks for accommodation which is almost always **luxurious**, in large en-suite walk-in tents, or small thatched rondavels, or – in the larger and most expensive lodges – plush rooms with air conditioning. A couple of places have "bush-showers" (a hoisted bucket of hot water with a shower nozzle attached) behind reed screens but open to the sky – one of the great treats of the bush is taking a shower under the southern sky. Some chalets or tents have gaslights or lanterns in the absence of electricity. **Food** is usually good and plentiful, and vegetarians can be catered for. Prices start at R1200 per person per night at a handful of places, but more commonly you can expect to pay upwards of R2000, rising to several times that amount at the most fashionable spots. It's worth remembering that, high as these prices are, all your meals and game drives are included, and as numbers are strictly limited, you get an exclusive experience of the bush in return.

Game viewing

Spotting game takes skill and experience. It's easier than you'd think to mistake a rhino for a large boulder, or to miss the king of the beasts in the tall grass – African game has after all evolved with camouflage in mind. Don't expect the volume of animals you get in wildlife documentaries: what you see is always a matter of luck, patience and skill. If you're new to the African bush and its wildlife, consider shelling out for at least two nights at one of the luxurious lodges on a private reserve (for example, those abutting Kruger); they're staffed by well-informed rangers who lead game-viewing outings in open-topped 4WDs.

The section on Kruger National Park (see p.710) gives more advice on how to go about spotting game and how to enjoy and understand what you do see – whether it's a brightly coloured lizard in a rest camp, head-butting giraffes at a waterhole or dust-kicking rhinos. For **books** that can enhance your visit to a game reserve – especially if you plan a self-drive safari – see p.924.

Self-drive safaris

The least expensive way of experiencing a game park is by renting a car and **driving** around a national park, taking advantage of the self-catering and camping facilities. You'll have the thrill of spotting game yourself and at your own pace, rather than relying on a ranger, and for people with **children**, a self-drive safari is the principal way to see a game reserve, as most of the upmarket lodges don't admit under-12s. The one real disadvantage of self-driving is that you can end up jostling with other cars to get a view, especially when it comes to lion-watching. Also, you may not know what animal signs to look for, and unless you travel in a minibus or 4WD vehicle you're unlikely to be high enough off the ground to be able to see across the veld.

The KwaZulu-Natal game reserves – foremost among them **Hluhluwe-Imfolozi**, **Mkhuze** and **Ithala** – offer rewarding opportunities for self-drive touring. The same applies to the **Pilanesberg Game Reserve** in North West Province, while the remote **Kgalagadi Transfrontier Park** that stretches across the border into Botswana promises truly exciting wilderness driving. You might choose to cover a route that combines the substantial Kruger National Park with the more intimate reserves of KwaZulu-Natal province.

If you plan to self-drive, consider investing in good animal and bird field guides, and a decent pair of **binoculars** – one pair per person is recommended if you want to keep your relationships on a friendly footing. Finally, whether you're cooking or not, it's worth taking a thermos for tea and a cool bag to keep water cold.

Escorted safaris

It's possible to book places on a **safari excursion** – such packages are often organized by backpackers' lodges located near reserves, and occasionally by hotels and B&Bs. On the downside, these don't give you the experience of waking up in the wild, and entail spending considerably more time on the road than if you were based inside a reserve. But during South African school holidays, when Kruger, for example, is booked to capacity, you may have no other option.

Mostly, you get what you pay for as regards game-viewing packages. Be wary of any cheap deals on "safari farms" in the vicinity of Kruger. These are generally fine if you want to see animals in what are essentially huge zoos and make an acceptable overnight stop en route to Kruger, but are no substitute for a real wilderness experience – sooner or later you hit fences and gates on your game drive. Some of the better places in this category are listed in the relevant chapters.

Safaris on private reserves

If you choose well, the ultimate South African game experience has to be in a **private reserve**. You can relax while your game-viewing activities are organized, and because you spend time in a small group you get a stronger sense of the wild than you ever could at one of the big Kruger rest camps. Best of all, you get the benefit of knowledgeable rangers, who can explain the terrain and small-scale wildlife as they drive you around looking for game.

Privately run safari lodges in concessions inside Kruger and some other national parks, such as Addo, operate along similar lines. The smaller private reserves accommodate between ten and sixteen guests; larger camps often cater to two or three times as many people, and resemble hotels in the bush. Many safari lodges have their own waterholes, overlooked by the bar, from which you can watch animals drinking. Nowhere are the private reserves more developed than along the west flank of the Kruger, where you'll find the top-dollar prestigious lodges as well as some places offering more bang for fewer bucks.

A **typical day** at a private camp or lodge starts at dawn for tea or coffee followed by guided game viewing on foot, or driving. After a mid-morning brunch/breakfast, there's the chance to spend time on a viewing platform or in a hide, quietly watching the passing scene. Late-afternoon game viewing is a repeat of early morning but culminates with sundowners as the light fades, and often turns into a night drive with spotlights out looking for nocturnal creatures.

Prices, which include accommodation, meals and all game activities, vary widely. The ultra-expensive camps offer more luxury and social cachet, but not necessarily better game viewing. You might find the cheaper camps in the same areas more to your taste, their plainer and wilder atmosphere more in keeping with the bush.

Activities and outdoor pursuits

South Africa's diverse landscape of mountains, forests, rugged coast and sandy beaches, as well as miles of veld and game-trampled national parks, make the country supreme outdoor terrain. This fact hasn't been overlooked by South Africans themselves, who have been playing in the outdoors for decades. The result is a well-developed infrastructure for activities, an impressive national network of hiking trails and plenty of commercial operators selling adventure sports.

Hiking trails

Over the past 25 years, **hiking** has taken off in a big way in South Africa, which now has the most comprehensive system of footpaths in Africa (inspired by the US Appalachian Hiking Trail). Wherever you are – even in the middle of Johannesburg – you won't be far from some sort of trail. The best ones are in wilderness areas, where you'll find way-marked paths that vary from half-hour strolls to major hiking expeditions of two to seven days that take you right into the heart of some of the most beautiful parts of the country.

Overnight hiking trails are normally well laid out, with painted footprints or other markers to indicate the route, and campsites or huts along the way (you'll need to carry all your own equipment). Numbers are limited on most, and many trails are so popular that you may need to **book** months in advance to use them (details are given in the Guide) – although you may be lucky enough to find that there is a last-minute vacancy just when you turn up.

If you want to do a fair amount of walking but don't want to launch out on a long expedition, consider basing yourself in one of the wilderness areas such as the **Drakensberg**, where you can stay in chalets and set off on a series of day-walks, returning each night.

Characteristic of Africa are **guided wilderness trails**, where you walk in game country (such as the Kruger National Park), accompanied by an armed guide. These walks should be regarded as a way to get a feel for the wild rather than actually see any wildlife, as you'll encounter far fewer animals on foot than from a vehicle. Specialist trails include mountain biking, canoeing, horseback trails and camel trails. A handful of trails have also been set up specifically for **people with disabilities**, mostly for the visually impaired or people confined to wheelchairs.

Watersports

South Africa has some of the world's finest spots for **surfing**. The country's perfect

Beach conditions

Don't expect balmy Mediterranean seas in South Africa: of its 2500km of coastline, only the stretch along the Indian Ocean seaboard of KwaZulu-Natal and the northern section of the Eastern Cape can be considered tropical, and along the entire coast an energetic surf pounds the shore. In **Cape Town**, sea bathing is only comfortable between November and March. Generally, the further east you go from here, the warmer the water becomes and the longer the bathing season. Sea temperatures that rarely drop below 18°C make the **KwaZulu-Natal** coast warm enough for a dip at any time of year.

A word of warning: dangerous **undertows** and riptides are present along the coast and you should try to bathe where lifeguards are present. Failing that (and guards aren't that common away from main resorts out of season) you should follow local advice, never swim alone, and always treat the ocean with respect.

wave at **Jeffrey's Bay** was immortalized on celluloid in the Sixties cult movie *Endless Summer*, but any surfer will tell you that there are equal, if not better, breaks all the way along the coast from the Namibian to the Mozambique border. Surfers can be a cliquey bunch, but the South African community has a reputation for being among the friendliest in the world and, provided you pay your dues, you should find yourself easily accepted. Some of the world's top shapers work here, and you can pick up an excellent board at a fraction of European or US prices. If you can face the humiliation of being regarded by the pro surfers as a "tea bag" or "doormat", boogie-boarding and body-surfing make easy alternatives to the real thing, require less skill or dedication and are great fun. **Windsurfing** (or sailboarding) is another popular sport you'll find at many resorts, where you can rent gear.

On inland waterways, South African holidaymakers are keen **speedboaters**, an activity that goes hand in hand with **waterskiing**. **Kayaking** and **canoeing** are also very popular, and you can often rent craft at resorts or national parks that lie along rivers. For the more adventurous, there's **whitewater rafting**, with some decent trips along the Tugela River in KwaZulu-Natal and on the Orange River.

Diving and snorkelling

Scuba diving is growing in popularity, and South Africa is one of the cheapest places in the world to get an internationally recognized open-water certificate. Courses start at R1600 (excluding rental of gear) and are available at all the coastal cities as well as a number of other resorts. The most rewarding diving is along the St Lucia Marine Reserve on the northern KwaZulu-Natal coast, where 100,000 dives go under every year for its coral reefs and fluorescent fish. You won't find corals and bright colours along the Cape coast, but the huge number of sunken vessels makes wreck-diving popular, and you can encounter the swaying rhythms of giant kelp forests. There are a couple of places along the southern Cape and Garden Route where you can go on **shark-cage dives** and come face to face with deadly great whites.

KwaZulu-Natal is also good for **snorkelling** and there are some underwater trails elsewhere in the country, most notable of which is in the Tsitsikamma National Park.

Other activities

Fishing is another well-developed South African activity and the coasts yield 250 species caught through rock, bay or surf angling. The confluence of the warm Indian Ocean and cooler Atlantic east of the Cape Peninsula brings one of the highest concentrations of game fish in the world, including longfin, tunny and marlin. Inland you'll find plenty of rivers and dams stocked with freshwater fish, while trout fishing is extremely well established in Mpumalanga, the northern sections of the Eastern Cape and the KwaZulu-Natal Midlands.

There are ample opportunities for aerial activities in South Africa. In the Winelands you can go **ballooning**, while **paragliding** offers a thrilling way to see Cape Town, by diving off Lion's Head and riding the thermals. More down-to-earth options include **mountaineering** and **rock climbing**, both of which have a huge following in South Africa. If you can't choose between being airborne or earthbound, you can always bounce between the two by **bungee jumping** off the Gouritz River Bridge near Mossel Bay – the world's highest commercial jump.

Horse-riding is a sport you'll find at virtually every resort, whether inland or along the coast, for two hours or two days. You can ride in the Drakensberg from the Natal parks, or go pony trekking for several days in Lesotho. Take your own hat, as not everyone provides them. **Bird-watching** is another activity you can do almost anywhere, either casually on your own, or as part of a guided trip with one of the several experts operating in South Africa. Among the very best bird-watching spots are Mkuzi and Ndumo game reserves in KwaZulu-Natal. **Golf** lovers will have a fabulous time in South Africa as courses are prolific and frequently in stunningly beautiful locations. Finally, if you decide to go **skiing** at one or two resorts in the Eastern and Western Cape, you'll be able to go home with a quirky experience of Africa.

Spectator sports

South Africa is a nation obsessed by sport, where heights of devotion are reached whenever local or international teams take to the field. Winning performances, controversial selections and scandals commonly dominate the front as well as the back pages of newspapers, and it can be hard to escape the domination of sport across radio, television and advertising media. The big spectator sports are soccer, rugby and cricket, and big matches involving the international team or big local clubs are well worth seeing live.

Soccer

Soccer is the country's most popular game, with a primarily black and coloured following, and it is now starting to attract serious money. The professional season runs from August to May, with teams competing in the **Premier Soccer League** (PSL) and a couple of knock-out cup competitions.

Unlike rugby teams, soccer teams do not own their own grounds and are forced to rent them for specific fixtures. In Gauteng, the heartland of South African soccer, all the big clubs use the same grounds, which has prevented the development of the kind of terrace fan culture found elsewhere. Nonetheless, soccer crowds are generally witty and good-spirited, and whites have no reason to feel uncomfortable going to a game. The very big games, normally involving Johannesburg's big two teams, **Kaiser Chiefs** and **Orlando Pirates**, do simmer with tension, though violence is rare. Although Chiefs and Pirates are both Sowetan clubs, they have a nationwide following, and their derbies are the highlight of the PSL's fixture list.

Games are played on weekday evenings (usually at 7.30pm or 8.30pm) and at 3pm on Saturdays. Tickets cost about R25. The national squad, nicknamed **Bafana Bafana** (literally "boys boys" but connoting "our lads") qualified for the World Cup finals in both 1998 and 2002. Bafana are imaginative and strong on spectacular athletic feats, but less impressive when it comes to team work and resilience. Even games the team should win have an element of unpredictability that makes for great spectator sport. In 2010 Bafana will have the particular honour of playing in the World Cup finals on home soil.

Rugby

Rugby is hugely popular with whites, especially Afrikaners, though attempts to broaden the game's appeal, particularly to a black audience, have struggled. The 1995 World Cup, hosted by South Africa, attracted fanatical attention nationwide, particularly when the national team, the Springboks, triumphed in the final and President Nelson Mandela donned a green Springbok jersey (long associated exclusively with whites) to present the cup to the winning side. Since then the goodwill has dissipated, to be replaced by an acrimonious struggle to transform the traditionally white sports (cricket and rugby) into something more representative of all race groups, particularly following the government's policy of enforcing racial quotas in national squads.

Despite this, the fact remains that South Africa is extraordinarily good at rugby, and you are likely to witness high-quality play when you watch either inter-regional or international games. The main domestic competition is the **Currie Cup**, with games played on weekends from March to October; admission to one of these matches costs around R50.

More recently this has been overshadowed by the **Super 12** competition, involving regional teams from South Africa, New Zealand and Australia. Matches are staged annually from late February to the end of May in all three countries, and in South Africa you'll catch a fair bit of action in the major centres of Johannesburg, Cape Town and Durban, though smaller places such as Port Elizabeth, East London, Bloemfontein and George sometimes get a look in.

International fixtures involving the Springboks are dominated by visiting tours by northern hemisphere teams and by the annual **Tri-Nations** competition, in which South Africa plays home and away fixtures against Australia and New Zealand. These are normally played from June to August, and you will need to get tickets well in advance to attend.

Cricket

Cricket was for some years seen as the most progressive of the former white sports, with development programmes generating support and discovering talent among black and coloured communities. The sport was rocked to its foundations in 2000, however, when it was revealed that the late South African national captain Hansie Cronje had received money from betting syndicates hoping to influence the outcome of matches. Cronje was banned for life, the credibility of the sport took a dive and the Proteas (formerly the Springboks), the national team, has been struggling to raise itself ever since.

The domestic season of inter-provincial games runs from October to April, and the main competitions are the four-day **Supersport Series** and the series of one-day matches, the **Standard Bank Cup**. Both contests see the eleven provincial teams slogging it out for national dominance. Games are played throughout the week, and admission is around R25 standing and R35 for a seat. In the international standings, South Africa are one of the world's top teams, and you stand a good chance of being around for an international test or one-day series if you're in the country between November and March.

Running and cycling

South Africa is very strong at **long-distance running**, a tradition that reached its apotheosis at the 1996 Atlanta Olympics when Josiah Thugwane won the marathon, becoming the first black South African ever to bag Olympic gold. The biggest single sports event in South Africa, the **Comrades Marathon**, attracts nearly 15,000 participants, among them some of the world's leading international ultra-marathon runners. The ninety-kilometre course crosses the hilly country between Durban and Pietermaritzburg, with a drop of almost 800m between the town and the coast. Run annually on May 31, the race alternates direction each year and is notable for having been non-racial since 1975, although it wasn't until 1989 that a black South African, Samuel Tshabalala, won it. Since then, black athletes have begun to dominate the front rankings. Almost as famous is the **Two Oceans ultra-marathon** which attracts 10,000 competitors each April to test themselves on the 56-kilometre course that spectacularly circuits the Cape Peninsula.

Traversing a 109-kilometre route, the **Pick 'n Pay Cape Argus Cycle Tour** also includes the Cape Peninsula in its routing. The largest individually timed cycle race anywhere, it attracts 35,000 participants from around the world each year in March.

Horse racing

You'll find huge interest among rich and poor South Africans in **horse racing**, with totes and tracks in all the main cities. Its popularity is partly due to the fact that for decades this was the only form of public gambling that South Africa's Afrikaner Calvinist rulers allowed – on the pretext that it involved skill not chance. The highlight of the racing calendar is the **Durban July Handicap** held at Durban's Greyville racecourse. A flamboyant event, it attracts huge crowds, massive purses, socialites in outrageous headgear and vast amounts of media attention.

Crime and personal safety

Despite horror stories of sky-high crime rates, most people visit South Africa without incident; be careful, but don't be paranoid. This is not to underestimate the issue – crime is probably the most serious problem facing the country. However, once you realize that crime is disproportionally concentrated in the poor African and coloured townships, the scale becomes less terrifying. Violent crime is a particular problem not just in the townships but also in Johannesburg, where the dangers are the worst in the country.

Protecting property and "security" are major national obsessions, and it's difficult to imagine what many South Africans would discuss at their dinner parties if the problem disappeared. A substantial percentage of middle-class homes subscribe to the services of armed **private security firms**. The other obvious manifestation of this obsession is the huge number of alarms, high walls and electronically controlled gates you'll find, not just in the suburbs, but even in less deprived areas of some townships.

Guns are openly carried by police – and often citizens. In many high streets you'll spot firearm shops rubbing shoulders with places selling clothes or books, and you'll come across notices asking you to deposit your weapon before entering the premises.

If you fall victim to a **mugging**, you should take very seriously the usual advice not to resist and do as you're told. The chances of this happening can be greatly minimized by using common sense and following a few simple rules.

Drugs and drink-driving

Dagga (pronounced like "dugger" with the "gg" guttural, as in the Scottish pronunciation of "loch") is cannabis in dried leaf form, South Africa's most widely produced and widely used drug. Grown in hot regions like KwaZulu-Natal (the source of Durban Poison), Swaziland (Swazi Gold) and as a cash crop in parts of the former Transkei, it is fairly easily available and the quality is generally good – but this doesn't alter the fact that it is illegal. If you do decide to partake, you should take particular care when

scoring, as visitors have run into trouble dealing with unfamilar local conditions.

Strangely, for a country that sometimes seems to be on one massive binge, South Africa has laws that prohibit drinking in public – not that anyone pays any attention to them. The **drink-drive laws** are routinely and brazenly flouted, making the country's roads the one real danger you should be concerned about. People routinely stock up their cars with booze for long journeys and even at filling stations you'll find places selling liquor. Levels of alcohol consumption go some way to explaining why during the Christmas holidays over a thousand people die in an annual orgy of carnage on the roads.

Sexual harassment

South Africa's extremely high incidence of **rape** doesn't as a rule affect tourists. In fact women are very unlikely to need to fend off the unwanted attentions of men. However, at heart the majority of the country's males, regardless of race, hold on to fairly sexist attitudes. Sometimes your eagerness to be friendly may be taken as a sexual overture – always be sensitive to potential crossed wires and unintended signals.

Women should avoid travelling on their own, nor should they hitchhike or walk alone in deserted areas. This applies equally to cities, the countryside or anywhere after dark. Minibus taxis should be ruled out as a means of transport after dark, especially if you're not exactly sure of local geography.

The police

For many black South Africans, the **South African National Police** (SANP) still carry

Safety tips

In general:
- try not to look like a tourist.
- dress down.
- don't carry a camera or video openly in cities.
- avoid wearing jewellery or expensive watches.
- leave your designer shades at home – they are sometimes pulled off people's faces.
- if you are accosted, remain calm and co-operative.

When on foot:
- grasp bags firmly under your arm.
- don't carry excessive sums of money on you.
- don't put your wallet in your back trouser pocket.
- always know where your valuables are.
- don't leave valuables exposed (on a seat or the ground) while having a meal or drink.
- develop an awareness of what people in the street around you are doing.
- don't let strangers get too close to you – especially people in groups.
- in big cities, travel around in pairs or groups.

On the road:
- lock all your car doors, especially in cities.
- keep rear windows sufficiently rolled up to keep out opportunistic hands.
- never leave anything worth stealing in view when your car is unattended.

On the beach:
- take only the bare essentials.
- don't leave valuables, especially cameras, unattended.
- safeguard car keys by pinning them to your swimming gear, or putting them in a waterproof wallet or splash box and taking them into the water with you.

At ATMs:
Cash machines are favourite hunting grounds for sophisticated conmen who use cunning rather than force to steal money. Never underestimate their ability and don't get drawn into *any* interaction at an ATM, no matter how well spoken, friendly or distressed the other person appears. If they claim to have a problem with the machine, tell them to contact the bank. Don't let people crowd you or see your personal identification number (PIN) when you withdraw money; if in doubt, go to another machine. Finally, if your card gets swallowed, report it without delay.

strong associations of collaboration with apartheid and a lot of public relations work has yet to be done to turn the police into a genuine people's law enforcement agency. Poorly paid, shot at (and frequently hit), underfunded, badly equipped, barely respected and demoralized, the police keep a low profile. If you ever get stopped, at a roadblock for example (one of the likeliest encounters), always be courteous. And if you're driving, note that under South African law you are required to carry your **driver's licence** at all times.

If you are robbed, you will need to report the incident to the police, who should give you a case reference for insurance purposes – though don't expect too much crime-cracking enthusiasm, or to get your property back.

Travellers with disabilities

Facilities for disabled travellers in South Africa are not as sophisticated as those found in the First World, but they're sufficient to ensure you have a satisfactory visit. By accident rather than design, you'll find pretty good accessibility to many buildings, as South Africans tend to build low (single-storey bungalows are the norm), with the result that you'll have to deal with fewer stairs than you may be accustomed to. As the car is king, you'll frequently find that you can drive to, and park right outside, your destination.

Planning a holiday

There are **organized tours** and holidays specifically for people with disabilities, and **activity-based packages** for disabled travellers to South Africa are increasingly available. These packages offer the possibility for wheelchair-bound visitors to take part in safaris, sport and a vast range of adventure activities, including whitewater rafting, horse-riding and parasailing. Tours can either be taken as self-drive trips or packages for large groups. The contacts below will be able to put you in touch with South Africa travel specialists.

If you want to be more independent on your travels, it's important to know where you can expect help and where you must be self-reliant, especially regarding transport and accommodation. It's also vital to know your limitations, and to make sure others know them. If you do not use a wheelchair all the time but your walking capabilities are limited, remember that you are likely to need to cover greater distances while travelling (often over rougher terrain and in hotter temperatures) than you are used to. If you use a wheelchair, have it serviced before you go and take a repair kit with you.

All the major **airlines** flying to South Africa can provide assistance for disabled passengers, but you should give them notice of your needs when booking. As far as domestic air travel is concerned, South African Airways provides passenger aid units at all principal airports.

Read your **travel insurance** small print carefully to make sure that people with a pre-existing medical condition are not excluded. A **medical certificate** of your fitness to travel, provided by your doctor, is also extremely useful, and some airlines or insurance companies may insist on it. Carry spares of any clothing or equipment that might be hard to find; if there's an association representing people with your disability, contact them early in the planning process.

Contacts for travellers with disabilities

South Africa

Eco-Access PO Box 1377, Roosevelt Park 2129 ☎011 477 3676, ⓦ www.eco-access.org. Non-profit agency working for improved facilities for disabled people to take part in eco-tourism in South Africa. The website has a page of useful links for disabled travellers.

KwaZulu-Natal Wildlife PO Box 13069, Cascades, Pietermaritzburg 3202 ☎033 845 1000, ⓦ www.kznwildlife.com. They can provide information about wheelchair-friendly accommodation and trails in game reserves and parks in KwaZulu-Natal.

National Council for the Physically Disabled in South Africa PO Box 426, Melville 2109 ☎011 726 8040,ⓦ www.ncppdsa.co.za. Advice on where to rent wheelchairs and other equipment in the major cities.

South African National Parks PO Box 787, Pretoria 0001 ☎012 343 1991, ⓦ www.parks-sa .co.za. Up-to-date information about access at rest camps in the national parks.

Titch Travel 26, Station Rd, Rondebosch 7700, Cape Town ☎021 689 4151, ⓦ www.titchtours. co.za. Travel agent whose portfolio includes programmes for physically disabled and visually impaired people.

UK and Ireland

Holiday Care 7th Floor, Sunley House, 4 Bedford Park, Croydon CR0 2AP ☎0845/124 9971, ⊛www.holidaycare.org.uk. Lists of accessible accommodation. Information on financial help for holidays available.

Irish Wheelchair Association Blackheath Drive, Clontarf, Dublin 3 ☎01/818 6400, ⊛www.iwa.ie. Useful information about travelling abroad with a wheelchair.

Tripscope Alexandra House, Albany Rd, Brentford, Middlesex TW8 0NE ☎08457/585 641, ⊛www .tripscope.org.uk. Registered charity whose telephone information service offers free advice on UK and international travel for those with a mobility problem.

US and Canada

Access-Able ⊛www.access-able.com. Online resource for travellers with disabilities.

Directions Unlimited 123 Green Lane, Bedford Hills, NY 10507 ☎1-800/533-5343 or 914/241-1700. Travel agency specializing in bookings for people with disabilities.

Society for Accessible Travel and Hospitality Suite 610, 347 5th Ave, New York, NY 10016 ☎212/447-7284, ⊛www.sath.org. Non-profit educational organization that has actively represented travellers with disabilities since 1976.

Australia and New Zealand

ACROD (Australian Council for Rehabilitation of the Disabled) PO Box 60, Curtin ACT 2605; ☎02/6282 4333 (also TTY), ⊛www.acrod.org.au. Provides lists of travel agencies and tour operators for people with disabilities.

Disabled Persons Assembly 4/173–175 Victoria St, Wellington, New Zealand ☎04/801 9100 (also TTY), ⊛www.dpa.org.nz. Resource centre with lists of travel agencies and tour operators for people with disabilities.

Facilities in South Africa

A growing number of popular tourist attractions, including national parks, are being designed to facilitate **disabled access**. For example, the Kirstenbosch Botanical Gardens in Cape Town have Braille and wheelchair trails, while trails aimed specifically at disabled visitors are on offer at Kamberg Nature Reserve in the Drakensberg and in the Karoo National Park. The longest trail so far is a six-kilometre walk with a tapping rail and guide ropes in the Palmiet Nature Reserve in Durban. Cape Town's Waterfront, one of the top national attractions, has specially designed parking bays as well as ramps and broad walkways around the development itself. Sun City in North West Province is also disability-friendly.

South Africa has a growing number of **hotels** with facilities for disabled people. South African Tourism publishes an accommodation guide, available from all their offices (see p.42), which includes up-to-date information about disability-friendly establishments. In the national parks, specially adapted huts are available in the Kruger and Karoo national parks. For further details of facilities in other parks, contact South African National and KwaZulu-Natal Wildlife.

Rental of cars with hand controls and automatic transmission can be arranged for no extra charge through Avis or Budget (see p.57) at all the major centres, but a month's prior notice is recommended. Many garages along the main routes, especially along the N1 between Johannesburg and Cape Town, have wheelchair-accessible **toilets**. A Special Parking Disc, which allows **parking** concessions to people with severe mobility impairment, can be obtained through through the local traffic department. You should bring any appropriate disc or badge from your home country, which can be used to get a temporary disc.

Gay and lesbian travellers

South Africa has the world's first gay- and lesbian-friendly constitution, and Africa's most developed and diverse gay and lesbian scene. Not only is homosexuality legal for consenting adults of 18 or over, but the constitution outlaws any discrimination on the grounds of sexual orientation. This means that, for once, you have the law on your side. Outside the big cities, however, South Africa is a pretty conservative place where open displays of public affection by gays and lesbians are unlikely to go down well; many whites will find it un-Christian, while blacks will think it un-African.

South African Tourism, on the other hand, has recently woken up to the potential of pink spending power and is actively wooing gay travellers – an effort that is evidently paying off, with the *Spartacus* gay guide ranking **Cape Town** among the world's top five gay destinations. The city is South Africa's – and indeed, the African continent's – gay capital. Like many things in the city, Cape Town's gay scene (see p.177 for more) is white dominated, though there are a few gay-friendly clubs starting to emerge in the surrounding townships. The gay scene is a lot more multiracial in **Johannesburg**, especially in the clubs. The **Pretoria** gay and lesbian scene has grown enormously over the past few years. There are also gay scenes in **Port Elizabeth** and **Durban** and you'll find a growing number of gay-run or gay-friendly establishments in small towns all over the country. Jo'burg has its own gay pride festival in September (@www.sapride.org), while the Gay and Lesbian Film Festival (@www.oia.co.za) takes place in Cape Town, Johannesburg and Durban every year in February and March.

Besides a substantial number of online gay resources, there are a number of gay print publications, including the *Exit* newspaper (www.exit.co.za) and *Gay Pages* (www.gaypagessa.co.za), a glossy monthly lifestyle magazine; both are available at newsagents in cities and the larger towns.

Contacts for gay and lesbian travellers

South Africa

capetown.tv @www.capetown.tv. Comprehensive site for gay travellers, with its focus on the Mother City. Covers everything from arts and theatre to cruising spots and travel information. Also info on gay Jo'burg and Durban.

Gay and Lesbian Association of Cape Town Tourism @www.galacttic.co.za. Cape Town directory covering gay businesses in the tourism industry, gay professionals, including dentists, doctors and lawyers, plus gay accommodation, clubs, restaurants and events.

Gay, Lesbian and Bisexual Helpline ☎021 422 2500. Helpline of the Cape Town-based Triangle Project (see below). Daily 1–9pm.

Gay Net @www.gaynetsa.co.za. Gay directory that covers the country.

Gay South Africa @www.gaysouthafrica.org.za. A slick, well-organized portal with links covering all topics of gay interest.

Lesbian and Gay Equality Project ☎011 487 3811, @www.equality.org.za. Johannesburg organization devoted mainly to lobbying and legal advice, but which can also provide basic information to gay visitors.

Our Way Travel and Safaris @www.ourway.co.za. Gay travel agency based in Cape Town.

Q @www.q.co.za. Excellent gay spin-off site of the daily *Mail & Guardian*, covering news and a variety of topics with a good travel section.

Triangle Project ☎021 448 3812, @www.triangle.org.za. Based in Cape Town, this is the longest-established gay organization in South Africa. A good first port of call for all types of information.

Wanderwomen @www.wanderwomen.co.za. Travel website for lesbians, where you can plan and book your entire South Africa itinerary.

UK

@www.gaytravel.co.uk Online gay and lesbian travel agent. Also lists gay- and lesbian-friendly hotels around the world.

US and Canada

Damron ☏1-800/462-6654 or 415/255-0404, ⓦwww.damron.com. The website allows you to search or purchase their gay travel publications.
gaytravel.com ☏1-800/GAY-TRAVEL, ⓦwww.gaytravel.com. International gay and lesbian travel; the website lists some accommodation in Cape Town and Jo'burg.
International Gay & Lesbian Travel Association ☏1-800/448-8550 or 954/776-2626,

ⓦwww.iglta.org. Trade group that can provide a list of gay- and lesbian-owned or -friendly travel agents, accommodation and other travel businesses.

Australia and New Zealand

Parkside Travel ☏08/8274 1222, ⓔparkside@herveyworld.com.au. Gay and lesbian travel worldwide.
Tearaway Travel ☏1800/664 440 or 03/9510 6644, ⓦwww.tearaway.com. Gay travel.

Travelling with children

Holidaying with children is straightforward in South Africa, whether you want to explore a city, relax on the beach, or find peace in the mountains. You'll find local people friendly, attentive and accepting of babies and young children. The following is aimed principally at families with under-5s.

Although children up to 24 months only pay ten percent of the adult airfare, the illusion that this is a bargain rapidly evaporates when you realize that they get no seat or baggage allowance. Given this, you'd be well advised to secure bulkhead seats and reserve a **basinet** or sky cot, which can be attached to the bulkhead. Basinets are usually allocated to babies under six months, though some airlines use weight (under 10kg) as the criterion. When you reconfirm your flights, check that your seat and basinet are still available. A child who has a seat will usually be charged fifty percent of the adult fare and is entitled to a full baggage allowance.

For getting to and from the aircraft, and for use during your stay, take a lightweight collapsible **buggy** – not counted as part of your luggage allowance. A child-carrier backpack is another useful accessory.

Given the size of the country, you're likely to be **driving** long distances. Aim to go slowly and plan a route that allows frequent stops – or perhaps take trains or flights between centres. The Garden Route, for example, is an ideal drive, with easy stops for picnics, particularly on the

section between Mossel Bay and Storms River. The route between Johannesburg and Cape Town, conversely, is tedious.

Game viewing can be boring for young children, since it too involves a lot of driving – and disappointment, should the promised beasts fail to put in an appearance. Furthermore, of course, toddlers won't particularly enjoy watching animals from afar and through a window. If they are old enough to enjoy the experience, make sure they have their own binoculars. To get in closer, some animal parks, such as Tshukudu near Kruger, have semi-tame animals, while snake and reptile parks are an old South African favourite.

Family accommodation is plentiful and hotels often have rooms with extra beds or interconnecting rooms. Kids usually stay for half-price. Self-catering options are worth considering, as most such establishments have a good deal of space to play in, and there'll often be a pool. A number of resorts are specifically aimed at families with **older children**, with suitable activities offered. The pick of the bunch is the Aventura chain (ⓦwww.aventura.co.za), which has resorts in beautiful settings, including Keurboomstrand near Plettenberg Bay, and two close to the Blyde River Canyon in Mpumalanga. Another excellent option is full-board family hotels, of which there are a number along the Wild Coast (see p.431), where not only are there playgrounds and canoes for paddling about lagoons, but also most provide nannies to look after the kids during meals or for the whole day if you want. Note that many safari camps don't allow children under 12, so you'll have to self-cater or camp at the national parks and those in KwaZulu-Natal.

Eating out with a baby or toddler is easy, particularly if you go to an outdoor venue where they can get on unhindered with their exploration of the world. Some restaurants have highchairs and offer small portions. If in doubt, there are always the ubiquitous family-oriented chains such as *Spur* or *Wimpy*.

Breast feeding is practised by the majority of African mothers wherever they are, though you won't see many white women doing it in public. Be discreet, especially in more conservative white areas – which is most of the country outside middle-class Cape Town, Johannesburg or Durban. There are relatively few **baby rooms** in public places for changing or feeding.

You can buy disposable **nappies** wherever you go (imported brands are best), as well as wipes, bottles, formula and dummies. High-street chemists and the Clicks chain are the best places to buy baby goods. If you run out of **clothes**, the Woolworths chain has good-quality stuff, while the ubiquitous Pep stores, which are present in even the smallest towns, are an excellent source of extremely cheap, functional clothes.

Malaria affects only a small part of the country, but think carefully about visiting such areas as the preventatives aren't recommended for under-2s. For toddlers, chloroquine is available as a syrup, while proguanil is only available in tablet form. Avoid most of the major game reserves, particularly the Kruger National Park and those in KwaZulu-Natal, Northwest and Limpopo provinces and Swaziland, and opt instead for malaria-free reserves – Addo Elephant National Park in the Eastern Cape is an excellent choice. Malarial zones carry a considerably reduced risk in winter, so if you're set on going this is the best time. For more advice on malaria, see p.48. **Tuberculosis** (TB) is widespread in South Africa, mostly (but by no means exclusively) affecting the poor, so make sure your child has had a BCG jab. For information on protection against the **sun**, see p.48.

Contacts for travellers with children

US

Family Holidays and Travel in South Africa
ⓦwww.go2africa.com/travel_ideas/family. Off-the-shelf and tailor-made family holidays in South Africa and neighbouring countries.

Rascals in Paradise ☏415/921-7000, ⓦwww
.rascalsinparadise.com. Itineraries in South Africa and neighbouring countries built around activities for kids.

The environment and ethical tourism

Tourism's growth in South Africa has been spectacular, even bucking the post 9/11 global trend that saw tourism falling off elsewhere, and the South African government is banking on tourism becoming one of the major sources of jobs and economic growth. However, the downside is the danger of serious and potentially disruptive effects environmentally, socially, culturally and economically.

Local issues have been covered throughout this book. If you are at all concerned about the impact of tourism or environmental matters, get in touch with the organizations mentioned in the text, or the ones listed below.

Contacts

Campaign for Environmentally Responsible Tourism (CERT) ⓦ www.c-e-r-t.org. Lobbies to educate tour operators and tourists in a sensitive approach to travel, focusing on immediate practical ways in which the environment can be protected.
Fair Trade in Tourism South Africa ⓦ www .fairtourismsa.org.za. Local non-profit organization that promotes equitable and sustainable tourism in South Africa. Website has links to accredited tour operators.

Partners in Responsible Tourism (PIRT) ⓦ www.pirt.org. An organization of individuals and travel companies promoting responsible tourism to minimize harm to the environment and local cultures. Their website features a "Traveler's Code for Traveling Responsibly".
Responsibletravel.com ⓦ www.responsibletravel .com. The site markets a huge variety of carefully screened holidays that are culturally and ecologically supportive of local communities as well as attempting to provide visitors with an "authentic" experience of the country they're visiting.
Tourism Concern ☏ 020/7753 3330, ⓦ www .tourismconcern.org.uk. Campaigns for the rights of local people to be consulted in tourism developments affecting their lives, and produces a quarterly magazine of news and articles. Also publishes a number of books including the *Good Alternative Travel Guide*.

Directory

AIRPORT TAX An arrival tax is charged on all flights, but it's included in all airfares.
BEGGING The coexistence of poverty and wealth in close proximity, and the absence of a social security safety net, make begging a widespread and inevitable phenomenon in South Africa. An extension of begging is people offering services you may not have asked for. Common examples are car "guards" – attendants who hang around parking places, direct you into your parking bay and offer to look

after your vehicle while you're away – essentially an offer you can't refuse. Agree to pay when you return (around R3–5 should do the trick) provided they've done their job.
CONTACT LENSES You can buy cleaning kits for most types of contact lenses in most towns big enough to have a chemist shop.
CONTRACEPTION Despite a serious HIV/AIDS problem, South Africa is remarkably coy about contraception and you shouldn't

expect to find condoms anywhere other than in pharmacies. The pill can also be bought through pharmacies, but only with a doctor's prescription. The safest option is to bring your own supply.

EDUCATIONAL TOURS For arranging specialist educational exchanges, cultural visits or fact-finding missions, there are few better operators than Ida Cooper Associates in Cape Town (℡021 683 4648, ✉idaca@iafrica.com), who facilitate contacts with a wide range of South Africans, including leading academics, artists, writers and government ministers.

ELECTRICITY 220/230V, 50Hz AC. Sockets take unique round-pinned plugs; see ⊛www.kropla.com for details. Most hotel rooms have sockets that will take 110V electric shavers, but for other appliances US visitors will need a transformer.

EMERGENCIES Police ℡10111, Ambulance ℡10177.

LAUNDRIES Most towns have self-operated launderettes where, for a reasonable sum, you can also often have a serviced wash which can include ironing.

SALES TAX AND REFUNDS Value-added tax (VAT) of fourteen percent is levied on most goods and services, though it's usually already included in any quoted price. Foreign visitors can claim back VAT on any goods over R250. To do this, you must present an official tax receipt for the goods, a non-South African passport and the goods purchased themselves, at the airport just before you fly out. You need to complete a VAT refund control sheet (VAT 255) which is obtainable at international airports. For further information contact the VAT Refund Administrator (℡011 394 1117, ⊛www.taxrefunds.co.za).

TIME There is only one time zone throughout the region, two hours ahead of GMT year round. If you're flying from anywhere in Europe, you shouldn't experience any jet lag.

Metric conversion table

1 centimetre (cm) = 0.394in
1 inch (in) = 2.54cm
1 foot (ft) = 30.48cm
1 metre (m) = 100cm = 39.37in
1 yard (yd) = 0.91m
1 kilometre (km) = 1000m
= 0.621 miles
1 mile = 1610m
1 hectare = 10,000 square metres
= 2.471 acres
1 acre = 0.4 hectares
1 UK gallon (gal) = 4.55 litres
1 litre = 0.26 US gallons
1 US gallon (gal) = 5.46 litres
1 gramme (g) = 0.035oz
1 ounce (oz) = 28.57g
1 kilogramme (kg) = 1000g = 2.2lb
1 pound (lb) = 454g

TIPPING Ten to fifteen percent of the tab is the normal tip at restaurants and for taxis – but don't feel obliged to tip if service has been shoddy. Keep in mind that many of the people who'll be serving you will be black South Africans, who rely on tips to supplement a meagre wage on which they support huge extended families. Porters at hotels normally get about R3–5 per bag. At South African garages and filling stations, someone will always be on hand to fill your vehicle and clean your windscreen, for which you should tip around R3–5. It is also usual at hotels to leave some money for the person who services your room. Many establishments, especially private game lodges, take (voluntary) communal tips when you check out – by far the fairest system, which ensures that all the low-profile staff behind the scenes get their share.

WEIGHTS AND MEASURES South Africa is fully metricated, and kilometres, grammes, kilogrammes, litres and degrees Celsius are the norm. Shoe sizes follow the British system.

Guide

Guide

1 Cape Town and the Cape Peninsula 93–185

2 The Western Cape 187–306

3 The Northern Cape 307–361

4 The Eastern Cape 363–456

5 KwaZulu-Natal 457–566

6 Free State.. 567–588

7 Gauteng 589–650

8 North West Province 651–681

9 Mpumalanga 683–726

10 Limpopo 727–757

11 Lesotho 759–807

12 Swaziland 809–839

1

Cape Town and the Cape Peninsula

CHAPTER 1 # Highlights

* **The Bo-Kaap** One of Cape Town's oldest residential areas, its streets characterized by colourful nineteenth-century Cape Dutch and Georgian terraces. See p.130

* **Golden Lion** Highlight of the Gold of Africa Museum, a major collection of historic African works of art. See p.131

* **Robben Island** The infamous island prison that was Nelson Mandela's home for nearly two decades. See p.137

* **Rotate up Table Mountain** Take the revolving cable car to the tabletop. See p.149

* **Chapman's Peak Drive** Enjoy spectacular views as Cape Town's most precipitous road winds along a cliffside above the pounding Atlantic. See p.155

* **The train to Simon's Town** Ride along the False Bay coast just metres from the crashing surf, with stunning views and the option of dining in the restaurant car. See p.157

* **Swim with penguins** Boulders Beach offers wonderful bathing and is home to a colony of African penguins. See p.160

* **Cape Point** The dramatically rocky southernmost section of the Cape Peninsula offers excellent hikes. See p.161

* **Long Street nightlife** Party till the early hours along the city-centre's café, pub and nightclub strip. See p.171

△ Boulders Beach

Cape Town and the Cape Peninsula

CAPE TOWN is southern Africa's most beautiful, most romantic and most visited city. Indeed, few urban centres anywhere can match its setting along the mountainous **Cape Peninsula** spine, which slides into the Atlantic Ocean. By far the most striking – and famous – of its sights is **Table Mountain**, frequently shrouded by clouds, and rearing up from the middle of the city.

More than a scenic backdrop, Table Mountain is the solid core of Cape Town, dividing the city into distinct zones with public gardens, wilderness, forests, hiking routes, vineyards and desirable residential areas trailing down its lower slopes. Standing on the tabletop, you can look north for a giddy view of the **city centre**, its docks lined with matchbox ships. To the west, beyond the mountainous Twelve Apostles, the drop is sheer and your eye sweeps across Africa's priciest real estate, clinging to the slopes along the chilly but spectacularly beautiful **Atlantic seaboard**. To the south, the mountainsides are forested and several historic vineyards and the marvellous Botanical Gardens creep up the lower slopes. Beyond the oak-lined suburbs of Newlands and Constantia lies the warmer **False Bay seaboard**, which curves around towards **Cape Point**. Finally, relegated to the grim industrial east, are the coloured **townships** and black **ghettos**, spluttering in winter under the smoky pall of coal fires – your stark introduction to Cape Town when driving in.

To appreciate Cape Town you need to spend time **outdoors**, as Capetonians do: they hike, picnic or sunbathe, often choose mountain bikes in preference to cars, and turn **adventure activities** into an obsession. Sailboarders from around the world head for Table Bay for some of the world's best windsurfing, and the brave (or unhinged) jump off Lion's Head and paraglide down close to the Clifton beachfront. But the city offers sedate pleasures as well, along its hundreds of paths and 150km of beaches.

Cape Town's rich urban texture is immediately apparent in its diverse **architecture** (see p.144): an indigenous Cape Dutch style, rooted in the Netherlands, finds its apotheosis in the Constantia wine estates, which were themselves brought to new heights by French refugees in the seventeenth century; Muslim slaves, freed in the nineteenth century, added their minarets to the skyline; and the English, who invaded and freed these slaves, introduced Georgian and Victorian buildings. In the tightly packed terraces of twentieth-century

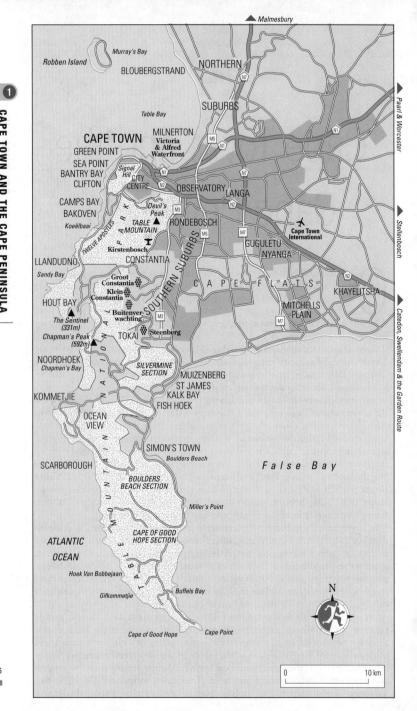

▲ *Malmesbury*

Robben Island

Murray's Bay

BLOUBERGSTRAND

NORTHERN

SUBURBS

Table Bay

► *Paarl & Worcester*

CAPE TOWN

MILNERTON

Victoria & Alfred Waterfront

GREEN POINT

SEA POINT

BANTRY BAY

CLIFTON

Signal Hill

CITY CENTRE

N1

OBSERVATORY LANGA

► *Stellenbosch*

CAMPS BAY

BAKOVEN

Koeëlbaai

Devil's Peak

TABLE MOUNTAIN ▲

RONDEBOSCH

M3

Cape Town International ✈

TWELVE APOSTLES

Kirstenbosch

GUGULETU

NYANGA

LLANDUDNO

Sandy Bay

CONSTANTIA

C A P E   F L A T S

Groot Constantia 🍇

Klein Constantia 🍇

SOUTHERN SUBURBS

KHAYELITSHA

HOUT BAY

The Sentinel (331m)

Chapman's Peak (592m) ▲

Buitenver-wachting 🍇

M3

Steenberg 🍇

TOKAI

MITCHELLS PLAIN

M7

NOORDHOEK

Chapman's Bay

SILVERMINE SECTION

MUIZENBERG

ST JAMES

KALK BAY

FISH HOEK

KOMMETJIE

OCEAN VIEW

SIMON'S TOWN

Boulders Beach

False Bay

SCARBOROUGH

BOULDERS BEACH SECTION

Miller's Point

ATLANTIC OCEAN

CAPE OF GOOD HOPE SECTION

Hoek Van Bobbejaan

Gifkommetjie

Buffels Bay

Cape of Good Hope *Cape Point*

N

0   10 km

► *Caledon, Swellendam & the Garden Route*

Bo-Kaap and the tenements of District Six, coloured descendants of slaves evolved a unique, evocatively Capetonian brand of jazz, which is well worth catching live – it's still played in the Cape Flats and some city-centre clubs.

Weather is an abiding obsession of Capetonians, and no climatic feature is more dominant in the mind of the city's inhabitants than the **southeaster**, the cool summer wind that blows in across False Bay. It can singlehandedly determine what kind of day you're going to have, and when it gusts at over 60kph you won't want to be outdoors, let alone on the beach. Conversely, its gentler incarnation as the so-called **Cape Doctor** brings welcome relief on humid summer days, and lays the famous cloudy tablecloth on top of Table Mountain.

Some history

San hunter-gatherers, South Africa's first human inhabitants, moved freely through the Cape Peninsula for tens of millennia before being edged into the interior some two thousand years ago by the arrival of sheep-herding **Khoikhoi** migrants from the north. Over the next 1600 years the Khoikhoi held sway over the Cape pastures. **Portuguese** mariners, in search of a stopoff point en route to East Africa and the East Indies, first rounded the Cape in the 1480s, and named it Cabo de Boa Esperanza (Cape of Good Hope), but their attempts at trading with the Khoikhoi were short-lived, and no Europeans seriously attempted to create a permanent stopping-off point until the **Dutch East India Company** (VOC) cruised into Table Bay in 1652 and set up shop.

The VOC, the world's largest corporation at the time, planned little more at the Cape than a halfway house, to provide fresh produce to their ships travelling between Europe and the East, in search of spices, slaves and profit. Their small landing party, led by **Jan van Riebeeck**, built a mud fort where the Grand Parade now stands and established **vegetable gardens**, which they hoped to work with Khoikhoi labour.

The Khoikhoi were understandably reluctant to exchange their traditional lifestyle for the restrictions of formal employment, so van Riebeeck began to import **slaves** in 1658. The growth of the Dutch settlement alarmed the Khoikhoi, who declared war in 1659 in an attempt to drive the Europeans out; however, they were defeated and had to cede the peninsula to the colonists.

During the early eighteenth century, Western Cape Khoikhoi society disintegrated, **German** and **French** religious refugees swelled the European population, and slavery became the economic backbone of the colony, which was now a minor colonial village of canals and low, whitewashed, flat-roofed houses. By 1750, Cape Town had become a town of over 1000 buildings, with 2500 inhabitants.

In 1795, **Britain**, deeply concerned by Napoleonic expansionism, grabbed Cape Town to secure the strategic sea route to the East. This move was not welcomed by the settlement's Calvinist Dutch burghers, but was better news for the substantially Muslim slave population, as Britain ordered the **abolition of slavery**. The British also allowed **freedom of religion**, and South Africa's first mosque was soon built by freed slaves, in Dorp Street in the Bo-Kaap.

By the turn of the nineteenth century, Cape Town had become one of the most cosmopolitan places anywhere and a sea port of major significance, growing under the influence of the British Empire. The Commercial Exchange was completed in 1819, followed by department stores, banks and insurance company buildings. In the 1860s the docks were begun, Victoria Road from the city to Sea Point was built, and the suburban railway line to Wynberg was laid. Since slavery had been abolished, Victorian Cape Town had to be built with **convict labour** and that of prisoners of war transported from the colonial frontier in Eastern Cape. Racial segregation wasn't far behind, and an outbreak of bubonic plague in 1901 gave the town council an excuse to establish **Ndabeni**, Cape Town's first black location, near Maitland.

In 1910, Cape Town was drawn into the political centre of the newly federated South Africa when it became the **legislative capital** of the Union. Africans and coloureds, excluded from the cosy deal between Boers and the British, had to find expression in the workplace. In 1919 they flexed their collective muscle on the docks, forming the mighty **Industrial and Commercial Union**, which boasted 200,000 members in its heyday.

Increasing industrialization brought an influx of black workers, who were housed in the locations of **Guguletu** and **Nyanga**, built in 1945. Three years later, the National Party came to power, promising a fearful white electorate that it would reverse the flow of Africans to the cities. In Cape Town it introduced a policy favouring coloureds for employment: among Africans, only men who had jobs were admitted (the women were excluded altogether), and the construction of family accommodation for Africans was forbidden.

Langa township became a stronghold of the **Pan Africanist Congress** (PAC), which organized a peaceful anti-pass demonstration in Cape Town on April 8, 1960. Police fired on the crowd, killing three people and wounding many more. As a result, the government declared a state of emergency and banned anti-apartheid opposition groups, including the PAC and ANC.

In 1966, the notorious **Group Areas Act** was used to uproot whole coloured communities from District Six and to move them to the desolate **Cape Flats**. Here, rampant gangsterism took vicious root and remains one of Cape Town's most pressing problems today. To compound the problem, the National Party stripped away coloured representation on the town council in 1972.

Eleven years later, at a huge meeting on the Cape Flats, the extra-parliamentary opposition defied government repression and re-formed as the **United Democratic Front**, heralding a period of intensified struggle to topple apartheid. In 1986, one of the major pillars crumbled when the government was forced to scrap influx control; blacks began pouring into Cape Town seeking work and erecting shantytowns, making Cape Town one of the fastest-growing cities in the world. On February 11, 1990, the city's history took a neat twist when, just hours after being released from prison, **Nelson Mandela** made his first public speech from the balcony of City Hall to a jubilant crowd spilling across the Grand Parade, the very site of the first Dutch fort. Four years later, he entered the formerly whites-only Parliament, 500m away, as South Africa's first democratically elected president.

Despite over a decade of non-racial democracy, Cape Town remains a divided city. On the one hand, the whites still enjoy a comfortable existence in the leafy suburbs along the two coasts and the slopes of Table Mountain. On the desolate **Cape Flats**, while some progress has been made in bringing electricity to the shantytowns, the shacks are still there – and spreading. Despite white fears about crime, it is still blacks and coloureds who are overwhelmingly and disproportionately the victims of protracted violence, much of it gang-related.

Orientation, arrival and information

Between two mountainous flanks, reaching away from the docks, encompassing the intense city centre and up the mountain is the **City Bowl** (made up of the Upper and Lower city centres and the Waterfront), where lively areas,

The language of colour

It's striking just how un-African Cape Town looks and sounds. Lying halfway between East and West, Cape Town drew its population from Africa, Asia and Europe, and traces of all three continents are found in the genes, language, culture, religion and cuisine of South Africa's coloured population. The dominant language of the city is **Afrikaans** (a close relative of Dutch), the only "European" language to evolve outside Europe. Although English is universally spoken and understood, Afrikaans is the mother tongue of a large proportion of the city's **coloured** residents, as well as a good number of whites. The term "coloured" is fraught with confusion, but in South Africa doesn't have the same connotations as in Britain and the US; it refers to South Africans of mixed race. This comes as a surprise to most visitors, who assume that it's all black and white in South Africa, when in fact issues of ethnicity and language are extremely complex. Most brown-skinned people in Cape Town (over fifty percent of the population), and many others throughout the country, are coloureds, with slave and Khoikhoi ancestry going back to the seventeenth to early nineteenth centuries.

In the late nineteenth century, Afrikaans-speaking whites, fighting for an identity, sought to create a "racially pure" culture by driving a wedge between themselves and coloured Afrikaans-speakers. They reinvented Afrikaans as a "white man's language", eradicating the supposed stigma of its coloured ties by substituting Dutch words for those with Asian or African roots. In 1925, the white dialect of Afrikaans became an official language alongside English, and the dialects spoken by coloureds were treated as comical deviations from correct usage.

For Afrikaner nationalists this wasn't enough, and after the introduction of apartheid in 1948, they attempted to codify perceived racial differences. Under the **Population Registration Act**, all South Africans were classified as white, coloured or Bantu (the apartheid term for Africans). The underlying assumption was that these distinctions were based on objective criteria. For the apartheid authorities, it seemed fairly clear who was "Bantu" and who was white, but the coloureds posed particular problems. Firstly, they weren't homogenous so, to accommodate this, the **Coloured Proclamation Act** of 1959 defined eight categories of coloured: Cape Coloured; Malay (Muslim); Griqua; Chinese; Indian; Other Indian; Other Asiatic; and Other Coloured. For reasons of expediency related to trade, Japanese people were defined as "honorary white".

The second difficulty surrounding coloureds was the fact that their appearance spans the entire range, from those who are indistinguishable from whites to those who look like Africans. A number of coloureds managed successfully to reinvent themselves as whites, and apartheid legislation made provision for the racial reclassification of individuals. Between 1983 and 1990, nearly five thousand "Cape Coloureds" were reclassified as "white" and over two thousand Africans were reclassified as "Cape Coloured". Notorious tests were employed – one, for example, where a pencil would be placed in a person's hair and twirled; if the hair sprang back the person would be regarded as coloured, but if it stayed twirled he or she was white.

Far more than mere semantics, these classifications became fundamental to what kind of life a person could expect. There are numerous cases of families in which one sibling was classified coloured, while another was termed white and could then live in comfortable white areas, enjoy good employment opportunities (many jobs were closed to coloureds), and have the right to send their children to better schools and universities. Many coloured professionals, on the other hand, were evicted from houses they owned in comfortable suburbs such as Claremont, which overnight were declared white.

With the demise of apartheid, the make-up of residential areas is shifting – and so is the thinking on ethnic terminology. Some people now reject the term "coloured" because of its apartheid associations, and refuse any racial definitions; others, however, proudly embrace the term, as a means of acknowledging their distinct culture, with its slave and Khoikhoi roots.

CITY CENTRE AND SUBURBS

Robben Island ◀

False Bay Seaboard ▶

Table Bay

THE FORESHORE

Duncan Dock

See City Centre

PAARDEN EILAND

MARINE DRIVE

TABLE BAY BOULEVARD (N1)

Salt River

Observatory

Mowbray

LIESBEEK PARKWAY

MAIN RD

N2

ROSEBANK

Rosebank

OBSERVATORY

MAIN RD

M3

SALT RIVER

VICTORIA RD

Woodstock

WOODSTOCK

EASTERN BOULEVARD (N2)

DE WAAL DRIVE (M3)

ZONNEBLOEM (DISTRICT SIX)

Cape Town Central Station

Castle of Good Hope

VICTORIA AND ALFRED WATERFRONT

See V&A Waterfront & De Waterkant map

CITY CENTRE

ADDERLEY ST

STRAND ST

LONG ST

BUITENGRACHT ST

BO-KAAP

SOMERSET RD

BUITENKANT ST

VREDEHOEK

KLOOF NEK ST

KLOOF ST

ORANJEZICHT

See City Bowl Suburbs map

Devil's Peak (1000m)

Rhodes Memorial

ROSEBANK

MOUILLE POINT

BEACH RD

MAIN RD

HIGH LEVEL RD

KLOOF RD

Signal Hill (350m)

TAMBOERSKLOOF

GARDENS

Kloof Nek Bus Terminus

Table Mountain

TAFELBERG RD

Cableway

The Pipe Track hiking route

CAMPS BAY DRIVE

THREE ANCHOR BAY

SEA POINT

BEACH RD

MAIN RD

Lion's Head (669m)

BANTRY BAY

CLIFTON

VICTORIA RD

CAMPS BAY

See Mouille Point, Green Point, Sea Point & Clifton map

N

0   1 km

such as Long Street, the Bo-Kaap and Gardens, rub shoulders with the wealth of suburbs such as Tamboerskloof and Oranjezicht. **Long Street** aptly runs the full length of the city centre and continues as lively **Kloof Street**, which cuts through the City Bowl suburbs to Kloof Nek, a junction that splays out to the lower cableway station, Sea Point, the Atlantic seaboard and Signal Hill. Straggling south from the centre along the eastern slope of the mountain, the predominantly white **southern suburbs** become progressively more affluent as you move from arty Observatory through the comfortably middle-class districts of Rondebosch and Newlands, culminating with the Constantia wine estates. Along the coastal belt, the **Atlantic seaboard** is drier and sunnier, with the wealthiest areas like Clifton and Camps Bay clinging to the mountainside above the sea, white sands and rocky beaches. The **False Bay** coast is wetter and greener, the sea here usually several degrees warmer than the western peninsula, making Muizenberg, Fish Hoek and Boulders Beach in Simon's Town the most popular bathing beaches in Cape Town. Curling northeast around Table Bay, the **northern suburbs**, taking in Parow, Milnerton and Bloubergstrand, are exceptionally dull, with a traditional Afrikaans flavour. South of these, and extending seemingly endlessly along the N2 into the interior, the coloured **Cape Flats townships** jostle with the desolate, litter-strewn **African ghettos** of Nyanga, Langa and Guguletu, which relentlessly overflow into kilometre after kilometre of iron, wood and cardboard shantytowns.

Arrival

Cape Town International Airport (flight information ☎021 934 0407) lies on the Cape Flats, 22km east of the city centre. Two **shuttle bus** companies, Legend Tours (☎021 936 2814) and Dumalisile (☎021 934 1660), have desks in the international arrivals hall outside the baggage reclaim area and run a door-to-door service throughout the peninsula. Although they don't operate to a strict schedule (they try to take three or four passengers travelling on the same route), you shouldn't have to wait more than fifteen minutes for your minibus to leave. The fare from the airport into the city centre is R130 for the first person and R30 for each additional passenger. An alternative is the similarly priced Magic Bus (☎021 505 6300), which must be **booked** a day ahead; the bus will meet you at the airport and take you anywhere on the peninsula. Babrius (☎021 788 6273), another thoroughly reliable and reasonably priced small transfer company, also needs to be booked ahead and is recommended if you want to head south to Muizenberg (R160) – where it is based – and beyond. Metered **taxis** operated by Touch Down Taxis, the company officially authorized by the airport, rank in reasonable numbers outside both terminals and charge about R150 per person for the trip into the city.

The major **car rental** firms have desks inside the international terminal. Prebooking a vehicle is essential, especially during the week when there is a big demand from domestic business travellers, and over the mid-December to mid-January and Easter peak seasons. A **bureau de change** is open to coincide with international arrivals; there are also **ATMs** and a basic tourist **information desk**.

Intercity buses and trains

Greyhound, Intercape and Translux **intercity buses** and mainline **trains** terminate in the centre of town around the interlinked central complex that includes the **train station** and **Golden Acre** shopping mall, at the junction of Strand and Adderley streets. Note that Intercape and Translux arrive on the northeast side of

CITY CENTRE

ACCOMMODATION
Ikhaya Lodge   A

**RESTAURANTS, CAFÉS,
BARS & CLUBS**
Biesmiellah   5
Caroline's Cape Kitchen   4
Charly's Bakery   8
Col'Cacchio   3
Drum Café   9
Jewel Tavern   1
Marimba's   2
Mercury Live and Lounge   6
The Shack   7

See V&A Waterfront
& De Waterkant Map

Duncan Dock

THE FORESHORE

DUNCAN ROAD

Cape Town
International
Conference Centre

COEN STEYTLER AVE

Artscape
Complex

HERTZOG BOULEVARD
HERTZOG BOULEVARD

HANS STRIJDOM AVE

THIBAULT
SQUARE

BREE
PRESTWICH

Gold
of Africa
Museum

Train
Station

STRAND STR EXTN

Castle of
Good Hope

Evangelical
Lutheran
Church

STRAND

CASTLE
HOUT

Cape Town Tourism
Visitors' Centre

See Around Long St & the
Company's Garden map

GRAND
PARADE

DARLING

ZONNEBLOEM
(DISTRICT 6)

BO-KAAP

CHURCH

LONGMARKET

City
Hall

LONGMARKET

CALEDON

CALEDON

Cape
Technikon

Bo-Kaap
Museum

WALE

DORP

District Six
Museum

UPPER LEEUWEN

PEPPER

HARRINGTON

DE VILLIERS

UPPER PEPPER

BLOEM

COMMERCIAL

UPPER BLOEM

BUITEN

ROELAND

MILITARY

BRYANT

NEWCHURCH

JORDAN

The
Company's
Gardens

DE WAAL DRIVE

ORPHAN

BUITENSINGEL

VREDEHOEK

BROOK

Bertram
House

JUTLAND AVE

PARK ROAD

ORANGE

ORANJEZICHT

GARDENS

0   500 m

Cable Station, Camps Bay & Atlantic Seaboard

the station, off Adderley Street, while Greyhound arrives on the northwest side
in Adderley itself. The Golden Acre shopping complex can be a confusing mud-
dle, but this is where all rail and bus transport (both intercity and from elsewhere
in the city) and most minibus taxis converge – if you use public transport at all,
you're bound to find yourself here at some stage. Everything you need for your
next move is within two or three blocks of here, including information.

Information

The best source of information about the city is **Cape Town Tourism** (ⓦwww.tourismcapetown.com), which has two excellent information bureaus: the city-centre visitor centre (March–Nov Mon–Fri 8am–6pm, Sat 8.30am–1pm & Sun 9am–1pm; Dec–Feb Mon–Fri 8am–7pm, Sat 8.30am–1pm & Sun 9am–1pm; ☏021 426 4260), at the corner of Burg and Castle streets, a five-minute walk two blocks west of the station; and the Clocktower Precinct visitor centre (daily 9am–9pm; ☏021 405 4500) in a fabulous office at the V&A Waterfront next to the Nelson Mandela Gateway to Robben Island. Both centres operate comprehensive accommodation and activity **booking services**, have a swanky coffee shop, a book shop and cybercafé as well as lots of brochures and very cheap city maps. Bookings for national parks can also be made here.

The best sources of **events listings** are the relatively unprepossessing supplements that appear in the mainstream press at the weekend. The *Top of the Times* supplement comes with Friday's *Cape Times* (ⓦwww.capetimes.co.za), and the *Good Weekend* pullout with the Saturday *Cape Argus* (ⓦwww.capeargus.co.za), but best of the bunch is the *Mail & Guardian*'s Friday supplement, which injects some attitude into its reviews and listings. A free two-pager, *48 Hours,* is handed out at city traffic lights on Fridays. *Cape Review*, a monthly listings magazine, gives a broad range of information on food, wine, gay venues, nightlife and sporting events. Also containing a fair amount of listings is *The Other Guide* (ⓦwww.otherguide.co.za)*,* a free monthly magazine aimed mainly at foreign tourists, and distributed at the airport.

If you're planning to explore beyond the confines of the city centre, you'll need to invest in one of the detailed **street atlases**, found at most bookshops, including the ubiquitous CNA chain. MapStudio's *A to Z Streetmap* is the cheapest; it's adequate for the centre and most of the suburbs, but doesn't cover Simon's Town. There are countless **guidebooks** on walks around Cape Town, hikes up Table Mountain, dive sites, fishing locations, surfing breaks and windsurfing spots. For the best-stocked shelves and nicest atmosphere, head for one of the Exclusive Books stores (see p.182). You'll also find useful books on all aspects of South Africa at the secondhand bookshops down Long Street (see p.122).

City transport

Although Cape Town's city centre is compact enough to get around on foot, many of the attractions are spread along the considerable length of the peninsula. To make the most of your visit you'll need to use **taxis**, **rent transport**, take a **tour**, or make do with the pretty skeletal public transport system. Inner-city areas west of the centre are better served by **buses** than other central suburbs, but transport north along the Atlantic coast is negligible. There is, however, a **train** service cutting through the southern suburbs and continuing all the way down to Simon's Town. It's fairly reliable and well used, though the rolling stock, which is gradually being upgraded, is looking a little battered.

Note that using public transport **after dark** is potentially risky. If you're forced to do so, take sensible precautions, such as travelling in a group (especially women) and avoiding third-class carriages on trains; otherwise, make every effort to take metered taxis at night.

Buses

The only frequent and reliable **bus** services are those from the centre to the Waterfront and Sea Point; infrequent buses also go down the Atlantic seaboard to Camps Bay and Hout Bay, and there are a couple to Kirstenbosch. Don't attempt to catch a bus to the southern suburbs: the train is much quicker and more efficient.

The principal bus station is the **Golden Acre bus terminal**, off Strand Street, wedged between Golden Acre Shopping Centre, the station and the Grand Parade. Buses depart from here to Green Point, Sea Point, Camps Bay and Hout Bay, while services for the Waterfront leave from Adderley Street outside the station. Note that the buses aren't numbered; you identify them from the destination on the front. All but the Waterfront buses are intended for use by workers, services beginning at 6.30am, and ending at 6.30pm. The Waterfront buses also start early, but continue until 10.30pm, and have the greatest frequency.

Tickets are sold by the driver: state your destination to the driver, and pay when you get on. A single ticket from the city costs around R4 to Sea Point, or about R6 to Camps Bay. Weekly and monthly tickets are also available. For **timetables**, enquire at the Golden Arrow **information booth** (℡021 408 1000 or toll-free ℡080 212 111, ⓦwww.gabs.co.za) at the Golden Acre bus terminal. It's advisable to check bus times and points of departure at the booth.

The open-top **bus tour** of Cape Tourism, the **Cape Town Explorer** (also called the Topless Tour; ℡021 511 1784, ⓦwww.hyltonross.co.za), is also an extremely useful, if slightly expensive (R90 per person per day), means of negotiating the city-centre sights and the Atlantic seaboard beaches. You can hop on and off throughout the day wherever you please along the route. **Departures** are hourly (April, Sept & Oct 9.30am–3pm, May–Aug 9.30am–2pm; Nov–March 9.30am–3.30pm & until 5pm Dec–Feb) from the **V&A Waterfront** outside *Ferryman's Pub*. The **route** is circular and takes in the Clock Tower at the Waterfront; the Cape Town Convention Centre on the Foreshore; the city centre (buses stop at Cape Town Tourism in Strand Street, the South Africa Museum, the South Africa Jewish Museum, the Castle of Good Hope and the Gold Museum); the City Bowl suburbs; the lower cableway station (for the cable car up Table Mountain) and the Atlantic Seaboard from Camps Bay to Sea Point, before returning to the Waterfront.

Useful city-bus routes

City centre to Waterfront Cape Town station–Riebeeck Street–Buitengragt Street–Waterfront (Mon–Fri every 10min, Sat & Sun every 15min).

City centre to Sea Point Golden Acre terminal–Mouille Point–Main Road Green Point–Main Road Sea Point (Mon–Sat 20 daily).

City centre to Hout Bay Golden Acre terminal–Lower Plein St–Darling Rd–Adderley Street–Green Point–Sea Point–Camps Bay–Hout Bay beach–Hout Bay harbour (Mon–Sat 6 daily, Sun 3 daily; 1hr).

City centre to Kirstenbosch Golden Acre terminal–Mowbray–Kirstenbosch at 7.30am, 12.35pm and 3.35pm, return only 9.35am and 3.30pm.

V&A Waterfront to Sea Point V&A Waterfront–Mouille Point–Green Point–Three Anchor Bay–Beach Road Sea Point (daily every 20min).

Taxis, minibus taxis and shuttle buses

The term "**taxi**" is no less ambiguous in Cape Town than elsewhere in South Africa: it's used to refer to conventional metered cars, jam-packed minibuses and their more upmarket cousins, Rikki's. **Metered taxis**, regulated by the Cape Town Municipality, don't cruise up and down looking for fares; you'll need to go to the taxi ranks around town, including the Waterfront, the train station and Greenmarket Square. Alternatively, you can phone to be picked up (see p.185). Taxis must have the driver's name and identification clearly on display and the meter clearly visible. Fares work out at around R10 per kilometre, expensive compared with other forms of transport, though definitely worth it at night, when metered taxis are the safest way of getting around.

Minibus taxis and Rikki's

Minibus taxis are cheap, frequent and bomb up and down the main routes at tearaway speeds. They can be hailed from the street – you'll recognize them from the hooting, loud music and touting – or boarded at the central taxi rank, adjacent to the train station. Once you've boarded, pay the *guardjie* (assistant), who sits near the driver, and tell him when you want to get off. Fares should be under R5 for most trips. As well as crazed driving, be prepared for pickpockets working the taxi ranks.

Rikki's are minibus taxis aimed principally at tourists (Mon–Sat 8am–4pm). Carrying no more than eight passengers, they are small open-backed vehicles, covered by a canopy but open at the rear; you need to book them by telephone (☎021 423 4888). In Cape Town, Rikki's zip about the City Bowl, the Waterfront and the Atlantic seaboard as far as Camps Bay, and go to Kirstenbosch (R60 for four passengers), as well as providing the cheapest transport to the airport (R120 for a group of four, plus R10 for each additional passenger up to a maximum of eight). There is also a regular Rikki's service in Simon's Town, operating between the station and other points in the village on request. Fares are kept down by picking up and dropping off passengers along the way (R10).

Shuttle buses

A growth area in Cape Town are **shuttle buses**, which have to be booked, and which will pick you up from your accommodation. In some cases they run to a schedule, or can be chartered. They tend to be cheaper than metered taxis and take you door to door. One of the most useful services runs on demand in co-operation with Cape Town Tourism from their city centre and Waterfront visitor centres during their opening hours, going to Kirstenbosch National Botanical Gardens (R35 one way), and also to the Table Mountain lower cableway station and other points of interest.

Reliable operators you can charter include: Sun Tours & Shuttle (☎021 797 4646), which offers a 24-hour service between any two points on the peninsula, including the city to the airport (R200 for the first three passengers, then R50 per additional person); and the similarly priced Boogey Bus (☎082 495 5698, ⓔsivada@telkomsa.net), which specializes in taking passengers to clubs, including those on the Cape Flats.

Trains

Cape Town's suburban train service is run by Metrorail (timetable information ☎0800 656 463, ⓦwww.capemetrorail.co.za). The only route likely to be useful to tourists is the relatively reliable if slightly run-down line going through the southern suburbs and all the way down to False Bay seaboard from Cape

A growing number of smaller companies offer niche cultural tours; the most popular of these are townships tours, which can safely get you around the African and coloured areas that were created under apartheid. Apart from this, a number of other outfits, listed below, can help you scratch beneath Cape Town's surface. Almost all companies will pick you up from your accommodation and drop you off again at the end of the day.

Besides the companies listed below, Cape Town Tourism offers a **city walking tour** (Mon–Fri 11am & 1.30pm; R100), which covers the main sights. The tour lasts an hour and departs from their visitor centre on the corner of Burg and Castle streets at 9.30am on Mondays, Wednesdays and Fridays (R50). There's a Bo-Kaap walk on Tuesdays and Thursdays at 9.30am (R75).

Tour operators

Ardis Tours ☎021 790 8864 or 082 655 0137, ⓦwww.ardis.co.za. Excursions to the Cape Peninsula excursions, as well as to Winelands, the West Coast, Hermanus, plus adventure sports tours. Reliable and restricted to small groups, though they need a minimum of three people to run. Half-day trips from R350.

Day Trippers ☎021 511 4766, ⓦwww.daytrippers.co.za. Cycling from Scarborough into the Table Mountain National Park, with hikes down to Cape Point and a picnic, as well as tours to the usual sights such as the Winelands (all R350). The peninsula day-trip includes Hout Bay, with the option of a boat trip to Duiker Island to see the seals and Boulders Beach for the penguins.

Grassroute Tours ☎021 706 1006, ⓦwww.grassroutetours.co.za. Half-day trips (R290) include a visit to African and coloured townships, and walking tours of the Bo-Kaap, covering the *kramats* (Muslim shrines). A day tour (R450) features a visit to Robben Island, with the cost of the ferry and island tour included in the price.

Hylton Ross Tours ☎021 511 1784, ⓦwww.hyltonross.co.za. Door-to-door tours which cover all the popular sights along the Cape Peninsula, and also scheduled guided day-tours to Hermanus (Wed & Sun), which cost R430.

Mother City Tours ☎021 448 3817. Half- and full-day tours of the city, Cape Point, Table Mountain and the Winelands. Also whale-watching trips in season (Aug–Oct; R350). Tours are limited to six people in a minibus; a full day for four, for example, works out at around R420 each.

Our Pride ☎021 531 4291 or 082 446 7974, ⓦwww.bonanitours.co.za. Highly recommended tours on which you get to meet the people of the Bo-Kaap and District Six as well as the African townships and squatter camps. They also do jazz outings in which you visit two clubs, and a "Township by Night" trip, which includes supper at a township restaurant and a visit to a *shebeen*. All these are half-day trips, costing R300.

Thuthuka Tours ☎021 433 2429 or 082 979 5831, ⓦwww.townshipcrawling.com. An outstanding range of half-day township tours, with the possibility of experiencing Xhosa rituals, authentic consultations with a traditional healer or night-time music outings. Gospel tours on Sunday mornings take visitors to township churches, while the Sunday breakfast/brunch outing takes you to a café in Guguletu where you listen to jazz and get to meet locals. On Thurs and Fri eves you get collected at 6pm and taken to a township music venue for supper. All outings R240.

Western Cape Action Tours ☎021 461 1371, ⓦwww.dacpm.org. Led by former Cape Town activists of Umkhonto we Sizwe (the ANC's armed wing), these tours focus on the fight against apartheid and the situation today. Visitors go to the townships, see sites of political resistance, as well as visit a traditional healer, housing projects and township markets. Half day R220, full day including lunch R450.

Town station. Three other lines run east from Cape Town to Strand (through Bellville), to the Cape Flats, and to the outlying towns of Stellenbosch and Paarl; however, the journeys aren't recommended, as they run through some less safe areas of the Flats.

The service to the False Bay seaboard is undoubtedly one of the great urban train journeys of the world. It reaches the coast at Muizenberg and continues south to Simon's Town, sometimes so spectacularly close to the ocean that you can feel the spray and peer into rock pools. The stretch of the line to Fish Hoek is well served, with several trains an hour (Mon–Fri 5.10am–7.30pm every 15min, Sat 6.20am–6.45pm every 20min, Sun 5.50am–6.30pm roughly hourly, though more frequently during the summer). Services to Simon's Town go every 40–60 minutes. By far the nicest way to travel is while savouring a meal in the **Biggsy's buffet car** (see p.157 for more).

Trains run overground, and there are no signposts to the stations on the streets. If you're staying in the southern suburbs, ask for directions at your accommodation. Tickets must be bought at the station before boarding. You're best off in the first-class carriages, which are reasonably priced (for example, Cape Town–Muizenberg is R10 one-way); curiously, there's no second class. Third class tends to be more crowded, and in the mornings can ring out with harmonies of domestic workers singing on their way to clean houses.

Driving

Cape Town has good roads and several fast freeways that, outside peak hours (7–9am & 4–6pm), can whisk you across town in next to no time. The obvious landmarks of Table Mountain and the two seaboards make orientation straightforward, particularly south of the centre, and some wonderful journeys are possible. The most notable are the drives along the Atlantic seaboard to Hout Bay and Chapman's Peak Drive, a narrow winding cliff-edge road with the Atlantic breaking hundreds of metres below; and around the Cape Point section of the Table Mountain National Park via the False Bay seaboard.

The usual precautions for defensive driving in South Africa are in order, especially since Cape Town has a few peculiarities all of its own. An unwritten rule of the road on the peninsula is that minibus taxis have the right of way – and will push in front of you without compunction. Don't mess with them: the vehicles are bigger than yours, drivers may carry handguns and will routinely run through amber lights as they change to red – as will many Capetonians. Take care approaching a freeway: the on-ramps frequently feed directly into the fast lane, and Capetonians have no compunction in exceeding the 100kph freeway and 120kph highway speed limits. There's often little warning of branches off to the suburbs, only the final destination of the freeway being signed. Your best bet is to plan your journey, and make sure you know exactly where you're going.

Car parks are dotted all over the place in this car-friendly city. To park on the street you'll need a prepaid ADO meter card, which you swipe in one of the green ADO Cash Card machines nearest to your parking space. There are also unofficial attendants who carry cards with them and whom you can pay directly. If you want to park in peace, head for one of the multistorey parking garages – there's one attached to the Golden Acre complex, and another at the north end of Lower Burg Street. Almost anywhere you park, bar the garages, you'll be expected to tip the car guards who are supposed to look after parked vehicles.

Car and motorbike rental

Given Cape Town's scant public transport, renting a vehicle is the only convenient way of exploring the Cape Peninsula, and needn't break the bank. There
are dozens of competing car rental companies to choose from (see p.184). To
get the best deal, either pick up one of the brochures at Cape Town Tourism
office or look in the *Yellow Pages*.

For motorbike rental, Le Cap Motorcycle Hire, 3 Carisbrook Street (℡021
423 0823 or 072 259 0009, ⓦwww.lecap.co.za), provides all the necessary
gear and rents out serious bikes (from R360 daily, plus R1/km; weekly rental
available). African Buzz, at 220 Long Street (℡021 423 0052), rents out 100cc
scooters with all the gear you need for R175 for 24 hours.

One of the most popular – and hair-raising – road routes for cyclists is along
the narrow hairpins of Chapman's Peak Drive (see p.155), which offer stupendous views of the Atlantic. There are also a number of dedicated mountain-
biking routes in the peninsula's nature reserves. For rental outlets, see p.184.

Accommodation

Cape Town has plenty of **accommodation** to suit all budgets, but to guarantee the kind of place you want, booking ahead is recommended, especially
over the Christmas holidays (mid-Dec to mid-Jan). The greatest concentration
of accommodation is in the City Bowl and the Atlantic seaside strip as far as
Sea Point.

Besides Cape Town Tourism's efficient accommodation booking desk,
there are a few accommodation **agencies** that may be able to help if you're
stuck: Bed 'n' Breakfast, PO Box 13640, Mowbray 7705 (℡021 686 9770,
ⓔbnb@mcaplan.co.za) has accommodation for R180–300 per person per
night, while A–Z Holiday Accommodation, 15 Winton Crescent, Woodbridge
Island 7441 (℡021 551 2785, ⓦwww.a-zholidayhomes.co.za) can provide
self-catering accommodation during December and January, ranging from a
two-person apartment for R500 a day to a R8000 super-luxury house.

City centre

The city centre's accommodation is highly concentrated along **Long Street**,
featuring more **backpacker lodges** per square metre than on any other street
in Cape Town and, in their wake, a growing number of student travel agencies,
cheap car-rental outfits and adventure-activity outlets. Long Street is also the
lively focus for restaurants, clubs and pubs. The heart of the city centre extends
four blocks east to take in the **Company's Gardens**. Accommodation in these
areas is marked on the map on p.120, except for the *iKhaya Lodge*, shown on
the map on p.102.

Cape Heritage Hotel 90 Bree St ℡021 424
4646, ⓦwww.capeheritage.co.za. An elegant and
tastefully restored hotel located in a row of houses
dating back to 1771, in Cape Heritage Square, just
below the Bo-Kaap. The rooms are spacious and
each is furnished according to a theme, among
them African, Japanese and Dutch. Although
there's no garden, there's a nice courtyard. ❻
Cape Town Hollow Hotel 88 Queen Victoria St
℡021 423 1260, ⓦwww.capetownhollow.co.za.

A smart multistorey hotel with a/c rooms, cable
TV, baths and showers. Two minutes from the
South African Museum and National Gallery, an
easy and pleasant walk away via the Company's
Gardens. ❺
Cat & Moose 305 Long St ℡021 423 7638,
ⓦwww.catandmoose.co.za. The most stylish of
the Long St lodges, housed in an eighteenth-
century building a couple of doors from the
steam baths at the south end of the city centre.

Timber floors with Turkish-style rugs, exposed beams, earthy reds and ochres as well as some African masks imbue it with a warm ethnic feel. The dorms, triples and double rooms are arranged around a small leafy courtyard, with a waterfall cascading into a plunge pool. Dorms ❶, rooms ❶

iKhaya Lodge Wandel Street, Dunkley Square ☎021 461 8880, ⓦwww.ikhayalodge.co.za. A guesthouse three short blocks away from the Company's Gardens and museums. Its eleven standard rooms in the main guesthouse, five luxury loft suites and two self-catering apartments, done out in ethnically inspired decor, have mountain or (cheaper) city views. The lodge's patio overlooks the outdoor eateries of trendy Dunkley Square. ❺

Long Street Backpackers 209 Long St ☎021 423 0615, ⓦwww.longstreetbackpackers.co.za. The oldest Long St backpacker lodge, on the top two floors of an unexceptional three-storey former apartment block arranged around a courtyard, with dorms, doubles and singles. Quieter than some of the other lodges in the vicinity, it's a well-organized place, with a laundry, Internet facilities and a travel desk; there's also a lively bar and a kitchen. ❶

Metropole Hotel 38 Long St ☎021 424 7247, ⓦwww.metropolehotel.co.za. Well-situated hotel that makes for a thoroughly urban stay. Done out in subtly contrasting oatmeal and beige shades, the rooms are comfortable if functional. The best parts are the public areas, bar and restaurant. Gay-friendly. ❺

Overseas Visitors' Club Hostel 230 Upper Long St ☎021 423 4477, ⓦwww.ovc.co.za. A well-organized lodge above some shops, run more along the lines of a guesthouse than a hostel. It's small by Long St standards, with three dorms, each sleeping six. There are high ceilings and airy spaces, while the absence of a bar makes it more tranquil than most lodges in the vicinity. A TV lounge leads onto a wraparound balcony that offers views of the street. ❶

St Paul's B&B Guest House 182 Bree St ☎021 423 4420, ⓕ021 423 1580. A charming, well managed and inexpensive guesthouse in a Georgian building (formerly a maternity hospital) in a calm street on the city-centre fringes, within easy striking distance of the sights. The rooms are large, comfortable and light with huge windows, and sharing bathroom and kitchen facilities. ❶

Travellers' Inn 208 Long St ☎021 424 9272, ⓦwww.travellers-inn.co.za. Pleasant budget accommodation in an early-twentieth-century building above a cybercafé. With no bar and no backpacker scene, this is a good bet for travellers wanting to avoid the hectic social atmosphere of the city-centre hostels. Apart from the light and spacious family rooms with twin beds and a double bunk, the rooms are small and sparely furnished; all rooms share bathroom facilities. Weekly and monthly discounts are available. ❷

Tudor Hotel 153 Longmarket St ☎021 424 1335, ⓦwww.tudorhotel.co.za. En-suite B&B rooms in a very central and reasonably priced hotel overlooking cobbled Greenmarket Square, and handy for taxis. ❹

V&A Waterfront and De Waterkant

In keeping with the gentrified ambience of the **V&A Waterfront** (usually referred to simply as the Waterfront), accommodation here tends to be upmarket; there are, however, a couple of reasonably priced places to stay, especially in the area just south of the Waterfront and **De Waterkant**. Accommodation here is marked on the map on p.134.

Breakwater Lodge Portswood Road, Waterfront ☎021 406 1911 (ask for Lodge Reservations), ⓦwww.breakwaterlodge.co.za. The most affordable place to stay on the Waterfront, this is a sparkling white hotel linked to Cape Town University's Graduate School of Business and partially housed in a nineteenth-century prison building. Although the lodge lacks personality, it does have thoroughly decent en-suite rooms with TV and phone, and there are over a hundred budget rooms sharing a bathroom with one other room. Rates exclude breakfast. ❸

The Cape Grace West Quay, Waterfront ☎021 410 7100, ⓦwww.capegrace.com. One of South Africa's most expensive and most exclusive hotels, this was Bill and Hillary Clinton's choice when they visited Cape Town in 1998. Spectacularly sited on a slender spit overlooking the Waterfront's small vessel marina to one side and the Alfred Basin to the other, the hotel's rooms have either harbour or Table Mountain views and are furnished in pared-back French period style. ❾

City Lodge On the corner of Alfred and Dock roads, Waterfront ☎021 419 9450,

@www.citylodge.co.za. A perfectly adequate if rather austere hotel, part of a national chain, less than 1km from both the Waterfront and the city centre. The rooms have TV and there's a small swimming pool. Rates are cheaper Fri–Sun nights, and you can also pick up discounts using their room auction site @www .bid2stay.co.za. ❺

De Waterkant Village and De Waterkant House Reception at 1 Loader St, De Waterkant ☎021 422 2721, @www.villageandlife.com. Attractively restored historic cottages in a villagey quarter of the eighteenth-century Waterkant district of Green Point, adjacent to the Bo-Kaap and less than 1km from the Waterfront and city centre. The luxury cottages in Waterkant, Loader, Dixon and Napier streets have up to three bedrooms; some have

garages, swimming pools and roof gardens with harbour or mountain views. Also part of the district is De Waterkant House, which has nine rooms sharing a pool and terrace with views over the Waterfront. ❺

St John's Waterfront Lodge 6 Braemar Rd ☎021 439 1404, @www.stjohns.co.za. The closest hostel to the Waterfront (a 15min walk away), well run by friendly and helpful staff. Accommodation is in four dorms sleeping eight to nine people, as well as some doubles, one of which is en suite. There are two swimming pools, a great garden and a bar, and the restaurant serves reasonably priced light meals till midnight. There's also Internet access, a coin-operated washing machine and a travel centre. Dorms ❶, rooms ❷

City Bowl suburbs

The **City Bowl suburbs** are popular for accommodation, and the most northerly sections are just five to ten minutes' walk from the Company's Gardens and the museums. A few backpacker lodges can be found along **Kloof Street**, the continuation of trendy Long Street. The further up you go, the leafier the suburbs become, and you'll find the pricier and more comfortable B&Bs, guesthouses and hotels along the lower slopes of Table Mountain, overlooking the city centre and Duncan Dock. There's no public transport to the City Bowl suburbs, but most accommodation listed is under 3km from Cape Town station.

Inexpensive

African Sun 3 Florida Rd, Vredehoek ☎021 461 1601, @afpress@iafrica.com. A small self-catering apartment, attached to a family house a little over 1km from the city centre. Furnished with pared-back ethnic decor, it's run by friendly, well-informed owners. A five percent discount is offered if you produce this book. Good value. ❷

Ambleside Guesthouse 11 Forest Rd, Oranjezicht ☎021 465 2503, @ambleside@bukhara.com. Comprising seven inexpensive, comfortable though slightly stuffy en-suite rooms, this guesthouse has been going for fifty years. All rooms have great views across the city to the harbour, plus cable-car watching from the back patio. A hot breakfast is served in the rooms, and you can prepare your own meals in a communal kitchen. ❷

Ashanti Lodge and Guest House 11 Hof St, Gardens ☎021 423 8721, @www.ashanti.com. King of the Cape Town lodges, this is a massive, superbly refurbished two-storey Victorian mansion. The details that give it the edge are stripped timber, chic marbling and ethnic decor, soaring ceilings, a beautifully kept front garden, cosy TV

lounge and a swimming pool with sun terrace. The private rooms (with twin or double beds) and dorms (sleeping six to eight) are furnished with custom-made wrought-iron bunks and beds. There is also have a quieter guesthouse around the corner in Union St, with keenly priced en-suite double/twin rooms with TVs and a communal kitchen. Dorms ❶, rooms ❷

The Backpack 74 New Church St, Tamboerskloof ☎021 423 4530, @www.backpackers.co.za. An excellent lodge in three interconnected houses, on the cusp of the City Bowl suburbs and the city centre, and easily walkable to both. Well run and with excellent service, it's furnished with bold colours and ethnic fabrics, with plenty of outdoor space, including a pool terrace in its own garden. Accommodation is in dorms (sleeping six to ten) and private rooms (several of which are en suite); some rooms are suitable for families. Dorms ❶, rooms ❷

Belmont House 10 Belmont Ave, Oranjezicht ☎021 461 5417, @www.capeguest.com. A tastefully restored 1920s house with seven fresh rooms, each with its own shower or bath. Either take the B&B option, or self-cater in the

CITY BOWL SUBURBS

RESTAURANTS, CAFÉS, BARS AND CLUBS

Amigos Mediterranean Restaurant	10
Café Paradiso	9
Chef Pon's Asian Kitchen	4 & 6
Kauai Juice	1
Limoncello	5
Melissa's	8
Mount Nelson Hotel Garden Room	D
Ocean Basket Southern Africa	3
Raith Gourmet	2
Yindees	7

ACCOMMODATION

African Sun	J
Ambleside Guesthouse	R
Ashanti Lodge and Guest House	K
The Backpack	A
Belmont House	N
Bergzicht	E
Blencathra	P
The Cape Colonial	L
Cape Milner Hotel	C
Leeuwenvoet House	H
Lezard Bleu	Q
Mount Nelson Hotel	D
Oak Lodge	I
Saasveld Lodge	G
Underberg Guest House	F
Villa Belmonte Hotel	O
Welgelegen Guest House	M
Zebra Crossing	B

communal kitchen. There's a five percent discount if you produce this book. ❸

Blencathra On the corner of De Hoop and Cambridge avenues, Tamboerskloof ☏021 424 9571, ⓦwww.blencathra.co.za. A large relaxed family house with stunning views on the slopes of Lion's Head, 2km from the city centre and 4km from the Atlantic seaboard beaches. There are peaceful, spacious self-catering rooms, four of which are en suite, attracting a young crowd who want to avoid the backpacker scene. The garden has seating and a swimming pool. ❷

Oak Lodge 21 Breda St, Gardens ☏021 465 6182, ⓦwww.oaklodge.co.za. More an event than a lodge, this highly recommended hostel in an 1860s Victorian house has dramatic dungeons, dragon murals, and a lively atmosphere; it's also spacious and well serviced, and has an immaculate kitchen. There are four dorms and sixteen rooms, one of which is en suite. ❷

Saasveld Lodge 73 Kloof St, Tamboerskloof ☏021 424 6169, ⓔsaasveld@icon.co.za. A rather impersonal 1950s-style, four-storey guesthouse on a buzzing thoroughfare lined with good eating places, less than 1km from the centre. The rooms are en suite and have TV and phone. The rate excludes breakfast. ❸

Zebra Crossing 82 New Church St ☏021 422 1265, ⓦwww.zebra-crossing.co.za. Cape Town's only backpacker lodge that actually boasts about being quiet. On the northern edge of the City Bowl suburbs, it's an easy walk to the Kloof St restaurants and pubs as well as those in the city centre. The café-bar serves full meals and decent coffee, and there are two pleasant terraces under vines. Accommodation is in three spacious dorms (sleeping eight), eleven doubles and three singles; the best rooms are the three doubles in the annexe, from whose balcony you can take in views of the mountain. Child-friendly. Dorms and rooms ❶

Moderate to expensive

Bergzicht 5 Devonport Rd, Tamboerskloof ☏021 423 8513, ⓦwww.bergzicht.co.za. Friendly and informal guesthouse with good views, caring hosts and a pool. Rooms are simply furnished with wicker furniture. ❹

The Cape Colonial 13 Union St, Gardens ☏021 426 2262, ⓦwww.capecolonial.com. A charming Victorian house decorated in colonial style, with friendly service. ❸

Cape Milner Hotel 2a Milner Rd, Tamboerskloof ☏021 426 1101, ⓦwww.capemilner.com. A smart, reasonably priced hotel, partly

incorporating an early eighteenth-century building, at the foot of Signal Hill.The airy rooms all boast views of Table Mountain and minimal decor, and the service is excellent. There's also a swimming pool, restaurant and bar on the premises. ❻

Leeuwenvoet House 93 New Church St, Tamboerskloof ☏021 424 1133, ⓦwww.leeuwenvoet.co.za. A tranquil restored Victorian guesthouse, with twelve en-suite rooms kitted out with pine and wicker and equipped with TV, phone and fan. Situated on a major thoroughfare with secure parking, it's a 15min walk from the city centre, with airport transfers available. ❺

Lezard Bleu 30 Upper Orange St, Oranjezicht ☏021 461 4601, ⓦwww.lezardbleu.co.za. Seven luxurious en-suite rooms, furnished with maple beds and cupboards in a spacious open-plan 1960s house. Sliding doors from each room open onto a garden. Located in a pleasant part of town, it's 1km from the centre and about half that distance to a nature reserve on the lower slopes of Table Mountain. ❻

Mount Nelson Hotel 76 Orange St, Gardens ☏021 483 1000, ⓦwww.mountnelson.co.za. Cape Town's *grande dame*: a fine and famous high-colonial Victorian hotel, built in 1899 (and extended in the late 1990s). Set in extensive established gardens, with arrival along a palm-lined colonnade, the hotel takes itself terribly seriously and charges accordingly; the rate excludes breakfast. ❾

Underberg Guest House 6 Tamboerskloof Rd, Tamboerskloof ☏021 426 2262, ⓦwww.underbergguesthouse.co.za. Located on the doorstep of the city centre, this Victorian guesthouse offers excellent value. Its high ceilings and compact size (there are only eleven rooms) create an atmosphere that is both intimate and airy. ❹

Villa Belmonte Hotel 33 Belmont Ave, Oranjezicht ☏021 462 1576, ⓦwww.villabelmontehotel.co.za. The Western Cape's smallest five-star hotel, on the lower slopes of Table Mountain and 1km from the city centre, feels like an elegant Italian country villa. The rooms, some of which lead onto a lovely garden, are individually decorated and rates vary according to size. Good value, given the level of comfort and style. ❻

Welgelegen Guest House 6 Stephen St, Gardens ☏021 426 2373, ⓦwww.welgelegen.co.za. A Victorian guesthouse with mountain views and furnished with considerable style – which is unsurprising, as the owner is an interior decorator. ❺

Southern suburbs

Cape Town's **southern suburbs** are the formerly whites-only areas closest to the mountain. **Rosebank**, **Claremont**, **Newlands** and **Rondebosch** are leafy, quiet and convenient for the Simon's Town train line, providing easy access to both the city centre and the False Bay seaboard. Lush **Constantia** is one of Cape Town's poshest suburbs, only twenty minutes' drive from either coast as well as the V&A Waterfront. Sharing the same valley is the adjoining suburb of **Tokai**, worth considering if you want to be well out of the centre; it's close to forest walks and ten minutes from the beach. Inexpensive accommodation is rare in Tokai, but if money's no object and you're looking for somewhere exceptional and romantic, you might just find it here in a Cape Dutch manor house. A car is essential if you're staying in Tokai or Constantia, as they're not served by public transport.

Allandale Holiday Cottages 72 Zwaanswyk Rd, Tokai ☎021 715 3320, ⊛www.allandale.co.za. Sixteen one-, two- and three-bedroom self-catering brick cottages on a smallholding adjoining Tokai Forest, on the slopes of Constantiaberg, 2min from the motorway and 20min from Cape Town. Each cottage has a garden area with a braai and outdoor seating, and the site boasts a pool and tennis courts. ❸

Carmichael House 11 Wolmunster Rd, Rosebank ☎021 689 8350, ⊛www.carmichaelhouse.co.za. A two-storey guesthouse in a building dating from the turn of the last century, with six big rooms equipped with phone, safe and hairdryer. There's a peaceful garden, swimming pool and secure parking, plus fax and email facilities. It's a 10min walk to Rhodes Memorial and the Contour Path, while the Rondebosch shops are 1km away. ❸

The Constantia Stables Chantecler Lane, Constantia ☎ & ℱ021 794 3653. Six en-suite doubles, each with their own entrance and patio, in converted stables. The six-course breakfasts are excellent, and you can relax around the pool in a large garden. ❹

Constantia Uitsig Country Hotel Spaanschemat River Rd, Constantia ☎021 794 6500, ⊛www.constantiauitsig.co.za. Sixteen custom-built and upmarket Cape Dutch-style cottages, in a garden setting on Constantia Uitsig wine estate, next door to Steenberg. There are a couple of excellent restaurants on site, including the *Uitsig* (see p.168). ❽

The Courtyard Liesbeek Ave, Mowbray ☎021 448 3929, ⊛www.citylodge.co.za. Exceptional value, considering the high level of luxury. A beautiful early nineteenth-century Cape Dutch homestead under thatch, with terracotta floors, brass chandeliers and large lawns in a semi-rural setting. There's a hotel minibus which you can pay to use. Breakfast is extra. ❺

Elephant's Eye Lodge 9 Sunwood Drive, Tokai ☎021 715 2432, ⊛www.elephantseyelodge.co.za. Half a dozen rooms at a friendly B&B family home in a converted Cape Dutch farmhouse, in its own large grounds with a pool, minutes' walk from Tokai Forest. Two of the rooms have basic self-catering facilities. ❸

Gloucester House Bed & Breakfast 54 Weltevreden Ave, Rondebosch ☎ & ℱ021 689 3894. A private house with two bedrooms, and a lounge/dining room for self-catering. Guests may use the large garden, swimming pool and barbecue area. The rate excludes breakfast. ❷–❸

Houtkapperspoort Hout Bay Main Rd, around 5km from Hout Bay and 15km from the city centre ☎021 794 5216, ⊛www.houtkapperspoort.co.za. Rustic one- and two-bedroom stone-and-brick self-catering cottages set up against the Table Mountain Nature Reserve, close to Constantia Nek. You can take paths straight from the estate up the mountain slopes, play tennis or take a dip in the solar-heated pool. Highly recommended. ❹

Ivydene Off Glebe Rd, Rondebosch ☎021 685 1747, ✉ivydene@mweb.co.za. Five flats in a delightful old house near the university, with a garden, swimming pool and friendly atmosphere. There are discounts for stays over a week or more. ❸

Kinloch Garden Apartment 3 Palm St, Newlands ☎021 683 5199, ✉marinella@mweb.co.za. Attached to a family home, this comfortably furnished self-catering apartment has a separate entrance and private garden with stunning views of Table Mountain. It's a 20min walk to Kirstenbosch and Claremont shops. Good value. ❷

Little Ruo 11 Willow Rd, off Spaanschemat River Rd, Constantia ☎021 794 2052, ⊛www.littleruo .co.za. Two pretty rooms in the home of the friendly architect owners, plus five self-catering suites set in a huge landscaped garden with willows, a stream and a saltwater pool. B&B ❺

Steenberg Hotel Corner Steenberg and Tokai roads, Tokai ℡021 713 2222, ⓦwww .steenberghotel.com. A luxurious place on South Africa's oldest wine estate at the foot of the Steenberg Mountain. Accommodation is in the original manor house and three other farm buildings (now national monuments), which are perfect examples of Cape Dutch architecture, dating back to 1682. Arranged around a large formal garden, the buildings have whitewashed walls, thatched roofs, ornate gables and are furnished with seventeenth- and eighteenth-century Cape antiques. ⑧

The Vineyard On the corner of Colinton and Protea roads, Newlands ℡021 657 4500, ⓦwww.vineyard.co.za. An excellent, classy hotel in a restored country villa built for Lady Anne Barnard in 1799. The public spaces are decorated in elegant Cape Dutch style, with an outstanding panorama of Table Mountain from the extensive garden. Outstanding value for the level of luxury. ⑥–⑦

Atlantic seaboard

Down the **Atlantic seaboard** lie the seaside suburbs of Mouille (pronounced "moo-lee") Point, Green Point, Three Anchor Bay and Sea Point. Historically Cape Town's hotel and high-rise land, this is now packed with a range of accommodation, making it a good alternative to the City Bowl if you want to be close to the city centre.

South from Sea Point along Victoria Drive, the well-heeled mountainside suburb of **Camps Bay** has soaring views over the Atlantic, with the advantage of being close to the city centre, and with its own restaurants and shops. Though nearby **Llandudno** lacks shops or restaurants, it can boast similar vistas and a supremely beautiful beach with clusters of granite boulders at either end. **Hout Bay** is the main urban concentration along the lower half of the peninsula, with a harbour, pleasant waterfront development and the only public transport beyond Camps Bay. South of Hout Bay is the semi-rural settlement of **Noordhoek**, close to the Table Mountain National Park, with good horseriding, beach walks and surfing.

RESTAURANTS, CAFÉS BARS & CLUBS

Chariots Italian Coffee Bar	6
Giovanni's Deliworld	8
Harveys at the Mansion	1
La Med Bar and Restaurant	11
Mano's	10
New York Bagels	4
Newport Market and Deli	5
Theo's Grill Butcher and Seafood	2
Tom Yum	3
Wakame	5
Wang Thai	7
Zeroninethreetwo	9

ACCOMMODATION

Altona Lodge	L	Lion's Head Lodge	C
Brenda's Guest House	J	Olive Branch Guest House	F
Dale Court Guest House	M	Stonehurst Guest House	D
David's	I	Villa Rosa	G
Don Suite Hotel	B	Waterfront Suites	K
Jambo Guest House	H	Winchester Mansions Hotel	A
Les Cascades de Bantry Bay	E		

0 — 500 m

Green Point

Altona Lodge 19 Croxteth Rd ☎ 021 434 2572, ⓦ www.altona.co.za. A quiet and friendly guest-house with a homely atmosphere in a Victorian house close to the city centre. Of the seventeen B&B rooms, five are en suite; the cheaper rooms share a bathroom, though each room has its own hand basin. The service is good, and there's also a small garden. ❸

Brenda's Guest House 14 Pine Rd ☎ 021 434 0902 or 083 627 5583, ⓦ www.brendas.co.za. Four rooms inside and another in the garden of a 1900s house, all brightly decorated, with wicker furniture. There's poolside seating on a bricked terrace. ❹

Dale Court Guest House 1 Exhibition Terrace Rd ☎ 021 439 8774, ⓦ www.dalecourt.co.za. Conveniently located, reasonable, though unremarkable B&B that accommodates children. The guesthouse manages the eight-storey block opposite, comprising functional, self-catering apartments for families (R695–895). ❸

David's 12 Croxteth Rd ☎ 021 439 464, ⓦ www.davids.co.za. An elegant and airy B&B in a quiet residential street just off the main road. Separate from the guesthouse are a selection of self-catering apartments which it manages. Gay-friendly. ❸

Jambo Guest House 1 Grove Rd ☎ 021 439 4219, ⓦ www.jambo.co.za. Small, atmospheric establishment with four double rooms in a quiet cul-de-sac off Main Rd, just over 1km from the V&A Waterfront. The lush leafy exterior and enclosed garden with pond are delightfully relaxing and the service is excellent. A luxury suite has a large sitting area, Jacuzzi and French doors opening onto the garden. ❹–❺

Olive Branch Guest House 9 Richmond Rd ☎ 021 434 9198, ⓦ www.olivebranch.co.za. Nine adequate en-suite rooms, reasonably priced for Green Point with easy access to the Waterfront. ❸

Waterfront Suites 153 Main Rd ☎ 021 439 5020, ⓦ www.waterfront-suites.co.za. Small four-storey block quite close to the waterfront, with modern, impersonal but extremely comfortable self-catering apartments offering brilliant value. The kitchens are well equipped, and the rooms are serviced daily. ❷

Sea Point and Bantry Bay

Don Suite Hotel 249 Beach Rd, Sea Point ☎ 021 434 1083, ⓦ www.don.co.za. A five-storey block of 27 self-catering apartments across the road from the beachfront promenade and 300m from the lively Main Rd restaurant strip. All the flats, studio apartments and one- and two-bedroom units are modern and well equipped; rates vary depending on whether or not you get a view. ❹

Les Cascades de Bantry Bay 48 De Wet Rd, Bantry Bay ☎ 021 434 5209, ⓦ www.lescascades.co.za. One of the most beautiful guesthouses in the country, in a prime location perched above the Atlantic. It's half the price of the much vaunted *Ellerman's*

House in the street below, and could not be more luxurious or relaxed. Every room has a full sea view and deck or balcony and features Balinese-influenced decor in warm earthy tones, and there are wonderful lounges, verandas and swimming pools. The Belgian owners cook up a storm. Unusually for such an upmarket place, they do take children. **⑥**

Lion's Head Lodge On the corner of Conifer and 319 Main Rd, Sea Point ☎021 434 4163, ⓦwww .lions-head-lodge.co.za. Plain but comfortable en-suite rooms that are well maintained, despite the weather-worn exterior of the four-storey building. Some face the busy main road at the heart of Sea Point's restaurant strip, while quieter rooms overlook the courtyard. All have phone and TV, and the lodge also has a swimming pool, bar, beer terrace and an à la carte restaurant. Also offers fully equipped apartments that sleep two. **②–③**

Stonehurst Guest House 3 Frere Rd, Sea Point ☎021 434 9670, ⓦwww.stonehurst.co.za. An airy tin-roofed Victorian residence with original fittings and Cape furniture. There's a pleasant front garden, a kitchen and guest lounge. Most rooms are en suite, and some rooms have balconies. **③**

Villa Rosa 277 High Level Rd, Sea Point ☎021 434 2768, ⓦwww.villa-rosa.com. A friendly eight-room guesthouse in a salmon-pink two-storey Victorian house on the lower slopes of Signal Hill, two blocks from the beachfront promenade. Decorated with simplicity and style, all rooms have TVs, phones and safes, but only some, on the upper floor, have sea views. **④**

Winchester Mansions Hotel 221 Beach Rd, Sea Point ☎021 434 2351, ⓦwww.winchester.co.za. A self-consciously colonial-style 1920s hotel, in a prime spot across the road from the seashore, with an atmosphere straight from the pages of Agatha Christie. Palm trees at the front of the three-storey Cape Dutch Revival building hint at the interior: rooms have ceiling fans, and a cool Italianate courtyard restaurant is overlooked by balconies draped in luxuriant creepers. There's a good restaurant, too. **⑦**

Camps Bay and points south

Bay Hotel Victoria Road, Camps Bay ☎021 438 4444, ⓦwww.thebay.co.za. Luxurious, glitzy five-star hotel on the fashionable beachfront strip. Its late-1980s construction blends neo-Cape Dutch with Mediterranean styles and cane furniture, to conjure up a laidback colonial fantasy. **⑧**

Beach House 7 Royal Avenue, Hout Bay ☎021 790 4228, ⓦwww.wk.co.za/beachhouse. A modern and friendly guesthouse with en-suite rooms and pleasant patio, a 5min walk from Mariner's Wharf and the beach. **③**

Camps Bay Backpack & Budget Inn 21 Central Drive, Camps Bay ☎021 438 2691. Less than 1km from the beach is this distinctive backpacker lodge, in a contemporary white house with lots of glass and pale beech wood floors . Fluffy white duvets, towels and toiletries are provided in dorms and doubles, there's a sparkling pool, bar and gym, and it's close to the trendy nightspots and restaurants frequented by the glitterati. Dorms **②**, rooms **③**

Leeukop 25 Sedgemoor Rd, Camps Bay ☎021 438 1361, Ⓔleeukopbb@hotmail.com. The most reasonably priced B&B accommodation in Camps Bay, near the beach and cafés, in two stylishly arty and comfortable apartments adjoining the cheerful proprietor's home. The flats are fully equipped, and you can either self-cater or stay on a B&B basis. **④–⑤**

Lichtenstein Castle Harbour Rd, Hout Bay ☎021 790 2213, ⓦwww.lichtensteincastle.co.za. A serious quantity of fantasy has been invested in this austere replica castle at the end of a winding mountainside drive. There's a vaulted wooden ceiling, chandeliers, armour, an enormous fireplace, comfy armchairs and a friendly hound; rooms are luxuriously furnished with carved period furniture, tapestries, brocade and velvet, and the leaded stained-glass windows frame awesome views of the harbour and ocean. Not quite in keeping with the medieval schloss imagery are the helipad, billiard room and swimming pool. **④**

Monkey Valley Resort Mountain Road, Noordhoek ☎021 789 1391, ⓦwww.monkeyvalleyresort.com. An attractive group of mainly wooden and thatched two-storey chalets spread over several acres of Chapman's Peak 40km south of the city centre. Overlooking the 7km of Noordhoek Beach, the site is surrounded by indigenous vegetation, with no other houses in sight, and there's an emphasis on natural products throughout. The cottages sleep six to eight people, and work out reasonably for a group. You can either eat in the restaurant, self-cater or stay on a B&B basis. **⑤**

Sleepy Hollow Farmyard 33 Sleepy Hollow Lane, Noordhoek ☎021 789 1201, Ⓔjjfrylinck@intekom.co.za. A simple self-catering cottage in a peaceful setting, next to a family home. The riding school next door has well-trained horses and can cater for disabled people. The beach is just a 15min walk away. Good value. **②**

Sunbird Mountain Retreat Boskykloof Road, Hout Bay ☎021 790 7758, ⓦwww.sunbirdlodge .co.za. Three pleasant, spacious self-catering apartments and a guesthouse that includes a family unit, all nestling in a forest high up on the mountainside. All the rooms have great views and there's a secluded swimming pool. **③**

False Bay seaboard

The Metrorail line to the handsome, historic village of Simon's Town reaches the coast at **Muizenberg**, the oldest of Cape Town's seaside suburbs. To its south, en route to Simon's Town, are a series of settlements, including salubrious **St James**, **Kalk Bay** with its working harbour and great cafés, and **Fish Hoek**, which is known for the best swimming beach along the False Bay seaboard. **Simon's Town** is regarded by most Capetonians as a separate village, which it originally was, although it's now quite definitely part of the metropolis. During the day, trains arriving in Simon's Town are met by Rikki's taxis, which will take you anywhere in the vicinity.

Muizenberg to Fish Hoek

Amberley Travellers Lodge 15 Amberley Rd, Muizenberg ☏021 788 7032, ⓦwww.amberleylodge .com. A lovingly restored two-storey house with gleaming wooden floors, and spacious rooms and kitchen. ❶

Blue Baboon Travellers 136 Main Rd, Kalk Bay ☏082 786 3629, ⓦwww.bluebaboon.co.za. A vibrant backpacker lodge opposite the colourful fishing harbour and above the excellent *Olympia Deli*. There are tiny sea-facing double rooms opening onto a balcony. ❶

Blue Oceans Backpackers 3 Church Rd, Muizenberg ☏021 788 9780, ⓔblueoceans@yebo .co.za. A cheerful, busy backpacker lodge in a two-storey Victorian house. Upstairs are three double rooms with their own kitchen, bathroom, and sharing a wraparound wooden deck. ❶

Chartfield Guest House 30 Gatesville Rd, Kalk Bay ☏021 788 3793, ⓦwww.chartfield.co.za. Unpretentious, newly refurbished accommodation, 100m from Kalk Bay station, in a well-kept rambling house halfway up the hill overlooking the harbour, with terrific panoramas of the Hottentots Holland Mountains across False Bay. The best rooms are the one in the loft with its own balcony, and the two semicircular corner ones with 180-degree views. You can eat in the bistro on the premises, or take the 3min walk to the Kalk Bay restaurant strip. ❷

Sunny Cove Manor 72 Simon's Town Rd, Fish Hoek ☏021 782 2274, ⓦwww.sunnycovemanor. com. Near Sunny Cove station, this cheerful B&B has four suites, three of them two-bedrooms affairs; all bar the back room have outstanding sea views, and there's secure on-site parking. If you cross the road and the railway line, you're on Jager's walkway, which leads after a short walk to Fish Hoek Beach. ❹

Tranquility Guest House 25 Peak Rd, Fish Hoek ☏021 782 2060, ⓦwww.tranquil.co.za. Warm and welcoming, with panoramic views of the mountainside and ocean (the beach is within walking distance). There are four cosy B&B en-suite rooms, plus a self-catering apartment with its own entrance. Guests can soak in the outdoor Jacuzzi. ❸–❹

Simon's Town and around

Boulders Beach Lodge 4 Boulders Place, Boulders Beach ☏021 786 1758, ⓦwww .bouldersbeach.co.za. Twelve B&B rooms and two self-catering flats above the Boulders Beach car park, a 2min walk from Boulders Coastal Park and the African penguin colony, and just over 1km from Simon's town. The self-catering units sleep two to six people. Meals are available at the adjacent restaurant (daily 8am–9.30pm). ❹

British Hotel Apartments 90 St George's St ☏021 786 2214, ⓦwww.british-hotel.co.za. Three-bedroom self-catering apartments in a grand 1898 Victorian hotel, that once had Cecil Rhodes and the nineteenth-century explorer, Mary Kingsley, as guests; there are also more modest doubles with baths. Part of a picturesque main street, this is an experience rather than just somewhere to stay, with Victorian colonial decor, high ceilings and huge balconies overlooking the street and the docks. ❹

Oatlands Holiday Village Froggy Pond, 3km from Simon's Town and 1km from the Boulders Beach penguin colony ☏021 786 1410, ⓦwww .oatlands.co.za. Across the road from the beach and near a golf course, this family resort is set in large grounds with its own pool and playground. There are over twenty self-catering chalets of various sizes, sleeping two to six people; there's also a pub and restaurant on the premises. ❷–❸

Simon's Town Backpackers 66 St Georges St ☏021 786 1964, ⓦwww.capepax.co.za. Conveniently located in the heart of Simon's Town, within walking distance of the station. The double rooms are fairly spacious and there's a large balcony with a view of the waterfront. You can rent one of their bicycles and ride to Cape Point or paddle in a kayak past the penguin colony. ❶

African township homestays

One of the best ways of getting a taste of the African townships is spending a night there. The number of township residents offering **B&B accommodation** in their homes is still small, but growing. You'll have a chance to experience the warmth of *ubuntu* – traditional African hospitality – by staying with a family with whom you'll generally eat breakfast and dinner; they can also usually take you around their area to *shebeens*, music venues or just to meet the neighbours.

A number of the township B&Bs will send someone to meet you at the airport, while many people are dropped off at their accommodation by tour operators. If you're driving, your accommodation will give you detailed directions or arrange to meet you at a convenient landmark, such as a garage or police station.

For information about township B&Bs other than the ones listed below, contact **Sivuyile Tourism Centre** in Guguletu (Mon–Fri 8am–5pm, Sat 8.30am–2pm; ☎021 637 8449, ⓦwww.sivuyile.co.za) or Thuthuka Tours (see p.106), which, aside from running township tours, also helps with finding township accommodation.

Kopanong Khayelitsha ☎021 361 2084 or 082 476 1278. One of the most dynamic B&B operations in the township, run by the tireless Thope Lekau, who has a mission to replace gawping tourists in their buses with guests who engage with township life. This former NGO worker will treat you to a history of the township, introduce you to local music and dish up a traditional family breakfast. A traditional dinner is available on request, as is a guided tour. B&B ❸

Majoro's Khayelitsha ☎021 361 3412 or 082 537 6882. Hosted by the charming Maria Maile in her family home, which has two rooms, sharing a bath and toilet. Dinner includes traditional fare such as *mielie pap*, and you'll be treated to an English breakfast with a difference, which may include bacon and egg with fish cakes, sausage and homemade steamed bread. B&B ❷

Malebo's Khayeletisha ☎021 361 2391. Three rooms sharing bath and toilet facilities in the welcoming home of Lydea Masoleng and her husband. In the morning you'll be served a continental breakfast; dinners, which combine Western fare with traditional African food, are available on request. You're welcome to join your hosts on outings to a *shebeen* or, on Sunday, to church. B&B ❸

Maneo Langa ☎021 694 2504. Friendly hostess Thandiwe Peter has two outside rooms and one inside the family house, in Cape Town's oldest township, and the closest to the city centre, so most guests drive here. She will take guests to some of the township highlights, including a local *shebeen* where you may see singing and dancing. B&B ❸

Vicky's Khayelitsha ☎021 387 7104 or 082 225 2986. Under the proprietorship of Vicky Ntozini, this three-room place was one of the first township homestays. Guests are offered a walking tour to meet local people. B&B ❷

Topsail House 176 St Georges St ☎021 786 5537. A converted old convent with more space than the average backpacker lodge, though a tad staid. It has various accommodation options including an extraordinary bedroom in a chapel, though it's the en-suite doubles upstairs that are the nicest rooms. ❷

The City Centre

Strand Street marks the edge of Cape Town's original beachfront (though you'd never guess it today), and all urban development to its north stands on reclaimed land. To its south is the **Upper City Centre**, containing the remains of the city's 350-year-old historic core, which has survived the ravages of modernization and apartheid-inspired urban clearance, and emerged with enough charm to make it South Africa's most pleasing city centre. The entire area from Strand Street to the southern foot of the mountain is a collage of Georgian, Cape Dutch, Victorian and twentieth-century architecture (see p.144), as well as being the place where Europe, Asia and Africa meet in markets, alleyways and mosques. Among the substantial drawcards here are **Parliament**, the **Company's Gardens** and many of Cape Town's major **museums**. North of Strand Street to the shore, the **Lower City Centre** takes in the still-functional **Duncan Dock**.

The Upper City Centre

Adderley Street, running from the train station in the north to the Gardens in the south, is the obvious orientation axis here. To its east, and close to each other just off Strand Street, are the **Castle of Good Hope**, the site of **District Six**, the **Grand Parade** and the **City Hall**. The district to the west of Adderley Street is the closest South Africa gets to a European quarter – a tight network of streets with cafés, buskers, bookstores, street stalls and antique shops congregating around the pedestrianized **St George's Mall** and **Greenmarket Square**. The **Bo-Kaap**, or Muslim district, three blocks further west across Buitengragt (which means the Outer Canal, but is actually a street), exudes a piquant contrast to this, with its minarets, spice shops and cafés selling curried snacks.

Southwest of Adderley Street, where it takes a sharp right into Wale Street, is the symbolic heart of Cape Town (and arguably South Africa), with **Parliament**, museums, archives and De Tuynhuys – the Western Cape office of the President – arranged around the **Company's Gardens**.

Adderley Street

Once *the* place to shop in Cape Town, **Adderley Street**, lined with handsome buildings from several centuries, is still worth a stroll today. Its attractive streetscape has been wantonly blemished by a series of large 1960s shopping centres, but just minutes away from crowded malls, among the streets and alleys around Greenmarket Square, you can still find some human scale and historic texture.

Low-walled channels, ditches, bridges and sluices once ran through Cape Town, earning it the name Little Amsterdam. During the nineteenth century, the canals were buried underground, and in 1850 Heerengracht (Gentlemen's Canal), formerly a waterway that ran from the Botanical Gardens down to the sea, was renamed Adderley Street (see box on p.121). There's little evidence of the canals today, except in name – one section of the street is still called Heerengracht and a parallel street to its west is called Buitengragt (sometimes spelled Buitengracht, after the Dutch style).

The destruction of old Cape Town continued well into the twentieth century, with the razing of many of the older buildings. One of the ugliest newcomers is the **Golden Acre** shopping complex, dominating the north (harbour) end of Adderley Street. Built in the 1970s, it's Cape Town's unavoidable public transport hub today, employing an unfriendly network of subways and walkways to draw together all the major road and rail services into town. Inside sit the **Golden Acre Ruins**, the remains of southern Africa's oldest colonial structure – a reservoir built in 1663 by the Dutch. All that's left is a small bit of wall behind glass, and you might easily walk past and think that the builders who worked on the complex forgot to finish the plastering.

ACCOMMODATION

Cape Heritage Hotel	**B**
Cape Town Hollow Hotel	**I**
Cat & Moose	**H**
Long Street Backpackers	**D**
Metropole Hotel	**A**
Overseas Visitors' Club Hostel	**F**
St Paul's B&B Guest House	**G**
Travellers' Inn	**E**
Tudor Hotel	**C**

0   50 m

CITY CENTRE: AROUND LONG ST & THE COMPANY'S GARDENS

RESTAURANTS, PUBS & CLUBS

Africa Café	2	Jo'burg	13	Mama Africa	9	The Purple Turtle	3
Bukhara	6	Kennedy's	14	M-Bar and		Rhodes House	12
Five Flies	7	Long Street		Lounge	**A**	Royale	16
Gallery Café	18	Café	15	Mexican Kitchen		Sutra	4
Ginja	1	The Lounge	10	Café	11		
Ivy Garden	5	Madame Zingara	17	Mr Pickwick's	8		

The naming of Adderley Street

Although the Dutch used Robben Island as a political prison (see p.137), the South African mainland only narrowly escaped becoming a second Australia, a **penal colony** where British felons and enemies of the state could be dumped. By the 1840s, "respectable Australians" were lobbying for a ban on the transportation of criminals to the Antipodes, and the British authorities responded by trying to divert convicts to the Cape.

In 1848, the British ship *Neptune* set sail from Bermuda for Cape Town with a cargo of 282 prisoners. When news of its departure reached Cape Town there was outrage; five thousand citizens gathered on the Grand Parade the following year to hear prominent liberals denounce the British government. When the ship docked in September 1849, governor Sir Harry Smith forbade any criminal from landing while, back in London, politician **Charles Adderley** successfully addressed the House of Commons in support of the Cape colonists. In February 1850, the *Neptune* set off for Tasmania with its full complement of convicts, and grateful Capetonians renamed the city's main thoroughfare **Adderley Street**.

Although the mall itself and its environs are anything but picturesque, here you do get an authentic taste of ordinary Capetonians doing their shopping, something you won't find at the sanitized Victoria and Alfred Waterfront. On Saturday mornings, if you exit onto Adderley Street, you'll often encounter the spirited sounds of busking brass bands or choirs. Among the sidewalks and pedestrianized sections outside, which run down to the station, there's a closely packed **flea market** offering curios, crafts and electronic goods (but watch your wallet).

A little further south lies a **flower market**, run by members of the Bo-Kaap Muslim community. Two grandiose banks stand on opposite sides of Adderley Street; the fussier of the two is the **Standard Bank**, fronted by Corinthian columns and covered with a tall dome – a temple to the partnership of empire and finance. The **First National Bank**, completed in 1913, was the last South African building designed by Sir Herbert Baker (see box, p.610). If you pop in for a quick look, still in place inside the banking hall you'll find a solid timber circular writing desk with the original inkwells, resembling an altar.

Slave Lodge

At the top corner of Adderley Street, just as it veers sharply northwest into Wale Street, you'll find **Slave Lodge** (Mon–Sat 8.30am–4.30pm, Sat 9am–1pm; R7), previously known as the Cultural History Museum. For nearly two centuries – more than half the city's existence as an urban settlement – Cape Town's economic and social structures were founded on slavery (see box, p.122), and the Slave Lodge was built in 1679 for the Dutch East India Company – the largest single slaveowner at the Cape – to house its human chattels. By the 1770s, almost a thousand slaves were held at the lodge. Under VOC administration, the lodge also became the Cape Colony's main brothel, its doors thrown open to all comers for an hour each night. Following the British takeover and the auctioning of the slaves, the lodge became the Supreme Court in 1810, and remained so until 1914. From 1914, the building was used as government offices, and in 1966 became a museum.

Slave Lodge houses an eclectic collection of antiquities and artefacts from around the world, as well as good displays on the Cape and an exhibition, still evolving, about slavery. A couple of small but interesting displays can be

Slavery at the Cape

Slavery was officially abolished at the Cape in 1838, but its legacy lives on in South Africa. The country's coloured inhabitants, who make up fifty percent of Cape Town's population, are largely descendants of slaves and indigenous Khoisan people, and some historians argue that apartheid was a natural successor to slavery. Certainly, domestic service, still widespread throughout South Africa, and certain labour practices such as the "*dop* system", in which workers on some wine farms are partially paid in rations of cheap plonk, can be traced directly back to slavery.

By the end of the eighteenth century, the almost 26,000-strong slave population of the Cape exceeded that of the free burghers. Despite the profound impact this had on the development of social relations in South Africa, it remained one of the most neglected topics of the country's history, until the publication in the 1980s of a number of studies on slavery. There's still a reluctance on the part of most coloureds to acknowledge their slave origins.

Few if any slaves were captured at the Cape for export, making the colony unique in the African trade. Paradoxically, while people were being captured elsewhere on the continent for export to the Americas, the Cape administration, forbidden by the VOC from enslaving the local indigenous population, had to look further afield. Of the 63,000 slaves imported to the Cape before 1808, most came from East Africa, Madagascar, India and Indonesia, representing one of the broadest cultural mixes of any slave society. This diversity initially worked against the establishment of a unified group identity, but eventually a **Creolized culture** emerged which, among other things, played a major role in the development of the Afrikaans language.

found on the ground floor, to the left of the entrance hall. The first deals with **Khoisan hunter-gatherers**, the original inhabitants of the Cape (and South Africa), focusing on their knowledge of plants and herbs, many of which are still in use today. An adjacent room houses "**186 Years of Slavery**", centred around a model of the lodge as it was 300 years ago. A poignant memorial plaque on one wall lists, by first name only, the slaves who endured the appalling conditions of the fortress-like structure, and a map on another wall refers to sites in the city centre with slave connections: where they worked, worshipped, were sold, punished and executed.

Behind Slave Lodge, on the traffic island in Spin Street, a simple and inconspicuous plinth marks the site of the **Old Slave Tree**, under which slaves were bought and sold.

Long Street

Parallel to Adderley Street, buzzing **Long Street** is one of Cape Town's most diverse thoroughfares, a great place for leisurely exploration, with views of Table Mountain, Signal Hill and Lion's Head, as well as glimpses of the sea. When it was first settled by Muslims some three hundred years ago, Long Street marked Cape Town's boundary; by the 1960s, it had become a sleazy alley of drinking holes and whorehouses. Miraculously, it's all still here, but with a whiff of gentrification. Mosques still coexist with bars, brothels trade above old-fashioned locksmiths, pawnbrokers function alongside porn shops, while gun shops sit next to delicatessens, antique dealers, craft shops and cafés. Also here are a number of excellent secondhand and Africana bookshops.

A Cape Town institution, established in 1906, the **Long Street Baths** (daily 7am–7pm) occupy the top of the road, where it hits Buitensingel (Outer Crescent). The steam rooms are great for relaxing on a winter's day and are open separately to women (Tues 9am–1pm, Thurs & Sat 9am–6pm) and men (Tues

1–7pm, Wed & Fri 9am–1pm, Sun 8am–noon). A four-hour session (R70) gets you a private cubicle and towel, access to the dry or wet steam rooms, the plunge pool and a short massage. Use of the pool costs R9.

Further north, an unmistakable landmark at no. 185, the **Palm Tree Mosque** (not open to the public) is fronted by a lone palm tree, its fronds caressing the upper storey. Significant as the only surviving eighteenth-century house in the street, it was erected in 1780 by Carel Lodewijk Schot as a private dwelling. The house was bought in 1807 by Frans van Bengal, a member of the local Muslim community, and a freed slave, Jan van Boughies, who became its imam, turning the upper floor into a mosque and the lower into his living quarters.

Across Wale Street is one of Cape Town's most intriguing places for African crafts, and one of the easiest to miss. The inconspicuous frontage of the **Pan African Market** (Mon–Fri 9am–5pm) at no. 76 belies the three-floor warren of passageways and rooms, which burst at the hinges with traders selling vast quantities of art and artefacts from all over the continent. Hidden among less inspiring offerings you'll find terrific masks from West Africa, brass leopards from Benin as well as contemporary South African art textiles. Also gathered here are leathersmiths, tailors, hair-braiders, a drum instructor and vendors selling CDs and musical instruments.

Further towards the harbour end of Long Street at no. 40, the **South African Missionary Meeting-House Museum** (Mon–Fri 9am–4pm; free) was the first missionary church in the country, where slaves were taught literacy and instructed in Christianity. This exceptional building, completed in 1804 by the South African Missionary Society, boasts one of the most beautiful frontages in Cape Town. Dominated by its large windows, the facade is broken into three bays by four slender Corinthian pilasters surmounted by a gabled pediment. Inside, an impressive Neoclassical timber **pulpit** perches high above the congregation on a pair of columns, framing an inlaid image of an angel in flight.

The society itself was founded in 1799 by Reverend Vos, who was alarmed that many slaveowners neglected the religious education of their property. The owners believed that once their slaves were baptized, their emancipation became obligatory – a misunderstanding of the law, which merely stated that Christian slaves couldn't be sold. Vos, himself a slaveowner, saw proselytization to those in bondage as a Christian duty, and even successfully campaigned to end the prohibition against selling Christian slaves, which he believed was "a great obstacle in this country to the progress of Christianity", because it encouraged owners to avoid baptizing their human chattels.

Greenmarket Square and around

Turning northeast from Long Street into Shortmarket Street, you'll skim the edge of **Greenmarket Square**, which is worth a little exploration to take in the cobbled streets, coffee shops and grand buildings. As its name implies, the square started as a vegetable market, though it spent many ignominious years as a car park. Human life has returned, and it's now home to a flea market, selling crafts, jewellery and hippie clobber. This is also one of the few places in Cape Town to buy from Congolese and Zimbabwean traders, selling masks and malachite carvings. On the western side are the solid limewashed walls and small shuttered windows of the **Old Town House** (Feb–Dec daily 10am–5pm; free), entered from Longmarket Street. Built in the mid-1700s, this beautiful example of Cape Dutch architecture, with its fine interior, has seen duty as a guardhouse, a police station and Cape Town's city hall. Today it houses the Michaelis collection of minor but interesting Dutch and Flemish landscape paintings. Small visiting exhibitions are also displayed, and good evening classical concerts are a regular event; pick up the town house's quarterly news-letter, which lists forthcoming events. Tickets are available at the door immediately prior to the shows.

Heading east of the square, you come to **St George's Mall**, a pedestrianized road that runs northeast from Wale Street to Thibault Square, near the train station. Coffee shops, snack bars and lots of street traders and buskers make this a more pleasant route between the station and the Company's Gardens than Adderley Street, while dancers, drummers, choirs and painters add a certain buzz to the place. At the southern end of the mall, at Queen Victoria and Wale streets, **St George's Cathedral** is interesting more for its history than for its Herbert Baker Victorian Gothic design; on September 7, 1986, **Desmond Tutu** hammered on its doors symbolically demanding to be enthroned as South Africa's first black archbishop. Three years later, he heralded the last days of apartheid by leading thirty thousand people from the cathedral to the City Hall, where he coined his now famous slogan for the new order: "We are the rainbow people!" he told the crowd, "We are the new people of South Africa!"

Church Street (which crosses the mall towards its southern end) and its surrounding area abound with antique dealers, and on the pedestrianized section at its northeastern end you'll find an informal antique market. Prices are competitive and you may pick up unusual pieces of jewellery, bric-a-brac, Africana and even old sheet music.

Government Avenue and the Company's Gardens

A stroll down **Government Avenue**, the southwest extension of Adderley Street, makes for one of the most serene walks in central Cape Town (all roads and paths in the Company's Gardens are pedestrianized). This oak-lined boulevard runs past the rear of Parliament through the Gardens, and its benches are frequently occupied by snoring *bergies* (tramps).

Looming on your right as you enter the north end of the avenue, the **South African Library** (Mon–Fri 9am–6pm, Sat 9am–1pm; free) houses one of the country's best collections of antiquarian historical and natural history books, covering southern Africa. Built with the revenue from a tax on wine, it opened in 1822 as one of the first free libraries in the world.

Stretching from here to the South African Museum, the **Company's Gardens** were the initial *raison d'être* for the Dutch settlement at the Cape. Established in 1652 to supply fresh greens to Dutch East India Company ships travelling between the Netherlands and the East, the gardens were initially worked by imported slave labour. This proved too expensive, as the slaves had to be shipped in, fed and housed, so the Company phased out its farming and granted land to free burghers, from whom it bought fresh produce. At the end of the seventeenth century, the gardens were turned over to botanical horticulture for Cape Town's growing colonial elite. Ponds, lawns, landscaping and a crisscross web of oak-shaded walkways were introduced. It was during a stroll in these gardens that Rhodes (a statue of whom you'll find here) first plotted the invasion of Matabeleland and Mashonaland (which together became Rhodesia and subsequently Zimbabwe). He also introduced an army of small, furry colonizers to the gardens – North American grey squirrels. Today the gardens are full of local plants, the result of long-standing European interest in Cape botany; experts have been sailing out since the seventeenth century to classify and name specimens. The gardens are still a pleasant place to meander, and feature an outdoor café.

Continuing along Government Avenue from the South African Library, past the rear of Parliament, you can peer through an iron gate to see the grand buildings and tended flowerbeds of **De Tuynhuys**, the office (but not residence) of the president. During Mandela's presidency, one party of tourists stood amazed as the great man, who is renowned for his common touch, strolled across the lawns for a friendly chat.

A little further along, the tree-lined walkway opens out into a formal gravel area with ponds and statues, around which are sited the National Gallery, the Jewish Museum and the Great Synagogue to the east, and the South African Museum and Planetarium to the west.

The South African National Gallery

Not far from the southern end of Government Avenue, where it's joined by the tiny Gallery Lane, the **South African National Gallery** (Tues–Sun 10am–5pm; R5) is an essential port of call for anyone interested in the local art scene, and includes a small but excellent permanent collection of contemporary South African art. You'll also find a fine display of traditional works from the southeast of the continent, based around a small collection donated by the German government. The exhibits, which include beadwork, carvings and craft objects, were chosen for their aesthetic qualities and rarity, and represent the gallery's policy of focusing on neglected parts of South Africa's heritage. One room contains minor works by various British artists including Pre-Raphaelites, George Romney, Thomas Gainsborough and Joshua Reynolds. The gallery has a good café serving light lunches, snacks, coffees and cakes, as well as an excellent shop.

The South African Jewish Museum

Next to the National Gallery but accessed from 88 Hatfield Street, the **South African Jewish Museum** (Mon–Thurs & Sun 10am–5pm, Fri 10am–2pm; R50; Ⓦwww.sajewishmuseum.co.za) is partially housed in South Africa's first synagogue, built in 1863. One of Cape Town's most ambitious permanent exhibitions, it tells the story of South African Jewry from its beginnings over 150 years ago to the present – a narrative which starts in the Old Synagogue from which visitors cross, via a gangplank, to the upper level of a new two-storey building, symbolically re-enacting the arrival by boat of the first Jewish immigrants at Table Bay harbour in the 1840s. Employing multimedia interactive displays, models and Judaica artefacts, the exhibition follows three threads: "**Memories**", looking at the roots and experiences of the immigrants; "**Reality**", covering their integration into South Africa; and "**Dreams**", examining a diversity of views about the role of Jews in South Africa, their relationship to Israel and their position in the world. Other displays examine anti-Semitism, apartheid and the Jews who opposed it, as well as Nelson Mandela's relationship with the Jewish community.

Drawing parallels between Judaism and the ritual practices and beliefs of South Africa's other communities, the "**Culture among Cultures**" display covers topics such as birth, marriage, circumcision and death. The **basement level** houses a walk-through reconstruction of a Lithuanian *shtetl* or village (most South African Jews have their nineteenth-century roots in Lithuania), as well as the **Discovery Centre**, an interactive computer with a genealogy bank, a searchable database on Jewish life and culture and a "glimpse into Israel". A restaurant, shop and auditorium are also housed in the museum complex.

Jewish immigration to South Africa

Today there are around twenty thousand Jews in Cape Town, the majority descended from **Eastern European refugees** who fled discrimination and pogroms during the late nineteenth and early twentieth centuries.

Since 1795, when the occupying British introduced freedom of worship at the Cape, Jews in South Africa have faced few legal impediments. However, there were instances of semi-official anti-Semitism during the twentieth century, the most notable being in the policy of the Nationalist Party while in opposition during the 1940s. Before World War II, elements in the party came under the influence of Nazi ideology, which was being poured into South Africa by the German foreign and propaganda offices, and began to attribute all the ills facing Afrikanerdom to a "British–Jewish capitalist" conspiracy. In 1941, the party adopted a policy of ending Jewish immigration and even repatriating "undesirable immigrants", as well as placing stronger controls over naturalization and the introduction of a "vocational permit" system to protect "the original white population against unfair competition".

Ironically, on the eve of taking power in 1947, the party of apartheid turned its back on anti-Semitism: one of its first acts after winning the 1948 election was to recognize the newly created state of Israel, with which South Africa maintained strong links until the National Party relinquished power in 1994. The ANC government is far more sympathetic to the Palestinian cause, and far more critical of Israel than its predecessors.

The Holocaust Exhibition and the Great Synagogue

Opened in 1999, the **Holocaust Exhibition** (Mon–Thurs & Sun 10am–5pm, Fri 10am–1pm; free) is one of the most moving and brilliantly executed museums in Cape Town. Housed upstairs in the Holocaust Centre (in the same complex as the Jewish Museum), it resonates sharply in a country that only recently emerged from an era of racial oppression – a connection that the exhibition makes explicitly. A densely layered narrative is related through text, photographs, artefacts (such as a concentration camp uniform), film clips, soundtracks, multimedia and interactive video, while the design uses modulated lighting, cobblestones reminiscent of the ghettos and pieces of barbed wire and railway track to evoke the death camps.

Exhibits trace the history of anti-Semitism in Europe, culminating with the Nazis' Final Solution; they also look at South Africa's Greyshirts, who were motivated by Nazi propaganda during the 1930s and were later absorbed into the National Party. There are accounts of heroism, often tragic, including acts of resistance by Jews, and a touch screen portrays many individuals in Europe who risked their lives to protect or rescue the victims of Nazism. To conclude, a twenty-minute video tells the story of survivors who eventually settled in Cape Town.

The **Great Synagogue** next door is one of Cape Town's outstanding religious buildings. Designed by the Scottish architects Parker & Forsyth and completed in 1905, it features an impressive dome and two soaring towers after the style of central European Baroque churches. To see the arched interior and the alcove decorated with gilt mosaics, you need to ask at the Holocaust Centre, and may be asked to provide some form of identification.

The South African Museum and Planetarium

The nation's premier museum of natural history and human sciences, the **South African Museum and Planetarium** (daily 10am–5pm; museum R8 for adults, free for kids; planetarium adults R20, kids R5; Ⓦ www.museums.org.za/sam)

stands at 25 Queen Victoria Street, west of Government Avenue. The museum's **ethnographic galleries** contain some very good displays on the traditional arts and crafts of several African groups, some exceptional examples of rock art (entire chunks of caves sitting in the display cases), and casts of the stone birds found at the archeological site of Great Zimbabwe, in Zimbabwe. Upstairs, the **natural history galleries** display mounted mammals, dioramas of prehistoric Karoo reptiles, and Table Mountain flora and fauna. The highlight is the four-storey "whale well", in which a collection of beautiful whale skeletons hang like massive mobiles, accompanied by the eerie strains of their song.

The attached **Planetarium** (shows Mon–Fri 2pm, Tues also 8pm; Sat noon, 1pm & 2.30pm) is recommended if you want to see the constellations of the southern hemisphere, accompanied by informed commentary. There's also a changing programme of shows covering topics such as San sky myths. Leaflets at the museum provide a list of forthcoming attractions, and you can buy a monthly chart of the current night sky – especially worthwhile if you're staying in an area without streetlights and can actually see the stars.

Bertram House

At the southernmost end of Government Avenue, you'll come upon **Bertram House** (Tues–Thurs 8.30am–4.30pm; R5), whose beautiful two-storey brick facade looks out across a fragrant herb garden. Built in the 1840s, the museum is significant as the only surviving brick Georgian-style house in Cape Town, and displays typical furniture and objects of a well-to-do colonial British family in the first half of the nineteenth century.

The site was bought in 1839 by John Barker, a Yorkshire attorney who came to the Cape in 1823. He named the house after his wife, Ann Bertram Findlay, who died in 1838, and was responsible for building it. Declared a National Monument in 1962, Bertram House was extensively restored to its current state in the 1980s: imported face brick and Welsh slate were used to recreate the original facade, while the interior walls were redecorated in their earlier dark green and ochre, based on the evidence of paint scrapings. The reception rooms are decorated in the Regency style, while the porcelain is predominantly nineteenth-century English, although there are also some very fine Chinese pieces.

Houses of Parliament

South Africa's **Houses of Parliament**, east of Government Avenue, on Parliament Street, are a complex of interlinking buildings, with labyrinthine corridors connecting hundreds of offices, debating chambers and miscellaneous other rooms. Many of these are relics of the 1980s reformist phase of apartheid when, in the interests of racial segregation, there were three distinct legislative complexes sited here to cater to different "races".

The original wing, completed in 1885, is an imposing Victorian Neoclassical building which first served as the legislative assembly of the Cape Colony. After the Boer republics and British colonies amalgamated in 1910, it became the parliament of the Union of South Africa. This is the old parliament, where over seven decades of repressive legislation, including apartheid laws, were passed. It's also where **Hendrik Verwoerd**, the arch-theorist of apartheid, met his bloody end, not at the hand of a political activist, but stabbed to death by Dimitri Tsafendas, a parliamentary messenger who inexplicably went off the rails, committing the act because, as he told police, "a tapeworm ordered me to do it." Due to his mental state, the assassin escaped the gallows to outlive apartheid – albeit in an institution. Verwoerd's portrait, depicting him as a man of vision and gravitas, used to hang over the main entrance to the dining room. In 1996 it was removed "for cleaning", along with paintings of generations of white parliamentarians.

The new chamber was built in 1983 as part of the **tricameral parliament**, P.W. Botha's attempt to avert majority rule by trying to co-opt Indians and coloureds – but in their own separate debating chambers. The "tricameral" chamber, where the three non-African "races" on occasions met together, is now the **National Assembly**, where you can watch sessions of parliament. One-hour **tours** (Mon–Fri 9am–noon on the hour; free) take in the old and new debating chambers, the library and museum, and should be booked in advance through the Tours Section (☏021 403 2201). This is also the place to contact for day tickets to the **debating sessions** – the most interesting of which is question time (Wed from 3pm), when you can hear ministers being quizzed by MPs. To join a tour, go to the Plein Street entrance to Parliament, opposite the Receiver of Revenue (it's the more southerly of the two entrances in this street); go through a security check, where you should ask for directions to the Poorthuis entrance. From there you'll see arrows indicating the starting point for tours.

Castle of Good Hope

From the outside, South Africa's oldest building looks somewhat miserable, and its position on Darling Street, behind the train station and city-bus terminal, does nothing to dispel this. Nevertheless the **Castle of Good Hope** (daily 9am–4pm; R18; ⊛www.castleofgoodhope.co.za) is well worth the entrance fee; inside, a meticulous ten-year restoration has returned the decor to the British Regency style introduced in 1798.

Completed in 1679, the Castle – as it's commonly known – replaced van Riebeeck's earlier mud and timber fort, which stood on the site of the Grand Parade. The Castle was built in accordance with seventeenth-century European principles of fortification, comprising strong bastions from which the outside walls could be protected by crossfire. Construction lasted over thirteen years, with work constantly coming to a standstill because of shortages of labour or materials. The original, seaward entrance had to be moved to its present position facing landward, because the spring tide sometimes came crashing in – a remarkable thought given how far aground it is now. This newer entrance is a fine example of seventeenth-century Dutch classicism, and in the tower above, the bell cast in Amsterdam by Claude Fremy in 1697 still hangs from its original wooden beams. For 150 years, the Castle remained the symbolic heart of the Cape administration, and the centre of social and economic life, but in the late nineteenth century – when the colony had expanded far beyond its walls – there were at least three attempts by the authorities to demolish it, as it was regarded as a white elephant.

Inside the Castle are three interesting collections. The **Military Museum** has displays on the conflicts that dogged the early settlement; the **Secunde's House** has furnishings, paintings and *objets d'art* that filled the living space of the deputy governor; and the **William Fehr Collection**, one of the country's most important exhibits of decorative arts, includes paintings of the settlement, eighteenth- and nineteenth-century Dutch and Indonesian furniture, and seventeenth- and eighteenth-century Chinese and Japanese porcelain. **Free tours** (daily 11am, noon & 2pm) are useful for orientation and cover the main features, including the prison cells and dungeons, with their centuries-old graffiti painstakingly carved by prisoners. In the elegant courtyard there is a very pleasant tea shop, with Table Mountain looming over the west wall. The Castle is also home to the Defence Force's Western Province Command; you may see armed soldiers marching through the courtyard.

The Grand Parade and the City Hall

To the west of the Castle, the **Grand Parade** is a large open area where the residents of District Six used to come to trade. On Wednesdays and Saturdays it still transforms itself into a **market**, where you can buy a whole array of bargains ranging from used clothes to spicy food.

The Grand Parade appeared on TV screens throughout the world on February 11, 1990, when 100,000 people gathered to hear **Nelson Mandela** make his first speech after being released from prison, from the balcony of **City Hall**. A slightly fussy Edwardian building dressed in Bath stone, City Hall manages, despite its drab surroundings, to look impressive against Table Mountain.

District Six

South of the Castle, in the shadow of Devil's Peak, is a vacant lot shown on maps as the suburb of **Zonnebloem**. Before being demolished by the apartheid authorities, it was an inner-city slum known as **District Six**, an impoverished but lively community of 55,000 predominantly coloured people. Once regarded as the soul of Cape Town, the district harboured a rich cultural life in its narrow alleys and crowded tenements: along the cobbled streets, hawkers rubbed shoulders with prostitutes, gangsters, drunks and gamblers, while craftsmen plied their trade in small workshops. This was a fertile place of the South African imagination, inspiring novels, poems, jazz and the blockbuster *District Six: The Musical*, by David Kramer, which in the late 1980s played to packed houses and spawned a series of hits.

In 1966 apartheid ideologues declared District Six a **White Group Area** and the bulldozers moved in, taking fifteen years to drive its presence from the skyline, leaving only the mosques and churches. But, in the wake of the demolition gangs, international and domestic outcry was so great that the area was never developed apart from a few luxury town houses on its fringes and the hefty Cape Technikon, a college that now occupies nearly a quarter of the former suburb. After years of negotiation, the original residents are moving back under a scheme to develop low-cost housing in the district.

The District Six Museum

Few places in Cape Town speak more eloquently of the effect of apartheid on the day-to-day lives of ordinary people than the compelling **District Six Museum** (Mon 9am–3pm, Tues–Sat 9am–4pm; R10). On the northern boundary of District Six, on the corner of Buitenkant and Albertus streets, the museum occupies the former **Central Methodist Mission Church**, which offered solidarity and ministry to the victims of forced removals right up to the 1980s, and became a venue for anti-apartheid gatherings. Today, it houses a series of fascinating displays that include everyday household items and tools of trades, such as hairdressing implements, as well as documentary photographs, which evoke the lives of the individuals who once lived here. Occupying most of the floor is a huge map of District Six as it was, annotated by former residents, who describe their memories, reflections and incidents associated with places and buildings that no longer exist. There's also an almost complete collection of original street signs, secretly retrieved at the time of demolition by the man entrusted with dumping them into Table Bay.

Cape Heritage Square

Back at Long Street, if you head northwest down Shortmarket Street, you'll come to **Cape Heritage Square**, the largest restoration project ever undertaken in Cape Town. The square is home to the *Cape Heritage Hotel* as well as a conglomeration of restaurants, wine merchants, art galleries, jewellers and fashion shops, many of which are housed in a complex dating back to 1771. Set around a courtyard, in which the oldest known (and still fruit-bearing) vine in South Africa continues to flourish, the square is worth visiting for a glimpse of the superb restoration work.

The Bo-Kaap

Minutes from Parliament, on the slopes of Signal Hill, is the **Bo-Kaap**, one of Cape Town's oldest and most fascinating residential areas. Its streets are characterized by brightly coloured nineteenth-century Dutch and Georgian terraces, which conceal a network of alleyways that are the arteries of its **Muslim community**. The Bo-Kaap harbours its own strong identity, made all the more unique by the destruction of District Six, with which it had much in common. A particular dialect of Afrikaans is spoken here, although it is steadily being eroded by English.

Bo-Kaap residents are descended from dissidents and slaves imported by the Dutch in the sixteenth and seventeenth centuries. They became known collectively as "**Cape Malays**", a term you'll still hear, even though it's a complete misnomer: most originated from Africa, India, Madagascar and Sri Lanka, with fewer than one percent actually from Malaysia.

The easiest way to get to the Bo-Kaap is by foot along Wale Street, which trails up from the south end of Adderley Street and across Buitengragt, to become the main drag of the Bo-Kaap. There's a deceptively quaint feel to the area: apart from Wale Street, this is not really a place to explore alone. It's better to join one of several **tours** that take in the museum and walk you around the district. The best (and cheapest, at R100) is run by Bo-Kaap Guided Tours (☎021 422 1554 or 082 423 6932; 2hr 30min) and operated by residents of the area, whose knowledge goes beyond the standard tour-guide script.

A good place to head for is the **Bo-Kaap Museum**, 71 Wale Street (Mon–Sat 9am–4pm; R5), near the Buitengragt end. It consists mainly of the family house and possessions of Abu Bakr Effendi, a nineteenth-century religious leader brought out from Turkey by the British in 1862 as a mediator between feuding Muslim factions. He became an important member of the community, founded an Arabic school and wrote a book in the local vernacular – now regarded as possibly the first book to be recognized in what can be recognized as Afrikaans. The museum also has exhibits exploring the local brand of Islam, which has its own unique traditions and nearly two dozen *kramats* (shrines) dotted about the peninsula. One block south of the museum, at Dorp Street, is the **Auwal**, South Africa's first official mosque, founded in 1795 by Tuan Guru, a Muslim activist. Ten more mosques, whose minarets give spice to the quarter's skyline, now serve its 10,000 residents.

A small Muslim shantytown, tucked away next to the old quarry below the cemetery, brings the immediacy of South Africa's housing crisis right to the edge of the city centre. Modern, low-cost developments, looking down from the heights of Signal Hill onto the photogenic Bo-Kaap townscape, have helped alleviate the community's housing shortage, but have added nothing to the architectural charm of the protected historic core bounded by Dorp and Strand streets, and Buitengragt and Pentz streets. Furthermore, many Bo-Kaap residents, tempted by the high prices their cottages can fetch, have sold them to outsiders who value the central location and picturesque quality of the area, a process which is seen to be diluting the Muslim lifestyle in the area.

Strand Street

A major artery from the N2 freeway to the central business district, **Strand Street** neatly separates the Upper from the Lower city centre. Between the mid-eighteenth and mid-nineteenth centuries, Strand Street was one of the most fashionable streets in Cape Town because of its proximity to the shore. Its former cachet is now only discernible from the handful of quietly elegant National Monuments left standing amid the roar of traffic: **Martin Melck House** (accommodating the **Gold of Africa Museum**), the **Evangelical Lutheran Church** and **Koopmans-De Wet House**.

Gold of Africa Museum

Since the discovery of gold near Johannesburg in the late nineteenth century, South Africa has been closely associated in the Western mind with the precious metal and the riches it represents. However, the outstanding **Gold of Africa Museum** at 96 Strand Street (Mon–Sat 9.30am–5pm; R20), just off Buitengragt, focuses on a completely different side to gold – the exquisite **artworks** crafted by nineteenth- and twentieth-century **African goldsmiths** from Mali, Senegal, Ghana and the Cote d'Ivoire. Arguably the most important such collection in the world, acquired in 2001 from the Barbier-Meuller Museum in Geneva, it traces Africa's ancient gold routes, and includes several hundred beautiful items – precious masks, crocodiles, birds, a gold crown and human figures; the highlight is the sculpted **Golden Lion** from Ghana that is the symbol of the museum. There's also a small auditorium with a continuous **film show**; a **wine cellar**, where you can have a snack, a coffee and quaff a glass of Cape wine; a **studio** where goldsmiths practise their art; and a **shop** selling postcards, gold leaf and beautiful little souvenirs.

Evangelical Lutheran Church

Next door to the Gold of Africa Museum, at the corner of Buitengragt and Strand Street, stands the **Evangelical Lutheran Church** (Mon, Wed & Fri 9am–noon; free). Converted by Anton Anreith (see box on p.144) in 1785 from a barn, its facade includes Classical details such as a broken pediment perforated by the clock tower, as well as Gothic features such as arched windows. Inside, the magnificent **pulpit**, supported on two life-size Herculean figures, is one of Anreith's masterpieces; the white swan perched on the canopy is a symbol of Lutheranism.

The establishment of a Lutheran church in Cape Town struck a significant blow against the extreme **religious intolerance** that pervaded under VOC rule. Before 1771, when permission was granted to Lutherans to establish their own congregation, Protestantism was the only form of worship allowed and the Dutch Reformed Church held an absolute monopoly over saving people's souls. The Lutheran Church's congregation was dominated by Germans, who at the time constituted 28 percent of the colony's free burgher population.

Koopmans-De Wet House

Sandwiched between two office blocks close to Cape Town Tourism, **Koopmans-De Wet House** at 35 Strand Street (Tues–Thurs 8.30am–4.30pm; R5) is an outstanding eighteenth-century pedimented Neoclassical town house and museum, accommodating a very fine collection of antique furniture and rare porcelain. An inexpensive **guide** booklet gives interesting contextual background to the house and its history, while a separate brochure describes items in the collection: both are available at the entrance.

The earliest sections of the house were built in 1701 by **Reyner Smedinga**, a well-to-do goldsmith who imported the building materials from Holland. The house changed hands more than a dozen times over the following two centuries, with minor additions made in the 1760s and a second storey added between 1774 and 1790. In 1806, it came into the hands of the De Wet family, eventually becoming the home of **Marie Koopmans-De Wet** (1834–1906), a prominent figure on the Cape social and political circuit.

The building's **facade** has been attributed to Louis Thibault and Anton Anreith (see box on p.144), but there's no proof of this. Whoever was responsible, the house represents a fine synthesis of Dutch elements (sash windows and large entrance doors) with the demands of local conditions; the huge rooms, lofty ceilings and shuttered windows reflect the high summer temperatures, while the front *stoep* has plastered masonry seats at each end. The **lantern** in the fanlight of the entrance to the house was a feature of all Cape Town houses in the eighteenth and early nineteenth centuries, its purpose to shine light onto the street and thus hinder slaves from gathering at night to plot.

The Lower City Centre

In the mid-nineteenth century, the city's middle classes viewed the **Lower City Centre** and its low-life activities with a mixture of alarm and excitement – a tension that remains today. **Lower Long Street** divides the area just inland from the docklands into two. To the east is the **Foreshore**, an ugly post-World War II wasteland of grey corporate architecture, among which is the **Artscape Centre**, Cape Town's prestige arts complex. The Foreshore is at last being redeveloped, its centrepiece being the **Cape Town International Convention Centre**, completed in 2003 and linked by a canal and pedestrian routes with the Waterfront.

The Foreshore

The Foreshore, an area of reclaimed land north of Strand Street, stretching to the docks and east of Lower Long Street, was developed in the late 1940s in a spirit of modernism – large highly planned urban spaces – that was sweeping the world. It was intended to turn Cape Town's harbour into a symbolic gateway to Africa; instead, it turned out as a series of large concrete boxes surrounded by acres of windswept tarmac parking lots. The opening in 2004 of the prestigious International Convention Centre in the area, and its promixity to some high rise hotels and parking garages, have opened up the area, but there is no street life at all, and no reason to explore the area.

Heerengracht, a truncated two-lane carriageway running from Adderley Street to the harbour, has massive roundabouts at each end solemnly guarded by statues of Jan van Riebeeck and Bartholomeu Dias. It was meant to be the ceremonial axis through this grand scheme, joining the city to the sea, but it never quite makes it to the water, coming to a disappointing standstill at the dock perimeter fence, before bearing east under the dismal shadow of the N1 and N2 flyovers.

The only building worth visiting here – when there's something on – is the **Artscape Complex** (previously known as the Nico Theatre Complex), Cape Town's major performance venue, in D.F. Malan Street just east of Heerengracht. Incorporating the large Main Theatre, it also houses the small Arena

Theatre, the opera house and a decent coffee shop; for more on events staged here, see p.174.

Duncan Dock

North of the Foreshore, **Duncan Dock** is Cape Town's working harbour. Work started on the dock in 1938, swallowing the city beachfronts at Woodstock and Paarden Island to cater for the growing supertanker traffic that was outstripping the capacity of the Victoria and Alfred Docks. The dock today is a forbidding industrial landscape of large ships and towering cranes cut off from the city by an enormous perimeter fence. It's a fabulous place to photograph gigantic hulks against Table Mountain, and has an excellent Taiwanese restaurant, the *Jewel Tavern* (see p.166), but is not the kind of area you'd want to linger in.

The V&A Waterfront, de Waterkant and Robben Island

The **Victoria and Alfred Waterfront**, usually known simply as the Waterfront, adjoins the west of Duncan Dock and is Cape Town's original Victorian harbour. After two decades of stagnation, it was redeveloped in the 1990s and is now the most popular attraction on the peninsula, incorporating the city's central shopping area, its most fashionable eating and drinking venues, the site of an excellent aquarium and the Nelson Mandela Gateway – the embarkation point for trips to **Robben Island**. Authentic nineteenth-century buildings, imitation Victorian shopping malls, piers with waterside walkways and a functioning harbour complement the wide range of restaurants, outdoor cafés, pubs, clubs, cinemas, museums and outdoor entertainment, with magnificent Table Mountain rising beyond.

West of the Foreshore and rubbing up against the west side of the city centre and the V&A Waterfront to its north is Cape Town's thriving clubland, incorporating **De Waterkant** and **Somerset Road**, the city's self-proclaimed "gay village". With its high density of **nightclubs** and **pubs**, the area around Somerset Road, which heads from the city centre into Green Point, has become the best place in Cape Town to club-crawl, one of the few places you're guaranteed action seven nights a week; for more, see pp.170–172. For coverage of the coast from Mouille Point onwards, see pp.152–156.

The Waterfront

Throughout the first half of the nineteenth century, arguments raged in Cape Town over the need for a proper dock. The Cape was often known as the **Cape of Storms** because of its vicious weather, which left Table Bay littered with wrecks. Many makeshift attempts were made to ameliorate the situation, including the construction of a lighthouse in 1823, and work was begun on a jetty at the bottom of Bree Street in 1832. Clamour for a harbour grew in the 1850s, with the increase in sea traffic arriving at the Cape, reaching its peak in 1860, when the Lloyds insurance company refused the risk of covering ships dropping anchor in Table Bay.

The British colonial government dragged its heels due to the costs involved, but eventually conceded; on a suitably stormy September day in 1860, at a huge ceremony, the teenage Prince Alfred tipped the first batch of stones into

V&A WATERFRONT & DE WATERKANT

N

RESTAURANTS, CAFÉS, BARS AND CLUBS

Anatoli	10	Green Dolphin	8
Andiamo	18	La Petite Tarte	18
Baia	1	Manenberg	
Bar Code	11	Jazz Café	7
Bayfront Blu	9	Mugg & Bean	2
Bossa Nova	12	The Nose	
Bronx	13	Wine Bar	18
Café Manhattan	18	On Broadway	15
Caffé Balducci	3	Opium	17
Caffé San Marco	5	Purgatory	16
Chilli 'n' Lime	14	Rosie's	19
Confession	13	Sliver	13
Den Anker Restaurant		Tasca de Belem	4
and Bar	6		

Mouille Point, Green Point & Sea Point

EAST PIER ROAD

Victoria Basin

❶ Baia

❷ Mugg & Bean

❸ Caffé Balducci

Victoria Wharf

JETTY WAY

BREAKWATER BOULEVAR

❹ Agfa Amphitheatre

❺ Caffé San Marco

Victoria Wharf

Swing Bridge

Nelson Mandela Gateway to Robben Island

Duncan Dock

Old Port Captain's Office

Pierhead

ⓘ

Market Square

❻ Den Anker

❼ Clock Tower Centre & Cape Town Tourism Visitors' Centre

Telkom Exploratorium

❽ Clock Tower & Waterfront Information Centre

Clock Tower & Waterfront Information Centre

BMW Pavilion & IMAX Cinema

Alfred Mall

Waterfront Buses

FISH QUAY ROAD

SOUTHARM ROAD

DUNCAN ROAD

PORTSWOOD ROAD

SA Maritime Museum

Taxi Rank ★

Two Oceans Aquarium

❾ Bayfront Blu

Ⓐ

Waterfront Marina

Ⓑ

DOCK ROAD

Ⓒ

City Centre

PORT ROAD

Green Point & Sea Point

UPPER PORTSWOOD ROAD

VESPERDENE ROAD

BRAEMAR ROAD

HIGH LEVEL ROAD

CHEPSTOW ROAD

CARREG CRESCENT

MERRIMAN ROAD

Ⓓ

HILLSIDE TERRACE

WESSELS ROAD

BOUNDARY ROAD

MAIN ROAD

GALLOWS HILL ST

BEAUMONT

HIGHFIELD ROAD

HIGHFIELD ROAD

EBENEZER ROAD

CARDIFF

BENNETT

BATTERY

PRESTWICH

LIDDLE

COBERN

❿ Anatoli

⓫ Bar Code

⓬ Bossa Nova

DE WATERKANT

DE SMIDT

JARVIS

NAPIER

WATERKANT

LOADER

DIXON

Ⓔ

⓭ Bronx/Confession/Sliver

⓮ Chilli 'n' Lime

⓯ On Broadway

⓰ Purgatory

⓱ Opium

⓲ Andiamo/Café Manhattan/La Petite Tarte/The Nose Wine Bar

⓳ Rosie's

SOMERSET ROAD

ALFRED

HOSPITAL

CHIAPPINI

HUDSON

VOS

STRAND

CHIAPPINI

Bo-Kaap ▼

ACCOMMODATION

Breakwater Lodge	B
The Cape Grace	A
City Lodge	C
De Waterkant Village	E
St John's Waterfront Lodge	D

0   100 m

Table Bay to begin the **Breakwater**, the westernmost arm of the harbour, which was subsequently completed with convict labour. In 1869, the dock – consisting of two main basins – was completed, and the sea was allowed to pour in.

The Waterfront is one of the easiest points to reach in Cape Town by **public transport**. Golden Arrow municipal buses leave for here from Adderley Street, from outside the train station and from Beach Road in Sea Point. The open-topped Cape Town Explorer bus (see p.104) also stops at the Waterfront. Arriving by **car**, you'll find yourself well catered for, with several car parks and garages. If you want to leave by taxi, head for the taxi rank on Breakwater Boulevard.

The Marina and the Victoria and Alfred basins

Victoria Basin, the smaller **Alfred Basin** to its west, and the **Marina** beyond, create the northwestern half of the Waterfront's geography of piers and quays. The shopping focus of the Waterfront is **Victoria Wharf**, an enormous flashy mall on two levels, extending along Quays Five and Six. It's here that most visitors to the Waterfront arrive. With outdoor seating, the restaurants and cafés on the mall's east side have fabulous views of Table Mountain across the busy harbour. On the west side of Victoria Wharf, and physically linked to it, the rather contrived **Red Shed Craft Workshop** (Mon–Sat 9am–9pm, Sun 10am–9pm) brings together craft workers such as glass-blowers, leatherworkers, township artists and jewellery-makers under one huge roof.

The outdoor action centres around **Market Square** and the **Agfa Amphitheatre**, where you can sometimes catch free rock, jazz or traditional African musical performances and occasionally hear the Cape Town Symphony Orchestra (details from the Visitor Centre).

South of here along the Alfred Basin's North Quay, **Alfred Mall Shopping Centre** is a complex of fifteen touristy curio shops, boutiques and restaurants. East of the Alfred Shopping Mall, the Pierhead is dominated by the **Old Port Captain's Office**, a gabled Arts and Crafts building erected in 1904, with an imposing presence that reflected its status as the nerve centre of the harbour in the early twentieth century. It's now the headquarters of the Victoria and Alfred Waterfront Company, which manages the Waterfront area.

Two Oceans Aquarium

One of Cape Town's highlights, the **Two Oceans Aquarium** (daily 9.30am–6pm; adults R55, children R25; ⓦwww.aquarium.co.za) on Dock Road at the Marina's North Wharf, showcases the Cape's unique marine environment, where the warm Indian Ocean mingles with the cold Atlantic. A designated route (which you're not obliged to follow) takes in the nine major galleries in sequence, starting on the **ground floor** with the **Indian Ocean**, where you'll see tank after tank of psychedelic fish. One of the most beautiful displays features scores of small gossamer jellyfish floating gently in their ultraviolet-lit cylindrical tank like parachutists. To the rear of the ground floor, the **Diversity Hall**, as its name implies, contains an astonishing variety of strange marine creatures, including giant spider crabs, octopuses, sea horses and the deadly devil firefish, whose lacy beauty disguises lethal spines. Also on the ground floor, the **Agfa Auditorium** shows videos on South Africa's marine life and related topics (such as underwater photography).

The **basement** houses the **Alpha Activity Centre**, a good place to keep kids occupied, with free organized activities such as puppet shows and face painting, and computers which allow youngsters to explore marine ecology.

The centre is combined with the **Diving Animals** display, where you can watch a group of resident Cape fur seals frolicking underwater.

The **top floor**, reached via a ramp, accommodates the **Story of Water**, which, in glorious reconstruction, traces the course of a river from its mouth to its source, via a salt marsh and lagoon. Not to everyone's taste, it features a small colony of African penguins (which you can see in their natural state at Boulders; see p.160), while captive sea birds fly about the rafters. In the **Kelp Forest** in an adjacent gallery a dense jungle of giant seaweed sways hypnotically with the rhythmic surge of the water; you can sit in the small amphitheatre and gaze at beautiful shoals of silvery fish shimmering through sunlit sea. From here, a ramp takes you in a gentle downward spiral through the **Predators** exhibit, for many visitors the most compelling attraction of all. A massive tank, open to the ocean, houses some large resident ragged-toothed sharks, which glide past as you walk through a glass underwater tunnel; other species confined here include rays and giant turtles.

Among the highlights of the aquarium is the **shark feeding** every Sunday at 3.30pm, when you can watch *raggies* – ragged-tooth sharks – being hand-fed by divers. Smaller sharks, stingrays and turtles get their turn on Monday, Wednesday and Friday at 3.30pm, and penguins are fed daily at noon and 3pm. If you have an Open Water 1 diving qualification, you can actually **dive** in the predators tank (book one day before on ℡021 418 3823; R400).

Fish Quay

From the Pierhead you can use the **swing bridge** to cross to **Fish Quay**, the **Clock Tower Precinct** and the **Nelson Mandela Gateway to Robben Island** (daily 7.30am–5.30pm; free). The embarkation point for ferries to Robben Island, this two-storey building also incorporates a restaurant with a great view and a small museum with hi-tech interactive displays, featuring a history of Robben Island, the voices of prisoners and resistance songs.

Rising up from Fish Quay, the **Clock Tower**, which houses a branch of the Waterfront Information Centre, is Cape Town's finest architectural folly. Built as the original Port Captain's office in 1882, this strange-looking octagonal structure with Gothic windows consists of three stacked rooms with a stairwell running through its core. The mirror room on the second floor enabled the Port Captain to survey all the activities of the harbour without leaving his office. Adjacent to the Clock Tower, the **Clock Tower Centre** is a compact two-storey shopping mall, with a substantial Cape Tourism visitor centre.

Robben Island tours

A number of vendors at the Waterfront sell tickets for cruises, which may go close to Robben Island, but only the official ones sold at the **Nelson Mandela Gateway** will get you onto it (R150, including catamaran fare, island entry and 3hr 30min tour). Book in advance with a credit card (℡021 419 1300, ⊛www.robben-island.org.za) as the catamarans are often full, especially around December and January. Be sure to present your booking reference number and arrive at least half an hour before departure to collect your ticket. In summer the boats operate hourly between 9am and 3pm; more boats are put on in December and January, including sunset trips at 5pm and 6pm, while in winter there are only four boats a day, at 9am, 11am, 1pm and 3pm.

Robben Island

Lying only a few kilometres from the commerce of the Waterfront, flat and windswept **Robben Island** is suffused by a meditative, otherwordly silence. This key site of South Africa's liberation struggle was intended to silence apartheid's domestic critics, but instead became an international focus for opposition to the regime. Measuring six square kilometres and sparsely vegetated by low scrub, it was Nelson Mandela's "home" for nearly two decades.

Some history

Nelson Mandela may have been the most famous Robben Island prisoner, but he certainly wasn't the first. In the seventeenth century the island became a place of banishment for those who offended the political order (initially the Dutch, later the British and the Afrikaner Nationalists). The island's first prisoner was the indigenous Khoikhoi leader **Autshumato**, who learnt English in the early seventeenth century and became an emissary of the British. After the Dutch settlement was established, he was jailed on the island by Jan van Riebeeck in 1658. The rest of the seventeenth century saw a succession of East Indies political prisoners and Muslim holy men exiled here for opposing Dutch colonial rule.

During the nineteenth century, the **British** used Robben Island as a dumping ground for deserters, criminals and political prisoners, in much the same way as they used Australia. Captured **Xhosa leaders** who defied the British Empire during the Frontier Wars of the early to mid-nineteenth century were transported by sea from the Eastern to the Western Cape to be imprisoned, and many ended up on Robben Island. In 1846, the island's brief was extended to include a whole range of the **socially marginalized**; criminals and political detainees were now joined by vagrants, prostitutes, lunatics and the chronically ill. All were victim to a regime of brutality and maltreatment, even in hospital. In the 1890s, a leper colony existed alongside the social outcasts. Lunatics were removed in 1921 and the lepers in 1930. During World War II, the **Defence Force** took over the island to set up defensive guns against a feared Axis invasion, which never came.

Robben Island's greatest era of notoriety began in 1961, when it was taken over by the **Prisons Department**. Prisoners arriving at the island prison were greeted by a slogan on the gate that read: "Welcome to Robben Island: We Serve with Pride." By 1963, when Nelson Mandela arrived, it had become a maximum security prison, and all the warders – but none of the prisoners – were white. Prisoners were only allowed to send and receive one letter every six months, and common-law criminals and political prisoners were housed together until 1971, when they were separated in an attempt to further isolate the politicals. Harsh conditions, including routine beatings and forced hard labour, were exacerbated by geographical location: there's nothing but sea between the island and the South Pole, so icy winds routinely blow in from across the Atlantic – and inmates were made to wear shorts and flimsy jerseys. Like every other prisoner, Mandela slept on a thin mat on the floor (until 1973, when he was given a bed because he was ill) and was kept in a solitary confinement cell measuring two metres square for sixteen hours a day.

Amazingly, the prisoners found ways of **protesting**, through hunger strikes, publicizing conditions when possible (by visits from the International Committee of the Red Cross, for example) and, remarkably, by taking legal action against the prison authority to stop arbitrary punishments. They won improved conditions over the years, and the island also became a university behind bars, where people of different political views and generations met; it was not unknown for prisoners to give academic help to their warders. The last political prisoners were released from Robben Island in 1991 and the remaining common-law prisoners were transferred to the mainland in 1996. On January 1, 1997, control of Robben Island was transferred from the Department of Correctional Services to the Department of the Arts, Culture, Science and Technology, which has now established it as a museum. In December 1999 the entire island was declared a **UN World Heritage Site**.

The island

The catamaran from the Waterfront takes about half an hour to reach this potent symbol of apartheid, where ex-prisoners and ex-warders work as guides, sharing their experiences. After arrival at the tiny Murray's Bay harbour, you are taken on a **bus tour** around the island and a **tour of the prison**.

The bus tour stops off at several historical landmarks, the first of which is the **kramat**, a beautiful shrine built in memory of Tuan Guru, a Muslim cleric from present-day Indonesia who was imprisoned here by the Dutch in the eighteenth century. On his release, he helped to establish Islam among slaves in Cape Town, where it has flourished ever since. The tour also passes a **leper graveyard** and **church** designed by Sir Herbert Baker, both of which are quiet reminders that the island was a place of exile for leprosy sufferers in the early twentieth century.

Robert Sobukwe's house seems to echo with loneliness, and is perhaps the most affecting relic of incarceration on the island. It was here that Sobukwe, leader of the Pan Africanist Congress (a radical offshoot of the ANC) was held in solitary confinement for nine years. He was initially sentenced to three years, but was regarded as so dangerous by the authorities that they passed a special law – the "Sobukwe Clause" – to keep him on Robben Island for a further six years. No other political prisoners were allowed to speak to him, but he would sometimes gesture his solidarity with other sons of the African soil by letting sand trickle through his fingers as they walked past. After his release in 1969, Sobukwe was restricted to Kimberley under house arrest, until his death from cancer in 1978.

Another stopoff is the **lime quarry** where Nelson Mandela and his fellow inmates spent countless hours of hard labour. The soft, pale stone is extremely bright under the summer sun, as a result of which Mandela and others have in later years suffered eye disorders. As the years passed, the lime quarry became a place of furtive study among the prisoners, with the help of sympathetic wardens.

The bus tour also takes in a stretch of coast dotted with shipwrecks and abundant seabirds, including the elegant **Egyptian sacred ibis**. You may also spot some of a recently expanded population of **antelope**: springbok, eland and bontebok.

The Maximum Security Prison

The **Maximum Security Prison**, a forbidding complex of unadorned H-blocks on the edge of the island, is introduced with a tour through the famous **B-Section**; you'll be guided by a former inmate, after which you're free to wander. B-Section is a small compound full of tiny rooms that has become legendary in South African history; initially a place of defeat for the resistance movement, it ironically came to incubate and concentrate the energies of liberation. **Mandela's cell** has been left exactly as it was, without embellishments or display, but the rest have been left locked and empty.

In the nearby **A-Section**, the "Cell Stories" exhibition skilfully suggests the sparseness of prison life; the tiny isolation cells contain personal artefacts loaned by former prisoners (including a functional saxophone made of found objects), plus quotations, recordings and photographs.

Towards the end of the 1980s, cameras were sneaked onto the island, and inmates took snapshots of each other, which have been enlarged to almost life size and mounted as the **Smuggled Camera Exhibition** in the D-Section communal cells. The jovial demeanour of the prisoners indicates their realization that the end was within sight; moreover, the warm camaraderie that evidently connects them suggests how people endured so many years of captivity. The **Living Legacy** tour in F-Section involves ex-political prisoner guides describing their lives here and answering your questions.

The southern suburbs

Away from Table Mountain and the city centre, the bulk of Cape Town's residential sprawl extends east into South Africa's interior. It's here that the **southern suburbs**, the formerly whites-only residential areas, stretch out down the east side of Table Mountain, ending just before Muizenberg on the False Bay coast. All the main suburban attractions are concentrated in this area and, not surprisingly, the best shopping areas and cinemas.

From anywhere in the southern suburbs you can see Table Mountain rising above Cape Town. The area offers some quick escapes from the city heat into forests, gardens and vineyards, all hugging the eastern slopes of the mountain, and its extension, the Constantiaberg. The suburbs themselves are pleasant enough places to stay, eat and shop, but sights are thin on the ground.

The quickest way of reaching the southern suburbs from the city centre, Waterfront or City Bowl suburbs is the **M3 highway**; indeed taking the tar is the only convenient way to get to Constantia, Kirstenbosch and Tokai. Outside rush hour, it takes about thirty minutes to get from the centre to Tokai, where the highway ends. Travelling by **train**, you can get to Woodstock, Salt River, Observatory, Mowbray, Rosebank and Rondebosch.

Woodstock, Salt River and Observatory

First and oldest of the suburbs as you take an easterly exit from town is **Woodstock**, unleafy and windblown, but redeemed by some nice Victorian buildings, originally occupied by working-class coloureds, and now yuppifying. To its east, **Salt River** is a harsh, industrial, mainly coloured area, built initially for workers and artisans, while **Observatory**, abutting its southern end, is generally regarded as Cape Town's bohemian hub, a reputation fuelled by its proximity to the University of Cape Town in Rondebosch and its large student population. Many of the houses here are student digs, but the narrow Victorian streets are also home to young professionals, hippies and arty types. The refreshingly unrestored peeling arcades on Observatory's Lower Main Road, and the streets off it, have some nice cafés and lively bars, as well as a wholefood shop, an African fabrics shop, and a couple of antiques emporiums. The huge Groote Schuur Hospital, which overlooks the freeway that sweeps through Observatory, was the site of the world's first heart transplant in 1967.

▲ Bloubergstrand

NYANGA

LANGA

GUGULETU

C A P E   F L A T S

PINELANDS

RONDEBOSCH

Mowbray
Rosebank
Rondebosch
Claremont
Harfield Road
Kenilworth
Wynberg
Wittebosch
Plumstead
Steurhof
Diep River
Heathfield

Woodstock
Salt River
Observatory

Mostert's Mill
University of Cape Town
Rhodes Memorial
Newlands
Groote Schuur

BISHOPS COURT

CONSTANTIA

Cape Town Central Station

Devil's Peak

Kirstenbosch Botanical Gardens

Groot Constantia
Klein Constantia
Buitenver-wachtung

CONSTANTIABERG

TOKAI

GREEN POINT

CITY BOWL

Signal Hill

Lions Head

Table Mountain

Lower Cable Station
CAMPS BAY
Upper Cable Station

T W E L V E   A P O S T L E S

SEA POINT

BANTRY BAY
CLIFTON
Camps Bay

World of Birds

CHAPMAN'S

P A R K

LLANDUDNO

Sandy Bay

H O U T   B A Y

A T L A N T I C   O C E A N

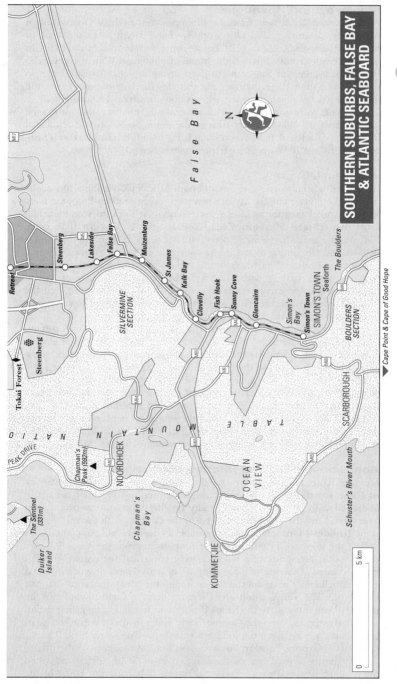

SOUTHERN SUBURBS, FALSE BAY & ATLANTIC SEABOARD

N

False Bay

Steenberg
Lakeside
False Bay
Muizenberg
St James
Kalk Bay
Clovelly
Fish Hoek
Sunny Cove
Glencairn
Simon's Bay
Simon's Town
SIMON'S TOWN
Seaforth
The Boulders
BOULDERS SECTION

Retreat
Steenberg
Tokai Forest
SILVERMINE SECTION

PEAK DRIVE
NATIO[N]
Chapman's Peak (592m)
NOORDHOEK
MOUNTAIN
TABLE
OCEAN VIEW
KOMMETJIE
Chapman's Bay
SCARBOROUGH
Schuster's River Mouth

The Sentinel (331m)
Duiker Island

▶ Cape Point & Cape of Good Hope

0   5 km

Mowbray and Rosebank

Along Station Road, away from the mountain and south of Observatory, is **Mowbray**, originally called Drie Koppen (Three Heads), after the heads of three slaves impaled there in 1724, but its name was changed in the 1840s. In the nineteenth century this was the home of philologist Willem Bleek, who lived with a group of San convicts given up by the colonial authorities so that he could study their languages and attitudes. Bleek's pioneering work still forms the basis of much of what we know about traditional Khoisan life.

Rosebank, to Mowbray's south, has a substantial student community, some staying in the so-called Tampax Towers, the unmistakable circular residential blocks on Main Road. Just beyond them is the brown-bricked **Baxter Theatre**, one of Cape Town's premier arts complexes (see p.174).

Irma Stern Museum

Irma Stern is acknowledged as one of South Africa's pioneering artists of the twentieth century, more for the fact that she brought modern European ideas to the colonies than for any huge contribution she made to world art. The **UCT Irma Stern Museum**, Cecil Road, Rosebank (Tues–Sat 10am–5pm; R8), was the artist's home for 38 years until her death in 1966. The museum is definitely worth visiting to see Stern's collection of Iberian, African, Oriental and ancient artefacts. The whole house, in fact, reflects the artist's fascination with exoticism, starting with her own Gauguinesque paintings of "native types", the fantastic carved doors she brought back from Zanzibar, and the very untypical garden that brings a touch of the tropics to Cape Town with its exuberant bamboo thickets and palm trees.

Born in a backwater town in South Africa in 1894 to German Jewish parents, Stern studied at Germany's Weimar Academy. In reaction to the academy's conservatism, she adopted **expressionist distortion** in her paintings, some of which were included in the Neue Sezession Exhibition in Berlin in 1918. Although Stern's work was appreciated in Europe when she returned to South Africa after World War II, critics claimed that her style was simply a cover for technical incompetence. Stern went on several expeditions into Africa in the 1940s and 1950s, where she found the source for her intensely sensuous work that shocked contemporary South Africa, but which has led historians to regard her as the towering figure of her generation.

Rondebosch and the Rhodes Memorial

South of Rosebank, neighbouring **Rondebosch** is home to the **University of Cape Town** (UCT), whose nineteenth-century buildings are handsomely festooned with creepers and sit grandly on the mountainside, overlooking Main Road and the M3 highway. Next to the campus north towards the city is the **Rhodes Memorial**, built to resemble a Greek temple and conspicuous against the slopes of Devil's Peak. The monument celebrates Cecil Rhodes' energy with a sculpture of a wildly rearing horse, and the empire-builder's bust is planted at the top of a towering set of stairs. Herds of wildebeest and zebra nonchalantly graze on the slopes around the Memorial, as cars fly past on the M3. The **Tea Garden** offers terrific views of Cape Town. From the memorial you can walk to the King's Blockhouse, formerly a signalling station to Muizenberg, and onto the Contour Path which follows the eastern side of the mountain, way above the southern suburbs to Constantia Nek. Rhodes' large estate, **Groote Schuur**, bordering on Main Road, became the official prime ministerial residence of the Cape, then of South Africa, and when the country switched to a presidential system it became the home of the president, though Nelson Mandela preferred to use a nearby residence named Genadendal (his private home is in Houghton, Johannesburg). Below the Memorial, alongside the M3, is the incongruous **Mostert's Mill**, a windmill built two centuries ago when there were wheat fields here.

Newlands, Claremont, Bishopscourt and Wynberg

Continuing south from Rondebosch along the Van der Stel Freeway (the M3) or along the more congested Main Road, you pass some of Cape Town's most prestigious suburbs. **Newlands**, almost merging with Rondebosch, is home to the city's famous rugby and cricket stadiums. Worth a stopoff here at 31 Newlands Avenue is **Montebello Craft and Design Centre** (Mon–Fri 9am–4.45pm, Sat & Sun 9.30am–3pm), a complex of exceptionally good craft shops and craftworkers studios, with a restaurant under shady oaks.

The well-heeled suburb of **Claremont**, south of Newlands, is an alternative focus to the city centre for shopping and entertainment, with two cinema complexes and plenty of shops at **Cavendish Square Mall**. Alongside the high-quality shops, hawkers sell clothes, vegetables and herbs; closer to Claremont station you can buy tasty *boerewors* from women cooking them outdoors on *skottel braais* (braziers).

A little further south, beyond the signpost to Kirstenbosch Gardens, is **Bishopscourt**. As its name suggests, it's home to the Anglican bishop of Cape Town, and it was in a mansion here that Archbishop Desmond Tutu lived even in the years when blacks weren't supposed to live in whites-only suburbs. Partly because of its prime siting – some plots have views of both Newlands Forest and the sea – this is one of the most prestigious areas in Cape Town; a number of consuls live here on huge properties behind high walls, which are about all you see as you pass through the area.

Further down the line, **Wynberg** is known for its Maynardville Shakespearean open-air theatre (see p.175) and its quaint row of shops and restaurants in Wolfe Street, known as **Little Chelsea**. By contrast Wynberg's Main Road offers a distinctly less genteel shopping experience, an interesting stroll past street vendors and fabric shops, as well as food outlets catering to the large number of workers travelling between Wynberg and Khayelitsha.

Kirstenbosch National Botanical Gardens

Five kilometres south of Rondebosch, in Rhodes Avenue, are the **Kirstenbosch National Botanical Gardens** (daily: April–Aug 8am–6pm; Sept–March 8am–7pm; ☎021 799 8899; R20, kids R5), the third most popular tourist attraction in Cape Town (surpassed only by the Waterfront and the cable-car trip up Table Mountain). Kirstenbosch is the oldest and largest botanical garden in South Africa, created by Cecil Rhodes in 1895 (his camphor and fig trees are still here). Today, over 22,000 indigenous plants – and a research unit and library – attract researchers and botanists from all over the world. There's a nursery selling local plants, while characteristic Cape plants, found nowhere else in the world, are cultivated on the slopes. In 2004 the gardens became part of South Africa's sixth UNESCO World Heritage site – the first botanical garden in the world to achieve this status, which in this instance recognizes the international significance of the *fynbos* plant kingdom (see box on p.161) that predominates at Kirstenbosch.

The gardens are magnificent, glorying in lush shrubs and exuberant blooms. Little signboards and paved paths guide you through the highlights of the gardens, with trees and plants identified to enhance the rambling. The most interesting route is the one created for blind visitors, with labels in Braille and an abundance of aromatic and textured plants. There is a free **walking tour** daily at 10am, and **golf-car tours** (R20) every hour on the hour. If you're visiting the gardens in summer, one of the undoubted delights is to bring a picnic for a Sunday evening **open-air concert**, where you can lie back on the lawn, sip Cape wine and savour the mountain air and sunsets. There's an outdoor coffee shop, open daily for breakfast, lunch and tea, plus a restaurant with a fire going for winter days. Eating out here is more about the fabulous location than the food or service.

The gardens trail off into wild vegetation, covering a huge expanse of the rugged eastern slopes and wooded ravines of Table Mountain. The setting is quite breathtaking – this is a great place to have tea and stroll around gazing up the mountain, or to wander onto the paths, which meander steeply to the top with

Cape Dutch architecture

Cape Dutch style, which developed in the Western Cape countryside from the seventeenth to the early nineteenth century, is so distinctively rooted in the Winelands that it has become an integral element of the landscape. The dazzling limewashed walls look stunning in the midst of glowing green vineyards, while the thatched roofs and elaborate curvilinear gables seem to mirror the undulations of the surrounding mountains. The style was embraced in the twentieth century as part of white South African identity, and elements appear on the facades of many **suburban homes**.

The **Posthuys** (1673) in Main Road, Muizenberg, is a rude thatch-roofed cottage consisting of a single rectangular space. Thought to be the oldest colonial dwelling in South Africa, it has tiny windows which served as a defence against feared attacks by the Khoikhoi, as well as protection from the fierce winds that lash the peninsula. One of the few surviving examples of the so-called "longhouse", it represents the primitive language from which a rich vernacular Cape Dutch architecture evolved during the first two hundred years of colonial settlement.

Although there were important developments in the internal organization of Cape houses during this period, their most obvious element is the **gable**. End-gables were common in medieval northern European and particularly Dutch buildings, but central gables set into the long side of roofs were more unusual, and became the quintessential feature of the Cape Dutch style. Large numbers of buildings in central Cape Town had gables during the eighteenth century, but they had disappeared from the urban streetscape by the 1830s, to be replaced by buildings with flush facades and flat roofs.

Arson appears to be a major reason for these developments. There was a succession of town fires believed to have been started by slaves, including one that razed Stellenbosch in 1710 and Cape Town's **great fires** of 1736 and 1798. The consequence was a series of measures that shaped the layout of central Cape Town as well as the design of its houses. Flat roofs, clad in fireproof materials, became compulsory on all VOC buildings, as exemplified by the **Old Town House** (1755) off Greenmarket Square. After the 1798 conflagration, alarmed officials studied reports from London's Great Fire of 1666 and introduced legislation based on the lessons learned. To retard the spread of flames, narrow alleys were provided between houses, there was a total ban on thatched roofs, and any protrusions on building exteriors – including shutters – were banned. This led to the flush facades and internal shutters that typify early nineteenth-century Cape town houses. With the disappearance of pitched roofs, the urban gable withered away, surviving symbolically in some instances as minimal roof decoration, one example being the **Bo-Kaap Museum** (1763–68) in Wale Street, which sports a wavy parapet.

Rural homesteads developed from the plain longhouse to become increasingly elaborate over time. As landowners became more wealthy, the size of homesteads no fences cutting off the way. Two popular paths, starting from the Contour Path above Kirstenbosch, are **Nursery Ravine** and **Skeleton Gorge** (see p.151); note that women should *not* walk alone in the isolated upper reaches of Kirstenbosch.

If you don't have a car and don't want to take an organized tour, the best way to get to Kirstenbosch is by Rikki or using one of the local taxi services. Additionally, there are three municipal buses daily from Cape Town Station at 7.30am, 12.35pm and 3.35pm. If you're driving, take the M3 and leave it at the signposted Rhodes Avenue turn-off, close to Newlands.

Constantia and its winelands

South of Kirstenbosch lie the elegant suburbs of **Constantia** and the Cape's oldest **winelands**. Luxuriating on the lower slopes of Table Mountain and the

grew, and the house plan became more complex. The spread of fire from one building to another wasn't a major consideration in the countryside, where VOC building regulations carried little weight. Consequently, the pitched roof survived here. Gables, similarly, became the hallmark of country manors, being an important element of the facade, positioned above the front door to provide a window admitting light into the loft. Because they were just above the front door, they could also provide protection for the entrance against burning thatch. From these functional origins gables evolved into important symbols of wealth, with landowners vying to erect the biggest, most elaborate and most fashionable examples.

Cape Dutch architects

Between 1750 and 1850 – the golden century of Cape architecture – three men were associated with some of the most highly regarded buildings in the colony. So elevated is their status that numerous apocryphal attributions exist, claiming their hand in various projects.

Anton Anreith (1754–1822) was born near Freiburg in Germany, where it is believed he was apprenticed to a Rococo master-sculptor. He joined the Dutch East India Company's army as a private in 1776, but quickly gained employment as a carpenter, later earning the commission to reconstruct the facade of the Lutheran Church in Strand Street. In 1786 he became the VOC's master-sculptor and was probably responsible for the Kat balcony at the Castle of Good Hope.

Hermann Schutte (1761–1844), born in Bremen, was apprenticed to an architect in Germany for seven years. After joining the Dutch East India Company as a stonemason, he came to the Cape in 1790 and worked on the Robben Island quarries, where he lost an eye and a hand in a blasting accident. He was discharged from the VOC and became a private building contractor, benefiting from numerous commissions from the influential Louis Michel Thibault. Schutte designed the Groote Kerk in Adderley Street and is also believed to have been responsible for the Green Point Lighthouse, the first lighthouse erected along the South African coast.

Louis Michel Thibault (1750–1815), a highly trained architect, was born near Amiens in France. Having held the honour of premier student at l'Academie Royale d'Architecture in Paris, he joined the Dutch East India Company as Lieutenant of Engineers, effectively making him the colony's principle military engineer and government architect, in which capacity he designed most of the major public buildings in Cape Town. Examples of his work include the Good Hope Masonic Lodge, which served as the parliamentary debating chamber prior to 1884, the current facade of the Slave Lodge, and the imposing gables at Groot Constantia.

Constantiaberg, with tantalizing views of False Bay, the winelands are an easy drive from town, not more than ten minutes off the Van der Stel Freeway (the M3), which runs between the centre and Muizenberg.

The winelands started cultivated life in 1685 as the farm of **Simon van der Stel**, the governor charged with opening up the fledgling Dutch colony to the interior. Thrusting himself wholeheartedly into the task, he selected for his own use an enormous tract of the choicest land set against the Constantiaberg, the section of the Peninsula just south of Table Mountain. He named the estate after his daughter Constancia, and this is now (with a minor change of spelling) the name of Cape Town's oldest and most prestigious residential area. Exuding the easy ambience of landed wealth, Constantia is a green and pleasant place, shaded by oak forests and punctuated with farm stalls, stables, the Cape Dutch-style Constantia Mall and shops and, of course, the vineyards.

Constantia grapes have been making wine since van der Stel's first output in 1705. After his death in 1712, the estate was divided up and sold off as the modern **Groot Constantia**, **Klein Constantia** and **Buitenverwachting**. In 1990, the nearby Steenberg Estate was bought up by a large Johannesburg mining conglomerate. All four estates are open to the public and offer tastings; they're definitely worth visiting if you aren't heading further afield to the Winelands proper.

There is no public **transport** to Constantia, but Groot Constantia features on most organized tours of Cape Town or the Peninsula. To get to it **by car**, take the signposted Groot Constantia exit from the M3 onto Ladies Mile Extension, and follow the signs to Groot Constantia. Buitenverwachting and Klein Constantia are on Klein Constantia Road, just off Ladies Mile Extension, and are clearly signposted.

Groot Constantia

The largest estate and the one most geared to tourists is **Groot Constantia** (Ⓦ www.museums.org.za/grootcon), Cape Town's fourth most-visited attraction. Its big pull is that it retains the rump of Van der Stel's original estate, as well as the original buildings, though its portrayal of life in a seventeenth-century colonial chateau makes scant reference to the slave labour that underpinned its operations. The **manor house**, a quintessential Cape Dutch building, was Van der Stel's original home, modified at the end of the eighteenth century by the French architect Thibault. Walking straight through it, down the ceremonial axis, you'll come to the cellar, fronted with a carved pediment, depicting a riotous bacchanalia, which represents fertility. Otherwise, there's a pretty average **museum** full of period furniture (daily 10am–5pm; R8), a gift shop, art gallery and two **restaurants**. **Cellar tours** start every hour on the hour (May–Nov 11am & 3pm; Dec–April 10am–4pm; R25 including five wines to taste; booking essential on ☎021 794 5128) and there's **wine tasting** (daily: May–Nov 10am–4.30pm; Dec–Apr 9am–5.30pm; R15).

Klein Constantia and Buitenverwachting

Smaller in scale than Groot Constantia, Klein Constantia and Buitenverwachting both offer free wine tasting in less regimented conditions than at the bigger estate and, although the buildings are far humbler, the settings are equally beautiful. **Klein Constantia**, Klein Constantia Road (free wine tasting & sales Mon–Fri 9am–5pm, Sat 9am–1pm; Ⓦ www.kleinconstantia.com) has a friendly atmosphere and produces some fine wines. Something of a curiosity is its **Vin de Constance**, the re-creation of an eighteenth-century Constantia wine that was a favourite of Napoleon, Frederick the Great and Bismarck. It's a delicious dessert wine, packaged in a replica of the original bottle, and makes an original souvenir. There's also wildlife here: look out for the guinea fowl that roam the estate munching on beetles that attack young vine leaves; in summer, migrant steppe buzzards prey on unsuspecting starlings, which eat the grapes.

Buitenverwachting (roughly pronounced "bay-tin-fur-vuch-ting", with the "ch" as in the Scottish rendition of loch), also on Klein Constantia Road (Mon–Fri 9am–5pm, Sat 9am–1pm; free; Ⓦ www.buitenverwachting.co.za) provides its workers with some of the best living conditions of any South African farm. Unusual labour practices include the provision of two social workers, weekly visits by a doctor to the farm clinic, and worker involvement in the selection of new staff. Buitenverwachting's expensive **restaurant** of the same name (Tues–Sat lunch & dinner; ℡021 794 3522) is regularly voted one of South Africa's ten best. For a day out on the farm (they have cattle and horses, too), they also do luxury **picnic lunches** (Nov–April Mon–Sat 12.30–2.30pm; R85; booking essential – contact Adrienne ℡021 794 1012 or 082 973 8543), which you can enjoy under the oaks in their fabulous gardens.

Tokai

Effectively the southern extension of Constantia, forested **Tokai** is an excellent area for leafy recreation away from the centre, with some relaxed and child-friendly places for eating and drinking, and sheltered from the southeaster. You can also take in some wine tasting at the nearby **Steenberg Vineyards**, which incorporates a luxury golfing resort. Across the road is Pollsmoor Prison, where numerous political prisoners did time during the apartheid era, including Nelson Mandela towards the end of his period of incarceration.

To drive to Tokai from the centre of Cape Town, head south along the M3 and exit north onto Ladies Mile Road; continue for 100m before turning south into Spaanschemat River Road (M42), signposted Tokai, which runs through the suburb. Along the M42 before Steenberg is an outstanding, if slightly pricey, lunch stop at the *Spaanschemat River Café* (closed Sun), part of the Constantia Uitsig Wine Estate. The food is imaginative and you can eat al fresco. You can easily combine Tokai with a trip to the seaside, as the suburb is fifteen minutes' drive from the False Bay seaboard.

Tokai Forest

Most people come out to Tokai for the well-marked hiking paths and mountain-biking trails in the pine plantations of the **Tokai Forest**. You can get here from Spaanschemat River Road M42, turning west towards the mountain, into Tokai Road, which leads straight to the forest. About 500m from Spaanschemat River Road, the road passes through pine forests, equipped with picnic tables, though this isn't the nicest part of the forest or the best place to picnic. Instead, keep on till you reach the arboretum. A little further along the road from the picnic sites, you can't fail to see the imposing **Tokai Manor House** (not open to the public). Designed by Louis Michel Thibault (see p.145) and built around 1795, this National Monument is an elegant gem of Cape Dutch architecture combined with the understated elegance of French Neoclassicism.

A hundred metres to its west lies the entrance to another National Monument, the historic tree plantation that constitutes the **Tokai Arboretum** (daily dusk to dawn; R5 donation). It's the work of Joseph Storr Lister, who was a nineteenth-century Conservator of Forests for the Cape Colony. In 1885 he experimented with planting 150 species of trees from temperate countries, with oaks and eucalyptus featuring extensively as well as some beautiful California redwoods. Storr discovered that conifers were best suited to the Cape, which is why the plantation to the west of the arboretum, owned by the Safcol timber company, consists mainly of pines. The arboretum is the best place to begin rambling and an ideal place to bring **children**, with outdoor seating, plenty of shade and logs to jump on and over. There's also a car park and a thatched **café** (closed Mon) close to the entrance gate for tea and scones.

Several tracks and trails crisscross the arboretum and plantation, providing easy walks and mountain-biking trails (bring your own bike). Longer hikes include the walk from the entrance gate to **Elephant's Eye Cave** (6km there and back), which can easily be completed in well under three hours. The route passes through pine forests before opening into montane *fynbos* that covers the slopes of the Constantiaberg, eventually leading to the cave, which offers terrific panoramas. Ask for a map and directions at the entrance gate or at the adjacent café.

Steenberg Vineyards

In a fabulous location at the foot of Steenberg mountain, the **Steenberg Vineyards** (Mon–Fri 8.30am–4.30pm; Sept–Feb also Sat 9am–1pm; free; Ⓦ www.steenberg-vineyards.com) comprise a fine Cape Dutch manor house and three other farm buildings, set around a large formal garden dating from 1695. This is South Africa's oldest wine estate: the lands were granted by Governor Simon van der Stel to the five-times widowed Catherina Michelse in 1682 and sold on in 1695 to Frederik Roussouw. That year Roussouw erected the first buildings and produced the first wine here. After his death, his widow Christina Diemer turned the estate into a highly profitable business, providing hospitality to travellers and provisions to the fleet (the VOC declared Simon's Town its winter port in 1741). Steenburg now boasts a luxury country hotel, using the refurbished buildings that were declared a National Monument in 1996. Of their wines, the Merlot, Sauvignon Blanc and Semillon stand out.

Table Mountain

The icon that for hundreds of years and from hundreds of kilometres announced Cape Town to seafarers, **Table Mountain**, a 1087m flat-topped massif with dramatic cliffs and eroded gorges, dominates the northern end of the Peninsula. Its north face overlooks the city centre with the distinct formations of **Lion's Head** and **Signal Hill** to the west and **Devil's Peak** to the east. The west face is made up of a series of gable-like formations known as the **Twelve Apostles**; the southwest face towers over Hout Bay and the east face over the southern suburbs.

The mountain is a compelling feature in the middle of the city, a wilderness where you'll find wildlife and 1400 species of flora. Indigenous mammals include baboons, dassies (see box on p.150) and porcupines. The animals that resemble mountain goats are Himalayan **tahrs**, descended from specimens introduced by Cecil Rhodes onto his estate, and which escaped to flourish on the mountain. A number of tahrs were controversially shot in 2004, in an attempt to allow native antelope species to flourish instead.

Reckoned the most-climbed massif in the world, Table Mountain has suffered under the constant pounding of **hikers** and wanton vandalism – although the damage isn't always obvious, certainly not from the dizzying vista at the top. Every year the mountain strikes back, taking its toll of lives. One of the

Table Mountain safety

Make sure you:

• Don't climb alone.

• Inform someone you're going up the mountain; tell them your route, when you're leaving and when you expect to be back.

• Leave early enough to give yourself time to complete your route during daylight.

• Don't try to descend via an unknown route. If you get lost in poor weather, seek shelter, keep warm and wait for help.

• Never leave even the tiniest scrap of litter on the mountain.

• Never make fires. No cooking is allowed, even on portable stoves.

Wear:

• Good footwear. Boots or running shoes are recommended.

• A broad-rimmed hat.

Take:

• A backpack.

• A water bottle. Allow two litres per person.

• Enough food.

• A warm jersey.

• A windbreaker.

• A raincoat.

• Sunglasses.

• High-factor sunscreen.

• Plasters for blisters.

• A map (available from Cape Union Mart at the Waterfront, or Cavendish Square Shopping Centre in Claremont).

commonest causes of difficulties is people losing the track (often due to sudden mist falling) and becoming trapped. If you plan to tackle one of the hundreds of walks and climbs on its slopes, go properly prepared (see box above). There are also **full-day guided hikes** which are thoroughly recommended, the price includes transport and packed lunches. These guided hikes are tailored to your level of fitness and can also include rock climbing (see p.179). You may choose to come back the easy way by cable car, or partially abseil.

The cable car

The least challenging, but certainly not least interesting, way up and down the mountain, is via the highly popular **cable car** at the western table, which offers dizzying views across Table Bay and the Atlantic. A state-of-the-art Swiss system was installed in 1997; the floor of the fishbowl-shaped cars is designed to complete a 360-degree rotation on the way, giving passengers a full panorama. Cars leave from the **lower cableway station** on Tafelberg Road (daily every 10–15 min: Jan & Dec 8am–9pm; Feb & March 8.30am–7.30pm; April 8.30am–5.30pm; May–Oct 8.30am–5pm; Nov 8.30am–7pm), with return **tickets** costing R110 for adults and R50 for kids, while under-4s ride for free. Operations can be disrupted by bad weather or maintenance work; for information on current schedules call ☎021 424 5148 or 021 424 8181, or check ⓦwww.tablemountain.net. You can make a real outing of it by going up for breakfast, or a sunset drink and meal at the restaurant, as the upper station is an incomparable spot to watch the sun go down.

You can get to the lower cableway station by Rikki, metered taxi, or in one of the minibus taxis that ply the route here from Adderley Street. The open-topped Cape Town Explorer bus also serves the cableway (p.104). If you're driving, you'll find parking along Tafelberg Road, but you may be in for a bit of a walk in peak season – the stretch of parked cars can extend several hundred metres.

Climbs and walks

Climbing the mountain will give you a greater sense of achievement than being ferried up by the cable car, but proceed with extreme caution: it may look sunny and clear when you leave, but conditions at the top could be very different. The weather is subject to rapid changes, both in general and in localized areas. The main hazards are sun, mist and violent winds. Unless you're going with a knowledgeable guide, attempt only the routes outlined here, which are the simplest.

Signal Hill and Lion's Head

From the roundabout at the top of Kloofnek, a road leads all the way along **Signal Hill** to a car park and lookout, with good views over Table Bay, the docks and the city. A cannon was formerly used for sending signals to ships at anchor in the bay, and the Noon Gun, still fired from its slopes daily, sends a thunderous rumble through the Bo-Kaap and city centre below. Halfway along the road is a sacred Islamic *kramat* (shrine), one of several dotted around the peninsula which "protect" the city. You can also walk up **Lion's Head**, an unstrenuous hike that seems to bring out half the population of Cape Town every full moon.

Platteklip Gorge and Maclear's Beacon

The first recorded ascent to the summit of Table Mountain was by the Portuguese captain Antonio de Saldanha, in 1503. He wisely chose **Platteklip Gorge**, the gap visible from the front table (the north side) which, as it turned out, is the most accessible way up. A short and easy extension will get you to Maclear's Beacon which, at 1086m, is the highest point on the mountain. The Platteklip route starts out at the lower cableway station and has the added advantage of ending at the upper station, so you can descend in a car.

Dassies

The outsized fluffy guinea pigs you'll encounter at the top of Table Mountain are **dassies** or hyraxes (*Procavia capensis*) which, despite their appearance, aren't rodents at all, but the closest living relatives of elephants. Their name (pronounced like "dusty" without the "t") is the Afrikaans version of *dasje*, meaning "little badger", given to them by the first Dutch settlers. Dassies are very widely distributed, having thrived in South Africa with the elimination of predators, and can be found in suitably rocky habitats all over the country. They live in colonies consisting of a dominant male and eight or more related females and their offspring.

Dassies have poor body temperature control and, like reptiles, rely on shelter against both hot sunlight and the cold. They wake up sluggish and seek out rocks where they can catch the early morning sun – this is one of the best times to look out for them. One adult stands sentry against predators and issues a low-pitched warning cry in response to a threat.

From the lower station, walk east along Tafelberg Road until you see a high embankment built from stone and maintained with wire netting. Just beyond and to the left of a small dam is a sign pointing to Platteklip Gorge. A steep fifteen-minute climb brings you onto the **Upper Contour Path**. About 25m east along this, take the path indicated by a sign reading "Contour Path/Platteklip Gorge". The path zigzags from here onwards and is very clear. The gorge is the biggest cleavage on the whole mountain, leading directly and safely to the top, but it's a very steep slog which will take two to three hours in total if you're reasonably fit. Once on top, turn right and ascend the last short section onto the **front table** for a breathtaking view of the city. A sign points the way to the upper cableway station – a fifteen-minute walk along a concrete path thronging with visitors.

Maclear's Beacon is about 35 minutes from the top of the Platteklip Gorge on a path leading eastward, with white squares on little yellow footsteps guiding you all the way. The path crosses the front table with Maclear's Beacon visible at all times. From the top you'll get views of False Bay and the Hottentots Holland Mountains to the east.

The Pipe Track

One of the most rewarding and easiest walks along the mountainside takes the **Pipe Track**, a service road which follows water pipes from the mountain reservoirs to Kloofnek. The track runs on the level for roughly 7km, on the west flank of Table Mountain, beneath the Twelve Apostles, following the mountain's contours and offering fantastic views of the Atlantic. The Pipe Track isn't a circular route, so you can turn back at any point; the whole walk can take up to three hours each way.

The route begins at some stone steps at Kloofnek opposite the bus terminus for the cable car, just to the west of the Tafelberg Road turn-off (if you're driving, park on Tafelberg Road). Steps lead up alongside forestry staff houses before the road levels off under some pines. The path intersects several climbs up the mountain, useful indicators as to how far you've come. The first, after about 45 minutes, is indicated by a sign to Blinkwater Ravine (closed to the public due to rockfalls). A further ten to fifteen minutes brings you to the Kasteelspoort ascent (signposted under gum trees) followed by Woody Ravine and finally, roughly 25 minutes after Kasteelspoort, the signpost at Slangolie Ravine, where the path ends. The rock bed on Slangolie is unstable and to be avoided. Turn back when you see the first of the Woodhead Tunnel danger signs.

Skeleton Gorge and Nursery Ravine

You can combine a visit to the gardens at Kirstenbosch with an ascent up Table Mountain via one route and a descent down another, ending at the Kirstenbosch National Botanical Gardens' **restaurant** for tea. Starting at the restaurant, follow the **Skeleton Gorge** signs, which lead you onto the **Contour Path**. At the Contour Path, a plaque indicates that this is **Smuts' Track**, the route favoured by Jan Smuts, the Boer leader and South African prime minister. The plaque marks the start of a broad-stepped climb up Skeleton Gorge, involving wooden steps, stone steps, wooden ladders and loose boulders. Be prepared for steep ravines and difficult rock climbs – and under no circumstances stray off the path. It requires reasonable fitness, but can take as little as an hour. Skeleton Gorge can be an unpleasant way down, especially in the wet season when it gets slippery.

Nursery Ravine is recommended for the descent. At the top of Skeleton Gorge, walk a few metres to your right to a sign indicating **Kasteelspoort**.

It's just 35 minutes from the top of Skeleton along the Kasteelsport path to the head of Nursery Ravine. The descent returns you to the 310-metre Contour Path, which leads back to Kirstenbosch. This entire walk lasts about five hours.

The Atlantic seaboard

Table Mountain's steep drop into the ocean along much of the western Peninsula forces the suburbs along the **Atlantic seaboard** into a ribbon of developments clinging dramatically to the slopes. The sea washing the west side of the Peninsula can be very chilly, far colder than on the False Bay seaboard. Although not ideal for bathing, the Atlantic seaboard offers mind-blowing views from some of the most incredible coastal roads in the world, particularly beyond **Sea Point**, and there are opportunities for whale-spotting (see p.156). The coast itself consists of a series of bays and white-sanded beaches edged with smoothly sculpted bleached rocks; inland, the Twelve Apostles, a series of rocky buttresses, gaze down onto the surf. The beaches are ideal for sunbathing, or sunset picnics – it's from this side of the peninsula that you can watch the sun sink into the ocean, creating fiery reflections on the sea and mountains behind as it slips away.

Mouille Point and Green Point

Just to the west of the V&A Waterfront, Mouille Point and its close neighbour, Green Point, are among the suburbs closest to the city centre. **Mouille** ("moo-lee") **Point** is known principally for its squat rectangular Victorian lighthouse, commissioned in the 1820s, and painted like a children's picture-book lighthouse, with diagonal red and white stripes.

Mouille Point merges with the far larger suburb of **Green Point**, which continues both inland from it and west along the ragged Atlantic shore. Over the last couple of years Green Point's proximity to the Waterfront – an easy ten-or-so minutes' walk away – and its position along the coast has turned it from a sleazy district into a humming area of excellent accommodation, eating places and clubs.

Sea Point and Bantry Bay

West along Main Road, Green Point merges with **Sea Point**, a long-established place for great restaurants. Middle-class couples, pram-pushing mothers, street kids, hookers and drunks create an uneasy blend of respectability and seediness that disappears as you move into Bantry Bay and the wealthier suburbs down the Atlantic seaboard. The closest seaside to the city centre is a block down from Main Road, although it's too rocky for swimming.

Halfway along the kilometre-long beach promenade, alongside Beach Road, you'll catch views of **Graaff's Pool**, an institutionalized and exclusively male nudist spot, while at the westernmost end is the only place in the vicinity to swim, at the unheated Olympic-sized **saltwater pool** (May–Nov 8.30am–4.30pm; Dec–April 7am–6pm; R10), alongside the crashing surf, with lawns for sunbathing. At the westernmost edge of Sea Point lies **Bantry Bay**, combining the density of Sea Point with the wealth of the Atlantic suburbs; here mansions are raked up on steep slopes above the Atlantic, guarded by the granite boulders of Lion's Head. The upmarket resort hotels and self-catering apartment blocks are just far enough for comfort from the sleaze of Sea Point, but close enough should you want to walk to a restaurant.

Clifton to Sandy Bay

Fashionable **Clifton**, on the next cove, along Victoria Road (the M6), sits on the most expensive real estate in Africa, studded with fabulous seaside apartments and with four sandy **beaches**, reached via steep stairways. The sea here is good for surfing and safe for swimming, but bone-chillingly cold. First Beach (they're all numbered) is frequented by muscular ball-players, surfers and their female counterparts, but is usually the least crowded of the four beaches. Second and Third beaches are split between the teenies and 30-somethings, with beautiful men and some cruising on Third; if in doubt, head for Fourth, which is suitable for families because it has the fewest steps. Hout Bay **buses** go to Clifton from the city centre several times a day (a 30min journey). Parking can be impossible along the M6 in summer, so you may be best off parking up in the residential area. Bring your own refreshments, as there's only one overpriced café on Fourth Beach and hardly any shops.

A little to the south, the suburb of **Camps Bay** climbs the slopes of Table Mountain and is scooped into a small amphitheatre, bounded by the Lion's Head and the Twelve Apostles sections of the Table Mountain range. This, and the airborne views across the Atlantic, make Camps Bay one of the most desirable places to live in Cape Town. The main drag, Victoria Road, skirts the coast and is packed with trendy restaurants, while the wide sandy beach is accessible by bus and is consequently enjoyed by families of all shapes and colours. Lined by a row of palms and some grassy verges with welcome shade for picnics, Camps Bay beach is very busy around the Christmas and Easter breaks. However, it's exposed to the southeaster, and there's the usual Atlantic chill and an occasional dangerous backwash.

There's little development between Camps Bay and the wonderful cove of **Llandudno**, 20km from Cape Town along Victoria Road (not served by public transport). Here a steep and narrow road winds down past smart homes to the shore, where the sandy beach is punctuated at either end by magnificent granite boulders and rock formations. This is a good sunbathing spot and a choice one for bring-your-own sundowners. The small car park frequently spills over into the suburban streets at peak periods.

Isolated **Sandy Bay**, Cape Town's main nudist beach, can only be reached via a twenty-minute walk from Llandudno. In the apartheid days, the South African police went to ingenious lengths to trap nudists, but nowadays the beach is relaxed, so feel free to come as undressed as feels comfortable. There are no facilities whatsoever – bring whatever supplies you may need. A path leads from the south end of the Llandudno car park, through *fynbos* vegetation and across some rocks, to the beach; it's a fairly easy walk, but watch out for broken glass if you're barefoot.

Hout Bay

Although no longer the quaint fishing village it once was, **Hout Bay** still has a functioning fishing harbour and is the centre of the local crayfish industry. Leopards no longer stalk its *kranse* and *koppies*, but their former presence is recalled by a bronze statue looking down from Chapman's Peak Drive. Despite ugly modern development and a growing shantytown, the natural setting is quite awesome, with the Sentinel and Chapman's Peak defining the entry to the bay. The best way to take in the landscape is on one of the short cruises just out of the bay, from the harbour to **Duiker Island**, home to a large seal colony. Drumbeat (℡021 790 5859) and Nauticat (℡021 790 7278) are reliable operators with departures at 9.45am, 11am, 12pm, 2pm and 3pm, the trip costing R50 there and back.

△ Hout Bay fishermen

The sea off the long slender **beach** is no good for swimming – not only is it too cold, it's also too close to the harbour and prone to have fish scales floating in the surf – but the beach is perfect for walks. Away from the harbour, the village is just managing to hang on to its historic ambience, with the **Hout Bay Museum**, 4 St Andrews Road (Tues–Fri 9am–4pm, Sat 8am–2pm; R5), offering good exhibits on Strandloper culture and the local fishing industry. The nearby **World of Birds**, Valley Road (daily 9am–5pm; R45, kids R30, under-3s free), requires at least two hours to see the more than three thousand birds and animals housed in surprisingly pleasant and peaceful walk-through aviaries. From Tuesday to Thursday, and at weekends, you can watch penguins being fed at 11.30am and 3.30pm, pelicans at 12.30pm and birds of prey at 4.10pm. A large walk-in monkey jungle (daily 11.30am–1pm & 2–3.30pm) includes among its inhabitants cute squirrel monkeys; visitors can handle and play with them. There's a café serving light lunches, or you can picnic at the Flamingo Terrace. Young children are well catered for with a couple of playground areas.

Hout Bay is at a convenient junction for the rest of the peninsula. From Cape Town, it's 20km away along either the coast or inland via Constantia; at a push you can get there by bus (see p.104) or use a minibus taxi. From Simon's Town across the peninsula spine, Hout Bay is 26km away via the Glencairn Expressway. The bay has the highest concentration of **places to stay** south of Sea Point, including hotels and bed and breakfasts. **Hout Bay Tourism** (Mon–Fri 9am–5pm, Sat 9am–1pm; ☎021 790 1264), adjacent to the museum, can book accommodation. Next to the harbour and car park, the little **Mariner's waterfront** development shelters the Seafood Emporium, selling fresh fish, including the Cape speciality of *snoek*, a bony but delicious fish. There's a decent fish **restaurant** upstairs with outdoor seating overlooking the beach. For straightforward fish and chips, use their downstairs takeaway facility.

Chapman's Peak Drive to Scarborough

East of Hout Bay, **Chapman's Peak Drive** is a thrilling journey. For 10km the road carves into the mountainside on the one side, dropping precipitously hundreds of metres to the ocean on the other. Unceasingly spectacular views take in the breadth of Hout Bay to the Sentinel on a curved outcrop. Viewpoints are provided along the route, but take care in high winds as there are occasional rockfalls – mostly contained in nets on the mountain side. Scores of cyclists sweat their way round, making considerate driving a necessity. Chapman's Peak Drive is a toll road (R20 per vehicle) with a single toll booth at the northern (Hout Bay) end of the road.

Noordhoek, a low-key settlement at the southern end of the descent from Chapman's Peak Drive, consists of smallholdings and riding stables in a gentle valley planted with oaks. From here, a long white untamed beach stretches 6km across Chapman's Bay to Kommetjie. The sands are fantastic for walking and **horse-riding**, but can resemble a sandblaster when the southeaster blows; Sleepy Hollow (☎021 790 5859) does ninety-minute rides daily at 9am and 1pm (R50). Swimming is hazardous, though surfers relish the rough waters around the rocks to the north. Signposted on the left if you're heading south is the excellent *Red Herring* restaurant and pub (see p.173), which has views of the beach; it's set back from the sea, about ten minutes' walk from the car park. Also signposted in the vicinity is *Monkey Valley Resort* (see p.116), which welcomes non-guests for reasonably priced meals with great views.

Although only a few kilometres south of Noordhoek along the beach, getting to **Kommetjie** by road involves a fifteen-kilometre detour inland. The beach's small inlet (*kommetjie*), which is always a few degrees above the surrounding sea temperature, is perfect for swimming. Just to the north, **Long Beach** is a favourite surfing spot, used by devotees even during the chilly winter months.

Almost 10km by road from Kommetjie, the developing village of **Scarborough** is the most far-flung suburb along the peninsula. A long wide beach edges temptingly to its south just beyond Schusters River Lagoon – resist its potentially treacherous sea and stick to the lagoon.

The False Bay seaboard

In summer the waters of **False Bay** are several degrees warmer than those on the Atlantic seaboard, which is why Cape Town's oldest and most popular seaside development is along this flank of the Peninsula. A series of village-like suburbs, backing onto the mountains, each served by a Metrorail station, is dotted all the way south from **Muizenberg**, through **St James**, **Kalk Bay**, **Fish Hoek** and down to **Simon's Town**. Each has its own character with restaurants, shops and places to stay, while Simon's Town, one of South Africa's oldest settlements, is worth taking in as a day-trip and makes a useful base for visiting the Cape of Good Hope section of the **Table Mountain National Park** and **Cape Point** (see p.161).

Driving here from Cape Town, you can take the M3 south, or the M5 via the less salubrious Cape Flats. From Muizenberg, Main Road and the railway

Cape Town's top whale spots

The commonest whales around Cape Town are southern rights, and the best **whale-watching spots** are on the warmer **False Bay** side of the Peninsula, from August to November. You could also try your luck on the **Atlantic seaboard** at **Chapman's Peak** towards Hout Bay, and between **Llandudno** and **Sea Point**, where the road curves along the ocean. Whichever seaboard you're visiting, remember to have **binoculars** handy.

Along the False Bay seaboard, look out for whale signboards, indicating good places for sightings. **Boyes Drive**, running along the mountainside behind Muizenberg and Kalk Bay, provides an outstanding vantage point. To get there by car, head out on the M3 from the city centre to Muizenberg, taking a sharp right into Boyes Drive, at Lakeside, from where the road begins to climb, descending finally to join Main Road between Kalk Bay and Fish Hoek.

Alternatively, sticking close to the shore along Main Road, the stretch between **Fish Hoek** and **Simon's Town** is recommended, with a particularly nice spot above the rocks at the south end of Fish Hoek Beach, as you walk south towards Glencairn. **Boulders Beach** at the southern end of Simon's Town has a whale signboard, and smooth rocky outcrops on which to sit and gaze out over the sea. Even better vantage points are further down the coast between Simon's Town and **Smitswinkelbaai**, where the road goes higher along the mountainside. Without a car, you can get the train to Fish Hoek or Simon's Town and whale-spot from the Jager's Walk beach path that runs along the coast from Fish Hoek to Sunny Cove, just below the railway line.

It's worth noting that there are more spectacular spotting opportunities further east, especially around Hermanus and Walker Bay (see p.241). Information on the locations of whale sightings in the past 24 hours is available from the MTN **Whale Route Hotline** (℡083 910 1028).

line spectacularly hug the shore all the way to Simon's Town; indeed, the **train** ride to Simon's Town, taking an hour from Cape Town, is reason enough to visit, and most stations are situated close to the surf. A particularly great outing is to take one of the **restaurant trains** pulling *Biggsy's Restaurant Carriage & Wine Bar*, on which breakfasts, lunches and salads are served. *Biggsy's* operates three trips a day from Platform 1 at Cape Town station (Tues–Sun 8.40am, noon and 3.10pm; reservations ☎021 449 3870). Fares are no different from those on normal trains, but space in the restaurant car is limited, so book ahead – particularly for the popular Sunday lunch service. The morning train is an ideal way to get to Simon's Town and have breakfast in style.

Muizenberg and the Historical Mile

Once boasting South Africa's most fashionable beachfront, **Muizenberg** is now rather run-down, though nothing detracts from the fact that it has a long, safe and fabulous beach. Brightly coloured bathing boxes are reminders of a more elegant heyday, when it was visited by the likes of Agatha Christie, who enjoyed riding its waves while holidaying here in the 1920s: "Whenever we could steal time off," she wrote, "we got out our surf boards and went surfing." Muizenberg's gently shelving, sandy beach is the most popular along the peninsula for swimming; the water tends to be flat and warm, and there's good **surfing** in its breakers, with the opportunity for grown-ups and children to take surfing lessons from Gary's Surf School on the beachfront (☎021 788 9839; R380 for two hours including gear rental). A waterslide and minigolf at the northern end of the beach help keeps kids well occupied. Away from the beach, there is a thriving Congolese community, as well as pale-skinned alternative types who get their organic veggie boxes from the *Olive Station* café and deli (see p.170) off Main Road.

A short stretch of the shore, starting at Muizenberg station, is known as the **Historical Mile**, dotted with a run of notable buildings and easily explored on foot. **Muizenberg station**, an Edwardian-style edifice completed in 1913, is now a National Monument, while the **Posthuys** is a rugged whitewashed and thatched building dating from 1673 and a fine example of the Cape vernacular style. **Rhodes' Cottage Museum** (summer Mon–Sun 9.30am–4pm; winter 11am–2pm; free) was bought in 1899 by the millionaire politician, who died here in 1902 before his grander dwelling next door (closed to the public) could be completed. The cottage contains memorabilia painting a distinctly rosy portrait of the man, with photographs, a model of the Big Hole in Kimberley (where Rhodes made his fortune at the diamond diggings), and a curious diorama of World's View in Zimbabwe's Matopos Hills, where he lies buried.

Plans are in the pipeline to upgrade and restore Muizenberg's neglected beachfront, which is one of the closest beaches to the populous Cape Flats. Several decent restaurants and cafés are leading the way, though there's a dearth of beachfront hotels; to book accommodation in the area, contact **Peninsula Tourism** (Mon–Fri 8.30am–5.30pm, Sat 9am–noon; ☎021 788 6193), housed in the pavilion on Beach Road.

St James and Danger Beach

St James, 2km south of Muizenberg, is more upmarket, its mountainside homes accessed mostly up long stairways between Main Road and Boyes Drive. The best reason to hop off the train here is for the **sheltered tidal pool** and the twenty-minute walk along the **paved coastal path** that runs along the rocky shore to Muizenberg – one of the peninsula's easiest and most rewarding walks, with panoramas of the full sweep of False Bay. Look out for the occasional seal that makes an appearance and, in season, whales.

The compact St James beach draws considerable character from its much-photographed Victorian-style bathing boxes, whose bright, primary colours catch your eye as you pass by road or rail. The beach tends to be overcrowded at weekends and during school holidays; far fewer visitors take the trouble to stroll along the short footpath that leads south along the lawned shore from St James to adjacent sandy stretch of **Danger Beach**, an excellent spot for sunbathing and building sand castles. As the name suggests, its surf should be treated with respect as there is a powerful undertow here – only go out as far as you see other bathers safely going.

Kalk Bay

One of the most southerly and smallest of Cape Town's suburbs, **Kalk Bay** centres around a lively working harbour with wooden fishing vessels, mountain views, and a tiny strip of shops packed with trendy coffee shops and antique dealers, plus a couple of places where you might catch some nightlife. Kalk Bay somehow managed to slip through the net of the Group Areas Act, making it one of the few places on the peninsula with an intact coloured community, and Kalk Bay and the larger Hout Bay are the only harbour settlements still worked by coloured fishermen.

The settlement is arranged around the small docks, where you can watch the boats come in; you can also buy fresh fish, which are flung onto the quayside and sold in spirited and noisy auctions. The harbour is busiest on Saturdays and Sundays when Capetonians descend to pick up something for a weekend braai or for lunch at *Kalky's*, an informal fish-and-chips **restaurant**. Other places to wine and dine here include *Harbour House*, the popular *Brass Bell* pub and restaurant and the *Olympia Deli* (see p.170).

Rising up behind the Kalk Bay settlement is **Silvermine Nature Reserve** (dawn–dusk; R10, kids R5), which runs across the Peninsula's spine, almost stretching to the west side at Chapman's Peak. Part of the Table Mountain chain, it offers walks and drives with fabulous views of False Bay, the mountains, indigenous forest and montane *fynbos*. It's most easily reached via the Ou Kaapseweg (Old Cape Road, the M64) through Tokai to Noordhoek and Simon's Town. Friends of Silvermine (☏021 785 1477) organizes free walks here on Thursday mornings and over the weekend. Alongside Silvermine runs **Boyes Drive**, a high-level alternative to Main Road, with spectacular views across to the Hottentots Holland Mountains on the east side of False Bay.

Fish Hoek

Fish Hoek, south of Kalk Bay, boasts one of the peninsula's finest family **beaches** along the False Bay coast. The best and safest swimming is at its southern end, where the surf is moderately warm, tame and much enjoyed by boogie boarders. Thanks to the beach, there's a fair amount of accommodation (see p.117), but this is otherwise one of the dreariest suburbs along the entire False Bay coast. An obscure bye-law banning the sale of alcohol in supermarkets or bottle stores boosts the town's image as the Mother Grundy capital of the Peninsula.

Facilities include a playground, changing rooms, toilets, fresh water, and the *Fish Hoek Galley Seafood Restaurant* right on the beach. From behind the restaurant, a picturesque concrete pathway called **Jager's Walk** skirts the rocky shoreline above the sea for 1km to Sunny Cove; from there, it continues for

6km as an unpaved track to Simon's Town. The walkway provides a good vantage point for seeing whales.

For drivers Fish Hoek is well placed for access to the Atlantic seaboard or for heading into the Constantia winelands. Just south of the suburb, you can strike west on the Glencairn Expressway (M6), or alternatively take the equally scenic Kommetjie Road (M65) about 4km further south (more convenient than the M6 if you're coming from Simon's Town). The two intersect halfway across the peninsula at Sun Valley, where Kommetjie Road continues west, veering slightly south to the coastal suburban village of Noordhoek. At Sun Valley, the M6 strikes north and splits about a kilometre after the intersection. The north-westerly branch hits the coast at Chapman's Point, and continues along the precipitously beautiful Chapman's Peak Drive, which eventually reaches the City Bowl along the Atlantic shore. The northeasterly branch heads along the winding treelined Ou Kaapseweg (M64, becoming the M42), passing through the Silvermine Nature Reserve and the winelands.

Simon's Town

The country's third-oldest European settlement, and also South Africa's principal naval base, **Simon's Town** isn't the hard-drinking, raucous place you might expect. It's exceptionally pretty, with a near perfectly preserved streetscape, slightly marred on the ocean side by the domineering **naval dockyard**, but this, and glimpses of naval squaddies square-bashing behind the high walls or strolling to the station in their crisp white uniforms, are what give the place its distinct character. Just 40km from Cape Town, roughly halfway down the coast to Cape Point, Simon's Town makes the perfect base for a mellow break along the peninsula, offering easy day-trips by train to Cape Town. A few kilometres to the south is the rock-strewn **Boulders Beach**, with its colony of nonchalant **African penguins** – reason in themselves to venture here.

Founded in 1687 as the winter anchorage of the Dutch East India Company, Simon's Town was one of several places in and around Cape Town modestly named by **Governor Simon van der Stel** after himself. Its most celebrated visitor was Lord Nelson, who convalesced here as a midshipman while returning home from the East in 1776. Nineteen years later, the British sailed into Simon's Town and occupied it as a bridgehead for their first invasion and occupation of the Cape. After just seven years they left, only to return in 1806. Simon's Town remained a British base until 1957, when it was handed over to South Africa.

There are fleeting hints, such as the occasional mosque, that the town's predominantly white appearance isn't the whole story. In fact, the first **Muslims** arrived from the East Indies in the early eighteenth century, imported as slaves to build the Dutch naval base. After the British banning of the slave trade in 1807, ships were compelled to disgorge their human cargo at Simon's Town, where one district became known as Black Town. In 1967, when Simon's Town was declared a White Group Area, there were 1200 well-established coloured families descended from these slaves. By the early 1970s, the majority had been forcibly removed under the Group Areas Act to the township of Ocean View, whose inspiring name belies its desolation. After their departure their dwellings were destroyed or allowed to rot, depriving the town of significant historic buildings. In 1973, town clerk Charles Chevalier complained that "the loss of the non-white population has had a depressing effect on the commercial life of the town".

The Town

Trains are met at Simon's Town by Rikki's (☏021 786 2136), which you can book for excursions to Boulders and on to Cape Point. A short way south of the station along St George's Street (the main drag), a signposted road to the left points to the museums. The building now housing the **Simon's Town Museum**, Court Road (Mon–Fri 9am–4pm, Sat 10am–4pm, Sun 11am–4pm; R5), was once the Old Residency built in 1772 for the Governor of the Dutch East India Company, and has also served as the slave quarters (the dungeons are in the basement) and town brothel. The museum's motley collection includes maritime material and an inordinate amount of information and exhibits on Able Seaman Just Nuisance, a much-celebrated seafaring Great Dane. He enjoyed drinking beer with the sailors he accompanied into Cape Town, and was adopted as a mascot by the Royal Navy in World War II. At the **South African Naval Museum** (daily 10am–4pm; free) next door, lively displays include the inside of a submarine, a ship's bridge that simulates rocking, and a lot of official portraits of South African Naval commanders from 1922 to the present.

In the centre of Simon's Town, a little over a kilometre south of the station, lies **Jubilee Square**, a palm-shaded car park just off St George's Street. Flanked by some good cafés, shops and a great fish-and-chips restaurant, the street has on its harbour-facing side a broad walkway with a statue of the ubiquitous Able Seaman Just Nuisance. A couple of sets of stairs lead down to the **Marina**, a modest development of shops and a couple of good restaurants set right on the waterfront.

Long and Seaforth beaches

Nearest to the station, **Long Beach** offers no shade and is therefore little used. However, on windless days it can be pleasant for long walks, with views of the Hottentots Holland Mountains, and its tidal pool is safe for bathing. Access is by a number of gaps in a brick wall alongside the main road and about midway along the beach (opposite Hopkirk Way), by a flight of steps. There are changing rooms and toilets nearby, and fresh water.

One of the best beaches for swimming is at **Seaforth**, where clear, deep waters lap around rocks. It's calm, protected and safe, but not pretty (bounded on one side by the looming grey mass of the naval base), but there's plenty of lawn shaded by palm trees and a restaurant with outdoor seating and fresh fish on the menu.

Boulders

Two kilometres from the station towards Cape Point lies **Boulders**, the most popular local beach (R10, kids R5), which offers a number of places to stay. The area takes its name from the huge rounded rocks that create a cluster of little coves with sandy beaches and clear sea pools which are gorgeous for swimming. However, the main reason people come to Boulders is for the **African penguins** (formerly known as jackass penguins), in the Boulders section of the Table Mountain National Park (open 24hr; April–Sept daily 8am–5pm; Oct–March daily 7am–7pm; R15 during official hours, free at other times R35 conservation fee plus), a fenced reserve on Boulders Beach. Passing sailors used to prey on the quirky birds and their eggs, and more recently they have fallen victim to vandals, and some locals who consider them pests; they're now protected by a guard. African penguins usually live on islands off the west side of the South African coast, the Boulders birds forming one of only two mainland colonies in the world. This is also the only place where the endangered species are actually increasing in numbers, and provides a rare opportunity to get a close look at them.

Miller's Point and Smitswinkelbaai

Almost 5km to the south is the popular **Miller's Point** resort, which has a number of small sandy beaches and a tidal pool protected from the southeaster. A **campsite** at the caravan park offers great sea views. Along Main Road, the notable *Black Marlin* seafood **restaurant** attracts busloads of tourists, while the boulders around the point attract rock agama and black zonure lizards and dassies. The last place before you get to the Cape of Good Hope Nature Reserve is **Smitswinkelbaai** (pronounced "smits-vin-cull-buy"). This little cove has a small beach safe for swimming, but feels the full blast of the southeaster. It's not accessible by car, as local property-owners fiercely guard their privacy. To get there, you must park next to the road and walk down a seemingly endless succession of stairs.

Table Mountain National Park – Cape of Good Hope

Most people come to **Cape of Good Hope section** of the Table Mountain National Park (daily: April–Sept 7am–5pm; Oct–March 6am–6pm; R35; ☎021 780 9100, ⊛www.tmnp.co.za) to see the southernmost tip of Africa and the place where the Indian and Atlantic oceans meet at **Cape Point**. In fact, it's the site of neither: the continent's real tip is at Cape Agulhas, some 300km southeast of here (see p.250), but Cape Point is a lot easier to get to and an awesomely dramatic spot, which should on no account be missed. The reserve sits atop massive sea cliffs with huge views, strong seas, and an even wilder wind, which whips off caps and sunglasses as visitors gaze southwards from the old lighthouse buttress.

Most people come to the Point as part of a circular trip, returning via Kommetjie and the especially scenic Chapman's Peak Drive (see p.155). Numerous

Fynbos

Early Dutch settlers were alarmed by the lack of good timber on the Cape Peninsula's hillsides, which were covered by nondescript, scrubby bush they described as *fijn bosch* (literally "fine bush") and which is now known by its Afrikaans name **fynbos** (pronounced "fayn-bos"). The settlers planted exotics, like the oaks that now shade central Cape Town, and over the ensuing centuries their descendants established pine forests on the sides of Table Mountain in an effort to create a landscape that fulfilled their European idea of the picturesque. It's only relatively recently that Capetonians have come to claim *fynbos* proudly as part of the peninsula's heritage.

Fynbos is remarkable for its astonishing variety of plants, its 8500 species making it one of the world's biodiversity hot spots. The Cape Peninsula alone, measuring less than 500 square kilometres, has 2256 plant species (nearly twice as many as Britain, which is 5000 times bigger). The four basic types of *fynbos* plants are **proteas** (South Africa's national flower); **ericas**, amounting to six hundred species of heather; **restios** (reeds); and **geophytes**, including ground orchids and the startling flaming red disas, which can be seen in flower on Table Mountain in late summer.

Cape fauna

Along with indigenous plants and flowers, you may well spot some of the animals living in the *fynbos* habitat. **Ostriches** stride through the low fynbos, and occasionally **African penguins** come ashore. A distinctive bird on the rocky shores is the **black oystercatcher** with a bright red beak, jabbing limpets off the rocks. You'll also see **Cape cormorants** in large flocks on the beach or rocks, often drying their outstretched wings. Running up and down the water's edge (where, as on any other beach walk in the Cape, you'll see piles of shiny brown *Ecklonia* kelp) are **white-fronted plovers** and **sanderlings**, probing for food left by the receding waves.

As for mammals, **baboons** lope along the rocky shoreline, and grazing on the heathery slopes are **bontebok, eland** and **red hartebeest**, as well as **Cape rhebok** and **grysbok**. If you're very lucky, you may even see some of the extremely rare **Cape mountain zebras**.

tours spend a day stopping off at the peninsula highlights; Day Trippers (☎021 511 4766) runs fun tours for R350 (including a picnic lunch), some of which give you the option of cycling part of the way. For general tours that take in the reserve see p.106.

There's no public transport to the reserve, although you can charter a Simon's Town **Rikki's** (☎021 786 2136) there and back. To **drive** there, take the M3 to Muizenberg, continuing on the M4 via Simon's Town to the reserve gates, where you'll be given a good **map** that marks the main driving and walking routes, as well as the tidal pools and other facilities. Go as early as you can in the day to avoid tour buses and the likelihood of the wind gusting more strongly as the day progresses. Worth a look is the **Buffelsfontein Visitors' Centre** (daily 7.30am–5pm; ☎021 780 9204), 8km from the entrance gate, which has attractive displays about the local fauna and flora as well as video screenings on the ecology of the area.

From the car park, the famous viewpoint is a short, steep walk, crawling with tourists, up to the original lighthouse. A **funicular** (R30 return) runs the less energetic to the top, where there's a curio shop. There's also a rather good **restaurant**, the *Two Oceans*, at the car park, which has outdoor seating (but it's usually too windy to be pleasant) and huge picture windows taking in the drop to the sea below.

Baboons can be a menace; keep your car windows closed, as it's not unknown for them to invade vehicles, and they're adept at slyly swiping picnics. Feeding them is provocative and can incur a fine.

Cape Point and around

Cape Point is the treacherous promontory of rocks, winds and swells braved by navigators since the Portuguese first "rounded the Cape" in the fifteenth century. Plenty of wrecks lie submerged off its coast, and at **Olifantsbos** on the west side you can walk to a US ship sunk in 1942, and a South African coaster which ran aground in 1965. The **Old Lighthouse**, built in 1860, was too often dangerously shrouded in cloud, and failed to keep ships off the rocks, so another was built lower down in 1914, not always successful in averting disasters, but still the most powerful light beaming onto the sea from South Africa.

Walking and swimming

Most visitors make a beeline for Cape Point, seeing the rest of the reserve through a vehicle window, but walking is the best way to appreciate indigenous Cape **flora**. At first glance the landscape appears rocky and bleak, with short, wind-cropped plants, but the vegetation is surprisingly rich. Amazingly, many bright blooms in Britain and the US, including varieties of geraniums, freesias, gladioli, daisies, lilies and irises, are hybrids grown from indigenous Cape plants.

There are several waymarked **walks** in the Cape of Good Hope Nature Reserve. If you're planning a big hike it's best to set out early, as shade is rare and the wind can be foul, especially during summer, often increasing in intensity as the day goes on. One of the most straightforward **hiking routes** is the signposted forty-minute trek from the car park at Cape Point to the more westerly **Cape of Good Hope**. For exploring the shoreline, a clear path runs down the Atlantic side which you can join at **Gifkommetjie**, signposted off Cape Point Road. From the car park, several sandy tracks drop quite steeply down the slope across rocks, and through bushes and milkwood trees to the shore, along which you can walk in either direction. Alternatively, take a copy of the Government Printer's 1:50,000 map *3318 C.D. Cape Town* for some more intrepid exploration. Take water on any walk in the reserve, as there are no reliable fresh sources.

You'll find the **beaches** along signposted side roads branching out from the Cape Point road through the reserve. The sea is too dangerous for swimming, but there are safe tidal pools at the adjacent **Buffels Bay** and **Bordjiesrif**, midway along the east shore. Both have braai stands, but more southerly Buffels Bay is the nicer, with big lawned areas and some sheltered spots to have a picnic.

Table Bay and the northern suburbs

The **northern suburbs**, middle-class and Afrikaner-dominated, curl around the edge of Table Bay, north from Duncan Dock, and east along the N1 freeway. Few tourists see more of this area than the strip along the coast from Milnerton to Blouberg, and with good reason: the main attraction here is the much-snapped view of Table Mountain across the bay. The sea in **Table Bay** is cold, and often windy, but windsurfers and kite-fliers do well here, and the long sandy beaches are ideal for a sunset walk, when you can watch the glowing orb slip into the sea close to Robben Island. Otherwise, the northern suburbs are an unappetizing sprawl of starter homes and new developments (this is one of the few areas of Cape Town where there's room for expansion).

The N1 from the city centre follows the coast to Milnerton, Tableview, Bloubergstrand and Melkbosstrand; use the Milnerton/Paarden Island exit off the N1 to get onto Marine Drive for these suburbs. The beachfront strip at **Milnerton**, closest to central Cape Town, is a banal, neon-lit fast-food haven, offering little reason to stop, unless you're one of the surfing devotees who brave the water for the break off the lighthouse, undeterred by the debris floating across from the docks.

To the west is **Table View**, noted for its easy access to the beach, beachside parking and its classic view of Table Mountain. Nearby **Bloubergstrand** (pronounced "blow-berg-strunt", though it's usually shortened to Blouberg), 25km from the city, is the only place to draw you out to Table Bay. Once a fishing village, this is a good place to walk and take in the views, and you can sample one of Blouberg's outdoor restaurants for meals or tea. **Big Bay**

(Grootbaai), close by, draws windsurfing enthusiasts from all over the world for annual competitions.

By the time you get to **Melkbosstrand** and find yourself driving through dry, low scrub, you'll feel well and truly out of Cape Town. **Melkbos**, 30km from Cape Town, has a caravan park and one or two places to stay, but few people choose to, perhaps because the settlement is so close to Koeberg, the country's only **nuclear power station**, which generates electricity for the Western Cape. It's said that the sea around Melkbos is a few degrees warmer than elsewhere around here, heated by the water used to cool the reactor.

The Cape Flats and the townships

East of the northern and southern suburbs, among the industrial smokestacks and the windswept **Cape Flats**, reaching well beyond the airport, is Cape Town's largest residential quarter, taking in the **coloured districts**, **African townships** and shantytown **squatter camps**. The Cape Flats are exactly that: flat, as well as being barren and windswept, with the M5 acting as a dividing line between it and the southern suburbs. Exclusively inhabited by Africans and coloureds in separate areas, the Flats can be both shocking and heartening, their abject poverty coexisting with a spirit of enterprise and stoicism.

The African townships were set up as dormitories to provide labour for white Cape Town, not as places to build a life, which is why they had no facilities and no real hub. The **men-only hostels**, another apartheid relic, are at the root of many of the area's social problems. During the 1950s, the government set out a blueprint to turn the tide of Africans flooding into Cape Town. No African was permitted to settle permanently in the Cape west of a line near the Fish River, the old frontier over 1000km from Cape Town; women were entirely banned from seeking work in Cape Town and men prohibited from bringing their wives to join them. By 1970 there were ten men for every woman in Langa.

In the end, apartheid failed to prevent the influx of work-seekers desperate to come to Cape Town. Where people couldn't find legal accommodation they set up the **squatter camps** of makeshift iron, cardboard and plastic sheeting. During the 1970s and 1980s, the government attempted to demolish these and destroy anything left inside – but no sooner had the police left than the camps reappeared, and they are now a permanent feature of the Cape Flats. One of the best known of all South Africa's squatter camps is **Crossroads**, whose inhabitants suffered campaigns of harassment that included killings by apartheid collaborators and police, and continuous attempts to bulldoze it out of existence. Through sheer determination and desperation its residents hung on, eventually winning the right to stay. Today, the government is making attempts to improve conditions in the shantytowns by introducing running water and sanitation; families and ad hoc traders are now moving in.

Langa is the oldest and most central township, lying just east of the white suburb of Pinelands and north of the N2. In this relentlessly grey place, without the tiniest patch of green relief, you'll find women selling sheep and goats' heads, alongside state-of-the-art public phone bureaus run by enterprising township businessmen from inside recycled cargo containers. Nuclear families live in smart suburban houses while, not far away, there are former men-only hostels where as many as three families share one room.

South of the African ghettos is **Mitchell's Plain**, a coloured area stretching down to the False Bay coast (you'll skirt Mitchell's Plain if you take the M5 to Muizenberg). More salubrious than any of the African townships, Mitchell's Plain reflects how under apartheid lighter skins meant better conditions, even if you weren't quite white. But for coloureds the forced removals were no less tragic, many being summarily forced to vacate family homes because their suburb had been declared a White Group Area. Many families were relocated here when District Six was razed (see p.129), and their communities never fully recovered – one of the symptoms of dislocation are the violent gangs which have become an everyday part of Mitchell's Plain youth culture.

Township tours and homestays

Several projects are underway to encourage tourists into the townships but, as a high proportion of Cape Town's nearly 2000 annual murders take place here, the recommended way to visit is on one of the **tours** listed in the box on p.106. All these tours are operated by residents of the Cape Flats, or in co-operation with local communities, and emphasize face-to-face encounters with ordinary people. They include visits to *shebeens*, nightclubs and a township restaurant, chats with residents of squatter camps and the Langa hostels, and meetings with traditional healers and music makers, township artists and craftworkers. Some tours also take in "sites of political struggle", where significant events in the fight against apartheid occurred. If you want to really get under the skin of the townships, there's no better way than staying in one of the **township B&Bs**; see box on p.118.

Eating

Cape Town has a large number of relaxed and convivial restaurants, which generally serve imaginative and healthy food of a high standard, with international cuisines readily available. Prices are inexpensive compared with much of the First World, and foreign visitors can eat in upmarket restaurants with outstanding chefs creating innovative food for the kind of money they'd spend on a pizza back home. This is the city to splash out in whatever takes your fancy, and you'll find the quality of meat and fish very high, with many vegetarian options as well. As far as **prices** go, expect to pay under R50 for a main course at an inexpensive restaurant, up to R75 at a moderately priced one, more than this at an expensive place.

There are a couple of restaurants dedicated to **Cape Cuisine** (see p.64), though it's not the thing to concentrate on when you're choosing somewhere to eat. As for **seafood**, you can expect fresh fish at every good restaurant. Cape Town itself offers cold-water fish such as kingklip, hake and *snoek*; the cold waters up the West Coast yield quantities of crayfish and mussels, while fresh fish, oysters and prawns are flown in from warmer waters, including Mozambique. **Cape wines** are the obvious accompaniment to your meals. For details of where to buy seafood, wines and other provisions to **self-cater**, see p.182.

City centre

Cape Town's once down-at-heel city centre is enjoying a renaissance, and its **restaurants** are being joined by plenty of continental-style **cafés**. Most cafés here stay open till around 11pm. The establishments reviewed in the Long Street area are marked on the map on p.120; for locations of the remaining places, see the map on p.102.

Around Long Street

Africa Café 108 Shortmarket St, Cape Heritage Square ☎021 422 0221. Probably the best restaurant in Cape Town for African cuisine, with a fantastic selection from around the continent. Given that you're served a communal feast of sixteen dishes, and can have as many extra helpings as you like, its R125 per head price tag is pretty reasonable. Booking essential. Inexpensive–moderate. Dinner daily from 6.30pm.

Bukhara 33 Church St ☎021 424 0000. A popular upmarket North Indian restaurant, with green marble floors and a show kitchen where you can watch chefs at work. The food is superb. Booking is essential to get into one of the two evening sittings (7pm & 9pm). Moderate–expensive. Mon–Sat lunch and dinner, Sunday dinner only.

Five Flies 14–16 Keerom St ☎021 424 4442. Wonderfully imaginative food, with a sophisticated blend of world cuisine which really works. The presentation delights, while the feel is elegant without being formal. Moderate–expensive. Mon–Fri lunch and dinner, Sat & Sun dinner.

Gallery Café South African National Gallery, Government Ave. Breakfast, lunch and tea with a good menu that includes a buffet, pasta, salads and sandwiches. Inexpensive. Tues–Sun 10am–5pm.

Ginja 121 Castle St ☎021 426 2368. Situated in a 160-year-old, stylishly renovated grain warehouse, this restaurant offers quality international fusion cuisine. Their specialty is the slow roasted duck breast. Expensive. Daily eves.

Ivy Garden Restaurant Old Town House, Greenmarket Square. Tucked away in the sheltered courtyard of the museum, this casual place is good for salads, *bobotie,* pickled fish, *potjiekos,* or just a beer. Inexpensive. Mon–Fri 8.30am–4pm, Sat 8.30am–1pm.

Long Street Cafè 259 Long St. Cool bar/deli/restaurant, with tasteful open-plan decor and fresh Continental-style food. They're famous for their cocktails. Inexpensive. Mon–Sat 9.30am–midnight.

Madame Zingara 192 Loop St ☎021 426 2458. A bohemian delight with decor as wild as the food. Try the fillet medallions with chocolate-chilli sauce. Moderate–expensive. Mon–Sat dinner.

Mama Africa 178 Long St ☎021 424 8634. Food from around the continent, including a mixed grill of springbok, impala, kudu, ostrich,even crocodile. You can also sit at the 12m bar – in the form of a green mamba – and listen to live African music. Moderate. Mon–Sat dinner.

Mexican Kitchen Café 13 Bloem St ☎021 423 1541. An excellent casual restaurant serving good-value burritos, enchiladas, nachos and calamari fajitas, with some fine vegetarian options and deli-style takeaways. Inexpensive. Daily until midnight.

Mr Pickwick's 158 Long St. Hearty and cheap "tin-plate" meals, including a challenging range of hot and cold "foot-long" sandwiches. Inexpensive. Mon & Tues 8am–2am, Wed–Sat 8am–4am.

Royale 273 Long St. Gourmet burgers that pack a surprise, with unusual combinations, such as brie or roasted vegetables in the bun. Choose from lamb, beef, chicken and vegetarian patties including tofu. Inexpensive. Mon–Sat from noon.

Elsewhere in the centre

Biesmiellah In the Bo-Kaap, on the corner of Upper Wales and Pentz streets ☎021 423 0850. One of the oldest and best-known restaurants for traditional Cape cuisine; especially recommended are the spicy stews and wickedly rich *malva* pudding. No alcohol. Inexpensive. Mon–Sat from 11am.

Caroline's Cape Kitchen 15 Long St ☎021 419 8984. Traditional Cape food in a casual country-style restaurant where you're surrounded by thousands of bottles of wine. Inexpensive–moderate. Mon–Sat noon–2pm.

Charly's Bakery 20 Roeland St. The most spectacular cakes and pastries in Cape Town, but don't expect anything from the decor. Try the Death by Chocolate – a very rich, moist cake – or the double chocolate cheesecake. Also does breakfasts and light lunches. Inexpensive. Mon–Fri 7.30am–4pm.

Col'Cacchio Seeff House, 42 Hans Strijdom Ave. An offbeat pizza restaurant, which also serves pasta and salads, and bills itself as low-fat and heart-friendly. Has over forty different designer pizza toppings, such as smoked salmon, sour cream and caviar. No bookings. Inexpensive. Lunch Mon–Fri, dinner daily.

Jewel Tavern Off Vanguard Rd, Duncan Docks ☎021 448 1977. An unpretentious Taiwanese sailors' eating house, now "discovered" by Cape Town's *bon viveurs.* Located in the middle of the docks, it serves superb food, including great hot and sour soup and spring rolls made while you watch. Moderate. Daily mid-morning till 10pm.

Marimba's Cape Town International Convention Centre, on the corner of Coen Steytler Ave and Heerengracht ☎021 418 3366. African and Continental cuisine – this is one of the few places to try crocodile carpaccio. There's an eclectic range of live music every night. Expensive, with a cover charge Sat and Sun. Mon–Fri noon till late, Sat & Sun 6pm till late.

V&A Waterfront and de Waterkant

The **Waterfront** offers a lot if you want to eat well and your budget is fairly generous, while **De Waterkant** has some nice places in a gentrified historic quarter; see the map on p.134 for locations.

The Waterfront

Baia Upper Level, Quay 6 ☎ 021 421 0935. Sit on the terraced balcony and take in the views of Table Mountain while dining on masterfully cooked fresh fish and seafood. The spicy seafood bouillabaisse is worth a try. Expensive. Lunch and dinner daily.

Bayfront Blu Two Oceans Aquarium ☎ 021 419 9068. All-day breakfasts and fine coffee in an unbeatable location attached to the aquarium, with seating on a quayside deck that gives views of boats cutting across the water and clouds drifting over Table Mountain. For something more substantial, there's traditional African fare as well as fusion dishes, with a good vegetarian selection and some exciting seafood options such as Swahili prawn curry. Moderate–expensive. Daily 9am–11.30pm.

Caffé Balducci Quay 6 ☎ 021 421 6002. An upmarket café-restaurant with lovely views, offering interesting Californian/Italian food with South African overtones. Inexpensive–moderate. Daily 9am–midnight.

Caffé San Marco Piazza level, Victoria Wharf ☎ 021 418 5434. A coffee shop/bar with umbrellas on the piazza, offering an all-day breakfast menu, good sandwiches on Italian breads and fresh salads. The grilled calamari with garlic and chilli is delicious. They also have 18 flavours of ice cream and sorbet. Inexpensive. Daily 8.30am–11.30pm.

Mugg & Bean Ground level, Victoria Wharf. A range of excellent coffees and light meals, including toasted sandwiches and salads, though their position in the mall doesn't benefit from the Waterfront setting. Inexpensive. Daily 9am–midnight.

Tasca de Belem Shop 154, piazza level, Victoria Wharf ☎ 021 419 3009. Portuguese specialities, with funky outdoor seating in summer. The flame-grilled Mozambican chicken is good, as are the *peri-peri* chicken livers. Moderate. Daily 11am–11pm.

De Waterkant

Anatoli 24 Napier St ☎ 021 419 2501. A Turkish restaurant in an early twentieth-century warehouse buzzing with atmosphere. The excellent *meze* include exceptionally delicious *dolmades*, and there are superb desserts such as pressed dates topped with cream. Moderate. Dinner Tues–Sun until 11pm.

Andiamo Cape Quarter piazza, Dixon St ☎ 021 421 3688. Italian deli with a courtyard restaurant serving salads, pastas and sandwiches. The deli itself does a great selection of meats, cheeses, salads, dips and fresh breads – phone ahead and they'll put a picnic together for you. Inexpensive. Daily 9am–11pm.

La Petite Tarte Cape Quarter, Dixon St ☎ 021 425 9077. Tiny, authentically French café whose menu includes sweet and savoury tarts, the latter including mushroom, and ham and blue cheese varieties. They also blend flavoured ceylon and herbal teas to create unusual flavours. Inexpensive. Daily 9am–11pm.

The Nose Wine Bar Cape Quarter, Dixon St ☎ 021 425 2200. Tastings from a wide selection of the Cape's finest wines (there's a nominal charge for the privilege), as well as light meals, stews, fish and steaks. Inexpensive. Mon–Sat 11am–late.

City Bowl suburbs

The vast majority of eating places in the City Bowl suburbs lie in a continuous strip along Kloof Street – or just off it – in Gardens. See the map on p.111 for the locations of the places reviewed here.

Amigos Mediterranean Restaurant 158 Kloof St, Gardens ☎ 021 423 6805. A tasty mixture of Greek *meze* combined with Italian and Spanish food. This is a lively joint, with some tables outside and a loyal clientele. Inexpensive–moderate. Daily 10am–midnight.

Café Paradiso 110 Kloof St, Gardens ☎ 021 423 8653. Good Greek and Mediterranean dishes, including a weigh-your-plate *meze* bar. The outside terrace has views up to the mountain and down over the city and docks. Moderate. Daily lunch & dinner.

Chef Pon's Asian Kitchen 12 Mill St, Gardens (next to the *Holiday Inn*) ☎ 021 465 5846; and 62a Kloof St ☎ 021 422 4033. A popular and noisy neighbourhood restaurant serving Thai, Vietnamese, Japanese and Chinese food. Moderate. Mon–Sat lunch and dinner.

Kauai Juice 50 Kloof St, Gardens. If you're in need of something healthy, this is the place to go. They're famous for their smoothies imbued with such exotics as ginseng, wheat grass or echinacea, and they also do low-fat Thai-influenced beef, chicken and veggie sandwiches, plus delicious salads. Inexpensive. Daily 8am–10pm.

Limoncello 8 Breda St, Gardens. Small Italian trattoria serving unfailingly excellent pastas and pizzas. Inexpensive–moderate. Mon–Fri lunch & dinner, Sat dinner only.

Melissa's 94 Kloof St, Gardens. Light meals and fine desserts in their small café, while the food emporium sells freshly made Mediterranean fare. Inexpensive. Mon–Fri 7.30am–9pm, Sat & Sun 8am–9pm.

Mount Nelson Hotel Garden Room 76 Orange St, Gardens. Colonial-style high tea in Cape Town's oldest and most gracious hotel is a definite culinary highlight of the city, the large tea table piled with hot and cold pastries, classic savouries like

smoked salmon sandwiches, and cakes. You can skip lunch and dinner after the R100 feast you get here. Daily 1.30–5.30pm.

Ocean Basket Southern Africa 75 Kloof St, Gardens ☎021 422 0322. Long queues and delicious aromas speak eloquently of the outstanding dishes – from humble fish and chips to prawns and calamari – at this slick, quick-in, quick-out seafood chain. Moderate. Mon–Sat lunch, daily for dinner.

Raith Gourmet Gardens Centre, Mill St, Gardens. Meat-focused deli and café with an exceptional selection of foods and some marvellous sandwiches; German specialities include sauerkraut fried with strips of bacon. Inexpensive. Mon–Fri 8.30am–6pm, Sat 8.30am–1pm.

Yindees 22 Camp St, Tamboerskloof ☎021 422 1012. This popular establishment was one of the first Thai restaurants in Cape Town, and has remained consistently good. Moderate. Mon–Sat lunch & dinner.

Southern suburbs

Woodstock to Wynberg

Don Pedros 113 Roodebloem Rd, Woodstock ☎021 447 4493. Since the 1980s, when it was a regular haunt for anti-apartheid activists, *Don Pedros* has been a place for good, cheap food – curries, stews, pasta, salads – and a scruffy Capetonian ambience, somewhere to linger all evening over a beer or coffee without feeling hassled. There are smoking and non-smoking rooms; it's also a gay-friendly place where people tend to hang out after shows. Inexpensive. Daily 10am–late.

Fiamma's 23 Wolfe St, Wynberg ☎021 761 6175. Innovative, colourful, Mediterranean-influenced creations that include egg-free, wheat-free and vegetarian dishes. The chickpea, coriander, spring onion and parsley patties are a firm favourite. Moderate. Mon–Sat lunch & dinner. Closed for two weeks in July.

Gardener's Cottage 31 Newlands Ave, Montebello Estate, Newlands. Serves hearty English breakfasts and light lunches – quiches, salads and lasagnes – as well as tea and coffee. It's set in a complex of old farm buildings under ancient pine trees, with neighbouring arts and crafts workshops at which to browse. Inexpensive. Tues–Fri 8am–4.30pm, Sat & Sun 8.30am–4.30pm.

Lupo's 19 Wolfe St, Wynberg ☎021 762 3855. An authentic Italian restaurant, with a vast antipasto spread followed by a limited if interesting range of pasta dishes and main courses. The fixed-price set menu options are a good deal for the full works:

antipasto, pasta, main dish and dessert. Moderate–expensive. Mon–Sat eves.

Constantia

Simon's at Groot Constantia Wine Estate Off Ladies Mile Extension ☎021 794 1143. Well-rounded menu offering salads, pastas, fish, meat and chicken with a South African flair. The setting is what makes this place stand out. The outdoor shaded patio has grand vistas of the Constantiaberg Mountains and it's a good place to get relief from the summer heat. Moderate. Daily lunch & dinner.

Spaanschemat River Café Constantia Uitsig Wine Estate, Spaanschemat River Rd ☎021 794 3010. This delightful venue, situated in the farm's old schoolhouse, serves sumptuous breakfasts, lunches and teas. Try the extravagant eggs benedict. Booking essential in high season. Moderate. Closed Sun.

Uitsig *Constantia Uitsig Country Hotel*, Spaanschemat River Rd ☎021 794 4480. Considered one of the finest restaurants (and one of the priciest) in South Africa for its Mediterranean-influenced cuisine. Expensive. Lunch & dinner daily. Closed July.

Wasabi Old Village Centre, Constantia Village ☎021 794 6546. Quality sushi bar in a stylish modern setting. The crab salad, *ramen* soups and Japanese noodles come up tops on the menu. Inexpensive–moderate. Daily lunch & dinner.

Atlantic seaboard

The places reviewed in Green Point, Mouille Point and Sea Point appear on the map on pp.140–141.

Green Point

Chariots Italian Coffee Bar 107 Main Rd. Stylish decor and great, reasonably priced food make this a fashionable haunt for Cape Town's yuppies. Inexpensive. Mon–Sat until 11pm, Sun until 5pm.

Giovanni's Deliworld 103 Main Rd. With indoor and pavement seating, this friendly Italian deli/coffee shop is handy for coffee, excellent made-to-order sandwiches, salads and dips. Inexpensive–moderate. Daily 8am–9pm.

Mano's 39 Main Rd ☎021 434 1090. Italian food, with exciting salads and one of the best *crème brûlées* in town. Moderate. Mon–Fri lunch & dinner, Sat dinner only.

Theo's Grill Butcher and Seafood Beach Rd ☎021 439 3494. Upmarket, and right on the beachfront, *Theo's* offers superb Greek-style meat and seafood dishes. Moderate. Mon–Fri lunch & dinner, Sat dinner only.

Wang Thai 105 Main Rd ☎021 439 6164. Cape Town's best Thai restaurant, serving such delights as hot and spicy prawn soup, steamed fish with lemon juice and chilli, and their special – thinly sliced, seared sirloin. Moderate. Mon–Fri & Sun lunch, daily for dinner.

Zeroninethreetwo Exhibition Building, 79 Main Rd ☎021 439 6306. Belgian cuisine and beer in funky minimalist surroundings – come here for mussels, excellent thin chips, prawns and salads. Moderate. Daily 11am till late.

Mouille Point

Newport Market and Deli 47 Beach Rd. A light, airy deli with views onto Table Bay, offering coffee, excellent sandwiches, salads and some hot dishes. Inexpensive. Mon–Fri 7.30am–8pm, Sat & Sun from 8am.

Wakame 47 Beach Rd ☎021 433 2377. Asian fusion food with killer desserts – try the chocolate and banana spring rolls. Every table has a view of the ocean. Booking essential. Moderate–expensive. Daily lunch & dinner.

Sea Point

Harveys at the Mansion *Winchester Mansion Hotel*, 221 Beach Rd ☎021 434 2351. The *nouvelle cuisine* menu includes combinations such as puréed peas with bone marrow, and there are great views of the sun setting over the Atlantic from the cool courtyard garden. Moderate–expensive. Daily breakfast, lunch & dinner.

New York Bagels 51 Regent Rd. A fantastic deli with a sit-down section. Choose from a dizzying array of bagels and homemade fillings, from chopped liver to herring, plus stir-fries, pasta and pastries. Inexpensive. Daily till late.

Tom Yum 72 Regent Rd ☎021 434 8139. A casual little eatery with friendly service and well-prepared, classic Thai food. Inexpensive–moderate. Tues–Sun lunch & dinner.

Camps Bay and points south

Café Caprice 37 Victoria Rd, Camps Bay ☎021 438 8315. Directly opposite Camps Bay beach, this lively Mediterranean-style restaurant is a great place to soak up street life and sunshine. Inexpensive–moderate. Daily 9am till late.

Fish on the Rocks Beyond Mariner's Wharf, Hout Bay (drive through the dock and past the factory). Delicious fresh fish and chips, served under red umbrellas or eaten on the rocks overlooking the bay. In season it's also a fabulous place to watch whales. Inexpensive. Daily 9am–8pm.

La Cuccina Food Store Victoria Mall, Victoria Rd, Hout Bay. High-quality deli and café food in pleasant surrounds. At lunchtime it has buffets of quiches, salads and lasagne. Inexpensive–moderate. Daily 8am–7pm.

Mariners Wharf Bistro The Harbour, Hout Bay. A relaxed, well-run place with terrace seating overlooking the harbour. Good for seafood to eat in or take away. Moderate. Daily 10am–6pm.

Red Herring Beach Rd/Pine Rd, Noordhoek ☎021 789 1783. A country restaurant that does grilled meats include springbok and kudu, plus a good choice of vegetarian options or fresh fish. Moderate. Tues–Sun dinner.

Theo's Grill Butcher and Seafood Promenade Building, Victoria Rd, Camps Bay ☎021 438 0410. Brilliant steaks sold by weight, plus seafood; the atmosphere is buzzy, and there's some outdoor seating. Moderate. Daily lunch & dinner.

Vilamoura 9 The Broadway, Victoria Rd, Camps Bay ☎021 438 1850. Cape Town's best seafood restaurant doesn't come cheap, but makes a fine choice for a special occasion. Slick and modern, it has fantastic views, superb service and features traditional Portuguese dishes on the menu, such as salt cod soup. Expensive. Daily noon–midnight or later.

False Bay seaboard

Muizenberg

Empire Café 11 York Rd. Surprising combinations of Mediterranean food with a hint of Asia in a casual, lively split-level restaurant. Staff amuse patrons by sliding down the spiral banister after taking orders. The menu changes regularly, but tends to include olive-oil roast vegetables and chocolate honey bread and butter pudding, both recommended. Inexpensive. Tues–Sun breakfast & lunch.

The Olive Station Muizenberg Station, Main Rd. Bright and friendly place where you can snack on delicious, Levantine-influenced food. Their olive bread, desserts and Lebanese cheese or lamb and pine-nut pies are especially good. There's a warehouse for curing olives on site, with other tasty bits on sale. Some seats overlook the station and beach. Inexpensive. Mon & Wed–Sun breakfast and lunch.

Kalk Bay

Brass Bell Kalk Bay station, Main Rd. Primarily an unpretentious drinking spot, *Brass Bell* has arguably the best location on the peninsula, with False Bay's waves breaking against the wall of its outdoor terrace. The views of both the peninsula mountains and the Hottentots Holland peaks are unbeatable, but the seafood meals don't always match the magnificent setting. Moderate. Daily until late.

Harbour House Restaurant At the harbour ⓣ021 788 4133. Freshly caught seafood and Mediterranean fare, at a venue situated spectacularly on the breakwater of Kalk Bay harbour; book a table with bay views. The winter specials are great value, and there's a fire inside. Moderate–expensive. Daily lunch & dinner.

Kalky's At the harbour. For years, this totally unpretentious eating place has been serving the fishing community the best traditional fish and chips on the peninsula, and great-value seafood

platters; fish is hauled off the boats and straight into the frying pan. You sit at benches to eat, though takeaway is available. Inexpensive. Daily.

The Olympia Café & Deli Main Rd. One of the few places that draws parochial uptown Capetonians down the False Bay seaboard, and has a regular meeting spot for residents of Kalk Bay and St James. Always buzzing, with views of the harbour, for breakfast *Olympia* offers great coffee or freshly squeezed orange juice, accompanied by freshly baked Danish pastries, filled croissants or delicious homemade biscuits. Gourmet lunch menus are chalked up on a board, with local fish often featured. Inexpensive–moderate. Tues–Sat 7am–7pm, Sun 7am–3pm.

Simon's Town and around

Bertha's 1 Wharf Rd ⓣ021 786 2138. Relax with views of False Bay and the harbour while enjoying a middle-of-the-road, child-friendly menu, with meat, chicken, fish and vegetarian dishes. Inexpensive–moderate. Daily from 7.30am until evening.

Bon Appétit 90 St George's St ⓣ021 786 2412. In the old *British Hotel*, *Bon Appetit* offers classic, beautifully presented French cuisine. Emmanuel, owner and chef, is Michelin-trained, so expect the best. Expensive. Tues–Sat lunch & dinner.

The Meeting Place 98 St George's St ⓣ021 786 1986. Enjoy funky Mediterranean café food while surveying harbour goings-on from the upstairs balcony. Inexpensive. Mon–Wed & Sun 9am–5pm, Thurs–Sat 9am–9pm.

Tibetan Teahouse 2 Harrington Rd, Seaforth Beach ⓣ021 786 1544. Traditional Tibetan recipes, served up in a venue signalled by its prayer flags. It's completely vegetarian, so don't expect yak meat in the lentil Sherpa Stew. Daily 10am–5pm. Inexpensive.

Drinking, nightlife and entertainment

Cape Town has finally shaken off its reputation as a place where **nightlife** was synonymous with hitting the sack. Things have become much more lively and cosmopolitan in recent years, the scene spiced up by thousands of African and European visitors and immigrants.

Bars and clubs

The city is well populated with **bars**, ranging from the hip to the eccentric to the seedy. Traditional pubs are not a big feature: where they do exist, they're

New Year, New Year – so good they do it twice

A longstanding tradition in Cape Town is **Tweede Nuwe Jaar** (second new year), January 2 – until recently an official public holiday. Historically this was the only day of the year when slaves were allowed off, and the day has persisted as a holiday of epic proportions. If you're in Cape Town over this period, Tweede Nuwe Jaar is the time to party, when Cape Minstrels from the coloured community dance through the streets of the city centre performing a traditional form of singing and riotous banjo playing. Expect each troupe to be dressed up in matching outfits, often featuring outrageous colour combinations. Some roads in the centre are blocked off during the day for the festivities, which process through the city and end up at Green Point Stadium.

generally depressingly empty dives or cod-Irish franchises. Most liquor licences stipulate that the last round is served at 2am, but this is far from strictly followed. Expect a cover charge if live music is featured.

Mainstream house is very popular in the **clubs**, but there are also strong followings for drum 'n' bass, trance, hip-hop, dub and Latin grooves, as well as **kwaito** (see p.885). Though *kwaito* is still predominately a black scene, coloured and white youth are gradually getting into it. Many clubs have a short lifespan – and many of the best regular parties hop from venue to venue. Some of the more enduring clubs are listed here, but watch the press for up-to-the-minute information. The daily *Cape Argus* newspaper runs a club column on Tuesdays, and the monthly listings magazine *Cape Review* is also useful. Backpacker hostels are often the most up-to-date sources of party information. Cover charges vary from R20 to over R100 for big events with international DJs. And if you find yourself wandering about at night in search of a party, head for the strip of clubs along Somerset Road in Green Point, where there's always something going on well into the early hours. It's worth remembering that all drugs are illegal in South Africa, and aggressive police raids on clubs are by no means unknown.

Some of the township tours (see box on p.106) offer **music outings**, which save you the hassle of negotiating badly lit areas at night, and allow you to hear authentic sounds in township clubs. In addition Thuthuka Tours (℡021 433 2429) does Sunday morning gospel excursions to township churches. Boogie Bus Tours (℡082 495 5698) specializes in transport to venues in the Cape Flats.

City centre

Around Long Street

Jo'burg 218 Long St ℡021 422 0142. A good place to schmooze to a funky soundtrack, in the company of a hip art-school and media crowd. There's a range of live music on Sun nights. Daily 5pm–4am.

Kennedy's Restaurant and Cigar Lounge 251 Long St ℡021 424 1212. A swanky bar offering cigars from all over the world, with brilliant martinis and margueritas, good food, an older crowd, and live jazz every evening. Mon–Fri noon till late, Sat 7pm till late.

The Lounge 194 Long St ℡021 424 7636. A longstanding, trendy refuge for Cape Town's smart and glamorous. Upstairs, make for the superb balcony and grab a table overlooking vibrant Long St. House and jungle dominate the turntables. Mon–Sat 8pm–2am.

Mama Africa 178 Long St ℡021 424 8634. A relaxed and spacious bar-restaurant in the heart of Long St clubland, *Mama Africa* boasts a 12m bar in the form of a green mamba. Traditional percussion groups perform regularly, and it's popular with European and North American visitors. Music Mon–Sat 8.30pm–late.

The Purple Turtle On the corner of Shortmarket and Long streets. A cavernous, vaguely seedy bar frequented by goths, metalheads and other creatures, with bands on Saturday nights. Daily 11am–late.

Rhodes House 60 Queen Victoria St ☎021 424 8844. A relaxed and fashion-conscious place, with a range of house sounds. Themed parties with designated dress codes also happen – call before turning up. Wed–Sat 10pm till late.

Sutra 86 Loop St ☎021 422 4219. Deep house and R&B sounds. Wed, Fri & Sat 9pm till late.

Elsewhere in the centre

Drum Café 32 Glynn St ☎021 461 1305. Every Monday and Wednesday at 9pm there's a facilitated drum circle lead by a South African or West African drum teacher, suitable for all levels of experience; the smaller Monday groups are better if you're a complete novice, while the Saturday afternoon sessions at 3pm are for families. For those who prefer to leave things to the professionals, there are often parties at the weekends; ring for the current schedule. Light meals available, and the café is fully licensed. Mon, Wed, Fri & Sat 9pm–late.

Marimbas Cape Town International Convention Centre, corner of Coen Steytler Ave and Heerengracht ☎021 418 3366. There's live music nightly, with an African marimba band on Thurs. Daily 10pm till late. Cover charge applies Sat & Sun.

Mercury Live and Lounge 43 De Villiers St, District Six ☎021 465 2106. Live music and underground hip-hop parties at a spacious venue with minimalist decor. Mon–Sat 8pm till late.

The Shack 45b De Villiers St, District Six ☎021 465 2106. Comprising a restaurant, bar and pool hall, with sounds from the Sixties up to the Eighties. Under the same management is the adjoining *Blue Lizard*, which plays acid jazz, house and trip-hop. Open till late: Mon–Sat from 1pm, Sun from 6pm.

V&A Waterfront and De Waterkant

As well as upmarket restaurants, the **Waterfront** and **De Waterkant** also offer reasonably good nightlife that's largely in keeping with the area's emphatically clean-cut atmosphere.

Bossa Nova 43 Somerset Rd ☎021 425 0295. Upmarket lounge and dance club, where evenings start off with commercial music and gradually shift into the rhythmic sounds of Latin America. Tues–Sat; drinks and light music from 5pm and DJs from around 9.30pm.

Chilli 'n' Lime 23 Somerset Rd, De Waterkant ☎021 426 4469. Painfully stylish upmarket club with two dance floors and four bars, which hosts pulsing house and hip-hop parties. Frequented by a 20-something left-field student crowd. Tues–Sat 8am–4am.

Den Anker Restaurant and Bar Pierhead. One of the liveliver Waterfront venues, a busy pub and Continental-style bistro, patronized by tourists and well-heeled locals. *Den Anker* specializes in imported Belgian beers, both on tap and bottled. Daily 11am–midnight.

Green Dolphin Pierhead ☎021 421 7471. A top-notch jazz venue (though a tad chilly in winter), hosting quality jazz bands nightly at 8.30pm. Dinner – there's excellent seafood – is served from 6pm. Daily noon–midnight.

Opium 6 Dixon St ☎021 425 4010. An über trendy club featuring acid jazz and funky house music. Wed–Sat 10pm–2am.

Purgatory 8b Dixon St ☎021 421 7464. The place to hang out with waiflike models and other good-looking people swaying to house music. Wed–Sat 11pm till late.

Southern suburbs

Boer and Brit Pub *Alphen Hotel*, Alphen Drive, off the M41, Constantia. A cosy English-style pub at a historic Cape Dutch hotel. It's gracious yet relaxed, with tables under oak trees, a warm hearth on cold nights and bar meals. Daily 10am–11pm.

Foresters' Arms 52 Newlands Ave, Newlands. Preppie students and professionals gather to quaff draught beer at the very popular and busy "Forries", in the heart of leafy Newlands. A big wood-panelled pub, it boasts a beautiful hedged-in courtyard where you can grab a bench for a drowsy afternoon pint. Mon–Sat 10am–11pm, Sun 9am–4pm.

Pedlars on the Bend Spaanschemat River Rd, Constantia. An upmarket bar at one of the posher restaurants in this ritzy suburb, with a delightful outdoor area shaded by oaks. Daily 11am–11pm.

Atlantic seaboard

Café Caprice 37 Victoria Rd, Camps Bay ☏021 438 8315. A lively restaurant by day, where the pace increases come evening when DJs play anything from Ella Fitzgerald to *kwaito*. Open morning till late; DJs feature nightly in summer, Fri–Sun the rest of the year.

Dizzy Jazz Café 41 Camps Bay Drive, Camps Bay ☏021 438 2686. A crowded and lively nightspot with a big veranda and sea views, featuring a variety of live music nightly and serving draught beer and quality seafood. R20 cover charge. Daily noon–4am (music from 8.30pm).

La Med Bar and Restaurant Glen Country Club, Victoria Rd, Clifton ☏021 438 5600. A great sundowner venue overlooking the rocks at Clifton Beach, drawing a sporty, mainstream crowd; it's a favourite spot for hang-gliders from Lion's Head to visit, after they've landed in the adjacent field. There's live music Wed, Fri & Sat. Daily noon till late.

Red Herring On the corner of Pine and Beach roads, Noordhoek. A pub above a smart restaurant with an outdoor deck overlooking the panoramic Noordhoek valley. Busy on warm weekend afternoons, when a clean-cut 20-something crowd gathers. Tues–Sun 11am–midnight.

Cape Flats

Dockside Ratanga Junction; take the N1 to Bellville, then exit 10 (Sable St exit) ☏021 552 7303. A massive three-storey warehouse holding individually styled venues whose featured sounds range from wild and wicked techno to jazz and Seventies hits; you can move freely between halls as you like. Wed–Sat 9pm–late.

West End and **Club Galaxy** College Rd, Rylands ☏021 637 9132. Definitely the most happening place on the Flats are these two nightclubs in one building, the former a top jazz venue with live and recorded sounds, the latter a straight-up dance club playing R&B and mainstream house to a smart young crowd. Thurs–Sat 8pm–late.

Theatre, comedy and live music

Despite scarce resources (state funds have been redirected to more pressing areas), theatre in South Africa is making a valiant attempt to lift itself out of its post-democracy doldrums. Protest theatre, a fertile genre in the oppressive 1970s and 1980s, is now obsolete, and it's no longer seen as self-indulgent for plays to deal with personal rather than political issues. As yet there is no real successor to the world-renowned playwright Athol Fugard, several of whose works were first staged here, though a steady trickle of new **plays** are being written and performed in Cape Town, some of them innovative and hard-hitting. Writers and directors to look out for include the brilliant Brett Bailey, Marthinus Basson, Reza de Wet, Fiona Coyne (who also hosts the South African version of *The Weakest Link*), Roy Sargeant and the duo of Heinrich Rosehofer and Oscar Petersen.

Comedy, too, is starting to shape up well with the annual Smirnoff International Comedy Festival, at the Baxter Theatre around October, showcasing global and local talent. Probably South Africa's best-known stage satirist is Pieter Dirk Uys, whose character Evita Bezuidenhout, South Africa's answer to Dame Edna Everidge, has relentlessly roasted South African society since apartheid days. New homegrown comedians to look out for include Marc Lottering, a coloured Capetonian, who derives his material from his own community, and David Kau, an African, who is as caustic about Jo'burg township dwellers as he is about white South Africans.

Classical music has a small but faithful following, with concerts tending to take place on Tuesdays and Thursdays. There are free lunchtime concerts, often showcasing the work of students from Cape Town University's South African College of Music, on Thursdays at 1pm during term time, and sometimes on Wednesday 2pm; these take place at the Baxter Theatre, or at

Drinking, nightlife and entertainment

Pop music and Cape jazz

Cape Town's greatest musical treasure is **Cape jazz**, a subgenre of South African township jazz. Its greatest exponent is the internationally acclaimed **Abdullah Ibrahim** (known as Dollar Brand before his conversion to Islam). Born and raised in District Six, Ibrahim is a supremely gifted pianist and composer, who for decades has produced a hypnotic fusion of African, American and Cape Muslim idioms. In his greatest recordings, *Mannenberg* and *African Marketplace*, the fluttering rhythms of *goema* – traditional Cape carnival music – are combined with the cascading call-and-answer structure of African gospel. This is emotional jazz, full of simple, euphoric melody and enchanting brass lines.

Other Cape Town jazz legends are the late Basil Coetzee, a phenomenal tenor saxophonist who played on *Mannenberg*; Robbie Jansen, another saxman with a raunchy, fiery style who worked with Afro-pop greats Juluka; and alto saxman Winston "Ngozi" Mankunku, an old-school hepcat whose gigs are an exercise in good vibes. Both Jansen and Mankunku can occasionally be heard live in the city – watch the press. Other veteran stars to look out for are guitarist Errol Dyers, pianist Hotep Galeta and bassist Spencer Mbadu. Two young stars stand out as talented heirs to the Cape jazz tradition: astronomically cool guitarist Jimmy Dludlu and subtle, mellow pianist Paul Hanmer; catch them live if you can. Also watch out for the powerful singer Judith Sephuma, and Jo'burg-based maestro McCoy Mrubata. Check the press for upcoming performances and venues, among which two reliable spots are *Green Dolphin* (p.172) and *Manenberg* (see below).

Cape Town is also well stocked with charismatic **rock**, **reggae** and **pop** bands. Notable exports include radical hip-hop crew Prophets Of Da City and R&B crooner Jonathan Butler.

---

the college itself (☎021 650 2640) just behind. Recitals by visiting soloists and chamber ensembles are put on by an organization called Cape Town Concert Series (⊛www.ctconcerts.co.za). It's always a treat to catch one of the performances by Cape Town Opera (⊛www.capetownopera.co.za) to hear black South Africans, who are coming to dominate opera in Cape Town, injecting some African spice into a programme that still predominantly features European works. As regards **musicals**, David Kramer and Taliep Petersen have produced several hit shows celebrating the history and culture of Cape Town. Their *Kat and the Kings* took Broadway and London's West End by storm a few years back, bagging the 1999 Olivier Award for the best new musical.

Artscape D.F. Malan St ☎021 421 5470. Once the Camelot of state-funded white performing arts, Artscape has reinvented itself as a less elitist theatre, though high-quality ballet and opera are still produced, while adventurous new dramas appear periodically. Don't be intimidated by the monumental 1970s architecture.

Baxter Theatre Centre Main Rd, Rondebosch ☎021 685 7880. This mammoth brick theatre complex, its design inspired by Soviet Moscow's central train station, mounts an eclectic programme – innovative plays, comedy festivals, jazz and classical concerts and kids' theatre.

Little Theatre University of Cape Town, Orange St ☎021 480 7129. A showcase for innovative work

from the University of Cape Town drama school; the productions range from self-indulgent to breathtaking. The drama school has a long tradition of producing fine actors, and counts Richard E. Grant among its graduates.

Manenberg Jazz Café Clock Tower Precinct, Waterfront ☎021 421 5639. One of Cape Town's premier venues for live music, specializing in Cape and African jazz and attracting some of the hottest names in the South African music. Open till late: Mon & Thurs–Sun from 8.30pm, Fri & Sat from 9.30pm.

Masque Theatre 37 Main Rd, Muizenberg ☎021 788 6999. Amateur theatre that comes up with quality productions year round.

Maynardville Open Air Theatre On the corner of Church and Wolfe streets, Wynberg. Under the summer stars in Maynardville Park, every year in January and February, an imaginative production of a Shakespeare comedy is staged by the cream of Cape Town's actors and designers. Book through Artscape.

On Broadway 21 Somerset Rd, De Waterkant ☎021 418 8338. One of the few venues committed to the city's small cabaret scene is this bar-restaurant with live performances for an ethnically mixed crowd every night. Drag shows on Tues & Sun, cabaret Wed–Sat, and satirist Pieter Dirk Uys performs Mon eve. Daily 7pm–late.

Theatre On The Bay Link St, Camps Bay ☎021 438 3300. An upmarket theatre catering to a mature audience, and staging accomplished – if rather predictable – productions of mainstream contemporary plays and farces, plus musical tributes and revues.

Cinemas

Despite the fact that Cape Town is booming as a film-production centre, local feature films are scarce. For an intelligent mix of art films, cult classics and new releases, try the Labia, 69 Orange Street, or the Labia on Kloof, Lifestyles on Kloof Centre, Kloof Street Gardens (both on ☎021 424 5927). Mainstream cinemas most convenient for visitors are the Nu-Metro (☎021 419 9700) and Ster-Kinekor Cinema Nouveau (☎021 425 8222) at the V&A Waterfront; the Ster-Kinekor Cavendish Commercial (☎0860 300 222) at Cavendish Square Shopping Centre, Claremont; and, at the same shopping centre, the Ster-Kinekor Cinema Nouveau (☎021 683 4063). The Ster-Kinekor complex at the Blue Route Mall in Tokai (☎021 713 1280) is convenient if you're staying along the False Bay seaboard. All the above cinemas advertise daily in the *Cape Times* and *Cape Argus*.

Cape Town for kids

Cape Town is an excellent place to travel with children. The city enjoys fine weather, and activities in its many nature reserves, gardens and historic estates let under-10s work off some energy in a safe environment. Many activities for kids are either free or inexpensive, although renting a car is pretty well essential, given the poor public transport. Where the prices in this section refer to children, they mean under-16s, unless specified.

Museums and sights

The **Two Oceans Aquarium** (see p.135) is not only one of Cape Town's most rewarding museums but also features loads of interest to kids. Apart from the excitement of just looking at the weird and wonderful sea creatures, kids can actually handle a few species in the touch pool – sometimes this includes a small shark or sea urchins – while the Apha Activity Centre usually has puppet shows or face painting as well as computer terminals where older kids can learn about marine ecology.

The **SA Museum and Planetarium** (see p.126) is great for rainy days, especially for 5- to 12-year-olds, who'll enjoy the four-storey whale well and African animal dioramas, as well as the dinosaur displays. Its Discovery Room (Mon–Fri 10am–3pm, Sat & Sun 11am–4.30pm) features live ants, massive spiders and a crocodile display. The Planetarium has special children's shows over weekends and in school holidays.

Beaches and swimming pools

Cape Town's **beaches** are a classic and easy destination for a summer weekend family outing. This selection is particularly suitable for toddlers and smaller kids and generally also offers something for parents. Most beaches are pretty undeveloped, so it's best to take what you need in the way of food and drinks with you. Sea water and swimming pool temperatures are published each day in the weather section of the *Cape Times*. Get to the beach as early as possible so you can leave by 10–11am before the sun gets too strong, and to avoid the wind which often gusts up in the late morning.

On the False Bay seaboard, **Boulders Beach** (see p.160) is one of the few beaches to visit when the southeaster is blowing. It has safe, flat water, making it ideal for kids – and its resident penguin breeding colony is an added attraction. **Fish Hoek** (see p.158) is one of the best Peninsula beaches, with gentle waves that are warm in summer, a long stretch of sand and a playground. The paved Jager's Walk which runs along the rocky coast here is suitable for pushchairs and offers beautiful views of the Hottentots Holland Mountains. **St James** (see p.157) boasts a safe tidal pool with a small sandy beach and photogenic bathing boxes. From here you can walk to Muizenberg along a pushchair-friendly coastal pathway, with more views of distant mountains across the water.

The **Atlantic seaboard** is too cold for serious swimming, but does have some lovely stretches of sand, boulders and rock pools – and astonishing scenery. The beaches here are excellent for picnics, and on calm summer evenings idyllic for sundowners and sunsets. In the summer they're less windy than the False Bay beaches, but the afternoons are often baking hot. The closest stretch of coast to the centre ideal for prams – and roller-blading – is the paved **Sea Point promenade**, stretching 3km from the lighthouse in Mouille Point to Sea Point Pavilion, with the draw of playgrounds and ice-cream sellers en route. The tidal pool and small rock pools of **Camps Bay** (see p.153) make this popular beach very child-friendly, and it's easily reachable from the centre by car or bus. Finally, the six-kilometre stretch of white sand from **Noordhoek** to **Kommetjie** (see p.155) provides fine walking, kite-flying and horse-riding opportunities, with stupendous views of Chapman's Peak. If you're heading for Kommetjie you can go camel-riding at Imhoff Farm Village (see below).

As regards child-friendly swimming pools, **Newlands Pool** (see p.143) has a toddlers' pool and little playground in large grounds, while the marvellous **Sea Point Pool** at Sea Point Pavilion (see p.152) has two paddling pools for children, and lawns to laze on.

Outdoor and picnic spots

The Barnyard Farmstall Steenberg Rd (M42), next to Steenberg Estate, between Tokai Rd and the Ou Kaapseweg. An excellent place for an outdoor snack or cup of coffee at a small farmyard, with ducks and chickens wandering around, and an unusually good kids' playground. For more on the farmstall, see p.183.

Imhoff Farm Kommetjie Rd, opposite the Ocean View turn-off ☎021 783 4545 or ☎083 735 5227. Great for camel rides (daily 11.30am–4.30pm; R15); toddlers can ride with a parent in the same saddle, while kids aged 4 and up can ride on their own. Tues–Sun 10am–5pm.

Kirstenbosch National Botanical Gardens See p.143. Top of the list for a family outing, with extensive lawns for running about, trees and rocks to climb and streams to paddle in. There's no litter, no dogs, it's extremely safe and you can push a pram all over the walkways; it's also great for picnics or to have tea outdoors at the café. For older kids there are short waymarked walks.

Newlands Forest 9km south of the centre, off the M3 to Muizenberg. Gentle walks in and around pine forests and streams on the wooded southern slopes of Table Mountain, with a flattish pathway suitable for pushchairs. It's good for picnics if you want to get out of the city and don't have time to go further afield. Safest at weekends and in the afternoons when the joggers and dog walkers are out. Use the access point off the M3 signposted "Forestry Office", where there's ample parking. Dawn–dusk; free.

Silvermine Nature Reserve See p.158. A good place to see *fynbos* vegetation at close quarters, stroll around the pine-fringed lake and picnic with small children; however, it is exposed, and

not recommended in heavy winds or mist. For older children there are some mountain-top walks with relatively gentle gradients, which give spectacular views over both sides of the Peninsula.

Tokai Forest Arboretum See p.147. Walks and mountain biking, as well as a thatched tea shop with outdoor seating. It's also a great place for young children to explore, with logs to jump off and a gentle walk to a stream.

Gay Cape Town

Cape Town is South Africa's – and indeed, the African continent's – gay capital. The city has always had a vibrant gay culture, and is on its way to becoming an African Sydney, attracting gay travellers from across the country and the globe. Cape Town's **gay village**, with B&Bs, guesthouses, pubs, clubs, cruise bars and steam baths, is concentrated along the entertainment strips of Somerset Road and Main Road in the interconnected inner-city suburbs of Green Point, Sea Point and De Waterkant, adjacent to the centre. The *Pink Map*, published by A&C Maps (☎021 685 4260, ⓦwww.capeinfo.com), lists gay-friendly and gay-owned places in Cape Town and is distributed at the visitor centre in town, the one in the Clock Tower at the V&A Waterfront, as well as the airport and hotels; they'll also send a copy free anywhere in the world on request.

Cape Town hosts a hugely popular annual **gay party**, organized by Mother City Queer Projects (ⓦwww.mcqp.co.za) and held on the second Saturday night in December. People dress as outrageously as possible according to the official yearly theme (past ones have included "kitchen kitsch", "the twinkly sea project" and "farm fresh") and the event seeks to rival Sydney's Mardi Gras. There's also an annual **gay pride festival** in February (ⓦwww.capetownpride.co.za).

Besides the South African gay **websites** and resources listed in Basics (p.85), it's worth having a look at ⓦwww.gaynetcapetown.co.za, aimed specifically at the gay traveller to Cape Town. For information on what's on, you can check out the gay section of the Western Cape listings magazine *Cape Review*, or the gay supplement published on the last Thursday of the month in the *Cape Argus*, Cape Town's daily afternoon newspaper. While in town, be sure to tune into Bush Radio's gay programme, called "In the Pink" (Thurs 8–10pm; 89.5FM).

Clubs and bars

Bar Code 18 Cobern St, De Waterkant. A leather uniform and jeans bar that attracts an older crowd, *Bar Code* has a darkroom and hosts monthly underwear and fetish parties. Daily 9pm till late.

Bronx 35 Somerset Rd, Green Point. A hugely popular bar with a dance floor and loads of energy. Attracts a mixed crowd. Daily 8pm till late.

Café Manhattan 74 Waterkant St, De Waterkant. A restaurant-bar which serves affordable food on an outside terrace beneath oak trees. There's live music every Thursday and Sunday night. Straight-friendly. Daily 10am–late.

Confession and **Sliver** 27 Somerset Rd, Green Point. Start with cocktails and relatively sedate house music at *Sliver* and then head upstairs to *Confession* for wild progressive house sounds, and an outdoor balcony where you can catch your breath. Daily 9pm till late.

M-Bar and Lounge *Metropole Hotel*, 38 Long St. An upmarket gay hangout par excellence is this sophisticated lounge and bar in a stylishly appointed hotel. Cocktails served from midday until late. Straight-friendly.

On Broadway 21 Somerset Rd, De Waterkant ☎021 418 8338. A great restaurant-bar with Mediterranean-style food and cabaret. Top comic and satirist Pieter Dirk Uys performs every Mon night, there are feature shows Wed–Sun, and drag shows Tues & Sun. All shows start at 9pm and cost R45. You can turn up earlier for dinner, but booking is essential. Mixed crowd, and definitely straight-friendly. Daily 7pm till late.

Rosie's 125a Waterkant St, De Waterkant, opposite *Café Manhattan*. A small, intimate pool bar attracting bears and leather boys, with a restaurant that's a popular after-work drinking

spot. Open till late: Tues–Fri from 4pm, Sat & Sun from 2pm.

Sauna

The Hothouse 18 Jarvis St, Green Point. A luxurious pleasure complex featuring Jacuzzis, sauna, a sundeck with a superb view, a full bar with a limited food menu, video room, fireplace and satellite TV. Luxury cabins R90. Entrance R35–50 depending on days and times. Mon–Fri noon–2am, Sat & Sun 24hr.

Outdoor activities and sport

One of Cape Town's most remarkable features is the fact that it melds with the Table Mountain National Park, a patchwork of mountains, forests and coastline – all on the city's doorstep. There are few, if any, cities in the world where outdoor pursuits are so easily available and affordable. You can try activities such as sea kayaking, abseiling, rock climbing and scuba diving for little more than the price of a night out back home. A notable activity locally is **kloofing**, which basically entails jumping into a deep river from a cliff above. Alternatively, just let everyone else get on with it while you sink a few beers and watch the cricket, rugby or soccer.

Spectator sports

Cricket This is keenly followed by a wide range of Capetonians. The city's cricketing heart is at Newlands Cricket Ground (also known after its sponsors as Sahara Park), 61 Campground Rd, Newlands (☎021 657 2003). One of the most beautiful grounds in the world, Newlands nestles beneath venerable oaks and the elegant profile of Devil's Peak, and plays host to provincial, test and one-day international matches.

Rugby The Western Cape is one of the world's rugby heartlands, and the game is followed religiously here. Provincial, international and Super 12 contests are fought on the hallowed turf of Newlands Rugby Stadium, Boundary Rd, Newlands (☎021 659 4600).

Soccer Though soccer matches aren't as well attended as cricket or rugby, Cape Town soccer is burgeoning with talent and is likely to get a huge boost now that South Africa is hosting the 2010 World Cup. The dusty streets of the Cape Flats have produced superb young footballers such as Benni McCarthy (Porto, Ajax Amsterdam, Celta Vigo) and Quinton Fortune (Atletico Madrid, Manchester United). The most ambitious and professional club in the city is Ajax (pronounced "I-axe") Cape Town (ⓦwww.ajaxct.org), jointly owned by its Amsterdam namesake. The most exciting games to attend are those between a local outfit and one of the Soweto glamour teams, Orlando

Pirates and Kaizer Chiefs. Matches take place at Green Point Stadium, off Beach Rd; Athlone Stadium, off Klipfontein Rd, Athlone; and Newlands Rugby Stadium (see above).

Participation sports and outdoor activities

Abseiling and kloofing You can abseil off Table Mountain with Abseil Africa (☎021 424 4760) for around R250 for a half-day trip (excluding cable-car fee). They also do full-day trips twice a week that include kloofing, hiking, abseiling, breakfast, lunch and a light supper, for R550. For half-day and full-day abseiling and kloofing trips in the region's lesser-known rugged landscapes, call Leading Edge (☎021 785 4016 & 082 321 3821).

Bird-watching The peninsula's varied habitats attract nearly four hundred different species of birds. Good places for bird-watching include Lion's Head, Kirstenbosch Gardens and the Cape of Good Hope Nature Reserve, as well as at Kommetjie and Hout Bay; you can find out about knowledgeable guides through the Cape Bird Club (☎021 559 0726). For a more institutionalized experience, try the World of Birds in Hout Bay.

Cycling Cycling (for rental outlets see p.184) is popular all over the peninsula, and is a great way to take in the scenery. For information about the Cape Argus Pick 'n Pay Cycle Tour, the largest individually timed bike race in the world, contact Pedal Power Associates (℡ 021 689 8420, 🅦 www.cycletour.co.za), which also organizes fun rides from September to May.

Golf The Milnerton golf course, Bridge Rd, Milnerton (℡ 021 552 1047), is tucked in between a lagoon and Table Bay, and boasts classic views of Table Mountain. Other popular local courses are at Rondebosch Golf Club, Klipfontein Rd, Rondebosch (℡ 021 689 4176), and Westlake Golf Club, Westlake Ave, Lakeside (℡ 021 788 2020). Prices are around R160/R260 for 9/18 holes; clubs can be rented for R120 and caddy fees are R100. Booking is essential.

Gyms Virgin Active clubs are upmarket, well-appointed gyms dotted around the peninsula. Contact their call centre (℡ 0860 200 911, 🅦 www.virginactive.co.za) to find out where the nearest one is to you and the rates.

Horse-riding Horse Trail Safaris, *Indicator Lodge*, Skaapskraal Rd, Ottery (east of Wynberg across the M5; ℡ 082 575 5669), offers riding through the dunes to Strandfontein and the False Bay coast as well as overnight trips; Sleepy Hollow Horse Riding, Sleepy Hollow Lane, Noordhoek (℡ 021 789 2341) covers the spectacular Noordhoek Beach. Both charge around R140 for 1hr 30min.

Kayaking Real Cape Adventures (℡ 021 790 5611 or 082 556 2520, 🅦 www.seakayak.co.za) offer a range of half- or full-day sea-kayaking packages that include trips around Cape Point, to the penguin colony at Boulders Beach and around Hout Bay. The company organizes trips of several days around the peninsula, on which you spend nights at guesthouses, and longer safaris all over South Africa and even further north. Half-days start at R300 per person.

Kite-flying At the Waterfront, the Kite Shop, Shop 110, Ground Floor, Victoria Wharf (℡ 021 421 6231), sells kites of all shapes, colours and sizes.

Mountain biking Day Trippers (℡ 021 511 4766, 🅦 www.daytrippers.co.za) offers expert mountain-bike tours, including one from Scarborough to Cape Point. Downhill Adventures, corner of Kloof and Orange streets in the city centre (℡ 021 422 0388), offer similar tours starting from their shop; for experienced mountain bikers it has a Tokai forest tour (R450 half day).

Paragliding Cape Town has great air thermals for paragliding. If you're tempted to leap off any of the surrounding mountains then contact Para-Pax (℡ 082 881 4724), who offer tandem flights for R750. A picture of your horrified face will cost R100. Dress warmly.

Rock climbing Leading Edge (℡ 021 785 4016 or 082 321 3821) will take you to unusual and

unique locations depending on your ability. Packages are tailor-made, with a minimum of two people. You can learn how to rock climb up Table Mountain's famous facade with Leading Edge (see under "Abseiling") or the Cape Town School of Mountaineering (℡ 021 531 4290), which charges R750 for a two-day rock-climbing course, usually over weekends; it also guide's experienced climbers.

Sand boarding Downhill Adventures (℡ 021 422 0388) are the pioneers of this latest adventure sport. Boards, boots and bindings are provided, as well as expert instruction for beginners. Half-day (R350) and full-day (R500) trips take you to the finest slopes in the area.

Scuba diving While the Cape waters are cold, they're good for seeing wrecks, reefs and magnificent kelp forests. False Bay is invariably warmer than the Atlantic seaboard and thus preferred in winter. Short dives cost R150 from the shore, up to around R220 from a boat; expect to pay R350 to rent all the gear. An internationally recognized PADI open-water diving qualification can be completed for around R2000. To arrange scuba-diving courses and equipment rental, contact Orca Industries, corner Herschel Rd and Bowwood Rd, Claremont (℡ 021 671 9673); or the Scuba Shack, Shop 3, Glencairn Shopping Centre, Glencairn (℡ 021 782 6279).

Skydiving The ultimate way to see Table Mountain and Robben Island is from a tandem jump 3000m up; contact Skydive Cape Town (℡ 082 800 6290, 🅦 www.skydivecapetown.za.net; R1200).

Surfing Top surfing spots include Big Bay at Bloubergstrand (competitions are held here every summer), Llandudno, Muizenberg, Kalk Bay and Long Beach bear Kommetjie and Noordhoek. For information on competitions contact Surfing South Africa (℡ 021 674 2972), or check out 🅦 www.wavescape.co.za, the best place on the Web for everything you want to know about surfing in SA, including what the waves are up to. To learn to surf, contact Downhill Adventures (℡ 021 422 0388; half day R350, full day R500, with all equipment provided) or Gary's Surf School on Muizenberg beachfront (℡ 021 788 9839).

Swimming In the summer there are surf life-saver patrols on duty at Milnerton, Camps Bay, Llandudno, Muizenberg and Fish Hoek beaches. For pools, try Long Street Baths, Long St (℡ 021 400 3302; daily 7am–7pm), Cape Town's only public heated indoor pool; or Newlands Swimming Pool, corner of Main and San Souci roads, Newlands (℡ 021 467 4197; daily: April–Sept

9am–5pm; Oct–March 7am–6.30pm; R7, kids R4), an Olympic-sized chlorinated pool, which isn't heated (the water temperature drops to an unappealing 15°C in winter). The excellent Sea Point Swimming Pool at Beach Rd, Sea Point (☎021 434 3341; adults R7, kids R4), is an Olympic-sized chlorinated seawater pool.

Walking The best places for gentle strolls are Newlands Forest, up from Rhodes Memorial, and the beaches. For longer walks, head for anywhere on Table Mountain, Tokai Forest, Silvermine Nature Reserve or Cape Point Nature Reserve. Leading Edge (see under "Abseiling") does guided hikes up Table Mountain, geared to your level of fitness and with experienced guides (half day R350, full day R500 including a packed lunch). If you want to go further afield, they'll arrange multi-day trips where you can opt to have your bags carried or have food prepared for you.

Windsurfing and kitesurfing While most Cape-tonians moan about the howling southeaster in summer, it's handy if you're into windsurfing; not much happens in the winter, as the winds just aren't as good. Langebaan, a 75min drive north of town, is one of the best spots. For further help, contact Cape Sport Centre, Langebaan (☎022 772 1114, ⊛www.capesport.co.za), which also does kitesurfing. Prices for windsurfing start at R220 for 2hr for rigs, while instruction for beginners starts at R200; a 10hr kitesurfing package costs R1650 including gear and instruction. Otherwise, the place to go in Cape Town is Bloubergstrand. Blouberg Windsurf and Leisure (☎021 554 1663 or 082 420 2990, ⊜blouwind@mweb.co.za) rents equipment, cars with racks and has long-term accommodation at Bloubergstrand, as well as being able to offer general advice to its clients, such as information on which airlines offer free carriage of windsurfing equipment.

Shopping

The **V&A Waterfront** is the city's most popular shopping venue, with good reason: it has a vast range of shops, the setting on the harbour is lovely and there's a huge choice of places to eat and drink when you want to rest your feet – but expect to pay above the odds for everything. The city centre also offers variety and, for some people's taste, a grittier and more interesting venue for browsing, especially if you're looking for collectables, antiques and secondhand books. Cape Town's suburbanites tend to do their shopping at the upmarket Cavendish Square Mall in **Claremont** or one of many other shopping centres. If you're staying in the inner-city suburbs of Green Point and Sea Point, adjacent to the V&A Waterfront, you'll find supermarkets and other functional shops along Main Road, and the City Bowl suburbs are served by the Gardens Shopping Centre. There are other smaller shopping areas dotted about the other suburbs.

Shopping hours have traditionally been Monday to Friday 8.30am to 5pm, and Saturday until 1pm, though lots of supermarkets, bookshops and other specialist outlets are now open beyond 5pm and also on Sundays.

Malls and shopping centres

South African shopping tends to follow an American model, with **malls** where you can browse in a bookshop as well as bank, buy clothes and groceries and go to the movies. Malls always have several coffee shops and restaurants.

Blue Route Mall Tokai Rd, Tokai. A functional single-storey centre with branches of Checkers Hyper and Woolworths, handy if you're staying in Constantia or along the False Bay. Mon–Fri 9am–5.30pm, Sat & Sun 9am–5pm.

Cavendish Square Claremont station, Vineyard Rd, Claremont. An upmarket multistorey complex, the major shopping focus for the southern

suburbs. Mon–Thurs & Sat 9am–6pm, Fri 9am–9pm, Sun 10am–4pm.

Constantia Village Shopping Centre Main Rd, Constantia. A small exclusive mall including two large supermarkets. Mon–Fri 9am–5pm, Sat 9am–2pm.

Gardens Shopping Centre Mill St, Gardens. Small shopping mall in the City Bowl, very close to the Company's Gardens and city centre, with a large supermarket, excellent deli and most of the shops you'll need. Mon–Fri 9am–6pm, Sat 9am–3pm; some shops also Sun 10am–2pm.

V&A Waterfront It would be possible to visit Cape Town and never leave the Waterfront complex, which has a vast range of upmarket shops packed into the Victoria Wharf Shopping Centre, including outlets of all the major South African chains, selling books, clothes, food and crafts. Mon–Sat 9am–9pm, Sun 10am–9pm.

Arts and crafts

Cape Town is not known for its indigenous **arts and crafts** in the way that Durban is, and many of the goods you'll buy here are from elsewhere in Africa, especially Zimbabwe and Zambia. There are several outlets in the city centre and the V&A Waterfront, but you'll often pick up the same arts and crafts for a lot less money at the pavement **markets** scattered around town. Don't expect exotic West African-style markets, however; Cape Town's markets are more like European or North American flea markets.

Craft shops

Africa Nova Cape Quarter, Dixon St, De Waterkant ☎021 425 5123. A better-than-average selection of ethnic crafts and curios as well as contemporary African textiles and artwork, with an emphasis on the individual and handmade. Mon–Fri 9am–5pm, Sat & Sun 10am–2pm.

African Image Branches at the corner of Church and Burg streets (☎021 423 8385); and Shop 6228, Victoria Wharf, V&A Waterfront (☎021 419 0382). One of the best places for authentic traditional and contemporary African arts and crafts, from fabrics and antique sculpture to beadwork, but goods are a little overpriced. Church & Burg branch Mon–Fri 9am–5pm, Sat 9am–1.30pm; Waterfront branch daily 9am–9pm.

Clementina Ceramics 20 Main Rd, Kalk Bay ☎021 788 8718. Unique contemporary South African ceramics. Tues–Sun 10am–5pm.

Ethno Bongo Mainstream Shopping Centre, Main Rd, Hout Bay ☎021 790 0802. A charming shop in the main shopping centre in Hout Bay, selling wonderful and well-priced crafts, jewellery and accessories made from recycled metal and wood, and also quirky kaftans and ethnic clothing – highly recommended for unique gifts and souvenirs. Mon–Fri 9.30am–5.30pm, Sat 9.30am–4pm, Sun 10am–2pm.

Kalk Bay Gallery 62 Main Rd, Kalk Bay ☎021 788 1674. Graphics, engravings as well as African art and artefacts – good value, with the chance of picking up something very collectible. Mon–Fri 9am–5pm, Sat & Sun 9.30am–5pm.

Rose Korber Art Consultancy 48 Sedgemoor Rd, Camps Bay ☎021 438 9152. This should be the first stop for the serious collector, with an exceptional selection of contemporary art and craft, including ceramics and beadwork from around the continent. Mon–Fri 9am–5pm.

Yellow Door Upper floor, Gardens Centre, Gardens ☎021 465 4702. One of the largest and best selections of local crafts and design, including ceramics, fabrics, jewellery, basketry, metalwork and interior decor. Mon–Fri 9am–6pm, Sat 9am–4pm, Sun 10am–2pm.

Markets

Cape Town Station Forecourt, Adderley St. Thronging ranks of market traders selling African crafts, as well as radios and leather goods. Not principally aimed at tourists, so it's pretty authentic. Mon–Fri 8am–5pm, Sat 8am–2pm.

Constantia Craft Market Alphen Common, corner of Spaanschemat River and Ladies Mile roads, Constantia. Sizeable outdoor flea market where you can pick up good local crafts and items from around the continent, ride a camel or a pony and have a cup of tea. First & last Sat & first Sun of the month.

Green Point Market Western Blvd, Green Point. A massive open-air market displaying everything from African arts and crafts to plants, car parts, and anything home made. Sun 9am–4pm.

Greenmarket Square Burg St. Open-air market where you can pick up knick-knacks, and the best place in town for colourful handmade Cape Town beachwear, from T-shirts to shorts and sandals. Mon–Fri 8am–5pm, Sat 8am–2pm.

The Pan African Market 76 Long St. A multicultural hothouse of township and contemporary art, artefacts, curios and crafts. There's music, a café specializing in African cuisine, a bookshop, a Cameroonian hairbraider and a West African tailor. Mon–Fri 9am–5pm, Sat 9am–3pm.

The Red Shed Craft Workshop Victoria Wharf, V&A Waterfront. A market where some two dozen craftworkers make and sell ceramics, textiles, candles and jewellery, and where you can see glass-blowers at work. Mon–Sat 9am–9pm, Sun 10am–9pm.

Sivuyile Craft Centre On the corner of NY1 and NY4, Guguletu, Cape Flats. Township market attached to an information centre close to the N2 freeway, where bead-workers, wire-workers and

other artists make traditional and modern crafts. Mon–Fri 8am–5pm, Sat 9am–2pm.

Victoria Rd Market Camps Bay. Carvings, beads, fabrics and baskets sold from a market spectacularly sited on a clifftop overlooking the Atlantic. Daily.

Books

South Africa produces a lot of **books** given the size of its reading population: you'll find good locally published novels and endless volumes on history, politics and natural history. For new books there are some pleasant places in the suburbs or at the Waterfront to browse for half an hour, while Upper Long Street has over half a dozen secondhand book and specialist comic shops in close proximity, interspersed with congenial cafés.

Clarke's Bookshop 211 Long St ☎021 423 5739. The best place in Cape Town for South African books, with a huge selection of local titles covering literature, history, politics, natural history and the arts, plus very well-informed staff. They also deal in collectors' editions of South African books. Mon–Fri 9am–5pm, Sat 9am–1pm.

Exclusive Books Branches at Victoria Wharf, V&A Waterfront ☎021 419 0905 (Mon–Fri 9am–10.30pm, Sat 9am–11pm, Sun 10am –9pm); Lower Mall, Cavendish Square, Clare-mont (☎021 674 3030; Mon–Thurs 9am–9pm, Fri & Sat 9am–10.30pm, Sun 9.30am–9pm); Constantia Village Shopping Centre, Main Rd, Constantia (☎021 794 7800; Mon–Sat 9am–8pm, Sun 9am–5pm). A friendly bookshop,

ideal for browsing; the reasonably well-stocked shelves include magazines and a wide choice of coffee-table books on Cape Town and South African topics.

Kirstenbosch Shop Kirstenbosch National Botanical Gardens ☎021 762 2510. A good selection of natural-history books, field guides and travel guides covering Southern Africa, as well as a range of titles for kids. You won't need a gardens ticket to browse. Daily 9am–7pm.

The Travellers Bookshop King's Warehouse, Victoria Wharf, V&A Waterfront ☎021 425 6880. Cape Town's only specialist travel bookshop stocks a decent range of titles, mainly about South Africa and especially the Cape, covering history, politics, natural history and the arts. Daily 9am–9pm.

Music

Look & Listen, Shop F14, Upper Level, Cavendish Square, Claremont (☎021 683 1810; daily 9am–10.30pm) is Cape Town's largest music store, with a selection of all kinds of sounds, including good local jazz and a respectable selection from all over the African continent. One of the best ranges of African music in the city is available at CD Warehouse, V&A Waterfront (next to the *V&A Hotel*; ☎021 425 6300). Also centrally located, African Music Store at 90a Long St (☎021 426 0867; Mon–Fri 9am–5pm, Sat 9am–2pm) is a small shop specializing in African music. The ubiquitous chains such as CNA and Musica tend to stock pretty unadventurous selections of mainly British and American sounds.

Food and provisions

Self-catering is the cheapest way to eat in Cape Town, and can also be good fun. **Braais** happen anywhere with any excuse, and there are countless places on beaches, in the forests or up Table Mountain where you can enjoy a terrific **picnic**. There are some excellent (if pricey) **delicatessens**, several of which are strung along Main Road, Green Point and Sea Point. You'll also find delicious food and some unusual fruit and vegetables at the more sophisticated **farm stalls**. The larger branches of the better **supermarkets** have fishmonger counters where you can buy fresh fish, though by far the most atmospheric places to buy seafood are the Hout Bay and Kalk Bay harbours (see p.153 & p.158 respectively).

Supermarkets tend to have decent **wine** at competitive prices, but for more interesting labels, there are some first-rate specialist wine merchants. Alcohol is not sold at retail outlets on a Sunday.

Supermarkets

Pick 'n Pay V&A Waterfront (daily 9am–8pm); Gardens Shopping Centre, Mill St, Gardens (Mon–Thurs 8am–7pm, Fri 8am–9pm, Sat 8am–5pm, Sun 9am–2pm); Main Rd, Camps Bay (daily 9am–7pm); Main Rd, Observatory (Mon–Thurs 7am–8.30pm, Fri & Sat 7am–10pm, Sun 8am–2pm); corner Main Rd and Campground Rd, Claremont (Mon–Thurs 8am–6pm, Fri 8am–7pm, Sat 8am–4pm, Sun 9am–2pm); Blue Route Mall, Tokai (Mon–Thurs 8.30am–6pm, Fri 8.30am–7pm, Sat 8am–2pm, Sun 9am–2pm); Constantia Village, Main Rd, Constantia (Mon–Fri 8am–8pm, Sat 8am–5pm, Sun 9am–4pm). One of the best places for groceries, considerably larger and cheaper than Woolworths, with a good deli counter and a choice of prepared meals, among which you'll find their excellent-value ready-grilled whole chickens.

Woolworths Adderley St (Mon–Fri 8.30am–5.30pm, Sat 8am–2pm); V&A Waterfront (daily 9am–9pm); Cavendish Square Mall, Claremont (Mon–Thurs 9am–6pm, Fri 8.30am–8pm, Sat 8am–6pm, Sun 9am–5pm); Blue Route Mall, Tokai (Mon–Thurs 9am–5.30pm, Fri 8.30am–7pm, Sat 8.30am–5pm, Sun 9am–2pm); Constantia Village, Main Rd, Constantia (Mon–Thurs 8.30am–7pm, Fri 8am–8pm, Sat 8.30am–6pm, Sun 9am–5pm). Excellent for quality fast-cook meals, fresh produce and cold foods, such as olives, hummus and various Mediterranean dips, but it can be pricey.

Delis and farm stalls

Andiamo Cape Quarter, Dixon St, De Waterkant. Italian Deli where you can select from meats, cheeses, salads, dips, meze and fresh breads to take on your mountain walk. Phone ahead and they'll put the picnic together for you. Daily 9am–11pm.

The Barnyard Farm Stall Steenberg Rd, adjacent to the well-signposted Steenberg Wine Estate, Tokai ☎021 712 6934. One of Cape Town's nicest farm stalls, with a selection of high-class cheeses, breads, home-baked cakes, wines, patés, coffee beans and many other delights. There's also the major attraction of a very good outdoor café with a children's playground attached. A good stop if you're doing the Constantia winelands. Daily 8.30am–5.30pm.

Giovanni's 103 Main Rd, Green Point. Excellent breads and delicious Italian foods to take away

and – if temptation overcomes you – there's always the option of sitting down for a coffee and a snack. Daily 8.30am–9pm.

Melissa's 94 Kloof St, Gardens; and Constantia Village. Highly delectable imported and local specialities, with the option of eating in. Gardens Mon–Fri 7.30am–8pm, Sat & Sun 8am–9pm; Constantia 7.30am–7pm, Sat & Sun 8am–6pm.

New York Bagel Deli 51 Regent Rd, Sea Point. The best bagels in town with a great selection of Eastern European Jewish fillings – salt beef, gherkins, chopped liver and pickled herring – and an array of delicious pastries. Daily 7am–9pm.

Fresh fish

Fish Market Mariner's Wharf, Hout Bay Harbour. Fresh seafood from South Africa's original waterfront emporium, but slicker and less atmospheric than Kalk Bay Harbour. Mon–Fri 9am–5.30pm, Sat & Sun 9am–6pm.

Kalk Bay Harbour Harbourside, Kalk Bay. Buy fresh fish directly from the fishermen and have it gutted and scaled on the spot. Your best bet is lunchtime, especially at weekends.

Wine

Caroline's Fine Wines 15 Long St ☎021 419 8984; and King's Warehouse, V&A Waterfront ☎021 425 5701. Caroline Rillema has been in the wine business since 1979 and offers daily tastings of the Cape's finest and most exclusive wines. Mon–Fri 9am–5pm, Waterfront also Sat 9am–5pm.

Vaughan Johnson's Dock Rd, V&A Waterfront ☎021 419 2121. One of Cape Town's best-known wine shops, which has a huge range of labels from all over the country, though it can be a bit pricey. Mon–Fri 9am–6pm, Sat 9am–5pm, Sun 10am–5pm.

Wine Concepts 50 Kloof St; and Castle Building, on the corner of Kildare Rd and Main Rd, Newlands. An excellent selection of South African and foreign wines from a knowledgeable and helpful outfit. Mon–Thurs 9am–7pm, Fri 9am–8pm, Sat 9am–5pm.

Woolworths See above. The own-label wines of South Africa's upmarket supermarket chain have come a long way since the days when you'd sneakily decant them so no one would know their source. Cognoscenti now happily flaunt these competitively priced wines.

Cape Town is South Africa's **holism** capital. The Fields Health Store at 84 Kloof Street, Gardens (℡021 423 9587), sells health and beauty products, with a juice bar serving a daily vegetarian lunch buffet and cakes. For homeopathic and herbal remedies try Natural Remedies, Pearce Street, Claremont (℡021 674 1692; Mon–Fri 9am–5pm, Sat 8.30am–1pm), or the central White's Chemist, 61 Plein Street (℡021 465 3332; Mon–Fri 7.30am–5pm, Sat 8am–12.30pm).

The best publications for more details are *Link-Up*, a free listings magazine, and the glossier *Odyssey*, which is also the place to track down sources of southern African crystals, gemstones and essential oils – disappointingly, though, there are few oils from Cape plants except for geraniums. Both are available from health-food shops and alternative health venues.

Listings

Airlines 1Time ℡0861 345 345; British Airways ℡0860 011 747; KLM Royal Dutch Airlines ℡0860 247 747; Kulula.com ℡0861 585 852; Lufthansa ℡021 415 3535; Nationwide ℡021 936 2050; Olympic Airways ℡021 419 2502; Qantas ℡011 441 8550; SA Airlink ℡021 936 1111; South African Airways ℡021 936 1111; Virgin Atlantic ℡011 340 3400.

American Express Lost Cards ℡0800 110 0929; traveller's cheque queries ℡0800 990 123.

Banks and exchange Main branches with ATMs are easy to find in the shopping areas of the city centre, the middle-class suburbs and at the Waterfront. For foreign-exchange transactions outside normal banking hours, try one of the following: American Express, Shop 11a, Alfred Mall, Waterfront (Mon–Fri 9am–7pm, Sat 9am–5pm, Sun 9am–5pm); Rennies Foreign Exchange, Victoria Wharf, V&A Waterfront (Mon–Sat 9am–9pm, Sun 10am–9pm); or Master Currencies, Cape Town International Airport (Mon–Sun 6.30am–10pm).

Bike rental Mountain bikes are available from Rent 'n' Ride, 243 Main Rd, Three Anchor Bay (℡021 434 2382; R85 a day including helmet and lock; R1000 credit card deposit required). Downhill Adventures (℡021 422 0388, ⓦwww .downhilladventures.co.za) has similar rentals for R100 for 24hr, and offers seven days' rental for the price of six.

Car rental Aroundaboutcars (℡0860 422 4022, ⓦwww.aroundaboutcars.com) is an independent national rental company based in Cape Town and offering great package deals and flexible pricing; the rate can be as low as R150 per day with unlimited mileage. It offers one-way rental (to drive down the Garden Route and fly back from

Port Elizabeth, for example), but as with all rental agencies, there is an additional charge for this. Another inexpensive option is Vineyard Car Hire (℡021 761 0671, ⓔvineyardcarhire@iafrica. com), which rents out vehicles for as little as R180 a day (including 200km per day free) for three to six days. Allen's Car Hire (℡021 701 8844) is reasonable, reliable and of a similar price. Staff can deliver a car to you, or meet you at the airport when you land. For details of the larger, national agencies, see Basics, p.57. To try to find the best deal, either pick up one of the brochures at Cape Town Tourism office or look in the *Yellow Pages*.

Consulates Canada, 60 St George's Mall ℡021 423 5240; Germany, St Martini Gardens, Queen Victoria St ℡021 464 3000; UK, Southern Life Centre, 8 Riebeeck St ℡021 405 2400; USA, 4th floor, Broadway Centre, Heerengracht ℡021 421 4280. The embassies for most countries are in Pretoria.

Dental care Dentists, listed in the *Yellow Pages* telephone directory, are well up to British and North American standards, and generally less expensive.

Emergencies See Basics, p.89.

Hospitals and doctors The largest state hospital is Groote Schuur, Hospital Drive, Observatory (℡021 404 9111), just off the M3. Nearer the centre and convenient for the City Bowl and Atlantic seaboard is Somerset Hospital, Beach Rd, Mouille Point (℡021 402 6911); it has outpatient and emergency departments, although it's generally overcrowded, understaffed and seemingly under-equipped. If you have medical insurance you might prefer to be treated at one of the well-staffed, efficient and well-equipped private hospitals listed in the phone directory. The two largest hospital groups are the Netcare (emergency response ☎ 082 911) and Medi-Clinic chains, with hospitals all over the Cape Peninsula. Most central of Netcare's hospitals is the Christiaan Barnard Memorial Hospital, 181 Longmarket Street (☎ 021 480 6111) – you'll get to see a doctor quickly and costs are not excessive.

Laundry Most backpacker hostels have coin-operated washing machines, while guesthouses, hotels and B&Bs will usually offer a laundry service for a charge. There are laundries offering service washes in the city centre and most suburban areas.

Left luggage Virtually every backpacker hostel provides luggage storage facilities, and most other accommodation will be happy to take care of your luggage for a day or two.

Mobile phone rental Available from Cellucity, Shop 6193, V&A Waterfront (☎ 021 418 1306) for around R30 per day for the handset, with calls charged at R2.70/min. You'll need to provide your credit card details. Rentals can also be done at the airport when you arrive.

Pharmacies Chemists with extended opening hours include: Hypermed Pharmacy, corner York and Main roads, Green Point (☎ 021 434 1414; Mon–Fri

8.30am–9pm, Sat & Sun 9am–9pm); Sunset Pharmacy, Sea Point Medical Centre, Kloof Rd, Sea Point (☎ 021 434 3333; daily 8.30am–9pm); and Tamboerskloof Pharmacy, 16 Kloof Nek Rd, Tamboerskloof (☎ 021 424 4450; daily 9am–9pm).

Police The central station is on Caledon Square, Buitenkant St ☎ 021 467 8000.

Post office The main branch, on Parliament St, (Mon, Tues, Thurs & Fri 8am–4.30pm, Wed 8.30am–4.30pm, Sat 8am–noon), has a poste restante and enquiry desk.

Taxis There are a number of reliable companies, including Marine Taxi Hire (☎ 021 434 0434), Sea Point Radio Taxis (☎ 021 434 4444), and Unicab (☎ 021 448 1720).

Ticket agencies Computicket (☎ 083 915 8000, ⓦ www.computicket.co.za) books most theatre, cinema and sporting events, as well as airline and bus tickets.

Travel agents The largest travel franchise in the country is Sure Travel, which has about two dozen offices across Cape Town (call ☎ 0800 221 656 for the nearest); try also One World Travel Centre, 309 Long St (☎ 021 423 0777). Cape Town Tourism can also book trips (see p.103).

Travel details

Trains

Cape Town to: Bloemfontein (1 weekly; 23hr); Durban (1 weekly; 36hr 25min); Johannesburg (1 daily; 24hr 55min); Kimberley (1 daily; 16hr 30min); Pietermaritzburg (every Mon; 34hr); Pretoria (1 daily; 26hr 20min).

Buses

Cape Town to: Bloemfontein (3 daily; 13hr); Calvinia (1 weekly; 6hr 30min); Cradock (1 daily; 10hr); Durban (3 daily; 20hr); East London (3 daily; 15hr 40 min); George (4 daily; 6hr); Graaff-Reinet (1–2 daily; 9hr); Grahamstown (1 daily; 12hr 25min); Johannesburg (4 daily; 17hr); Kimberley (1 daily except Wed; 11hr 45min); Knysna (4 daily; 6hr 50min); Montagu (3 weekly; 4hr); Mossel Bay (4 daily; 5hr 15min); Oudtshoorn (3 weekly; 6hr 15min); Paarl (4 weekly; 1hr 30min); Pietermaritzburg (3 daily; 18hr 40min); Plettenberg Bay (4 daily; 7hr 30min); Port Elizabeth (4 daily; 10hr); Pretoria (4 daily; 18hr); Sedgefield (1 daily; 6hr 45min); Springbok (6 weekly; 6hr 30min); Stellenbosch (1–2 daily; 1hr); Storms River (4 daily; 10hr 10min); Umtata (1 daily; 18hr); Upington

(5 weekly; 10hr 30min); Vanrhynsdorp (1 daily; 5hr); Wilderness (4 daily; 6hr 30min); Windhoek (Namibia; 4 weekly; 16hr 30min).

Baz buses

All services below operate daily. For details of onward services from Port Elizabeth, see p.456.
Cape Town to: Bot River (1hr 30min); George (7hr; change here for shuttle bus to Oudtshoorn); Jeffrey's Bay (12hr 15min); Knysna (8hr 30min); Mossel Bay (6hr); Nature's Valley (10hr); Plettenberg Bay (9hr 30min); Port Elizabeth (13hr 30min); Storms River (10hr 30min); Swellendam (3hr); Wilderness (7hr 30min).

Domestic flights

Cape Town to: Bloemfontein (2–3 daily; 1hr 35min); Durban (10 daily; 2hr); East London (4 daily; 2hr); George (3–4 daily; 1hr); Hoedspruit (1 daily; 3hr); Johannesburg (16 daily; 2hr); Kimberley (1 daily; 2hr); Nelspruit (1 daily; 2hr 15min); Port Elizabeth (4 daily; 1hr 30min); Sun City (1 daily; 2hr); Upington (6 weekly; 1hr 50min); Walvis Bay (2 weekly; 2hr); Windhoek (5 weekly; 5hr 25min).

The Western Cape

CHAPTER 2 # Highlights

✱ **The Winelands** Quaff fine vintages on some of South Africa's most beautiful wine estates. See p.192

✱ **Route 62** This mountainous inland route takes you through dozy villages, across spectacular passes and through semi-desert. See p.211

✱ **De Hoop Nature Reserve** Massive dunes and edge-to-edge whales in season make this arguably the most exciting provincial nature reserve in the county. See p.253

✱ **Ocean safaris** Learn about whales and dolphins on an excursion around Plettenberg Bay. See p.282

✱ **Canopy Tour** Swing from tree to tree among the highest boughs of the Tsitsikamma Forest's arboreal giants. See p.288

✱ **Storms River Mouth** One of the most dramatic sections of coast, where hillside forests drop away to rocky coastline and the Storms River surges out of a gorge into the thundering ocean. See p.288

✱ **Seafood** Feast on endless courses of fish, lobster and whatever else the ocean yields at one of the casual beachside eating places along the West Coast. See p.291

✱ **Oudrif** An exceptional and remote retreat lodge on the edge of a gorge in the dry and dramatic redstone back country of the Cederberg. See p.305

△ Cape Dutch architecture

The Western Cape

The most mountainous and arguably the most beautiful of South Africa's provinces, the **Western Cape** is also the most popular area of the country for foreign tourists. Curiously, it's also the least African province. Visitors spend weeks here without exhausting its attractions, but frequently leave slightly disappointed, never having quite experienced an African beat. Of South Africa's nine provinces, only the Western Cape and the Northern Cape don't have an African majority; one person in five here is African, and the largest community, making up 55 percent of the population, are coloureds – people of mixed race descended from white settlers, indigenous Khoisan people and slaves from the East. Although the Western Cape appears to conform more closely to the First World than any other part of the country, the impression is strictly superficial. Beneath the prosperous feel of the Winelands and the Garden Route lies a reality of Third World poverty in **squatter camps** on the outskirts of well-to-do towns, and on some farms where nineteenth-century labour practices prevail, despite the end of apartheid.

Nevertheless, you can't fail to be moved by the sensuous physical beauty of the province's mountains, valleys and beaches. The **Winelands**, less than an hour from Cape Town, give full reign to the sybaritic pleasures of eating, drinking and visual feasting. Dutch colonial heritage reaches its peak in this region of gabled homesteads sitting among vineyards against a backdrop of slaty crags.

The best-known feature of the Western Cape is the **Garden Route**, a drive along the N2 that technically begins at **Mossel Bay**, where the freeway hits the coast, and continues east for 185km to **Storms River**. In reality it is taken as part of a journey between Cape Town and Port Elizabeth (see p.369), simply because these are the easiest places to catch flights and to pick up and drop off rental cars. The Garden Route proper can be driven in half a day, but to cover it so quickly would mean missing its essence, which can be found off the road in its coastal towns, lagoons, mountains and ancient forests, the highlight being the **Tsitsikamma National Park**, where the dark Storms River opens spectacularly into the Indian Ocean. **Public transport** along the Garden Route is better than anywhere in the country, partly because the route is a single stretch of freeway, and tour operators along the way have begun turning it into the country's most concentrated strip for packaged **adventure sports** and **outdoor activities**.

To the east of the Winelands, the **Breede River Valley** is a region usually bypassed along the N1 en route to Johannesburg, but featuring among its faceless fruit-farming towns some hideaways, such as Greyton and McGregor,

De Aar

N10

Carnarvon

R384

R63

R63

R308

R353

R356

R381

Victoria West

N12

R63

N1

C A P E

G R E A T   K A R O O

Three Sisters

R63

R356

KAROO NATIONAL PARK

Beaufort West

WITTEBERG

GROOTRIVI

N9

Leeu-Gamka

R332

Laingsburg

N1

N12

SWARTBERG

E A S T E R N

C A P E

BAVIAANSKLOOF MOUNTAINS

R327

R329

Prince Albert

Swartberg Pass

Meringspoort Pass

R407

R332

GROENFONTEIN VALLEY

Cango Caves

De Rust

R341

Uniondale

KOUGA MOUNTAINS

T E R N   C A P E

K A R O O

Calitzdorp

Oudtshoorn

R62

R323

R327

R328

N12

OUTENIQUA MOUNTAINS

N9

WILDERNESS NATIONAL PARK

R62

TSITSIKAMMA MOUNTAINS

Tradouws Pass

LANGEBERG

Gourits

George

Sedgefield

Knysna

N2

Keurbooms

Bloukrans

Storms

Port Elizabeth

Riversdale

N2

OVERBERG

Mossel Bay

Plettenberg Bay

TSITSIKAMMA NATIONAL PARK

I N D I A N   O C E A N

N

0 ──────── 100 km

favoured by Capetonians as weekend retreats. Though the region has been almost totally neglected by visitors in the past, some creative marketing has now literally put it on the map as the **Route 62**, most of which consists of the intriguing R62 back road tracing its way through the interior, linking **Little Karoo** towns between Cape Town and Port Elizabeth. The timeless landscapes of the Little Karoo, the curtain-raiser to the semi-desert covering one-third of South Africa's surface, is nowhere more rewarding nor more easily accessed than here. Less visited than it deserves, the Little Karoo is skirted by the N1 to the north and the N2 to the south, and offers a succession of dramatic – sometimes hair-raising – **passes** switch-backing across one mountain range after another.

The **Overberg** – roughly the area between **Arniston** and **Mossel Bay** along the coast, and as far inland as Swellendam – is another region that remains hidden behind the mountains during a hasty journey through. West of here, the **Whale Coast**, an angry stretch of Indian Ocean that has claimed hundreds of ships, is known for being the best area in the country for shore-based **whale-watching**, and there are a couple of pleasant coastal towns off the main routes along here. North of Cape Town, the less popular, remote and windswept **West Coast** is usually explored during the wild-flower months of August and September, when visitors converge on its centrepiece, the **West Coast National Park**. Its other major draw, 200km north of Cape Town on the N7, is the **Cederberg** mountain range, a rocky wilderness with hikes and hidden rock-art sites.

Apart from the annual explosion of wild flowers in the north, the Western Cape, as South Africa's **fynbos** region, really scores on wilderness and flora. The plants you'll glimpse from afar all along the coast and up every mountainside look like a nondescript grey-green blur of vegetation, but on closer examination reveal a rich kingdom of delicate flowering species rivalling the Amazon rainforest for biodiversity. Several national parks and nature reserves make excellent places to explore *fynbos*, as do all the hikes mentioned in this chapter, but you shouldn't expect to see much African wildlife here, apart from a few game sanctuaries off the Garden Route. Though most reserves have a few zebra or antelope, the big game disappeared many years ago – reflecting the fact that South Africa's longest-colonized province was also the first to taste the destructive power of firearms. By the same means, indigenous **Khoikhoi and San people** were virtually extinguished in the nineteenth century and **Africans** kept at a distance, some 1000km away on the "Eastern Frontier", which accounts for their relatively small numbers in the Western Cape.

The Winelands

South Africa has over a dozen recognized wine routes extending to the Karoo and way into the Northern Cape, but the area known as the **Winelands** is restricted to the oldest wineries outside the Cape Peninsula, within a sixty-kilometre radius of Cape Town. The district contains the earliest European settlements at Stellenbosch, Paarl, Franschhoek and Somerset West, each with

Tackling the Winelands

With over one hundred estates in the **Winelands**, the big question is which ones to visit. The wineries in our selection were chosen not primarily because they produce the best wine (although some are in the first rank), but for general interest – beautiful architecture or scenery – or because they are entertaining in some way. When planning your trip, bear in mind that although all the wineries offer tastings, many offer a lot more, such as restaurants, picnics and horse-riding. Choose an area to explore and don't try to visit too many wineries in a day unless you want to return home in a dizzy haze. Note also that most wineries are **closed on Sundays**.

Wine tasting and buying are supposed to be fun, so don't take them too seriously. If you aren't a wine buff, you'll often find staff at tasting rooms are happy to talk you through a wine, which can be especially interesting once you begin to pick up the characteristics of different wines. Most estates charge a fee for a wine-tasting session (typically R2–8) and some only have tastings at specific times; see the individual accounts for more details.

If you plan on anything more than the briefest of tours, think about buying the annually updated *John Platter's South African Wine Guide* (ⓦwww.platteronline .com), which provides ratings of the produce of every winery in the country. *Wine* magazine, published every month and available from all newsagents, has useful features on wineries, places to eat, wine reviews, information on latest bottlings and a diary of events.

Recommended estates

Boschendal Estate Franschhoek (see p.209). The best-organized estate aimed at tourists, offering conducted tours, beautiful buildings, shops and a choice of restaurants.

Cabrière Estate Franschhoek (see p.209). Here you can see the most eccentric uncorking using sabrage – slicing clean through the neck of a bubbly bottle with a sabre.

Delaire Stellenbosch (see p.200). Offering the best mountain view across the Helshoogte Pass.

Fairview Estate Paarl (see p.205). A great family venue with a famous goat tower, peacocks, cheese and wine.

La Motte Estate Franschhoek (see p.210). The best tasting room, decorated with marble, glass and oak barrels.

Rhebokskloof Estate Paarl (see p.205). This estate offers the trendiest restaurant, overlooking a lake of swans.

Rustenberg Estate Stellenbosch (see p.199). The most bucolic setting, with a historic gabled milking shed.

Vergelegen Somerset West (see p.200). The estate that has it all: fabulous buildings, a small museum, beautiful gardens, good wines to taste and a choice of restaurants.

its own **wine route**, on which you travel from one estate to the next to taste the wines. On the hillsides and in the valleys around these towns you'll find a flawless blending of traditional Cape Dutch **architecture** with the landscape. The Winelands are best covered in a car, as half the pleasure is the drive through the countryside; without your own transport, you could take a day-trip to the Winelands with one of several Cape Town-based companies (see p.106).

The most satisfying of the Wineland towns is **Stellenbosch**, which enjoys an easy elegance, beautiful streetscapes, a couple of decent museums and plenty of visitor facilities. One of the region's scenic highlights is the drive along the R310 through the **Helshoogte Pass** between Stellenbosch and **Paarl**. The workaday farming town of the region, Paarl is credited as the place where Afrikaans first sprang to recognition, and has an Afrikaans language monument and a museum to honour the fact. Smallest of the Wineland towns, with a rural yet sophisticated feel, **Franschhoek** has the most magnificent setting at the head of a narrow valley, and has established itself as the culinary capital of the Cape. By contrast, the sprawling town of **Somerset West** has only one drawcard, but it's an outstanding one – **Vergelegen**, by far the most stunning of all the Wineland estates, which can be tacked onto a tour of the Stellenbosch wine route.

Summer is the best time to visit, when days are longer (as are opening hours), the vines are in leaf and there's activity at the wineries. In winter the wine has been made and there are fewer cellar tours, though the landscape is still gorgeous, and many upmarket guesthouses sell their rooms at half-price. Several estates offer lunches, while some allow picnics in their grounds – a great idea if you're travelling with children or simply want to drink in the mountainous views in a bucolic haze.

Stellenbosch

Dappled avenues of three-century-old oaks are the defining feature of **STELLENBOSCH**, 46km east of Cape Town – a fact reflected in its Afrikaans nickname Die Eikestad (the oak city). Street frontages of the same vintage, sidewalk cafés, water furrows and a European town layout centred on the Braak, a large village green, add up to a well-rooted urban texture that invites casual exploration. The city is the undisputed heart of the Winelands, having more urban attractions than either Paarl or Franschhoek, while at the same time being at the hub of the largest and oldest of the Cape **wine routes**.

The city is also home to Stellenbosch University, Afrikanerdom's most prestigious educational institution, which does something to enliven the atmosphere. But even the heady promise of plentiful alcohol and thousands of students haven't changed the fact that at heart this is a conservative place, which was once the intellectual engine room of apartheid, and fostered the likes of Dr H.F. Verwoerd, the prime minister who dreamed up Grand Apartheid.

Some history

One of the first actions of **Simon van der Stel** after arriving at the Cape in November 1679 to take over as Dutch East India Company commander was to explore the area along the Eerste River (first river), where he came upon an enchanting little valley. Less than a month later it appeared on maps as Stellenbosch (Stel's bush), the first of several places dotted around the Cape which the governor was to name after himself or members of his family; another was Simonsberg overlooking the town.

Charged by the Dutch East India Company directors in the Netherlands with opening up the Cape interior, van der Stel soon settled the first **free burghers** in Stellenbosch. Within eight years, sixty freehold grants had been made; within the next two decades, Stellenbosch had established itself as a prosperous, semi-feudal society dominated by landowners, and in 1702 the Danish traveller, Abraham Bogaert, admired how it had "grown with fine dwellings, and how great a treasure of wine and grain is grown here". By the end of the century there were over a thousand houses and some substantial burgher estates in and around Stellenbosch, many of which still exist.

Arrival and information

Metrorail **trains** (℡021 449 2991) travel between Cape Town and Stellenbosch roughly every two hours during the day, and take about an hour. Infrequent (and expensive) intercity buses from Cape Town and Port Elizabeth pass through Stellenbosch, calling at the train station.

The busy **tourist office**, about 1km from the station at 36 Market Street (May–Aug Mon–Fri 9am–5pm, Sat 9.30am–2pm, Sun 10am–2pm; Sept–April Mon–Fri 8am–6pm, Sat 9am–5pm, Sun 10am–4pm; ℡021 883 3584, Ⓦwww.stellenboschtourism.co.za), can provide basic information on local attractions, and can supply the *Discover Stellenbosch on Foot* leaflet, which describes a walking tour covering a daunting 62 sites, or direct you to another walking tour. Easy Rider Wine Tours, based at *Stumble Inn* backpacker lodge (see below), offers daytime packages to four cellars (R220), plus reasonably priced pub crawls.

Accommodation

Stellenbosch has no shortage of **places to stay**, from backpacker lodges to total luxury. Apart from a handful of out-of-town farmstays, all the accommodation is within easy walking distance of the town centre.

Backpackers Inn De Wet Centre, corner of Bird and Church streets ℡021 887 2020, Ⓔbacpac1@global.co.za. Stellenbosch's most central backpacker lodge has a squeaky-clean atmosphere, attracting travellers of all ages and making it highly suitable for families. Dorms ❶, rooms ❶

Bonne Esperance 17 Van Riebeeck St ℡021 887 0225, Ⓦwww.bonneesperance.com. An easy walk from the centre, this is an excellently run Victorian guesthouse, complete with Scottie dogs. Simply furnished, it has a gracious dining room and veranda overlooking a lovely front garden, plus a courtyard and swimming pool at the rear. ❸

De Oude Meul 10a Mill St (off Dorp St) ℡021 887 7085 or 082 923 0744, Ⓦwww.deoudemeul.snowball.co.za. Located in the middle of town on a fairly busy street, above an antique shop, these pleasing rooms are good value. ❸

Glenconner Jonkershoek Rd, 4km from centre ℡021 886 5120, Ⓦwww.winelands.co.za/glenconner. Pretty cottages on a farm in a spectacular valley, tranquil and close to the walks in the Jonkershoek Nature Reserve. Breakfast can be taken under an old oak tree. Self-catering or B&B ❸

Natte Valleij On the R44, 12km north of town ℡021 875 5171, Ⓔmilner@intekom.co.za. Guests have a choice of a large cottage sleeping six, or a smaller and less expensive family unit attached to an old whitewashed homestead. There's a swimming pool, and breakfast is served on the veranda. ❷–❸

River Manor 6–8 The Ave ℡021 887 9944, Ⓦwww.rivermanor.com. A totally romantic stay with rose-petal strewn beds, oil lamps, plush dressing gowns and wicker chairs to laze on in the sun around the pool, with spa facilities on site for extra pampering. Discounts in the winter. ❺

Ryneveld Country Lodge 67 Ryneveld St ℡021 887 4469, Ⓦwww.ryneveldlodge.co.za. Gracious late-nineteenth-century building, now a National Monument and furnished with Victorian antiques. The rooms are spotless, with the two best rooms upstairs leading onto a wooden deck. There are also five family cottages which sleep up to four, and a pool. ❹

Stumble Inn 12 Market St ℡ & Ⓕ021 887 4049, Ⓦwww.jump.to/stumble. The town's best and oldest established hostel in two houses from the turn of the last century, with friendly, switched-on staff and a relaxed atmosphere. Just down the road from the tourist office, the hostel offers doubles, dorms and camping, and is also noted for its good-value tours (see above). Dorms and rooms ❶

Taylor's 6 Verreweide Rd ℡ & Ⓕ021 883 3427, ⒺDjlt@mweb.co.za. Unexceptional but functional self-catering accommodation in three flatlets, a cottage and a house, a 10min walk from town in the vicinity of the university. ❷

Villa Merwe 6 Cynaroides Rd, Paradyskloof ℡021 880 1185, Ⓔdeidre@iafrica.com. Three immaculate and comfortable rooms in the owner's modern house, each with its own entrance and bathroom, with a lounge, pool and garden. It's a 5min drive from the centre. ❸

195

STELLENBOSCH

ACCOMMODATION
Backpackers Inn — F
Bonne Esperance — E
De Oude Meul — G
Glenconner — D
Natte Valleij — A
River Manor — I
Ryneveld Country Lodge — C
Stumble Inn — H
Taylor's — B
Villa Merwe — J

RESTAURANTS & BARS
Al Frascati — 6
Bukhara — 7
Decameron — 3
De Oewer — 8
The Fishmonger — 2
The Greek Kitchen — 1
Spice Café — 5
Wijnhuis — 4
Volkskombuis — 8

The Town

Stellenbosch's attractions lie principally in its setting and streetscape; it's a lovely place to simply wander around and safe at night. The tourist office is a good place to start your explorations. Heading east up this road, you'll soon reach a whitewashed block that was the **VOC Kruithuis** (Jan–May & Aug–Dec Mon–Fri 9.30am–1.30pm & 2–5pm) – the Dutch East India Company's powder magazine – which houses a small and unprepossessing collection of four British uniforms, assorted rifles, some intriguing but unexplained laptop-sized cannons and powder kegs. From here, a right turn south down the side of the **Braak**, the large green occupying the centre of town, will take you past the **Rhenish Church** in Bloem Street, built in 1823 as a school for slaves and coloured people.

The Village Museum and Dorp Street

Head north up Ryneveld Street, and you'll encounter Stellenbosch's highlight, the extremely enjoyable **Village Museum** at no. 18 (Mon–Sat 9am–5pm, Sun 2–5pm), which cuts a cross section through the town's architectural and social heritage by means of four fortuitously adjacent historical dwellings from different periods. They're beautifully conserved and furnished in period style, and you'll meet the odd worker dressed in period costume. Earliest of the houses is the homely **Shreuderhuis**, a vernacular cottage built in 1709, with a small courtyard garden filled with aromatic herbs, pomegranate bushes and vine-draped pergolas – bearing more resemblance to the early Cape settlement's European aesthetics than to modern South Africa. Across the garden, **Blettermanhuis**, built in 1789 for the last Dutch East India Company-appointed magistrate of Stellenbosch, is an archetypal eighteenth-century Cape Dutch house, built on an H-plan with six gables. **Grosvenor House**, opposite, was altered to its current form in 1803, reflecting the growing influence of English taste after the 1795 British occupation of the Cape. The Neoclassical facade, with fluted pilasters supporting a pedimented entrance, borrows from high fashion then current at the heart of the growing Empire. The more modest **O.M. Bergh House**, across the road, is a typical Victorian dwelling that was once similar to Blettermanhuis, but was "modernized" in the mid-nineteenth century on a rectangular plan, with a simplified facade without gables.

From the Village Museum, head back south into **Dorp Street**, Stellenbosch's best-preserved historic axis, well worth a slow stroll just to soak in the ambience of buildings, gables, oaks and roadside water furrows. Look out for **Krige's Cottages**, an unusual terrace of historic town houses at nos. 37–51, between Aan-de-Wagenweg and Krige Street. The houses were built as Cape Dutch cottages in the first half of the nineteenth century; Victorian features were added subsequently, resulting in an interesting hybrid, with gables housing Victorian attic windows and decorative Victorian verandas with filigree ironwork fronting the elegantly simple Cape Dutch facades.

Eating and drinking

You'll be spoilt for choices of good places to eat in Stellenbosch, both in the centre and on some of the surrounding estates. Many places have outdoor seating, and in the evenings the student presence ensures a relaxed and sometimes raucous drinking culture.

Al Frascati Mill St. The best coffee and panini in town, plus pasta, salads and sandwiches. Mon–Sat 9am–10pm.

Bukhara Dorp and Bird streets ☎021 882 9133. Succulent North Indian dishes prepared in a kitchen behind a glass wall, in full view of diners. Prices are moderate or even steep, though portions are large. Favourites include butter chicken and tandoori lamb chops. Service is excellent and the ambience relaxed. Daily 11am–11pm.

Decameron 50 Plein St ☎021 883 3331. Honest, energetic Italian restaurant, offering pasta and gnocchi, as well as seafood and wood-fired pizza. You can watch the street life from the glassed-in pavement tables. Young children not welcome. Daily 11am–11pm, though closed Sunday eves.

The Fishmonger Sanlam Building, Ryneveld St ☎021 887 7835. A superb seafood restaurant, reasonable value and with outdoor seating, though lacking in ambience. Daily lunch & dinner.

The Greek Kitchen 42 Ryneveld St ☎021 887 7703. A cosy place serving, as its name suggests, Greek fare, including delicious herb and garlic

infused meze, and traditional desserts. The halva ice cream is great. Mon–Sat eves.

Spice Café Church St ☎021 883 8480. In a relaxed garden setting and with a play area for kids, the *Spice Café* is popular for weekend brunches, and also offers fresh cakes, sandwiches, salads and heavy veggie bakes. Mon–Fri 9am–5pm, Sat 9am–2pm, Sun 10am–2pm.

Volkskombuis and **De Oewer** Aan-de-Wagenweg, off Dorp St ☎021 887 2121. On the banks of the Eerste River, these venues have the same management. There's an eclectic range of dishes from North Africa and the Mediterranean at *De Oewer*, while platters of reasonably priced Cape Cuisine are the speciality of *Volkskombuis*. Daily lunch & dinner, except Sun lunch only.

Wijnhuis Church and Andringa streets ☎021 887 5844. At a place whose name translates as "wine house", it's no surprise that the wine list is longer than the menu. Regulars come to enjoy their tipple with Mediterranean seafood dishes, grilled meat or pastas, served in an old building with a light, contemporary feel. Wine tasting and buying wines is all part of the experience. Daily 8am–11pm.

The Stellenbosch wine estates

Stellenbosch was the first locality in the country to wake up to the marketing potential of a **wine route**. It launched its wine route in 1971, a tactic which has been hugely successful; today tens of thousands of visitors from all over the world are drawn to its wineries annually, making this the most toured area in the Winelands. Although the region accounts for only fifteen percent of South Africa's land under vine, its wine route is the most extensive in the country and offers some of the Cape's best reds and the greatest diversity of wines.

The wineries are all along a series of roads that radiate out from Stellenbosch; the selection below covers three of these roads, with the wineries arranged from Stellenbosch outwards. All the wineries have wine-route signposts along the main road.

Along the R44

North out of Stellenbosch towards the N1, Klapmuts Road (the **R44**) leads you after around 4km to **Morgenhof** (May–Oct Mon–Fri 10am–4.30pm, Sat 10am–3pm; Nov–April Mon–Fri 9am–5pm, Sat & Sun 10am–5pm; R10; ⓦwww .morgenhof.com), a French-owned chateau-style complex overlooked by the vine-covered Simonsberg. Morgenhof has a light and airy tasting room with a bar; among the numerous top-ranking wines worth sampling are the Merlot, Cabernet Sauvignon, Pinotage, Sauvignon Blanc, Chardonnay and Chenin Blanc. Delicious light lunches are served outside, topped off with ice cream on the lawns.

Drive north along the Klapmuts Road for about another 4km and you'll reach the left turn-off to **Simonsig**, located just over 2km down Kromme Rhee Road (Mon–Fri 8.30am–5pm, Sat 8.30am–4pm; cellar tours Mon–Fri 10am & 3pm, Sat 10am; R10; ⓦwww.simonsig.co.za). The winery has an outdoor tasting area under vine-covered pergolas, offering majestic views back

Lievland

R304 Simonsig
R44

Morgenhof

Rustenburg

Wedge
Farm
HELSHOOGTE
PASS
Stellenbosch
Station R310

Jordan Neethlingshof

Overgaauw Delaire

R310

Stellenbosch

R306

Eerste River

R300 R102

Franschhoek

ANNANDALE RD R44

R310

Blaauwklippen N

STRAND RD

0 5 km

STELLENBOSCH WINE ROUTE

Somerset West

to Stellenbosch of hazy stone-blue mountains and vineyards. Their first-class wines include a cutting-edge Pinotage Red Hill, a Kaapse Vonkel sparkling wine and an extremely good value Chardonnay.

Back on the main road, Lievland (Mon–Fri 9am–5pm, Sat 10am–4pm; R10), 4.5km north of the Simonsig turn-off, is the last of the Stellenbosch wineries on this section of the R44 (wineries beyond are covered under Paarl; see p.201). Lievland is an informal place, with a Cape Dutch tasting room which dates back to 1823. Its small variety of wines include an ace Shiraz and a Bordeaux-style blend; for a good quaffer at a reasonable price, give their Lievlander red blend a shot.

South of Stellenbosch, 4km from town along the Strand Road (R44 south), you'll come to **Blaauwklippen** (Mon–Fri 9am–5pm, Sat & Sun 9am–4.30pm; R20; ⓦwww.blaauwklippen.com), at the foot of the Stellenboschberg. Although big enough to take tour buses, Blaauwklippen isn't overly commercialized. Apart from the usual Cape Dutch buildings, there's a museum housing antique horse-drawn carriages, a little shop sells soft drinks and knick-knacks, and a veranda where a coachman's lunch is served daily. Their wines are generally of middling quality, but include a celebrated Zinfandel, of which they are one of the few local producers. If you continue south along the R44, you'll eventually reach Somerset West, centre of the Helderberg wine route, the highlight of which is Vergelegen (see p.200).

Along the R310

One of the closest wine estates to central Stellenbosch, **Rustenberg Wines** (Mon–Fri 9am–4.30pm, Sat 9am–12.30pm; free) is also one of the most alluring.

To get there, join the R310 to Franschhoek from the R44 to Paarl, just north of town. After just under 2km along the R310, turn into Ida's Valley along Lelie Road for a further 2km which, after a drive through orchards, sheep pastures and tree-lined avenues, brings you to the estate. An unassuming working farm, Rustenberg has a romantic pastoral atmosphere, in contrast to its hi-tech tasting room. The first vines were planted here in 1692, but the viniculture looks to the future. Most of their wines under the Rustenberg label are worth tasting, but also look out for highly drinkable and less expensive reds and whites under the Brampton brand – their second label.

For the best views in the Winelands, head for **Delaire** (Mon–Sat 10am–5pm; R15; ☎021 885 1756), on the **Helshoogte Pass**, 6km east of Stellenbosch along the R310. The restaurant here has views through oaks across the Groot Drakenstein and Simonsig mountains and down into craggy valleys; in the tasting room, their flagship Merlot is particularly worth sampling.

Along the R306

Moddergat Road (the R310) heads southwest out of Stellenbosch beside the train tracks, branching off 5.5km later onto Polkadraai Road (the **R306**). Half a kilometre later you'll come to the driveway leading to **Neethlingshof** (Mon–Fri 9am–5pm, Sat & Sun 10am–4pm; tasting R25 including a glass you take away; ⓦwww.neethlingshof.co.za), the first vines at whose site were planted in 1692. Neethlingshof produces very good wines, consistently hitting the high notes with its stunning Noble Late Harvest sweet dessert wines. The winery has a beautifully restored Cape Dutch manor dating back to 1814, and two good restaurants. A further 500m along the R306 takes you to another turn-off to the north, along which after a short distance you'll reach **Overgaauw** (Mon–Fri 9am–12.30pm & 2–5pm, Sat 10am–12.30pm; R10), notable for its elegant Victorian tasting room. A pioneering estate that produces reds and ports of excellent quality, Overgaauw was the first in the country to produce Merlots, and it's still the only one to make Sylvaner, a well-priced, easy-drinking dry white.

Further north along the same road, **Jordan Vineyards** (Mon–Fri 10am–4.30pm, Sat 9.30am–2.30pm; R10, of which R7.50 refundable with purchases) is part of the new wave of Cape wineries, with a hi-tech cellar, modern tasting room and friendly service. The drive there is half the fun, taking you into a *kloof* bounded by vineyards that get a whiff of the seas from both False Bay and Table Bay, which has obviously done something for their outstanding Chardonnay and Blanc Fumé.

Somerset West and Vergelegen

The only compelling reason to trawl out to the unpromising town of **SOMERSET WEST**, 50km east of Cape Town along the N2, is for **Vergelegen** on Lourensford Road (daily 9.30am–4pm; entrance R10; wine tasting R2–10 per glass; ⓦwww.vergelegen.co.za), an absolute architectural treasure as well as an estate producing a stunning range of wines. Officially part of the Helderberg wine route, Vergelegen can easily be included as an extension to a visit to Stellenbosch, just 14km to the north.

Vergelegen represents a notorious episode of corruption and the arbitrary abuse of power at the Cape in the early years of Dutch East India Company rule. Built by Willem Adriaan van der Stel, who became governor in 1699 after the retirement of his father Simon, the estate formed a grand Renaissance complex in the middle of the wild backwater that was the Cape at the beginning of the eighteenth century. Van der Stel acquired the land illegally and used Dutch East India Company slaves to build Vergelegen, as well as company resources to farm vast tracts of land in the surrounding areas. At the same time he abused his power as governor to corner most of the significant markets at the Cape. When this was brought to the notice of the Dutch East India Company in the Netherlands, van der Stel was sacked and Vergelegen was ordered to be destroyed to discourage future miscreant governors. It's believed that the destruction was never fully carried out and the current building is thought to stand on the foundations of the original.

Vergelegen was the only wine estate visited by the British queen during her 1995 state visit to South Africa – a good choice, as there's enough here to occupy even a monarch for an easy couple of hours. The **interpretive centre**, just across the courtyard from the shop at the building entrance, provides a useful history and background to the estate. Next door, the **wine-tasting centre** (open Nov–April) offers a professionally run sampling with a brief talk through each label. The **homestead**, which was restored in 1917 to its current state by Lady Florence Phillips, wife of a Johannesburg mining magnate, can also be visited. Its pale facade, reached along an axis through an octagonal garden that dances with butterflies in summer, has a classical triangular gable and pilaster-decorated doorways. Massive grounds planted with chestnuts and camphor trees and ponds around every corner make this one of the most serene places in the Cape.

Paarl

Although **PAARL** is attractively ensconced in a fertile valley brimming with historical monuments, at heart it's a parochial *dorp*, lacking either the sophistication of Stellenbosch or the striking setting and trendiness of Franschhoek. It can claim some virtue, however, from being a prosperous farming centre that earns its keep from the agricultural light industries – grain silos, canneries and flour mills – on the north side of town, and the cornucopia of grapes, guavas, olives, oranges and maize grown on the surrounding farms. Despite its small-town feel, Paarl has the largest municipality in the Winelands, with its most exclusive areas on the vined slopes of **Paarl Mountain** overlooking the town. In stark contrast with the cliquey conservatism of the predominantly white centre, the coloured townships on its periphery bear racy American names such as Chicago and New Orleans.

Some history

In 1657, just five years after the establishment of the Dutch East India Company refreshment station on the Cape Peninsula, a party under **Abraham Gabbema** arrived in the Berg River Valley to look for trading opportunities with the Khoikhoi, and search for the legendary gold of Monomotapa. They obviously had treasure on the brain, because on waking after a rainy night to the sight of the silvery dome of granite dominating the valley, they dubbed it Peerlbergh (pearl mountain), which in its modified form, **Paarl**, became the name of the town.

Thirty years later, the commander of the Cape, Simon van der Stel, granted strips of the Khoikhoi lands on the slopes of Paarl Mountain to French Huguenot and Dutch settlers. By the time Paarl was officially granted town status in 1840, it was still an outpost at the edge of the Drakenstein Mountains, a flourishing wagon-making and last-stop provisioning centre. This status was enhanced when the first **train line** in the Cape connected it to the Peninsula in 1863. Following in the spirit of the first Dutch adventurers of 1657, thousands of treasure-seekers brought custom to Paarl as the gateway to the interior during the diamond rush of the 1870s and the gold fever of the 1880s.

The town holds deep historical significance for the two competing political forces that forged modern South Africa. **Afrikanerdom** regards Paarl as the hallowed ground on which their language movement was born in 1875 (see box on p.204), while for the **ANC** (and the international community), Paarl will be remembered as the place from which Nelson Mandela made the final steps of his long walk to freedom, when he walked out of **Drakenstein Prison** (then called Victor Verster) in 1990.

Arrival, information and accommodation

Metrorail and Spoornet **trains** from Cape Town pull in at Huguenot Station in Lady Grey Street at the north end of town, near to the central shops. Greyhound and Intercape intercity **buses** stop at the Shell Garage, on the main road at the south end of town. The garage is about 2km from the **tourist office**, 216 Main Street (Mon–Fri 9am–5pm, Sat 9am–1pm & Sun 10am–1pm; ☎021 872 3829, ℻021 872 9376), which has a selection of good **maps** and can help with finding **accommodation**.

Most places to stay in town are either along or just off Main Street, many in historic buildings, with camping and chalets just outside town for the cheapest stay. At the other end of the scale is *Roggeland Country House.*

RESTAURANTS	
Cattle Baron	2
De Malle Madonna	4
Il Campanelli	1
Marc's Mediterranean Cuisine & Garden	3
Roggeland Country House	A

ACCOMMODATION	
De Waenhuis	D
Lemoenkloof	C
Nantes Vue	B
Queenslin	E
Rodeberg Lodge	F
Roggeland Country House	A

De Waenhuis 8 Patriot St, on the corner of Second St ☎ 021 872 6643, ✉ droelf@iafrica.com. A couple of blocks down from the tourist office, this tiny but fully equipped self-catering cottage has TV, swimming pool and a private entrance. ❷

Lemoenkloof 396a Main St ☎ 021 872 3782, ✉ lemkloof@adept.co.za. A comfortable and tranquil owner-run guesthouse in a National Monument, with 1820s' Cape Dutch and Victorian features, a TV and fridge in each room, and a secluded swimming pool. ❺

Nantes Vue 56 Mill St ☎ 021 872 7311, ⓦ www.nantes-paarl.co.za. En-suite doubles and a cottage that sleeps three, decorated with artistic flair in a friendly Cape Dutch guesthouse, also a National Monument. Breakfast is served on the veranda overlooking a small garden. ❸

Queenslin 2 Queen St ☎ & 🖷 021 863 1160 or ☎ 082 577 0635. Two en-suite rooms with their own entrances and garden spaces, and three double rooms that share a bathroom, in a split-level family home set in a quiet part of town, bounded on one side by vineyards and towered over by Paarl Rock. Limited self-catering is possible – they have a fridge and microwave. Breakfast can be provided as an extra. ❷

Rodeberg Lodge 74 Main St ☎ 021 863 3202, ⓦ www.rodeberglodge.co.za. Plain period furnishing gives the five en-suite rooms in this huge, centrally located Victorian town house a cool, spacious atmosphere. Ask for a room at the back if traffic noise bothers you. ❸

Roggeland Country House Roggeland Rd, Dal Jospehat Valley, just northeast of Paarl ☎ 021 868 2501, ⓦ www.roggeland.co.za. The accolades keep rolling in for this family-run inn, which somehow manages to combine good service, outstanding food (see p.207) and informality. The homestead is an eighteenth-century masterpiece of Cape Dutch architecture, with bedrooms in outbuildings. The rate includes dinner with wine tasting, and is a third cheaper May–Aug. ❼

The Town and around

Unlike Stellenbosch and Franschhoek, which are ideal for wandering, the best preserved and oldest historical frontage in Paarl stretches for some 2km down oak-lined **Main Street**. It's here you'll find the **Paarl Museum** at no. 303 (Mon–Fri 9am–5pm, Sat 9am–1pm; R5), in a handsome, thatched Cape Dutch building with one of the earliest surviving gables (1787) in the "new style", characterized by triangular caps. The contents don't quite match up to the exterior, but include some reasonably enlightening panels on the architecture of the town, and several eccentric glass display cases of Victorian bric-a-brac. Post-apartheid transformation has introduced some coverage of the indigenous Khoisan populations of the area and the changes that came with European colonization, including slavery.

South down Main Street away from the museum, a left turn into Van der Lingen Street and then a right into Pastorie Street brings you to the **Afrikaans Taal Museum** (Mon–Fri 9am–5pm; R2), which chronicles the development of the Afrikaans language (see box on p.204). Located in the house of Gideon Malherbe (1833–1921), one of the founders of the League of True Afrikaners, the museum's displays are in Afrikaans, and a leaflet available from the reception desk gives an English summary of exhibits. Some brief material gives an alternative history of Afrikaans, placing new emphasis on the role of slaves and coloured South Africans in its evolution.

The only other sight of any interest in Paarl itself is the grandiose **Taal Monument** (daily 9am–5pm), the controversial memorial to the Afrikaans language, standing just outside the centre on the top of Paarl Mountain. To get there, drive south along Main Street past the head office of the KWV, and follow the signs to your right up the slope of the mountain. The monument used to be as important a place of pilgrimage for Afrikaners as the Voortrekker Monument in Pretoria, although when it was erected in 1973 critics joked that monuments were usually erected to the dead. From the coffee and curio shop you can admire a truly magnificent panorama across to the Cape Peninsula and False Bay in one direction and the Winelands ranges in the other.

The history of Afrikaans

Afrikaans is South Africa's third mother tongue, spoken by fifteen percent of the population and outstripped only by Zulu and Xhosa. English, by contrast, is the mother tongue of only nine percent of South Africans, and ranks fifth in the league of the eleven official languages.

Signs of the emergence of a new southern African dialect appeared as early as 1685, when H.A. van Rheede, a Dutch East India Company official from the Netherlands, complained about a "distorted and incomprehensible" version of Dutch being spoken in the Drakenstein Valley around modern-day Paarl. By absorbing English, French, German, Malay and indigenous words and expressions, the language continued to diverge from mainstream Dutch, and by the nineteenth century was widely used in the Cape by both white and coloured speakers, but was regarded by the elite as an inferior creole, unsuitable for literary or official communication. Even the first attempts by dominee **Stephanus du Toit** and the Genootskap van Regte Afrikaners (League of True Afrikaners) to have Afrikaans recognized as a separate language from Dutch, and their launching in 1875 of *Die Patriot*, the first white Afrikaans **newspaper**, made little impact outside Paarl.

Ironically, it was the British defeat of the Afrikaner republics in the second Anglo-Boer War at the turn of the twentieth century that provided the catalyst for a mass white Afrikaans movement. The scorched-earth policy of the British had driven many Boers from the lands and produced a demoralized and semi-literate Boer underclass, while the official British policy of anglicizing South Africa helped to unite the white Afrikaner proletariat and elite against the common English enemy.

In 1905, **Gustav Preller**, a young journalist from a working-class Boer background, set about reinventing Afrikaans as a "white man's language". He aimed to eradicate the stigma of its "coloured" ties by substituting Dutch words for those with non-European origins. Preller began publishing the first of a series of populist magazines written in Afrikaans and glorifying Boer history and culture. Through this **Second Language Movement**, whites took spiritual control over Afrikaans and the pressure grew for its recognition as an official language, which came in 1925.

When the National Party took power in 1948, its apartheid policy went hand in hand with promoting the interests of its Afrikaans-speaking supporters and a concerted programme of the **upliftment of poor whites** began. Afrikaners were installed throughout the civil service and filled most posts in the public utilities. Despite the fact that there were more coloured than white Afrikaans speakers, the language quickly became associated with the **apartheid** establishment. This had electrifying consequences in the Seventies, when the government attempted to enforce Afrikaans as the sole medium of instruction in African schools, leading directly to the **Soweto uprising** in 1976, which marked the beginning of the end for Afrikaner hegemony in South Africa. The repressive period throughout the Seventies and Eighties and the forced removals under the Group Areas Act led many coloured Afrikaans speakers to adopt English in preference to their mother tongue, which they felt was tainted by apartheid.

There are few signs that Afrikaans will die out. Under the new constitution, existing **language rights** can't be diminished, which effectively means that Afrikaans will continue to be almost as widely used as before. It is now as much with coloured as white people that the future of the *taal* (language) rests.

Groot Drakenstein (Victor Verster) Prison

Roughly 9km south of the N1 as it cuts through Paarl, along the R301 (the southern extension of Jan van Riebeeck Street), stands the **Victor Verster Prison**. Renamed **Groot Drakenstein** in 2000, this was Nelson Mandela's last place of incarceration. It was through the gates at Victor Verster (not Pollsmoor in Cape Town or Robben Island as many people believe) that Mandela walked to his freedom on February 11, 1990, and it was here that the first images of him in 27 years were bounced around the world – under the Prisons Act not even old pictures of him could be published throughout his incarceration. The working jail looks rather like a boys' school fronted by rugby fields beneath hazy mountains, and there's something bizarre about seeing a prison sign nonchalantly slipped in among all the vineyard and wine-route pointers.

The wineries

Retracing your route to town, and turning left into Langenhoven Street and left again into Main Street, will bring you to the entrance of **Laborie**, Taillefert St (Mon–Sat 9am–5pm; tasting R9 for five wines), one of the most impressive Paarl wineries, all the more remarkable for being right in town. The beautiful manor is fronted by a rose garden, acres of close-cropped lawns, historic buildings and oak trees – all towered over by the Taal Monument. There's a truly wonderful tasting room balcony, jettying out over the vineyards trailing up Paarl Mountain.

Back towards the centre along the main drag, a dirt track, Jan Phillips Mountain Drive, takes a detour along the hillside past **Paarl Mountain Nature Reserve**, emerging 11km later at the north end of town to rejoin Main Street. If you take a left turn from Jan Philips back into Main Street, after nearly 2km you'll reach the magnificently set **Rhebokskloof** (daily 9am–5pm; tasting R8 which includes a cellar tour; ⓦwww.rhebokskloof.co.za), a highly photogenic wine estate at the foot of sculptural granite koppies overlooking a shallow *kloof* that borders on the mountain nature reserve. The estate's renowned restaurant (see p.207) overlooks an artificial lake with swans. You can also reach Rhebokskloof by heading out of town along Main Street, where you'll meet Jan Phillips Drive. Also based at Rhebokskloof is **Wine Valley Horse Trails** (ⓣ021 869 8687 or 083 226 8735, ⓦwww.horsetrails-sa.co.za), which offers one- to four-hour equestrian trails for novices and experts through the surrounding countryside – a choice spot for some riding. Prices start from R120 for a one-hour trail. Longer trails are restricted to experienced riders, but a four-hour package of a ride plus a conducted wine-tasting at the estate is available to novices.

Back on the southern fringes of town, **Fairview** (Mon–Fri 8am–5pm, Sat 8.30am–1pm; R10; ⓦwww.fairview.co.za) promises the most fun of all the Paarl estates, with much more than just wine tasting on offer. To get there, take the R101 (the southwest extension of Main Road) out of town, turning right at the sign and continuing for about 2.5km down a minor road to the estate entrance. Your arrival is marked by the emblem of the estate, a spiral tower which the estate's famous goats climb. A deli sells sausages and cold meats for picnics on the lawn, and you can also sample and buy the goat's, sheep's and cow's cheeses made on the estate. As far as wine tasting goes, Fairview is an innovative, family-run place, but it can get a bit hectic when the tour buses roll in, so try to phone ahead to find out when they're expected.

From here the **Backsberg estate** (Mon–Fri 8.30am–5pm, Sat 9am–1pm; R10), south of the R101 along the very minor WR1, can be reached easily by backtracking from Fairview, turning right into the R101, and continuing a short way before turning left. After passing the Simonsvlei winery, go a short way till you strike a T-junction at the WR1, where you turn left and almost immediately get to the winery entrance. Outdoor seating with views of the rose garden and vineyard makes this busy estate a nice place to while away some time. Just a little further afield is the **Boschendal** estate (see p.210).

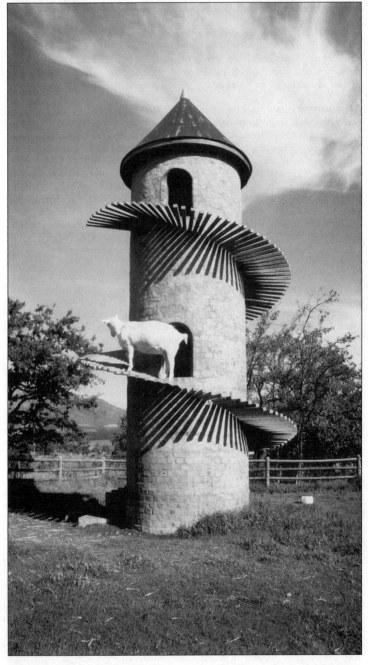

△ Goat Tower, Fairview Estate

Eating and drinking

A working town, Paarl has none of the Winelands foodie pretensions of Franschhoek, but you'll find a number of places along the main street for a decent snack and coffee or a meal, as well as a couple of outstanding places in the surrounding countryside, with great views of the vineyards and mountains.

Cattle Baron Gymnasium St ☏ 021 872 2000. Reliable family-oriented steakhouse that specializes in beef, chicken and fish. Mon–Fri noon–3.30pm & 6–11.30pm; Sat 6–midnight; Sun noon–3.30pm & 6–10.30pm.

De Malle Madonna 127 Main Rd ☏ 021 863 3925. Interestingly eccentric and vibey spot for a relaxed coffee, breakfast or light lunch with seating indoors and on a veranda with mountain views. Take up the challenge of playing Scrabble with an Afrikaans set (the distribution of letters is different to an English game) while sipping your cappucino on the veranda. Menu includes salads, quiches, pasta and burgers. Tues–Sun 8.30am–5.30pm.

Il Campanelli 62 Breda St ☏ 021 872 4397. Popular with locals, this low-key family-friendly Italian restaurant does pizzas and pasta as well as seafood, veal and steaks. Tues–Fri & Sun lunch; Mon–Sat dinner.

Marc's Mediterranean Cuisine & Garden 129 Main St ☏ 021 863 3980. Simple but tasty menu that includes paella, meze, couscous, seafood and lamb, served in a converted historic house with a large outdoor area dotted with sun umbrellas and lemon trees. Tues–Sun lunch; Mon–Sat dinner.

Rhebokskloof Restaurant Rhebokskloof winery, Rhebokskloof Minor Rd ☏ 021 869 8386. Intimate outdoor established recommended for the outstanding setting as well as the food. Overlooking a lake, it has a shaded terrace for summer lunches, offering gourmet meals with thrilling combinations of flavours, both Cape and international. It's also a good place for morning or afternoon teas. Daily breakfast, lunch & tea daily; Mon & Thurs–Sun also dinner.

Roggeland Country House See p.203. The imaginative and ever-changing set menu here (lunch is three courses and dinner four) is inspired by the regional produce of Paarl, using vegetables and herbs grown in Roggeland's own gardens. Beautifully prepared dishes are accompanied by a selected wine, each of which you are talked through. Booking essential and forewarning required for children.

Franschhoek

Between 1688 and 1700 about two hundred **French Huguenots**, desperate to escape religious persecution in France, accepted a Dutch East India Company offer of passage to the Cape and the grant of lands. They made contact with the area's earliest settlers, groups of **Khoi herders**. Conflict between the French newcomers and the Khoi followed familiar lines, with the white settlers gradually dispossessing the herdsmen, forcing them either further into the hinterland or into servitude on their farms. The establishment of white hegemony was swift and by 1713 the area was known as *de france hoek*. Though French-speaking died out within a generation because of explicit Company policy, many of the estates here are still known by their original French names. **FRANSCHHOEK** itself, 33km from Stellenbosch and 29km from Paarl, occupies parts of the original farms of La Cotte and Cabrière and is relatively young, having been established around a church built in 1833.

If sybaritic indulgence – eating, drinking and memorable lodgings – is what the Winelands is really about, then Franschhoek is the place that does it best. Despite being a fairly small dorp, it has managed to establish itself as the culinary capital of the Western Cape, if not the whole country. Its late Victorian and more recent Frenchified rustic architecture, the terrific setting (it's hemmed in on three sides by mountains), the vineyards down every other backstreet, and some vigorous myth-making have created a place you can really lose yourself in, a set piece that unashamedly draws its inspiration from Provence.

Arrival, information and accommodation

There's no public transport to Franschhoek or in the town itself. The buzzing **tourist office** is on Huguenot Road (summer Mon–Fri 9am–5pm, Sat & Sun 10am–5pm; winter Mon–Fri 9am–5pm, Sat & Sun 9am–4pm; ℡021 876 3603, ⓦwww.franschhoek.org.za), the main road through town. At no. 68, just north of the junction with Kruger Street, it can provide activities in the area and some excellent maps of the village and its winelands.

Accommodation

Guesthouse **accommodation** tends to be a bit pricey here, but the rooms are of high quality and frequently in unparalleled settings; Franschhoek is a place where you'll eat and sleep well.

Auberge Bligny 28 Van Wijk St ℡021 876 3767, ⓔbligny@mweb.co.za. A centrally located Victorian house furnished in country style and with a nice guest lounge, veranda, pool and garden. ❸

Auberge Clermont Robertsvlei Rd, signposted just west of the Huguenot Monument along Lambrecht Rd ℡021 876 3700, ⓦwww.clermont.co.za. Six luxury rooms decorated in French country style (two have hand-painted ceilings) in a Provencal-inspired inn, right in the middle of a vineyard, with views of the surrounding mountains. ❺

Klein Dassenberg Cottages Off Huguenot Rd ℡021 876 2107, ⓦwww.kleindassenberg.co.za. Self-catering cottages in a peaceful and beautiful setting. Two of the cottages are ideal for a couple, while the other pair sleeps four and can accommodate families. ❸

Le Ballon Rouge Guest House 7 Reservoir Rd ℡021 876 2651, ⓦwww.ballon-rouge.co.za. Comfortable, though small-roomed B&B with some rooms leading onto a veranda, in a Victorian town house with its own restaurant. ❹

La Provence Vineyard Cottages La Provence Farm, signposted south off Huguenot Rd ℡021 876 3603, ⓕ021 876 2768. Three cottages set in gardens, with large fireplaces, use of tennis courts and a spring-water pool. Self-catering and B&B ❷

Le Quartier Français 16 Huguenot Rd ℡021 876 2151, ⓦwww.lequartier.co.za. A luxurious place with two suites (one with its own pool) and fifteen huge rooms decorated with sunny fabrics, all arranged around herb and flower gardens and a swimming pool. Child-friendly. Also has one of the consistently best restaurants in the country (see p.211). ❽

Paradise Cottages Roberstvlei Road ℡ & ⓕ021 876 2160. Some of the valley's cheapest rooms, in two small, basic, self-catering cottages on a working farm with riding stables, 5km from the centre. ❶

Plumwood Inn 11 Cabriére St ℡021 876 3883, ⓦwww.plumwoodinn.com. Boutique guesthouse which makes a break from Franschhoek's Franco-philia with its ethnic African-inspired decor. Detail is everything – from the custom-made cotton tablecloths to the luxurious beds covered with a sea of cushions, and impeccable service from Dutch owners Roel and Lucienne Rutten. ❺

ACCOMMODATION		RESTAURANTS	
Auberge Bligny	C	Boschendal	
Auberge Clermont	G	Bread & Wine	8 La Fromagerie at La
Klein Dassenberg		Col'Cacchio	9 Grange	10
Cottages	F	Delicious	4 Le Bon Vivant
Le Ballon Rouge		French Connection Bistro	6 Le Quartier Français	3
Guest House	A	Haute Cabrière Cellar	5 Ralf's Country Restaurant	B
La Provence Vineyard		Restaurant	& Village Pub	2
Cottages	D		1 Topsi and Company	7
Le Quartier Français	B		
Paradise Cottages	H		
Plumwood Inn	E		

The Town and around

Away from the wining and dining, Franschhoek's attractions include hiking, horse-riding or cycling in the valley, or visiting the institutionalized Huguenot Monument and adjacent museum, which together occupy a prime position at the head of Huguenot Road, where it forms a T-junction with Lambrecht Street. The **Huguenot Monument** consists of three skinny, interlocking arches symbolizing the Holy Trinity, while the **Huguenot Memorial Museum** (Mon–Sat 9am–5pm & Sun 2–5pm; small entrance fee) gives comprehensive coverage of Huguenot history, culture and of their contribution to modern South Africa.

The best **hike** in the vicinity is the Cat se Pad (Cat's Path), which starts on your left just under a kilometre from the museum as you head out of town up the Franschhoek Pass. The walk leads into *fynbos* with proteas, and gives instant access to the mountains surrounding the valley, with good views. The first two-kilometre section gets you to the top of the pass, and you can keep going for another 10km in the direction of Villiersdorp (though you don't actually reach it).

The wineries

Franschhoek's **wineries** are small enough and sufficiently close together to make it a breeze to visit two or three on foot, by mountain bike or even on horseback. Heading north through town from the Huguenot Monument, you'll find virtually all the wineries signposted off Huguenot Road and its extension, Main Road.

Close to the monument, **Cabrière Estate**, on Berg Road (Mon–Fri 9am–4.30pm, Sat 11am–3pm; tastings Mon–Fri 11am & 3pm, Sat 11am; Ⓦwww.cabriere.co.za), is reached through groves of fruit trees leading up to the homestead and tasting room. The winery is notable for its Pinot Noirs and colourful wine-maker Achim von Arnim, whose presence on Saturdays guarantees an eventful visit; try to catch him when he slices off the upper neck of a bubbly bottle with a sabre, sending flying the neatly detached cork encased in the severed top ring of glass. Next door, **Mont Rochelle**, on Daniel Hugo Road (Mon–Sat 11am–5pm, plus Sept–April 11am–3pm; cellar tours Mon–Fri 11am, 12.30pm & 3pm; Ⓦwww.montrochelle.co.za), has one of the most stunning settings in Franschhoek and an unusual cellar in a converted nineteenth-century fruit-packing shed, edged by eaves decorated with fretwork, stained-glass windows and chandeliers.

Horseback wineland outings

A great way to take in the beauty of Franschhoek (and some wine) is in the saddle – several operators offer guided equestrian tours, for about R100 an hour.

Mont Rochelle Equestrian Centre Mont Rochelle Estate ☎083 300 4368. Their ride lasts about two-and-a-half hours and takes in three cellars, at each of which you taste one wine, except at Mont Rochelle itself, where you get to try their whole range. Longer rides or purely scenic rides can be arranged.

Paradise Stables Roberstsvlei Rd ☎ & ℻021 876 2160. Horseback cellar tours and straightforward outrides.

Steinmetz Arabians Le Belle Dauphine Farm, Excelsior Road, 1500m from Hugenot Memorial ☎021 876 2570. Three-hour wine tours on horseback, stopping at two wineries (R300), as well as lessons for beginners.

Back on Huguenot Road, keep heading north and turn right into Uitkyk Street to get to **Chamonix** (daily 9.30am–4.30pm; Ⓦwww.chamonix.co.za), which holds its tastings in the cosy Blacksmith's Cottage (where you can also get a light meal). The estate's most consistent wines are their Chardonnays, but they also produce Chamonix schnapps from pear, peach, plum, apple and nectarine, and, for teetotallers, Eau de Chamonix. There's a restaurant here too.

Retrace your route back to Huguenot Road and past the Pippin Farm Stall to **La Motte Estate** (Mon–Fri 9am–4.30pm, Sat 10am–3pm; Ⓦwww.la-motte .com), further along Huguenot Road (here called the R45), which presents a supremely cool front, with a superb designer tasting room looking into the cellar through a sheer wall of glass. This was the estate that put to rest once and for all the long-held notion that Franschhoek was a poor region for producing red wines: La Motte offers an excellent Shiraz and Chardonnay and an elegant Merlot–Cabernet blend known as Millennium, which sells out quickly.

For something less formal, make for newcomer **GlenWood** (Mon–Fri 9am–1pm plus Sept–April Sat & Sun 11am–3pm; Ⓦwww.glenwoodvineyards.co.za), down Robertsvlei Rd, signposted off the R45 a couple of hundred metres back towards the village from La Motte and on the opposite side of the main road. About ten-or-so minutes' drive from the village throng, it feels surprisingly remote; vineyard and cellar tours are frequently conducted by the owner.

At the opposite end of the scale, **Boschendal** (Mon–Sat 8.30am–4.30pm; plus Nov–April Sun 8.30am–4.30pm; Ⓦwww.boschendal.com) is the obvious choice if you have time for only one winery. Almost equidistant from Franschhoek, Paarl and Stellenbosch at the junction of the R45 and R310, it is geared to the busloads of tourists who lap up its impressive Cape Dutch buildings, tree-lined avenues, choice of restaurants and cafés (see below), and of course its wines. Boschendal is one of the world's longest-established New World wine estates, dating back to 1685, when its lands were granted to Huguenot settler Jean Le Long. The Cape Dutch manor was built in 1812 by Paul de Villiers and his wife, whose initials appear on the front gable. Wine tasting takes place at the Taphuis, where you can sit indoors or sip under shady trees.

Eating and drinking

Eating and drinking is what Franschhoek is all about, so plan on sampling at least one or two of its excellent **restaurants**, some of which rate among the Cape's best. Franschhoek's cuisine tends to be French-inspired, but includes salmon trout as a local speciality. Restaurants in town are concentrated along Huguenot Road, but there are a number of excellent alternatives in the more rustic environment of the surrounding wine estates. **Booking** is essential.

Restaurants

Boschendal Pniel Rd, just after the junction of the R45 and R310 to Stellenbosch ☏021 870 4274. Boschendal is legendary for its pricey, exhaustive daily buffet lunch, which will set you up for the rest of day – you can eat as much as you can from the spread of soup, oysters, calamari, roasts, casseroles, salads, Cape specialities, cheeseboard and desserts. Le Café does light, sit-down lunches, while Le Pique Nique offers de luxe picnic hampers daily (May–Oct) under the shady pines. Children get a special picnic wrapped in a cloth and tied to a stick, Dick Whittington style. Booking essential.

Bread & Wine Môreson Farm, Happy Valley Rd, La Motte ☏021 876 3692. Signposted off the R45 is this genial and child-friendly venue surrounded by lemon orchards and vineyards. It serves imaginative modern country cuisine lunches (try the Gazpacho sorbet with onion and brinjal compote) accompanied by a variety of breads and the estate's own wines. Oct–June Wed–Sun lunch only.

Col'Cacchio 66 Huguenot Rd ☏021 876 4222 Highly imaginative wood-fired pizzas available as full or half portions, which can be eaten in, taken away or delivered. Daily lunch and dinner.

Delicious 38 Huguenot Rd ☏ 021 876 4004. Humming deli and espresso bar that does salads, buns and breads with imaginative fillings as well as daily hot specials. You can also buy take-away ingredients to put together your own picnic. Daily 7.30am–5pm and Wed dinner.

French Connection Bistro Huguenot and Bordeaux Streets ☏ 021 876 4056. Simple yet interesting food that includes tandoori chicken wrapped in a pancake. There's a bustling French country-style interior as well as pavement seating. The children's menu makes this an obvious choice for families. Daily lunch & dinner.

Haute Cabrière Cellar Restaurant Cabrière Estate, Franschhoek Pass ☏ 021 876 3688. A bunker-like venue with an interesting menu planned around Cabrière wines, available by the glass or bottle. The food, available as half or full portions, include mousses and terrines, wonderful desserts and homemade chocolates. Book ahead and ask for one of the two window seats. Lunch daily, dinner daily summer and Fri & Sat in winter.

La Fromagerie at La Grange 13 Daniel Hugo St. Sample platters of South African cheeses accompanied by local wines in the gardens here, overlooking vineyards, or sit down for tea or lunches that include savoury tarts, terrines and soufflés. Daily for lunch and tea as well as cheese tasting 9am–noon and 3–5pm. On Friday eves in summer this family-friendly spot becomes a buzzing jazz venue.

Le Bon Vivant 22 Dirkie Uys St ☏ 021 876 2717. Well-priced and consistently excellent establishment serving two-to-five course nouvelle cuisine set meals as well as an à la carte menu with a splash of Dutch influence. Mon & Wed–Sun lunch & dinner.

Le Quartier Français 16 Huguenot Rd ☏ 021 876 2151. The place that made Franschhoek synonymous with food remains consistently one of South Africa's best restaurants, offering excellent formal evening meals, or informal and imaginative lunches with a Cape/Provençal flavour. There are always vegetarian options and delicious desserts. In winter you can sit by the fire inside, while on fine days there are pavement tables for lunch. Book ahead. Daily breakfast to dinner.

Ralf's Country Restaurant & Village Pub 5 Main Rd ☏ 021 876 3360. A relaxed and inexpensive bistro with a good pub and beer garden, serving pizzas, trout and German specialities such as schnitzels, eisbein and apple strudel. Mid-morning till late: summer Mon–Sat, winter Tues–Sat.

Topsi and Company 7 Reservoir St West ☏ 021 876 2952. Run by one of South Africa's most eccentric and best-known chefs, Topsi Venter, this is a bag of surprises. There's no set menu, but you'll always find unlikely flavours being combined to great effect. A talking parakeet wanders around checking that everything is all right. Mon & Wed–Sun lunch and dinner.

Route 62 and the Little Karoo

One of the most rewarding journeys in the Western Cape is an inland counterpart to the Garden Route (see p.254) – the **mountain route** from Cape Town to Port Elizabeth, largely along the R62, and thus often referred to as **Route 62**. Nowhere near as well known as the coastal journey, this trip takes you through some of the most dramatic passes and *poorts* (valley routes) in the country and crosses a frontier of *dorps* and drylands.

Beyond the Paarl and Stellenbosch winelands, a vast hinterland fans out away from Cape Town. Just outside Paarl, the Huguenot Tunnel on the N1 punches through the Dutoitsberg mountain range to emerge in the fruit-growing and wine-making country of the **Breede River Valley**, where mountains give way to a jigsaw of valleys, each quite distinct in character. It's here rather than in the more developed Winelands proper that so many calendar shots are taken of isolated whitewashed homesteads dwarfed by vine-covered hills.

Although the Breede River Valley is part of a through route to the Eastern Cape via Oudtshoorn, its towns also make convenient excursions from Cape Town. **Worcester**, the large functional hub of the region, is on the N1 just 110km from Cape Town, while to its north, **Tulbagh**, a more promising destination, with a perfectly restored provincial Cape Dutch street, is an easy 130km from the city. South from Worcester, the R60 shadows the groove cut by the

Passes and poorts of the Little Karoo

The **Little Karoo** is hemmed in to the north by the Langeberg range and to the south the Outeniqua (the range separating it from the Garden Route). In between lies a gauntlet of mountains and valleys that for centuries made this area virtually impassable for wheeled transport. In the nineteenth century, the British began to tackle the problem and dozens of **passes** were built through the Cape's mountains, 34 of which were engineered by the brilliant road-builder Andrew Geddes Bain and his son Thomas. In 1878, Anthony Trollope commented that the **Outeniqua Pass**, just north of George on the way to Oudtshoorn, equalled "some of the mountain roads through the Pyrenees", a description which just as easily applies today to any number of other Little Karoo passes. In fact, whatever the Little Karoo lacks in museums and art galleries is amply compensated for by the towering drama of these Victorian masterpieces.

In **Afrikaans** there are two words for pass: *pas*, meaning "a route over the mountains", and *poort*, meaning "a valley route", often following a river. Most passes are narrow, winding and steep, and frequently untarred, so they need to be driven slowly. In any case, you won't want to rush past such fantastic views, so it's worth bringing along food and drink to enjoy at the numerous picnic spots along the way. We've listed a selection of some of the best of the passes and *poorts* below.

Bain's Kloof Pass On the R303 northeast of Paarl, with spectacular switchbacks.

Cogman's Kloof Pass Between Ashton and Montagu. A five-kilometre route that's at its most dramatic as it cuts through a rock face into the Montagu Valley (see box on p.29).

Du Toit's Kloof Pass Between Paarl and Worcester. The more exciting alternative to the Huguenot Toll Tunnel, with 1:9 gradients (see "Worcester" opposite).

Gamkaskloof Pass Also called Die Hel (The Hell; see box on p.227), reached from the summit of the Swartberg Pass. Arguably the most awesome of all the passes leading into a dramatic and lonely valley.

Meiringspoort Just north of De Rust. A tarred road through a gorge in the Swartberg, which keeps crossing a light-brown river, while huge slabs of folded and zigzagging rock rise up on either side. There's a picnic spot at each fording place and a waterfall at Ford 17 (they're all numbered). You can walk from here for 12km into the mountains.

Prince Alfred's Pass On the R339, between the N2 just east of Knysna and Avontuur on the R62. A dramatic dirt road twisting through mountains, past a few isolated apple farms.

Swartberg Pass Between Oudtshoorn and Prince Albert. Over-the-Swartberg counterpart of Meiringspoort, with 1:7 gradients on narrow untarred roads characterized by precipitous hairpins. Not recommended in poor weather or if you suffer from vertigo.

Breede River and provides access to the rather dull little town of **Robertson**, centre of yet another wine route. Some 19km south lies **McGregor**, a small, laid-back village with a rural feel, and an excellent choice for a weekend stay. Nearby, and a similar distance from the Cape Peninsula, the pleasant historic spa town of **Montagu** is towered over by precipitous red-streaked cliffs that attract serious mountaineers from all over the country.

Continuing east from Montagu, the R62 meanders into the Garden Route's backyard, the **Little Karoo** (or Klein Karoo), a vast and brittle khaki-coloured hinterland (the name is a Khoi word meaning "hard and dry"). The Little Karoo provides the easiest access to the semi-desert covering one-third of South Africa's surface. Open treeless plains, sporadically vegetated with low, wiry scrub, and dotted with flat-topped hills, dissolve eventually into the Great Karoo, which extends into the southern Free State and well into the Eastern and Northern Cape provinces. The Great Karoo is the harsh frontier which a succession of South Africans occupied by turns: San hunters, Khoi herders, Griqua (coloured) farmers and Afrikaner trekkers. Today Afrikaans is the dominant language, used by white and coloured speakers, the latter having absorbed what remained of the Khoi.

The unsung surprise along the way is **Calitzdorp**, a rustic little *dorp*, five to six hours' solid driving from Cape Town, down whose backstreets a few unassuming wine farms produce some of South Africa's best port. Around here you'll find neglected valleys where some of the old Karoo clings on tenuously in an almost feudal relationship between farmsteads and faded scatterings of coloured workers' cottages. By contrast, the well-trumpeted attractions of **Oudtshoorn**, half an hour further on, are the ostrich farms and the massive **Cango Caves**, one of the country's biggest tourist draws. Less than 70km from the coast, with good transport connections, Oudtshoorn marks the convergence of the mountain and coastal roads and is usually treated as a leisurely day-trip away from the Garden Route.

The N1 beyond Worcester slices up through the northernmost third of the Klein Karoo, slipping past **Matjiesfontein**, a wonderfully preserved Victorian railway town, and the unassuming, undervalued **Karoo National Park**, both just off the main road and definitely worth breaking a trip for (see p.228).

Worcester

The fastest way to cross the mountains from Paarl into the Breede River Valley is via the **Huguenot Toll Tunnel** on the N1, which burrows straight through to the other side, but misses the wonderful scenery of driving over the **Du Toit's Kloof Pass**. Much slower, but far more interesting, the pass works its way through a series of wonderful mountain ranges with views onto distant farms and villages in the valleys.

WORCESTER, 31km from Paarl through the tunnel, is a relatively large town for this part of the world, an agricultural centre with a number of factories and smelly chicken farms. It's at the centre of a wine-making region, consisting mostly of co-operatives producing bulk plonk that makes up about a fifth of national output. There isn't much reason to dally here, apart from driving down Chruch Street, which has attractive historical frontage, and visiting the absorbing **Kleinplasie Living Open Air Museum** (Mon–Sat 9am–4.30pm; R12), which depicts life on the Karoo frontier between 1690 and 1900. The museum is made up of about two dozen reconstructed buildings, with staff in old-style workshops engaged in crafts and home industries. Keep a lookout in particular for the corbelled shepherd's hut, which represents a vernacular style unique to the Karoo, using domed stone roofs rather than beam and lintel construction – a response to the dearth of timber in the treeless expanse. There's a **restaurant** and **café** on site, and next door a wine shop selling a good selection from the Worcester wineries. The museum is just outside the centre of town – to get there, head east along High Street and turn right onto the road to Robertson.

Tulbagh

The most rewarding destination in the northern section of the Breede River Valley is **TULBAGH**, easily visited in a day from Cape Town, 120km away, though there's no public transport to Tulbagh. Driving up from the south, you can get here on the **R43** from Worcester or the **R301** from Paarl. If you've time, you could also attempt to cross the beautiful **Bain's Kloof Pass**, on the R303 connecting these two routes.

You could drive into town, down Van der Stel Street and out the other end, and assume from this unexceptional main street that Tulbagh was just another humdrum *dorp*. But one block west, on **Church Street**, is the most perfectly restored eighteenth- and nineteenth-century streetscape. Only a fraction of what you see here is original (the town was flattened in 1969 by an earthquake), yet this is no Disneyland; the restoration of the buildings used salvaged materials from the ruins, following photographic and hand-drawn records.

The best way to enjoy Tulbagh is to stroll up Church Street and take in the houses, gardens and gables that are an essential element of Cape Dutch architecture. At least six different styles can be distinguished just along this short road. At no. 23, **Paddagang** (frog passage) was originally a *taphuis* (wine house); today it's a restaurant with a wine house attached (see opposite), recommended for its wonderful labels all featuring comical frogs rather than for the liquor itself. Although the gabled Old Church, built in 1743, is of some interest, you won't miss much if you don't spend long over the collection of bric-a-brac inside that constitutes the **Oude Kerk Volksmuseum**, 2 Church Street (Mon–Fri 8.30am–5pm, Sat 9am–4pm, Sun 11am–4pm; R5). The museum has three annexes (included in entry fee) at nos. 4, 14 and 22, which won't keep you busy for too long, either. No. 4 has photographs of old houses in Tulbagh before the earthquake and traces the histories of the families who lived in them.

Just outside town, **De Oude Drostdy Museum** (Mon–Fri 10am–5pm & Sat 10am–12.30pm), 4km to the north on the extension of Van der Stel Street, is an impressive Cape Dutch spectacle designed by the French architect Louis-Michel Thibault. Each town in the Cape, under the Dutch, had a *drostdy*, or courthouse, where justice was dispensed. These days, in Tulbagh, the dark prison quarters have become candle-lit tasting rooms.

Practicalities

The town's **tourist office**, 14 Church Street (Mon–Fri 9am–5pm, Sat 10am–4pm, Sun 11am–4pm; ☎023 230 1348, ⓦwww.tulbaghtourism.org.za), can give advice on activities and accommodation in the area. Better than the tourist bureau's site, though, is ⓦwww.tulbagh.net.

There's a good range of **accommodation** in Tulbagh, from camping or self-catering on farms to roomy guesthouses, and there's also a surprising range of good **restaurants**, most of which specialize in Cape country cuisine.

Accommodation

Acre Laan Farm Cottages 5km south of town, 1km off the Wolseley Rd ☎023 230 2991, ⓕ023 230 2762. Two self-catering cottages sleeping four on a farm. ❷

Danie Tron 21 Church St ☎084 742 3704. A designated National Monument, with three bedrooms and two bathrooms, in a quiet spot a stone's throw from the *Paddagang* restaurant where you have breakfast (included in the rate). The best value accommodation in town. ❷

De Oude Herberg 6 Church St ☎023 230 0260, ⓔingham@mweb.co.za. A well-positioned inn

offering gorgeous, country-style rooms with French doors opening onto the veranda, and a pool for hot days. Meals served for guests and drop-ins in the courtyard. ❸

Die Ster 7km north of town ☎023 230 0545 or 083 629 3339. Two self-catering farm cottages perfectly situated on a mountainside, with great views and hiking opportunities. ❷

Hunter's Retreat Roughly 1500m north of town along the main road ☎023 230 0582, ⓦwww.lando.co.za/HuntersRetreat. Airy B&B rooms and spacious two-storey thatched cottages with lounges, on a working farm that rears cattle, ostriches and sheep. A chapel on the farm makes this a favourite for weddings. ❸

Wild Olive Farm 6km south of town, heading towards Wolseley; a signposted turn-off leads you 2km down a bumpy track ☎ 023 230 1160, ⓦ www.wildolivefarm.com. Family-oriented farm accommodation in six fully equipped, self-catering cottages with fireplaces and braai stands. Grassy campsites with spotless ablution facilities are also available. Guests receive complimentary milk and free-range eggs, and you can swim in a mountain-stream dam. ❷

Eating and drinking

Ballotina 43 Church St ☎ 023 230 1694. Italian food – and arias delivered by owner Michael Kenny. Mon–Sat lunch & dinner.

Bloemkombossi Church St. Great steaks and a grassed area with swings to keep the whole family happy. Tues–Sun breakfast & lunch.

Epicentre Church St. Coffee shop-cum-art gallery.

Paddagang Restaurant and Wine House 23 Church St ☎ 023 230 0242. Tulbagh's biggest attraction, apart from its historic streetscape. Established in 1821 as one of the first taverns in the Cape, it serves moderately priced regional cooking, including *waterblommetjiebredie*, *smoersnoek* and *bobotie*, and locally produced wines. You can sit outside under vines in the lovely garden. Daily breakfast, lunch and tea, plus Wed & Fri dinner.

Readers 12 Church St ☎ 023 230 0087. Small, elegant eating place and art gallery in the eighteenth-century cottage once used by the church's sick comforter or "reader". The lunch and dinner menu consists of country cuisine with a touch of sophistication – so you'll find lamb cooked with citrus and served with roasted garlic, and gazpacho with avocado sorbet. Closed Tues.

Robertson

ROBERTSON, approached either from the N1 or N2 from Cape Town, is the largest town in the attractive stretch of the Breede River Valley, known as the Robertson Valley hereabouts. The acidity level of the soil is ideal for growing grapes – indeed the Robertson Valley is responsible for some ten percent of South Africa's vineyards – but irrigation is necessary as the climate is hot and dry. The best wines here tend to be Chenin Blancs and Colombards, and some good Muscadels are conjured up too.

The only conceivable reason for visiting this fruit-picking town is the **Robertson Winery** (Mon–Thurs 8am–5pm, Fri 8am–4.30pm, Sat 9am–1pm) just off the R60, which produces some good-value and fairly quaffable Chardonnays and Colombards that are cheaper here than in the shops. The valley, however, has its own **wine route**, which extends to McGregor and Bonnievale in the south; we've picked out the best of its roughly two dozen wineries below.

Along the R317 from Robertson to Bonnievale

About 8km southeast of Robertson, **Bon Courage** (Mon–Fri 8am–5pm, Sat 9.30am–1pm; free) is notable for its sweet whites, especially Muscadel, and has a tasting room in a beautiful old homestead along the Breede River. The *Café Maude* here (Mon–Sat 9am–4pm) serves breakfast and light lunches. Roughly 8km further south, and also on the right-hand side of the road, **Van Loveren** (Mon–Fri 8.30–5pm, Sat 9.30am–1pm; free; ⓦ www .vanloveren.co.za) offers wine tasting in a lovely garden and is known for its great-value wines, especially the River Red. **De Wetshof**, 500m south of Van Loveren on the left of the road (Mon–Fri 8.30am–4.30pm, Sat 9.30am–12.30pm; free; ☎ 023 615 1853), is a top-notch estate with photogenic mountain and vineyard views, producing several excellent whites, including their flagship Bateleur Chardonnay.

Along the R60 from Robertson to Worcester

About 7km north of Robertson, **Graham Beck** (Mon–Fri 9am–5pm, Sat 10am–3pm; free; ⓦ www.grahambeckwines.co.za) is a high-flying estate making an international splash, with orders from British supermarket giants for their vast range of reds and whites, many of them in the top rank. Their tasting room is daringly modern.

McGregor

If you're not stocking up on wine, press straight on from Robertson to **McGREGOR**, fifteen minutes to the south at the end of a minor road signposted off the R60. Although it's been described as South Africa's best-preserved Victorian Karoo village, you shouldn't expect anything like a quaint English hamlet – a description that might just about apply to Greyton on the well-watered side of the mountains (see p.233). Still, dry as it is, McGregor is an attractive place, with thatched, whitewashed cottages glaring in the summer daylight amid the low rusty steel-wool scrub, and a quiet, relaxed atmosphere that has attracted a small population of spiritual seekers and artists. Residents are being urged to build in harmony with existing style and thus maintain the town's character.

McGregor gained modest prosperity in the nineteenth century by becoming a centre of the whipstock industry, supplying wagoners and transport riders with long bamboo sticks for goading oxen. There aren't too many ox-drawn wagons today, and tourism, though developing, is still quite limited. The main reason people come here, other than to take in the town's spare beauty (it's worth taking a late-afternoon stroll down one of the dirt roads out of town), is to walk the **Boesmanskloof Traverse** (see box on p.234), which starts 14km from McGregor and crosses to Greyton on the other side of the mountain.

Practicalities

You'll find most of what you want down Voortrekker Street, McGregor's main thoroughfare, dominated by a Dutch Reformed church. In the same street you'll also find the small, clearly signposted **tourist office** (Mon–Fri 9am–1pm & 2–4.30pm, Sat & Sun 9am–1.30pm; ☎023 625 1954; ⓦ www.mcgregor .org.za). They can book you accommodation, and issue permits for walking the Boesmanskloof Traverse. They will also direct you to artists' studios in town, and to complementary health practitioners, offering massage and yoga; Pilates is available with outstanding teacher Corrie van der Walt (☎023 625 1951).

Accommodation

All the central **accommodation** is in Voortrekker Street or clearly indicated off it. There are also a couple of nice places in the atmospheric Karoo semi-desert outside town, including *Whipstock Farm*, which is a good base on this side of the hills if you're hiking the Boesmanskloof Traverse.

Green Gables Country Inn Voortrekker St ☎023 625 1626, ✉grgables@telkomsa.net. Tastefully furnished rooms in a former late-Victorian country trading store, which retains its original ambience through the use of period pieces. All the rooms have doorways onto a Frenchified English country garden. There's also a pub and highly rated restaurant. ❸
McGregor Country Cottages Voortrekker St ☎023 625 1816, ✉countrycottages@lando

.co.za. Tranquil self-catering in a complex of cottages with traditional reed ceilings and fireplaces, surrounded by gardens, orchards and vegetable patches. There's also a pool. A separate honeymoon house is available and worth the price. Wheelchair- and child-friendly. ❷
McGregor Country House B&B Voortrekker St ☎023 625 1656, ✉mcgcountry@telkomsa.net. Friendly guesthouse with three attractive en-suite

rooms, one of which is available on a self-catering basis. B&B ❸

Mr Oosthuizen On the McGregor side of the Boesmanskloof Traverse ☎023 625 1735. Basic semi-equipped huts – bring your own sleeping bag, towels and supplies. ❶

Old Mill Lodge On the southern outskirts of town, at the end of Voortrekker St, ☎023 625 1841, ⓦwww.oldmilllodge.co.za. A set of appealing cottages at a historic country lodge, with a tranquil ambience, surrounded by vineyards and gardens. There's also a swimming pool and a good restaurant. B&B ❹, half board ❺

Rhebokskraal Farm Cottages 2km south of town ☎023 625 1787, ⓔrhebokskraal@hermann .co.za. Secluded cottages, each on a different part of this beautiful fruit, olive and grape farm, which

is within easy reach of the restaurants in town. It's best to make a reservation and get directions then, though you could at a pinch just turn up at *Villagers*, their shop selling the farm's organic products in the main street, and ask if a cottage is available. ❷

Whipstock Farm 8km from the centre on the southerly continuation of Voortrekker St ☎ & ⒻЛ023 625 1733. Restored cottages on an old citrus, almond and grape farm in the mountains. *Whipstock* is 5km from the McGregor side of the Boesmanskloof Traverse (see box on p.234), and the owners will pick you up from the trail for free. Swimming, bikes and canoes are available free to guests, and there's reasonably priced horse-riding, too. Great for kids. Full board ❸

Eating and drinking

All the establishments mentioned here are along or off Voortrekker Street; Sundays are noticeably quiet. *Café Temenos* (Tues–Sun breakfast and lunch) offers a tranquil garden setting and first-rate Italian deli fare, including bruschetta, ciabatta and focaccia filled with cold meat or cheese. *Villagers* (Mon–Sat) sells olives, preserves and fruit nectars and is good for daytime snacks and teas, with a veranda from which to watch the passing scene. In summer, only, the *Malmani Craft Shop* does teas, coffees and toasted sandwiches.

Light lunches are on offer at the *Old Mill Lodge*, where you can also splash out on a four-course set evening meal (though make a reservation for this by lunchtime). You can sit by the fire in the winter, or enjoy their veranda's views on summer evenings. Decidedly convivial is the *Green Gables Country Inn*, for delicious and well-priced three-course dinners, including offerings such as roast lamb with Mediterranean vegetables, plus coffee and cake during the day. There's also a friendly **pub** here. Two other pubs, in Voortrekker Street, are the *Jack and Grape* (Mon–Sat) in the *McGregor Haus Hotel*, which has a large TV screen for watching sport, and serves steaks to a clientele of local farmers; and the Irish pub at the *McGregor Country House*, which really hums on Friday and Saturday night.

Montagu

The ultimate Breede River Valley destination, 190km from Cape Town, is **MONTAGU**. The approach from the south through Cogman's Kloof Gorge numbers among the most dramatic arrivals in the country: a short five-kilometre winding road cuts through a rock face into a narrow valley dramatically opening out to Montagu. Soaring mountains rise up in vast arches of twisted strata that display reds and ochres, and from September to October the gentler tints of peach and apricot blossoms flood the valley. Not only is Montagu very pleasing, with sufficient Victorian architecture to create an historic character, but there's enough to do here to more than justify an overnight stay.

The town was named in 1851 after **John Montagu**, the visionary British Secretary of the Cape, who realized that the colony would never develop without decent communications and was responsible for commissioning the first mountain passes connecting remote areas to Cape Town. The grateful farmers of Agter Cogman's Kloof (literally: "behind Cogman's Kloof") leapt at the chance of a snappier name for their village and named it after him.

Montagu is best known for its **hot springs**, but serious **rock climbers** come for its cliff faces, which are regarded as among the country's most challenging. You can also explore the mountains on a couple of trails or, easiest of all, on a tractor ride onto one of the peaks. Montagu is also conveniently positioned for excursions along both the Robertson and Little Karoo **wine routes** (see p.215).

Arrival, information and accommodation

Buses to Montagu are restricted to a service from Belville in Cape Town via Paarl and Worcester, operated by Munniks (☎021 637 1850), departing Cape Town on Wednesday, Friday, Saturday and Sunday. Montagu's **tourist office**, 24 Bath Street (Mon–Fri 8.45am–4.45pm, Sat 9am–5pm, Sun 9.30am–noon & 3–5pm; ☎023 614 2471), is useful for picking up information about local attractions. Even if you're here for the springs, it is far nicer to find somewhere to **stay** in town rather than at the spa, which amounts to little more than a large crowded resort, especially at weekends and school holidays.

Accommodation

Aasvoelkrans 1 Van Riebeeck St ☎023 614 1228, ⓦwww.aasvoelkrans.co.za. Three exceptionally imaginative garden rooms at a guesthouse situated on a Arabian stud farm, in a pretty part of town. ❸

Cynthia's 3 Krom St ☎023 614 2760, ⓔcyncots@lando.co.za. Nine self-catering cottages dotted around the west side of town, all in old houses, with gardens and braai areas, and near the starting point for hiking trails. ❶

John Montagu Victorian Guest House 30 Joubert St ☎023 614 1331, ⓦwww.johnmontagu.co.za. En-suite rooms at an elegant guesthouse with enough period furniture and knick-knacks to create a historic ambience without being oppressive. ❺

Mimosa Lodge Church St ☎023 614 2351, ⓦwww.mimosa.co.za. A handsome Edwardian-era two-storey house just off Bath St. Rooms are en suite, with either shower or bath – the best are upstairs, with a balcony. There's an emphasis on food – which they characterize as South African fusion – using venison or seafood, and local ingredients. Half board ❻

Montagu Caravan Park At the west end of Bath St, across the Keisie River ☎023 614 2675, ⓔmontagu@telkomsa.net. A friendly municipal caravan park offering campsites and basic timber cabins sleeping four, with personal touches such as fresh flowers. The units have cooker and fridge, with the nicest cabins boasting thatched roof,

TV and microwave. Ablution facilities are shared; bring your own towels. Bedding can be rented. ❷

Montagu Country Hotel 27 Bath St ☎023 614 3125, ⓦwww.montagucountryhotel.co.za. Rooms with Art Deco-inspired decor, plus a restaurant, bar and heated mineral pool. ❹

Montagu Rose Guest House 19 Kohler St ☎023 614 2681, ⓔbenvr@lantic.net. In a modern home, with personalized service. All rooms have baths and mountain views. Well run and good value. ❸

Montagu Springs ☎023 614 1050, ⓦwww.montagusprings.co.za. Large resort with fully equipped self-catering chalets, some more luxurious than others, that sleep four. Prices start at R300 per chalet though note that you pay an extra fifty percent during school holidays, or to stay Fri and Sat at any time of year.

Seven Church Street 7 Church St ☎023 614 1186, ⓔmwjones@yebo.co.za. A lovely central Victorian house, offering a romantic stay. Enticements include embroidered pure cotton linen, clawfoot baths and a gorgeous garden popular for bridal photography. Friendly and well run. ❹

Squirrel's Corner On the corner of Bloem and Jouberts streets ☎ & ⓕ023 614 1081, ⓦwww.squirrelscorner.co.za. B&Bs with four comfortable, spotless en-suite rooms in a friendly family house, as well as a garden suite which is two blocks from the main road. ❸

The Town and around

Highly photogenic, Montagu is ideal for seeing on foot, taking in the interesting buildings or simply enjoying the setting, with its mountains, valleys and farms. There are also a couple of museums, neither of which is outstanding. The best thing about the **Montagu Museum**, 41 Long Street (Mon–Fri 9am–1pm & 2–5pm, Sat & Sun 10.30am–12.30pm; R3),

Montagu activities

Three **hikes** begin from the Old Mill at the north end of Tanner Street, where there's also a small park at the foot of cliffs; **maps** for the hikes are available from Montagu's tourist office. Shortest is the Lover's Walk, a stroll of just over 2km through Bath Kloof (or Badkloof; daily 7am–6pm) that follows the Keisie River to the hot springs. More substantial is the twelve-kilometre **Cogman's Kloof hiking trail**, which can be completed in three to six hours; only the first 2km are steep, after which it's an easy walk with nice views of Montagu, the ravines and mountains. Most ambitious is the **Bloupunt hiking trail**, at around 15.5km, which gets you up to an altitude of over 1000m and can be completed in six to nine hours; the terrain en route encompasses ravines, mountain streams, craggy cliffs and rock formations. From the summit of Bloupunt you can see as far as McGregor and Robertson. Throughout the year, you will see dassies and klipspringers as well as a large variety of wild flowers because of the presence of perennial streams. The *fynbos* vegetation includes proteas, ericas, aloes, lilies, watsonias and wild orchids. Carry a waterbottle to fill up at a waterpoint about halfway up the mountain.

If you don't feel like walking up the Langeberg Mountains, you can still get to the top on a highly recommended three-hour **tractor ride** (Wed & Sat 10am & 2pm; book at the Montagu tourist office) from Protea Farm, which is 29km along the Koo/Touws River road (R318). Remember to take warm clothes. Further along the same route, on Eendracht Farm, 45km from Montagu (☏023 614 1991), you can try your hand at **archery** or **quad bike riding**. The farm rents out a basic stone cottage (❷) with no electricity, which makes a great retreat from the city lights.

housed in a pleasant old church, is its herbal project, which traces traditional Khoisan knowledge about the medicinal properties of local plants. Work is being done in conjunction with the Pharmacology Department at the University of Cape Town and you can buy their booklet *Herbal Remedies: Montagu Museum*, which details some of the findings. The herbs themselves are also on sale, some of them grown in the gardens of the **Joubert House Museum** (Mon–Fri 9.30am–1pm & 2–5pm, Sat 10.30–noon; R3), one block west at 25 Long Street. Built in 1853, this was one of the first houses standing in a vast plot which was originally a town farm, and has peach-pip floors fixed with beeswax, characteristic of the area, and period furniture on display in each of the rooms.

Montagu's main draw is the **Montagu Springs Resort** (daily 8am–11pm; R30; ⓦwww.montagusprings.co.za), about 3km northwest of town on the R318 (or reached on foot by following the Keisie River, which flows along the north edge of town). Several chlorinated open-air pools of different temperatures and a couple of Jacuzzis are spectacularly situated at the foot of cliffs – an effect slightly spoilt by the neon lights of a hotel complex and fast-food restaurant. It's a fabulous place to take kids, but the weekends become a mass of splashing bodies. If you want a quiet time, go first thing in the morning or last thing at night; when the outside air is cooler, the steaming waters provide a wonderfully relaxing alcohol-free nightcap.

Eating and drinking

Montagu has a couple of good **restaurants** (evening meals must be reserved in advance); two farm stalls along Bath Street to pick up fresh and dried fruit, *biltong* and *boerewors*; a pleasant out of town tea-garden; as well as a couple of coffee shops along Bath Street.

Die Stal 8km out of town on the R318 ☎082 324 4318. A pleasant venue on a farm serving lunches and teas, en route to the obligatory tractor ride.

Four Oaks 46 Long St ☎023 614 2778. With a shaded courtyard, this top-quality restaurant serves South African country-style food with a European influence (the chef is German). Tues–Sun lunch and dinner.

Jessica's 28 Bath St ☎023 614 1805. Small and friendly, named after the proprietors'

boxer dog and decorated with period dog prints. Here you'll get cosmopolitan bistro-style dishes and a top selection of Robertson wines; the cajun-roasted baby chicken on wild rice with *peri-peri* cream is recommended. Daily eves.

Preston's Restaurant & Thomas Bain Pub Bath St ☎023 614 1633. Small, intimate nightspot that remains open till late and is recommended for its sole and oxtail.

Oudtshoorn and around

OUDTSHOORN has been called the "ostrich capital of the world"; the town's surrounds are indeed crammed with ostrich farms, several of which you can visit, and the local souvenir shops keep busy dreaming up 1001 tacky ways to recycle ostrich parts as comestibles and souvenirs. But Oudtshoorn has two other big draws: it's the best base for visiting the nearby **Cango Caves** (see p.223), and the town is known for its sunshine and pleasant climate. Only 63km of tar and a range of mountains separate Oudtshoorn from Wilderness on the coast, yet the weather couldn't be more different; this is especially good news in winter, when a cold downpour along the Garden Route can give the lie to the idea of "sunny South Africa".

Some 50km west of Oudtshoorn, **Calitzdorp** is a delightfully unassuming Victorian village that can be seen as part of a circular excursion incorporating the scenic **Groenfontein Valley**. Its wineries and one or two tea shops offer the chance of a breather if you're travelling on the R62 through the Little Karoo. **De Rust**, a town with similar origins to Calitzdorp but 35km in the opposite direction, has benefited greatly from lying on the N12 connecting the N1 to the Garden Route, but is little more than a pleasant pit stop.

Some history

Oudtshoorn started out as a small village named in honour of Geesje Ernestina Johanna van Oudtshoorn, wife of the first civil commissioner for George. By the 1860s **ostriches**, which live in the wild in Africa, were being raised under the ideal conditions of the Oudtshoorn Valley, where the warm climate and loamy soils enabled lucerne, the favourite diet of the flightless birds, to be grown. The quirky Victorian fashion for large feathers had turned the ostriches into a source of serious wealth, and by the 1880s hundreds of thousands of kilogrammes of feathers were being exported, and birds were changing hands for up to £1000 a pair – an unimaginable sum in those days. On the back of this boom, sharp businessmen made their fortunes, ignorant farmers were ripped off, and labourers drew the shortest straw of all. The latter were mostly coloured descendants of the Outeniqua and Attaqua Khoikhoi and trekboers, who received derisory wages supplemented by rations of food, wine, spirits and tobacco – a practice that still continues on some farms. In the early twentieth century, the most successful farmers and traders built themselves "feather palaces", ostentatious sandstone Edwardian buildings that have become the defining feature of Oudtshoorn.

Arrival and information

Of the **intercity buses**, Intercape pulls in at Stanmar Motors, 187 Langenhoven Road, and Translux at Queens Riverside Mall, off Voortrekker

Street. Oudtshoorn's **tourist office** (Mon–Fri 8am–5pm, Sat 9am–1pm; ☎044 279 2532, ⍟www.oudtshoorn.com), next to the *Queens Hotel*, Baron van Reede Street, is good for information about the caves, ostrich farms and local accommodation. *Backpackers Paradise* rents out **bikes** and also arranges spectacular **adventurous cycling trips** down the Swartberg Pass, chaperoned with motor vehicle backup. Oudtshoorn has several **Internet cafés**, the most convenient of which is *Internet@café*, 62 Baron van Reede Street.

Accommodation

Oudtshoorn has a number of large hotels catering mainly to tour buses, plus plenty of good-quality B&Bs and guesthouses, a centrally located campsite with chalets, and one of the country's best-run backpacker lodges. Some of the nicest places to stay are in the attractive countryside en route to Cango Caves. **Rates** fall dramatically during the winter months following the arts festival. The tourist office offers a free accommodation booking service.

Backpackers Paradise 148 Baron van Reede St ☎044 272 3436, ⍟www.backpackersparadise.hostel.com. A friendly and well-run two-storey hostel along the main drag, which makes an effort to go the extra few centimetres with three-quarter beds, en-suite doubles and family rooms as well as three small dorms – and, in season, a portion of ostrich egg on the house for breakfast. If you're travelling on the Baz Bus or the Outeniqua Choo-Tjoe to George (see p.262) and intend to stay at *Backpackers Paradise*, you can arrange for them to pick you up (R50). Their on-site adventure centre organizes cycle trips in the Swartberg Pass. ❶

Berluda On the R328, 15km from Oudtshoorn, en route to Cango Caves ☎ & Ⓕ044 272 8518, Ⓔjpsch@mweb.co.za. Farmhouse with three bedrooms and two family units on a working ostrich ranch run by friendly owners whose family have been in the tranquil Schoemanshoek Valley for generations. They can organize ostrich farm tours too, and there is a pool to cool off in. ❸

De Opstal Country Lodge 12km north of Oudtshoorn on the R328 ☎044 279 2954, ⍟www.deopstal.co.za. Most luxurious and biggest of the Schoemanshoek establishments with restored farm buildings from 1830. Rooms have a/c and fireplaces, and there is a saltwater pool in lovely gardens, as well as a restaurant. ❸–❻

De Oude Meul Signposted off the R328 to Cango Caves, 18km north of Oudtshoorn ☎ & Ⓕ044 272 7190, Ⓔdeoudemeul@mweb.co.za. A row of pleasant B&B rooms and some family units facing onto a small lake and hills in Schoemanspoort, on an ostrich nursery farm which also has a few tame kudu, eland and blesbok. ❸

De Oue Werf Signposted off the R328 to Cango Caves, 12km north of Oudtshoorn ☎ & Ⓕ044 272 8712, Ⓔouewerf@mweb.co.za. B&B in an old Schoemanshoek Valley farmstead, with good walks, bird-watching and a swimming pool. The dam has a raft and swinging slide. A good option if you're visiting the caves and want to stay in the country. ❸

Gum Tree Lodge 139 Church St ☎044 279 2528, ⍟www.oudtshoorn.com/gumtree. Two houses opposite each other with B&B rooms, a 10min walk from the centre. There's sherry on arrival and electric blankets for the cold winter nights. ❸

Kannaland Lodge 126 St John St ☎044 279 2685, Ⓕ044 279 2686. Reliable if predictable modern hotel-style rooms conveniently located in the centre. You can buy meat packs and braai in the garden. ❷

Kleinplaas Holiday Resort 171 Baron van Reede St ☎044 272 5811, ⍟www.kleinplaas.co.za. Shady camping and fully equipped brick chalets sleeping four, conveniently close to town, with a swimming pool and launderette. ❷

Old Parsonage 141 High St Ⓔgvs74@xsinet.co.za. Rooms, some en suite, in a two-storey sandstone Dutch Reformed Church parsonage that's still in use, and has a very pleasant garden. ❷

Queen's Hotel Baron van Reede Street ☎044 272 2101, ⍟www.queenshotel.co.za. Nicest of the smart hotels in Oudtshoorn, and geared to tour buses, with all the facilities and right in the centre, next to the museum. *Queen's* offers style and cool relief in the summer, with marble floors, a fountain and swimming pool. The expensive *Colony* restaurant has an upstairs terrace and ostrich on the menu. ❺

The Town and the ostrich farms

Oudtshoorn's town centre is a pretty straightforward place to negotiate, and has little more than a couple of museums worth checking out if you've time to kill. The town's main interest lies in its Victorian and Edwardian sandstone buildings, some of which are unusually grand and elegant for a Karoo *dorp*.

The **C.P. Nel Museum** (Mon–Sat 8am–5pm, Sat 9am–5pm; R8), on the corner of Baron van Reede Street and Voortrekker Road, is a good place to start your explorations. A handsome sandstone building, it was built in 1906 as a boys' school, but now houses an eccentric collection of items relating to ostriches. Nearby, **Le Roux Town House**, on the corner of Loop and High streets (Mon–Fri 9am–1pm & 2–5pm), is a perfectly preserved family town house, and the only way to get a glimpse inside one of the much-vaunted feather palaces. The beautifully preserved furnishings were all imported from Europe between 1900 and 1920, and there is plenty to stroll around and admire.

Many people come to Oudtshoorn to see, or even ride, **ostriches**. You don't actually have to visit one of the ostrich farms to view Africa's biggest bird, as you're bound to see flocks of them as you drive past farms in the vicinity or past truckloads of them on their way to the slaughterhouse (feathers being no longer fashionable, these days ostriches are raised for their low-cholesterol flesh). A number of show farms offer **tours** (45–90min) costing around R20 a person, which include the chance to sit on an ostrich and the spectacle of jockeys racing the birds. Best of the bunch is Cango Ostrich and Butterfly Farm on the main road between Oudtshoorn and the Cango Caves, which takes only one group of visitors (or individuals) at a time.

Eating and drinking

Oudtshoorn has a choice of several places to eat, mostly strung out along Baron van Reede Street and catering to the tourist trade, with the obligatory ostrich dish.

Bernard se Taphuis Baron van Reede St ☎044 272 3208. Large, central restaurant opposite the tourist office, with a pleasant outdoor terrace upstairs. A good place to sample ostrich, game dishes, steaks and Afrikaner specialities at moderate prices. Mon–Sat eves.

Fijne Keuken Restaurant Baron van Reede St ☎044 272 6403. In a house converted into a cosy restaurant with tables in several rooms as well as on the veranda, this is the nicest spot in town for a drink or for a reasonably priced meal, with enormous salads, pasta and ostrich dishes. Mon–Sat lunch & dinner, Sun dinner.

Friedl's Baron van Reede St, opposite the museum. A central coffee shop that does nice salads, sandwiches, burgers, pitta pockets and decent coffee. Daily 8.30am–10pm, though closed Sun eves.

Godfather Restaurant 61 Voortrekker Rd ☎044 272 5404. A popular eating place with a huge menu, noted for its medium-priced pizzas, venison

and ostrich steaks; also good just for a drink. It's an excellent spot in winter, when there's a roaring fire. Closed Sun.

Jemima's 94 Baron Reede St ☎044 272 0808. The best place to eat in town, with an imaginative and good-value menu including *boerewors*-stuffed ravioli. Mon & Sun dinner only, Tues–Sat lunch & dinner.

Paljas Baron van Reede St ☎044 272 0982. One of the town's best eating places, with a contemporary South African menu that brings together Cape cuisine, Karoo cooking and African flavours from the Eastern Cape and KwaZulu-Natal. The emphasis is heavily on meat. Dinner daily.

The Rock Art Café Baron van Reede St ☎044 279 1927. The only place in town consistently open after midnight, where they serve a reasonably priced and varied menu including local specialities such as venison pie, *bobotie* and ostrich *potjie* and coffee spiked with liquor. Mon–Sat 11am–2am, Sun 6pm–2am.

Cango Caves

The **Cango Caves** number among South Africa's ten most popular attractions, drawing a quarter of a million visitors each year to gasp at their fantastic cavernous spaces, dripping rocks and rising columns of calcite. In the two centuries since they became known to the public, the caves have been seriously battered by human intervention, but they still represent a stunning landscape growing inside the Swartberg foothills. Don't go expecting a serene and contemplative experience, though: the only way of getting inside the caves is on a guided tour accompanied by a commentary.

Cango is a Khoi word meaning "a wet place" – accurate enough, given that the caves' awesome formations are the work of water constantly percolating through rock and dissolving limestone on the way. The solution drips from the roof of the cave and down the walls, depositing calcium carbonate which gradually builds up. Although the caves are many millions of years old, the calcite formations that you see today are geological youngsters, dating back a mere 100,000 years.

San hunter-gatherers sheltered in the entrance caves for millennia before white settlers arrived, but it's unlikely that they ever made it to the lightless underground chambers. **Jacobus van Zyl**, a Karoo farmer, was probably the first person to penetrate beneath the surface, when he slid down on a rope into the darkness in July 1780, armed with a lamp. Over the next couple of centuries the caves were visited and pillaged by growing numbers of callers, some of whom were photographed cheerfully carting off wagonloads of limestone columns.

In the Sixties and Seventies the caves were made accessible to mass consumption when a tourist complex was built, the rock-strewn floor was evened out with concrete, ladders and walkways were installed and the caverns were turned into a kitsch extravaganza with coloured lights, piped music and an indecipherable commentary that drew hundreds of thousands of visitors each year. Even apartheid put its hefty boot in: under the premiership of Dr Hendrik Verwoerd, the arch-ideologue of racial segregation, a separate "non-whites" entrance was hacked through one wall, resulting in a disastrous through-draft that began dehydrating the caves. Fortunately, the worst excesses have now ended; concerts are no longer allowed inside the chambers, and the coloured lights have been removed.

Practicalities

The **drive** here from Oudtshoorn involves heading north along Baron van Reede Street, and continuing 32km on the R328 to the caves. The visitors' complex includes an interpretive centre with quite interesting displays about geology, people and wildlife connected with the caves; the decent *Marimba* **restaurant**; and a souvenir shop. Below the complex you'll find shady picnic sites at the edge of a river that cuts its way into the mountains and along which there are hiking trails. Two **tours** leave every hour (daily 9am–4pm). The one-hour Standard Tour (on the hour; R40) gets you through the first six chambers, but if you're an adrenaline junkie, the ninety-minute Adventure Tour (on the half-hour; R55) is a must; this takes you into the deepest sections open to the public, where the openings become smaller and smaller. Squeezing through tight openings with names like Lumbago Walk, Devil's Chimney and The Letterbox is not recommended for the overweight, faint-hearted or claustrophobic, and you should wear oldish clothes and shoes with a grip to negotiate the slippery floors.

The nearest **accommodation** is set beautifully on the river at *Cango Mountain Resort* (☏044 272 4506; ❷), signposted off the R328 27km north of

Oudtshoorn, and 3km off the main road. This is the best self-catering accommodation in the area, with especially nice timber chalets and a small shop. *Wilgewandel*, a cheap place to **eat** after seeing the caves, has the draw of camel rides on the property; it's 2km from the caves on the road back to Oudtshoorn and offers burgers, steak and sandwiches.

Calitzdorp

The tiny Karoo village of **CALITZDORP** hangs in a torpor of midday stillness. After the bustle of the "ostrich capital", it comes as a welcome surprise, with its attractive, unpretentious Victorian streets and handful of wineries. There's nothing much to do here, apart from have tea, taste some wine and wander through the streets. As in many of these inland towns, you'll find Afrikaans dominating.

The low-key **tourist office** at JS Motors in Voortrekker Street (℡044 213 3312) has some brochures about the village and its surroundings, as well as information about the wineries and accommodation. Some of South Africa's best ports are produced at the three modest wineries signposted down side roads, a few hundred metres from the centre. The most highly recommended is **Die Krans Estate** (Mon–Fri 8am–5pm, Sat 9am–3pm; free), where you can sample their wines and ports (their vintage reserve port is reckoned to be among the country's top three), and stretch your legs on a thirty-minute vineyard walk in lovely countryside. Boplaas Estate (Mon–Fri 8am–5pm, Sat 9am–3pm; free tasting; ⓦwww.boplaas.co.za) also produces some fine ports and is worth a quick look to see their massive reed-ceiling tasting room, like a cantina that fell off the set of a spaghetti western. If you've time, head for the **Calitzdorp Wine Cellar** (Mon–Fri 8am–1pm & 2–5pm, Sat 8am–noon; free), where the main attraction is the stunning view from the tasting room into the Gamka River Valley.

The best **guesthouse** in town is the very friendly *Port-Wine Guest House* (℡044 213 3131, ⓦwww.portwine.net; ❹), in a renovated early nineteenth-century homestead on the corner of Queen and Station streets and overlooking the Boplaas Estate. There's also the comfortable, country-style *Welgevonden Guest House* (℡ & Ⓕ044 213 3642, Ⓔwelgevon@telkomsa.net; ❷), St Helena Road, on a small Chardonnay farm 300m from the main road. Airy rooms with verandas are available at *Die Dorpshuis* (℡044 213 3453, Ⓔdorphuis@mweb .co.za; B&B ❷), which is centrally located at 4 Van Riebeeck Street, opposite the church, and also has self-catering. *Die Dorpshuis* is a good place to **eat** (Mon–Sat), serving reasonably priced sandwiches, teas, light meals and heavier traditional Karoo food, such as stews and lamb.

The Groenfontein Valley

A circuitous minor route diverts just east of Calitzdorp and drops into the highly scenic **Groenfontein Valley**. The narrow dirt road twists through the Swartberg foothills, past whitewashed Karoo cottages and farms and across brooks, eventually joining the R328 to Oudtshoorn. Winding through these back roads is also an option to reach Cango Caves and Prince Albert, one of the best drives you'll do in South Africa. Many of the roads are unsealed but are navigable in an ordinary car if taken slowly.

An excellent reason to take this back route is to spend a couple of nights at the *Retreat at Groenfontein* (℡ & Ⓕ044 213 3880, ⓦwww.groenfontein .com; ❺), 20km from Calitzdorp and 59km from Oudtshoorn. This isolated Victorian colonial farmstead borders on the 2300 square kilometre Swartberg Nature Reserve, an outstandingly beautiful area of gorges, rivers and dirt tracks.

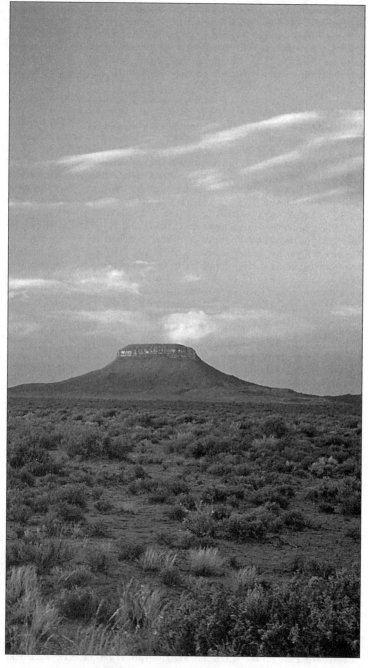

△ Karoo scenery

Accommodation is in comfortable en-suite rooms, each with its own fireplace, and rates include a very good dinner, with vegetarians well catered for.

Two good self-catering establishments are *Red Stone Hills* (℡044 213 37783, ⓌWwww.redstone.co.za) which has four lovely period-furnished Victorian cottages on a working farm 6km off the R62 (turn off 14km east of Calitzdorp), and the cheaper, homely *Kruis Rivier Guest Farm* (℡044 213 3788; ❶), further along the same road as *Red Stone Hills*.

De Rust

DE RUST is a drive-through town on the N12, which accounts for the fact that most of the buildings along the town's small main road seem to be selling something – teas, crafts, *biltong* and ostrich products galore. You'll need to reach for your phrasebook (or consult our language glossary on p.937) in this very Afrikaans village, which has a calm atmosphere and gardens that make a bright contrast with the surrounding dry hills. De Rust is a nice enough place to stop to stretch your legs and have a drink, but there's little reason to spend the night here.

Translux intercity **buses** between Gauteng and Knysna stop at the *De Rust Hotel* in the centre. The **tourist office**, 29 Schoeman Street (Mon–Fri 8.30am–5.30pm, Sat 8.30am–12.30pm; ℡044 241 2109), can supply details of accommodation other than the places reviewed here. In town, the *Avondrust B&B*, 1 Vrede Street (℡044 241 2459, ✉orbitestates@yahoo.co.uk; ❷), has en-suite **rooms** in a two-storey house a couple of streets back from the main road, as well as a self-catering flat in the garden at the back. *Oulap Country House*, some 15km east of town off the R341 to Uniondale (℡044 241 2250, ✉oulap@mweb.co.za; half board ❼), is an unusual place to stay, a Karoo farm in the Swartberg Mountains run by Jans Rautenbach, film producer and storyteller, and his wife. Rooms are eclectically furnished with antiques, *objets d'art* and South African paintings, each of them worth a story over an excellent dinner with the host.

For outdoor **eating**, there are two tea shops in the main road, both with gardens: *Herries*, marked by a purple elephant outside, has pleasant seating under shady trees, does reasonably priced food and is licensed; and *Mulberry Inn*, an acceptable tea garden. For fresh bread, cakes, indoor **teas** and light meals, *Die Groen Bliktrommel*, on the same road, is recommended. For superb meals cooked by a top city chef come to live in the country, there's the *Plough* on Schoeman and Burger streets (℡044 241 2020; Tues–Sat lunch and dinner, Sun lunch only).

Prince Albert and around

Isolation has left intact the traditional rural architecture of **PRINCE ALBERT**, an attractive little town 70km north of Oudtshoorn, across the loops and razorbacks of the Swartberg Pass – one of the most dramatic drives and entries to a town imaginable. Although firmly in the thirstlands of the South African interior, on the cusp between the Little and Great Karoo, Prince Albert is all the more striking for its perennial spring, whose water trickles down furrows along its streets – a gift that propagates fruit trees and gardens. Visitors mostly come to Prince Albert for the drive through its two southerly gateways – the **Swartberg Pass** on the R328 and **Meiringspoort** on the N12 – generally driving in one way, spending the night in town, and driving out the other.

Go to Hell

Prince Albert is one of the best places to begin a trip into **Die Hel** (also known as Hell, The Hell or Gamkaskloof), a valley that's part of the Swartberg Nature Reserve. Die Hel is not on the way to anywhere and, although it doesn't look very far on the map, you'll need to allow two and a half hours in either direction to make the spectacular but tortuous drive into it along a dirt road. A 4WD vehicle isn't needed, but you should definitely not attempt the drive in the killing heat of December or January without a/c.

There's **accommodation** here in the form of caravans and restored farm cottages, (☎044 802 5310, ✉george@cnc.org.za; ❷), with camping facilities also available. The valley has no electricity supply, though, and you'll have to heat water using a wood-fired boiler; there are also no shops or any other facilities, though you can order picnic baskets and cooked breakfasts and dinners.

Prince Albert is small enough to explore everywhere on foot. Supremely old-fashioned displays make window-shopping as much fun as the interior of any country museum, but the essence of Prince Albert is in the fleeting impressions that give the flavour of a Karoo *dorp* like nowhere else: the silver steeple of the Dutch Reformed church puncturing a deep-blue sky, residents sauntering along or progressing slowly down the main street on squeaky bikes. The town's beauty has attracted a number of artists to live here, and there are good guesthouses with mountain biking and hiking trips on offer at reasonable prices. One of the best trips is run by *Dennehof Guest House*, who can drive you up one of the mountains, at which point you're on your own two wheels for the 18km down; they charge R65 a day for bike rental. Alternatively, you can rent motorized wheels through Karoo Scooter Rental (☎023 541 1330) to explore the Swartberg Mountains.

One of the most exciting things you can do in Prince Albert, if not in South Africa, is to watch the **night skies** with resident astronomer Hans Daehne (☎084 776 4414 or 072 732 2950, ✉astrarea@absamail.co.za). The Karoo sky is literally heaven for astronomers with no pollution and few lights, and you get some of the Southern Hemisphere's sharpest views of the firmament from here. From 2005 South Africa will have the biggest telescope in the Southern Hemisphere at Sutherland, deeper in the Karoo.

Practicalities

Most people get to Prince Albert through the mountains by **car**, but you can get off the Cape Town–Johannesburg **train** at Prince Albert Road station, 45km from the hamlet, and arrange to be collected by *Onse Rus* B&B (even if you don't intend to stay with them). The trains are often late, and Prince Albert Road Station has absolutely no facilities. A courier service runs from Oudtshoorn to Prince Albert and back on Monday, Wednesday and Friday. While mostly intended for delivering goods, they do take passengers, and will do the run to Prince Albert Station (☎082 493 9535).

The **tourist office** in Church Street (☎023 541 1366) has maps with accommodation, restaurants and craft shops, and can point you to other activities in the area, as well as rent out bikes.

Accommodation

There's plenty of stylish accommodation in Prince Albert, mostly in historic limewashed and thatched Karoo cottages, Cape Dutch homesteads or colonial Victorian houses.

Bijlia Cana Wellness Retreat De Beer St ☎ &
℻ 023 541 1872, ⓦ www.karooretreat.com. An
excellent-value Karoo retreat with three en-suite
bedrooms. The hosts pamper you with
aromatherapy, reiki and reflexology, and take guests
on walks and outings to local points of interest. The
food served includes healthy continental breakfasts,
homemade bread and Karoo lamb, though veggies
can be catered for. Full board ❹

Collins House 63 Church St ☎ 023 541 1786.
The town's top place to stay consists of three
beautifully done out, a/c en-suite guest rooms in
a two-storey Victorian house, with a swimming
pool. The owner does evening meals and is a great
cook, but you may feel rather over-directed. ❸

Dennehof Guest House Off Christina de Wit St, on
the outskirts of town ☎ 023 541 1227, ⓦ www
.home.intekom.com/dennehof. Three self-contained
cottages and suites in a homestead that is a National
Monument. The owner does hiking and mountain-
biking trips. Self-catering and B&B. ❷

Hoogenoeg Holiday Houses ☎ 023 541 1455.
The cheapest accommodation in town is run by

Tannie ("Aunt") Alta, who rents out a number of
sparsely furnished but adequate old houses in
Prince Albert. ❶

Karoo Lodge 66 Church St ☎ 023 541 1467
or 082 692 7736. Reasonably priced, spacious
accommodation in a B&B run by keen hosts who'll
show you the ropes. ❸

Onse Rus 47 Church St ☎ 023 541 1380,
ⓔ lisass@intekom.co.za. Cool, thatched
B&B rooms attached to a restored Cape Dutch
house with welcoming and informed owners,
and lunches on the veranda. Tours to
Gamkaskloof and into the Swartberg range
are also offered, including ones on foot or by
bike, and children are welcome. There are
horses to pet on the property, or ride if you're
experienced. ❷–❸

Swartberg Hotel 77 Church St ☎ 023 541 1332,
ⓦ www.swartberg.co.za. A Victorian two-storey
National Monument, fully refurbished following a
fire in 2001. Traditional Karoo dinners are served
in an atmospheric dining room, and there's a
swimming pool. ❸

Eating

CJ's Church St, a few doors down from the *Swartberg Hotel*. Good value for no-nonsense evening
meals, including lamb chops, fish and chips and
other deep-fried delights, served with a singular
lack of flair. Daily from 5pm.

Die Ou Kelder 5km out of town on a very rough
road ☎ 023 541 1908. Traditional Afrikaans catering in a 100-year-old barn. Offerings including
braaivleis and, by prior arrangement, a cold buffet
on Sundays for a minimum of six people.

Karoo Kombuis 18 Deurdrift St
☎ 023 541 1110. Traditional fare from this part
of the country, with a home-cooked feel. Daily
eves only.

Sampie se Plaasstal At the south end of
the main road. A great place for snacks,
with excellent dried fruit and rusks, as well
as local olives which are among the best in
South Africa. Open for breakfast, light lunches
and tea.

The N1 from Worcester to Beaufort West

The **N1** is the main highway between Cape Town and Johannesburg, and with
the majority of flights still arriving in Johannesburg it's common for visitors
to arrive there and drive down to the coast. This account, however, assumes
you'll be starting your journey in Cape Town and heading north. While this
route isn't particularly inspiring, and won't take you through the diversity of
the country, it does lead you into the Karoo, the huge semi-desert filling the
centre-west of South Africa. The various towns along the way have a couple of
interesting historic buildings and some of the flavour of the isolated Karoo in
their street scenes – enough to fill an hour if you're looking for a break from
the long journey. The most compelling places are undoubtedly the Victorian
village of **Matjiesfontein** and **the Karoo National Park** just outside Beaufort West, both of which are destinations in their own right.

Matjiesfontein

One of the quirkier manifestations of Victorian colonialism lies 250km east of Cape Town at the historic village of **MATJIESFONTEIN** (pronounced "Mikey's-fontayn"). Little more than two dusty streets beside a train track, the village resembles a film set rather than a Karoo *dorp*: every building, including the grand train station, is a classic period piece, with tin roofs, pastel walls, well-tended gardens and Victorian frills. At the eastern end of the main street is the centrepiece, the *Lord Milner*, a hotel decked out with turrets and balconies and fountains by the entrance. If you're passing by, make sure you stop at least for a look around; at less than three hours' drive from Cape Town the village is worth considering as a two-day trip in its own right.

The origins of this curious place lie in the tale of a young Scottish entrepreneur, Jimmy Logan, who came to Cape Town to work on the railways and obtained the concession to sell refreshments to passengers all the way along the line from Cape Town to Bulawayo. He built Matjiesfontein as a health resort – making much play on the clean Karoo air – and it became a gathering point for the wealthy and influential around the turn of the last century.

Today the village is doing brisk trade as a treasured relic. You can still come here in the classical manner on the mainline **train** from Cape Town to Jo'burg/Pretoria (a leisurely rather than direct journey), and **stay** at the *Lord Milner* (☎023 561 3011, ⓦwww.matjiesfontein.com; ❷), either in one of the comfortable rooms in the hotel itself, or in one of the annexes in the surrounding houses; the cheapest rooms are in a separate section in the garden and don't include breakfast. The gardens themselves and the large swimming pool are delightfully restorative. Inside the hotel there are huge portraits on the wall, grand staircases, polished brass fittings and, perhaps taking the theme a touch too far, rather surly service from waitresses dressed in black and white, with doilies on their heads. For **eating and drinking**, the hotel has a dimly lit dining room and a wonderfully aged and creaking bar. Along the main street you'll find a tea room, souvenir shop and post office, all in attractive Victorian houses.

Laingsburg and Leeu-Gamka

There's little incentive to stop at **LAINGSBURG**, a town only 27km further along the N1, which marks the start of the long, lonely spaces of the Karoo. There's a service station at the spot where the road pulls around the Buffels River, and there are a couple of nondescript hotels and a cosy **caravan park** just up behind the service station, with tiny rondavels (❶). As you drive through town, look out for the sign on the central reservation showing the water level during the catastrophic flood here in 1981 – it's level with (if not higher than) the roof of a car. Just outside Laingsburg, beside the road, is one of the best surviving examples of a Anglo-Boer War **blockhouse**. In all the British built some eight thousand blockhouses (at £16 each) at frequent intervals along the railway line to protect their main supply route, prompting Boer General Christiaan de Wet to pass comment on the British "blockhead" system.

One of the longest empty stretches is along the next 124km until you reach **LEEU-GAMKA**, with a filling station and a tiny Anglo-Boer War cemetery that just about has room for the grave of Private Schultz, the tallest man in the British army. Both barrels of the name Leeu-Gamka mean "lion", the first of which is Afrikaans, the second Khoi. But the acquaintanceship of the hamlet with its namesake ended some time ago through the barrel of a gun.

Beaufort West

For over 100km on either side of **BEAUFORT WEST**, the scenery from the N1 is far away and hazy, so the appearance of the Nieuwveld Mountains, which rise up behind town, give the place a certain distinction. Beyond that, however, Beaufort West is not a pretty place, with the N1 traffic trundling through its centre (watch out for speed traps and remember to stop at traffic lights), and it devotes most of its attention to servicing road-weary travellers.

As befits a town which is the oldest municipality in South Africa, most of the old buildings have a very municipal stolidity to them. Principal among these is the town's **museum**, 87 Donkin Street (Mon–Fri 8.30am–12.45pm & 1.45–4.45pm, Sat 9am–noon; R6), in the old town hall, which houses an exhibition honouring the glamorous life and achievements of Beaufort West's Professor Christiaan Barnard, who performed the world's first human heart transplant operation at Groote Schuur Hospital in Cape Town in 1967. He died in 2001 and his burial place, in the garden of the parsonage, is part of the museum.

Practicalities

Intercity **buses** pull into the Engen garage complex in Donkin Street. The town's helpful **tourist office** is at 63 Donkin Street (Mon–Fri 8am–4.45pm; ℡023 415 1488), one block along from the museum.

For **eating**, you could do worse than the breakfasts and lunches in the *Clyde House Coffee Shop and Guest House* on Donkin Street, though the best breakfasts are to be had at the *Matoppo Inn*, which is open to non-guests (7–9am). They also do four-course, set menu Karoo-style dinners, if booked earlier in the day. Otherwise evening meals come down to *Mac Young's*, a Scottish-themed restaurant at 156 Donkin St (it's nestled behind a Caltex service station) and popular with Afrikaners. Opposite the *Formula 1* hotel is the predictable but reliable *Saddles Steak House*.

Accommodation

Beaufort West has no shortage of **accommodation**, though much of it is on the busy main road. There's a municipal camping and caravan park under some trees on the right as you come into the main part of town on Donkin Street, but, as with other camping options along the N1, it's a bit scruffy and unappealing. If you want to **camp**, you're far better off going to the Karoo National Park, just a few kilometres out of town, and certainly the park's accommodation is tranquil and lovely, if you're doing more than just dossing down late at night in town. This requires booking well in advance.

Donkin Country House 14 Donkin St ℡023 414 4287. This simple guesthouse has en-suite rooms with TV and fridge, the requisite a/c, a swimming pool and some communal space to hang out in. ❷

Hotel Formula 1 144 Donkin St ℡023 415 2421, ⓦwww.hotelformula1.co.za. Part of a chain that delivers slick if tiny budget rooms that resemble a ship's cabin. Breakfast is extra. ❷

Matoppo Inn On the corner of Bird and Meintjies streets ℡023 415 1055, ⓦwww .matoppoinn.mrinfo.co.za. Elegant rooms with brass beds and antique furniture, as well as standard rooms in the town's old *drostdy*, or magistrate's house. The gardens are beautiful, and there's a pool, good food and a relaxed atmosphere. ❸

Wagon Wheel Country Lodge Off the N1 on the northern fringe of town ℡023 414 2145, ⓦwww .infobeaufortwest.co.za. En-suite motel rooms, plus camping faciiities, with a splash pool for kids. Meals are extra. ❷

Karoo National Park

With an unusually mountainous setting for the generally flattish and parched Karoo, the **Karoo National Park** (daily 5am–10pm; ☎023 415 2828; R60) has emerged in recent years as a reserve with much more to offer than first meets the eye. The themes of the semi-desert are undoubtedly here, and after a night gazing at the dazzling sky, or a hot day walking on some trails and learning about the unexpectedly intricate flora of the region, you'll start to appreciate this park's special value.

Much of the experience here is in the landscape and the serene atmosphere: despite the recent introduction of some **black rhino**, big game is limited, although there are some impressive raptors, including the **black eagle**. The designated drives around a limited section of the 600-square-kilometre park aren't terribly exciting; however, there is a wider-ranging 4WD trail, with the opportunity to overnight out in the veld in a remote mountain hut, for around R200 per person. For bookings, contact South African National Parks (see p.71).

Near the main restcamp there is an environmental **education centre**, along with three **trails**: an eleven-kilometre day-walk; a short but informative tree trail; and a very imaginative fossil trail (designed to accommodate wheelchairs and incorporating Braille boards), which tells the fascinating 250-million-year geological history of the area and shows fossils of the unusual animals that lived here in the times when the Karoo was a vast inland sea. Information about these is available at camp reception.

Practicalities

The entrance gate to Karoo National Park is right on the N1, 2km south of Beaufort West. The **reception and restcamp** are 10km into the park, hidden among the appealing flat-topped mountains in a way that makes you feel as though you're a million miles from the town and the highway. At reception there's a shop selling basic foodstuffs and a **restaurant** (Mon–Sat 8am–8.30pm, Sun 8am–7pm), with a pool nearby. Accommodation is in thirty fully equipped **chalets** and **cottages** that sleep three people (❸), strung out on either side of the main complex; the rate is for a minimum of two people and includes breakfast in the restaurant. The **campsite** is hidden away over a rise.

The Overberg interior and the Whale Coast

East of the Winelands lies a vaguely defined region known as the **Overberg** (Afrikaans for "over the mountain"). In the seventeenth century, when Stellenbosch, Franschhoek and Paarl were remote outposts, everywhere beyond them was, to the Dutch settlers, a fuzzy hinterland drifting off into the arid sands of the Karoo. These days it extends to an imprecise point between Arniston and Mossel Bay on the coast and somewhere east of Swellendam in the interior.

Of the two main routes through the Overberg, the **N2** strikes out across the less interesting interior, a four- to five-hour stretch people endure rather than enjoy to get to the Garden Route – but you can make it less of a chore with a couple of well-chosen stops along the way. North of the N2 is **Greyton**, a pleasant village used by Capetonians as a relaxing weekend retreat, and the starting point of the **Boesmanskloof Traverse** – a terrific one-day trail across the mountains into the Karoo. The historic Moravian mission station of **Genadendal**, five minutes down the road from Greyton, has a strange Afro-Germanic ambience that offers a couple of hours' pleasant strolling. Along the N2 itself, the only places that justify a restorative stop are **Caledon**, for its thermal springs, and **Swellendam**, for its well-preserved streetscape as well as one of South Africa's best country museums.

The real draw of the area is the **Whale Coast**, close enough for an easy outing from Cape Town, yet surprisingly undeveloped. The exception is popular **Hermanus**, which owes its fame to its status as the whale-watching capital of South Africa. The whole of this southern Cape coast is, in fact, prime territory for land-based whale-watching. Also along this section of coast is **Cape Agulhas**, the southernmost point on the continent, which sadly fails to deliver the drama its location promises. Nearby, and far more worthwhile, is **Arniston**, one of the best-preserved fishing villages in the country, and a little to its east the **De Hoop Nature Reserve**, an exciting wilderness of bleached dunes, craggy coast and more whales.

Caledon

The first impression of **CALEDON** is of huge, cathedral-like grain silos that dwarf its church spires. A low-key farming town some 111km east of Cape Town, Caledon built its former prosperity on the wheat, barley and malt trade. Now the town is gambling on making its fortune through a casino and family entertainment complex, built around the town's one natural asset, its thermal springs. When the Dutch arrived here in the eighteenth century, Khoi people were already wallowing in steaming holes dug in the ground – a practice imitated by the settlers. The Victorians built a wrought-iron structure around the main rectangular pool, replaced in 2001 by a timber one that retains the feel of the original.

Today, Caledon **spa** (daily 6am–midnight; R100) offers a gamut of physical indulgences in a tasteful, yet tired, setting. The so-called Khoisan spa consists of a fake waterfall tumbling down the mountainside into a series of rocky pools, getting progressively cooler as they approach the foot of the hill (the one at the top clocks 40°C). Use of the saunas, a steam room, frigidarium and gym are all included in the price; towels are provided and robes can be rented. A **treatment centre** offers a huge variety of expensive massages and beauty treatments, from aromatherapy massage to thalassotherapy (using seaweed).

The town's **casino** forms part of a small mall with a couple of family restaurants and a few shops. If you fancy a flutter, you can try your luck at one of the scores of slot-machines lined up inside the large gambling hall, which also has a number of gaming tables.

Caledon has a couple of other decent attractions. The **House Museum** at 11 Constitution Street (Mon–Fri 8am–1pm & 2–4.30pm, Sat 9am–12.30pm) consists of displays of mainly domestic items in a house faithfully restored to "Victorian Caledon style" (1837–1901). A photographic display – also part of the museum – is housed with the information bureau at the old town hall. The town's outdoor attraction is the **Wildflower Garden and Nature Reserve**, where you can wander through *fynbos*, aloes and succulents on a lovely long amble along a rocky, wooded *kloof* into the mountains, or head out on the ten-kilometre Meiring trail, which goes deep into the nature reserve.

Practicalities

You can reach Caledon with only a minor detour from the N2. To get to the spa, follow the sign displaying the hotel and spa symbols which, if you're coming from Cape Town, is a little way beyond the town centre indicator.

Intercity **buses** stop off at the Spar supermarket on Market Square (corner Plein St and Prince Alfred Rd) in the centre of town. Caledon's **tourist office**, in the old town hall, 22 Plein Street (Mon–Fri 8am–5pm, Sat 9am–1pm; ☎028 212 1511), has literature about the area, details of places to stay, and an attached crafts shop.

As regards **accommodation**, the *Painted Lady*, 3 Donkin Street (☎083 468 8192; ❷), has beds in two Victorian self-catering cottages, and also offers B&B. Similarly priced are *Nana Cottage*, 41 Meul Street; and *Kelkiewyn*, 22 Prince Alfred Street. Signposted 1km east of the centre, *Caledon Hotel* (☎028 214 1500, ⓦ www.caledoncasino.co.za; ❺) offers the best accommodation and dining in town, though that's not saying much – it's a tired affair catering to weekenders and the conference market. The *Venster Restaurant* at the Wildflower Garden serves snacks and traditional Afrikaner fare, such as *bobotie* and *bredie*, during the day. To self-cater, besides the Spar supermarket you can try the House Museum's shop at 22 Plein Street, which sells fresh bread and other home-baked products, every Friday.

Greyton, Genadendal and the Boesmanskloof Traverse

Greyton, a small, peaceful village 46km north of Caledon, is based around a core of Georgian and Victorian buildings, shaded by grand old oaks, and tucked away at the edge of the Riviersonderend (meaning "river with no end") Mountains. In recent years, it has changed from being a retirement village to a place where young city families come to seek a more peaceful life. The town's big attraction is the superb **Boesmanskloof Traverse** hike, which crosses the mountains to a point 14km from McGregor. There's another worthwhile hike beginning near South Africa's oldest mission station, **Genadendal**, a six-kilometre excursion west of Greyton.

Greyton

GREYTON is a great place to unwind, stroll and potter about in the handful of galleries, antique and tea shops. The town's **Dolls' House Museum**, at the tourist office, is filled with miniature handmade dolls' houses showing attention to the minutest details, right down to cakes and pastries.

There's no public transport to Greyton. The best route to drive here is the sealed R406 from just west of Caledon; don't attempt the untarred route from Riviersonderend, which will hammer your suspension. The **Greyton**

The Boesmanskloof Traverse

The fourteen-kilometre **Boesmanskloof Traverse** takes you from the gentle, oak-lined streets of **Greyton** across the Riviersonderend mountain range to the glaring Karoo scrubland around the town of **McGregor** (see p.216). The stark contrast over so short a distance is staggering, made all the more so by the fact that no direct roads connect the two towns; to drive from one to the other involves a circuitous two-hour journey.

The classic way to cover the Traverse is to walk from Greyton to **Die Galg** (14km from McGregor), where people commonly spend the night, returning the same way to Greyton the following day. The Traverse rises and falls a fair bit, so you'll have to contend with a lot of uphill walking, but the route can easily be completed in a day if you're reasonably fit, and you can still have a rewarding outing venturing only part of the way and returning to Greyton for the evening. A decent day's walk takes you to **Oak Falls**, 9km from Greyton. Composed of a series of cascades, it's the highlight of the route, its most impressive feature being a large pool where you can rest and swim in cola-coloured water.

The walk takes you through numerous species of wonderful montane *fynbos*, and between July and October you can find yourself walking through magnificent groves of flowering king proteas. Mammals include small antelope, caracals, baboons and dassies, though it's unlikely you'll see many of them.

Trail practicalities

You're free to walk the first 5km of the trail and back, but to complete the whole route from Greyton to Die Galg – numbers are limited to fifty people per day – you will need a **permit** (R25 per person per day). Over weekends, the trail gets extremely full and permits must be arranged in advance through the Greyton Tourism Bureau or through Cape Nature Conservation (☎028 425 5020, ✉capenature@tiscali.co.za). You get a **map** when you buy the permit, although you don't really need one as the Traverse is very clearly marked out. The walk can be strenuous, so make sure you're fit and have good shoes. It's also worth noting that this is an area of winter rainfall; summers are hot and dry.

As for **accommodation**, there's *Whipstock Farm* (see p.217) 4km beyond Die Galg (the owner can collect you free of charge from Die Galg), or the overnight dorms at Die Galg (☎023 625 1735; ask for Mr Oosthuizen), equipped with a fridge, cooker and beds (but no bedding).

Tourism Bureau at 29 Main Street (Mon–Sat 10am–5pm, Sun 10am–3pm; ☎ & ✆028 254 9414, ⓦwww.greyton.net), along the main road as you come into town, has lists of accommodation and rents out bicycles for R15 an hour.

Accommodation

It's worth staying somewhere with a fireplace if you're here in winter, as it can be cold in this mountainous terrain. Besides the places to stay reviewed below, there is a municipal **campsite** signposted off Main Rd (☎028 254 9620), in a lovely setting 2.5km out of town on the banks of the Riviersonderend. Amenities are limited to an ablution block with hot water.

Acorns On Oak 2 Oak St ☎028 254 9567, ⓦwww.acorns-on-oak.co.za. Three luxurious rooms each with underfloor heating, espresso machine, loft lounge, private balcony and spectacular mountain views.

There's also a 12m heated pool and free use of bicycles. ❹
Auberge Greyton Corner Oak St and Main Rd ☎028 254 9192. Simple, uncluttered farm-style rooms – if you're planning on hiking and just need

a bed for the night, this friendly B&B is a good bet. **②**

Guinea Fowl Ds Botha St ☎028 254 9550. Guesthouse with en-suite rooms and serving a full English breakfast. **②**

High Hopes 89 Main Rd ☎ & ⓕ028 254 9898. One of the best B&Bs in town, in a beautiful country-style home set in magnificent gardens with a huge ornamental pond and a swimming pool. Besides three rooms, there's a self-contained unit with a kitchen, which can be taken on a B&B or self-catering basis. Afternoon tea and biscuits as well as delicious breakfasts are included in the rate. **④**

Post House Main Rd ☎028 254 9995, ⓦwww .posthouse.co.za. En-suite rooms, each named after a Beatrix Potter character. The dining room and lounge are filled with warmth and character, but somehow the rooms don't seem to carry that through. **③**

Eating and drinking

The town has a short-lived Saturday **market** at the corner of Main Road and Cross Market Street (10–11am), to which locals bring their produce: organic vegetables, dairy products, decadent cakes, breads, biscuits and preserves; also on sale are secondhand books and bric-a-brac. Otherwise, there is a limited range of food on sale at the small deli at the *Oak and Vigne Café*. There is a small country **pub** at the *Post House*.

Café Herbert Main Rd. There's a simple lunch menu of pastas, salads and sandwiches, and you can also sample the products of the small Belgian chocolatier here, which boast some unusual flavours – masala chai, *crème brûlée* and chilli, to name just three.

Greyt-on-Main 31 Main Rd ☎028 254 9722. Tasty authentic German food in a well-appointed restaurant, though the lighting is almost oppressively bright.

Jam Tin In the township 2km south of town ☎028 254 9075. From her humble 200-year-old family home, Dora cooks a traditional three-course Cape Malay meal in the evening (R50). You can find her daily at her other job at Mfala Textiles, Main Rd (next to *Café Herbert*). Directions are given when you book.

Oak and Vigne Café Ds Botha St ☎028 254 9037. Highly popular, situated in an old cottage with an oak-shaded terrace where you can savour reasonably priced Mediterranean-influenced country breakfasts, teas and lunches daily.

Plum 7 Ds Botha Street ☎028 254 9730. Chef and owner Eve puts together ever-changing, creative menus, with North African and Mediterranean flavours a predominant influence. Thurs–Sun dinner, plus Sat & Sun lunch.

Post House Main Rd. A lively evening venue serving Asian and European-influenced fare. The dining is better over the weekend when city slickers from Cape Town come to stay.

Rosie's High St, off Main Rd ☎028 254 9640. The only place in the village for steaks, pastas and pizzas.

Genadendal

GENADENDAL, whose name means "valley of grace", was founded in 1737 by Moravians, and some of the ochre and earthy-pink architecture hints at Central European influences. The village's focus is around **Church Square**, dominated by a very Germanic church building dating back to 1891. The old bell outside dates back to the eighteenth century, when it became the centre of a flaming row between the local farmers and the mission station. The scrap broke out when missionary Georg Schmidt annoyed the local white farmers by forming a small Christian congregation with impoverished Khoi – who were on the threshold of extinction – and giving refuge to maltreated labourers from local farms. What really got the farmers' goat was the fact that while they, white Christians, were illiterate, Schmidt was teaching native people, whom they considered uncivilized, to read and write. The Dutch Reformed Church, under the control of the Dutch East India Company, waded in when Schmidt began baptizing converts, and prohibited the mission from ringing the bell which called the faithful to prayer.

At one stage during the eighteenth century, Genadendal was the largest settlement in southern Africa after Cape Town. Although it never became more than a village, Genadendal experienced a golden age in the nineteenth century, with a flourishing economy based on home industries. In 1838 it established the first teacher training college in the country, which the government closed in 1926, on the grounds that coloured people didn't need tertiary education and should be employed as workers on local farms – a policy that effectively ground the community into poverty. In 1995, in recognition of the mission's role, Nelson Mandela renamed his official residence in Cape Town "Genadendal".

Today, the population of this principally coloured town numbers around four thousand people, adhering to a variety of Christian sects – no longer just Moravianism. The **Mission Museum** (Mon–Thurs 9am–1pm & 2–5pm, Fri 9am–3.30pm, Sat 9am–noon), adjacent to Church Square, is moderately interesting and provides some clues as to why Moravians came here. You should allow up to two hours to explore the museum and wander through the town, down to the rural graveyard, spiked with tombstones dating back to the early nineteenth century.

The Genadendal **tourist office** (Mon–Thurs 8.30am–5pm, Fri 8.30am–4pm, Sat 10am–2pm; ☎028 251 8291) is on Church Square in the centre of the mission. Basic budget **accommodation** aimed principally at hikers doing the Genadendal trail is available at the Hester Dorothea Conference Centre (☎028 251 8346; ❶), on the square, in dormitories and a few private rooms, sharing bathrooms and kitchen facilities. Genadendal offers few other visitor amenities, but there is a **tea room** just off Church Square, where you can get refreshments.

The Genadendal trail

A short way from the village in the surrounding countryside is the **Genadendal trail**. The full twenty-five-kilometre, circular trail, usually covered in two days, requires a high level of fitness, particularly for the first 2km of the second day. But much of the rest is fairly easy-going, passing through montane *fynbos* inhabited by a variety of small antelope, caracals and the odd leopard. Only 24 people are allowed on the trail at one time, so reservations are essential. **Bookings and permits** (R50) are arranged through Cape Nature Conservation (☎028 425 5020, ✉dehoopinfo@sdm.dorea.co.za). Overnight **accommodation** can be booked in a self-catering hikers' cottage on De Hoek, a flower farm halfway along the trail (☎023 626 2176; ❶); you'll need to bring your own bedding and eating utensils. The farm is home to antelope and a wide variety of birds, and you can swim in the farm dam.

Swellendam and around

On the N2, 97km east of Caledon, **SWELLENDAM** is an attractive historic town at the foot of the Langeberg. With one of the best country museums in South Africa, it's a congenial stop along the N2 between Cape Town and the Garden Route. And because of its ample supply of good accommodation and its position – poised between the coastal De Hoop Nature Reserve and the Langeberg – it's a suitable base for spending a few days exploring this part of the Overberg, with the Bontebok National Park, stomping ground of an attractive type of antelope, close at hand to the south.

South Africa's third-oldest white settlement, Swellendam was established in 1745 by Baron Gustav van Imhoff, a visiting Dutch East India Company bigwig. He was deeply concerned about the "moral degeneration" of burghers who were trekking further and further from Cape Town and out of Company control. Of no less concern to the Baron was the loss of revenue from these "vagabonds", who were neglecting to pay the company for the right to hold land and were fiddling their annual tax returns. Following a brief hiccup in 1795, when burghers declared a "free republic" (quickly extinguished when Britain occupied the Cape), the town grew into a prosperous rural centre known for its wagon-making, and for being the last "civilized" port of call for trekboers heading out into the interior. The income generated from this helped build Swellendam's gracious homes, many of which went up in smoke in the fire of 1865, which razed much of the town centre.

The Town

The only building in the centre to survive the town's ravages is the Cape Dutch-style **Oefeningshuis**, 36 Voortrek Street, which now houses the tourist office. Built in 1838, it was first used as a place for religious activity, then as a school for freed slaves, and has surreal-looking clocks with frozen hands carved into either gable end, below which there's a real clock above the entrance. Diagonally opposite and slightly east at no. 11, the **Dutch Reformed Church**, dating from 1910, incorporates Gothic windows, a Baroque spire, Renaissance portico elements and Cape Dutch gables into a wedding cake of a building that agreeably holds its own, against the odds.

On the east side of town, a short way from the centre, is the excellent **Drostdy Museum**, 18 Swellegrebel Street (Mon–Fri 9am–4.45pm, Sat & Sun 10am–3.45pm; R10). It's a collection of historic buildings arranged around large grounds, with a lovely nineteenth-century Cape garden. The centrepiece is the *drostdy* itself, built in 1747 as the seat of the *landdrost*, a magistrate-cum-commissioner sent out by the Dutch East India Company to control the outer reaches of its territory. The building conforms to the beautiful limewashed, thatched and shuttered Cape Dutch style of the eighteenth century, but the furnishings are of nineteenth-century vintage. From the rear garden of the *drostdy* you can stroll along a path and across Drostdy Street to **Mayville**, a middle-class Victorian homestead from the mid-nineteenth century with an old rose garden. Also part of the complex are the **Old Gaol**, the **jailer's cottage**, and an interesting display of eighteenth- and nineteenth-century farm implements and tools. Look out, too, for the circular threshing floor old, made out of dung and mud, in a low-walled enclosure into which horses were driven to tramp the wheat.

On a far flightier note, the **Sulina Faerie Sanctuary**, 33 Buitenkant Street (Thurs–Sun 9am–4.30pm; R10), is the result of one Swellendam resident's obsession, housing hundreds of fairy statuettes and images. Its mystical garden has gnomes, pixies and miniature castles hidden in the overgrowth.

Practicalities

Greyhound, Intercape and Translux **buses** between Cape Town and Port Elizabeth pull in diagonally opposite the *Swellengrebel Hotel*, 91 Voortrek Street, in the centre of town, while the Baz Bus will drop you off at any of the central accommodation. Swellendam has a very switched-on **tourist office** at 36 Voortrek St (Mon–Fri 9am–1pm & 2–5pm, Sat 9am–noon; ☎ & ℱ 028 514 2770, ⓔ infoswd@sdm.dorea.co.za), which provides frank and helpful advice about local attractions and can book accommodation. You can easily cover the town centre on foot; there's no public transport, anyway.

Out of town, Two Feathers Horse Trails (℡082 494 8279, ⓦwww .twofeathers.co.za) offers Western-style and English **horse-riding** by the hour, or you can do a full-day outing with lunch included. They also offer **wilderness trails** with accommodation in tepees or self-catering log cabins (R400 for four people). The landscape is varied and ranges from forest tracks past waterfalls and mountain streams to riverside trails, meandering country roads and open grass plains.

Accommodation

Anyone who enjoys the atmosphere of historic houses will be spoilt for choice in Swellendam, where places to stay in Cape Dutch and Georgian houses are ten a penny, and rates tend to be pretty reasonable.

Augusta de Mist 3 Human St ℡028 514 3325 or 083 261 1923, ⓦwww.augustademist.co.za. A 200-year-old homestead with three beautifully renovated cottages and seven en-suite rooms, most with fireplaces. A rambling terraced garden and a pool complete the picture. ❺

Babette's B&B 13 Drostdy St ℡028 514 2406 or 083 824 2406, ⓔebbie@dorea.co.za. Tuscan-style B&B that seems rather out of place in Swellendam, but its manicured garden, swimming pool and individually styled bedrooms make it a pleasant place to stay. ❸

The Coachman 14 Drostdy St ℡028 514 2294, ⓦwww.coachman.co.za. An old coach house close to the Drostdy Museum, offering three comfortable en-suite bedrooms with private entrances off a courtyard and two luxury thatched cottages in the garden. Rooms ❸, cottages ❺

Cypress Cottage 3 Voortrek St ℡028 514 3296. Five charming rooms, decorated with antiques, in the back garden of a grand house, one of the oldest in town. Good value. ❸

Eenuurkop Huisie 8km from town on the Ashton road ℡ & ℱ028 514 1447. Two self-catering cottages, one with three bedrooms, the other with one, in a stunning setting with great views and access to mountain walks. ❷

Herberg Roosje Van De Kaap 5 Drostdy St ℡028 514 3001, ⓔroosje@dorea.co.za. A popular

B&B in a beautiful house; service is first-rate, though some of the rooms are rather small. ❸

Hermitage Huisies 3km from town on R60 to Ashton ℡ & ℱ028 514 2308. Two wonderful self-catering cottages, one with one bedroom, the other with two rooms, on a smallholding with a duck pond and grazing sheep. ❷

Klippe Rivier Homestead Off the western end of Voortrek St, just outside the centre ℡028 514 3341, ⓦwww.klipperivier.com. Swellendam's most formal and luxurious accommodation, in a beautiful 1825 Cape Dutch homestead with six opulent bedrooms, a secluded cottage and saltwater swimming pool. No under-10s. ❼

Lulu's B&B 10 Voortrek St ℡028 514 2202 or 082 847 9523. A well-run B&B, centrally located, with two en-suite rooms and a self-catering loft apartment (sleeping up to eight) above. ❷

Swellendam Backpackers 5 Lichtenstein St ℡028 514 2648, ⓔbackpack@dorea.co.za. Swellendam's only hostel is a friendly place with camping, dorms and doubles; staff can also arrange activities including horse-riding, mountain biking and canoeing. ❶

Swellendam Country Lodge 237 Voortrek St ℡028 514 3629, ⓦwww.swellendamlodge.com. Six rooms with separate entrances, reed ceilings, and elegant, uncluttered decor in muted hues. ❸

Eating

There's no shortage of decent places to eat in Swellendam – ranging from snack bars to formal restaurants where you can enjoy a romantic candle-lit dinner – many of them in delightful old buildings.

The Connection 132 Voortrek St ℡028 514 1988. In an eighteenth-century town house, this restaurant serves tasty light meals such as toasted sandwiches and main courses featuring, among other delicacies, game fowl and venison. Tues–Thurs.

Koornlands 5 Voortrek St ℡028 514 3567. Elegant restaurant famous for traditional South African fare such as *bobotie* and Cape Malay curries, as well as delicious desserts, at reasonable prices. Mon & Wed–Sun eves only.

La Belle Alliance Swellengrebel St ☎028 514 2252. Near the museum, this serves sandwiches and light meals and is housed in a spectacular old church, with outdoor seating under trees by a river. Open daily, daytime only.

The Old Mill 241–243 Voortrek St ☎028 514 2790. Pleasant and inexpensive outdoor spot, with ducks and chickens wandering about, where you can order tea, coffee and light meals. Daily daytime only.

Roosje Van De Kaap 5 Drostdy St ☎028 514 3001. A highly rated restaurant offering traditional Cape food, with a great wine list – a good choice for a romantic candle-lit dinner. Booking essential. Tues–Sun 7–11pm.

Bontebok National Park

Just 6km south of Swellendam along the Breede River, the **Bontebok National Park** (May–Sept 7am–6pm; Oct–April 7am–7pm; ☎028 514 2735; day visitors R20, overnight visitors free) is a compact 28-square kilometre reserve at the foot of the Langeberg range that makes a relaxing overnight stop between Cape Town and the Garden Route. The park was established in 1931 to save the Cape's dwindling population of bontebok, an attractive antelope with distinctive cappuccino, chocolate-brown and white markings on its forehead and hindquarters. By 1930, hunting had reduced the number of animals to a mere thirty. Their survival has happily been secured and there are now three hundred of them in the park, as well as populations in other game and nature reserves in the province. There are no big cats in the park, but **mammals** you might encounter include rare Cape mountain zebra, red hartebeest and grey rhebok, and there are more than 120 **bird species**. It's also a rich environment for **fynbos**, with nearly 500 species here, including erica, gladioli and proteas. Apart from game viewing, there are opportunities to swim in the Breede River, hike a couple of short nature trails and fish.

Self-catering **accommodation** is available in inexpensive six-berth caravans with timber anterooms along the river, or you can camp in your own tent. Basic kitchen equipment, bedding, towels and soap are provided, and there are communal ablution facilities. A **shop** at the park entrance sells commodities such as meat and booze, while fresh fruit and vegetables are available in Swellendam.

The coast from Strand to Kleinmond

The main reason you'd take the coastal route that skirts the eastern shore of False Bay is to get to Hermanus, but scenically the drive has much to recommend it, especially once you get past the commuter settlements close to Cape Town. Leaving the N2 from Cape Town at Somerset West, the first coastal settlement you hit is **Strand**, a massive industrial centre on the edge of Cape Town. Although it has a good beach, this isn't sufficient reason to stop off and the R44 quickly takes you to the ongoing commuter development of **Gordon's Bay**, your last chance for a decent sea swim for some distance. After here, the mountains bear down on the sea and the road winds its way around the folding mountainside, with the sea crashing against the rocks below – without a tree in sight, the barren landscape has a raw dramatic quality. **Cape Hangklip**, the tip of False Bay, earned its name from the fact that Hangklip frequently fooled Portuguese mariners into thinking they were rounding the Cape of Good Hope. A dirt road takes you down to **Hangklip** itself, where a succession of dwellers have made their homes since humans left stone axes here over 20,000 years ago. In the nineteenth century, outlaws lived in Hangklip's remote caves, but were flushed out in 1852, leaving the area to its present population of baboons.

Betty's Bay and around

Cape Hangklip roughly marks the point at which the commuters become holidaymakers. Just around the corner to the east, **BETTY'S BAY** was developed as a seaside retreat for Capetonians wanting to get away from the city. This collection of private holiday cottages was prosaically named after Betty Youlden, daughter of the director of the first company to try to develop the area, and is rather boring. Its saving grace is that it hosts a colony of **African (jackass) penguins**, best seen in the morning or evening between April and June. African penguins mate for life and return to the same nest every year, but here are suffering from interference with their turf by perlemoen (abalone) poachers. Residents urge you to tell local shopkeepers if you see poaching taking place. Otherwise, Betty's Bay is not geared up to visitors, though you can **eat** at the Harold Porter Botanical Garden.

Harold Porter National Botanical Garden

Creeping up the mountains just above Betty's Bay, **Harold Porter National Botanical Garden** (Mon–Fri 8am–4pm, Sat & Sun 8am–5pm; R7) is a wild sanctuary of coastal and montane *fynbos* that makes a good stop along the R44, if only to picnic or have tea at its outdoor **café**. The relatively compact botanical garden extends over two square kilometres from the mountains, through marshland down to coastal dunes. Once here, you'll probably get lured at least some of the way up the *kloof* that runs through the reserve; as you get higher up, you're treated to sea views in one direction and rugged mountains in the other.

Although wildlife in the form of small **antelope**, **baboons** and **leopards** are present, they are rarely sighted and it's more worthwhile to look out instead for the birds and blooms. In January you can see brilliant red disas in all their glory, while the nerine lilies flower in March. Keep an eye open for colourful, nectar-loving sunbirds and scores of other bird **species** that are found here. Four **trails** of between one and three hours meander through the gardens, but you can just as easily take yourself off on an impromptu stroll, up and across the red-stained waters (the colour stems from phenols and tannins leaching from the *fynbos*) running through Disa Kloof.

Kleinmond

Because of its isolation, **KLEINMOND**, roughly 12km northeast of Betty's Bay, was an outlaws' stronghold for some two hundred years. In the twentieth century, however, relatively easy access turned the town into a holiday spot for Capetonians and for farmers from the surrounding areas. An impressive confluence of sea, dune, tidal estuary and mountain waterfalls combines with a ten-kilometre crescent **beach** curving across the Bot River Mouth to Mudge Point, a promontory that completes the vista as you look east. Swimming is safest close to the *Beach House Hotel*, but take care not to venture beyond where you see other bathers. A newish strip of craft and coffee shops that includes a deli, sports bar and an **abalone hatchery** (R8) is reached down the road signposted "Harbour" off the main coastal road.

The cheapest **accommodation** is at the couple of caravan parks, signposted from the main road, where you can **camp**. The better of the two is the *Palmiet* (℡028 271 4050), which is quieter and closer to the safely swimmable river. *Beach House* on Beach Rd (℡028 271 3130, ⓦwww.relaishotels.com; ❻) is a small **hotel** whose spacious rooms have king-size beds, white wicker furniture and tastefully understated floral fabrics. Here you can look out over Sandown Bay, the lagoon and mountains and enjoy the sound of the endlessly pounding surf; if you are going to fork out to stay here, you may as well stay in one of the luxury sea-facing rooms. *Beach House* is also the best place for eating, with its expensive formal **restaurant**, *Tides*, which serves seafood and meat dishes.

Hermanus and the Whale Coast

On the edge of rocky cliffs and backed by mountains, **Hermanus**, 112km east of Cape Town, sits at the northernmost end of Walker Bay, an inlet

Whale-watching

The Southern Cape, including Cape Town, provides some of the easiest and best places in the world for **whale-watching**. You don't need to rent a boat or take a pricey tour to get out to sea; if you come at the right time of year, whales are often visible from the shore, although a good pair of binoculars will come in useful for when they are far out.

All nine of the great whale species of the southern hemisphere pass by South Africa's shores, but the most commonly seen off Cape Town are **southern right whales** (their name derives from being the "right' one to kill because of their high oil and bone yields and the fact that, conveniently, they float when dead). Southern right whales are black and easily recognized from their pale, brownish **callosities**. These unappealing patches of raised, roughened skin on their snouts and heads have a distinct pattern on each animal, which helps scientists keep track of them.

Female whales come inshore to calve in sheltered bays, and stay to nurse their young for up to three months. **July to October** is the best time to see them, although they start appearing in June and some stay around until December. When the calves are big enough, the whales head off south again, to colder, stormy waters, where they feed on enormous quantities of plankton, making up for the nursing months when the females don't eat at all. Though you're most likely to see females and young, you may see **males** early in the season boisterously flopping about the females, though they neither help rear the calves nor form lasting bonds with females.

What gives away the presence of a whale is the blow or spout, a tall smoky plume which disperses after a few seconds and is actually the whale breathing out before it surfaces. If luck is on your side, you may see whales breaching – the movement when they thrust high out of the water and fall back with a great splash.

Probably the best **whale watching tour** in Hermanus is with Ivanhoe Sea Safaris (℡028 384 0556, @balaena@kingsley.co.za), whose owner, Rudy Hughes, has for years assisted scientists researching the whales in Walker Bay.

The Whale Coast's hottest whale spots

In **Hermanus**, the best vantage points are the concrete cliff paths which ring the rocky shore from New Harbour to Grotto Beach. There are interpretation boards at three of the popular vantage points (Gearing's Point, Die Gang and Bientang's Cave). At their worst, the paths can be lined two or three deep with people.

Although Hermanus is best known and most geared up for whale-watching, it's also the most congested venue during the whale season and there are equally good – if not better – spots elsewhere along the Walker Bay coast. Aficionados claim that **De Kelders** (see p.249), some 39km east of Hermanus, is even better, while **De Hoop Nature Reserve** (see p.253), east of Arniston, is reckoned by some to be the ultimate place along the entire southern African coast for whale-watching, with far greater numbers of southern rights breaching here than anywhere else.

whose protective curve attracts calving whales as it slides south to the promontory of Danger Point. From about July, southern right whales (see box on p.241) start appearing in the warmer sheltered bays of the Western Cape, and the town trumpets itself as the **whale capital** of South Africa. To prove it, an official whale crier (purportedly the world's only one) struts around armed with a mobile phone and a dried kelp horn through which he yells the latest sightings. The hype aside, **Walker Bay** does provide some of the finest shore-based whale-watching in the world and, even if there are better spots nearby, Hermanus is the best geared-up place in the country to exploit it.

North of Hermanus are some **wineries** you can visit, while due east of Walker Bay, the inland hamlet of **Stanford** on the banks of the Klein River has managed to retain its historic village feel; it's a quieter base than Hermanus, while being near enough to the whale capital for a meal and sightseeing. Southeast down the bay from Hermanus, the unprepossessing town of **De Kelders** outshines its smarter neighbour as a whale-watching spot, but at nothing much else; and, just inland of it, the wonderful and very upmarket **Grootbos Nature Reserve** is one of the best places in the country to learn about *fynbos*. Heading further down the bay, you hit the fishing town of **Gansbaai** (Afrikaans for "goose bay"), which these days is far better known for its shark-cage diving than its waterfowl. Curving back to Hermanus, Danger Point is the promontory that indicates Walker Bay's southern extent, and marks the spot where HMS *Birkenhead* literally went down in history (see p.250).

An easy excursion from Hermanus takes you through attractive and relatively untrammelled farming country to **Bredasdorp**, a junction town on the R316 that gives you the choice of branching out to Africa's southern tip at **Cape Agulhas**; the well-preserved Moravian mission town of **Elim**; or the fishing village of **Arniston**, which is the least-developed and nicest town along the Whale Coast.

Hermanus

There is still the barest trace of a once-quiet cliff-edge fishing village around the historic harbour and in some understated seaside cottages, but for the most part **HERMANUS** has gorged itself on its whale-generated income that has produced modern shopping malls, supermarkets and craft shops. Hermanus also has good swimming and walking **beaches**, opportunities for **activities** and makes a good base for exploring the rest of the Overberg.

Arrival and information

Of the two routes here from the Cape Town, taking the N2 and heading south onto the R43 at Bot River is the more direct (a 1hr 30min drive), but the winding road that hugs the coast from Strand, leaving the N2 just before Sir Lowrie's Pass, is the more scenic (2hr). Scant public transport passes through Hermanus, the exception being the **Splash bus** (T082 658 5375, E splash@hermanus.co.za), which runs at least once daily between Cape Town train station and Hermanus. The **Baz Bus** drops people off at **Bot River**, 28km to the north on the N2, from where you can arrange to be collected by a shuttle operated by *Moby's Travel Lodge*, whether you're staying there or not – booking is recommended, but the Baz carries a mobile phone and can call ahead while you're en route.

HERMANUS

ACCOMMODATION

The Artist's House	**A**
Auberge Burgundy	**H**
Eastbury Cottages	**C**
Forty Five Marine Drive	**E**
Marine Hotel	**G**
Moby's Travellers Lodge	**D**
Pat's Place	**F**
Robin's Nest	**B**

Walker Bay

Pick'n Pay

Kwikspar

Delis Halian Delicatessen

Old Harbour

Museum

N

RESTAURANTS & CAFÉS

Annie se Kombuis	8	Hermanus Fish Shoppe	9	
B's Steakhouse	1	Marimba Café	6	
The Burgundy	10	Meditarranea	11	
The Café	4	Milkwood Restaurant	2	
Fisherman's Cottage	7	Mogg's Country		
Harbour Rock Seagrill		Cookhouse	3	
& Bar	12	Rossi's Italian Restaurant	5	

0   500 m

There's a helpful **tourist office** (Mon–Sat 9am–5pm, plus in summer Sun 10am–3pm; ☏028 312 2629, ⓦwww.hermanus.co.za) at the old station building in Mitchell Street, with maps, useful brochures about the area and an **Internet café**. They operate a free accommodation-finding service and can take bookings for boat-based and aerial whale-watching, as well as shark-cage diving trips.

Over the last weekend in September the town puts on a fun show of anything that's got a whale connection, even tenuously. To find out what's on – events range from ecology talks to classical recitals – check ⓦwww.whalefestival.co.za.

Accommodation

Unsurprisingly, accommodation on the shore is in high demand and tends to be more expensive than places set back. If there are more than two of you, the best option may be to rent a whole house or apartment through Hermanus Accommodation Centre, on the corner of Church and Myrtle lanes (☏028 313 0004, ⓦwww.hermanusaccom.co.za).

The Artist's House Hemel-en-Aarde Valley ☏028 313 0533, ⓦwww.artistshouse.co.za. Tranquil and luxurious house 12km from Hermanus (head along the R320 to Caledon, then left at Karwydeskraalpad) built from quarried stone, with views of the valley from each en-suite room. Breakfast is included in the rate. Good value. **❹**

Auberge Burgundy 16 Harbour Rd ☏028 313 1201, ⓦwww.auberge.co.za. An imitation Provençal

country house in the town centre, projecting a stylish Mediterranean feel, with imported French fabrics and a lavender garden. Breakfast is served across the road at the *Burgundy* restaurant. **❺**

Eastbury Cottages 36 Luyt St ☏082 658 4945. Three very reasonably priced, fully equipped self-catering cottages close to the *Marine Hotel*. Prices are in the R200–500 range depending on how many people there are. No credit cards.

243

Forty Five Marine Drive 45 Marine Dr ☎028
312 3610, ⓕ028 313 1125. Cliffside self-
catering luxury apartments next to the *Windsor
Hotel*, with two bedrooms, two bathrooms, a
kitchen and terrific views across the bay. Overflow
guests may be shunted off to its far less comely
relative, the *Esplanade*. R600 per apartment.

Marine Hotel Marine Dr ☎028 313 1000,
ⓦwww.marine-hermanus.co.za. A grand, rather
formal seafront hotel, unquestionably Hermanus's
best and easily up to the standard of the top
establishments in the country. If you're shelling
out, you may as well book early and pay extra for
a sea-facing room. There's a Jacuzzi and an indoor
swimming pool. ❻

Moby's Travellers Lodge 9 Mitchell St ☎028
313 2361, ⓦwww.mobys.co.za. Centrally located
hostel with doubles, dorms and a family suite as
well as a cosy pub and inviting relaxation areas,

including a rock pool. They provide breakfast and
dinner at reasonable rates, or you can self-cater.
They'll organize all tours and outings, and arrange
transport to and from the Baz Bus drop off in Bot
River. Dorms ❶, rooms ❸

Pat's Place 245 Main St ☎083 270 5213. Four
simple yet elegant en-suite rooms, with private
courtyards and outdoor showers. There's also a
self-catering unit that sleeps four. The thatched
home has a secluded garden, and a pool with
mountain views. ❸

Robin's Nest Meadow Ave ☎072 512 3830,
ⓔrobinsnest@hermanus.co.za. Three fully
equipped, self-catering studio flats in the gardens
of what was once Rheezicht Farm, 4km west of
the centre. Reached through the Hemel-en-Aarde
shopping village, these purpose-built, two-storey
flats sleep two and open onto a communal courtyard. A semi-rural alternative to staying in town. ❷

The Town
Main Road, the continuation of the R43, meanders through Hermanus,
briefly becoming Seventh Street. **Market Square**, just above the old harbour and to the south of Main Street, is the closest thing to a centre, and it's
here you'll find the heaviest concentration of restaurants, craft shops and flea
markets – the principal forms of entertainment in town when the whales are
taking time out.

Just below Market Square is the **Old Harbour Museum** (Mon–Sat
9am–4.30pm, Sun noon–4pm; R3) where, among the uncompelling
displays, you'll find lots of fishing tackle and some sharks' jaws. Outside,
a few colourful boats, used by local fishermen from the mid-eighteenth

Hermanus activities

There's more to Hermanus than whales. The surrounding Raednagael Mountains
serve as a great launching pad for **paragliding**; Para-Pax offer tandem flights (☎82
881 4724; R750). The coastline, a marine reserve stretching 500m out to sea, boasts
some of the best **coral reefs** in Southern Africa, viewed by flashlight because of the
lack of light permeating the plankton-rich water. **Scuba Africa**, The New Habour,
Westcliff Drive, ☎028 316 2362 ⓔaron@scubaafrica.co.za) runs **diving tours** (R330
for a dive and full gear rental) for anyone who arrives with proof of certification and
a log book. The water is too cold for tropical fish, but if you're lucky a whale might
come over to see what you're up to. You can also see the whales from horseback;
Horse Trail Safaris (☎082 729 7776) and **African Horse Co** (☎082 667 9232) both
offer half-day beach and lagoon tours (R250), as well as *fynbos* mountain tours and
overnight trails.

After indulging in all the activities on offer, you may want to relax for a half-day at
the luxury *Arabella Sheraton Western Cape Hotel & Spa* (take the R43 in the direction of Cape Town and the N2, and turn left at the Kleinmond turn-off). The **spa** here
is worth a visit: for R250 you get four hours of sheer pleasure in the Turkish bath-
house with its flotation pool, Jacuzzis, steam rooms and saunas. All the regular body
treatments are available at hefty prices (R330 for a one-hour Swedish massage, for
instance); booking is essential (☎028 284 000, ⓦwww.arabellasheraton.co.za).

to mid-nineteenth centuries, create a photogenic vignette in the tiny harbour.

An almost continuous five-kilometre cliff path through coastal *fynbos* hugs the rocky coastline from the old harbour to Grotto Beach in the eastern suburbs. For one short stretch the path heads away from the coast and follows Main Street before returning to the shore. East of the Old Harbour, just below the *Marine Hotel*, a beautiful tidal pool offers the only **sea swimming** around the town centre's craggy coast; it's big enough to do laps. For **beaches**, you have to head out east across the Mossel River to the suburbs, where you'll find a decent choice, starting with secluded **Langbaai**, closest to town, a cove beneath cliffs at the bottom of Sixth Avenue that has a narrow strip of beach and is excellent for swimming. **Voëlklip**, at the bottom of Eighth Avenue, has grassed terraces, toilets, a nearby café for tea and is great for picnics if you prefer your sandwiches unseasoned with sand. Adjacent is **Kammabaai**, with the best surfing break around Hermanus, and 1km further east, **Grotto Beach**, which despite its name is not a rocky cove, and marks the start of a twelve-kilometre curve of dazzlingly white sand that stretches all the way to De Kelders.

Also on the east side of town, the **Fernkloof Nature Reserve** (dawn–dusk; free) encompasses fifteen square kilometres of mountainous terrain and offers sweeping views of Walker Bay. This highly recommended wilderness area is more than just another nature reserve on the edge of town – it has some 40km of **waymarked footpaths**, including a 4.5-kilometre circular nature trail. Visiting is an excellent way to get close to the astonishing variety of delicate montane coastal *fynbos* (over a thousand species have been identified in the reserve), much of it flowering species that attract scores of birds, including the brightly coloured sunbirds and sugarbirds endemic to the area.

A couple of kilometres west of town along Westcliff, the **New Harbour** is a working fishing harbour, dramatically surrounded by steep cliffs, projecting a gutsy counterpoint to the more manicured central area. The whales sometimes enter the harbour – and there's nowhere better to watch them than from the *Harbour Rock* (see p.246).

On the eastern edge of Hermanus, **Rotary Way** is a fantastic ten-kilometre drive that follows the mountain spine through beautiful montane *fynbos* offering sweeping views of the town, the Hemel-en-Aarde Valley and Walker Bay from Kleinmond to Danger Point. To get there from town, turn right just after the sports ground, and take a track straddled by a pair of white gateposts labelled "Rotary Way". The road is tarred for part of the way, then becomes a dirt track, eventually petering out altogether, which means you have to return the same way.

Eating and drinking

Although **seafood** is the obvious thing to eat in Hermanus – and you'll find plenty of good restaurants serving it – there's a wide range of cuisine available here, with some gourmet **restaurants** to try.

There's no nicer way to eat on a beautiful day in Hermanus than to do a bit of self-catering or buy some fish and chips and eat out on the wall of the old harbour. *Hermanus Fish Shoppe* in Market Square does takeaway fish and chips – the best in town – as well as seafood salads and fresh seafood to cook yourself. *Ethne's*, 17B Royal Centre, Main Road, is a tiny café best known for its tasty ready-to-microwave meals (with good vegetarian options), though it also does sandwiches on homemade bread as well as takeaway coffees. Grub features large at the **market** held every Saturday morning on Market Square, where you'll find excellent homemade cheeses from Bot River as well as homemade pasta, pesto, marinated cheeses, muffins, houmus and baked goods. As for **delis**, try *Deli's Italian Delicatessen*, 181 Main Road, a pukka Italian place selling pastas, sauces, cheeses, meats and good Italian coffee. Central **supermarkets** include Kwikspar at 247 Main Road (daily 7am–7pm) and Pick 'n Pay at 81 Main Street (Mon–Sat 8am–6pm, Sun 9am–4pm).

Restaurants and cafés

Annie se Kombuis Warrington Pl, Harbour Rd ☎ 028 313 1350. Small, simple place serving traditional South African fare, such as *bobotie* and *koeksisters*, at reasonable prices. Tues–Sat lunch & dinner, Sun lunch only.

B's Steakhouse Hemel-en-Aarde Village ☎028 316 3625. A friendly, buzzing steakhouse – not part of a chain – serving brilliantly prepared, reasonably priced, slabs of beef (they hasten to tell punters they don't do burgers). Its formidable wine list and child-friendliness makes it an obvious choice for families. Tues–Sun dinner, Fri & Sun also lunch.

The Burgundy Marine Dr ☎028 312 2800. Above the old harbour, in one of the town's oldest buildings, this fairly expensive Mediterranean-influenced restaurant has a seafood-dominated menu, with some shady outdoor seating. Daily lunch, tea & dinner.

The Café 14 Aberdeen St. Fresh salads, quiches and breads in summer, soups and stews in winter, charged by the weight of your plate. Order your coffees and drinks from the counter, and help yourself to delicious cakes and desserts. Mon–Sat 8.30am–5pm, Sun 10am–5pm.

Fisherman's Cottage Lemms Corner. An excellent spot for drinks, though the food – salads, fish and chips, and burgers – is pretty average. It's housed in an old rustic cottage off Market Square, with veranda seating. Tues–Sat 11am–11pm, Sun lunch only.

Harbour Rock Seagrill & Bar New Harbour ☎ 028 312 2920. Reasonably priced fish and chips and other seafood dishes; stunning views from the

cliffs make it an excellent place for sundowners. Daily breakfast, lunch & dinner.

Marimba Café 9 Royal Centre, Main Rd ☎028 312 2148. Lively place with a constantly changing mid-priced menu from across Africa – the likes of Ethiopian roast lamb seasoned with cardamom and ginger, and *yassa* – Senegalese-style chicken. Booking essential. Daily eves.

Mediterranea Marine Dr ☎028 313 1685. One of the best restaurants in town, with good views of Walker Bay. The Mediterranean-style food is expensive, but worth the treat. Tues–Sun eves.

Milkwood Restaurant Atlantic Drive, Onrus ☎028 316 1516. A 15min drive west of Hermanus, *Milkwood* is especially recommended for its deck in an unsurpassed setting on a seaside lagoon, and does medium-priced steaks and excellent freshly caught fish. A good family venue. Daily noon–10.30pm.

Mogg's Country Cookhouse Hemel-en-Aarde Valley, 12km from Hermanus along the R320 to Caledon ☎028 312 4321. A most unlikely location for one of Hermanus's most successful restaurants – on a working farm in the back country – with superb views across the valley. Mogg's is an intimate, mid-priced place that's always full and unfailingly excellent, serving whatever country-cooking surprises take the fancy of chefs Jenny Mogg and her daughter Julia, but there's always a choice of three starters, main courses and desserts. Booking essential. Wed–Sun lunch, plus Fri & Sat eves.

Rossi's Italian Restaurant 10 High St ☎028 312 2848. A inexpensive, child-friendly establishment with reliable pastas and furnace-baked pizzas seven nights a week.

Listings

Emergencies Fire ☎028 361 0000; police (enquiries) ☎028 312 2626. See also p.89.
Hospital Hermanus Private Hospital, Hospital St, off Main Rd (☎028 313 0168), has a 24hr casualty service.
Internet access There's an Internet café at 69 Main Rd (Mon–Fri 7.30am–6pm, Sat 9am–4pm, Sun 10am–2pm).

Pharmacy Hermanus, 145 Main Rd (☎028 312 4039 or 312 233) is open Mon–Fri 8am–6.30pm, Sat 8am–1pm and Sun 10am–noon & 6.30–7.30pm.
Taxis Bernardus shuttle service (☎028 316 1093 or 083 658 7848) runs buses to and from Cape Town (R140 per person sharing one way), and can get you around town.

Hemel-en-Aarde Valley: the Walker Bay wineries

Some of South Africa's top wines come from the **Hemel-en-Aarde Valley**, about fifteen minutes by car west of Hermanus. Vineyards in the area date back to the early nineteenth century, when the Klein Hemel-en-Aarde Vineyard was part of a Moravian mission station, but winemaking has been established here for more than a decade. Four small **wineries** are dotted along a few gravel kilometres of the R320 to Caledon, which branches off the main road to Cape Town 2km west of Hermanus, and are worth popping into for their intimate tasting rooms and first-class wines, with views of the stark scrubby mountains just inland.

Closest to town, **Whalehaven Winery** (Mon–Fri 9.30am–5pm, Sat 10.30am–1pm; free; ⓦ www.whalehavenwines.co.za) has seen its reputation grow since its first vintage was released a decade ago; it's a couple of hundred metres after the Caledon turn-off. The longest established of the Walker Bay wineries is **Hamilton Russell** (Mon–Fri 9am–5pm, Sat 9am–1pm; free), which produces some of South Africa's priciest wines. Adjacent to Hamilton Russell, towards Caledon, **Bouchard Finlayson** (Mon–Fri 9am–5pm, Sat 10.30am–12.30pm; ⓦ www.bouchardfinlayson.co.za) is another establishment with a formidable reputation, and a wider range of wines than its neighbour. Furthest from town and newest of the wineries is **Cape Bay** (Mon–Fri 9am–4pm & summer only Sun 9am–noon), just under 7km from the Hemel-en-Aarde turn-off and about half a kilometre after the tar ends.

Across the road from Whalehaven Winery, in Hemel-en-Aarde Village, is possibly the best wine shop in South Africa, the **Wine Village** (Mon–Sat 9am–6pm & Sun 10am–3pm), with a staggering selection of labels from all the country's various wine-producing districts, covering a vast price range.

Stanford

East of Hermanus the R43 takes a detour inland around the Klein River Lagoon, past the pretty riverside hamlet of **STANFORD**, fifteen minutes away. Despite its proximity to hyped-up Hermanus, this historic village, established in 1857, has become something of a refuge for arty types seeking a tranquil escape from the urban rat race. To keep visitors racing around Stanford, the hamlet's residents have created an **arts and crafts route** that takes in over a dozen artists' studios. But apart from the town's excellent micro-brewery, Stanford's principal attraction is its travel-brochure streetscape of simple **Victorian architecture** that includes lime-washed houses and sandstone cottages – as well as an Anglican church – with thatched roofs that glow under the late afternoon sun.

Although the **Birkenhead Brewery** (tasting Mon–Sat 11am–4pm, free tours Mon–Fri) just across the R43 from the village (along the R326) bills itself as a "craft brewery estate", the gleaming stainless steel pipes and equipment inside soon dispel any images of bloodshot hillbillies knocking up a bit of moonshine on the quiet. This is a very slick operation and a great place to go for a pub lunch (daily 11am–3pm) or to sample and buy beers which put those of SAB, South Africa's big brewing near-monopoly, in their place.

Two kilometres beyond the brewery is the **Klein River Cheese Farm** (Mon–Fri 9am–5pm, Sat 9am–1pm), which offers tastings of its famous Gruyère, Leiden, Colby and Dando cheeses. Buy a slab to have with a glass of wine from **Erica Vineyards** (Mon–Fri 9am–6pm), Stanford's first winery, 4km further along the R326.

Practicalities

There is no public transport to Stanford, but once there you'd have no problem getting around this tiny hamlet on foot. The **tourist office** (Mon–Fri 8am–4pm & Sat 10am–5pm; ℡028 341 0340), next to the library and opposite the Spar **mini-supermarket** in the middle of the village, has brochures about Stanford and can help with finding **accommodation**, of which Stanford has a fair selection – well-run B&Bs and self-catering cottages at reasonable prices.

Accommodation

B's Cottage 17 Morton St ℡028 341 0430, ℮milkwood@hermanus.co.za. A small open-plan self-catering thatched house, sleeping two, in an English-style country garden. ❷

Galashiels Lodge 10 King St, ℡028 341 0181, ℮gslodge@hermanus.co.za. A Scottish-themed lodge in a restored Victorian house with more reception rooms than bedrooms, all opulent and full of character. There's a pub, library and rambling terraced garden. ❸

Pizbrooke Shortmarket St ℡028 341 0900, ℮reservations@standfordvillage.co.za. Self-catering house that sleeps four, simply decorated with old Cape furniture, large, comfortable wrought-iron beds and polished wooden floors. R650 per night.

Stanford Hotel 18 Queen Victoria St ℡028 341 0900, ℮reservations@stanfordvillage.co.za. Five-room guesthouse in a 1920s house with uncluttered, minimalist decor that includes white linen drapes and period country-style beds. They occasionally host evenings of music and entertainment in keeping with the period feel of the place. ❷

Restaurants

Marianne's Bistro and Home Deli Du Toit St ℡028 341 0272. In a Victorian cottage, good enough to draw Cape Town gourmands out for the day and recommended for its cream teas, homemade fare and carefully prepared and delicious lunches. Fri–Sun 9am–4pm.

Paprika Shortmarket St ℡028 341 0662. Delicious Mediterranean-style dinners and Sunday lunches in a convivial cottage. Tues & Sun dinner, plus Sun lunch.

Peregrine Farm Stall Queen Victoria St ℡028 341 0386. Besides selling vegetables and breads, they have a café serving breakfast and light lunches, including a traditional Sunday roast. Daily 8.30am–4pm.

The Ploughman's Pantry Queen Victoria St ℡028 341 0444. Pastas, lasagne and quiche served throughout the day, and pizza in the evenings. Mon & Thurs–Sun 8.30am–4pm & 6–9pm, Tues & Wed 8.30am–4pm.

Grootbos and De Kelders

It's not hyperbole to say that the **Grootbos Private Nature Reserve** (℡028 384 0381, ℗www.grootbos.co.za; half board including all activities ❽; minimum stay two nights) is unique. A highlight of the area, 33km from Hermanus, this luxury reserve has superb middle-distance views of the coast, and is promoted as a "*fynbos* lodge", where experts guide you through the Western Cape's unique and richly varied plant kingdom. Accommodation is in self-contained stone cottages with ethnic-chic furnishings, polished granite kitchen surfaces, imported fittings, temperature-controlled showers, multiple sun decks and views of the mountain from one side and the sea from the other. The rate includes a three-course dinner served in the main lodge, breakfast in your own cottage and a choice of activities, including guided horse-rides, walks or drives through the *fynbos* and conducted beach hikes. If you don't want to stay, you can experience the place on one of their **day excursions** from Grootbos (R650), led by a professional guide; morning and afternoon tea and a gourmet lunch are included in the price.

The nearest coast is a couple of kilometres to the east at **DE KELDERS**, a haphazard and treeless hamlet that stares from bleak cliffs across Walker Bay to Hermanus. Despite surpassing fashionable Hermanus as a whale-watching venue and having a marvellous, long, sandy beach, De Kelders remains a backwater, devoid of facilities apart from a few rentable **rooms**. Best value of these is *Liesje's Lodge*, 77 Hoof Road (℡028 384 1277 or 072 222 0885; self-catering ❶, B&B ❷), where some of the units offer sea views. The friendly owner Liesje van Voorkom, takes guests whale-watching and can give advice on the local **shark-cage diving** operations (see also Gansbaai, below).

At the end of Cliff Road is a car park from which you can clamber down to the **Klipgat Strandloper Caves**, excavated in the early 1990s, when evidence was unearthed of modern human habitation from 80,000 years ago. The caves became unoccupied for a few thousand years after which they were used again by Khoisan people, 20,000 years ago. Shells, middens, tools and bones were uncovered, some of these now displayed in the South African Museum in Cape Town (see p.126). From the caves, the waymarked **Duiwelsgats hiking trail** goes east for 7km as far as Gansbaai and is a good way to explore this beautiful coastline.

Gansbaai and Danger Point

GANSBAAI is a workaday place, economically dependent on its fishing industry and the seafood canning factory at the harbour. This gives the place a more gutsy feel than the surrounding holidaylands, but there's little reason to spend time here unless you want to engage in **great white shark safaris**, Gansbaai's other major industry, an appropriately competitive and cut-throat business with operators engaged in a blind feeding frenzy to attract punters. Boats set out from Gansbaai to **Dyer Island** (see box below), east of Danger Point, where great white sharks come to feed on the resident colony of seals. Sharks are baited, but while you do stand a chance of seeing one, sightings are certainly not guaranteed, especially over December and January when the abundance of seal pups keeps the sharks well fed and less inclined to show up for tourists. Even if a shark does appear, it may not stay long enough for all the people on the boat to get into the cage for a viewing (only two can fit in at a time). For more information, contact the Gansbaai **tourist office** (Mon–Fri 9am–1pm & 2pm–5pm, Sat 10am–2pm; ℡028 384 1439, ⓦwww .gansbaaiinfo.com).

Dyer Island and Shark Alley

How a black American came to be living on an island off South Africa in the early nineteenth century is something of a mystery. But, according to records, **Samson Dyer** arrived here in 1806 and made a living collecting guano on the island that subsequently took his name.

Dyer Island is home to substantial **African penguin** and **seal breeding colonies**, both of which are prized morsels among great white sharks. So shark-infested is the channel between the island and the mainland at some times of year that it is known as **Shark Alley**, and these waters are used extensively by operators of great white viewing trips. In 1996, a group of West African castaways washed up here having been put out to sea by the unscrupulous skipper of a Taiwanese merchant vessel whom they had paid to take them to the Far East, where they hoped to find work. One of them drowned in the process, but the rest (amazingly) survived five days at sea, including a stint down Shark Alley, clinging to pieces of timber and barrels.

Danger Point, the southernmost point of Walker Bay, is where British naval history was allegedly made. True to its name, the Point lured the ill-fated HMS *Birkenhead* onto its hidden rocks on February 26, 1852. As was the custom, the captain of the troopship gave the order "Every man for himself". Displaying true British pluck, the soldiers are said to have lined up in their ranks on deck where they stood stock-still, knowing that if one man broke ranks it would lead to a rush that might overwhelm the lifeboats carrying women and children to safety. The precedent of "women and children first", which became known as the **Birkenhead Drill**, was thus established, even though 445 lives were lost in the disaster.

Elim

A good reason to venture along the network of dirt roads that crisscrosses the Whale Coast interior is to visit **ELIM**, a Moravian mission station 40km northwest of Agulhas, founded in 1824. The whole village is a National Monument of streets lined with thatched, whitewashed houses and fig trees. There's nothing twee about this very undeveloped and untouristy place – there isn't even a bottle store, and facilities amount to a couple of tiny shops.

The **tourist office** in Church Street (Mon–Sat 9am–12.30pm & 1.30–5pm; ☎028 482 1806) provides brochures about the area. **Tours** (R35, by arrangement) of the village start at the tourist office and take in the oldest house in the settlement, the church, the restored water mill where wheat is still ground, and the pottery studio. There's also a memorial commemorating the **emancipation of slaves** in 1834, the only such monument in South Africa; its presence reflects the fact that numerous freed slaves found refuge in mission stations like Elim.

The only **accommodation** is the community-run *Elim Guesthouse* (☎028 482 1715; ❷; dinner available on request), a newly renovated 1901 thatched home. For a cup of tea or a **snack**, try the *Old Mill Tea Room* (also run by the community, and open by arrangement; contact the tourist office).

Bredasdorp

BREDASDORP, the commercial centre of the Overberg farmlands, lies on the main routes to Cape Agulhas, Arniston and De Hoop Nature Reserve. Although it doesn't merit an overnight stay it does offer two good reasons to stop off. One is **Kapula Candles**, at the corner Petterson Road and First Avenue, which started as a cottage industry and now supplies its beautifully crafted candles to shops throughout South Africa, with outlets in Germany. The factory shop has a café where you can get a decent cup of coffee surrounded by colourful candles, or outside in the herbarium. The **Shipwreck Museum** at 6 Independent Street (Mon–Fri 9am–4.45pm, Sat & Sun 11am–4pm; R10) displays an interesting array of items retrieved from the many dashed vessels that have gone down off the treacherous coastline.

Cape Agulhas

Along the east flank of the Danger Point promontory, the rocky and shallow coastline with heavy swells and strong currents makes this one of South Africa's most treacherous stretches of coast – one that has claimed over 250 wrecks and around 2500 lives. Its rocky terrain also accounts for the lack of a coastal road from Gansbaai and Danger Point to **Cape Agulhas**, the southernmost tip of Africa.

The plain around the southern tip has been declared the **Agulhas National Park** to conserve its estimated 2000 species of indigenous plant and marine and intertidal life as well as a cultural heritage which includes shipwrecks and archeological sites – stone hearths, pottery and shell middens have been discovered. There are no facilities apart from a basic **tea shop** inside the terrific **Agulhas Lighthouse** (daily 8am–5pm; R10), commissioned in 1849. At the top, reached by a series of steep ladders, there are vertiginous views and some interesting exhibits about lighthouses around South Africa and elsewhere in the world.

Three-hour **tours** taking in the coast, *fynbos* as well as history and archeology of the area are operated by the well-informed Riaan Pienaar of Coastal Safaris (☎028 435 7148 or 082 331 6819, ✉coastaltours@isat.co.za).

Practicalities

L'AGULHAS, the rather windblown settlement associated with the southern tip, consists of a small collection of houses and a few shops. It's reached from Hermanus by heading inland on the R316 to Bredasdorp, where the road splits, the more westerly branch (the R319) continuing 43km on to Agulhas.

The smartest **accommodation** in town is the *Agulhas Country Lodge* on Main Road (☎028 435 7650, ⓦwww.agulhascountrylodge.com; ❺), in a relatively grand stone building perched halfway up a hillside. All rooms have sea views from private balconies; excellent seafood **dinners** provide another inducement to stay. Uniquely positioned on the edge of the Agulhas National Park is the sea-facing *Pebble Beach Vlei Laan*, Suiderstrand (☎028 435 7270 or 082 774 5008; ❸; follow signs to the Southern Tip of Africa and then 5km beyond, turn left at Suiderstrand), with two rustic en-suite rooms. The thatched *Sea House B&B*, Van Breda Street (☎028 435 6542, ✉pfm@isat.co.za; ❸) has lime-washed floors and three cool rooms in front of a tidal pool. As its name implies, the *Southernmost*, on the corner of Van Breda and Lighthouse streets (☎028 435 6565, ✉cowper@isat.co.za; ❸), has the most southerly beds for rent in Africa, but doesn't welcome kids, mobile phones, smokers or pets.

Arniston

After the cool deep blues of the Atlantic to the west, the tepid azure of the Indian Ocean at **ARNISTON** is truly startling, made all the more dazzling by the white dunes interspersed with rocky ledges. Reached on the R316, 24km southeast of Bredasdorp, this is one of the best places to stay in the Overberg and is refreshingly underdeveloped compared to Hermanus and places closer to Cape Town. The village is known to locals by its Afrikaans name, Waenhuiskrans ("wagon-house cliff"), after a cliff containing a huge cave 1500m south of town, which *trekboers* reckoned was spacious enough for a wagon and span of oxen (the largest thing they could think of). The English name derives from a British ship, the *Arniston*, which hit the rocks here in 1815.

The shallow seas, so treacherous for vessels, provide Arniston with the safest swimming waters along the Whale Coast. Apart from sea bathing, the principal attraction is **Kassiesbaai**, a district of starkly beautiful limewashed cottages, now declared a National Monument and home to coloured fishing families that have for generations made their living here. Its beautifully simple dwellings invariably show up in coffee-table books whenever picturesque images of fishing villages are called for. But Kassiesbaai sits a little uneasily as a living community, as it's also a bit of a theme park for visitors stalking the streets with their cameras. More positively, all the holiday accommodation is in the adjacent new section of town, which has managed to blend in with the spirit of the old village.

The only regular entertainment here is wandering down to the harbour at high tide to watch fishing boats being shoved down the slipway by a tractor that ends up half submerged. Otherwise, swimming and beach walks offer a break from the supreme languor. You can swim next to the slipway or at **Roman Beach**, the main swimming beach, just along the coast as you head south from the harbour. In season, keep your eyes open for **southern right whales**.

Heading north through Kassiesbaai at low tide, you can walk 5km along an unspoilt beach unmarred by buildings until you reach an unassuming fence – resist the temptation to climb over this, as it marks the boundary of the local testing range for military materiel and missiles. Heading south of the harbour for 1500m along spectacular cliffs, you'll reach the vast **cave** after which the town is named. The walk is worth doing simply for the *fynbos*-covered dunes you'll cross on the way. From the car park right by the cave, it's a short sign-posted walk down to the dunes and the cave, which can only be reached at low tide. The rocks can be slippery and have sharp sections, so be sure to wear shoes with tough soles and a good grip.

Practicalities

There's no public transport to Arniston. For food, the choice is limited to three **restaurants**, all of which serve fresh fish caught locally. *Die Waenhuis* on Du Preez Street (a continuation of the national road), is decorated to resemble a fishermen's tavern and serves butter-soft calamari. The Arniston fishermen's wives have opened a small eating place in the Kassiesbaai Craft Shop (booking required on ☎028 445 9760; ask for Lilian Newman), where they'll cook up a three-course traditional fisherman's meal with the catch of the day brought in by their menfolk. The *Arniston Hotel* has a dining room and a more relaxed pub (the bar counter is a U-shaped fish tank) serving light meals.

You can buy fresh fish from the fishermen at the slipway near the hotel. There's a small **supply store** attached to *Die Waenhuis* selling basics, but if you're self-catering it's best to stock up at the Super Spar on Church Street in Bredasdorp.

Accommodation

Accommodation is limited to one hotel, some self-catering cottages and a handful of B&Bs, which get snapped up quickly during school holidays and over weekends. You might want to book through Etna's Accommodation (☎028 445 9757), an agency with over thirty self-catering properties on its books. The village is small and not all properties are numbered, so be sure to get directions from the main road if you're renting a house.

Arniston Hotel ☎028 445 9000, ⊛www .arnistonhotel.com. A luxurious and well-run hotel in a central position along the seafront, the only place to stay in the village with sea views, at least from some rooms. ⑥

Arniston Seaside Cottages Well signposted from the national road, along the street behind the hotel ☎028 445 9772, ⊜cottages@arniston-online

.co.za. Limewashed self-catering cottages, fully equipped and serviced. Out of season rates are per person, but in season (Jan, Easter school holidays & Dec) you pay for the number of beds in the unit. ❸

Kassiesbaai Cottage Kassiesbaai ☎028 445 9760. Lilian Newman rents out her modestly furnished traditional fisherman's cottage, which contains three double rooms. On a self-catering basis, the cottage costs R350 a night.

Southwinds Huxham St, just behind the hotel ☎028 445 9303, ✉southwinds@kingsley.co.za. Four well-appointed double suites, with goose-down duvets and crisp linen, looking onto a courtyard garden. The hosts, Marc and Annie, will prepare picnics and dinners on request. Annie is a registered reflexologist, and practises from the house. B&B ❸

Waenhuis Caravan Park Along the main road into Arniston, 300m from the centre ☎028 445 9620. Pitch your own tent or stay in one of the basic, four-bed en-suite bungalows. Cooking equipment is available at a small charge, but you'll need to bring your own bedding and towels. The place can get crowded and noisy over weekends and peak season. ❷

De Hoop Nature Reserve

It's surprising that **De Hoop** (daily 7am–6pm; R20) isn't a national park, when it's probably the wilderness highlight of the Western Cape. Although the reserve makes a relatively easy day-trip from Hermanus, you'll find it far more rewarding to come here for a night or more.

The breathtaking coastline is edged by bleached sand dunes standing 90m high in places, and rocky formations that at one point open to the sea in a massive craggy arch. The flora and fauna are impressive, too, encompassing 86 species of mammal, 260 different birds and 1500 varieties of plants, and it's reckoned to be the ultimate place in South Africa (surpassing even Hermanus and De Kelders) to see **southern right whales**. If you're here for a couple of days in season, chances are you'll be lucky – occasionally dozens of whales are in evidence at one time. July to September is the best time, but you stand a very good chance of a sighting from June through to November. Inland, rare **Cape mountain zebra**, **bontebok** and other **antelope** congregate on a plain near the reserve accommodation. Apart from swimming and strolling along the length of white sandy beach, there are mountain-biking trails (bring your own bike as there's nowhere to rent one) and hikes, including a seventy-kilometre trail consisting of three days' hiking along the coast and two days along the Potberg Mountains; overnight huts are provided along the way and numbers are limited to twelve people (book through the reserve).

Practicalities

De Hoop is along a signposted dirt road that spurs off the R319 as it heads out of Bredasdorp, 50km to its west. Accommodation, usually booked up at weekends, includes a **campsite** and two-bedroomed **self-catering cottages** (Mon–Thurs & Sun R285, Fri & Sat R350) with a cooker, fridge and kitchen utensils, with bedding available to rent. The choicest places to stay are the three luxury thatched cottages on the lip of the estuary (Mon–Thurs & Sun R430, Fri & Sat R535), also with two bedrooms, but with more privacy and a large comfortable living room. Bookings should be made through the reserve's manager (☎028 425 5020, ✉dehoopinfo@sdm .dorea.co.za). Overnight visitors must report to the reserve office (☎028 542 1253), about 4km into the reserve, by 4pm. Be sure to stock up on supplies before you come – the nearest shop is 15km away, in the hamlet of Ouplaas.

There's good privately run accommodation just outside the entrance gate at *Buchu Bushcamp* (☎028 542 1602, ✉info@buchu-bushcamp.com; B&B ❸) in six open-plan timber and thatch chalets, as well as a **restaurant** where guests can get meals. The owner is a conservationist who is extremely knowledgeable about the local flora and fauna and leads tours.

The Garden Route

The **Garden Route**, a slender stretch of coastal plain between Mossel Bay and Storms River Mouth, has a legendary status as South Africa's paradise – reflected in local names such as **Garden of Eden** and **Wilderness**. This soft, green, forested swath of nearly 200km is cut by rivers from the mountains to the north, tumbling down to its southern rocky shores and sandy beaches.

The **Khoi** herders who lived off its natural bounty considered the area a paradise, calling it Outeniqua ("the man laden with honey"). Their Eden was quickly destroyed in the eighteenth century with the arrival of Dutch **woodcutters**, who had exhausted the forests around Cape Town and set about doing the same in Outeniqua, killing or dispersing the Khoi and San in the process. Birds and animals suffered too from the encroachment of Europeans. In the 1850s, the Swedish naturalist Johan Victorin shot and feasted on the species he had come to study, some of which, including the endangered narina trogon, he noted were both "beautiful and good to eat".

Despite the dense appearance of the area, what you see today are only the remnants of one of Africa's great **forests**; much of the indigenous hardwoods have been replaced by exotic pine plantations, and the only milk and honey you'll find now is in the many shops servicing the Garden Route coastal resorts. **Conservation** has halted the wholesale destruction of the indigenous woodlands, but a huge growth in tourism and the influx of urbanites seeking a quiet life in the relatively crime-free Garden Route towns threatens to rob the area of its remaining tranquillity.

The Garden Route coast is dominated by three inlets – Mossel Bay, the Knysna lagoon and Plettenberg Bay – each with its own town. Oldest of these and closest to Cape Town is **Mossel Bay**, an industrial centre of some charm, which marks the official start of the Garden Route. **Knysna**, though younger, exudes a well-rooted urban character and is the nicest of the coastal towns, with one major drawback – unlike **Plettenberg Bay**, its eastern neighbour, it has no beach of its own. A major draw, though, is the **Knysna forest** covering some of the hilly country around Knysna, the awe-inspiring remnants of once vast ancient woodlands.

Between the coastal towns are some ugly modern holiday developments, but also some wonderful empty beaches and tiny coves, such as **Victoria Bay**, **Buffels Bay** and **Nature's Valley**. Best of all is the **Tsitsikamma National Park**, which has it all – indigenous forest, dramatic coastline, the pumping **Storms River Mouth** and South Africa's most popular hike, the **Otter trail**.

Most visitors take the Garden Route as a **journey** between Cape Town and Port Elizabeth, dallying for little more than a day or two for shopping, sightseeing or a taste of one of the many adventure sports on offer. The rapid passage cut by the excellent **N2** makes it all too easy to have a fast scenic drive – and end up disappointed because you don't see that much from the road. To make the journey worthwhile, you'll need to slow down, take some detours off the highway and explore a little to find secluded coves, walks in the forests or even mountain passes in the Karoo (see p.212).

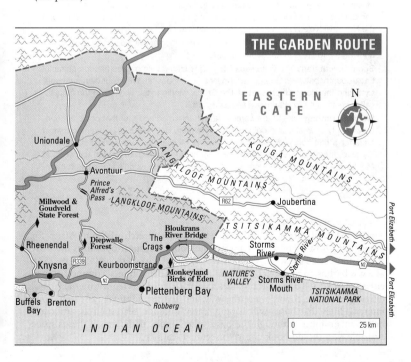

Garden Route adventure activities: the highlights

The Garden Route is fast losing its reputation as the place to go for sun-soaking idleness or to commune with nature. Adrenaline and adventure are elbowing out these passive pursuits and now thrill-junkies go expressly to throw themselves off bridges, to gape into the jaws of great white sharks and to freewheel down scary mountain passes. The choice is broad – and widely spread across the entire length of the Garden Route. To help you plan, here are some highlights.

Abseiling Drop down a cliff face at the private Featherbed Nature Reserve (box on p.273), the entrance to the Knysna lagoon, or along the Kaaimans River gorge in Wilderness (p.265).

Blackwater tubing Float down the spectacular Storms River Gorge (box on p.288) in inflatable tubes.

Bungee jumping The world's highest commercial jump is at Bloukrans Bridge (see p.285); you can also try bungee swinging, a jump with a twist, at Gouritz River Bridge near Mossel Bay (see box on p.261).

Canopy tours Monkey around swinging from tree to tree in an indigenous forest, thirty metres above the forest floor (see box on p.288).

Hiking There's a terrific circular one-day hike along the edge of the Robberg Penin-sula (see p.282), with a chance of seeing whales, dolphins and seals. Otherwise, there are quite a few longer and more challenging trails to attempt; see the box on pp.258–259.

Horse-riding Sit cowboy-style in a deep saddle at *Southern Comfort Western Horse Ranch*, between Knysna and Plettenberg Bay (see p.272). Or head out with an English saddle through African countryside near Plettenberg Bay, for *fynbos* and forest trails.

Mountain biking Tear down the hair-raising Swartberg Pass, starting out from Kny-sna or Oudtshoorn (see p.221), or pedal your way in a slightly calmer fashion round the Homtini Cycle Route in the Knysna forest (see p.277).

River boat Go for a leisurely ferry ride down the spectacular Keurbooms river estu-ary where bird life is in abundance (p.284).

Scenic excursions The Outeniqua Choo-Tjoe steam train passes through beautiful back-country between George and Knysna (see opposite). With your own transport, try taking the old road just east of The Crags, winding your way down the fantasti-cally scenic route to Nature's Valley (see p.287).

Wildlife-spotting Take to the water on a well-informed eco-tour that could encoun-ter a variety of whales and dolphins at Plettenberg Bay (see p.282), or enter a shark cage for a first-hand encounter with Jaws at Mossel Bay (see opposite). Back on dry land, there's family fun in the forest, looking for apes from around the world at Monkeyland (see p.285) or coming face to face with the world's largest land mam-mal at the Knysna Elephant Sanctuary (see box on p.278).

Travel practicalities

The **Garden Route** is probably the best-served stretch of South Africa for **transport**. Most user-friendly among the public transport options is the daily **Baz Bus** service between Cape Town and Port Elizabeth (℡021 439 2323, ⊛www.bazbus.co.za), which picks up passengers daily from accommodation at either end (7.15–8.30am). It provides a door-to-door service within the central districts of all the towns along the way, and has the advantage over the large intercity lines that buses will happily carry outdoor gear, such as surfboards or mountain bikes. Although the buses take standby passengers if there's space available, you should book ahead to secure a seat.

Intercape, Greyhound and Translux **intercity buses** from Cape Town and Port Elizabeth are better for more direct journeys, stopping only at Mossel Bay, George, Wilderness, Sedgefield, Knysna and Storms River (the village, but not the Mouth, which is some distance away). These buses often don't go into town, letting passengers off at filling stations on the highway instead.

More of a day out than serious transport, the **Outeniqua Choo-Tjoe** is a goods train with passenger carriages attached, running the 30km between George and Knysna (Mon–Sat: summer 2 daily, less frequently at other times; 2hr 45min; R65 single, R75 return) in both directions, via Wilderness, Sedgefield and Goukamma. You need to book your tickets a day ahead on ☏044 382 1361 or 044 801 8202. And finally, if time is tight, you may want to go by **air** to George at the west end of the Garden Route, served by scheduled flights from Cape Town, Johannesburg, Durban and Port Elizabeth. The only other centre served by regular flights is Plettenberg Bay, which is connected to Cape Town and Johannesburg.

Mossel Bay

MOSSEL BAY, a midsized town 397km east of Cape Town, gets an undeservedly bad press from most South Africans, mainly because of the huge industrial facade it presents to the N2. Don't panic – the historic centre is a thoroughly pleasant contrast, set on a hill overlooking the small working harbour and bay, with one of the best **swimming** beaches along the southern Cape coast and an interesting museum. The town takes on a strong Afrikaans flavour over Christmas, when Karoo farmers and their families descend in droves to occupy its caravan parks and chalets. While Mossel Bay's modest attractions are unlikely to hold you for more than a night, it has some decent accommodation and a first-class restaurant, which make it a good place to pause before launching out along the Garden Route.

Mossel Bay bears poignant historical significance as the place where indigenous Khoi cattle herders encountered the Europeans in a bloody spat that symbolically set the tone for five hundred years of race relations on the subcontinent. A group of Portuguese mariners under captain **Bartholomeu Dias** set sail from Portugal in August 1487 in search of a sea route to the riches of India, and months later rounded the Cape of Good Hope. In February 1488, they became the first Europeans to make landfall along the South African coast, when they pulled in for water to the safety of an inlet they called Aguado de São Bras ("watering place of St Blaize"), now Mossel Bay. The Khoikhoi were organized into distinct groups, each under its own chief and each with territorial rights over pastures and water sources. The Portuguese, who were flouting local customs, saw it as "bad manners" when the Khoikhoi tried to drive them off the spring. In a mutual babble of incomprehension the Khoi began stoning the Portuguese, who retaliated with crossbow fire that left one of the herders dead.

Arrival, information and accommodation

The N2 bypasses Mossel Bay and, of all the buses, only the **Baz Bus** comes right into town, dropping you off anywhere on request. The large **intercity buses** all stop at Shell Voorbaai Service Station, 7km from the centre, at the junction of the national highway and the road into town. The town itself is small enough to negotiate on foot, but should you need transport Jordaan runs

Major Garden Route hikes

If you're keen on walking and the outdoors, and want to schedule in at least one long walk somewhere in the country during your holiday, the Garden Route provides some fine possibilities. Indeed, walking is the only way to really experience the Garden Route's forests and coast and escape the clutter of holiday homes and the noisy N2.

The waymarked **hikes** listed below are two to five days long. You'll need to carry all your food, a sleeping bag for use in the communal hiking huts (mattresses are provided), lightweight cooking utensils and stove, and waterproofs. You should also wear proper worn-in hiking boots. For day-hikes and walks lasting only a couple of hours, consult Judith Hopley's *On Foot in the Garden Route*, available from Knysna's tourist office and several other outlets on the Garden Route.

Dolphin trail

Start: Sandrif River Mouth, Tsitsikamma National Park
End: Storms River Mouth, Tsitsikamma National Park
Distance: 20km
Duration: two and a half days
Cost: Storms River Adventures (see box on p.288) charges R2700 per person, including food, accommodation and permits
This is the Garden Route's luxury trail. Backpacks are transported to overnight stops where you're greeted with comfortable accommodation and cooked meals. The terrain through the Tsitsikamma National Park is breathtaking, covering the rugged coastal edge and the natural forest. The price includes a guide, a boat trip up the Storms River Gorge, and a 4WD drive through the Storms River Pass.

Harkerville Coast hiking trail

Start and end: Harkerville Forestry Station, 12km west of Plettenberg Bay, signposted off the N2
Distance: 26.5km
Duration: two days
Permit: Department of Forestry and Water Affairs, Knysna (℡044 382 5466)
Cost: R60 per person per day
Closer to the roads, this circular trail doesn't feel as remote as the Otter trail, but is a good second-best, taking in magnificent rocky coastline, indigenous forest and *fynbos*. Lots of rock scrambling and some traversing of exposed, narrow ledges above the sea is required, so don't attempt this if you're unfit or scared of heights. Monkeys, baboons and fish eagles are commonly seen, and you may also spot dolphins or whales.

a **taxi** service (℡082 673 7314). The busy **tourist office** (Mon–Fri 8am–6pm, Sat 9am–4pm; ℡044 691 2202, @www.visitmosselbay.co.za), bang in the centre on the corner of Church and Market streets, has shelves of brochures about Mossel Bay and the rest of the Garden Route, and a **map** of the town.

Accommodation

Mossel Bay has a broad range of **accommodation**, including a number of reasonable B&Bs that can be booked through the tourist office should our recommendations be full. There's **camping** at the municipal site, *De Bakke*, at George Road just back from the beach (℡044 691 2915, ✉iti26097@mweb.co.za), which also has good self-catering chalets sleeping four (R400). *Point Caravan Park* at Bland St (℡044 690 3501; ❶), along the rocky point, is not as nice as the bay's main beach for swimming, but it's close to the start of the St Blaize hiking trail.

Otter trail

Start: Storms River Mouth, Tsitsikamma National Park
End: Nature's Valley, Tsitsikamma National Park
Distance: 42km
Duration: five days
Bookings: Through South African National Parks, up to twelve months in advance. The maximum number of people on the trail is twelve.
Cost: R450 per person.
South Africa's first established hiking trail, this is a coastal walk crossing rivers, tidal pools and indigenous forest. You may see dolphins, whales and seals, and the spoor of the Cape clawless otter – although virtually impossible to spot, the creatures are certainly around. The short stretches between log-hut nightstops mean you can take things slowly, and enjoy the vegetation and birds. The Bloukrans River has to be crossed by wading or swimming: go at low tide and waterproof your backpack. Some parts of the hike are steep, so you need to be fit.

Outeniqua trail

Start: Beervlei (the old forest station – eight overnight huts); directions are given when you book
End: Harkerville Forestry Station, 12km west of Plettenburg Bay
Distance: 108km
Duration: seven days (shorter versions possible)
Permit: Department of Forestry and Water Affairs, Knysna (℡044 382 5466)
Cost: R30 per person per day
The main draw here is the indigenous forest, including giant yellowwood trees, pine plantations and gold-mining remains at Millwood in the Goudveld State Forest.

Tsitsikamma trail

Start: Nature's Valley Caravan Park, Tsitsikamma National Park
End: Storms River Bridge, Tsitsikamma National Park
Distance: 64km
Duration: five days (shorter versions possible)
Permit: South Africa National Parks
Cost: R47 per person per night
Features: Not to be confused with the Otter trail, this is an inland walk through indigenous forest, long stretches of open *fynbos* and the Tsitsikamma mountain range. Five overnight huts accommodate thirty people. It's not a difficult hike, and you won't cover more than 17km or so per day – although after heavy rains the rivers can be hard to cross.

Barnacles Econo Lodge 112 High St ℡044 690 4584 or 082 670 5259, ✉bismos@mweb.co.za. A sparkling backpacker hostel that's a cut above the average with an excellent kitchen and a helpful adventure desk that can book activities in the area. Dorms ❶, rooms ❷

Edward Charles 1 Sixth Ave ℡044 691 2152 or 082 441 7242, ℻044 691 1759. A comfortable guesthouse with a heated pool, mini-gym and Jacuzzi. ❺

Green Door 49 Marsh St ℡044 691 3820, ✉dirbb@lantic.co.za. Central B&B in a charming 100-year-old sandstone building. The older family rooms, which sleep four, are less attractive than the newer doubles, but are good value if there are more than two of you. ❸

Highview Lodge 76 Rodger St ℡044 691 9038, ⓦwww.highviewlodge.co.za. Luxury self-catering and B&B rooms with exceptional views of the bay and the mountains. Self-catering ❸, B&B ❹

Mossel Bay Guest House 61 Bruns Rd ℡044 691 2000, ℻044 690 4900. Comfortable rooms in a suburban home. ❸

Old Post Office Tree Manor Bartholomeu Dias Museum Complex, Market St ℡044 691 3738, ⓦwww.oldposttree.co.za. Opposite the tourist office, in an old Cape Dutch manor house, this quaint place is by far the best hotel in town, with breakfast served at *Café Gannet*, Mossel Bay's nicest restaurant. ❺

Santos Express Santos Beach ℡044 691 1995. A stationary train with a great location – on the beach, just metres from the surf. Accommodation is in four-person train compartments, but you'll have one to yourself if you're a couple or a family.

Morning coffee and continental breakfast is included. The restaurant is good value. ❷

Valhalla Guest House 86 Montague St ℡044 691 1075 or 082 658 2532, ✉cranbar@yebo .co.za. An inexpensive B&B with six rooms set back from the shore, but with sea views owing to its elevation on the hillside. ❸

The Town

Mossel Bay's main urban attraction is the **Bartholomeu Dias Museum Complex**, housed in a collection of historic buildings well integrated into the small town centre, all near the tourist office and within a couple of minutes' walk of each other. The highlight is the **Maritime Museum** (Mon–Fri 8.15am–4.45pm, Sat & Sun 9am–4pm; R10), a spiral gallery with displays on the history of European, principally Portuguese, seafaring, arranged around a full-size replica of Dias' original caravel. The ship was built in Portugal and sailed from Lisbon to Mossel Bay in 1987 to celebrate the five hundredth anniversary of Dias' historic journey. You can't fail to be awed by the idea of the original mariners setting out on the high seas into terra incognita on such a small vessel – particularly as the crew were accommodated above deck with only a sailcloth for protection against the elements.

The one Mossel Bay attraction that most South Africans have heard of is the **Post Office Tree**, just outside the Maritime Museum. Sixteenth-century mariners used to leave messages for passing ships in an old boot under a milkwood tree somewhere around here, and the plaque claims that "this may well" be the same tree. You can post mail here in a large, boot-shaped letterbox and have it stamped with a special postmark.

Of the remaining exhibitions, the **Shell Museum and Aquarium** (Mon–Fri 9am–4.45pm, Sat & Sun 10am–4pm; donation) next to the Post Office Tree is the only one worth taking time to visit. This is your chance to see some of the beautiful shells found off the South African coast, as well as specimens from around the world. The fascinating displays of living shellfish include cowries with their inhabitants still at home.

A short walk north down the hill from the Maritime Museum gets you to **Santos Beach**, the main town strand, and purportedly the only north-facing beach in South Africa – which gives it exceptionally long sunny afternoons. Adjacent to the small town harbour, the beach provides some of the finest swimming along the Garden Route, with uncharacteristically gentle surf, small waves and a depth perfect for practising your crawl.

East of the harbour, the coast bulges south towards the **Point**, which has several restaurants and a popular bar/restaurant (see opposite) with a deck at the ocean's edge, from which you may see dolphins cruising past, as well as a surreal five-hundred-metre rocky channel known as the aquarium, which is used as a natural **tidal pool**. Adjacent to this, the Department of Marine and Coastal Management has installed an **Aquarium** (Mon–Fri 9am–4pm, Sat & Sun 9am–12.30pm; donation) under *Tidals* pub, which showcases local lobsters, crabs and fish found off this coast in a handful of small tanks, as well as a pair of Amazon piranhas.

A couple of hundred metres to the south at the top of some cliffs, the **St Blaize Lighthouse**, built in 1864, is still in use as a beacon to ships. Below it, the **Cape St Blaize Cave** is both a marvellous lookout point and a significant archeological site. A boardwalk leads through the cave past three information panels describing the history of the interpretation of the cave as well as the modern understanding of it. In 1801 Sir John Barrow insisted that shells found at the site had been brought by seagulls, while others argued that they were relics of human habitation. It turned out that Barrow's opponents were right, but it wasn't till 1888 that excavations uncovered stone tools and showed that people had been using the cave for something close on a 100,000 years. The path leading up to the cave continues onto the Cape St Blaize trail (see below).

Activities

Given that the seals of **Seal Island**, about 10km northwest of Santos Beach, are a popular delicacy for great white sharks, you'd be forgiven for wondering why scuba diving remains so popular off Mossel Bay. In 1990, the unfortunate Monique Price became the first fully kitted scuba diver to die in a great white attack – just off the island – and divers are warned to avoid its immediate environs. There are, however, several rewarding **diving and snorkelling** spots around Mossel Bay, and full facilities, including open-water certification courses (from R1100) and one-off dives are available from Electro Dive (☎ & ℻044 698 1976 or ☎082 561 1259) or the tourist office. Electro Dive rents out gear (R100 per day), and provide shore-based and boat-based dives (R80–140). These aren't tropical seas, so don't expect clear warm waters (although temperatures tend to be warmer than at other Garden Route resorts), but with visibility usually between 4m and 10m you stand a good chance of seeing octopus, squid, sea stars, soft corals, pyjama sharks and butterfly fish.

For those who want to see **great white sharks** face to face there are a couple of outfits offering cage dives. The best months for sightings are March to November, and the worst January and February, but at no time are encounters guaranteed. One of the better operations in the country is Shark Africa, located on the corner of Church and Market streets (☎044 691 3796, ⓦwww.sharkafrica.co.za), with whom you can either observe from a boat (R600) or go underwater in a cage for R900, with the assurance that if the sharks don't show you get half your money back. If you're unlucky the first time and choose to try again on another day, you'll only be charged the amount you were refunded.

Cruises around Seal Island to see the African penguin and seal colonies can be taken on the *Romonza* (hourly 10am–4pm; R50; ☎ & ℻044 690 3101) a medium-sized yacht that launches from the yacht marina in the harbour. On the mainland you can check out the coast on the **St Blaize hiking trail**, an easy fifteen-kilometre walk (roughly 4hr each way; a map is available from the tourist office) along the southern shore of Mossel Bay. The route starts from the Cape St Blaize Cave, just below the lighthouse at the Point, and heads west as far as Dana Bay, taking in magnificent coastal views of cliffs, rocks, bays and coves.

If jumping off bridges is your bag, **bungee jumping** at the old Gouritz River Bridge, about 40km west of Mossel Bay along the N2, offers a considerably cheaper alternative (R180) to the Bloukrans Bridge (see p.285) near Nature's Valley. If you're interested, just turn up and talk to Face Adrenalin at the bridge (☎044 697 7161). Gouritz also offers the option of a bungee swing with Wildthing Adventures (☎083 299 9900; single R150, tandem R110) in which the bungee is attached to the back of the same bridge causing you to swing down and under.

Eating and drinking

With the notable exception of the *Café Gannet*, the **Lighthouse Restaurant** at the Point Hotel is the nicest place for food and drinks, mainly because of the large stretch of sea frontage it offers, though there has been an upsurge of development here. The small Point Village shopping development at the north end has a couple of inexpensive to mid-priced family restaurants, opening daily from the morning until 11pm-ish.

Café Gannet Market St ☎044 691 1885. Close to the Bartholomew Dias Museum Complex is, Mossel Bay's top restaurant, with moderately priced seafood lunches and dinners, served in a stylish garden with glimpses across the harbour. Daily.
Delfino's Point Village. Italian food at reasonable prices, plus a view.
King Fisher Point Village ☎044 690 6390. A relaxed joint above *Delfino's*, specializing in seafood and offering good views.
Lighthouse Restaurant *Point Hotel*, Point Rd ☎044 691 3512. A wide-ranging à la carte menu in a fabulous setting, with some veggie options.

Red Rooster Green Door, 49 Marsh St. Burgers, fish and chips and toasted sandwiches, at reasonable prices, with kerbside seating.
Santos Express Santos Beach. The restaurant attached to the accommodation is a lively venue with good calamari and burgers, at keen prices.
Tidals Waterfront Tavern & Pub The south side of the Point. Mossel Bay's liveliest drinking spot buzzes until the early hours on Fridays and Saturdays, in a stunning seaside location overlooking cliffs and the open sea.

George, Victoria Bay and Wilderness

There's little reason to visit **GEORGE**, 66km northeast of Mossel Bay, unless you're starting or finishing a trip on the Outeniqua Choo-Tjoe. This large inland working town, surrounded by mountains, is a five-kilometre detour northwest off the N2, and 9km from the nearest stretch of ocean at Victoria Bay. Sadly, all that's left of the forests and quaint character that moved Anthony Trollope, during a visit in 1877, to describe it as the "prettiest village on the face of the earth", are some historic buildings, of which the beautiful **Dutch Reformed Church**, in Davidson Street at the top end of Meade Street, is the most notable. Completed in the early 1840s, the church is definitely worth a stop if you happen to be passing through, with its elegantly simple classical façade, Greek-cross plan with an impressive centrally placed pulpit and wonderful domed ceiling, panelled with glowing yellowwood. **St Mark's Cathedral**, in Cathedral Street, consecrated in 1850, is also worth seeing, but unlike the Dutch Reformed Church which is open to the public it can only be visited by appointment. Other than that, George's claim to recent fame (or notoriety) is the fact that it was the parliamentary seat of former State President **P.W. Botha** (see box opposite), the last of South Africa's apartheid hardliners. The George Museum once housed the P.W. Botha collection, an exercise in blind adulation for one of the most ruthless proponents of apartheid. The collection was regarded as unsuitable for a museum in the "New South Africa" and was removed in the 1990s, but if you look hard you can still spot the odd fragment here and there that the authorities failed to expunge.

Practicalities

The small George **airport** is 10km west of town on the N2. A Zeelie's **taxi** (☎044 874 6707) into town will set you back R50 from the airport; most tourists flying in rent a car from one of the rental companies here and set off down the Garden Route. Outeniqua Choo-Tjoe **trains** (see p.257) arrive at the Outeniqua Railway Museum, 2 Mission Road, just off Knysna Road (☎044 801 8202). Intercape, Translux and Greyhound **intercity buses** pull

President Botha: the King Canute of apartheid

Pieter Willem Botha is credited with setting up an autocratic "Imperial Presidency" in South Africa, but in retrospect he was actually the King Canute of apartheid, closing his eyes to the incoming tide of democracy and believing that by wagging his finger (his favoured gesture of intimidation) he could turn it back.

A National Party hack from the age of 20, Botha worked his way up through the ranks, getting elected an MP in 1948 when the first apartheid government took power. He became leader of the National Party in the Cape Province and was promoted through various cabinet posts until he became **Minister of Defence**, a position he used to launch a palace coup in 1978 against his colleague, Prime Minister John Vorster. Botha immediately set about modernizing apartheid, modifying his own role from that of a British-style prime minister, answerable to parliament, to one of an executive president taking vital decisions in the secrecy of a President's Council heavily weighted with army top brass.

Informed by the army that the battle to preserve the apartheid status quo was unwinnable purely by force, Botha embarked on his **Total Strategy**, which involved reforms to peripheral aspects of apartheid and the fostering of a black middle class as a buffer against the ANC, while pumping vast sums of money into building an enormous military machine that crossed South Africa's borders to bully or crush neighbouring countries harbouring groups opposed to apartheid. South African refugees in Botswana and Zimbabwe were bombed, Angola was invaded, and arms were run to anti-government rebels in Mozambique, reducing it to ruins – a policy that has returned to haunt South Africa with those same weapons now returning across the border and finding their way into the hands of criminals. Inside South Africa, security forces enjoyed a free hand to murder, maim and torture **opponents of apartheid** on a scale that only fully emerged between 1996 and 1998, under the investigations of the Truth and Reconciliation Commission.

Botha's intransigence led to his greatest blunder in 1985, when he responded to international calls for change by hinting that he would announce significant reforms at his party congress that would irreversibly jettison apartheid. In the event, the so-called **Rubicon speech** was a disaster, as Botha proved to have insufficient steel to resist pressure from white right-wing extremists. The speech shrank away from meaningful concessions to black South Africans, the immediate result of which was a flight of capital from the country and intensified sanctions. Perhaps worst of all for the apartheid regime, the **Chase Manhattan Bank** refused to roll over its massive loan to South Africa, leaving the country an uncreditworthy pariah.

Botha blustered and wagged his finger at the opposition through the late 1980s, while his bloated military sucked the state coffers dry as it prosecuted its dirty wars. Even National Party stalwarts realized that his policies were leading to ruin, and in 1989, when he suffered a stroke, the party was quick to replace him with **F.W. de Klerk**, who immediately proceeded to announce the reforms the world had expected four years earlier from Botha's Rubicon speech.

Botha lives out his retirement near George where, it is reported, he still harbours deep resentments against his National Party colleagues, whom he believes betrayed him. Unrepentant, he has declined to apologize for any of the brutal actions taken under his presidency to bolster apartheid.

in at George station, adjacent to the railway museum. The **Baz Bus** drops off at *McDonald's* on Courtenay Street. George's excellent **tourist office**, 124 York Street (Mon–Fri 8am–5pm, Sat 9am–1; ☎044 801 9295, ⊛www .georgetourism.co.za), can provide town **maps** and help with accommodation bookings.

Accommodation

10 Caledon Street 10 Calendon St ℡044 873 4983, ⓦwww.10caledon.co.za. The pick of the mid-priced B&Bs, in a spotless guesthouse in a quiet street around the corner from the museum, featuring balconies with mountain views and a garden. ❸

Arbour Lodge On the corner of Davidson and Arbour roads ℡044 874 7592 or 082 412 4114, ⓦwww.ashmole.com. A modern suburban home with three large en-suite rooms with kitchenettes, close to the centre on the busy road to Oudtshoorn. It's hosted by an extremely friendly and obliging couple, who welcome children. ❸

Die Waenhuis 11 Caledon St ℡044 874 0034, ⓔdiewaenhuis@lantic.net. Mid-nineteenth-century home that has retained its period character. English breakfasts are served in a sunlit dining room. ❸

George Tourist Resort York St ℡044 874 5205, ⓕ044 874 4255. En-suite chalets (R620/R910 sleeping four/eight) and rondavels (R500 sleeping four) in well-kept pleasant gardens, with a swimming pool, children's playground, shop and laundry facilities.

Oak Tree 30 Caledon St ℡082 563 9952. This Victorian home has two comfortable rooms, with white linen and well-appointed bathrooms. Both rooms have separate entrances. ❸

Eating and drinking

Copper Pot 12 Montagu St ℡044 870 7378. One of George's best restaurants, an intimate and formal place on the west side of town that draws its culinary inspiration from all corners of the globe. Daily noon–2.30pm & 6.30pm–late.

Fong Ling Taiwanese On the corner of York and Fichat streets ℡044 884 0088. Quick mid-priced lunches or evening marathons. Daily.

Herman's Pub and Grill Next to the museum, in two old railway carriages, serving an inexpensive daily special such as a mixed grill or spare ribs and chips. It's also a good central place for a drink, with some outdoor seating overlooking the busy main drag. Daily lunch and dinner.

Red Rock Café Red River Centre, Arbour Rd. Excellent value at a lively venue a few blocks from the centre, serving pizzas, seafood, ribs and a number of vegetarian options. Its lawn and small playground makes it great for kids. Daily eves, plus lunchtime in summer.

Victoria Bay

Some 9km south of George and 3km off the N2 lies the minuscule hamlet of **VICTORIA BAY**, on the edge of a small sandy beach wedged into a cove between cliffs, with a grassy sunbathing area, safe swimming and a tidal pool. During the December holidays packs out with day-trippers, and rates as one of the top **surfing** spots in South Africa. Because of the cliffs, there's only a single row of buildings along the beachfront, with some of the most dreamily positioned guesthouses along the coast (and therefore some of the priciest for what you get).

There's no public **transport** to Victoria Bay, although many people hitch the few kilometres from the N2. Arriving by **car**, you'll encounter a metal barrier as you drop down the hill to the bay, and you'll have to try and park in a car park that's frequently full (especially in summer). If you're staying at one of the B&Bs, leave your car at the barrier and collect the key from your lodgings to gain access to the private beach road. The only places to buy **food** are a small beachside kiosk selling light refreshments and a casual restaurant. However, the resort's B&Bs are served by Mr Delivery, a service that will collect from about ten fast-food joints in George and will also fetch groceries and even videos.

Accommodation

Besides the places to stay reviewed here, there's magnificently located **camping** on the clifftop overlooking the beach, at the *Victoria Bay Caravan Park*, on the left as you approach the beach (℡044 889 0081).

Land's End Guest House The Point, Beach Rd ☎044 889 0123, ⓦwww.vicbay.com. Two self-catering studio apartments at the end of the road, sleeping two, plus two flats on a B&B basis. ❺
Pier Plesier Beach Rd ☎044 889 0051, ⓔianwesson@mjvn.co.za. A modern brick building with upstairs and downstairs en-suite flats overlooking the sea, just 6m from the high-water mark. The flats have either one or two rooms, and can sleep four. Self-catering ❸, B&B ❺

Sea Breeze Holiday Resort Along the main road into the settlement ☎044 889 0098, ⓔseabreeze@pixie.co.za. A variety of budget self-catering units, including modern two-storey holiday huts and wooden chalets, sleeping two, four or eight people. The huts have no sea views, but it's an easy stroll to the beach. ❷
The Waves 7 Beach Rd ☎ & ⓕ044 889 0166, ⓔthewaves@intekom.co.za. Two suites in a high-ceilinged Victorian house. ❺

Wilderness

East of Victoria Bay, across the Kaaimans River, the beach at **WILDERNESS** is so close to the N2 that you can pull over for a quick dip with barely an interruption to your journey. Unfortunately, the position of the national road leaves the village and lakes stranded inland. Wilderness village earned its name, so the story goes, after a young man called Van den Berg bought the property in 1830 for £183 as a blind lot at a Cape Town auction. When he got engaged, his fiancée insisted that their first year of marriage should be spent out of town in the wilderness, so he romantically (or perhaps opportunistically) named his property Wilderness and built a hut on it.

If the hut still exists, you'll struggle to find it among the sprawl of retirement homes, holiday houses and thousands of beds for rent in the vicinity. Take your life in your hands and cross the N2 to get to the beach, which is renowned for its long stretch of sand, backed by tall dunes, rudely blighted by holiday houses competing to outdo each other. Once in the water, stay close to the shoreline: this part of the coast is notorious for its unpredictable currents.

Practicalities

The tiny **village centre**, on the north side of the N2, has a filling station, a few shops, restaurants and a **tourist office** in Leila's Lane (May–Sept Mon–Fri 8am–5pm, Sat 9am–1pm; Oct–April Mon–Fri 8am–6pm, Sat 8am–1pm, Sun 3–5pm; ☎044 877 0045, ⓦwww.wildernessinfo.co.za).

Eden Adventures (☎044 877 0179 or 083 628 8547) run half-day **canoeing**, **cycling**, **abseiling** or **kloofing** trips along the nearby Kaaiman's River and its gorge (R200). Explore the river yourself by renting a two-seater canoe from them (R110 per day including park fees). Wilderness Adventures (☎044 850 1008) runs beach and mountain **horse-riding** tours (R100 an hour). To see it all from the air, sign up with Cloudbase for a tandem **paragliding** jump that clocks in at R370.

For **seafood**, the *Albatross* on George Road (☎044 877 0288; daily lunch & dinner) in the village centre is the place to come; they also serve spare ribs and ostrich. Combining middle-European and local flavours, at moderate prices, *Palms* is the best restaurant at the Swiss-owned *Palms Wilderness Guest House*, Owen Grant Road (☎044 877 1420; Aug–May eves), 3km from town. For an informal meal that might include smoked salmon omelette, pizza or steak, try the **Wilderness Grill** on George Road (open daily for breakfast, lunch & dinner), with seating outside under parasols or indoors by the fire.

Accommodation

The Albatross Sixth Ave, take South St exit off the N2 ☎044 877 1716. Guesthouse in easy walking distance from the beach, with large balconies and perfect dolphin watching views. ❹

Fairy Knowe Backpackers ⓣ & ⓕ 044 877 1285, ⓔ fairybp@mweb.co.za. The oldest home (built 1897) in the area, with a wraparound balcony and set in the quiet woodlands near the Touws River, though nowhere near the sea; to reach the site, 6km from the village, follow signs from the N2 east of Wilderness. The Baz Bus will drop off here. Dorms ❶, rooms ❷

Island Lake Holiday Resort Lakes Rd, 2km from the Hoekwil/Island Lake turn-off on the N2 ⓣ & ⓕ 044 877 1194. Camping and self-catering bungalows that sleep four (R485), on one of the quietest and prettiest spots on the lakes.

Mes-Amis Homestead Buxton Close, signposted off the N2 on the coastal side of the road, directly opposite the national park turn-off ⓣ 044 877 1928, ⓔ mesamis@mweb.co.za. Nine double rooms, each of which has its own terrace, offering some of the best views in Wilderness. ❹

The Tops Hunts Lane, on a hill about 500m from the tourist office ⓣ & ⓕ 044 877 0187 or ⓣ 083 631 2339. Four airy en-suite bedrooms, three of which have sea views and French doors opening onto a deck. ❸

Wilderness Bush Camp Heights Rd (follow Waterside Rd west for 1600m up the hill) ⓣ 044 877 1168, ⓔ wildernessbushcamp@mweb.co.za. Six self-catering timber units with loft bedrooms, thatched roofs and ocean views. The camp is part of a conservation estate that you're free to roam around. ❷

Wilderness Retreat Heights Rd ⓣ 044 877 0262 or 082 555 6424, ⓔ wildretreat@mweb.co.za. Perched on the hillside above Wilderness (follow Waterside Rd west for 1200m up the hill) are these two fully equipped cottages decorated with wicker and white linen, each sleeping four people. R750.

Wilderness National Park

Stretching east from Wilderness village is the **Wilderness National Park** (reception open 24hr; ⓣ 044 877 1197; R60), the least aptly named national park in South Africa, as it never feels very far from the rumbling N2. Although the park takes in beach frontage, it's the **forests** you should come for, as well as the 16km of inland waterways; the variety of habitats here include coastal and montane *fynbos* and wetlands, attracting 250 species of **birds** – as well as many holidaymakers.

There are two **restcamps**, both on the west side of the park and clearly signposted off the N2. *Ebb and Flow North* (❷), right on the river, is cheap, old-fashioned and away from the hustle. It offers camping, fully equipped two-person bungalows with their own showers, and slightly cheaper huts with communal washing and toilet facilities. *Ebb and Flow South* (❷), signposted close by, has camping and modern accommodation in spacious log cabins on stilts and brick bungalows which, although dearer than *North* camp, represent good value if there are more than two of you (you pay for a minimum of four people): the fully equipped, self-contained family brick bungalows go for R400 and the log cabins on stilts for R420. There are also cheaper en-suite forest huts with communal kitchens for two people and cheaper still, huts with shared ablution facilities. Seasonal discounts of twenty percent are offered on accommodation (apart from the forest huts and camping) from mid-January to mid-March and from May to November. There is a **shop** selling milk, bread and basic groceries at reception, a coin-operated **laundry**, and a small children's playground.

Activities

To take advantage of all the water, you can rent **canoes** and **pedaloes** from reception. There are also several waymarked walking trails, well worth doing to get a feeling of the indigenous vegetation and escape the N2 and holiday homes – the reception issues trail **maps**. The **Giant Kingfisher trail** is an easy seven-kilometre walk that starts at *Ebb and Flow North* camp and passes through the forest along the eastern bank of the Touws River to some rock pools teeming with little sea creatures, returning along the same route, taking three hours for the round trip. Another hike of about three hours is the six-kilometre **Cape Dune Molerat trail**, a circuit along the dunes separating

Rondevlei and Swartvlei lakes, with good views onto both. It offers excellent birding opportunities and you'll see wild flowers during winter and spring. To get there, take the N2 east towards Sedgefield for 16km, take the Swartvlei turn-off and continuing down a dirt road; after 2.8km turn right and continue for just over a kilometre to the conservation station and trail starting point.

Sedgefield, Goukamma and Buffels Bay

The drive between Wilderness and Sedgefield gives glimpses on your left of dark-coloured lakes which eventually surge out to sea, 21km later, through a wide lagoon at **SEDGEFIELD**, a lacklustre holiday village a few kilometres off the road, with a safe swimming **beach** that makes a refreshing pit stop. Until recently Sedgefield's unpromising appearance of shops, restaurants and B&Bs lining the highway hid a gloriously undeveloped beachfront. But the resort's authorities have woken up to the economic potential of development, and turned parts of the beachfront into a building site. At least accommodation prices are more reasonable here than at Knysna half an hour away (see p.268), making Sedgefield a potential base for exploring the area.

Sedgefield could be used as a base from which to explore **Goukamma Nature and Marine Reserve** (℡044 383 0042) and the western extent of **Groenvlei**, a freshwater lake that falls within the reserve's boundaries. An unassuming sanctuary of around 220 square kilometres, Goukamma ranges from near Sedgefield east as far as the small seaside resort of **Buffels Bay** to absorb 14km of beach frontage, some of the highest vegetated dunes in the country, and walking country covered with coastal *fynbos* and dense thickets of milkwood, yellowwood and candlewood trees.

The area has long been popular with anglers for Groenvlei's six **fish** species. Away from the water, you stand a small chance of spotting one of the area's **mammals**, including bushbuck, grysbok, mongoose, vervet monkeys, caracals and otters. Because of the diversity of coastal and wetland habitats, over 220 different kinds of **birds** have been recorded here, including fish eagles, Knysna louries, kingfishers and very rare African black oystercatchers. Offshore, southern right **whales** often make an appearance during their August to December breeding season, and bottlenose and common **dolphins** can show up at any time of year.

Apart from angling and bird-watching, the Goukamma offers a number of self-guided activities, including safe **swimming** in Groenvlei. There are several day-long hiking **trails** that enable you to explore different habitats – if you plan on hiking you should pick up the Cape Nature Conservation map from your guesthouse. A beach walk, which takes around four hours one way, traverses the 14km of crumbling cliffs and sands between the Platbank car park on the western side of the reserve and the Rowwehoek one on the eastern side. Alternatively, you can go from one end of the reserve to the other via a slightly longer inland trek across the dunes. There's also a shorter circular walk from the reserve office through a milkwood forest, as well as **horse-riding** trips run by Cheri's Riding Centre (℡082 962 3223; R100/hr).

Two roads off the N2 provide **access** to the reserve. At the westernmost side, a dirt road that runs down to Platbank Beach takes you past the tiny settlement of **Lake Pleasant** on the south bank of Groenvlei, which consists of little more than a hotel and holiday resort. On the eastern side, access is via the Buffels Bay road, halfway along which is the reserve office. There are no public roads within the reserve.

Accommodation

Among the forest of holiday homes in **Sedgefield**, you'll find some decent accommodation away from the N2. Another inexpensive alternative to Knysna is **Buffels Bay**, a haphazard little development at the east of the reserve; it's 10km down a turn-off along the N2, 13km east of Sedgefield.

At Goukamma Nature Reserve (bookings ☎044 802 5310), you can choose to stay at a basic bushcamp that sleeps eight (R1080) on the southern shore of the Lake Pleasant, reached by a road past the Lake Pleasant turn-off; or, on the Buffels Bay side, three thatched rondavels that sleep five (R600) and a river lodge that sleeps up to nine (R730), overlooking the Goukamma River. All have fully equipped kitchens, but you must bring your own bedding.

Sedgefield

Coral Reef Guesthouse 28 Coral Reef Crescent, Cola Beach ☎ & ⓕ044 343 3133, ⓔcoralref@mweb.co.za. Two rooms and a family unit, all brightly decorated. There's a saltwater pool and a comfortable relaxing area. ➋

Landfall Resort Kingfisher Dr ☎ & ⓕ044 343 1840. A low-key and old-fashioned place which allows camping and rents out caravans sleeping up to six people (R450), with attached kitchens, toilets and showers. The resort also rents out more spacious two-bedroom fully equipped cottages that sleep six for R800.

Warthog Wallow 11 Begonia St ☎ & ⓕ044 343 1965, ⓔwarthogw@iafrica.com. Peaceful timber guesthouse with views of the nearby mountains. ➋

Lake Pleasant and Buffels Bay

Buffalo Bay Apartments 160 Walker Dr ☎044 383 0218, ⓔbuffalobayletting@absamail.co.za. Overlooking the bay, this is probably the best accommodation in the resort. Apartments sleep six (R950–1300 per day).

Lake Pleasant Chalets & Lodges East of Sedgefield, south of the N2 ☎ & ⓕ044 383 1985, ⓦwww.lake-pleasant.co.za. Shady campsites with six-person self-catering timber chalets (R1500) and slightly smaller four-person garden lodges (R930). The resort has a restaurant, a pub and a store selling basics, and rents out mountain bikes, rowing boats and canoes.

Knysna and the Knysna forests

South Africa's 1990s tourist boom rudely shook **KNYSNA** (pronounced "Nize-na") from its gentle backwoods drowse, which for decades made this the hippy and craftwork capital and quiet retirement village of the country. The town, 102km east of Mossel Bay, now stands at the hub of the Garden Route, its lack of ocean beaches compensated for by its hilly setting around the **Knysna lagoon**, its handsome **forests**, good opportunities for **adventure sports** – and some hot marketing.

Knysna's distinctive atmosphere derives from its small historic core of Georgian and Victorian buildings, which gives it a character absent from most of the Garden Route holiday towns. Coffee shops, craft galleries, street traders and a modest nightlife add to the attractions, and you may find yourself tempted to stay longer than just one night. That the town has outgrown itself is evident from the cars and tour buses which, especially in December and January, clog Main Street, the constricted artery that merges with the N2 as it enters the town.

Some history

At the beginning of the nineteenth century, the only white settlements outside Cape Town were a handful of villages that would have considered themselves lucky to have even one horse. Knysna, an undeveloped backwater hidden in the forest, was no exception. The name comes from a Khoi word meaning "hard to reach", and this remained its defining character well into the twentieth century. One important figure was not deterred by the distance – **George Rex**, a colourful colonial administrator who placed himself beyond the pale of decent colonial society by taking a coloured mistress. Shunned by his peers in Britain, he headed for Knysna at the turn of the nineteenth century in the hope of making a killing shipping out hardwood from the lagoon.

By the time of Rex's death in 1839, Knysna had become a major **timber centre**, attracting white labourers who felled trees with primitive tools for miserly payments, and looked set eventually to destroy the forest. In 1872, **Prince Alfred**, on his visit to the Cape, made his small royal contribution to this wanton destruction when he made a special detour here to come elephant hunting. The forest only narrowly escaped devastation by far-sighted and effective conservation policies introduced in the 1880s.

By the turn of the twentieth century, Knysna was still remote, and its forests were inhabited by isolated and inbred communities made up of the impoverished descendants of the woodcutters. As late as 1914, if you travelled from Knysna to George you would have to open and close 58 gates along the 75-kilometre track. Fifteen years on, the passes in the region proved too much for **George Bernard Shaw**, who did some impromptu off-road driving and crashed into a bush, forcing Mrs Shaw to spend a couple of weeks in bed at Knysna's *Royal Hotel* with a broken leg.

Arrival and information

Knysna wraps around the lagoon, with its oldest part – the town centre – on the northern side. The lagoon's narrow mouth is guarded by a pair of steep rocky promontories called **The Heads**, the western side being a private nature reserve and the eastern one an exclusive residential area (confusingly, it's also called The Heads), along dramatic cliffs above the Indian Ocean.

Greyhound and Intercape **buses** drop passengers off at Bern's Service Station in Main Street, right in the centre of town, while Translux pulls into the **train station** in Remembrance Avenue opposite Knysna Quays; the **Baz Bus** will drop passengers off at any of the town's accommodation. The steam-driven **Outeniqua Choo-Tjoe** (see p.257) operates between George and Knysna. For those who only want to go one way, Kontours (☏082 569 8997) runs road transport in conjunction with the train timetable (R150 for a one-way train ticket and return transfer by road). For local transport, there are a couple of **taxi** services (see "Listings" on p.275).

The **tourist office**, Knysna Tourism, at 40 Main Street (Mon–Fri 8am–5pm, Sat 9am–1pm; slightly longer hours during the season; ☏044 382 5510, ⓦwww.knysna-info.co.za), provides maps and runs a desk for booking **adventure activities** around Knysna – from abseiling down The Heads to bungee jumping from the Bloukrans River Bridge.

Accommodation

Knysna has hundreds of accommodation establishments to choose from, though rates have become expensive over the years. The best places to stay in town are away from the main road, with views of the lagoon and The Heads. Out of town there are some excellent and very reasonably priced self-catering cottages right in the **forest**, where you can get well away from the town buzz. For somewhere quieter on the lagoon, make for the western edge at **Brenton-on-Sea**. It is possible to stay here or a few kilometres inland in

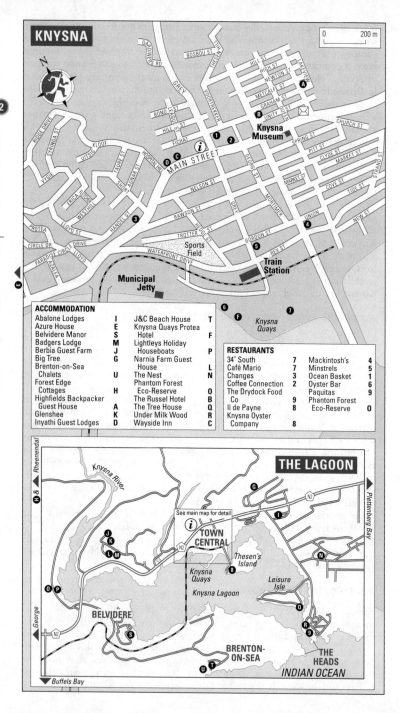

KNYSNA

0   200 m

Knysna Museum

Sports Field

Train Station

Municipal Jetty

Knysna Quays

ACCOMMODATION

Abalone Lodges	I	J&C Beach House	T
Azure House	E	Knysna Quays Protea	
Belvidere Manor	S	Hotel	F
Badgers Lodge	M	Lightleys Holiday	
Berbia Guest Farm	J	Houseboats	P
Big Tree	G	Narnia Farm Guest	
Brenton-on-Sea		House	LN
Chalets	U	The Nest	
Forest Edge		Phantom Forest	
Cottages	H	Eco-Reserve	O
Highfields Backpacker		The Russel Hotel	B
Guest House	A	The Tree House	Q
Glenshee	K	Under Milk Wood	R
Inyathi Guest Lodges	D	Wayside Inn	C

RESTAURANTS

34° South	7	Mackintosh's	4
Café Mario	7	Minstrels	5
Changes	3	Ocean Basket	1
Coffee Connection	2	Oyster Bar	6
The Drydock Food		Paquitas	9
Co	9	Phantom Forest	
Il de Payne	8	Eco-Reserve	0
Knysna Oyster			
Company	8		

THE LAGOON

Rheenendal

Knysna River

See main map for detail

TOWN CENTRAL

Thesen's Island

Knysna Quays

Knysna Lagoon

Leisure Isle

BELVIDERE

BRENTON-ON-SEA

THE HEADS

INDIAN OCEAN

George

Buffels Bay

Plettenberg Bay

the quaint and very upmarket settlement of **Belvidere**, through which visitors are prohibited from driving.

For something different, you can rent a houseboat from Lightleys, moored at the Belvidere turn-off from the N2 (☎044 386 0007, ℮sandpoint@pixie .co.za; ❹). Their four-berth houseboats let you explore the lagoon's 20km of navigable water and are fully equipped, with interiors resembling those of caravans. Another option is a **township homestay**, arranged through Knysna Tourism; they run a busy accommodation office (☎044 382 6960, ℮booking@mweb.co.za) and can help you book homestays and any other type of accommodation in the vicinity.

Town centre and Knysna Quays

Highfields Backpacker Guest House 2 Graham St ☎044 382 6266, ⓕ044 382 5799. The best of the backpacker lodges, with stylish decor, a friendly atmosphere, a swimming pool and sun deck. Dorms and double rooms are available, and reasonably priced excursions can be arranged to The Heads, Mitchell's Brewery and Brenton. ❶

Inyathi Guest Lodges 52 Main St ☎ & ⓕ044 382 7768, ⓦwww.inyathi-sa.com. The most imaginative accommodation in the town centre, ten quirky, en-suite timber lodges – think J.R.R. Tolkien meets safari camp – arranged around a beautiful courtyard garden. Each of the lodges is individually designed and has its own entrance and a deck overlooking the garden. Try to ask for a cottage away from the noisy main road. ❸

Protea Hotel – Knysna Quays Waterfront Dr ☎044 382 5005, ℮knysres@mweb.co.za. A luxury hotel on the waterfront, within walking distance of the centre. Most rooms have views of the lagoon and the yacht basin. ❺

The Russel Hotel Cnr Unity, Long and Graham St ☎044 382 1052, ⓦwww.russelhotel.co.za. Small hotel with spacious, comfy rooms, some allocated to smokers. It's fairly quiet considering its proximity to the main road. On the same property is a renovated 130-year old B&B cottage that sleeps five. ❺

Wayside Inn Pledge Square, 48 Main Rd ☎ & ⓕ044 382 6011. A smart place done out in sisal matting and white linen on black wrought-iron bedsteads. Right in the centre, it makes a pleasing enough night stop. A continental breakfast is served in your room or on the deck outside. ❹

Eastern suburbs, Leisure Isle and The Heads

Abalone Lodges 30 Heron Way, Lower Old Pl ☎ & ⓕ044 382 2943, ⓦwww.abalonelodges.co.za. Self-catering timber cabins decorated with white linen. Each cabin has a kitchenette, spa bath and views of the setting sun. ❸

Big Tree 54 Milkwood Dr, Old Pl ☎044 384 3421 or 082 369 0966, ℮surfculture@mweb.co.za. A large self-catering double-storey timber home with three en-suite rooms, an extensive balcony and good views of the lagoon. R700 for the house.

The Nest 9 Bolton St, Hunters Village ☎044 384 0937, ⓦwww.thenestknysna.co.za. Three cottages with five rooms, including one family unit, all comfortably furnished and tucked away in a lush garden. Saltwater pool, breakfast daily. ❸

The Tree House 37 Cearn Dr ☎ & ⓕ044 384 0777 or ☎082 432 5180, ℮saltdog@mweb .co.za. On Leisure Isle, connected to the eastern suburbs on the shore by a narrow causeway, this lovely self-catering cottage has two bedrooms, two bathrooms, TV, video and a large sun deck screened by a huge tree. It's near an excellent swimming spot. R1500.

Under Milk Wood George Rex Dr, The Heads ☎044 384 0745, ⓦwww.milkwood.co.za. Luxury self-catering accommodation on the lagoon at the foot of The Heads with its own private beach – safe for swimming – and terrific views of the mountains and water. The two-bedroom self-catering units, with their own sun decks, are surrounded by milkwood trees; rates vary depending on whether the unit is on the lagoon, the hillside or between. There are also three B&B rooms. ❺

West of town

Azure House 65 Circular Dr ☎044 382 1221, ⓦwww.azurehouse.com. Lime-washed whites, blues and pale yellows are the signature colours in these upmarket self-catering rooms, each en suite, with a small lounge. Breakfast (optional) is served on a wicker tray on your private balcony overlooking the lagoon. ❸–❹

Badgers Lodge 1km down Welbedacht Lane, 1km west of Knysna off the N2 ☎044 382 2840, ⓦwww.badgers-africa.com. B&B rondavels with private entrances, and three self-catering timber bungalows that sleep two or four people, facing onto a wooded creek. There's a pool. Self catering ❷, B&B ❸

Berbia Guest Farm 5km down Welbedacht Lane, which lies 1km west of Knysna off the N2 ☎ & ⓕ044 382 5429. Four en-suite rooms, attractively furnished in warm colours, leading onto a swimming pool, from which you can see the lagoon and The Heads. Braai stands are the only catering facilities. ❹

Glenshee Eastford Downs, 4km down Welbedacht Lane, 1km west of Knysna off the N2 ☎044 382 3202 or 082 789 5062, ✉glenshee@mweb.co.za. Immaculately run B&B that enjoys views of the Knysna River Valley, with two well-appointed rooms on the edge of the Eastford Nature Reserve. ❸–❹

Narnia Farm Guest House Signed off Welbedacht Lane, 3km west of Knysna ☎044 382 1334, ⓦwww.narnia.co.za. On a hillside with views of the lagoon, this is an immensely fun stone and rough-hewn timber farmhouse in a glorious garden, set among protea plantations. Two en-suite B&B rooms upstairs have their own balconies and swinging chairs and are decorated in a rustic-chic style, as is a comfortable semi-detached two-bedroom cottage downstairs which has a lounge, fireplace and kitchenette. Walks on the property include one down to a small lake; mountain bikes are available and there's a delightful treehouse and children's play area next to a hen run. Self-catering ❸, B&B ❹

Phantom Forest Eco-Reserve Phantom Pass Rd, west of town off the N2 ☎044 386 0046, ⓦwww.phantomforest.com. Breathtaking, tranquil forest lodge making extensive use of timber and glass, set on a hill in indigenous forest, with fabulous lagoon views. African fabrics and pure cotton linen help reinforce the sense of unbridled luxury. Timber boardwalks wind through the forest to connect the suites to the main buildings, which feature a safari-style dining room, an open-air hot tub, a massage suite and a Jacuzzi. The swimming pool teeters on the edge of the hill, cocooned by vegetation, with vervet monkeys frolicking in the forest canopy. Half board ❾

The forest

Forest Edge Cottages Rheenendal turn-off, 16km west of Knysna on the N2 ☎044 388 4704 or 082 965 5765, ✉forest.edge@knysna.co.za. Ideal if you want to be close to the forest itself, these traditional tin-roofed, two-bedroomed cottages have verandas built in the vernacular tin-roofed style. Self-contained, fully equipped and serviced, the cottages sleep four. Forest walks and cycling trails start from the cottage, and you can also rent mountain bikes. ❸

Southern Comfort Western Horse Ranch 3km along the Fisanthoek road, 17km east of Knysna en route to Plettenberg Bay ☎044 532 7885, ✉schranch@mweb.co.za. Very basic double rooms, dorms and a tree house, on a farm adjacent to the eastern section of the Knysna forest; staff can pick you up from the N2. Horse-riding (R110/hr, R500 for overnight forest trails) – and massages for the saddle-weary – are on offer. You can self-cater or take the meals provided. ❶

Belvidere and Brenton-on-Sea

Belvidere Manor Duthie Dr, Belvidere Estate ☎044 387 1055, ⓦwww.belvidere.co.za. Thirty-four tin-roofed repro Victorian cottages, nicely positioned on the water's edge. Although they're spacious and were once quite smart, the feel now is of Laura Ashley let loose in a *Holiday Inn*. However, this is the only accommodation in this unique area. ❻

Brenton-on-Sea Chalets C.R. Swart Dr, Brenton beachfront ☎044 381 0081, ⓦwww.abalonelodges.co.za. A 15min drive from Knysna and overlooking the long curve of Brenton Beach, which swings round to Buffels Bay. The chalets, which sleep six people, are well equipped and comfortably furnished. R950. They can also be taken on a B&B basis. Self-catering ❺

J&C Beach House 116 Watsonia Ave, Brenton ☎044 381 0107, ⓦwww.jcbeachhouse.co.za. Simple and elegant rooms, each with views of the ocean from the balcony. You can sun yourself at their pool or on nearby Brenton beach. ❹

The Town and beaches

Main Street is the hub of the city centre. The **Knysna Museum** (Mon–Fri 9.30am–4.30pm, Sat 9.30am–noon; entry by donation, includes Angling Museum) on the corner of Queen and Main streets contains a complex of minor exhibits that can comfortably occupy an undemanding half-hour. Attractions here include South Africa's first **Angling Museum**, an extensive collection of antique nets and rods, tracing the changing technology of the activity. Look out for the preserved coelacanth, one of several specimens in the country of a fish long thought to have been extinct, until one turned up in a fishing net in 1939 (see p.394).

Knysna cruises and activities

One of the obligatory excursions around Knysna is a **cruise** across the lagoon to The Heads. Knysna Waterfront Ferries (℡044 382 1693 or 382 1697) runs several 75-minute trips a day from Knysna Quays to The Heads (R60), a ninety-minute trip on the double-decker M/V *John Benn* (R75) as well as a dinner cruise (R220) on the only paddle-driven vessel in the country. For travel beyond The Heads, Zakat Yachting (book through Waterfront Ferries) offer a sailing trip (1hr 30min; R140) and a sunset cruise (2hr 30min; R380) with a delicious food spread. The only way to reach the private **Featherbed Nature Reserve** on the western side of the lagoon is on a four-hour Featherbed Nature Tour (R250), which includes the boat there and use of a 4WD shuttle to the top of the western Head, with the option of walking 2km back downhill to enjoy spectacular views and see flora and fauna, including Knysna louries; a buffet meal is included as well. **Bookings** are essential, and can be made at the kiosk on the north side of Knysna Quays; **departures** are from the Waterfront Jetty and municipal jetty on Remembrance Avenue, 400m west of the quays and station.

Activities and adventure sports

Seal Adventures (℡044 382 5599) runs **abseiling** and **rap jumping** trips (the latter involving running down a mountainside while harnessed; R280) in the Featherbed Nature Reserve, **canoeing** trips on the lagoon, and **quad biking** (R350) in the forests. You can cycle remote forest paths with Mountain Biking Africa (℡044 382 0260 or 082 783 8392). Besides half-day trips (R250), they also offer two-, three- and five-day tours (R1000–4000), the price including comfortable accommodation, good food, equipment and a backup vehicle. Both the above firms operate from the *Protea Hotel*.

Customized tours can be arranged by Deep South (℡044 382 2010 or 083 250 9441), allowing you to combine, for example, mountain biking and a lagoon cruise (R500 per person for two and six people; cost includes lunch). For hikes in Knysna's forests, contact Knysna Forest Tours (see p.275).

About 500m south of Knysna Tourism, at the end of Grey Street lies the **Knysna Quays**, the town's waterfront complex and yacht basin. Built at the end of the 1990s, this elegant two-storey steel structure with timber boardwalks resembles a tiny version of Cape Town's V&A Waterfront – but probably owes its inspiration as much to New England or Seattle, and blows away Knysna's hippy cobwebs with a breath of upmarket supercool. Here you'll find the luxury *Protea Hotel*, some clothes and knick-knack shops and a couple of good eating places, including a stunning deli-style bistro, *34° South*, with outdoor decks, from which you can watch yachts drift past.

A short way from the centre in the industrial area, **Mitchell's Brewery** offers thirty-minute tours (Mon–Fri 10.30am) on which you get to sample their beers for next to nothing, including Foresters Draught, a Pilsner-type lager, and Bosun's Bitter, an ale modelled on Yorkshire bitter (tastings Mon–Fri 8am–5pm & Sat 9am–1pm). The brewery is in Arend Road, off George Rex Drive via Vigilance and Sandpiper roads, a twenty-minute walk away.

The main reasons to head for **Leisure Isle** off the eastern suburbs are the excellent swimming in the lagoon and the views out to sea through the gap between The Heads. The best bathing spots are along the southern shore of the island, particularly the western section along Bayswater Drive, but the swimming is only good around high tide in summer.

Continuing south along George Rex Drive brings you to the web of roads winding through the small suburban areas of The Heads and Coney Glen to the top of the **eastern Head**. Around *Paquitas* restaurant (see opposite) there are fantastic views out to sea; for an even better viewpoint head along the short walkway starting outside the restaurant, taking you along the cliff edge.

The beaches

Don't come to Knysna for a beach holiday: the closest beach is 20km from town at **Brenton-on-Sea**. A tiny settlement on the shores of Buffels Bay, it does admittedly have a quite exceptional beach. Although **Buffels Bay** (see p.267), the next beach to the west, is along the same continuous stretch of sand as Brenton-on-Sea, there's no direct route there; you have to return to the N2 and proceed from there. In the opposite direction from Knysna, the closest patch of sand is at **Noetzie**, a town known more for its eccentric holiday homes built to look like castles than for its seaside.

Eating, drinking and nightlife

As far as food goes, oysters are an obvious choice, with the Knysna Oyster Company here being one of the world's largest oyster farms, but you'll also find a lot of good **restaurants** catering to other palates and one or two excellent **coffee shops**. With so many forests, waterways and beaches, you may be tempted to have a **picnic**, and there's no shortage of tempting deli food in town.

Knysna has a livelier atmosphere than you might expect from a Garden Route town. At night *Tin Roof Blues*, on the corner of St George's and Main roads, is where to head for local and visiting **bands** from across the country.

34° South Knysna Quays ☏ 044 382 7331. An outstanding deli and eating place, with imported groceries, homemade fare and seafood; from here you can watch the drawbridge open to let yachts sail through. Daily 9am–1pm.

Café Mario Knysna Quays ☏ 044 382 7250. A small Italian restaurant with good pizza and pasta. Daily from 9am.

Changes Pledge Square, 48 Main St ☏ 044 382 0456. A reasonably priced gay-run restaurant that plugs itself as "your pink triangle on the square". The menu is imaginatively eclectic, featuring seafood and vegetable tempura, and duck and cherry pie among the seafood, steak and vegetarian courses. Tues–Sat from 7pm.

Coffee Connection Main Rd. Breakfast and light lunches are available at this shop selling a range of fine coffees, a firm favourite with the locals. Daily 8am–5pm.

The Drydock Food Co Knysna Quays ☏ 044 382 7310. A good seafood place where starters include coastal oysters and local salmon trout and main courses prawns and East Coast sole. Daily lunch & dinner.

Il de Payne Thesen Island ☏ 044 302 5707. Trendy restaurant in a bakery, with a menu of salads, baguettes, oysters and pastas, written

up on a blackboard. Tues–Sat 7am–5pm & Sun 9am–1.30pm.

Knysna Oyster Company Thesen Island ☏ 044 382 6941. Run by the firm of the same name which has been in operation since 1949, this restaurant serves oysters harvested by the parent company from beds in the Knysna River Estuary. Don't worry if you're not an oyster eater – they also serve steaks, chicken and fine fish. Daily lunch & dinner.

Mackintosh's 6 Long St. A café serving breakfast and lunch daily, in a large traditional country store with everything a foodie could want, including fresh breads.

Minstrels 3 Grey St. Set in a quaint tin house serving salads, quiches and open sandwiches in generous sized portions. Breakfast, lunch and teas daily from 9am.

Ocean Basket Memorial Square, Main Rd. A family-friendly seafood restaurant chain with everything from freshly caught fish to hake and chips, at reasonable prices.

Oyster Bar Knysna Quays. On the far side of the boat moorings, this outdoor restaurant serves oysters and inexpensive light meals. Don't expect too much from the food, but the setting is great.

Paquitas Knysna Heads ☎044 384 0408. Burgers, ribs and pizzas in a restaurant fabulously located on the rocks beneath The Heads, where kids can run onto the beach. Daily lunch & dinner.

Phantom Forest Eco-Reserve Phantom Pass Rd ☎044 386 0046. Eating is secondary to being in one of the most beautiful places in South Africa, in a forest with views of the whole estuary. The expensive Pan-African set menu ranges from ostrich medallions marinated in orange and ginger to forest mushrooms with garlic rocket and Knysna cheese, and tempting desserts such as brandy snap baskets. Dinner daily.

Listings

Bike rental Oldies Pub & Grill, 14 Grey St, charges R15/hr (R75 for 24hr).

Car rental Avis 68 Main Rd ☎044 382 2222; Tempest, 14 Gray St ☎044 382 0354.

Emergencies Fire ☎044 382 6400 or 044 382 5066. See also p.89.

Hospitals and doctors Knysna Private Hospital, Hunters Dr (☎044 384 1083), is well run and has a casualty department open to visitors. For malaria prophylaxis and vaccinations, go to the SAA Net-care Travel Clinic in Marine Pharmacy (see below), (Mon–Fri 8am–12pm, afternoons by appointment only ☎044 382 6366 or 083 416 0613), which is geared to travellers, and operates an affordable service and up-to-date information.

Laundry The Knysna Wash Tub, 20 Gray St (Mon–Fri 7.30am–5.30pm, Sat 7.30am–1pm); and The Laundry Bin, 12 Main St (Mon–Fri 7.30am–5.30pm, Sat 8am–1pm).

Pharmacy Marine Pharmacy, on the corner of Main and Grey streets ☎044 382 5614 (Mon–Fri 8am–9pm, Sat & Sun 8am–8pm); and Village Pharmacy, Spar Centre, 41 Main St (Mon–Fri 8am–6pm, Sat & Sun 8am–2pm).

Taxis Glory's Cab (☎044 382 4223 or 083 226 4720) and Benwill Shuttle (☎083 728 5181; after hours ☎044 384 0103) are handy for transport around town, but take care to agree the fare before getting inside.

The Knysna forests

The best reason to come to Knysna is for its **forests**, shreds of a once magnificent woodland that was home to **Khoi** clans and harboured a thrilling variety of wildlife, including elephant herds. The forests attracted European explorers and naturalists, and in their wake woodcutters, businessmen like George Rex and gold-diggers, all bent on making their fortunes here.

The French explorer Francois Le Vaillant was one of the first **Europeans** to sample the delights of these forests. He travelled through in the eighteenth century with Khoi trackers, who shot and cooked an elephant; the explorer found the animal's feet so "delicious" that he wagered that "never can our modern epicures have such a dainty at their tables". Two hundred years later, all that's left of the Khoi people are some names of local places. The legendary Knysna elephants have hardly fared better and are teetering on certain extinction.

Eleventh-hour **conservation** has ensured that some of the hardwoods have survived to maturity in reserves of woodland that can still take your breath away. A number of walks have been laid out in several of the forests – yet the effects of the nineteenth-century timber industry means that all these reserves are some distance from Knysna itself and require transport to get to. Knysna Forest Tours (☎082 921 1480) run guided **walking tours and hikes**, such as an easy two-and-a-half hour Big Tree Walk (R240) and a four-hour walk through the Millwood Goldfields, South Africa's first gold mine, at Rheedendal and Jubilee Creek; the latter costs R360, including a picnic and use of Wellington boots and transport. For the more energetic there are eight-to-ten-kilometre hikes that take you deep into the forest. For self-guided trips, buy the second edition of the excellent book by Judith Hopley, *On Foot in the Garden Route*, available from Knysna's tourist office.

THE KNYSNA FORESTS

Goudveld State Forest

The beautiful **Goudveld State Forest** (daily sunrise–sunset; R4 if attendant is present, otherwise by self-issued free permit), just over 30km northwest of Knysna, is a mixture of plantation and indigenous woodland. It takes its name from the gold boom (*goudveld* is Afrikaans for goldfields) that brought hundreds of prospectors to the mining town of **Millwood** in the 1880s. The six hundred small-time diggers who were here by 1886, scouring out the hillsides and panning Jubilee Creek for alluvial gold, were rapidly followed by larger syndicates, and a flourishing little town quickly sprang up, with six hotels, three newspapers and a music hall.

However, the singing and dancing was shortlived and bust followed boom in 1890 after most of the mining companies went to the wall. The ever-hopeful diggers took off for the newly discovered Johannesburg goldfields, and Millwood was left a deserted **ghost town**. Over the years, its buildings were demolished or relocated, leaving an old store known as Materolli as the only original building standing. Today, the old town is completely overgrown, apart from signs indicating where the old streets stood. In **Jubilee Creek**, which provides a lovely shady walk along a burbling stream, the holes scraped or blasted out of the hillside are still clearly visible. Some of the old mine works have been restored, as have the original **reduction works** around the cocopan track, used to carry the ore from the mine to the works, which is still there after a century.

The forest itself is still lovely, featuring tall, indigenous trees, a delightful valley with a stream, and plenty of swimming holes and picnic sites. To get there from Knysna, follow the N2 west toward George, turning right onto the Rheenendal road just after the Knysna River, and continue for about 25km, following the Bibby's Koep signposts until the Goudveld sign.

Hiking in the Goudveld

A number of clearly **waymarked hikes** traverse the Goudveld. The most rewarding (and easy going) is along **Jubilee Creek**, which traces the progress of a burbling brook for 3.5km through giant woodland to a gorgeous, deep rock-pool – ideal for cooling off after your effort. It's also an excellent place to encounter **Knysna louries**; keep an eye focused on the branches above for the crimson flash of their flight feathers as they forage for berries, and listen out for their harsh call above the gentler chorus provided by the wide variety of other birdlife here. You can pick up a **map** directing you to the creek from the entrance gate to the reserve; note that the waymarked trail is linear, so you return via the same route. There's a pleasant **picnic site** along the banks of the stream at the start of the walk.

A more strenuous option is the circular **Woodcutter Walk**, though you can choose either the three- or the nine-kilometre version. Starting at **Krisjan se Nek**, another picnic site not far past the Goudveld entrance gate, it meanders downhill through dense forest, passing through stands of tree ferns and returns uphill to the starting point. The picnic site is also where the nineteen-kilometre **Homtini Cycle Route** starts, taking you through forest and *fynbos* and offering wonderful mountain views. Be warned though; you really have to work hard at this, with one particular section climbing over 300m in just 3km. The tourist office has maps of the area.

Diepwalle Forest

The **Diepwalle Forest** (daily 6am–6pm; small entry fee), just over 20km northeast of Knysna, is the last haunt of Knysna's almost extinct elephant population. The only elephants you can expect to see here are on the painted markers indicating the three main hikes through these woodlands. However, if you're quiet and alert, you do stand a chance of seeing vervet monkeys, bushbuck and blue duiker. To get there from Knysna, follow the N2 east towards Plettenberg Bay, after 7km turning left onto the R339, which you should take for about 16km in the direction of Avontuur and Uniondale. The **forest station** is 10.5km after the tar gives way to gravel. All trails begin at the forest station, which provides a map of them.

Diepwalle ("deep walls") is one of the highlights of the Knysna area and is renowned for its impressive density of huge trees, especially **yellowwoods**. Once the budget timber of South Africa, yellowwood was considered an inferior local substitute in place of imported pine, and found its way into the structure, floorboards, window frames and doors of thousands of often quite modest nineteenth-century houses in the Western and Eastern Cape. Today, its deep golden grain is so sought after that it commands premium prices at the annual auctions.

The Knysna elephants

Traffic signs warning motorists about elephants along the N2 between Knysna and Plettenberg Bay are rather optimistic: there are few indigenous pachyderms left and, with such an immense forest, sightings are rare. But such is the mystique attached to the **Knysna elephants** that locals tend to be a little cagey about just how few they number. By 1860, the thousands that had formerly wandered the once vast forests were down to five hundred, and by 1920 (twelve years after they were protected by law), there were only twenty animals left; the current estimate is three. Loss of habitat and consequent malnutrition, rather than full-scale hunting, seems to have been the principal cause of their decline.

An attempt was made in 1995 to create a breeding herd by introducing three young cows from the Kruger National Park, who it was hoped would breed with the forest's lone bull. The "bull" turned out also to be a cow and fled in terror when confronted with the three teenagers. In the chase that followed, one young elephant died from pneumonia, brought on by stress. By 1997, the two surviving aliens had moved east and were causing destruction to farmland near Plettenberg Bay. South African National Parks, working with local wildlife organizations, decided to relocate them to Shamwari Game Reserve (see p.379), some 300km to the east near Port Elizabeth, where they are doing well. The only elephants you're guaranteed to see near Knysna are at the **Knysna Elephant Park** close to Plettenberg Bay (see p.281).

The three main hiking routes cover between 7km and 9km of terrain, and pass through flat to gently undulating country covered by indigenous forest and montane *fynbos*. If you're moderately fit, the hikes should take two to two-and-a-half hours. The nine-kilometre **Arboretum trail**, marked by black elephants, starts a short way back along the road you drove in on, and descends to a stream edged with tree ferns. Across the stream you'll come to the much-photographed **Big Tree**, a 600-year-old Goliath yellowwood. The easy nine-kilometre **Ashoekheuwel trail**, marked by white elephants, crosses the Gouna River, where there's a large pool allegedly used by real pachyderms. Most difficult of the three hikes is the rewarding seven-kilometre **Veldboeksdraai trail**, marked by red elephants, which passes along the foothills of the Outeniquas. Take care here to stick to the elephant markers, as they overlap with a series of painted footprints marking the Outeniqua trail, for which you need to have arranged a permit to use. Just before the Veldboeksdraai picnic site stands another mighty yellowwood regarded by some as the most beautiful in the forest.

Plettenberg Bay

Over the Christmas holidays, forty thousand residents from Johannesburg's wealthy northern suburbs decamp to **PLETTENBERG BAY** (usually called Plett), 33km east of Knysna, and the flashiest of the Garden Route's seaside towns. It's wise to give it a miss at this time, with prices doubling and accommodation impossible to find. Yet, during low season, sipping champagne and sucking oysters while watching the sunset from a bar can be wonderful – the banal urban development on the surrounding hills somehow doesn't seem so bad because the bay views really are stupendous. Further afield, the deep-blue **Tsitsikamma Mountains** drop sharply to the inlet and its large estuary, providing a constant vista to the town and its suburbs. The bay generously curves over several kilometres of white sands separated from the mountains by forest, which makes this a green and temperate location with rainfall throughout the year.

Southern right whales appear every winter, and are a seriously underrated attraction, while **dolphins** can be seen throughout the year, hunting or riding the surf, often in substantial numbers. **Swimming** is safe, and though the waters are never tropically warm they reach a comfortable temperature between November and April. River and rock **fishing** are rewarding all year long. One of the Garden Route's best short **hikes** covers a circuit round the Robberg Peninsula – a great tongue of headland that contains the western edge of the bay.

Arrival, information and accommodation

SA Airlink (℡044 533 9006) **flights** from Johannesburg, George and Cape Town arrive daily at Plettenberg Bay airport. There's no transport from the airport into town, so make arrangements with your accommodation to be picked up. Intercape and Greyhound **intercity buses** stop at the Shell Ultra City service station, just off the N2 in Marine Way, 2km from the town centre. As there's no transport around town, you'll need to arrange for your guesthouse to collect you. The **Baz Bus** drops passengers off at accommodation in town. Plett's **tourist office**, Shop 35, Mellville Corner, Main Street (Mon–Fri 8.30am–5pm, Sat 9am–1pm; ℡044 533 4065, ⊛www.plettenbergbay.co.za), has maps of the town and can help with finding accommodation.

Because of the hilly terrain, much of the **accommodation** in Plettenberg Bay has views of the sea and mountains, though you're likely to have to put up with views of holiday developments as well. Accommodation in the town has become expensive, so staying just outside has its benefits.

Guesthouses, B&Bs and hotels

An Ocean Watch 21 Plettenberg St ℡& ℻044 501 8092, ℮info@anoceanwatchguesthouse .co.za. A beautifully decorated beach-style home with views from the sea-facing rooms and the heated swimming pool. ❺

Hunter's Country House Off the N2, 10km west of Plett on the way to Knysna ℡044 532 7818, ⊛www.hunterhotels.co.za. Set in a woodland area, this is one of the best upmarket places to stay on the Garden Route, with an emphasis on country comfort rather than seaside glitz, at half the price of the much-vaunted *Plettenberg*. Accommodation is in thatched cottages set in well-established gardens, each with an open fireplace and private patio. ❾

The Lodge on the Bay 77 Beachy Head Dr ℡044 501 2800, ⊛www.thelodge.co.za. Unquestionably one of the hippest – and most expensive – places to stay in South Africa, the *Lodge* was voted one of the world's 101 best hotels in 2001 by Britain's style-conscious *Tatler* magazine. With just six suites, it's the embodiment of cool style and comfort, boasting wonderful views of the Robberg Peninsula across

the sea, meticulous interior design and highly personalized service. Despite the initial feeling that you've walked into the pages of a design mag, the atmosphere is anything but stuffy and total relaxation is encouraged, with a massage room and sauna. A hot choice for blowing your honeymoon budget. ❾

Pat's Place 4 Meeding St ℡044 533 3180. Two rooms in one of the cheapest B&Bs in Plett, in an old timber and iron house a 3min walk from Hobie Beach. The rooms don't have baths, but they're pleasantly decorated. ❸

The Plettenberg 40 Church St, Lookout Rocks ℡044 533 2030, ⊛www.plettenberg.com. Plett's prestige hotel is a large, luxurious establishment offering unbeatable views straight onto the ocean. But despite the sky-high rates you could still end up in a room overlooking the car park. ❽

Southern Cross Beach House 1 Capricorn Lane, Solar Beach ℡044 533 3868. Situated on Robberg Beach this colonial style home has rooms that either open onto the balcony or the patio. Each room has a kitchenette. ❺

Self-catering

Anlin Place 33 Roche Bonne Ave ℡044 533 3694, ⊛www.anlinplace.co.za. Two garden

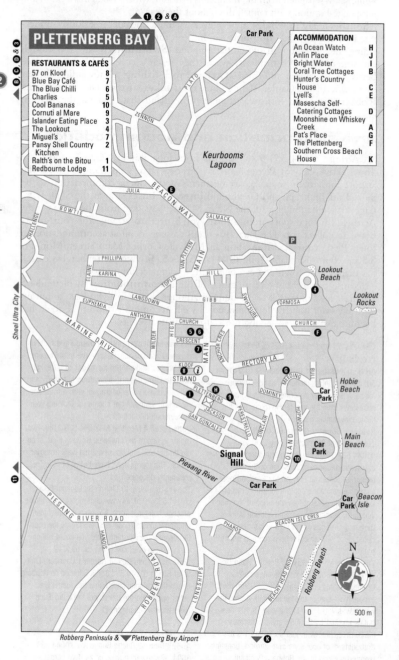

PLETTENBERG BAY

RESTAURANTS & CAFÉS

57 on Kloof	8
Blue Bay Café	7
The Blue Chilli	6
Charlies	5
Cool Bananas	10
Cornuti al Mare	9
Islander Eating Place	3
The Lookout	4
Miguel's	7
Pansy Shell Country Kitchen	2
Ralth's on the Bitou	1
Redbourne Lodge	11

ACCOMMODATION

An Ocean Watch	H
Anlin Place	J
Bright Water	I B
Coral Tree Cottages	B
Hunter's Country House	C
Lyell's	E
Masescha Self-Catering Cottages	D
Moonshine on Whiskey Creek	A
Pat's Place	G
The Plettenberg	F
Southern Cross Beach House	K

Car Park

Keurbooms Lagoon

Lookout Beach

Lookout Rocks

Hobie Beach

Main Beach

Beacon Isle

Signal Hill

Piesang River

Car Park

Car Park

Car Park

Car Park

Robberg Beach

N

0   500 m

Robberg Peninsula & ▼*Plettenberg Bay Airport*

studios with kitchenettes, and a larger family unit with three bedrooms and a kitchen, in a garden setting close to Robberg Beach. Units are serviced daily. ❸

Bright Water 15 Jackson St ☎ & ℱ 044 533 0467, 🌐 www.brightwater.co.za. Three en-suite doubles in a centrally located, homely suburban house where you can rent the whole place or just a room, with use of the kitchen. ❸

Coral Tree Cottages Off the N2, 11km west of Plettenberg Bay ☎ 044 532 7822, 🌐 www.coraltree .net. High-quality, spacious thatched cottages that sleep up to four, though unfortunately the roar of the N2 is never absent. R650 per cottage.

Lyell's 59 Beacon Way ☎ 044 533 5692. Five simple rooms, two with shared bathrooms, on a self-catering or B&B basis. The upstairs living area has sea views. ❸

Masescha Self-Catering Cottages 1km north off the N2, signposted 12km west from

Plettenberg Bay ☎ 044 532 7647, ℱ 044 532 7645. Three plainly furnished, whitewashed cottages on a farm, with outdoor sitting areas surrounded by pleasant gardens and a forest. Good for families or couples, it has a swimming pool, and also on site are an indigenous plant nursery and natural-history bookshop. Breakfast is available as an extra. R400 per cottage.

Moonshine on Whiskey Creek 14km east of Plettenburg Bay along the N2, signposted north of the N2 ☎ 044 534 8515 or 072 200 6656, 🌐 www.whiskeycreek.co.za. Fully equipped bungalows, three wooden cabins and one creatively renovated labourers' cottage, nestled in indigenous forest, with a children's play area. One of the best reasons to come here is the access to a secluded natural mountain pool and waterfall at the bottom of nearby the gorge. ❸

The Town and around

Plett's town **centre**, at the top of the hill, consists of a conglomeration of supermarkets, swimwear shops, estate agents and restaurants aimed largely at the holiday trade. Visitors principally come for Plett's **beaches** – and there's a fair choice. Southeast of the town centre on a rocky promontory is **Beacon Island**, dominated by a 1970s hotel, an eyesore blighting a fabulous location. Beacon Island Beach, or **Main Beach**, right at the central shore of the bay, is where the fishing boats and seacats anchor a little out to sea. The small waves here make for calm swimming, and this is an ideal family spot. To the east is **Lookout Rocks**, attracting surfers to the break off a needle of rocks known as the Point and the predictable surf of **Lookout Beach**, to its east, which is also one of the nicest stretches of sand for bathers, body-surfers or sun lizards. Lookout Beach has the added attraction of a marvellously located restaurant (see p.284), from which you can often catch sight of **dolphins** cruising into the bay. From here you can walk several kilometres down the beach towards Keurbooms and the **Keurbooms Lagoon**.

If you just fancy a bit of an adrenaline rush, you can go tandem **skydiving** (no experience required) with Skydive Plettenberg Bay (☎082 905 7440, 🌐www.skydiveplett.co.za). They charge R1300 for a jump, with the option of paying extra for a DVD or video of the event.

Knysna Elephant Park

Nine kilometres west of Plett on the N2, the **Knysna Elephant Park** (☎044 532 7737, 🌐www.knysnaelephantpark.co.za; R100, children R50) was established in 1994 to provide a home for abandoned, orphaned and abused young elephants, and opened to the public in 2003. The youngest of its charges are reared by park staff, who hand feed them forty litres of baby formula a day, and sleep next to them at night. The park offers **accommodation** in upmarket self-catering units (❸–❹), which, as the management points out, are "situated on the second level of the elephant *boma* and as a result the sounds of the elephants and the cleaning of their stalls in the morning will be audible".

Robberg Marine and Nature Reserve

One of the Garden Route's nicest walks is the four-hour, nine-kilometre circular route around the spectacular rocky peninsula of **Robberg**, 8km southeast of Plett's town centre. Here you can completely escape Plett's development and experience the coast in its wildest state, with its enormous horizons and lovely vegetation. Much of the walk takes you along high cliffs, from where you can often look down on seals surfacing near the rocks, dolphins arching through the water and, in winter, whales further out in the bay.

If you don't have time for the full circular walk, there is a shorter two-hour hike and a thirty-minute ramble. A **map** indicating these is available at the reserve gate when you pay to enter (daily: Feb–Nov 7am–5pm; Dec & Jan 7am–8pm; R14). You'll need sturdy walking shoes, as the terrain is rocky and steep in parts, and the walk involves some serious rock-hopping on the west side. Bring a hat and a bottle of water, as there's no drinking water for much of the way and no tea rooms.

There's no public transport to the reserve; if you're staying at a backpacker lodge, ask about their transfers, which are generally reasonably priced. To **drive** there, take Strand Street towards Beacon Isle, turn right into Piesangs Valley Road, and 200m further on turn left into Robberg Road. Follow the airport signs, continuing for 3.5km and then turning left toward *Robberg Holiday Resort*; you'll find the gate to the reserve 500m beyond the resort.

Whale- and dolphin-watching

Elevated ocean panoramas give Plettenberg Bay outstanding vantages for watching **southern right whales** during their breeding season between June and October. Phone the **Whale Hotline** (☎044 533 3743) at the Whale Shop, Boekenhout Centre, Piesangs Valley Road, for information about their current whereabouts. An especially good vantage point is the area between the wreck of the *Athene* at the southern end of Lookout Beach and the Keurbooms River. The Robberg Peninsula is also excellent, looming protectively over this whale nursery and giving a grandstand view of the bay. Other good town viewpoints are from Beachy Head Road at Robberg Beach; Signal Hill in San Gonzales Street past the post office and police station; the *Beacon Isle Hotel*; and the deck of the *Lookout* restaurant on Lookout Beach. Outside Plett, the Kranshoek viewpoint and hiking trail offers wonderful whale-watching points along the route. To get there, head for Knysna, taking the Harkerville turn-off, and continue for 7km. It's also possible to view the occasional pair (mother and calf) at Nature's Valley, 20km east of Plett on the R102, and from Storms River Mouth. For more information about whales, see box on p.241.

One of the best ways to **whale-watch** is in a kayak with Dolphin Adventures (☎083 590 3405). Experienced and knowledgeable guides will take you on an unforgettable journey from Plett in two-person kayaks, to view whales, dolphins and seals (R200 including all equipment). Other wildlife-spotting options include their trips in Polynesian-style catamarans across the bay towards Nature's Valley (R300), or a tri-cat ride (R300; 2hr) with The Explorer, Shop 20, Melville's Corner, Main St (☎082 377 3348). Ocean Safaris, Shop 1, Hopwood St (☎044 533 4963), can arrange tailor-made cruises, the advantage over shore-based watching being that you stand a chance of encounters throughout the year, including species that you'd be unlikely to spot from land. Apart from southern rights, their trips run into common, bottlenose, Indo-Pacific and humpback dolphins, as well as Bryde's and humpback whales – and the occasional minke and killer whale. Viewing the coastline with its whales, bays, river inlets and forests is quite spectacular from the **air**; African

Whaling and gnashing of teeth

For conservationists, the monumental 1970s eyesore of the *Beacon Island Hotel* may not be such a bad thing, especially when you consider that previously the island was the site of a whale-processing factory established in 1806 – one of some half-dozen such plants erected along the Western Cape coast that year. Whaling continued at Plettenberg Bay until 1916. Southern right whales were the favoured species, yielding more oil and **whalebone** – an essential component of Victorian corsets – than any other. In the nineteenth century, a southern right would net around three times as much as a humpback caught along the Western Cape coast, leading to a rapid decline in the southern right population by the middle of the nineteenth century.

The years between the establishment and the closing of the Plettenberg Bay factory saw worldwide whaling transformed by the inventions of the industrial revolution. In 1852, the explosive harpoon was introduced, followed by the use of steam-powered ships five years later, making them swifter and safer for the crew. In 1863, Norwegian captain Sven Foyn built the first modern whale-catching vessel, which the inventive Foyn followed up in 1868 with the **cannon-mounted harpoon**. In 1913 Plettenberg Bay was the site of one of seventeen shore-based and some dozen floating factories between West Africa and Mozambique, which that year between them took about 10,000 whales.

Inevitably, a rapid decline in humpback populations began; by 1918, all but four of the shore-based factories had closed due to lack of prey. The remaining whalers now turned their attention to fin and blue whales. When the South African fin whale population became depleted by the mid-1960s, to twenty percent of its former size, they turned to sei and sperm whales. When these populations declined, the frustrated whalers started hunting minke whales, which at 9m in length are too small to be a viable catch. By the 1970s, the South African whaling industry was in its death throes and was finally put out of its misery in 1979, when the government harpooned it by banning all activity surrounding whaling.

Ramble (☎083 375 6514) flies trips from Plett airport in a Piper tri-pacer (from R400 for half an hour).

Eating, drinking and nightlife

Plett has a respectable supply of good restaurants and some pleasant beachside pubs with terrific views. Locally caught fresh fish is the thing to look out for.

57 on Kloof Melville's Centre, Main St ☎044 533 5626. One of the best restaurants in town, elevated above the rooftops, with great views of the bay. The sandwiches, salads, burgers and steaks are excellent, the portions generous, and the prices reasonable. Daily breakfast & lunch.

Blue Bay Café Lookout Centre, Main St ☎044 533 1390. A good, moderately priced place to eat throughout the day in a courtyard tucked away under trees and overlooking both the main drag and the sea. Their offerings include a poached egg, salmon and croissant breakfast, Thai prawn dishes and ostrich fillet with mango. Daily.

The Blue Chilli Pick 'n Pay Centre, Main St ☎044 533 5104. This bistro has a superb Mexican menu, though beware of their "hot" dishes, which

positively sizzle. Meals can be washed down with a glass of tequila, with or without worm. Mon–Sat lunch & dinner.

Charlies Yellowwood Centre, on the corner of Main and Crescent streets ☎044 533 1420. A cosy restaurant serving moderately priced, tasty seafood, steaks and baked potatoes. Daily breakfast, lunch & dinner.

Cool Bananas Central Beach ☎044 533 0973. On the beach, in one of the best settings in town, this place does a straightforward range of burgers, salads and pizzas. Daily lunch & dinner.

Cornuti al Mare Shop 1, Seaview Properties, Perestrella St ☎044 533 1277. Terrific pizzas – the best along the Garden Route – and also great pasta dishes that won't break the bank. Daily noon–11pm.

Islander Eating Place 8km away on the N2 between Plett and Knysna ☎044 532 7776. A popular, high-quality seafood restaurant with a South Sea theme. Eat as much as you like for a set price from a seafood buffet that will blow you away. Booking essential. Daily breakfast, tea & lunch.

The Lookout Lookout Beach ☎044 533 1379. Marvellous bay views – if you're lucky, you'll see whales and dolphins rollicking in the surf – at this casual bar-restaurant focusing on seafood, including crayfish. Daily 9.30am–late.

Miguel's Melville's Corner, Main and Marine streets ☎044 533 5056. Medium-priced English cooking, at a stunning location with views of the ocean and passing trade. Daily breakfast & eves.

Pansy Shell Country Kitchen Old Nick Village, 2km east on the N2 ☎044 533 6061. In a quiet country garden, they offer curries, pastas and salads. The village features craft shops, a gallery and a weaving factory. Daily breakfast & lunch.

Ralth's on the Bitou On the Bitou River, just off the N2 between Plettenberg Bay and Keurbooms ☎044 535 9445. Reasonably priced meals are served at this pleasant pub with outdoor seating on the edge of the calm lagoon. Their fish and chips are especially recommended. Daily 11am–10pm.

Redbourne Lodge On the corner of Piesang Valley and Country roads ☎044 533 5037. An exceptional, stylish family-run restaurant with an eclectic menu – Mediterranean-style seafood dishes, oven-charred sole and butternut risotto cakes served with smoked ostrich. Booking essential. Daily breakfast, lunch & dinner. Closed June.

Keurboomstrand and around

Some 14km east of Plettenberg Bay, across the Keurbooms River, is the uncluttered resort of **KEURBOOMSTRAND** (Keurbooms for short), which shares the same bay and has equally wonderful beaches, but is less safe for swimming. The safest place for swimming is at **Arch Rock**, in front of the caravan park, though **Picnic Rock Beach** is also pretty good. A calm and attractive place, Keurbooms has few facilities, and if you're intending to stay here you should stock up in Plettenberg Bay beforehand.

If you can tear yourself away from the beach, **canoeing** up the Keurbooms River gives an alternative perspective on the area. Cape Nature Conservation on the east side of the Keurbooms River Bridge along the N2 (☎044 533 2125) rents out fairly basic craft (R70 per day for a two-person canoe). Keurbooms River Ferries (☎083 254 3551) run guided upriver **boat trips** (R75) with knowledgeable guides skilled at spotting rare birds, and also rent motorboats (R60/hr; minimum 2hr). Be sure to bring a **picnic** for any of the boat trips; the river is dotted with little beaches that are a good place to stop for a swim and walk. The indigenous forest comes right down to the river edge, and the journey gets better the higher up you go, the gorge narrowing and the pleasure boats and water-skiers now left behind. Don't be put off by the river's cola colour (which comes from harmless oxides in the water): the water is quite fresh, and wonderful to swim in during the summer. While you're here, keep an eye out for the pink-flowering keurboom trees that give their name to the river and resort.

Keurbooms has one of the country's best family-oriented **resorts**, the *Keurbooms Aventura*, 6km east of Plett and signposted off the N2 (☎044 535 9309, ⓦwww.aventura.co.za; family chalets R960). Here you can choose between campsites on the shady banks of the river, away from the sea, or self-catering chalets sleeping two adults and two children. Canoes and motorboats are available to rent, and there's a swimming pool. On the beach, *Arch Rock Chalets and Caravan Park* (☎044 535 9409; ②) is packed in summer, with families staying at the shady campsite or in the self-catering accommodation – either old, standard units or serviced "luxury" affairs (③). *Dune Park* on Keurbooms Strand Road (leading off the N2 and running along the shore to Keurbooms;

T 044 535 9606, W www.dunepark.co.za) has four luxury self-catering timber chalets (⑤) on the beach and ten budget ones (②) behind the dunes, just a short walk to the sea. The only place in Keurbooms for **eating and drinking** is the reasonably priced *Rafiki's*, which has an unbeatable location right on the beach and makes a great whale- and dolphin-spotting venue.

Monkeyland and Tsitsikamma Forest Village

Little more than a satellite of Plettenberg Bay, **The Crags**, 16km to its east, comprises a collection of smallholdings along the N2, a bottle store and a few other shops on the forest edge, as well as a primate and bird sanctuary, **Monkeyland** (daily 8am–6pm; free entry to viewing deck, safaris into the forest R100; W www.monkeyland.co.za). Look out for the BP filling station, then take the Kurland Village/Forest Hall turn-off for 2km to reach the site. The animals, from several continents, are free to move around the reserve, looking for food and interacting with each other and their environment in as natural a way as is possible. Guides take visitors on walking "**safaris**", during which you come across water holes, experience a living indigenous forest and have chance encounters with creatures such as including lemurs from Madagascar and squirrel monkeys from South America. The safaris are not only entertaining but also feature a commentary covering issues such as the differences between monkeys and apes, primate communication and social systems. One of the sanctuary's highlights is crossing the Indiana Jones-esque **rope bridge** (at 128m, it's purportedly the longest such bridge in the southern hemisphere) spanning a canyon to pass through the upper reaches of the forest canopy, where a number of species spend their entire lives. For refreshments or meals, there's a **restaurant** with a forest deck at the day lodge.

Part of Monkeyland is in fact a bird sanctuary, **Birds of Eden** (R100), the creation of which took four years to complete, as great effort was taken to place netting over the indigenous forest with as little impact as possible. A wheelchair-friendly timber walkway winds its way a gorge where over a thousand exotic bird specimens from around the world live. On the edge of the bird sanctuary is the **Raptor Centre** (R50), looking after eagles, hawks and other raptors which have little chance of being reintegrated back into the wild because of injuries or too much human contact.

For all the attractions and good work of Monkeyland, there has been criticism from nature lovers who believe that the presence of exotic primates and birds affects on the migration and breeding habits of the indigenous fauna.

Tsitsikamma Forest Village

If you want to try your hand at swinging through the air, then pull in at the **Tsitsikamma Forest Village**, 20km east of The Crags and the Monkeyland turn-off along the N2, where the registration office for the world's highest commercial **bungee jump** is based. The jump takes place off the 216-metre **Bloukrans River Bridge**, 2km beyond the village down a signposted road that also brings you to a viewpoint. There's no need to book ahead for the jump, which costs R550 (including video) for the seven-second descent. For the not so brave there's a mesh catwalk that takes you over the jump site (R80), and a 160-metre flying fox – a cable along which you slide while harnessed – that will run half the length of the bridge is planned. For further information, contact Bloukrans Bungy (aka Face Adrenalin) at the bridge (T 042 281 1458).

At the entrance to the site, the **Khoisan Cultural Village** is a mockup of a traditional khoi village, where guides teach you about Khoisan history and spirituality, and their tragic demise with the arrival of European colonization. The **information office** here (daily 9am–5pm; ☎042 281 1450, ⓦwww.tsitsikamma.org.za) is run by the Tsitsikamma Forest Village Trust, a non-profit community project aimed at keeping what remains of Khoisan culture alive.

Accommodation

You could do a lot worse than stay the night near the jump site, as all the accommodation (book through the tourist office) is in the midst of verdant indigenous forest. There's a well-maintained **caravan park** halfway down the road to the bridge with camping and, at the end of the road, a well-equipped log-cabin **backpacker lodge**, with two eight-bed dorms and four doubles (❶), a couple of hundred metres from the jump site. There are also some **self-catering chalets** sleeping four (R450). The **Baz Bus** pulls into the village and will usually take passengers as far as the backpacker lodge and jump site.

For a touch of luxury, there's the *Hog Hollow Country Lodge*, on a private reserve on Askop Road 18km east of Plettenberg Bay (turn south off the N2 at the signpost; ☎044 534 8879, ⓦwww.hog-hollow.com; ❾). Each of the chalets, done out in earthy colours and spiced up with African artefacts, has a bath or shower and its own wooden deck with vistas across the forest and Tsitsikamma Mountains; superb food is served as well. From here you could hike for a couple of hours through forest to Keurbooms Beach, or drive there in fifteen minutes.

Tsitsikamma National Park

The **Tsitsikamma National Park** (daily 7am–9.30pm; R80 per person; ☎042 281 1607), roughly midway between Plettenberg Bay and Port Elizabeth, is the highlight of any Garden Route trip. Starting from just beyond Keurboomstrand in the west, the national park extends for 68km into the Eastern Cape along a narrow belt of coast, with dramatic foamy surges of rocky coast, deep river gorges and ancient hardwood forests clinging to the edge of tangled, green cliffs. You'd be crazy to pass up its main attraction, the **Storm's River Mouth**, the most dramatic estuary on this exhilarating stretch of coast. Established in 1964, Tsitsikamma is also South Africa's oldest marine reserve, stretching 5.5km out to sea, with an **underwater trail** open to snorkellers and licensed scuba divers.

Tsitsikamma has two sections: **De Vasselot** in the west and **Storms River Mouth** in the east. Each section can only be reached down a winding tarred road from the N2 (there's no way of getting from one to the other through the park itself). De Vasselot incorporates **Nature's Valley**, the only resort in the park, and the most low-key settlement on the Garden Route, with a fabulous sandy beach stretching for 3km. South Africa's ultimate hike, the five-day **Otter trail**, connects the two sections of the park (see box on p.259).

De Vasselot and Nature's Valley

The **De Vasselot** section, at the western end of Tsitsikamma, extends inland into a rugged and hilly interior incised with narrow valleys and traversed by a series of footpaths. In fact De Vasselot is not a name that trips readily off South African tongues – most people know the section for **Nature's Valley**, a pleasingly old-fashioned settlement on the Groot River Lagoon with 20km of beach. Bypassed by the N2, and by intercity buses and tour parties, Nature's Valley is the place to go if you're after a quiet time along the Garden Route.

There are plenty of good **walks** at Nature's Valley, many starting from the De Vasselot campsite, 1km north of the village, where you can pick up maps and information about birds and trees. One of the loveliest places to head for is **Salt River Mouth**, 3km west of Nature's Valley, where you can swim and picnic – though you'll need to ford the tannin-dark river at low tide. This walk starts and ends at the café at Nature's Valley. Also recommended is the circular six-kilometre **Kalanderkloof trail**, which starts at the De Vasselot campsite, ascends to a lookout point, and descends via a narrow river gorge graced with a profusion of huge Outeniqua yellowwood trees and Cape wild bananas.

Practicalities

Public transport to Nature's Valley is limited to the **Baz Bus**, which deposits passengers at the De Vasselot restcamp or the backpacker lodges. The village centre is little more than an all-in-one restaurant, pub and small trading store that acts as an informal, but excellent, **information** bureau (☎044 531 6835, ⓦwww.natures-valley.co.za), and can help you find the limited **accommodation** available.

If you're **self-catering**, stock up on supplies before you get to Nature's Valley. The only place to buy a meal is at the **restaurant**, on the corner of Forest and St Michael streets, which serves seafood, steaks, burgers and toasted sandwiches, and provides the only nightlife apart from gazing at the stars.

Accommodation

Apart from the places listed below, self-catering accommodation can be rented through Clare Carr in Plettenberg Bay (☎ & ⓕ044 533 0743), who handles around eight cottages (R400–800 per cottage) in and around Nature's Valley – most of which sleep between six and eight people.

De Vasselot restcamp 1km to the north of the village. Bookings through South African National Parks (see p.71), or if you're already in Nature's Valley, the camp supervisor ☎044 531 6700. Campsites tucked into indigenous forest, and basic two-person forest huts with communal ablution facilities. ❷

Froggy Pond Second house on the right as you enter Nature's Valley ☎044 531 6835, ⓦwww .natures-valley.co.za. Self-catering accommodation in a two-storey timber and brick cottage. Downstairs is a self-contained flatlet with a double bedroom and living area that can sleep two adults and two children; upstairs there are two double rooms with en-suite showers. ❷

Nature's Valley Guest House & Hikers' Haven ☎044 531 6805, ⓔpatbond@mweb.co.za. A well-located hostel just 200m from the sea and the lagoon, offering backpacker and B&B accommodation. The choice encompasses a fourteen-bed backpacker dorm, three doubles sharing a bathroom, two very reasonably priced en-suite rooms – one of which is a family unit – and probably the least expensive honeymoon suite in the country, under thatch and with its own balcony and a sunken bath surrounded by mirrors. The backpacker section has a self-catering kitchen, and there's a snooker table, TV lounge and a payphone. Bikes, a canoe, rowing boat, surfboard and windsurfer are available for guests, and you can set out from the guesthouse on two- to six-hour hikes along the beaches or through the forests. Breakfast is extra. Dorms ❶, rooms ❷

Tourist Lodge 28 St Georges St, in the village ☎044 531 6681. Comfortable and immaculately clean unit that sleeps three and can be taken on a self-catering or B&B basis. ❷

Storms River Mouth

In contrast to the languid lagoon and long soft sands of Nature's Valley, **Storms River Mouth**, 55km from Plettenberg Bay, presents the elemental face of the Garden Route, with the dark Storms River surging through a gorge to battle with the surf. **Storms River Mouth Restcamp**, sited on tended lawns, is poised between a craggy shoreline of black rocks pounded by foamy white surf and steeply raking forested cliffs, and is without a doubt the ultimate location along the southern Cape coast. Don't confuse this with **Storms River Village** just off the N2, which is nowhere near the sea.

Walking is the main activity at the Mouth, and at the visitors' office at the restcamp you can get **maps** of short, waymarked coastal trails that leave from here. These include steep walks up the forested cliffs, where you can see 800-year-old yellowwood trees onto a wide stretch of ocean. Most rewarding is the **three-kilometre hike** west from the restcamp along the start of the Otter trail to a fantastic **waterfall** pool at the base of fifty-metre-high falls where you can swim right on the edge of the shore. Less demanding is the kilometre-long **boardwalk stroll** from the restaurant to the suspension bridge to see the river

---

Storms River activities

Storms River Adventures (☎042 281 1836, ⓦwww.stormsriver.com), which has its main office next to the post office in Storms River Village, and another office next to reception at the Storms River Mouth section of the Tsitsikamma National Park, has helped put the village on the map with its range of activities. The best known of which is so-called **blackwater tubing** (R380) down the Storms River Canyon through the Tsitsikamma National Park to the sea, ending at the suspension bridge. The price for a half-day trip includes all your gear, transfers to and from the Storms River adventure centre and lunch. Be sure to bring shoes that you don't mind getting wet. Alternatively, you can experience the otherwise inaccessible Storms River Gorge on one of their **Marine Tours** (R140) which takes in the suspension bridge over the gorge, Khoisan caves and a boat trip. A half-hour cruise up the gorge costs R50.

The **Canopy Tour** (R420) is the first of its kind in Africa, in which you get a bird's eye view of the forest trees by swinging 30m above ground on a series of interconnected steel wires attached to the tallest trees. The system has been constructed in such a way that not a single nail has been hammered into any tree. Also recommended is their relaxed **Woodcutters Journey** (teatime trip R105, lunch trip R190) down the old Storms River Pass through the forest depths in a specially designed trailer, drawn by a tractor down to the river.

Guided hikes lasting up to five days through the Tsitsikamma Mountains can be arranged (R450 per person per night including meals, minimum four people). Or there's the luxury **Dolphin trail**, 20km covered in two-and-a-half days and three nights, with luxury accommodation and no carrying of backpacks (R2700).

Other activities include **abseiling** 35m into the Storms River gorge (R190) and two-and-a-half-hour **mountain-bike trails** (unguided R105, guided R180) in the Tsitsikamma Forest. For the highly energetic, the **Awesome Storms River Gorge Challenge** involves a 110-metre abseil, blackwater tubing and mountain biking, all in one day (R580).

If you want to concentrate on the marine reserve, you could go **scuba diving** here; Storms River Adventures charge R300 for day rental of full diving kit with a guided dive (tank fills R40). Visibility ranges from 5m to 12m and corals and some fifty species of fish are on show, though don't expect the fluorescent colours you get in tropical waters. **Snorkelling** costs R95 for gear; add an extra R40 if you want a guide to go with you.

mouth. On your way to the bridge, don't miss the dank *strandloper* (beachcomber) **cave**. Hunter-gatherers frequented this area between 5000 and 2000 years ago, living off seafood in wave-cut caves near the river mouth. A modest display shows an excavated midden, with clear layers of little bones and shells.

If you're desperate to walk the **Otter trail** (see box on p.259), which begins at Storms River, and have been told that it is full, don't despair. A single person or a couple do stand a chance of getting in on the back of a last-minute cancellation, so it may be worth hanging out at the Mouth for a night or two.

Swimming at the Mouth is restricted to a safe and pristine little sandy bay below the restaurant, though conditions can be icy in summer if there are easterly winds and cold upwellings of deep water from the continental shelf. Hikes and other outdoor pursuits can be arranged through Storms River Adventures (see opposite).

Practicalities

Storms River Mouth is 18km south of **Storms River Bridge**. Most people stop at the bridge, on the N2, to gaze into the deep river gorge and fill up at the most beautifully located filling and service station in the country. Even if your time is limited and you can't spend the night at Storms River Mouth, it's still worth nipping down for a meal, a restorative walk or a swim in the summer. You'll need your own wheels, though, as there's no public transport to the Mouth. The only **eating** place is the restcamp restaurant, serving breakfasts and à la carte meals which, alas, are less memorable than the startling views.

A wide variety of **accommodation**, all with sea views, is available at **Storms River Mouth Restcamp** (☎042 281 1607; ❷–❹), including superb campsites just metres from where the surf breaks on the rocks; incredibly good-value two-person cabins, which provide bedding and towels, share ablutions and have communal catering facilities; comfortable one-bedroom self-catering log cottages, including breakfast; oceanette mini-apartments close to the sea, also including breakfast; and family oceanettes and cottages for a minimum of four people. All are heavily subscribed in season, so advance booking through South African National Parks is essential (see p.71).

Storms River Village

About a kilometre south of the national road, **STORMS RIVER VILLAGE** is a tranquil place crisscrossed by a handful of dirt roads and with about forty houses, enjoying mountain vistas. It offers a number of places to stay, a couple of general dealers selling basics, a liquor store, a fish-and-chips shop and an adventure centre which organizes activities in the area, though note that there's no public transport to Storms River Mouth and the national park.

Accommodation

The Armagh Fynbos Ave ☎042 281 1512, ⓦwww.thearmagh.com. A hospitable guesthouse in a beautiful garden that drifts off into the *fynbos*. The rooms include a rather tired looking honeymoon suite and four standard rooms, all of which open onto the garden. ❺

Ploughman's Rest 31 Formosa St ☎ & ⓕ042 541 1726. A reasonably priced farm-style B&B, with five en-suite rooms with their own entrances onto a small forested verandah. ❷

Tsitsikamma Lodge A couple of kilometres east of town along the N2, 8km east of the Storms River Bridge ☎042 280 3802, ⓦwww.tsitsikamma.com. Thirty cosy A-frame cabins with their own decks and connected by boardwalks that traverse beautifully kept gardens. Most cabins have their own Jacuzzi, and there are a number of forest walks, including their famous nudist hiking trail along the river. There's also a restaurant serving South African cuisine. ❻

Tsitsikamma Village Inn Along the road into the village and left at the T-junction ☎ 042 281 1669, ⓦ www.village-inn.co.za. The best place to stay in the village – eleven cottages, each differently themed, and surrounding a manicured garden. Each room is tastefully decorated. ❹

Tube 'n Axe On the corner of Darnell and Saffron streets ☎042 281 1757, ⓔtube-n-axe@telkomsa .net. A wacky place that works hard to compete with the bright lights of Knysna and Plett by offering backpackers drumming nights, a pool table and loads of laughs. You can camp in your own tent or in one they supply, or choose to sleep in the dorms or twin rooms. Meals are served at the bar (self-catering is possible), and there's a laundry service available. ❶

The West Coast and the Cederberg

The **West Coast** of South Africa – remote, windswept and bordered by the cold Atlantic, demands a special appreciation. For many years the black sheep of Western Cape tourism (a fact borne out by the prominence of industries such as fishing, and the iron-ore terminal at Saldanha Bay), it has been set upon by developers who seem all too ready to spoil the bleached, salty emptiness which many people had just begun to value. The sandy soil and dunes harbour a distinctive **coastal fynbos** vegetation, while the coastline is almost devoid of natural inlets or safe harbours, with fierce southeasterly summer winds and dank winter fogs, though in spring **wild flowers** ever-miraculously appear in the veld. The southern 200km of the region, by far the most densely populated part of the coast, has many links to Namaqualand to the north – not least the flowers.

Bird-watching on the West Coast

The West Coast is a twitchers' dream, where you can tick off numerous wetland species. The most rewarding viewing time is just after flower season in early summer, which heralds the arrival of around 750,000 migrants on their annual pilgrimage from the northern hemisphere, many from as far off as the Arctic circle. They spend about eight months fattening up on delicacies from the tidal mudflats before their arduous journey back to their breeding grounds. **Langebaan** in the West Coast National Park is the best place in the country for such sightings and is considered the fifth most important wetland in the world, hosting over 250 bird species, more than a quarter of South Africa's total. The Berg River estuary and saltworks at **Velddrif** are another vital feeding ground for waders. The coastal lake of **Verlorenvlei**, meaning "the lost marsh", is one of the most important wetlands in South Africa; it stretches 13.5km from its mouth at Eland's Bay (25km south of Lambert's Bay) to its headwaters near Redelinghuys. Look out here for the Purple Gallinule, a colourful, shy wader, and the African Marsh Harrier, a raptor which may be declining in numbers. Here species more fond of arid conditions merge with the waders, and there have been some rare sightings including a Black Egret and a Palm-nut Vulture. At **Bird Island**, Lambert's Bay, a sunken hide makes it convenient to view the garrulous behaviour of the breeding colony of Cape gannets.

Outside the flower months of August and September, this part of the West Coast has a wide range of attractions, particularly during summer when the lure of the sea and the cooler coast is strong. The area is well known for a wide range of activities, most popularly hiking and horse-riding along the coast or in the mountains, various types of watersports, whale-spotting and some excellent **bird-watching** (see box opposite).

A highlight of a number of West Coast towns is the casual but sumptuous **seafood** feast served in **open-air restaurants**, with little more than a canvas shelter held up with driftwood and lengths of fishing twine or a simple wind-cheating brush fence as props. The idea is to serve up endless courses of West Coast delicacies right by the ocean, in the style of a beach braai; you eat with your fingers and stand or perch on a rock, and you're likely to hear the waves crashing on the strand a few metres away and feel the sea air rolling in. A typical menu includes several different kinds of fish cooked in different ways – *bokkoms* (dried fish), mussels, lobster, paella, plus homemade breads with jams. Expect to pay around R120 per person for such a meal, excluding drinks. It's essential that you **book** in advance.

Immediately inland is the unusually fertile **Swartland** region; north of Swartland, the impressive **Cederberg mountain range** is an area of distinctive beauty, and a striking feature on the N7 highway, the main artery between Cape Town and Namibia. **Clanwilliam** is the attractive town at the northern end of the Cederberg, north of which the N7 connects with **Vanrhynsdorp**, within the Western Cape but for practical purposes covered with the flower routes of Namaqualand in the Northern Cape (see p.346).

Swartland

The N7 highway north from Cape Town leads quickly into the pleasing and fertile **Swartland** landscape. Swartland means "black country", but while the rolling countryside takes on some attractive hues at different times of year, it's never really black. The accepted theory is that before the area was cultivated, the predominant vegetation was a grey-coloured bush called *renosterbos* (rhinoceros bush) which, seen from the surrounding ranges of hills, gave the area a complexion sufficiently dark to justify the name.

Bordered to the west by the less fertile coastal *strandveld* and to the east by the tall mountain range running from Wellington to the Cederberg, Swartland is known best as a wheat-growing area, although it also supports dairy farms, horse studs, tobacco crops and vineyards famous for earthy red wines.

The N7 skirts a series of towns on its way north, including the largest in the region, **Malmesbury**. If you're travelling south towards Cape Town, look out for some unusual views of Table Mountain, and also for tortoises, which you should take care to avoid as they cross the road.

Darling and around

The small country town of **DARLING** lies caught between Swartland and the West Coast; it's famous for its rolling countryside and dairy products, and also for its displays of wild flowers in spring. Easily reached from Cape Town via the coastal R27 route, Darling boasts some handsome old buildings and has developed recently as an **artists' colony**. One of South Africa's best-loved comedians, Pieter Dirk-Uys, has established his most famous character, **Evita Bezuidenhout** (South Africa's answer to Dame Edna Everidge), as the hostess

West Coast flowers

During August and September you'll find displays of **wild flowers** across the West Coast region, with significant displays starting as far south as the inland town of Darling, just 80km north of Cape Town off the main R27 coastal route. Excellent displays are also found in the West Coast National Park and the hazy coastal landscapes around Cape Columbine and Lambert's Bay, while inland Clanwilliam is the centre of some good routes. An incredible four thousand flower species are found in the region, most of them members of the daisy and mesembryanthemum groups. For up-to-date advice and guidance, contact the helpful tourist offices in Darling, Saldanha and Clanwilliam; for further tips on flower-viewing, see pp.344–345.

of a weekend cabaret show at *Evita se Perron*, the tiny **old train station** in the centre of town (☎022 492 2831 or ⓦwww.evita.co.za for details and reservations). Local painters are displayed at the well-cared-for **Darling Museum** (daily 9am–1pm & 2–4pm; small entry fee) on the corner of Pastorie and Hill streets, and an "Art Walk" to the homes and studios of local artists, photographers and jewellers is organized on the first weekend of every month (details from the museum).

Just under 20km to the south of Darling at **Mamre**, near the coloured commuter town of Atlantis, an old Moravian **mission station** stands on the northern edge of town. Still active (call ☎021 576 1579 for details of tours), it includes a series of old thatched mission cottages, a huge church and a working water mill, and remains one of the finest examples in the Western Cape of these pragmatic but bold early nineteenth-century outposts.

Practicalities

Darling's **tourist office** is located inside the museum (Mon–Fri 9am–1pm & 2–4pm, Sat 10am–3pm, Sun 11am–3pm; ☎022 492 3361). Although Darling is well within the scope of a day-trip from Cape Town, it's also a good spot for a short **stay**. *Trinity Guest Lodge*, 19 Long Street (☎022 492 3430; ❸), is a charming Victorian guesthouse set in gracious large grounds; while *Darling Lodge*, 22 Pastorie Street (☎022 492 3062; ⓦwww.darlinglodge.co.za; ❸–❹), a Cape cottage, has a lush garden and six en-suite rooms. As well as *Evita se Perron* (see above), good **places to eat** include *Trinity Guest Lodge* for gourmet country fare (dinner Thurs–Sun, booking essential), *Zum Schatzi*, a German restaurant on Long Street (closed Mon & Sun) or, for pub lunches, *Bistro 7* on Main Road. An excellent place to have lunch just out of town is at *Hilda's Kitchen*, Groote Post Wine Estate, upon Darling Hills (☎022 492 2825; Wed–Sat).

Riebeek West

To the northeast of Malmesbury lies an impressive island of hills, **Kasteelberg** (castle mountain), on the far side of which lie two small settlements, **Riebeek Kasteel** and, a little to the northwest, **RIEBEEK WEST**. Roughly 3km north of Riebeek West on the road towards Moorreesburg lies a turning to a PPC Cement works. It's here, rather incongruously set among rumbling conveyor belts and grey dirt heaps, that you'll find the whitewashed cottage where **Jan Smuts**, the South African statesman and soldier, was born in 1870. There isn't a great deal to see other than a simple old house with wooden floors and some contemporary artefacts inside but, if you can ignore the fact that it has been all

The life of **Jan Christiaan Smuts**, one of South Africa's greatest figures, perhaps embodies more than any other this country's strained relationship with itself in the first half of the twentieth century. Born to an Afrikaner farming family, Smuts spoke English with the distinctive linguistic burr of Swartland and excelled as a scholar at Stellenbosch and then Cambridge universities. During the Anglo-Boer War he waged a wide-ranging and ultimately undefeated guerrilla campaign as the leader of a Boer commando. However, he came to believe in a unified South Africa under a British flag, and was appointed commander in chief of imperial forces in East Africa during World War I, attending meetings of the British War Cabinet in the final phases of the war.

Smuts served as **prime minister** of South Africa between 1919 and 1924, and again between 1939 and 1948, when he led South Africa into World War II on the British side. Like his fellow leader and statesman Winston Churchill, he failed to hold together support at home and in 1948 lost the postwar general election to the hardline Afrikaner D.F. Malan who, coincidentally, grew up on the farm Allesvoloren, a few kilometres from Smuts' birthplace.

Smuts spent much of his career in domestic politics trying to hold together disparate political and social moralities among English and moderate Afrikaans-speaking whites. He is remembered by white South Africans as a wily, tainted politician rather than as a great humanitarian. Yet he was, like very few South Africans before or since, a man of global vision and influence who as a 76-year-old played an important role in drafting the United Nations charter in 1946. He also published a philosophical treatise and was known for his love of nature and the outdoors, in particular Table Mountain in Cape Town – one of the popular routes up the mountain carries his name.

but gobbled up by an industrial site, there are some pleasant lawns, flowerbeds and a handful of outbuildings to wander around – one of which displays an interesting series of storyboards about the eventful life and times of the man (see box above).

Accommodation in Riebeek West is available in a luxurious Victorian villa, *Riebeek Valley Hotel*, 4 Dennehof Street (☎022 461 2672; ❺–❻), which also has a good restaurant (daily breakfast, lunch & dinner). Good meals and rooms can also be found in the renovated *Royal Hotel*, 33 Main St (☎022 448 1378; ❸), in neighbouring Riebeek Kasteel. Between Riebeek Kasteel and Tulbagh is *Bartholomeus Klip*, (☎022 448 1820; full board and activities ❾), a historic wheat farm and nature reserve with extensive herds of antelope. The gracious Victorian farmhouse has five en-suite rooms, elegantly decorated and furnished with heirloom antiques.

For **food**, *L'Attitude* is a friendly offbeat place on Sarel Cilliers Street (Wed–Sat lunch, Fri–Sun dinner); and *Twist at the Barn* (☎022 448 1377; Tues–Sun lunch, plus Fri & Sat dinner), in a converted rustic barn on Church Street, which makes a great place for an alfresco meal – booking is advised.

Groot Winterhoek

Situated within the often hazy, fortress-like line of mountains on the eastern fringe of Swartland is the three-hundred-square-kilometre **Groot Winterhoek Wilderness Area**, an excellent place for lonely hiking and camping, with sparkling swimming pools, typical Cape mountain fauna such as klipspringer, rhebuck and elusive felines, distinctive *fynbos* vegetation and – as the name suggests – rather formidable winter conditions. It is also an area well worth exploring if you're a mountain biker or paraglider.

As this is a wilderness area, you're free to walk and camp where you wish, although there are a number of suggested trails varying in length from a few hours to a few days, and you must carry a **permit** (R25 entrance fee plus R20 overnight). For details and **bookings**, contact the Cape Nature Conservation Office in Porterville (☎022 931 2900; Mon–Fri 7.30am–4pm).

Saldanha Bay and around

To the west of rural Swartland, and immediately north of Cape Town's fast-developing northern coastal suburbs of Bloubergstrand and Table View, the West Coast of South Africa starts off much as it continues for many hundreds of kilometres north: isolated fishing settlements and windswept dune vegetation of bleak but alluring beauty. Other than river mouths, the only sea inlet and protected deep-water harbour on the entire South African Atlantic seaboard is some 100km north of Cape Town at **Saldanha Bay**. The bay is connected to Langebaan Lagoon, the attractive centrepiece to the small but precious **West Coast National Park**.

While the holiday town of **Langebaan**, just to the north of the park on the eastern shore of the lagoon, has managed to keep its focus relatively frivolous and beach-oriented, industrial development has muscled into the northern part of the bay. This has brought in its wake a 1500-metre causeway, an iron-ore railway terminal and a fast-rising steel and concrete works, which come as an ugly intrusion after the delicate simplicity of the national park. They also mean that the town of **Saldanha**, once a sturdy fishing port with historic naval and military ties, is now grim, sullied and eminently avoidable.

Langebaan

Once the home to the largest whaling station in the southern hemisphere, and for a while Cape Town's long-haul passenger flight terminus (when seaplanes from Europe touched down on the lagoon during World War Two), **LANGEBAAN** now sells itself as the gateway to the West Coast National Park in the vicinity. One of the best reasons to spend time in Langebaan is for the excellent conditions for various wind sports. If you're into windsurfing, kitesurfing or sailing and have been wondering how to harness the big southeasterly summer winds, Langebaan could be just your thing. Right off the beach the water is flat, the sailing winds – as the ragged flags above the centre testify – anywhere from fresh to fearsome and, unless you catch a fast-running tide out towards the Atlantic, it's all reasonably safe.

If you want to try your hand at any of the watersports on offer, the friendly Cape Sport Centre (daily: summer 9am–7pm; winter 10am–6pm; ☎022 772 1114), on the beach on the northern edge of town, is the place to head to for gear rental and **windsurfing** and **kitesurfing** tuition, though they also rent out **mountain bikes**. **Sailing** courses are offered by Ocean Sailing Academy (☎021 425 7837, ⓦwww.oceansailingacademy.co.za).

Tourist **information** is available in the municipal building in Bree Street (Mon–Fri 9am–5pm, Sat & Sun 9am–1pm; ☎022 772 1515).

Accommodation

Accommodation is plentiful – it's what the town exists on. The municipal **caravan park** is a couple of blocks from the beach on Suffrens Street, and though it claims not to allow tents without permission, you probably won't need to ask when you arrive.

Club Mykonos Just north of Langebaan, on the road tracing the edge of Saldanha Bay ☎0800 22 6770. A burgeoning Greek-village-style holiday development offering one-, two- and three-bedroom units, the place to go if you're missing a Costa del Cape flavour in your holiday. Mon–Thurs & Sun ❹, Fri & Sat ❺

The Farmhouse Hotel ☎022 772 2062. A luxuriously restored farmhouse set up on the hill among some new houses on the southern end of town. It has a good restaurant and impressive cellar. ❻

Friday Island Conveniently situated next to Cape Sport, on the beach ☎022 772 2506. Perfect for the watersport enthusiast, the units are fresh and light with small kitchenettes, wooden decks and outdoor courtyards opening from the bathroom to hang up wet gear. There's also an in-house restaurant and pub. ❸

Langebaan Beach House On the lagoon's edge ☎022 482 1101. A guesthouse with spacious, airy rooms. It's a quick stroll to restaurants and shops. B&B ❸–❹

Olifantskop Opposite the *Club Mykonos* turn-off on the coast road, halfway between Langebaan and Saldanha ☎022 772 2326. A guesthouse that has both rooms and self-contained cottages, plus a restaurant, bar, pool and equestrian centre. ❷

Puza Moya North and Suffern streets, Langebaan ☎022 772 1114. Cheerful en-suite rooms with a shared kitchen and courtyard for braais. A good option if you like to socialize in a relaxed environment after an active day. Self-catering or B&B ❷

Eating

As with accommodation, there's a wide selection of **places to eat** in town. *Die Strandloper* (☎022 772 2490 or 083 227 7195; booking essential), on the beach just beyond the West Coast Centre on the road to Saldanha, is a good example of the West Coast's open-air seafood restaurants. On the main beach in town, *Pearly's* and *Driftwood* are crowded eating, drinking and ogling spots in a prime location. The gourmet's choice is *Froggy's*, 29 Main Road (summer Wed–Sun lunch & dinner, plus Tues dinner; winter Tues–Sun dinner, plus Sun lunch; ☎022 772 1869), which offers delicious and unusual seafood and curries, with some vegetarian options.

West Coast National Park

The **West Coast National Park** (April–Sept 7am–7pm, R20; Oct–Mar daily 6am–8pm, R30; ☎022 772 2144) is one of the best places to savour the simple, unspoilt charm of the West Coast. The park protects over 40 percent of South Africa's remaining pristine strandveld and 35 percent of the country's salt marshes, and incorporates both the majority of Langebaan Lagoon and a Y-shaped area of land immediately around and below it.

Much of the park's appeal lies in uplifting views over the still lagoon to an olive-coloured, rocky hillside; the sharp, saline air; the calling gulls and Atlantic mists vanishing in the harsh sunlight. This isn't a game park – a few larger antelope are located in the Postberg section of the park, an area open only during the spring flower season – but there are huge numbers of **birds**, including some 70,000 migrating waders. A number of well-organized interpretive walking trails lead through the dunes to the long, smooth, wave-beaten Atlantic coastline, offering plenty of opportunity to learn about the hardy *fynbos* vegetation which so defines the look and feel of the West Coast region. The best time to visit the park is in spring, when the sun is shining and the flowers are out, although this is, inevitably, also the busiest period. Like much of the West Coast, the national park is chilly and wet in winter, and hot and wind-blasted in summer.

On the southern tip of the lagoon is a large old farmhouse and steading called **Geelbek**. There are a number of bird hides nearby, and all the main **trails** (up to a total of 30km) start from here. If you continue from Geelbek up the peninsula on the western side of the lagoon you'll come to **Churchhaven**, a tiny village where there are some simple private cottages and where you can swim in the still, relatively warm water of the lagoon.

A little further on is the demarcated **Postberg area**, open only during flower season (see box on p.292), but worth visiting at that time to see **zebra**, **gemsbok** and **wildebeest** wandering through fields of wild flowers. The tip of the peninsula overlooking the mouth of Saldanha Bay is owned by the South African National Defence Force and inaccessible. The reserve also includes a number of islands around the mouth of the bay, home to gannets, penguins, seals and, on one, a colony of albino rabbits.

Practicalities

There are two **entrance gates** to the park: one on the R27, roughly 10km north of the turning to Yzerfontein, and the other south of the town of Langebaan. The park isn't huge; if you're driving you'll cover the extent of the roads in a couple of hours. You can see a good chunk if you enter at one gate and come out at the other – but it's worth taking the roads slowly to enjoy the views, and a visit to Geelbek, where there's an **information centre, booking office** and **restaurant** (℡022 772 2134; daily 9am–6pm), will allow you to appreciate a bit more of what you're seeing. Overnight **accommodation** is available here in a self-catering cottage with three bedrooms for R750 per night, and dormitories set attractively near the edge of the lagoon (❶). There are also two houseboats on the lagoon, one that sleeps four adults and two children and a larger one that can sleep up to eighteen (book through Tony and Cleo Drayton; ℡021 689 9718 or 082 258 0929; R800 for four people).

Cape Columbine

The coastline north of Vredenburg is classical West Coast territory: isolated fishing settlements with small, whitewashed cottages and a salty haze over the lazy, glinting ocean. Despite the quaint image, most of the settlements possess alarmingly expanding holiday developments, offering (naturally) whitewashed cottages in classical West Coast style. Although you can still find the odd lonely coastline and some genuine character in the old villages and their coloured inhabitants, the area feels as though it has reached that sad moment of changing from "best-kept secret" to an over-subscribed building site.

Vredenburg and the West Coast Fossil Park

North of Saldanha lies a sizeable inland farming centre, **VREDENBURG**, an unremarkable town in a featureless setting. Vredenburg has well-stocked supermarkets and a **tourist office**, the West Coast Peninsula Tourism Bureau (Mon–Fri 9am–4pm; ℡022 715 1142, ✉vredenburg@telkomsa.net), in the Atrium Building on Main Road. The town is also a good place to buy fuel – many of the smaller towns nearby don't have filling stations.

About 10km southeast of Vredenburg, the **West Coast Fossil Park** (Mon–Fri 9am–4pm, Sat & Sun 10am–1pm; R10) was founded in 1998 on the site of a decommissioned phosphate mine. In the process of being developed, it's still a relatively small and low-key affair, but interesting nevertheless, with guided tours of the museum and dig daily at 11.30am (R20). Displays include thousands of fossils and modern animal bones, and also information panels about the extinct species from about five million years ago found on site. Finds include fossils from sabre-toothed cats, two species of extinct elephant and *sivatheres* – long-horned, short-necked giraffe-like browsers. Perhaps strangest of all are the extinct giant bears, *Agriotherium africanum*, which weighed in at 750kg (compared to 150kg for a large lion), making them the heftiest predators – and the only known bears – to have roamed sub-Saharan Africa in the past 65 million years.

Budget **accommodation** is available on the adjacent property at *Windstone Backpackers* (☏022 766 1645 or 083 477 1756, ⓦ www.sawestcoast.com /windstone; ❶), just past the main crossroads of the R45 from Vredenburg and the R27 from Cape Town. The lodge has four- and six-bedded dorms and one room suitable for families. *Windstone* makes a friendly base for exploring the region and also has a **horse-riding centre** run by owners Andy and Brenda Winder, the latter a qualified riding instructor who will take on novices as well as organize horse trails along the coast or up in the Cederberg. The lodge is on the route of the daily Elwierda bus (☏021 418 4673), between Cape Town and Saldanha; the Winders can provide mountain bikes and transport to Langebaan (around R35 for both).

Paternoster

The best of the coast is to be found 20km northwest of Vredenburg around the village of **PATERNOSTER** (whose name derives from the fact that prayers were uttered by Portuguese sailors crawling ashore from a shipwreck in the adjacent bay). Small-scale angling and crayfish netting is the principal economic activity of the village, and most of the fishermen live in the whitewashed cottages of the coloured district to the west of the hotel. When they're not out at sea, their small, brightly painted boats lie beached at the water's edge.

An adventure highlight of Paternoster is **sea kayaking** with former game ranger Hannes Kleynhans of the *Beach Camp* at Columbine Nature Reserve (☏082 926 2267, ⓦ www.ratrace.co.za). Trips last from two hours (R180 per person) to several days (two nights costs R900 per person, including meals) and are as much about observing and learning about birds, whales, dolphins and seals as about paddling. Kleyhhans also operates kayak trips from a yacht moored off Dassen Island and leads hiking trails. His brother, André (same contact details), a professional diver and licensed divemaster, leads **scuba trips** through multicoloured kelp forests and can take people on traditional fishing trips.

Accommodation

Baywatch Villa 8 Ambyl Rd ☏022 752 2039. Four self-catering thatched fishermen's-style cottages, luxuriously kitted out. ❷–❸

Blue Dolphin 12 Warrelklip St, right on the beach ☏022 752 2001. Four en-suite rooms in a modern building. The owner, George, is very informative and prepares excellent breakfasts. B&B ❸

Die Opstal Sonkwasweg ☏022 752 2648. Three quaint self-catering flats and a B&B loft with separate entrances. The owner, Francois, is a multitalented, true West Coast character, who created the paintings, mosaics and furniture about the place. ❷

Mosselbank Corner of Trappiesklip and Mosselbank streets ☏022 752 2632. Hospitable B&B in a suburban development, with sea views from four en-suite rooms. ❸

Oystercatchers' Haven 48 Sonkwasweg ☏022 752 2193. A beautiful guesthouse with three rooms situated on the beach and the edge of Columbine Reserve. The views are wonderful, and the place has an air of the old romance of Africa, where everything you touch tells a story. ❹

Paternoster Hotel St Augustine's Rd ☏022 752 2703. A rather old-fashioned hotel in the approximate centre of the village. There are ten en-suite rooms, four with balconies for sea views; they also have a number of self-catering cottages. ❷

Eating

Eating and **seafood** are virtually synonymous in Paternoster. Here you'll find probably the best fish (braaied) and chips along the West Coast, and crayfish in season, at the informal *Ahoy Galley* (daily noon–3pm, Wed, Fri & Sat evenings) just east of the hotel in the old general dealer's store building. Next door is Op ve Koep Winkel, a bric-a-brac store with tea garden that's almost an institution. Spectacularly sited on the beach, the *Voorstrand* (daily 10am–10pm) in a corrugated iron building at the bottom of Malgas Road, serves similar fare.

Columbine Nature Reserve

If you get as far as Paternoster, be sure not to miss the **Columbine Nature Reserve** (daily sunrise to sunset; R8), 3km to its west. A small area set aside to conserve the indigenous sandveld-*fynbos* heathland indigenous to the region, it makes a stunning change from the salty flats that typify the West Coast. Large vegetated dunes sweep down to a shoreline of massive pink granite boulders and little coves, with beaches that are blue-tinged, a result of oyster shells being washed up and finely crushed into the sands.

There are some excellent coastal **hiking trails** through these reserves, including two long day-trails (details from Vredenberg tourist office). There are also some very basic but highly attractive **campsites** along the shore (❶). On the edge of a small bay surrounded by huge granite boulders and *fynbos*, the *Beach Camp* (☎082 926 2267, ⓦwww.ratrace.co.za; ❶–❷) is run by Hannes, an adventurer extraordinaire who organizes kayaking, diving, hiking and yacht trips (see p.297). Seafood meals, fish braais, a basic pub, comfortable beds and hot showers are on offer, and mountain bikes can be hired for exploring the reserve and village.

Along the road from Paternoster to the reserve you'll pass the **Cape Columbine lighthouse** (open to the public for tours; Mon–Fri; R10), built in 1936 on Castle Rock. Usually the first lighthouse to be sighted by ships from Europe rounding Africa, it emits a single white flash every fifteen seconds. **Self-catering accommodation** (☎021 449 2400; ❷–❹) is offered in two former lighthouse keeper's cottages and a condominium, kitted out with all mod cons.

St Helena Bay

St Helena Bay was the point where **Vasco da Gama** set foot in what is now South Africa during his epic voyage around the Cape and through to India in 1497. He wasn't the first European to round the Cape of Good Hope, nor the first to land, but his voyage did open up the route to the East, which was to give the Cape its strategic importance for four centuries. Three granite lumps on the shore between the fishing villages of St Helena Bay and Stompneus Bay serve as a memorial to his landing, and a no-expenses-spared **Da Gama Museum** (daily 9am–4.30pm; free) has also been established within the largest of the new housing developments in the area at **Shelley Point**. The museum is more a rainy-day affair than a must-see, but does include some well-devised storyboards, a collection of model ships and some early navigation devices.

Throbbing away in the background of the granite memorial is a **lobster factory**, where you can usually buy fresh or frozen specimens if you enquire at reception. It's illegal to buy the lobsters if they're offered to you on the street, though in season you can obtain a permit, available from post offices, to catch them for personal consumption. Strangely enough, fishermen once regard the lobsters that got entangled in their nets as a pest, and during the nineteenth century sold wagonloads of them to farmers to be ground up and used as fertilizer.

Velddrif

At the northern end of the R27 from Cape Town and 15km east of St Helena Bay is **VELDDRIF**, a fishing town situated at the point where the Great Berg River meets the sea. Each year the Berg River **canoe marathon** (which starts near Ceres, 49km north of Worcester) ends here at a marina development called Port Owen. During the last few years, the town has outgrown its fishing industry origins and is now dominated by a modern suburbia of brick bungalows. The town's setting on the meandering Berg River and the surrounding wetlands – as well as the vision of some locals, who have managed to stay the eager hand of the demolition crews – has resulted in Velddrif retaining a little of its historic character.

In the quieter backwaters near the Velddrif bridge, you can still see individual fishermen in small boats landing catches of mullet or horse mackerel. The fish are then dried and salted to make **bokkoms**, called by some a delicacy, but essentially a source of cheap protein for fishermen and farm workers on the West Coast. To see the rickety wooden jetties where the boats tie up, and the frames and sheds by the shore where *bokkoms* are strung up to dry, turn right at the roundabout just over the bridge coming into town on the R27, and after a kilometre or so take the first right-hand turn down to the riverside.

Heading straight on at the roundabout onto Church Street and then right up a dirt driveway will bring you to the **West Coast Gallery** (Mon–Fri 9am–5pm, Sat 9am–3.30pm), one of the best of its type in the area. Essentially a shop run by a local artist, it displays a wide selection of art and crafts, including some interesting driftwood collages. You can also have a cup of coffee here, explore the reed maze or have a game of petanque in the grounds. Look out for the selection of sea-salt products, including flavoured salts, seaweeds and bath salts, produced on a small pan by the coast nearby.

There is a wealth of **birdlife**, including pelicans and flamingoes along both banks of the river (see box on p.290). You can take a pleasant **boat trip** into the wetlands with well-informed birder Dan Ahlers (☎022 783 0698 or 082 951 0447), who takes excursions up the Berg River. A two-hour trip costs R60 per person. He also leads bay cruises on which you stand a chance of seeing marine mammals, including Heaviside's dolphins, distinguished from their commoner bottlenosed cousins by their stocky bodies and short beaks.

Practicalities

The *Riviera Hotel* (☎022 783 1137; ❷) has ten new, well-equipped self-catering **chalets** near the bridge and on the water's edge. Flamingoes and many other waterbirds can be seen from the balcony. There are two pleasant self-catering cottages and rooms in the farmhouse on the historic farm of *Langrietvlei* (☎ & ⓕ022 783 0856; ❶), halfway between Velddrif and Hopefield, which also offers walking trails. Just 5km from town on the other side of the river is *Kuifkopvisvanger* (☎ & ⓕ022 783 0818; ❶), with three B&B rooms and five charming, rustic fisherman's cottages with views of the river and marshlands.

Best of the lot though, 25km south of Velddrif on the Berg River, is *Kersefontein Guest Farm* (☎022 783 0850; ⓦwwwkersefontein.co.za; ❹). A definite highlight of the West Coast region, this is a working farm dating back to the eighteenth century, and boasts several handsome Cape Dutch listed buildings, some of which have been converted into stylish accommodation. All the rooms have antiques from the original homestead, and dinners are served in a chandelier-lit dining room. The atmosphere is anything but formal, though, with Julian Melck, the eighth generation owner, treating guests to lively tales of life on a South African farm. There are delightful gardens and miles of farmland to explore, the latter grazed by domestic as well as wild horses.

Velddrif has no shortage of waterside **restaurants**, one of the most charming of which is the low-key *Vishuis*, about 3km west along the atmospheric riverside dirt road from the Velddrif bridge. Housed in a restored traditional fish-drying factory, with outdoor seating offering views across the wetlands, it serves extremely well-priced English breakfasts and excellent fish-and-chips lunches. Next to bridge, the *Riviera Hotel* does good seafood and steaks, while the *Laaiplek Hotel* is a relaxed place for a **drink** in close proximity to large boats, fish factories and cranes.

Lambert's Bay

The only settlement of any note between Velddrif and Port Nolloth, the latter almost at the Namibian border, is **LAMBERT'S BAY**, 75km north of Velddrif (by indirect dirt road) and 70km due west of Clanwilliam (by tarred road). This is an important **fishing port**, although by the sights and sounds of the harbour you soon become aware that even the fishermen have to stand aside for the impressive colony of **gannets** on Bird Island, in the centre of the bay. You can walk out to the island on the causeway which encloses the fishing-boat harbour for a closer look at the tightly packed, ear-piercing mass of petulant gannets, along with a few disapproving-looking penguins and cormorants.

Lambert's Bay itself is rather short on charm; the fish-processing plant sits on the edge of the harbour, right in the town centre, giving you the feeling you're in a seat behind a pillar at the theatre. Nevertheless, its isolation means that there's some deserted coastline and nature nearby. During the breeding season (July–Jan), the bay plays host to a resident pod of around seven **humpback whales**. This is also the southernmost area ranged by **Heaviside's dolphins** – small, friendly mammals with wedge-shaped beaks (rather than the longer ones more commonly associated with dolphins), with a white, striped patterning reminiscent of killer whales. You can view the cavorting mammals on trips from the fishing port.

Practicalities

The **tourist office** is in Main Road (Mon–Fri 9am–5pm, Sat 9am–12.30pm; ☎027 432 1000). There are a couple of **caravan parks** at either end of town, and no shortage of self-catering apartments, but nothing much by way of charm or character. In Voortrekker Street in the centre of town, the neat *Lamberts Bay* (☎027 432 1126, ✉marinelb@kingsley.co.za; ❸) offers comfortable **hotel** rooms with breakfast.

Eating is one of Lambert's Bay's specialities. *Bosduifklip* (☎027 432 2735), an open-air restaurant set inland among some big rock formations 6km out of town along the R364, is a reasonable option, while the original West Coast open-air restaurant, *Muisboskerm* (☎027 432 1017), scores on location – right on the edge of the ocean, 5km south of the town. For a more conventional seafood restaurant, try *Kreefhuis* (☎027 432 2235; closed Sun evenings) at the entrance to the harbour on Strand Street. Right on the harbour, *Isabel's Coffee Shop* does the whole gamut from light meals to prawns, but is renowned for its blowout "West Coast breakfast".

The Cederberg

A bold and jagged outcrop of the Western Cape fold escarpment, the Cederberg mountain range is one of the most magical wilderness areas in the Western Cape. Rising with a striking presence on the eastern side of the Olifants river valley, around 200km north of Cape Town, these high sandstone mountains and long, dry valleys manage to combine accessibility with remote harshness, offering something for hikers, campers, naturalists and rock climbers.

The **Cederberg Wilderness Area**, flanking the N7 between Citrusdal and Clanwilliam, was created to protect the silt-free waters of the Cederberg catchment area, but also provides a recreational sanctuary with over 250km of hiking trails. In a number of places, the pink-hued sandstone (which can glow with heartbreaking beauty in the light of a low sun) has been weathered into grotesque, gargoyle-like shapes and a number of memorable natural features. Throughout the area there are also numerous **San rock-art** sites, an active array of Cape mountain fauna, from baboon and small antelope to leopard, caracal and aardwolf, and some notable montane *fynbos* flora, including the gnarled and tenacious Clanwilliam cedar and the rare snow protea.

The Cederberg is easily reached from Cape Town by way of the N7: the towns of **Citrusdal** and **Clanwilliam** lie just off the highway near, respectively, the southern and northern tips of the mountain range. Both make attractive bases from which to explore the area, particularly during spring flower season, although you can find simple accommodation right in the mountains themselves. From Clanwilliam, set beside a man-made dam, there are worthwhile routes out to Lambert's Bay on the coast (see opposite) and over a spectacular mountain pass to the remote and unique mission at **Wuppertal. Weather conditions** are often extreme in the Cederberg, with frost and snow during winter, and blistering heat in summer. However, a number of rivers are safe for **swimming**.

Citrusdal

North of Piketberg on the N7, a long, flat plain reaches out to the line of Olifantsrivierberg Mountains, which the highway crosses by way of the impressive **Piekenierskloof Pass**, forged in 1857 by the indomitable road engineer Thomas Bain. Down the northern side of the pass, the humdrum town of **CITRUSDAL** appears in the rolling countryside of the Olifants River Valley, with the dramatic mountainscape of the Cederberg behind. Strange as it may seem now, early Dutch explorers saw huge herds of elephants here as they travelled north towards Namaqualand, hence the river's name.

There are no roads from Citrusdal itself into the heart of the Cederberg Wilderness Area nearby to the north, although there are various routes leading into the foothills, which are justifiably popular with mountain bikers. You can get a **map** outlining these at the town's upbeat **tourist office** at 39 Voortrekker, the town's wide main street (Aug & Sept Mon–Sat 8am–5pm, Sun 9am–1pm; Oct–July Mon–Fri 8.30am–12.30pm & 1–5pm, Sat 9am–1pm; ☎022 921 3210, ⓦwww.citrusdal.info). The staff here can provide useful information about self-catering cottages and guesthouses in the area.

In town, there's a pleasant **campsite** with a pool (☎022 921 3145) on the left-hand side as you come in over the bridge from the N7, and en-suite **rooms** at the garishly coloured *Cederberg Lodge* on Voortrekker Street (☎022 921 2221; ❶–❷). The lodge boasts the family-friendly *Tangelo's* **restaurant**, serving Afrikaner farm-style food in a garden setting; a little further along the road at no. 66, you can get light meals at the distinctive yellow and purple *Uitspan Coffee Shop*.

If you're making a lunch stop along the N7, the obligatory port of call is *Craig-Royston* (☎022 921 2963), on a working orange farm signposted off the N7, about 500m south of the Citrusdal turn-off. Housed in a former trading store, post office and hotel from the 1860s (predating Citrusdal by about forty years), it serves unpretentious meals and snacks. The hugely atmospheric rural Victorian building still functions as a general store, and also sells a large selection of wines from the Olifants river valley, as well as local liqueurs and spirits.

Citrusdal hot springs

Surrounding Citrusdal is some attractive countryside and farmland including, as the town's name suggests, plenty of citrus groves. One of the principal attractions of this area is *The Baths* (☎022 921 8026; ❷), a pleasantly old-fashioned, if rather rule-bound, mineral **spa resort** with one large hot pool (43°C), a cold pool and several large indoor Jacuzzis. The place is set in a beautiful wooded glen with campsites, chalets and self-catering rooms in some large old stone buildings. It's a good spot to relax, particularly if you've been hauling over mountain and rock for a few days. To get there, turn right (south) off the road leading into Citrusdal from the N7 and drive 16km down a good tarred road past the airfield – incidentally, one of the best places in the Western Cape for parachuting.

Along the same road, but 6km closer to Citrusdal, the smaller and more upmarket *Elephant Leisure Resort* (☎022 921 2884, ⓦwww.elephantleisure .co.za; ❸) is a complex of four two-bedroom and six one-bedroom self-catering chalets in a beautiful valley festooned with *fynbos* and arranged around a little artificial lake. Each of the chalets is finished to a high standard with air conditioning, TV and its own Jacuzzi. Meals and drinks are available at the reception complex, where there's also a heated swimming pool.

The Cederberg Wilderness Area

A dirt road 28km north of Citrusdal and 25km south of Clanwilliam leads east off the N7 to the 710-square-kilometre **Cederberg Wilderness Area**, featuring many designated **trails**, including routes to the main rock features and the two main peaks, **Sneeuberg** (2027m) and **Tafelberg** (1969m). Among the rock formations are the huge **Wolfberg Arch** in the southeast of the reserve, and a thirty-metre-high free-standing pillar shaped like (and known as) the **Maltese Cross**, to its south – both reward heading out into the wilderness on foot.

The **permit** system here allows a certain number of people to be in each of three separate parts of the wilderness area; you can hike or camp where you like within the areas you hold a permit for (arrange permits in advance through the Cape Nature Conservation Office at the forest station at **Algeria**, 5km inside the reserve; ☎022 931 2088, ⓦwww.capenature.org.za; entry R25 per person, plus an additional R25 to overnight).

Camping is available at a pretty riverside site at Algeria, where there are also seven unsophisticated but fully equipped **self-catering chalets** (R380) that sleep four; the stone cottages are the nicest. Cheaper ones 4km away at the bottom of Uitkyk Pass are unequipped and you must bring your own bedding and cooking utensils; contact the Cape Nature Conservation Office in Algeria for bookings and information.

Apart from the Cape Nature Conservation accommodation, there are several private places to stay south of Algeria on farms in the reserve, reached along the single main road passing through this section of the Cederberg. *Sanddrif* (☎027 482 2825, ⓦwww.cederbergwine.com; ❶), about 26km south of Algeria, offers fully equipped chalets with one to three rooms (bring your own bedding), on a farm where there are natural river pools and good walks. At

Kromrivier (☎027 482 2807; ❷), some 50km south of Algeria, there are thirteen fully equipped chalets, some with their own baths and cheaper ones without, that sleep four, with bedding available for a small charge. Another 12km south is the hospitable *Cederberg Oasis* (☎027 482 2819; ❷), the only licensed B&B and restaurant in the area. Accommodation is in basic rooms or a stone cottage that sleeps four, plus reed huts to camp in. Further south along the road on Grootrivier Farm is *Mount Ceder* (☎023 317 0113, ⓦwww.mountceder .co.za; ❷–❹), the most luxurious place to stay in the reserve, with B&B rooms in the lodge and six self-catering cottages. It's set along a perennial river, and there are some good horse-riding trails. If you're coming from Cape Town, it's better to approach Grootrivier via Worcester (see p.213), 95km to the south, passing through Ceres and Prince Alfred Hamlet, as this entails a shorter section of dirt road.

Clanwilliam and the Boskloof

Also on the N7, but at the northern end of the Cederberg, **CLANWILLIAM** is an attractive and assured town. It carries off with some aplomb its various roles as a base for the majestic Cederberg Wilderness Area, as a centre for spring flowers, as a holiday resort focused on the neighbouring dam, and as a service centre for some of the irrigation schemes of the Olifants River Valley to the north.

Established in the last years of the eighteenth century, Clanwilliam is one of the older settlements north of Cape Town, and features a number of historic buildings around town, including a tourist office (Mon–Fri 8.30am–5pm, Sat 8.30am–12.30pm, though mid-Aug to mid-Sept daily 8am–5pm; ☎027 482 2024, ⓦwww.clanwilliam.info) and **museum** (Mon–Sat 8am–1pm; R5) situated in the old jail at the far end of Main Road. There are some genuinely interesting attractions in town, including **Kunshuis**, a good commercial art gallery on Main Street; a traditional leather **shoemaking factory** on Ou Kaapseweg; and the country's main **rooibos tea-processing factory** next door, which has a window through which you can peer in from the street, and videos of the manufacturing process (Mon–Fri 10am, 11.30am, 2pm, 3.30pm).

Just to the south of town is **Ramskop**, a wild-flower reserve set on a hillside inside the entrance to the dam resort. The *Clanwilliam Dam Resort* is the only

---

Rooibos tea

Few things in South Africa create such devotion, derision, hype and, among visitors, bemused suspicion as **rooibos** (literally, "red bush") **tea**. Still sown and harvested by hand on many farms, *rooibos* is a type of *fynbos* plant grown only in the mountainous regions around Clanwilliam and Nieuwoudtville. The caffeine-free tea brewed from its leaves has been a staple South African drink ever since it was developed by Asian slaves two centuries ago, but it is only in the last twenty or so years that it has broken free of health-food-shop earnestness and established some mainstream credibility. In homes and tea rooms throughout South Africa, *rooibos* is now firmly entrenched alongside regular tea and coffee. Mild in flavour, it can be drunk with milk and sugar, or just with a slice of lemon and a teaspoon of honey.

Should you want to see how the tea is grown and processed, take one of the **tours** offered by Elandsberg Eco Tours (☎027 482 2022; R50); trips start from their premises 14km west of Clanwilliam on the Lambert's Bay road. They also have accommodation in two simple self-catering chalets (❷). Ysterfontein Farm (☎027 482 2512), just 10 km further along the same road, offer similar tours and accommodation in cottages under thatch next to the farmstead (❷).

public access point to the **dam** – one of the country's top water-skiing venues – which in summer and at weekends is often monopolized by speedboat louts.

Reinhold's (see below) has the best reputation in town as a place to **eat**, but for something more casual, head for *Olifantshuis Pizzeria* (closed Sun), on the corner as you turn into Main Road off Augsburg Drive. For daytime meals and snacks, try the tea room at *Strassberger's Clanwilliam Hotel*, or *Nancy's Tea Room* (daily 9am–4pm) opposite.

Accommodation

Bulshoek Dam Resort 17km north of the village, along the R363 ☎027 482 2635. Hilda, the hospitable owner, comes from a long line of Compions, a family that farmed in the area for generations, and has vast knowledge of the plants and local lore. Apart from an unusual camping site on an island in the middle of the Olifants River, there are self-catering stone cottages near the river and a characterful, secluded mountain cottage that was an artist's home for 25 years and has its own solar power supply. **❷**

Ceder Sun ☎083 465 5757. A spacious self-catering house on the edge of the Clanwilliam dam, with views and a private jetty. **❸**

Clancourt B&B 2 Arnold St ☎027 482 1143. Four en-suite rooms arranged around a swim-ming pool. The hosts are interesting former media personalities. **❸–❹**

Daisy Cottage ☎027 482 1603. A quaint thatched cottage in a quiet street within strolling distance of the main road. The friendly owner is a journalist with the town's newspaper. **❷**

Ndedema Lodge At the end of Park St ☎027 482 1314. A romantic Victorian B&B with an upmarket feel, four antique-filled rooms and a charming garden. **❸**

Strassberger's Clanwilliam Hotel On the main street ☎027 482 1101. A South African institution, dignified and well run, with rooms and chalets, an open-air pool, a tea room and an excellent restaurant, *Reinhold's*. **❸**

The Boskloof

About a kilometre east of town along the Pakhuis Pass road, a good dirt road heads south and drops into the **Boskloof**, through which the Jan Dissels River traces its course. Although less than 10km from the town, the valley feels a hundred miles from anywhere and is a relaxed spot where you can spend time lolling about along the riverbank, swimming in its natural pools or just walk along the dirt road which twists through the mountains. If you're up for something more energetic, you can go on two-hour or two-day horse-riding expeditions at Karukareb farm, 13km down the Boskloof road (☎027 482 1675), or head into the Cederberg on the **Krakadouw hiking trail**, which starts at *Krakadouw* cottages in the valley (permits available via *Krakadouw* cottages if you're staying there, or from the reserve's Algeria forest station; see p.302). Hikes can last up to a week, though you can also do shorter day or half-day hikes along a section of the trail.

There are a number of good **places to stay** along the quiet road, which terminates in the valley. *Klein Boschkkloof Chalets*, 9km from Clanwilliam (☎027 482 2441; **❶**), is a very reasonably priced collection of 250-year-old Cape Dutch farm buildings converted into guest cottages. The thatched chalets stand in the middle of fragrant citrus groves, and are finished to a high standard, with cooking gear, bed linen and towels. Breakfast and dinner can be provided by prior arrangement. Some 4km further down the valley, *Krakadouw* (☎027 482 2507; **❷**) has three fully equipped secluded cottages; it's also the starting point for the Krakadouw hiking trail. At the end of the road, 13km from Clanwilliam, *Karukareb* (☎027 482 1675, ⓦwww.karukareb.co.za; full board and activities **❽**) is a luxury bushcamp and guest lodge along the river. They're best known for their eco-safaris on **horseback**: there are trails for novice and experienced riders along the river and into the mountains, in one of the loveliest and wildest valleys in the Western Cape.

The R364 to Wuppertal

The untarred **R364** northeast from Clanwilliam winds through the northern Cederberg over the **Pakhuis Pass**, a drive worth taking for its lonely roadside scenery and inspiring views. A couple of places on the road, about 2km before the turn-off to the historic **Wuppertal** mission station, offer excellent access to ancient San **rock art**. If you keep straight along the R364 for another 100km or so beyond the Wuppertal turn-off, you will go though some remote and beautiful landscapes, renowned for their spectacular **wild flowers** in spring, to Soetwater, on the R27 between Nieuwoudtville and Calvinia.

Good-value **accommodation** is available at *Traveller's Rest* 36km northeast from Clanwilliam on the R364 (T & F 027 482 1824, W www.travellersrest .co.za; ❷). Situated on a farm, *Traveller's Rest* offers various self-catering cottages and the well-regarded *Khoisan Restaurant*, which serves South African farmstyle home cooking. The main attraction, apart from its Cederberg setting, is the four-kilometre **Sevilla bushman painting trail**, starting right beside the farm. The trail takes in nine separate rock-art sites, and provides an easy and varied introduction to rock art; if you're pushed for time, you can restrict yourself to the first six, which are the best. Enquire at the farmhouse or restaurant for **permits** (R20) and a leaflet and book covering the trail.

About a kilometre beyond *Traveller's Rest* is *Bushman's Kloof* (T 027 482 2627; bookings T 021 685 2598, W www.bushmanskloof.co.za; ❸), a **luxury lodge** set in a wilderness area. The focus here is on rock art, with over 125 recorded sites on the property; the rangers are trained in both wildlife guiding and rock-art interpretation. The rate includes all meals, game drives and guided rock-art trails.

Two kilometres beyond *Bushman's Kloof*, a turn-off from the road after it drops into the Doring River Valley takes you to **WUPPERTAL**. Set deep in the tunefully named Tra-tra Valley, the Moravian mission station is one of the oldest in the Western Cape and, with a tiny collection of thatched cottages, it remains one of the most untouched settlements in South Africa. The mission is famous for making *velskoene* (literally "hide shoes"), the suede footwear commonly known as *vellies* and part of Afrikaner national dress. You can see the shoes being made and, of course, buy them.

Oudrif

Oudrif (booking essential; T 027 482 2397, W www.oudrif.co.za; full board weekdays ❹, weekends ❺) is an exceptional retreat lodge in the Cederberg backcountry, 48km from Clanwilliam, some of it along rough dirt roads. It occupies inspiring countryside in the transitional zone between the foothills of the mountains and the dry Karoo, with redstone gorges and a wide valley incised by the Doring River. You can pick up early marine fossils on nearby hills, from the days when the area was flooded by an inland sea.

More recently, the area was once inhabited by San hunter-gatherers, who left their mark on a number of painted rock-faces in the area. Although there are wonderful walks through *fynbos* to **rock art**, this is as much a place to chill out – the only rule enforced by the co-owner and manager Bill Mitchell is that there are no rules. The multi-talented Mitchell is also a qualified chef and does all the cooking at this full-board establishment. The river has beaches for sunbathing and there are some fine spots for cooling off in its flow on hot days; as a former river-rafting guide, Mitchell can take you onto the water in a boat.

Accommodation is in five straw-bale houses, built using a traditional North American method in which bales are sandwiched between solid facings

– in this case concrete. The earth-red chalets have an uneven hewn quality that befits their isolation on the edge of the gorge that falls away to the Doring River. Each is stylishly equipped with retro furniture and has a double and a three-quarter bed; the power for lighting is provided by solar panels and showers are heated.

If you want some more sustained adrenaline, the best **whitewater rafting trips** in the Western Cape set out a short walk downstream from *Oudrif* from mid-July to mid-September, operated by River Rafters (℡021 712 5094, Ⓦwww.riverrafters.co.za; weekend trips R950 per person).

Travel details

Trains

The most useful trains in the Western Cape are the two Metrorail services connecting Cape Town with Stellenbosch and Paarl (all a 1hr journey). Outside peak morning and evening hours, trains are irregular, but run at approximately two-hour intervals.

Paarl to: Cape Town (18 daily; 1hr 15min).
Stellenbosch to: Cape Town (6–7 daily; 1hr 10min).

Buses

Principal routes are Cape Town–Port Elizabeth along the N2 coastal route, with an inland alternative along the Little Karoo mountain route; Cape Town–Johannesburg/Pretoria along the N1; Knysna–Johannesburg/Pretoria via Mossel Bay and the N12; and Cape Town–Windhoek via the N7.
Clanwilliam to: Cape Town (6 weekly; 3hr 45min); Citrusdal (6 weekly; 25min); Windhoek (Namibia; 6 weekly; 16hr 10min).
George to: Cape Town (6–7 daily; 6hr); Durban (1 daily; 18hr); Johannesburg (1–2 daily; 15hr); Knysna (6–7 daily; 1hr); Mossel Bay (6–7 daily; 45min); Oudtshoorn (3–4 daily; 1hr 30min); Plettenberg Bay (6–7 daily; 1hr 30min); Port Elizabeth (6–7 daily; 4hr 30min); Pretoria (1–2 daily; 16hr).
Knysna to: Cape Town (6–7 daily; 7hr); Durban (1 daily; 17hr); George (6–7 daily; 1hr); Johannesburg (1–2 daily; 16hr); Mossel Bay (6–7 daily; 1hr 15min); Oudtshoorn (1–2 daily; 2hr); Plettenberg Bay (6–7 daily; 1hr 30min); Port Elizabeth (6–7 daily; 4hr 30min); Pretoria (1–2 daily; 17hr).
Mossel Bay to: Cape Town (6–7 daily; 5hr 30min); Durban (1 daily; 18hr 30min); George (6–7 daily; 45min); Johannesburg (1–2 daily; 14hr); Knysna (6–7 daily; 1hr 15min); Oudtshoorn (1–2 daily; 1hr 15min); Plettenberg Bay (6–7 daily; 2hr 15min); Port Elizabeth (6–7 daily; 4hr 30min); Pretoria (1–2 daily; 15hr).
Oudtshoorn to: Cape Town (3 weekly; 6hr 15min); George (3–4 daily; 1hr 30min); Johannesburg (1–2 daily; 13hr 30min); Knysna (1–2 daily; 2hr); Mossel Bay (1–2 daily; 45min); Pretoria (1–2 daily; 14hr 30min).
Paarl to: Beaufort West (4–5 daily; 5hr); Cape Town (4 weekly; 1hr 30min); Durban (2 daily; 18hr); East London (daily; 11hr 30min); Johannesburg (4–5 daily; 14hr); Pretoria (4–5 daily; 15hr).
Plettenberg Bay to: Cape Town (6–7 daily; 7hr 30min); Durban (1 daily; 16hr); George (6–7 daily; 1hr 30min); Knysna (6–7 daily; 1hr 30min); Mossel Bay (6–7 daily; 2hr 15min); Port Elizabeth (6–7 daily; 2hr 30min).

Baz Bus

The Baz Bus travels once daily in both directions along the N2 between Cape Town and Port Elizabeth. You can be let off anywhere along the national road, and the bus pulls into all the major destinations along the way (with the notable exception of Storms River Mouth); see "Travel details" for chapter 1 on p.185.

Domestic flights

George to: Cape Town (2–4 daily; 1hr); Durban (daily; 2hr 15min); Johannesburg (2 daily; 1hr 30min); Port Elizabeth (3 weekly; 1hr).
Plettenberg Bay to: Johannesburg (1 daily; 2hr 15min).

3

The Northern Cape

CHAPTER 3 # Highlights

* **Kimberley Diamond Tour** Head 1km underground into a working mine, then visit the hand-diggings on the Vaal River, in the steps of Cecil Rhodes and the pioneer diamond hunters. See p.320

* **Augrabies Falls** Africa's second-biggest waterfall, where the Orange River thunders into an echoing gorge. See p.333

* **Kgalagadi Transfrontier Park** Discover lion, gemsbok and suricate among the parched red sand dunes of the Kalahari. See p.336

* **Pella Mission** One of the country's most improbable sights, a towering yellow cathedral in the middle of a tiny, dusty mission village. See p.336

* **Kuruman Mission** Built by pioneering missionaries Robert and Mary Moffat, the starting point for David Livingstone's exploration into the interior, and still a venerable and tranquil spot. See p.342

* **Namaqualand flowers** In August and September the veld puts on a superb natural floral display. See p.344

* **Richtersveld Transfrontier Park** South Africa's only mountain desert, a hot, dry and forbidding place which can only be explored by 4WD or by drifting down the Orange River in an inflatable canoe. See p.360

△ Richtersveld landscape

3

The Northern Cape

The vast **Northern Cape**, the largest and most dispersed of South Africa's provinces, is not an easy region to tackle as a visitor. From the lonely Atlantic coast to **Kimberley**, the provincial capital on its eastern border with the Free State, it covers over one-third of the nation's landmass, an area dominated by heat, aridity, empty spaces and huge travelling distances. The miracles of the desert are the main attraction – improbable swaths of flowers, diamonds dug from the dirt and wild animals roaming the dunes.

The most significant of these surprises is the **Orange** (or Oranje) **River**, flowing from the Lesotho Highlands to the Atlantic, where it marks South Africa's border with Namibia. The river, often with parched land stretching for hundreds of kilometres on either side, separates the **Kalahari** and **Great Karoo** – the two sparsely populated semi-desert ecosystems that fill the interior of the Northern Cape. It was by the Orange that **diamonds** were first discovered in the 1860s, although it was in the Vaal River's alluvial deposits and the nearby dry diggings around Kimberley that the story of diamonds would unfold in its most compelling detail.

Large **irrigation schemes** have created a stretch of incongruous green along the course of the Orange, principally around the isolated northern centre of **Upington**, the main town in the Kalahari region. A small but important town, Upington acts as a major gateway to the magnificent **Kgalagadi Transfrontier Park**, one of the finest game-viewing parks in South Africa, and the smaller **Augrabies Falls National Park**, where the Orange plunges dramatically into a large granite gorge.

In **Namaqualand**, on the western side of the province, the brief winter rains produce one of nature's truly glorious transformations, when in August and September the land is carpeted by a magnificent display of **wild flowers**. A similar display of blossoming succulents can be seen at the little-visited **Richtersveld Transfrontier Park**, a mountain desert tucked around a loop in the Orange River, either side of the Namibian border.

Despite these impressive natural attractions, the most commonly visited part of the Northern Cape is its southeastern corner, through which the two main routes between Johannesburg and Cape Town, the **N1** and the **N12**, pass. While the N12 provides a good opportunity to spend a day or so in Kimberley, neither route offers particularly inspiring scenery or sights, and so the southeast of the province isn't covered in this book. A less obvious option is to take the **N14** from Johannesburg through Upington, passing the atmospheric old mission station at **Kuruman**, and on to **Springbok** and the **N7** to Cape Town. This route is around 400km longer than the N1 or N12 and, while it doesn't

offer respite from long, empty landscapes, the sights on the way are more interesting; it also puts the Augrabies, Kgalagadi and Richtersveld national parks within striking distance.

Getting around by **public transport** can be a pain. While the main towns of Kimberley, Springbok and Upington lie on Intercape's bus routes (with connections to Windhoek in Namibia), many services arrive and depart at night and thus miss the scenery. Minibus taxis cover most destinations several times a day during the week, but are much reduced or nonexistent at weekends. Taxis don't serve the national parks (take an organized tour instead). As ever, early starts (6–7am) are best. Details of the most useful routes are given in the text.

Some history

The history of the Northern Cape area is intimately linked to the **San**, South Africa's first people whose hunter-gatherer lifestyle and remarkable adaptations to desert life exert a powerful fascination. Although no genuine vestiges of the San way of life can be found in South Africa (only tiny pockets remain in the Namibian and Botswanan sections of the Kalahari desert), their heritage is most visible in the countless examples of **rock art** across the province, and to a lesser extent in their ancient legends and place names. The movement of Africans from the north and east, and Europeans from the southwest, drove the San from their hunting grounds and eventually to extinction; yet for both sets of newcomers, the semi-desert of the Karoo and the Kalahari at first appeared to offer little more than hopelessness and heartbreaking horizons. What it did provide – wealth under the dusty ground – the Europeans pursued without restraint, beginning in 1685 with an expedition into Namaqualand to mine for copper, led by **Governor Simon van der Stel** soon after the Dutch first established their settlement in the Cape. The other Europeans who made an early impression on the province were **trekboers**, Dutch burghers freed from the employment of the Dutch East India Company in the Cape who wanted to find new lands to farm away from the authoritarian company rule, and **missionaries**, who established a framework of settlement and communication used by all who came after.

Within a few years of the discovery of **diamonds** in the area, a settlement of unprecedented size had grown up around Kimberley. The town soon boasted more trappings of civilization than most of the southern hemisphere, with public libraries, electric streetlights and tramways, as well as South Africa's first urban "location" for Africans and coloureds. The British authorities in the Cape were quick to annexe the new diamond fields – a move which didn't endear them to either the Orange Free State or the mainly coloured **Griqua**

Diamonds are forever

Diamonds originate as carbon particles in the earth's mantle, which are subjected to such high pressure and temperature that they crystallize to form diamonds. Millions of years ago the molten rock, or magma, in the mantle burst through weak points in the earth's crust as volcanoes, and it is in the pipe of cooled magma – called **kimberlite**, after Kimberley – that diamonds are found. Finding kimberlite, however, isn't necessarily a licence to print money – in every one hundred tonnes there will be about twenty carats (4g) of diamonds.

The word "carat" derives from the carob bean – dried beans were used as a measure of weight. (Carat has a different meaning in the context of gold, where it is a measure of purity.) De Beers estimates that fifty million pieces of diamond jewellery are bought each year, which represents a lot of marriage proposals.

people (see box on p.579), who both claimed this ill-defined region. It was no surprise, therefore, that at the outbreak of the **Anglo–Boer War** in 1899, rich and strategic Kimberley was one of the first towns besieged by the Boer armies, and many reminders of the war can still be seen in the area. In some ways, the province today is little changed. Kimberley is still the largest town, farming is tempered by the lack of water, wealth is still gathered greedily from the ground and anyone travelling into the interior is regarded as adventurous.

Kimberley and around

The **N12** highway, running from Johannesburg through **Kimberley** and then down to meet the N1 link to Cape Town, is the main reason most visitors find themselves in this area. Although the term might suggest a wonderland of romance and riches, the surrounds of Kimberley and its **Diamond Fields** are mostly dry and uninspiring, and the city will never again know the importance and glamour it had for two heady decades at the end of the nineteenth century.

Despite being the provincial capital, Kimberley does not really act as a gateway to the Northern Cape – it's far nearer to Bloemfontein and the Free State. For those passing through, however, there is enough in the area to justify spending a day or two here, especially if you're interested in the complex history of South Africa. The biggest draw is Kimberley itself, but trips to the nearby **Anglo–Boer War battlefields** and the **alluvial diamond diggings** around the Vaal River are well worth the effort.

Kimberley

Despite being a provincial capital and the centre of production of one of the world's most valuable materials, **KIMBERLEY** itself is neither large nor glamorous. During the diamond rush, it was the fastest-growing city in the southern hemisphere and **Cecil Rhodes** held in his grip not only the fabulously wealthy diamond industry, but the heart and mind of the British Empire – yet status and sophistication have been draining from Kimberley ever since. Even the all-controlling **De Beers Group** (sometimes called the "grandfather" of Kimberley for the number of people it directly and indirectly employs) is largely controlled from Johannesburg, and the city lives in the chilly shadow of the day when the diamonds finally dry up.

However, Kimberley's legacy gives it an historic flavour few other cities in South Africa can match. It's worth spending a few hours seeking out some of the many old buildings, not forgetting to peer into the depths of the **Big Hole**, the remarkable, hand-dug chasm taking up almost as much land area as the city's central business district (CBD). With a little more time, an **underground tour** of a working diamond mine, or a visit to the diamond miners who make a living on the Vaal River's alluvial diamond diggings, are fascinating opportunities to experience some of the grit and excitement which made the city famous.

A short history of the Diamond Fields

The area now known as the Diamond Fields was once unpromising farmland, marked by occasional *koppies* inhabited by pioneer farmers and the Griquas, an independent people of mixed race (see box on p.579). In 1866 this changed forever, when a 15-year-old boy noticed a shiny white pebble on the banks of the Orange River near Hopetown, about 120km southwest of Kimberley. Just as word of that discovery was spreading, another Hopetown resident, Schalk van Niekerk, acquired from a Griqua shepherd a massive 83.5-carat diamond. These two stones became known, respectively, as "Eureka" and "The Star of South Africa"; the latter was described at the time – with some justification – by the British Colonial Secretary as the "rock on which the future success of South Africa will be built". Certainly in the short term, the discoveries provoked wild optimism: thousands of prospectors made the gruelling trek across the Karoo to sift through the alluvial deposits along the banks of the Orange and Vaal rivers, and by 1873 there were an estimated fifty thousand people living in the area.

Although plenty of diamonds were found in the rivers, prospectors also began scratching around in the dry land between them, encouraged by tales of diamonds found in farmhouse bricks made from local earth. Two of the most promising "dry diggings" were on a farm owned by two brothers, Johannes Nicolas and Diederick Arnoldus de Beer. In 1871 the brothers sold the farm, which they had bought a few years previously for £50, to prospectors for the sum of £6300. The two sites subsequently became the Kimberley Mine, or **Big Hole**, and the **De Beers Mine**, situated on either side of the centre of Kimberley. The Big Hole was the focus of the most frenetic mining activity of the early years, and the shantytown that grew up around it, New Rush, was the origin of the present city.

Kimberley in those days was a heady, rugged place to live, with little authority or structure, but with prizes rich enough to attract bold men with big ideas. Of these, two very different, if equally ambitious, men rose to prominence in the new settlement. **Barney Barnato**, a flamboyant Cockney, established his power base at the Kimberley Mine, while **Cecil Rhodes** (see p.319), a parson's son who had come out to join his brother in South Africa to improve his health, gradually took control of the De Beers Mine. The power struggle between the two men was intense, culminating in the formation in 1888 of the De Beers Consolidated Mines Limited, an agreement involving the transfer from Rhodes to Barnato of over £5 million, an astronomical sum in those days. This consolidation laid the foundation for De Beers' monopoly, still intact, of the diamond industry in South Africa.

The rise of the gold fields on the Witwatersrand soon overshadowed Kimberley's importance, however. Although three of the five large mines in the area still produce diamonds, and the alluvial claims along the Vaal are still worked, the firm hand of De Beers has stifled the enterprise which initially gave the area its character.

Arrival, information and city transport

Kimberley's **airport** lies 7km to the west along the N8 Upington road. There's no regular transport into town, so phone for a cab (see p.316). **Intercity buses** stop outside the tourist office, which is handy when arriving on overnight Greyhound and Translux services from Cape Town, but to be avoided on other routes, which arrive at night when the place is deserted. You can arrange for a hotel to pick you up, or ask to be dropped off at one of the hotels along the N12 (Bishops Avenue) just south of the centre, or alight at the Ultra City service station 6km north of town, which is a much safer place to call a cab. The **train station** is just off Quinn Street on the northeastern edge of town. Note that the daily Cape Town train pulls in around 3.30am, while those from Johannesburg arrive around 9pm and 4am (p.316).

KIMBERLEY

ACCOMMODATION

Big Hole Caravan Park	A
Bishop's Lodge	K
Carrington Lodge	M
Cecil John Rhodes Guest House	D
Edgerton House	F
Estate Private Hotel	E
Formula 1	L
Gum Tree Lodge	C
Halfway House Pub	H
Holiday Inn	I
Garden Court	B
Milner House	J
Stay-a-day	G
Sundowner Lodge	G

RESTAURANTS, CAFÉS, BARS & CLUBS

Barnato's	9
Danskraal	3
George & Dragon	7
Halfway House Pub	H
Heaven's Delight	5
Mario's	6
Star of the West	1
Tasty Eats	2
Tiffany's	4
Umberto's	8

Moving on from Kimberley

South African Airlink, based at the airport (☎053 838 3337), operate **flights** to Johannesburg and Cape Town. **Trains** (station ☎053 838 2631) run daily to Cape Town, Mafikeng, Pretoria and to Johannesburg via Klerksdorp and Potchefstroom. There's also a weekly service to Durban via Bloemfontein (Tues 12.25pm), and a Bloemfontein service (Mon, Thurs & Sat 4.50am).

Information and tickets for most **intercity buses** are available at the Tickets for Africa bureau inside the Diamantveld Visitor Centre (Mon–Fri 8am–4.30pm, Sat 8–11.30am; ☎053 832 6040); most buses depart from outside or from the Shell garage nearly opposite. Seats on Big Sky, which runs some of the buses to Bloemfontein and Upington, must be reserved at the office at 5 Kelvin Street (☎053 832 2006–7).

Minibus taxis operate from Pniel Road (the northern extension of Bultfontein Road), 1500m from the tourist office. To be sure of a ride in daylight, arrive at 6.30am (7am winter); most destinations also have early afternoon departures, but on these you risk being dropped off at night. Except to Barkly West, fares are paid at an office on Pniel Road beside the long-distance rank.

Kimberley's helpful tourist office, the **Diamantveld Visitor Centre**, is at 121 Bultfontein Road (Mon–Fri 8am–5pm, Sat 8am–noon; ☎053 832 7298, ⒺＥ tourism@kbymun.org.za). The staff can provide city plans, lists of places to stay, detailed driving itineraries in the province, information on local tours (see box on pp.320–321) and an excellent listings booklet. For more information about the province, particularly wildlife parks and reserves, visit the **Northern Cape Tourism Authority** on Dalham Road, a few hundred metres east of the tourist office (☎053 832 2656, Ⓦwww.northerncape.org.za).

There are a couple of reliable **metered-taxi** outfits: AA Taxis (☎053 861 4015 or 083 283 0558) and Rikki's (☎053 842 1764 or 083 342 2553).

Accommodation

The bulk of the town's hotels, guesthouses and B&Bs lie in the southern suburbs, most within a kilometre or two of the centre. The most atmospheric places – occupying historic buildings – are clustered in and around the upmarket **Belgravia** suburb, close to the museum. It's even possible to stay in Galeshewe township (see p.321). Most hotels have safe parking.

Hotels and guesthouses

Bishop's Lodge 9 Bishops Ave ☎053 831 7876, Ⓦwww.bishopslodge.co.za. Close to the visitor centre, this quiet modern affair offers spotless twin rooms and keenly priced self-catering apartments, plus a suite with wheelchair access. There's a swimming pool, but no meals. ❷

Carrington Lodge 60 Carrington Rd, corner with Oliver Rd ☎053 831 6448, Ⓦwww.carringtonlodge .co.za. A friendly guesthouse on the edge of Belgravia, with a pool and pleasant garden with braai area. Two other perfectly reasonable and marginally cheaper guesthouses are on the same street: *Carrington B&B* at no. 55, and *Carrington Guest House* at no. 32. ❷

Cecil John Rhodes Guest House 138 Du Toitspan Rd ☎053 830 2500, Ⓦwww .ceciljohnrhodes.co.za. The most central of the historic guesthouses, built in 1895, with seven airy and elegantly furnished rooms with all mod cons, and a shady tea garden (dinner on request) facing the road. ❸

Edgerton House 5 Egerton Rd ☎053 831 1150, Ⓔedgerton@kimberley.co.za. An elegant Belgravia option in an attractive black-and-white Edwardian house, now a National Monument, kitted out with crystal chandeliers and gold-plated bathroom fittings. There are eleven rooms, plus a pool and a tea room; it also offers expensive dinners. ❹

Estate Private Hotel 7 Lodge Rd ☎053 832 2668, Ⓦwww.theestate.co.za. Seven wheelchair-friendly rooms with all mod cons in the Oppenheimers' former Belgravia home, open to visitors by day (see p.322). There's also a pool, tea garden and restaurant. Good value. ❸

Formula 1 Memorial Dr (N12), 1500m south of the tourist office ☎053 831 2552, ⓦwww.hotelformula1 .co.za. The rooms are the chain's usual diminutive prefab units, each with a double bed, bunk and TV. Prices are per room, with keen rates for doubles and triples. Breakfast is extra. It's a safe place to be dropped at if you're arriving by bus at night. There's a *Choctaw Spur Steakhouse* adjacent. ❷

Halfway House Pub Du Toitspan/Egerton Rd ☎053 831 6324, ⓔhalfwayhouse@intekom.co.za. Large and airy, if basic, en-suite rooms around a paved beer garden behind the historic boozer, handy for crashing after sampling the pub's nocturnal delights. ❶

Holiday Inn Garden Court 120 Du Toitspan Rd ☎053 833 1751, ⓦwww.southernsun.com. The town's largest hotel has bright, well-appointed rooms over six floors, including one wheelchair-friendly room. ❸

Milner House 31 Milner St ☎053 831 6405, ⓦwww.milnerhouse.co.za. Another Belgravia guesthouse, this one more down-to-earth than the others, with six comfortable rooms and a swimming pool. ❷

Sundowner Lodge 1 Bishops Ave ☎053 831 1145, ⓔsundowner@telkomsa.net. Within shouting distance of the tourist office, this friendly family-run place has a vaguely colonial feeling (perhaps it's the boggle-eyed wildlife trophies adorning the walls), and offers fourteen huge rooms in rows of chalets. Book ahead. Breakfast included. ❷

Campsites and budget lodging

Big Hole Caravan Park West Circular Rd ☎053 830 6322. The only central campsite, located among the old mine heaps over the road from Big Hole. Lush, neat and relatively quiet, with a pool, although the shade from the trees isn't generous. The office is open daily 6am–8pm.

Gum Tree Lodge Boshof Rd (R64) ☎053 832 8577, ⓔlawrie@global.co.za. Kimberley's only backpackers' lodge, with 150 beds, is inconveniently located 5km east of town, but is pleasantly shady and has a swimming pool, a bar, kitchen and fun "jungle playground" for kids. Dorms and more comfortable self-catering units are available. There's an inexpensive restaurant next door. ❶

Stay-a-day 72 Lawson St ☎053 832 7239. Basic dorms, stark doubles, some wheelchair accessible, and a couple of self-catering flats. Run as a revenue earner by a Dutch Reformed Church orphanage, it's 1km south of the tourist office in the residential Labram district. Dorms ❶, rooms ❷

The City

Many of Kimberley's main sights lie on or near **Du Toitspan Road**, which slices diagonally across the city centre and becomes one of the main arteries out of town to the southeast. The must-see **Big Hole** lies just west of the centre, while the more open central business district (CBD) lies to the south of Lennox Road. The fact that Big Hole is underground doesn't make orientation immediately easy; a useful landmark is the stern-looking skyscraper, **Harry Oppenheimer House** (often referred to as HOH), near the tourist office.

The Big Hole: Kimberley Mine Museum

Although the **Big Hole**, just west of the city centre, is neither the only nor even the biggest hole in Kimberley, it remains the city's principal attraction. The only official way to see it is from inside the **Kimberley Mine Museum** (daily 8am–6pm; R20), spread out along the western side of the hole along West Circular Road. You can take a delightfully rickety, open-sided **tram** there from the City Hall (hourly 9.15am–4.15pm, returning on the hour 9am–4pm; R7 one-way).

The museum has two viewing platforms, from which you can peer down into nothingness, where once mountains were moved in the quest for wealth. On the opposite side of the crater, the now diminutive outline of the city is almost swallowed up by the size and silence of the hollow below. There's also a "museum village", actually a large collection of **historic buildings**, many originating from the days of Rhodes and Barnato; they were moved here from the city centre when development and demolition threatened. With old shops, churches, a pub,

Kimberley's Big Hole

Where there is now a gaping 500-metre-wide cavity, there was once a small hill on a typically dry, Northern Cape farm, which belonged to the brothers Diederick Arnoldus and Johannes Nicolas de Beer. In the early 1870s, with diamonds known to be in the area, various work parties scratched around in the hope of a lucky find. One such group, known as the Red Cap Party, were working at the base of **Colesberg koppie** in July 1871. The story goes that they sent one of their cooks to the top of the hill as a punishment for being drunk, telling him, with a laugh and a clip round the ear, not to return until he'd found a diamond. The unnamed servant duly came back with a peace offering, and within two years there were over fifty thousand people in the area frantically turning Colesberg *koppie* inside out.

In its heyday, tens of thousands of miners swarmed over the mine to work their ten-square-metre claim, and a network of ropes and pipes crisscrossed the surface; each day saw lives lost and fortunes either discovered or squandered. Once the mining could go no further from the surface, a shaft was dug to allow further excavations beneath it to a depth of over 800m. Incredibly, the hole was dug to a depth of 240m entirely by pick and shovel, and remains one of the largest manmade excavations in the world. By 1914, when De Beers closed the mine, some 22.6 million tonnes of earth had been removed, yielding over 13.6 million carats (2722kg) of diamonds.

banks and sundry other period institutions, including Barney Barnato's Boxing Academy and a skittle alley, there's enough here to create a fairly complete settlement, and most of the fixtures, fittings and artefacts are genuine. One of the more engaging features is an area where you can buy a bucket of alluvial river diggings and sift through it on old sorting tables, in the hope of finding one of the mock diamonds planted among the gravel. Your chances of striking lucky are about one in five – much better odds than the original miners faced.

Market Square and around

At the heart of the city centre is **Market Square**, dominated by the white, Corinthian-style **City Hall**. During the early diamond days, the square was the hub of buying and selling. It was also the scene of two occasions significant in South Africa's history: the public crushing of gold-bearing rock from the Witwatersrand that persuaded Rhodes, Barnato and others to further their investments in gold-mining; and the departure in 1890 of the Pioneer Column, which effectively established "white" Rhodesia by pursuing Rhodes' expansionist claims to the territory north of the Limpopo. Around the square, the sense of movement and commerce is perpetuated by a large taxi rank and an assortment of scruffy but colourful stalls and traders.

One block west of Market Square along the tram line, at 36 Stockdale Street, lies the head office of **De Beers**, a dignified but unremarkable old building rather swallowed up by the city around it. You can read the brass plates by the door, but the building is not open to the public.

The Kimberley Club and the Africana Library

Not far southwest of Market Square, at 70–72 Du Toitspan Road, is the two-storey **Kimberley Club**, founded in 1881 by the new settlement's movers and shakers. The club was modelled on London's gentlemen's clubs, but its colourful, enterprising members made the place dynamic rather than stuffy. It was claimed that there were more millionaires to the square foot here than any other place in the world, and acceptance within the club was allegedly a significant carrot in Rhodes' wooing of Barnato in 1888 – together with a cheque for £5 million.

The present building – the third on the site – was completed in 1896 and would have been known by Rhodes, whose presence dominates even today, with countless portraits, busts and other memorabilia of the man in all parts of the building. As well as leather armchairs in the smoking lounge and marble in the hallway, there are plenty of fine antiques and a few quirky pieces, such as a weighing chair presented to the club by Lord Randolph Churchill, Winston Churchill's father. It's possible to look around or go for a drink in the **bar**, though you'll get a much less chilly welcome if you introduce yourself at the reception and respect the club's rules – which include no jeans or T-shirts, and no women in the bar.

Across the road is the small but engrossing **Africana Library** (Mon–Fri 8am–12.45pm & 1.30–4.30pm), specializing in historical material relevant to Kimberley and the Northern Cape. Opened in 1887, it retains many original features, and one of the librarians will show you around if you ask nicely. The excellent Kimberley Ghost Tour (see p.320) visits the library; although you don't enter the building, you'll hear about the restless spirit of its first librarian, whose presence explains why books and files keep getting mysteriously muddled.

The CBD

At the junction of Du Toitspan and Lennox roads stands a statue of **Cecil Rhodes**. He is portrayed astride a horse, and the tributes around the plinth are rich with the swagger common to most Rhodes memorials. Across the road in the grounds of the red-brick, Neo-Gothic **St Cyprian's Cathedral**, and a little more humble in tone, stands a statue depicting **Sister Henrietta Stockdale**, a pioneer of nursing in South Africa.

Moving south of Lennox into the CBD area, you'll come to the **Oppenheimer Memorial Gardens**, which contain a bust of mining magnate Sir Ernest Oppenheimer and the **Diggers Fountain**; the latter depicts five miners holding aloft a massive sieve, and looks particularly impressive when floodlit after dusk. The gardens host an eclectic flea market on the last Saturday of the month. The tall building overlooking the gardens is **Harry Oppenheimer**

Cecil John Rhodes

When **Cecil Rhodes** first arrived in the Kimberley Diamond Fields he was a sickly 18-year-old, sent out to join his brother for the sake of his health. Soon making money buying up claims, he returned to Britain to attend Oxford University, where his illnesses returned and he was given six months to live. He came back out to South Africa, where he was able to improve both his health and his business standing, allowing him to return to Oxford and graduate in 1881, by which time he had already founded the **De Beers Mining Company** and been elected an MP in the Cape Parliament.

Within a decade, Rhodes controlled ninety percent of the world's diamond production and was champing at the bit to expand his mining interests north into Africa, with the British Empire in tow. With much cajoling, bullying, brinkmanship and obfuscation in his dealing with imperial governments and African chiefs alike, Rhodes brought the regions north of the Limpopo under the control of his South African Company. This territory – now Zimbabwe and Zambia – became known as Rhodesia in 1895, the same year as a Rhodes-backed invasion of the Transvaal Republic, the Jameson Raid, failed humiliatingly. Rhodes was forced to resign as prime minister of the Cape Colony, a post he had assumed in 1890 at the age of 37, while the Boers and the British slid towards war. He spent the first part of the war in besieged Kimberley, trying to organize the defences and bickering publicly with the British commander. A year after the end of the war, aged only 49 and unmarried, Rhodes died at Muizenberg near Cape Town; he was buried in the Matopos Hills near Bulawayo in Zimbabwe.

House (HOH), the offices of De Beers' DTC (Diamond Trading Company; not open to the public), on the upper floors of which all of the company's South African-mined diamonds are assessed for caratage, colour, clarity and shape. To allow this to take place in the best natural light, the building faces south, with special windows to eliminate glare; there are no windows on the other faces other than small ones along the stairwell.

On the opposite side of the gardens to HOH, in the Civic Centre, lies an unexpected gem, the **William Humphreys Art Gallery** (Mon–Sat 10am–5pm, Sun & holidays 2–5pm; R2), South Africa's only Grade One art gallery. Although dominated by European Old Masters when it opened in 1952, the collection has always moved with the times and now houses an impressively well-balanced representation of South African art, with traditional and contemporary work, including some excellent modern sculpture. The gallery was one of the first places in the world to display San **rock paintings** as works of art rather than museum pieces. At the back of the gallery is a very pleasant **tea room**, the *Palette*, which serves breakfasts, light lunches and snacks on a terrace beside a small garden.

On Angel Street, across from the City Civic Complex, stands **Sol Plaatje House** (Mon–Fri 8am–1pm & 2–4pm; R2), a two-room museum in the

---

Kimberley tours

Kimberley offers a series of informative and entertaining local tours. The Diamantveld Visitor Centre maintains a list of accredited guides; alternatively, contact Diamond Tours Unlimited (℡053 861 4983, ⓦwww.diamondtours.co.za) or In-Roads Tours (℡084 689 7251 or 083 398 8176), both of which are recommended. Tours follow more or less predefined routes, although both guides and tour companies are flexible. For a radical view of the Big Hole, contact Andrew Conroy (℡053 591 0364) for information about **microlight flights**.

De Beers' diamond mines

If you join an **underground tour** of one of De Beers' working diamond mines – **Bultfontein** and **Du Toitspan**, both on the southeastern outskirts of the city along Molyneaux Road – instead of being whisked around a sanitized visitor centre, you get right to the heart of the mine, amid the noise of turbines and engines, the dust, the mud, the heat and thick air. After an introductory video and safety talk, visitors are kitted out with overalls, hard hats, torches and emergency oxygen packs – the same gear as the miners wear – and then taken down by the shaft lift to a depth of 825m. Once down, you'll be shown around caves where kimberlite (see p.312) is loosened by explosions, dragged out into trolleys, crushed and then taken to the surface for cleaning and sifting. In the event you spot a diamond while underground, De Beers will give you twenty percent of its value, more (they claim) than it would fetch on the black market. Don't get too excited, though; mostly all you'll see is grey clay dirt.

Tours (Mon, Tues, Thurs & Fri 8am; R80) last three and a half hours, and you have to book beforehand on ℡053 842 1321. They're not a good idea for the timid or claustrophobic, and De Beers won't allow anyone under the age of 16 underground. Ninety-minute **surface tours** of the same mines are also available (same days at 9am & 11am; R15).

Ghost tours

As the light fades in early evening and the city centre empties, the many restless spirits produced by over a century of surreptitious diamond wheeling and dealing begin to make their presence felt. If you're brave enough to hear the stories, or simply like the idea of poking around some of Kimberley's most interesting former home of the author and activist. Born near Barkly West, Plaatje was the first black South African to publish a novel in English; he's also known for the diary he kept during the siege of Mafikeng in the Anglo–Boer War, describing a very different experience to that popularized by British hero Sir Robert Baden-Powell (see p.671). Plaatje returned to Kimberley in 1910, editing newspapers and helping to establish the South African Native National Congress, a forerunner of the ANC. He died in this house in 1932.

Just south of the CBD, in the middle of a roundabout where Dalham Road and Memorial Drive meet, is the **Honoured Dead Memorial**, a monument to the victims of the Kimberley siege during the Anglo–Boer War, and also the tomb of 27 British soldiers. Beside is the British gun known as **Long Cecil**, used in the siege; it was built in the De Beers' workshops to respond to the Boers' Long Tom cannon.

Belgravia

About 1km southeast of the CBD, along Du Toitspan Road, lies **Belgravia**, the residential suburb where most of Kimberley's wealthy families lived. A stroll around these streets is a good way to get a feel for the more refined side of

buildings after hours, join a **Ghost Tour** (R70) in the company of Dr Le Sueur, the city's resident ghost expert, who will show you scenes of strange encounters such as the Africana Library (p.319), the Regimental headquarters and the spooky Rudd House in Belgravia. Tours begin just before sunset at the Honoured Dead Memorial, and last three to four hours.

Township tours
Kimberley was the first settlement in South Africa to establish "locations" on its fringes to house the African and coloured labourers working in the mines. A tour of **Galeshewe**, named after a rebellious nineteenth-century chief, offers an insight into a typical modern South African township with its mix of shacks, simple government houses and the more ostentatious homes of locals-made-good. In contrast to townships attached to places like Jo'burg and Cape Town, Galeshewe has a very unintimidating atmosphere, allowing an easy introduction to township life, including *spaza* shops, African restaurants, *shebeens* and music. The tour also takes in some alternative historic sights – including the grave of Sol Plaatje and the house where Robert Sobukwe (see box on p.406), founder of the Pan-African Congress, lived under house arrest after his release from Robben Island in 1969. Most tours finish with the post-apartheid **Northern Cape Provincial Legislature** complex – an extraordinary construction combining elements of traditional African design (the conical tower is a delight) with silver polygonal slabs; it occupies part of the "buffer strip" that used to separate black and white communities. Apart from the tour operators mentioned above, also recommended are Pulane Tours (℡053 872 1180, ℻053 832 7211), who manage a couple of guesthouses in the township (❶).

Tours in the Kimberley area
Organized tours of the area around Kimberley include visits to the controlled area on the banks of the Vaal River where **alluvial diamond digging** takes place (see p.325); **Kamfersdam**, a reservoir north along the N12 with 180 bird species to its name, including a resident flock of several thousand flamingoes; the Anglo-Boer War battlefield at **Magersfontein** (p.325); and a series of **archeological sites**, including San rock engravings at Wildebeest Kuil (p.324).

the diamond age. The focus of the area is at the junction of Du Toitspan and Egerton roads, where you'll find the historic **Halfway House Pub**. Originally located on the site now occupied by the McGregor Museum, it was shifted in 1897 when the museum was built. The pub takes its name from its location halfway between the De Beers and Bultfontein mines, and gained fame as a drive-in (or, in those days, ride-in) pub, a custom started by Cecil Rhodes who like to tipple while in the saddle. Nowadays you blow your horn to attract the bartender. Next door is **Edgerton House** (Mon–Sat 10am–4pm), built in 1901 and now an upmarket guesthouse, complete with tea room in its courtyard.

Across the road, the fabulous **McGregor Museum** (Mon–Sat 9am–5pm, Sun 2–5pm, holidays 10am–5pm; R10; ⓦwww.museumsnc.co.za), named after an early mayor of Kimberley, is housed in a magnificent Victorian mansion. Built in 1897 as a sanatorium, but never used as one, it saw action during the 1899 siege of Kimberley when it served as the headquarters of Cecil Rhodes, and was later a hotel and a convent school. The museum is highly respected in South Africa for its dedicated conservation work and research throughout the Northern Cape, with satellite museums at places such as Magersfontein (see p.325) and Wonderwerk Cave (see p.344). The highlight here is the extensive and imaginative **Ancestors Display**, which draws on archeological evidence to piece together an absorbing and – unusual still in South Africa – well-balanced exhibition on the various ancestral roots of today's inhabitants of the Northern Cape, going right back to evidence of the earliest hominids millions of years ago. There's also an evocative section on the siege of Kimberley, including two rooms with period furniture where Rhodes stayed during the siege, and a sensitive display tracing the implementation of apartheid and subsequent resistance to it.

Adjacent to the museum is the **Duggan-Cronin Gallery** (Mon–Fri 9am–5pm, Sat 9am–1pm & 2–5pm, Sun 2–5pm, holidays 10am–5pm; donation expected), which includes over 8000 endearingly unsophisticated photographs portraying the lifestyles of the indigenous people of South Africa between the two world wars. They were taken by Alfred Duggan-Cronin, a nightwatchman for De Beers.

Still in Belgravia, you can visit a trio of restored houses, all on Lodge Road: **Rudd House** (also called "The Bungalow") at no. 5 was the mansion of mining magnate and partner of Rhodes, Charles Dunnell Rudd; at no. 10, **Dunluce** is an elegant late-Victorian home in Hollywood's favoured "haunted house" style. To see inside either house, make arrangements with the museum (weekdays only; R15). Easier to visit is the Edwardian **estate** at #7, birthplace of Harry Oppenheimer and the family's last Kimberley home before they moved to Johannesburg in 1915. It's now a hotel, best visited at lunchtime for its tea garden and restaurant. These and many other historic homes and points of interest are included in the **Belgravia Historical Walk**, which you can do self-guided or accompanied; details from the tourist office.

Eating, drinking and nightlife

Beyond the familiar range of franchised steakhouses, including *Mohawk Spur Steakhouse* at the *Holiday Inn* on Du Toitspan Road, Kimberley offers a reasonable selection of locally run, mid-priced **restaurants**, many with good **wine** lists, too. Apart from a handful of historic **pubs**, which can be entertaining for their atmosphere and clientele (use a cab at night), there's little in the way of **nightlife**. For live music, ask at the tourist office for *Magambo's* and *Destiny*, two township nightclubs that host old time jazz bands. Those with bursting wallets can relieve themselves at *Flamingo Casino* (℡053 830 2600) on Transvaal Road (the N12), 6km north of town.

Restaurants, cafés, bars and clubs

Barnato's 6 Dalham Rd, close to the tourist office. The poshest restaurant in town, friendly and refined without being snobbish, and serving decent French- and Cape-inspired nosh (mainly meat and fish), washed down with excellent wine. The works might put you back R100–200. Closed Sat lunch.

Danskraal Old De Beers Rd. A popular dance hall for almost a century, particularly on Friday nights. Saturdays tend to be taken over by the satellite TV sports crowd, while Wednesdays may feature live Afrikaans rock.

George & Dragon Du Toitspan Rd. Popular English theme pub and sports bar, serving exceptionally good grub, including old favourites like cottage pie, and fancier stuff like snails and mussels (and some vegetarian dishes). Prices are reasonable and portions huge. Also features the the town's best selection of draught beers.

Halfway House Pub Corner of Du Toitspan and Egerton roads. Cecil Rhodes' old refreshment stop, known as "the Half" and still a popular, unpretentious local. Pretty quiet by day, it's popular on Wed, Fri and Sat nights, and the Monday karaoke gets the place heaving. There are more tables in a paved courtyard out the back, and two pool tables. Also serves cheap and decent British pub lunches with a nicely old-fashioned twist. Closed Sun.

Heaven's Delight *Victoria Guest Lodge*, 16 West Circular Rd. Opposite the Big Hole, this handy café does good snacks, a huge and aptly named "Big Hole breakfast" (R35), and gorgeous homemade desserts, including cinnamon pancakes. Licensed. Closed Sun.

Mario's 159 Du Toitspan Rd. Bright and cheery Italian place that's one of the most popular restaurants in town, with friendly staff and a big menu, including light lunches and a good if expensive wine list. Closed Sat lunch and all day Sun.

Star of the West West Circular Rd, corner with North Circular Rd. Kimberley's oldest pub still serves beer to diggers after the diamond markets on Saturdays, and does decent cheap pub meals throughout the day, too. Despite the tourist trade, it remains a defiantly local dive, complete with characterful regulars propping up the bar. Tends to host live bands on Friday or Saturday nights. Daily from 9am to way past your bedtime.

Tasty Eats Market Square, facing the tram terminus. No frills halal meals, including dirt cheap curries.

Tiffany's *The Savoy* hotel, 15 De Beers Rd. Formerly Kimberley's foremost dining experience, this formal place lacks windows and is ageing fast, though the food – with plenty of vegetarian dishes loosely based on Chinese – is still good and affordable.

Umberto's Du Toitspan Rd, next to *Halfway House Pub*. A regular Italian restaurant serving decent pizza and pasta, and with a pleasant roof terrace. Closed Sun.

Listings

Banks Quickest for changing money is the foreign exchange counter at Absa, corner of Bultfontein Rd and Long St. Standard has branches on Chapel St and Old Main Rd.

Bookshops The Bookbin, bottom of Jones St, has a huge selection of secondhand novels. The stationers at Game Shopping Centre sells new titles.

Car rental All the agencies are based at the airport: Avis ℡053 851 1082–3; Budget ℡053 851 1182; Hertz ℡053 830 2200 or 086 160 0136; Imperial ℡053 851 1131; and Tempest 053 851 1516.

Cinema Four screens at the cinema in the Pick 'n Pay Centre.

Couriers DHL is at 41 De Beers St, near Quinn St ℡053 832 3516.

Emergencies Call ℡053 831 1954 for an ambulance; for other emergency services, see p.89. The tourist office operates a 24hr emergency and help line (℡053 861 1481 or 053 861 1483).

Hospitals and doctors Best-equipped is the 24hr Medi-Clinic, 177 Du Toitspan Rd (℡053 838 1111 or 053 831 1453). There are good doctors at Medicross (℡053 830 4200), corner of Long St and Stone St.

Internet access Small World Net Café, 42 Sidney St, near the tourist office opposite the library (Mon–Fri 8.30am–6pm, Sat 9am–2pm).

Pharmacies Piet Muller Pharmacy, 52 Market Square ℡053 831 1787 (daily to 9pm); Medpack, 142 Du Toitspan Rd ℡053 831 1737.

Post The post office is a little east of Market Square.

Shopping For diamond jewellery, try Jewel Box, 18 West Circular Rd next to *Victorian Guest Lodge*, or any of the jewellers along Jones St. The best place for arts and crafts is Africa Now, 37–39 Du Toitspan Rd, close to Jones St. There are gift shops at Big Hole, at the McGregor Museum, and antiques at *Victorian Guest Lodge*.

Swimming The open-air Karen Muir Pool is in Queen's Park (Sept–April); the entrance is on Park St, opposite Lyndhurst Rd.

Around Kimberley

The handful of interesting places around Kimberley includes **Barkly West**, the town where some of the first diamond camps sprung up in the 1860s, **Vaalbos National Park**, and some fascinating San rock art at **Wildebeest Kuil**. All these lie on or near the **R31**, which runs northwest out of Kimberley in the direction of Kuruman. South of Kimberley along the N12, the mostly unremarkable landscape around **Magersfontein** was the setting for one of the most dramatic campaigns of the Anglo-Boer War.

Wildebeest Kuil

Around 15km from Kimberley along the road to Barkly West is a small *koppie* of ancient andesite rock, **Wildebeest Kuil** (Tues–Fri 10am–5pm, Sat & Sun 11am–4pm; ⓦ www.museumsnc.co.za/wildebeestkuil.htm; R20, recorded audio tour R5). This is an important **rock art** site, unusual in that the images are engraved (rather than painted) and are found on loosely scattered rocks and small boulders, rather than cave walls or overhangs. Coming from Kimberley, you can catch one of the frequent minibus taxis to Barkly West and ask to be dropped at the signposted turning; the site is close by.

There are more than four hundred engravings here, the most recent from the 1800s, the oldest possibly dating back 1000–2000 years. They depict elephant, rhino, dancing human figures and, most commonly of all, the eland, a central shamanic metaphor in San art representing mediation between spirit realms, and also strongly associated with rain. A number of boardwalks have been built to allow access without disturbing the engravings and trained guides from the local community are on hand to show you around. The **visitor centre** at the base of the *koppie* provides an introductory display and shows a video.

Under South Africa's programme of land restitution, ownership of the site has been given to the local **!Xun** and **Khwe San communities**. Originally from Angola and Namibia, they were recruited as trackers by the South African Defence Force during the war fought in those countries in the 1970s and 1980s. When Namibia became independent in 1990, 370 of these soldiers and their families chose to relocate to South Africa. Largely ignored and forgotten thereafter, and subsisting on meagre military pensions, they established various projects to generate income. The most successful of these have been to do with **art**: some vivid and attractively designed ceramics and art work, mostly drawing on traditional San images and motifs, are on sale in the shop.

Barkly West

The small town of **BARKLY WEST**, originally a convenient crossing point of the Vaal River known as Klipdrif, lies 35km northwest of Kimberley. It was the first important focus of the diamond rush, out of which rose the short-lived **Klipdrif Diggers' Republic**, proclaimed by militant miners when British, Boer and Griqua authorities squabbled about who was to control the area. Later, political representation came in the form of Cecil Rhodes, who was the MP for the town up to and including his time as prime minister of the Cape Colony.

The alluvial beds along the river on the fringes of town are still being worked, and on Saturday mornings diggers come to sell their week's findings to licensed buyers at the **Diamond Market**. Some of the older diggers still prospect by hand, always hopeful of one "big one" despite finding perhaps just five good stones in a year. It can't be denied that a rough romance still surrounds the whole business, though Barkly West is visibly poor and snooping around on your own is inadvisable. The best way to explore is to join one of the fascinating insider **tours** of the alluvial diggings with Diamond Tours Unlimited (see box on p.320), on which you meet both the old hand-prospectors and the more modern operators.

For a bit more about the diamond-digging history of the area, visit the small **museum** (daily 9am–5pm; R5) located at the old toll house for the 1884 bridge over the Vaal River. Displays cover the Diggers' Republic and life in the early days, and archeological finds, including two enormous hand-axes unearthed at Canteen Kopje, an early diamond working site south of town. To get there, turn right towards the town's campsite/resort just after crossing the new bridge over the Vaal as you approach Barkly West from Kimberley.

Vaalbos National Park

Further along the Vaal River, about 20km from Barkly West on the R31, **Vaalbos National Park** (dawn–dusk) is a 230-square-kilometre reserve protecting a unique confluence of distinct ecological zones: Karoo, Kalahari thornveld, grassveld and river. While it's fairly unremarkable compared to many of the country's national parks, and the facilities are limited, it features some very African-looking camelthorn plains which look particularly attractive at sunrise or sunset. You have a good chance of seeing game here, such as buffalo, giraffe, zebra and plenty of buck, particularly around the waterholes – though the resident **rhino**, both black and white, are seldom seen from the park's gravel roads. Game hides and a walking trail are being developed, and the park offers night game drives and an "Eco-Adventure" trail for 4WDs (for which it has a vehicle available).

Near the entrance are three self-catering **chalets** (❶), each with solar-powered lights and fans, and beds in their lofts for children; there's also a **campsite**. The nearest supplies are at Longlands, 5km outside the gate.

Magersfontein

The Anglo-Boer War battlefield at **Magersfontein** (ⓦ www.museumsnc.co.za), 32km south of Kimberley along the N12, provides a poignant reminder of the area's blood-spattered past. This is where Boer forces put trench warfare into effect against British troops, with devastating results (see box on p.326). Signs point the way to the **visitor centre** (daily 8am–5pm; R5) with a small **museum**, which has some vivid exhibits, including an audiovisual re-creation of the battle. You can also hike up to various monuments situated on the western end of the line of hills. Out on the battlefield itself – now open veld with springbok grazing and the occasional car throwing up a plume of dust along the dirt road – the lines of **trenches** can still be seen, along with other memorials, including a pair of granite crosses marking the graves of Scandinavian soldiers who fought on the Boer side. Local legend has it that at least two ghosts have lingered: a saddled but riderless horse, and a lone Scottish piper.

One of the most enjoyable ways of finding out more about the history is to book a one-day **battlefield tour** with Steve Lunderstedt (☏053 831 4006 or

The Kimberley campaign

At the outbreak of the **Anglo-Boer War**, the Boer forces identified diamond-rich Kimberley as an important strategic base and quickly besieged the city, trapping its residents, including Cecil Rhodes, inside. In response, the British deployed an army under **Lord Methuen** to relieve the city. The size of the army and lack of knowledge of the terrain compelled them to advance from the coast along the line of the railway so that a supply of troops, water, food and equipment could be ensured.

Methuen first encountered Boer forces at Belmont, just across the Orange River. This was followed by further battles at Graspan and the Modder River, from which the Boers made a tactical withdrawal to Magersfontein. Here the Boer generals, under the leadership of General Cronjé and the tactical direction of **Koos de la Rey**, decided to dig a line of **trenches** along the bottom of the *koppie* rather than defend the top of the ridge of hills, as was their usual tactic.

In the early hours of December 11, 1899, the British advanced on Magersfontein, fully expecting the enemy to be lined along the ridge. The British were led by the Highland Regiment fresh from campaigns in North Africa and India, and considered the elite of the British army. Just before dawn, as they fanned out into attack formation, four thousand Boers in the trenches just a few hundred metres away opened fire. The use of trenches was, at that point, a rare tactic in modern warfare, and the element of surprise caused devastation in the ranks of Highlanders. Those not killed or wounded in the first volleys were pinned down by snipers for the rest of the day, unable to move in the coverless *veld* and suffering appallingly under the hot sun. The next day the British withdrew to the Modder River, and the relief of Kimberley was delayed for two months. The defeat was one in a series of three the British suffered within what became known as "Black Week", news of which sent shock waves through the British public expecting their forces to overrun the "crude farmers" before Christmas.

083 732 3189) or Frank Higgo (℡053 839 2722 or 082 963 6657), both enthusiastic and entertaining military historians. Their tours provide a vivid picture of the campaign, with trips to battlefields, fortifications and gun positions, and walks to get a sense of the terrain and look for old shells and other evidence of the fighting. Alternatively, pick up a "Diamond Fields Battlefields Route" brochure from the tourist office in Kimberley for detailed self-drive directions.

The museum runs the closest place to **stay** hereabouts, *Bagpipe Lodge*, next to the site (℡053 833 7115, Ⓦwww.museumsnc.co.za/bagpipe.htm; ❷), with three smallish rooms and meals on request. Much better, however, 11km towards Kimberley, is *Langberg Guest Farm* (℡053 832 1001, Ⓦwww.langberg.co.za; ❷), a hospitable family-run game farm at the western end of the battlefield, set in several Cape Dutch horse stables and cottages. They offer sports facilities and activities such as hikes and trips to feed the farm's antelopes, buffalo and giraffe.

The Kalahari

While the Northern Cape has no shortage of dry, endless expanses, the most emotive by far is the **Kalahari**. The very name holds a resonance of sun-bleached, faraway spaces and the unknown vastness of the African interior, both harsh and magical. The name derives from the word *kgalagadi* (salt pans, or thirsty land), and describes the semi-desert stretching north from the Orange River to the Okavango delta in northern Botswana, west into Namibia and east until the bushveld begins to dominate in the catchment areas of the Vaal and Limpopo rivers.

The Kalahari in the Northern Cape is characterized by surprisingly high, thinly vegetated red or orange sand dunes, scored with dry river beds and large, shimmering saltpans. Although this is, strictly speaking, semi-desert, temperatures are searingly hot by day in summer and numbingly cold at night in winter. North of the Orange, South Africa's largest river, the land is populated by tough, hardworking farmers and communities largely descended from the indigenous San hunter-gatherers and nomadic Khoi herders. For many land-users, there is an increasing realization that **eco-tourism** may be the only viable option on huge areas where stock farming and hunting provide at best a marginal living.

Upington, the main town in the area, stands on the northern bank of the Orange at the heart of an irrigated corridor of intensive wheat, cotton and,

Kalahari tours

To save yourself driving the vast distances of the Kalahari region – and to take advantage of specialized knowledge of the region's distinctive flora, fauna, landscapes and climate – it's worth considering joining a guided tour. Most of the tours incorporate a visit to the Augrabies Falls and the Kgalagadi Transfrontier Park, although customized itineraries are available. Prices start at R800 per person per day for a party of two, double that for upmarket trips, and include entrance fees, night game drives and guided walks. Costs can be kept to a minimum by asking to join a prebooked safari. And for a bird's eye view of the Kalahari, it's possible to go paragliding at Kuruman (see p.341) or get airborne in a microlight in Upington (see p.328).

Tour operators

Diamond Tours Unlimited 71 Jacobson Avenue, Kimberley ⓣ053 861 4983, ⓦwww.diamondtours.co.za. A knowledgeable and enthusiastic Northern Cape specialist offering a range of tours in the Kgalagadi, Augrabies, Richtersveld and – in August – Namaqualand (where a luxury week-long trip costs around R10,000–14,000 per person sharing). Tours can depart from Upington if required.

Kalahari Adventure Centre *Augrabies Falls Backpackers*, Upington (see p.334) ⓣ054 451 0177, ⓦwww.kalahari.co.za. An energetic backpacker outfit offering a budget five-day "Kalahari Backroads Safari", with two nights in Kgalagadi and one in the rarely explored Riemvasmaak area, whose highlight is a swimming pool fed by a hot spring. They also offer rafting on the Orange River and the "Augrabies Rush" whitewater experience.

Kalahari Safaris *Kalahari Junction Backpackers*, Upington ⓣ054 332 7874 or 054 332 5653, ⓦwww.upington.co.za/kalahari-junction.htm. A personable and knowledgeable outfit specializing in tailor-made Kalahari trips, for backpackers or in more luxurious style. Their five-day tour of Kgalagadi, Riemvasmaak and Augrabies is particularly recommended, and rafting can be incorporated. Minimum two people per tour, never more than five.

Kalahari Tours and Travel ⓣ054 338 0375 or 082 493 5041, ⓦwww.kalahari-tours .co.za. Well-organized Upington operator whose tours are mid-priced. They offer two-day trips to Kgalagadi and desert camping experiences; longer trips to other parts of the Kalahari, the Richtersveld, and rafting on the Orange are also available, plus bird-watching and flower tours.

most prominently, grape farms. At the far end of the farming belt, about an hour's drive west, the Orange picks up speed, and froths and tumbles into a huge granite gorge at **Augrabies Falls**, the focus of one of the area's two national parks. The other is the undoubted highlight of this area, the **Kgalagadi Transfrontier Park**. A vast desert sanctuary rich in game and boasting a magnificent landscape of red dunes and hardy vegetation, it's well worth the long trek to get there. If you're coming to it from Gauteng along the N14 highway, you can either turn onto the R31 (a long, bleak dirt road which should only be tackled in a sturdy vehicle) at **Kuruman**, site of a famous nineteenth-century **mission station** established by Robert and Mary Moffat, or travel on to Upington, from where the road is tarred for all but the last 45km.

The main reason to visit the **Witsand Nature Reserve** (℡053 313 1061–2, ⓦwww.witsandkalahari.co.za; R20 entry, R30 picnic site) is to hear its pristine white "**roaring**" **dunes**: in summer a curious rumbling sound occurs when the dunes, 9km in extent, are disturbed, possibly by ground water. While the reserve isn't exactly teeming with wildlife, it does have an abundance of desert bird species, and with patience you may also be rewarded by springbok, duikers and ground squirrels. There are some superb self-catering air-con **chalets** to stay in (❷), plus a campsite. The park is some 130km due east of Upington, and not that much further from Kuruman and Kimberley. It can be reached off the N8 or by heading south off the N14 from Olifantshoek; organized trips are available from Kalahari Safaris in Upington.

Upington and around

As an inevitable focus of trips to Kgalagadi and Augrabies, as well as those to and from Namaqualand and Namibia, **UPINGTON** is a good place to stop for supplies, organize a park tour or onward accommodation, or simply draw breath. Situated on the banks of the Orange River, it can also be a mellow spot, although the savage summer temperatures mean you probably won't want to linger.

Arrival and information

All **buses** stop at Intercape's office on Lutz Street, in the town centre. **Minibus taxis** use the rank north of Mark Street, between Le Roux and Park streets. The **train station** is 1km north of the centre, while the **airport**, which has no public transport, lies 7km north of town along Diedericks Road (℡054 337 7900). If you're likely to arrive at night, it's best to reserve a room and get your accommodation to pick you up when you arrive (usually R20). That said, some enterprising drivers are usually on hand to meet tourists arriving by rail or bus, or you could try ringing Peter Bens (℡054 339 0422) or Blue Line Shuttle (℡054 332 7993), who operate minibuses.

Central Upington is compact and easy to get around, with most of the activity on the three main streets running parallel to the river. Upington has two **tourist offices**. The one at the Kalahari-Oranje Museum on Schröder Street (Mon–Thurs 8am–5.30pm, Fri 8am–5pm, Sat 9am–noon; ℡ & ℻054 332 6064) deals only with the town and its immediate surroundings, and provides brochures, an accommodation list and details of local tours. For regional information, including details of Augrabies and Kgalagadi, head to the Green Kalahari tourist office at the start of Swartmodderweg (Mon–Fri 7.30am–4.30pm, Sat

South African Airlink, based at the airport (℡054 332 2161), **flies** from here to Cape Town and to Johannesburg. There's no public transport to the airport; arrange a lift via your hotel. Passenger **trains**, operated by TransNamib (⊛www.transnamib.com .na) are limited to twice-weekly runs into Namibia (change at Keetmanshoop).

The only major **bus** company operating from Upington is Intercape, based at Lutz Street (daily 6am–5.45pm or longer, except Sat when closed 1–4pm; ℡054 332 6091). It serves Johannesburg and Pretoria via Kuruman, Vryburg and Klerksdorp; Cape Town via Springbok or Calvinia; and Windhoek in Namibia. The only bus to Kimberley and Bloemfontein is the weekly Big Sky service (Sun 1pm at the time of writing), leaving from the Intercape office (book on ℡054 331 1123 or 072 290 4849).

There are regular **minibus** services (except Sun) to Springbok, Vryburg, Calvinia, Kimberley and Cape Town. Bays are marked for local destinations; it's a question of asking around for long-distance runs. There's no ticket office.

9–11am; ℡054 337 2885, ⊛www.greenkalahari.co.za), which has even more brochures, including detailed driving itineraries.

Accommodation

Upington has accommodation for all tastes and pockets, including a couple of quiet **backpackers' lodges** within walking distance of the centre. The busiest months are August and September, when Upington receives through traffic bound for Namaqualand; book ahead at this time. Particularly recommended – so long as guard dogs and a sometimes starchy neocolonial tenor don't phase you – are the **riverfront guesthouses** on Budler Street and Murray Avenue; reservations are advisable to secure a room and to ensure that someone's there when you arrive. For more options, pick up the *Upington Accommodation Collection* booklet at the tourist office. All hotels reviewed below have their own parking.

Affinity Guest House 4 Budler St ℡054 331 2101, ⊛www.affinityguesthouse.co.za. The largest of the riverfront choices, offering reasonable en-suite rooms in a functional pink two-storey building, all with TV, a/c and fridge. There's also a small swimming pool and braai area, and staff can arrange tours and safaris. ❷

Die Eiland On an island opposite the town centre ℡054 334 0286–8. This huge, busy holiday resort has a pleasant campsite and self-catering chalets, cottages, huts and rondavels, the best of which are right by the river and sleep four. No credit cards. ❶–❷

Kalahari Junction 3 Oranje St ℡054 332 7874. The busier and more compact of the town's two backpacker hostels. Camping and doubles are available, with some odd triple-storey bunk beds and outside beds for the hot summer nights. Also has a kitchen, a small swimming pool and TV in the main house. No credit cards. Dorms ❶, rooms ❶–❷

Le Must Guest Manor 12 Murray Ave ℡054 332 3971, ⊛www.lemustupington.com. Two Cape

Dutch houses on the riverbank with elegant and comfortable rooms, minimalist decor and large gardens, offering luxury and sophistication rarely encountered in the Northern Cape. ❸

Oranje Hotel Scott St ℡054 332 3177, ℗054 332 2612. An excellent three-star hotel one block from the taxi rank, handy for night-time arrivals (reception is 24hr), and with large, well-appointed rooms and a pool. The rate includes a huge buffet breakfast (R40 for non-residents). ❷

Protea Hotel Upington 24 Schröder St ℡054 337 8400, ⊛www.proteahotels.com. Decent but mundane rooms, the main draws being a nice swimming pool and sun deck with river views, and similar vistas from the "superior" rooms, which have lounges. There's no restaurant (though the *Totem Creek Spur* steakhouse is next door), and the large bar is often deserted. Breakfast costs extra. ❸

River Lodge B&B 4 Murray Ave ℡054 332 6327 or 082 821 1025, ℗054 332 4283. One of the most attractive places along the river, in an old

Cape Dutch house guarded by particularly noisy dogs. There are just three beds in two bright rooms, plus a swimming pool, braai area, canoes and fishing equipment. ❷

Yebo Backpackers & Guest House 21 Morant St ☏ 054 331 2496 or 072 473 1115, ✉ yebo@lantic.net. Run by a charming couple, this quiet compound has an eight-bed dorm and three attractive doubles. Facilities include two kitchens, braai area and Internet access; camping is allowed. They're particularly good value for lone travellers. Dorms ❶, rooms ❶–❷

The Town and around

Upington's obvious highlight is the **Orange River**, but unless you're staying at one of the riverside guesthouses, it tends to be hidden from view. The terraces behind *O'Hagan's* (see p.332) and the *Kalahari Dried Fruit & Coffee Shop* in the museum grounds, both on Schröder Street, are good places to admire the river and its swans. Better still, take a **cruise** with Sakkie se Arkie on their strange two-tier barge (daily Sept–April, by prior arrangement in winter if the river

RESTAURANTS, CAFÉS, BARS AND CLUBS
Dros	3
Eljays Sports Bar	7
Fantasy	9
Kalahari Dried Fruit & Coffee Shop	8
Le Must Restaurant	6
Le Raisin	1
O'Hagan's Irish Pub & Grill	5
Rio's	2
Saddles Steak Ranch	4
Totem Creek Spur	G

ACCOMMODATION
Affinity Guest House	C
Die Eiland	D
Kalahari Junction	A
Le Must Guest Manor	E
Oranje Hotel	H
Protea Hotel Upington	G
River Lodge B&B	F
Yebo Backpackers & Guest House	B

UPINGTON

is sufficiently high; ☎082 564 5447 or 082 575 7285; R25). They're based on the riverbank at the east end of Park Street, but can also pick up clients from the *Affinity Guest House*.

At the south end of Schröder Street at the 1875 mission church, the **Kalahari-Oranje Museum** (daily 8am–5pm; free) tells a fairly predictable history of isolated missionaries, hardy pioneer farmers and less-than-perfect race relations, and there are now a couple of very cursory displays on Bushmen and traditional blacksmiths. You won't miss much if it's closed. The museum grounds contain a quirky bronze sculpture of a donkey drawing water from a well. This alludes to the **irrigation** which allows Upington to be surrounded by vineyards, producing ten percent of the country's grapes – mostly table grapes and for dried fruit, though wine is also produced. The introduction of irrigation here apparently has its origins with a former slave named Abraham September. In 1882, he was granted a desolate patch of land 12km west of town, and duly set to work digging a channel from the river to his land. September is commemorated by a stone pillar at the corner of Scott and Mutual streets.

Wine tasting is offered by Oranjerivier Wine Cellars (Mon–Fri 8am–12.45pm & 2–5pm; free; ⊛www.owk.co.za) in the industrial estate west of the town centre off Dakota Road. Alternatively you can sample or buy their output at the restaurant at *Le Must*, or at the **Kalahari Dried Fruit & Coffee Shop** (Mon–Fri 7.30am–5pm, Sat 7.30am–1pm) in the museum grounds, which also sells other local produce, including raisins (the biggest export crop), conserves and pickles, and *mampoer* firewater.

Consumables of another kind entirely can be found at the remarkable **Skaapland** (Sheepland; open daily), a huge modern butchery which stands testimony to the devotion locals have for red meat. Located on the corner of Brug and Le Roux streets, it's worth a visit for all but the most devout vegetarian simply to see this vast, bright and spotless emporium selling everything from whole lamb carcasses (which can be cut up to your specific requirements at a special bay) to *biltong*, which hangs in dark forests in one corner of the shop.

Plans are afoot to establish a series of local tours in Upington, along the lines of those in Kimberley (p.320). **Township tours** to Paballelo and Progress should be up and running by the time you read this, and will include local **shebeens**. Local **craft co-operatives** will also feature; especially worth a visit is the Paper Craft and Design co-operative in **Raaswater** village, 16km from Upington, which makes cool papier-mâché animals. For more information and bookings contact the municipal tourist office. In early October, the *Die Eiland* resort plays host to the **Kalahari Kuierfees** (first Thursday to Saturday) combining flea markets and craft stalls with a triathlon, arts, live music and dance.

Spitskop Nature Reserve

With a limited array of rather skittish plains game, the **Spitskop Nature Reserve** (dawn–dusk; ☎ & ℻054 332 1336; R12) is just 13km north of town along the R360. The name Spitskop refers to the small rocky hill near the entrance with decent views of the surrounding plains. At its base is a quiet **campsite** and a simple four-bed **chalet** (●). Deeper into the reserve is a more basic hut with five bunks but no electricity (bring your own bedding; ●). The reserve contains three hiking and mountain-bike trails, and 37km of gravel roads for game-viewing. There's no public transport to the reserve, though Kalahari Safaris (see box on p.327) offers half-day trips here for around R65 per person.

Eating, drinking and nightlife

As the only large centre for hundreds of kilometres, Upington seems like culinary heaven compared to the towns you pass through to get here. If you were ever going to appreciate a franchised **steakhouse**, it would be here and, sure enough, they are lined up in anticipation in the town centre: the best ones are *Saddles Steak Ranch* on Mark Street and *Totem Creek Spur* on the corner of Schröder and Lutz streets, next to the *Protea Hotel Upington*.

The best place to down a **beer** is *O'Hagan's Irish Pub & Grill*, 20 Schröder Street, with real Guinness and a lovely terrace at the back overlooking the river. Popular with blacks is *Eljays Sports Bar* on Mark Street (daily mid-afternoon until 2am, closed earlier on Sun), a friendly little billiards place with a large TV screen for sports. The town's main **nightclub** is *Fantasy*, less than 1km southwest of the centre in the Lemoen Drie area, just off Old Keimoes Road, and good for contemporary music. Go with a local; *Eljays* is a handy place to find volunteers.

Restaurants

Dros Pick 'n Pay Centre, off Le Roux St. A swanky franchise decked out as a German wine cellar. Good service, a cosy ambience (despite its size), and excellent food – mostly meat – make it the town's most popular restaurant. Also has tables outside, a bar, and an extensive wine list. Mains R30–70.

Le Must Restaurant 11a Schröder St ☏054 332 3971. Reason enough to stop over in Upington, this exquisitely sophisticated place is one of South Africa's leading restaurants, with a menu as weird as it is imaginative and mouth-watering – smoked mussels and litchis wrapped in bacon with garlic, for example. Game and fish feature prominently, though there are vegetarian dishes, delicious salads and lighter meals. A three-course slap-up with wine might set you back R200. Closed Sat lunch.

Le Raisin 67 Mark St (Zelco Plaza). A cool, rather dark interior, popular for its cheap lunchtime buffets, mainly Afrikaans specialities, grills, and one or two vegetarian dishes. Licensed. Closed Sun & Mon evenings.

Rio's (The Diner) River/Scott St. The decor features funky 1960s retro kitsch, including old LPs as place mats. Light meals and snacks are available, plus takeaways, including pizzas, ribs, waffles and ice cream. Functions as a bar in the evenings. Closed Sun.

Listings

Banks Standard, Absa and First National are all on Hill St.

Car rental You need a 4WD to visit Kgalagadi under your own steam. Recommended local rental outfits include Kalahari 4x4 Hire, Caltex garage, 66 Scott St (☏054 332 3098 or 082 490 1937, ⓦwww.kalahari4x4hire.co.za); Kgalagadi 4x4 Hire, corner Mark St and Park St facing the taxi rank (☏054 337 7133 or 082 820 5376, ⓦwww.kgalagadi4x4.com), and Walker's Midas, 53 Mark St (☏054 337 5200, ⓔwalkermidas@cybertrade.co.za). All three can provide vehicles with camping gear. The international agencies are Avis, at the airport (☏054 332 4746); Europcar at *River City Inn*, corner of Scott and Park streets (☏082 426 8489); and Hertz, Le Roux St (☏054 337 3600).

Cinema Four screens at Ster Kalahari, Pick 'n Pay Centre (☏054 332 2107), showing pretty obscure movies.

Courier Postnet, Mark St, opposite *Saddles Steak Ranch*.

Doctors There are several surgeries at the north end of Scott St and Mark St, especially at Medpro Arcade.

Hospitals Best is Upington Private Hospital (☏054 338 8900); the public hospital is the Gordonia (☏054 331 1580). Both are out of town off the northern continuation of Schröder St.

Internet access BSA, corner of River St and Le Roux St; Café de Net, Pick 'n Pay Centre.

Microlight flights The long-established Upington Microlight Training Centre (ⓦwww.microlightkalahari .co.za), based at the *Islandview House* hotel on Murray Avenue in Upington, offers introductory tandem flights on microlights and hang-gliders.

Pharmacies De Duine Pharmacy, Pick & Pay Centre (☏054 331 1458; open daily to 8pm); Upington Pharmacy, 33 Schröder St (☏054 332 3071).

Police Corner of Schröder St and Hill St
☎054/332 1121.
Post The post office is on Mark St.
Shopping Good places for local handicrafts include *Friends Coffee Shop*, 51 Scott St (Markstraat Arkade; closed Sun); the new Mill Community Craft Centre along the southern extension of Mark St, where you'll also see the creators at work; and – for the widest choice – Living Interiors, opposite St Augustine Cathedra on Le Roux St.

Supermarkets Pick 'n Pay, west end of Rivier St, off Le Roux St, is open daily 8am–8pm.
Swimming pool The open-air Olympic-size municipal pool is off Borcherd St, the northern extension of Le Roux St (summer only, daily to 8pm).
Travel agent Club Travel, 11 Schröder St (☎054 332 3971, ⓦ www.clubtravel.co.za), run by the same people as *Le Must*, is clued up and efficient, handling airline ticketing and alterations, plus safari packages and trips to Botswana, Namibia and elsewhere.

Augrabies Falls National Park

One of the undoubted highlights of any trip to the Northern Cape is **AUGRABIES FALLS NATIONAL PARK**, 120km southwest of Upington. Roaring out of the barren semi-desert, sending great plumes of spray up above the brown horizon, the falls are the most spectacular moment in the two-thousand-kilometre progress of the Orange River. Rafting along the 18km granite canyon is another draw, while the fairly inhospitable northern section of the park sustains game, including reptiles, klipspringers and springbok. The best time to visit Augrabies is from March to May, when the temperatures are slightly cooler and the river is at its maximum flow after summer rainfall up in the Lesotho catchment areas, though water levels have reduced noticeably since the diversion of some water into the Vaal River (see p.790). With your own transport, the falls are easily visited as a day-trip from Upington, although

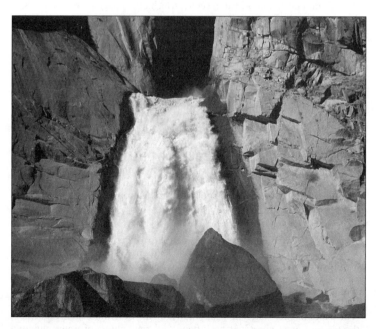

△ Augrabies Falls

there's plenty of reasonable accommodation both in the park itself and nearby. The closest you can get to the park on public transport is **Alheit**, on the N14 at the start of the turning to the park, 28km short of the entrance; however, most of the Kalahari **tours** out of Upington and elsewhere in Northern Cape (see box on p.327) incorporate a visit to the falls.

En route to the park

The route from Upington is west along the **N14**, following the Orange River and its rich fringe of vineyards, orchards and alfalfa fields. Eighty kilometres southwest of Upington, **KAKAMAS** is the last town before the park, and a handy base for visiting Augrabies if you're driving. The settlement was founded in 1897 by the Dutch Reformed Church as a colony for livestock farmers rendered destitute by a prolonged drought; each farmer contributed manpower for a system of **irrigation** canals and tunnels, and were rewarded with a plot of irrigated land. Considered primitive by the experts of the day, their handiwork still funnels water to the land today. The inhabitants' ingenuity also saw expression in South Africa's first hydro-electric power station, modelled on an Egyptian temple and completed in 1914, and which now houses a small museum. It's at the top of Voortrekker Street as you come in along the N14.

Good **places to stay** in Kakamas include the friendly *Lapa Side B&B* at 1 Voortrekker Street (℡083 332 5127, ℻054 431 1362; ❷), with a cottage and kitchen; the large *Kalahari Gateway Hotel* (℡054 431 0838, ⓦwww.kalaharigateway.co.za; ❷) two blocks along at no. 19, with a swimming pool, two bars, restaurant and car rental; and – best of the lot – *Vergelegen Guesthouse & Restaurant* (℡054 431 0976, ⓦwww.augrabiesfalls.co.za; ❷) on a farm by the main road about 3km east of Kakamas. It has ten neat and attractive rooms, a swimming pool, a restaurant and a small farm shop and information centre, which can arrange tours and safaris.

On the north bank of the Orange (reached via a turn-off just east of Kakamas) is **Khamkirri Private Game Reserve** (℡054 451 0325, ⓦwww.khamkirri.co.za; ❶–❷), offering a flavour of the dry, rocky landscape that fringes most of the Orange River. You can overnight here in a bushcamp (bring your own equipment), at a number of plain chalets at the river's edge, or in the main homestead. Activities available include game drives, horse-riding, gentle river-rafting trips, abseiling and safaris into the national park.

There's pleasant backpacker accommodation, with dorms, doubles and a campsite at *Augrabies Falls Backpackers* in **Augrabies village** (℡054 451 0177, ⓦwww.kalahari.co.za; ❶), 11km before the park gate, which acts as the base for the Kalahari Adventure Centre (see p.327). It has a bar, great food, a communal *boma* under an ancient camelthorn tree, and staff are happy to shuttle you in from Upington. Only a couple of kilometres from the park's main gate is the *Falls Guesthouse* (℡082 928 7938; ❸), a renovated farmhouse with big, cool rooms, nice furnishings and a veranda overlooking rows of vines.

The park

The park's **reception**, a little way inside the park entrance (daily 7am–7pm; ℡054 452 9200, ℻054 451 5003; R60), has a shop, a self-service snack bar and a **restaurant** with views towards the gorge. Self-catering **accommodation** is available at cottages and bungalows (❷–❸) close to the gate and the falls (two of which have wheelchair access), and at a large shaded camping and caravan area. There are swimming pools at each site.

The park's mighty waterfall is still known by its Khoikhoi name, Aukoerabis, "the place of great noise". At peak flow, the huge volume of water plunging

Activities at Augrabies Falls

Various adventure activities are promoted within the park, though none really matches the adrenaline surge of the falls themselves. The half-day **3-in-1 Gariep Trail** (R120) combines a short canoeing trip in the gorge with a walk and an eleven-kilometre mountain-bike ride back to the restcamp. The **Dassie Nature Trail** is a half-day hike out from the main restcamp, while the popular three-day **Klipspringer Trail** (April–September only; R125) involves two overnight stops at simple huts; advance booking is essential. **Night game drives** are also on offer (R50), **abseiling** is currently being developed, and there's a 56-kilometre **self-drive tourism route** (4WD only) in the park's northwestern section for viewing plains game. Reservations for all these activities must be made before 4pm the day before.

Perhaps more instantly gratifying is the "**Augrabies Rush**", a half-day trip on small rafts down 8km of increasingly swift river immediately above the falls, run by the Kala-hari Adventure Centre (p.327; R275 per person for a minimum of four). The Adventure Centre also runs four-day rafting trails taking you deep into the empty country downriver of the falls, while another two-day trip surges down the exciting rapids of the Oneepkans Gorge near Pella. Khamkirri Private Game Reserve (see opposite) also offers a range of activities, including gentle canoe trips and horse-riding.

through a narrow channel at the head of a deep granite gorge actually compares with the more docile periods at Victoria Falls and Niagara, although Augrabies lacks both the height and the soul-wrenching grandeur of its larger rivals. However, it is free of rampant commercialization, and in its eerie desert setting under an azure evening sky, the falls provide a moving and absorbing experience. The sides of the canyon are shaped like a smooth parabola, and there are many tales of curious visitors going too far in their quest to peer at the falls, and sliding helplessly into the seething maelstrom below. Despite the odd miraculous survival – most famously a Scandinavian who was stripped of all his clothes by the force of the water before he was plucked out – several dozen people have died here since the national park was created in 1966.

There is now a large fence from behind which you view the falls. A boardwalk currently nearing completion will allow wheelchair access to the viewpoint. To see more of the gorge, walk the short distance to Arrow Point or drive on the link roads round to Ararat or Echo Corner. The atmosphere is at its best near **sunset**, when the sun shines straight into the west-facing part of the gorge.

The rest of the park covers 184 square kilometres on both sides of the river. The land is dry and harsh, with sparse plants typical of arid areas, such as *kokerboom* (quiver tree), camelthorn and Namaqua fig. There are various striking rock formations, notably **potholes** scoured out by the river when it ran a different course to its present one, and **Moon Rock**, a huge dome of smooth, flaking granite rising out of the flat plains. If you drive on the (unsurfaced) roads in the park you'll probably spot some of the resident fauna, notably eland, klipspringer and other small antelope. On foot around the falls and the camp you're likely to see the smaller animals, including dassie, mongoose and lizards.

From Augrabies Falls to Springbok

West of Augrabies Falls National Park, the N14 highway becomes increasingly straight, spooling across largely flat and featureless semi-desert, the flanking telegraph poles stretching off to a shimmering horizon. The scarcity of trees means that a number of poles have been adopted as hosts for huge brown **sociable weaver nests**, a distinctive feature of these arid northern regions.

There's almost no sign of human habitation for hundreds of kilometres along this road, which is one of the reasons why the tiny, hot and famously remote town of **POFADDER** has a reputation in South Africa for being a little way past the back of beyond. Roughly midway between Upington and Springbok, Pofadder won't delay you for long, except perhaps to take a photo to prove you've been there. The name, much ridiculed by South Africans (it's Afrikaans for puff adder, the highly venomous snake which is found around the country), in fact refers to the nineteenth-century Koranna chief, **Klaas Pofadder**, who spent most of his time on an island in the Orange River near Upington but had a base here; his grave is in the town's cemetery. There is a **hotel** in town, the pleasant two-star *Pofadder* on Main Street (℡054 933 0063, ℻054 933 0061; ❷), and a caravan park a couple of blocks away (℡054 933 0056).

Pella

Around 15km west of Pofadder – 150km short of Springbok – is a turning to **PELLA**, an intriguing settlement established around a mission station founded by the London Missionary Society in 1814, then abandoned in 1872 and taken over by the Roman Catholic Church in 1878. After turning off the N14, take the right-hand fork after 3km and follow the dirt road for another 10km towards the range of mountains which follow the course of the Orange River.

Pella is a simple gathering of shacks, sandy roads and a few stone or brick buildings, in the midst of which a striking yellow **cathedral** stands in an open, dusty-white plot surrounded by stately date palms. The cathedral was built over seven years by two French missionaries in the 1880s who, lacking an experienced cathedral-builder in their group, used the *Encyclopédie des Arts et Métiers* for guidance. The surrounding mission buildings are attractive and still home to a community of nuns, and the cathedral itself is in continual use. The two small **museums** among the mission buildings are of some interest; if they're not open, ask at the mission office (℡027 718 2986, ℻027 712 1421).

On the corner where the road into Pella swings left to pass the mission, the *Kultuur Koffie Kroeg* is a **coffee shop** run from a flimsy-looking reed house by a local woman and her daughters. With *kokerboom* trunks for stools and coffee brewing on an open fire in the back yard, it's a triumph of local enterprise appreciated by the few visitors who make it this far. Ask there for the **Pella Community Tourism project** (℡054 971 0062), who offer various short walking tours in the area. Very basic but relatively authentic **accommodation** is available at the back of the *Koffie Kroeg* in *matjies* houses, the traditional domed reed huts of the Nama people (℡054 971 0040, ask for Elizabeth; ❶). They also have more modern chalets (❶), and evening meals, normally a *potjie* stew, will be rustled up if you're staying. The only real alternative is the excellent *Klein Pella Guest House* (℡054 972 9712, ⊛www.karsten.co.za; ❷), 24km away on a working farm beside the banks of the Orange River, with both chalets and camping.

Kgalagadi Transfrontier Park

The result of the formalization of a long-standing joint management arrangement between South Africa's Kalahari-Gemsbok National Park and Botswana's neighbouring Gemsbok National Park was the creation, in 1999, of Africa's first official transfrontier park, named **KGALAGADI TRANSFRONTIER PARK** after the ancient San name for the Kalahari (it's pronounced "kha-la-khadi", the *kh* as in the Scottish "loch"). The park is run as a single ecological unit and gate receipts are shared, although the tourist facilities in the two areas are still run autonomously. Almost all visitors to the park will, however, encounter only the South African section, where all the established tourist facilities are found.

In another development, the park entered into an agreement with the local **Mier** and **San** communities, under South Africa's programme of restitution of land rights to communities which had lost land under apartheid. The Mier and San communities have in turn agreed that their land be jointly managed by themselves and South African National Parks, so the land remains part of the wildlife sanctuary. The agreement also states that tourism opportunities for the local community will be explored. While these cover obvious areas such as jobs within the park and the sale of local crafts, locals have also been employed as trackers on a lion-monitoring project and to work on dune rehabilitation and alien plant eradication.

The park covers an area of over 37,000 square kilometres – nearly twice the size of Kruger National Park – and although the South African side is by far the smaller section, it still covers a vast 9500 square kilometres, bounded on its western side by the Namibian border, and to the south by the dry Auob River and a strip of land running parallel to this. The national boundary with Botswana is along the dry Nossob river bed, along which one of the few roads in the park runs, but no fences exist along this line, allowing game to move freely along the ancient **migration routes** that are so necessary for survival in the desert.

The best time to visit the park is between **March** and **May**, when there is still some greenery left from the summer rain and the sun is not so intense. Winter can be very cold at nights, while spring, though dry, is a pleasant time before the searing heat of summer.

Practicalities

The longer approach via the **R31** is surfaced only between Kuruman (see p.341) and Hotazel. From Upington (see p.328), the **R360** is surfaced all the way to Andriesvale, about 200km, after which it becomes a sand road for the 45km to the park entrance at **Twee Rivieren**. Whichever way you travel, the journey is a long, hot and weary one. You'll see plenty of the classic **red dunes** of the Kalahari, and every so often a huge, crazily paved grey saltpan, but the vegetation has been largely denuded, and the landscape is filled with desolate images, such as broken windmills and rusting frames of motor cars, drowning in the desert sand.

The **park roads** are also sand. While you can travel in a normal car, bear in mind that the higher the clearance the better – a car packed with four adults might struggle. It's also a good idea to reduce the pressure in your tyres by about half a bar before setting off, and to play the steering to maintain traction. You might find it's often easier to drive either side of the "road" along tracks left by other drivers. If you're in a rental car, check the small print as it may exclude cover for damaged wheels, undercarriage and paintwork. In the event of a **breakdown** you just have to sit it out until someone else passes; a park vehicle patrols most roads each day. **Fuel** is available at the restcamps at Twee Rivieren, Mata Mata and Nossob. Entry to the **Botswana** side of Kgalagadi is only allowed by 4WD, and you must exit through same gate you entered. The Botswana section has 974km of dirt roads comprising two access routes, two self-guided 4WD trails and a game-viewing trail.

The two alternatives to making the long drive to Kgalagadi are to go on a **package tour** (see p.327), or to **fly** to Twee Rivieren by private charter plane (arrange this

through Walker Flying Service in Upington; ℡054 332 3685, Ⓦwww.walkerflying
.com), from where you can pick up a car by prior arrangement with Avis (weekdays only, ℡054 561 0021 or c/o their Upington office, p.332).

Opening hours vary from month to month, roughly following first and last
light. **Entrance fees** are R120 per day; if you stay longer than anticipated
(unlikely, as accommodation is often fully booked), pay for the additional time

when you leave. The **visitor centre** at Twee Rivieren (℡054 561 2000, ℻054 561 2005) has exhibitions and slide shows worth checking out. For safety reasons you'll be given a **permit** on arrival, and you have to sign in and out whenever you are leaving or arriving at a restcamp.

Accommodation

On the approach road to Kgalagadi there are a number of **places to stay**. However, with morning being the best time for game viewing, staying en route to the park isn't really an option if you're on a tight schedule. The closest accommodation to the entrance, 30km south of Twee Rivieren, is the **campsite** at the community-run *Rooidun Guest Farm* (℡082 589 6659), which has become famous for **sand-surfing** – a bit like snow-sledging, sitting on a strip of plastic – down the face of one of the large nearby red sand dunes. Five kilometres beyond Rooidun is the *Kalahari Trails Nature Reserve* (℡082 448 2945 or 082 786 7712, ℺www.kalahari-trails.co.za; ❶), with a guesthouse overlooking the Nossob River, as well as tented chalets and a camping area. There's a small shop with basic supplies, but you should bring fresh food with you. Day visitors are welcome; entrance is R15, and activities go for R25–40 each. The reserve offers guided morning walks over the dunes with a desert ecologist or bushman tracker, plus game drives, night drives and walks (summer only).

Still further south, 55km from Twee Rivieren, is **ANDRIESVALE** and the *Molopo Kalahari Lodge* (℡054 511 0008, ℺www.molopolodge.co.za; ❶), a smart, well-run place with over thirty comfortable en-suite chalets arranged around a pool, as well as luxury bush tents, a bar and a decent **restaurant**. Andriesvale also has a **filling station** and a small shop. Alternatively, the nearby settlement of **ASKHAM** has the *Askham Post Office Guesthouse* (℡054 511 0040; ❷), which offers B&B in three spacious and clean en-suite rooms on the site of the old post office.

Inside the park

On the South African side, it's vital to **book park accommodation**, even for campsites, as early as you can, through South Africa National Parks (see p.71). The park has a choice of cottages and camping in two broad types of site: **fenced restcamps** at Twee Rivieren, Mata Mata and Nossob, which have electricity and creature comforts such as kitchens, fans or air conditioning, braai areas and shops, and the far more basic and remote **unfenced wilderness camps**, for which you need to be completely self-sufficient. It's worth staying at least a night at a park restcamp away from Twee Rivieren to taste the raw flavour of the desert. If time is limited, the shorter distance to Mata Mata makes more sense, but Nossob is better for atmosphere and game viewing: as well as hearing the lions roaring at night, you'll probably have your best chance of seeing them in this area. The roads to Nossob and Mata Mata follow riverbeds, and so are good for spotting game. On the **Botswana side**, facilities are limited to campsites at Mabuasehube, Two Rivers, Rooiputs and Polentswa. Visitors need to be completely self-sufficient. For reservations, contact the Botswana *Parks and Reserves Reservation Office* in Gaborone (from South Africa, ℡09 267 3918 0774, ℻09 267 3918 0775, ℮dwnp@gov.bw).

In addition to the restcamps below, three new sites should be functioning by the time you read this. The *Gharagab Wilderness Camp* is in the remote far north (access by 4WD), giving elevated views of the dunes and thornveld; *Kieliekrankie Wilderness Camp* is sunk into a dune in the Twee Rivieren region and is accessible in ordinary vehicles, as is *Urikaruus Wilderness Camp* in the Mata Mata region, set among camelthorn trees overlooking the Auob River.

Bitterpan Wilderness Camp Near the centre of the park on a 4WD trail between Nossob and Mata Mata, this has four unfenced reed cabins overlooking a saltpan. ③

Grootkolk Wilderness Camp Near Union's End at the very northern tip of the South African section, this unfenced camp in prime predator country is small, fully equipped and exclusive – and usually booked solid months in advance. ④

Kalahari Tent Camp Guarded by an armed guide, this unfenced site has fully equipped self-catering tents built of sandbags and canvas, giving views over the Auob River. There's also a swimming pool. ④

Mata Mata Camp A fenced restcamp 120km from northwest of Twee Rivieren on the (closed) Namibian border, at the end of the road that follows the course of the Auob River. Accommodation is in fully equipped family cottages, comfortable two-person bungalows (all with power) and campsites (no power). Other amenities include a water hole lit up at night, a shop and fuel. ②

Nossob Camp On the Botswana border, 160km along the Nossob River road, this is the most remote of the three fenced restcamps. It has fifteen simple chalets, and better family-size guesthouses and a cottage (all with electricity), and a campsite (no power). There's also a supply shop, fuel, plus a predator information centre (the place is famed for nocturnal visits by lions). Night game drives and guided day walks are available. ②

Twee Rivieren Camp The first, and most developed, of the three fenced restcamps, right by the entrance, offering over thirty pleasant self-catering chalets with thatched roofs and nice patio areas, a sizeable campsite, a mediocre restaurant, fuel, and a shop selling souvenirs and simple foodstuffs. Night game drives and guided day walks can be organized. ③

The park

Following the long slog to get to Twee Rivieren, be prepared to clock up even more mileage inside the park – the shortest circular game drive is over 100km long, not far short of the distance to Mata Mata restcamp. The main roads follow the **river beds**, and this is where the game – and their predators – are most likely to be. Water flows very rarely in the two rivers, but frequent **boreholes** have been drilled to provide water for the game. Larger **trees** such as camelthorn and *witgat* (shepherd's tree) offer a degree of shade and nutrition, and desert-adapted plants, including types of melon and cucumber, are a source of moisture for the animals.

Much of the park is dominated by **red sand dunes** which, when seen from the air, lie strung out in long, wave-like bands. From a car, the perspective is different, as you are in the valley of the river bed, but this doesn't prevent the path from offering one of the finest **game-viewing** experiences in South Africa – not only for the animals, but for the setting, with its broad landscapes, the crisp light of morning and the huge open skies. The clear viewing and wonderful light are ideal for **photography**, as shown by the exhibition at the visitor centre at Twee Rivieren camp or in any number of glossy coffee-table wildlife books.

The focus in Kgalagadi Transfrontier Park is on self-guided **game drives**. **Activities** inside the park are limited to the exacting three-day Nossob 4WD trail over the duneveld (book this in advance), and night game drives and day walks, which can be booked on arrival at Nossob or Twee Rivieren. Look out for details posted at the restcamp offices about what's happening on any given day. There are no guides for hire other than for these activities.

Seeing the animals

The game-viewing highlights in Kgalagadi Transfrontier Park are, inevitably, the predators, headed by the **Kalahari lion** and, enjoying rare status alongside the Big Five, **gemsbok**, the large, lolloping antelope with classically straight, V-shaped horns. You won't find buffalo, elephant or rhino, but the other animals more than compensate. Of the remaining Big Five, the **leopards**, as elsewhere, are not uncommon, but remain elusive. Kalahari lions commonly have much darker manes than those found in the bushveld, and studies have shown their behavioural and eating patterns to be distinctively well adapted to the semi-desert conditions here. Beyond the Big Five, there are various species of **antelope**, **hyena**, **jackal**, **bat-eared fox**, **cheetah** and some extravagant **birdlife**, including vultures, eagles, the dramatic bateleur (which takes it's name from the French word for an acrobatic tumbler), bustards and ostrich. There's also a good chance you'll see family groups of **suricate**, a relative of the mongoose and squirrel, striking their characteristic pose of standing tall on their hind legs, looking round nervously for signs of danger.

The best time to take your game drives is as early as possible in the **morning**, when you're more likely to see animals out in the open. Drives normally take at least four to five hours, so an early start means you can avoid the desert sun at its zenith. The last couple of hours of light in the afternoon are also a good time for game (and for taking photographs), but it's a lot more relaxing to go out for a little foray from your base than to be en route for a new camp, destined to arrive just as it's getting dark. The middle of the day, especially during summer, is a necessarily inactive time for both animals and humans, so don't plan too full a programme.

Kuruman and around

Lying near the border between the Northern Cape and Northwest provinces, the historic settlement of **KURUMAN** is an important landmark along the main N14 route to or from Gauteng. The settlement grew up around **The Eye**, a natural spring which, since time immemorial and through drought and flood, has consistently delivered twenty million litres a day of crystal-clear water. The Eye was the focal point for a rather unsettled Tswana clan called the **Batlhaping**, whose chief, Mothibi, first invited missionaries to live among his people in the early nineteenth century, a decision that led to the building of the famous **Mission Station** by Robert Moffat, and the establishment of Kuruman as the "Gateway to the Interior" of darkest Africa.

In addition to the historical charm of the mission and the natural beauty of the Kalahari, the area around Kuruman boasts important minerals, with iron, manganese and asbestos **mines** in the region. The associated infrastructure includes a single-track railway line running from **Sishen**, a vast open-cast iron-ore mine just to the east of Kuruman, all the way to Saldanha on the west coast, some 850 very lonely kilometres away. More exciting than any of this though is **paragliding**, for which Kuruman has gained a worldwide reputation – it's one of very few places where a 150-kilometre unpowered flight leaves your peers unimpressed. Winter is the best time, as in summer dust devils and turbulence make things dangerous. For more information, see the website of the South African Hang Gliding and Paragliding Association, Ⓦwww.sahpa.co.za.

The Town

Kuruman's centre is pretty scruffy, dominated by cut-price chain stores, faceless supermarkets and litter-strewn minibus-taxi ranks. The only central sight

The Moffats and their mission

Robert and Mary Moffat, newly married and envoys of the London Missionary Society, arrived in the Kuruman area in 1820, initially at a place rather charmingly mistranslated by early explorers as Lattakoo, about 14km from Kuruman. As a former market gardener, however, Moffat soon saw the advantages of irrigating the flow of The Eye of Kuruman, and began to build his mission on the closest land wide and flat enough to plough.

Moffat didn't clock up too many converts – by the time he had built his eight-hundred-seater "Cathedral of the Kalahari", in 1838, he had just nine – but the challenge of preaching and establishing a school inspired him not only to learn the local language, which he did by living for a period in a remote Tswana village, but also to attempt the daunting task of **translating the Bible** into Tswana, which he then published on an imported iron printing press, now on display in the old mission schoolroom.

The late nineteenth century was a time when the popular imagination of Victorian Britain about "Darkest Africa" was at its height, and the most famous of the missionaries had the status of movie stars today. The Moffats were treated as celebrities when they retired back to Britain in 1870, not least because of the continuing exploits of their son-in-law, David Livingstone. The mission at Kuruman, meanwhile, carried on until the passing of the Group Areas Act of 1950, which brought about the end of the school and the church as a functioning place of (multiracial) worship. The old mission, neglected and forgotten, was revived in the 1980s as an interdenominational trust; a retreat and educational centre has been built behind the old village, under the supervision of a permanent director and volunteer staff.

of interest is **The Eye** ("Die Oog" in Afrikaans), behind the office, but there's not much to look at: a moss-covered slab of rock dribbling water and a lily-covered pond surrounded by a high green fence, which you'll be charged a nominal sum to get past (daily 8am–8pm). The tourist office has details of the **Kuruman Hiking Trail**, which leads from The Eye to another natural spring, Second Eye, 11km to the east, past Anglo-Boer War forts and dolomite caves.

Some 4km north of town along Tsening Road (the R31) lies the wetland **Billy Duvenhage Nature Reserve and Bird Sanctuary** (Sat & Sun: summer 3–7pm, winter 2–6pm), a gorgeously tranquil location in which to escape the heat. Some 115 bird species have been counted here so far, mainly ducks, ibis and heron, and there's some plains game, too. Opposite is Moffat Lane and Kuruman's main attraction, **Moffat Mission Station** (Mon–Sat 8am–5pm, Sun 3–5pm; R5; ⓦwww.kuruman-mission.org.za). It was here that a large, often gruff, energetic Scot, **Robert Moffat**, and his demure but equally determined wife, **Mary**, established a mission station (see box above) where they lived for fifty years. During this time they produced and printed the first Tswana Bible, and saw their eldest daughter, also called Mary, married to the missionary/explorer **David Livingstone**. Charmingly overgrown and shaded by tall acacia and camelthorn trees, the old village includes the Moffat homestead, with furniture and exhibits inside, the schoolroom housing the Tswana printing press, and the large rough-stone church, with rows of pews standing on an uneven dried-dung floor, huge rafters holding up a thatched roof and shafts of sunlight angling in through the small windows and split wooden door. In front of the homestead is the furrow that carried water from The Eye, and beyond that, in Mary Moffat's garden, is the stump of the almond tree (destroyed by lightning) under which David Livingstone proposed to his future wife. Livingstone, who would go on to become one of the greatest explorers of his age, used Kuruman as an initial stepping stone for his first explorations of the interior.

Practicalities

Main Street, running east–west, is the N14 Upington–Vryburg highway. Bisecting it north–south is the R31 Kimberley–Kgalagadi road, which south of Main Street is called Voortrekker Street, and to the north becomes Tsening Road. The **tourist office** (Mon–Fri 8am–4.30pm, Sat 8am–12.30pm; ☎053 712 1095–7, ⓦwww.kurumankalahari.co.za) occupies the old *drostdy* (magistrate's house) at their intersection. After hours, there's a board outside with various accommodation options displayed.

Getting to Kuruman is easiest from Upington or North West Province, with daily Intercape **buses** running to and from Jo'burg and Pretoria via Vryburg, Klerksdorp and Potchefstroom. The buses stop at Leach Toyota on Main Street (☎053 712 1031), which also sells bus tickets. From Kimberley, **minibus taxis** are the only option; in Kuruman they stop at the rank just up from the tourist office along Tsening Road.

To change **money**, try Absa bank at the corner of Main and Livingstone streets; other banks also have central branches. The **hospital** is on Main Street 1km east of the tourist office (☎053 712 0044); the **post office** is on Church Street, two blocks north and one block west of the tourist office.

Accommodation and eating

The cheapest **rooms** are at the Moffat Mission (☎053 712 1352, ⓦwww .kuruman-mission.org.za; ❶), in the conference centre just behind the old homestead. Self-catering facilities are provided, although meals can be arranged in advance. Closer to town, the brightly coloured *Janke Gasthaus*, 16 Chapman Street (☎053 712 0949; ❷), is obvious from the road as you head out towards the mission; it has six en-suite rooms, a swimming pool and braai area. Not as characterful, but with a gorgeous swimming pool, shady gardens and restaurant, is *Riverfield Guest House* at 12 Seodin Road (☎053 712 0003, ⓦwww.riverfield.co.za; ❷), 2km northeast of the centre: from the tourist office, walk east along Main Street, then left up Livingstone Street.

You can **camp** at *Kuruman Caravan Park* (☎053 712 1479, Ⓕ053 712 3581; ❶), on Voortrekker Street 500m south of the tourist office. A much more pleasant option outside weekends and school holidays is *Red Sands Country Lodge* (☎053 712 0033 or 082 801 4414–5, ⓦwww.redsands.co.za; ❷), set among the Kuruman Hills 15km along the N14 towards Upington. Besides camping facilities, they have a characterful thatched stone rondavel and comfy self-catering chalets sleeping up to four. There's also a good German/South African restaurant.

Almost all of Kuruman's **restaurants** lie along Main Street. Particularly pleasant are *De Oude Drostdy Tea Garden* by the tourist office, *Melissa's Coffee Shoppe* – which sells curios – and, for the town's most upmarket culinary experience, the *Red Ox Restaurant*.

Around Kuruman

The upmarket **Tswalu Kalahari Reserve** (☎053 781 9311, ⓦwww.tswalu .com; ❾) centres on an impeccably stylish game lodge not far from the tiny settlement of **Sonstraal**, on the R31, 100km northwest of town. Tucked under the 1500-metre Korannaberg Mountains, this is the largest privately owned game reserve in South Africa, and was created by an English businessman, the late Steven Boler. He spent R50 million bringing over nine thousand head of game to this desert setting, including some highly endangered **desert black rhino**, sable, roan antelope and cheetah. Now owned by the Oppenheimer family, it remains part rich man's dream, part dedicated wildlife protection project, and part glamorous safari experience. Along with the wide desert panoramas, serious luxury and sumptuous meals, game viewing on foot or on horseback is on offer.

Also along the R31, but in the opposite direction from Kuruman, is a major archeological site, the intriguing **Wonderwerk** (Miracle) **Cave**. It has yielded important evidence of human occupation in various eras dating back over 800,000 years, including fossils, animal teeth, San rock paintings and engraved stones. There is a small visitor centre on the site, 43km south of Kuruman, and a **campsite** and self-catering **chalet** run by the Nieuwoudt family (☎053 384 0680 or 082 832 7226; ❷). Sometimes there are archeologists working in the cave, but if there's no one around, you'll have to ask at the farm for the gate to be unlocked. Admission is R5.

Viewing the flowers of Namaqualand

The seeds of the spectacular **flowers of Namaqualand** – multicoloured daisies, mesembryanthemums (*vygies*), aloes, gladioli and lilies – lie dormant under the soil through the harshest droughts of summer, waiting for the rain that sometimes takes years to materialize. About four thousand floral species are found in the area, a quarter of which are found nowhere else on earth. With different species reacting to different conditions, the flowers in any given place will come at different times from one year to the next, and attempting to predict where the best displays will occur is fraught with uncertainty. For more or less guaranteed displays, however, head for the Skilpad section of **Namaqua National Park** (p.352). And don't forget Richtersveld Transfrontier Park (p.359), whose ocean-mist-fed succulents blossom at this time.

One of the clues to where the displays will occur is **winter rainfall**, unusual in semi-desert ecosystems, which is why the flowers appear only in August and September; they follow the rainfall, so early in the season they will be out near the coast, moving steadily inland. Don't expect anything in July – early rains are extremely rare, and if the rains fail or come later, displays will be below par. **Temperature** is also a factor – flowers rarely open before 10am and on cool or cloudy days the displays are muted. While most of Namaqualand's flowers are wind-pollinated, temperatures below 15°C or so indicate that the wind is likely to be too strong (usually blowing straight towards the Atlantic), so flowers stay closed to protect their pollen.

Practicalities

Flower-viewing anywhere in Namaqualand means you spend a lot of time in a **car**, simply because the distances in this region are so great and flowers can never be guaranteed – you may spend some time tracking them down. **Cycling** is an option, although it can become a frustrating business if the best displays turn out to be 20km away from where you're based. As for **accommodation** (which needs to be booked well in advance), you should decide whether you'd rather stay on a farm (especially viable if you don't have your own transport, as you can take a guided walk around the farm's own flower fields), or in one of the main centres, such as Calvinia or Springbok, from where you can follow a wider range of routes. Tourist offices in the area can offer guidance and help organize accommodation; you can

Namaqualand

NAMAQUALAND is another Northern Cape region with a name that conjures a blend of desolation and magic. According to an oft-quoted saying about the area, in Namaqualand you weep twice: once when you first arrive and once when you have to leave. It is the land of the **Nama** people, Khoikhoi herders comprised the Little Nama, who lived south of the Orange River, and the Great Nama, who lived north of the river in what is now Namibia. Sparsely populated, the region stretches south from the Orange to the empty **Knersvlakte** plains around Vanrhynsdorp, and from the **Atlantic coast** to the edge of the **Great Karoo**. Above all, Namaqualand is synonymous with the incredible annual display of brightly coloured **wild flowers** which carpet the landscape in August and September, one of South Africa's most compelling spectacles. Even outside the flower season, swathes of orange, purple and white daisies emerge, and there is a tenacious beauty about the dry, empty landscape, with mountain deserts, mineral-bearing granite hills, and drought-defiant succulents.

also contact the **Flower Hotline** (late July to early October; ☎083 910 1028) for updates on the best floral displays and a weather forecast. The following **tactics** are also worth keeping in mind.

• Day by day, plan your route before heading out. Your hosts will often have inside information about the best spots on a particular day. Be warned, however, that you sometimes get "gold rush" situations, with everyone flocking to certain places.

• As the flowers open up around 10am and close between 3pm and 4pm, you have plenty of time for a good breakfast and to get yourself where you want to be. Because the flowers orientate themselves to face the sun, it's best to drive westwards in the morning, eastwards in afternoon, and generally from north to south.

• Get out of your car – all the most dedicated flower-watchers have muddy patches on their knees.

• Although it goes without saying, don't pick the flowers. Take pictures, or buy a book such as the *Garden of the Gods* by Freeman Patterson, or *Namaqualand: A Succulent Desert* by Richard Cowling.

• Pack warm clothes, as it gets chilly at night.

Flower tour operators

IN CAPE TOWN

Cape Rainbow Tours Suite 16, Millpark, Ixia St, Milnerton ☎021 551 5465, ⓦwww .caperainbow.com.

Landscape Tours Somerset West ☎021 851 7706, ⓦwww.africa-adventure.org/l /landscape.

IN NORTHERN CAPE

Diamond Tours Unlimited 71 Jacobson Ave, El Toro Park, Kimberley ☎053 861 4983, ⓦwww.diamondtours.co.za.

Richtersveld Challenge Voortrekker St, Springbok ☎027 718 1905, ⓔrichtersveld .challen@kingsley.co.za.

Virosatours Springbok ☎027 712 3650 or 073 229 5014, ⓦwww.virosatours.com.

The area is most easily reached from Cape Town along the **N7** highway. Flowers occur as far south as Darling, a mere 60km north of Cape Town, with the start of the northern section of the flower area marked by the small agricultural town of **Vanrhynsdorp**. To the east of it, up in the mountains beyond the coastal plain, the intriguing settlements of **Nieuwoudtville** and **Calvinia** offer a more intimate flower-viewing experience plus some attractive rustic accommodation. Further north, warranting more than a day-trip from Cape Town, is **Namaqua National Park** – part of which opens during the flower season, providing reliable displays even in years of low rainfall, when displays elsewhere may be muted. Further north, at the junction with the dusty **N14** from Upington and the Kalahari, lies Namaqualand's capital, **Springbok**. This is a handy base both for flowers and for visiting the Province's remote northwestern corner: the **Diamond Coast**, stretching from **Port Nolloth** to the Namibian border, and, inland, the harsh but spectacular **Richtersveld Transfrontier Park**, bisected by the Orange River – rafting on which ranks high among the region's attractions.

Southern Namaqualand and the Bokkeveld

Not strictly part of Namaqualand, the small agricultural town of **Vanrhynsdorp** in Western Cape province is the gateway to the Northern Cape flower routes. It marks the crossroads between the N7 Cape Town–Namibia highway and the R27, which connects via the glorious Bokkeveld Escarpment with Calvinia and ultimately Upington, on the northern fringe of the Great Karoo. Beyond the escarpment are the agricultural *dorps* of **Nieuwoudtville** and **Calvinia**, which make great bases for exploring the fertile region and its nature reserves.

Vanrhynsdorp

Set in the lee of the spectacular flat-topped Maskam mountain, **VANRHYNSDORP** is pretty much deserted out of flower season. The town is dominated by the tall spire of its church, 500m east of the N7 highway at the end of Van Riebeeck Street. The town's **museum** is just before it (Mon–Fri 8am–4pm & 2–4.30pm; also Sat & Sun during flower season; free), featuring a collection of old domestic and military pieces and the obligatory Voortrekker wagon. On the same side of Van Riebeeck Street is the former **prison** (Mon–Fri 8am–1pm & 2–5pm), an attractive, low yellow building built in 1895; it now contains a small coffee shop and, making use of the old cells, various small crafts stalls displaying the woodwork and needlework of older members of the local Afrikaner population. Also in town is the quirky **Latsky Radio Museum** at the corner of Kerk and Olive streets behind the church (Mon–Sat 9am–noon & 2–5pm), nurturing a collection of some 200 valve radios dating back to the 1920s.

Five blocks east of the church, along Voortrekker Street, **Kokerboom Kwekery** is a nursery specializing in succulents (℡027 219 1062 or 082 811 5474). Around a third of the world's succulent species grow in this area, many of them endemic. Here you can obtain a permit for the three-kilometre **succulent hiking trail**, situated 25km north of town off the N7 – a worthwhile diversion if you're travelling that way.

Practicalities

The first thing you come to after turning off the highway into town are two 24-hour service stations at the start of Van Riebeeck Street. The Shell garage is the stop for **buses and taxis** running to and from Cape Town, Springbok or Upington. Onward travel to Cape Town is easiest by taxi, best at 9am when the early ones from Springbok pass through; ring ahead to be sure of a seat (see p.354). If you're going to Springbok, afternoons are better, when vehicles return from Cape Town. Taxis east for Nieuwoudtville, Calvinia and beyond into the Great Karoo are infrequent and mostly travel this way at night. Intercape **buses** (tickets at Shell) run daily to Cape Town and Upington, via Springbok or Calvinia depending on which day you're travelling.

There's a simple and friendly **tourist office** (Mon–Fri 8am–1pm & 2–5pm; ☎027 219 1552) in the museum. You can change **money** at Absa on Troe-Troe Street or Standard on Voortrekker Street, both close to the church. The post office is on Kerk Street; **Internet access** is available at the supermarket at the top of Van Riebeeck Street, facing the church.

Accommodation, eating and drinking

The best place to **stay** is the calm and welcoming *Van Rhyn Guest House*, Van Riebeeck Street (☎027 219 1429, ⓦwww.vanrhyngh.co.za; flower season half-board ❹, at other times B&B ❷). The eight rooms, in converted outhouses, are dark if decent enough, and excellent meals can be provided. The town's main hotel is the plain *Namaqualand Country Lodge*, on Voortrekker Street next to the church (☎027 219 1633, ⓦwww.namaqualand.co.za; flower season ❸, otherwise ❷), where the rooms come with TV and, in most cases, a/c. A kilometre south of here along Gifberg Road, *Vanrhynsdorp Caravan Park* (☎027 219 1287) is reasonably quiet out of season and has a cheap **campsite** and basic en-suite chalets (❶), two of them with kitchenettes. If you're planning on staying more than one night, you're probably best off looking for **farm-based accommodation** in the nearby mountains, for which you'll need a vehicle. Some 29km south of town, on the plateau of the Maskam mountain, *Gifberg Holiday Farm* (☎027 219 1555, ⓦwww.gifberg.co.za; ❷) has various self-catering cottages to rent; the older two-bed *Kliphuis* is particularly pleasing. From the farm there's a network of paths and trails leading to San rock paintings and swimming holes.

The cute *Rock Art Café*, next to the Shell garage, is the best **restaurant** (closed Sat eve and all day Sunday). Less attractive but open daily is *Meet & Eat* at *Namaqualand Country Lodge*, which also has the only **bar**.

Nieuwoudtville and around

Heading east from Vanrhynsdorp on the R27 you have a very clear impression of the sudden elevation of the land from the plains up to the Bokkeveld escarpment, which the road tackles by way of **Van Rhyn's Pass**, complete with a couple of neck-achingly tight hairpins near the top. There's an excellent viewpoint overlooking the plains, signposted soon after you reach the plateau. You'll notice (as the early settlers did, much to their relief, after hauling their ox wagons up the escarpment) that the vegetation on top of the plateau is suddenly more fertile.

Eight kilometres on from the top of Van Rhyn's Pass, just over 50km from Vanrhynsdorp, the R27 passes just to the north of **NIEUWOUDTVILLE** ("Knee-voet-vil"), with an attractive collection of tin-roofed, honey-coloured

Glenlyon

An old Bedford bus, called Flora, is one of the great characters of Nieuwoudtville. Behind the wheel is another, **Neil MacGregor**, a man whose love and knowledge of the botany of the land he has farmed all his life has won him admiration not just in Namaqualand, but around the world. The visitors' book at **Glenlyon**, Neil and Neva MacGregor's farm just outside town, includes such names as David Attenborough, who came with the BBC Wildlife team to film *The Private World of Plants*, and Sir Ghilleam Prance, a former director of Kew Gardens in London.

Each flower season, during August and September, Neil and Flora take tours around the farm, a 65-square-kilometre property where he breeds pure merino sheep and has been striving for three decades to prove that farming and the spectacular natural flora can flourish successfully alongside one another. The house special at Glenlyon are orange bulbinellas, but Neil's enthusiasm and expertise soon have you down on your hands and knees examining all kinds of fascinating flowers. Tours lasts for two and a half hours and depart each day during season at 2pm (℡027 218 1200); book well in advance.

sandstone buildings, and the sombre **ruins** of early settler homesteads on the outskirts. Founded just over a century ago, it's by far the most atmospheric place to stay at in the region, full of character and history. The soil here has the highest concentration of **bulb** species on earth, and there are several appealing nature reserves in the vicinity. Although most of the flowering species appear in August and September, a time of spectacular colourful display, you're likely to find something in flower here any time between March and October. The flower season here is also notable for the highly recommended **tours** run by Neil MacGregor, one of the gurus of Namaqualand flowers (see box on pp.344–345).

Practicalities

Public transport to Nieuwoudtville is extremely limited. Buses from Upington and Vanrhynsdorp all arrive at night, while taxis are infrequent, and tend also to travel at night. Look out for a grand **church** set in a large plot of attractively unkempt ground on Voortrekker Road (the only sealed road); it's on the left if you're arriving from Vanrhynsdorp. During the flower season, an **information centre** operates out of the house in the church grounds (℡027 218 1336). Reliable advice is available year-round at the *Smidswinkel Restaurant & Information Centre* (℡027 218 1535, ⓦwww.nieuwoudtville.co.za) in a large sandstone building on Neethling Street, who can point you to the various hiking trails in the region, and to rock art sites.

The restaurant is also the place for booking one of the town's atmospheric *Van Zijl* **guesthouses** (❷), beautifully restored traditional sandstone buildings stuffed with characterful old furniture and located within walking distance of the restaurant. There's also the *Green Door* (❷), a snug loft above the restaurant. Just over 1km outside town is a pleasant **campsite**; book through the municipality office (℡027 218 1316).

Some of the farms around Nieuwoudtville offer accommodation in classic, old, thatched Karoo cottages, ranging from typically hearty farmhouse B&Bs to more basic self-catering rooms. Particularly recommended as bases for visiting Oorlogskloof Nature Reserve (see opposite) are those run by the Van Wyk family. They're based at Papkuilsfontein Farm, 23km south of town off the dirt road to Clanwilliam (℡ & ⓕ027 218 1246; half board ❷). Activities include hikes, mountain-bike trails, birding (black and martial eagles are present) and trips to the reserve. Each of their four cottages has its own charm, but the best for hiking are Papkuilsfontein, De Hoop and Gert Boom, all within two hours' walk of the canyon.

For somewhere to **eat**, you can't do better than the excellent *Smidswinkel Restaurant*, whose leg of lamb and springbok shanks are famously good, especially when washed down with the local wine. For less common Afrikaans specialities like baked sheeps' heads and stuffed heart, give them a day's notice.

Around Nieuwoudtville

The area receives unusually high rainfall thanks to its location at the edge of the escarpment, and consequently boasts over three hundred different floral species; flowering starts after the first rains in April or May, and peaks in August and September. The flowers are best seen at the **Nieuwoudtville Wildflower Reserve** some 3km east of town on the R27, with an unparallel variety of bulbs, notably the orange-flowered bulbinellas.

The **Bokkeveld Nature Reserve** and its thirty-metre waterfall lie 7km north from town, towards the settlement of **Loeriesfontein**. When the Doring River is flowing between April and October, the waterfall tumbles down into an impressive gorge where large raptors can sometimes be seen soaring around the tall cliffs. A few kilometres beyond on the R357, a dirt road leading towards Gannabos will take you to another of the area's botanical oddities, an extensive **quiver tree forest**, containing some of the tallest specimens of *Aloe dichotoma* (the *kokerboom*) found in South Africa. They flower in June and July.

Worthwhile for those who have a bit of time in the area, especially out of flower season, the **Oorlogskloof Nature Reserve** (Mon–Fri 8am–4pm) encompasses a series of deep ravines and natural swimming pools carved out by the Oorlogskloof River. Perched on the edge of the escarpment, it gives breathtaking views over the Knersvlakte plain to the northwest, the surrounding mountain ranges and the river. The reserve is known for rare breeding colonies of black booted eagles, and is paradise for hikers and mountain bikers. Access is via a ten-kilometre gravel road that starts at the R27 near the top of Van Rhyn's Pass, 6km west of town. Before going, notify the Department of Nature Conservation on Goedehoop Street in Nieuwoudtville (☎ & ⓕ027 218 1159), where you can also get a map and brochure. Good bases for visiting the reserve are the cottages run by the Van Wyk family.

Calvinia and on to the Great Karoo

Despite its stern name, bestowed by an early dominee, **CALVINIA** has quite an appealing setting beneath the impressive Hantam Mountains. The town acts as a service centre for the western part of the Great Karoo, but it isn't a place you'll want to spend a lot of time in, unless you're here for the flowers in the surrounding area (*hantam* is Khoi for "where the red bulbs grow"). Outside flower season, the climate can make the area fairly unwelcoming, with temperatures climbing towards 40°C during summer and dipping below freezing in winter, when snow is sometimes seen on the mountains.

The centre of Calvinia is dominated by the Neo-Gothic **Dutch Reformed Church**, although it now vies for your attention with a cylindrical water storage tank dressed up as a huge red postbox, just along on Hoop Street. The idea behind this was to create a tourist attraction, and however crass the concept it does turn heads; letters and postcards posted in the box are stamped with a special postmark. Immediately opposite the postbox is a more serious attraction, the Cape Dutch **Hantam Huis** (Mon–Sat 7.30am–5pm, also Sun during flower season), the oldest building in Calvinia (1853) and a national monument, which has won various awards for its restoration. It now functions as a restaurant, gift shop and information centre.

The large **Calvinia Museum** (Mon–Fri 8am–1pm & 2–5pm, Sat 8am–noon; R5) is housed in a 1920 Art Deco synagogue on Church Street, a link to the once sizeable Jewish community here, now melted away (one of its more famous sons is the Shakespearean actor Antony Sher, born in nearby Middlepost). Inside are some extensive displays on settler life, including old wooden flour mills, printing presses, huge forge bellows and no fewer than six pianos. There are also some bizarre exhibits, which include a black wedding dress and a display of *dagga* (marijuana) pipes. Predictably, a display cabinet displaying the memorabilia of two of the town's rugby Springboks is as large as that showing San artefacts.

Practicalities

Minibus taxis and Intercape **buses** travelling between Upington and Cape Town stop at the Total garage on Paul Kruger Street. While catching a minibus taxi toward Vanrhynsdorp and Cape Town is easy early in the morning (except Sunday), heading up towards Upington by taxi can mean a night-time departure or arrival. If you're thinking of heading east across the Great Karoo by public transport, count on several days – services here are few and far between.

The **tourist office** (Mon–Fri 8am–1pm & 2–5pm, Sat 8am–noon; ☏027 341 1712 or 027 341 8100, ℻027 341 8128) in the museum provides details of **flower routes**, various 4WD trails in Hantam district, and two hiking trails in the magnificent Akkerendam Nature Reserve, just north of town in the lee of the mountains. More information is available from the congenial proprietors of *Hantam Huis* at 42–44 Hoop Street (☏027 341 1606, ⓦwww .calvinia.co.za), who also offer **accommodation** in a characterful collection of old town houses (❸). Opposite Hantam Huis, another nineteenth-century building, 35 Water St, houses *Pionierslot Guesthouse* (☏027 341 1263 or 027 341 1484, ℻027 341 8204; ❷), where the most pleasant rooms here are in the side annexe. The **camping and caravan park** (☏027 341 1011) is on the corner of Station and Hofmeyr streets, on the way through town towards the Upington road.

Hantam Huis is the place to head for fresh bread, cakes, tea and coffee, and – in a separate dining room – traditional Afrikaans **food**, served all day but doused in candlelight and soppy music in the evenings. *Die Blou Nartjie* restaurant (closed Sat lunch & all day Sun) is a rather grander affair within *Pionierslot Guesthouse*.

The Great Karoo

Strange though it may seem, the **Great Karoo**, the vast, dry, empty interior of South Africa, was an equally vast inland lake some 250 million years ago. It was populated by tiny marine creatures and, around its fringes, dinosaur-like amphibians, some of which left footprints in the mud that have been preserved as fossils. The contrast now could hardly be greater, with slow creaking windmills struggling to bring water to the surface and the baked, brown-red earth roamed only by small herds of antelope or tough merino sheep. Farmers here talk about the terrain in terms of hectares per sheep rather than sheep per hectare. The summer heat is fierce, the winter biting cold, the rain elusive, and the soil all but barren. Yet the Karoo has a special place for many South Africans, who take an almost perverse joy in the crisp air, the colours of the scattered *koppies* at sunset, the vastness of the pale sky, the depth of the darkness at night and the jostling galaxies of stars.

Just east of Calvinia, the R27 goes north through **Brandvlei** and **Kenhardt** towards Upington, while the R63 goes east through **Williston** and **Carnarvon** to **Victoria West** on the N12 Cape Town–Kimberley–Johannesburg road. Other than their sheer isolation, these Karoo settlements offer the odd interesting feature, such as ancient fossil remains and corbelled houses – whitewashed, beehive-like constructions, built because of the lack of timber available for roofs.

Central Namaqualand

Travelling south from Springbok is a stimulating experience, thanks to the spectacular pink flat-topped mass of the **Matzikama Range** that increasingly dominates the southern skyline. But if you're heading north from Vanrhynsdorp, with the Matzikama behind you, the bleak plains stretching along the first 100km or so can seem bleak and grey, particularly out of flower season; this is the pebble-strewn **Knersvlakte** – the "plains of the gnashing teeth", referring to the sound made by wagon wheels toiling across the harsh terrain. The N7 eventually becomes attractive among the **Kamiesberg Mountains**, where **Kamieskroon** and **Garies** are good bases for the flower season. Kamieskroon in particular is handy for visiting the Skilpad section of **Namaqua National Park**, the stage for some of Namaqualand's most reliable and spectacular floral displays.

Garies

GARIES is the first town inside the Northern Cape you encounter on the N7 north of Vanrhynsdorp. A sleepy *dorp* for much of the year, Garies comes to life during the flower season, when the **town hall** (☎027 652 1014) is used as a flower information centre and casual market.

The town's three **hotels** are on the central Main Street. The best is *Garies Hotel* (☎027 652 1042 or 072 396 1752, ⓕ027 652 1141; ❶), with reasonable rooms, a simple restaurant and swimming pool. *Sophie's Guesthouse* at no. 33 (☎ & ⓕ027 652 1069; ❶–❷) has rooms with kitchenettes. Further along Main Street, a left turn – if you're coming in from the N7 – leads to the pleasant *Garies Municipal Caravan Park* (☎027 652 8000, ⓕ027 652 8006), with space for **camping** and some nice views up the nearby Green Valley. **Buses and taxis** leave from the garage next to *Garies Hotel*; as ever, mornings are the best time to catch them, especially to Cape Town, though you should be able to catch a ride in the afternoon towards Springbok.

Kamieskroon and Namaqua National Park

About 50km north of Garies, and 67km short of Springbok, the village of **KAMIESKROON** is set among the Kamiesberg Mountains, beneath the

Kamieskroon photographic workshops

Capturing on film the immensity and spectacle of the Namaqualand landscapes is no easy task. One way of improving your technique is to book a place on one of the popular **photography workshops** at the *Kamieskroon Hotel*. The residential courses last a week, and involve lectures, tuition and field work under the instruction of the dynamic Colla Swart (whose family runs the hotel) and the internationally renowned Canadian photographer **Freeman Patterson**, whose coffee-table book on the flowers of Namaqualand, *The Garden of the Gods*, is a classic portrait of the region. You'll also learn more about the inspiring landscape and flora of Namaqualand, and hear the odd epiphany about the meaning of life. Although the flowers are the principal focus, workshops are also held in March and May, when field work takes place around the dunes on the Atlantic coast near Hondeklip Bay. The workshops are often fully booked, so contact the hotel as far in advance as you can. Full board with tuition starts at around R4000 per person per week.

rocky peak – or *kroon* – from which it takes its name. There isn't much to the village other than a pretty setting, the crisp air of the mountains and, in flower season, a sense of being at the heart of the garden of the gods.

As you come off the highway, the village is to the right, while to the left is the *Kamieskroon* (☎027 672 1614, ⓦwww.agape.co.za; ❷), seemingly an inauspicious wayside **hotel** but in fact a vibrant and creative place. The hotel has become famous for running photographic workshops during the flower season (see box above), and is the centre for a growing number of activities in the surrounding Kamiesberg. Also good and informative about the region is *Randspaar Guest House*, 25 Church Street (☎ & Ⓕ027 672 1604 or ☎027 672 1729; self-catering ❶, half board ❸), actually two guesthouses, one with en-suite bedrooms, bar and dining room, the other self-catering apartments. Other reasonable but unexciting options include *Gousblom B&B*, 95 De Waal Street (☎ & Ⓕ027 672 1004 or ☎082 962 3213; ❷), and *Kamieskroon B&B*, Charlotte Street (☎ & Ⓕ027 672 1652 or ☎082 898 2759; ❶). The **campsite** at *Kamieskroon Hotel* is more pleasant than *Verbe Caravan Park*, on Kordon Street (☎ & Ⓕ027/672 1176).

Deeper into the mountains, at places east of Kamieskroon such as **Nourivier** and the old Moravian mission station of **Lelifontein**, the land is owned and farmed as a community project by the local Nama people. In places you'll see families living in traditional *matjieshuise* (reed huts); these settlements, many of which are still based around a mission, are connected by dirt roads, and so make good flower-viewing routes. It's possible to arrange to stay overnight in a *matjies* house, through the Lelifontein community project (☎027 672 1808).

Namaqua National Park

A place worth going to in flower season, even if you're just passing through on the highway, is the **Skilpad section** of **Namaqua National Park** (Aug & Sept daily 8am–5pm, sometimes Oct if rains are late; ☎027 672 1948; R60), 17km northwest of Kamieskroon along a signposted gravel road. The displays here tend to be more reliable than elsewhere, even in years with low rainfall, with great swathes of orange colour. Butterfly fanatics and twitchers should be in for a treat, too. There's a circular five-kilometre drive around the reserve, two short walking trails and a scenic picnic site, but facilities are limited to toilets and a farm stall offering light meals.

Springbok and around

The semi-arid expanse of northern Namaqualand is where the Karoo merges into Kalahari, and both meet the ocean. If it wasn't for the discovery of **copper** in the 1600s, and more recently of alluvial and offshore **diamonds** washed down from the Kimberley area by the Orange River, the region might well not have acquired any towns at all. Fresh water is scarce, and its presence here ensured the survival of **SPRINGBOK**, the region's capital, after its copper mines were exhausted.

The Town

Hemmed in by hills, Springbok is the main commercial and administrative centre of Namaqualand, and an important staging post at the junction of the N7 and N14 highways. Lying 550km from Cape Town, and just over 100km south of the border with Namibia, it makes a pleasant base for visiting northern Namaqualand's flower fields in August and September, to arrange trips to the Richtersveld Transfrontier Park (see p.360), and as a springboard for visiting the coast.

Springbok's main action is centred on the mound of granite boulders next to the taxi rank. Called **Klipkoppie** ("rocky hill"), this was the site of a British fort blown up by General Jan Smuts' commando during the Anglo-Boer War. A short walk up Monument Street brings you to the town's **museum** (Mon–Fri 8am–5pm; donation expected) in a 1929 synagogue, a sadly uninteresting collection of household bric-a-brac, including whips and clothes, but with little real information about the town or the region. A little way along from this, at the back of town, a gash in the hillside marks the **Blue Mine**, the first commercial copper mine in South Africa, sunk in 1852. Recent activity here has been in search of gemstones – previously ignored in the search for copper ore – and zinc. A short trail wends up to a good viewpoint over town. You'll find a good selection of gemstones for sale at *Springbok Lodge*, together with an excellent display of mineralogical specimens from all over the globe.

Practicalities

The town's main road, Voortrekker Street, comes in from the south and veers east at the taxi rank to rejoin the N7. Almost all buses and taxis pull in at the **taxi rank** in the centre of town on Voortrekker Street, next to Klipkoppie. Intercape buses stop 200m south of here next to the *Melkboschkuil* restaurant, also on Voortrekker Street. The helpful **tourist office**, doubling as the headquarters of the Namaqua Region Tourism Board (flower season Mon–Fri 7.30am–6pm, Sat & Sun 9am–6pm; rest of year Mon–Fri 7.30am–4.15pm; ℡027 712 2011, ⓦwww.namaqualand.com) is on Voortrekker Street 700m south of the taxi rank. Another source of local wisdom (and dour wit) is the *Springbok Lodge & Restaurant* on the corner or Voortrekker and Kerk streets. A hub for travellers and locals alike, this also sells an excellent selection of **books**, including plenty of titles on Namaqualand and its flowers, the history of copper mining and the Nama, the Richtersveld and rock art.

For **Internet** access, try Something Online (Mon–Thurs 8am–1pm & 2–5pm, Fri 8am–1pm & 2–4pm), next to *Melkboschkuil* restaurant. You can **change money** at the Absa bank, on Namakwa Street facing the taxi rank. Fully equipped 4WDs and camping gear can be rented from Richtersveld Challenge, facing the tourist office (℡027 718 1905,

Moving on from Springbok

Most **buses and minibuses** leave from the taxi rank at Klipkoppie, but will pick you up at your hotel if you ring ahead (it's recommended in any case). **Intercape buses** serving Upington, Cape Town and Windhoek leave from Voortrekker Street, next to *Melkboschkuil* restaurant. Well-established bus companies for **Cape Town** include Titus (T027 712 1381), Van Wyk's (T027 713 8559) and Carsten's (T027 712 1847). Van Wyk's also run to Okiep and Nababeep. VIP Taxis (T027 851 8780) have a 3pm weekday service to Port Nolloth and Alexander Bay, and weekday runs to Upington. For **Windhoek** in Namibia, Bailey's Reo Liner (T021 939 9777) – arriving from Cape Town – runs every two days from KFC next to *Springbok Lodge*. Covering the same route three times a week is Namibian company *Econolux* (T+264 811 248 137).

Erichtersveld.challen@kingsley.co.za); other 4WD rental agencies include Tempest and Imperial, who share an office next to the *Melkboschkuil* restaurant (T027 718 1600 or 083 644 6406).

Accommodation

There's no shortage of **rooms** in Springbok, but you're still advised to book ahead in flower season. The noticeboard outside the tourist office has details and prices for most properties in and around town, and a map. The closest **campsite** is the plain and shadeless *Springbok Caravan Park* (T & F027 718 1584), 2km southeast of town along the R355 towards Goegap. The caravan park also has some cabins, double rooms and caravans for hire (❶), and a swimming pool.

In town

Annie's Cottage 4 King St, signposted from Klipkoppie T027 712 1451, Wwww.springbokinfo .com. Extremely stylish, comfortable and colourful rooms (including one that's wheelchair accessible) in a restored colonial house. There's plenty of local artwork, a swimming pool under jacaranda trees, and hiking and biking trails in the vicinity. Flower season ❹, otherwise ❷–❸

Cat Nap Voortrekker St, facing the tourist office T027 718 1905, Erichtersveld.challen@kingsley .co.za. Very attractive African-themed rooms, two with bathrooms, and twelve rudimentary pull-down bunks in the garage, with a kitchenette – there's even room for you to park your vehicle beside your bed. Bunks ❶, rooms ❷

Elkoweru 1 Bree St T027 718 1202, Wwww .elkoweru.co.za. A modern two-storey guesthouse in vaguely Mediterranean style. Rooms are a bit small but nothing special, but good value at the price, and there are also self-catering flats. The owners can arrange flower tours and other trips. ❶

Masonic Hotel Van Riebeeck St T027 712 1505, Ejcb@mynet.co.za. The town's only package/business class hotel, with well-kept if bland rooms, as well as a restaurant and bar. An annexe has some cheaper singles. ❷

Mountain View Guest House 2 Overberg Ave (follow the signs off Kerk St) T027 712 1438, Wwww.mountview.co.za. Eight tasteful, colourfully African-themed rooms in this stylish four-star guesthouse, pleasantly situated on the fringe of the town, right by a short trail offering views over Springbok and the surrounding countryside. There's also a swimming pool and braai areas, and two self-catering flats. ❹

Springbok Lodge & Restaurant 37 Voortrekker St, entrance on Kerk St T027 712 1321, Esbklodge@intekom.co.za. Operates twenty guesthouses, all in distinctive white and yellow livery, and within walking distance. The rooms are plain but reasonable, and there are also some self-catering apartments. ❷

Outside town

Môrewag Guest Farm 12km northwest of town T083 627 6423 or 084 408 0135, Ekillerpcs@webmail.co.za. A pleasant working farm with plentiful flowers and succulents in season, some small game, three fully furnished guest rooms and a comfortable, old-fashioned cottage. Activities include petting farm animals, biking, walking trails, a swimming pool, and there's also a campsite. They're happy to pick you up from Springbok. If you're driving, take the Kleinzee road and turn right after 8km towards Nababeep. Breakfast included. ❷

Naries Guest Farm 27km west of town along the Kleinzee road ☎ 027 712 2462, ℗ 027 718 1300. A homely, comfortable place to stay, this has five somewhat plain rooms in an atmospheric Cape Dutch farmhouse, and a self-catering cottage with two doubles and one single. No under-12s allowed in the main farmhouse. The candlelight dinners are a big draw, and hiking and horse-riding can be arranged. ❹

Eating and drinking

There are a couple of pizza places and takeaways on Voortrekker Street near the taxi rank. As for proper **restaurants**, *Carne Casa* on Voortrekker Street is a fine steakhouse with a Portuguese touch, also featuring fish and vegetarian dishes (mains around R40; closed Sun). The main attraction is its sunny street-facing balcony, which doubles as a **bar**. Also on Voortrekker Street is one of the province's leading restaurants, *Melkboschkuil*, 300m south of *Springbok Lodge* (☎ 027 718 1789; closed Sun lunchtime). The mouth-watering menu includes vegetarian dishes such as lasagna, pies and wood-fired pizzas, and look out too for the day's specialities, often featuring game; eat inside or out on the shaded veranda. A three-course splurge with wine will set you back R150–200. Another good place for a drink is *Alysium*, a chilled-out cocktail bar with white-draped sofas, good music and a youthful clientele (Mon–Sat 7pm–2am); it's at 35 Voortrekker Street two blocks east of the taxi rank.

Around Springbok

Following the R355 east out of Springbok for around 15km, you arrive at the entrance to **Goegap Nature Reserve** (daily 8am–6pm; R10; no public transport), which proclaims itself "Namaqualand in miniature". The privately managed reserve boasts a surprisingly high species count – close to 600 indigenous flower species, 45 flavours of mammal (including springbok, gemsbok and Hartmann's mountain zebra), and 94 bird species. Activities include three hiking trails, a mountain-biking trail, and – inevitably – a 4WD route; the visitor centre (closes 4pm) can provide details. If you haven't got your own transport, you could take a day-trip here from Springbok with Virosatours (see box on p.345).

Okiep and Nababeep

Lying 8km north of Springbok on the N7 is the slightly scruffy little town of **OKIEP** (or O'Okiep), which took over from Springbok as the copper-mining centre of Namaqualand in the 1880s. Until production ceased temporarily in 1919, it was the world's richest copper mine, and a major prize during the 1902 Anglo-Boer War, in which 900 defenders – mostly employees of the Cape Copper Company – repulsed a 53-day siege by Jan Smuts' forces. The ruins of one of the block houses built during the siege can still be seen on a hill northeast of town.

The mines were established under the expertise of Cornish tin mine engineers, and you can still visit both the easily identified **smokestack** (actually a ventilation shaft) and **Cornish beam pump** beside it. Visits are arranged through the three-star *Okiep Country Hotel* (☎ 027 744 1000, 🖥 www.okiep.co.za; ❷), under the palm trees on the main street. The hotel itself is a delight, a low colonial structure with green gabled roof and white wooden verandas, with rooms (all en suite and with satellite TVs) in the main building or in an annexe.

Another old mining town, **NABABEEP**, lies 7km west of Okiep. There's a small **museum** here (daily 9am–1pm, in flower season until 5pm; donation expected) charting the copper boom – and bust. The highlight is "Clara", a sweet narrow-gauge steam loco that used to haul copper ore to Port Nolloth. There are **minibus taxis** from Springbok to Nababeep daily except on Sundays; they can drop you outside the museum.

Steinkopf

Some 44km north of Okiep, **STEINKOPF** marks the junction of the N7 with the R382 to Port Nolloth and the Richtersveld Transfrontier Park. An otherwise nondescript little settlement founded in 1819 as a mission station, Steinkopf is a good example of how grassroots tourism initiatives are trying to take root in South Africa. The **Kookfontein Information Centre** (daily 8am–5pm; ☎027 721 8162 or 027 721 8841, ✉steininfo@lantic.net), 500m north of the turn-off on the N7, provides details of the local sights, which include lookout points, a succulent nursery, reconstructed *matjies* houses, and **Kinderlê**, the grave of 32 Nama children massacred by Khoisan in the mid-1800s while the adults were attending church. The centre provides clued-up **guides** to accompany you to these sights. Self-catering **accommodation** is available at the community-run *Kookfontein Chalets* (book through the information centre; ❷), and traditional Nama meals can be provided.

The Namibian border

For 50km north of Steinkopf, the N7 crosses some fairly bleak plains before descending through a band of rocky hills, burnt black and ochre in the heat, and into a haunting pass with the Scrabble-winning name of **Vwfmylpoort**. The road then breaks through into the green floodplain of the **Orange River**, which marks South Africa's border with Namibia. The gathering of buildings on the South African side of the river is called **Vioolsdrift**; there isn't much here apart from a filling station, a dusty store and a high-fenced government building.

A turning here along a dirt road traces the south bank of the Orange, 10km along which is the *Fiddlers Creek* **campsite** (☎027 761 8953, ⓦwww.bushwhacked.co.za), on the grassy riverbank with a bar and braai area. This is the base of one of the companies offering rafting trips down the Orange (see opposite), as well as arranging 4WD excursions, sunset cruises and fishing. Day visitors are welcome; expect to pay R25 entrance plus the cost of activities. Sadly, the more luxurious *Peace of Paradise* campsite, 10km further downstream, burned down in 2004; it was too early at the time of writing to tell whether it would be resurrected.

If you're going on **into Namibia** from Vioolsdrift, you have to clear immigration and customs on both sides of the bridge; the border is open 24 hours a day. The town on the Namibian side, **Noordoewer**, has several service stations, and simple rooms plus camping facilities at the *Orange River Lodge* (☎+264 63 297 012, ⓦwww.orlodge.iway.na; ❷).

The west coast and the Richtersveld

North from St Helena Bay, the hook of land 100km north of Cape Town, the long, lonely **west coast** of South Africa has two simple components: the cold, grey Atlantic Ocean, and the dominant sandveld vegetation, hardy but infertile. There isn't much more to the region: between the mouth

Canoeing trips on the Orange River

One way to enjoy the majesty of the mountain-desert landscape of the Richters-veld is to take a canoe down the Orange River. The canoes are of the inflatable variety, more akin to **rafts**, and you'll find the words used interchangeably. This is not, as sometimes portrayed, white-water rafting – by the time it reaches northern Namaqualand the river is broad, the few rapids tending to rouse you from slumber rather than quicken the pulse. The highlights are the dramatic rock formations and varied birdlife – but above all relaxation is the key. Trips range from half-day tasters to full-on six day expeditions, with camps set up by the riverbank en route; costs start at around R220 for a full day including lunch, or R400 overnight with all meals. For more exciting rapids, try the stretch of the Orange in the Onseepkans Gorge, north of Pofadder.

A recommended **rafting company** is Bushwhacked Outdoor Adventure (T027 761 8946, Wwww.bushwhacked.co.za), based at *Fiddler's Creek* campsite near Vioolsdrif. More upmarket operators, both in Cape Town, include Felix Unite River Adventures (T021 425 5181, Wwww.felixunite.com) and River Rafters (T021 712 5094, Wwww.riverrafters.co.za). Most companies offering tours of the region can also arrange the rafting side of things.

of the Olifants River near Vanrhynsdorp, and the Orange River over 400km to the north, there is just one sealed road connecting the N7 highway to the coast, which leads to the only settlement of significance, **Port Nolloth**.

Namaqualand's first **diamonds** were discovered in 1925, confirming that diamonds could be carried the length of the Orange, washed out into the ocean, and then dispersed by currents and the processes of longshore drift. Although initial prospecting was carried out along the course of the Orange and in the coastal dunes, the diamonds lying offshore on the sea bed are now the more eagerly chased, mostly by boats operating with huge underwater "vacuum cleaners" and divers working in often dangerous conditions. Whereas much of Namaqualand's coast remains off-limits thanks to the presence of diamonds, the "**Diamond Coast**" from Port Nolloth to Alexander Bay, the mouth of the Orange River, is visitable.

During the flower season, the rains fall first on the coastal areas, and you can often see displays beginning about 20km inland, making the few roads down to the coast from the N7 worthwhile detours. The dirt R355 road through the **Spektakel Pass** between Springbok and Kleinzee is one of the most spectacular drives in Namaqualand, and the **Anenous Pass** on the tarred R382 between Steinkopf (see opposite) and Port Nolloth is also impressive. Along this road you'll also see wandering herds of goats belonging to the pastoral **Nama** people living in the area, as well as the peaks and valleys of the **Richtersveld Transfrontier Park**, the mountain desert occupying the area immediately south of the Orange River. The area surrounding the park is home to several developing **community tourism** initiatives, providing an excellent introduction to the life of the Nama.

The only public transport for Port Nolloth and Alexander Bay is the weekday **minibus**, run by VIP Taxis (T027 851 8780), between Sanddrif on the border and Springbok. This passes through Alexander Bay at 7.45am, then Port Nolloth at 9am en route to Springbok, and turns around there at 3pm. Note that the border crossing to Oranjemund on the Namibian coast is closed; the only open border post is at Vioolsdrift (see opposite).

Port Nolloth

PORT NOLLOTH is an odd but delightful place. In the hazy sunshine the horizons are never quite in focus, while the heavy morning mists shroud the town in a quiet eeriness. Populated by an eclectic mix of races and professions, including fishermen, diamond-boat owners, fortune-seeking commercial divers, diver-seeking girls and a significant Portuguese and Nigerian community, Port Nolloth is a place with a whiff of mystery and excitement, and tales are thick about "IDB" (illegal diamond buying). You should take care when broaching the subject – paranoia and illegal firearms make a volatile combination.

Attractions are limited and the Atlantic too cold for swimming, but a stroll to the **harbour** is always interesting, and there's a small **museum** (Mon–Fri 9am–5pm) on the corner of the main road and Beach Road, where you can view an ad-hoc collection of flotsam, jetsam, photographs and newspaper articles about Port Nolloth, and find out about some of the local plant and sea life. There are no tours on the diamond boats, but the guesthouses at **McDougall's Bay**, 5–6km to the south, have canoes and small boats for their guests.

The **tourist office** (℡027 851 1111, ℻027 851 1101) is at the museum; another good source of information is the laid-back *Bedrock Lodge* next door (℡027 851 8865, Ⓔbedrock@icon.co.za; ❷), a stylish old beach house with period furniture that's a great place to **stay**. There are simpler rooms in several beachfront houses at McDougall's Bay (ask locally for advice about walking there with luggage, as there have been muggings in the past), such as *McDougall's Bay Beach House Accommodation* on Haarder Street (℡027 851 8856, Ⓔbeachaccom@telkomsa.net; ❷), and the similar *Port Indigo* on Kamp Street (℡027 851 8012, Ⓦwww.portindigo.co.za; ❷).

There are several good places for **eating**. *Bedrock Tea Garden* at the back of the lodge is good for lunch (closed evenings). Alternatively, Port Nolloth Fish Shop has a tiny and very pleasant restaurant attached. More formal meals can be found in the cosy *Anita's Tavern*, opposite the *Scotia Inn Hotel* and offering plain fish, meat and pasta dishes. The main **drinking** hole is *Diamond Hunters Pub*, along from Port Nolloth Fish Shop.

Alexander Bay

The most western point of South Africa is **ALEXANDER BAY**, at the mouth of the Orange River within a stone's throw of Namibia. Alluvial **diamonds** are the town's *raison d'être*, their discovery in 1927 leading to the site's appropriation by the state, which still runs the place. The largest stone ever found here, in 1944, was the Merensky Diamond, weighing in at a cool 211.5 carats; more recently, a 111-carat stone was found by divers contracted by the state **Alexkor** mining company, which still controls most commercial activity in and around town. Alexkor offers visitors a four-hour **diamond mine tour** on Thursday mornings (R120; no under-18s), which includes a visit to a small museum, and can be extended to include a seal colony. Local guides can show you to a (fenced-off) **lichen "forest"** on a hilltop east of town, which boasts 29 different species, or accompany you on a **desert walk** through the barren-looking landscape surrounding the town. But the main attraction is the ample **birdlife** at the mouth of the river, where over 75 species of water bird are recorded.

When you arrive, you'll have to **sign in**, giving a plausible reason for your visit, and your departure time; diamond-smuggling paranoia means you're not allowed to leave after 5pm. Information and bookings for pretty much everything, including the mine tour (book at least a day in advance), are done through Alexkor's **Tourist Information Centre** (Mon–Fri 8.30am–4.30pm; ☎027 831 1330, ⊛www.diamondcoast.co.za).

Alexkor maintains three decent **guesthouses** (weekdays ☎027 831 1330 extension 2121, weekends ☎027 831 1655): the *Af-en-Toe* (❶), *Frikkie Snyman* (❷) and the *Uitsig* (❸). There are also four rooms at the community-run *Beauvallon Ostrich Farm* (☎027 831 1592), with meals rustled up by the local women's group. En route to Richtersveld Transfrontier Park, there's also the company-run *Brandkaros Holiday Resort* on a farm 27km east of Alexander Bay (☎027 831 1856 or 082 323 9556, ⓔhanny@alexkor.co.za; ❶), with simple rondavels with kitchens, sleeping four each, plus rooms in a guesthouse and a grassy **campsite** 400m from the river. The town's best **restaurant** is *Merensky Coffee and Curio Shop*, decked out with mining memorabilia.

The Richtersveld

The area of northwestern Namaqualand known as the **Richtersveld** covers an area roughly bounded by the Orange River to the north, the N7 to

---

Community tourism in the Richtersveld

A rarity in South Africa, the Richtersveld area has become something of a testing ground for **community-based tourism initiatives**, combining basic accommodation (all in the ❶ bracket) – sometimes in the traditional *matjies* huts of the Nama – with opportunities to get to know the locals, eat traditional food, and hike around the hills. **Access** – or lack thereof – is the main problem, as for most places you need your own wheels, and you'd do well do arrange things a week or so in advance by phone to be sure that places are open and food and water are available. Still, the projects at **Sanddrif** and **Steinkopf** (p.356) are accessible by **minibus taxi and bus**, respectively, and organized trips in the Richtersveld are nowadays likely to include a visit to at least one of these projects. For more information, ask at the tourist office in Springbok.

Eksteenfontein (Xhobes) ☎027 851 7108. The oldest and most wide-ranging of the projects, this was started by local women whose husbands were away working in mines. It features the comfortable *Eksteenfontein Guesthouse*, with kitchen and shower, *matjies* huts to stay in (not all with beds or linen), a coffee bar, 4WD trail, meals, and plenty of excitable kids.

Kuboes (Khubus) ☎027 831 2095 or 027 831 1212. A diminutive Nama settlement just outside the park's southwestern boundary, with a late nineteenth-century church, a small museum, guides for hikes (book on ☎027 831 1185), traditional dance on request, a two-room guesthouse, and the *Plantasie* campsite, where it's possible to stay in a *matjies* hut (which is put up especially for you). Bring water and supplies, or give them a few days' notice if you'd like meals provided.

Lekkersing ☎ & ⓕ027 851 8580. Over the hills west of Eksteenfontein, this offers the modern, self-catering *Lekkersing Guesthouse*, hiking, horse-riding, donkey cart rides and even caving. The project also maintains a campsite at Koerdap.

Rooiberg ☎027 851 8755 or 027 851 8772. A few kilometres from Eksteenfontein at the base of a mountain, perfect for that miles-from-anywhere wilderness experience (bring water from Eksteenfontein). There's a guesthouse, campsite and hiking trails, for which you'll need a guide.

Sanddrif ☎027 831 1457 or 083 538 9585. On the Orange River off the road from Alexander Bay to Sendelingsdrift, this is the departure point for the weekday *VIP* minibus taxi to Springbok (see p.354), and is thus easily accessible. The local Nama and Xhosa communities run the modern *Sanddrif Guesthouse*. A 4WD trail starts here, canoeing is possible and a campsite is planned. Basic provisions are available but no petrol.

the east, the R382 to Port Nolloth to the south and the Atlantic Ocean on its western side. Here, the starkly beautiful **AI-AIS RICHTERSVELD TRANSFRONTIER PARK** – to give it its full title – was formed in 2003 by the merger of South Africa's Richtersveld National Park (by which name the new park is still known in South Africa) and Namibia's Ai-Ais Hot Springs Game Park. Tucked along either side of a loop in the Orange, the landscape is fierce and rugged; names such as Hellskloof, Skeleton Gorge, Devil's Tooth and Gorgon's Head indicate the austerity of the inhospitable brown mountainscape, tempered only by a broad range of hardy succulents, mighty rock formations, the magnificence of the light cast at dawn and dusk, and the glittering canopy of stars at night. Annual rainfall in parts of the park is under 50mm, making this the only true desert – and mountain desert at that – in South Africa. In summer the daytime heat can be unbearable – temperatures over 50°C have been recorded – while on winter nights temperatures drop below freezing.

The best time to visit is August and September, when the area's **succulents** – representing almost one third of South Africa's species – burst into flower. There's little **fauna** in the park other than lizards and klipspringers, although leopards are present if characteristically shy. Along the Orange you'll find surprisingly rich **birdlife**.

The wider Richtersveld area outside the park is largely inhabited by Nama people herding sheep and goats, though some of the settlements offer accommodation and hiking guides for travellers as part of a slew of community development programmes. Two settlements can be visited by public transport, but the rest of the area – including the park – is only feasible in a 4WD vehicle or as part of an organized tour.

Practicalities

Facilities are extremely limited – this is not the place for a casual visit, and there's no public transport either. Ordinary cars are not allowed inside the park; the only way to explore is in a 4WD or a pick-up with a high enough clearance to handle the sandy river beds and rough mountain passes between the designated campsites. Unless you're an experienced driver, probably the best way of seeing Richtersveld is as part of a **tour**. The most experienced operation is Richtersveld Challenge (see p.353), offering expeditions of varying lengths into the park as well as to Kgalagadi, Namibia and Botswana; also recommended are Virosatours (see p.345). Both outfits can include hiking, abseiling or rafting along the Orange in their tours.

If you are driving, it's recommended that you travel in a group of two vehicles, but note that no driving is allowed at night; fuel and limited supplies are available at the park headquarters at **Sendelingsdrift** (daily 8am–4pm; ☏027 831 1506, ℻027 831 1175; R80), 94km from Alexander Bay. **Maps and guidebooks** are sold at the gate, and at *Springbok Lodge* (p.353) and Richtersveld Challenge (p.353) in Springbok. Though the park must be entered at Sendelingsdrift, visitors can exit at Helskloof Gate in the south, handy for the nearby community tourism projects.

At the time of writing, the South African and Namibian sections of the park remained separated, the border closed other than for rafters camping along the Orange. Plans are afoot to establish a pontoon bridge at the park headquarters to ferry vehicles across, and once in place it would be reasonable to assume that tourists will be allowed to enter the Namibian side of the park so long as they return via the same route, as happens at Kgalagadi Transfrontier Park.

Park **accommodation** includes decent chalets (❷) at the park-run guesthouse by the gate at Sendelingsdrift, and very basic **campsites** at De Koei,

Kokerboomkloof, Potjiespram, Richtersberg and De Hoop inside the park; all except De Koei have ablution facilities. Between April and September it's possible to **hike**, accompanied by a guide, along designated trails, and also into the park with the help of the community tourism project at Kuboes.

Travel details

Trains

De Aar to: Beaufort West (1 daily plus Thurs; 3hr 45min–3hr 55min); Bloemfontein (Tues; 6hr 50min); Bloemhof (1 daily; 6hr 25min); Cape Town (1–2 daily; 13hr 15min–13hr 55min); Christiana (1 daily; 5hr 30min); Durban (Tues; 23hr 20min); Johannesburg (1 daily; 12hr 30min); Kimberley (1–2 daily; 3hr 40min–3hr 50min); Klerksdorp (1 daily; 8hr 30min); Krugersdorp (1 daily; 11hr 35min); Ladysmith (Tues; 17hr 10min); Laingsburg (1 daily plus Thurs; 7hr 10min–7hr 30min); Pietermaritzburg (Tues; 21hr); Potchefstroom (1 daily; 9hr 25min); Pretoria (1 daily; 14hr 25min); Worcester (1–2 daily; 10hr).
Kimberley to: Beaufort West (1 daily; 8hr); Bloemfontein (4 weekly; 2hr 45min–3hr 15min); Bloemhof (1–2 daily; 2hr 20min); Cape Town (1–2 daily; 17hr 30min–18hr); Christiana (1–2 daily; 1hr 30min); De Aar (1 daily; 4hr); Durban (Tues; 19hr 15min); Johannesburg (1–2 daily; 8hr 30min–9hr); Klerksdorp (1–2 daily; 4hr 30min); Krugersdorp (1–2 daily; 7hr 35min–8hr); Ladysmith (Tues; 13hr); Laingsburg (1–2 daily; 11hr 45min); Mafikeng (1 daily; 9hr); Pietermaritzburg (1 weekly; 17hr); Potchefstroom (1–2 daily; 5hr 30min); Pretoria (1 daily; 10hr 25min); Worcester (1 daily; 14hr 30min).
Upington to: Windhoek (Namibia; 2 weekly; 25hr 20min).

Buses

Calvinia to: Cape Town (1 weekly; 6hr 30min); Johannesburg (3 weekly; 15hr 30min); Upington (3 weekly; 4hr 45min); Vryburg (3 weekly; 10hr).
Kimberley to: Bloemfontein (4 weekly; 2hr 30min); Bloemhof (2–3 daily; 2hr); Cape Town (3–4 daily; 11hr–11hr 30min); Christiana (2–3 daily; 1hr 30min); George (4 weekly; 9hr 30min–9hr 55min); Johannesburg (2–3 daily; 6hr 10min–7hr 40min); Klerksdorp (2–3 daily; 3hr 45min); Mossel Bay (4 weekly; 9hr–9hr 30min); Oudtshoorn (4 weekly; 7hr 30min); Potchefstroom (2–3 daily; 4hr 30min); Pretoria (2–3 daily; 7hr–8hr 40min); Upington (1 weekly; 5hr).
Kuruman to: Johannesburg (1 daily; 7hr 20min);

Pretoria (1 daily; 8hr 20min); Upington (1 daily; 3hr 30min); Vryburg (1 daily; 1hr 40hr); Windhoek (Namibia; 1 daily; 15hr 10min).
Springbok to: Cape Town (6 weekly; 6hr 30min); Johannesburg (4 weekly; 16hr); Klerksdorp (4 weekly; 13hr); Kuruman (4 weekly; 8hr 30min); Potchefstroom (4 weekly; 13hr 45min); Pretoria (4 weekly; 17hr); Upington (4 weekly; 5hr); Vryburg (4 weekly; 10hr 30min); Windhoek (8 weekly; 12hr).
Upington to: Bloemfontein (4 weekly; 7hr); Calvinia (1 weekly; 4hr 45min); Cape Town (1 daily; 11hr 30min–12hr 45min); Johannesburg (1 daily; 10hr 15min); Kimberley (Sun; 5hr); Klerksdorp (1 daily; 7hr 20min); Kuruman (1 daily; 2hr 45min); Potchefstroom (1 daily; 8hr); Pretoria (1 daily; 11hr 15min); Springbok (4 weekly; 5hr 10min); Vryburg (1 daily; 4hr 40min); Windhoek (Namibia; 4 weekly; 11hr 30min).
Vanrhynsdorp to: Calvinia (3 weekly; 2hr); Cape Town (1 daily; 5hr); Springbok (4 weekly; 4hr 30min); Upington (3 weekly; 7hr).

Minibus taxis

Services on all routes are reduced on Saturday, and often nonexistent on Sunday. Frequencies given below refer to weekdays.
Kimberley to: Barkly West (hourly; 30min); Kuruman (2–4 daily; 5hr); Upington (2–4 daily; 5hr).
Springbok to: Alexander Bay (1 daily Mon–Fri; 1hr 10min); Cape Town (3–4 daily; 6hr 30min); Port Nolloth (1 daily Mon–Fri; 4hr); Sanddrif (1 daily Mon–Fri; 3hr 30min); Upington (3 daily; 5hr).
Upington to: Calvinia (1–2 daily; 5hr); Cape Town (1–2 daily; 10hr); Kimberley (2–3 daily; 5hr); Kuruman (2–3 daily; 4hr 30min); Springbok (2–3 daily; 5hr).

Domestic flights

Kimberley to: Cape Town (Mon–Fri 2 daily, Sun 1 daily; 2hr); Johannesburg (1 daily; 1hr 15min).
Upington to: Cape Town (1 daily; 1hr 50min); Johannesburg (1–2 daily; 1hr 50min).

The Eastern Cape

CHAPTER 4 # Highlights

* **Port Elizabeth township tour** Several guides run very accessible tours into the African areas of the province's largest city. See p.372

* **Addo Elephant National Park** See pachyderms and the rest of the Big Five in the best game reserve in the malaria-free southern half of the country. See p.377

* **Grahamstown Festival** Africa's largest arts festival wakes up this pretty colonial university town. See box on p.395

* **The Tuishuise** Accommodation in a street of beautifully restored and furnished Victorian houses in the historic frontier town of Cradock. See p.403

* **Karoo farmstays** Experience the sharp light and panoramic landscape of the Karoo semi-desert that sweeps across South Africa's interior. See p.406

* **Fort Hare art gallery** A superb collection of black South African art buried in the remote university that educated many of the country's leaders, including Nelson Mandela. See p.420

* **Wild Coast family hotels** Terrific hotels occupying isolated spots along ravishing subtropical coastline. See p.433

* **Amadiba Horse Trail** Explore unspoilt areas inaccessible by car on this riding excursion, led by members of the local Pondo community. See p.434

* **Bulungula Backpacker Lodge** In a remote Wild Coast village, this brilliant base offers a vivid experience of Xhosa life and culture. See p.441

△ Sunset on the Wild Coast

The Eastern Cape

Sandwiched between the Western Cape and KwaZulu-Natal, South Africa's two most popular coastal provinces, the **Eastern Cape** tends to be bypassed by visitors – and for all the wrong reasons. The relative neglect it has suffered as a tourist destination and at the hands of the government is precisely where its charm lies. You can still find traditional African villages here, and the region's 1000km of undeveloped **coastline** alone justifies a visit, sweeping back inland in immense undulations of vegetated dunefields. For anyone wanting to get off the beaten track, the province is, in fact, one of the most rewarding regions in South Africa.

Port Elizabeth is the province's commercial centre, principally used to start or end a trip along the Garden Route, though it's a useful springboard for launching out into the rest of South Africa – the city is the transport hub of the Eastern Cape, well served by flights, trains, buses and car rental companies. **Jeffrey's Bay**, 75km to the west, has a fabled reputation among surfers for its perfect waves. East of Port Elizabeth the **R72** coastal road, a great rolling journey, provides easy access to a series of unassuming resorts, all gloriously sited on euphorbia-clad hillsides at the mouths of lazy rivers. Around an hour's drive inland are some of the province's most significant game reserves, the only places in the southern half of the country providing serious game viewing, among them **Addo Elephant Park**, a Big Five reserve where sightings of elephants are virtually guaranteed. Addo and the private reserves nearby are among the few game reserves in South Africa that are malaria-free throughout the year. The hinterland to the north takes in areas appropriated by English immigrants shipped out in the 1820s as ballast for a new British colony. Here, **Grahamstown** glories in its twin roles as the spiritual home of English-speaking South Africa and host to Africa's biggest arts festival. Close by, the giraffe, antelope and hippo country of the **Great Fish River Reserve Complex** comprises stony hills vegetated by monumental candelabra-like succulents and river courses lined with thorn trees.

The northwest is dominated by the sparse beauty of the **Karoo**, the thorny semi-desert stretching across much of central South Africa. The rugged **Mountain Zebra National Park**, 200km north of Port Elizabeth, is a terrific place to watch herbivorous game in a stirring landscape of flat-topped mountains and arid plains stretching for hundreds of kilometres. A short step to the west, **Graaff-Reinet** is the quintessential eighteenth-century Cape Dutch Karoo town, with its serene whitewashed streetscape.

The eastern part of the province, largely the former Transkei, is by far the least developed, with rural Xhosa villages predominating. **East London**, the province's only other centre of any size, sits on the cusp of the former "white" South Africa and the African "homelands", and also serves well as a springboard for heading north into the central region, where the principal interest derives from political and cultural connections. **Steve Biko** was born here, and you can visit his grave in **King William's Town** to the west. Further west is **Alice**, less well known than its university, **Fort Hare**, which educated many contemporary African leaders, including Nelson Mandela.

The only established resorts in this section are in the **Amatola Mountains**, where indigenous forests and mossy coolness provide relief from the dry scrublands below. Tucked into the northeastern corner of the province, the **Drakensberg range**, more commonly associated with KwaZulu-Natal, makes a steep ascent out of the Karoo and offers trout-fishing, skiing in winter and ancient San rock art. The focus of the area is the remote, lovely village of **Rhodes**, a long journey down a rough road, which rewards you with absolute tranquillity and exceptional views.

Further east, the **Wild Coast region** remains one of the least developed and most exciting regions in the country. It's also the poorest part of the poorest province, a fact reflecting its historic role as a dumping ground for black South Africans. Despite this, the region is blessed with fabulously beautiful subtropical coast. From here, all the way to the KwaZulu-Natal border, dirt roads trundle down to the coast from the N2 to dozens of remote and indolent hillside resorts, of which **Port St Johns** is the biggest and best known. West of Port St Johns, the **Wild Coast Hotel Meander**, an organized walking trail, takes in a deserted stretch of cliffs and sands with convenient stops at small family resort hotels. Along the coast to the east of town you can explore beaches and rural villages on horseback as part of the community-run **Amadiba Trail**, which starts near the KwaZulu-Natal border. In the rugged goat-chewed landscape inland, Xhosa-speakers live in mud-and-tin homesteads, scraping a living herding stock and growing crops. Most visitors pass as quickly as possible through **Umtata**, the ugly former capital of the Transkei – but if you're following in the footsteps of Nelson Mandela, the **Nelson Mandela Museum** in the centre of Umtata and **Qunu**, his birthplace southwest of the town, are obvious ports of call.

Some history

The Eastern Cape was carved up into black and white territories in a more consolidated way than anywhere else in the country. The stark contrasts between wealth and poverty were forged in the nineteenth century when the British drew the Cape colonial frontier along the **Great Fish River**, a thousand kilometres east of Cape Town, and fought over half a dozen campaigns (known as the **Frontier Wars**) to keep the **Xhosa** at bay on its east bank. In the 1820s the British shipped in thousands of settlers to bolster white numbers and reinforce the line. West of the Kei River, which subsequently became the colonial boundary, you'll encounter fenced-off white farms, pretty historic towns and industrial development. Across the river, the scourges of imperialism and apartheid have left little but overgrazed communal lands dotted with traditional huts and skinny cattle.

Even for a country where everything is suffused with politics, the Eastern Cape's identity is excessively **political**. South Africa's black trade unions have deep roots in its soil, which also produced many anti-apartheid African leaders, including former president **Nelson Mandela**, his successor **Thabo Mbeki**, and Black Consciousness leader **Steve Biko**, who died in 1977 at the hands of Port Elizabeth security police. The Transkei or Wild Coast region, wedged between the Kei and KwaZulu-Natal, was the testing ground for grand apartheid when it became the prototype in 1963 for the Bantustan system of racial segregation. In 1976 the South African government gave it notional "independence", under the puppet leadership of the Matanzima brothers, in the hope that several million Xhosa-speaking South Africans, surplus to industry's needs, could be dumped in the territory and thereby become foreigners in "white South Africa". When the Transkei was reincorporated into South Africa in 1994 it became part of the new Eastern Cape province, which is struggling for economic survival under the weight of its apartheid-era legacy.

Port Elizabeth and the western region

A city of flyovers and sprawling townships, **Port Elizabeth** is the industrial centre of the Eastern Cape, where African shanty dwellers scrape a living on the dusty fringes of well-tended middle-class suburbs. In 1820 it was the arrival point for four thousand British settlers, who doubled the English-speaking population of South Africa. Today, their descendants risk the hellish national roads from Gauteng every Christmas to speed down to the "Friendly City" and holiday along the institutionalized beachfront, with its burger bars and performing dolphins. The port's industrial feel is mitigated by some outstanding city beaches, and should you end up killing time here (and you could certainly do worse), you'll find diversion in beautiful **coastal walks** a few kilometres from town and in the small **historical centre**. There are also a couple of excellent township tours, which offer valuable insight into apartheid and the new South Africa, and are a welcome contrast to the Garden Route's beach focus.

The main reason most people wash up here is to start or finish a tour of the **Garden Route** – or head further up the highway to **Addo Elephant National Park** (see p.377), the most significant game reserve in the southern half of the country. Also within easy striking distance are several other smaller, private and utterly luxurious game reserves such as **Shamwari**, **Amakhala** and **Lalibela**.

To the east of Port Elizabeth, a handful of **resorts** are found along the **R72 East London coast road**, where the roaring surf meets enormously wide sandy beaches, backed by mountainous dunes. The inland route to East London deviates away from the coast to pass through **Grahamstown**, a handsome university town, worth at least a night (more if you're interested in English settler history and the frontier conflicts with the Xhosa). Nearby, pretty settler villages trace the spread of the 1820 settlers into the interior.

A couple of hundred kilometres north from Port Elizabeth, an area of flat-topped hills and treeless plains opens out to extend across a third of South Africa. Its name, the **Karoo**, means "hard and dry" in the tongue of the Khoikhoi pastoralists, the region's original inhabitants, who were exterminated by Dutch frontiersmen. The oldest and best known of the settlements here is the picture-postcard town of **Graaff-Reinet**, a solid fixture on bus tours. Just a few kilometres away is the awesome **Valley of Desolation**, and the village of **Nieu Betheseda**, best known for its eccentric Owl House museum. Nearly as pretty as Graaff-Reinet, though not as architecturally rich, the town of **Cradock**, to its east, has the added attractions of mineral baths and the rugged **Mountain Zebra National Park**. Some of the best places to stay in the *platteland*, or interior, are on sheep farms or in historically listed guesthouses.

Port Elizabeth

At the western end of Algoa (aka Nelson Mandela) Bay, **PORT ELIZABETH**, commonly known as **PE**, is not a place to visit if you're looking for cosmopolitan urban culture or beautiful buildings. The smokestacks along the N2 bear testimony to the fact that the Eastern Cape's largest centre has thrived on heavy industry and cheap African labour, which accounts for its deep-rooted trade unionism and strong tradition of African nationalism. So it may come as a surprise that this has long been a popular holiday destination for white Gauteng families – but then the town beachfront, stretching for several kilometres along Humewood Road, has some of the nicest, safest and cleanest **city beaches** in the country, thoroughly geared up with waterslides, performing dolphins and snakes to keep the kids occupied.

As a city, PE is pretty functional. There's enough reason to linger for a couple of days, however, and the city has some terrific accommodation and good restaurants in a relatively crime-free environment. Although the town has been ravaged by industrialization and thoughtless modernization, one or two buildings do stand out in an otherwise featureless **city centre**, and a couple of classically pretty rows of Victorian terraces still remain in the suburb of **Central**. Holiday-makers head for the beachfront suburbs of **Humewood** and **Summerstrand** where there are places to stay, bars, restaurants and clubs in abundance. There are also some excellent **tours** around PE and into the townships.

Arrival and information

Port Elizabeth's **airport** (☏041 581 2984 & 041 507 7319) is conveniently situated on the edge of Walmer suburb, 4km south from the city centre. From here, a minibus shuttle (☏041 582 3720) stops at all the main hotels, and makes other unscheduled stops on request. The fare from the airport to the city centre is around R60 one-way, considerably less than the cost by metered taxi.

The **train station** (☏086 000 888) is centrally located, with buses departing from the rank directly across the road. The **Baz Bus** will drop you off at any central location or accommodation. Arriving by **intercity bus**, you alight at Greenacres shopping mall in Newton Park suburb, 3km from the centre, served by Translux (☏041 392 1333), Greyhound (☏041 363 4555) and Intercape (☏086 128 7287). As for regional bus services, Minilux (☏043 741 3107) runs buses between Grahamstown or East London and PE most days of the week. The Sunshine Express (☏082 956 2687) offers a door-to-door shuttle bus from PE to Jeffrey's Bay and Cape St Francis.

The extremely helpful **Nelson Mandela Bay Tourism** office (Mon–Fri 8am–4.30pm, Sat & Sun 9.30am–3.30pm; ☏041 585 8884, ⓦwww.nmbt.co.za) is in the Donkin Lighthouse Building (a National Monument with a good view from the top) on the Donkin Reserve in Belmont Terrace, Central suburb.

City transport and tours

If you're staying in Central, exploring the city **on foot** is a realistic possibility – try the self-guided **Heritage Walk**, shown on a map available at the tourist office). However, for any serious exploration of PE, or for getting to and from the beachfront, **renting a car** is your best option (see "Listings", p.376), as the city's transport system leaves much to be desired. **Buses** operated by the municipal Algoa Bus Company (☏041 404 1200) are infrequent, running from the Market Square bus depot to the suburbs, the beaches and Greenacres shopping mall. PE's **minibus taxis** run from town to the beachfront on a regular basis, but are the least recommended way to travel. **Metered taxis** don't have ranks so you'll need to phone to find a taxi (see p.376); if you're going to the airport or the bus or train stations, it's advisable to book ahead.

PORT ELIZABETH
BEACHFRONT & SUBURBS

◄ Cape Town, East London & Grahamstown

Humewood Road Station
(Apple Express Terminal)

King's Beach

Dolphinarium
Oceanarium

Snake Park
& Museum

Bay
Tourism

HUMEWOOD

HAPPY VALLEY

Hobie Beach

Humewood Beach

A l g o a
B a y

See Inset for detail

Humewood Road Station

NORTH END

Harbour

LAKE VIEW

GOVAN MBEKI STREET

CENTRAL

Train
Station

See Central Port Elizabeth map

St George's
Park

SETTLERS PARK
NATURE RESERVE

WESTERN ROAD

FOREST HILL
DRIVE

MILL
PARK

Greenacres
& The Bridge
Shopping Malls

Baakens River

NEWTON
PARK

Port Elizabeth
Airport

W A L M E R

Apple Express Narrow Gauge Railway

SIXTH AVE
SEVENTH AVE
EIGHTH AVE
NINTH AVE
TENTH AVE

ALISTER MILLER DRIVE

Summer-
strand

MARINE DRIVE

BRIGHTON DRIVE

WINCHESTER WAY

Schoenmakerskop, ⑤, ⑥, ⑧ & ⑨ ▶

ACCOMMODATION

Admiral's Lodge	H
Beach Hotel	F
First Avenue Lodge	G
The Humewood	D
Kelway Hotel	B
King's Beach Backpacker	
Hostel	A
Lungile Backpackers	E
Pine Lodge Resort	I
Windermere	C

N

RESTAURANTS,
BARS AND CLUBS

Blue Water Café	2
Café Brazilia	4
Castro's	3
The Island Seafood	
Grill & Bar	5
Sacramento	6
Sugar Rays	1
Tapas Al Sol	1
Toby Joe's	1

0   1 km

The best way to see Port Elizabeth is on one of the excellent **bus tours**, which shed light on the culture and history of a city shaped by layers of political history. Calabash Tour (℡041 585 6162 or 083 303 7553, ⓦwww.calabashtours.co.za) operates excellent "Real City Tours" by day and *shebeen* tours by night; Tanaqua Indigenous Tours (℡083 270 9924/083 995 6345; ⓔwaldoadams@hotmail.com) offers the same packages as well as whale-watching. Both operators also offer day-trips to Addo, as do many others. B&Bs and hotels carry an extensive range of tour brochures and are generally happy to make bookings for guests. Polani offers breakfast and sunset sailing **cruises** around Algoa Bay (from R125; book on ℡041 583 2141), leaving from the harbour next to the dry dock (signed from the harbour entrance).

Accommodation

The obvious place to stay is the **beachfront**, with a vast choice of hotels, self-catering suites and hundreds of B&Bs. During the December and January peak holiday period the beachfront becomes the focus for most of the city's action, while February, March and April are much quieter yet offer perfect beach weather. Note that PE can be subject to excoriatingly **strong winds**, especially between September and December, which makes going to the beach unpleasant. **Central PE** has some good places to stay, too, including guesthouses and backpacker lodges (for the locations of which, see the map opposite). Bay Tourism & Tours is a central **booking agency** (℡041 584 0622 or 083 369 4722, ⓕ041 584 0016).

If you fancy a slice of **African township life**, *Fundani Lodge* (℡041 454 2064/6 or 082 964 6563) offers an opportunity to enjoy football matches, traditional ceremonies and good African cooking, while you stay with a family in the New Brighton, Zwide or Motherwell townships (❷).

Beachfront

Admiral's Lodge 47 Admiralty Way, Summerstrand ℡041 583 1894 or 083 455 2072, ⓔadmiralslodge@mweb.co.za. Spacious and stylish rooms at a good B&B, at the far end of Summerstrand about 7km from the centre. There's a braai area, communal lounge, pool and trampoline for the kids. Airport transfers are available. ❺

Beach Hotel Marine Dr, Humewood ℡041 583 2161, ⓔresbeach@pehotels.co.za. Across the road from popular Hobie Beach, and sited at the centre of the beachside action, the hotel has a great patio bar overlooking the sea, offering snacks, cocktails and cold beer, and *The Bell*, a very decent à la carte restaurant. Recent renovations have included a sun deck and pool. Ask about the weekend specials. Breakfast extra. ❹

First Avenue Lodge 3 First Ave, Summerstrand ℡041 583 5173, ⓕ041 583 5176. Fourteen en-suite rooms close to the beach with their own entrances, offered on a B&B or self-catering basis, in a popular and pleasant establishment with a pool and entertainment area. Airport transfers are available. ❺

The Humewood 33 Beach Rd, Humewood ℡041 585 8961, ⓕ041 585 1740. A large, old-fashioned hotel that reeks nostalgically of 1950s family seaside holidays. The rooms are large rooms and feature wicker furniture and summery floral prints. Service is excellent and includes laundry facilities and babysitting. There's a good bar and sun deck. Airport transfers available. ❹

Kelway Hotel Brookes Hill Dr, Humewood ℡041 586 0638, ⓦwww.thekelway.co.za. Spanking new and stylishly upmarket hotel kitted out with timber panelling, seagrass chairs and handcrafted wooden tables. Standard, luxury and family rooms available. Breakfast included. ❺

King's Beach Backpacker Hostel 41 Windermere Rd, Humewood ℡041 585 8113, ⓔkingsb@agenet.co.za. Spotless, well-established hostel, a block away from the beach, with camping facilities, dorms and double rooms, plus an outside bar and braai area. Although principally for self-catering, it lays on tea, coffee, bread and jams in the morning. The travel desk can book township, game park and other tours. Dorms ❶, rooms ❷

Lungile Backpackers 12 La Roche Dr, Summerstrand ℡041 582 2042, ⓔlungile@netactive.co.za. Large and popular beachfront hostel where you can party indoors or step out into the heart of PE's beachfront nightlife strip. Perched on a hill, it has facilities for camping, a large lawn to relax on, sea views, a pool table, bar and swimming pool. Self-catering only. Dorms ❶, rooms ❷

Pine Lodge Resort Off Marine Dr, Humewood ☎041 583 4004, ⊛www.pinelodge.co.za. Right on the beach near the wonderful historic lighthouse and next to the Cape Recife Nature Reserve, where owls, mongooses and antelope make appearances. Offers various log cabin units, some with full kitchens, sleeping from four to eight people. Besides a popular bar and restaurant, the lodge boasts a swimming pool, a gym and a games room. Cabins for four from around R270.

Windermere 35 Humewood Rd, Humewood ☎041 582 2245, ⊛www.thewindermere.co.za. Stylish hotel with just eight suites, given an almost Zen-like feel through the subtle use of off-white to oaty colours contrasted with dark hues, such as chocolate brown, and materials that include timber and granite. ❻–❽

Central

Calabash Lodge 8 Dollery St ☎041 585 6162 or 083 303 7553, ⊛www.calabashlodge.co.za. Cotton sheets and African-inspired decor in a multi-level house in one of Central's oldest areas. Rooms are en suite and great breakfasts are available, as are secure parking and airport transfers. Beats the rest of the town's budget accommodation hands down. ❷

Jikeleza Lodge 44 Cuyler St ☎041 586 3721, ⒺWinteam@hinet.co.za. Friendly backpacker place with dorms, doubles and a family room. Their adventure centre can help you sort out tour and travel bookings. Dorms ❶, rooms ❷

Millbrook House 2 Havelock Square, Havelock St ☎041 585 3080, ⒻO41 582 3774. Charming B&B in a Victorian house with plunge pool and braai area. It's on Central's prettiest street, with some worthwhile British colonial architecture to take in. Airport transfers can be arranged. ❸

The City

Port Elizabeth's **city centre** is marred by a network of freeways that cuts a swath across the south of town, blocking off the city from the harbour. The city's white population retreated to the suburbs some time ago, leaving the centre to African traders and township shoppers, who are slowly resuscitating its commercial spirit. The **suburbs** offer little to draw you away from the beachfront, unless you're a shopaholic, in which case you should make a

▲ Cape Town, East London & Grahamstown

CENTRAL PORT ELIZABETH

ACCOMMODATION
Calabash Lodge ... A
Jikeleza Lodge ... C
Millbrook House ... B

RESTAURANTS AND CLUBS
52 Parliament ... 2
Natti's Thai Kitchen ... 3
Nine Yards ... 1

0 300 m

beeline for **Newton Park**, 5km west of the centre and home to **Greenacres** and **The Bridge**, vast shopping malls to which the city-centre department stores have relocated en masse.

Central

The city's main street, which runs parallel to the freeway as it sweeps into town, has been renamed **Govan Mbeki Avenue** in honour of the veteran activist (father of Thabo Mbeki, South Africa's president), who died in 2001. African traders dealing a pretty standard line in crochet tat and leather goods line up along the pavements giving the precinct a lively feel, but it's not safe after dark. Despite some nice old office blocks, the area is marred by several miserable high-rises housing the government departments they were built for in the apartheid era.

The symbolic heart of town is the **City Hall**, standing in **Market Square**, a large empty space surrounded by some striking mid-Victorian buildings, adjacent to the train and bus stations on the edge of the harbour. But the dejection of the quarter, under the grimy shadow of a flyover, conspires against it ever pumping any real life into the district. Nevertheless, the **City Library**, across the road from the City Hall, is a genuine attraction, especially the second floor, with its beautiful stained-glass dome and windows and magical little balconies of bookshelves. Cultural battle lines have been drawn around the dour statue of **Queen Victoria** in front of the library, and she may not be around much longer. Wezandla, at 27 Baakens Street, has a wide selection of African arts and crafts for sale.

Heading west up hilly **Donkin Street**, you'll come upon a curious stone pyramid commemorating **Elizabeth Donkin**, after whom PE was named. Elizabeth was the young wife of the Cape's acting governor in 1820, Sir Rufane Donkin; she died of fever in India in 1818. West from here, Lawrence Street has some browsable antiques and collectables shops, including Books and Bygones, which has an outstanding stock of books, magazines and kitsch relating to South Africa.

Further west, you reach St George's Park and the **Nelson Mandela Metropolitan Art Museum**, 1 Park Drive (formerly the King George VI Art Gallery; Mon–Fri 8.30am–5pm, Sat 9am–4.30pm, Sun 2–4.30pm; free), which has a collection of contemporary local work, visiting exhibitions and a small shop selling postcards and local arts and crafts. At 30 Park Drive, the **Ron Belling Art Gallery** (Mon–Fri 10am–4pm, Sat & first Sun of the month 10am–1pm; R5), is housed in one of the city's finest examples of Art Deco architecture, and displays Belling's detailed paintings of aircraft and ships, a must if you're interested in military aviation.

St George's Park itself is a huge circular green, dominated by the St George's Cricket Ground. It contains a public swimming pool, and the tiny iron-and-glass **Pearson Conservatory**, an elegantly bulbous Victorian hothouse whose components were shipped out from Scotland and erected in Port Elizabeth in 1882. Across Park Drive, at the junction of Rink and Cape roads, stands the **Horse Memorial**, commemorating the gallant horses who fell during the Anglo-Boer South African War. Below a larger-than-life British soldier kneeling to feed a horse is a quintessentially English inscription: "The greatness of a nation lies not so much in the number of its people or the extent of its territory but in the extent and justice of its compassion."

The beachfront and around

PE's wonderful **beaches** are its main attraction. The protection provided by Algoa Bay makes them safe for swimming (that said, it's best to do so

The Apple Express

Just southeast of the harbour, on Humewood Road, **Humewood Road station** is the starting point for the **Apple Express**, a beautifully restored steam train that, during the holiday season, usually runs at 9.30am to **Thornhill** village and other destinations. En route it stops on Van Staden's River Bridge, the highest narrow-gauge railway bridge in the world. After a leisurely lunchtime break at Thornhill, the train trundles back to Humewood, arriving at 4pm. Tickets (R120 return for adults, R60 for children) can be booked through Spoornet (℡041 507 2333) or at the tourist office.

between the lifeguard beacons), and clean enough to make **beachcombing** a pleasure.

The beachfront strip, divided from the harbour by a large wall, starts about 2km south of the city centre. En route to the beaches, the **South End Museum** on the corner of Humewood Road and Walmer Boulevard (Mon–Fri 9am–4pm, Sat & Sun 2–5pm) is worth a visit. Based in the old Seamen's Institute, it recalls the bygone days of the South End, a vibrant multicultural neighbourhood the growth of which had much to do with PE's then booming harbour. As a result of the Group Areas Act it was razed street by street in the 1960s, save for a handful or churches and mosques. Today, the area is full of pricey townhouses.

The first of the beaches is beautiful, wide **King's Beach**, which is somewhat marred by a jumble of coal heaps and oil tanks behind it. To the southeast lies **Humewood Beach**, where the recently upgraded **McArthur's Pool and Leisure Centre** (daily 8.30am–6pm; R30, children half-price) offers heated pools as well as a tidal one, children's water chutes and splash pools, and restaurants. Across the road from here is a complex housing **Bayworld Museum, Oceanarium and Snake Park** (daily 9am–4.30pm; R33); the Oceanarium (performing dolphin and seal shows 11am & 3pm) brings huge pleasure to hordes of excited children during the holidays. **Brookes Pavilion** next door and **Dolphin's Leap** nearby are complexes of restaurants, pubs and clubs with great views. Beyond, to the south, **Hobie Beach** and **Summerstrand** are great for walking and sunbathing, with one dive operator based at the latter (see "Listings", p.376). Summerstrand's **Boardwalk Casino Complex** has some pleasing shops, including an indigenous crafts market, cinemas and some reasonable eating places.

Marine Drive continues 15km down the coast as far as the village of **Schoenmakerskop** (Schoenies to the locals), along impressive coastline that alternates between rocky shores and sandy beaches. From here you can walk the eight-kilometre **Sacramento Trail**, a shoreline path that leads to the huge-duned **Sardinia Bay**, the wildest and most dramatic stretch of coast in the area. To get there by road, turn right at the Schoenmakerskop intersection and follow the road until Sardinia Bay is signed, on the left.

Eating, drinking and nightlife

Port Elizabeth has no great culinary reputation, but there are some decent **eating places** to suit most budgets, especially along the beachfront. Apart from the hotel bars mentioned in the accommodation section, there are a few other passable joints for a drink, and a couple of **nightclubs**.

Many of the **bars** listed below feature lively local bands playing jazz, rock and pop. The hub of the pub and club universe is Brookes Pavilion on Humewood Beach. The daily *Eastern Province Herald* lists the occasional **concerts** at the PE Opera House, next to the Donkin Memorial, and the odd **cabaret** event, most notably Centrestage at the Boardwalk Casino (℡041 581 2245).

A good range of **films** is screened at the Kine Park Cinema, 3 Rink Street. For the usual Hollywood fare, try Nu Metro, Walmer Park Shopping Centre, Walmer (℡041 367 1102); Ster Kinekor in The Bridge shopping complex; or Cinema Starz at the Boardwalk Casino Complex – check the *Herald* for programme details.

Restaurants

Blue Water Café Hobie Beach ℡041 583 4110. Great sea views, good pasta and light snacks at this pleasant eating place. Daily 8.30am–11pm.

Café Brazilia Humerail Centre, Humewood ℡041 585 1482. A beachfront café and eating place with a Portuguese-inspired menu, friendly service and great harbour views. Daily from 10am.

Castro's 13 Eastbourne Rd ℡041 373 6615. Very cool late night bar and eating place popular with the smart set. The fare comprises hot and spicy Cuban/Mediterranean fusion food, leaning heavily towards seafood and poultry. Daily from noon. Closed Sun.

The Island Seafood Grill & Bar *Pine Lodge Resort*, Marine Dr ℡041 583 3789. A patio bar with an indoor restaurant serving a decent range of snacks and full meals. Every dish is named after an island, though the food is in fact fairly predictable pastas, burgers and so forth, all nicely presented.

Natti's Thai Kitchen 21 Clyde St, Central ℡041 585 4301. Excellent restaurant serving authentic Thai cuisine in a relaxed atmosphere. Eves only.

Sacramento Marine Dr. A range of pastas, steaks and toasted sandwiches, set along a stunning piece of coastline. Closes at 5pm.

Bars and clubs

52 Parliament 52 Parliament St, Central. Late-night bar in a Victorian building decked out with interesting metal sculptures. DJs play house and other sounds, with occasional live music. Food is available. The R30–40 deters impecunious teenagers. Wed, Fri & Sat.

Nine Yards Chapel St, Central. Cocktail and dance place with lots of drinks specials. Wed, Fri & Sat.

Sugar Rays, Tapas Al Sol & Toby Joe's Brookes Pavilion, Marine Dr ℡041 586 2159. Brookes is a multilevel complex where you can dine, drink and party, the hub of late-night beachfront clubbing. The dance floors can be packed, but there are wooden decks with sea views to provide relief. This is also the only place in PE where you might just get to hear local indie bands, who play here sporadically.

Listings

Airlines SAA ℡041 507 1111.

Car rental All at the airport: Avis ℡041 501 7200; Budget ℡041 581 4242; Hertz ℡041 581 6550; Imperial ℡041 581 1268; Tempest ℡041 581 1256.

Consulates UK, First Bowring House, Ring Rd, Greenacres (Mon–Fri 9am–12.30pm; ℡041 363 8841).

Diving Although the Indian Ocean around PE isn't tropically clear and warm, the diving here is good, especially for soft corals. For dive courses, try Pro Dive, at the Red Windmill, Beach Road, Summerstrand (℡041 583 5316 or 368 7880, ⊛www.prodive.co.za), which offers a one-day scuba diving course and refresher courses.

Emergencies Fire ℡041 585 1555; see also p.89.

Hospitals St George's (private), Park Dr, Settlers Park ℡041 392 6111; Provincial (state), Buckingham Rd, Central ℡041 392 3911.

Internet access Try Axxess Africa, 66a Westbourne Rd, Central, or the Humerail Centre, Humewood.

Laundries Automat, 6a Parliament St, Central; Rub & Tub, Rink House, 70d Clyde St, Central.

Pharmacy Mount Road Medicine Depot, Govan Mbeki Ave, is open daily until 11pm (℡041 484 3838).

Post office Brookes Pavilion, Humewood (Mon–Fri 9am–3.30pm & Sat 8.30–11am).

Taxis Reliable firms include Magic Cabs (℡041 582 2800) and Hurters Taxis (℡041 585 5500).

Travel agents Atkinsons, 50a Pickering St, Newton Park (℡041 365 2344; Pentravel, Walmer Park Shopping Centre, Walmer ℡041 368 6151.

The reserves around Port Elizabeth

A Big Five reserve, **Addo Elephant National Park** is just 73km north of Port Elizabeth, and should be your first choice for a relaxing few days' excursion from PE, though it is close enough to town to take in on a day-trip. If park accommodation is full, you may decide to stay at one of the nearby **private reserves** – especially if you just want to be pampered. On the N2 highway between PE and Grahamstown, alone, there are three: **Shamwari**, **Amakhala** and **Lalibela**, while **Schotia**, a kilometre off the N10/N2 interchange, has exciting night drives. One big attraction of Addo and these private reserves is that, unlike the country's other major game parks, they benefit from the fact that the Eastern Cape is **malaria-free**.

Addo Elephant National Park

Addo Elephant National Park (daily 7am–7pm; R80; Ⓦwww .addoelephantpark.com) is undergoing an expansion programme that will see it become one of South Africa's three largest game reserves, and the only one including coastline. Its PR people are talking in terms of a "Big Seven" reserve, as the denizens of the future coastal section (adjoining the Alexandra State Forest/Woody Cape section of the park; see p.383) include whales and great white sharks. **Elephants** remain the most obvious drawcard of Addo, but with the re-introduction in 2003 of a small number of **lions**, in two prides (big cats last roamed here over a century ago), as well as the presence of the rest of the Big Five – **buffalo**, **hippos** and **leopards** – it has become a game reserve to be reckoned with. Eight **spotted hyenas** have also been introduced as part of a programme to re-establish predators in the local ecosystem. Other species to look out for include **cheetah**, **black rhino**, **eland**, **kudu**, **warthog**, **ostrich** and **red hartebeest**.

The Addo bush is thick, dry and prickly, making it difficult sometimes to spot any of the 200–300 elephants and other game; when you do, though, it's often thrillingly close up. The best strategy is to ask where the pachyderms and the other four of the Big Five have last been seen (enquire with staff at the park reception), and also to head for the water hole in front of the restaurant to scan the bush for large grey backs quietly moving about. It also makes sense to go on a **guided game drive** in an open vehicle with a knowledgeable national parks driver. Two-hour outings leave throughout the day and cost R140 a person for day drives, R220 for sunset trips (including snacks and drinks), and R160 for night drives; book at Main Camp. The vehicles used are higher off the ground than a normal sedan to improve viewing opportunities.

Addo also offers a couple of **activities** to spice up your visit, with more in the pipeline. Two-hour **horse rides**, suitable for the not-so-experienced, leave at 8am from just outside the main gate and run along the exterior of the park fence (R100; book at Main Camp). **Elephant-back safaris** are operated from a farm abutting the northern boundary of Addo (Ⓣ & Ⓕ042 235 1400, Ⓦwww.addoelephantbacksafaris.co.za), 90km from Port Elizabeth, off the R335. Excursions last two to three hours and cost R650 per person, with air transfers possible from Port Elizabeth or nearby private lodges.

Practicalities

By far the most straighforward way of getting to Addo is via the new southern gate, which is accessed off the N2 at the village of Colchester, 43km northeast of Port Elizabeth. The gate is about 5km from **Matyholweni Camp**. To get to **Main Camp**, Addo's older and more established base, which is north of Matyholweni, you can either take a slow game drive through the park, which will take at least an hour, or use the R335 road that runs outside the western flank of the park – take the N2 from Port Elizabeth east towards Grahamstown for 5km, branching off at the Addo/Motherwell/Markman signpost onto the R335 through Addo village. Narina bush camp is 22km north of Main Camp along a gravel road. The network of roads within the section of the park between Main Camp and Matyholweni is untarred, but in good condition.

Maps of the park are available at reception and indicate the location of **picnic** and braai sites. A **restaurant** (daily 6am–8pm) at Main Camp offers three meals a day, while the shop is well stocked with food and drink. Until the park is consolidated (expected to be completed by 2010), you won't be able to reach the coastal section that includes the Alexandria State Forest from inside the national park.

Accommodation

Addo's two major public restcamps, **Main** and **Mathyolweni**, provide comfortable national park accommodation in a range of thatched, fully equipped self-catering units, while **Narina bush camp** has four safari tents. **Reservations** are essential in the high season, and can be made through SANParks or, less than 72 hours in advance, directly with Addo (☎042 233 0556, ℉041 233 0196). At the time of going to press a programme of reintroducing big game to the section of the park around Matyholweni had begun and was expected to be completed by the end of 2006. In addition to the national parks accommodation, there are some **luxury private lodges** inside the park – most notable of which is *Gorah Elephant Camp*.

Outside the park, but within easy striking distance, private B&Bs and guesthouses are in abundance around Addo, especially among the citrus groves of the Sundays River Valley. Many offer day and night drives in the game reserve.

Inside the park

Gorah Elephant Camp 9km west along the Addo Heights road leading from the N10 to Addo village ☎044 532 7818, ⊛www.gorah.com. Ultra-luxurious outfit based around a Victorian homestead decked out with the appropriate paraphernalia (mounted antelope skulls above the fireplace, evocative African landscapes, and polished tabletops you can see your reflection in) to play up those colonial-era safari fantasies. The suites are plush, there are opportunities to dine under the stars and there's a beautifully landscaped swimming pool. The steep price tag includes exclusive conducted game-viewing trips. ❾

Main Camp The oldest and largest of the National Parks camps. Besides camping facilities, there are forest cabins that share cooking facilities in communal kitchens; and more luxurious chalets with their own kitchenettes. Some of these units sleep up to four people (but the minimum charge is for two occupants). Also available are well-designed, spacious safari tents, perfect for summer, with decks right next to the perimeter fence; and for up

to six people there are larger standard (R680) and luxury (R1540) family units. Two chalets have been adapted to accommodate the disabled. ❷–❸

Mathyolweni Camp National Parks accommodation in a dozen fully equipped self-catering chalets with showers, and sleeping two. Set in a secluded valley surrounded by thicket that supports a wealth of birdlife, the chalets have decks from which you will be able to view game once a planned waterhole is completed. There is no restaurant, but Colchester, a 15min drive away, has shops and basic places to eat. ❸

Narina Camp Small National Parks bush camp in the mountainous Zuurberg section of Addo with four safari tents that share ablution and cooking facilities; bring your own provisions. Horse-riding is available. ❷

Outside the park

Avoca River Cabins 13km northwest of Addo village on the R336 ☎ & ℉042 234 0421 or 082 677 9920, ℮avocafrm@mweb.co.za. Reasonably priced B&B and self-catering accommodation on a farm in the Sundays River Valley. There are budget cabins, more comfortable thatched huts (some on the banks of the river), and a timber chalet on stilts nestled among trees; canoes are available to rent. ❷

Chrislin 12km south of Addo main gate, off the R336 ☎ 042 233 0022 or 082 783 3553, ⓦ www .africanhuts-addo.co.za. Quirky B&B with thatched huts built using traditional Xhosa construction techniques, with a lovely *lapa* (courtyard) and pool, and hearty country breakfasts, as well as dinners on request. ❹

The Elephant House 5km north of Addo village on the R335 ☎ & ⓕ 042 233 2462 or ☎ 083 799 5671, ⓦ www.elephanthouse.co.za. On a stud farm just minutes from Addo is one of the Eastern Cape's top places to stay, a stunning thatch-roofed lodge filled with Persian rugs and antique furniture. The five bedrooms, two of which are in garden cottages, open onto a lawned courtyard. Candlelit dinners available, as a tours into the surrounding reserves. ❽

Geelhoutboom 26 Market St, Kirkwood ☎ 042 230 1837 ⓦ www.kirkwood.co.za/geelhoutboom. Homely B&B with a/c rooms, a 20min drive from Addo main gate and shaded by a large yellowwood tree. Good value. ❷

Hitgeheim Country Lodge 20km southwest of Addo main gate ☎ 042 234 0778, ⓦ www .hitgeheim-addo.co.za. Small exclusive lodge set high above the Sundays River Valley on a working buffalo and ostrich farm. The thatched chalets, each with a private deck, overlook verdant countryside; rooms boast leather-upholstered chairs, white linen and antique furniture. Great five-course dinners can be arranged on request by energetic owners Archie and Maritjie Hitge, or you can order a picnic for a day outing to Addo. ❽

Kronenhoff On the R336 as you enter Kirkwood ☎ 042 230 1448, ⓦ www.kronenhoff.co.za. In a small farming town, this is a hospitable, high-ceilinged Cape Dutch-style home, with spacious suites, polished wooden floors, large leather sofas and a sociable pub. In summer the sweet scent of orange blossom carries from the surrounding citrus groves. ❻

Woodall Country House About 1km west of Addo main gate ☎ & ⓕ 042 233 0128, ⓦ www .woodall-addo.co.za. Luxury B&B on a working citrus farm. Accommodation ranges from a garden cottage to self-contained suites and rooms inside the beautiful homestead with a swimming pool, gymnasium, spa and sauna (massages are available, and there's a resident beautician). A lovely sundowner deck overlooks a small lake full of swans and other waterfowl. Three-course dinners are available. ❼

The private game reserves

Shamwari, 65km north of Port Elizabeth on the N2 (☎042 203 1111, ⓦwww.shamwari.com; ❾), is cultivating an image as a jetsetter destination, hosting the rich and famous, such as Tiger Woods and John Travolta. Accommodation is the colonial-style Long Lee Manor and an ever-growing number of attractive lodges dotted around the reserve, furnished with every conceivable comfort. While the reserve certainly excels at opulence, it's questionable whether this relatively small tract delivers the kind of wilderness experience you'll find in more substantial reserves.

Two kilometres north of the Shamwari turn-off, **Amakhala Game Reserve** (☎042 235 1608, ⓦwww.amakhala.co.za) is altogether a better option. The area is stocked with a variety of game, such as cheetah, giraffe, zebra, wildebeest and many antelopes; the absence of predators means you aren't confined to game drives, and paths make hiking among the aloes and other beautiful indigenous flora a great way to get close to the landscape. The Bushman's River meanders through the reserve and there is a river boat on which you can make game-viewing trips, accompanied by a ranger. **Accommodation** here comprises six indepedendently owned lodges that make use of the existing farmhouses on the reserve, as well as a camp where there are beds inside restored ox-wagons with private bathrooms – all with wonderful views. *Carnarvon Dale*, *Reed Valley Inn* and the *Witmos Oxwagons* have a half-board rate (❻), while rates at *Woodbury Lodge*, *Leeuwenbosch Country House*, *Shearers Lodge* and *Safari Lodge* are for full board and two safari activities a day (❽).

Lalibela Game Reserve

Preferable to Shamwari if you want more affordable luxury and game viewing is the **Lalibela Game Reserve**, 90km northeast of Port Elizabeth on the N2 to Grahamstown (☎041 581 8170, ⓦ www.lalibela.co.za; ❾). It's home to the Big Five and a diversity of flora and fauna, which you can see on day or evening safaris (R650). There are three fabulous **lodges** with private viewing decks, swimming pools and *bomas* to choose from: *Tree Tops* offers luxury safari tents on thatched platforms; *Lentaba Lodge* houses visitors in thatched chalets; and *Mark's Camp*, the largest of the three (it takes up to twenty people), consists of stone and thatch cottages. You can dine on terrific Eastern Cape fare and contemporary cuisine.

Schotia Private Game Reserve

Schotia Private Game Reserve (☎042 235 1436, ⓦ www.schotia.com), on the eastern flank of Addo, provides the perfect ending to a day-trip at Addo or any of the other parks. It's the smallest of the private reserves, a fact for which it compensates by offering a highly personalized experience, with three chalets for a maximum of just six guests, and thrilling night outings to see its three resident **lions**, zebra and twelve species of antelope. These night excursions are full of shining eyes caught by powerful lamps, with a delicious dinner to follow up, cooked on an open fire in a thatched courtyard. Visitors can arrange to be collected from Port Elizabeth or anywhere in the Addo vicinity; if you're driving, you're collected from a secure car park 2km up the N10 from the N2/N10 intersection.

Between Port Elizabeth and Storms River

Among the few reasons to turn off the 186-kilometre stretch of the N2 between Port Elizabeth and Storms River to the west are the resorts of **Jeffrey's Bay** and **St Francis Bay**. Of the two, Jeffrey's Bay is the more famous, at least if you happen to be a surfer; more than anywhere in the country, it has dedicated itself to having fun and making money from its pumping surf. Although St Francis Bay has some fine surfing breaks, it's thanks to its tranquil atmosphere and beauty that it's become a popular spot with upcountry South Africans. For travellers heading along the coast, both are good places to break a journey.

A useful mode of transport along this part of the coast is the **Sunshine Express** (☎082 956 2687), which operates like a taxi between Port Elizabeth and Jeffrey's and St Francis. This is a door-to-door service, meaning you can be collected and deposited wherever you specify. From PE to the other end of the route, the fare is R60 per person, for a minimum of two passengers.

Jeffrey's Bay

Some 75km west of Port Elizabeth, off the N2, **JEFFREY'S BAY** (known locally as **J Bay**) is jammed during the holiday seasons, when thousands of visitors throng the beaches, surfing shops and fast-food outlets, giving the place a real tacky seaside resort feel. Mansions dot the town's hill, but there's not much by way of grace and beauty here.

Surfing etiquette

Jeffrey's Bay's legendary reputation with international surfers was built on the Sixties cult movie *Endless Summer*, featuring surfer Bruce Brown trotting the globe in search of perpetual sunshine and the perfect wave. Although J Bay is by no means the best place to surf in South Africa – there are hundreds of good breaks up and down the coast between Cape Town and Durban – it is probably the place most single-mindedly devoted to the sport.

If you come here to surf, paddle-ski or boogie-board (aka "shark biscuit"), you should take care to observe the fundamentals of **surfing etiquette**. On arriving at a new spot, always hang around the margins sussing out the scene, never intruding on someone else's patch and always remembering that you are a visitor. Surfers are highly territorial and there are clearly defined rules – which often come down to proficiency – governing who takes precedence in the water. If you observe these conventions, the chances are you'll find South African surfers exceptionally friendly, ready to talk and happy to offer tips. And beginners will find it easy to locate someone willing to get them started for a small fee.

In the surfing pecking order, the 16- or 17-year-old rising stars are "grommets" or "surf rats", challenging the "old bullets" – the 20- or 30-somethings whom they consider to be over the hill. Half-crazed rodeo-riders of the swell, who take on seven-metre waves, are known as "hell men", while at the other end of the spectrum you'll find "doormats", "spongers" and "tea bags", who take to the sea on boogie- or knee-boards, and receive only marginally less contempt from surfers than paddle-skiers, who are termed "egg whippers" or "deckchairs".

For **surfing aficionados**, however, these are trifling details; J Bay is said by some to be one of the world's top three surfing spots. If you've come to surf, head for the break at **Super Tubes**, east of the main bathing beach, which produces an impressive and consistent swirling tube of whitewater, attracting surfers from all over the world throughout the year. Riding inside the vortex of a wave is considered the ultimate experience by surf buffs, but should only be attempted if you're an expert. Other key spots are at Kitchen Windows, Magna Tubes, the Point and Albatross. Surfing gear, including wet suits, can be rented from the multitude of surfing shops along Da Gama Road, while Jeffrey's Bay Surf School (☎082 939 1138) will show you the finer points of both surfing and sand-boarding.

Dolphins regularly surf the waves here, and **whales** can sometimes be seen between June and October. The main **bathing areas** are Main Beach (in town) and Kabeljous-on-Sea (a few kilometres north), with some wonderful seashells to be found between Main and Surfer's Point.

Practicalities

The **Baz Bus** stops at J Bay on its daily trek in either direction between Cape Town and Port Elizabeth. The **tourist office** (Mon–Fri 8.30am–5pm, Sat 9am–noon; ☎042 293 2588, ⓦwww.jeffreysbaytourism.com), on the corner of Da Gama and Dromedaris roads, publishes a wide-ranging list of places to stay.

J Bay has the usual collection of pizza joints, burger bars and steak houses. The resort's top **restaurant** is the *Walskipper*, incongruously housed in a weather-beaten wooden shack on the beach in Marina Martinique Harbour. Here you can tuck into lovely homemade bread and patés and jams while the main courses – including luxurious seafood – are cooked on an outside fire. The *Sunflower*, 20 Da Gama Road, does good breakfasts.

Accommodation

With lots of **hostels** to choose from, J Bay is definitely backpacker territory – but if communal living isn't your scene, you're still in luck, as there are numerous good and inexpensive **B&Bs** and some self-catering places in town. There's also camping right near the beach at the municipal caravan parks, *Kabbeljous* (T & F 042 293 3330) and *Jeffrey's Bay* (T 042 200 2214) in Da Gama Road, but the price is barely cheaper than a backpacker dorm.

To stay in December, January, Easter or July it's essential to book accommodation in advance. The off-season is very quiet except during the the the Billabong world-championship surfing competition, usually staged in July.

A1 Knyaston 23 & 27 Chestnut Ave T 042 296 1845, E a1knyaston@xsinet.co.za. Friendly establishment offering rooms in two houses and a self-contained flat, with great views and mega-breakfasts. **②–③**

Island Vibe 10 Dageraad St T & F 042 293 1625, E ivibe@lantic.co.za. Backpacker lodge built on a dune, with a wooden walkway onto the beach. Offers camping, dorms and doubles, with spectacular views. There's a lounge, bar, pool table and self-catering facilities. Breakfasts are available. **①**

Jeffrey's Bay Backpackers 12 Jeffrey St T & F 042 293 1379, E backpack@netactive.co.za. Two blocks away from the beach, this functional establishment has been going for some time. The dorms and doubles have good facilities for self-catering, and guests can chill out in the bar, lounge and swimming pool. Board rental is available. **①**

Lazee Bay 25 Mimosa St T & F 042 296 2090, W www.travelsa.co.za/lazeebay. Light and airy B&B with panoramic views and lots of marine murals indoors. An informal place, it has a spacious communal lounge, a kitchen, plus a pool, sun deck and airy African-inspired decor. **②**

Mount Joy Guest House 31 Mimosa St, reached up a steep narrow pathway T & F 042 296 1932. B&B with five elegant en-suite bedrooms. The fabulous view makes breakfast on the terrace pretty much obligatory. **③**

Super Tubes Guest House 12 Pepper St St T & F 042 293 2957, W www.supertubesguesthouse .co.za. A modest mansion in J Bay-style. Rooms are en suite, with old wooden bedsteads, and open onto a patio or garden. The Super Tubes beach is practically on the doorstep. **④**

St Francis Bay

A short hop south of Jeffrey's Bay, **ST FRANCIS BAY** is much more genteel than its neighbour. Part of the town is built around an attractive network of canals leading to the river, the houses here whitewashed and thatched, with some fine B&Bs among them. Further towards **Cape St Francis**, the houses feature a Mediterranean influence, as does the **Port St Francis** harbour, both holiday resort and haven for the fleet of *chokka* (squid) boats. The town is ringed by a series of small nature reserves, offering beautiful **walks**, some of which are trails through the *fynbos*. During the holiday season the town seethes with thousands of upcountry South Africans who own holiday homes here, but at other times peace and tranquillity reign. The commanding **lighthouse**, now a National Monument, was once described as the loneliest in Africa.

Practicalities

St Francis is easily reached **by car**; turn off the N2 at Humansdorp and continue 15km south to the coast. The **tourist office** at the Village Centre on the main thoroughfare, St Francis Drive (Mon–Fri 8.30am–4.30pm & Sat 9am–12.30pm, T 042 294 0076, W www.stfrancistourism.com) can help find accommodation. For **food**, there are lots of pubs, coffee shops and restaurants; calamari has to be pick of the menu. Both *The Dock o' the Bay* at Port St Francis and *Kamwaki*, 173 St Francis Drive, are highly recommended.

Accommodation

Accommodation at Port St Francis ranges from modern chic resorts along the harbour to thatched rural cosiness.

Cape St Francis Resort ℡ 042 298 0054, ⓦ www.capestfrancis.co.za. B&B and self-catering thatched cottages, with a pub and a restaurant on site. Excursions are available – among them canal trips, a sunset bay cruise and a 4WD visit to archeological sights in the Shark Point Nature Reserve. ❷
The Cottage ℡ & ⓕ 042 294 0328 or 082 465 2288, ⓔ thecottage@isat.co.za. Pleasant, functional B&B with just two rooms. ❸
Port St Francis Resort ℡ 042 294 1223, ⓦ www.coastcountry.co.za. A Mediterranean-style harbour complex of self-catering apartments, some facing the ocean, with panoramic views of the bay in front and the marina to the rear. All are beautifully decorated, with stunning patios, and some have their own plunge pools. ❻
The Sands ℡ 042 294 1888. Utter luxury in a beach house where each suite comes complete

with Jacuzzi and private timber deck. Breakfast is included in the rate; light meals are available on request. ❽
Thatchwoods 63 Lyme Rd, off St Francis Dr ℡ 042 294 0082, ⓦ www.thatchwood.com. Supremely comfy B&B where each room has its own private garden or sun deck. It's positioned on the edge of the popular golf course, and can arrange golf rounds for guests. Good value. ❺
Waterways 37 Shore Rd ℡ 042 294 0282 or 083 660 8909, ⓔ waterwaysbb@webmail.co.za. Of the many Port St Francis B&Bs under thatch, *Waterways* is recommended for its friendliness as well as its situation at the confluence of the canals and river, with a beautiful beach nearby. There are two en-suite bedrooms with their own outdoor living areas and spectacular views. Cruises can also be arranged. ❸

Between Port Elizabeth and Port Alfred

One of South Africa's most undeveloped stretches of coast, with wide beaches and exhilarating surf, stretches east from Port Elizabeth for a sandy 150km to **Port Alfred**. The sea temperature here is several degrees higher than around Cape Town (though not as warm as KwaZulu-Natal, and never tropically clear), and the deserted beaches are a walker's paradise, with shells, birds and rock pools. The only problem is the summer **wind**, which often affects the whole Eastern Cape coast – particularly in the afternoon, so set out as early as you can. The weather is at its calmest from April to September, and while it's not hot enough to tan, you'll certainly be comfortable picnicking or walking along the beaches. April to July is the optimum season for scuba diving, with the water at its clearest.

The resort of **Kenton-on-Sea** is one of the most arresting spots along this coast, with two rivers dotted with boats, rocky coves and fabulous beaches for swimming and walking. Most of the houses are holiday homes, unoccupied much of the year, belonging to white South Africans, but there is a fair bit of **accommodation** – good B&Bs in beautiful locations, at much lower prices than along the sometimes overrated Garden Route.

The most deserted section of the coast, once difficult to access, is now administratively part of the Addo Elephant Park (see p.377), and includes some spectacular and enormous sand dunes. Staying at Cannon Rocks or Alexandria is a good way to explore this area.

Alexandria State Forest

A fifty-kilometre tract of Eastern Cape beachfront is protected by the **Alexandria State Forest**. Part of the **Woody Cape** section of the Addo Elephant Park, it can be walked on the circular two-day **Alexandria Hiking Trail**, one

THE EASTERN CAPE | Between Port Elizabeth and Port Alfred

of South Africa's finest coastal hikes, which winds through indigenous forest and crosses a landscape of great hulking sand dunes to the ocean.

You'll need to **book** one of the places on the trail through Addo Elephant Park (T041 468 0916, E matyholweni@sanparks.org; R70 per person per day), especially to walk it at weekends, when the trail tends to be full. The 35-kilometre trail starts at the Woody Cape office, 8km from the R72 (and not served by public transport), where you collect permits. If you're heading east, the signposted turn-off is on the right, just before you reach Alexandria, 86km from Port Elizabeth. There's an **overnight hut** at the Woody Cape office (●), for use at the beginning or end of the trail (alternatively, stay in Alexandria or Cannons Bay nearby), and another on the coast, both with mattresses and drinking water, but no cooking facilities. The hike is quite tough going, especially along the windy dunes – the markers in the sand can get blown over, obscuring the route – but in fine weather the isolated beaches are magnificent. The **forest** can also be accessed on the seven-kilometre Tree Dassie Trail from the Woody Cape offices (R20).

Alexandria and Cannons Bay

ALEXANDRIA, a pineapple- and chicory-growing centre with a strip of shops and an imposing Dutch Reformed Church, is the closest town to Woody Cape. *Heritage Lodge*, along the main street (T046 653 0024, W www.heritage-lodge .co.za; ●), is one of the few **places to stay**, and although its reasonably priced rooms are nothing special, the *Gordons* **restaurant** (closed Sun eves) has a good reputation. Better still, you can stay at the recommended *Quins Sculpture Garden and B&B* at 5 Suid Street (T046 653 0121 or 082 770 8000, W www.quin-art .co.za; ●). Animal sculptures peep through the foliage and in a section of the main house there's a lovely, two-bedroomed apartment linked by a sitting room.

From Alexandria, a good dirt road takes you 18km southeast through the State Forest and farmland to the coast at **Boknes**. This tiny resort is the start of an hour-long beach walk eastwards to the monument of **Diaz Cross**, commemorating the Portuguese adventurer and explorer Bartholomeu Diaz, who rounded the South African coast in 1487 in search of a profitable new sea route between Europe and the East. The first European to make recorded contact with the Khoikhoi, Diaz was also the first to kill one of them. The cross, on a rocky promontory, marks the spot where he was forced by his crew to turn back to Cape Town, rather than face the journey eastwards.

The only place to stay nearby is **CANNON ROCKS**, 2km west of Boknes and linked to Alexandria by a tarred road. At the thoroughly family-oriented *Cannon Rocks Holiday Resort* (T046 654 0043, E cannonrocks@telkomsa.net; ●–●), you can pitch a tent or rent a two-bedroom chalet or luxury flat. The resort, which has a simple restaurant, is protected from the wind by trees, and is a five-minute walk to the beach. *Sandon B&B*, 187 Alice Road (T046 654 0217 or 082 594 4699, E sandon@cybertrade.co.za; ●), a large, modern house right on the beach, has two en-suite rooms and a separate flat in the same section of the property, with two double bedrooms where you can self-cater. Although there's a small shop, you're best off buying **supplies** from Alexandria. As Cannon Rocks adjoins the boundary of Woody Cape, it is possible to walk straight into the park along the beach, and a two-hour walking trail has been laid out.

Kenton-on-Sea

Some 26km from Alexandria and 56km from Grahamstown, the resort of **KENTON-ON-SEA** lies along two river valleys, perfect for a short beach holiday. A conglomeration of holiday houses served by a few shops and places to eat, Kenton is a good choice if you want to be somewhere undemanding and very beautiful. There's little to do here except enjoy the surf, sandy beaches and dunes (horse-riding here is fabulous; arrange this through Beachcombers, ☎046 648 1533) or wallow in big shallow tidal pools. While you can swim in the rivers, avoid getting close to the entrance to the sea, as strong **riptides** occur. There are also a couple of good **game lodges** on the Kariega River (see p.397), which can be accessed from either Kenton or Grahamstown, and a nature haven in **Kasouga**, a totally unspoilt scattering of cottages a few kilometres eastwards along the coast. The area doesn't see many foreign visitors and South Africans pack in principally during the school holidays, so the rest of the year, especially during the week, you're assured a quiet time.

If you want to spend time on Bushman's River, you can rent small **motor boats** from Kenton Marina (☎ & ☎046 648 1223; from R80/hr), well signposted off the R72, 300m up the R343 to Grahamstown. The marina also rents out two-person beaver **canoes** for paddling the fifteen-kilometre upriver **Bushman's River Trail**, on which you pass through countryside lined with cycads and euphorbias, and filled with chattering birdlife. The trip takes between two and five hours depending on your fitness, the direction of the tide and weather conditions. At the end of the trail is a **hut** sleeping sixteen in bunks (book at the marina; ❶). Mattresses, cooking utensils, braai facilities and outdoor cold showers are provided, but you must bring your own sleeping bag and provisions.

Practicalities

Kenton is a very small place, though it has a couple of restaurants, mini-supermarkets, a bank and cash machine, post office and a filling station – all along the main street, Kenton Road. Many people do their shopping fifteen minutes' drive away in Port Alfred. The **tourist office**, signposted on the main road (Jan–Nov Mon–Fri 9.30am–1pm & 2–4pm, Sat 9.30am–1pm; Dec daily 9am–5pm; ☎046 648 2418, ⓦwww.kenton.co.za) has information about most accommodation options in and around Kenton, and can certainly find you a bed. Erica McNulty, who runs the tourist office, also runs **Kenton township tours** and is the co-ordinator of an interesting sustainable community project, Masithandane, run by Xhosa women in Grahamstown.

Accommodation

Kenton has reasonably priced self-catering cottages and B&Bs, most of which provide breakfast as an extra. The nicest places to stay are close to the river. You can **camp** at the well-kept *Bushman's River Caravan Park*, 2 Loerie Road (☎046 648 1227) right in the centre of Bushman's River Mouth, a resort that's effectively an extension of Kenton. It's a few minutes' drive west of Kenton – follow the signs from the R72 turn-off to Bushman's River.

Berribridge B&B 28 Oxford St ☎046 648 1048. In a fine location, a 5min walk from the Kariega River, this family home has three doubles sharing two bathrooms, set apart from the main house. ❷
Burke's Nest 38 Van der Stel Rd ☎046 648 1894 or 082 577 2142. Garden cottage and a flatlet connected to a family home away from the beach, a short amble from the Kariega River. ❷
Oribi Haven Kasouga Farm, 9km from Kenton, on a gravel road off the R72 ☎046 648 2043,

ⓦwww.oribihaven.co.za. A 10min drive east of Kenton takes you to the Kasouga turn-off, where Kasouga farms sits on a hillside overlooking one of the best and least known beaches in the country. The farm, which has been declared a natural heritage site for its large population of Oribi antelope, has a two-bedroom cottage, which can be taken on a B&B or self-catering basis. ❷
Wings 21 Elliot Rd ☎046 648 1834, ⓔwings@casbusol.co.za. The bottom floor

of this upmarket home overlooking the Bushmans River has three bedrooms and a kitchen with the option of B&B or self-catering. There are garden chairs and braai facilities to enjoy the view. ❷

Woodlands Country House and Tea Garden 2km from the centre along the R343 to

Grahamstown ☎ & ℻ 046 648 2867, ✉ woodlands@compuscan.co.za. Acres of garden and bush leading down to the Bushman's River, with little cottages dotted along pathways cut through the vegetation. Birdlife thrives here and it's a very relaxing place to have teas or meals at the small restaurant. ❷

Eating and drinking

The best-located **eating and drinking** place in Kenton is *Homewoods*, 1 Eastbourne Road (closed all day Mon & Sun eves), a restaurant and pub at the mouth of the Kariega River. It has two decks and grand views, but the fare is run-of-the-mill, including steaks, fish and burgers. In the village centre, *The Local*, a pub and grill joint, is a reliable place for evening meals (closed Sunday eves), while during the day you can usually get coffee, teas and cake at *The Garden* on the main road.

Outside town, 2km along the R67 Grahamstown Road, *Woodlands Tea Garden* is the best place for teas and light lunches, serving good cheesecake, apple pie, quiches and fish and chips, with the option of eating outdoors. A kilometre further on along the same road, the child-friendly *Stanley's* (Mon–Sat lunch & dinner, Sunday lunch only; ☎046 648 1332) is an unpretentious farmhouse which offers nicely cooked English-style roasts, fish, steaks and ribs; you can eat on the deck, while taking in views of the Kariega River. Booking is essential, especially during holiday season and on Sundays.

Upstream along the Bushman's River, the *Sandbar Restaurant* (☎046 648 2192; closed Mon) is a modest pontoon that doubles as a pub, serving hamburgers, chips and calamari. The views of the steep cliffs, thick with euphorbia, amply compensate for any lack of flair. To get there, head out on the R67, taking the Riversbend turn-off west of Bushman's River Mouth.

Port Alfred

Of all the settlements between Port Elizabeth and East London, only **PORT ALFRED**, midway between the two, can make any claims to a town life outside the holiday season, when for a few weeks the small centre is transformed into a hectic bustle of cars and people. For the rest of the year, the town's population is swelled every weekend by wet-suited surfers and partying students from Rhodes University in Grahamstown, less than an hour away. Besides beach walking and swimming, it's an excellent place to do some **canoeing**: the Kowie Canoe Trail is an overnight jaunt up the Kowie River, or you do a day's paddle up the Lynedoch River to the east of Port Alfred. There is also an active dive school which doubles up as an adventure centre offering water-skiing, abseiling, deep-sea fishing and horse-riding, among others.

Nicknamed "Kowie" by locals, after the river, Port Alfred was named in honour of the second son of Queen Victoria, although he never actually made it here. The prince, who visited the Cape in 1870, cancelled a trip to Port Alfred at the last minute, because the prospect of an elephant hunt seemed more appealing. Although Port Alfred started life as a port for settler enterprises in the 1840s, it was never quite suitable (the river kept silting up) and it quickly faded away into a resort. No large ships navigate the river, but plenty of **fishing boats** brave its turbulent mouth every day, watched by fascinated bystanders on the end of the pier.

Arrival and information

The **Kowie River** slices through Port Alfred, creating an east and west bank, with the town and most popular swimming **beaches** to the west, and the less-developed dunes stretching east. The river is traversed by two **bridges**: a concrete bowstring-arch bridge that has become Port Alfred's symbol, and an older one, which leads straight into **Main Road**, lined with banks and small shops. Sadly, the natural lagoon was blasted away in the 1980s and replaced by a marina, floating with dozens of boats and artificial islands dotted with toytown holiday homes.

On Tuesdays and Thursdays, the Minilux **bus service**, connecting Port Elizabeth to East London via Grahamstown, pulls into the *Halyards Hotel*, off the main coastal road on the east side of the Kowie River. The **Baz Bus** stops daily at the backpackers' hostel at the old train station, as well as at *Beaver's Restaurant* on the west bank, which is good for getting to the self-catering places

PORT ALFRED

0 — 500 m

INDIAN OCEAN

Kelly's Beach

West Beach

East Beach

Pier

Royal Alfred Marina

Children's Beach

Kowie River

Bow-arch bridge

Kowie Museum

MAIN ROAD

SOUTHWELL ROAD

WHARF ROAD

PASCOE CRESCENT

ALFRED ROAD

JACKS CLOSE

YORK LANE

PARK ROAD

ALBANY ROAD

SPORTS ROAD

HIGH ROAD

PUTT ROAD

MILES BOWKER DRIVE

WEST BEACH DRIVE

ORIOLE ROAD

GLENEAGLES DRIVE

GRAND STREET

BEACH ROAD

WESLEY HILL

STEWART ROAD

HARDS

VROOM ROAD

ST ANDREWS

SMITH ROAD

DICKINSON ROAD

GEORGE STREET

FAIRLIE ROAD

HERON ROAD

TERN

A HERSTONE HILL

HERON ROAD

SOUTHWELL ROAD

STOCKS AVE

MASONIC STREET

CAMPBELL STREET

VANDER RIET STREET

CAUSEWAY

HALSTEAD

PARK AVENUE

YORK ROAD

▲ Grahamstown

◀ Port Elizabeth

▶ East London

Ten Burke Street & ◀

RESTAURANTS

Butlers	**1**
Buck & Hunter	**3**
Guido's on the Beach	**4**
Trainspotting	**B**

ACCOMMODATION

Coral Guest Cottage	**C**
The Halyards	**D**
Medolino Caravan Park	**E**
The Residency	**G**
Royal St Andrews	**F**
Riverside Caravan Park	**A**
Rugged Rocks	**K**
Settler Sands	**J**
Spinning Reel Holiday	
Cottages and B&B	**H**
The Station Backpackers	**B**
Villa de Mer	**I**

in Salt Vlei, a secluded beach 3km from the main beaches. From the former station, it's a minute's walk to the helpful **tourist office** and *Mama Temba* tea shop, on the riverfront as you cross the bridge into Main Street (Mon–Fri 8.30am–4.30pm, Sat 8.30am–noon; ⊤046 624 1235).

Accommodation

Outside school holidays you should have no problem finding a place to stay. The tourist office publishes a useful accommodation list, including B&Bs and self-catering cottages. The priciest and most sought-after places are on **West Beach**, while you'll find more affordable options back from the seafront and particularly in the older, slightly more characterful areas on the hill on the east side of town. Most B&Bs are indicated from the main roads with official brown signs, making them relatively easy to find. If you're on a budget and value seclusion, it's worth considering the self-catering cottages at Salt Vlei.

Hotels, guesthouses and B&Bs

Coral Guest Cottage Jack's Close ⊤ & ⓕ046 624 2849, Ⓦwww.coralcottages.co.za. Reasonably priced B&B on one of the East Bank hills, a 20min walk from East Beach. Comfortable rooms with bath in a restored corrugated-iron settler cottage, though the walls are not at all soundproof. You can expect to be pampered by the ebullient owner. ❷–❸

The Halyards Royal Alfred Marina, Albany Rd ⊤046 624 2410, Ⓦwww.halyardshotel.com. The smartest hotel in town, with marine-themed decor, swimming pool and wooden deck area. ❹

The Residency 11 Vroom Rd ⊤046 624 5382, Ⓦwww.theresidency.co.za. Spacious, beautifully restored Victorian house with yellowwood panelling, large comfortable beds and breakfasts on the veranda. There are views across the dunes to the sea. ❸

Royal St Andrews 19 St Andrews Rd ⊤046 624 1379, Ⓦwww.compushop.co.za/standrew. The Tudor-style exterior and conservative image cunningly disguise thoroughly modern refurbished interiors. Besides rooms, there are apartments which represent the town's best self-catering option. Outside, the pool has a wooden deck and terraced seating under trees. The hotel is across the road from the golf course, a 10min walk from Kelly's Beach. ❸

Spinning Reel Holiday Cottages and B&B Freshwater Rd, Salt Vlei, 3km west of West Beach ⊤046 624 4281, Ⓦwww.spinningreel.co.za. B&B rooms with sea views. ❷

Villa de Mer 22 West Beach Dr ⊤ & ⓕ046 624 2315, Ⓦwww.villademer.co.za. Kitsch postmodern guesthouse in the best location in town, right across the road from the beach. There are four en-suite rooms, a family unit, a courtyard swimming pool and huge windows through which to take in the views. ❸

Backpackers' lodges, campsites, chalets and apartments

Medolino Caravan Park Prince's Ave, Kowie West ⊤046 624 1651, Ⓦwww.medolino.caravanparks .com. A very efficiently run place, in shady grounds behind the dunes, protected from the wind by its trees. A 10min walk from Kelly's Beach. Good camping facilities, excellent wooden self-catering chalets and swimming pool. ❷

Riverside Caravan Park Mentone Rd ⊤046 624 2230. Small caravan park where you can rent two-bedroomed chalets (no camping). Peacefully set next to the river (but 3km from the town and beach), it faces onto a wetland, and boats are available to rent to explore the waterways. Bed linen can also be hired, but you must bring your own towels. ❷

Rugged Rocks Salt Vlei ⊤046 624 3112 or 082 781 4682, Ⓦwww.ruggedrocks.co.za. A beachside property in sizeable grounds 4km from the town centre. Six fully equipped cottages, either tucked in the coastal bush or with sea views. There are significant discounts for week-long stays outside the school holidays. Self-catering ❷

Settler Sands West Beach ⊤046 624 1110, Ⓦwww.remaxkowie.co.za. Self-catering units, sleeping two to six, in duplexes very close to the river mouth and a stone's throw from the sea. ❷–❸

Spinning Reel Holiday Cottages and B&B See under "Hotels". Relaxed, self-catering beach cottages where you can spend the day in your swimming gear. ❷

The Station Backpackers In the converted old train station ⊤046 624 5869, Ⓦwww.thestation .co.za. Bang in the centre, with a good, well-priced restaurant and mellow pub. Accommodation comprises three dorms and one double room. Tours and activities can be arranged. ❶

The Town and beaches

Port Alfred's attractions are firmly rooted in its **beaches** and the **Kowie River**. The town itself has little else to offer. The *Halyards Hotel* and a pub constitute the town's ersatz caged-in waterfront; far more authentic, the river frontage on **Wharf Street**, next to the old bridge, has been revamped and the row of Victorian buildings spruced up. Of passing interest is the tiny **Kowie Museum**, in Pascoe Crescent (Tues–Sat 9.30am–12.30pm; free), on the east side of the old bridge, featuring sepia photographs of Port Alfred before the marina and its mansions gobbled up the magnificent lagoon.

Beach life is focused on popular **West Beach**, where the river is sucked out to sea and the breakers pound in. From the café and stone pier you can watch the surfers and see fishing boats make dramatic entries into the river from the open ocean. Fifteen minutes' walk west along the beach lies **Kelly's Beach**, where you can swim safely in a gentle bay. **East Beach**, reached from the signposted road next to *Halyards Hotel*, is the nicest beach for walking, with a

Between Port Elizabeth and Port Alfred

Activities around Port Alfred

Divers shouldn't expect to see crystal waters and fluorescent fish around Port Alfred (the Indian Ocean isn't tropical here), though the slightly murky water contains colourful underwater denizens, as well as beautiful corals and sponges. Port Alfred is home to the reputable **Keryn's Dive School** (⊤082 692 6189 or 046 624 4432), based next to the *Halyards*. You can qualify here in a week for an internationally recognized diving certificate. They also offer a host of **adventure activities**, some of them geared specifically for children, such as Kids Scuba, kite flying and a climbing wall. Other activities, all reasonably priced, include water-skiing and tubing, and they rent out a range of gear, including dune boards to ski down the big sand dunes.

The Kowie Canoe Trail

The two-day **Kowie Canoe Trail**, a 21-kilometre paddle up the Kowie River, is a much-sought-after trip and one of the few self-guided canoeing and hiking trails in South Africa. Much of its charm is the colourful bird life, and the landscape – hills of dense, dry bush that slope down to the river. **Booking** is essential (⊤046 624 2230; R75 per person, including accommodation and a double canoe) and, while the trip is almost always full at weekends, it's easy to find a weekdays out of school holidays place on.

On the trip, you **stay overnight** in a hut in the **Horseshoe Bend Nature Reserve**, from where you can explore the forest on foot, and climb the steep escarpment to get an impressive view over the horseshoe. The biggest difficulty on this trip is the tide – make sure you check the tide table in the local *Kowie Announcer*, and paddle with the flow, going up the river when the tide is coming in, and back to Port Alfred when the river is flowing out. If it's windy, stay close to the shore and ensure your gear is in waterproof bags.

Horse-riding

Port Alfred has two horse-riding establishments. **Glenhope Riding**, off the Bathurst Road (⊤046 625 0866), is based on a pineapple farm and has first-rate horses and fabulous views to the sea. The other company is the Three Sisters Horse Trail, signposted 14km east of Port Alfred off the R72 towards East London road (booking essential ⊤046 675 1269 or 082 645 6345). They have access to one of the loveliest stretches of the coast in the region, and are recommended for children. Besides beach outrides, Three Sisters does more adventurous two- to three-day horse safaris where you overnight in a treehouse in riverine forest, and at a small game farm (if you extend the ride).

backdrop of hilly dunes stretching to the horizon. For toddlers, the safest and most popular spot is **Children's Beach**, a stretch of sand close to the town centre along a shallow section of river, reached from Beach Road, a few hundred metres from the arched bridge.

When the weather is blowy (or should you want to swim laps or join a water aerobics class), head for the heated indoor **swimming pool** next to *Halyards Hotel* (daily from 7.30am for laps and aerobics, otherwise 9.30am–7pm; R5). There's a small pool for toddlers.

Eating

Port Alfred is not noted for its cuisine. The town's swankiest **restaurant** is *Butlers*, 25 Van der Riet Street (Tues–Sat lunch & dinner, plus Sun lunch; ☎046 624 3464), which enjoys a riverside setting and is good for fish. Nearby on Main Street, at no. 9, *Buck & Hunter* (Mon–Sat 11.30am–10pm) is a restaurant and bar offering pizzas, fish, prawns, kudu steaks and a number of vegetarian dishes, with some outdoor seating at the back. On West Beach, *Guido's on the Beach* (open daily) does pizzas and pasta dishes, plus booze, attracting an early-20s crowd, with an upstairs deck. Service isn't their strong point, though the location certainly is in their favour. For keenly priced meals, including prawns and calamari, and excellent sandwiches, try *Trainspotting*, part of the *Station Backpackers* (see p.388); it's open daily from breakfast through to dinnertime. The biggest supermarket is Pick 'n Pay , in a small mall at the end of Main Road.

Grahamstown

Just over 50km inland from Port Alfred, but worlds apart in terms of ambience, **GRAHAMSTOWN** projects an image of a cultured, historic town, quintessentially English, Protestant and refined. Dominated by its cathedral, university and public schools, this is a thoroughly pleasant place to wander through, with well-maintained colonial **Georgian** and **Victorian buildings** lining the streets, and pretty suburban gardens. Every July, the town hosts an **arts festival**, the largest of its kind in Africa, and purportedly the second largest in the world (after Edinburgh; see box on p.395).

As elsewhere in South Africa, there are reminders of conquest and dispossession. Climb up Gunfire Hill, where the fortress-like 1820 **Settlers Monument** celebrates the achievement of South Africa's English-speaking immigrants, and you'll be able to see Makanaskop, the hill from which the **Xhosa** made their last stand against the British invaders. Their descendants live in desperately poor ghettos here, in a town almost devoid of industry. Marking the gap are the Kowie Ditches (which you'll cross if you take the old East London Road out of town), a waterway that ran red with Xhosa blood in the 1819 battle of Grahamstown.

Despite all this, and the constant reminders of poverty, Grahamstown makes a good stopover, and is the perfect base for excursions: a number of **historic villages** are within easy reach, some **game parks** are convenient for a day or weekend visit and, best of all, kilometres of **coast** are just 45 minutes' drive away. Cupped in a valley surrounded by hills, Grahamstown itself is compact; you'll only need a car to get out of town.

Some history

Grahamstown's sedate prettiness belies its beginnings as a **military outpost** in 1811. **Colonel Graham** made his name here (and gave it to the town), driving the Xhosa out of the Zuurveld, an area between the Bushman's and Fish rivers. The Fish River, 60km east of Grahamstown, marked the eastern boundary of the frontier, with Grahamstown as the capital. The ruthless expulsion of the Xhosa sparked off a series of nineteenth-century **Frontier Wars**.

A line of **forts** was built to defend the frontier, subsequently developing into the settlements, which now include Fort Beaufort, Fort Hare and Peddie, but these alone were not enough to hold the line, and the British decided to reinforce the frontier with a human barrier. With the promise of free land, they lured the dispossessed from a depressed Britain to occupy the lands west of the Fish River. In the migration mythology of English-speaking whites, these much-celebrated **1820 Settlers** came to take on a larger-than-life status as ancestors to whom many trace back their origins. However, far from discovering the hoped-for paradise, the ill-equipped settlers found themselves in a nightmare. The plots given them were unsuitable for crops and too small for cattle in the harsh Eastern Cape; drought, floods and disease were a constant problem, and the threat of Xhosa attack was never far away.

Not surprisingly, many settlers abandoned their lands and headed to Grahamstown in the early 1820s. This brought prosperity and growth to the town, which enjoyed a boom in the 1840s, when it developed into the emporium of the frontier. Xhosa traders came to barter ivory and hides for beads, buttons and brass wire, while some colonists, who had persisted with farming in the surrounding district, traded **wool** from Spanish merino sheep which thrived in the Eastern Cape.

Arrival and information

Grahamstown is on the N2, 127km inland from Port Elizabeth, roughly twelve hours by bus from Cape Town, Johannesburg or Durban. Translux, Intercape and Greyhound **buses** stop outside the *Frontier Country Hotel* on the corner of Bathurst and High streets. The Minilux **minibus**, which connects Grahamstown with the airport at Port Elizabeth daily, and goes on to Port Alfred and East London on Tuesdays and Thursdays, stops at Settler City Motors in Beaufort Street. The **train station** at the bottom of High Street sees only one train a day, a branch-line service connecting to the Johannesburg–Port Elizabeth line.

Grahamstown is easily covered on foot, but if you want a **taxi**, use the reliable Beeline (℡082 651 6646), the only licensed company in town. Their main trade is zipping up and down to Port Elizabeth airport. The helpful **tourist office** on the High Street (Mon–Fri 8.30am–5pm, Sat 9am–1pm; ℡046 622 3241, ⓦwww .grahamstown.co.za), next to the City Hall, has information on accommodation.

Accommodation

Grahamstown has the distinction of hosting the country's only backpackers' lodge that is housed in a historic jail, where you sleep in a former cell. Other than that, the most notable and choicest places to stay are in historic houses, and there's a good selection of hotels. If you've just arrived from the Garden Route or one of the more popular tourist areas of South Africa, accommodation rates will seem very reasonable here.

Nicely located next to wooded hills, and an easy walk to town, the **caravan park** (℡046 622 9112) is on the right of the N2 if you're coming into town from Port Elizabeth. Besides camping, it has basic rondavels with bunks and modest self-catering chalets sleeping five (bring your own linen).

Grahamstown provides the ideal opportunity for a **township homestay** (B&B ❶–❷) without having to traipse far – the townships are less than ten minutes' drive from the centre. Thabisa Xonxa (℡082 932 1304) can place you with a hospitable Xhosa family in Grahamstown East. The rooms are mostly en suite, in proper brick houses with secure off-street parking.

The only time you may have difficulty finding accommodation is during the festival in July, for when you'd be well advised to book as early as March. Several agencies specialize in finding accommodation during this period (to look for B&B accommodation, call Festival B&B on ℡046 622 2589).

7 Worcester Street 7 Worcester St ℡046 622 2843, ⒲www.worcesterstreet.co.za. Ten huge, extremely comfortable rooms furnished extravagantly with eclectic decor in a 1888 stone mansion. Managed by a trained chef, this establishment offers excellent three-course dinners on Wed & Fri nights, for which you need to book ahead. ❻

The Cock House 10 Market St ℡046 636 1295, ⒲www.cockhouse.co.za. Plush rooms in a beautiful Victorian house with a good reputation for food. It counts Nelson Mandela among its satisfied guests. ❹

Hotel Victoria Mews 8 New St ℡046 622 7261, ⒲www.hotelvictoria.co.za. Decent central hotel, with B&B as well as self-catering units. They have an annex across town in Market St. ❷–❸

Lantern Hill 2 Thompson St ℡046 622 8782, Ⓔlanternhill@imaginet.co.za. The most central of Grahamstown's B&Bs, across the road from the university. There are six en-suite rooms in two Victorian semi-detached houses, modestly furnished with a nice garden, and ramps for wheelchairs. Well run and efficient. ❷

Old Gaol Backpackers Somerset St ℡046 636 1001 or 083 982 5966, Ⓔoldgaol@imaginet.co.za.

Dorms and doubles in the cells of an old jail built in 1824 – a genuinely atmospheric place to stay. Trips are available to Addo Elephant Park and the Fish River. ❶

Settlers Hill Cottages 8 Bartholomew St & 1 Sheblon Lane, off Cross St ☎ 046 622 9720 or 082 809 3395, ⊛ www.settlershillcottages.co.za. A couple of reasonably priced, two-person settler cottages (both National Monuments) in the old part of town, with yellowwood floors. ❷

The Town

Reminders of the **colonial past** are everywhere in central Grahamstown, not just in the architecture, but also in streets named after Cape governors and soldiers: Cradock, Meyer, Somerset, Stockenstrom and Cuyler. **High Street** is Grahamstown's major shopping axis, with terraces of nineteenth-century buildings lending it a graceful air. Running from the station at its seedier east end, High Street continues past the cathedral at the junction of Hill Street, terminating at the 150-year-old Drostdy Arch, the whitewashed entrance gate to Rhodes University, of course named after Cecil John Rhodes (see box on p.315). Hawkers on the pavements sell small bags of fruit and vegetables, and you may see young Xhosa men in new caps and jackets, with red clay on their faces, signifying that their initiation period is over. At the centre of the street is the **Cathedral of St Michael and St George**, opened in 1830 and which, like many churches in the area, became a refuge for women and children during the Frontier Wars. Inside, on the right as you come in, is a quietly ironic memorial tablet to Colonel John Graham, who commanded the frontier.

While the High Street has most of the shops you'd need, many businesses have relocated, or opened up in the **Pepper Grove mall**, five minutes' walk north of High Street, with entrances in African and Allen streets. Pepper Grove also has the town's best-stocked supermarket, a chemist, cinemas, doctor, cafés, and a natural food store selling herbal remedies.

One of Grahamstown's rewarding short walks starts at the **Old Provost** in Lucas Avenue, on the edge of the Botanical Gardens and university. Built as a prison in the nineteenth century, the whitewashed stone Provost is now a craft shop; next to it are the graves of some British soldiers killed by Xhosa warriors. The walk heads up through the gardens to the **1820 Settlers Monument**, looming on Gunfire Hill above. Built in 1974 to commemorate the British settlers, it's an ugly fortress-like building, supposedly fashioned to look like a ship. The best reason to trudge up here is for the panoramic views, or for a performance at the Monument Theatre (see p.396). Avoid wandering around the gardens alone, especially in the evenings, as there has been the occasional mugging.

Rhodes University and the museums

Strung along Somerset Street, which runs at right angles to the top (west end) of High Street, is **Rhodes University** and a succession of modest museums – all are covered by a convenient multi-entry ticket, and can take up a pleasant morning. If you've time for only one, head for the **Natural Science Museum** (Mon–Fri 9.30am–1pm & 2–5pm, Sat 9.30am–1pm; R6), just south of the university entrance on the same side of the street. The display of Eastern Cape fauna and flora from 250 million years ago is excellent, with intriguing plant fossils and the bones of dinosaurs which once roamed these parts. Also worth a look is the **gallery** of the curator who worked for 48 years at the museum, containing his personal collection of objects in beautiful old teak display cases. The **History Museum** next door houses a dusty collection of 1820 settler memorabilia, nineteenth-century paintings and antique firearms.

Beyond the Drostdy Arch, tucked behind some buildings at the corner of Somerset and Prince Alfred streets, is **ILAM**, the International Library of African Music (Mon–Fri 8.30am–12.45pm & 2.15–4.45pm; free; ⓦilam .ru.ac.za). The library is an absolute treasure trove of recordings of **traditional African music** from southern Africa, as well as Zaire, Rwanda, Uganda and Tanzania. It also sells cassettes on request, and there's a collection of over two hundred traditional instruments on view. Contact them beforehand to be shown around (from R80), and to get a demonstration and also the chance to play some instruments with African music expert Andrew Tracey. Reasonably priced kalimbas, handmade using high-quality timber by Hugh Tracey (Andrew's father), and many other instruments can be bought from African Musical Instruments on the corner of Cloncourt and Jarvis streets (ⓦwww.kalimba.co.za), *the* place in South Africa to buy an authentic instrument.

On the same side of the road as ILAM, the **SA Institute of Aquatic Biodiversity** (Mon–Fri 8.30am–1pm & 2–5pm; free) is named after the Rhodes University scientist who shot to fame in 1939 after identifying the coelacanth, a "missing link" fish, caught off the East London coast and thought to have become extinct fifty million years ago. Plenty of coelacanths, their preferred dwelling in the pitch-dark depths of the Indian Ocean, have now been spotted by deep-sea divers; in the foyer are two huge stuffed specimens, with fins that look like budding arms and legs.

Heading back down High Street and right onto Bathurst Street brings you to the **Observatory Museum** (Mon–Fri 9.30am–1pm & 2–5pm; Sat 9.30am–1pm; R6), a fun display in a restored building that was the home and shop of a notable watchmaker and jeweller during the mid-1850s. Also well worth a visit is the rooftop Victorian **camera obscura**, which projects onto a wall magnified images of the streets below. It's best seen on a clear day, when the reflections are crisp and clear.

Xhosa Grahamstown

Xhosa Grahamstown starts buzzing around **Market Square**, off Beaufort Street, where you'll see hawkers by the dozen and a busy minibus-taxi rank. In the late 1820s, the square was the trading venue for ivory, hides, wool and farm produce. If you're in the area, it's worth walking west of Market Square to see the restored **1820 settlers' cottages** in Cross and Bartholomew streets, some flat-roofed and two-storeyed, others with pitched tin roofs.

Beaufort Street, the main through road, leads up the hill towards the townships on the eastern side of town. At the top, the road cuts through a hill of white clay, where Xhosa people scratch out pigment for face markings. From this cutting, looking into the valley, well away from the squatters' shacks, you'll see some roughly made traditional huts, used during the seclusion period, when young men, **amakweta**, are initiated. All over the Eastern Cape, it's not unusual to see *amakweta* on the roadside wearing very little and smeared in white clay, which signifies they've just been circumcised and initiated into manhood (Nelson Mandela went through the same ordeal).

Beyond the cutting lies the treeless **Kings Flats** township, where the **Umthathi Self-help Project** teaches people how to grow vegetables and raise chickens. Umthathi's office, in the train station (☎046 622 4450), can arrange **township tours** that include a traditional Xhosa lunch in a township house.

Eating, drinking and entertainment

Eating prospects in Grahamstown are far from exciting, but there's at least one good pub, a decent coffee shop and a couple of restaurants with pleasant settings. For **self-catering**, the Home Industries shop at the Pepper Grove mall is great for homemade pies, seasonal fruit and vegetables, and venison and ostrich eggs for gigantic omelettes (all produce comes from local farms).

137 High St 137 High St, close to the Drosdty Arch and university. Come here for good coffee and great cheesecake, in a Georgian building with an outdoor courtyard. Daytime only from 7.30am; closed Sat afternoon & Sun.

The Cock House Corner of Market and George streets ☎046 636 1295. Grahamstown's best restaurant, serving country cuisine; their speciality is local lamb shank, braised and marinated. There's home-baked bread, and after-dinner rum and chocolate truffles. Mon–Sat lunch & dinner.

Gino's Hill St, cnr New St, attached to the *Hotel Victoria Mews*. Serves pizzas (in or out), steaks and pasta, with some vegetarian options. Daily 11am–11pm.

La Galleria 13 New St ☎046 622 2345. This Italian place with high ceilings, wooden floors and (in keeping with its name) walls bedecked with paintings is one of the town's top restaurants. It has a reputation for its homemade pasta dishes, and also excels at red meat and poultry, plus tempting starters and desserts. Mon–Sat 7pm–midnight.

The Rat & Parrot 59a New St. Jekyll and Hyde venue that's a lively student bar and restaurant by day, but can become yobbish by night. Mon–Sat from noon.

Redwood Spur 97 High St, near the cathedral. Open long hours, this serves reliable American-style food, mainly burgers and beef, with generous salads and late-night bottomless coffee, served with a smile by clean-cut young waiters. Daily 8am till late.

Entertainment

Despite being the home of the country's premier **arts festival** (see box below), and dominated by Rhodes University, Grahamstown's nightlife and entertainment scene is far less exciting than you might expect. Outside the hectic festival fortnight in July, the town relies on the **cinema** at the Pepper Grove Mall

---

The Grahamstown Festival

For eleven days every July, Grahamstown bursts to overflowing as the town's population doubles, with visitors descending for the annual National Arts Festival – usually called the **Grahamstown Festival**, or more simply The Festival. At this time, seemingly every home is transformed into a B&B and the streets are alive with colourful food stalls. Church halls, parks and sports fields become flea markets and several hundred shows are staged, spanning every conceivable type of performance.

This is the largest arts festival in Africa, and even has its own fringe festival. The hub of the event is the 1820 Settlers Monument, which hosts not only big drama, dance and operatic productions in its theatres, but also art exhibitions and free early evening concerts. Grahamstown's festival began in 1974 when the Monument building was opened. While work by African performers and artists is well represented, and is perhaps the more interesting aspect of the festival for tourists, the festival-goers and performers are still predominantly white.

The published **programme** – spanning jazz, classical music, drama, dance, cabaret, opera, visual arts, crafts, films and a book fair – is bulky, but absolutely essential; it's worth planning your time carefully to avoid walking the potentially very cold July streets without seeing much of the festival proper. If you don't feel like taking in a show, the free art exhibitions at the museums, Monument and other smaller venues are always worth a look. For more **information and bookings**, contact the Grahamstown Foundation (☎046 622 7115, ⓦwww.nafest.co.za).

to deliver its only regular evening entertainment. The two main venues for **live performances** are the Monument Theatre and the Rhodes University Theatre, where the Drama Department puts on productions from time to time. Well worth catching is anything staged by Andrew Buckland, a local actor with an international reputation in physical theatre. The university's Music Department puts on eclectic and fairly regular **classical concerts**. Black musicians also sometimes hit town, performing at the town hall or venues in the townships.

Thanks to the university connection, the town is periodically treated to a better selection of events than you'd be likely to find in the average Karoo *dorp*. To find out what's on, check the flyposters down High Street and also look in *Grocott's Mail*, the local rag, which comes out on Tuesday and Friday afternoons. Another source of information is *GOG – Good Old Grahamstown*, a monthly booklet available from the tourist office.

Around Grahamstown

From Grahamstown, it's a short journey to the **coast**: Port Alfred and Kenton-on-Sea (see p.384) are both less than an hour's drive away, and each has a historic settler village en route – **Bathurst** and **Salem** respectively. A bit further afield, you can meander down dirt roads, pausing at old settler churches and graves, and end up at the **Great Fish River Wetland Reserve** (see opposite), which has magnificent beach and river frontage.

Grahamstown is also close to a couple of fine **wildlife reserves**, especially good for experiencing the striking, dry bush particular to this area and the animals that little over a century ago roamed the land freely. The highlight is the **Great Fish River Reserve Complex** (distinct from the wetland reserve), a rambling wilderness slaked by the Great Fish and its tributary, the Kap. Its appeal lies in its backwoods feel and the beauty of its landscape, offering a different experience to that found in the well-organized Addo Elephant Park, though if you want luxury, it can be had nearby at the pricey **Kwande private reserve**. There are also a couple of lodges on the **Kariega River**, south of Grahamstown.

Twenty minutes' drive north of Grahamstown is the **Valley of the Ancient Voices** (℡046 622 8511, ⓦwww.ancientvoices.co.za), where you can take a four-hour tour (daily 9.30am & 2.30pm; R150 including picnic lunch; booking required) to explore ancient Bushman **cave paintings**, rock pools and see some of the birds and antelopes in the area.

Bathurst and around

A significant centre in the nineteenth century, **BATHURST**, 45km south of Grahamstown, is today little more than a picturesque straggle of houses, gardens and curiosity shops. The *Pig and Whistle Hotel*, on the corner of the Grahamstown road as you drive into Bathurst, started life as a smithy in 1821, with an inn attached a few years later; they can provide maps and directions to historical sites. A pleasant two-kilometre walk from the *Pig and Whistle,* the water-powered **Bradshaw's Wool Mill** marks the spot where South Africa's wool industry started.

The setup at **Summerhill Farm** (see opposite) should keep kids occupied for a while, with an outsized museum of pineapples housed inside a yellow-and-green plastic pineapple, in turn plonked in the middle of a field full of the genuine article. There are also a pool, playground and mini-farm.

Accommodation, eating and drinking

All the accommodation in Bathurst is strung along the **R67**, the main road between Grahamstown and Port Alfred that runs through the hamlet. *Cosy Corner* on Hill Street (☎ & ⓕ046 625 0955; B&B ❶, with the option of self-catering) has two reasonably priced cottages with a pool and braai facilities. The *Pig and Whistle* on the R67 (☎046 625 0673; ❷) is a colonial Victorian village inn where the old rooms upstairs, furnished with period pieces, are especially recommended. Finally, Summerhill Farm plays host to the *Protea Hotel Bathurst* (☎046 625 0833, ⓦwww.protea-hotels.co.za; ❸), landmarked by its enormous plastic pineapple. The farmstead houses B&B units with double beds, bunks for kids (it's very child-friendly) and sitting areas, overlooking pineapple plantations.

Summerhill Farm offers a bar and a mid-priced **restaurant**, open daily for lunches and dinners, including English-style fish, chicken and meat, plus veggie meals. On Sundays they do a self-service carvery (booking essential). The atmospheric *Pig and Whistle*, on the corner of the Grahamstown road and the main road through the village, is a favourite weekend spot for locals downing a **beer** or five. Across the road, *Bleak House*, with veranda and garden seating, serves salads cut from the garden and reasonably priced lunches.

Thomas Baines and Kariega reserves

Grahamstown's closest nature reserve, **Thomas Baines Nature Reserve** (daily dawn–dusk; free), is a hilly area 15km south of town on the road to Kenton-on-Sea. The main attraction here is **Settler's Dam**, good for picnics, braais and wandering around the vicinity of the dam. Walking elsewhere isn't permitted as rhino and buffalo live in the thick, prickly bush. During late afternoons you're very likely to see antelope grazing on open spaces, but not much else.

Just 14km from the coast, upmarket **Kariega Park** (☎046 636 7904, ⓦwww.kariega.co.za) is a delightful privately run Big Five game reserve reached along the R343. Its balconied family lodges feature three or four bedrooms (full board ❽, self-catering ❻), and they also have more exclusive luxury units sleeping two (❾); all rates include game drives. There's a restaurant on site, and in the evening river booze cruises are organized. It's worth coming as a day visitor (Wed & Sun only; R650) if you want to get close to zebras and grazing antelope, as they are used to cars, and hopefully see the big draw of lions and elephants. The entrance fee includes lunch, a game drive and river cruise.

Another private reserve, **Sibuya Camp** (☎046 6482020, ⓦwww.sibuya.co.za; ❼), collects guests by boat along the Kariega River from Kenton-on-Sea. While this isn't a Big Five reserve, you will see zebra, giraffe and plenty of antelope here. Activities include game drives, fishing and bush walks.

The Great Fish River Reserve Complex

On the Fort Beaufort Road (the R67) 34km north of Grahamstown, the huge **Great Fish River Reserve Complex** (office daily 8am–5pm, gate open 24hr; R20 per vehicle plus R6 per person) is an amalgamation of three separate reserves covering 430 square kilometres. A far cry from the well-tended game parks of Mpumalanga or KwaZulu-Natal, it has no shops or restaurants and the roads are often horrible, but, provided you're ready to rough it, Great Fish is the Eastern Cape's most rewarding wildlife destination after Addo, despite the notable absence of lions. Along the banks of the Fish and Kat rivers, stands of thorn trees afford welcome shade during the

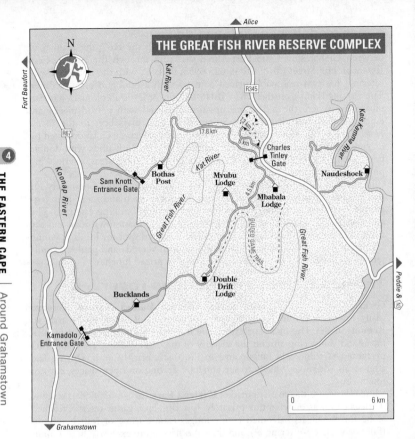

summer heat, while in the parched areas away from the rivers, the striking landscape of cliffs and dense valleys is overgrown with scrubby bush, thick with succulents, euphorbias and aloes.

The varied terrain supports an abundant range of **game** (although not in large numbers) including black-backed jackals, hyenas and rarely seen leopards. Among the trees and bushes are several species of browsers and grazers, from blesbok to nyala, including numerous white rhinos, a handful of elephants, and warthogs by the dozen. A few snorting hippos while away their days in the rivers, and along the banks you may see waterbuck; look out for vervets in the trees.

Practicalities

The only way to reach the complex is to drive, and the easiest route is the tarred **R67**, which provides access to the two entrances on the western flank: **Kamadolo Gate** in the south and **Sam Knott Gate** in the north. The other route is the **R345**, a reasonable dirt road through the eastern section of the reserve, connecting the N2 70km east of Grahamstown (just beyond the town of Peddie) with Alice (see p.420); this takes you to **Charles Tinley Gate**, the park headquarters, though the gate is often unattended.

Kwandwe Private Game Reserve

Adjoining the Great Fish River complex is the very exclusive **Kwandwe Private Game Reserve** (℡046 603 3400, Ⓦwww.ccafrica.com; ❾ – upwards of R5000 per person per night), with 30km of Fish River frontage and the Big Five in attendance. There are three lodges, each with its own staff and rangers, ensuring a highly personalized experience: *Kwandwe Main Lodge*, a classic safari-style thatch and stone complex with nine suites; *Uplands Homestead*, an historic farmhouse dating back to 1905 evoking colonial Edwardian life, with three bedrooms; and *Kwandwe Ecca Lodge*, a funky boutique-hotel-in-the-bush.

Apart from twice-a-day game drives, Kwandwe's safari activities include guided river walks, canoeing on the Great Fish, rhino tracking, in which you follow one of the large mammals on foot, and aerial whale-watching (June–November). They also run cultural tours with a resident historian who looks at the fascinating social and archeological past of the area. Children are welcome at *Ecca Lodge* and *Uplands*, and special activities are laid on for them, including family game drives, short bush walks, and frog safaris.

It's easy to drive to the game reserve, which is 160km from Port Elizabeth and is reached along the R67 that runs between Grahamstown and Fort Beaufort. Road or air transfers are available from Port Elizabeth airport.

The Great Fish River and its tributary, the Kat, flow in a series of sinuous oxbows to segment the reserve into three; you can't always count on getting from one section to another in an ordinary vehicle, particularly when the river levels rise to flood the fords. If you do intend driving through the reserve, either enquire at headquarters about conditions before leaving or take a direct route to your destination. Roads in the reserve are dirt tracks and are frequently poor, so you'll have to drive carefully and slowly.

Accommodation

There's a limited selection of **lodges** and **cabins** (❷ including meals), booked through the Eastern Cape Parks Board (℡040 635 2115, Ⓦwww .ecparksboard.co.za). In the **eastern section** (east of the Fish River), *Mbabala Lodge*, 2km south of Charles Tinley Gate, offers five doubles and is rented out to a single party at a time. Thirteen kilometres east of the gate, on the banks of the Keiskamma River, *Naudeshoek* has a single log cabin sleeping six. At Mvubu, 9km southwest of the gate, four twin-bedded chalets share a communal kitchen, dining area and plunge pool. Another six rustic maisonette-style family chalets, each sleeping two adults and two children, sit on the banks of the Great Fish. In the **southwestern section** (the closest to Grahamstown), *Double Drift Lodge*, 16km northeast of Kamadolo Gate, is a basic place with five doubles, perched on the north bank of the Great Fish.

Game viewing and activities

Most people coming to the reserve want to see **hippos**, a relatively rare sight in the Eastern Cape. To do so, report to Charles Tinley Gate and ask for an armed ranger to take you on the **guided game trail**, which runs along the northern bank of the Great Fish from *Double Drift Lodge*. Despite their cumbersome appearance, hippos – with a top speed of 30kph and the ability to turn on a sixpence – can easily outmanoeuvre a human, and can be extremely dangerous if they feel threatened.

If you're **driving**, your best bet is to make for the **Nyathi loop**, in the north-eastern section of the reserve, where game tends to concentrate. Midday, when animals tend to duck into the deep shade of trees and bushes, is your cue to head for the terrific picnic spot near Double Drift, on the south bank of the Great Fish, under the shade of huge acacia trees.

Inland to the Karoo

Travelling between Grahamstown and the towns of Cradock and Graaff-Reinet (the Eastern Cape's two most-visited Karoo towns), you'll be heading into **sheep-farming country**, with the occasional *dorp* rising against the horizon, offering the experience of an archetypal Eastern Cape one-horse outposts. The roads through this vast emptiness are quiet, and lined with rhythmically spaced telephone poles. Dun-coloured sheep, angora goats and the occasional springbok graze on brown stubble, and you'll often see groups of charcoal-and-grey ostriches in the veld, once farmed to satisfy an Edwardian feather fetish, and now reared to cater for a fashion for lean and healthy meat.

Cradock, 240km north of Port Elizabeth, lies in the **Karoo** proper, the semi-desert heartland of South Africa, with knee-high bush, clear dry air and an enormous sense of open space. It makes a great stopover on the Port Elizabeth to Johannesburg run, not least because of the excellence of its accommodation in historical houses (a stay at the *Tuishuise* in particular is reason enough to visit Cradock), and also for its proximity to **Mountain Zebra National Park**, one of the country's most beautiful game parks.

Some 100km due west of Cradock, **Graaff-Reinet** is one of the oldest towns in South Africa, and much of its historical centre is intact. Exploring its charms takes at least a day, and many people stop over here en route between Johannesburg and the Garden Route. Surrounding the town is the **Karoo Nature Reserve**, and if you want to get more of a sense of the Karoo's dry timelessness, head to **Nieu Bethesda**, 50km to the north of town.

Bedford and Somerset East

In the foothills of the Kaga Mountains, on the R63 and the R350, 87km north of Grahamstown, lies **BEDFORD**, the former realm of Xhosa Chief Phato. This was one of the little "English" towns Cape governor Sir Harry Smith promised to create in the nineteenth century, and has some attractive settler buildings. In the mountainous backdrop you'll find some **farm-stays**, most notably *Cavers*, 16km north of Bedford (T & F 046 685 0619, E ckross@intekom.co.za; 4), a working settler dairy farm tucked away in a pretty valley. It has an 1850 refurbished two-storey stone manor house with four en-suite bedrooms, and a thatched two-bedroom cottage with its own garden, and the use of a swimming pool and tennis courts; walks on the property give you the chance to see antelope and myriad birds. Reservations are required if you want to stay; the owners will give you directions.

Just under 60km west of Bedford on the R63 lies **SOMERSET EAST**, a town that gets chewing during its *biltong* festival in June, and where Afrikaans matrons with tight perms, cardigans and plump brown arms stroll the main street. The historical part of the town merits a visit; down Beaufort Street, on an axis with the white-spired Dutch Reformed Church, is the **Somerset East Museum** (Mon–Fri 8am–5pm; donation), once the home of a Victorian pastor. One block from the museum is Somerset East's second attraction, the

Walter Battiss Art Gallery (Mon–Fri 9am–1pm & 2–4pm, Sat & Sun by arrangement through the museum), in a handsome two-storey house on the corner of Beaufort and Poulet streets. Batiss is one of South Africa's most well-known modern artists, noted for his sense of humour, which shines out even in this uneven collection of drawings and paintings (his best work hangs in galleries elsewhere).

Cradock

The silvery windmills on the surrounding sheep farms of **CRADOCK** have become an unofficial symbol of the town; Xhosa hawkers (often kids) stand along the main road around the city limits, selling intricately crafted wire model windmills, their blades spinning in the breeze. Poverty has overshadowed Cradock since the Frontier Wars of the nineteenth century and the subjugation of the Xhosa people that continued right up to the 1990s. Against this history of conquest the town has provided fertile grounds for **resistance**: some members of the ANC were based in and around the town, and almost single-handedly kept the organization alive during the 1930s. In 1985, Cradock hit the headlines when anti-apartheid activist **Matthew Goniwe** and three of his colleagues were murdered (see box on p.402).

Political controversy is also the theme at Cradock's biggest attraction, **Schreiner House**, 9 Cross Street (Mon–Fri 8am–4.30pm; donation). The

CRADOCK

Mountain Zebra National Park & Bloemfontein

East London & Port Elizabeth

0   200 m

N

DEARY AVE
MILNER STREET
ALBERT ST
HOSPITAL ST
NAESTED STREET
ALBERT ST
FRERE STREET
ADDERLEY STREET
BEERENS STREET
DUNDAS STREET
STOCKENSTROOM STREET
CAWOOD STREET
SPRIGG STREET
VICTORIA STREET
DURBAN
DURBAN

Great Fish River

★ Translux Intercape Bus Stop

✝ Dutch Reformed Church

CHURCH STREET

Great Fish River Museum ⓘ

VOORTREKKER STREET

COMMISSIONER ST

Train Station

HARE ST

BREE STREET

HIGH STREET

MARKET STREET

CAWOOD STREET

SPRIGG STREET

CROSS STREET

ACCOMMODATION
Cradock Spa   **A**
Heritage House   **D**
Tuishuise   **C**
Victoria Manor   **B**

RESTAURANTS
1814   1
Fiddler's Grill 2
Schreiner Tea
Room   3

Schreiner House

▼ Olive Schreiner's Grave

house is dedicated to the life of the writer Olive Schreiner, best known for her ground-breaking novel *The Story of an African Farm* (1883), made into a film in 2004. It was remarkable enough for a woman from the conservative backwoods of nineteenth-century Eastern Cape to write a novel (it was published under the pseudonym Ralph Iron), but even more amazing that she espoused ideas considered dangerously radical even a century later. While in London looking for a publisher, Schreiner mixed with the likes of Havelock Ellis and Eleanor Marx, returning to South Africa at the turn of the last century to campaign for universal franchise for men and women irrespective of race. After a life of campaigning, Schreiner died in Cape Town in 1921 and is buried near Cradock on the Buffelskop peak, with her one-day old daughter and favourite dog, overlooking the Great Fish River Valley. Her **burial site** has become something of a place of pilgrimage, and details of how to get there are available from Schreiner House, along with a photocopied Ordnance Survey map. You'll need to drive to the starting point, and should allow a good half-day for the trip, which involves a very stiff climb.

Cradock's other points of interest include the **Dutch Reformed Church** at the upper end of Church Street, based on London's St Martin's-in-the-Fields and completed in 1868, and a warm sulphur spring-fed **swimming pool** at the Cradock Spa on Marlow Road, 4.5km from town (daily 7am–6pm; R8). It has indoor and open-air pools, though it is getting a bit run-down. Behind the town hall, the **Great Fish River Museum** (Tues–Fri 8am–1pm, Sat 8am–noon) is housed in an 1849 Dutch Reformed Church parsonage and depicts the early history of Eastern Cape pioneers.

Practicalities

Cradock is small and easily covered **on foot**, but you'll need your own transport to get to the nearby Mountain Zebra National Park. Translux and Inter-

---

Matthew Goniwe and the murder of the Cradock Four

Even by apartheid standards, 1985 was a dark year for South Africa. In July, the hawkish President P.W. Botha declared a state of emergency in response to a nationwide wave of popular resistance; by the end of the year, over five hundred people had been killed in police action. In this maelstrom of repression, **Matthew Goniwe** and three other Eastern Cape leaders from Cradock died in "mysterious" circumstances.

Goniwe was a prominent member and rural organizer for the United Democratic Front (UDF), a proxy organization for the then banned ANC. Early on June 27, 1985, he left Vergenoeg township on the outskirts of Cradock, heading for a UDF meeting in Port Elizabeth. He was accompanied by **Fort Calata**, **Sparrow Mkhonto** and **Sicelo Mhlauli**. The four were never to return. On their way home, they were ambushed, murdered and their bodies burnt and spread several kilometres apart.

The nature of the murder indicated considerable planning and resources. A highly publicized inquest in 1989 could not find the evidence necessary to incriminate apartheid government forces. In May 1992, a chilling document leaked to the anti-apartheid *New Nation* newspaper revealed that a signal had been sent by Commandant du Plessis to General van Rensberg calling for Matthew Goniwe to be "permanently removed from society".

Although there was now proof that the Port Elizabeth security police were responsible, the identities of the men were protected. It wasn't until 1997, during the **Truth and Reconciliation Commission** hearings, that the whole sickening story came out, including the identities of the five security police officers who confessed to the killings. The policemen were granted amnesty, despite the bitterness this caused.

cape **buses** pull in daily at Shoprite Checkers on Voortrekker Street, where you can buy tickets and get information for onward travel to Cape Town, East London, Port Elizabeth and Johannesburg. Cradock is a daily stop on the Port Elizabeth–Johannesburg rail line; the station is on the west bank of the Great Fish River. The very helpful but overworked one-person **tourist office** in Stockenstroom Street (Mon–Fri 8.30am–12.30pm & 2–4.30pm; ☏048 881 2383, ⓦwww.cradock.co.za) can supply maps, accommodation lists and information on farmstays and local attractions.

Accommodation

For a small town, Cradock offers some delightful accommodation; if you want to taste some Karoo country style, the *Tuishuise* is especially recommended.

Cradock Spa 4.5km north of town on the road to the signposted Mountain Zebra National Park ☏048 881 2709. The best bet for budget accommodation, with self-catering, fully equipped chalets sleeping two to four. ❶

Heritage House 45 Bree St ☏048 881 5251. Large Victorian home with a pool landscaped into rocks in the garden and a menagerie of animals, including a tame springbok. The owner is the curator of the Olive Schreiner Museum and will pack you picnic for an early morning hike up to the tomb. ❷

Tuishuise Market St ☏048 881 1322, ⓦwww .tuishuise.co.za. Staying in this street of comfortable and very stylish one- to four-bedroomed Victorian houses for rent gives an authentic sense of colonial domestic life over a century ago. Prices are very reasonable given that you get what amounts to a mini-museum to yourself, each house kitted out with antique furniture and crockery. There's dining close at hand at the *Victoria Manor*, though you can also self-cater. ❸

Victoria Manor 36 Market St ☏048 881 1650, ⓦwww.tuishuise.co.za. Effortlessly gracious, old-fashioned hotel with excellent service, bags of character and period fittings. The rooms are en suite, dining is off silverware and the breakfasts are among the best in the country. ❸

Eating

The *Schreiner Tea Room* (Mon–Sat 8.30am–5pm) next to the *Victoria Manor* in Market Street is the nicest place for tea, sandwiches and hot lunches. The *Manor* itself does dinners of very tasty meat dishes and vegetables, including favourites like Karoo lamb and *malva* pudding, in a crimson Victorian dining room, and is open for teas on Sundays. The *1814* (☏048 881 5390), with a distinctive sloping red roof standing out on Main Road, offers tasty breakfasts, lunches and teas with an Afrikaans slant. A favourite with local families is the *Fiddler's Grill*, in the Total filling station complex on Voortrekker Street (daily lunch & dinner).

Mountain Zebra National Park

When the **Mountain Zebra National Park** (daily: May–Sept 7am–6pm; Oct–April 7am–7pm; R60; ☏048 881 2427), 26km west of Cradock, was created in 1937, there were only five Cape **mountain zebras** left on its 65 square kilometres. If that wasn't bad enough, four were males. At the time, environmental issues were far from being vote-winners; indeed, one cabinet minister dismissed the threatened animals as "a lot of donkeys in football jerseys". Miraculously, conservationists managed to cobble together a breeding herd from the few survivors on surrounding farms, and the park now supports several hundred, while also translocating healthy numbers to various corners of South Africa.

For **game viewing**, the park has a couple of good part-tar, part-gravel loop roads forming a rough figure of eight. Most rewarding is the northernmost route, 14.5km long, which circuits the Rooiplaat section where the plains game tends to congregate. As well as zebra, keep an eye out for **springbok**, blesbok and **black wildebeest**. The introduction of **buffalo** in 1998 and plans to bring in cheetahs and rhinos adds to the wildlife interest, but means that hiking across the park isn't possible. Unlike their docile Asian water buffalo cousins, the African buffalo have a reputation for extreme aggression. There are, however, two **waymarked walks** near the camp, one of them taking you high onto rocks above the camp. Allow an hour and a half for this circular trail.

Practicalities

To reach the park, head north out of Cradock on the N10, turning west after about 6km onto the Graaff-Reinet Road. After a further 5km, you turn left at the National Park sign onto a good gravel road, which reaches the park gate after a further 16km.

The park has **accommodation** in twenty comfortable two-bedroomed cottages (❷), all of which have outstanding mountain views and their own kitchens and bathrooms. The price includes breakfast in the camp restaurant. There's also a good **campsite**, but the unrivalled highlight of the park's lodgings is the self-catering **Doornhoek Guest House** (R700 for a minimum of four people), a beautifully restored Victorian homestead set in splendid isolation, with great Karoo views across a small lake to the surrounding chain of scrubby hills. Extremely comfortable, it has three en-suite double rooms furnished with antiques. A twenty-percent discount on accommodation and camping is available from June to September, excluding school holidays (when the park is always booked out).

A small **shop** at reception sells basics, souvenirs, alcohol and soft drinks, but if you're staying for a few days you should stock up in Cradock. There's a reasonable licensed **restaurant**, a post office, a filling station and a lovely swimming pool set among huge rocks, all near reception.

Graaff-Reinet and the Karoo Nature Reserve

It's little wonder that tour buses pull in to **GRAAFF-REINET** in their numbers; this is a beautiful town, one of the few places in the Eastern Cape where you'd want to wander freely day and night, taking in historical buildings and the occasional little museum, and have a meal or a drink before strolling back to your accommodation.

Graaff-Reinet has a large population of Afrikaans-speaking coloured people, mostly living on the south side of town, some of slave origin, others the descendants of indigenous Khoi and San who were forced to work on frontier farms. The dry mountains surrounding the town are part of the **Karoo Nature Reserve**, whose main attraction is the **Valley of Desolation**, a B-movie name for an impressive site. The rocky canyon, echoing bird call and expansive skies of the valley, shouldn't be missed.

Some history

By the late eighteenth century, Dutch burghers had extended the Cape frontier northwards into the Sneeuwberg Mountains, traditionally the stomping ground of Khoi pastoralists and San hunter-gathers. Little more than brigands, the settlers raided Khoi cattle and attacked groups of San, killing the men and abducting women and children to use as farm and domestic labourers. Friction escalated when the Khoi and San retaliated and, in 1786, the Cape authorities sent out a *landdrost* (magistrate) to **establish Graaff-Reinet**, administer the surrounding area and pacify the frontier.

Nine years later, *landdrost* Honoratus Maynier, following orders to stop vigilante rule by white settlers and to curb the maltreatment of Khoi and San servants, was forced out of town at gunpoint by a group of burghers, bandying catchphrases from the recent French revolution. Declaring South Africa's **first Boer republic**, they complained that Maynier was "protecting the Hottentots and Kafirs against the Boers".

In 1800 Maynier was again put in charge of Graaff-Reinet, and colonial control over the district was slowly consolidated, with vast tracts turned over to grazing sheep. The **wool boom** of the 1850s brought prosperity to the town and established a pattern of farming and land ownership which continues to this day.

Arrival and information

Translux **buses** between Johannesburg and Port Elizabeth, and Intercape buses connecting Jo'burg with the Garden Route towns, pull in daily at Kudu Motors, 84 Church Street (a stone's throw south from the historical centre),

Karoo Nature Reserve & ▲ *Valley of Desolation*   **A**, **B**, **C**, *Cradock &* ▲ *Bloemfontein*

N

GRAAFF-REINET

ACCOMMODATION
Andries Stockenstroom Guest House	I
Bloemhof Bed & Breakfast	A
Camdeboo Cottages	G
Cypress Cottage	J
Drostdy Hotel	H
Ganora Farm	C
Karoopark Holiday Cottages	F
The Red Geranium	E
Trymore Cottage	B
Urquhart Caravan Park	D

RESTAURANTS
Coral Tree	1
Kliphuis	2
Number 8 Pub & Grill	3

0   200 m

Train Station

▼ *Port Elizabeth*

Robert Sobukwe and the Africanists

One of Graaff-Reinet's most brilliant but often-forgotten sons is **Robert Managaliso Sobukwe**, founder of the Pan Africanist Congress (PAC). Unlike some followers of the PAC, who have not always held back from anti-white rhetoric, Sobukwe maintained that whites were capable, in time, of becoming genuine Africans. Born in 1923, Sobukwe won a scholarship to Healdtown, a boarding school near Fort Beaufort, going on to Fort Hare University (see p.419), where he joined the African National Congress Youth League. After graduating in 1947, he became a schoolteacher and then a lecturer at the University of the Witwatersrand. A charismatic member of the Africanist wing of the ANC – even the ultra-apartheid prime minister B.J. Vorster acknowledged him as "a man of magnetic personality" – Sobukwe questioned the organization's strategy of co-operating with whites, and formed the breakaway PAC in 1959. The following year he launched the nationwide **anti-pass protests**, which ended in the Sharpeville massacre and his imprisonment on Robben Island for nine years. In 1969, Sobukwe was released under a banning order to Kimberley, where he died in 1978. Five thousand people attended his funeral in Graaff-Reinet.

You can visit the Sobukwe home and grave on a **township tour** with Xolile Speelman (T082 844 2890), who also accompanies people to traditional events, with music and the chance to meet members of Graaff-Reinet's African community.

or on the opposite side of the street at the Engen garage. For bus tickets and timetables you need to go to the **tourist office** at 13 Church Street (Mon–Fri 8am–5pm, Sat & Sun 9am–noon; T049 892 4248, Wwww.graaffreinet.co.za). This is also the place for **maps** and accommodation lists. **Umasizakhe township tours** are a recommended way to experience the other side of Graaff-Reinet; contact Xolile Speelman (see box above).

Accommodation

Graaff-Reinet has plenty of decent **places to stay** in the centre; the nicest are in listed historic buildings. If the Karoo landscape grabs you, you might want to head for one of the **farmstays** around here and Nieu Bethesda (see p.409), to witness some of the country's most dazzling night skies and spacious landscape. December is the busiest month, and you should definitely book well ahead if you want to stay then.

Andries Stockenstroom Guest House 100 Cradock St, a couple of streets back from the *Drostdy Hotel* T & F049 892 4575, Wwww .stockenstrom.co.za. A handsome listed house that has several times won the Automobile Association award for the best guesthouse in South Africa. It's worth staying just for the evening meals (only for guests) – outstanding French-Karoo cuisine with imaginative game and mutton dishes and scrumptious desserts. You're unlikely to eat better anywhere in the Karoo. Half board **6**

Camdeboo Cottages 16 Parliament St T049 892 3180, F049 891 0919. Bang in the historical centre are these eight smallish, fully equipped (though rather basic) nineteenth-century self-catering cottages, built around a courtyard. **2**

Cypress Cottage 80 Donkin St T049 892 3965 or 083 456 1795, Wwww.cypresscottage.co.za. A restored Karoo cottage rented out as a whole, with six double en-suite rooms and a communal lounge and dining room. Families are welcome and the garden makes it good for kids. **3**

Drostdy Hotel 30 Church St T049 892 2161, Edrostdy@intekom.co.za. Elegant Cape Dutch landmark in a prime location, with a candle-lit dining room, shady gardens and fountains. The rooms, in terraced artisan cottages behind the hotel, are comfortable but small; larger rooms are pricier. **4**

Karoopark Holiday Cottages 81 Caledon St T049 892 2557, Einfo@karoopark.co.za. Complex of self-catering cottages set in a garden with a pool, plus dinky B&B units that are adequate for an overnight stay. **2**

The Red Geranium 52 Stockenstrom St T049 892 2332. Three decent cottages run by a friendly owner. They're equipped for self-catering, though breakfast can be provided. ❶–❷

Urquhart Caravan Park On the outskirts of town, at the extension of Stockenstroom St, next to the Karoo Nature Reserve ☎049 892 2136. Large and well maintained, with campsites and good-value rondavels, chalets and bungalows, next to the Sundays River. The bungalows are more roomy than the stuffy rondavels and have linen, but you must bring your own towels. ❶

Farmstays

Bloemhof Bed & Breakfast 27km north of Graaff-Reinet on the N9, and 5km down a good gravel road ☎ & ⓕ049 840 0203, ⓔmurraybloemhof@yebo.co.za. Grand homestead from the turn of the last century, built on ostrich-feather money, with enormous, yellowwood-floored rooms. It's part of a large sheep and game farm, and serves Karoo lamb dinners. Children are welcome. ❸

Ganora Farm Off the N9, 7km east of Nieu Bethesda ☎049 841 1302 or 082 698 0029, ⓦwww.owlhouse.co.za. The advantage of staying in this self-contained Karoo cottage on a sheep farm is that the owners arrange trips to climb Compassberg (see p.410) and see Bushman rock shelters and Anglo-Boer War engravings. You can also be shown how sheep farming works or view their small fossil collection. Meals can be arranged if you're not up to cooking. ❷

Trymore Cottage Wellwood Farm, 31km north of town, on the road to Nieu Bethesda off the N9 ☎ & ⓕ049 840 0302, ⓔwellwood@wam.co.za. Self-catering, comfortable, four-bedroomed house on a long-established, beautiful farm with a merino sheep stud and an orange grove. Braai packs are available on request as are evening dinners, with Karoo lamb or venison on the menu. Their well-known private collection of Karoo reptile fossils is absolutely stunning and not open to the public, but residents may view it. Half board ❸, self-catering ❷

The Town and the reserve

Graaff-Reinet centres around the imposing 1886 **Dutch Reformed Church**, with its pointy steeple and cake-icing decoration. The main

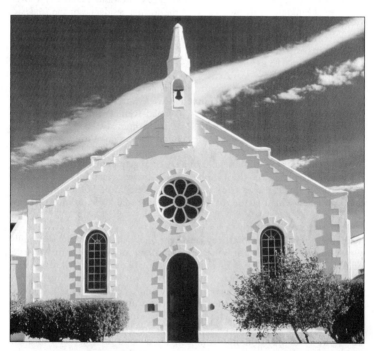

△ Graaff-Reinet church

thoroughfare, **Church Street**, splits at either side of the church, heading northwest to the Valley of Desolation and northeast to Nieu Bethesda, Middelburg and eventually Johannesburg. On either side of Church Street, little roads fan out, lined with whitewashed Cape Dutch, Georgian and Victorian buildings – it's in these parts that you'll find the town's museums, restaurants and most attractive buildings.

Church Street itself bustles with antique shops and businesses with Karoo-inspired names, such as Merino Pharmacy and Kudu Motors. One block south of the church is the **Old Library Museum** (Mon–Fri 8am–12.30pm & 2–5pm, Sat 9am–3pm, Sun 9am–noon & 2–4pm; R5). The only attraction here is the excellent collection of **fossil skulls** and skeletons of reptiles that populated the marshes, lakes and pools of prehistoric Karoo, some 230 million years ago. These Karoo dinosaurs were entombed in mud, and their bones became embedded in the present-day Karoo shale; the fossils were collected from the hills and river channels in the surrounding area. There's an even better collection on Wellwood Farm (see *Trymore Cottage* on p.407), but you'll have to stay there to see it as it is not open to the public.

Next door, in a restored 1821 mission church with Dutch gables, is the **Hester Rupert Art Museum** (Mon–Fri 9am–12.30pm & 2–5pm, Sat 9am–3pm, Sat & Sun 9am–noon; R1), which features a representative selection of work by South African artists (primarily white) active in the mid-1960s. Much of it is dreary and derivative of European art, but a few pieces stand out. Look out in particular for Cecil Skotnes's woodcuts, the strong expressionistic work of Johannes Meintjies, and Irma Stern's very appealing paintings.

Opposite the Art Museum stands the graceful, whitewashed **Drostdy Hotel**, a historical building in its own right, as the former residence of the *landdrost*. Most of the hotel guests are housed behind the main building, in Stretch's Court, a cobbled lane of nineteenth-century cottages with brightly coloured shutters. It hasn't always been so twee: Drostdy's slaves lived here, and after slavery ended in 1838 their descendants stayed on until they were kicked out under the 1950 Group Areas Act.

From the front steps of the Drostdy, you can look down Pastorie Street, lined with Cape Dutch buildings, to **Reinet House** (Mon–Fri 8am–12.30pm & 2–5pm, Sat 9am–3pm, Sun 9am–4pm; R7), Graaff-Reinet's finest museum. Formerly a parsonage, it was built in 1812 in the traditional Cape Dutch H-plan, with six gables and a spiral stairway leading to the garden. With wooden floors and airy rooms, it's essentially a period house museum, filled with covetable furniture and intriguing household objects. Strangely enough, the museum is the only place allowed to distil an illicit home-brewed spirit called "Withond" (white dog), which has an exceptionally sharp bite. Little bottles of the clear liquor, labelled with a picture of a bull terrier, are sold at the front desk.

Karoo Nature Reserve

The low-lying **Karoo Nature Reserve** (daily dawn–dusk; free) totally surrounds the town, with its entrance 5km north of Graaff-Reinet's centre, off the Murraysburg Road. Its indisputable highlight is the strikingly deep **Valley of Desolation**, which you can gaze down into by driving the narrow tarred road from the reserve's entrance and ascending the bush-flecked mountainside; you'll pass a series of viewpoints up to the cliffs overlooking the valley. Late afternoon is the best time to enjoy the scenery, when the sun saturates the ochres and reds of the rock towers soaring from the valley floor. The views from the lip of the canyon, beyond the rocks and into the plains of Camdeboo, are truly thrilling, and even better if you tune into the echoing bird calls, especially when black eagles circle the dolomite towers, scanning the crevices for prey.

There's a 45-minute looped **walk** along the canyon lip, well marked with a lizard emblem. To undertake longer trails, or **overnight** in one of the hiker's hut (which have a braai area), book at the Department of Nature Conservation on Bourke Street in Graaff-Reinet (☎049 892 3453), where you can also pick up detailed **maps**.

Eating and drinking

You'll find only a couple of centrally located **restaurants** and **tea shops** catering for Graaff-Reinet's many visitors, and the town is pretty dead on Sundays. The culinary highlight is unquestionably the *Andries Stockenstroom Guest House* (see p.406), but you need to be staying there to enjoy its cooking, which attracts gourmets from across the country.

Coral Tree 3 Church Square. Best place for light lunches such as pitta pockets, venison pies and open sandwiches. In the evening it's a good place to sample local meats such as Karoo lamb, pork loin or springbok steaks. Mon–Fri 9.30am–1pm & 6.30pm till late.

Drostdy Hotel 30 Church St. The hotel has an unrivalled garden for drinks or tea, and a grand dining room for rather formal dinners, with a pricey English-style set menu and the odd Afrikaans speciality thrown in; better value are the buffet lunches and breakfasts. There's also an atmospheric pub here. Daily.

Kliphuis 46 Bourke St. Come here for tea and sandwiches or a light lunch at pavement tables. Mon–Sat daytime only.

Number 8 Pub & Grill Somerset St. Restaurant and pub primarily patronized by locals, with a pleasant atmosphere and tortoise-slow service, and a big screen for sports broadcasts. They serve steaks, toasted sandwiches, burgers and fish and chips. Mon–Sat daytime and eves.

Nieu Bethesda

In the mountains north of Graaff-Reinet, **NIEU BETHESDA** is drier and dustier than you might wish, especially in midsummer when it boils with harsh, bright light. There are no streetlamps, and on winter nights temperatures plummet to zero, the sky filled with icy stars. Most people who come here do so in order to marvel – or shudder – at the **Owl House** on River Street (April–Sept 9–5pm; Oct–March 8am–6pm; R12; ⊛www.owlhouse.co.za), once the home of Helen Martins, a reclusive artist who expressed her disturbing and fascinating inner world through her work. Every corner of the house and garden has been transformed to meet her vision. The interior walls glitter with crushed glass, owls with large eyes gaze from the tin-roofed veranda, while at the back of the house, trapped by a stone wall and high chicken wire, are hundreds of glass and cement sculptures: camels, lambs, sphinxes and human figures. Martins never exhibited her work or courted publicity, though since her death in 1976 many have visited the museum and pondered on her life in this Karoo backwater. South African playwright Athol Fugard, who loves the Karoo and has a house in Nieu Bethesda, used her life and creative toil as inspiration for his celebrated play *The Road to Mecca*.

Owl House aside, the whitewashed **village** has plenty of charm. It's a tranquil place, accessible on a good gravel road, with the sound of spring water flowing down furrows into the little windmilled allotments. Once an archetypal conservative Karoo *dorp*, the town has reinvented itself as a tiny artists' colony, attracting a growing number of visitors. Nearby, a few hundred coloured residents somehow manage to eke out a living in this harsh environment. The Nieu Bethesda Community Art Group's gallery, opposite the police station, also exhibits local artwork.

The **Compassberg Mountain**, one of the highest peaks in the Eastern Cape and part of the Sneeuberg range, dominates the Nieu Bethesda skyline. You'll need local guidance to scale it; organized **hikes** up here are arranged at Ganora Farm (see p.407).

Practicalities

Nieu Bethesda is 23km off the N9 between Graaff-Reinet and Middelburg. There's a **village shop** and butcher on the main road, but if you're self-catering you should stock up elsewhere, especially for fresh fruit and vegetables, which are scarce in the Karoo. No petrol is available in Nieu Bethesda, so fill up in Graaff-Reinet; neither is there an ATM or a tourist office.

Given how tiny Nieu Bethesda is, it's surprising to find any **restaurants** at all. You can pop into *Egbert's Place*, on the main road, Martin Street, as you arrive in the village from Graaff-Reinet, for light meals and tea where you can sit on the *stoep*. Egbert himself is a mine of **information** about the area, and you pay him what you think the food was worth – there are no set prices. A little further along on the left is *Outsiders*, which is open for breakfast, lunch and teas, and for dinner by arrangement.

During the day you can eat at the *Village Inn*, along from the Owl House in New Street, whose cold ginger beer, cakes and homemade bread go down well. *The Brewery*, across the dry Gats River off New Street, serves their own cold beer accompanied by homemade cheese, bread, olives and salami.

Accommodation

There's an excellent selection of cheap **places to stay**, mostly self-catering cottages, with one party per house, at around R120 per person; see Ⓦwww .nieubethesda.co.za for additional recommendations. *Huis Nommer Een*, Murray Street (book through Suzette Pienaar on Ⓣ049 841 1700; ❷), has three spacious rooms furnished in South African country style, a farm-style kitchen, and a handsome veranda. The only **backpacker lodge**, *Owl House*, Martin Street (Ⓣ049 841 1642, Ⓦwww.owlhouse.info; ❷), is friendly, laidback and well organized, with dorm beds, B&B rooms, two self-contained cottages and a restaurant, *Outsiders*. They will collect you if you arrive in Graaff-Reinet by public transport. If you want to stay on a **farmhouse**, try the friendly *Doornberg Farm* (Ⓣ & Ⓕ049 841 1401, Ⓦwww.nieubethesda.co.za; ❷), which has a pub and serves evening meals, or you can self-cater; there's also a trampoline, pool, riding and hiking.

East London and the central region

Between Port Alfred and East London lies some of the Eastern Cape's least-developed **coastline**, saved from the hands of developers because it fell into the neglected Xhosa Bantustan of the Ciskei. **East London**, wedged uncomfortably between two ex-Bantustans, is the largest city in the central region of the province, with excellent beaches for surfing and swimming and good transport links to Johannesburg and along the coast. Inland, **Fort Hare University** near Alice has educated political leaders across the subcontinent, including Nelson Mandela, and has the country's finest collection of contemporary black South African art.

Sweeping up from Fort Hare's valley, the gentle, wooded **Amatola Mountains** yield to the dramatic landscapes of the **Eastern Cape Drakensberg**, which offer hiking, horse-riding and even skiing opportunities. Before white settlers (or even the Xhosa) arrived, these towering formations were dominated by **San hunter–gatherers**, who decorated the rock faces with thousands of ritual **paintings**, many of which remain surprisingly vivid.

The coast: Fish River Mouth to East London

Heading 30km east of Port Alfred, along the R72, you'll come to the **Great Fish River**, the boundary across which the British drove the Xhosa in the Fourth Frontier War of 1811–12. It's a major landmark, cutting through a steep-sided valley shrouded in thick prickly bush. During apartheid, the river became the frontier of the notionally independent Ciskei Bantustan, whose multi-million-rand border post on the east bank of the river stood unused until the 1990s, when it became a rather pleasant roadside tea room and Shell Ultra City Garage.

The **Great Fish River Wetland Reserve** between the R72 and the river mouth is noted for its beautiful plants and prolific birdlife. There's nowhere to stay in the reserve, but just across the Great Fish is the luxurious *Fish River Sun Hotel* (☎040 676 1102, ⓦ www.sun-international.com; ❹). Conforming to the bizarre logic of apartheid, this is where Eastern Cape whites could nip over the border to the Bantustan and the South African-owned **hotel** where they could enjoy a spot of gambling, which was banned in "White South Africa". The *Sun* has arguably the best **golf** course in the country (open to non-residents) with stunning views of the river and beach. A few kilometres further east, the *Mpekweni Beach Resort* is very comfortable, but not as glitzy (☎040 676 1026, ⓔ nicolette@mpekweni.co.za; half board ❹). Its position couldn't be better, though, with rooms close to the beautiful lagoon and beach, which the hotel has managed to nab for its own exclusive use.

Hamburg

One of the few resorts along the Pineapple Coast – the stretch between Port Elizabeth and East London – that feels like real Africa is **HAMBURG**, a low-key village on a good dirt road, 14km off the R72. The route passes through **Xhosa settlements** and shanties, where you'll see traditionally decorated thatch-and-mud huts. Look out for stock animals wandering perilously into your way and strolling around Hamburg itself, lending the town a truly rural feel. Hamburg is renowned for **fishing**, and the muddy-bottomed Keiskamma River is excellent for catching prawns. The sea offers a good beach break for **surfers**, but otherwise there's not much else to do here except laze on the beach, go for walks and bird-watch.

There are a couple of **places to stay**, both with views over the wide, brown Keiskamma River and high olive-green hills, but a three-kilometre walk to the beach. *Sampie's Landing* (℡040 678 1032; half board ❷) rents out rooms, and the owner takes guests fishing. There's a little shop but no restaurants. The beach itself offers nothing but a car park, broken-down toilets and miles of sand and sea.

East London and around

EAST LONDON, the second-largest city in the Eastern Cape, is the obvious jumping-off point for exploring the Transkei or the coast west to Port Elizabeth. It has good **connections** to the rest of the country by air, rail and bus, and you don't need a car to enjoy the beach life. But without fine, warm weather, the city can be dreary. What does happen takes place along the beachfront, where there's a plethora of places to stay, eat and drink. **Nahoon Beach** is a great **surfing spot**, and the town has a dedicated and lively surfing scene. It's also gradually becoming a place for black holiday-makers – a post-apartheid phenomenon. The beaches to the east of town are very beautiful, with long stretches of sand, high dunes, estuaries and luxuriant vegetation, and good swimming. Although definitely not a fashionable city, it's small and easy to drive around, with some good restaurants and accommodation.

Before the British, and even the Xhosa, this was home to the **Khoikhoi** people, who called it Place of the Buffaloes. The Buffalo River once teemed with game, but the animals were gradually killed off with the arrival of British hunters. East London began life as a permanent British settlement during the nineteenth-century **Frontier Wars**, when it was used as a beachhead to land military supplies needed to push back the Xhosa. Taken by its strategic possibilities as a port, the British governor Sir Harry Smith optimistically called it **London** in 1848, after the capital of the empire. Later it was changed to the Port of East London, not after London's East End, but because the port was on the east side of the Buffalo River. British connections are still obvious, though: East London's main thoroughfare is called Oxford Street and there's a Fleet Street and even a Belgravia suburb.

Away from the holiday strip, East London is dominated by an industrial centre served by **Mdantsane**, a huge African township 20km from the city towards King William's Town. Apart from the active river port, there are several large factories, including a Mercedes-Benz plant, whose workers presented Nelson Mandela with a bright red, top-of-the-range Mercedes as a coming-out-of-prison present.

Arrival, information and orientation

East London's small **airport** (℡043 706 0211), a few kilometres west of the centre on the R72, connects the city to all major centres. The **airport shuttle**, the Little Red Bus (℡082 569 3599), meets all flights and drops off at the *Holiday Inn* near the beachfront (R65–100 depending on your destination). The **train station** (℡043 740 2126) is on the eastern edge of East London's small business and shopping district. From here, it's a thirty-minute walk to the backpacker hostel at Eastern Beach, and a slightly shorter stroll to Orient Beach. Buses are scarce, but there are metered **taxis** outside the station.

All three of the **intercity buses** – Translux (℡043 700 1999), Intercape (℡0861 287 287) and Greyhound (℡083 915 9000) – offer a frequent,

4

THE EASTERN CAPE | East London and around

ACCOMMODATION

Dolphin View Lodge	F
Holiday Inn Garden Court	E
Loerie Hide B&B	C
Meander Inn	B
St Andrews' Lodge	A
Sugar Shack	D
Windsor Cabanas & Courtyard	G

RESTAURANTS AND BARS

Buccaneer's Pub	1
Ernst Chalet Suisse	4
Imbizo's Jazz Café	3
Quarterdeck	5
Shenanigans	2

EAST LONDON

Airport, coastal road, Port Alfred & Port Elizabeth ◄

0   500 m

▼ Coastal Road

comprehensive and inexpensive service connecting East London to major centres in the coastal provinces of Northern, Western and Eastern Cape, and KwaZulu-Natal, as well as to Johannesburg and Pretoria. The buses drop off at the coach terminal at Windmill Park on Moore Street.

Like many South African cities, central East London is gridded; with uncongested roads and easy parking, it's far more geared to **driving** than walking. **Minibus taxis** connect the townships to the centre, and buses link the **city centre** and **beachfront**. For a **taxi**, call Springbok Taxis (☎043 722 4400).

Maps and a comprehensive list of B&Bs are available from the helpful **tourist office** at the Esplanade on the beachfront (Mon–Fri 8am–4.30pm, Sat 9am–2pm; ☎043 722 6015, ⓦwww.visitbuffalocity.co.za). In the same building is the head office for the **Eastern Cape Tourism Board** (ⓦwww.ectourism .co.za), where you can pick up information on the rest of the province. Imonti Tours (☎043 741 3884 or 083 487 8975, ⓔimontitours@absamail.co.za) conducts **tours** of the city centre and townships, including a visit to the Khaya La Bantu Cultural Village 30km east of town (see p.417), where there's a storyteller, Xhosa dancing and traditional food.

Accommodation

East London fills up over the Christmas period, when prices rise sharply. The **beachfront** sports graceless blocks of holiday apartments and functional hotels, redeemed only by their fabulous views of the Indian Ocean. The really cheap hotels are mostly filled with long-term residents, and are often rough drinking hangouts – best avoided. If the urban nature of the main beachfront doesn't appeal, your best bet is to head for the mostly white suburbs of **Beacon Bay**, **Bonza Bay** or **Gonubie**, close to the river and sea and reached via the N2 east of the city; without your own transport, you'll need to take a taxi or arrange to be picked up. Besides a couple of old-fashioned hotels, these areas have a good selection of smart B&Bs in private houses. East London's **campsites** are out this way, too, near the water. There are also places to stay in the suburb of Selborne, 3km north of the centre off Oxford Street, near the Vincent Park Centre. For **backpackers**, the best lodge is *Sugar Shack*, at Eastern Beach, spectacularly situated in a former lifeguard's lookout.

Beachfront and northern suburbs

Dolphin View Lodge 6 Seaview Terrace ☎043 702 8600, ✉dolphin.view@mweb.co.za. Luxury guesthouse on the edge of cliffs above the beach with two budget double rooms; six well-appointed standard rooms with limewashed furniture and crisp white linen; a suite with lounge and dining room furnished with rich dark wood antiques and thick brocade curtains; and a self-catering family suite that sleeps four (R700). ❸–❺

Holiday Inn Garden Court Close to Eastern Beach ☎043 722 7260, �🌐www.southernsun .com. Comfortable without offering any surprises in terms of price or decor. ❹

Meander Inn 8 Claredon Rd, Selborne ☎043 726 22310, ✉meanderinn@telkomsa.net. Five spacious, tastefully furnished rooms with white linen and ceiling fans, in a luxurious yet relaxed two-storey building. The garden is manicured and there's a swimming pool, patio and bar, and dinner on request. Often used as the starting or finishing point of the Wild Coast Hotel Meander (see box on p.434); they will do free airport transfer. ❸

Quarry Lake Inn Quartzite Dr, off Pearce St, The Quarry ☎043 707 5400, �🌐www.quarrylakeinn .co.za. Spacious, well-appointed rooms on the edge of a flooded disused quarry which has become home to an abundance of vegetation and bird life. ❹

St Andrews Lodge 14 St Andrews Rd, Selborne ☎043 743 5131, ✉sandrews@iafrica.com. Four basic en-suite B&B units with separate entrances and TV inside a suburban house, as well as a garden cottage with cooking facilities. Swimming pool. ❸

Sugar Shack Eastern Beach ☎ & 📠043 722 8240, �🌐www.sugarshack.co.za. Brilliantly located hostel, right on the beach, with terrific views and an outdoor relaxation area. Free pick-up is available from town, and there's transport from the hostel to the mountain resort of Hogsback (see p.421). ❶

Windsor Cabanas & Courtyard George Walker Parade ☎043 743 2225, �🌐www.windsorcabanas .co.za. Spanish-style block near Orient Beach, offering great views. The *Cabanas* has comfortable one-, two- and three-bedroom self-catering apartments (❹) with breakfast available as an extra. The adjacent *Courtyard* offers B&B (❸).

Eastern suburbs and resorts

Blue Lagoon Hotel Blue Bend Pl, Beacon Bay ☎043 748 4821, ✉blhotel@iafrica.com. Very pleasant accommodation surrounded by palm trees and close to the beach. Rooms are quiet and spacious, with balconies looking onto the river, which you can reach via a short path that also leads to the beach. ❹

Dolphin Hotel 85 Harewood Dr, Nahoon ☎043 735 1435, ✉dolphinhotel@telkomsa.net. A plain 1950s suburban hotel, whose prim style gives no hint of the lush vegetation and wonderful beach just a 15min walk away. ❸

Gonubie Resort & Caravan Park 19km east of the city off the N2 ☎043 740 2021. The best camping place in East London, well maintained and near the beach and lovely estuary, which are both safe for swimming. There are also self-catering wooden chalets, fully equipped if also a little run-down. ❷

Habitat 2 Cane St, Gonubie, one block away from Gonubie Beach ☎043 740 3703. Two basic self-catering units with private entrances, one in the garden, the other on the ground floor of the main house. No children. ❷

The Loerie Hide B&B 2B Sheerness Rd, off Beach Rd, Nahoon ☎043 735 3206, ⌀www .loeriehide.co.za. Four reasonably priced en-suite rooms in the vicinity of Nahoon Beach, decorated in ethnic African and English country-cottage style, at the bottom of a garden that gives way to indigenous bushland. ❸

Montrose Valley 4 Montrose Pl, Bunkers Hill, 3km northeast of Orient Beach along the M13 ☎043 735 3418, ✉montrosevalley@mweb.co.za. Notable for its quiet location on the edge of Blind River Valley rather than its comfortable but somewhat ordinary rooms set in lush gardens. One room is separate from the main house and has its own entrance. They also have a log cabin and a thatched cottage to rent. ❸

The City

East London's drab city centre is dominated by **Oxford Street**, once the main shopping precinct, parallel to Station Street and the train station. Although a major traffic thoroughfare, it is largely deserted at night, when you shouldn't wander around alone. White East Londoners have abandoned the centre, preferring to shop at the **Vincent Park Centre** on Devreux Avenue, 5km north of the city centre (leave the centre on Oxford Street, and turn right into Devreux just beyond the museum), in the midst of the salubrious suburbs of Vincent and Stirling. This is the best place for shopping, or to find anything practical such as banks and the post office.

Apart from a couple of handsome buildings, East London's Victorian heart has progressively been demolished. From the station you can walk a few blocks north up Cambridge Street to the city centre's principal landmark, the splendid terracotta and lace-white **City Hall**, opened in 1899. Its tall, colourful clock tower amid the otherwise dreary modernish buildings is a useful orientation point. Over the road is a rather lifeless statue of martyred Black Consciousness leader **Steve Biko** (see box on p.419), a minor point of pilgrimage for visitors, unveiled by Nelson Mandela in 1997. Staying with the Biko theme, the **Daily Dispatch Building**, with a surrounding colonial-style veranda, is also worth taking in, at the corner of Caxton Street and Cambridge Road. Founded in 1879, the newspaper made national headlines in the 1970s, when the then editor, the late Donald Woods, earned the wrath of the apartheid government for being involved with Biko, who contributed to the newspaper under a pseudonym. After endless police harassment, Woods fled the country dramatically, a story told in the book and 1987 movie *Cry Freedom*.

One street north of here, Terminus Street leads to the Victorian **Gately House** (Tues–Thurs 10am–1pm & 2–5pm, Fri 10am–1pm, Sat & Sun 3–5pm; entry by donation). This was the home of the city's first mayor, John Gately, and contains some fine period furniture. You can also enter Gately House via **Queen's Park & Zoo** (daily 9am–5pm; R10), a good spot to take children, with its farmyard, reptiles and birds, as well as a playground and refreshment kiosk. At weekends there are pony rides (10am–3pm) and a little train all day (on weekdays it operates at 11am and 2.30pm).

East of the city's train station is **Quigney**, a racially mixed area of small colonial-style Victorian houses, some nicely restored with verandas and corrugated-iron roofs, others run-down. Quigney slopes downhill to the **Esplanade** and **Orient Beach**, the safest place to swim and most easily reached along Currie Street, off Fleet Street. Here you'll find the city's best curio outlet, Umzi Wethu Curio Shop, stocking handmade **African crafts**; it's at 110 Moore Street, up the hill from the *Holiday Inn*. Near the station, African Culture at 46 Station Street has ceramics, sculpture, drawings, batiks and tie-dyed products made on the premises; nearest the beach is the consistently reliable Africa Curio Shop in Lock Street Gaol, Fleet Street which sells curios, leather and woodwork.

Two kilometres uphill from the centre is **Latimer's Landing**, the working dockland waterfront on the Buffalo River. Never the success it was hoped to be, it appears a little deserted, and business is slow – but there's a pub, and it's good for a wander around to see the boats. To get there, head west along Fleet Street towards the airport, and just before Buffalo Bridge head steeply down Pontoon Road. **Boat trips** from here head through the Buffalo harbour out to sea and along the beachfront shore; Yacht Miscky (℡043 735 2232) offers trips by arrangement.

A few kilometres north of the city centre, the **East London Museum**, Upper Oxford Street (Mon–Fri 9.30am–5pm, Sat 2–5pm, Sun 11am–4pm; R8), has a stunning collection of South Nguni beadwork and contemporary wire sculpture, including an inventive wire car made by Mdantsane resident Phillip Ntliziywana. The museum's pride and joy, however, is its stuffed coelacanth (see p.394), caught off the coast in the 1950s.

The beaches

East London's **Esplanade** loops from Orient Pier in a wide and beautiful sweep of rocks, beach and sand dunes to Eastern Beach, marred only by the motley assortment of holiday apartments, hotels and restaurants lining the beachfront. It's about thirty minutes' walk from the city centre; buses here are sporadic, but it's easy enough to stroll from one end to the other.

Tucked in next to Orient Pier, with dockland cranes poking their necks above the water, **Orient Beach** is a wonderful place to swim, though it looks a bit grim and industrial. The waves are gentle, the water and sandy beach clean. Red-hatted lifeguards lend a sense of security, and there are changing rooms, and a couple of little pools for kids. You pay a small fee to enter the beach area during the day, but it's free after 5pm.

From Orient Beach, the sea-walled Esplanade continues northeast, along sand and black rocks, to **Eastern Beach**, with its high, bush-capped sand dunes. Although far more attractive, Eastern Beach is not really safe for swimming, and muggings have been reported. Don't leave your belongings unattended, and give the beach a wide berth at night.

Northeast beyond Bat's Cave – a distinctive chunk of rock jutting out to sea – is popular **Nahoon Beach**, a long stretch of sand, backed by dunes. This wonderful natural setting is superb for swimming and surfing, with some of the best waves in the country. Public transport is scant, but there are three **buses** a day from the Esplanade, or you can walk the 5km from the centre if you're feeling energetic. East of the Nahoon River, 10km from the centre, the coast curves into **Bonza Bay**, with kilometres of beach walks and a lazy lagoon at the mouth of the Quinera River. Further on, **Gonubie Beach**, 18km northeast of the centre, at the Gonubie River Mouth, is still close enough to be considered part of East London, with some good accommodation, a beautiful beach and walks.

Eating, drinking and nightlife

East London has several surprisingly good restaurants and a couple of very decent places serving **fresh fish** in an outdoor setting. **Drinking** spots abound, from beachfront sleaze at lowlife hotels to lively surfers' hangouts or swanky places overlooking the ocean. Some of the pubs double up as **live music** venues, as well as offering a bite to eat.

Buccaneer's Pub Eastern Beach, next to *Sugar Shack*. Lively bar that buzzes till the early hours, with occasional live music (Wed, Fri & Sat). During the day there are fantastic views of the rodeo riders of the surf. Good pub fare includes fish and chips and, best of all, chicken schnitzel. Daily lunch & dinner.

Emzini Hemingway's Casino Complex, Vincent ☏043 726 9169. Traditional Xhosa cuisine and African pub fare – samp and beans and braaied meat. Daily breakfast, lunch & dinner.

Ernst Chalet Suisse Upstairs at the paying entrance to Orient Beach ☏043 722 1840. One of East London's top restaurants, whose outstanding Swiss chef cooks up a seafood storm and delectable desserts. Smart yet reasonably priced. Daily except Sat for lunch and daily except Sun for dinner.

Imbizo's Jazz Café Curie St ☏043 722 0155. Traditional Southern African cuisine – *bobotie*, Malay curries, kudu steak – with occasional live music. Daily lunch & dinner.

Le Petit 54 Beach Road Shopping Centre, Nahoon ☎043 735 3685. Highly regarded eating place serving rich Mediterrean/French-inspired food, with an emphasis on game, seafood and veal. Mon–Fri lunch & dinner, Sat also dinner.

Quarterdeck Orient Beach, overlooking the paddling pool ☎043 743 5312. The informal counterpart of *Ernst Chalet Suisse*, served by the same kitchen. It's one of the best beachside places for a quiet drink, with reasonably priced catch of the day served daily. Closed Sat lunchtime & all day Sun.

Shenanigans Esplanade, next to the aquarium. The food and service are unexciting at this bar-restaurant; the real attraction is the setting, on a terrace jutting out over the waves. You can watch the surfers through the huge picture windows, even in poor weather. Daily.

Listings

Car rental Avis ☎043 736 2250, Imperial ☎043 736 2230.

Emergencies Fire ☎043 705 9000; see also p.89.

Garages Stirling Motors, 8 Old Transkei Rd (☎043 735 1580), is open 24hr.

Hospitals Frere Hospital (state), Amalinda Dr ☎043 709 1111; St Dominics (private), 45 St Mark's Rd ☎043 743 4303.

Internet access Try Cyberlink, 58 Beach Rd, Nahoon (Mon–Sat 10am–1pm, 3–6pm & Sun 3–6pm).

Laundries There is a coin-operated launderette at the Edcott Centre, Oxford St.

Pharmacies John Forbes, 205a Oxford St (☎043 722 2062; till 10pm); Berea Pharmacy, Pearce St (☎043 721 1300; Mon–Sat 8am–10pm, Sun 9am–1pm & 2–9pm).

Travel agents Rennies Travel, 33 Chamberlain Rd, Berea ☎043 726 0698; Let's Travel, Kennaway Building, Esplanade ☎043 743 2983.

Around East London

Several worthwhile excursions detailed below are within an hour's drive from East London. If you don't have your own wheels, you can cover the same ground with Imonti Tours (☎043 741 3884 or 083 487 8975, ✉imontitours@absamail .co.za) which offers half-day trips from R200 per person.

The privately run **Inkwenkwezi Game Reserve** lies 35km from East London (book in advance for a safari; ☎043 734 3234, ⊛www.inkwenkwezi .co.za), set in an appealing landscape, encompassing bushveld, grassland, forest and two rivers, with views of the Indian Ocean. The reserve offers luxury tented **accommodation** with full board (⊚), and you can view the wildlife, including rhino, giraffe, zebra, wildebeest, various antelope and some rare birds, on early morning or afternoon/evening game drives in one of the reserve's 4WD vehicles. The centrepiece is a magnificently sited, thatched *lapa* (enclosure or corral) with spacious decks where food is served. To get there, drive north out of East London along the N2, taking the Brakfontein off-ramp onto the East Coast Resorts Road; then travel east for about 20km, until you see the Inkwenkwezi Entrance Gate on the left.

Xhosa and township cultural tours

KHAYA LA BUNTU, near Mooiplaas, 30km east of East London, signposted off the N2 (☎043 851 1011; visits by prior arrangement, R140 including lunch), is a **Xhosa village** which sees only twenty or thirty tours a year – it's not one of the dressed-up villages deemed suitable for tourists. It's best visited for a traditional lunch, and being a group encourages dancing and storytelling.

It's possible to have a more casual **lunch** at the *Emzini Traditional Food Restaurant*, 14 Station St, Berlin, 45km northwest of East London. Follow the N2 in the direction of King William's Town, take exit 19 and turn right at the stop sign towards Border Technikon, which brings you to the little town of Berlin. At the four-way stop, turn right into Immigrant Road, then right into Station Street.

The Amatola Mountains

Most visitors drive quickly through the scrubby, dry impoverished area between East London and the **Amatola Mountains** proper, to reach the cool forests and holiday lands at **Hogsback**. However, it's worth deviating en route, to see the marvellous collection of African art at **Fort Hare University**, close to the little town of Alice, and to visit apartheid martyr Steve Biko's grave in **King William's Town**. King, as it's usually called, has a couple of worthwhile museums which help you absorb some of East Cape's settler history and Xhosa culture.

One of South Africa's least-explored game reserves, **Mpofu**, lies in this region, with hiking trails and cheap self-catering accommodation. If you want to do the reserve in style, stay in the fabulous settler farmhouse at Waylands, 40km north of **Fort Beaufort**, the region's farming centre.

King William's Town

KING WILLIAM'S TOWN, more commonly known simply as **King**, lies 56km northeast of East London. It started life as a military frontier and missionary outpost, and today has a large population drawn from the former Ciskei. There's enough historical interest here to satisfy at least half a day's visit. To get a feel for **Xhosa history**, head for the **Amatola Museum** in Alexandra Road (Mon–Fri 9am–4.30pm, Sat 9am–1pm; R5, includes the Missionary Museum); the Xhosa Gallery has unusually good displays, including full accounts of the British tactics and campaigns which crushed the Xhosa. Traditional culture is well represented, with contemporary exhibitions on current building styles. Don't miss Phillip Ntliziywana's imaginative bus and car sculptures made from wire and discarded bits and pieces.

Two blocks north of the museum, off Albert Road, is the nineteenth-century **Edward Street Cemetery**, notable for the story it tells of the conflicts in the area. Besides a memorial to those killed in the innumerable Frontier Wars against the Xhosa, there is an open piece of ground on the far side of the cemetery which marks a mass grave where hundreds of Xhosa were buried; they died of starvation as a result of the disastrous 1857 **Cattle Killing**, when many Xhosa people destroyed their cattle at the behest of the false prophetess Nongqawuse (see box on p.437).

About fifteen minutes' walk north of the Amatola Museum, the **Missionary Museum** in Berkeley Street (arrange a visit through the museum) is mainly of interest for the glimpse it gives into early educational institutions in the Eastern Cape. South Africa's first black professionals were schooled here, including many of the new nation's heavyweights such as Nelson Mandela.

King's only other attraction of note is **Steve Biko's grave** in the Ginsberg Cemetery. It's a moving place, and the grave is much humbler than you'd expect for such an important figure in black politics. The polished, charcoal-coloured tombstone sits midway through the graveyard, among the large patch of paupers' graves. To get there, take Cathcart Street south out of town (towards Grahamstown), turning left onto a road signposted to the cemetery, after the bridge (just before the Alice turn-off to the right).

Rob Speirs of Speirs Tours (☎043 642 1747, ⓦwww.speirstours.co.za) offers affordable **battlefield tours** around King William's Town, visiting various forts and battle sites from the Frontier Wars and grave sites of Xhosa chiefs. Also worthwhile is the Liberation Tour which takes you through the history of the struggle against apartheid. King is also the place to set out on all or part of the

Amatola Hiking Trail, which starts from Maiden Dam, just outside town, and continues as a five-night/six-day hike into the mountains (see box on p.422).

Practicalities

Alexandra Road is the town's main drag, where you'll find a 24-hour filling station and a few takeaway restaurants. The **minibus taxis** rank is in Cathcart Street, with connections to East London and the rest of the Eastern Cape.

Accommodation in King William's Town is principally geared to business travellers; at weekends, you'll find a greater choice and often discounted rates. A pleasant B&B is the *Dreamers Guest House,* 29 Gordon Street (T & F 043 642 3012, W www.dreamersguesthouse.com; ❷), in a centrally located Victorian building with a lovely garden, pool and real log fires in winter. The *Grosvenor Lodge*, Taylor Street, near the Amatola Museum (T 043 604 7200; ❸), is a business-class hotel with cable TV; they also run the *Grosvenor Guest House* around the corner (❷). For **eating and drinking**, *Archie's Pub & Pizzeria* in Taylor Street is popular, while the *Castle* on Queens Road serves good steaks and salads. *Nando's*, which offers spicy grilled chicken, and *Steers*, which does burgers, are handy fast-food joints on Alexandra Road.

Fort Hare University and Alice

Despite decades of deliberate neglect, and its relegation after 1959 to a "tribal" **university** under apartheid, **Fort Hare** (W www.ufh.ac.za), 64km west of

---

Steve Biko and Black Consciousness

Steve Biko's brutal interrogation and death while in police custody triggered international outrage and turned opinion further against the apartheid regime. His death was followed by the banning of the Black Consciousness organizations, and was a major factor in the imposition of a mandatory **arms embargo** against South Africa by the United Nations Security Council.

Steven Bantu Biko was born in 1946 in King William's Town. His political ascent was swift, due in no small part to his eloquence, charisma and focused vision. While still a medical student at Natal University during the late Sixties, he was elected president of the exclusively black South African Students' Organization (SASO) and started publishing articles in their journal, fiercely attacking white liberalism, which they saw as patronizing and counter-revolutionary. In an atmosphere of repression – both ANC and PAC leaders were serving hefty sentences at the time – Biko's brand of Black Consciousness immediately caught on. He called for blacks to take destiny into their own hands, to unify and rid themselves of the "shackles that bind them to perpetual servitude". He became honorary president of the Black Peoples' Convention, an umbrella organization which attracted mainly young intellectuals and professionals. From 1973 onwards, Biko suffered banning, detention and other harassment at the hands of the state. In 1974, he defended himself in court, presenting his case so brilliantly that his profile in the international press soared.

Barred from leaving King William's Town, Biko continued working and writing, frequently escaping his confinement. In 1976, black outrage burst into the open with the **Soweto riots**. The police response was brutal, and the search for "agitators" led to Biko's 101-day detention. In August the following year, he was stopped at a roadblock near Grahamstown (outside his restricted area), taken to Port Elizabeth and intensively interrogated and tortured. On September 12, 1977, he died from a brain haemorrhage, sustained at the hands of security police. No one was held accountable. Diplomats from thirteen Western countries joined the thousands of mourners at his funeral in King William's Town.

King William's Town, is assured a place in South African history. Established in 1916 as a multiracial college by missionaries, it became the first institution in South Africa to deliver tertiary education to blacks, and was attended by many prominent African leaders, including Zimbabwe's president Robert Mugabe and Tanzania's former president, Julius Nyerere.

The most famous former student is **Nelson Mandela** (see box on p.447), making this an essential port of call if you're following his footsteps. Sadly, though, the Wesley Residence, from whose window the young Mandela reputedly used to climb to go ballroom dancing, has been pulled down. The spot it occupied is now the lawn just to the right as you enter through the main gate. **Freedom Square**, at the centre of the campus, was the scene of many protests at the university – this is the spot where several members of the present government cut their political teeth.

Virtually all students live on campus as **Alice**, the adjacent town, is too undeveloped to offer much in the way of digs. It's possible to visit **Beda Residence** where Mugabe studied, though the dormitory where he stayed has been converted into single rooms. This is one of the pleasanter old residences; some of the others are pretty dilapidated owing to underfunding during the apartheid years.

If you have even the slightest interest in African art, Fort Hare's **De Beers Art Gallery** (Mon–Fri 8am–4.30pm; free) is well worth a visit. From the outside, the cylindrical gallery resembles a high-security bank vault. Once inside, you're faced with a treasury of contemporary black southern **African art** – one of the most significant and least publicized collections anywhere. Pioneers of black painting, including Gerard Sekoto and George Pemba, are represented, and you should look out for the lively oils of Dan Rakgoate. There are some stunning sculptures: Uneas Sithole's elongated *Is My Friend the Chameleon Hiding?*, Percy Konqobe's *Ntsikana and his Cow*, and Sydney Kumalo's *Robot Man*. Also unmissable is the sequence of fifteen woodcuts by Lucky Sibiya called *Umabatha*, the Zulu adaptation of *Macbeth*. The gallery also houses Fort Hare's **ethnographic collection** – a major museum of traditional crafts and artefacts, with many rare and valuable pieces. The best way to see the gallery is to take a free tour with the gallery's erudite curator, Reggie Letsatse. The university library houses the **ANC's archives** (Mon–Fri 8am–4.30pm; Ⓦwww.liberation.org.za), which include historic documents and photographs.

All **tours** of the university, its art gallery and ANC archives should be arranged beforehand through the public relations department (Mon–Thurs 8am–4.30pm, Fri 8am–3.30pm; Ⓣ040 602 2239; free).

Alice

A handful of photogenically decaying colonial houses with peeling corrugated-iron roofs and balconies smothered in creepers constitute the main interest in **ALICE**. It's the closest town to Fort Hare University, but can in no way be called a university town. The lengthy decay of the town reflects the second-class status accorded the university under Afrikaner Nationalist rule. There's one hopelessly tiny bookshop, a depressing reflection of local poverty and the high cost of books in South Africa, which puts them beyond the reach of the majority of the population. Alice's two hotels are little more than run-down carousing joints. Of the two, the *Amatola* is favoured for drinking by university staff and students.

Just 1km east of the town centre is **Lovedale College**, older than Fort Hare, and no less significant in educating Africans. Built in 1842 as a Presbyterian mission station, it was soon educating the country's first black professionals, and became an important publishing centre. The Xhosa language was first transcribed here, and one of Lovedale's students, J. Tengo Jabavu, was the founder of South Africa's first weekly African-language paper, *Zabantsundu*. With the passing of the Bantu Education Act under the apartheid government, Lovedale was closed. Now the college is in use again as a high school, you can drive in and look at the Victorian buildings. The actual site doesn't have any displays or information – for that, visit the Missionary Museum in King William's Town (see p.418).

Practicalities

The university is a couple of kilometres east of Alice on the R63; from King William's Town there are **minibus taxis** to Alice that drop off passengers at the university gates. With the virtual absence of accommodation in Alice, you're better off staying making a day-trip here from Grahamstown, East London, Fort Beaufort or Hogsback.

Hogsback

Made sweeter by the contrast with the hot valleys below, the village of **HOGSBACK** in the Amatola Mountains, 32km north of Alice and 145km from East London, offers cool relief after hauling through prickly, overgrazed country. The name "Hogsback" applies to the area as much as to the village, and comes from the high rocky ridge (actually three peaks) resembling a bushpig's spine, which runs above the settlement.

Hogsback represents a corner of England, a fantasy fed by mists, pine plantations and exotic trees such as oak, walnut and azaleas, and guaranteed snowfalls each winter. It's a great place to spend a relaxing couple of days, with plenty of walks and good air among the flowers, grasslands and forests, and there are many places to stay. The real attraction is the **Afro-montane cloud forest**, singing with bird calls and gauzy waterfalls, and populated by the odd troop of **samango monkeys**, which survive on the steep slopes above the pine plantations. Note that Hogsback can be wet and cold, even in summer, so bring a warm pullover, sturdy shoes and rain gear.

Winding your way up the mountains on the road from Alice, you'll have a good view of the forest, dense with yellowwood, stinkwood and Cape chestnut. The hamlet itself is strung out along 3km of gravel road, with lanes branching out on either side to hotels and cottages. The closest thing to a **centre** is the small conglomeration of a general store, post office, filling station and some nearby craft shops. Hogsback has its own **indigenous craft** found nowhere else in the country: prepare to be pestered by Xhosa kids selling the characteristic unfired clay horses and hogs with white markings.

Hogsback is prime **rambling** country, with short, relatively easy trails indicated by hogs painted onto trees. For a rewarding taste of indigenous forest, the Contour Path above the campsite makes an easy, one-hour walk. From this path, a route goes steeply up **Tor Doone**, which overlooks the settlement, and is the easiest summit to climb. One of the most rewarding waterfall trails is the one-hour steep downhill walk to the lovely **Madonna and Child Waterfall**. A number of short and long routes, including the Amatola Trail and Zingcuka Loop (see box on p.422), are detailed in inexpensive **guidebooks** available at the village shops.

Practicalities

It's worth spending a couple of nights in Hogsback. A cheap shuttle (☎043 722 8240) connects *Sugar Shack* in East London (see p.414) and Cintsa (see

Ranked among South Africa's best forested mountain walks, the **Amatola Trail** is a tough but fabulously beautiful five-night trail, with numerous waterfalls, rivers and bathing pools en route. Starting at Maiden Dam in the Pirie Forest, some 21km north of King William's Town, it stretches 105km to end at Hogsback. There are huts with mattresses and braai facilities, some also with showers, at each designated night stop along the way.

There are a number of shortened versions of the trail, but these can only be done outside school holidays, or at short notice if the huts are not filled. Best of the shortened trails is the 36-kilometre **Zingcuka Loop** from Hogsback, which scales the Hogsback itself, and follows streams much of the way, past idyllic waterfalls and pools. Right in the forest at the base of a cliff, the overnight hut has the luxury of a primitive shower, and firewood.

To go on one of these trails, **book** through the Department of Forestry (☎043 642 2571, ✉amatola@dwas.gov.za; R200 for the complete trail). You'll need well-broken-in boots, plus waterproofs and warm clothes.

p.435) with Hogsback three days a week; the *Away With The Fairies* hostel in Hogsback can make arrangements, whether or not you intend to stay there. On the main road, Storm Haven Crafts is also the town's **tourist office** (Mon–Fri 8am–4.30pm; ☎045 839 2265, ⓦwww.hogsback.co.za), and can supply accommodation details, **hiking maps**, and information on activities like mountain-bike trails (bikes can be rented from the hostel). Lowestoff (☎045 843 1716) offers **horse trails** for beginners and experienced riders alike.

Places to stay are plentiful, but the village tends to fill up during holidays and weekends, when you'll need to book ahead. The *Hog Island Country House* is well known for its gourmet **food**; the *Kings Lodge* has a good restaurant and bar, while the *Hogsback Inn* is much better for drinks than food. The best place for afternoon tea is *Tea Thyme* at the *Edge*. Hogsback has a general **shop** selling basic supplies.

Accommodation

Away With The Fairies Hydrangea Lane; down the first turning on your right and signposted as you drive into Hogsback ☎045 962 1031, ✉hogsback1@iafrica.com. Unequivocally geared to the backpacker scene, this a large converted house on a sizeable property, with fabulous views of the Tyumi Valley. Small dorms sleep three to eight guests, and there's a double room in the house and another in a garden cottage. Mountain bikes are available to rent, horse-riding can be arranged, and the owners offer free guided hikes in the forests and mountains. One of the nicest features of the hostel is a platform in a tree for drinks and hanging out. ❶
The Edge ☎ & ⓕ045 962 1159, ⓦwww.theedge-hogsback.co.za. The best of the self-catering accommodation, nine cottages in separate locations a couple of kilometres

off the main road. There are superb valley and forest views, and a herb patch from which meals are garnished – the owners grow 25 kinds of lavender on the property. They also have space for twenty tents. Booking is essential for the cottages, which range in price from R300 to R700, sleeping two to four people. ❷
Hog Island Country House Wolfridge Rd ☎045 962 1088 or ☎082 335 4625, ⓦwww .hogisland.co.za. Thatched guesthouse with three elegant en-suite rooms decorated with white linen and Oregon pine furniture. A river with a waterwheel runs through the large tranquil property. ❸
Kings Lodge Signposted along the main road ☎045 962 1024, ⓦwww.kingslodge.co.za. The best of the hotels, with wood-panelled interiors and en-suite rooms. They also have self-catering units sleeping two to six. ❹

Fort Beaufort

A farming town at the heart of a citrus- and wool-producing district, **FORT BEAUFORT**, 80km west of King William's Town, and roughly the same distance north of Grahamstown, is nothing to get excited about. The most likely reason for a close encounter is because you're passing through on your way from Grahamstown or East London to Katberg or Mpofu Game Reserve. Having said that, Fort Beaufort does have a reputation throughout the Eastern Cape for its lusciously sweet **oranges**; should you find yourself here in winter, look out for African traders selling them by the sackful for a song, at the main crossroads out of town.

Founded as a link in the chain of forts built along the eastern frontier to form a buffer against the Xhosa, Fort Beaufort's moment in history came in 1845, when Tsili, a Xhosa man, stole an axe from a shop here, precipitating the bloody **War of the Axe** – the Seventh Frontier War. The theft provided a pretext for the British to act on a growing and expedient belief among whites that Xhosa land would be put to better use in their own hands. In 1847, after literally bringing the Xhosa chiefs to their knees (forcing them at bayonet point to kiss his boots), Governor Harry Smith told the vanquished that their land would be divided into counties, towns and villages bearing English names. "You may no longer be naked and wicked barbarians," he informed them, "which you will ever be unless you labour and become industrious."

The axe shop is still here, as is the 1830 officer's mess, now the highly eccentric **Fort Beaufort Museum**, which doubles as a tourist office and resembles a bric-a-brac shop. Interesting items include a painting by the Victorian documentary oil colourist, Thomas Baines. There's also a proclamation by Sir Harry Smith inviting anyone with a gun to take pot shots at the Xhosa, with the incentive that they could keep any cattle they rustled. The other notable historical building is a **Martello Tower**, still intact and exactly the same as those built two hundred years ago along the British coastline to keep out the French. The underworked tourist office will direct you there and fill you in on local history.

Practicalities

The **tourist office** in Fort Beaufort Museum (Mon–Fri 8am–5pm, Sat 8.30am–12.45pm; ☎046 645 1555) can provide lists of **places to stay**, of which the unexceptional *Savoy Hotel* (☎046 645 1146, ℗046 645 2082; ❷) is on Durban Street, not far west of the museum on the other side of the road, with a couple of reasonable **B&Bs** nearby. **Eating** places are limited to *Savoy Hotel* and the *Country Club*, north of town on the R67; the latter is a farmers' hangout that does good steaks and pizzas, and also has a bar and outdoor seating with views of the golf course and the surrounding hills.

Mpofu Game Reserve and Katberg

If you want somewhere like Hogsback, only even less developed, you'll find it in the mountainscapes of **Mpofu** and **Katberg**. Both are within spitting distance of Fort Beaufort, yet less than an hour's drive transports you dramatically from parched scrubby lowlands into high country, broken with cliffs and draped with indigenous forests. Facilities are fairly basic, but the area feels far more pristine than the Hogsback and draws far fewer visitors.

Mpofu Game Reserve

Mpofu Game Reserve is a 75-square-kilometre tract of land northwest of Fort Beaufort, with spectacular views over the Katberg Mountains. To get there, take the Lower Blinkwater/Post Retief turn-off to the west, 13km from Fort Beaufort, and continue for a further 8km to the entrance gate. The steep terrain and changing rainfall generates a varied habitat, supporting a respectable cross section of **wildlife**, such as white rhino, giraffe, waterbuck and warthog, plus a wealth of antelope such as springbok, kudu, eland, reedbuck and lechwe. Baboons, vervet monkeys, black-backed jackals, caracals and ostriches are also found. A number of **trails** are on offer, taking from ninety minutes to a full day to complete.

There is **accommodation** at two houses in the game reserve: *Mpofu* in the north, a six-bedroom house (minimum charge for four people R630), and in the south, the four-bedroom *Ntloni* (minimum charge for four people R600). These should be booked through the Eastern Cape Parks Board (☎040 635 2115, ⓦwww.ecparksboard.co.za).

Waylands Farm

Outside Mpofu, you can stay in an Art Nouveau farmhouse – a historic monument – at **Waylands Farm** (☎046 684 0151 or 072 289 8468, ⓔwaylands@procomp.co.za; full board ❾), on a north-facing slope of the Katberg, 40km north of Fort Beaufort. A large, organic livestock farmstead, it boasts some very upmarket guest suites with four-poster beds, yellowwood floors and period furniture. The farm arranges hikes and game drives in Mpofu, guided horse trails and mountain biking on its grounds, occasional art and music workshops, and has resident natural health practitioners.

If you're driving, continue for 30km from the Mpofu entrance through the game reserve; at the T-junction, turn right towards Post Retief and continue for about 10km to Post Retief Country Club. From here take the right fork and continue for another 10km and you'll see the farm signposted to your left. Alternatively, the farm can pick you up by prior arrangement from Adelaide or Fort Beaufort.

Katberg

KATBERG, an area of mountains and indigenous forest west of Hogsback, is a sort of poor relation of that village, since it fell into the former Ciskei and never developed into a residential area. To get there, take the R67 from Fort Beaufort north towards Queenstown; after 40km, follow the dirt road signposted to the *Katberg Hotel* for 13km. It's essentially a weekending spot, with only one **place to stay** – the *Katberg Hotel* itself (☎040 864 1010, ⓦwww.katleisure.co.za; during school terms half board ❹, school holidays full board ❾), a mountain resort that's great for families, offering walking trails, horse-riding, tennis and pleasant, shady gardens. Maps and information are available from the hotel, which is also worth visiting for tea or a **meal** – it has a good reputation for food.

East London to Aliwal North

Besides the mountainous scenery of the Amatolas, there's little to encourage a stop along the **N6** East London–Bloemfontein highway until you reach the inviting **hot springs** of **Aliwal North**. The road traverses a region which was once home to **German settlers**; between 1857 and 1859, over four thousand Germans arrived in the Eastern Cape, initially drawn from a German regiment fighting for the British in the Crimea, and brought in by the Cape Governor to act as a buffer against the Xhosa. The once-cohesive German-speaking community has long been diluted, and the last settler farms were abandoned in the 1980s when the area came under the auspices of the Ciskei government.

Queenstown and around

There's no reason at all to pause in **QUEENSTOWN**, 190km north of East London, a sizeable workaday shopping and administrative centre serving a large and poor black rural community and white stock-farmers. However, if you're here for the night on a cross-country journey, the **Lawrence de Lange** and **Longhill nature reserves**, just out of town in the mountains, are worth a visit. From Cathcart Road, the main street, head out of town on Kingsway and Hangklip roads, and look out for signs to the reserve.

Intercity **buses** stop at the Ultra City, 2km southeast of town on the N6. The **tourist office** at the Pick 'n Pay Mall, Cathcart Road (Mon–Thurs 8.30am–4.30pm, Fri 8.30am–4pm; ☎045 839 2265), represents the surrounding Stormberg region, and can help with finding accommodation (after hours, it posts up an emergency B&B list). The best **places to stay** are in the middle-class suburbs above the rail line, where you'll find some excellent B&Bs. *Carthews Corner*, 1 Park Avenue, Blue Rise (☎ & ℱ045 838 1885 or ☎082 492 7547; ❷), has garden cottages, a pool and braai facilities, and secure off-street parking.

The *Black Swan* (☎045 839 7475; closed Sun), in an old restored sandstone house in Grey Street, is the nicest of the **restaurants** in town. The menu is varied with light lunches, delicious tea-time treats, and a good selection of meat and fish dishes for dinner. For steaks, you could do worse than the *Spur* (open daily) in Cathcart Road and the *Parlour and Grill* (closed Sun) in Ebden Street right in the centre, which also serves pasta and bar meals.

Dramatic scenery surrounds Queenstown, with tawny grass-covered mountains and rocky outcrops. *Carnarvon Estates* (☎ & ℱ045 966 0408, ⓦwww .carnarvon-estate.com; half board ❹), 50km north of town on the N6, is the longest-established of several **game farms** in the area. Here you can go on botanical walks and view seventeen species of antelope and 250 bird varieties. There's accommodation in a luxury farmhouse lodge with seven en-suite bedrooms, or a garden cottage suitable for a couple. There is also the plus of seeing Bushmen paintings on the farm.

Aliwal North

Bordering Free State province, and with a distinctly Afrikaner flavour, **ALIWAL NORTH** lies on the Orange River 158km north of Queenstown (and roughly the same distance south of Bloemfontein). The town's name celebrates the smashing of the Sikhs at Aliwal in India in 1846 by the governor of the Cape Colony, Sir Harry Smith (Mossel Bay in the Western Cape was formerly Aliwal South). More relevant to its Afrikaans character is the town's role in the Second Anglo-Boer War, when the Boers under General Olivier occupied the town and declared the Republic of Oliviersfontein in 1900. What remains of the short-lived republic is a sobering memorial to the Boers who died in concentration camps set up by the British. Historic interest aside, the main reason to come to Aliwal North is for its curative **mineral springs**, 3km from the centre, which merit a restorative stop.

The town is effectively divided into two: the central area dominated by the N6 traffic, and the area built up around the spa which, although ugly, has the best places to stay, shop and eat. The **spa** (daily 7am–10pm; R15), signposted off the N6 and R58, centres around an Olympic-sized outdoor pool with palm trees and green lawns – perfect for swimming and relaxation. The indoor pools are much warmer, but not quite hot enough in winter. Admission gives you access to the modest gym and tennis courts, but you'll have to bring your own gear.

At the southern edge of town, signposted off the N6, is a **Boer War Concentration Camp Memorial**. On the site of two camp cemeteries, the memorial looks from the outside like a prison or crematorium. Inside, the walls are plastered with handmade gravestones of the 716 people (many of them Afrikaner children) who died as a result of the terrible conditions in the tented camps set up by the British.

Practicalities

Translux and Greyhound **buses** between Port Elizabeth or East London and Johannesburg pull in at the *Balmoral Hotel* in Somerset Street. **Tickets** for Translux buses can be bought at the Shoprite Checkers supermarket (☎051 634 2592) in Robinson Street, while Greyhound tickets should be booked through their East London office (☎043 743 9284). The **tourist office**, 97 Somerset St (Mon–Fri 8am–4.30pm; ☎051 633 3567), can supply **maps** and lists of places to stay in the North Eastern Cape and over the river in the Eastern Free State mountains.

Most of the town's **accommodation** is clustered around the spa; rates are modest since the springs are essentially for a local market. Opposite the spa entrance, adjoining the *Spa Hotel* in Dan Pienaar Avenue, the smart *Pink Lady* **steakhouse** serves reasonably priced fish and steak main courses (closed Sun). Back in the centre, the nicest place is *Three Treat*, Somerset Street, serving good teas and light lunches.

Accommodation

Aliwal Spa De Wet Dr ☎051 633 2951, ℱ051 634 1307. Municipal outfit with a huge caravan park, camping and run-down bungalows. Set on a lake 8km beyond the campsite are *Islands*, two-bedroom self-catering timber cottages – the best places to stay in Aliwal North. ❷

Buffelsbron Chalets 35 Dan Pienaar Ave ☎ & ℱ051 633 3129. Fully equipped, spotless self-catering brick chalets sleeping four to six people. ❶

Spa Hotel 14 Dan Pienaar Ave ☎051 634 2189, ℮spahotel@cybertrade.co.za. Over the road from the spa, offering the best-value hotel rooms in town with a fair bit of comfort, including electric blankets in winter, satellite TV and tea-making facilities in the en-suite rooms. ❷

Umtali Motel Dan Pienaar Ave ☎051 633 2400, ℮umtali@getaway-gateway.co.za. At the end of the avenue, this is the smartest hotel, but it's a bit characterless and a long walk from the spa. ❷

The Eastern Cape Drakensberg

The **Eastern Cape Drakensberg** is the most southerly section of southern Africa's highest and most extensive mountain chain, stretching east across Lesotho and up the west flank of KwaZulu-Natal into Mpumalanga. Although known misleadingly as South Africa's "little Switzerland" in tourist brochures, they are wonderful African mountains, full of **San rock paintings**, sandstone **caves** and craggy sheep farms. **Rhodes**, one of the country's best-preserved and prettiest Victorian villages, is the obvious goal in the region, a good base for riding, walking, skiing and trout fishing. While it's very cold, dry and sunny in the winter, summer is idyllically green, with river pools to swim in. There are some appealing cottages for rent on farms, and a number of **hiking trails**, many of which offer the opportunity to see rock paintings and sleep in enormous caves. Since there is no national park in the Eastern Cape Drakensberg, activities are all arranged through private farms. For **bird-watchers**, the region is especially good for raptors (notably the rare lammergeier and Cape vulture), as well as orange-breasted rock jumpers and ground woodpeckers. Unfortunately, there's no public transport in the area.

From Aliwal North to Rhodes

LADY GREY, 50km east of Aliwal North and 5km off the R58, is the only place worth a stop en route to Rhodes. It has one **hotel**, the *Mountain View Country Inn*, signposted from Botha Street (℡051 603 0421, ⓦ www.ladygrey .co.za; ❷), which has nice old-fashioned rooms with great views. Staff keep a list of **walks** to help you explore the surrounding peaks, and the owners can organize **fly-fishing**. The town offers a tiny **museum** at the Dutch Reformed church, dominated by a Victorian horse-drawn hearse and more of a curiosity shop under dust covers than anything else; it's open by arrangement only, through the hotel. The first minister of the Dutch Reformed church was a Scot, **David Ross**, who used to preach both in Afrikaans and English. His antiimperialist views got him imprisoned by the British during the Anglo-Boer War, after which he is said to have never spoken his native tongue again.

Some 79km southeast of Lady Grey, **BARKLY EAST** serves a large surrounding farming community. If your destination is Rhodes, it's the last place to get money and fill up your car. Don't expect much help from the **tourist office**, which doubles as the manual telephone exchange in the municipal offices. The very comfortable *Judy's Guest House*, 17 Jameson Street (℡045 971 0302, Ⓔpfjjkot@absamail.co.za; ❷), in a Victorian house filled with antiques and four-poster beds, provides the best **accommodation** in Barkly East. There's also a little-used **campsite** 100m off to the right as you hit town from Lady Grey.

There's nothing at all to do in Barkly East, so unless night is falling, push on for another ninety minutes to Rhodes. The sixty-kilometre dirt road to Rhodes is tortuous and rough with sheer, unfenced drops – definitely not recommended in the dark or mist.

Rhodes and around

Some 60km northeast of Barkly East, **RHODES** is almost too good to be true – a remote and beautiful village girdled by the Eastern Cape Drakensberg. Few people actually live here: like other villages in this region, Rhodes was progressively deserted as residents gravitated to the cities to make a living, leaving its Victorian tin-roofed architecture stuck in a very pleasing time warp. Today, its *raison d'être* is as a low-key holiday place for people who appreciate its isolation, wood stoves and restored cottages. Although electricity reached the village a few years ago, very few establishments have it, and paraffin lamps and candles are the norm. Given that Rhodes is not on the way to anywhere (on some maps it doesn't even appear), it is a place to dwell in for a few days, rather than for an overnight stop. While nights are cool even in summer, in winter they are freezing, and there's no central heating, so pack warm clothes.

The village itself is not much more than a few crisscrossing gravel roads lined with pine trees. The trees were donated in the 1890s, so the story goes, after a group of scheming townsfolk hoped to extract a large donation from **Cecil Rhodes**, by changing the village's name in his honour. All they got from the astute entrepreneur was a sackful of seeds. At the heart of the

Tiffendell Ski Resort

Tiffendell, South Africa's only ski resort, promotes itself as a little Switzerland, with Alpine ski lodges and European instructors on the slopes. However, it's essentially a venue for conspicuous South African consumers in search of a nonstop party. The resort is enormously successful, and for foreign visitors it provides, if nothing else, a quirky experience of Africa.

Skiing at Tiffendell is on **artificial snow** – despite regular winter falls, the real snow melts too quickly to provide a reliable piste. The **season** runs from May 20 to September 12. You can rent everything you need (except gloves) at the resort for about R250 per day, slightly cheaper out of school holidays. A four-hour beginner's lesson costs R220; three-night fully inclusive packages, including on-site accommodation, work out at around R2000–3500 per person, much less out of school holidays. **Rooms** at the resort's lodge are small and functional, with shared washing facilities, though the higher-priced packages provide en-suite rooms. The lodge is usually full, and many people stay at Rhodes village instead. Day visitors need to book, as there is a maximum of 180 people on the slopes per day. **Bookings** are made through the Snowscape shop in Jo'burg, at the Decor Centre, Forest Road, Fourways (⊕011 787 9090, ⊛www.snow.co.za).

Out of the ski season, Tiffendell runs as a **summer holiday** location, with trout fishing, mountain biking, grass skiing, horse-riding and hiking. Bookings for summer holidays are done locally (⊕045 974 9005), and cost R280 per person per day for half board.

The shortest **route** to Tiffendell is via Rhodes, but the road is steep and needs a 4WD at all times. The alternative route starts 23km north of Barkly East, and if the road is wet or snowy needs a 4WD vehicle for the last 19km. In Rhodes, the *Rhodes Hotel* and *Walkerbouts Inn* provide daily transfers to the resort (around R120 return).

village is the *Rhodes Hotel*, a general shop and a garage; there's also a post office and payphone, but no banking facilities and no public transport in or out of the village.

Rhodes is busiest in the winter, when **skiers** use it as a base for the Tiffendell slopes (see box above), an hour's 4WD drive into the highest peaks of the Eastern Cape Drakensberg. December to May are the best months for swimming and hiking; this is one of the best places in the country for **fly-fishing**, with all the solitude and glorious landscape you could hope for and rivers jumping with rainbow and brown trout, stocked in the 1920s. The *Rhodes Hotel* can give advice about where to fish, or you could check out ⊛www.wildtrout.co.za; better still, you can go out for a day or longer with Dave Walker of *Walkerbouts Inn* (see opposite), who can organize permits giving you access to 150km of river, but you'll need all your own gear. Dave also runs **Highlands Information** (⊛www.highlandsinfo.co.za), a service which can be used to book any sort of holiday in the area.

Rock-art sites

Rhodes is a good base for exploring millennia-old **San rock paintings**, the majority of which are on surrounding private farms which can be visited with the farmers' permission (some farms also take guests). The South African Heritage Resources Agency (⊕021 462 4502, ⊕021 462 4509) in Cape Town has a comprehensive list, and Rhodes locals can point you to nearby farms, such as Buttermead and Hillbury, which have their own paintings. Sue Tonkin in Maclear (⊕082 686 4468) does fully guided **rock-art tours**.

Close to Rhodes, **Martin's Hoek** farm, 16km from the village, is worth a visit, not just for the well-preserved, photogenic paintings, but for the lovely, lonely valley you have to drive through to get there. Make an appointment with Russie or Lookie Schmidt to see them (℡045 974 9201). The signposted turn-off to Martin's Hoek is 8km from Rhodes on the road to Barkly East. From the turn-off it's another 8km to the site, with parking and a couple of picnic tables. The paintings are fenced off on the cliff face opposite the parking area; it's a ten-minute uphill scramble to reach them, much easier than it first appears, with views out onto the rough and streaky sandstone peaks. A second site, at **Denorben Farm**, 32km southeast of Barkly East, offers the longest series of San paintings in the country. It's only 1km to the farm from the main road. A nominal entry fee is charged and there's a helpful information sheet on the images, many of which are confusing. Don't miss the impressive (unpainted) cave in the farmyard – it's common practice for farmers in the area to use overhangs as cosy sheep pens and sheds.

Rock art had an essentially religious purpose, usually recording experiences of trance states (see p.517 for more); shamans' visions often included powerful animals like the eland, which you can see depicted at both Denorben and Martin's Hoek, and whose power shamans were able to access for healing. A dying eland is a metaphor for the shaman who enters a **trance** and takes on aspects of an animal. At Denorben there's a half-animal, half-human figure, an image of transformation during the trance state. Also at Denorben are painted figures dancing, clapping and singing, in the process of inducing trance.

Accommodation

Gateshead Lodges ℡045 971 9303. Several farmhouses and excellent cottages on huge properties in marvellously remote and rugged territory, all within a large radius of Rhodes. Some cater specifically for fly-fishing, river swimming, hiking, riding or bird-watching, while a few have caves and rock paintings on the property. All are clearly detailed in a brochure available from PO Box 267, Barkly East 5580. ❷
Rhodes Hotel Main Rd ℡045 947 9305. Decorative exterior and charming Victorian furnishings. Quiet horses are available for hire, there are tennis courts and the owner is a trout-fishing guide. Full board ❸

Rubicon Flats ℡045 974 9268, ℯ rubicon@telkomsa.net. The best-value, and the warmest, place in town, this handsome old schoolhouse has been converted into self-catering rooms, each with an anthracite burner, and simple dorms. The owner, Mrs Reeders, also rents out self-catering cottages in the village and provides meals, but you need to book ahead for dinner. ❷
Walkerbouts Inn Signposted off the main road ℡045 974 9290, ℗ www.walkerbouts.co.za. Relaxed house with six en-suite guest rooms, with room-only, B&B and half board rates. The friendly owner, Dave Walker, knows a good deal about the area and can organize almost any activity, including fly-fishing and horse-riding. B&B ❸

Eating and drinking

For **eating**, your best choice is *Walkerbouts*, which does home-cooked meals, with two wood-burning pizza ovens on site. Cheapest of all are the ready-cooked meals, such as curry and rice, from local farmer's wife Marian Henning (℡045 974 9273), who'll deliver to your door. For **drinking**, the hotel bar is one of the most atmospheric pubs in the country. It's decorated with the horns of Wydeman, the lead ox of the supply wagon from Barkly East, who dropped dead outside the hotel in 1896. Also lining the walls are smoky relics of the days when this was a frontier town of gamblers, cattle rustlers and bar-room shoot-outs.

Naude's Nek

The most exhilarating drive out of Rhodes is on the R396 along **Naude's Nek**, the highest mountain-pass road in South Africa, connecting Rhodes with **Maclear** to the south, in a series of snaking hairpin bends and huge views. If you're chiefly looking for scenery, it's not essential to do the whole route to Maclear. Many people go from Rhodes to the top of the pass and back as a half-day trip, during which you can make a call from the highest phone (with a crank handle) in the country, in a corrugated-iron booth in the middle of a sheep pen at the top of the pass.

While it's only 30km from Rhodes, the journey can take a couple of hours to the Nek because so many changing vistas en route demand stops. You don't need a 4WD, but if you feel precious about your car don't attempt this route, as the road is harsh. The surface deteriorates from the top of the pass to Maclear, with sharp stones and a hump down the centre of the road, which may scrape the bottom of your vehicle, and is definitely impassable after snow. If you're wanting to use this route into the Transkei and KwaZulu-Natal, check with the *Rhodes Hotel* as to the current state of the road, and take two spare tyres.

The R56 from Maclear to Dordrecht

If you're not aiming for the Transkei, you can head **west from Maclear**, at the bottom of the escarpment, and take the tarred **R56** towards **Dordrecht** and the N6. The string of small towns along the R56 from Maclear to Dordrecht

---

Trails and hikes in the northeast of Eastern Cape

The northeastern part of Eastern Cape province is prime **walking** country, with expansive skies and long views across the mountains. There is no national park here, so all walks have to be done (and booked) on private property, but are very reasonably priced. Three of the best trails are listed below.

Ben Macdhui Hiking Trail Beginning and ending at Rhodes village, this is a three-day circular trail along a 51-kilometre route, involving about eight hours' walking each day. It takes in magnificent mountain scenery, wild flowers and waterfalls, and affords the chance to see rare mountain birds (such as the bearded vulture) and climb Ben Macdhui (3000m), the highest mountain in the Eastern Cape. Accommodation is in an old farmhouse and a mountain hut, both equipped with beds, mattresses, drinking water, long-drop toilets, a gas stove, kettle, pans, basin and a coal stove for heating. Book through Gideon van Zyl, PO Box 299, Barkly East, 5580 (☎045 971 0446).

Kranskop Hiking Trail One- to two-day hike on a farm, 33km north of Dordrecht, on the Barkly East Road. The highlights include some beautiful *kloofs*, the chance to overnight in a sandstone cave, and San rock art. Accommodation at the start or finish of the trail is in a comfortable rustic farm cottage sleeping twelve. Beds, mattresses, pillows, hot water, stove, fridge, lamps, candles and a coal stove are provided. Book through Frans Slabbert, PO Box 85, Dordrecht 5435 (☎045 944 1014).

Woodcliffe Farm A variety of one- to four-day trails on a farm, 22km north of Maclear, on the Naude's Nek Road. The trails take in stunning Drakensberg scenery, rock art, dinosaur footprints on the Pot River and cover terrain inhabited by 185 bird species. Accommodation is available in a self-catering cottage, which can be used as a base for day-walks or at the start of a longer hike, while cave overhangs can be used on longer hikes. Maps are provided and advice can be given to help you plan a route matching your fitness and time available. Book through Phyll Borrowdale (☎045 932 1550, ℮psephton@intekom.co.za).

are unmemorable trading centres, with nowhere to stay. All along the route though, the high Drakensberg march along, providing a dramatic backdrop to the journey. **Sheep farming** is the mainstay of white farmers in the region, though rampant stock theft is putting many out of business. One farmer has employed armed San ex-trackers from a defunct unit of the South African army to patrol his farm.

The R56 gives access to a couple of **hiking trails** with farm cottages for rent in the southern part of the Cape Drakensberg, notably **Woodcliffe** near Maclear, and **Kranskop** near Dordrecht, both of which have caves and rock paintings (see box opposite).

The Wild Coast region

The **Wild Coast region** is aptly named: this is one of South Africa's most unspoilt areas, a vast stretch of undulating hills, lush forest and spectacular beaches skirting a section of the Indian Ocean. Its undeveloped sandy beaches stretch for miles and miles, punctuated by rivers and several wonderful, reasonably priced hotels geared to family seaside holidays. The wildness goes beyond the landscape, for this is the former **Transkei** homeland, a desperately poor region that during apartheid was disenfranchised and turned into a dumping ground for Africans too old or too young for South African industry to make use of.

Few whites live in the Wild Coast region; nearly everyone is Xhosa, and those in rural areas live mostly in traditional rondavels dotting the landscape for as far as the eye can see. This neglect lives on in the negative image most white South Africans still have of the Transkei. Unless they have actually visited the area and come to appreciate it, most people have an exaggerated image of its dangers: legendary (and wildly overstated) tales of crime, hostile locals (quite untrue) and shocking roads (these are being upgraded).

Also in the Transkei's favour, this is the "Africa" completely missed by those who restrict their holiday to Cape Town and the Garden Route. One or two of the hotels – and most of the backpacker lodges – offer a chance to experience traditional **Xhosa life**, with village visits to healers or overnight stays with a Xhosa family (see the box on p.439 for some background on Xhosa traditions). In all of South Africa, this is the best and easiest place to experience authentic African rural life as a tourist. Despite the obvious hardship, it's refreshing – at least for visitors – to find that rural areas are still communally owned rather than parcelled up into private farms. Instead of the fenced-off spaces edged by squatter camps found in most of rural South Africa, here the land is unfenced and fully inhabited.

The **N2** highway runs through the middle of the region, passing through the old Transkei capital of **Umtata** and a host of scruffy, busy little towns along the way. Northwest of the N2, towards the Lesotho border and the Drakensberg Mountains, you'll find beautiful mountainous country and endless little villages, but the lack of accommodation and poor roads make travelling here difficult.

THE WILD COAST

0 ————— 50 km

ACCOMMODATION

Anchorage	**E**	Haga Haga	**P**	The Kraal	**C**	Ocean View	**F**	Wavecrest	**L**
Buccaneers	**Q**	The Haven	**I**	Mazeppa Bay	**K**	Seagulls	**N**	Wild Coast	**M**
Bulungula		Hole in the Wall	**G**	Mbotyi River Lodge	**B**	Trennery's	**O**	Umngazi River Bungalows	Sun Hotel **A**
Backpackers Lodge	**H**	Kob Inn	**J**	Morgan Bay			**D**		

Far more accessible is the **coastal region**, which runs from just north of East London to the mouth of the **Mtamvuna River**. With its succession of great beaches, hidden reefs, patches of subtropical forest, rural Xhosa settlements and the attractive little towns of **Coffee Bay** and **Port St Johns** (both popular with backpackers), this region, along with northern KwaZulu-Natal, offers the most deserted and undeveloped beaches in the country. While there are some beautiful, state-run **nature reserves** along the coast, they are totally underfunded and poorly run. **Mkambati Nature Reserve**, however, has a good system operating, and is nothing short of totally fabulous, with outstanding beaches, lagoons and wildlife, though some of the accommodation is very shabby. There are plans to hand over the accommodation to a private company who aim to convert it into a five star facility. Until then a good way to see it is on the **Amadiba Horse Trails**, which finish at the reserve.

Wild Coast practicalities

The Wild Coast, unlike the Western Cape Garden Route, is not a stretch that you can easily tour by car; there's no coastal road, and no direct route between one seaside resort and the next. Yet in this **remoteness** lies the region's charm. Resorts are isolated down long, winding gravel roads off the N2, which sticks to the high inland plateau. Choose one or two places, and stay put for a relaxing few days. Apart from Port St Johns, none of the places on the coast has a **bank** or ATM, so be sure to organize money in East London or Umtata.

Although some of the southern Wild Coast roads are being surfaced as part of an upgrading programme, most in the region remain **untarred** and, while generally passable in an ordinary car, they invariably take a mechanical toll. Always carry a tool kit, a spare tyre (or two), and take the roads slowly. When you choose a resort, phone to ask for the best road route, as road conditions change. Watch out for livestock on all Wild Coast roads, including the N2, and avoid driving in rainy weather and at night. **Car theft** at night, or the removal of tyres or wheels, even in remote areas, is the biggest crime problem in the Transkei. All the hotels are surrounded by fences and lock up their gates at night to counter this problem.

Public transport in minibuses links villages throughout the region – easiest from Umtata to Port St Johns and Coffee Bay along the tarred roads. The **Baz Bus** stops in Cintsa West and Umtata; you can arrange to be met by hostels in Port St Johns and Coffee Bay, or in Butterworth for Mazeppa.

The **hotels** here are typically run along old-fashioned, colonial lines, with set meals – old-fangled British fare features prominently – and tea at specific times. Most of the hotels offer full board – outside Port St Johns and Umtata, there are no restaurants besides those provided by the accommodation establishments (as for **self-catering**, you'll need to buy groceries at a big centre on the N2). Many hotels offer the services of experienced **Xhosa nannies** who can be employed for the whole day or for short stretches while you take a break to go the beach or have a meal. Some hotels even have separate meal times for children, and recommend that children stay with their nannies during adult meal times.

There a number of good **backpacker lodges** along the coast, and plenty of campsites. Although security is no longer the worry it once was, **camping** in rural areas is not advisable, even if a beach looks idyllically deserted. If you want to stay among rural Xhosa people, the safest way to do so is with a guide.

It's wise to **book accommodation** in advance: the Umtata-based Wild Coast Reservations (see p.445) is useful if you are planning to stay in several places on your journey. Even better is the superbly well-informed and efficient Wild Coast Holiday Reservations (℡043 743 6181, 🌐www.wildcoastholidays.co.za),

A walk and a gallop on the Wild Coast

Since there's no coastal road, the only way to explore stretches of the Wild Coast is **on foot** or **horseback**. Booking a package is a sensible option, not least because in most cases the tour operator takes care of transfers at the start and end of the package.

Wild Coast hiking trails

Walking packages includes transfers between East London and the Wild Coast, accommodation, all meals, picnic lunches, and the services of guides. Expect to pay around R600 per night per person for a group of four. Hotels dotted along the coast where you might stay include the *Kob Inn*, *Mazeppa Bay*, *Wavecrest*, *Trennery's*, *Seagulls* and *Morgan Bay Hotel*. All you have to carry is your day pack as porters and transport are available to take your luggage to the overnight stops. **Book** through Wild Coast Holiday Reservations (℡043 743 6181, ⓦwww .wildcoastholidays.co.za).

Wild Coast Hotel Meander A 55-kilometre section of the coast from Qora Mouth to Morgan Bay, covered at an easy pace over five days (six nights). There are some modest challenges en route, such as river crossings and hiking over headlands, which will pose no problems for those of average fitness.

Wild Coast Amble Starting north of Kei River and heading south, this ends in Cinsta, covering terrain of moderate difficulty in 56km in five days (four nights). The trail includes a three-hour boat cruise up the Kei River, some canoeing and, if you don't wish to walk the whole way, horse-riding.

Wild Coast Pondo Walk Five nights based at the *Mboyti River Lodge* near Luisikisiki. Transfers aren't included, though you will given maps and information to help you drive there and back. The hike entails two coastal walks and two inland trails that take in indigenous forest, sandy bays, escarpments and local settlements; there's also a sixteen-kilometre strenuous walk to the Magwa Falls. You might have to cover anything from 13km to 26km a day.

Strandloper There is no luxury along this four-night 59-kilometre trail. Accommodation is in basic hikers' huts with toilets and cold showers, but no electricity. You'll need to bring camping gear, including a sleeping bag and cooking equipment (for use on the third night). There are places along the way to have pub lunches, and small stores where you can purchase basic foodstuffs. For all this roughing it you get to experience remote beaches and rivers, and panoramic views from Kei Mouth south to Gonubie. For a surcharge, porters can be hired to carry your pack.

The Amadiba Horse Trail

A Wild Coast highlight, the **Amadiba Horse Trail** is a fifty-kilometre, four- to six-day excursion from the *Wild Coast Sun* casino and hotel (served by shuttles from Durban which can be booked through the hotel) to the exquisitely beautiful Mkambati Nature Reserve, with plans to extend the trip as far as Port St Johns. The package, run entirely by members of the local Pondo community, is probably the best way to spend time with Xhosa speakers and travel in unspoilt areas that you can't reach in a vehicle. Beginner riders will find the trail not unduly daunting: well-schooled horses are used, the going is easy and distances between the **tented camps** on the banks of the Kwanyana and Mtentu rivers are manageable. From these bases you while away gentle days exploring the coast, rivers and inland, sometimes visiting villages on horseback, on foot or in canoes with the guides. Fully inclusive trips cost R2500 per person for four days, R3800 for six days; the maximum group size is ten. To book, contact Amadiba Adventures (℡039 305 6455, ⓔamadiba@euwildcoast.za.org).

based in East London which, apart from being able to arrange places to stay, is unsurpassed when it comes to organizing **activities** in the region, including hiking (see box opposite).

The hotels themselves offer a variety of activities, from canoeing to horse-riding. To visit the region's **nature reserves** you'll usually need to book in advance. However, the post-apartheid reorganization in the Wild Coast, combined with a bankrupt provincial administration and a disintegrating civil service, can make it exceedingly difficult to make arrangements. Provided you are resourceful, you should overcome these bureaucratic obstacles – an effort worth making, as the region's wildernesses are exceedingly beautiful. We have provided the most up-to-date booking information available at the time of writing for each reserve.

For some people, one attraction of the Wild Coast region, especially the Port St Johns area, is the ready availability of high-quality **cannabis** (*insango* in Xhosa). Be warned, though, that cannabis is illegal here as anywhere else in South Africa, and that the former Transkei police are trying to prove their worth to the national force with regular busts.

Cintsa and Haga-Haga

Of the smattering of resorts between East London and the Kei River, the best are at Cintsa and Morgan Bay, where endless sandy beaches back up into forested dunes sliced through by lagoons and rivers. Cintsa is actually two places with distinct characters, Cintsa East and Cintsa West, divided by a river.

CINTSA EAST, 45km from East London, is an upmarket holiday village of some two hundred houses, reached on a tarred road: turn off the N2 at the East Coast Resorts Road (30km out of East London) then, after 8km, turn left at the sign to Cefane Mouth and *Michaela's Restaurant*, from where the village is 7km away. The *Cintsa East B&B* (℡043 738 5021; ❷) here offers two modestly priced **rooms** in the owners' two-storey house with sea views, a five-minute walk from the glorious eight-kilometre-long sandy beach; while *The Gables* (℡043 738 5353 or 083 676 0213, ❹), facing inland onto a valley, is an upmarket, luxurious country lodge with five en-suite bedrooms, which also does dinner. Of the handful of **eating** places, *Michaela's* restaurant (daily except Tues 10.30am until late; ℡043 738 5139) is an excellent spot for seafood and salads, and is built spectacularly on a giant sand dune, which can be ascended on a short funicular ride. More modest fare is served at the popular and friendly *Fred's Pub & Grub* in Cintsa Drive (Tues–Sun lunch & dinner). Takeaways are available from the shop next door.

Across the river, on the **Baz Bus** route, **CINTSA WEST** is home to *Buccaneer's* (℡043 734 3012, ⓦwww.cintsa.com; dorms ❶, rooms ❷), one of South Africa's most popular hostels. *Buccaneer's* has built its reputation on the excellence of its **backpacker accommodation** in eight cottages of varying sizes, with fantastic sea and lagoon views, unspoilt beaches, and a plethora of activities such as hiking, surfing (free boards) and horse-riding. You can self-cater, or eat inexpensive breakfasts and dinners in the café and pub. It also lays on trips to a local African school and township, and its adventure company will take you for surfing lessons, out kloofing, or for day-trips deeper into the Wild Coast. Game drives in neighbouring Inkwenkwezi Nature Reserve cost R250. Finally, there's transport from here to the mountain resort of Hogsback (see p.421) and on to East London.

Just northeast of Cintsa, **HAGA-HAGA** (72km from East London, 27km of this along a dirt road off the N2) is dominated by the box-like but perfectly positioned *Haga-Haga Resort* (T043 841 1670, Ehaga@intekom.co.za). It offers reasonably priced half board in hotel rooms (❹), and self-catering in fourteen flatlets sleeping two or four people (❸). A tidal swimming pool is sculpted into the rocky shoreline in front of the hotel; to reach a sandy beach, take the two-kilometre path to Pullens Bay, which is ideal for swimming among the breakers. A four-kilometre walk takes you to Bead Beach, where vendors sell beads made from carnelian, and bits of pottery.

Morgan Bay to Qora Mouth

MORGAN BAY, 90km from East London, lies magnificently in an estuary at the confluence of two rivers carving their passage through forested dunes. The friendly, well-run *Morgan Bay Hotel* (T043 841 1062, Wwww.morganbay.co.za; full board ❹) overlooks a gorgeous beach and is one of the best hotels along the Wild Coast, particularly for family holidays. It offers good food and fresh, airy rooms (the cheaper ones aren't en suite) with beachside motifs and furnished with limewashed furniture, and there's also **camping**. A hike from the hotel leads over some grassy knolls to the fifty-metre Morbay Cliffs, an excellent vantage point for spotting dolphins and, in season, whales. The bay is pounded by massive breakers, but the estuary provides a safe and tranquil place for toddlers to paddle.

Kei Mouth and Qholorha Mouth

From Morgan Bay, it's a short, rough drive to the village of **Kei Mouth** (it's not signposted, so get directions from *Morgan Bay Hotel*), with some self-catering places, a post office and small shops, though there's little point dallying. From Kei Mouth, a six-kilometre walk along the beach leads to beautiful **QHOLORHA MOUTH** (roughly pronounced "kalocha" – the "rh" in Xhosa is like the "ch" in loch). The easiest way to get here is to cross the Kei River on a small pontoon (which you can take your car on) that operates from 6am to 6pm in summer and from 7am to 5.30pm in winter; after disembarking, continue for another 17km to *Trennery's* (signposted), the marvellous family **hotel** which dominates this resort. Founded in 1928, *Trennery's* (T047 498 0004, Etrennerys@border.co.za; full board ❹) still has its heart somewhere in the Fifties or Sixties. Uniformed nannies accompany children around the playground and the separate children's dining room, where the little darlings need neither be seen nor heard by their parents. The self-contained thatched bungalows are slightly worn, while the English-style food is wholesome and well cooked, if unrevelatory; the seamless organization and attentive service make up for these. From the hotel, it's a steep walk through luxuriant vegetation to the spectacular beach, while canoes and rowing boats are available for outings on the lagoon. The more modest *Seagulls* hotel (T & F047 498 0044, Wwww.seagulls.co.za; half board ❹) has the advantage of being right on the beach. Both offer seven-night specials, and are a bit cheaper outside school holidays.

A recommended excursion is **Trevor's Trail**, a three-hour bush walk and boating trip to the "The Gates" – the short corridor of rock-face towering above the Qholorha River; it's run every morning by local resident Trevor Wigley (T072 225 5492 or book through your hotel; R100). Other trails run by Trevor include an exploration of the enormously varied shell life of

The great cattle killing

The 1850s were a low point for the Xhosa nation: most of their land had been seized by the British, drought had withered their crops, and cattle-sickness had decimated their precious herds. In 1856, a young woman called **Nongqawuse**, whose uncle Mhlakaza was a prophet, claimed to have seen and heard ancestral spirits in a pool on the Gxara River. The spirits told her the Xhosa must kill all their remaining cattle and destroy their remaining crops; if they did this, new cattle and crops would arise, along with new people who would drive the whites into the sea.

As news of her **prophecy** spread, opinion was sharply divided amongst the Xhosa. Those whose herds had been badly affected by cattle-sickness were most inclined to believe her. A turning point came when the Gcaleka paramount chief Sarili visited Nongqawuse, became convinced she was telling the truth and ordered his subjects to start the cull. Thousands of cattle were killed, but when the "new people" failed to materialize on the expected day, the unbelievers who had not killed their herds were blamed. By February 1857, the next date for the appearance of the new people, over 200,000 cattle had been slaughtered, their corpses left decomposing everywhere. When the new people failed once more to materialize, it was too late for many Xhosa. By July there was **widespread starvation**; 30,000 of an estimated population of 90,000 died of hunger.

The British administration saw the famine as a perfect way to force the destitute Xhosa into working on white settlers' farms. To speed up the process, the Cape governor Sir George Grey closed down the feeding stations established by missionaries and laid the blame for the disaster on the Xhosa chiefs, imprisoning many of them on Robben Island. Not surprisingly, the 1856 cattle killing is often used by whites as evidence of the folly of black superstition. The Xhosa, however, have a different interpretation: "*Intombi kaMhlakaza yathetha ubuxoke*" goes the song – "Mhlakaza's girl told lies".

the seashore and some of the coastline's many **shipwrecks**; a visit to a local *igqirha*, or **traditional healer**; a trip to the **Gxara River**, where the prophetess Nongqawuse's disastrous visions induced the Xhosa to kill their cattle (see box above); and a visit to the major **battlefields** of the last Frontier War between the Xhosa and the British in 1878. These trails involve a 4WD vehicle, so are more expensive than the daily jaunt.

Nxaxo Mouth and Wavecrest Hotel

NXAXO MOUTH, just north of Qholorha (though not drivable from there), is a tranquil location with mangrove swamps teeming with wildlife. It's an ideal place for hiking, shoreline fishing and general relaxation, as well as the more strenuous **activities** – canoeing, water-skiing and deep-sea fishing. All of this can be arranged through the resort's only **accommodation**, the *Wavecrest* (☎047 498 0022, ⊛www.wavecrest.co.za; full board ❹), a cluster of pleasant bungalows and family rooms – arguably the most beautifully positioned of all the Wild Coast hotels. To get there, follow the 34km of tarred road to Centani from the N2 at **Butterworth**. At Centani, take the signposted road (to the left) to Nxaxo for 8km, then the road to *Wavecrest* (on the right) for 24km. This road is in poor condition, so go slowly.

Mazeppa Bay and Qora Mouth

Two good **fishing** and general chill-out spots on the Wild Coast, **MAZEPPA BAY** and **QORA MOUTH**, lie northeast of Nxaxo. Mazeppa Bay, a lovely spot surrounded by dunes and coastal forest, is reached along the signposted road from Centani (34km of tarred surface from Butterworth, and about 45km further of dirt road). Since there are two routes to complete the journey, it's advisable to contact the hotel when you're about to travel for advice about road conditions. The slightly downmarket *Mazeppa Bay* **hotel** here (℡047 498 0033, ℻047 498 0034; ❹) offers full board in comfortable cabanas or family rooms in the hotel, 39 steps up from the beach. It has the added attraction of its own island (reached along a bridge), on which there's an unexcavated Khoisan midden. Swimming in the bay is safe, and the surfing is good.

Just northeast of Mazeppa, **QORA MOUTH** is the site of the *Kob Inn* (℡ & ℻047 499 0016, ⓦwww.kobinn.co.za; ❹), set away from the beach on a rocky shore close to the wide Mbashe River. The hotel has well-kept thatched bungalows, a good bar with views of the sea, and a breathtaking swimming pool built into the tidal rocks. Staff can arrange a boat and fishing tackle, or equip you for canoeing, water-skiing and boardsailing. A small ferry traverses the river mouth and takes you to some good hiking trails along the coast, through grassland and into nearby forest patches. To get to Qora Mouth, take the signposted dirt road heading east for 34km from Idutywa (see p.440), passing through grassy rolling hills and Xhosa villages.

Butterworth and Idutywa

Butterworth, 110km from East London on the N2, and **Idutywa**, 35km further on, are places you pass through rather than visit. Both are busy centres, barely distinguishable from each other, although Butterworth is the larger. They serve the vast rural communities on either side of the N2 and each has a reasonable hotel – useful if you find yourself stranded at nightfall.

Butterworth

BUTTERWORTH, the oldest town in the Transkei, is located near the site of the Gcaleka chief Hintsa's Great Place, and was founded by Methodist missionaries in 1827. The town, known to Xhosa as Gcuwa (after the river running through it), derives its English name from the then-treasurer of the Wesleyan Mission Society, Reverend Butterworth. It was selected as the focal point of Transkeian industrial development in the 1970s, with its new industries drawing thousands of workers from the surrounding countryside. Most of the industries have now closed, but the people are still living in sprawling townships and squatter camps around the town, where unemployment is alarmingly high.

While Butterworth itself is unattractive and a bit chaotic, with tatty department stores and supermarkets, the nearby **Bawa Falls** on the Qholorha River, which have a sheer drop of nearly 100m, are spectacular and worth a visit if you're not pressed for time. The poorly maintained twenty-kilometre dirt track leading to them is just west of town past the Shell filling station, but numerous twists and turns make the falls quite hard to find, so you will need to ask directions.

The well-signposted road to Centani and the Wild Coast is at the eastern end of Butterworth, past the Gcuwa Bridge, and winds through the sprawling Zitulele Industrial Township, where the tar stops and gives way to a potholed dirt road. Butterworth's **bus station** is at the western end of town, next to the Shell garage, from which numerous buses and increasing numbers of **minibus**

Some Xhosa traditions

The Wild Coast region is largely populated by **rural Xhosa**, who still practise traditions and customs that have faded in more urban areas. Many people, for example, still believe that the sea is inhabited by strange people who do not always welcome visitors, which explains the relative scarcity of the activities you would normally find thriving among seashore-dwelling people, such as fishing and diving.

Initiation for teenage boys and young men is still common. Young men usually leave their homes to stay in "circumcision lodges", dress in distinctive white paint and costumes and learn the customs of their clan. At the circumcision ceremony the young men are expected to make no sound while their foreskin is cut off (with no anaesthetic) with a single slice of a knife. After the ceremony, they wash off the paint and wrap themselves in new blankets, and all their possessions are thrown into a hut and set alight – they must turn away from this and not look back. There follows a feast to celebrate the beginning of manhood and the start of a year-long intermediary period during which they wear ochre-coloured clay on their faces. After this, they are counted as men. Boys who have gone through the experience of initiation together are supposed to remain bonded at a deep level for the rest of their lives.

Like other African peoples, although they believe in one God, uThixo, or uNhkulukhulu (the great one), many Xhosa also believe that their **ancestors** play an active role in their lives. However, the ancestors' messages are often too obscure to be understood without the aid of specialists, or *amagqira*.

The Xhosa are patriarchal by tradition, with women's subordinate status symbolized by *lobola*, the **dowry** payment in cattle and cash that a prospective husband must make to her parents before he can marry her. If the woman is not a virgin, the man pays less. Married Xhosa women have the same right as men to smoke tobacco in **pipes**, and can often be seen doing so, the pipes' long stems designed to prevent ash falling on babies suckling at their breasts. Pipes are shared, but each person must have their own stem, not just for matters of hygiene but also to prevent witchcraft: bits of the body make the most effective poisonous medicines against people, and that includes hair, skin and spittle.

The Xhosa did not wear **cloth** until it was introduced by Europeans, when it was quickly adopted. Today, what is now seen as traditional Xhosa cloth is almost always worn by women, mostly in the form of long skirts, beautifully embroidered with horizontal black stripes placed at varying intervals, which are displayed to subtle effect when the wearer is walking. Bags in matching colours with long shoulder straps are popular accessories, especially at weddings, when people put cash gifts inside them. The breasts of unmarried women were traditionally uncovered, while those of married women were usually covered with beads or matching cloth. These days, most women wear T-shirts, though almost all women still cover their heads with scarves intricately tied to form two peaks above the forehead. The **traditional colours** of the Thembu and Bomvana clans are red or orange, while the colour of the Pondo and the Mpondomise clans is light blue. In practice, these traditions are not always observed, and married women from a number of clans often wear white instead.

---

taxis run to East London, Umtata and Centani. Daily Greyhound and Translux **buses** stop off the main road on Merriman Street, which is just before the Gcuwa Bridge.

The N2 highway runs through Butterworth and is lined with **takeaways**, beer halls and filling stations. The only slightly decent **accommodation** in town is the *Wayside* (☎047 491 4615, ✉wayside@cybertrade.co.za; ❷), reached by turning right down King Street off the main road, and taking the first right into Sauer Street, where you'll see the hotel on your left. The rooms are comfortable and a fair bit cheaper over weekends. The hotel has safe underground parking, and a good **restaurant** serving lunchtime buffets and à la carte evening meals. The one drawback is that it's right next to a busy taxi rank swarming with people until late into the evening.

Idutywa

The small town of **IDUTYWA**, 35km north of Butterworth on the N2, is only a place to head for if you are short of fuel, or very hungry and tired. On the main road going through town you'll find a passable *KFC* and the unassuming, old hotel *Idutywa* (☎047 489 1040; ❸), the only decent place to stay on the noisy main road between Butterworth and Umtata. Their restaurant, the only one in town, serves a typical South African selection of steaks and grills.

A few kilometres east of town, a right-hand turn leads to **Colleywobbles**, the name given by British soldiers to a particularly tortuous and fascinating stretch of the Mbashe River about 10km down an exceedingly difficult dirt track. The river reaches the sea 50km further east, disgorging between the **Cwebe** and **Dwesa** nature reserves, but the best way for you to reach these two beautiful places is by continuing for another 60km or so along the N2 until **Jojweni** (formerly Viedgesville), and turning right down the Coffee Bay road. Another possible diversion is the open-air museum at **Mveso**, where Nelson Mandela spent the first couple of years of his life (see p.448).

Dwesa and Cwebe reserves and Nqileni

Between Qora Mouth and Coffee Bay, the **Dwesa Nature Reserve** (daily 6am–6pm) is undeveloped and remote, yet very much visitable and safe. With basic, well-sited self-catering wooden chalets (❶) and a campsite, Dwesa is one of the best places to stay on the coast, boasting rare animals such as tree dassies and samango monkeys, as well as red hartebeest, blesbok, blue wildebeest and buffalo, pristine forest, grassland and coastline. To stay at Dwesa you should ideally book ahead (☎047 499 0078), but the system is not entirely reliable. That said, during the week the reserve is hardly visited and there's a good chance you'll get accommodation if you just show up. Either way, make sure you have enough time to drive on to another resort if necessary. To get to the reserve, turn east off the N2 at Idutywa towards the coast and continue for 73km or so; the road forks right to *Kob Inn* and left to Dwesa.

Cwebe Nature Reserve

North of the Mbashe River from Dwesa, the **Cwebe Nature Reserve** (daily 6am–6pm) makes up for its lack of big game with dense subtropical forest, brimming with flora and fauna. Stinkwood and samango monkeys, both of which have all but disappeared from most of southern Africa's east coast, are to be found here along a rough network of trails. Thankfully, the trail to the beautiful **Mbanyana Waterfall** is in good shape, easily walkable from the *Haven* (see below) if the ground is dry. The remainder of the reserve comprises rolling grassland and a long stretch of wonderful dune-filled shoreline lying in the shadow of the Mbashe lighthouse. The reserve was returned to the local community in 2001.

To get to **Cwebe**, take the Coffee Bay turn-off from the N2 at **Jojweni** (the town itself is not signposted but there is a Coffee Bay sign), turn right 27km later at Gogoswayo Trading Store, and follow the tarred road another 17km to the small hamlet of **Elliotdale**, the main administrative centre in the communal lands of the Bomvana people. (Avoid the route off the N2 south of Qunu to Elliotdale, as this section requires a high-clearance vehicle.) From Elliotdale it's 47km of generally good-quality dirt road to the privately owned *Haven* (☎047 576 0006 or 083 996 5343, ⓔwinhaven@wildcoast.com; full board ❹). Its **bungalows** are dotted fairly close together on the fringes of a small golf course regularly grazed by wildebeest and zebra, only a short walk through milkwood groves to the sea. The swimming pool has sea views, as does the main hotel building.

Nqileni and Bulungula Lodge

Idyllically located at the mouth of the Bulungula River, the spread-out village of **NQILENI** gives you the opportunity to experience rural Transkei life. The river winds its way to the sea through rolling green hills dotted with rondavels, maize fields, and livestock, ending at a tranquil river mouth. The coastline is carpeted in dense forest stretching into kilometres of soft, white beach. On a walk through the village you'll invariably be invited into a someone's home to have your face painted with traditional clay, to try your hand at grinding maize for the evening meal or to see traditional beer being brewed. Other possibilities include spending the day with a traditional fisherman, taking a canoe trip along the river, horse-riding across the beach or consulting a *sangoma*.

If you're looking for relaxation and an authentic cultural experience, you'll be hard pressed to find a better **place to stay** than the well-run *Bulungula Backpackers Lodge* (booking essential; ☎047 577 8900, ⓦwww.bulungula.com; ❶), which has ten brightly painted rondavels (sleeping two or four) with shared ablutions. It's a joint venture between the community and seasoned traveller Dave Martin, who spent many of his student years involved in community development projects. The lodge buys most of its vegetables from an organic farming project run by the villagers, and is equipped with solar electricity, satellite telephone and eco-friendly toilets.

The lodge runs a **shuttle** service from the Shell Ultra City in Umtata (arrange this when booking). To **drive** to the lodge, make for **Elliotdale** (turn off the N2 at Jojweni; see opposite), then about 500m beyond the edge of town, turn left onto a dirt road signposted for *Bulungula Lodge* and Madwaleni Hospital. Continue for another 30km until you reach the hospital, where you leave your car (secure parking costs R10 per day). Lodge staff will collect you from there.

Coffee Bay and around

The densely populated, gentle hills of **COFFEE BAY**, known to the Xhosa as Tshontini after a dense wood that grows there, mark the traditional boundary between the Bomvana and Pondo clans of the Xhosa nation. Coffee Bay, with its laid-back, relaxed atmosphere, draws a growing number of visitors – yet retains its feeling of idyllic obscurity. It's easily reached on a tarred road which leaves the N2 14km south of Umtata's Shell Ultra City, and there are a number of nearby attractions such as **Hole in the Wall** village.

The **landscape** at Coffee Bay, dramatic high cliffs dropping to sandy beaches speckled with black pebbles, contrasts with the grasslands, forested sand dunes and lagoons further south. The main attraction here is the **coastal hikes**; the walk to Hole in the Wall is particularly outstanding. To start the trail, head south along the track from Coffee Bay, and turn left at a small sign just past the Telkom tower, from where it's another 5km along the coast.

The **huts** here are also very distinctive: many are thatched with a topknot made from a tyre, coloured glass or even an aloe plant – said to discourage owls, harbingers of ill-omen, from roosting on roofs. An excellent community-run **village tour** can be organized through the impressive ANC Women's League veteran, Betty Madlalisa (☎083 339 0454; R50). Apart from visiting homesteads, the outing takes in the **Masizame Women's Project** (daily 8am–5pm), housed in a colourful building opposite the Bayview Store, 5km out of Coffee Bay on the Umtata Road. If you're not taking the tour, it's still definitely worth visiting the project – it's one of the very few outlets in South Africa where you can buy traditional Xhosa craftwork, including beaded bags and belts, traditional clothing, baskets, mats and blankets. With advance notice, they also offer **Xhosa meals** – based mostly around meat stews, maize meal, and homegrown vegetables like spinach and pumpkin, washed down with traditional beer.

Practicalities

The smartest **accommodation** is the *Ocean View* hotel right on the sandy bay (☎047 575 2005, ⓦwww.oceanview.co.za; full board ❹). It's an exceptionally friendly and well-run place, with bright rooms decorated in floral motifs, terraced gardens, a pool area, and a trampoline and playground right next the beach. The restaurant and bar, open to day visitors, serves good food, with seafood splurges on Saturday nights, and fresh oysters among the bar snacks. Of the **backpacker lodges**, the best is *Coffee Shack* (☎047 575 2048, ⓦwww.coffeeshack.co.za; ❶), with dorms, a double room and camping, and well located on the Bomvu River. It offers seafood suppers, day-trips and homestays with the local community, and activities such as surfing (with free lessons and boards), hiking, canoeing and abseiling. Its **shuttle bus** plies the route between Umtata and Coffee Bay, meeting the Baz Bus on request. One bay west of Coffee Bay, and set on a cliff high above the water, *White Clay* (☎ & ⓕ047 575 0008; self-catering ❷, half board available) has double rooms with shared bathrooms, and camping facilities. No one else lives on this bay, so you have it all to yourself, and the location couldn't be better, with gorgeous views. Whales can be seen literally a stone's throw away in the bay between August and November, and dolphins all year round.

There are no grocery shops, banks or ATMs in Coffee Bay, so make sure you come prepared. Petrol is available at the hotel, and food basics can be purchased at the expensive Bayview Trading Store, 5km out of Coffee Bay towards Port St Johns.

Hole In The Wall

The village of **HOLE IN THE WALL** has grown up on the shoreline near the large cliff that juts out of the sea a short distance from the Mpako River Mouth, from which it gets its name. The cliff has a tunnel at its base through which huge waves pound during heavy seas, making a great crashing sound that has led the Xhosa to call it esiKhaleni (the place of sound). As well as good fishing, safe swimming and snorkelling, there are several spectacular hikes, including a coastal walk northeast to Coffee Bay. A nine-kilometre gravel road – a **scenic drive** through traditional villages and along cliffs with sea views – links Coffee Bay with Hole in the Wall, a trip definitely worth making if you're based at Coffee Bay. It's a very pleasant one-kilometre walk from the village to **the hole**, a lovely spot ideal for picnics or just relaxing.

Dominating the tiny settlement, the *Hole In The Wall* **hotel** (☎047 575 0009, ⓔholeitwh@iafrica.com; self-catering ❶–❷, half board ❹) is a conglomeration of white thatched rondavels situated on a small sandy bay and surrounded by lawns, with a pool, bar and playground. The hotel doesn't have a great reputation for food, accommodation or organization, though you can self-cater (a rare option for a Wild Coast hotel; the best place for supplies is Umtata). There are well-equipped self-catering units sleeping two to six people, plus basic bedsit units. The hotel owns the quiet *Hole In The Wall Backpackers* on the same site (℡083 317 8786, ℻047 575 0010; dorms and doubles ❶), and allows residents to use hotel facilities. There isn't the same social scene here as at the Coffee Bay hostels, but you can get free surfing lessons, and there are reasonably priced day excursions to hard-to-reach and spectacular spots along the coast, such as Umdumbi. The *Hole In The Wall* can collect you from Coffee Bay.

Umtata River Mouth

The **Umtata River** disgorges 6km north of Coffee Bay into another soothing lagoon. This is the site of a **hotel**, the *Anchorage* (℡ & ℻047 575 9884, ✉anchorage@wildcoast.co.za; self-catering ❷, half board ❸), 70km from the N2, offering old-fashioned bungalow accommodation, plus camping. While it's no great shakes as a resort – there are better for the same price – it's worth considering for its setting between two rivers. The hotel is a three-kilometre walk along the beach from the Umtata River Mouth, and also 3km from the Mdumbi River Mouth, with good fishing at both. The *Anchorage* has a **general dealer** and liquor store, where you can buy bread, milk, eggs and braai packs. An excellent way to see the surrounding area's gentle hills, coastal forest and shoreline is on **horseback**, which the hotel can arrange. The best **route** to the *Anchorage* is the tarred Coffee Bay road: around 6km before you reach Coffee Bay, there's an *Anchorage* sign where you turn left and continue 14km on an extremely rough dirt road.

Hluleka Nature Reserve

One of the loveliest of the Wild Coast reserves, **Hluleka Nature Reserve** (daily 6am–6pm; R5) consists of coastal forest whose coral trees flower scarlet in July and August, a strip of grassland and outstanding sandy beaches interspersed with rocky outcrops tattooed with extraordinary wind-shaped rock formations. Although Hluleka's trails are poorly maintained and frequently dead ends, the reserve is sufficiently small to make getting lost for a while no great disaster. In the grassland strip, you're likely to encounter wildebeest, zebra and blesbok.

You can reach Hluleka along the difficult coastal road from Coffee Bay. Heading towards the N2 from Coffee Bay for a short distance, take the Mdumbi turn on the right, and continue for some 30km, when signs to Hluleka appear. Alternatively – and more easily – take the Hluleka turning 30km along the R61 from Umtata to Port St Johns, and continue for another 57km to the coast.

There are plans to privatize the reserve but at present **accommodation** (book through the Eastern Cape Parks Board; ℡040 635 2115, 🌐www.ecparksboard.co.za) is in two sets of chalets which sleep up to six people, one on stilts overlooking the sea (R320), the other further up the hill in the forest (R220). Both are spacious but poorly equipped and subject to electricity blackouts, so bring candles. You'll also need all your own food, though you may be able to buy fish from local fishermen if you tell the reserve's staff, who will tip them off. **Fishing permits** should be arranged via the Nature Conservation Office in Umtata (see p.445).

Umtata and around

Straddling the Umtata River and the N2 highway 235km from East London, the fractious, shambolic town of **UMTATA** is the former capital of the Transkei and is the Wild Coast region's largest town. Unfortunately, it's a pretty ugly place, its litter-strewn streets lined with nondescript 1970s office buildings and crowded with people. However, the town is useful for stocking up and drawing money, all of which can be done at the Spar Centre or Shell Ultra City on the edge of town. The best reason to venture into the town centre is to visit the **Nelson Mandela Museum**.

The Umtata River was traditionally the boundary between the Thembu and Pondo clans of the Xhosa nation, with the Thembu to the south and the Pondo to the north. Whites farmed by the river from the 1860s, and when Britain acquired Thembuland in 1875, Umtata was established as the site of one of its four magistracies. From 1976 until 1994, Umtata was the capital of the Transkei homeland, with a smattering of showcase large buildings and a reputation for some of the most corrupt officialdom in South Africa.

Arrival and information

The small Umtata **airport** (☎047 536 0121) lies 10km west of town on the Queenstown Road. There is no public transport from the airport, but you can rent a car here (see p.448). Given the crowds, traffic and fear of crime in Umtata, most motorists, and backpackers on the Baz Bus, orientate from **Shell Ultra City**, 6km from the centre, on the N2 towards East London. This is where the Greyhound and Translux **buses** pull in, and is served by the Baz Bus. It's a convenient place to refuel, **eat** at the reasonably pleasant *Whistle Stop Restaurant* and buy basic groceries – milk, bread, cheese, chicken and soup – from the

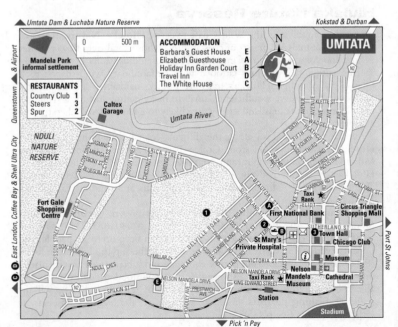

Select Shop. There's an ATM here, and in the car park a little **Eastern Cape Tourism Board** caravan provides maps and basic information.

Umtata's **tourist office** at 64 Owen Street in the town centre (Mon–Fri 8am–4.30pm; ☎047 531 5290) has useful **maps** and knowledgeable staff. The **Nature Conservation Office** on the corner of York and Victoria (Mon–Fri 8am–4.30pm; ☎047 531 1191) is the place to book accommodation in Silaka and Hluleka nature reserves, both south out of town on the R61. Here you can also pick up **maps** of the areas you want to visit and buy a helpful booklet about the whole coastal strip. **Wild Coast Reservations**, 3 Beaufort Street (daily 8am–6pm; ☎047 532 5344), can arrange accommodation at resorts and hotels throughout the region.

Accommodation

Umtata is not somewhere you'd choose to spend a night, but there's some decent accommodation catering mostly to people on business, predominately on the quieter fringes of the city. Weekend nights are always less expensive and you'll find it almost impossible to get a bed on a Monday night in particular, when the place is crawling with businessmen. The cheapest B&B, half an hour out of the centre, is at the Cultural Centre in Qunu (see p.448).

Barbara's Guest House 55 Nelson Mandela Dr, near the centre ☎047 531 1751, ℻047 531 1754, ✉barbp@cybertrade.co.za. A decent establishment with thirty neat en-suite rooms with TV, a swimming pool, nice garden and a bar with a pool table, where you can have good pub lunches. Half board ❹, B&B ❸

Elizabeth Guesthouse 19 Cumberland St ☎ & ℻047 531 5631 or ☎083 755 5425. A well-run, friendly establishment in a family home in a quiet part of town. ❸

Holiday Inn Garden Court Along the N2 in the town centre ☎047 537 0181, ⊛www.southernsun .com. Large 1970s building with a stylish pool, slot machines, a chic cocktail bar and restaurant. The rooms are unremarkable; all the singles face the car park. ❹

Travel Inn Adjoining Shell Ultra City ☎047 537 0761. A totally impersonal place set behind gates and fences with no public spaces or meals; it's suitable only for a stopover, but the en-suite family rooms are comfortable and clean. Very much cheaper over weekends. ❸

The White House 5 Mhlobo St, South Ridge Park ☎047 537 0580 or 083 458 9810, ✉whitehouse @intekom.co.za. Seventeen rooms, eight en suite, in two adjoining suburban houses in a quiet area just off the N2, opposite the Shell Ultra City. An evening meal can be provided if booked beforehand, and there is a communal lounge and pool table. ❸

The Town and around

Central Umtata comprises a small grid of crowded streets lined with dull office buildings, interspersed with the odd older architectural gem. One of these is the elegant **town hall** on Leeds Street, which looks down onto a war memorial and pleasant gardens. One block south, opposite the tourist office, stands the town's small and neglected **museum** (Mon–Fri 8am–4.30pm; free), which has fairly informative displays of traditional Xhosa costume, local geology and an exhibit on the ANC that stops before the 1994 elections.

Continue further south to the corner of Owen and Nelson Mandela Drive for the **Nelson Mandela Museum** (Mon–Fri 9am–4pm, Sat 9am–12.30pm; free), housed in the old **parliament**, or *bunga*, built in 1927. The museum is divided into three sections, the most interesting of which is the central section, "The Long Walk to Freedom", which traces the great man's life with photos and other visual material. The other two rooms house the

△ Nelson Mandela Museum, Umtata

extraordinary number of gifts given to Mandela from all over the world. The museum also offers free guided trips to **Qunu** and **Mveso** (see below), Mandela's birthplace; contact the museum, or the tour co-ordinator Miss Tetani (☎082 933 6264).

One block east of the museum, on the corner of Alexandra and York streets, is an elegant sandstone Anglican **cathedral**, sadly permanently closed. A major taxi rank straggles along the opposite side of Alexandra Street, and behind it is the small **stadium** used by the Umtata Bucks soccer team. If you are in town for a few days and the weather is good, head for the pleasant open-air **swimming pool** at the western end of Sutherland Street (daily 9am–12.30pm & 2–4.45pm), near the junction with Stanford Terrace.

Qunu and Mveso

Thirty kilometres south of Umtata are the scattered dwellings of **Qunu**, where Mandela grew up (see box below). The N2 thunders through it,

Nelson Mandela and the Qunu connection

Nelson Rolihlahla Mandela was born near tiny **Qunu** in the even tinier village of **Mveso** on July 18, 1918. His father was a member of the Xhosa royal house and a custodian of Xhosa history – he was also chief of Mveso, until he crossed swords with the local white magistrate over a minor dispute concerning an ox. After his sacking, the family moved to a small kraal in Qunu, which Mandela remembers as consisting of several hundred poor households.

Mandela is often called **Madiba** – the name of his family's subclan of the Thembu clan. The name Nelson was given to him by a schoolteacher, and Rolihlahla means "pulling the branch of a tree" or, more colloquially, "troublemaker". Mandela has said that at home he was never allowed to ask any questions, but was expected to learn by observation. Later in life, he was shocked to visit the homes of whites and hear children firing questions at their parents and expecting replies.

Shortly after his father died, Mandela was summoned from Qunu to the royal palace at Mqhakeweni, where he sat in on disputes in court and learnt more about Xhosa culture. At 16 he was **initiated** – and burnt with shame for a long time afterwards over the cry he let slip out when circumcised. He enrolled in Clarkebury, a college for the Thembu elite, then the Wesleyan college of Healdtown at Fort Beaufort, and finally the celebrated **Fort Hare** in Alice (see p.419), which has educated generations of African leaders. Mandela was expelled from Fort Hare after clashing with the authorities, and returned to Mqhakeweni. In 1941, faced with the prospect of an arranged marriage, he ran away to Johannesburg and there immersed himself in politics.

It was only upon his released from prison in 1990 (at the age of 72) that Mandela was able to return to Qunu, visiting first the grave of his mother, who had died in his absence. He noted that the place seemed poorer than he remembered it, and that the children were now singing songs about AK47s and the armed struggle. However, he was relieved to find that none of the old spirit and warmth had left the community, and he arranged for a palace (or "country house" as he called it) to be built there. This palace has become the venue for Mandela's holidays and family reunions and has a floor plan identical to that of the house in Victor Verster prison where Mandela spent the last few years of his captivity. In his autobiography he writes:

The Victor Verster house was the first spacious and comfortable home I ever stayed in, and I liked it very much. I was familiar with its dimensions, so at Qunu I would not have to wander at night looking for the kitchen.

but his large and rather plain mansion, which you may photograph but not enter, is clearly visible on the roadside 28km from Shell Ultra City in Umtata (it's on the left if you're heading south), 52km from Idutywa. A tunnel under the N2 connects his house with the village, built so that visiting children especially could cross the road in safety. You can also visit the remains of Mandela's primary school, the rock where he used to slide down with friends, and the graveyard where his parents, son and daughter are buried. The best way to appreciate Qunu is to take one of the **guided tours** run by the Mandela museum.

Seven kilometres north of Mandela's house, the **Jonopo Cultural Village** (☎083 503 3890; daily 8am–5pm; R10) has basic **B&B accommodation** in rondavels (❷) with a washbasin in each room and shared outside toilet. A Xhosa dinner can be cooked if ordered in advance, and there are also good crafts for sale and some exhibitions of rural life. You can also have a traditional Xhosa outfit made, which can be posted to you if you aren't able to come back to collect it.

Mandela spent his first two years at **Mveso**, on a hillside facing the Mbashe River, an hour-and-a-half south of Umtata. The **open-air museum** here contains the remains of the rondavels where he was born and raised, and a photographic exhibition with images that include Mandela burning his pass – the infamous identity document Africans were forced to carry under apartheid. If you're approaching from Umtata, Mveso is signed after 32km on the N2, though the route is a rough and eroded dirt road. It's better to continue 8km further down the N2, beyond Qunu, to the Elliotdale turning, on which you head 11km east on a good gravel road, until the unmarked Madondile Junction. Here you turn south for 19km to the museum, at the end of the road.

Eating

The hotel restaurants apart, there aren't many **places to eat** in Umtata. *Spur* in Sutherland Street has a range of salads, burgers and steaks; the *Country Club Restaurant* on Delville Road (☎047 531 0795; closed Sun) is open to non-members and has a thatch-covered deck overlooking the golf course. Umtata has a thriving **nightlife**, with bars and *shebeens*, but exploring it without a local escort isn't recommended.

If you're self-catering, pick up **groceries** at the Spar Centre (daily 7am–9pm), two-and-a-half kilometres away towards town on the N2 (next to the *Wimpy* restaurant), or Pick 'n Pay (Mon–Fri 8.30am–7pm, Sat & Sun 9am–4pm) at the Southernwood Shopping Centre on Errol Spring Avenue. These supermarkets are far better stocked than the shop at the Shell Ultra City, and have an ATM.

Listings

Banks First National Bank, corner of Sutherland St and York Rd; Standard Bank, corner of York Rd and Leeds St. Expect large queues – it's better to use the ATMs at the Spar Centre or at Shell Ultra City.

Car rental Avis, at Umtata airport ☎047 536 0066.

Emergencies Ambulance ☎10177 or 047 532 2222; see also p.89.

Garages Fort Gale Motors ☎047 532 3882, on Queenstown Rd.

Hospital St Mary's Private Hospital, 30 Durham St ☎047 531 2911.

Pharmacy Triangle Pharmacy, Circus Triangle Centre, Port St Johns Rd ☎047 531 0215.

Travel agents Sure Travel Centre, Metropolitan Place, Leeds St ☎047 531 2011.

Port St Johns and around

The ninety-kilometre drive on the R61 to **PORT ST JOHNS** from Umtata is one of the best journeys on the Wild Coast. After passing tiny **Libode**, with its small hotel and restaurant, you start the dramatic descent to the coast, past craggy ravines and epic vistas of forest and rondavel-spotted grassland. The road runs alongside the Mzimvubu River for the last few kilometres, giving you a perfect view of the Gates of St John, before reaching the town square and taxi rank. The big surprise, coming from the sparse hillsides around Umtata, is how dramatic, hilly, lush and steamy it all is.

Port St Johns is a favoured destination for backpackers, drawn by its stunning location at the mouth of the Mzimvubu River, dominated by Mount Thesiger on the west bank and Mount Sullivan on the east. A further attraction for some visitors is the strong cannabis grown in the area, and the town's famously laid-back atmosphere may tempt you to stay for longer than you intended. Port St Johns also has good fishing and swimming beaches, a wider choice of accommodation than anywhere else on the Wild Coast, and a good tarred road all the way into town.

Some history

The origins of Port St Johns' name is something of a mystery but may derive from the sixteenth-century Portuguese ship, *São João*, which was wrecked nearby, leaving around four hundred survivors to complete a seven-hundred-kilometre walk to Mozambique. Only eight survived, and one of those was shipwrecked again near the Umtata River Mouth two years later. He reportedly died of despair, unable to face the trek to Mozambique once more.

In 1878, in an effort to reduce gun-running from the harbour, a representative of the Cape governor bought a fifteen-kilometre stretch of the river from the shore inland, and the land on the western side from the Pondo for R2000. While he was waiting for the money, an armed force arrived from Natal and annexed the eastern side of the river. A compromise was found by making Port St Johns a crown colony in its own right, though this was rescinded when the whole of Pondoland was annexed by Britain in 1895.

The area was then known for its **tobacco**, which was exported from Durban and East London. During the negotiations for the Act of Union, the Transvaal demanded the cessation of the trade to allow its white tobacco growers to expand their business without competition. The Cape Colony obliged and in 1906 stopped exporting tobacco. Local farmers responded by switching to **cannabis**, supplying the growing numbers of men from the area working in the Gauteng mines. Today, the cultivation and trade are as strong as ever, which may explain the presence of so many white South African hippies in the town.

Arrival and information

Initially the town is quite confusing – it meanders into three distinct localities, some kilometres apart. **First Beach**, where the river meets the sea, is along the main road from the post office and offers good fishing, but is unsafe for swimming. Close to First Beach is the rather run-down town centre, where you'll find shops and minibus taxis. **Second Beach**, 5km west along a tarred road off a right turn past the post office, is a fabulous swimming beach with a lagoon; it has a couple of nice places to stay close by, and a number of alternative folk living locally. The area along the river around the **Pondoland Bridge** has some accommodation popular with anglers.

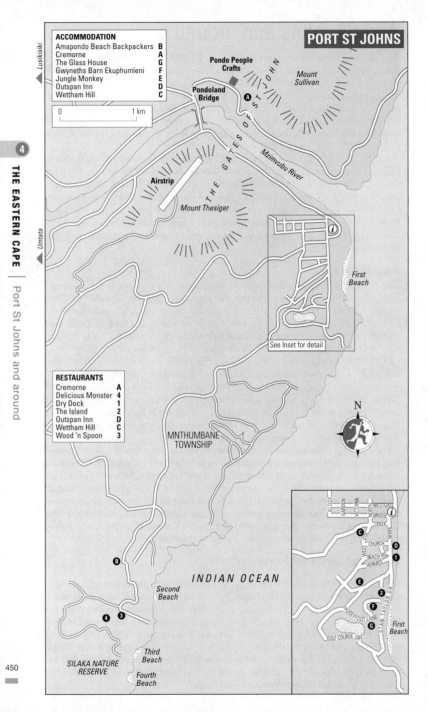

PORT ST JOHNS

ACCOMMODATION
Amapondo Beach Backpackers	B
Cremorne	A
The Glass House	G
Gwyneths Barn Ekuphumleni	F
Jungle Monkey	E
Outspan Inn	D
Wettham Hill	C

0   1 km

Lusikisiki

Umtata

Pondo People Crafts

Pondoland Bridge

Mount Sullivan

Mzimvubu River

THE GATES OF ST JOHN

Airstrip

Mount Thesiger

First Beach

See Inset for detail

RESTAURANTS
Cremorne	A
Delicious Monster	4
Dry Dock	1
The Island	2
Outspan Inn	D
Wettham Hill	C
Wood 'n Spoon	3

MNTHUMBANE TOWNSHIP

N

INDIAN OCEAN

Second Beach

Third Beach

Fourth Beach

SILAKA NATURE RESERVE

KLOOF
GARDEN
VICTORIA
WESTGATE
BRIDGE
CREEK
CHURCH
WEST DR
BEACH RD
HERMES
MAIN
PUSSYFOOT LANE
STAN TAILOR DR
GOLF COURSE DR
First Beach

The Baz Bus drops off in Port St Johns, which is also easily reached by **minibus taxi** from Umtata: plenty run from the *Steer's* restaurant at the Circus Triangle Mall. If you're travelling **from KwaZulu-Natal** to Port St Johns by public transport, an alternative route is via Port Edward, the *Wild Coast Sun* (see p.455), Bizana and Lusikisiki on the R61. This journey is most easily done by catching the Grimboys bus from Durban, which runs daily directly to Port St Johns. This is also the route you should take if you're driving **from Durban**.

There's a **tourist office** (daily 8am–4.30pm) in an obvious building at the roundabout as you enter town. As well as maps, they provide information about local Xhosa homestays. Jimmy Gila from the tourist office (℡082 507 2256) runs **tours** in the area. Also in the centre you'll find a post office, a bank with an ATM and a Shoprite supermarket.

Accommodation

Port St Johns has the best selection of **accommodation** on the Wild Coast, with a healthy number of backpacker lodges, B&Bs and resort complexes. Neither of the hostels in Port St Johns itself is in a particularly exciting location, although there are some other well-positioned budget options, among which is the accommodation at the Silaka reserve (see p.452). The most spectacular view is high above the Mzimvubu River, on Mount Thesiger. For a **hostel** offering a beach and rural experience, head for Mpande, some way out of town.

Amapondo Beach Backpackers Second Beach ℡047 564 1344, ⊛www.amapondo.co.za. Lively hostel situated on a hilltop with a sea view, but some way from Second Beach. A free shuttle heads into the centre each morning, 5km away, and the hostel liaises daily with the Baz Bus to collect passengers. Accommodation comprises dorms, double rooms and permanent tents mounted on decks; Internet access is available to residents, and evening meals can be ordered. Staff can organize trips to the Silaka Nature Reserve, or to spend the night in a rural village and meet a traditional healer. ❶

Cremorne Estate 5km from the centre on the Mzimvubu River, signposted from the Pondoland Bridge ℡ & ℻047 564 1113, ⊛www.cremorne.co.za. One of Port St John's few upmarket places, offering self-catering timber cottages on stilts set on tidy lawns running down to the Mzimvubu River, with views of Mount Thesiger's red-slabbed cliffs. The cottages have two en-suite bedrooms, making them very affordable for a party of three or four. A less expensive row of small B&B doubles shares the view; cheaper still are some tiny cabins equipped with double bunks, where you can also camp. There's a restaurant, bar and a relaxing swimming pool area. ❸

The Glass House Marine Dr; follow the signs to Second Beach ℡ & ℻047 564 1242. Nestled in the bushes within walking distance of First Beach, these comfortable wooden bungalows are raised to give good ocean views. Each unit has two rooms with separate entrances. ❸

Gwyneths Barn Ekuphumleni Marine Dr; follow signs to Second Beach ℡ & ℻047 564 1506. A delightful, Robinson Crusoe-style guesthouse with three self-catering wooden cabins, all raised on stilts, and tucked away in the forest near first beach. The cabins all converge on a central shaded deck, which has a shared bathroom, open air shower and communal kitchen. On the adjoining property, a larger, brightly painted cottage and a renovated barn each sleep six (R450). ❷

Jungle Monkey Berea Rd, second right off the main road after the post office ℡047 564 1517, ⊛junglemonkey@iafrica.com. Adequate hostel in a converted house near the centre. It can arrange guided trips into the villages and overnight visits to a traditional healer as well as drive you to the Silaka Nature Reserve. Camping, dorms & doubles ❶

The Kraal Near Mpandi ℡082 871 4964, ⊛www .thekraalbackpackers.co.za. Four traditional huts, each sleeping four people, on community land well off the beaten track. Efficiently run and wonderfully set right on the beach, it has no electricity or flushing toilets (enviroloos are used), and showers and washing facilities are in reed huts. Meals are available, often featuring crayfish, oysters and mussels; activities include beach hikes, snorkelling, surfing and dolphin-watching (also whale-watching in season). A hostel bus connects with the Baz Bus at Shell Ultra City in Umtata (book in advance by phone); driving, turn off at Tombo Stores, 70km from Umtata on the Port St Johns

Road, and travel another 30min to the little village of Mpandi. ❶

Outspan Inn In the centre, past the town hall on the road to First Beach ☎047 564 1057, ⓦwww .outspaninn.co.za. Two-storey ochre B&B with en-suite rooms set in an appealing large garden. Some rooms have unusually high beds that give a view of nearby First Beach. The restaurant and pub is open daily and there's a swimming pool. Frequently used by aid workers and business people, it's cheaper at weekends. ❸

Umngazi River Bungalows Umngazi rivermouth, west of Port St Johns ☎047 564 1115, ⓦwww .umngazi.co.za. Unsurpassed as a Wild Coast holiday resort, Umngazi delivers probably the best beachside family holiday in the country. It's frequently fully booked, especially during school holidays, so book as far in advance as possible. The beach and pool are inviting and the lunchtime buffet spread is particularly good. It's signposted off the R61, about 10km before you reach Port St Johns from Umtata; from the sign, continue another 11km along a potholed road. Alternatively, guests can arrange a private plane into Port St Johns and get picked up. Full board ❹

Wettham Hill 2 Mountain Dr, signposted from the tourist office ☎082 453 3944, ⓦwww.wetthamhill .co.za. Port St Johns' nicest mid-range guesthouse with panoramic views of the town and a small restaurant open to the public. The rooms are comfortable and pleasantly furnished with white linen and curtains and the odd Art Deco piece. ❸

The Town and around

Although there is nothing much to see town, Port St Johns is still a nice place to take a leisurely stroll, particularly in the early evening, when many residents are doing the same. Most people rarely go anywhere besides First and Second beaches and Pondoland Bridge, though the rocky coastline into the **Silaka Nature Reserve** and as far as the **Umngazi River Mouth** provides wonderful walks, as do the endless stretches of pristine beach east of the Mzimvubu River. The river is muddy in summer, disgorging topsoil washed down the Drakensberg from Lesotho, but cleans up dramatically in winter, when it is clear and good for fishing.

Both the mountains of the **Gates of St John** merit a stiff climb to the top, from where you get a superb view of the lush surrounding landscape. The Gates are two sentinel-like mountainous outcrops on either side of the Mzimvubu River, marking the point where it flows out to the Indian Ocean. By car, drive up to the aircraft landing strip at the top of Mount Thesiger. Look out for the birds of prey, making use of the updrafts.

For **crafts**, check out Pondo People on the east side of the Mzimvubu River across the Pondoland Bridge, easily the best craft shop on the Wild Coast, with wooden sculptures, baskets, carved wooden animals, and immaculate bead jewellery and clothing – all at affordable prices.

Silaka Nature Reserve

Just south of town, the **Silaka Nature Reserve** (daily 6am–6pm; R10) is a small reserve with a dramatic coastline, and comprises the idyllic **Third Beach**, dense and beautiful tropical-forest areas with huge trees (through which there are good **trails**) and a handful of animals, including zebra and wildebeest. **Accommodation** is in spacious self-catering chalets surrounded by grassland, sleeping four (R300); bookings are through Nature Conservation in Umtata (☎047 532 1191). To get to the reserve, head down the Second Beach road from Port St Johns and then up the treacherously steep dirt road to the reserve's office. Some of the backpacker lodges can drop you in the reserve, and you can walk back along the coast.

Eating and drinking

There are a couple of decent places to **eat** and **drink** in Port St Johns. If you're self-catering, you can buy tempting local fruits which are sold by the roadside, and sometimes fresh fish is available too. In the centre, Boxer Supermarket has most foodstuffs you'll need, while Green Foods is the place for vegetables.

Cremorne Mzimvubu River; follow the signs from the Pondoland Bridge ⊕047 564 1113. Port St John's poshest eating place. Very good fish, steaks and puddings, a pizza oven, pub, and seating both indoors and out. Daily lunch & dinner.
Delicious Monster Near Second Beach. A couple of tables in the owner's garden, where you can get breakfast, lunch and dinner made with fresh herbs from the garden, and home-baked goodies for tea. There's a little craft shop, too, in a caravan with nice postcards.
Dry Dock On the road to First Beach, next to *Outspan Inn*. A lively pub and restaurant filled with memorablia from the owner's sea ferrying days. A local policeman regularly plays on the untuned piano in the corner of the restaurant. Daily 10am–late.
The Island Signposted off First Beach ⊕047 564 1958 or 082 813 611. Funky, fun place where you sit to eat, Japanese-style, with the food anything from toasted sandwiches to Thai vegetable stir-fry, reasonably priced, nicely

cooked and well presented. You can watch videos on a giant screen in one room while large speakers blast out in another. Takeaways and deliveries possible. Daily except Tues noon–midnight.
Outspan Inn See opposite. The restaurant at this B&B is a great place for blow-out breakfasts, and has an interesting and inexpensive lunch and dinner menu. Closed Sun eves.
Wettham Hill 2 Mountain Dr, signposted west of the town centre. A smart restaurant by Port St John standards, with fantastic views from its wraparound balcony. The menu changes every day, with offerings such as balsamic chicken and Mediterranean roast vegetables.
Wood 'n Spoon Near Second Beach. Operating from a red floral caravan in the owners' garden, this serves up unusual dishes like apple and bacon macaroni cheese. Tables are laid out in the garden and at night the area is lit with candles and lanterns. Breakfast, lunch and dinner daily in summer, opening erratically in winter.

The northern Wild Coast and the KwaZulu-Natal enclave

For many visitors to the northern part of the Wild Coast, the main draw is the **Wild Coast Sun**, a hotel and casino on the border of KwaZulu-Natal. However, the stretch of coast from Port St Johns to the Mzamba River by the *Sun* is outstandingly beautiful, with three of only five waterfalls in the world that fall over 100m directly into the sea, as well as countless deserted beaches and cosy bays. The best way to see it is to walk, though it's possible to drive – with some difficulty – to the **Mkambati Nature Reserve**, which contains a good portion of this coast.

The road from Port St Johns to the *Wild Coast Sun* via **Lusikisiki** and **Bizana** makes an interesting alternative to the N2 for getting from the Eastern Cape to KwaZulu-Natal. Inland, the road through the Eastern Cape enclave in KwaZulu-Natal takes you into the rolling hills of **Ixopo**, made famous by Alan Paton's novel, *Cry the Beloved Country.*

North to the Wild Coast Sun

The tarred road north from Port St Johns heads to the small unremarkable town of **LUSIKISIKI**, continuing on to the *Wild Coast Sun*. East of Lusikisiki lies the **Magwa Falls** and, tucked away in indigenous forest at the mouth of the **Mbotyi River**, the recently refurbished *Mbotyi River Lodge* (⊕039 253 8822, ⊛www.mbotyi.co.za; ➎). With it's numerous hiking trails (it's used as the base for the Wild Coast Pondo Walk; see box on p.434), horse-riding, stretch of unblemished coastline and ideal swimming conditions, the lodge makes a good place to stop and rest for a few days. Full-board **accommodation** is in rustic thatched chalets or timber bungalows; the standard rooms have balconies and views of the forest, the luxury ones views of the sea and lagoon. The nearby *Mbotyi Campsite* (℡039 235 8295, Ⓔcamping@mbotyi.co.za), run separately from the lodge as a joint venture with the local community, offers clean and comfortable self-catering rondavels (sleeping four/six R450/700), with communal kitchens, ablution facilities and a dining area (you'll need to supply your own cutlery, crockery and linen). There's also ample space for **camping**, and a small **store** for basic supplies. The first 6km of the Magwa/Mbotyi road from Lusikisiki are tarred, after which it's 20km of well-maintained gravel to the lodge.

Mkambati Nature Reserve

Beyond Lusikisiki, the hills of Pondoland seem to stretch for miles, punctuated 50km later by the small village of **Flagstaff**, where you can turn east for the largest of the Wild Coast reserves, the eighty-square-kilometre **Mkambati Nature Reserve** (daily 6am–6pm; ℡040 635 2115). The park consists almost entirely of grassland, flanked by the forested ravines of the Msikaba and Mtentu rivers, and a **ravishing coastline** of rocky promontories and deserted beaches. There's **plenty of game**: you're likely to see eland, hartebeest, wildebeest and blesbok, as well as Cape vultures. The highlight, though, is the Mkambati River itself, which cuts through the middle of the reserve down a series of striking waterfalls, of which the **Horseshoe Falls** near the sea are the most spectacular. **Horse-riding** is on offer and there's plenty of fine walking. **Swimming** is idyllic: a warm sheltered lagoon is flanked by steep dunes down which you can slide into the water; trees offer some shade along the wide, clear river, and there's the rolling surf itself. There are no facilities at the beach, so bring whatever you need for a picnic, including drinking water.

To get to Mkambati, turn towards the coast at the Mkambati signpost at **Flagstaff** on the tarred R61. From Flagstaff, the reserve is 70km away on dirt road, which is very variable in quality; when it has been raining hard you'll need a 4WD vehicle. From Port St Johns, count on two to three hours for the trip. Although the road to the reserve restcamp is fine, **driving** anywhere in the park except to the beach requires a high-clearance vehicle to negotiate the crumbling roads. The beach road itself is poor, and passable in an ordinary car only with considerable care in good weather and when the road is dry. Fortunately, the footpath to the beach through tropical forest is not too long.

There are plans to develop luxury **accommodation** here, but at present all the places to stay are a bit run-down, though they do have cooking facilities (no meals are provided). Bring all you need, as there are no shops. The prime place to stay, not far from the reception, is *The Lodge*, built as the doctor's stone house when the restcamp was a sanatorium some years ago. It has a veranda set on a hilltop overlooking the sea and its own swimming pool. Paths slither through thick vegetation, down to the lagoon, river and sea. With several bedrooms, it's ideal for a family or group and costs R500 per night. Around reception, there are some basic cottages (❶), the best of which are the two stone houses with a couple of bedrooms each – try for one of these when you book, rather than the one-bedroomed cottages which are pretty tatty. All this accommodation is fully equipped with electricity. At the beach, in another dreamy location, is a three-bedroom thatched house, **The Point**, the only place on the beach for miles. There is no mains electricity here, just solar power and gas lamps.

Bizana and the Wild Coast Sun

Roughly 30km north of Flagstaff is a junction where you can head northwest to the N2. If you continue 20km northeast instead, through heavily populated hillsides, you reach the busy town of **BIZANA**, 60km from the coast in an area where both former ANC president **Oliver Tambo** and **Winnie Madikizela-Mandela** were born. The *Bizana Hotel* on the left side of the main road has a quiet **restaurant** serving good-value steaks and curries, but is not recommended as a place to stay.

Some 50km southeast of Bizana is the glitzy *Wild Coast Sun* (℡039 305 9111, Ⓦwww.suninternational.co.za; ❼) in a well-chosen location by the Mzamba River Mouth. The hotel marks the start of the **Amadiba Horse Trail** (see box on p.434) down the coast to Mkambati Nature Reserve and is quite pleasant in parts, despite its tacky Pacific island-themed decor. Most people are here to gamble, but an impressive games arcade, ten-pin bowling, pony rides and mini-golf are also on offer. **Accommodation** is in small, well-equipped, yet very expensive, rooms, with some suites looking onto the sea. You can **eat** tasty (if overpriced) fish steaks at the *Driftwood Terrace*, which has a fantastic sea view.

Opposite the complex is the **Mzamba Crafts Market**, arranged in a circle to resemble a traditional kraal. The central shop sells authentic crafts from all over southern Africa for reasonable prices, with local ones the cheapest, particularly the grasswork. Reject goods are on sale in the outlying huts for even better prices.

There's a daily shuttle here **from Durban airport** run by Margate Mini Coach (℡039 312 1406 or 082 455 9736; 2hr). **Taxis** and **buses** stop outside the market on their way to or from Bizana and **Port Edward** in KwaZulu-Natal (see p.498).

The N2 north of Umtata

The quickest and busiest way from the Eastern Cape to KwaZulu-Natal is on the **N2**, passing by the scraggy towns of Mount Frere and Mount Ayliff, before reaching **Kokstad** and the provincial boundary. From the road you'll see hillsides dotted with densely packed dwellings. Closer inspection reveals that the hillsides are not coping well with the strain, as there are massive *dongas* (eroded gullies) creating scar-like craters in many places where huge volumes of topsoil have simply been washed away.

Mount Frere is about 100km from Umtata, and is called kwaBhaca in Xhosa, meaning "the place of the Bhaca" – for many of those fleeing south from the Zulu king Shaka settled here, earning themselves the name *amaBhaca*, "the people who hide". Today, Mount Frere is a fairly rough town and you'd be wise to pass swiftly through.

The Eastern Cape enclave

The **Eastern Cape enclave** in KwaZulu-Natal for many years sat uncomfortably with the crass ethnic categorizations of past regimes, and the legacy of this lives on today. The people living in the enclave, whose main town is uMzimkhulu, are a mixture of Zulu, Pondo, Bhaca and Griqua, economically tied in the main to Pietermaritzburg and Durban. The apartheid regime yoked them with the Transkei, ostensibly on the grounds that most were Pondo, and thus part of the Xhosa nation, but in fact to tap them as a cheap labour reserve. Controversially, the area was included in the Eastern Cape when the boundaries were redrawn after the 1994 elections, in part because many in the area support the ANC and did not want to be part of a province ruled by the Zulu nationalist Inkatha Freedom Party.

The enclave is reached by turning off the N2 onto the R56 at the Stafford's Post junction towards **Ixopo**. It's scenic and pleasant enough to pass through, though not a good place to travel around – there's nowhere to stay or any infrastructure for tourists, and it's desperately poor. **uMzimkhulu** is a busy transport centre, with a large taxi rank by its Shell garage and plenty of fast-food outlets to feed hungry passengers, most of whom are going to and from Pietermaritzburg and Durban. After passing the remnants of a small border post just east of the town, you'll find yourself back in KwaZulu-Natal, a short distance from Ixopo.

Travel details

All major transport in the Eastern Cape runs between Port Elizabeth and East London – the two hubs of the province – or from these centres to other major cities: Johannesburg, Cape Town and Durban. Two mainline trains, the Amatola from East London, and the Algoa from Port Elizabeth, connect the Eastern Cape with Johannesburg and Pretoria, both stopping along the way. The main bus routes run from Port Elizabeth (up the N10) and East London (up the N6) to join the N1 via Bloemfontein to Johannesburg and Pretoria; and along the coast to Cape Town in the west and Durban in the east. An alternative route goes inland through the Little Karoo to Cape Town.

Trains

East London to: Bloemfontein (daily; 13hr); Johannesburg (daily; 20hr); Pretoria (daily; 21hr 30min); Queenstown (daily; 4hr 30min).
Port Elizabeth to: Bloemfontein (daily; 11hr 30min); Cradock (daily; 4hr 30min); Johannesburg (daily; 18hr); Pretoria (daily; 19hr 30min).

Buses

East London to: Alexandria (5 weekly; 3hr 15min); Aliwal North (daily; 5hr); Bloemfontein (daily; 7hr 30min); Cape Town (1–2 daily; 14hr); Durban (2 daily; 9hr); Grahamstown (2 daily; 2hr); Johannesburg (daily; 13hr); Kenton-on-Sea (5 weekly; 3hr); King William's Town (2–3 daily; 45min); Knysna (1–2 daily; 7hr 30min); Mossel Bay (1–2 daily; 9hr); Paarl (5 weekly; 14hr 30min); Plettenberg Bay (1–2 daily; 7hr); Port Alfred (3 daily; 2hr 30min); Port Elizabeth (3 daily; 4hr); Port Shepstone (2 daily; 8hr); Pretoria (daily; 14hr); Sedgefield (1–2 daily; 8hr); Storms River (1–2 daily; 6hr); Swellendam (1–2 daily; 11hr) Umtata (2 daily; 3hr 30min); Wilderness (1–2 daily; 8hr 30min).
Port Elizabeth to: Alexandria (5 weekly; 1hr); Bloemfontein (1–2 daily; 10hr); Cape Town (6–7 daily; 11hr); Durban (2 daily; 13hr 30min); East London (3 daily; 4hr); George (6–7 daily; 4hr 30min); Graaff-Reinet (5 weekly; 3hr 30min); Grahamstown (2 daily; 1hr 30min); Jeffrey's Bay (2 daily; 45min); Johannesburg (3–4 daily; 16hr); Kenton-on-Sea (5 weekly; 1hr 30min); Knysna (6–7 daily; 3hr 30min); Mossel Bay (6–7 daily; 4hr 30min); Paarl (4 weekly; 10hr); Plettenberg Bay (6–7 daily; 3hr); Port Alfred (5 weekly; 1hr 45min); Port Shepstone (2 daily; 12hr); Pretoria (1–2 daily; 17hr); Sedgefield (6–7 daily; 3hr 30min); Stellenbosch (6 weekly; 10hr); Storms River (6–7 daily; 2hr); Umtata (2 daily; 7hr 30min); Wilderness (4 daily; 3hr 30min).
Umtata to: Cape Town (1–3 daily; 17hr 30min); Durban (3 daily; 5hr 50min); East London (1–2 daily; 3hr); Johannesburg (2 daily; 12hr 45min); Port Elizabeth (daily; 5hr 40min); Pretoria (daily; 13hr 45min).

Baz Buses

The Baz Bus plies the coastal route daily between Port Elizabeth and Cape Town. It also goes all the way through to Durban five times a week.
Port Elizabeth to: Durban (5 weekly; 15hr 30min); East London (5 weekly; 2hr 30min); George (daily; 7hr 45min); Jeffrey's Bay (daily; 1hr 45min); Knysna (daily; 6hr 30min); Mossel Bay (daily; 10hr 15min); Nature's Valley (daily; 4hr 30min); Oudtshoorn (daily; 9hr); Plettenberg Bay (daily; 5hr 30min); Port Alfred (5 weekly; 2hr 15min); Port Shepstone (5 weekly; 14hr); Umtata (5 weekly; 8hr 30min); Wilderness (daily; 7hr 15min).

Domestic flights

East London to: Cape Town (2–3 daily; 2hr); Durban (2–4 daily; 1hr); Johannesburg (7 daily; 1hr 20min); Port Elizabeth (2–4 daily; 45min).
Port Elizabeth to: Bloemfontein (1 daily Mon–Fri & Sun; 1hr 20min); Cape Town (3–4 daily; 1hr 15min); Durban (4 daily; 1hr 10min); East London (1–4 daily; 45min); George (1 weekly; 1hr); Johannesburg (6 daily; 1hr 30min).
Umtata to Johannesburg (2 daily; 1hr 30min).

5

KwaZulu-Natal

CHAPTER 5

Highlights

✳ **Indian culture** The Hindu temples and tangy food of KwaZulu-Natal's second-largest ethnic group can be experienced in the heart of Durban. See p.475

✳ **Ukhahlamba Drakensberg Park** Towering peaks and ancient San (Bushman) rock paintings in one of KwaZulu-Natal's two World Heritage Sites. See p.512

✳ **Hluhluwe-Imfolozi Park** One of the best places in the world to see rhinos. See p.529

✳ **Greater St Lucia Wetland Park** Declared a World Heritage Site in 1999, this reserve is home to five ecosystems, marine and wildlife. See p.532

✳ **Authentic Zulu Culture** Be a guest at a traditional Zulu wedding or coming of age ceremony in Eshowe. See p.555

✳ **Zulu baskets** The Vukani Collection in Eshowe includes some of South Africa's most beautiful woven artefacts. See p.555

✳ **Battlefield tours** Experience the drama of the Anglo-Zulu wars with world-renowned storytellers and guides. See p.558

△ Rhinos are a Big Five attraction

KwaZulu-Natal

KwaZulu-Natal, South Africa's most African province, has everything the continent is known for – beaches, wildlife, mountains and accessible ethnic culture. South Africans are well acquainted with KwaZulu-Natal's attractions; it's the leading province for domestic tourism, although foreign visitors haven't quite cottoned on to the incredible amount packed into this compact and beautiful region.

Among white South Africans, KwaZulu-Natal is well known for its subtropical **coastline**, which offers a temperate climate even in the winter, when the Cape can be showered by an icy downpour. This is where you'll find Africa's most developed beaches, in a 250-kilometre ribbon of holiday homes stretching along the shore from the Eastern Cape border in the south to the Tugela River in the north.

At the ribbon's centre lies **Durban**, the industrial hub of the province and the country's principal harbour. Apart from Cape Town, Durban is the only major city in South Africa that warrants a visit in its own right. British in origin, it has a heady mixture of cultural flavours deriving from its Zulu, Indian and white communities. You'll find palm trees fanning Victorian buildings, African squatters living precariously on truncated flyovers, high-rise offices towering over temples and curry houses, overdeveloped beachfronts, and everywhere an irrepressible fecundity.

Paradoxically, while the coasts immediately on either side of Durban – known as the **North and South coasts** – are South Africa's busiest and least enticing, north of the Tugela River are some of the most pristine shores in the country. Here, in the **Elephant Coast**, a patchwork of wetlands, freshwater lakes, wilderness and Zulu villages meets the sea at a virtually seamless stretch of sand that begins at the St Lucia Estuary and slips across the Mozambique border at Kosi Bay. Apart from southern **Lake St Lucia**, which is fairly developed in a low-key fashion, the Elephant Coast is one of the most isolated regions in the

---

KwaZulu-Natal Wildlife

All the public game parks and wilderness areas described in this chapter fall under the auspices of **Ezemvelo KwaZulu-Natal Wildlife**, also known as Ezemvelo KZN Wildlife or KZN Wildlife (PO Box 13069, Cascades, Pietermaritzburg 3202; ☎033 845 1000, ⊛www.kznwildlife.com). **Accommodation** in these areas is best booked in advance through them (exceptions or alternative ways of booking are noted in the text); if you want to do so in person, one convenient location is their head office at Tourist Junction in Durban (☎031 274 1150; see p.465).

country, though it does reward visitors with South Africa's best snorkelling and scuba diving along the coral reefs off **Sodwana Bay**.

KwaZulu-Natal's marine life is matched on land by its **game reserves**, some of which are beaten only by the Kruger National Park, and easily surpass the latter as the best place in the continent to see both black and white rhinos. Concentrated in the north, the reserves tend to be compact and feature some of the most stylish game-lodge accommodation in the country. Most famous and largest of the reserves is the **Hluhluwe–Imfolozi Park**, trampled by a respectable cross section of wildlife that includes all of the Big Five.

Since the nineteenth century, when missionaries were homing in on the region, the **Zulu** have captured the popular imagination of the West and remain one of the province's major pulls for tourists, despite the fact that you're more likely to encounter a Zulu dressed in jeans in Jo'burg than someone in traditional garb in KwaZulu-Natal. You'll find constant reminders of the old Zulu kingdom and its founder Shaka, including an excellent reconstruction of the beehive-hutted capital at **Ondini** and the more touristy **Shakaland**, near **Eshowe**. The interior north of the Tugela River was the heartland of the Zulu kingdom and saw gruesome battles between Boers and Zulus, British and Zulus, and finally Boers and British. Today, the area can be explored through **Battlefield tours**, a memorable way of taking in some of South Africa's most turbulent history. The political violence that has divided the province's Zulu majority in a low-key but deadly war of attrition and vendetta is something you're unlikely to encounter, as it occurs in remote rural villages.

The area south of the Tugela, designated "white man's country" in the mid-nineteenth century and consolidated a century later under apartheid, represents the most English area of South Africa. Though it is very pretty and has some fabulous accommodation in country houses, the **Midlands'** rolling green sugar estates, polo clubs and rather contrived arts-and-crafts routes pale by comparison with the drama of the rest of the province.

From the Midlands, South Africa's highest peaks sweep west into the soaring **Ukhahlamba Drakensberg** range, protected by a chain of KwaZulu-Natal Wildlife reserves. The area's restcamps are ideal bases for walking in the mountains or heading out for ambitious hikes; with relatively little effort, you can experience crystal rivers tumbling into marbled rock pools, peaks and rock faces enriched by ancient San paintings.

KwaZulu-Natal experiences considerable variations in **climate**, from the occasional heavy winter snowstorms of the Ukhahlamba Drakensberg to the mellow, sunny days and pleasant sea temperatures a couple of hundred kilometres away along the coast. This makes the region a popular winter getaway, but in midsummer the low-lying areas, including Durban, the coastal belt and the game reserves, can experience an uncomfortably high humidity.

Durban

Until the 1970s, **DURBAN** was regarded as white South Africa's quintessential seaside playground – a status fostered by its tropical colours, oversized vegetation and an itinerant population of surfers, hedonists and holidaying Jo'burg families. Then, in the 1980s, the collapse of apartheid population-influx controls saw a growing stream of Africans flood in from rural KwaZulu-Natal – and even from as far afield as central Africa – to stake their claims in the city centre, with shantytowns and cardboard hovels revealing the reality of one of the most unmistakably African conurbations in the country.

South Africa's third-largest city – and reputedly the fastest-expanding city in the southern hemisphere – is a thriving industrial centre and the largest port in Africa. Its **beachfront** pulls thousands upon thousands of white Jo'burgers down to "Durbs" every year, while the **harbour** remains a photogenic place for meandering or eating and drinking at the dockside. Another unmistakable feature of Durban is a legacy of the city's **Indian population** (its second-largest group): mosques, bazaars and temples, festooned with wildly coloured deities, stand juxtaposed with the Victorian buildings marking out the colonial centre.

The city's main interest lies not in its seaside, but its gritty urbanity, a seemingly endless struggle to reconcile competing Indian, African and English cultures and to keep the rampant vegetation at bay. There's enough here to keep you busy for a few days, looking at mosques, exploring the Indian area around Grey Street, or passing by the Dalton Road Zulu Market. However, most people come to Durban because it provides a logical springboard for the KwaZulu-Natal game parks, the Ukhahlamba Drakensberg and the Battlefields. Durban is well connected to the rest of South Africa, and some international flights call here.

Some history

Less than two hundred years ago, Durban was known to Europeans as **Port Natal**, a lagoon thick with mangroves, eyed by white adventurers who saw business opportunities in its ivory and hides. In 1824, a British party led by **Francis Farewell** persuaded the Zulu king, **Shaka**, to give them some land. Not long after, the British went on to rename the settlement **Durban** after Sir Benjamin D'Urban, governor of the Cape Colony, whose support, they believed, might not go amiss later.

Britain's tenuous toehold looked threatened in 1839, when **Boers** trundled over the Ukhahlamba Drakensberg in their ox wagons and declared their Republic of Natalia nearby. The threat was compounded the following year, when a large force of now-hostile Zulus descended on the settlement and razed it, forcing the British residents to take refuge at sea in the brig *Comet*. Capitalizing on the British absence, a group of Boers annexed Durban, later laying siege to a British detachment. This provided the cue for a much-celebrated piece of Victorian melodrama, familiar until recently to every English-speaking school child in South Africa – when teenager **Dick King** heroically rode the 1000km from Durban to Grahamstown in ten days to alert the garrison there, which promptly dispatched a rescue detachment to relieve Durban.

While Cape Town was becoming a cosmopolitan centre by the 1840s, Durban's population of barely one thousand lived a basic existence in a near wilderness roamed by lions, leopards and hyenas. Things changed after Britain formally annexed the **Colony of Natal** in 1843; within ten years, a large-scale immigration of settlers from the mother country had begun. Over the next couple of decades all the niceties of English life – horse racing, postal deliveries, two-storey houses and newspapers – started to appear.

The promise of the industrial age, heralded in 1852 with the arrival in Durban of the first steamship, the *Sir Robert Peel*, actually pointed to the settlement's Achilles heel: the sand bar across the harbour mouth which prevented large vessels from entering. Work to clear it continued through the 1850s and beyond, while in 1860 the first railway tracks in town were laid. More than three hundred indentured **Indian labourers** arrived to work in the KwaZulu-Natal cane fields, planting the seeds for South Africa's lucrative **sugar industry** and the city's now substantial Indian community.

The British **conquest of the Zulus** in 1879, and the imposition of taxes on the defeated warrior nation, paved the way for their enforced entry into South Africa's growing cash economy. Many Zulus headed north in the 1890s to work on the Gauteng goldfields, while others were drawn south to enter Durban's expanding economy. In 1895, the completion of the railway connecting Johannesburg and Durban – which still carries hundreds of thousands of Zulu workers to Johannesburg every year – accelerated the process of migrant labour. This link to South Africa's industrial heartland, and the opening of Durban's harbour mouth to large ships in 1904, ensured the city's eventual pre-eminence as South Africa's principal harbour.

In 1922, in the face of growing Indian and African populations, Durban's strongly English city council introduced **legislation** controlling the sale of land in the city to non-whites, predating Afrikaner-led apartheid by 26 years. During the boom years of World War II, Africans flooded into the city in even greater numbers, leading to calls (which were ignored) for their recognition as permanent residents.

With the strict enforcement of **apartheid** in the 1950s, Durban saw a decade of ANC-led **protests**. These started with the country-wide Defiance Campaign in 1952, and reached a peak in 1959 when *shebeen* queens – the African women who ran speakeasies – took to the streets and attacked municipal beer halls in protest at police harassment. The ANC was quick to seize this local momentum, steering it towards nationwide marches and protests that led to nearly three years of turmoil, culminating in the government clampdown of 1961, when the authorities swamped the streets with troops, declared a state of emergency, and banned the ANC. Left with no peaceful option, the ANC formed its armed wing, with plans for a nationwide **bombing campaign** that was initiated with an explosion in Durban on December 15, 1961. Durban scored another first in 1973, when workers in the city initiated a wildcat strike, despite a total ban on black industrial action. This heralded the rebirth of South Africa's **trade unions** and reawakened anti-apartheid activity, sparking the final phase of the country's road to democracy.

Arrival and information

Durban International airport (☎031 451 6667) is 14km south of the centre on the Southern Freeway. The domestic and international terminals are in the same building, with arrivals on the south side and departures on the north side. Bus services leave every half hour (daily 8am–8pm; ☎031 465 1660; R25) for the twenty-minute journey from outside the arrivals terminal to the SAA building on Aliwal Street in the city centre. A metered taxi to the city costs around around R150. Julnic Tours run a shuttle service between the airport and city accommodation (R150 one-way; ☎031 205 9119).

There's an excellent **tourist information desk** in the arrival terminal (daily 6.30am–9pm), plus ten car rental companies, including Hertz and Avis. Windermere Car Hire (see p.490) will collect you from the airport free of charge if

KwaMashu & Gandhi Settlement ▲ ▲ Umhlanga Rocks

DURBAN SUBURBS

0   2 km

INDIAN OCEAN

Umgeni Canal

UMGENI ROAD

MORNINGSIDE

Battery Beach
♦ Snake Park
♦ Amphitheatre
North Beach

WINDERMERE
B E R E A

West St Jetty   North   South
South Beach   Pier   Pier
Addington   The
Beach   Point   The
Bluff

BEREA

Botanical
Gardens

CITY
CENTRE

MUSGRAVE

uShaka
Marine
World

♦ Shree
Ambalvanar
Alayam Temple

♦ Natal Society
of Arts Gallery

☐ Pleasure
Cruises
Yacht Mole

Marine
Terminal

♦ Sugar Terminal

Bay of Natal

CATO
MANOR

UNIVERSITY

MAYDON
WHARF

CONGELLA

WESTVILLE

UMBILO

Umbilo

BELLAIR

Umhlatuzana

N

Valley of a Thousand Hills

▼ Chatsworth, Durban International Airport & Port Edward

you're hiring a car from them. Absa Bank in the arrival terminal opens daily from 7am to 8pm, and there's a 24-hour ATM next to it.

By train

The Trans-Natal service from Johannesburg and the Trans-Oranje service from Cape Town via Free State both arrive at the grim **New Durban station** off NMR Avenue (☎031 361 7609), just north of the main commercial centre. The best option from here is to take one of the metered taxis that rank inside the station complex; a ride to the beachfront costs around R50.

By bus

Intercape (☎0861 287 287), Greyhound (☎031 334 9700) and Translux (☎031 308 8111) end their runs at the **Motorcoach Terminal** attached to the New Durban station complex. The Margate Mini Coach (☎039 312 1406) from the South Coast pulls in here, and also outside domestic departures at

Durban airport. Baz Bus (☎031 304 9099, ⓦwww.bazbus.com) stops at most of the Durban backpackers' lodges.

Two **minibus shuttles**, Rollercoaster Taxi (☎031 464 5858 or 072 101 7353) and Rasool's (☎031 208 0803), each run a door-to-door service twice a day between Johannesburg and Durban (picking up 5–6.30am & 4–5pm; 6–7hr) and will drop you anywhere in Durban. A number of other small companies operating limited routes within the province use other arrival points: the Cheetah Coach from Pietermaritzburg (☎033 342 2673) lets passengers off at the airport and outside the Local History Museum on Aliwal Street; the Umhlanga Express from Umhlanga Rocks (☎082 268 0651) drops off at a number of points in Durban, the most central of which is opposite Tourist Junction (see below). The Umhlanga Express will taxi you as far north as Ballito, by prior arrangement.

By minibus taxi

Long-distance **minibus taxis** from Gauteng arrive opposite the Umgeni Road entrance to the train station, while those from the South Coast and Transkei terminate at Berea Road in the Warwick Triangle area at the west of the city centre. Both are very busy points, rife with pickpockets, so take care of your baggage – and bear in mind that the city-centre and beachfront accommodation are a fairly brisk walk away. If you intend to stay in the Berea, catch a Mynah bus to Smith Street and the main bus depot, from where you'll be able to get another Mynah bus connection.

Information

The obvious first port of call for information is the central **Tourist Junction** at Old Station Building, 160 Pine Street (Mon–Fri 8am–4.30pm, Sat 9am–2pm; ☎031 304 4934, ⓦwww.durbanexperience.co.za), which houses Durban Africa (the city's tourist bureau) and Tourism KwaZulu-Natal (the province's excellent tourist bureau, ⓦwww.kzn.org.za). Also here are **KZN Wildlife** and **South African National Parks** booking offices, accommodation agents, and a couple of travel agents who can book intercity coaches and **tours** (including walking tours of the Grey Street area, city centre and historical tours; for other recommended local tour operators, see box on p.467).

Durban Africa and Tourism KwaZulu-Natal (who both also have offices at uShaka Marine World; see p.476) provide comprehensive brochures and free maps of the city and province. If you're planning to stay a while, it's worth investing in one of the several **street map directories** covering the city and suburbs in detail. MapStudio produces a range of maps, from mid-priced fold-out plans of the city to pricier charts that include the surrounding area. The best selection is at Adams Bookshop, 341 West Street (☎031 304 8571), in the centre, or at Exclusive Books, Lower Level, Pavilion Shopping Centre, in the suburb of Westville (☎031 265 0454). You can also pick up maps at any branch of the CNA chain.

City transport

The easiest way to explore Durban is by **car**. The city's freeways are well signposted, and with careful map-reading getting around is straightforward. You need to plan ahead, though, as Durbanites drive fast and there's no time to dither at lane changes and junctions. **Cycling** is safe along the beachfront, but hazardous on any major road. There are several car and bicycle **rental companies** in Durban; to find out where to get the best deal, either pick up one of the brochures at Tourist Junction or look in the *Yellow Pages*. We've recommended some larger operators in "Listings" (see p.490).

Buses

Durban's most useful urban transport is the cheap and regular **bus** system operated by Mynah and Aqualine (enquiries ☎031 309 5942), which cover the central districts, including the city centre, the beachfront, the Berea and Florida Road. If you want to get to the more far-flung suburbs, Durban Transport Municipal Buses (☎031 309 4126) is quite functional, although slightly the worse for wear and not as frequent. For quick and easy reference to **times and routes**, pop into the **Pine Street bus depot**, which is adjacent to The Workshop mall and is the starting point for most local bus services, or pick up a bus schedule from the Tourist Junction (see p.465).

Taxis and minibus taxis

There are several several reputable **taxi companies** in central Durban, including Aussies (☎031 309 7888), Eagle (☎031 368 1706), Swift Falcon (☎031 309 6771) and Zippy ☎031 202 7067. Mozzies (☎0860 669 943) has minibuses which can take up to fifteen people, making them good value to ferry a group around.

Minibus taxis can be hailed along any busy road. Although they bear no obvious identification, you can usually recognize them by the frighteningly loud music blaring from their sound systems; they also have a high accident rate. To get to town or the beachfront from any of the suburbs, stand along the sidewalk and signal assertively with an index finger. Minibuses follow set paths (you can get off at any point by asking the driver); once in the city centre, they follow West Street to the beachfront, but turn south into Marine Parade as far as Addington Beach.

Useful bus routes from the city centre

To North/South Beach Mynah buses leave from St Andrews Street, on the north side of Albert Park, which stretches down to the Victoria Embankment at the western edge of the city centre (an inner-city strip of high-rise apartments best avoided at night, especially if you're carrying luggage or cameras). From here they turn north into Russell Street, before running all the way east along West Street to Marine Parade, where they either strike north as far as Battery Beach, or south as far as Addington Beach. Boards on the front of the bus indicate whether they're bound for North or South Beach. On their return trip, buses head through the centre along Smith instead of West Street. Daily to South Beach: every 10min 6am–5pm, then hourly until 11pm; daily to North Beach: every 10min 6.10am–10.15pm.

To the Berea (Musgrave/Mitchell Park Circle) Mynah buses leave from the Pine Street bus depot, heading west down Smith Street to the Berea, taking in the restaurants and bars of Florida Road, and Musgrave Road, before returning to the city centre via Berea Road. Mon–Fri every 15min 6am–5pm, then hourly until 11pm, Sat slightly less frequent, Sun hourly 6.30am–7pm.

To Natal Society of Arts Gallery Aqualine buses (route #86/87) leave from the Pine Street bus depot and go to Glenmore, via Bulwer Road, for the NSA Gallery. Mon–Fri every 30min 6.45–8.30am, hourly 8.30am–5pm; Sat hourly; Sun 2 daily 7am and 5.30pm.

Durban tours and harbour rides

One of the safest and easiest ways to get under the skin of ethnic Durban is to take a **guided tour**, which can get you into African and Indian areas or out-of-the-way places. Standard three-hour tours cost around R250 per person and R400 for a full day tour.

Cycle Tours De Durban ☎031 564 0730. Relaxed two-wheeled tours around the city, including a trip to the Hindu temple and museums (R150 including guide).

Gailforce Tours ☎031 468 8609 or 083 643 1923, ⓔgailsnyman@hotmail.com. Tours of the coloured townships of Durban.

Strelitzia Tours ☎031 266 9480, ⓦwww.strelitziatours.com. Daily minibus trips around the major sights, the centre and the Berea, as well as trips further afield to the game parks, the Battlefields and up Sani Pass in the Ukhahlamba Drakensberg.

Tekweni Eco Tours ☎031 312 8727 or 083 468 9526, ⓦwww.tekweniecotours .co.za. Visits to Zulu villages in the Valley of a Thousand Hills for a Zulu meal and beer, traditional dancing and an encounter with a traditional healer. Also available are camping safaris into the Ukhahlamba Drakensberg.

Thuthuka Tours ☎082 264 2556, ⓦwww.thuthukatours.co.za. Discover the roots of resistance to apartheid by taking a township tour in the company of Langa Dube, whose late grandfather was the first president of the ANC. Langa can also take you on an overnight trip to his family homestead in a remote part of central Zululand.

Tours of Remembrance ☎031 337 7879 or 083 560 9999. A community-based tour company that can take you to the townships, the Gandhi settlement and Hindu temples.

Harbour rides

Ferry and Bay Services (☎031 301 1953) offers rides around the harbour (hourly 10am–5pm on the half-hour; R35). Sarie Marais Pleasure Cruises (☎031 305 4022) also runs reasonably priced rides around the harbour (Nov–April 10am–4pm hourly in school holidays on the half-hour; R35).

Accommodation

Durban's high-rise **accommodation** is concentrated along the **beachfront**, where you're close to the action, the city centre and public transport (though note the warnings on see box on p.477 about beachfront security). Far more affordable than the sleek towers of chain hotels offering sea views and swimming pools are self-catering **apartments**, largely on the beachfront, which offer good value if there are several of you sharing. It's always worth checking out the apartment before agreeing to stay, as the promotional brochures can be misleading. Expect to pay R30 per night for secure parking, plus R55 per person for a full buffet breakfast, where available.

While the **city centre** hotels are conveniently located, the area isn't great at night, when the deserted streets are potentially menacing; taking taxis to your doorstep is recommended after dark. An alternative to the city centre and beachfront is the **Berea** residential area west and north of the centre. It boasts the best backpackers' lodges in town, while its guesthouses and B&Bs are often housed in beautifully renovated old homes. There are plenty of restaurants and bars in the area too, in particular on Florida Road in **Morningside**.

Durban has a selection of **township homestays** where you can experience the warmth of urban Zulu hospitality. Durban Africa at Tourist Junction can arrange your accommodation as well as transport into the townships. And if you fancy basing yourself within an easy drive of the city, appealing possibilities include Umhlanga Rocks (see p.499) and Warner Beach (see p.493).

Beachfront and city centre establishments reviewed here appear on the map on pp.470–471; see the map on pp.480–481 for establishments in the Berea.

City centre

Durban Hilton 12–14 Walnut Rd ☎ 031 336 8100, ⓦ www.hilton.com. Conveniently located next to the International Convention Centre, and providing all the creature comforts you'd expect from this chain. **❼**

Hotel Formula 1 Near the train station, on the corner of NMR Ave and Jeff Taylor St ☎ 031 301 1551, ⓦ www.hotelformula1.co.za. No-frills chain hotel in a noisy area that's also potentially rough. If you arrive late at night by train or bus, though, the hotel is worth considering. **❸**

The Royal Hotel 267 Smith St ☎ 031 333 6000, ⓦ www.theroyal.co.za. Once Durban's finest hotel, but now feels a little oldfangled. Used mainly by business visitors, it's worth considering if you can afford five-star splendour and fancy the liveried service and its legendary *Ulundi* Indian restaurant. Discounts are often available. **❼**

Beachfront

The Balmoral 125 Marine Parade ☎ 031 368 5940, ⓦ www.raya-hotels.com. Dark timbers and historical photographs of Durban create a serious, colonial atmosphere. The rooms are large and feature classy fittings; most also have glorious sea views, and there's Internet access in the more expensive suites. The veranda is magnificent for sipping drinks on balmy summer nights while watching the buzz along the Marine Parade and the ocean beyond. **❺**

Banana Backpackers 61 Pine St, 1st floor, Ambassador House, city centre ☎ 031 368 4062, ⓔ aroutes@iafrica.com. Clean dorms and doubles in an old Durban building with a congenial courtyard, very close to the beach, Tourist Junction and the Pine St bus terminal. Dorms and rooms **❶**

The Blue Waters Hotel 175 Snell Parade ☎ 031 332 4272, ⓕ 031 337 5817. A delightful 1950s Durban landmark opposite Battery Beach, with mangroves on the pavement and leisure lounge with great views onto the oceanfront. **❹**

The Edward On the corner of Marine Parade and Seaview Rd ☎ 031 337 3681, ⓦ www.proteahotels .com. Crystal chandeliers, a colonial-style ambience, sea-view balconies and a ladies' bar leading onto a cool veranda make this Art Deco mansion the *grande dame* of the beachfront. Breakfast not included. **❹**

Holiday Inn Garden Court – Marine Parade 167 Marine Parade ☎ 031 337 2231,

ⓦ www.southernsun.com. All the rooms face the sea (those on the top floors are best); the view from the thirtieth-floor swimming pool is fabulous. A cool through-breeze and tropical vegetation offer respite against the summer heat, and a back entrance across from Victoria Park provides handy access to the city centre. **❸**

Silversands 16 Erskine Terrace, South Beach ☎ 031 332 7391, ⓔ silversands@worldonline .co.za. Along the far end of Addington Beach, near the Addington Hospital, these clean, comfortable and spacious apartments sleep two to eight people (cheaper for more sharing). **❸**

The Berea

Morningside

The Benjamin 141 Florida Rd ☎ 031 303 4233, ⓦ www.benjamin.co.za. A swish boutique hotel with stylish rooms and a swimming pool, in the heart of the Florida Rd action. Good value. **❹**

Goble Palms 120 Goble Rd ☎ 031 312 2598, ⓦ www.goblepalms.co.za. Exquisitely decorated home built in 1900, featuring a pool and a sunny patio with sea views. It's within walking distance of restaurants, and there's an intimate English-style pub below the house. **❹**

La Bordello 47 Campbell Rd ☎ 031 309 1001, ⓔ denise.beanbag@worldonline.co.za. A funky Moroccan-themed B&B housed in a former brothel, hence the name; the clientele consists largely of models and film-makers. It's next to the popular *Bean Bag Bohemia* restaurant and a block away from *Marco's* (see p.485). **❹**

Madeline Grove 116 Madeline Rd ☎ 031 303 5425, ⓦ www.madeline.co.za. Six charming self-contained units, each with a kitchenette stocked with all you need for a healthy breakfast. Florida Rd is only a short walk away. **❸**

McAllisters 11 Eighth Ave ☎ 031 303 4991, ⓦ www.mcallisterson8th.co.za. Well-appointed rooms with white linen and African artwork, built around a courtyard pool. **❸**

Meg's B&B 12 Nuttall Gardens ☎ 031 312 9045, ⓔ maasdyk@mweb.co.za. Home-away-from-home comforts in one of Durban's longest-established B&Bs. Meg's speciality is her lavish, beautifully presented breakfasts. **❸**

Rosetta House 126 Rosetta Rd ☎ & ⓕ 031 303 6180, ⓦ www.rosettahouse.co.za. Just four rooms with lush fabrics and loads of style, all with a/c and satellite TV, and there's a tranquil garden to relax in. ❸

Sommersby 17 Claribell Rd ☎031 312 8667 or 072 529 2594, ⓦwww.sommersby.co.za. Within walking distance of Florida Rd, this B&B is in a renovated Edwardian house, with wooden floors and Oregon pine furniture. ❸

Tekweni Backpackers 169 Ninth Ave ☎031 303 1433, ⓦwww.tekwenibackpackers.co.za. The cheapest accommodation around Florida Rd, with relaxing communal areas, pool table, a pool, bar and a shady veranda. Dorms ❶, rooms ❷

Elsewhere in the Berea

20 Palm Grove 367 Ridge Rd ☎031 240 9140, ⓦwww.20palmgrove.co.za. Well-equipped and comfortable self-catering units and B&B rooms, all with separate entrances, set in lush tropical gardens with two swimming pools. It's close to public transport and restaurants, and excellent value. ❸

Clyde Cottage 23 Clyde Ave ☎031 202 7577, ⓔjhopper@saol.com. Shaded by tall trees, this charming and comfortable B&B has four rooms and two self-catering units. It's within walking distance of shops and restaurants and on the main bus route. ❷

The Elephant House 745 Ridge Rd ☎031 208 9580, ⓔelephanthouse@mweb.co.za. A B&B in Durban's oldest house, built in 1850 as a hunting lodge, in the tranquil part of the ridge where the vegetation has won the day. The owners have a

good collection of African literature and love showing travellers around. ❸

Hippo Hide Lodge and Backpackers 2 Jesmond Rd ☎031 207 4366, ⓦwww.hippohide.co.za. A stunning, imaginative and cosy lodge in a beautiful garden with a rock pool. It's clean and quiet, with a guesthouse feel, and conveniently located on the bus route to the centre (10min). Some of the doubles are en suite, and there are also log cabins. Dorms ❶, rooms ❷

Laletsa Lodge 21/25 South Ridge Rd ☎031 201 0785, ⓦwww.laletsa.co.za. A restored old home with good views and African-flavoured decor, within walking distance of the Musgrave Centre mall, and a 10min bus ride to town. There's also a saltwater pool, barbecue facilities, halal buffet breakfasts and a/c rooms. ❷

Napier House 31 Napier Rd ☎031 207 6779. A stone's throw from the scenic Botanic Gardens, and offering charming rooms with the ambience of a country estate and an expansive view over the city. ❸

Nomad's Backpackers 70 Essenwood Rd ☎031 202 9709 or 082 920 5882, ⓦnomads.durban.co.za. A short walk from Musgrave Centre, on a main bus route (a 10min ride from the beach and Golden Mile). A black-bottomed swimming pool, a pool table, the *Bambooza Pub*, and friendly hosts who cook up a mean Durban curry, all add to the appeal. ❶

Windmill Ridge 81 Windmill Rd ☎031 201 4972 or 082 462 2927, ⓦwww.windmill-ridge.co.za. Five comfortable rooms, all en suite. Close to Musgrave Centre. ❸

The City

Durban's **city centre**, confined by the Bay of Natal to the south and the beaches of the Indian Ocean to the east, grew around the arrival point of the first white settlers; the remains of the historical heart are concentrated around **Francis Farewell Square**, five minutes' walk north of the bay. Today the central business area, studded with high-rise buildings and packed with traffic, lacks views of the ocean and gives no hint you're in a seaside city.

On the western side of the city centre, around Grey and Victoria streets, lies Durban's most fascinating area, the **Indian district**. This is where you'll find a pulsing warren of bazaars, alleyways, the Juma mosque and Victoria Street market, as well as Zulu traders selling *umuthi*, traditional herbal medicines. Although the laws enforcing the divide between the white-dominated business centre and the Indian district have gone, each area still has a distinct feel. Further west and deeper downtown, situated in the hub of taxi ranks and bus depots, the **Warwick Triangle** seethes with ceaseless activity; the *shebeens* do a brisk trade while the poorest of the poor spend the nights on their market stalls under plastic and cardboard.

RESTAURANTS, CAFÉS, BARS & CLUBS

The Brasserie Smorgasbord	5
Cargo Hold	17
Charlie Crofts Wharfside Diner	16
Cool Runnings	6
The Dockyard Theatre	20
The Famous Fish Co	18
Franko's	11
Imbizo	19
Jewel of India	1
Joe Kool's Bar & Grill	2
Little Gujarat	7
Model Dairy	10
New Café Fish	14
Oriental	9
Roma Revolving Restaurant	12
Saagries House of Curries	4
Tilt	3
TransAfrica Express	13
Victoria Bar	15
Victory Lounge	8

KWAZULU-NATAL

5

470

DURBAN CITY CENTRE & BEACHFRONT

M4

A & Battery Beach

Amphitheatre
Flea Market

Amphitheatre

Mini
Town

Fitzsimmons
Snake Park

Bay of Plenty
Beach

INDIAN
OCEAN

North Beach

Kingsmead
Cricket
Ground

Rachel Finlayson
Baths

International
Convention
Centre

Exhibition
Centre

Dairy Beach

Sea View

Natural Science Museum
& Durban Art Gallery

Old Courthouse
Museum

SAA Building (Airport
Shuttle arrivals &
departures)

South Beach

BAT
Centre

VICTORIA EMBANKMENT

Natal
Bay

QUAYSIDE ROAD

Addington Beach

ACCOMMODATION	
Balmoral	F
Banana Backpackers	G
Blue Waters	A
Durban Hilton	C
The Edward	E
Holiday Inn	
Garden Court	D
Hotel Formula 1	B
Royal Hotel	H
Silversands	I

471

The Point, uShaka Marine World, 17 , 18 , 19 & 20

Durban's **beachfront** on the eastern edge of the centre has one of the city's busiest concentrations of restaurants and a surfeit of tacky family entertainment – and a growing reputation for crime. South of the centre, skirting the north of the bay, **Victoria Embankment** was once one of Durban's most desirable residential areas but it, too, is witnessing a decline. The Embankment provides access to the northern side of the **harbour**; despite its handful of trendy pubs and restaurants, this compelling industrial marinescape is still the real economic hub of the city. Enclosing the northern half of the harbour, the **Point**, a seedy peninsula protruding south from the city centre, is slowly transforming itself. The bottom end has now been restored, and a couple of decent pubs and clubs have moved in as well as some excellent restaurants – and it has the best view of the city across the water. Rising above the flat city centre and harbour is the **Berea**, a desirable residential district on a cooler ridge which, despite its proximity to the centre, has luxuriant gardens alive with the sounds of birds, and fashionable restaurants, cinemas and shopping malls.

Much further afield lie dormitory towns for blacks who commute vast distances to work every day. Among these areas are the apartheid **ghettos** of KwaMashu, Inanda and Clermont to the northwest. **Cato Manor**, the closest township to the city, provides an easily accessible vignette of South Africa's growing urban contradictions.

The centre

Standing at the heart of colonial Durban, **Francis Farewell Square** is hemmed in by the centre's two main thoroughfares, West Street and Smith Street. A sultry palm-fringed garden overlooked by some fine old buildings, the square marks the site where the British adventurers Francis Farewell and Henry Fynn set up Durban's first white encampment to trade ivory with the Zulus. Today, down-and-outs enjoy its lawns, dotted with statues of city fathers, while the yellows and blues of the **Cenotaph**, a marvellous Art Deco monument to the fallen of World War I, creates an eye-catching focus for the square. The granite obelisk is decorated with ceramics depicting angels delivering the soul of a dead soldier. Regarded initially by Durban's prim citizens as improperly vibrant, it clearly also offended an anti-apartheid activist, who bombed it in 1984 – but today the monument is intact. North of here at 160 Pine Street are the remnants of the **Natal Great Railway Station**, built in 1894 and recycled a century later as shops and the Tourist Junction information centre.

City Hall and the Old Courthouse Museum

East of the Cenotaph, the imposing neo-Baroque **City Hall** is the monumental centrepiece of the area. Erected in 1910, it now houses the **Natural Science Museum** on its ground floor (Mon–Sat 8.30am–4pm, Sun 11am–4pm; free). Along with an array of stuffed animals (useful if you want to brush up on your mammals before heading north to the game reserves) is the "KwaNunu" section, featuring oversized insect specimens such as cockroaches – all a little too close to home for anyone living in Durban, where such creatures, known as "Durban prawns", are an ongoing menace and a constant topic for urban legends.

A far better reason to cross the City Hall's threshold is to visit the **Durban Art Gallery** upstairs (Mon–Sat 8.30am–4pm, Sun 11am–2pm; free). This fine collection includes Art Nouveau glassware by Lalique, bronzes by Rodin and Victorian paintings, but is most notable for its pioneering vision back in the 1970s in becoming the first gallery in the country to collect **black South**

African art. This approach has since been expanded into the recognition of indigenous craft as an art form of equal status with painting or sculpture, which is why the gallery has an outstanding collection of **hlabisa** baskets. In no way to be confused with cheap souvenirs bought at roadside stalls, the traditional craft of *hlabisa* was revived in the province around two decades ago, and is now highly sought after by galleries and collectors worldwide.

Entered from Aliwal Street, the **Old Courthouse Museum** (Mon–Sat 8.30am–4pm, Sun 11am–4pm; free) east of City Hall was Durban's first two-storey building, erected in 1866 in the Natal Veranda style, characterized by wide eaves to throw off heavy subtropical downpours. Housed here in a somewhat austere atmosphere is a reconstruction of Henry Francis Fynn's wattle-and-daub hut, Durban's first European structure.

Tourist Junction, Workshop Mall and Central Park

The **African Art Centre** on the first floor of Tourist Junction is the heart of Durban's artistic life. Primarily a gallery and shop where many rural artists sell their work, the centre is also involved in work to move rural craftsmen away from the production of curios and towards artistic expression. Among the artists who have gained recognition through the centre are Tito Zungu, who draws pen-and-ink aeroplanes and boats; Bheki Myeni, who sculpts wooden insects; and Mzwakhe Mbatha, originally an airline cook and now a carver of wooden aircraft. North of here is the **Workshop Mall**, which sounds more interesting than it proves to be, although it does provide parking and every type of shop you're likely to need, conveniently close to Tourist Junction. **Central Park** on the north side of the mall offers a large green space, with a lovely mosaic water fountain as its focus.

The Exhibition Centre and the Kwa Muhle Museum

Nearby to the east, the **Exhibition Centre** in Walnut Road is the venue for a busy Sunday flea market, where you can pick up trinkets, authentic didgeridoos and (a hot tip if you need footwear) handmade leather shoes and hiking boots from the Ground Cover workshop in the KwaZulu-Natal Midlands. The market's popularity is also its drawback – you'll need to shop quickly to avoid getting smeared by *boerewors* rolls or getting crushed.

The **Kwa Muhle Museum** at 130 Ordnance Road (Mon–Sat 8am–4pm; free), also known as the Apartheid Museum, should not be missed if you have the slightest interest in understanding modern South Africa. Permanent exhibitions include one on the Durban System, which enabled the city council to finance the administration of African affairs without ever spending a penny of white ratepayers' money. It achieved this by granting itself a monopoly on the brewing of sorghum beer, which it sold through vast, African-only municipal beer halls. The resulting revenue was used to ensure that blacks lived in an "orderly" way. The exhibit also illustrates the Pass System, one of the most hated aspects of apartheid, through which constant tabs could be kept on Africans and their influx into the urban areas. Look out, too, for photographs of life in the single-sex, artificially tribalized worker hostels, which deliberately sowed divisions among blacks by creating separations and divisions, and so played its part in much of the current violence in South Africa.

Grey Street and around

Where **Grey Street** draws a north–south line across the city, the pace accelerates perceptibly, and you leave behind the formal city centre for the densely packed warren of shops and living quarters of Durban's central **Indian**

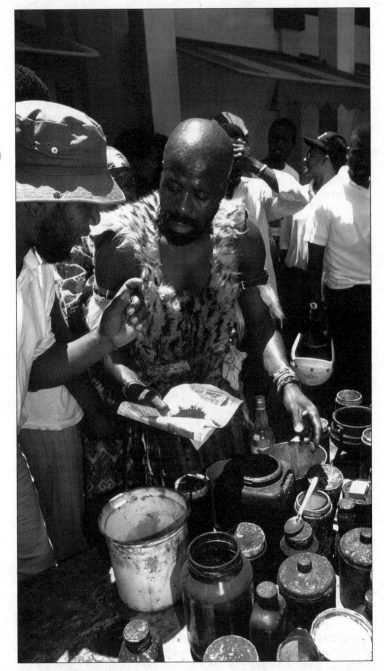

△ Victoria Street Market

district. Post-1910 Union-style architecture is well preserved here and, along with minarets and steeples, punctuates the skyline with an eclectic roofscape. Down at street level, the rich cultural blend includes African street vendors selling herbs, fruit and trinkets outside the Indian general dealers and spice merchants. If the crowds feel too intimidating, you can always explore this area on one of the reasonably priced daily **walking tours** from Tourist Junction (see box on p.467).

On the corner of Grey and Queen streets stands the **Juma Musjid** and its gilt-domed minarets, completed in 1927. It's the largest mosque in the southern hemisphere, and the area's focal point, although Durban's Indian population is predominantly Hindu. You're welcome to enter the mosque, but make sure you leave your shoes at the door. The colonnaded verandas give way to the alley of the bazaar-like **Madressa Arcade** next door, which provides tantalizing glimpses through mountains of coloured plastic bowls and draped bolts of cloth into general dealers cluttered with aluminium pots and kettles, and Indian traders peddling kerosene lamps, tailor-made outfits and beads. The arcade emerges with a start into Cathedral Street, dominated by the **Emmanuel Cathedral**, built in 1902 in Gothic Revival style.

North across Queen Street, the **Victoria Street Market** is a bright building with purple minarets, where traders sell curios and spices with labels that include "mother-in-law exterminator". The hectic fish market downstairs can provide drama, particularly on Saturdays when the stall holders compete to sell their stocks before the Sunday close-down.

A little further west, African hawkers unable to afford official stalls gather on **Russell Street**, where they scrape an existence trading *umuthi*, used goods or anything that might raise a few bucks. Extreme poverty dictates that they spend nights on their market pitches in plastic and cardboard hovels: the minibus-taxi fare to any of the township areas would cost an entire day's takings. West of Russell Street and jammed between the railway tracks to the west and the N3 into town on its northern side, **West Street Cemetery** is zoned according to religion, with many of the city's colonial big names buried here, such as Durban's first mayor, George Cato, and the Victorian documentary painter, Thomas Baines. In the Muslim section some tombstones are inscribed "*hagee*" or "*hafez*", the former indicating someone who has been to Mecca and the latter an individual who managed to memorize the entire Koran.

Warwick Triangle

In an Africanized *Bladerunner* setting west of Grey Street, concrete freeways run overhead chaotic roadways and minibus taxi ranks; here you'll find Durban's real urban heart of hawkers, shacks and *shebeens*. You'll need to be bold to explore the **Warwick Triangle**, which lies between Berea Road, Brooke Street and Cannongate – police advise tourists to go in a group, to leave cameras behind and to wear nothing easily snatched.

The gateway to the triangle is across Brook Street – known until 1988 as Slaughterhouse Road, because butchers slaughtered livestock here – and then through the Berea station concourse and across the Market Road footbridge. The station concourse, which serves most of the African townships, pumps with reggae and the music of popular South African musicians, while hawkers sell baseball caps, patent leather shoes and tortoise shells. As you move across the footbridge, take a look at the truncated flyover alongside the station, going nowhere, but now the site for shacks. On a buttress at the end of the flyover, an eight-metre mural of the African goddess Nomkhubulwana stretches out her arms in a gesture of greeting and protection.

Durban's major fruit, vegetable and flower **market**, operating in the early morning only, lies between Warwick Avenue and Market Road, extending well beyond its walls in a dense mass of vendors. The shopping is frenetic; take your own basket and load up with the cheapest produce in town, from aubergines and jackfruit to betel nut for red-stained lips and a two-minute rush.

Victoria Embankment

The **Victoria Embankment**, or the Esplanade, is Durban's palm-lined city avenue, connecting Point Road in the east to Maydon Wharf Road (which leads to the container terminal piers and the dry dock off Bay Road) in the west. The Embankment was the prime residential area during the city's early development in the nineteenth century, and it's here, one block north at the east end of the road, that the **Old House Museum**, 31 St Andrews Street (Mon–Sat 8.30am–4pm, Sun 11–4pm; donation invited), is sited. Once the home of Sir John Robinson, who became Natal's first prime minister in 1893, the renovated settler house serves as a reminder of Durban's colonial heritage.

Along the Embankment is the entrance to the **Yacht Mole**, a slender break-water jutting into the bay and home to the Point and Royal Natal Yacht clubs, with an amazing variety of craft. Here you'll also find the upmarket *The New Café Fish* bar and restaurant, which specializes in great seafood (see p.485). A walk along here provides both a photogenic view of Durban from across the water and a breather from the city traffic. A little further east along the dockside, a statue of **Dick King** celebrates his heroic ride to save Durban (see p.462). Further east still is the **BAT (Bartle Arts Trust) Centre** (ⓦ www .batcentre.co.za; access is via the Yacht Mole), an industrial-chic arts devel-opment and community venue boasting a concert hall, practical visual art workshops, classes and exhibition galleries. The *Trans African Express Restaurant* upstairs (see p.485) provides a magnificent lookout for watching the passing harbour scene. Regular drum circles as well as jazz and *maskanda* performances are also staged here (see p.487).

Back on the Esplanade, heading east towards the Stanger Street intersection, enter the Harbour at Port Entrance no. 3 and follow the signs to the **Ocean Terminal Building**, which harks back to the romantic days of sea travel and is one of Durban's architectural masterpieces. Formerly the harbour reception building, this is now the headquarters for Portnet, the public utility that main-tains South Africa's harbours. Although you can't enter the building, the view from outside it at night, looking back onto the city, is spectacular.

The Point

Striking south from the city centre, **Point Road** was known in its heyday – in the early 1900s – as Africa's most exciting thoroughfare and Durban's hottest red-light district. It cuts down the **Point**, the northernmost of the two arms that enclose Durban's harbour in the Bay of Natal. At the city end of the road, tawdry hotels rent out rooms by the hour and scantily clad women linger by the roadside, but with the opening in 2004 of **uShaka Marine World** at the opposite end of Point Road and an upmarket residential area being built next to it, the Point has started to change for the better. This impressive water adventure wonderland is a tropical African theme park, with palm trees, fake rock formations and thatched *bomas*. The most appealing section is **uShaka Sea World** (daily 9am–5pm; R90), designed in and around a superb mockup of a wrecked 1920s cargo ship. The main entrance leads you down to the darkened hull with its broken wood, battered engine room, ropes and slop-ing floors. The walls of the hull serve as windows into the "ocean" (actually a series of large tanks) where you can see turtles, pipe fish, octopus, sharks and a host of other marine life. Aquarium guides are available to answer questions and take you **snorkelling** in one of the tanks (R50 for 45min including gear). Also part of the complex are **Dolphin and Seal World**, with daily shows (12pm and 3pm) and **uShaka Wet 'n Wild** (daily 9am–5pm; R65), a series of pools and water slides.

The **uShaka Village Walk** development and **uShaka Beach** (the southern section of Addington beach) are open from 9am until late. The Village Walk has plenty of restaurants, making it a great nighttime venue, and an excellent **tourist office** (daily 9am–9pm) with an Internet café. Here you can catch jazz at *Imbizo Restaurant and Jazz Bar* (see p.487) or have a meal with the shark tank in view at the *Cargo Hold* (see p.484).

Maydon Wharf and Dalton Road

Maydon Wharf wraps around the harbour's western edge in a photogenic complex of functional industrial architecture, most notable of which are the three dramatic sugar silos at the **Sugar Terminal**, 57 Maydon Wharf Road. The terminal, whose design has been patented and used internationally, has become something of a tourist attraction; a tour (Mon–Fri 8.30am, 10am, 11.30am, 2pm; R15) gives you one hour of sugary history and access to half a million tons of sugar (head to the SA Sugar Association Tour Centre; ☎031 365 8153).

Inland from the Sugar Terminal, across the Southern Freeway, the Dalton Road area clings closer to the city centre than any other African residential area. Craftsmen toil in the dingy hive of activity that constitutes **Dalton Road Market**, turning out traditional Zulu regalia including *amabheshu* (leather aprons), shields, *izimboko* (staffs), dancing sticks and beadwork. Every Saturday night, the *Dalton Road Men's Hostel* comes alive with *iscathamiya* concerts, which start around midnight and continue into the small hours, with competing groups singing in unaccompanied harmony. This genuine Durban experience would be worth catching, but it's inadvisable to come to this ropey part of town at night unless you know someone involved.

The beachfront

Durban's **beachfront**, a high-energy holiday strip just east of the centre, is South Africa's most developed seaside, one to avoid unless you enjoy unabashed kitsch and garish amusement parks. This six-kilometre stretch from the Umgeni River in the north to the Point in the south was traditionally called the **Golden Mile**, but it's becoming known as Mugger's Mile, which is why so many middle-class Gauteng families are breaking the habit of generations and deserting the beachfront for the safer (white, middle-class) sands north and south of Durban.

Beachfront safety

With tourists venturing onto beaches wearing expensive watches and jewellery and carrying large wads of cash, Durban's beaches are notorious hunting grounds for sharks – not of the piscean variety. **Muggings** here, though common, are usually avoidable: stay in a group, and don't go out alone at night, no matter how enticing the seafront seems on a balmy evening. **Street children** positively thrive on the rich pickings of Durban's beachfront: no matter how small they look, many are skilful pickpockets and accomplished bag-snatchers.

Addington Beach, the southernmost swimming strand, draws Durban families to its wide expanse of sand and lawns, and is a favourite spot for apprentice surfers. Just north lies **South Beach**, the busiest beach in South Africa, which nets visitors with the start of the beachfront tourist tack. Further along Marine Parade, you'll find paddling pools, stepping stones, an aerial cableway and amusement rides. The only redeeming feature along here is the saltwater **Rachel Finlayson Baths** (daily: summer 6am–8.30pm, winter 6am–4.30pm; R4), which offer sheltered swimming and sunbathing. Next is **Dairy Beach**, so called because of the milking factory that once stood here; now regarded as one of the country's best surfing beaches, it's also home to the Oceans Entertainment Centre, whose bars and restaurants are popular with the surfer-groupie crowd.

Dairy Beach adjoins **North Beach** and the adjacent **Bay of Plenty**, both of which host the international professional surfing contest held every July. North Beach is Durban's prime angling, bathing and surfing beach, made even more popular by the presence of hip bars and restaurants. Between Snell Parade and the pedestrian walkway at the Bay of Plenty is the **Amphitheatre**, the venue for Sunday flea markets. Here, local hawkers are joined by travelling merchants from Zimbabwe, Malawi and as far afield as Kenya, who trundle down the continent to sell their wares for two weeks before returning to restock. Rickshaws also gather here, their ornate carriages pulled by Zulus elaborately decked out in beads and streamers.

Just north of the Bay of Plenty, near the corner of Snell Parade and Old Fort Road, **Mini Town** is scale replica of Durban's landmarks (daily 9am–4.30pm; R15), great fun for kids; walkways lead you past hotels, beaches and the airport, giving you a bird's-eye view of the city. A kilometre further north is the massive **Suncoast Casino**, a mock Art Deco entertainment complex with restaurants, gambling tables, eight cinemas and a pristine private beach (R5). Attached to the casino is **Waterworld**, a water extravaganza of pools and slides. Further north, the beachfront hype steadily diminishes with **Battery Beach**, which has good swimming.

The Berea

West of the city centre, high on a north–south ridge, the **Berea** is Durban's oldest and most desirable residential district, where mansions and apartment blocks enjoy airy views to the harbour and the sea. Its palmy avenues provide an alternative to the torrid city centre and beachfront for accommodation, eating and entertainment. The term Berea actually has two meanings locally; the suburban area immediately north and west of the city centre is called the Berea, though within this is a suburb known as the Berea, as well as suburbs such as Morningside and Musgrave.

Undulating **Ridge Road** cuts a six-kilometre axis through the Berea from the Umgeni River in the north to the University of KwaZulu-Natal. South of the N3, which passes through the Berea to the city, and east of Ridge Road, in Bulwer Road, the **Natal Society of Arts Gallery** (Tues–Fri 11am–5pm, Sat 10am–4pm & Sun 11am–3pm; free), or NSA, adjacent to Bulwer Park, provides a breezy venue for taking in fortnightly exhibitions by local artists. Designed for the local climate, the 1990s building is a mass of interlinked spaces, divided by a timber screen that forms a veranda. The gallery shop has a good collection of original art pieces and cheaper, jazzy creations, and there's a great coffee shop (longer hours than the gallery) to relax in.

A little way northwest of the centre and east of Musgrave, Durban's **Botanical Gardens** (daily: mid-April to mid-Sept 7.30am–5.15pm; mid-Sept to mid-April 7.30am–5.45pm) were established in 1849. They're famous for their cycad collection, which includes *Encephalartos woodii*, one of the rarest specimens in the world. The gardens also boast cool paths, excellent picnic spots, a lovely tea house and a magnificent array of orchids. A notice board outside the entrance advertises forthcoming events, including regular KwaZulu-Natal Philharmonic Orchestra **concerts**.

Head several blocks north from here and west into Mariott Road, and you'll find another magnificent garden at **Muckleneuk** on the corner of Essenwood Road (Mon–Fri 8.30am–4.30pm or by appointment; ☎031 207 3432, ✆harkness@nu.ac.za; tours R15). The Cape Dutch–revival former homestead of sugar baron Sir Marshal Campbell, it's also Durban's premier museum, with one of the finest private collections of Africana in the country, including material relating to KwaZulu-Natal's ethnic heritage. The **Killie Campbell Africana Library and Musuem** at 229 Mariott Road (Mon–Fri 8.30am–4.30pm, Sat 9am–noon) is well known for its comprehensive collection of books, manuscripts and photographs, while the **William Campbell collections** (same times) comprise artworks and excellent examples of Cape Dutch furniture. Also here is the **Mashu Museum of Ethnology** (same times), consisting of a superb collection of Zulu crafts, including tools, weapons, beadwork and pottery.

Cato Manor

A short drive west of the city centre takes you through **Cato Manor**, offering a graphic cross-section of Durban's twentieth-century history, where you can see a juxtaposition of African squatter camps, Hindu temples and vegetation mingling in the heart of the city's middle-class suburbs. A large area in a valley below the Berea, Cato Manor was named after Durban's first mayor, **George Cato**, who arrived here in 1839. During the first half of the last century, the district was home to much of Durban's Indian community, who built temples on its hills. They were later joined by Africans, who were forced into crowded slums because of the shortage of housing. In 1949, an incident in which an Indian trader assaulted a Zulu man flared up into Durban's worst **riot**, with thousands of Africans attacking Indian stores and houses, leaving 142 people dead.

Because Cato Manor was right in the middle of white suburbs, the apartheid government began enforcing the Group Areas Act in the 1960s, moving Africans north to KwaMashu and Indians south to Chatsworth, leaving a derelict wasteland guarded only by the handful of Hindu temples left standing. The vacuum was filled again in the late 1980s, when Africans pouring into Durban built the closely packed tin shacks that line Bellair Road, winding its way through Cato Manor's valley.

Along this interesting, but not altogether safe, drive (carjackers are a potential hazard), it's well worth stopping to visit the **Shree Ambalvanar Alayam Second River Hindu Temple**, a National Monument in Bellair Road (something you can safely do on a tour; see box on p.467). Leave the city centre on the M13, take the Brickfield Road exit and then turn left into the M10, which becomes Bellair Road; the temple is on the right if you're coming from town, just before the Edwin Swales freeway. The building is a 1947 reconstruction of the first Hindu temple in Africa, built in 1875 on the banks of the Umbilo River and subsequently destroyed by floods. The beautifully carved entrance

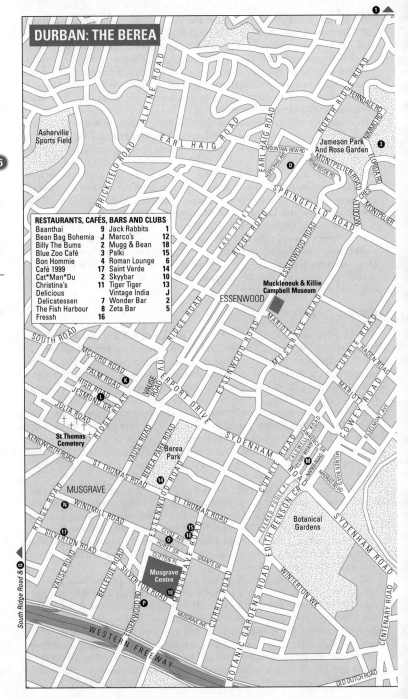

DURBAN: THE BEREA

RESTAURANTS, CAFÉS, BARS AND CLUBS

Baanthai	9	Jack Rabbits	1
Bean Bag Bohemia	J	Marco's	12
Billy The Bums	2	Mugg & Bean	18
Blue Zoo Café	3	Palki	15
Bon Hommie	4	Roman Lounge	6
Café 1999	17	Saint Verde	14
Cat*Man*Du	2	Skybar	10
Christina's	11	Tiger Tiger	13
Delicious		Vintage India	J
Delicatessen	7	Wonder Bar	2
The Fish Harbour	8	Zeta Bar	5
Fressh	16		

Asherville
Sports Field

Jameson Park
And Rose Garden

Muckleneuk & Killie
Campbell Museum

ESSENWOOD

St Thomas
Cemetery

Berea
Park

MUSGRAVE

Botanical
Gardens

Musgrave
Centre

South Ridge Road & ⓒ

N

Mitchell
Park

WINDERMERE

Sutton
Park

Absa
Stadium

STAMFORD
HILL

Ike's Books
Collectables

GREYVILLE

Train
Station

Blue Waters Hotel & Battery Beach

ACCOMMODATION

20 Palm Grove	K
The Benjamin	H
Clyde Cottage	O
The Elephant House	D
Goble Palms	A
Hippo Hide Lodge and Backpackers	L
La Bordello	J
Laletsa Lodge	Q
Madeline Grove	E
McAllisters	I
Meg's B&B	B
Napier House	M
Nomad's Backpackers	P
Rosetta House	C
Sommersby	F
Tekweni Backpackers	G
Windmill Ridge	N

0   500 m

Tourist Junction

doors are originals salvaged from the flood, while the facade is adorned with a pantheon of wonderfully garish Hindu deities. Around Easter every year the temple hosts a **firewalking festival** in which unshod devotees walk across red-hot coals, emerging unscathed. Visitors are welcome to join the thousands of worshippers who come to honour the goddess Draudpadi.

KwaMashu, Shembe and Inanda

Even though they're not hard to reach with your own wheels, some quintessential Durban experiences rarely make it into the pages of tourist brochures. Driving, you can visit the place where Gandhi dreamed up passive resistance, witness the epic religious ceremonies of the Zulu-Christian Shembe sect and walk among the serene buildings of Inanda, a nineteenth-century seminary for Zulu girls. A word of **warning**: driving through some of the areas covered here carries a certain risk, and you're advised to go with someone familiar with the road and local customs. Be particularly aware of the national penchant for car-jacking, and check with Tourist Junction as to the best **maps** to use. Alternatively, take one of the trips organized by Thuthuka Tours, Tours of Remembrance and Strelitzia Tours (see box on p.467).

Heading out of town towards the North Coast on the R102, take the Inanda Phoenix exit along the M25. As you leave the R102 you'll see the suburb of Duff's Road on the left; look up the hillside for Dookie Ramdaari's **Aeroplane House** and his son's **Ship House** a few metres away. An affluent Indian bus builder with a taste for the unconventional, Ramdaari was a voracious traveller, a passion reflected in his first home built in the form of a ship, sailing east out of Duff's Road Indian township. Poised for take-off, the Aeroplane House – his current abode – has wings, an undercarriage, a television room with row seats in the tail and a superb lounge in the cockpit.

KwaMashu and the Gandhi Settlement

Further on to Inanda, you'll pass the African township of **KwaMashu** on the left, established in the late 1950s to house residents of Cato Manor who had been forcibly resettled. It displays all the unimaginative planning typical of such low-cost housing schemes. The area is a sea of hills, vegetation and colour, which makes it tempting to romanticize the locality's poverty.

A well-signposted right turn off the M25 takes you to the **Gandhi Settlement** (daily 8.30am–5pm; donation expected). On the eastern edge of the vast Inanda squatter camp, it's the site of a self-help scheme established by Mohandas Gandhi soon after his arrival in Durban in 1903. It was from here that Gandhi began to forge his philosophy of passive resistance; in a sad irony, violence brought it to ruin in 1985 when squatters from the adjacent camp looted and razed the settlement. With the help of the Indian Government the settlement was rebuilt in time for its centenary celebration. A bronze bust of Gandhi now stands near the entrance to his house, **Sarvodaya** ("a place for the upliftment for all"), the building now a **museum** focusing on his time in South Africa and on Indian resistance to segregation. The area now hums with roadside traders selling anything from water to hair makeovers or "Durban poison" – a highly sought-after type of *dagga* (marijuana).

Shembe

The M25 continues to **Ekupakumeni** ("the elated place"), where two "stars" laid in stone in the hilly landscape mark the spots where meteorites from the 1906 appearance of Halley's Comet struck the earth. This is also the site of the

Shembe settlement, established by the Holy Church of Nazareth as a refuge for Africans dispossessed as a result of the Land Act of 1913. According to the founding history of the church, its prophet Isaya Shembe was "called" in 1910 to the summit of a mountain outside Durban, where he vowed before God to bring the Gospel to the Zulus. The church drew membership from rural people whose lives had been devastated by colonization and who were eager to embrace Christianity, but were unwilling to give up traditional customs. Shembe brought about a rich religious synthesis that rejected drinking, smoking and cults, while encouraging a work ethic that centred around crafts, giving rise to a sect that now has tens of thousands of adherents.

Continuing to the Inanda police station at the top of the hill, turn left to descend into the valley and cross the Umhlanga River bridge. At the next intersection, take the dirt road to the left, past the sports field, and turn left again to view **Ebuhleni**, where every July devotees of the Holy Church of Nazareth gather for a month of worship. Ignoring the dirt road turn-off, head straight on to reach the Inanda Dam. The deep gorge to your left is the **Inanda Falls**, where the Shembe have baptismal ceremonies, which visitors are welcome to attend.

The settlement resembles an emerging medieval city, replete with winding pathways negotiating the narrow spaces between buildings. Many homes are owned by believers who come to Ebuhleni only at festival times, timeshare Zulu-style. On these occasions, the men and women live on different sides of the village, and the unmarried maidens live in a separate enclosure. At the entrance gates to the settlement, rows of tables display what appear to be religious knick-knacks for sale to tourists, but which are actually religious artefacts revered by the converted of Shembe. Among the items are holographic images of Isaya Shembe, and key rings with religious icons embedded in perspex. A range of traditional outfits are sold in the village, from men's ceremonial skirts to magnificent women's headdresses.

The Inanda Seminary

It's strongly recommended that you visit Inanda in the company of a guide who knows the area well. From Ebuhleni, make your way back to the M25, and continue to the **Inanda Seminary** along a well-indicated route. The seminary, whose dignified old buildings give it an air of serenity, was established in 1869 by Daniel Lindley, an American missionary and pastor of the Voortrekkers. It's also the oldest secondary school for African girls in southern Africa, and played a pioneering role in the liberation of Zulu women. Staff members have always been drawn from all racial groups, which is why the school received no funding from the apartheid educational authorities after 1957. The story of Inanda between 1869 and 1969 is recounted in a book by Agnes Wood, *Shine Where You Are*. To return to Durban, simply turn tail and head east along the M25.

Eating

Eating out is a favourite pastime in Durban, whether you're a suburbanite relishing the seafood of a swanky restaurant, or an African worker shelling out a few rand for a filling Indian takeaway. Although all types of cooking are found here, **Indian** food is what Durban excels at – hardly surprising for a city with one of the largest Indian populations outside Asia. The Indian takeaways of the city centre are good places to try *bunny chow* – Durban's big contribution to the national fast-food scene – and the not-dissimilar *rotis* (Indian bread) stuffed with curries. *Shisanyama* outlets at the African markets and around the taxi ranks offer hunks of meat cooked over an open fire. For a city that prides itself on its dedication to hedonism, Durban turns in disappointingly early; **closing time** for most restaurants is around 10.30pm.

If you're **self-catering**, you can buy groceries at any of the supermarket chains in shopping malls. Tropical fruit is available in season from supermarkets and street traders, and also at the Indian market off Warwick Avenue; in summer, try masala pineapple here – cubes of the skewered fruit sprinkled with red-hot spices. Finally, *Mozarts* at uShaka Marine World is recommended for terrific **ice cream** and sorbet concoctions, in forty flavours (daily 9am–9pm).

City centre

Inexpensive Indian **takeaways** abound in this part of Durban. *Little Gujarat* at 107 Prince Edward Street, the *Model Dairy* in Gardiner Street, *Patel's Vegetarian House* in Rama House, Grey Street and *Victory Lounge* on the corner of Grey and Victoria streets are all noted for their *bunny chow*; all open very early and tend to be shut by 5pm. *Patel's* is also recommended for its traditional sweetmeats. Otherwise, the *Oriental* takeaway opposite Tourist Junction does a hotchpotch of fare – delicious Lebanese *shawarmas*, plus pies and curries. If you're hankering for something a little slicker in the heart of town, try *Franko's* at 300 Smith Street, an unpretentious café which serves great pepper steak and light snacks (Mon–Fri 7am–3.30pm, Sat 8am–12.30pm.)

Beachfront

Restaurants

The Brasserie Smorgasbord *The Edward*, 149 Marine Parade ☎031 337 3681. This beachfront hotel has delicious breakfasts on the terrace and very good smorgasbord lunches comprising a magnificent spread of seafoods, including crayfish, oysters and calamari. Come here for a splurge. Daily noon–10pm.

Jewel of India *Holiday Inn Durban*, 63 Snell Parade ☎031 362 1300. A plush North Indian venue with authentic Eastern decor and an adjoining informal lounge, where you can recline on cushions at low tables. The food is varied and includes a superb list of vegetarian offerings. Mon 6.30–10.30pm, Tues–Sun 12.30–2pm & 6.30–10pm.

Joe Kool's Bar & Grill 137 Lower Marine Parade. A trendy, inexpensive eating place and pub right on the beach, with pool tables and first-class live music. Daily 8am–late.

Saagries House of Curries *Holiday Inn Garden Court*, Marine Parade. This grand Durban landmark offers some ultra-tangy curries and side dishes, at decent prices. Daily except Tues lunch & dinner.

Victoria Embankment and the Point

Restaurants

The Cargo Hold uShaka Marine World. Italian, Mexican and north African and Asian-influenced dishes are available here, though the best thing about this restaurant is its location next to the shark tank. Daily noon–10.30pm.

Charlie Crofts Wharfside Diner 18 Boatsman Rd, Wilson's Wharf, west of the Yacht Mole ☎031 307 2935. Boasting one of the best waterfront settings in Durban, this place does delicious seafood and meat dishes at reasonable prices. The spicy calamari grill is first-class, as is the *eisbein*. A great place for takeaways. Daily noon–10pm.

The Dockyard Theatre Shotblast Shed, Point Waterfront ☎031 332 1086. A two-course set menu with four main dishes to choose from, as the prelude to a stage show which could be anything from an Abba tribute to a stand-up comic playing a musical instrument. Dinner is served Tues–Sat at 7pm, Sun 6pm.

The Famous Fish Co North Pier, end of Point Rd ☎031 368 1060. Perfectly positioned at the port entrance, this pricey seafood restaurant has wonderful views of ships navigating the harbour mouth. Daily lunch & dinner. Expensive.

The New Café Fish Yacht Mole, Victoria Embankment ☎ 031 305 5062. A beautiful restaurant looking out onto the harbour, which specializes in great seafood, with prices to match. Ordering the catch of the day is *de rigueur*. Daily lunch & dinner.

Roma Revolving Restaurant John Ross House, Victoria Embankment ☎ 031 368 2275. No visitor to Durban should miss the view from the *Roma* as it revolves above the city. The international menu includes great mussel starters and Italian specialities, like gnocchi and veal dishes. Prices aren't outrageous. Mon–Sat lunch & dinner.

TransAfrica Express BAT Arts Centre, Small Craft Market, Victoria Embankment. This lively value dishes up modern African fusion food like creamed spiced *samp* (coarse maizemeal) and beans, and steamed Zulu bread pudding. With regular live music, it's a great place to meet the locals. Daily 10am–midnight.

The Berea

Restaurants

Baanthai 138 Florida Rd, Morningside ☎ 031 303 4270. The unfailingly excellent Thai food here includes *tom yum* soup and steamed mussels, outshone only by their honeyed duck. Prices can be a little steep. Daily noon–2.30pm, 7–10.30pm.

Bean Bag Bohemia 18 Windermere Rd, Morningside ☎ 031 309 6019. A trendy eating place in a two-storey house, with an informal bar/bistro downstairs and a more formal restaurant above. Expect unusual combinations like Thai soup with African maize dumplings. The restaurant hosts art exhibitions and changes its menu to suit the art being shown. Mon–Sat till 1am, Sun till midnight.

Blue Zoo Café 6 Nimmo Rd, Morningside. A varied and unusual menu features delicious Cajun chicken, lamb shank in a port wine sauce, steaks, fish and salads with mango and chilli dressings. Beautifully located in Mitchell Park Gardens and great for kids; not expensive either. Tues–Sat lunch & dinner, Sun dinner only.

Café 1999 Silvervause Centre, Silverton Rd ☎ 031 202 3406. An excellent, if pricey, fusion restaurant which is also good for late night coffees. Mon–Sat 12.30–2.30pm & 5.30–10.30pm.

Cat*Man*Du 411 Windermere Rd, Morningside. A cosy, moderately priced restaurant, actually Middle Eastern-influenced despite its name. The meze platter, with fiery olives, is recommended, as are the "Turkish Tigers" – vodka, condensed milk, cream and cinnamon. Mon dinner, Tues–Sat lunch & dinner.

Christina's 134 Florida Rd, Morningside ☎ 031 303 2111. Excellent, if pricey, meals prepared by the students of Christina Martin's acclaimed cookery school – expect fare such as smoked trout with apple mousse, or beetroot, radish and cucumber tzatziki with roast lamb. Tues–Sat 8.30–4pm plus Wed–Sat eves.

The Fish Harbour 144 Florida Rd, Morningside ☎ 031 312 5379. A speciality shellfish restaurant with unbeatable prices, mainly because the owners are also fishmongers. Tues–Sat lunch & dinner. Moderate.

Marco's 45 Windermere Rd, Morningside ☎ 031 303 3078. A classy, moderately priced trattoria, with fresh pasta made daily and delectable pizzas. Mon–Fri lunch & dinner, Sat dinner only.

Palki 225 Musgrave Rd ☎ 031 201 0019. The South African representative of a chain of restaurants based in the East, this has mouthwatering, authentic North and South Indian foods, created by chefs shipped in from other branches. Vegetarians are well catered for and prices decent. Mon dinner only, Tues–Sun lunch & dinner.

Vintage India 20 Windermere Rd, Morningside. Less formal than some of the other Indian restaurants in town, *Vintage* offers both North and South Indian fare. There's a great range of inexpensive starters, a comprehensive vegetarian selection and some unusual dishes. The stuffed chicken legs are good, and their "Bombay crush", a traditional Indian milkshake invented for "cooling the palate", is a must after a fiery curry. Daily lunch & dinner.

Cafés

Delicious Delicatessen and Coffee Shop Windermere Centre, Windermere Rd, Morningside. Seriously delicious, healthy noodle dishes, salads and sandwiches, including green Thai chicken bagels. Excellent coffees too, and takeaways are available. Mon–Fri 8am–6pm, Sat 7am–2pm.

Fressh 141 Musgrave Rd, next to Musgrave Centre. A great bagel and coffee shop, popular with the Berea's upper crust. Mon–Sat 7.30am–5pm, Sun 8am–3pm.

Mugg & Bean Musgrave Centre. A good place for endless coffee refills, breakfast, light lunches, cakes and muffins, all in gigantic portions. Daily 8am–11.30pm. Inexpensive.

Saint Verde Corner Essenwood and St Thomas roads ☎ 031 201 9176. Housed in a former power station, this fashionable establishment has some outdoor seating and does salads, ciabatta sandwiches and pastas. The French pastry chef makes a mean Opera Slice, a moist chocolate/coffee cream cake. Mon–Sat 7.30am–9pm, Sun 7.30am–5pm.

Drinking, nightlife and entertainment

Durban has a healthy nightlife scene, with a decent number of bars, clubs and music venues. For entertainment and nightlife **listings**, the *Mercury* is the better of Durban's two English-language dailies, while the *Sunday Tribune* has a thorough and comprehensive section on forthcoming events in its *SM* magazine. Durban Africa publishes a monthly events brochure available from tourist offices. The Johannesburg-based weekly *Mail & Guardian* also covers Durban nightlife in its *What's On* supplement.

Bars

Billy The Bums 504 Windermere Rd, Morningside. Acrobatic barmen juggle bottles while mixing highly imaginative cocktails at this popular singles' watering hole, which also does good food. Mon–Sat noon–midnight.

Cool Runnings 39 Milne St, near the beachfront. A brilliant rasta/reggae hangout. Daily noon–6am.

Jack Rabbits 1 McCarthy Centre, North Ridge Rd, Morningside. Sports bar with a wonderful outside deck, inexpensive meals and nightly happy hours with cheap booze. Daily 10am–late.

Victoria Bar Point Rd. A seedy but highly popular Portuguese venue, good for boozing and watching sport on TV. *Catembe* (cola and wine) is a house speciality, as is the excellent prawn curry and *peri-peri* chicken. Bar: Mon–Sat 10.30am–11pm; restaurant: Mon–Sat 12.30pm–3pm & 6.30–10pm.

Wonder Bar Windermere Rd, Morningside (next to *Billy The Bums*). An increasingly popular bar/club, with hi-tech stainless steel decor, lava lamps and a good vibe. Front bar: daily 6pm; inside area: Tues, Thurs, Fri & Sat 2.30pm–2.30am. There's a small cover charge Fri between 10pm and midnight.

Zeta Bar 263 Florida Rd. A fun place to hang out, with a good mix of contemporary music and house. Mon–Sat 7pm till late.

Clubs

80s Absa Stadium, off Walter Gilbert Rd, Stamford Hill. Hugely popular, particularly on Wednesday nights, when local students are on the loose. There's a large dance floor with top DJs, several bars, pool tables and an outdoor area. Wed, Fri & Sat 8pm–4am; Wed & Fri R10, Sat R15.

Tiger Tiger 15 Mitchell Crescent, Greyville. Frequented by the young and trendy, and spinning house, hip-hop and other current sounds. Wed–Sat 8pm until late; R30.

Tilt 11 Walnut Rd, opposite the *Hilton*. Central nightspot appealing to an upmarket crowd who enjoy funky R&B and contemporary music in a sophisticated, but relaxed, environment. Fri & Sat 9pm–7am; R40.

Skyybar 25 Silver Ave. Minimalist decor and a focus on house music, with a fabulous outdoor deck. Sat & Sun 8pm–4am; R50.

Durban gay venues

Durban has a fairly well-established and lively **gay scene**, with a handful of excellent clubs where heteros are also welcome. Worthwhile venues include the mixed *Bon Hommie*, 264 Florida Road (Tues–Sat 8pm till late) and the upmarket gay bar *Roman Lounge*, 202 Florida Road (open till late: Mon, Tues & Thurs from 4pm, Wed & Fri–Sun from 2pm). The *Bean Bag Bohemia* bar-restaurant (see p.485) is very gay-friendly, frequented by young beautiful things of both sexes. For more venues, check out the brochure produced by the KwaZulu-Natal Gay & Lesbian Tourism Association; it's available at the Tourist Junction.

Live music

You'll find plenty of live **indie music** on offer in Durban, much of it derivative of European or North American trends. More interesting, but less accessible, are some of the **Zulu forms** such as *iscathamiya* and *maskanda*. On the **jazz** scene, the city's most indigenous offering is a spicy combination of American mixed with township jazz and Zulu forms. The late Durban-born guitarist Sipho Gumede used to perform regularly, often at *Transafrica Express*, while Jimmy Dludlu is another hot favourite.

The best place to hear **classical concerts** by the KwaZulu-Natal Philharmonic is at a sundowner concert held in the Botanical Gardens or the Kingsmead Cricket Grounds. Check for listings and adverts in the press, or on the notice board in the gardens.

Imbizo Restaurant and Jazz Bar uShaka Marine World ☎ 031 337 0312. Offering a complete array of jazz styles Wed & Fri 7–10pm, and Sun noon–3pm. No cover charge.
The Rainbow 23 Stanfield Lane, Pinetown, northwest of Durban ☎ 031 702 9161. From Afro-fusion to jazz, occasional Sundays at lunchtime.

TransAfrica Express BAT Centre, Small Craft Harbour; entrance opposite Hermitage Lane, off Victoria Embankment. Probably the best jazz venue in Durban; don't miss sundowner time here on Friday eves, when local musicians hold alternating jazz and *maskanda* sessions (5–7pm; free). There's also a drum circle by top local drummers, performing in the *Bat Café* most Tuesdays (7.30–9.30pm; cover charge).

Theatre and cinema

There are two major **theatres** in town: the Playhouse Drama Theatre, a mock-Tudor building at 231 Smith Street (☎ 031 260 2296) that tends to host middle-of-the-road productions, but also sees performances by the resident progressive Playhouse Dance Company; and the Elizabeth Sneddon Theatre at the University of KwaZulu-Natal on South Ridge Road (☎ 031 260 2296), a modern venue for university and visiting productions. The Dockyard Theatre, Shotblast Shed, Point Waterfront (☎ 031 332 1086), puts together good quality musicals with supper served an hour and a half before the show begins (show starts 8.30pm Tues–Sat; 6pm Sun). The Catalina Theatre, Wilson's Wharf (☎ 031 305 6889), is another supper theatre club, with performances by local actors.

The best and most convenient **cinemas** are the multiscreen complexes at the Musgrave Centre on Musgrave Road, The Workshop Mall in the city centre and the Suncoast Casino on Battery Beach. The only place to see art-house movies is 15km north of town at the Gateway Mall (see p.499).

Outdoor activities

More than a pastime, **surfing** in Durban is a way of life. Night surfing competitions draw enormous crowds, as does the annual Mr Price Pro (the world's longest-running professional surfing competition, formerly the Gunston 500), held here every July. The favourite spot for surfers is **North Beach**, while a good place to pick up gear is the Safari Surf Shop, 43 Brickhill Road (☎ 031 337 2176), where Spider Murphy, South Africa's top board-shaper, will custom-build a world-class board for much less than a comparable order would cost in Europe or North America. Island Style Surf Shop, 121 Old Fort Road, Marine Parade (☎ 031 304 2393), is a good bet for accessories. Beach & Bush Adventures (☎ 031 569 1397, ⓦ www.beachandbush.co.za)

offer one-day **surfing lessons** with experienced instructors (R900, equipment supplied).

Diving is an obvious and pleasurable activity in KwaZulu-Natal's subtropical waters, but is somewhat limited immediately around Durban, where the best diving sites are Vetches Pier, at the southern tip of the beachfront, and Blood Reef at the tip of the Bluff (opposite the Point). Further along the coast, Aliwal Shoal along the South Coast (see p.494), and Sodwana up the Elephant Coast (p.543), are superb. Beach and Bush Adventures runs full-day diving trips for certified divers (R720 including gear). **Scuba courses** can be arranged through Underwater World, 251 Point Road (℡031 332 5820); a full six-day internationally recognized NAUI course with them costs R1700, including use of the main gear you'll need.

Bird-watching

Bird-watching, a major activity in the green fringes of the city, is being aided by the Durban Metropolitan Open Space System (DMOSS), a project linking all the city parks via narrow green corridors. Promising spots include the Manor Gardens area; the Botanic Gardens; the Berea; Burman Bush, to the north of the city; Pigeon Valley, below the University of KwaZulu-Natal; the Umgeni River Mouth; Virginia Bush, on the road to Umhlanga Rocks; and the Havana Forest in Umhlanga, where the spotted thrush and green coucal have been seen.

Worth a visit is the **Umgeni River Bird Park**, 490 Riverside Road, Durban North (daily 9am–5pm; R25; ⓦwww.umgeniriverbirdpark.co.za), which has a fantastic free-flight bird show (Tues–Sun 2 daily), with spectacular specimens as well as a vast collection of indigenous and exotic birds, including flamingos, finches, magpies and macaws.

Hiking, climbing and airborne activities

You can arrange **hiking** and **rock climbing** in the Ukhahlamba Drakensberg through one of several hiking clubs. Contact them through the Mountain Club of South Africa (℡082 9202287, ⓦwww.mcsa.org.za), which itself organizes a variety of bush outings from gentle walks to rock climbing and, in winter, **ice-climbing**; non-members are welcome. Beach and Bush Adventures (see p.487) operates a one-day Drakensberg trip featuring bushmen paintings, wildlife-spotting and gentle hiking (R900 for a group of at least seven), while 180 Degrees Adventures (℡031 566 4955, ⓦwww.180.co.za) has a six-day hiking tour to the Mnweni valley (see p.520) in the Northern Drakensberg with its dramatic scenery, rock art and wildlife (R6100). They also run a one-day rock–climbing trip to Monteseel Crag and Kloof Gorge (R415) where they'll teach you the basics of the sport if you're a beginner. For hiking equipment, head for Cape Union Mart, 306 Musgrave Centre, Musgrave Road (℡031 201 0231).

To see Durban and its surrounds from the air, try a tandem **skydive** with Skydive Durban (℡072 214 6040; R1200) or **microlighting** with 180 Degrees Adventures (R185/hr).

Rafting, kayaking and dolphin-spotting

From October to March, 180 Degrees Adventures (see above) run **white-water rafting** trips to the Umkomaas River (R450), lasting anything from four to seven hours, depending on the water level. For a more challenging whitewater run, contact Four Rivers Rafting and Adventures (see p.514), a Winterton-based firm who offer trips on the Tugela River near the Ukhahlamba Drakensberg.

Beach & Bush Adventures (see p.487) offers one-day **ocean kayaking** trips where there's a good chance you'll see **dolphins** (R420). Dolphin-spotting boat excursions are offered by 180 Degrees Adventures, whose trips are led by a knowledgeable skipper (1hr; R150).

Shopping

As one of South Africa's major cities, Durban is a good centre to pick up general supplies and local books and records. But it's for **crafts and curios** that it scores particularly highly, with a dazzling range of handmade Zulu goods (see box below). The best places to browse for crafts are in the downtown markets, the weekend flea markets and the specialist shops around the city.

Durban is littered with shopping **malls** of varying sizes, the two largest being the Workshop Mall on the corner of Commercial and Aliwal streets in the centre, and the upmarket Musgrave Centre in Musgrave.

Books and music

Adams & Co 341 West St ⓦ www.adamsbooks
.co.za. In the city centre, this is Durban's oldest
book store, and has an excellent selection of
books on the history of Durban and KwaZulu-Natal.
There's also a branch at the Musgrave Centre.
Mon–Fri 8.30am–4.30pm.

Exclusive Books Lower Level, Pavilion Shopping
Centre, Westville. Durban's flashiest general book
store, where browsers pore over coffee-table
books. Mon–Fri 9am–6pm, Sat 9am–10pm, Sun
10am–4pm.

Ike's Books and Collectables 48a Florida Rd,
Greyville. A fascinating secondhand bookshop, with

Zulu crafts and curios

Durban's huge range of galleries, craft shops and markets makes it one of the best centres in the country to pick up **Zulu crafts**. Traditional works include functional items such as woven beer strainers and grass brooms, and basketry that can be extremely beautiful. Other traditional items are beadwork, pottery and Zulu regalia, of which *assegais* (spears), shields, leather kilts and drums are a few examples. However, the availability of cheap plastic crockery and enamelware has significantly eroded the production of traditional ceramics and woven containers for domestic use. Cheap facsimiles of these personal household items are now churned out for sale to curio hunters who are indifferent to the authenticity or quality of what they are buying.

Fortunately, the news isn't all bad. Although urbanization has stifled the production of much traditional craft, it has thrown up **creative adaptations**: the use of new materials, or new ways of using old materials. Among these are beautifully decorated black and white sandals made from recycled rubber tyres, wildly colourful baskets woven from telephone wire and *sjamboks* (whips) decorated with bright insulation tape. On the more frivolous side, there's a whole genre of affordable curios that break away from stereotypical tribal woodcarvings and masks, and marry industrial materials with rural life or rural materials with industrial life. Attractive tin boxes made from flattened oil cans, chickens constructed from sheet plastic, and aircraft and little 4WD vehicles carved from wood are some of the results.

An entire movement of **master craftspeople** draws on traditional forms to produce objects of the highest quality, many of which are sought after by art collectors. Among these many excellent craftworkers are woodcarver Vuminkosi Zulu, scrap-metal car sculptor Nkosinathi Gumede and potter Nesta Nala – contact them through the Natal Society of Arts shop in the Berea (see p.490).

an interesting range of items covering KwaZulu-Natal's history and the fauna and flora of the area. Speciality areas include Africana and the Boer War, travel and exploration, and left-wing classics. Mon–Fri 8.30am–5.30pm, Sat 9am–1pm.

Look and Listen Lower Level, Pavilion Shopping Centre, Westville. Durban's best-stocked music shop, with a comprehensive range of indigenous music from the whole continent, including local favourites such as Ladysmith Black Mambazo and Hugh Masekela. Mon–Fri 9am–6pm, Sat 9am–10pm, Sun 10am–4pm.

Crafts and curios

African Art Centre Tourist Junction, 160 Pine St ☏031 304 7915. A gallery and shop well worth visiting for its traditional and modern Zulu and Xhosa beadwork, beaded dolls, wire sculptures, woodcuts and tapestries. Mon–Fri 8am–4.30pm, Sat 9am–2pm.

The BAT Shop The BAT Centre, off Victoria Embankment. Contemporary pieces, including an excellent collection by African artists, in a bright and colourful venue with masterful wireworks and robust ceramics. Mon–Fri 8am–5pm, Sat 8am–2pm.

NSA Gallery Shop NSA Gallery, Bulwer Rd ☏031 202 3686. This menagerie of contemporary hand-crafted goods includes a wonderful selection of functional art, including pewter cutlery, etchings and paintings; there are fortnightly exhibitions and an outdoor coffee shop.

Tourist Junction Shop 160 Pine St. Quality African artefacts, from Zulu basketwork to tribal masks and weaving. Mon–Fri 8am–4.30pm, Sat 9am–2pm.

Markets

Amphitheatre Fleamarket Snell Parade, Beach-front. For local crafts and bead work. Daily.

Dockside 17 Market King's Battery, The Point. An interesting harbour venue where you can pick up handmade clothing, spicy pineapples, marsala green mangoes, silver jewellery and African arts and curios. Sun.

Essenwood Fleamarket Berea Park, Essenwood Rd. Upmarket stalls in a beautiful setting. Sat.

South Plaza Fleamarket Durban Exhibition Centre, Walnut Rd. Centrally situated, this is the largest flea market in town. Sun 6.30am–5pm.

Listings

Airlines British Airways ☏860 011 747; Kulula .com ☏861 585 852; SA Airlink ☏031 250 1111; South African Airways ☏031 250 1111.

Banks First National Bank, 32 West St, Marine Parade, has extended hours for changing foreign currency (Mon–Fri 9am–6pm, Sat 8.30am–6pm, Sun 10am–3pm).

Bicycle tours Cycle Tours De Durban (see box on p.467) offers leisurely guided trips around the city, though at the time of writing there was nowhere to rent bikes.

Camera repairs Camera Clinic, Shop 4, Standard Bank Centre, 135 Musgrave Rd ☏031 202 5396.

Car parks The most convenient and central are those at Pine Arcade, at the west end of Pine Street, and in the Workshop Mall, on the corner of Commercial Road and Aliwal Street.

Car rental Avis ☏0861 021 111; Berea ☏031 202 3333; Budget ☏031 304 9023; Europcar ☏031 469 0667; Hertz ☏0861 600 136; Imperial ☏0800 13 10 00; Rent & Drive ☏031 332 2803; Tempest ☏031 368 5231; and Windermere ☏031 312 0339 (they have seven-seater mini vans).

Consulates Germany, 2 Devonshire Place, Smith St ☏031 305 5677; UK, 124 Davenport Rd, Glenwood ☏031 202 6823; USA, Durban Bay House, 333 Smith St ☏031 305 7600.

Emergencies AA ☏082 16111. See also p.89.

Hospitals and medical centres The main state hospital is the Addington, Erskine Terrace, South Beach (☏031 327 2000), which offers a 24hr emergency ward. A better alternative is Entabeni Private Hospital, 148 South Ridge Rd, Berea (☏031 204 1300), which has a casualty unit and can also treat minor conditions, but where you will have to pay a deposit on admission and settle up before leaving town. A convenient option, open 24hr, is South Beach Medical Centre, Rutherford St (☏031 332 3101), which has a pharmacy, doctors, an optician, a dentist, a physiotherapist, as well as aromatherapy, reflexology and homeopathy. Travel Doctor at 45 Ordnance Rd, International Convention Centre (☏031 360 1122, ⊛www.traveldoctor .co.za) is a clinic offering information and advice on local and international destinations, as well as on malaria and the necessary jabs for venturing into African countries to the north.

Internet access Both the Workshop Mall and Musgrave Centre have Internet cafés.

Laundries Convenient for the Berea are Musgrave Laundromat, 2nd Level, Musgrave Centre and Econ-O-Wash, ground floor, Berea Centre, Berea Rd. South Beach Wash-Tub, 428 Point Rd, is located on the beachfront.

Left luggage Durban station has inexpensive left-luggage facilities on the first floor (Mon & Wed–Fri 6am–6pm, Tues 6am–4pm, Sat 6am–noon).

Pharmacies Sparkport, corner Smith and Broad streets (☎031 304 9767; Mon–Sat 7.30am–9.30pm, Sun 9am–9pm), offers a doctor on call 24hr as well as a range of specialist treatments and all pharmaceutical travel requirements. Medicine Chest, 155 Berea Rd, Berea (☎031 305 6151; daily 8am–midnight), offers free deliveries, as does Daynite Pharmacy, corner of West St and Point Rd (☎031 368 3666; Mon–Thurs 7.30am–10.30pm, Fri–Sun 7.30am–11.30pm); Mediquick Pharmacy, 88 Overport Dr, outside Overport City Shopping Centre, Berea (☎031 209 3456; daily 8am–10pm), can deliver anywhere in town for a nominal charge.

Post The main post office, on the corner of Gardiner and West streets, has a poste restante and enquiry desk (Mon–Fri 8am–4.30pm, Sat 8am–noon).

Spectator sport Not surprisingly for a city with such a British heritage, cricket and horse racing are high on the agenda. The Kingsmead Cricket Ground in the centre (☎031 335 4200) is the principal venue for local and international cricket matches and is home to the provincial cricket team. You'll also have plenty of opportunity to watch rugby in season at Absa Stadium, Walter Gilbert Road, Stamford Hill (☎031 308 8400), home to the local Sharks. Horse racing is popular: the main season runs from May to August, and centres around the course at Avondale Road, Greyville (☎031 314 1651). The annual "July at Greyville" is South Africa's premier horse-racing event, drawing bets from across the length and breadth of the country and wildly exhibitionist fashions in the spectator boxes.

Swimming Durban's largest pool is the heated King's Park Olympic Swimming Pool on NMR Ave, between Argyle and Battery Beach roads in Stamford Hill (☎031 312 0404). Convenient for the Berea are Sutton Park Baths, Stamford Hill Rd (☎031 303 1823), while the seawater Rachel Finlayson Baths, Lower Marine Parade (☎031 337 2721), are handy if you're staying near the beachfront.

Around Durban

If you're looking for quieter beaches out of the city, the **North** or **South coasts** around Durban make an obvious and easy day-trip or weekend jaunt. The coasts around Durban, with easy access to Johannesburg, the warmest waters in the country and a decidedly tropical feel, have primarily been developed for white South African families on holiday, and can seem rather bland in a country with so many spectacular landscapes. Having said that, there are kilometres of uncongested sandy beaches backed by wild banana trees, and the chance to spot dolphins, especially along the North Coast.

The South Coast draws diving enthusiasts to **Aliwal Shoal**, one of the country's top dive spots near Umkomaas, and is also notable for two nature reserves: **Oribi Gorge**, where you can try out some adventure sports in the gorge or visit it by steam train; and **Umtamvuna**, which offers day-walks along the Umtamvuna River. Unless you're travelling to or from the Eastern Cape, the North Coast is preferable to the South Coast – it's a lot less built-up and tacky. **Umhlanga Rocks**, an upmarket resort less than half an hour's drive from Durban, offers beach walks as well as great places to have a drink or meal. Further up the coast is a string of resorts which get more low-key the further north you go, all with sandy beaches and large tidal rock pools to swim in. Inland is sugar-cane country, with a couple of upmarket guesthouses reflecting the colonial-style grandeur of the early sugar barons.

Northwest from Durban is **Pietermaritzburg**, the provincial capital, with an excellent art gallery and some interesting red-brick Victorian architecture plus a vibrant mix of Zulu and Indian culture. Pietermaritzburg can be combined with the all-time favourite day-trip out of Durban, the scenic **Valley of a Thousand Hills**. Beyond Pietermaritzburg, and definitely more of a weekend stay than a day-trip, are the KwaZulu-Natal **Midlands**, with appealing scenery in the Ukhahlamba Drakensberg foothills, trout fishing, numerous craft shops, and a number of hotels, guesthouses and cottages catering especially for the weekend trade.

The South Coast

The South Coast, the 160-kilometre seaboard from Durban to Port Edward on the Eastern Cape border, is a ribbon of seaside suburbs linked for most of its length by the **N2** and **R102** roads, running side by side. Thousands of upcountry families have built holiday homes here along the closest stretch of sand to Johannesburg, and although in wilderness terms the area is unexciting, it does have some lovely beaches and ample accommodation. In the winter months it's much warmer and sunnier along this stretch than on any of the beaches between here and Cape Town. Away from the sea, the land is very hilly and green, dotted with sugar-cane fields, banana plantations and palm and pecan nut trees. Gardens are bright with exuberant flowering trees and shrubs, and in some places alive with monkeys. Note that many beaches shelve steeply into the powerful surf, so only swim where it's indicated as safe.

Transport from Durban and Johannesburg to the South Coast is good (see p.466) and there are plenty of caravan parks next to the beaches, a couple of backpacker lodges and a number of mid-priced places to stay. **Margate**, 133km from Durban, is the transport and holiday hub of the area, with plenty of resorts lying to the east and west of it. **Port Shepstone**, 117km south of Durban, is the grim industrial and administrative centre, while **Oribi Gorge Nature Reserve**, just 21km inland from Port Shepstone, has lovely forest hikes, breathtaking views and good-value accommodation.

There are daily direct **flights** from Johannesburg on SA Airlink (☎031 250 1111) to Margate airport (☎039 312 0560). **Driving**, head for the N2, which runs south from Durban as far as Port Shepstone, before heading inland to Kokstad. From Port Shepstone to Southbroom, the South Coast Toll Road is even faster and less traffic-clogged. Margate Mini Coach, Gird Mowat Building, Marine Drive, Margate (☎039 312 1406), has a daily **bus** service from Durban station (Translux terminal) via Durban's *Royal Hotel*), Durban

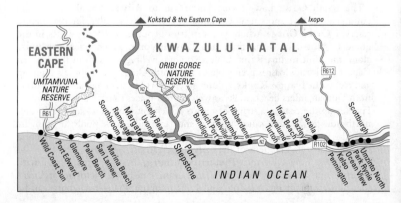

The sardine run

The South Coast is witness to the extraordinary annual migration of millions of **sardines**, moving northwards along the coast in massive shoals. Around June or July, the shoals leave their feeding ground off the Southern Cape coast, and move up the coast towards Mozambique. They are followed by about 23,000 dolphins, 100,000 Cape gannets and thousands of sharks and game fish, attracting fishermen from all over the province to join in the jamboree. The shoals appear as dark patches of turbulence in the water, and when they are cornered and driven ashore by game fish, hundreds of people rush into the water either to scoop them out with their hands or to net them. For updates on shoal co-ordinates and other information of use for sardine-spotting, call the Sardine Hotline on ☎082 284 9495.

airport (domestic arrivals), Amanzimtoti (prebooked only), Hibberdene (prebooked only), Hibberdene (Super Tube), Port Shepstone (LSC Motors) and Margate (Dennisons Funworld). There are also buses daily from Pretoria with Luxliner (☎039 315 7206 or 315 7306), running through Pietermaritzburg and Durban and passing through Amanzimtoti, Scottburgh, Hibberdene, Port Shepstone, Shelly Beach and Margate. The **Baz Bus** (☎031 304 9099, ⓦwww .bazbus.com) between Port Elizabeth and Durban pulls in at major South Coast resorts, although you can ask to be put off at intermediate destinations.

Amanzimtoti, Warner Beach and Umkomaas

Some 27km south of Durban and just minutes from Durban airport, **AMANZIMTOTI** (Zulu for "sweet waters") earned its name, according to tradition, because it was here in the river of this name that King Shaka slaked his thirst. Toti, as the resort is known to locals, is the largest town along the upper South Coast, yet feels more like a beachside suburb. Outside weekends and school holidays – when its high-rise holiday developments are full to bursting point – it's worth coming here for a day's swimming and lounging on Nyoni Rocks Beach.

If you're looking for somewhere to stay, **WARNER BEACH**, 3km further south, is the place to head for. Far less developed than Amanzimtoti, Warner Beach offers some excellent surfing spots, as well as good swimming and a large tidal pool that's safe for children. Overlooking the beach, the supremely relaxed *Angle Rock Backpackers*, 5 Ellcock Road (☎031 916 7007, ⓦwww.anglerock .co.za; dorms and rooms ❶), is a cut above the average **hostel**, with a swimming pool, dorms and three doubles – one of which is en suite with a marble bathtub. The lodge offers free use of surfboards and canoes.

Roughly 16km further down the coast, **UMKOMAAS**, a faded town of buildings with corrugated-iron roofs, exudes an atmosphere that is more laid-back still. Perched on a headland with outstanding views across the sea, this is essentially a retirement village with beaches that are periodically discoloured by effluent washing down the Mkomazi River from the Saiccor cellulose mill, just upriver. For diving enthusiasts, Umkomaas is the perfect point to set out for **Aliwal Shoal**, a scattered reef quite close to the shore and one of southern Africa's top dive sites. Meridian Dive Charter (☎039 973 2813, ⓦwww .scubadivesouthafrica.co.za) run trips to Aliwal Shoal (R200, kit R180). On the beachfront, *Umkomaas Lodge Dive Centre*, Roland Norris Drive (☎039 973 2542, ⓔumkomaas@netactive.co.za; dorms and rooms ❶), offers a wide range of **diving activities** with self-catering **accommodation**, from dorms to luxury en-suite rooms. Their four-day Open Water diving course leads to a PADI certificate and costs around R1400 if they provide the gear. It's possible to do the same type of course here with Amatikulu Tours (☎039 973 2534, ⓦwww .amatikulu.com) for R1800 (includes all equipment). Rewards for experienced divers include sightings of whale sharks, ragged-tooth sharks, potato bass, manta rays and eels, as well as shoals of tropical fish, corals and anemones; enthusiasts can also go wreck-diving to three stunning sites. The ideal time to dive is between June and October, when visibility is at its best.

Scottburgh to Port Shepstone

A further 9km south is **SCOTTBURGH**, the oldest town along the South Coast and one of the most appealing because of its sheltered, lawn-covered beach fringes. The *Cutty Sark* on Beachfront Road (☎039 976 1230, ⓦwww .cuttysark.co.za; ❹) has rather tired, old-fashioned rooms, though discounts off-season are available, while camping and self-catering six-bed cottages (R450) are available at *Scottburgh Caravan Park*, also on Beachfront Road (☎039 976 2135, ⓔcaravanpark@scottburgh.co.za).

Turn off the N2 at **HIBBERDENE**, continue south along the R102 for a couple of kilometres, and you'll come to *Mantis Moon Backpackers*, 7/178

The Banana Express

A steam train, the **Banana Express** (☎039 682 4821, ⓦwww.bananaexpress .co.za), chugs south from Port Shepstone along a scenic narrow-gauge railway, bound for either Paddock (39km) or Izotsha (13km). The station in Port Shepstone is on Princess Elizabeth Drive. The longer **Paddock** return trip leaves at 10.30am and takes six hours, meandering along the coastline and then inland through hilly country covered with banana and sugar-cane plantations, and costs R140. The trip includes a visit to the Zakhele Homecraft Training Centre and a ninety-minute stop for a DIY braai lunch on the lawns of the Paddock stationmaster's garden. The stationmaster's wife sells braai packs with salad for R40. The shorter **Izotsha** return trip leaves at 11am and takes about two hours and costs R80 in first class (recommended) or R50 in tourist class (a bit windy, as the coaches have no glass in the windows). Out of season the train runs on Thursday, Saturdays and Sundays, with additional services in December and January.

Station Road, Umzumbe (℡039 648 6256, ✉travelsa@saol.com; ❶). A friendly, laidback place, it's two minutes' walk from the beach and boasts an outdoor Jacuzzi and rooftop deck for relaxing, as well as drumming workshops and mouthwatering fish braais.

Some 15km further south along the R102 in **UMTENTWENI** is another beachfront backpackers' lodge, *The Spot*, at 23 Ambleside Road (℡039 695 1318, ✉spotbackpackers@netactiveco.za; dorms and rooms ❶), with camping, dorms and doubles, as well as free use of surf boards and boogie boards. From here, one resort after another follows the shoreline to gritty, sprawling **PORT SHEPSTONE**, a dismal place where you won't want to linger for long, although there are a couple of reasonable beaches just south of the town centre, and it's the gateway to the nearby Oribi Gorge Nature Reserve (see below). The town is also the place to hop on one of the Banana Express steam-train journeys (see box opposite).

The warm ocean water hereabouts makes **diving** a pleasant experience, with soft and hard corals, sharks and game fish viewing. March to September are the best months for **dolphin-** and **whale-watching**; Adventures Extreme Ocean Safaris (℡039 695 2714) offers two-hour trips for R450.

Oribi Gorge Nature Reserve

The South Coast's most compelling attraction is KZN Wildlife's **Oribi Gorge Nature Reserve** (daily 8am–4.30pm; ℡039 679 1644; R12), about 21km inland from Port Shepstone. A highly scenic area with cliffs rising from vast chasms and forest, it's traversed by the fast-flowing Umzimkulu and Umzimkulwana rivers. There are numerous idyllic picnic spots on the riverbanks (though avoid swimming here, as bilharzia parasites are present in the water) and waymarked **hikes** ranging from thirty-minute to day-long excursions, leading to dizzying look-out points or through the forest. A fine one-hour **walk** starts from the Umzimkulu car park and picnic site, crosses the river and heads immediately up some steps into the forest. You can hear the river through the dense vegetation, but you'll only see it when it opens out quite dramatically to reveal **Samango Falls** and a perfect little rock-bounded sandy beach.

Wildlife in the reserve includes bushbuck, common reedbuck, blue and grey duiker, but not oribi, which have left for the succulent shoots of the surrounding sugar-cane plantations. You're more likely to hear than to see the shy samango monkeys, hiding in the high canopy of the forest, and although leopards are present it's probable that they'll see you before you catch sight of them.

There are a few adventure activities that you can do in the reserve, all run by Wild 5 (℡039 687 0253 or 082 337 3746, ⓦwww.oribigorge.co.za), who operate from the *Oribi Gorge Hotel* (see p.496). There's an **abseil** (R210) with a tough half-hour walk out of the gorge afterwards; a **gorge swing** that requires you to leap off the top of the Lehrs Falls (R320); a Flying Fox gorge **slide** (R195), erected 160m above the gorge floor; plus horse-riding, mountain-bike rental and **rafting** trips down the Umzimkulu River.

Practicalities

Travelling by car to Durban from the Eastern Cape along the N2, you'll find the reserve just a few hundred metres off the main road (it's signposted). You can also get here by train from Port Shepstone on the Banana Express (see box opposite), though this is more of an excursion than a convenient means of transport.

The nicest accommodation is in the KZN Wildlife huts (**❷**) in the **restcamp** at the head of the Umzimkulwana Gorge, peering into the chasm of Oribi Gorge itself. There's a swimming pool here, and all crockery, cutlery and bedding is provided. Alternatively, you can stay in the colonial-style *Oribi Gorge Hotel* (℡039 687 0253; **❸**) some 16km from the restcamp, off the Oribi Flats road, which has spectacular views, including the famous overhanging rock and offers spacious rooms, meals to suit most budgets and a pleasant outdoor tea area. They can accommodate backpackers in a separate cottage (**❶**).

The Hibiscus Coast

The 44km of coast from Port Shepstone to Port Edward has been dubbed the **Hibiscus Coast** because of its luscious, bright gardens, luxury suburbs, beachside developments and attractive caravan parks. It's also known as the **Golf Coast**: there are nine top courses on this short stretch of coastline, and many people come specifically for its golfing opportunities. Although the whole area, centred on Margate, is built up, the Hibiscus Coast gets nicer the further south you go, escaping the development.

Uvongo

Some 12km south of Port Shepstone, the Vungu River narrows into a gorge and crashes down a **waterfall** before opening out onto a broad sandy beach at **UVONGO**. The waterfall is definitely the town's biggest attraction; elsewhere, tatty clifftop developments have destroyed much of the natural vegetation. To see the falls, take the path from the bottom of the cliffs to the rear of the beach and follow the steps in the corner away from the river, following the path through some undergrowth until you reach the viewpoint on a ledge. Uvongo's pleasant beach is the site of a daily market, where Zulu women sell fruit, crafts and good-quality basketwork.

One of the most comfortable **places to stay** is *Ebenezer Palms*, 1 Emthunzi Drive (℡039 317 1128, ✉ hoatson@venturenet.co.za; **❸**), with Mediterranean-style rooms, pool, and an extensive continental breakfast. Nearby, the *Uvongo Beach Lodge*, Pioneer Road (℡039 315 0013, ℻039 315 5194; **❸**), is a bit old-fashioned, but it's only a three-minute stroll from the beach. For something smarter, the very appealing thatched *Shaka's Inhlaba Lodge*, 15 Riviera Crescent (℡039 315 5171, ✉ shakas@venturenet.co.za; **❹**), to the west of *Uvongo Beach Lodge*, offers B&B and excellent, inexpensive home-cooked pub lunches and dinners. Even if you're not staying, the pub is recommended. The Shelly Beach Information Centre (℡039 315 0265) can help you find other accommodation in Uvongo itself and also all the way down to Ramsgate.

The best **places to eat** are the *Pavilion*, a restaurant right on the beach with a curving glazed frontage looking out to sea, and the *Edelweiss* in town, which serves excellent food at reasonable prices.

Margate and Ramsgate

The brash, built-up holiday town of **MARGATE**, 2km south of Uvongo, is as far as you'll get down the South Coast using public transport. With its highrise apartments, fast-food outlets and ice-cream parlours, Margate offers little in the way of undiscovered coves or hidden beaches; its big plus point is the wide choice of good-value places to stay, especially out of season. The **tourist office** on the beachfront (Mon–Fri 8.30am–4pm, Sat 9–11am; ℡039 312 2322) has details of accommodation and general information for the whole South Coast area. Five minutes' drive south of Margate, across the lagoon in

RAMSGATE, the Gaze Gallery (9am–4.30pm; free) displays some reputable work by local artists, and serves the best waffles in the province at the attached waterside *Waffle House*.

Accommodation

Beachcomber Bay 75 Marine Dr, Ramsgate ☏039 317 4498, ✉beachcomberbay@mweb.co.za. With views of the sea front and private access to the beach, this comfortable guesthouse has five rooms, a family unit and a sauna. ❸

The Courthouse 2079 Buck Drive, Ramsgate ☏ & Ⓕ 039 314 4046, ⓦwww.thecourthouse.co.za. Four beautiful upmarket self-catering apartments along the water, all with four-poster beds and some with Jacuzzis. ❹

De Wet Caravan Park St Andrews Avenue, along the beachfront ☏039 312 1022. Fully equipped four-berth caravans, park homes and grassy campsites. ❶–❷

Margate Backpackers 14 Collis Rd, Manaba Beach, Margate ☏039 312 2176, ✉ulrike@venturenet.co.za. Dorms, doubles and camping are offered at this hostel that's practically on the beach and only 200m from a great tidal pool. The hostel has a big self-catering kitchen, as well as a pool table; shark diving and deep-sea fishing can be arranged. Dorms and rooms ❶

Margate Hotel Marine Drive ☏039 312 1410, ✉info@margatehotel.co.za. Very comfortable accommodation near the centre of town, right on the beach, with discounts offered out of season. ❸

Suntide Resort and Cabanas 5 Duke Road ☏039 317 4010, ✉ bookings@anytimeholidays .co.za. Excellent-value self-catering apartments in a quiet stretch right on the beach. The only drawback is that most doubles face onto the car park; you're better off paying a little extra and, even if there are only two of you, taking a larger, sea-facing four-bed apartment. ❷

Southbroom, Palm Beach and Port Edward

Some 7km beyond Margate, **SOUTHBROOM** is known disparagingly as "Houghton-by-Sea" after Johannesburg's wealthiest suburb, which allegedly relocates here en masse in December. The town is predominantly a sumptuous development of large holiday houses set in expansive gardens; out of season, it can feel quite deserted. Huge dunes covered by lush vegetation sweep down to the sea, and there are good long walks along the shore – although heading out alone isn't advisable along this coastline for safety reasons. The best place for swimming is **Marina Beach**, 3km south of Southbroom Beach. Near Southbroom is one of the area's most upmarket **hotels**, the tranquil *Country Lodge* (☏039 316 8380, ⓦwww.thecountrylodge.co.za; ❹). Signposted off the R61 (the Port Edward road), it's a romantically secluded place surrounded by forest, away from the beachfront buzz. Champagne breakfasts and light meals are served at their marvellous *Treehouse Restaurant* on the premises. You can also eat at the *Cycad Restaurant*, adjoining the *Lodge* building, with a menu that includes delicacies like curried kudu and saffron and sweet potato gnocchi.

On the R61 at the sign for *Country Lodge*, S'khumba Crafts is a recommended stopoff where you can have a coffee in soothing forest surrounds and look at the finely crafted leather footwear. Besides *Country Lodge*, other **places to eat** are the *Riptide Restaurant*, which is highly rated for its excellent well-priced seafood; the *Trattoria La Terrazza*, which – no surprises here – serves Italian food; or the *Bistro*, known for its Beef Wellington. As for **pubs**, the *Pistols Saloon*, adjoining the *Old Bavaria* restaurant on the road to Port Edward is notable for its resident pet pig, Bandit, which has a penchant for crisps and beer.

Heading on to Port Edward, which marks the border with the Eastern Cape, you'll soon arrive at **Palm Beach**, a rocky beach bordered with banana palms with a tidal pool for swimming, and one of the quietest spots along the South Coast. The main attraction of **PORT EDWARD**, 9km further on, is its proximity to the Umtamvuna Nature Reserve (see p.498), though there are some nice sandy beaches at this resort and some good **places to stay**. The *Ferryman's*

Inn, 14 Old Pont Road (☎039 311 2308; ❷), is a comfortable colonial-style place nestled in the forest overlooking the Umtamvuna River. Further inland, on a hilltop with sweeping views of the ocean, is the excellent *Ku-boboyi Back-packers*, Old Main Road, Leisure Bay (☎039 319 1371, ✉kuboboyi@saol.com; ❶–❷), a pleasant establishment where evening meals can be ordered.

The only public transport heading west from Port Edward is the minibus taxis that form a lively rank on the R61 just outside town, collecting passengers for the Eastern Cape, many heading across the old Transkei border to gamble at the *Wild Coast Sun* casino (see p.455).

Umtamvuna Nature Reserve

Some of the best nature walks in the whole of KwaZulu-Natal are to be found at the **Umtamvuna Nature Reserve** (daily: April–Aug 7am–5pm; Sept–March 6am–6pm; R5), about 8km north of Port Edward. Extending 19km upriver along the tropical Umtamvuna River and the forested cliffs rising above it, the reserve is well known for its spring flowers, and the sunbirds and sugar birds feeding on the nectar. It's home to three hundred species of birds, including a famous colony of rare Cape **vultures**, though to see where they nest you'll have to be prepared for a whole day's walk. Waymarked paths are dotted throughout the reserve.

Umtamvuna is off the R61 to Izingolweni, signposted near Port Edward. There are pleasant **places to stay** nearby. *Umtamvuna River Lodge*, Holiday Road (☎039 311 2313, ⓦwww.riverlodge.co.za; B&B ❸), has ten rooms in tranquil forested surroundings on the banks of the river inside the reserve, and canoeing and water-skiing are available. Also on the river bank is *Old Pont Holiday Resort*, Old Pont Road, Banners Rest (☎039 313 2211, ⓕ039 313 2033; ❶–❷). With caravans, camping and rondavels, it's a good spot for fishing, with jetskis for rent. There's a useful shop selling basics.

A few hundred metres along the same road, turn right to the highly recommended *Vuna Valley Backpackers*, Michelle Road (☎039 311 1676, ✉vunavalley@hotmail.com; dorms and rooms ❶), which has attractive dorms and a double. Meals can be provided on request, and horse-riding, hiking, canoeing, surfing and dolphin-watching can be arranged.

North of Durban: the Dolphin Coast

The **Dolphin Coast** is the appealing name given to the eighty-kilometre stretch along the coast north of Durban, from Umhlanga Rocks to the mouth of the Tugela River. The combination of a narrow continental shelf and warm, shallow waters creates ideal conditions for attracting bottle-nosed dolphins all year round to feed. Though the chances of sighting a cetacean are fairly high, you'd be unwise to base a visit solely around this possibility.

Less tacky and developed than the South Coast, the North Coast attracts an upmarket breed of holidaymaker, especially to the main resorts of **Ballito** and **Salt Rock**. If you're after an easy beachside holiday close to Durban, **Umhlanga Rocks** is the best choice. Less than half an hour's drive up the N2 from the city centre, and served by public transport, the beaches here are long, steep and sandy, backed by banana palms, with warm strong surf, and shark nets to protect swimmers.

Rolling in from the coast are hills of sugar-cane plantations, the main industry of the area (it was sugar barons who established the first holiday retreats along the coastline). Driving along here, you'll be competing with long transport trucks, which litter the tarmac with dry stalks and strands of cane. While the Dolphin Coast is still pretty well dominated by whites, the inland towns of **Verulam**, **Tongaat** and **Dukuza**, linked by the old **R102** road, have substantial Zulu and Indian populations, with Indian temples at Tongaat and the Shaka memorial at Duzuku. Also on the R102 is the grave of one of the ANC's best-loved leaders, Albert Luthuli, at **Groutville**.

Besides the usual transport companies, Zulu Sun Safaris (☎082 552 5745, ⓔzulusun@absamail.co.za) provides transport by arrangement, up and down the Dolphin Coast and to Durban airport. Based in Ballito, they also run day-trips throughout the area.

Umhlanga Rocks

With a permanent population of around 100,000, **UMHLANGA ROCKS** is 20km from the centre of Durban and merges with the suburb of Durban North. A swish resort, the town makes a good day out from the city, with a pleasant, sandy beach dominated by a red and white lighthouse. The town's shopping area along Chartwell Drive has a collection of smart, well-stocked malls as well as the monster **Gateway Mall** at Umhlanga Ridge, with four hundred shops and fourteen cinemas. To find it, follow the N2 from Durban and take the Umhlanga/Mount Edgecombe off ramp, then follow the signs.

Nearby, also a couple of kilometres north of Umhlanga's centre, signposted off the N2, the **KwaZulu–Natal Sharks Board**, 1a Herrwood Drive (☎031 566 0400; R20), shows a multiscreen audiovisual about sharks and conducts a dissection of a recently caught shark (Tues, Wed & Thurs 9am & 2pm, Sun 2pm), which disabuses any notions of sharks as the hooligans of the oceans. It also plugs the board's work in maintaining the province's **shark nets**: although these nets protect swimmers all along the coast, they are controversial, as not just sharks but also endangered turtles and dolphins die in them, thus affecting the balance of the inshore ecosystem. The Sharks Board is investigating an electronic shark barrier that might improve the situation, while ensuring safe swimming. Without your own transport, the best way to get to the Sharks Board is by minibus taxi or shuttle, from outside Sugar Coast Tourism (see below).

A trip on a Sharks Board ski boat allows you to look out for dolphins and whales. The trips, departing at 6am, cost R150 per person (book on ☎082 403 9206), and a minimum of eleven passengers are needed for the trip to run.

Practicalities

Sugar Coast Tourism, 14 Chartwell Drive (Mon–Fri 8am–4.30pm, Sat 9am–noon; ☎031 561 4257), is a useful source for **maps and information** about attractions up the coast. Outside, you'll find the departure point for the Umhlanga Express minibus service (☎082 268 0651), which runs trips on request to the Musgrave Centre in Berea and to Durban city centre.

Accommodation

Beverly Hills Sun Lighthouse Rd ☎031 561 2211, ⓦwww.southernsun.com. The flashest place to stay in Umhlanga, but you'll get better value at the more characterful *Oyster Box*. ❼
Honeypot 11 Hilken Dr ☎031 561 3795, ⓔsugarfld@iafrica.com. Five B&B units decorated

in rustic style with limewashed furniture and African fabric. Each room sleeps two and there's a swimming pool. ❹
Jessica's B&B 35 Portland Dr ☎ & ⓕ031 561 3369. Two self-contained garden flats accommodating four people in each. ❸

Oyster Box Lighthouse Rd ☎031 561 2233, ℮oysterbox@iafrica.com. The oldest hotel on the Dolphin Coast oozes established elegance with a choice of rooms. The *Box* is also a great place for tea or drinks on the outside terrace overlooking the ocean. ❺

Sylvan Grove 49 Sylvan Grove ☎031 561 5137, ℮sylvangrove@mweb.co.za. Four rooms in a sea-facing guesthouse in a tropical garden, offering great breakfasts and also convenient transfers from Durban airport. ❺

Teremok 49 Marine Dr ☎031 561 5848, ⓦwww.teremok.co.za. An intimate guesthouse with contemporary decor. It has a small wellness centre, free laundry service and free airport shuttle. ❽

Eating

Ambrosia Chartwell Dr. A recommended Greek eating place, with exceptionally friendly staff.

Cottonfields 2 Lagoon Dr. A popular local bistro and bar serving up *potjiekos* and regular live music. Daily noon till late.

Il Maurice 9 McCausland Crescent ☎031 561 7609. Serving French and Mauritian food, this pricey restaurant has received rave reviews locally. Open Tues–Sun noon–2.30pm & 6.30–10.30pm.

Oyster Box Grill Room *Oyster Box Hotel*. First-class curries and great seafood at one of the few eating places here offering dancing on a Saturday night. Daily noon–3am.

Razzmatazz *Cabana Beach Hotel*, Lagoon Dr. If you can afford to splash out, look no further than this restaurant specializing in seafood and game; come here to treat yourself to springbok fillet or roast guinea fowl, and savour the ocean views from their great outdoor deck. The three-course set menu is great value (R75). Daily lunch & dinner.

Umdloti, La Mercy and Tongaat

North of Umhlanga, the blur of development unexpectedly opens out into sugar-cane hills and subtropical coastal vegetation. **UMDLOTI**, just 6km north of Umhlanga, has a safe swimming beach, as well as a fabulous natural rock pool, great for swimming or snorkelling on the calm inside of the shallow reef. A couple of kilometres further along at **LA MERCY** is a highly recommended **restaurant** – the long-established *Sea Bell*, a slightly tatty curry house under a dingy hotel, which is noted for its piquant prawns.

Three kilometres north of the restaurant, you'll come to **Casuarina Beach**, the location of *Beachbums Backpackers Lodge*, 65 Casuarina Drive (☎032 943 1401 or 082 4458 951, ℮bsbeach@iafrica.com; dorms and rooms ❶). Right on the beach and the only **backpacker lodge** in the area, it's conveniently on the Baz Bus route. The two-storey home has double rooms, dorms and space to camp. You can chill out on sun decks overlooking the ocean, and the lodge can provide free surfboards and bodyboards, as well as famously good pizzas. Five minutes away lies **Westbrook Beach**, good for swimming, dolphin viewing and with a popular surfing break. Set in a secluded part of the beach is *Sea Villa* (☎031 568 1839, ℮seavilla@iafrica.com; ❹), where each room has a private balcony for you to enjoy the view.

TONGAAT lies a few kilometres inland from here across the N2 highway, a barrier between the coastal resorts and the workings of KwaZulu-Natal's sugar industry. Arriving in town, you're confronted by a massive sugar mill pumping pungent white smoke from its towering chimneys, and by pedestrians chewing sticks of sugar cane. The town, fronted by neglected imitation Cape Dutch cottages, has long associations with South Africa's Indian community and boasts a handful of garish temples. The most distinguished of these, a National Monument, is the small **Shri Jugganath Puri Temple**, dedicated to Vishnu. A whitewashed, phallic building tipped by deities on each corner, and surrounded by mango trees, the temple was built at the turn of the last century by the Sanskrit scholar Pandit Shrikishan Maharaj, who came to

KwaZulu-Natal in 1895. To get to the temple, take the R102 towards Durban, turn right into Ganie Street at the first traffic lights after the police station, then left into Plane Street and left again into Catherine Street; the temple is at the junction of Catherine and Plane streets.

Ballito

There's nothing very African about **BALLITO**, a Mediterranean-style resort 43km up the coast from Durban, with a splurge of time-shares, high-rise holiday apartments and shopping malls by the sea. Nevertheless, it's a pleasant enough place, with a beach offering safe swimming and full-time lifeguards, and a couple of natural rock pools for bathing – one at Ballito itself, and the other at the far northern end of Ballito Beach, near the Santorini development. The area is also well known for its luxury guesthouses on wealthy sugar estates, set back from the coast and all signposted from the N1.

The excellent Dolphin Coast Publicity Association (Mon–Fri 8.30am–5pm, Sat 9am–1pm; ☎ & ℉ 032 946 1997), just before the BP service station as you enter town, has an up-to-date list of B&Bs and can supply **information** about the surrounding area. Even if you choose not to stay in the vicinity, it's worth stopping off at the *Zimbali Lodge* for a **meal** or, best of all, a sundowner in the bar, which is raised on stilts overlooking the fourteenth fairway of the golf course, and rewards you with soaring views across the Indian Ocean. In Ballito itself, one of the best places to eat is *Al Pescatore*, 14 Edward Place, which serves outstanding Italian seafood and has great ocean views. Another good option is *Foodmatters*, in the Well Building, Albertina Way, open daily for breakfast, lunch and tea. They do excellent café-style fare – try the French toast with halloumi cheese, sun-dried tomatoes and syrup.

Accommodation

Ballito Manor Compensation Beach Rd ☎032 947 1140, ⓦwww.threecities.co.za. Elegant accommodation in a historic colonial homestead, with fourteen luxury rooms surrounded by wonderful gardens. ❽
Dolphin Holiday Resort On the corner of Compensation Beach Rd and Hillary Dr ☎032 946 2187, ⓦwww.dolphinholidayresort.co.za. A well-shaded campsite and collection of self-catering cottages; there's no sea view, but it's only a 5min walk from the beach. ❶
The Vineyard 11 Ashley Road ☎032 946 1204, ⓦwww.vineyardonballito.co.za. A well-run, elegant B&B with worthwhile afternoon teas. ❻

Zimbali Lodge 1km south of Ballito ☎032 538 1007, ⓦwww.sun-international.com. The swishest establishment in the vicinity is set in lush subtropical coastal forest in the heart of a network of wetlands. Antelope are frequently seen, the butterflies, such as the citrus swallowtail, are larger than life, and the birdlife is prolific – you might even see the rare spotted narina trogon. Accommodation is in luxury suites attended by butlers, and you can avail yourself of clay-pigeon shooting, beach or forest walks, steam rooms, massages, and pedicures. ❽

Shaka's Rock

Some 49km north of Durban, the rather tame coastal resort of **SHAKA'S ROCK** feels at odds with the name of Shaka, whose warrior reputation reverberated across southern Africa in the nineteenth century. More or less a continuation of Ballito, Shaka's Rock has a small selection of **accommodation**, one of the nicest being *Lalaria Lodge*, 25 Dolphin Crescent (☎032 525 5789, ⓦwww.lalaria.co.za; ❹), with king-sized beds, ocean views, and within walking distance of the beach. Excellent value for money is *Sundance* at 18 Dolphin Drive (☎032 525 5342, ⓦwww.sundanceguesthouse.co.za; ❸). It has just three rooms, each with its own private garden. Adjoining the old-fashioned *Salt Rock Hotel* on Basil Hulett Drive is its **caravan park (❶)**, situated on grassy terraces. Built into the rocks below the hotel are two tidal pools, great for swimming, and where Zulu women are reputed to have collected salt in King Shaka's day.

There's an even better tidal rock pool at Thompson's Bay, built on an elevated rocky platform with changing rooms and big enough for anyone wanting to swim serious lengths. To get to Thompson's Bay, simply walk back along the beach towards Ballito, about 2km from the *Salt Rock Hotel*.

Dukuza and Groutville

You'll get far more of a sense of Shaka's legendary status as founder of the Zulu state by heading inland along the R102 to **DUKUZA** (still widely known by it's pre-1994 election name, **Stanger**), which has a special place in the cosmology of Zulu nationalists. Roughly 70km north of Durban, Dukuza is the site of the Zulu king's last kraal and the place where he was treacherously stabbed to death in 1828 by his half-brother Dingane, who succeeded him. Shaka used his exceptional military talents to build up the Zulu state into the greatest power in southeast Africa by the mid-1820s – creating disquiet even among the British. The warrior-king is said to have been buried upright in a grain pit, and is commemorated by a small park and memorial in Couper Street, right in the centre of town. Near the memorial is a rock with a groove worn into it – supposedly where Shaka sharpened his spears. These days, the park is the venue for a semi-religious pilgrimage by modern-day **Zulu warriors** from all over the country – members of the fiercely Zulu nationalist Inkatha Freedom Party (IFP). Every year, on September 24, known to Zulus as Shaka's Day and now falling on a public holiday, Heritage Day, they gather here to be addressed by **Chief Mangosuthu Buthelezi**, a mercurial figure who started his political life as an ANC member but fell out with the organization. Those attending Buthelezi's speech are often colourfully clad in traditional Zulu garb and armed with traditional weapons.

At the rear of the memorial park, the **Dukuza Interpretative Centre** (Mon–Fri 8am–4pm, Sat & Sun 9am–4pm; free) has a small display on Shaka and a very good fifteen-minute audiovisual display; you can also see craftspeople at work and sample traditional meals in an attached café. Nearby, the lively **Dukuza Market** in Market Road, off King George Road, is where Zulu and Indian traders sell fresh spices, herbs, fruit and vegetables.

Some 8km southwest of Dukuza on the R102, just across a rusty bridge over the Mvoti River, tiny **GROUTVILLE** is remarkable mainly for the grave of **Albert Luthuli**, one of South Africa's greatest political leaders. A teacher and chief of the Zulus in Groutville, Luthuli became President General of the ANC in 1952. Advocating a non-violent struggle against apartheid, Luthuli was awarded the Nobel Peace Prize in 1960, which at home earned him a succession of banning orders restricting him to the Dukuza area. In 1967, he died in mysterious circumstances in KwaDukuza, apparently knocked down by a train. He is buried next to a whitewashed, nineteenth-century corrugated-iron mission church. Luthuli's life is recounted in the moving autobiography, *Let My People Go*.

Blythedale

The closest stretch of sand to Dukuza is at **BLYTHEDALE**, some 8km away, where a ban on high-rise construction has preserved the deserted appearance of its endless beach and kept buildings screened behind the curtain of thick coastal vegetation. Swimming here is possible; shark nets are in place between December and April, and lifeguards are on duty in season. As with many spots along the KwaZulu-Natal coast, you're likely to see local fishermen trying their luck for shad, garrick, kingfish and barracuda.

Accommodation

Baroque B&B 14 Dolphin Crescent ℡ 032 551 5272, ℮ leonklopper@telkomsa.net. Attractive rooms with en-suite showers, 150m from the beach. ❸

Bush and Beach 71 Umvoti Dr ℡ 032 551 1496, ℻ 032 551 1546. Pleasant cottages in a nice garden setting. ❷

La Mouette Caravan Park 1 Umvoti Dr ℡ 032 551 2547, ℮ lamoutte@iafrica.com. Camping and a small self-catering log cabin, just back from the beach. ❶–❷

Mini Villas Just across the road from the caravan park ℡ 032 551 1277, ℻ 032 551 1628. Simple budget cottages. ❶

Palm Dunes Umvoti Dr ℡ 032 552 1588, ℮ palmdunes@maggie.co.za. Self-catering or B&B at an upmarket resort and conference centre, where you can opt for a classy three-bedroomed chalet or a double room. The resort also offers jetskis, canoes, a theatre (in season), and can arrange guided hiking and mountain biking in the nearby forests. ❹

Harold Johnson Nature Reserve

Abutting the Tugela River is KwaZulu-Natal Wildlife's **Harold Johnson Nature Reserve** (daily dawn–dusk; R12; ℡ 032 486 1574), signposted 24km north of Dukuza off the N2 (take the Zinkwazi turn-off and turn left at Darnall). With its well-preserved coastal bush, steep cliffs and gullies, this is a fine place to come for a day's visit or to camp overnight (❶; there are no shops or facilities, so be sure to stock up before arrival). At the main picnic site and parking area you'll find a cultural museum housed in huts and featuring good displays of Zulu beadwork and aspects of Zulu society. You can follow the two-kilometre "Remedies and Rituals" **trail** from the picnic site taking you past plants whose medicinal uses you can read about. Alternatively, pick up the Tugela Trail booklet and follow a walk which highlights various historical sites in the reserve, most of them connected to the Anglo-Zulu War of 1879 and **Ultimatum Tree**. This wild fig tree, all but demolished in a cyclone in 1987, was where the British issued their ultimatum to King Cetshwayo in 1878, part of which required the Zulus to demobilize their standing army. The British used his non-compliance as an excuse to attack the Zulus and crush their independence. Also on the trail are the remains of Fort Pearson, from which the British launched their invasion of Zululand.

Valley of a Thousand Hills

The evocatively named **Valley of a Thousand Hills** (ⓦ1000hills.kzn.org .za), 45km from Durban, makes for a picturesque drive along the edge of densely folded hills where Zulu people still live in traditional homesteads, and which visitors rarely venture into. The spectacular landscape goes some way to soothing any misgivings you might have about ethnographic "game viewing", but it's only worth a special effort if you're not exploring the KwaZulu-Natal interior, where scenes like this occur in abundance. While the valley is best suited to touring in your own car, there are **daily tours** from Durban offered by Tekweni Eco Tours (see box on p.467) which take in the highlights. Alternatively, if you're in Durban on the last Sunday of the month, take a **vintage train trip** with Umgeni Steam Railways (☏082 353 6003; R45), which boasts one of the largest collections of historic locomotives and coaches in the southern hemisphere. There are two trips, at 8.45 and 12.30pm, from the Kloof station, Stockers Arms, Old Main Road.

The trip to the valley and back can be done in half a day, but there are sufficient attractions laid on along the route to extend it to a full day's outing. If you're driving, head inland from Durban along the N3, following the Pinetown signs. At the Hillcrest/Old Main Road turn-off, turn right over the freeway onto the Old Main Road (M31) and continue along here following the Thousand Hills Experience Route sign. Within a kilometre you'll pass the thriving Victorian-styled **Heritage Market**, with craft shops, restaurants and jewellery stores. Continue for several kilometres, past the Fainting Goat, a small shopping centre, and turn left to the appealing *Pot & Kettle* restaurant and gallery, which offers unparalleled views of the Thousand Hills. Just around the bend is **Phezulu Safari Park** (daily 8.30am–4.30pm; R40; ☏031 777 1000), which brings you close to deadly serpents – tucked away in cramped little glass boxes – plus crocodiles and other penned animals. There's also a reconstruction of a pre-colonial Zulu village, where you can watch tourist-geared – but nonetheless spirited – displays of **Zulu dancing**, set against the dramatic horizon of the valley (daily 10am, 11.30am, 2pm & 3.30pm; price included in R60 entrance fee).

One of the nicest places to stop is *The View* **restaurant** (daily 9am–4.30pm) at 330 Old Main Road, with magnificent views over the valley (into which you can walk from here) and a shaded patio. It's a good stop for tea or lunch, with savoury and sweet pancakes on offer. Attached is The Loom, a Zulu women's weaving project selling brightly coloured handwoven crafts, though not traditionally styled.

Pietermaritzburg

Although **PIETERMARITZBURG** (often called Maritzburg) sells itself as the best-preserved Victorian city in South Africa, with strong British connections, little of its colonial heritage remains, and it's actually a very South African city. Zulus make up the largest community, with people of Indian descent coming second, and those of British extraction a minority – albeit a high-profile one. This multiculturalism, together with a substantial student population, adds up to a fairly lively city that's also relatively safe and small enough to explore on foot. Only 80km inland from Durban along the fast N3 freeway, Pietermaritzburg is an easy day's outing from the coastal city, and one you can combine with visiting the Valley of a Thousand Hills (see p.503) along the Old Main Road (R103). The city is also well positioned for an overnight stop on your way to the Ukhahlamba Drakensberg (see p.512) or the Battlefields in the vicinity of Ladysmith (see p.562).

Pietermaritzburg's Afrikaner origins are reflected in its name; after slaughtering three thousand Zulus at the Battle of Blood River, the Voortrekkers established the fledgling Republic of Natalia in 1839, naming their capital in honour of the Boer leaders **Piet Retief** and **Gerrit Maritz**. The republic's independence was short-lived; only four years later, Britain annexed it and spent the rest of the century transforming Pietermaritzburg into an English town stamped with all the grandeur and pomposity of empire. Even as the Afrikaners trekked north to escape the irksome British, English settlers were arriving from the south to swell the city's population, and during the closing decade of the nineteenth century Maritzburg was the most important centre in the colony of Natal, with a population of nearly 10,000 (more than Durban at that time).

Indians arrived at the turn of the last century, mostly as indentured labourers, but also as traders. Among their number was a young, little-known lawyer called Mohandas Gandhi, who went on to change the history of India. He later traced the embryo of his devastatingly successful tactic of passive resistance to an incident in 1893, when as a non-white he was thrown out of a first-class train compartment at Pietermaritzburg station.

Pietermaritzburg is the provincial capital of KwaZulu-Natal, but its exact status is ambiguous, as Ulundi, in the former KwaZulu Bantustan, is currently striving for recognition as the political centre of the province.

Arrival and information

Flights from Johannesburg, used mainly by business travellers, arrive at the city's **Oribi airport** (℡033 386 9577), about 6km south of the town centre. The only means of getting to town from here is by taxi. If you buy your ticket some time in advance, it can be much cheaper to fly into Durban airport, connected twice daily to Pietermaritzburg by the Cheetah intercity shuttle bus (℡033 342 0266). The journey takes about 75 minutes and the bus drops off outside the *Imperial Hotel*, 224 Loop Street. (The Cheetah also picks up passengers in the centre of Durban, outside the Old Courthouse Museum in Aliwal Street and at the motorcoach terminal at Durban Station.) Intercape **buses** pull in at the centrally located bus terminal on the north side of the information bureau, on the corner of Longmarket Street and Commercial Road. Greyhound buses also stop nearby, at *MacDonald's* in Burger Street, while Translux pulls in at the Premier Caltex garage on the corner of Commercial and Burger streets. If you're staying at the backpacker lodge, you can arrange for staff to pick you up; alternatively, the **Baz Bus** drops off at any of the central places to stay.

The **train station** (℡033 897 2350) lies at the unsavoury southwest end of Longmarket Street, one of the main city thoroughfares, from where it's advisable to arrange beforehand to be collected, particularly at night. The hectic **minibus taxi rank** lies outside the tourist office, and stretches from the bus terminus right down the block (destinations are posted outside the taxis). Metered taxis should be booked in advance (see "Listings" on p.510), and in this compact city are unlikely to break the bank.

The **tourist office** at Publicity House, on the corner of Longmarket Street and Commercial Road (Mon–Fri 8am–5pm, Sat 8am–3pm; ℡033 345 1348), stocks an excellent selection of books and accommodation leaflets; you can buy tickets for Translux and Greyhound buses in the same building. The best place to find a fold-out map of the whole city is at Shuter & Shooter, 230 Church Street, which also sells travel guides, natural history field guides and books covering KwaZulu-Natal history.

Accommodation

Maritzburg has a good selection of reasonably priced accommodation, including some good-value luxury places. If you need help with B&B accommodation, try Pietermaritzburg B&B Network (℡073 154 4444).

PIETERMARITZBURG

5

WILLOWTON ROAD

DU TOIT VILJOEN ROAD

Durban

Johannesburg

Howick

GRETOWN ROAD

MANNING AVENUE

OHRTMANN ROAD

QUEEN
CHUTNEY RD

EAST   EAST

JAMES   WILLIAMS

THOMAS   GEORGE   LYTTON

PIETERMARITZ   CHURCH

GINMAN   KNIPE
VERNON   DERWENT   COLLIER   FLEET
HENRY

PRINCE ALFRED
BULWER
MASON ROAD
MAPLE ROAD

RETIEF   RETIEF

GARFIELD
IRENE TERR.
BOURKE   BURGER   WATT LANE
SLATTER   MURPHY   LONGMARKET   LOOP   HOLIDAY
DAVIS   DOIG

BOSHOFF   BOSHOFF

Voortrekker
Museum

FRANCIS
CLAYBOURNE   AKERMAN
ST. ANDREW
STANTIAL   DRUMMOND
SMITH   MAY   THRASH   ASSURANCE   OLD
OWEN   MARKET

ARCHBELL
HENRIETTA
Upper Crust   STRAPP
Publicity
House   6
Tatham Art Gallery

BRAID
PAYN

COMMERCIAL ROAD
Supreme Court
Gardens
City Hall
OTTO

MILLER

MACLEAN
Gandhi Statue
Old Natal   Natal Museum
Parliament Building
STRANACK   Imperial
Reid's Building
St Peter's Church   First National Bank

COMMERCIAL ROAD

CHAPEL

EBENEZER   LEIGHTON
Victoria
Mall   DEANERY
LANE   TEMPLE

PRINCE CHARLES DRIVE

BALMORAL DRIVE

ORMOND
GARRICK   RAVEN
OXFORD   WILSON   BURGER
BURROWS   STEAD   LOOP
LANE   TROY   DEANE   PRINCESS MARGARET DR
WALKER

NORTH   FIRST AVE

PERTH   POLO   SCOTT   FLEMING   COLLEGE ROAD
AVE
SYNDICATE
CURRAN
Macrorie House Museum
QUARRY RD

KEATE   KEATE

Train Station

GRIFFIN RD

LOGAN RD

0   500 m

BALE RD

NAPIER RD

Durban Road

HOWICK ROAD
HOSSIP RD
CHATTERTON RD
SANCTUARY RD
ARMITAGE RD
ROBERTS ROAD
VICTORIA ROAD
GREYLING STREET
BOOM STREET
BERG STREET
PIETERMARITZ STREET
CHURCH STREET
LOOP STREET
BURGER
PRINCE ALFRED
GERTRUDE
ZEEDER-
BURG
MAYOR'S WALK
WINSTON ROAD
HOWARD ROAD
DOULL ROAD
KERSHAW HAVELOCK RD
EUGENE MARAIS RD

N

Johannesburg
Howick
Durban
A
G, D, E, F & 5
C, D, E, F
G & H
13, 12 & 11
Durban Road, 8, 9 & 10

ACCOMMODATION

African Dreamz	**G**	Crossways Country Inn	**C**
Ascot Inn	**A**	Duvet and Crumpets	**E**
Brevisbrook	**I**	Greenlands	**H**
Briar Ghyll Lodge	**D**	Redlands Hotel & Lodge	**F**
City Royal Hotel	**B**		

RESTAURANTS, CAFÉS, BARS AND CLUBS

9Bar	**C**	Kara Nichha's	**6**	Stagecoach	**8**
The Artists Palate		Le Gourmet	**11**	TAPS	**4**
The Butchery	**13**	McGinty's Irish Pub	**9**	Tropicana	**2**
Crowded House	**10**	Pesto Deli &		Turtle Bay	**5**
Els Amics	**3**	Trattoria	**12**		

African Dreamz 30 Taunton Rd, Wembley ☎ & ⓕ033 394 5141. One mini-suite in a family home on a large property 2km from the centre, where you can self-cater or get breakfast. Guests have use of the garden, tennis court and swimming pool. ❶

Ascot Inn 210 Woodhouse Rd, Scottsville ☎033 386 2226, ⓦwww.ascot-inn.co.za. A complex of comfortable mock-colonial cottages with a swimming pool, set on a large lawned property next to Scottsville race course and the N3, about 4km east of the city centre. You can self-cater or eat in their dining room. ❷

Brevisbrook 28 Waverleydale Rd, Boughton ☎033 344 1402 or 072 244 9766, ⓦwww.brevisbrook .co.za. Old-fashioned hospitality and attention to detail make a stay here memorable. All four rooms have a private entrance and bathroom, and access to the swimming pool. ❸

Briar Ghyll Lodge George MacFarlane Lane, off Howick Rd, Town Hill ☎033 342 2664, ⓦwww .bglodge.co.za. A magnificent Victorian homestead 5km northwest of the city centre, on rolling lawns, with a tennis court and swimming pool. You can choose between spacious suites within the main homestead or two self-contained cottages. ❹

City Royal Hotel 301 Burger St, City Centre ☎033 394 7072, ⓦwww.cityroyalhotel.co.za. A modernized 1930s building catering mainly to business travellers. It's worth asking about their substantial discounts during weekends and school holidays. ❺

Crossways Country Inn Old Howick Rd, Hilton ☎033 343 3267, ⓦwww.futurenet.co.za. Roughly 9km north of Pietermaritzburg, *Crossways* is a fine choice if you want to stay out of town. Modelled on an English country pub, with nice old furniture, it's also a good place to stop off for teas and lunches. ❹

Duvet and Crumpets 1 Freelands Pl, Wembley, 2km north of the centre ☎ & ⓕ033 394 4133, ⓔduvetb&b@lantic.net. Simple but pleasantly furnished self-catering or B&B rooms and cottages in a 1930s family home. ❸

Greenlands 15 Hosking Rd, Wembley ☎033 342 6233 or 082 444 9292, ⓔgreenlands@mjvn.co.za. A small, comfortable B&B with en-suite rooms, each with a separate entrance. ❷

Redlands Hotel & Lodge 1 George MacFarlane Lane, Wembley ☎033 394 3333, ⓔredlands@mweb.co.za. This upmarket boutique hotel has luxury finishes, a swimming pool and tennis court. Besides rooms, they offer self-catering one- and two-bed apartments. ❹

The City

Most places of interest in Pietermaritzburg are within easy walking distance of the centre's heart, which is crossed by the junction of **Commercial Road** and **Longmarket Street**. The inevitable old apartheid divisions are marked out by roads and railways, with the African majority crammed into townships south of the station, as they used to be excluded from the city centre. By contrast, Indians were allowed to bring their business into the city fringes, but only as far as Boshoff Street, northeast of Commercial Road. Around here, and in the nearby Asian suburbs of Woodlands, Mountain Rise and Willowton, you'll find the greatest concentration of shops selling cheap spicy snacks like *rotis* and *bunny chows*, as well as the city centre's mosques and Hindu temples. On the hills northwest of the centre, the predominantly white and affluent suburbs of Wembley, Athlone and Montrose look down from their heights at the sweaty buzz in the valley below, while south of the centre, the Pietermaritzburg campus of the **University of KwaZulu-Natal** in Scottsville attracts large numbers of students to set up digs in the suburban houses.

City Hall, Tatham Art Gallery and around

The **City Hall**, on the corner of Commercial Road and Church Street, is a great example of late Victorian red-brick civic architecture, self-assuredly holding the prime spot in town, with wonderful detailing and an impressive fifteen-metre clock tower. Across Commercial Road, the **Tatham Art Gallery** (Tues–Sun 10am–6pm; donation), another fine brick edifice, is the highlight of Pietermaritzburg's formal attractions, housing one of the country's best collections of international and local art. Completed in 1871 as the

Supreme Court of the Colony of Natal, the building formed the central complex of the capital's defences when an invasion was feared during the Zulu War of 1879. In 1990, the building became home to the Tatham collection and the Zulus finally made it inside, with artworks by black South Africans exhibited alongside those by Pablo Picasso, Graham Sutherland, Edgar Degas, David Hockney and Henri Matisse.

Adjacent to the Tatham, the **Old Natal Parliament Building** represents a typical piece of imperial architecture. Started in 1889 for Queen Victoria's Jubilee, it borrows the grand language of columns and pediments from the Roman Empire. Standing amid the formal front gardens is a statue of the unamused "Queen Empress" wielding a distinctly Freudian combination of a sceptre and orb. From here, heading down Longmarket Street as far as Chapel Street, you'll pass a series of attractive period buildings. Most notable of these are the **post office**, a solid dressed stone pile built in 1903; the three-storey **Reid's Building**, a little further along and considered a daringly tall skyscraper in its day; and the **First National Bank**, even further along, which dates from 1903 and had its facade chosen from an Edwardian catalogue and shipped out from the mother country. Between this section of Longmarket and Church streets is the tightly gridded warren of alleyways known as **the Lanes**, a mostly pedestrianized quarter of lawyers' offices, takeaways, shops and an inordinate number of hairdressers. The area, which was the financial hub of Natal from 1888 to 1931 and housed four separate stock exchanges, is enjoyable to explore during the day, but is a notorious stamping ground of pickpockets, so stay alert and don't come here after dark.

Any of the Lanes will bring you through to Church Street, which is worth wandering along to take in some more period buildings. **St Peter's Church**, completed in 1857, was the base for Bishop John Colenso after he was kicked out of the Church of England for his liberal theological ideas and his role in championing the Zulu cause against the British. As you head up Church Street, back toward the City Hall, you can't miss the **Gandhi Statue**, unveiled on June 6, 1993, on the centenary of his ejection from a first-class train carriage at Pietermaritzburg station because he wasn't white. Adjacent to Gandhi, the **Supreme Court Gardens** on the corner of Commercial Road and Church Street are filled with monuments to Britons who died fighting against the Zulus, the Boers and other European powers in two world wars.

The museums

On Boshoff Street, the **Voortrekker Museum** (Mon–Fri 9am–4pm, Sat 9am–1pm; R3) centres on the original Church of the Vow, built in 1838 by Boers in honour of their victory over the Zulus three years earlier at the Battle of Blood River. The church was their part of a bargain allegedly struck with God (see p.562). The museum connects with the Voortrekker roots of Pietermaritzburg and is worth a fleeting visit to gain some insight into life on trek. The most interesting items are the homemade children's toys and beautifully embroidered *kappies* (hats) which the women used to shield themselves from the sun. New additions include a replica of a Hindu Shiva temple and a Zulu hut, as well as a display relating to the French Prince Imperial, who died during the Zulu War of 1879. Across the lovely courtyard garden is the reconstructed house of **Andries Pretorius**, leader of the Voortrekkers at Blood River and the driving force behind the establishment of the Boer Republic of Natalia. The thatched house, originally built in 1846, is appealing for its sheer simplicity, which stands in contrast to fussy Victorian fashion.

Alan Paton

Writer, teacher and politician **Alan Paton** was born in Pietermaritzburg in 1903. His visionary first novel, *Cry, the Beloved Country*, focused international attention on the plight of black South Africans and sold millions of copies worldwide. The book was published in 1948 – the same year the National Party assumed power and began to establish apartheid – and Paton subsequently entered politics to become a founder-member of the non-racial and fiercely anti-apartheid Liberal Party. He was president of the party from 1960 until 1968, when it was forced to disband by repressive legislation forbidding multiracial political organizations.

Paton died in Durban in 1988, having published a number of works, including two biographies and his own autobiography. The following year, the Alan Paton Centre was established at the University of KwaZulu-Natal's archives building at 165 King Edward Avenue (visits by appointment; ☎033 260 5926). The Centre includes a re-creation of Paton's study, as well as personal memorabilia and documents.

Less inspiring is the **KwaZulu-Natal Museum**, 237 Loop Street (Mon–Fri 9am–4.30pm, Sat 10am–4pm, Sun 11am–3pm; R4), one block east of the Old Natal Parliament, with a collection of stuffed animals, dioramas, a small dinosaur display and a reconstruction of a late Victorian Maritzburg street. The best reason to visit is for the display of African sculpture, crafts and masks from across the continent, the highlight of which is a golden stool taken by British invaders as booty from the Asante people of Ghana. The museum also boasts the third largest butterfly collection in the world.

Continuing down Loop Street for about 1km, you'll reach Pine Street, on the corner of which is the **Macrorie House Museum** (Mon 11am–4pm, Tues–Fri 9am–1pm; R5), a beautiful two-storey Victorian house with intricate wrought-iron detailing. Built in 1862, the house became the home of Bishop Macrorie from 1869 to 1891, after he arrived to take over from Bishop Colenso. Today it houses furniture and other relics of early British settlers.

Striking northwest up Pine Street brings you to the classically Victorian **train station** at the end of Church Street. Although a little neglected in this now seedy part of town, the station is notable for its alternating courses of red-brick and stone facings and for its fine wrought-iron lacework dripping from the forecourt eaves. As you enter the concourse, a small plaque on your left, just before the platform, records (yet again) that this was where Gandhi was thrown off the train.

Eating, drinking and nightlife

Pietermaritzburg has a fairly good choice of **restaurants**, as well as a handful of decent nightclubs and pubs, particularly along Commercial Road. If you want to self-cater, you'll find home-baked pastries and pies, and a good range of breads and imported foods such as olive oil and Swiss chocolate, at Upper Crust, a **delicatessen** on Longmarket St (open daily until 9pm), opposite the taxi rank.

The three **cinema** complexes – the Nu Metro, in the Cascades Centre, McCarthy Drive; the Cine Centre at the Liberty Midlands Mall, Chatterton Road (both of these in the northern suburbs); and Ster-Kinekor, 50 Durban Road, in Scottsville – show mainstream releases. The university's Hexagon Theatre hosts occasional **drama** productions (bookings on ☎033 260 5537); check the *Witness* newspaper for details.

Restaurants and cafés

The Artists Palate Tatham Art Gallery, Commercial Rd. The best place in town for coffee and light lunches. Closed Mon.

The Butchery 101 Roberts Rd, Wembley ☏033 345 5239. A good place not just for steaks, ribs and chicken, but also for salads and vegetarian dishes. Daily from noon.

Els Amics 380 Longmarket St ☏033 345 6524. Set in a colonial house, Maritzburg's oldest restaurant is a popular place with a pleasant atmosphere, good prices and varied menu. Tues–Sat 11am–9pm.

Kara Nichha's 470 Church St. An excellent, very cheap Indian takeaway, particularly good for filled *rotis* and Indian sweets.

Le Gourmet 80 Roberts Rd, Wembley ☏033 342 3280. Pricey, suitably elegant restaurant serving fusion cuisine – duck with cumin-infused plum sauce, or sun-dried tomato and camembert filo parcels, to name but two worthwhile items on the menu. Mon–Sat lunch & dinner.

Pesto Deli & Trattoria 101 Roberts Rd, Wembley ☏033 342 2778. A good-value Italian restaurant serving everything from pizzas to fish and veal. Daily from noon.

Stagecoach 44 Durban Rd. Close to the university, this popular eating place offers good pub food, plus live music on Wednesday nights.

Tropicana 418 Longmarket St. Popular with Indian families, serving cheap curries as well as an extensive range of burgers and steaks with chips.

Turtle Bay 7 Wembley Terrace, Wembley, just off the N3 circle ☏033 394 5390. A decent seafood restaurant in the northern suburbs. Closed Sun.

Bars and clubs

Crowded House 124 Balhambra Way & Commercial Rd. Pleasant indoor and outdoor bars attracting a late-20s crowd. Wed, Fri & Sat; R25.

McGinty's Irish Pub 50 Durban Rd, Scottsville. A fairly smart pub with occasional live Irish music.

9Bar 121 Commercial Rd. A trendy club playing house and funk music. Thurs, Fri & Sat; R25.

TAPS Royal Show Grounds, Chatterton Rd. A restaurant and pub serving fifteen types of draught beer. It's a popular watering hole with office workers, and has a large outdoor deck. Daily from 12am until late.

Listings

Emergencies AA ☏082 16111; see also p.89.
Hospital For medical emergencies, contact the Med 24 hospital, Payn St ☏033 342 7023 or 033 342 7024.
Internet access The Hive Media Café, Scottsville Mall, 50 Durban Road, Scottsville (daily 10am–9pm)

Laundry The Wash Tub, Shop 2, Park Lane Centre, 12 Commercial Rd (daily 7am–6pm, Sat 8am–4pm, Sun 8am–3pm).
Pharmacy Medpharm, Victoria Mall, 157 Victoria Rd (24hr).
Taxis Junior Taxi Service, Echo Garage, Echo Rd ☏033 394 5454; Unique Taxis, 524 Khans Rd ☏033 391 1238.

The Midlands

For most travellers, the verdant farmland that makes up the **Midlands** is picture-postcard terrain, to be whizzed through on the two-hour journey from Durban or Pietermaritzburg to the Ukhahlamba Drakensberg. There's little reason to dally here, unless you fancy taking in the region's quaint, English-style country inns, tea shops and craft shops. From 1842 to 1897, battalion after battalion of British troops marched through the Midlands during a succession of wars to pacify first the Zulus and later the Boers. The region plays up its British connections, with clubs dedicated to trout-fishing or polo, posh boarding schools and old-fashioned country hotels. The cosy image is deceptive: security fences erected around most farms indicate deep levels of black resentment, with theft common and the murder of white landowners not unusual.

As you head north out of Pietermaritzburg on the N3 through the Midlands, you're roughly tracing the last journey of **Nelson Mandela** as a free man before his arrest in 1962. On the run from the police, Mandela had been continuing his political activities, often travelling in disguise – a practice that earned him the nickname of the "Black Pimpernel". **Howick**, 18km northwest of Pietermaritzburg, is recorded as the place where his historic detention began; the actual spot is on the R103, 2km north of a side road heading to the Tweedie junction. On this occasion, he was masquerading as the chauffeur of a white friend, when their car was stopped on the old Howick road, apparently because of a tip-off. A memorial unveiled by Mandela himself in 1996 marks the unassuming spot, along farmland between a railway line and the road.

Public relations consultants have dreamt up the **Midlands Meander**, a route that weaves its way around the N3 on back roads between Pietermaritzburg and the **Mooi River** 60km to the northwest. The route takes in a number of dispersed craft shops, hotels and other minor attractions; the scenery and little stopoffs are more appealing than the Midlands towns themselves, which you can comfortably bypass in the certainty that you're not missing much. If you want to see traditional Zulu beadwork being applied in contemporary ways, try to visit **Decadence**, a community-based **beadwork project** supporting over a hundred Zulu women in **Lidgetton**, off the N3, 20km west of Hawick. The project has had a constant fight for survival, but the women are beginning to reap the rewards.

For a more vigorous experience of the Midlands there are a couple of adventure activities on offer, both of which involve dangling from cables and ropes. In Howick, Over The Top Adventures (℡082 736 3651, ⓦwww.overthetop .co.za; R250 for a group of at least four) organize a 107-metre **abseil** down along the Howick Falls. North of Howick at the Karkloof Nature Reserve, you can undertake a **canopy tour** with Karkloof Canopy Tours (℡033 330 3415, ⓦwww.karkloofcanopytour.co.za; R450), on which you're strapped into a harness and glide along steel cables that link platforms erected high above the forest floor.

Practicalities

A free **map** outlining the attractions on the trip is available from most tourist offices in the vicinity, and there's a range of **accommodation** in the Midlands, including some upmarket country hotels; we review a selection below. For lists of self-catering accommodation hereabouts, contact KwaZulu-Natal Wildlife or the Midlands Meander Association (℡033 330 8195, ⓦwww.midlandsmeander.co.za).

Granny Mouse Country House Old Main Rd, Balgowan ℡033 234 4071, ⓦwww .grannymouse.co.za. Some 28km northwest of Howick on the R103, this has been stylishly renovated and offers sixteen rooms in thatched cottages, and decorated with rich textured fabrics. There's a swimming pool, restaurant and loads of small lounges with large comfortable chairs to relax in. Midweek discounts are available. ➍

Loxley House South off the Lonteni/Sani Pass Rd in the hamlet of Nottingham Rd, 30km northwest of Howick on the R103 ℡033 266 6362, ⓔloxley @futurenet.co.za. Comfortable rooms in a small B&B with its own restaurant. ➌

Rawdon's Old Main Rd, Nottingham Rd ℡033 266 6044, ⓦwww.rawdons.co.za. Set in a gracious country estate looking onto its own trout lake, with welcoming log fires for cool misty days and airy verandas for hot summers. It has an atmospheric pub with its own brewery on site. ➍

Stonehaven On the R103 (Old Main Rd) between Mooi River and Estcourt, south of the Hidcote turning and 3km northeast of the N3 ℡ & ℱ033 263 2632, ⓦwww.natalafrica.co.za. Comfortable self-catering cottages and B&B rooms and warm hospitality at this reasonably priced guesthouse on the farm of Anglo-Boer War specialist Ron Gold (see box on p.558). ➌

The Ukhahlamba Drakensberg

Hugging the border with Lesotho, South Africa's premier mountain wilderness and is mostly a vast national park, officially known as the **Ukhahlamba Drakensberg Park**. The tallest range in southern Africa, the "Dragon Mountains" (or, in Zulu, the "barrier of spears") reach their highest peaks along the border with Lesotho. The range is actually an escarpment separating a high interior plateau from the coastal lowlands of KwaZulu-Natal, and is the source of many streams and rivers which flow out to the Indian and Atlantic oceans. Although this is a continuation of the same escarpment that divides the Mpumalanga highveld from the game-rich lowveld of the Kruger National Park, and continues into the northern section of the Eastern Cape, when people talk of the Berg, they invariably mean the range in KwaZulu-Natal.

For elating scenery – massive spires, rock buttresses, wide grasslands, glorious waterfalls, rivers, pools and fern-carpeted forests – the Ukhahlamba Drakensberg is unrivalled. Wild and unpopulated, it's a paradise for **hiking**. While the southern section of the Ukhahlamba Drakensberg lacks the drama and varied landscape found further north, it does have an outstanding highlight in the hair-raising **Sani Pass**, a precipitous series of hairpins that twist to the top of the escarpment, up to the highest point in southern Africa reachable on wheels. The Ukhahlamba Drakensberg is also a World Heritage Site, one of the richest **San rock-art** repositories in the world. There are more than six hundred recorded sites hidden all over the mountains (three easily accessible ones are at **Giant's Castle**, **Injisuthi** and **Kamberg**), featuring more than 22,000 individual paintings by the original inhabitants of the area.

Visitors to the Ukhahlamba Drakensberg can **stay** either in the self-catering and camping options provided by KwaZulu-Natal Wildlife, or in hotels or backpacker lodges outside the park, which are the most feasible option if you don't have your own transport. The highest concentration of hotels and resorts is in the Central Berg, midway between Johannesburg and Durban. As for the **weather**, summers are warm but wet, and sees dramatic thunderstorms, with lightning flashing across huge charcoal skies, as well as misty days that block out the views. Winters tend to be dry, sunny and chilly, and you can expect freezing nights and, on the high peaks, occasional snow. The best times for hiking are probably spring and autumn. As the weather can change rapidly at any time of year, always take sufficient clothing and food, and don't forget a hat – the sun is fierce and bright, even in winter.

Reaching the Ukhahlamba Drakensberg

Most roads to the mountains branch off westwards from the **N3** between Pietermaritzburg and the Ladysmith area, and come to a halt at various Kwa-Zulu-Natal Wildlife camps. There is no public transport to any of these. You can reach the Southern Drakensberg using the **R626** or **R612/R617**, both routes putting you within striking distance of Sani Pass. With no connecting road system through the Ukhahlamba Drakensberg, it's not possible to drive from one end to the other.

Nearly all hotels in this area offer transfers from the Greyhound or Translux **intercity bus terminals** in Estcourt (see p.514) or Ladysmith (see p.562). The **Baz Bus** Durban–Jo'burg service goes via Winterton for the Northern Drakensberg; or Mooi River and Estcourt for the Central Drakensberg. **Sani Pass Carriers'** shuttle service (see p.523) connects Pietermaritzburg at least daily with Underberg and, further south, Kokstad.

There are no towns close to the mountains. Instead the park is hemmed in by rural African areas – former "homeland" territory, unsignposted and unnamed on many maps, but interesting to drive through and take in a slice of traditional **Zulu life**, complete with beehive-shaped huts.

En route to the Northern and Central Drakensberg

The nearest commercial centres lie on or just off the N3, and are useful for stocking up on supplies, filling up your car or arranging transport into the mountains. Largest and least appealing of these is **ESTCOURT**, 88km north of Pietermaritzburg, home to a cold-meat factory that processes bacon which, when the wind blows, perfumes the town with the smell of an all-day fry up. It's worth stopping off here to see the superb little museum housed at **Fort Durnford**, Cemps Road, off the R103 (daily 9am–noon, 1–4pm; donation). The museum re-creates an old Estcourt street, complete with pawn shop, blacksmith, wholesale merchant and even rail ticket office, and has some displays on local military history as well as an impressive collection of wild bird eggs.

WINTERTON, 43km north of Estcourt along the R74 as it deviates west off the N3, is a tiny hamlet with some interesting little shops and eating places, filling stations and banks. The **museum** (Mon–Fri 9am–3pm, Sat 9am–noon; donation), signposted from Colenso Road, the main drag next to the municipal offices, justifies a stop for its excellent displays on San rock art and coverage of the Boer War Battlefields in this vicinity, notably Spioenkop and Vaalkrans. If you need a place to stay hereabouts, there's the pleasant *Lilac Lodge* (☎036 488 1025; ❷), 8 Springfield Road, the main drag as you drive into the town. It has accommodation in small cottages and its own coffee and arts and crafts shop. Another appealing choice is *Ukuthula Bush Camp* at Rolling M Ranch (☎082 773 9914, ✉rollingmranch@saol.com; ❷), a working farm outside town on the banks of the Tugela River. Accommodation includes B&B rooms and self-catering cabins and cottages. The camp organizes plenty of activities, including walks up the river and into the mountains, plus, as they're on the Battlefields route, they also have trails to Spioenkop and Buller's Cross monuments. To get there, head 2km north from Winterton on the R600, then turn right at the signposted Skietdrift road; the camp is around 20km down this route. Alternatively, they can collect you from Winterton. If you fancy **whitewater rafting**, the Tugela River east of the Drakensberg can be accessed from Winterton on trips run by Four Rivers Rafting and Adventures (☎ & ℻036 468 1693, ⓦfourriversadventures.co.za). Their inflatable-raft forays into the river gorge last from half a day to three days; a half-day trip in a two-person inflatable raft costs R370.

BERGVILLE, 23km north of Winterton, is another tiny and rather ugly village, notable only for being the last place to stock up before heading on to the Royal KwaZulu-Natal National Park. Apart from the helpful **Ukhahlamba Drakensberg Tourism Association** (Mon–Fri 9am–5.30pm, Sat 9am–1pm; ☎036 448 1557, ⓦwww.drakensberg.org.za) at the Sunbird Nursery in Winterton Road, there's not much to keep you here.

En route to the Southern Drakensberg

UNDERBERG on the R617 is the main gateway to the Southern Drakensberg, with a good supermarket for stocking up and some emergency services should you run into difficulties in the mountains. It also has a selection of good craft shops and attractive pubs. At the *Underberg Hotel* a few metres from the supermarket is the Major Adventure offices (☎033 701 1628), where you can book overnight, three- and five-day **tours to Lesotho**. There's also a

pharmacy, the Sani (☎033 701 1034, after hours ☎033 701 1955 or 033 702 1210), and a **private hospital**, the Riverview (☎033 701 1331). The Automobile Association offers a 24-hour breakdown service (☎082 16111).

HIMEVILLE, 4km north of Underberg, is the last village you'll find before heading up Sani Pass. At the centre of the village, Sani Saunter Publicity (Mon–Fri 8am–4pm; ☎033 701 1471, ⓦwww.sanisaunter.com) is the best place to get **information** about the region. Opposite is the decent *Himeville Arms* (☎033 702 1305; ❶–❸), a country **inn** which makes a good stopover before the final haul to the mountains, organizing 4WD trips, horse-riding, tennis and golf. There's a plethora of **B&Bs** along this road, one of the nicest being *Yellowwood Cottage* (☎ & Ⓕ033 702 1065; ❷); set in a spectacular garden with wonderful Berg views, it has three en-suite rooms and a fully equipped kitchenette.

Hiking and other activities

Whether you choose to take your time on easy walks or embark on a challenging three- or four-day trip into the mountains, **hiking** in the Ukhahlamba Drakensberg remains one of South Africa's top wilderness experiences. The marvel of setting out on foot in these mountains is that you're unlikely to encounter vehicles, settlements, or even other people, and the scenery is sublime.

The Ukhahlamba Drakensberg is divided into the High Berg and Little Berg, according to altitude. In the **High Berg**, you're in the land of spires and great rock buttresses, where the only places to sleep are in caves or, in some areas, huts. You'll need to be totally self-sufficient and obey wilderness rules, taking a trowel and toilet paper with you and not fouling natural water with anything – which means carrying water away from the streams to wash in. Both mountaineers' huts and caves must be booked with the KwaZulu-Natal Wildlife office you start out from, and you'll also need to write down your route details in the mountain register. Slogging up the passes to the top of the mountains requires a high degree of fitness, some hiking experience and a companion or guide who knows the terrain.

The **Little Berg**, with its gentler summits, rivers, rock paintings, valleys and forests, is equally remote and beautiful. It's also safer, and easy enough to explore if you're of average fitness. If you don't want to carry a backpack and sleep in caves or huts, it's feasible to base yourself at one of the KZN Wildlife camps and set out on day hikes, of which there are endless choices. It's also possible to do a two-day walk from one of the camps, spending one night in a cave. Two highly recommended bases for walking are **Injisuthi** in the Giant's Castle Game Reserve (see p.518), or **Thendele** in the Royal KwaZulu-Natal National Park (see p.520). If you want the luxury of spending the nights in a hotel, base yourself in the **Cathedral Peak** area at the *Cathedral Peak Hotel* (see p.520). With extensive grasslands, the Southern Berg is the terrain of the highly recommended **Giant's Cup Hiking Trail**, an exhilarating introduction to the mountains (see p.523).

KZN Wildlife offices sells books on Ukhahlamba Drakensberg walks, as well as *Slingsby* **maps** (1:150,000), though note that some of the paths you'll find indicated are no longer in existence. If you don't feel confident to tackle the terrain, or are alone, you could contact Stef Steyn (☎033 330 4293, ⓦwww.kzntours.co.za), who specializes in **guided hikes** across the Ukhahlamba Drakensberg, as well as scenic tours all over the province. Another option is Ukhahlamba Drakensberg Spectacular Tours (☎036 631 3630 or 084 301 5701).

As for other activities, **angling** at Lotheni, Kamberg, Cobham or Giant's Castle costs R80 per day by permit only from KwaZulu-Natal Wildlife, with a bag limit of three trout per day. You'll need to bring all your own gear.

The Central Drakensberg

The **Central Drakensberg** incorporates four distinct areas, all clearly signposted from the N3. **Giant's Castle**, the site of a beautiful game reserve, is where you'll find the popular Lammergeyer bird hide and access to important San rock paintings. More San art is at **Injisuthi** to the north, principally a hiking destination and the place to head for if you're after complete wilderness. Far more accessible and tourist-trammelled is **Champagne Valley**, which offers a healthy number of hotels with ample sporting facilities, while to the north, and out on a limb, the hotel at **Cathedral Peak** is the best place to base yourself for some serious walking.

Giant's Castle Game Reserve

Giant's Castle Game Reserve (daily: April–Sept 6am–6pm; Oct–March 5am–7pm; R20) was created to protect the dwindling numbers of **eland**, which occurred in great numbers in the Ukhahlamba Drakensberg before the arrival of colonialists. Antelope of the montane zone are also found here – oribi, grey rhebuck, mountain reedbuck and bushbuck – as well as four dozen mammal species and around 160 bird species. The reserve is bordered to the west by three of the four highest peaks in South Africa: Mafadi (the highest at 3410m), Popple Peak (3325m) and the bulky ramparts of Giant's Castle itself (3314m).

This is not a traditional game park – there are no roads inside the reserve apart from access routes, which terminate at the two main KZN Wildlife accommodation areas, **Giant's Castle** and **Injisuthi**; the way to see the wildlife here is by walking or hiking through the terrain. One of the big attractions at the Giant's Head peak is the thrilling **lammergeier hide** (May–Sept), where you may see the rare lammergeier, a giant, black and golden bird with massive wings and a diamond-shaped tail. A scavenger, the lammergeier is an evolutionary link between eagles and vultures and was thought extinct in southern Africa until only a couple of decades ago. The bird is found only in mountainous areas such as the Himalayan foothills, and in South Africa only in the Ukhahlamba Drakensberg and Maloti mountains. In the locality you may also spot Cape vulture, black eagle, jackal buzzard and lanner falcon, attracted by the carcasses of animals put out by rangers during the winter. To visit the hide (R115 per person, minimum three people), you'll have to **book** as much as a year in advance through KZN Wildlife.

Giant's Castle has one of the three major **rock-art sites** open to the public in the Ukhahlamba Drakensberg, with more than five hundred paintings at **Main Caves**, about a half-hour's easy walk up the Bushman's River Valley. There's a R15 entry fee to the caves, which are fenced in, and self-guided tours with some interpretative materials on site.

If the KZN Wildlife accommodation below is full, you'll have to head for the one **hotel** that gives access to the reserve: *White Mountain Lodge* (T & F 036 353 3437 or 084 758 6531; ❷), along the road to Giant's Castle hutted camp, 34km on a tarred road from Estcourt and 32km from the reserve. The

The San and their rock paintings

Southern Africa's earliest inhabitants and the most direct descendants of the late Stone Age, the **San**, or Bushmen, lived in the caves and shelters of the Ukhahlamba Drakensberg for thousands of years before the arrival of the Nguni people and later the white farmers. There is still some disagreement over what to call these early hunter-gatherers. Many liberal writers use the word "Bushmen" in a strictly non-pejorative sense – though the word was originally deeply insulting. Several historians and anthropologists have plumped for "San" but, as the term refers to a language group and not a culture, this isn't strictly accurate either. Since there is no agreed term, you'll find both words used in this book.

The San hunted and gathered on the subcontinent for a considerable period – paintings in Namibia date back 25,000 years. In the last two thousand years, the southward migration of Bantu-speaking farmers forced change on the San, but there is evidence that the two groups were able to live side by side. However, serious tensions arose when the white settlers began to annex lands for hunting and farming. As the San started to take cattle from farmers, whites came to regard these people as vermin, and felt free to hunt them in genocidal campaigns in the Cape, and later in other areas, including the Ukhahlamba Drakensberg, until they were wiped off the South African map.

San artists were also **shamans**, and their paintings of hunting, dancing and animals mostly depict their religious beliefs rather than realistic narratives of everyday life in the Ukhahlamba Drakensberg. It's difficult to **date** the paintings with accuracy, but the oldest are likely to be at least 800 years old (although Bushmen lived in the area for thousands of years before that) and the most recent are believed to have been painted after the arrival of the whites towards the end of the nineteenth century. However, it's easy and rewarding to pick out some of the most significant elements in San paintings. The **medicine** or **trance dance** – journeying into the spiritual world in order to harness healing power – was the Bushmen's most important religious ritual and is depicted in much of their art. Look out for the postures which the shamans adopted during the dance, including arms outstretched behind them, bending forward, kneeling, or pointing fingers. Dots along the spine often relate to the sensation of energy boiling upwards, while lines on faces or coming out of the nose usually depict nosebleeds – a common side effect of the trance state. Other feelings experienced in trance, such as that of elongation, attenuation or the sensation of flight, are expressed by feathers or streamers. The depictions of horses, cattle and white settlers, particularly in the Southern Berg, mark the end of the traditional way of life for the Ukhahlamba Drakensberg Bushmen, and it is possible that the settlers were painted by shamans as a supernatural technique to try to ward off their all-too-real bullets.

To enter the spirit world, shamans often tapped into the spiritual power of certain animals. You'll see the spiral-horned **eland** depicted in every cave – not because these antelope were prolific in the Berg, but because they were considered to have more power than any other animal. Sometimes the elands are painted in layers to increase their spiritual potency. In the caves open to the public, you can see depictions of human-like figures in the process of transforming into their power animal. Besides antelope, other animals associated with trance are honeybees, felines, snakes and sometimes elephants and rhinos.

Paintings weather and fade, and many have been vandalized. Well-meaning people dabbing water on them to make them clearer, or touching them, has also caused them to disappear – so never be tempted. One of the best and most up-to-date introductions to rock art is the slim **booklet** by David Lewis-Williams, *Rock Paintings of the Natal Ukhahlamba Drakensberg*, published by the University of KwaZulu-Natal Press and available from most decent bookshops.

hotel offers full board as well as self-catering cottages, and is in the foothills and close to Zulu villages and farmlands, so while the area is pretty, it's neither grand nor remote.

Giant's Castle

The most comfortable of the reserve's **accommodation**, *Giant's Castle Lodge* has comfortable self-contained chalets, sleeping two to eight (❸), with wonderful picture windows looking out to the peaks, and cosy fireplaces. There's also a luxury lodge with three rooms (full board ❼), but the *Lodge* has no campsite. For food, there's the pleasant *Izimbali* buffet-style **restaurant**, and you can buy frozen meat for braais and some tinned food at the curio shop in the reception area, though it's preferable to stock up before getting here. The reserve's only **filling station** is at the main entrance. There are fabulous **hiking trails** from the camp, with some of the Berg's best-located, though basic, hiking **huts** – Meander Hut, Giant's Hut and Bannerman's Hut (all ❶).

Injisuthi

Some 50km from both Winterton and Estcourt, **INJISUTHI** (April–Sept 7am–6pm; Oct–March 6am–7pm; R15 entrance fee) is a hiker's dream. You can walk straight out into the mountains (there are ten different day hikes, lasting 1–7hr), swim in the rivers or take in rock art. One of the best day walks, albeit a tough one, is up Van Heyningen's Pass to the viewpoint – the friendly staff at reception will direct you. To get there, take the indicated turning off the R615, which takes you along 30km of dirt road, passing through **Zulu villages** with traditional beehive huts along roads frequently blocked by groups of Nguni cattle. **Accommodation** includes self-catering comfortable chalets (❷) and more basic huts (❶) as well as campsites. Most people come here with the express purpose of taking to the hills and camping in one of the designated **caves**, which have absolutely no facilities and must be booked at reception.

If you have even a passing interest in rock art, don't miss the paintings at **Battle Cave**, so named because of a series of paintings that apparently depict an armed conflict between two groups of Bushmen. San art authority David Lewis-Williams has argued that these paintings are unlikely to depict a conflict over territory because there is no evidence that such conflicts took place in a society that was very loosely organized and unterritorial. Instead, he claims, the paintings are about the San spiritual experience and shamanic trance, the battles taking place in the spiritual realm where marauding evil shamans shoot arrows of "sickness", while good shamans attempt to fight them off.

There are more than 750 beautifully painted people and animals in this extensive cave, though many are faded. The paintings are fenced off, and can be visited only in the company of a KZN Wildlife guide, who sets out most days at 8.30am on the three- to four-hour walk (bookings a day in advance through the Injisuthi office on ☎036 431 7848; R35 per person; minimum four people). Once at the cave, the guide plays a recorded commentary on the paintings. A **fossil trail** is also planned, to open up some valuable fossil finds made in 2001.

Champagne Castle and Champagne Valley

Champagne Castle, the second-highest peak in South Africa, provides the most popular view in the Ukhahlamba Drakensberg, with scores of resorts in the valley cashing in on the soaring backdrop. The name, so the story goes, derives from an incident in 1861, when a Major Grantham made the first recorded ascent of the peak accompanied by his batman, who inadvertently dropped the bottle of bubbly and christened the mountainside.

These days, champagne tends to be enjoyed within the confines of the hotels down in the **Champagne Valley**, by cityslickers who refuse to follow in the major's footsteps. The valley is an easy 32km from Winterton, and has shops, restaurants and facilities absent in other parts of the Ukhahlamba Drakensberg, all indicated along the route. This overcivilized but extremely pretty area, which lies outside the KwaZulu-Natal Wildlife reserve, is best avoided if you want to hike from your doorstep – you'll have to drive west along the R600 through the valley to **Monk's Cowl** (R15 entrance fee, overnight hiking R30; campsite can be booked on ☏036 468 1103), from where plenty of hikes set off into the mountains.

The **Ardmore Ceramic Art Studio**, 20km from Winterton off the R600 (daily 9am–4.30pm; ⊛www.ardmore.co.za) and signed between the *Nest Hotel* and the *Drakensberg Sun*, is one of the area's highlights. The studio was started in the 1980s by fine-arts graduate **Fée Halsted–Berning** with trainee **Bonnie Ntshalintshali**, a young Zulu girl suffering from polio. By 1990 they had collected a clutch of awards for their distinctive ceramic works, and the studio now has around forty people creating beautiful sculpture and crockery with wildly colourful and often impossibly irrational motifs that have included rhinos dressed as preachers, administering the sacrament to a congregation of wild animals. Bonnie died of AIDS, as have at least eight other artists at the studio, but the distinctive style she pioneered has been continued here, and the works are well worth seeing and buying. There's also a less pricey local **curio shop** on the premises, selling works by other local artists.

Accommodation

You shouldn't have any problem finding a **place to stay** in Champagne Valley, as numerous hotels, family resorts and B&Bs are signposted off the R600. There are no KZN Wildlife chalets, only a campsite at **Monk's Cowl** (☏036 468 1103).

Ardmore Guest Farm Signposted off the R600, midway between Winterton and Monk's Cowl ☏036 468 1314, ✉ardmore@futurenet.co.za. A thoroughly hospitable farmstay, with accommodation in en-suite rondavels or inside the main house, attached to the Ardmore Ceramic Art Studio. Guests eat together from marvellous hand-crafted crockery made on the farm. Staff can arrange horse trails into Spioenkop Game Reserve through the Battlefields. ❸

Cayley Lodge Along the R600, west on D53, north on D227 ☏036 468 1222, ⊛www.planethotels.co.za/cayleylodge. Pleasant and well managed, and featuring sweeping visits of the mountains, a swimming pool and restaurant. ❺

Champagne Castle Along the R600 ☏036 468 1063, ℉036 468 1306. This old-fashioned hotel, the closest accommodation to the hiking trails beginning at Monk's Cowl, has comfortable en-suite chalets set in lovely gardens with a swimming pool. Half board ❹

Graceland Cottage Signposted off the R600 ☏ & ℉036 468 1091. A three-bedroomed self-catering cottage with TV and fireplace (R500 per night), as well as a larger cottage, the Homestead (R600 per night), perched right on the edge of a mountain with spectacular views.

Inkosana Lodge Halfway along the R600 from Winterton to Monk's Cowl ☏ & ℉036 468 1202, ⊛www.inkosana.co.za. Backpacker and B&B accommodation in unpretentious, ethnic-style rooms, with beautiful indigenous gardens and a retreat-centre feel. Self-catering is available, and the lodge can provide free transfers from Winterton and up to the Berg trailheads. Dorms ❶, rooms ❶

Cathedral Peak

North of Monk's Cowl and the Champagne Valley resorts are the Mlambonja River Valley and **Cathedral Peak**, a freestanding pinnacle sticking

5

KWAZULU-NATAL | The Central Drakensberg

out of the five-kilometre-long basalt Cathedral Ridge. The peak looks nothing like a cathedral (its Zulu name, Mponjwane, means "the horn on a heifer's head").

The only **hotel** here is the excellent *Cathedral Peak* (☎036 488 1888, ⓦwww.cathedralpeak.co.za; full board ⑥), the closest hotel in the Ukhahlamba Drakensberg to the mountains, and within the KZN Wildlife protected area. The views are perfect and the rooms in thatched two-storey wings are comfortably furnished with pine and country-style floral fabrics. The *Cathedral Peak* is well signposted, 44km from either Winterton or Bergville.

There are **hiking trails** starting right from the hotel, which can provide maps and books. One of the most popular day walks is to the beautiful **Rainbow Gorge**, an eleven-kilometre round trip (4–5hr) following the Ndumeni River, with pools, rapids, falls, lichens, mosses and ferns to detain you. The hike can be wet, so wear proper walking boots. The hotel also operates guided trips up to Cathedral Peak, taking nine hours, which includes plenty of time at the top to revel in the views. It's a very steep climb, and the final section beyond Orange Peel Gap should only be tackled by experienced climbers – you'll probably be quite satisfied to stop at this point.

The only other places to stay are the small KZN Wildlife **campsite** (☎036 488 1880), opposite the Mike's Pass guardhouse, about 4km before the hotel, or at **Didima**, a new KZN Wildlife camp offering chalets (④), with San rock-art as its major theme.

The guardhouse itself is the place to buy a permit to drive up **Mike's Pass** (R15 per person, R35 per vehicle), a ten-kilometre twisting forestry road which takes you to a car park from where, on a clear day, you'll get outstanding views of the entire region. There's a scale model on top to help identify the peaks. An ordinary car will make the journey when the weather is dry and the road is hard, but you'll need a 4WD when it's wet.

The Northern Drakensberg

The dramatically beautiful **Northern Drakensberg** consists mainly of the **Royal Natal National Park** (daily 24hr; R25) with a few resorts scattered around the fringes. The Tugela River and its bouldered gorge offer some of the most awe-inspiring scenery in the area, its most striking geographical feature being the **Amphitheatre**, the crescent-shaped five-kilometre rock wall over which the Tugela plunges. With a complete cross section of accommodation, the Northern Berg is a very desirable area to visit. The best place to get a real feeling of these pristine mountains and valleys is at **Thendele**, the main KZN Wildlife camp, with chalets but oddly enough no camping.

The **Mnweni Cultural Centre** (☎072 712 2401; R15), in the Mnweni Valley 30km west of Bergville along the Woodstock Dam/Rookdale roads, is home to the amaNgwane community, who own the land of this breathtaking valley and have opened it up to tourism. The centre has **accommodation** in simple two-bed thatched cottages (upmarket rondavels are planned), with shared ablutions and kitchen facilities, and meals on request (❶). Aside from hiking in the mountains (R20 per night), there are craft stalls, horse-riding and some San rock paintings to keep you busy for a few days.

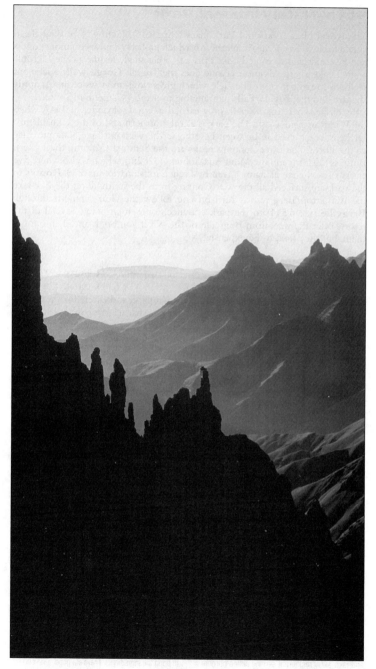

△ Mnweni Valley, Drakensberg

Royal Natal National Park

The **Royal Natal National Park** (daily 24hr; R15), 46km west of Bergville, is famed for its views of the Amphitheatre, which probably appears on more posters and postcards and in more books than any other single feature of the Ukhahlamba Drakensberg. Almost everyone does the **Tugela Gorge walk**, a fabulous six-hour round trip from Thendele, which gives close-up views of the **Amphitheatre** and the **Tugela Falls** plummeting over the 947-metre rock wall.

Established in 1916, the park only earned its royal sobriquet in 1947, when the Windsors paid a visit. The park is at the northern end of the Ukhahlamba Drakensberg, tucked in between Lesotho to the west and Free State province to the north. The three defining peaks are the Sentinel (3165m), the Eastern Buttress (3048m) and the Mont Aux Sources (3282m), which is also where five rivers rise – hence its name, given by French missionaries in 1878. **Routes** to the park are surfaced all the way. Coming from the south along the N3, take the Winterton/Berg resorts turn-off and follow the clear signposts through **Bergville** (see p.514) to the park entrance, some 46km away. Several of the resorts offer transfers from Bergville or the N3 if you book ahead and notify them, but they tend to be expensive.

Accommodation

KZN Wildlife accommodation consists of two campsites and the *Thendele Hutted Camp*. The huge *Mahai Campsite* (☎036 438 6303, ℱ036 438 6231) is set along the river adjacent to the national park, and caters for up to four hundred campers, attracting hordes of South Africans over school holidays and weekends. From here you can strike straight into the mountains for some of the best walks in the Berg. Smaller and quieter, the *Rugged Glen Campsite* is signposted 4km from Mahai (☎036 438 6303, ℱ036 438 6231; ❶). The views and walks here aren't as good, though conveniently the *Mont-Aux-Sources Hotel* is an easy walk away – handy if you want a substantial meal. While you can book the KZN Wildlife chalets through their usual reservation system (see box on p.459), use of campsites here is best arranged by calling the sites concerned.

Outside the park, a well-signposted dirt road heading north, just before you reach the entry gate from Bergville, is the location for the handful of resort-style hotels in the area, including all the places listed below except the *Cavern*.

The Cavern ☎036 438 6270, �🌐www.cavernberg .co.za. Off the R74, about 20km from the Royal KwaZulu-Natal. The most tucked-away of the hotels, the *Cavern* is family-run and has an old-fashioned feel, with adequate rooms. It's very much a South African weekend getaway with a swimming pool, horse-riding, Saturday night dances and a TV room. There are discounts during the week. Full board ❺

Hlalanathi Berg Resort ☎036 438 6308, �🌐www.halanathi.za.net. Some 10km from the Royal KwaZulu-Natal, this family resort offers camping and self-catering thatched chalets, which sleep two to six people. There's also a swimming pool, trampolines, a TV room as well as a sit-down and take-away restaurant serving cheap burgers, sandwiches and more substantial meals. ❷

Orion Mont-Aux-Sources Hotel ☎036 438 6230, �🌐www.orion-hotels.com. Roughly 4km from the park, this smart but impersonal hotel has views of the Amphitheatre behind scrawny villages and cattle-chewed hillsides. ❻

Thendele Hutted Camp ☎033 845 1000, ℱ033 845 1001. At the end of the road into the park, right in the mountains, this is one of the most sought-after places to stay in South Africa, with splendid views of the Amphitheatre and excellent walks right from your front door. Accommodation is in comfortable two-, four- or six-bed en-suite units, the cheapest of which have hotplates, fridges, kettles, toasters and eating utensils. If you opt for the more luxurious cottages or lodge, chefs are on hand to cook, though you need to bring the ingredients. There's a good curio and supply shop. ❸–❺

The Southern Drakensberg

From Pietermaritzburg and the N3, the main access to the Southern Berg is along the R617 (take the Bulwer/Underberg exit west off the N3). KZN Wildlife offers campsites and cottages at **Cobham**, **Lotheni** and **Kamberg**, and plenty of opportunity for trout fishing. Sani Pass is accessible by public transport and has a couple of hostels. For **information** about the area, contact Sani Saunter in Himeville (see p.515).

Sani Pass

Sani Pass is the only place in the KwaZulu-Natal Ukhahlamba Drakensberg range where you actually can drive up the mountains, using the only road from KwaZulu-Natal into Lesotho, connecting to the tiny highland outpost of **Mokhotlong** (see p.795). It's the pass itself, zigzagging into the clouds, that draws increasing numbers into the High Berg.

For all its isolation, Sani Pass is fairly straightforward to get to. Sani Pass Carriers, based in Underberg (℡033 701 1017, ℮spc@y.co.za), operates a Pietermaritzburg–Underberg **bus** service (Mon–Fri 2 daily; Sat 1 daily; R120 one way, R200 return) timed to connect with the Cheetah Coach and other intercity buses. They also run a service to Kokstad where you can pick up the **Baz Bus**. They can shuttle passengers to any of the accommodation in the Southern Berg subject to demand (charge depends on destination with minimum fee for two people).

If you intend to **drive** up to Sani Pass, it's preferable to use a 4WD vehicle, and you'll need your passport. The South African and Lesotho border posts are both open daily from 8am to 4pm. As for **organized trips**, Thaba Tours in Underberg (℡033 701 2888, ℮thabatours@futurenet.co.za) does a daily jaunt into Lesotho, on which they take you by 4WD to the highest point on

---

Giant's Cup Hiking Trail

The sixty-kilometre, five-day **Giant's Cup Hiking Trail** (R35 per person per night, including entrance fee of R20), part of which traverse a depression which explains the trail's name, is the only laid-out trail in the Ukhahlamba Drakensberg. It starts at the Sani Pass road, then leads through the foothills of the southern Ukhahlamba Drakensberg and winds past eroded sandstone formations, overhangs with San paintings, grassy plains, and beautiful valleys with river pools to swim in. No single day's hike is longer than 14km and, although there are some steep sections, this is not a difficult trail – you need to be fit to enjoy it, but not an athlete.

The **mountain huts** at the four overnight stops have running water, toilets, tables and benches, and bunks with mattresses. It's essential to bring a camping stove, food and a sleeping bag. The trail can be shortened by missing the first day and starting out at Pholela Hut, an old farmhouse where you spend the night, then terminating one day earlier at Swiman Hut, close to the KZN Wildlife office at Garden Castle. You can also lengthen the trail by spending an extra night at Bushmen's Nek Hut, in an area with numerous caves and rock-art sites.

The trail is restricted to thirty people per day and tends to get booked out during holiday periods; **bookings** should be made through the KwaZulu-Natal Wildlife who provide a map and a trail booklet. **Transport** at the end of the hike to get back to where you started should be arranged through Sani Pass Carriers (see above), who can pick you up at Himeville or Underberg, or move and store your car if you're driving.

the Sani–Mokhotlong Road to visit shepherds and learn about their lifestyle; they also organize horse-riding trails and walking trips to see rock art. It's also possible to do Sani Pass as a worthwhile, though very long, day-trip from Durban, with Strelitzia Tours (see box on p.467), which includes a visit to a Lesotho village, where you get to taste homemade sorghum beer and lunch at the *Sani Top Chalets*.

Accommodation

Most accommodation is at the foot of the mountains, just before the pass hair-pins its way up to the top. Closest to the start of the pass is *Mkomazana Lodge*, while the highest up is *Sani Top Chalets*.

Mkomazana Lodge 25km northwest of Underberg along the Sani Pass road ℡033 702 0340, ⓔwendy@mkomazana.co.za. Self-catering in four- and six-bed dorms, a huge thirty-bed dorm, doubles with shared toilets and washing facilities, plus two fully equipped houses sleeping eight. The lodge is near the start of Giant's Cup Hiking Trail, and you can safely leave your car here before setting out on the trek. Less ambitious walks into the mountains begin on the property, which has its own river and waterfall, and a private dam with trout. Dorms and rooms ❶

Sani Lodge Backpackers Hostel 19km north-west of Underberg along the Sani Pass road ℡033 702 0330, ⓦwww.sanilodge.co.za. Dorms, doubles and self-catering cottages at this establishment with pleasant verandas and lawns where meals are served all day, and a mean reputation for chocolate cake. It's a good base for walking

to waterfalls and rock paintings – they can supply packed lunches – and there's horse-riding and mountain biking. Tours up Sani Pass and into Lesotho are also on offer, or you can stay in a nearby homestead to experience ordinary Zulu life. Dorms ❶, rooms ❶

Sani Pass Hotel A little beyond *Sani Lodge Backpackers* ℡033 702 1320, ⓔreservations @sanipasshotel.co.za. A comfortable hotel offering full board and plenty of extras, including horse-riding and tennis facilities. ❺

Sani Top Chalets ℡033 701 1064 ℻033 702 1069. Double rooms as well as backpacking facilities at the top of Sani Pass, just inside Lesotho. Recommended if you're after a serious hiking vibe, but with a relaxed atmosphere, spectacular views and the highest pub in Africa. Meals and teas are available. Dorms ❶, rooms ❷

Lotheni and Kamberg

Well off the beaten track, along dirt roads and seldom explored by foreign visitors, the two **KZN Wildlife camps** at Lotheni and Kamberg (both daily: April–Sept 6am–6pm; Oct–March 5am–7pm; R15) are worth venturing into for their isolated wilderness, good trout fishing and, at Kamberg, some exquisite San rock paintings.

In a valley in the foothills of the Berg, **LOTHENI** is tranquil and beautiful, with waterfalls, grasslands and the lure of fishing in the Lotheni River, which flows through the reserve and is stocked with brown trout. The **Settler Museum** is worth a quick look (Mon–Fri 9am–4pm, Sat 9am–noon; R10); it's housed in the original stone buildings belonging to the Root family who left Britain in the nineteenth century and farmed here for two generations before the area was proclaimed a reserve, and Arnold Root became the first warden. Displays include wagons, farm tools and period furniture, re-creating early settler life.

It's possible to get to Lotheni by car either via Nottingham Road (see p.511) to the northeast or from Himeville to the southeast. Lotheni offers a small campsite and twelve comfortable self-catering **chalets** (❷), eight of which sleep two, while the rest have three beds. All chalets have their own well-equipped kitchen and bathroom. Best of all here is *Simes Cottage* (❷), a stone farmhouse with a majestic outlook, its own trout lake and grounds traversed by bushbuck and eland. The cottage sleeps ten, and there's a minimum charge for six people. You'll need to bring all your own supplies, which you could buy at the trading store 10km before you reach the restcamp (☎033 702 0540).

The best reason to visit **KAMBERG**, 42km west of **Rosetta**, apart from the superb fishing, is for the rock art. At **Game Pass Cave** (one of the three caves in the Ukhahlamba Drakensberg open to the public, also known as Shelter Cave), images of stylized figures in trance states and large, polychrome eland dance across the wall. The paintings can only be visited with a guide; arrange this beforehand, or join one of the guided tours departing daily from the restcamp (R35) at 9am. The walk there and back takes around three hours, following a contour path through grasslands. There are other less distinct paintings (free), which you can visit at will, near the waterfall. There's also a **rock-art centre** at the rest camp that's worth a visit. **Walks** from Kamberg are undemanding and very scenic, and include a four-kilometre trail with handrails for wheelchair-users and the visually impaired.

Kamberg's **restcamp** (☎033 263 7251; **❶–❷**) consists of chalets, huts and a rustic cottage; there's a communal kitchen but no campsite. The nearest major supplies are at Rosetta, so it's best to bring all your own food and drink, though there's a basic supply store just before you reach the reserve.

The Elephant Coast and Zululand game reserves

In startling contrast to the intensely developed 250-kilometre ribbon of the South Coast, which runs north and south of Durban, the seaboard to the north of the Dolphin Coast drifts off into some of the wildest and most breathtaking sea frontage in South Africa – an area known as the **Elephant Coast**.

If you've travelled along the Garden Route and wondered where stereotypical Africa was, the answer is right here, in the northern reaches of the Elephant Coast – traditionally known as **Maputaland** – with its tight patchwork of wilderness and **ancestral African lands**. The figures speak for themselves: the area, hemmed in by Swaziland and Mozambique, has more *nyangas* and *sangomas* (traditional healers and spirit mediums) than anywhere else in the country. With one traditional healer for every 550 people – compared with one Western-style doctor to 18,000 people – **traditional life** continues in this forgotten corner of sub-Saharan Africa's most industrialized country. There's only one tarred road leading all the way from the N2 to its 200km of virtually uninterrupted beachfront, most of which is still only accessible with a 4WD vehicle – although this will probably change in the next few years.

Further south, less than three hours' drive north on the N2 from Durban, is the big game country of **Hluhluwe-Imfolozi**, which rivals even the Kruger National Park in beauty and a sense of the wild. Drive the same distance, but turn right instead of left at the Mtubatuba junction, and you'll hit the

Manzini   Manzini

NDUMO
GAME RESERVE   MOZAMBIQUE

Big Bend

Hlathikulu   Ndumo   TEMBE
ELEPHANT
PARK   Kosi Bay

Border
Caves   Lake Nhlage

S W A Z I L A N D   Kwa-Ngwanase

Piet Retief

Ingwavuma   M A P U T A L A N D

ONVERWACHT   Rocktail Bay
Lala Nek

GOLELA   Lake
Sibaya   Mabibi &
Thonga Beach

N2

Pongola   Jozini   Baya

ITHALA GAME
RESERVE

R66

Louwsburg   R69   Ubombo   Mbazwana   Sodwana Bay

Mkuze

Vryheid

MKHUZE
GAME
RESERVE

GREATER

PHINDA PRIVATE
GAME RESERVE   ST LUCIA

Nongoma   WETLAND

Hluhluwe

K W A Z U L U - N A T A L

FALSE BAY PARK   Lake
St Lucia   PARK

Hluhluwe

Dundee

Hlabisa   Fanies Island   N

R66

Charter's Creek   Cape Vidal

HLUHLUWE-
IMFOLOZI
PARK

Nyalazi

Mission Rocks

R618

Ulundi   R618   St Lucia

Mtubatuba

0   50 km   Cape
St Lucia   **ELEPHANT COAST &
THE GAME RESERVES**

Kwambonambi

Empangeni, Gingindlovu & Richards Bay

southernmost extent of South Africa's most satisfyingly "tropical" coast, protected all the way up to Mozambique by wetland reserve and marine sanctuaries – the St Lucia Reserve, St Lucia Park, False Bay Park, St Lucia Marine Reserve, Sodwana Bay National Park, Cape Vidal State Forest, Mkhuze Game Reserve, and other interlinked areas, with few roads linking one area to another. All the reserves fall under the umbrella of the **Greater St Lucia Wetland Park**, a 2750-square-kilometre patchwork encompassing five distinct ecosystems and a UNESCO World Heritage Site; planned developments will make this South Africa's third-largest protected area. Vastly popular here for its outstanding scuba diving and fishing opportunities is **Sodwana Bay**. The coast gets remoter and more exhilarating the further north you head, with two of South Africa's best upmarket beachside stays near Mozambique at **Rocktail Bay** and **Kosi Bay**.

So far, the only major development blighting the area is the large modern industrial port of **Richards Bay**, 185km north of Durban, nudging the southern edge of the Elephant Coast. But with the possibility of a continuous strip of resorts all the way from Durban to the Mozambique border, there are real fears for the whole of this fragile ecosystem. Conservation and poverty sit uncomfortably here. In the past, African farmers were banned from planting crops in the wetlands, traditional fishermen were arrested for casting their nets on waters they believed to be theirs, and cattle herders had their livestock confiscated if they wandered into certain areas. It's not surprising that for some local people, struggling to sustain a livelihood, tourism equals dispossession. That said, a number of locals have responded positively to the influx of visitors, and this is one of the best areas to buy **crafts**. Even on remote roads, you'll come across stalls with beautiful carvings, often suspended like windchimes from roofs or trees. Objects produced include platters, sticks or, in a more contemporary vein, models of little 4WD vehicles. More positive still is the growth of eco-tourism projects in the vicinity that involve partnership with the community. An example of this is **Phinda Private Game Reserve**, a seriously upmarket park near Mkhuze Game Reserve that has brought tangible benefits to the local community and suggests a way in which business, communities and the environment can gain mutual benefit from tourism.

The **Baz Bus** service between Durban and Swaziland along the N2 stops in Kwambonambi, Mtubatuba, St Lucia, Hluhluwe and Mkhuze. Note that the northern KwaZulu-Natal coastal region is **malarial**.

Richards Bay to Hluhluwe

There's no reason to spend time in either **Empangeni**, 173km north of Durban, or **RICHARDS BAY**, on the coast 12km east of Empangeni, on the coast. Two modern industrial sprawls that are the only urban centres of any size in the vicinity, they are completely at odds with the remote and pristine coast to the north.

You might, however, fly into Richards Bay and rent a car there to make a quick getaway. SA Express flights from Johannesburg (☎035 786 0301) touch down at **Richards Bay airport** (☎035 786 0301), 6km north of the town centre. **Car rental**, including 4WD, can be arranged from the airport through Avis (☎086 102 1111) and Imperial (☎0800 131 000). The rental companies make their money from daily rentals to businessmen, so don't expect to get a special rate for a long rental, which is anything longer than one day. Greyhound **intercity buses** (☎031 334 9700) arrive at the *Steers* restaurant, next to the Total filling station in Anglers Rod Street and the *Richards Bay Hotel*. If you're stuck here for the night, **Umhlathuze Tourism** at Reptile City, John Ross Highway (Mon–Fri 8am–4pm, Sat & Sun 10am–2pm; ☎035 753 3909, ⓦwww.tourismassociation.org.za), can help find accommodation.

Kwambonambi and Mtubatuba

Some 26km north of Richards Bay, the tiny, predominantly African village of **KWAMBONAMBI** (known locally as Kwambo) is safe and friendly, and preferable to Hluhluwe as a base for exploring St Lucia and the Hluhluwe-Imfolozi game reserve. Kwambo has a small supermarket, a bottle store, post office and filling station and an excellent **backpacker lodge**, the congenial *Cuckoo's Nest*, 28 Alibizia Street (☎035 580 1001, ⓔcuckoos@mweb.co.za; ❶), which has A-frame doubles, teepees, camping, some dorms, plus a great treehouse. The lodge can organize diving at Sodwana and overnight trips to the Hluhluwe-Imfolozi reserve, boat tours on the St Lucia estuary, and visits to a traditional Zulu village.

Another 25km further north, **MTUBATUBA** (often shortened to Mtuba) is likewise a more attractive base than Hluhluwe, and features lots of herbalists, traditional healers and a Zulu market. It's also a thriving centre for the local sugar-cane industry – both large commercial farms and small-scale African growers. Situated where the R618 intersects the N2, it is just twenty minutes from both the Hluhluwe-Imfolozi Park and the St Lucia estuary. Among its facilities, the hamlet has some banks, pharmacies, supermarkets and filling stations. There are also a couple of good **places to stay**: *Wendy's Country Lodge*, 3 Riverview Drive (☎035 550 0407 or 083 628 1601, ⓦwww.wendybnb.co.za; ❸), has six luxurious rooms in a house set in tropical gardens, with a swimming pool. *The Circle*, 92 Umkuhla Crescent (☎035 550 0660, ⓕ035 550 1209; ❸), is a tranquil place with two two-bedroom cottages, one of which is self-catering, as well as double and single rooms. From here you can go on forest walks and experience an array of wildlife activities organized by the host, who's fluent in Zulu and has excellent local knowledge.

Some 35km north of Mtubatuba there's another good place to stay, the *Emdoneni Lodge and Game Farm* (☎035 562 2256 or 083 654 1161, ⓦwww .emdonenilodge.com; ❻), a family-friendly place with accommodation in chalets and rondavels. There's also a **restaurant** and bar serving home-cooked meals, plus a swimming pool and some big cats in enclosures. To get there, take the Bushlands turn-off on the east side of the N2; from here turn left, then immediately right over the motorway bridge and continue for another kilometre.

Hluhluwe

Just off the N2 nearly 60km north of Mtuba is the straggling village of **HLUHLUWE** (rendered "shla-shloo-wee"), which has a few shops and the friendly **Elephant Coast Tourism Association** office at the Engen filling station on Main Street (Mon–Fri 8am–5pm, Sat & Sun 9am–4pm; ☎035 562 0353, ⓦwww.elephantcoast.org.za), providing details of numerous lodges and game farms in the vicinity. Though Hluhluwe makes a perfectly adequate base, you may prefer the more attractive False Bay Park (see p.538), 15km to the east on the western shore of Lake St Lucia.

Hluhluwe has a couple of **places to stay**, one of which is a Zulu **homestay** organized by Mbonise Cultural Concepts and Safaris (☎035 562 1329 or 082 953 5601, ⓦwww.mbonise.com; ❻). Staying with the Mdaka family in their homestead, you'll also be taken to visit the Nompondo Community adjacent to the Hluhluwe-Imfolozi park; the price includes meals, walking tours and the services of a Zulu guide. Otherwise, there's comfy, en-suite **B&B** accommodation at the *Hluhluwe Guest House* in the residential area behind the Engen garage (☎035 562 0838 or 082 629 1462, ⓔhluguest@iafrica.com; ❹), with a pool and small bar and meals on request. The guesthouse can arrange trips into the Hluhluwe-Imfolozi Game Reserve and Sodwana Bay. Five minutes' drive from Hluhluwe, *Ilala Weavers and Savanna Restaurant* is a hub of community projects selling well-priced traditional **crafts** in a cheerful atmosphere, with a **restaurant** serving decent breakfasts, lunches and dinners, and cold beers.

En route to Hluhluwe from the south, you could stop over at **Dumazulu Traditional Village**, 14km from Hluhluwe, with displays of energetic Zulu dancing, beer brewing, spear and basket making. Nearby are two more places to **stay**. *Isinkwe Backpackers Wetlands Lodge* (☎035 562 2258, ⓔisinkwe@saol.com; ❷) is a well-run rustic hostel offering camping, wooden cabins for four and a traditional Zulu-style beehive hut dorm, as well as more comfortable doubles in the lodge. They serve reasonably priced meals (or you can self-cater), arrange tours to Hluhluwe-Imfolozi, Mkhuze, Cape Vidal and the St Lucia Wetlands and can organize transport to and from Sodwana Bay. Just 1km to the north, *Dumazulu Kraal and Lodge* (℡035 652 2260, @dumazulu@iafrica.com; half board ❻) has comfortable en-suite cottages on a farm done out with ethnic African decor. The lodge has a restaurant and bar, and next door is a Zulu traditional village and a snake park.

Hluhluwe-Imfolozi Park

Hluhluwe-Imfolozi (daily: April–Sept 6am–6pm; Oct–March 5am–7pm; R70 per person per day) is KwaZulu-Natal's most outstanding game reserve, considered by some even better than the Kruger. While it certainly can't match Kruger's sheer scale (Hluhluwe is a twentieth of the size) or its teeming game populations, its relatively compact 960 square kilometres have a wilder feel. This has something to do with the fact that, apart from **Hilltop**, an elegant hotel-style restcamp in the northern half of the park, none of the other restcamps is fenced off, and wild animals are free to wander through. The vegetation, with subtropical forest in places, adds to the sense of adventure. The park also offers the best **trails** in the country.

The park used to be two distinct entities – hence its tongue-twisting double-barrelled name (pronounced something like "shla-shloo-wee-oom-fa-low-zee") – and the two sections retain their separate characters, reinforced by a public road slicing between them. The southern **Imfolozi section** takes its name from a corruption of *mfulawozi*, a Zulu word that refers to the fibrous bushes that grow along its rivers. The topography here is characterized by wide, deep valleys incised by the Black and White Imfolozi rivers, with altitudes varying between 60 and 650 metres. Luxuriant riverine vegetation gives way in drier areas to a variety of woodland, savanna, thickets and grassy plains. The notable feature of the northern **Hluhluwe section** is the river of the same name, so called because of the dangling monkey ropes that hang from the riverside forest canopy. A slender, slithering waterway, punctuated by elongated pools, the Hluhluwe rises in the mountains north of the park and passes along sandbanks, rock beds and steep cliffs in the game reserve before seeping away into the St Lucia Wetlands to the east. The higher ground is covered by veld and dense thicket, while the well-watered ridges support the softer cover of ferns, lichens, mosses and orchid.

Some history

Despite Hluhluwe-Imfolozi being the oldest proclaimed national park in Africa (it was created in 1895), its future as a game refuge has hung by a thread on several occasions in the last two hundred years. In the nineteenth century, the park lay at the very centre of the **Zulu kingdom** and Imfolozi was the private hunting preserve of the Zulu king, Shaka. During Shaka's reign between 1818 and 1828 the area saw the most sustained campaign of hunting in Zulu history, but this was nothing compared to the destruction caused by white men in the twentieth century, when the park was twice de-gazetted under pressure from neighbouring farmers whose cattle were being infected by **nagana**, a disease transmitted by tsetse flies from wild to domestic stock. Between 1929 and 1950, a crusade of game **extermination** was launched to wipe out the disease and saw 100,000 head of game from sixteen species fall to the gun, with rhinos alone spared.

It was only in 1952, when the park was handed over to the newly formed organization now known as **KwaZulu-Natal Wildlife**, that the slow process of resuscitating the threadbare game reserve began. The sense of pristine wilderness you now get at Hluhluwe-Imfolozi is the result of careful management, crowned by the brilliant success of re-establishing its white rhino population from twenty animals at the start of the twentieth century to nearly two thousand today. In 1994, the **white rhino** became the first species to be removed from the World Conservation Union's endangered list, their survival down mostly to conservationists in the Hluhluwe-Imfolozi Park, which has become the world's breeding bank for these animals.

Arrival and information

There is no public transport to Hluhluwe-Imfolozi. Without your own car, you can choose from any of the day-trips offered by accommodation within an hour's drive of the park, or from the tours operated by the Durban firms listed in the box on p.467.

Access to the park is via three gates. Just north of Mtubatuba, the R618 to Hlabisa and Nongoma reaches **Nyalazi Gate** after 21km, providing access to the southern section of the park. Further north, on the N3, an unclassified but signposted and tarred road near the turning for Hluhluwe takes you via **Memorial Gate** into the northernmost section of the park. A third gate, **Cengeni**, is accessible along a thirty-kilometre tarred road from Ulundi to the west. Maps and **information**, including details of guided walks, night drives and boat trips, are available at the receptions of the *Hilltop* and *Mpila* camps. The gates are open from 6am to 6pm between March and October, inclusive, and from 5am to 7pm the rest of the year.

Accommodation

Accommodation is available in both the Imfolozi and Hluhluwe sections of the game reserve. Imfolozi is the less developed of the two sections. Hluhluwe's *Hilltop* camp has a pleasant **restaurant**, the *Mpunyane*, and a bar lounge, the *Uzavolo*, both attached to the central block. *Hilltop* also has a small store selling basics, but it's best to stock up before you enter the park. Hluhluwe village and Mtubatuba have well-stocked supermarkets. In Imfolozi you'll find the Centenary Centre (daily 8am–4pm) which has a small takeaway restaurant, a craft centre, and *bomas* which house animals brought from other parks to be introduced here. **Bookings** for accommodation are made through KwaZulu-Natal Wildlife as usual, though camping should be arranged locally.

Hluhluwe section

Hilltop Probably the best publicly run safari camp in South Africa, set high on the edge of a slope, with sweeping views across the park's hills and valleys. The camp has modern, comfortable and varied accommodation: budget two-bed rondavels that share communal ablutions and kitchen facilities; en-suite chalets with bar-fridges, tea- and coffee-making facilities, and some kitchenettes; and en-suite chalets without kitchens. *Hilltop* is surrounded by an electric fence, which keeps out most animals. You may, however, come across nyala, zebra and other herbivores grazing around the chalets – remember that all wild animals are potentially dangerous and should be treated with respect. ③–⑤

Mthwazi Lodge Near *Hilltop*. Four luxurious en-suite rooms in a secluded private garden. A chef and game ranger are available to cater for your every need. Full board ⑥

Muntulu and Munyawaneni Four bedrooms with secluded verandas at each of two upmarket bush lodges overlooking the Hluhluwe River, rented out to whole groups. A cook is on hand to cater and a field ranger is available to take guests on walks. Minimum charge for six people. ⑥

Imfolozi section

There are no fences around the Imfolozi camps, so take care when walking around, particularly at night. If there are four or more of you, the **lodges** offer good value.

Gqoyeni and Hlatiku Bush Lodges Each lodge has four two-bed units which are elevated above the Black Imfolozi River and linked to the living area by wooden walkways. Their field ranger can conduct walks in the area, and they have a chef to cook meals (you bring the ingredients). ⑤

Masinda Lodge Near the Mambeni Gate, this secluded upmarket lodge has nine bedrooms, with service of the highest standard. Full board ⑥

Mpila In the centre of Imfolozi. Excellent views of the surrounding wilderness from twelve one-roomed huts with four beds each and communal ablutions; two self-contained three-bedroom cottages for seven people (minimum charge for three people); and six self-catering chalets that accommodate five people (minimum charge for three people). There is also a safari camp with seven tents with two beds, and two with four. ③

Nselweni Bush Camp A rustic but very comfortable camp with four two-bed units and a communal ablution block. You can self-cater or have the chef prepare whatever you've brought. ④

Game viewing and activities

Despite its compact size, Hluhluwe-Imfolozi is home to 84 mammal species and close on 350 varieties of birds. The Big Five are all here, and it's no exaggeration to say that this is the best place in the world to see **rhinos**, both black and white. **Lions** had become extinct in Imfolozi until 1958, when a black-maned male made an appearance, apparently having traversed the 400km from Mozambique. Females were later introduced, and today there are around seventy of the big cats in the reserve, although they're not easy to see and their future hangs in the balance. Other **predators** present are cheetah, leopard, spotted hyena and wild dog. **Herbivores** include blue wildebeest, buffalo, giraffe, hippo, impala, kudu, nyala and zebra. When it comes to **birds**, there are over a dozen species of **eagle**, as well as other **raptors** including hawks, goshawks and honey buzzards. Other larger birds include ground hornbills, vultures, owls and herons, and there are hundreds of other beautiful species to look out for. **Reptiles** species number in the sixties, including crocodiles and several types of venomous snake, none of which you're likely to see. Along the Hluhluwe River, keep an eye open for the harmless monitor lizards.

Where Hluhluwe-Imfolozi really scores over the Kruger is in the variety of activities on offer. Apart from **self-driving** around the park, there are also **self-guided walks** near several of the restcamps, **guided trails** in the company of an armed field ranger, guided **night drives**, and a **boat trip** on the Hluhluwe Dam. South Africa's first **wilderness trail** started in Imfolozi, and the reserve has remained the best place in South Africa for these. There are two four-night trails, both starting from the Mndindini base camp not far from Mpila. The **Traditional Trail** comes with pack donkeys to carry your gear and accommodation in four satellite camps that are moved every three months to protect the environment (R2700 per person); the **Primitive Trail** requires you to carry your own gear and sleep under the stars, wherever the ranger chooses (R2900). Also available is the **Weekend Trail**, starting from Mpila at lunchtime on Friday and ending on Sunday at Mndindini (R1600). These trails, which must be booked through the KwaZulu-Natal Wildlife, can be undertaken year round except December. You'll be accompanied by an armed ranger and all gear – including linen and food – is included in the price.

Lake St Lucia

The most striking feature of the **Greater St Lucia Wetland Park** is the 360-square-kilometre **Lake St Lucia**, South Africa's largest inland body of water, formed 25,000 years ago when the oceans receded. The lake is flanked by mountainous **dunes** covered by forest and grassland, whose peaks soar to an astonishing 200m above the beach to form a slender rampart against the Indian Ocean. Aside from the lake and dune ecosystems, the reserve protects a **marine zone** of warm tropical seas, coral reefs and endless sandy beaches; the **papyrus and reed wetland** of the Mkhuze swamps, on the north of the lake; and, on the western shore, dry **savanna** and **thornveld**. Any one of these would justify conservation, but their confluence around the lake makes this a world-class wilderness.

Since 2002, low rainfall has put the park under severe strain. By 2004 the estuary through which the lake drains into the ocean had all but dried up, and areas like Charter's Creek and Fanies Island, usually on the lake shore, stood a few hundred metres from the receding shoreline. Unless there is exceptional rainfall in the next few years, the lake is unlikely to recover quickly.

St Lucia and Cape Vidal

Once a rough and out-of-the-way anglers' hangout, **ST LUCIA**, which lies at the mouth of the **St Lucia Estuary** in the extreme south of the park, is in the process of reinventing itself as a well-organized eco-destination. At the end of the R618, 32km east of Mtubatuba, the town can become pretty hectic in midsummer when the **angling** fanatics descend on the town for the school holidays; you can't miss the plethora of tackle and bait shops, seafood restaurants and vehicles buzzing up and down the main street bristling with fishing rods, beers and men. The real prize of the area, however, is **Cape Vidal** inside the wetland park, though the limited accommodation there may necessitate your making a day-trip from St Lucia town.

The Town

St Lucia's best feature is the **estuary**, whose mouth was reached by Portuguese explorers in 1576, and which they named Santa Lucia. During the second half of the eighteenth century, landlocked Boers made attempts to claim the mouth as a port, but were pipped at the post by the British, who sent HMS *Goshawk* in 1884 to annex the whole area, which then developed as a fishing resort. In the 1920s the town got its first hotel, and in the 1950s it was connected to the mainland by a bridge. The estuary is hidden behind the buildings along the main drag, and easy to miss if you drive quickly through.

There's not much to do in St Lucia itself, but it does provide an excellent base for a number of activities (see box on pp.534–535). Fishing aside, the main way of killing time in the village is at the **St Lucia Crocodile Centre** (daily 7.30am–4.30pm, crocodile feeding Sat 3pm; R40), at the park gate about 2km north of town on the road to Cape Vidal. This isn't another of the exploitative wildlife freak-shows common throughout South Africa, but a serious educative spin-off of KwaZulu-Natal Wildlife's crocodile conservation campaign. Up until the end of the 1960s, "flat dogs" or "travelling handbags" were regarded as pests, and this led to a hunting free-for-all that saw them facing extinction in the area. Just in time, it was realized that crocs play an important role in the ecological cycle, and KZN Wildlife began a successful **breeding programme**, returning the crocs to the wild to bolster numbers. The Crocodile Centre aims to rehabilitate the reputation of these maligned creatures, with informative displays and an astonishing cross section of species lounging around enclosed pools (only the Nile crocodile occurs in the wild in South Africa). There's also an impressive collection of snakes and a very good **bookshop** at the centre, with items on natural history and cheap, informative booklets about the local coastal and wetland ecology, as well as the *Zulu & I* restaurant (see p.536).

Practicalities

The **Baz Bus** comes into town several times a week and drops passengers off anywhere in town. The main drag is McKenzie Street, which runs parallel to the estuary. For **information**, the most helpful places are St Lucia Tours & Charters at the Dolphin Centre on McKenzie Street (daily 7am–7pm; ☏035 590 1259) and its sister company, Advantage Tours (same times; ☏035 590 1180), next to *St Pizza* on McKenzie Street. **KZN Wildlife** has an office at the south end of Pelican Road (daily 8am–4.30pm; ☏035 590 1340), which is two blocks east of and parallel to McKenzie. You can access the **Internet** in St Lucia at *Bib's International Backpackers*.

The local black village of **Khula**, 7km west of St Lucia on the Mtuba road, has an excellent **tourist office** specializing in responsible eco-tourism on the

Small as it is, St Lucia is the biggest settlement around the Greater St Lucia Wetland Park, and the best place to organize activities. Other than booking through the activity operators themselves, you can make reservations through St Lucia Tours & Charters in McKenzie Street (☎035 590 1259).

Biking

Birders on Bikes is the best-value cycling package in town, and one of the most interesting tours available. A two- to three-hour gentle cycle leads you through the southern part of the estuary, along the beach and into the Cape Vidal reserve. Knowledgeable Zulu guides teach you about flora and fauna and the use of plants in Zulu culture and medicine. Book through Shaka Barker Tours (43 Hornbill St; ☎035 590 1162, ✉info@shakabarker.co.za; R85 including bike rental).

Fishing

Deep sea fishing trips for novices and seasoned anglers with a skipper, guide, experienced fisherman and tackle supplied. Either tag and release your game fish or take it home to cook. The approximately five-hour trip run by St Lucia Tours & Charters (☎035 590 1259) costs from R400. Bring your own lunch and refreshments.

Hiking

There are a number of short and longer hikes in the St Lucia/Cape Vidal area, organized under the auspices of KZN Wildlife: a full-day Wetland Walk (R60); the five-day/four-night Emoyeni Trail (R35 per person per night); the three-day/two-night Mziki Trail (R40 per person per night); and the excellent, fully catered and portered four-night Wilderness Trail (R1400 per person). For further information contact KwaZulu-Natal Wildlife.

Horse-riding

Bhangzi Horse Safaris (☎035 550 4438 or 083 668 7693) offers rides through bushland, forests and lakes where you can view wildlife. The four hour trip costs R395.

Kayaking

Kayaking in the lake system gives an unparalleled experience of the wetland. St Lucia Kayak Safaris (☎083 463 3253) runs half- and full-day outings which

---

Elephant Coast. Facilities in town include filling stations, a couple of well-stocked supermarkets, self-service laundries, an ATM and two banks (Mon–Fri 9am–3.30pm).

Accommodation

Out of season, accommodation across a range of budgets isn't hard to find in St Lucia. KZN Wildlife has three excellent **campsites**: *Eden Park*, on the banks of the estuary, across the road from the KZN Wildlife office; *Sugarloaf*, a sizeable camp on the best site in St Lucia, also along the estuary and a few hundred metres north of Eden Park on the same road; and *Iphiva*, the quietest and most rustic of the camps, reached off McKenzie Street, north of the R618.

For a chance to experience warm Zulu hospitality, there's a worthwhile **homestay** in Khula village (❷). Accommodation is with the *Mngo B&B* (☎082 714 9444; ask for Jane), *Funokwakhe B&B* (☎072 62 8456; Thandi) or *Igugulamandlouv* (☎083 437 8089; Mr Nkosi).

cost R200–375 including all gear, transfers to the launch site, a light lunch and refreshments.

Khula Village tours

Trips operated by Veyane Cultural Tours (☎083 525 0228 or 082 958 1237) or Fafa Cultural Tours (☎082 344 0309) depart St Lucia for nearby **Khula village**, where you can visit the local church, a *shebeen* and a *sangoma*. Tours cost around R200 per person, though you can visit independently.

Lake cruises

If you spend any time in St Lucia, it's well worth going on a lake cruise with St Lucia Tours & Charters (☎035 590 1259; R180; 2hr), departing from the eastern shore at the jetty next to *Für Elize* (see p.536) or with KwaZulu-Natal Wildlife on their vessel *Santa Lucia* (☎035 590 9002; R100; 1hr 30min), departing from the west side of the estuary next to the bridge. You stand a good chance of seeing crocodiles and hippos, as well as pelicans, fish eagles, kingfishers and storks.

Wetland wildlife tours

An outstanding range of tours in the wetland are led by Kian Barker, a qualified zoologist and marine biologist, including the full-day St Lucia World Heritage Tour; the Turtle Tour (Nov–Feb) to watch the annual turtle egg-laying migration; and the interesting and unusual Chameleon Night Drive, which goes out in search of the sixteen chameleon species of the St Lucia region (a staggering fourteen of which are endemic). Book through Shaka Barker Tours (see opposite); the trips cost R200–600 depending on duration.

Whale-watching

Humpback and Southern Right whales cruise along the wetland's shore, and in season (June–Nov) you can join a boat excursion to look for them. Book through Advantage Tours & Charters (☎035 590 1180; R480; 2hr 30min); the trips leave from their office on McKenzie St (next to *St Pizza*; see p.533). There's no jetty down at the beach and launching the boat into the waves is an adventure in itself; if the ocean is choppy, expect to get soaked.

Bib's International Backpackers 310 McKenzie St ☎035 590 1056, ⓦwww.bibs.co.za. Firmly on the Baz Bus route, this thatched lodge offers camping, dorms, doubles and self-catering en-suite private rooms, and facilities such as Internet access, microwaves, laundry and pool tables. They also offer a range of excursions, including boat trips, cultural visits and overnight trails and drives. Dorms ❶, rooms ❶

Elephant Lake Hotel 3 Mullet St ☎035 590 1001, ⓔelephantlake@mweb.co.za. St Lucia's only hotel, recently renovated, with a pool, a fantastic deck for evening drinks and good views of the estuary. ❹

iGwalagwala Guest House 91 Pelican St ☎035 590 1069, ⓔigwala@mweb.co.za. Spacious en-suite rooms in a quiet part of town, with a large garden and swimming pool. ❸

Jo a Lize McKenzie St ☎035 590 1224, ⓔjoalizelodge@futurenet.co.za. Self-contained, self-catering flats and tiny en-suite units on a B&B basis. ❸

Kingfisher Lodge McKenzie St ☎035 590 1015, ⓔstluciakingfisherlodge@mweb.co.za. One of the most comfortable B&Bs in town, with seven stylish chalets. It's the only guesthouse with views of the estuary. ❹

Seasands 135 Hornbill St ☎035 590 1082, ⓔseasands@saol.com. Comfortable suites with patios and balconies overlooking shaded gardens. Each unit has a fully equipped kitchen, and there's also a small restaurant. ❹

St Lucia Wetlands Guest House 20 Kingfisher St ☎035 590 1098, ⓦwww.stluciawetlands.com.

Offers five large en-suite rooms and exceptional service and comfort. ❹

Sunset Lodge 154 McKenzie St ☏035 590 1197, ✉info@sunsetstlucia.co.za. Self-catering log cabins, sleeping two or four, with balconies and views of the estuary. Hippos occasionally feed on the grasslands in front of the wooden pool deck. ❷

Eating

The freshest **seafood** in town, as well as curries, can be had at *Für Elize* on McKenzie Street, while elsewhere on the same street, *Alfredo's* is best for pastas and lasagnas. Another option is the *Zulu & I Restaurant and Tea Garden* at the St Lucia Crocodile Centre (daily till about 9pm), a family restaurant where you can eat reasonably priced sandwiches, pasta, pizzas, chicken and meaty dishes while watching birds, crocs and 25 species of snake (not on the menu). The *Boat House Gallery Fish Grill*, at the ski-boat club at the end of Pelican Street, has pleasant views of the estuary, but don't expect too much from the food. If you want to catch your own fish, head for the Bait and Tackle Shop in McKenzie Street, which sells rods, tackle and (should you fail to hook anything) fresh fish, as well as all the spices and condiments you'll need for a fish braai.

Cape Vidal

Another popular fishing spot, **Cape Vidal** (daily: April–Sept 6am–6pm; Oct–March 5am–7pm; R30 per vehicle, R25 per person) can only be reached via St Lucia, from where you take a tarred road north (the extension of McKenzie St) for 32km, navigating a narrow land bridge between the lake and the Indian Ocean. En route you'll pass through grassland and wetlands populated by small game, rhino, birdlife and the occasional leopard.

There's enough stunning wilderness at Cape Vidal to keep you chilling out for several days, even if you aren't a keen angler. The sea is only minutes from the KZN Wildlife accommodation, and an offshore reef shelters the coast from the high seas, making it safe for **swimming**. If you're keen on **snorkelling**, an underwater extravaganza of hard and soft corals and colourful fish awaits. Go gazing into the tiny **rock pools** and you'll be rewarded with sightings of seaweeds, snails, crabs, sea cucumbers, anemones, urchins and small fish, though burly anglers who use the rocks for casting their lines into the wide ocean may look on you in disbelief.

Large mammals and fish move just offshore in the open seas beyond the reef. Cape Vidal is an excellent place for shore sightings of **humpback whales**, which breed off Mozambique, not far to the north, in winter. In October they move south, drifting on the warm Agulhas current with their calves. If you're lucky you may see these and other whales from the dunes, but without binoculars they'll just look like specks on the horizon. A **whale-watching tower**, reached through the dune forest south of the restcamp, provides an even higher viewpoint. Eighteen-metre plankton-feeding whale sharks, the largest and gentlest of the sharks, have been sighted off this coast in schools of up to seventy at a time, and manta rays and dolphins are also common in these waters.

Practicalities

There's no public transport to Cape Vidal. On **arrival** at Cape Vidal, you'll need to report to the Conservation Services office (daily 8am–4.30pm). If you're planning to stay overnight (highly recommended), book **accommodation** in advance. There are eighteen five-bed chalets (R230 per person, for a group of at least three) and twelve eight-bed Swiss-style log cabins, all of which are en suite and provided with linen and cooking utensils, and an eight-bed bush lodge at Bhangazi (**❹**). There's also a campsite with space for fifty tents in the dune forest near the beach, with ablution facilities, and four cabins which are let out to large groups (**❶**).

Reservations for cabins and chalets should be made through KZN Wildlife. Bookings for the campsite in particular are vital during school holidays and over long weekends. There's a small store selling basics and a petrol pump at the beach. St Lucia is close enough to stock up on anything else you should need.

The western shore

Accessible only with your own transport, the **western shore** of Lake St Lucia marks the old seashore, harking back aeons to a time when the ocean level was 2m higher than it is today. Decayed matter from marine animals has created a rich soil that once supported an extensive array of animal life, and although the Big Five were shot out ages ago, **birdlife** and over a hundred species of **butterfly** still flit about. Among the **herbivores** are suni – Africa's smallest antelope – as well as nyala and red duiker. With no dangerous predators apart from **crocodiles** (take care along the shore), the inland bushveld and woodlands are safe for walking without a guide.

The main activities here are **fishing** and **bird-watching**; most camps have enjoyable **waymarked trails** from which to discover the lakeside vegetation and birdlife. Keep an eye open for game, especially the water-loving reedbuck that take refuge in the swamps.

The only privately run **accommodation** in the Greater St Lucia Wetland Park is here, in the seriously luxurious *Makakatana Bay Lodge* (☎035 550 4189, **Ⓦ**www.makakatana.co.za; **❾**) near the Charter's Creek KZN Wildlife camp. The lodge has five suites located on the lake's edge or in tangled forest, and connected by wooden walkways. All meals and activities – canoe safaris, boat trips, beach safaris and game drives – are included in the rate.

Charter's Creek

At the southern end of the lake, **CHARTER'S CREEK** (daily: April–Sept 6am–8pm; Oct–March 5am–8pm; R20) is primarily an anglers' retreat, though it's also excellent for **bird-watching** and has two half-day **trails**. The major attraction here is the **camp**, situated on a cliff edge with views across the lake. From here you can spot waterfowl and flamingos – even pelicans make an appearance – while permanent residents include hippos and crocodiles. The seven-kilometre **Isikhova Trail** and the five-kilometre **Umkhumbe Trail** both leave from the camp and take in typical coastal forest, providing the opportunity to spot small **game**, including the tiny red duiker, with its short, backward-pointing horns. Other species occasionally encountered include mongooses, bushbuck, jackals, bushbabies and, commonest of all, vervet monkeys.

To get there, turn off the N2 some 20km north of Mtubatuba and follow the signs all the way to Charter's Creek, via the Nyalazi River halt. KZN Wildlife **accommodation** comprises a seven-bedded cottage (R190 per person; minimum charge for four people) and chalets (**❷**) – ten four-bedded, fourteen three-bedded and one two-bedded, plus fourteen campsites. You must bring your own provisions as there are no restaurants, shops or other facilities. Although you can't swim in the lake, there's a pool at the camp for cooling off in.

Fanies Island

Not an island at all but part of the western shore, approximately 20km north of Charter's Creek as the crow flies, **Fanies Island** (daily: April–Sept 6am–8pm; Oct–March 5am–8pm; R20) once looked out onto reeded islands between networks of waterlogged paths worn away by hippos. The views are magnificent across the reed beds to the grasslands, forests and misty hill-like dunes of Cape Vidal on the coast; however, the large croc population here makes bathing or paddling out of the question. Like all the western shore camps, Fanies Island is much favoured by anglers, but this is one of the most secluded, and attractively positioned.

It's a tranquil enough place to hang out or fish, with a couple of walking trails to help you explore. The five-kilometre **Umkhiwane Trail** goes through forest, open grassveld and swamp forest, and is highly recommended for bird-watching. Hippos, vervet monkeys, bushbuck, warthog, reedbuck and waterbuck are among the common mammals you stand a good chance of seeing. The **Umboma Trail** is shorter, wending its way through forest and back to camp along the lake shore. You can arrange two-hour boat trips (R65 per person) on the lake with Imvubu Launch Tours, through KwaZulu-Natal Wildlife central reservations.

To **get there**, take the undesignated tarred road that runs east from the N2 20km north of Mtubatuba. Eleven kilometres from the N2 the route splits into two dirt roads, the more northerly one reaching Fanies Island after 14km; the route is well signposted. KZN Wildlife **accommodation** here comprises a seven-bedded cottage (R190; minimum charge for four people) and twelve fully equipped two-bedded rondavels (❷) with their own fridge, but sharing an ablution block and a self-catering kitchen. There are twenty shaded **campsites**, reservations for which should be made on ☎035 550 9035. **Fuel** is available at the camp, as is a limited range of basic foods, but you're better off stocking up in Hluhluwe or Mtubatuba.

False Bay Park

Situated about 20km north of Fanies Island, **False Bay Park** (daily: April–Sept 6am–8pm; Oct–March 5am–8pm; R20) doesn't see many tourists or even anglers, despite offering opportunities to fish for both freshwater and marine species, as well as Cape salmon. The park is also excellent for **bird-watching**, and local **birding guides** can show you pink-throated longclaws and lemonbreasted canaries. If the water levels are right, flocks of pelicans and flamingos can also be seen. You can arrange guides through the Zululand Birding Route (☎035 753 5644, ⓦwww.zbr.co.za; R160 half day).

False Bay Park perches on the west shore of a small, lozenge-shaped waterway which is connected to Lake St Lucia by a narrow steep-sided channel known colourfully as "Hell's Gates". The park gives an excellent, low-key experience of the lake, which you can get onto with **launch tours**. There's also the opportunity to get out into the bush: the eight-kilometre **Dugandlovu Trail** and the ten-kilometre circular **Mpophomeni Trail** are clearly waymarked, pass through a variety of terrain and offer the opportunity of seeing birds and a decent variety of antelope and other small mammals such as jackals, mongooses, servals, genets, warthogs and vervet monkeys. If you're not so energetic, there's the shorter six-kilometre **Ingwe Trail** alongside the lake.

You reach the park **via Hluhluwe** (see p.528); continue east through the village to a T-junction at the end of the road and follow the signposts for 15km to the False Bay Gate. There's a **campsite** at Lister's Point about midway down the west shore of False Bay, which has communal ablutions, but you must supply everything else. About 8km to the south, *Dugandlovu* **hutted camp** has four basic, four-bed chalets (R120 per person; minimum charge R240) with cold showers (you can heat water over the fire in pots provided), toilets, gas cookers and paraffin lamps. You must bring all your own gear, including linen and sleeping bags. **Bookings** for both camps are through KwaZulu-Natal Wildlife.

A couple of places to stay lie just outside False Bay Park and are signposted from Hluhluwe. The *Sand Forest Lodge* (☎035 562 2509, ✉info@sandforestlodge .co.za; ❷–❸) has more campsites plus self-catering bungalows and chalets. The lodge is located on a small reserve with antelope, zebra and wildebeest, and meals are available on request. For a touch of luxury, the *Falaza Game Park* (☎035 562 2319, ⓦwww.falaza.co.za) has slick tented accommodation in another small reserve, and also boasts a reasonably priced health spa and a pool which the rhino enjoy lounging around at. Activities such as guided walks and boat trips, or game drives into Hluhluwe-Imfolozi (see p.532) can be arranged.

Mkhuze and Phinda game reserves

Reached across the Lebombo Mountains, 28km east of **Mkuze** village on the N2, **Mkhuze Game Reserve** has a rich cross section of mammals covering 78 species, though it's for its varied and highly beautiful countryside and its birdlife that the reserve really rates. The reserve is a major part of the Greater St Lucia Wetland Park, connected to the coastal plain by a slender corridor through which the Mkhuze River flows before emptying itself in Lake St Lucia.

At Mkhuze's southern end is the **Phinda Private Game Reserve**, open only to resident guests. Not one of the great South African game-viewing destinations, it makes up for this abundantly by the sheer panache with which it provides fine-tuned hospitality to the upmarket clientele.

Mkhuze Game Reserve

Defined to the west by the Lebombo Mountains, **Mkhuze Game Reserve** (daily: April–Sept 6am–6pm; Oct–March 5am–7pm; R35 per vehicle, R30 per person) marks the final haul of the coastal plain stretching down the east of the continent from Kenya. The landscape varies from the **Muzi Pans**, wetlands consisting of seasonal flood plains floating with waterlilies, reed beds and swamps, to savanna. Elsewhere you'll come across stands of acacias, and in the south across the Mkuzi River you can wander through the cathedral-like fig forest that echoes to the shriek of trumpeter hornbills.

If you're **driving**, the easiest way to get to the reserve is to leave the N2 at **MKUZE** village and follow the signs along a good dirt road to **Emshopi Gate**. An alternative route, which leaves the N2 further south, 35km north of Hluhluwe, involves a lot more driving on dirt and doesn't knock much off the distance. There's no public transport into Mkhuze, and if you don't have your own vehicle you'll need to join one of the daytime or night time **excursions** into the park from Mkuze village. The village has a few shops for supplies, a garage and the excellent *Ghost Mountain Inn*

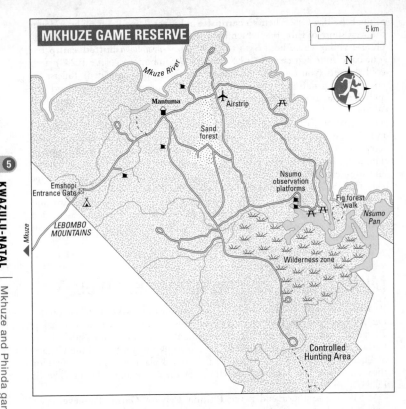

MKHUZE GAME RESERVE

0   5 km

N

Mkuze River

Mantuma

Airstrip

Sand
forest

Nsumo
observation
platforms

Fig forest
walk

Nsumo
Pan

Emshopi
Entrance Gate

Mkuze

LEBOMBO
MOUNTAINS

Wilderness zone

Controlled
Hunting Area

(☎035 573 1025, ⓦwww.ghostmountaininn.co.za; ❺) signposted off the
N2, which is great for a drink or meal and a dunk in their pool, even if you
aren't staying. Operating from the hotel, Tribe Africa (☎035 573 1474) runs
four-hour day and night **game drives** in Mkhuze (from R250 per person;
minimum three people). If you have time to climb **Ghost Mountain**,
which overlooks Mkuze, you can combine the experience with tales of the
battles associated with the peak, as told by local guides (hikes 3–4hr; R160
per person; book through Elephant Coast Tourism Association in Hluhluwe
– see p.528).

For navigating your way around the park, the **reception office** (☎035
573 9004) provides a clear **map** that shows all routes and distances and
gives general information about the park. You can buy fuel at the entrance
gate, and there is a **shop** selling basic supplies and books at reception,
but you should stock up on provisions in Mkuze village before heading
out here.

A **campsite** is situated right at Emshopi Gate, while **Mantuma**, the main
public restcamp, 9km into the park in the northern section, has a range of
accommodation. Cheapest are the three-bed rest huts with shared ablution
facilities and a kitchen (❷). There are also larger chalets that sleep two (❷),
four or seven. The most enticing units are the large two- or four-person safari
tents, each with its own roof and ablutions (❸). **Reservations** should be made

through KZN Wildlife (see box on p.459). The small **Crafts Centre**, marked on the map you pick up at reception, offers some excellent and inexpensive Zulu crafts made by local people.

Game viewing and activities

Some 84km of road traverse Mkhuze, but one of the best ways to see game is to stay put and wait for the animals to come to you. Several **hides** have been erected at artificial waterholes and on the edge of pans. All animals have to drink at some time, particularly in the drier months when naturally occurring water is scarcer, so you're bound to have a relaxed and interesting time at a hide if you chill out with a pair of binoculars and a good field guide.

Mkhuze is among the top spots for **bird-watching** in the country, with an impressive 430 species on record. Some of the prizes include Pels fishing owl and Rudd's apalis, a small insect-eating bird with a very restricted distribution. Even if you know nothing about birds, you're likely to appreciate one of Africa's most colourful here – the lilac-breasted roller. The two hides at **Nsumo Pan**, in the southern section of the park, apart from overlooking a very beautiful natural waterway, are superbly placed for observing **waterfowl**. Between July and September, if conditions are right, you can catch up to five hundred birds on the water at one time. Flocks of pelicans and flamingos make their appearance, as do kingfishers, fish eagles, waders, ducks, geese and countless other species. To arrange a specialist birding guide, contact the Zululand Birding Route (☎035 753 5644, ⓦwww.zbr.co.za; R160 half day). Nsumo's picnic site is one of the few places in the game reserve where you may leave your car, and it makes a great place to stop and eat.

Of the predators, there are no lions, while **cheetah** and **leopard** are present but rarely glimpsed; you stand a better chance of seeing fox-like black-backed **jackals**. The obvious draw of Mkhuze, however, is its black and white **rhinos**. The **impala** antelope will also be hard to miss, and you should catch sight of the large, spiral-horned **eland** and **kudu**. **Baboons** and **vervet monkeys** are generally found rustling around in the trees and making a nuisance of themselves on the ground, while at night you could be treated to the eerie call of the thick-tailed **bushbaby** from the canopy.

KZN Wildlife offers a number of activities, including recommended **night drives** from Mantuma (R150). During the day, you can explore Mkhuze on foot on a two-hour conducted **walk** (R75) with a field ranger. Many of the older rangers speak very little English, and their main function is to protect you. Current KZN Wildlife policy, however, is to employ younger guides who speak English well and have a knowledge of the environment, so check out the situation when you book your walk at the restcamp reception. One of the areas you can explore with a guide is the three-kilometre **Mkhuze Fig Forest Trail** – another highlight of the reserve. Sycamore fig forest is one of the rarest types of woodland in South Africa, and the stands of massive trees give the forest a gentle green glow. Look out for the flashing red flight feathers of fruit-eating **birds** like the purple-crested lourie or green pigeons, and listen for the tap-tap of golden-tailed woodpeckers on the trees. Monkeys and baboons, which pass through from time to time, pose no threat though they might steal your food, but you should keep alert to the possibility of encountering black rhinos or hippos.

The only way to see the Muzi Pans is with Muzi Pan Canoeing Adventures (book through the Elephant Coast Tourism Association in Hluhluwe; see p.528), a community-based initiative with well-trained guides.

Phinda Private Game Reserve

On a 150-square-kilometre ranch, **Phinda Private Game Reserve** offers a good chance of seeing **lion**, **cheetah** and both varieties of **rhino** on game drives, but it's hard not to feel that it's all a bit too well managed. At the moment the property is too small to sustain a self-regulating wildlife ecology, but if, as is hoped, it becomes integrated with surrounding parks (as has happened around the Kruger National Park) this could change dramatically.

Accommodation is at four lodges (⑨ including all meals and game activities), with *Mountain Lodge* providing vistas of the Lebombo range and the nearby St Lucia coastal plain; *Rock Lodge* embracing a more intimate experience, with just six glass chalets chiselled into rock; *Forest Lodge* offering stunning Afro–Japanese-style timber houses on stilts, each tucked away discreetly among bush and trees; and *Phinda Vlei Lodge*, in a sand forest on the edge of a pan system, featuring highly polished timber and glass chalets. The **food**, described as "eclectic pan-African", is excellent. All game drives or walks are accompanied by well-informed expert guides, who are as good as any you'll find in South Africa.

Bookings should be made through Conservation Corporation Africa (☎011 809 4300 or 021 425 0222, ⓦwww.ccafrica.com), or through one of the specialist travel agents listed in Basics. Detailed instructions on how to get there are provided when you make your booking.

The far north of the Elephant Coast

Also known as **Maputaland**, the extreme northeast section of the Elephant Coast is the remotest tract of South Africa, mostly accessible only along dirt roads that work their tortuous way to the coast. Some 11km north of **Mkuze** village, the longest tarred road in the area snakes north and then east for 133km, passing through **Jozini**, a small, dog-eared town that will seem like a thriving metropolis next to anything you'll encounter beyond. Some 40km beyond Jozini is a turning for the border village of **Ingwavuma**, home to a fascinating women's crafts project and the base for some excellent hikes.

As it turns toward the sea, the main road brushes past a short track that leads to **Ndumo Game Reserve** and 8km later the entrance gate to **Tembe Elephant Park** (ⓦwww.tembe.co.za), both reserves reaching down from the Mozambique border. The elephant park is not described here, as it's a very underdeveloped conservation area to which only the dedicated go in 4WD vehicles. The road stops 26km beyond Tembe and 24km short of the coast at the busy, run-down settlement of **Kwa-Ngwanase** (Manguzi on some maps), from where an unsurfaced road heads for **Kosi Bay** and the Mozambique border.

The tiny settlement of **Mbazwana** is a springboard for **Sodwana Bay National Park** to the south and **Lake Sibaya** to the north. Mbazwana can be reached by striking east off the Kwangwanese road at Jozini, or from **Hluhluwe** village, where a tarred road passes through Mbazwana to Sodwana Bay.

For much of this area, a **4WD** vehicle is essential and it's best to travel in two vehicles as there's nowhere to get repairs done and facilities are poor. It's also essential to carry an inflated spare tyre, jack and wheel spanner and spare water. Watch out for unattended stray animals and school children wandering onto the roads; never resort to speeding on dirt roads to make up time, and watch out for potholes on all roads.

Sodwana Bay

A tiny scoop in the Zululand Coast, **SODWANA BAY** (daily 24hr; R20), 19km east of Mbazwana, is the only breach in an almost flawless strand extending 170km from St Lucia to Kosi Bay. It's the fortuitous convergence of the bay (which makes it easy to launch boats) with the world's southernmost coral reefs that makes Sodwana the most popular base in the country for **scuba diving** and the most popular KwaZulu-Natal Wildlife resort. Because the continental shelf comes extremely close to shore (near-vertical drops are less than 1km away), it offers very deep waters, much loved by anglers who gather here for some of South Africa's best deep-sea **game fishing**, mostly tag and release. The abundance of game fish also makes for some of the best surf fly-fishing in the country.

When there's no one around, Sodwana Bay is paradise, with tepid waters, terrific sandy beaches, relaxed diving or snorkelling and plenty of basic accommodation. Over weekends and during school holidays, however, fashion-conscious Jo'burgers tear down in their 4WDs trailing boats to show off their designer wet suits, while thick-set anglers from Gauteng, Free State and Mpumalanga come here and drink themselves into a stupor. Thankfully, government regulations now limit the number of 4WDs using the beach as a car park. A gentler presence from mid-November to February are the leatherback and loggerhead **turtles**, who make their way onto Sodwana's beaches to reproduce, as they've been doing for the last 60,000 years (see box on p.547).

Practicalities

There is no public transport to Sodwana other than the **Baz Bus**, which drops off at Hluhluwe, and can arrange for you to connect with a bus to Sodwana (ask when booking). Some of the dive outfits provide transport from Hluhluwe to Sodwana. **Hitching** is possible, but even if you succeed in thumbing a lift here, the place is so spread out that getting around on foot is a major hassle.

The national park takes in the bay itself, while the desultory collection of shops and an upmarket lodge that pass for the **town** are 8km to the west, back along the Mbazwana road. The KwaZulu-Natal Wildlife office, park entry gate, campsites, chalets and two of the dive lodges are up the hill past the town. Here you'll also find a small shop selling **food** and other camping basics (closes 5pm; no liquor available), and a clinic (daily 8–9am and 4–5pm; for emergencies call ☏035 571 0283). **Petrol** is available at the entry gate from 6am till 6pm. There is no ATM, but the shop may allow you to draw cash on your credit card.

The best place to **eat**, though they only do café-style fare and snacks, is *Tomboti* (daily except Tues 9am–5pm), on the right as you approach the town from the west. Set in a rustic art and craft village, this excellent establishment offers pancakes, smoothies and rich chocolate cake at unbeatable prices. A regular hangout for divers is *Jabu Takeaways*, an old caravan parked next to the craft market, and dishing out cheap, filling half-loaves of bread stuffed with fried potatoes, fried egg or curry.

Accommodation

Most **accommodation** at Sodwana lies inside the KZN Wildlife conservation area along the bay's beaches, though the most upmarket place to stay, *Sodwana Bay Lodge*, is outside. Rates tend to be on the high side because of the lack of competition in the area.

Staggeringly, there are more than four hundred KZN Wildlife **campsites** here (☏035 571 0051, ℱ035 571 0115), with a minimum fee of R140 per site during public and school holidays as well as on Friday and Saturday nights. The seasonal population explosion allegedly makes Sodwana the largest campsite in the southern hemisphere. There are also twenty KZN Wildlife **chalets**, fully equipped log cabins with either five beds (R210 per person; minimum charge for three people) or eight (R210; minimum charge for four people).

If you're staying inside the park at the privately run *Coral Divers* or *Mseni*, you must pay a R35 daily camping fee to KZN Wildlife. *Mseni* includes the fee in their rate; to stay at *Coral Divers*, pay the fee at the KZN Wildlife office.

Coral Divers ☎035 571 0290, ⊛www.coraldiver .co.za. The largest dive outfit at Sodwana is a basic, rather tired, backpacker haunt with a variety of two-bed safari tents, two-bed cabins with shared ablutions, and two-bed en-suite cabins. You can self-cater or pay for half board, and takeaways are available throughout the day. Their PADI-certified courses range from the one-day Discovering Scuba through Open Water certification up to instructor level. All equipment for training and subsequent dives is provided, and scuba gear is available to rent. They lay on transport to and from the beach to coincide with dives and meal times. ❷–❹
Mseni Lodge ☎035 571 0284, ⊛www.mseni -lodge.com. The only establishment to have direct access to the beach, this is a comfortable lodge of twenty en-suite log cabins spread out amid thick coastal forest. There's a restaurant, bar, satellite TV and swimming pool. The lodge has a full-time registered dive operation, Amoray Divers, and offers a variety of dive packages. Land excursions include

4WD day-trips to Sibaya and Bangazi lakes in the park's wilderness area, and to Mkhuze, plus trips to secluded beaches. Half board ❻
Sodwana Bay Lodge In the village ☎035 571 6000, ⊛www.sodwanadivelodge.co.za. En-suite two-bed B&B chalets (insist on getting a renovated one), and six- or eight-bed self-catering cottages. The reasonably priced *Leatherback Restaurant and Bar* offers decent food, including the best pizzas around and carvery fare most evenings. A groovers' bar downstairs has pool tables, music, a swimming pool and a sun deck that attracts both visitors and locals. The registered dive operation here offers instruction from open water to instructor level, and rents out scuba equipment. Half board ❻
'Vis' 'Agie's' Camp 500m beyond *Sodwana Bay Lodge*, towards the bay ☎035 571 0104 or 082 440 4141, ⓔvisa1234@iafrica.com. Basic accommodation in cabins sleeping from two to eight people, with a restaurant and bar on site. Half board ❹

Diving and snorkelling

Unless you're a keen angler, the principal reason to come to Sodwana is for the diving off its **coral reefs** which, along with bright tropical fish, thrive here in the warm waters carried down the coast by the Agulhas current. Delicate convolutions of both soft and hard corals cover the rocks with a range of textures, shades and colours. The waters are clear, silt-free and perfect for spotting some of the 1200 varieties of **fish** that inhabit the waters off northern KwaZulu-Natal, making it second only to the Great Barrier Reef in its richness.

The closest reef to the bay, and consequently the most visited, is **Two Mile Reef**, 2km long and 900m wide, offering excellent dives. Among the others is **Five Mile Reef**, which is further north and is known for its miniature staghorn corals, while beyond that, **Seven Mile Reef** is inhabited by large anemone communities and offers protection to turtles and rays, which may be found resting here.

There's excellent **snorkelling** at Jesser Point, a tiny promontory at the southern end of the bay. Just off here is **Quarter Mile Reef**, which attracts a wide variety of fish, including moray eels and rays. Low tide is the best time to venture out – a sign on the beach indicates daily tide times. You can buy competitively priced snorkels and masks from the dive shop at *Sodwana Bay Lodge* (see above), and they may be prepared to rent these as well as wet suits during off-peak periods.

The Mngobolezeni Trail

The five-kilometre circular **Mngobolezeni Trail** winds its way from just across from the park reception through a variety of habitats, including woodland, to the coastal lake that gives the hike its name. Arrows and signs indicate the way – but take care not to get sidetracked down one of the many game paths that crisscross it. The walk takes around three hours and there's no drinkable water along the way, so you should bring refreshment. **Crocodiles** live in the lake, as do hippos, who leave the water to feed, usually at dusk. If you encounter a hippo on land, treat it with the utmost respect: hippos are responsible for more human deaths than any other African mammal. Avoid getting between a hippo and its line of retreat, which will generally be the most direct route to the safety of the water. If you do disturb one, find a tree to hide behind or, even better, to climb.

Apart from hippos, you may be lucky enough to see some of the other animals that inhabit the dune forest and its surrounds, among them bushbuck, duiker (red and common), reedbuck and Tonga squirrels. A trail **booklet** available from the park reception interprets points of interest along the way.

Other activities

There's more to do in Sodwana than diving. Down Wind (☏035 571 0560) run **kite boarding** lessons in the area (R320 for 1hr 30min); all gear is supplied except a wet suit. Exodus Adventures, whose office is opposite the park reception (☏083 349 8575), have a number of **horse-riding** trails that take you through forest and beach (from R160). **Quad bikes** can be rented from a nearby outlet (☏082 785 7704; R180 per hr) to ride within the bay area or, more ambitiously, for the three-hour cycle to Lake Sibaya. It's also possible to go **microlighting** over the pristine beaches and wilderness (book on ☏072 211 6662; R130 for 15min).

During December and January, when loggerhead and leatherback turtles (see box on p.547) come to nest and lay their eggs on the beach, you can join one of the guided **turtle tours** from Sodwana. As a limited number of licences are issued each year for these, the operators change from year to year, so enquire locally.

Lake Sibaya

Lake Sibaya, South Africa's largest natural freshwater lake, covers 77 square kilometres, and is fringed by white sandy beaches disappearing into dense forest. On a windless day the lake, 10km due north of Sodwana, appears glassy, azure and flat; the waters are so transparent that when KZN Wildlife take a hippo census they just fly over and count the dark blobs clearly visible from the air. From the margins, timid crocodiles cut the lake surface, exchanging the warmth of the sun for the safety of the water. This is not an unpopulated wilderness: the lake fringes are dotted with traditional African lands and villages.

There's an exceptionally easy-going three-kilometre **circular walk** that starts from the viewing platform behind KZN Wildlife's now closed *Baya Camp*. **Bird-watching** can be rewarding (there are two hides) with close on three hundred species present. Needless to say, with crocs and hippos lolling about, swimming in the lake is most unwise.

Entrance into the lake is free. On the edge of the lake is *Sibaya Lake Lodge* (☏011 616 9950, ⓦwww.lake-sibaya.co.za; ❾ including food and activities) with sixteen luxury chalets sleeping two, each featuring rustic reed walls and timber floors. From here you can explore the lake in the lodge's Arab-style dhow. Another highlight is the evening entertainment from a community choir and local dancers.

Mabibi

MABIBI is probably the most remote and idyllic campsite in South Africa (daily: April–Sept 6am–8pm; Oct–March 5am–8pm; R20 per person, R15 per vehicle). Situated in luxuriant subtropical forest, about 20km from Sodwana up the coast towards Mozambique, the ten **campsites** (❶) perch on a plateau at the top of monumental dunes that descend sharply to the sea. The camp is protected from the winds by the dune forest and a boardwalk leads down the duneside to the **sea** – a walk that takes about ten minutes. This is one of the most undisturbed sections of coast in KwaZulu-Natal, and outside school holidays you stand a fair chance of having a perfect tropical beach all to yourself. You won't get the frenetic activity of outboard motors and 4WD vehicles found at Sodwana and other spots to the south – they're banned within the Maputaland Coastal Forest Reserve, which Mabibi falls under.

The sea here offers **surf angling** and **snorkelling** matching that at Sodwana, with rich tropical marine life thriving on the coral reefs offshore. A number of mammals live in the forest, but most of them – bushbabies, large-spotted genets and porcupines – only come out after dark, while others like suni and samango monkeys tend to be shy. Vervet monkeys, on the other hand, are fairly bold and you're bound to encounter a troop if you stay for more than a day.

One approach to Mabibi is the tarred Kwa-Ngwanase (also called Manguzi) road from the N2, some 11km north of Mkuze. At the Manzengwenya intersection, turn right and follow the (poorly marked) signboards to Mabibi. Because this final 45km from the junction is along gravel and thick sand tracks, a 4WD vehicle, or at least one with high clearance such as a *bakkie* (pick-up truck), and competent driving are essential. You can also reach Mabibi on the coastal forest link road from Mbazwana; turn right at the Manzengwenya road and follow the signs.

The campsites should be booked through Isibindi Africa (☏035 474 1473, ⓦwww.isibindiafrica.co.za), which also runs the luxury Robinson Crusoe-style *Thonga Beach Lodge* (❾), its thatched suites secluded in the coastal dune forest. The lodge has a wellness centre, dive operation, turtle tracking tours, and dolphin boat trips. If you are staying at *Thonga Beach Lodge* you'll be collected at the end of the tarred road, beyond the Manzengwenya intersection. The closest **shops and fuel** are at **Mbazwana** (see p.542).

Rocktail Bay

South Africa's most sublime beachstay lies about 20km north of Mabibi along the coast at **ROCKTAIL BAY**, a stretch of sand and sea that is restricted to guests who are prepared to pay for the privilege of staying at the *Rocktail Bay Lodge* (book through Wilderness Safaris; ☏011 883 0747, ⓦwww.wilderness-safaris.com; full board ❾). **Accommodation** is in ten en-suite reed-and-thatch chalets raised on stilts into the forest canopy, each with its own wooden deck. This is the ideal place to get away: there's no phone, limited solar electricity, and the last few kilometres are so heavy-going that you leave your vehicle at the Coastal Forest Reserve office on the dirt road from Mabibi, and get ferried in by 4WD.

Few parts of the South African coastline are as unspoilt as the beaches around here, and although there's no big game to pull in the punters, there's excellent **scuba diving** offshore and a dive centre with a qualified PADI instructor, a

Turtles

Sea turtles from as far afield as Malindi in Kenya (3500km to the north) and Cape Agulhas (2000km west along the South African coastline) come ashore on the beaches of the northern Elephant Coast every year between October and February to lay their eggs. The turtles have survived virtually unchanged for almost a hundred million years and it's reckoned that loggerhead turtles have been using Maputa-land's beaches to lay their eggs for 60,000 years.

It is believed that the turtles are lured onto the beach by a hormone that oozes from the beach, a scent that they follow and which is thought to have been pro-grammed into their subconscious while they were themselves in their eggs. The myopic turtle, whose eyes are adapted to underwater vision, pulls herself along the beach in the dark until she encounters an obstruction such as a bank or a log, where she begins digging a pit using her front flippers until she has scooped out a nest big enough to hold her own volume. She then digs a flask-shaped hole about 50cm deep and lays her eggs into this, a process which takes about ten minutes. The turtle fills the hole with sand using her front flippers, disguising the place where the eggs are stored, and returns to the sea. After about two months the eggs hatch, and the entire clutch of hatched turtles will simultaneously race down the beach. Once in the ocean, the hatchlings swim out to sea where they are either carried away by the Agulhas current into the Atlantic or along the Indian Ocean coast. Only one in five hundred will survive to return.

The whole of the northern Elephant Coast is excellent for spotting loggerhead and leatherback turtles, with **Rocktail Bay** probably the best spot of all. As the turtles are easily disturbed, only a few licensed operators are allowed to escort visitors to watch the turtles at night.

boat and skipper. You can also go **snorkelling** in the bay at low tide (fins and snorkels are available to guests). The **bird–watching** here is excellent; among a number of rare species are the green twinspot, green coucal, grey waxbill, purple-crested and Livingstone's louries as well as the Natal robin, emerald cuckoo and – particularly prized – the palmnut vulture.

Supreme idleness is one of the big attractions of the place, but you can walk in the coastal forest, join an excursion to Black Rock or Lake Sibaya and watch turtles during the summer egg-laying season. **Surf fishing** for shad, springer, kingfish, bonefish, stumpnose, barracuda and blacktail is another possibility.

Ingwavuma

A small village high up in the Lebomba Mountains, on the border with Swaziland, **INGWAVUMA** is home to the **Ingwavuma Women's Cen-tre**, a poverty alleviation project started in 2001. The project (arrange a visit through Maryna Heese on ☏035 591 0027 or 072 279 2962) employs nearly three hundred women to undertake basket weaving, embroidery, wire work and beading, and you can get informal instruction in these traditional Zulu art forms. The most fascinating craft to learn is sisal-basket weaving, which requires you to know how to collect the correct grass. The centre offers simple B&B **accommodation** in three en-suite rooms (booking is essential; ☏035 591 0133 or 082 296 0942, ✉stembenivw@xsinet.co.za; ❷).

The area offers a rich mix of Zulu and Swazi culture, where you can experi-ence the foods and dances of both nations. Guides are available to take you on mountain **nature walks** and to visit **caves** spectacularly overlooking a five-hundred-metre drop into Swaziland (daily 9am–4pm; free).

Ndumo Game Reserve

One of the most beautiful of the KwaZulu-Natal reserves, **Ndumo** (daily dawn–dusk; R35 per vehicle, R30 per person) looks across the flood plain into Mozambique to the north and up to the Lebombo Mountains in the south. Its northern extent hugs the **Usutu River**, which rises in Swaziland and defines South Africa's border with Mozambique. The turn-off to the reserve is 56km north of Jozini, with the final 15km along a rough gravel track.

No great volume of animals trammel the reserve, but the beauty, solitude and prolific birdlife here make this a good place to head for if you're not simply into ticking off your check list of **mammals**. That's not to underplay the 62 species here (including buffalo, jackal, wildebeest, giraffe, hippo, hyena, zebra and both species of rhino), but they may be more difficult to see than elsewhere. For twitchers, however, Ndumo ranks among the country's **bird-watching** top spots. The staggering 420 different varieties recorded here include the African broadbill, pink-throated twinspot, Pels fishing owl, gorgeous bushshrike, cuckoo hawk, southern banded snake eagle and the palmnut vulture.

You can **drive** around some areas, one of the highlights being the trip to **Redcliffs**, where there's a picnic site with a towering vantage point offering soaring views across the Usutu River into both Swaziland and Mozambique. KwaZulu-Natal Wildlife offers open-topped 4WD outings in the mornings and evenings to the lovely **Inyamiti pan**, which is inhabited by hippos and crocodiles and receives visits from an array of waterfowl; guided **walking trails** are also available.

The small KZN Wildlife **restcamp** (☎035 591 0032) is sited on a hill and has a number of campsites and seven well-maintained, two-bed **huts** (❷), each with a fridge and shared ablutions. A shop near the entrance gate sells basic **supplies**, but you're better off stocking up en route in Mkuze village. In an area of the reserve closed to the general public, the private *Ndumo Wilderness Camp* (book through Wilderness Safaris; ☎011 883 0747, ⓦwww.wilderness -safaris.com; ❽ including meals and activities) consists of a series of luxury en-suite safari tents on decks overlooking a beautiful pan, and connected by boardwalks on stilts. The lounge area is an open-sided deck that juts out towards the water, offering fabulous views of its crocodile-infested waters and the perfect vantage from which to watch water birds with a pair of binoculars. The lodge organizes game drives and informative guided walks. Just outside the park is another pleasant place to stay, the *Ndumu River Lodge* (☎035 591 0011, ⓦwww.ndumu.com; ❷) which offers accommodation on a self-catering or B&B basis; directions are given when you book.

Kosi Bay

The northernmost place along the KwaZulu-Natal coast, **KOSI BAY** (daily: April–Sept 6am–8pm; Oct–March 5am–8pm; R15 per vehicle, R20 per person) is at the centre of an enthralling area of waterways fringed by forest. Despite the name, this is not a bay at all, but a system of four lakes connected by narrow reed channels which eventually empty into the sea at Kosi Mouth.

One of the most striking images of Kosi Bay is of mazes of reed fences in the estuary and other parts of the lake system. These are **fish kraals**, or traps, built by local Tonga people, a practice that has been going on for hundreds of years. Custom has made the method of harvesting sustainable, because trap numbers are strictly controlled; the traps are passed down from father to son and capture only a small fraction of the fish that pass through.

Staying at Kosi Bay, you're likely to feel frustratingly land-locked – you won't so much as glimpse the coast unless you sign up for the four-day **Amanzimnyama Trail**. This circular hike begins at the base camp on the west shore of Nhlange, the largest lake in the area, and passes through beautiful coastal forest, along the beach, through groves of cycad and giant raffia palm. In summer, there's the chance of seeing turtles on the beach. Beds, pots, cookers, ablution facilities and limited water are available at night stops along the route, but there's no electricity or refrigeration, and you must bring your own utensils, food, bedding, torches and snorkelling gear. Mosquito repellent is recommended, and this is one of the few parts of the country where it's advisable to use water purification tablets. **Bookings** for the trail, which costs R250 per person, should be made through KwaZulu-Natal Wildlife central office.

A highly recommended alternative way to explore the area is on a **tour** guided by members of the local community, who can show you the lakes and the fish traps. Trips start just outside the restcamp from the reserve **office** (☎035 592 0236), where you can gather more **information**. Horse-riding safaris in the area can be arranged through Maputaland Horse Safaris (☎083 556 6609, ⓔmail@maputaland.net; R225 for 2hr, with longer trips possible).

Accommodation

A number of locally owned and operated restcamps have opened in recent times, the proprietors all enthusiastic hosts and knowledgable guides. Directions to the camps are given when you book, and 4WD transfers from Kwa-Ngwanase can be arranged for an additional charge.

Hlalanathi Forest Camp ☎072 345 6260. Campsites, huts and tented accommodation, with a communal kitchen (bring your own provisions) and dining area. It's uniquely positioned in the sand forest at Bhanga Nek. ❷

Kosi Forest Lodge Inside the reserve ☎035 474 1504, ⓦwww.zulunet.co.za. Arguably the most dreamy place to stay in KwaZulu-Natal, featuring eight reed-and-thatch suites in a remote landscape of palms, lakes, sand forest and bleached white beaches. There is no electricity, and you have to be collected by 4WD from the Kwanganase police station and taken along sandy tracks to the lodge. Activities include guided canoeing trips, reef snorkelling and forest walks; there's a good chance you'll see hippos, crocodiles and marine turtles. The rate is inclusive of all meals and activities. May–Aug ❻, Sept–April ❼

KwaZulu-Natal Wildlife restcamp Inside the reserve, on the west shore of Nhlange, the largest of the lakes. Two-bed, five-bed (minimum charge for three people) and six-bed chalets (minimum charge for four people), with a small campsite nearby; an upmarket lodge is in the pipeline. ❷

Siphiwe's Camp ☎082 731 2096. The only dorm accommodation in the area, and also offering two two-sleeper units and camping. ❶

Utshwayelo Campsite ☎084 303 2040 or 035 592 9626. Situated in a prime position close to the river mouth with rustic ablution facilities and a kitchen. ❶

Victor's Camp ☎073 150 9350. Six well-run rondavels sleeping two, with shared ablution facilities, a communal kitchen, and good views. ❷

Ithala Game Reserve

West of Maputaland and close to the Swaziland border, the small **Ithala Game Reserve** (daily: April–Sept 6am–6pm; Oct–March 5am–7pm; R30 per vehicle, R30 per person) is little known, despite being one of the country's most uncrowded and spectacularly scenic places to watch wildlife. The reserve's relative youth (it was only proclaimed in 1972) may be one reason why it is frequently bypassed by visitors. This could soon change, especially as Ithala's main camp, **Ntshondwe**, is one of the best game-reserve restcamps in South Africa. Ithala is largely mountainous, and the terrain extremely varied, with numerous cliffs and rock-faces contained within a protective basin.

Like the rest of the KwaZulu-Natal game reserves, Ithala is excellent for white **rhinos** and there's plenty of **plains game**, including zebras and giraffes. Of the **predators**, you could, if you're very lucky, encounter brown hyenas, cheetahs and leopards. If you're obsessed with seeing the Big Five, however, Ithala is not the place to visit – the king of the beasts is notably absent here, even though the other four make periodic appearances. But the best idea is to throw away your mammal check list and take a slow drive around the mountains into the valleys and along the watercourses. As there are no lions, the game is relaxed, and on a quiet weekday watching **animal behaviour** can be fascinating. Slow down, keep your eyes open, and you may see a rhino male defending his territory, or two young giraffes testing their strength with neck wrestling. One of the most rewarding **drives** is along Ngubhu Loop, with a detour to Ngubhu picnic site.

There are some **self-guided trails** into the wooded mountainside above *Ntshondwe Restcamp*, which give the chance to stretch your legs if you've spent a morning driving around. **Day and night drives** in open vehicles can be booked through the restcamp's reception at a cost of R100 per person.

Practicalities

There's no public **transport** to the park or near it, so driving here is your only option. All accommodation here is run by KwaZulu-Natal Wildlife. The main restcamp, **Ntshondwe**, 7km beyond the entrance gate, is ingeniously camouflaged against a high plateau with views at the foot of huge cliffs. The camp's reception can provide **information** and **maps**. There are no lawns or gardens; each chalet is surrounded by indigenous bush through which paved walkways weave their way around granite rocks and trees to the main reception area, which has a small shop, a restaurant, and bar with a deck overlooking a waterhole.

Ntshondwe has a **restaurant** serving a surprisingly varied range of foods from *escargot* to steaks – though meat-free meals aren't always on the menu – and a cosy **bar** whose sundeck looks out over the waterhole and across the valleys. If you want to self-cater, you'll need to get **supplies** before you come – the camp shop specializes in beer and frozen meat and hasn't much by way of fresh food. **Louwsburg**, signed from the surfaced road along the southern section of the reserve, has a very small general store that's a little better and, further afield, Vryheid, Pongola or Mkuze are better still.

Accommodation

Mbizo Campsite If you want an extremely pared-down bush experience, you can't beat this marvellous campsite with space for just sixteen people, shaded by thorn trees and ilala palms, on the banks of the Mbizo River. Expect no frills here – it's cold showers in reed enclosures and cooking over wood fires, the only concession to civilization being a flushing toilet. ❸

Mhlangeni, Mbizo and Thalu bush camps A wonderful choice if you want something a bit wilder, these camps are all in beautiful secluded settings and cater for four to ten people, with no minimum occupancy charge. The camps are staffed by an attendant and you can make arrangements to have a field ranger to take you on walks. ❸

Ntshondwe Lodge Next to the restcamp, yet completely secluded, this luxury lodge has beautifully decorated rooms, a restaurant and a small plunge pool overlooking the reserve. ❽

Ntshondwe Restcamp Offers 37 extremely comfortable two- and four-bed self-catering chalets with fully equipped kitchens, lounge areas and verandas, and 28 non-self-catering units. Also features a pool and restaurant. ❸

Central Zululand and the Battlefields

Central Zululand – the Zulu heartland – radiates out from the unlovely modern town of **Ulundi**, some 30km west of the Hluhluwe-Imfolozi Park. At the height of its influence in the 1820s and 1830s, under King Shaka, the core of the Zulu state lay between the **Black Imfolozi River** in the north, and in the south, the **Tugela**, which discharges into the Indian Ocean roughly 100km north of Durban.

Despite being a beautiful area of dry thornveld, large hills and impressive views, Central Zululand tends to be visited as a series of routes taking in museums and **Battlefield sites**. The Zulu heartland, where you'll find **museums** relating to local history and culture, is concentrated just to the west of the Hluhluwe-Imfolozi Park, King Shaka's personal hunting preserve. The heartland can be taken as a side trip from a visit to Hluhluwe-Imfolozi or Ithala Game Reserve, which lies about 150km north of Ulundi.

Contained in a relatively small area to the west of the heartland are a series of sites of nineteenth-century battles, first between Zulus and Boers, then Zulus and the British, and finally between the Boers and Brits. Don't attempt to visit this area on your own: all you'll see is empty veld with a few memorials. Far better is to join a tour with one of the several excellent guides who make it their business to bring the region's dramatic history alive (see box on p.558).

The Zulu heartland

Don't expect to see "tribal" people who conform to the Zulu myth outside theme parks such as Shakaland, near Eshowe. Traditional dress and the **traditional lifestyle** are largely a nineteenth-century phenomenon, deliberately smashed by the British a century ago, when they imposed a poll tax that had to be paid in cash – thus ending Zulu self-sufficiency, generating urbanization and forcing the Africans into the modern industrial economy, where they were needed as workers.

You will find beautiful Zulu crafts in this part of the country, the best examples being in museums such as the little-known but outstanding **Vukani Collection** in Eshowe. Also worth checking out is the reconstructed royal enclosure of Cetshwayo, the last king of the independent Zulu, at **Ondini**, near Ulundi.

Some history

The truth behind the Zulus is difficult to separate from the mythology, which was fed by both the Zulus themselves as well as white settlers. Accounts of the Zulu kingdom in the 1820s rely heavily on the diaries of the two adventurers, **Henry Fynn** and **Nathaniel Isaacs**, who portrayed King Shaka as a mercurial and bloodthirsty tyrant who killed his subjects willy-nilly for a bit of fun. Despite their attempts to cover up their profligate disregard for the truth, a

THE ZULU HEARTLAND
& THE BATTLEFIELDS

0   25 km

FREE
STATE

Newcastle

Ermelo

Harrismith

Harrismith

N11

R103

R74

N3

Bergville

Cathedral
Peak

Champagne
Castle

UKHAHLAMBA-
DRAKENSBURG
PARK

R600

Winterton

Chievely

SPIOENKOP
NATURE
RESERVE

Spioenkop

Battle of
Spioenkop
1900

Colenso

Capture of
Winston
Churchill 1899

Estcourt

Weenen

Mooi River

Pietermaritzburg

Siege of Ladysmith
1899-1900

Ladysmith

Glencoe

Dundee

Battle of Talana
1899

Helpmekaar

Newcastle

R602

R68

N11

R103

Utrecht

R34

R33

Piet Retief

Vryheid

ITHALA
GAME
RESERVE

R69

Louwsburg

R66

Pongola

Tembe, Kosi Bay
& Ndumo

Nqutu

Battle of
Blood River
1838

Battle of
Isandlwana
1879

Battle of
Rorke's Drift
1879

Buffalo River

Tugela River

Greytown

R74

R33

R74

Dukuza

Pietermaritzburg

Babanango

R68

R34

Nongoma

R66

Black Imfolozi River

Ulundi

Ondini

Battle of Ulundi
1879

Spirit of
eMakhosini

Melmoth

White Imfolozi

Hlabisa

R618

HLUHLUWE-
IMFOLOZI PARK

Mtubatuba

Hluhluwe

St Lucia

N2

Nkwalini

Shakaland

Eshowe

R66

R34

Empangeni

Richards
Bay

INDIAN OCEAN

Battle of
Gingindlovu
1879

Gingindlovu

R102

N2

Dukuza & Durban

N

Zulu festivals

In September and October KwaZulu-Natal is host to three significant Zulu **festivals** that until recently were only attended by the actual participants, though it's now possible to witness these with the Eshowe-based Zululand Eco-Adventures (Ⓦwww .eshowe.com).

The Royal Reed Dance

In the second week of September, the Zulu King hosts a four-day celebration at his royal residence at **Nongoma**. The event is both a rite of passage to womanhood for the young maidens of the Zulu nation, and a chance for them to show off their singing and dancing talents. The festival, known as **Umkhosi woMhlanga** in Zulu, takes its name from the riverbed reeds that play a significant role in Zulu life. Young women carry the reed sticks, which symbolize the power of nature, to the king. According to Zulu mythology, only virgins should take part, and if a woman participant is not a virgin, this will be revealed by her reed stick breaking.

King Shaka Day

In honour of King Shaka, a celebration is held yearly on September 24 at **Dukuza** (see p.502), Shaka's original homestead and the place where he was murdered in 1828 by his brothers Dingane and Mhlangana. It was Shaka who brought together smaller tribes and formed them into the greatest worrier nation in Southern Africa. Today, the celebration is attended by a who's who of South African Zulu society, and there are speeches, music and fantastic displays of warrior dancing, the men decked out in full ceremonial gear.

Shembe Festival

Held in mid- to late October in **Judea**, near Eshowe, the Shembe Festival is the culmination of weeks of endless rituals, dancing and prayers held throughout Kwa-Zulu-Natal. Some thirty thousand members of the Shembe church (see p.483) return here every year to meet their leader and celebrate their religion, with prayer dances and displays of drumming.

letter from Isaacs to Fynn was uncovered in the 1940s. In it he encourages his friend, who was en route to London to publish his memoirs, to depict the Zulu kings as "bloodthirsty as you can, and describe frivolous crimes people lose their lives for. It all tends to swell up the work and make it interesting."

A current debate divides historians about the real extent of the **Zulu empire** during the nineteenth century. Some now question the conventional wisdom that Shaka was the "African Napoleon", a military genius who transformed the politics of nineteenth-century South Africa. What we do know is that in the 1820s Shaka consolidated a state that was one of the most powerful political forces in the subcontinent, and that internal dissent to his rule culminated in his assassination by his half-brothers **Dingane and Mhlangana** in 1828.

In the 1830s, pressure from whites exacerbated internal tensions in the Zulu state and reached a climax when a relatively small party of Boers defeated Dingane's army at **Blood River**, leading to a split in the Zulu state, with one half following **King Mpande**. Collapse threatened when Mpande's sons Mbuyazi and Cetshwayo led opposing forces in a pitched battle for the succession. **Cetshwayo** emerged victorious and successfully set about rebuilding the state, but too late. Britain had already determined that its own interest would best be served by a confederated South Africa under its own control and a powerful Zulu state wasn't going to be allowed to stand in the way. On the banks of the Tugela River, the high commissioner, Sir Bartle Frere, delivered a Hobson's choice of an **ultimatum** that Cetshwayo should dismantle his polity or face invasion.

In January 1879, the British army crossed the Tugela, and suffered a humiliating disaster at **Isandlwana** – the British army's worst defeat ever at the hands of native armies. However, the tide turned against the Zulus after just over a hundred British soldiers repulsed a force of between 3000 and 4000 Zulus at Rorke's Drift. By the end of July, Zulu independence had been snuffed, when the British lured the reluctant (and effectively already broken) Zulus, who were now eager for peace, into battle at Ulundi. The British set alight Cetshwayo's capital at Ondini – a fire which blazed for four days – and the king was taken prisoner and held in the Castle in Cape Town.

Gingindlovu

There's nothing much to see in **GINGINDLOVU** (shortened to Ging by local whites), which is 50km north of Dukuza along the R102, but it makes as good a base as any to explore the Zulu heartland and the Battlefields, and has the advantage of being near the coast. It was here at Gingindlovu that the Zulus attacked a British relief column on April 2, 1879, as it was marching on Eshowe to relieve a siege. In one of the decisive battles of the Anglo-Zulu War, the colonial invaders delivered a crushing defeat to the Zulus that destroyed their morale, with the loss of only thirteen British lives. The following day, the British column continued its advance, and successfully raised the Eshowe siege.

The Baz Bus can drop you off at either of the two excellent **places to stay**, the cheaper being the eccentric and thoroughly entertaining *Inyezane Backpackers* on a sugar farm just outside town (☎035 337 1326, ✉inyezane@ethniczulu .com; dorms ❶, rooms ❷). Accommodation consists of a series of eclectically decorated rondavels, with dorms, doubles and camping available. The hostel is well known for its herbal baths, Zulu mud baths and classes in fabric painting and the playing of traditional instruments. Also on a sugar estate, but at the opposite extreme with its old-fashioned elegance, is *Mine Own Country House* (☎035 337 1262, ✉remark@netactive.co.za; ❹), 4km north of Gingindlovu on the R102. It's fifteen minutes' drive from the beach in a grand homestead resembling something out of *Gone with the Wind*, and offers en-suite rooms, well-tended gardens, a golf course, a swimming pool and tennis courts.

Eshowe

The name **ESHOWE** has an onomatopoeic Zulu derivation, evoking the sound of the wind blowing through the trees. Though visitors generally give the town a miss on the way to the more obvious drama of Ondini and the Battlefields, the place deserves more than a passing glance, as it offers a gentle introduction to the Zulu heartland. Apart from its attractive setting 22km inland from Gingindlovu, interlacing with the **Dlinza Forest**, the town is home to one of the world's finest collections of Zulu crafts and has a tour operator offering excellent excursions that take you under the skin of a Kwa-Zulu-Natal provincial town.

The Town

Containing more than 3000 examples of traditional Zulu arts and crafts, the brilliant **Vukani Collection Museum** is housed in a purpose-built structure in the grounds of Fort Nongqayi on Nongqayi Road (daily 9am–4pm; R25;

035 474 5274), a few minute's walk from the city centre. The best way to see the museum is to arrange a 45-minute guided tour, which is included in the price. On display is a huge range of **baskets**, something Zulu culture excels at (and examples of which are held in many major international art collections), each made for a specific purpose. There are also carvings, clothing, beadwork, tapestries and some outstanding ceramics, including works by **Nesta Nala**, one of the leading contemporary proponents of the form. The benchmark examples here allow you to form an idea of the quality of basketry and crafts you'll see for sale as you work your way around Zululand. There are plans to run an artist-in-residence scheme in which craftworkers will live and work in the grounds of Vukani.

Also inside Fort Nongqayi is the **Zululand Historical Museum** (daily 9am–4pm; R10), a collection that is eccentric and informative by turns, but never dull. Among the displays is furniture belonging to **John Dunn**, the only white man to become a Zulu chief and, incidentally, also to take 49 wives, so becoming the progenitor of Eshowe's coloured community, many of whom still carry his last name. You can also see Zulu household artefacts, the replica of a silver beer mug given by Queen Victoria in London to Cetshwayo, the last king of the free Zulus in 1882, and displays on Zulu history. One of these covers the **Bambatha Rebellion**, in which Fort Nongqayi saw action, when Natal's colonial forces put down the last armed resistance by Africans till the formation of the ANC's armed wing in the 1960s. Also on site are the *Adams Outpost Restaurant* and the **Zululand Missionary Museum** in the fort's chapel.

Dlinza Forest and aerial boardwalk

A must for bird-watchers, **Dlinza Forest** is also a great place for picnics or trekking along the impressive **Dlinza Forest Aerial Boardwalk** off Kangella Street (May–Aug 8am–5pm; Sept–April 6am–6pm; R25), on the southwestern side of Eshowe (it's accessed from the museums complex at Fort Nongqayi). Wheelchair-friendly, the boardwalk spans 125m and is raised 10m into the air just under the forest canopy, giving visitors a chance to experience a section of the woodland normally restricted to birds. The boardwalk leads to a twenty-metre-high stainless-steel **observation tower**, offering stunning panoramas across the treetops to the Indian Ocean shimmering in the distance. A **visitor information centre** at the foot of the boardwalk provides information about forest ecology. Among the birds you might see here are black sparrowhawks, crowned eagles and green coucals, while seventy species of butterfly have also been recorded in the forest.

Practicalities

The Translux **intercity bus** stops in front of the City Hall on its way between Pretoria/Johannesburg and Richards Bay, and the Durban–Johannesburg **Baz Bus** also passes through town. The **Vukani shop** on Main Street, near the *George Hotel*, sells examples of contemporary Zulu craftwork.

Based at the *George Hotel* are Zululand Eco-Adventures (035 474 4919, www.eshowe.com), whose **tours** offer an authentic experience of local Zulu life. They can take you to rural Zulu communities where you'll have the opportunity to attend a Zulu wedding, naming ceremony or divining ritual, and see markets and *shebeens* without feeling as if you're in a theme park. The company also organizes **hikes** along the Dabulamanzi trail, taking in sugar-cane fields and indigenous forest, plus day-trips to Imfolozi game reserve, battlefield tours and some adventure activities.

Amble Inn 116 Main St ☎035 474 1300,
ⓔambleinn@corpdial.co.za. Simple rooms and a
restaurant serving English-style meals. ❷
The Chase ☎035 474 5491,
ⓔthechase@netactive.co.za. From the N2, head
northwest on the R66 for Eshowe, turn left at the
first Eshowe sign, and continue for 1800m until
the large white gates on the left. This comfortable
hotel has two large en-suite rooms and views of
the surrounding sugar-cane fields. There's also a
small cottage sleeping four, with the option of B&B
or self-catering. ❷

Chennells Guesthouse 36 Pearson Ave ☎035
474 2894, ⓔchennells@iafrica.com. A beautiful colonial home built over a century ago, with
a large garden and views of the surrounding
countryside. It's run by Graham and Meg Chennells, who also own Zululand Eco-Adventures, the
George Hotel and *Zululand Backpackers*. ❸
Zululand Backpackers 36 Main St, next to the
George ☎035 474 4919, ⓦwww.eshowe.co.za.
The cheapest beds in town, with dorm rooms,
doubles and camping, and sharing a compound
with the Zululand Brewery. Dorms and rooms ❶

Shakaland and Simunye

North of Eshowe, the winding R66 leaves behind the softer vistas of the
Dlinza Forest, the citrus groves and green seas of cane plantations and looks
across huge views of the valleys that figure in the creation mythology of the
Zulu nation. In no time you're into thornveld (acacias, rocky *koppies* and
aloes) and **theme park** country. Most accessible of these "Zulu-village hotels"
is **Shakaland**, Norman Hurst Farm, Nkwalini (☎035 460 0912, ⓦwww
.shakaland.com), 14km north of Eshowe off the R68.

Built in 1984 as the set for the wildly romanticized TV series *Shaka Zulu*,
Shakaland was taken over in 1988 by the Protea hotel chain. What the brochures
don't tell you is that the village is a reconstruction of a nineteenth-century Zulu
kraal and quite unrepresentative of how people live today. However, Shakaland
just about manages to remain on the acceptable side of exploiting ethnic culture,
and does offer the chance to sample **Zulu food** in a spectacular dining area.
Tours for day visitors (daily 11am & 12.30pm; R170) begin with an audiovisual
presentation about the origin of the Zulus, followed by a guided walk around
the huts, an explanation of traditional social organization, a beer-drinking ceremony and a buffet lunch with traditional food (including vegetarian fare). The
finale is probably one of the best choreographed Zulu **dancing** shows in the
country, with the dramatic landscape as the backdrop; it's worthwhile putting
up with all the other stuff just to see it. You also get to see a Zulu courting
ritual, stick fighting and spear throwing, all of which are included in the price.
Accommodation is available in comfortable traditional beehive huts (❻), with
untraditional luxuries such as electricity and en-suite bathrooms.

In a different league, **Simunye Zulu Lodge**, along the D256, off the R34,
and 6km north of Melmoth, offers a far more authentic experience of Zulu
culture, introducing guests to contemporary ways of life as well as traditional
customs. Visitors are conveyed to the camp by horse, ox wagon or 4WD, and
get to see dancing, visit a working kraal and meet local people. There's **accommodation** here (☎035 450 3111, ⓦwww.protea-hotels.co.za; full board ❻),
encompassing stone-and-thatch cottages carved into the cliffside overlooking
the Mfule River, as well as a beehive hut or rondavels at a kraal (for those who
need mod cons, five of the rooms have electricity).

Ulundi and Ondini

Some 83km north of Eshowe on the R66, and served by domestic flights,
ULUNDI is the former capital of the KwaZulu Bantustan and lies at the

centre of the **Emakhosini Valley** (Valley of the Kings). The latter holds a semi-mythical status among Zulu nationalists as the birthplace of the Zulu state and the area where several of its founding fathers lived and are now buried. A memorial to them was erected in 2003, the Spirit of Emakhosini, on a hill 3km up the R34, beyond the junction with the R66 for Ulundi. The circular memorial is surrounded by seven large aluminum horns representing the kings that came before Shaka, while in the centre is an impressive six-hundred-litre bronze traditional beer pot. A local guide is available to explain the significance of the site (daily 8am–4pm; donation expected).

Now that KwaZulu has been reintegrated with Natal, this rather unattractive modern town is tussling with Pietermaritzburg for pre-eminence in the province, but for the moment the two are joint capitals with most of the action taking place in Pietermaritzburg. Aside from Ulundi's historical connections, the only thing worth stopping for is the **tapestries** at the KwaZulu-Natal Legislature building (Mon–Fri 9am–4pm; free), 1km north of the city centre on King Dinuzulu Highway (the R66). The twenty tapestries are colourfully and intricately woven, and tell stories of Zulu life, traditions and history over the centuries.

The **Battle of Ulundi Memorial**, just outside town on the tarred road to the Cengeni Gate of the Hluhluwe-Imfolozi Park, is the poignant spot marking the final defeat of the Zulus. An understated small stone structure with a silver dome houses a series of plaques listing all the regiments on both sides involved in the last stand of the Zulus on July 4, 1879. The rectangular park around the memorial marks the site of the hollow square formation adopted by the British infantry and supported to devastating effect by seven- and nine-pounder guns.

By far the most interesting sight around here is the **Ondini Historical Reserve** (Mon–Fri 8am–4pm, Sat & Sun 9am–4pm; R12), a few kilometres further along the road, which houses the reconstruction of the royal residence of **King Cetshwayo**, a site museum and a cultural museum. After the decisive Battle of Ulundi, the royal residence at Ondini was razed to the ground and Cetshwayo was captured. Still puzzled by Britain's actions, Cetshwayo wrote to the British governor in 1881 from his exile at the Castle in Cape Town: "I have done you no wrong, therefore you must have some other object in view in invading my land." The *isigodlo*, or **royal enclosure**, has been partially reconstructed with traditional Zulu beehive huts, which you can wander round, while the site museum has a model showing the full original arrangement. Among the items in the **Cultural Museum** is a major bead collection.

A **picnic site** has been provided in the extensive grounds of the reserve and there's **accommodation** at the well-run *uMuzi Bushcamp*. Here you can stay in a traditional Zulu hut, the choice ranging from beehives to grass and reed rondavels and more modern concrete huts, some en suite (❷–❸). All the huts are located in a traditional *umuzi* (homestead) with a central fire area for night-time gatherings. The camp offers tours to eMakhosini Valley, the surrounding battlefields, and Imfolozi Game Park, booked through Tinta Safaris (☎035 450 2531, ⓦwww.tintasafaris.co.za).

The Battlefields

Most of the major KwaZulu-Natal Battlefields lie in the northwestern corner of the province, where first the Boers came out of the mountains from the northeast into Zulu territory and inflicted a severe defeat on the Zulus at

Visiting the **Battlefields** with a qualified guide will infinitely enhance the experience. The guides below specialize in different battle sites, usually those closest to their base. Most guides have negotiable fees; expect to pay in the region of R350–700 for a day-trip, and to have your own transport.

The next best thing to hiring a guide is buying an **audio tour** to listen to in your car; these are available from reception at the Talana Museum (see p.561). David Rattray's excellent set of tapes/CDs *The Day of the Dead Moon*, covering Rorke's Drift and Isandlwana, is available from Exclusive Books or directly from Rattray (see below). As for reading matter, one of the most authoritative **books** about the Anglo-Boer War is the highly entertaining *Boer War* by Thomas Pakenham (see p.920).

Recommended guides

Alain Delvilani *Villa Prince Imperial*, 201 Deputation Street, Vryheid (T034 983 2610, Wwww.etictours.net). Delvilani specializes in the Battle of Blood River.

Elisabeth Durham 39 Tatham St, Dundee T034 212 1014. Informative English and French tours (R400–800) of Rorke's Drift, Isandlwana and the route followed by the French Prince Imperial, who fell at Nqutu.

Ron Gold Stonehaven Tours, Mooi River T083 557 4068, Eron.gold@iafrica.com. Gold specializes in the battles of Spioenkop, Willow Grange and Colenso, and the site of Churchill's arrest. He has reasonably priced accommodation on his farm in Mooi River (see p.511).

Evan Jones T & F034 212 4040, Ebattlepackers@futurenet.co.za. Extensive tours of the Battlefields by a guide with a vast repository of knowledge, who breathes life into the battles.

David Rattray *Fugitive's Drift Lodge* (see p.560) T034 642 1843, Efugdrift@trustnet .co.za. Rattray and his guides are consummate storytellers, who infuse their accounts of Rorke's Drift and Isandlwana with more emotion than anyone else. Their Isandlwana and Rorke's Drift tours leaves the lodge at 7.30am and 2.30pm, respectively; each trip costs R600 per person.

Pat Rundgren T034 212 4560, Egunners@trsutnet.co.za. A large, burly man of Scandinavian/Irish decent, Pat provides an alternative perspective on the battles around the Dundee area.

John Turner PO Box 10, Babanango T035 835 0062, F035 835 0160. With a degree in animal behaviour, Dr Turner is able to combine tours of Hluhluwe-Imfolozi Game Reserve and ecological topics, including birding and basic tree identification, with Zulu historical sites and the Anglo-Zulu Battlefield.

Foy Vermaak PO Box 1358, Dundee 3000 T & F034 642 1925, Efoy@pennyf .co.za. Based close to Isandlwana and Rorke's Drift sites, in which he specializes; he also covers Helpmekaar and Fugitive's Drift.

Blood River in 1838, 13km southeast of the tiny town of Utrecht. Some four decades later, the British spoiled for war and marched north to fight a series of battles against the Zulus, the most notable being at **Isandlwana** and **Rorke's Drift**, southeast of Dundee. If you're only planning to take in one battlefield site, then Isandlwana should be the one, and you really should take in Rorke's Drift as well to complete the day; both sites are eerily beautiful.

Twenty years on, Britain again provoked war, this time against the **Boers** of the South African Republic and the Orange Free State to the north and west. The Second Anglo–Boer War (also known as the South African War) was fought over control of the Gauteng **goldfields**. British troops were landed at Durban, in the British colony of Natal, and boldly marched north. Britain believed the campaign would be quick, cheap and over by Christmas. But in the early stages of the war, the huge, lumbering British machine proved no match for the mobile Boers who fought a guerrilla campaign that checked the British advance in northern KwaZulu-Natal.

At **Ladysmith**, the British endured months of an embarrassing siege, while nearby, at **Spioenkop**, bungling British leadership snatched defeat from the jaws of victory. Although the empire successfully struck back, it took three years to subdue the South African Republic and the Orange Free State, two of the smallest states in the world, after committing half a million troops to the field in an operation that was the costliest campaign since the Napoleonic Wars nearly, a century earlier.

There is more to do in the area than just tour battlefields. From September to April, Isibindi Adventures (☏035 474 1473, ⓦwww.paddlesa.com) offers **whitewater rafting** down the Buffalo River, a nineteen-kilometre journey on two-man inflatable rafts that winds its way through private reserves and traditional homelands. The day-trip costs R375 per person, and you can arrange a suitable departure point when booking.

Isandlwana and Rorke's Drift

On January 22, 1879, the British suffered the most humiliating defeat in their colonial history when virtually their entire force of 1200 men at Isandlwana was obliterated by warriors armed with spears. Dominated by an eerie hill, the **Isandlwana Battlefield**, off the R68 just over 130km northwest of Eshowe and 70km southeast of Dundee (daily 8am–5pm; R8), remains unspoilt and unchanged apart from some small homesteads and the graves of those who fell. A small **interpretation centre** houses artefacts and mementos.

The monumental bungling and the scale of the Zulu victory over the British sent shock waves back to London. Following the British ultimatum to the Zulus, three colonial columns were sent to invade Zululand. King Cetshwayo responded by sending a force against each of these. On January 21, 1879, Zulu troops encamped 6km from Isandlwana Hill, where one of the British columns had set up camp. Unaware of the Zulus over the brow, the British commander took a large detachment to support another British force, leaving the men at Isandlwana undefended and unfortified.

Meanwhile, a British scouting party rode to the brow of a hill and were stunned to find the valley filled with some 25,000 Zulu warriors sitting in utter silence. Because of a superstition surrounding the phase of the moon, the Zulus were waiting for a more propitious moment to attack. On being discovered, they rose up and converged on the British encampment using the classic Zulu "horns of the bull" formation to outflank the unprotected British, whom they completely overran.

The British press at the time demonized the Zulus for disembowelling the dead. In fact, the practice had a religious significance for the Zulus, who believed that it released the spirit of the dead. The custom also had a less spiritual significance; a Zulu warrior was required to "wash his spear" (ie kill an enemy) before he was allowed to marry.

Rorke's Drift

The same evening as the Isadlwana battle, tattered British honour was restored when a group of British veterans and sick successfully defended the field hospital at **Rorke's Drift**, just across the Buffalo River from the site of the earlier disaster, against four advancing Zulu regiments. Despite Cetshwayo's express orders not to attack Rorke's Drift, 3000–4000 hot-headed young Zulu men were so fired up by the Isandlwana victory and so eager to "wash their spears" – they were part of a reserve force and had not yet seen action – that they launched the assault. For twelve hours spanning January 22 and 23, 1879, just over a hundred British soldiers (many of whom were ill) repulsed repeated attacks by the Zulus and so earned eleven Victoria Crosses – the largest number ever awarded in one battle.

Connected by the D30 road with Isandlwana, 15km to the east, Rorke's Drift is the most rewarding Battlefield to visit on your own, thanks to its excellent **field museum** and interpretation centre (daily 8am–4pm; R10). While you're here, it's also worth taking in the **Rorke's Drift ELC Craft Centre** (Mon–Fri 8am–4.30pm, Sat 10am–3pm), known for its hand-printed fabrics and tapestries depicting rural scenes.

Practicalities

For somewhere to stay in the vicinity, you could do worse than the blink-and-you've-missed-it village of **BABANANGO**, 92km northwest of Eshowe, which consists of a shop or two and not much else. The only decent option here is *Babanango Valley Lodge* (☎035 835 0062, ⊛www.babanangovalley.com; half board ❼), signposted 4km west of Babanango on the R68. It's situated on a Natural Heritage Site deep in a beautiful valley, where you can be taken on walks to explore the veld, rocks and river. **Accommodation** is in pleasant en-suite rooms, and there's a swimming pool. Under the same ownership is the luxury tented *Rockpools Bush Camp*, which consists of nine units along the edge of a stream, each with its own private patio and rock pool (❺). The proprietor, Dr John Turner, is a registered guide (see box on p.558).

Near the minuscule settlement of **HELPMEKAAR**, along the R33 south of the Rorke's Drift Battlefield and 30km south of Dundee, *Penny Farthing* (☎ & ℻034 642 1925, ✉foy@pennyf.co.za; ❹) is a historic pioneer farm still furnished with a lot of original objects and generations of hunting trophies, set in an area of big open grasslands and hills, crisscrossed with hiking trails. The host Foy Vermaak is a Battlefields guide (see box on p.558) who enjoys fireside chats on the subject, and has a personal collection of memorabilia.

The ultimate Battlefields place to stay, however, is at *Fugitives' Drift Lodge & Guesthouse* (☎034 642 1843, ⊛www.fugitives-drift-lodge.com; full board ❽; battlefield tours R600), 9km north of Rorke's Drift along the D31 dirt road. Located on a huge game farm, this luxury lodge overlooks the drift where the few British survivors of Isandlwana fled across the Buffalo River. The colonial-style rooms are in individual cottages that open onto lawns and gardens, and guests eat together in a central dining room among the world's largest Zulu battlefield memorabilia collection. Your hosts here are David and Nicky Rattray (see box on p.558); David is occasionally away lecturing, so you may find yourself in the capable hands of Rob Caksie or Pete Wenham, each accomplished raconteurs in their own right. If the *Lodge* is beyond your budget, you can always stay in Dundee and book one of the tours.

Dundee and the Talana Museum

Some 32km west of the Rorke's Drift turn-off, along the R68, **DUNDEE** has little to offer except shops, supermarkets and pharmacies, catering to a population suffering from the effects of large industries who have left the area in recent years. Dundee does, however, serve as a good base to explore the surrounding areas, and features the excellent **Talana Museum** (Mon–Fri 8am–4.30pm, Sat & Sun 10am–4pm; R12), 2km outside town on the R33 to Vryheid.

Under shady blue gums, the museum consists of ten historic whitewashed buildings from the time of the Battle of Talana Hill, the first engagement of the Anglo-Boer War, in 1899. The most interesting of these is **Talana House**, which gives information about northern KwaZulu-Natal conflicts, including Anglo-Zulu, Zulu-Boer and Anglo-Boer wars. The displays include weapons and uniforms, but most evocative are the photographs, which really personalize the wars and provide fascinating details such as the POW camps Boers were exiled to in far-flung parts of the British Empire, including St Helena and the Far East. Often-neglected aspects of the Anglo-Boer War, including the roles of Africans and Indians, also get some coverage. In a photograph of Indian stretcher-bearers, you may be able to spot the youthful Mohandas Gandhi, who carried wounded British soldiers off the Spioenkop and Colenso Battlefields. Arrangements can be made with the curator for guided tours of the museum and surrounding Battlefields (☏034 212 2654). The museum also has the lovely *Miners Rest Tea Shop*.

There's backpacker **accommodation** in the vicinity at *Battlefields Country Lodge*, 5km north of Talana Hill and close to the Battlefields (☏034 218 1641, ⒲www.battlefieldslodge.co.za; ❶–❷). By day, you can take a tour with guides (English, German and French spoken) organized by the hostel; in the evenings, chill out and enjoy traditional Zulu beer and good food at the lovely Zulu-style *Lapa Ukhamba*. Another option is *Battlefields Backpackers*, 90 Victoria Street (☏034 212 4040, Ⓔbattlepackers@telkomsa.net; ❶–❷), a small lodge run by Evan Jones (see box on p.558) and his wife Moira, where you can self-cater or order home-cooked meals. Advance booking is essential at *Lennox Guest Cottage* 3km east of town on the R68 (☏ & Ⓕ034 218 2201, Ⓔlennox@dundeekzn.co.za; ❹), run by former rugby Springbok Dirk Froneman and his wife, Salome. This excellent B&B is unpretentious and comfortable, and Salome serves a four-course **dinner** (R130) that rivals the fare at any sophisticated city restaurant. You can stay in a cottage on a B&B or self-catering basis at *Chez Nous*, 39 Tatham Street (☏034 212 1014; ❷), run by charming French hostess and Battlefields guide Elisabeth Durham (see box on p.558).

Ncome Blood River and Vryheid

You can't fail to be amazed by the monument at the **Blood River Battlefield** (daily 8.30am–4.30pm; R10), 48km from Dundee on the way to Vryheid off the R33. Of all the Afrikaner quasi-religious shrines across the country, this

The unknown soldiers

Africans are rarely mentioned in the context of the Anglo-Boer war, a confrontation fought in a theatre where eighty percent of the population was black. Although both sides denied that Africans served on their side, the British employed around 100,000 blacks both as labourers and under arms, while the Boers had at least 10,000 blacks on their side – often press-ganged into service. After the war, the British denied recognition to Africans who had seen service with them, to the extent that Sir George Leuchars, Natal Minister for Native Affairs, blocked them from receiving their campaign medals on the grounds that it would "irritate" the Boers – to whom the British were now nuzzling up.

definitely takes the biscuit, comprising a replica laager of 64 life-size bronze wagons on the site where the Boers defeated a Zulu army on December 16, 1838. During the apartheid years, this date was celebrated by Afrikaners as the **Day of the Vow**, a public holiday honouring a supposed covenant made by the Boers with God himself that if he granted them victory, they would hold the day sacred. Afrikaners still visit the monument on this day, but under the new government the public holiday has been recycled as the **Day of Reconciliation**, with Blood River also referred to by its Zulu name, Ncome. On the eastern side of the river, the **Ncome Monument and Museum Complex** (daily 8.30am–4.30pm; free) contains a display about the Zulu martial pincer formation, and a reed garden relating the importance of river reeds in Zulu life.

Back on the R33, it's 56km east to **VRYHEID** (Freedom), one-time capital of the Nieuwe Republiek, which still represents some kind of Boer stronghold for many whites who refuse to fly the new South African flag. Unless you're stopping for the night at the highly recommended *Villa Prince Imperial*, 201 Deputation Street (☎034 983 2610, ⓦwww.etictours.net; ❹), clearly signposted from the main street, there's little reason to dally. The villa is a breath of French air in the heart of redneck country, offering thirteen en-suite rooms with baths or (less expensively) showers, a swimming pool, billiard room and bar. The owner, Alain Delvilani, is a knowledgeable Battlefield guide. There is also a **Zulu art gallery** on the premises, with the only display in northern KwaZulu-Natal of authentic and very beautiful antique Zulu beadwork, as well as works by young Zulu artists.

Ladysmith and around

LADYSMITH, 61km south of Dundee on the N11, owes its modest fame to one of the worst sieges in British military history nearly a century ago, and more recently to **Ladysmith Black Mambazo**, the local vocal group that helped Paul Simon revive a flagging career in the mid-1980s. Now one of South Africa's best-known black groups, Mambazo are rarely at home, but the new Cultural Centre and Museum honours their status as local heroes, and a Mambazo trail has been created around the town. The longer-established reason to hang out here is to explore the Anglo-Boer War in the Ladysmith Siege Museum, monuments and the surrounding Battlefields.

"[Ladysmith] is famous to the uttermost ends of the earth: centre of the world's attention, the scene of famous deeds," wrote Winston Churchill as a young, gung-ho journalist covering the Anglo-Boer War for the *London Morning Post*. Some 40km south of Ladysmith, near **Chievely**, is the spot where an armoured train carrying Churchill was blown up by Boers.

The Town

It's easy enough to walk around Ladysmith's small centre. Along Murchison Street, the main artery running through Ladysmith, you'll find banks, the post office and shops as well as the main tourist attractions. Adjacent to the Town Hall, the **Ladysmith Siege Museum** on the corner of Queen and Murchison streets (Mon–Fri 9am–4pm, Sat 9am–1pm; R2) is the obvious starting point for any tour of the Anglo-Boer Battlefields. The siege began on November 2, 1899, and lasted 118 days, with 12,000 British troops suffering the indignity of being pinned down by undisciplined farmers. This compelling little museum tells the story of the war through text and photographs, conveying the appalling conditions during the siege as well as key points in a war that helped shape twentieth-century South Africa, paving the way for its unification. The museum is also a good place to browse books about the war, written from both the British and Boer points of view. The **Town Hall** itself, where the British were to "thank God we kept the flag flying" after the siege, is also worth a peek for its collection of photographs depicting the town's history up to the present.

Right behind the Town Hall and Siege Museum stands the **Cultural Centre and Museum**, 25 Keate Street (Mon–Fri 9am–4pm; R2). Housed in a lovely classic Victorian colonial house, it was opened in 1997, when Ladysmith Black Mambazo were granted the freedom of the town. Life-size cut-outs of the group dominate a mock stage in the Ladysmith Black Mambazo Hall – the first room to the left of the foyer, which is filled with the strains of their stirring choral music. Other rooms display artefacts from the town's various cultures, tributes to local high-fliers – such as world boxing champion Sugarboy Malinga – and work by local artists. For kids, the Jungle/Discovery room offers an adventure into a tropical world with bugs and all, where they are encouraged to touch the exhibits.

Back on Murchison Street, 600m southwest of the Town Hall, **All Saints** Anglican church is a Victorian Gothic edifice built from chiselled shale in 1882 after the contemporary English style, with extensions carried out in 1902 as a memorial to those who died during the siege. Take a step inside to see a plethora of military memorials and some nice stained-glass windows.

Retrace your steps to the Town Hall, and diagonally opposite stands the **Royal Hotel**, where the more privileged of the besieged passed their time, including Leander Starr Jameson and Frank Rhodes (brother of the more famous Cecil), who routinely lunched there. In 1895, both had been involved in the Jameson Raid, an attempt to overthrow the Boer government, which was why some believed that the Boers regularly shelled the hotel around lunchtime.

Head down Queen Street away from the *Royal Hotel* to Forbes Street, where a **statue of Gandhi** stands in front of the unprepossessing Vishnu Temple. Although the monument depicts Gandhi in his later role as the saintly Mahatma, his associations with Ladysmith go back to the Boer War, when he enrolled in the British army as a stretcher-bearer and trained members of Ladysmith's Indian community to do likewise. Gandhi, still at an early stage of his political education, believed that by showing the British that Indians were loyal subjects, they would grant independence to India.

Ladysmith presents an altogether more African face around the **Forbes and Lyell streets** areas, near the temple. Here you'll find people thronging the taxi ranks and informal market stalls on empty plots dotted between run-down Indian shopping malls, while people jive to the rhythm of backstreet music bars and mothers shop with babies strapped to their backs. The Muslim side of Ladysmith is represented by the **Soofie Mosque**, across the Klip River in Mosque Road, in the Indian suburb of Rose Park, said (most notably by the Publicity Association) to be the most beautiful mosque in the southern hemisphere.

Practicalities

Greyhound Johannesburg–Durban **buses** (℡083 915 9000) pull into Ladysmith at *BJ's Restaurant*. The **train station** (℡036 637 7273) is 500m east of the town hall, but arrival and departure times make the train an unrealistic option. The **tourist office** at the Town Hall (Mon–Fri 9am–4pm, Sat 9am–1pm; ℡036 637 2992) has a good selection of literature on the Battlefields. Local battlefields tour guide Liz Spiret (℡036 637 7702 or 072 262 9669,

Ⓔ lizs@telkom.net) charges R600 for up to four people (you need to have your own transport).

As for dining, the siege is over and horse is off the menu, but the *Royal Hotel*, with its three **restaurants**, is still the best place to eat in town. Less formal are the *Guinea Fowl Steakhouse* on Alfred Street, noted for its spare ribs; and *Spur*, Oval Shopping Centre, Murchison Street (next to the Siege Museum), which does a wide selection of burgers, steaks, chicken and a salad buffet (daily 10am–10pm).

Accommodation

There are plenty of **places to stay** in and around Ladysmith, some of them plugging right into the Battlefields scene, with proprietors offering themselves as "Battlefields hosts".

In town

Budleigh House 12 Berea Rd ⓣ 036 635 7700, Ⓔ slabb12@telkomsa.net. A newly built guesthouse overlooking the town, with a pool and sunny patio. Rooms are pleasantly decorated, featuring wooden floors and a subtle African feel. ❸

Bullers Rest Lodge 59/61 Cove Crescent ⓣ 036 637 6154, Ⓔ info@bullersrestlodge.co.za. A smart thatched establishment with a large wooden deck overlooking town. The pub is filled with original battlefield artefacts. ❹

Hunters' Lodge 6 Hunter St ⓣ 036 637 2359 or 083 627 8480, Ⓔ jem@futurenet.co.za. This lovely old home is located in a peaceful neighbourhood and has three single and three double rooms, all en suite. ❹

Royal Hotel 140 Murchison St ⓣ & Ⓕ 036 637 2176, Ⓦ www.royalhotel.com. In the heart of town, this is the hotel that harboured the town's most privileged during the siege – and was regularly shelled by the Boers. Now a three-star establishment catering mainly to travelling reps, it's full during the week, which makes booking essential at any time of year. It can be noisy, thanks to traffic. ❸

Around town

The Aloes Game Farm and B&B 33km from Ladysmith, signposted a further 6km south of Colenso on the R103 ⓣ 036 422 2834, Ⓕ 036 422 2592. The thatched cottage here sleeps five; breakfast costs extra. You can go fishing and mountain biking in the vicinity, and the farm is close to a small game reserve. Breakfast costs extra. ❶

Mac's Nest Heronmere Farm, 5km from town on Windsor Dam Road, off the R103 to Harrismith ⓣ 036 635 4093 or 082 802 1645. A homely B&B on a smallholding with scenic sunsets, first-rate cooking and a small brass foundry; there's also prolific birdlife and small antelope. ❷

Tugela Game Ranch Bush Camp 33km south of Ladysmith ⓣ & Ⓕ 036 422 2592. Fully equipped rondavels overlooking a bass dam with game drives, game viewing, nature walks, fishing and bird-watching. ❷

Spioenkop

Spioenkop Battlefield (daily 9am–5pm; R10) lies 35km west of Ladysmith and is set in the **Spioenkop Nature Reserve** (daily: April–Sept 6am–6pm; Oct–March 6am–7pm; R10). The bloodiest of all the Boer War battles, Spioenkop took more British lives than any other and taught the British command that wars fought by means of set-piece battles were no longer viable. After this, the guerrilla-style tactics of modern warfare were increasingly adopted.

Some 1700 British troops took the hill under cover of a mist without firing a shot, but were able to dig only shallow trenches because the surface was so hard. When the mist lifted they discovered that they had misjudged the crest of the hill, but their real failure was one of flawed command and desperately poor intelligence. Had the British reconnoitred properly, they might have discovered that they were facing a motley collection of fewer than 500 Boers with only seven pieces of artillery, and they could have called in their 1600 reserves to relieve them. Despite holding lower ground, the Boers were able to keep the

British, crammed eight men per metre into their trenches, pinned down for an entire sweltering midsummer day. Around six hundred British troops perished and were buried where they fell on the so-called "acre of massacre".

Meanwhile the Boers, who were aware of the British reinforcements at the base of the hill, had gradually been drifting off and, by the end of the day, unbeknownst to the British, there were only 350 Boers left. In the evening the British withdrew, leaving the hill to the enemy.

Spioenkop has a number of places to **stay** adjoining the nature reserve. Cheapest is the *Mambasa Hutted Camp*, with traditional Zulu beehive huts on the banks of the Tugela River. The huts are basic, with communal ablutions and open fires for cooking; canoes are available for use on the river. Tours of the battlefield and outdoor activities, including wildlife-spotting, can be arranged at either the *Spioenkop Game & Safari Lodge* (℡036 488 1404, ⓦwww.spioenkop.co.za; ◉), with rooms in two cottages, or the colonially stylish *Three Tree Hill Lodge* (℡036 448 1171, ⓦwww.threetreehill.co.za; ◉).

Travel details

Trains

Durban to: Cape Town (1 weekly; 36hrs); Bloemfontein (1 weekly; 17hr); Johannesburg (1 daily; 15hr); Pietermaritzburg (1 daily; 2hr 10min).

Buses

The main **bus lines** serving the principal routes from Durban to Johannesburg or Cape Town are Translux and Greyhound. Supplementary services are offered daily down the South Coast as far as Margate by Margate Mini Coach (℡039 312 1406). Super Shuttle (℡0860 333 444) offers a 24-hour door-to-door service anywhere in the province.

Durban to: Ballito (2 daily; 35min); Bloemfontein (3 daily; 10–12hr); Cape Town (4 daily; 20hr); Dukuza (6 weekly; 1hr); East London (2 daily; 9hr); Empangeni (1 daily; 2–3hr); Grahamstown (2 daily; 12hr); Harrismith (4 daily; 4hr 30min); Johannesburg (8 daily; 11hr 30min); Knysna (2 daily; 15hr); Ladysmith (2 daily; 3hr 30min); Margate (2 daily; 2hr); Melmoth (1 daily; 4hr); Pietermaritzburg (10 daily; 2hr 15min); Plettenberg Bay (2 daily; 14hr 30min); Port Elizabeth (2 daily; 13hr 30min); Port Shepstone (2 daily; 1hr 30min); Pretoria (5 daily; 9hr); Richards Bay (1 daily; 2hr 30min); Sedgefield (2 daily; 15hr); Umhlanga Rocks (1 daily; 15min); Umtata (2 daily; 6hr); Vryheid (2 daily; 6hr).

Margate to: Durban (1–2 daily; 2hr); Johannesburg (5 weekly; 8hr 30min); Pretoria (5 weekly; 10hr).

Pietermaritzburg to: Bloemfontein (2–3 daily; 8hr 30min); Cape Town (4 daily; 19hr); Durban (9 daily; 2hr 15min); Johannesburg (6–7 daily; 7hr); Kimberley (3 weekly; 10hr); Ladysmith (2 daily; 2hr); Pretoria (6–7 daily; 8hr).

Richards Bay to: Durban (2–3 daily; 2hr 30min); Johannesburg (6 weekly; 9hr 30min); Pretoria (6 weekly; 10hr).

Baz Buses

Baz Buses north from Durban to Johannesburg and Pretoria travel either via the Drakensberg or via Swaziland, the latter being an overnight journey. For more about Baz Bus routes, see p.52.

Durban to: Amphitheatre (3 weekly; 5hr); Ballito (3 weekly; 45min); Cintsa (5 weekly; 6hr 30min); Coffee Bay (5 weekly; 8hr); East London (5 weekly; 9hr 45min); Eshowe (3 weekly; 2hr); Gingindlovu (3 weekly; 1hr 30min); Hamburg (5 weekly; 10hr 45min); Harrismith (3 weekly; 7hr); Howick (3 weekly; 2hr 30min); Johannesburg (3 weekly via the Drakensberg; 10hr); Kokstad (5 weekly; 3hr 40min); Kwambonambi (3 weekly; 4hr); Manzini (Swaziland; 3 weekly; 10hr 30min); Mkuze (3 weekly; 8hr); Mliliwane (Swaziland; 3 weekly; 10hr 30min); Mooi River (3 weekly; 3hr); Mtubatuba (3 weekly; 6hr 15min); Pietermaritzburg (3 weekly; 2hr); Port Alfred (5 weekly; 11hr 45 min); Port Elizabeth (5 weekly; 13hr 30min); Port Shepstone (5 weekly; 1hr 30min); Pretoria (3 weekly; 11hr); Richards Bay (3 weekly; 3hr); St Lucia (3 weekly; 5hr); Umtata (5 weekly; 5hr 45min); Warner Beach (5 weekly; 30min); Winterton (3 weekly; 4hr).

Pietermaritzburg to: Amphitheatre (3 weekly; 3hr); Durban (3 weekly; 2hr); Harrismith (3 weekly; 4hr); Johannesburg (3 weekly; 8hr); Mooi River

(3 weekly; 1hr); Pretoria (3 weekly; 9hr); Winterton (3 weekly; 2hr).

Domestic flights

Durban to: Bloemfontein (12 weekly; 1hr 20min); Cape Town (10 daily; 2hr 15min); George (7 weekly; 3hr); Johannesburg (32 daily; 1hr 10min); Nelspruit (1 daily; 1hr 20mins); Pietermaritzburg (10 weekly; 25min); Plettenberg Bay (3 weekly; 2hr 50min); Port Elizabeth (5 daily; 1hr 20min); Ulundi (10 weekly; 40min).

Margate to: Johannesburg (1 daily; 1hr 30min).

Pietermaritzburg to: Durban (2 daily; 25min); Johannesburg (7 daily; 2hr 15min); Ulundi (2 daily; 1hr 30min).

Richards Bay to: Johannesburg (6 daily; 1hr 20min).

6

Free State

CHAPTER 6

Highlights

* **Basotho vernacular architecture** See the decorative adobe huts typical of the Eastern Free State and Lesotho at the Basotho Cultural Village. See p.580

* **Highlands Route** A scenic drive past massive rock formations, cherry orchards and sandstone farming towns. See p.580

* **Drakensberg Escarpment** Catch some of South Africa's most spectacular mountain views by climbing to the highest point on the escarpment via a chain ladder. See p.582

* **Golden Gate Highlands National Park** A stunning reserve dominated by the beautiful Maluti Mountains with their stripy red sandstone outcrops. See p.583

* **Street Café Restaurant** Sample one of 107 varieties of beer, sitting outdoors in the delightful town of Clarens. See p.585

* **Rustler's Valley Easter Festival** A legendary festival in a beautiful valley, which draws hordes of young South Africans to listen to music and chill out. See p.586

△ Landscape near Clarens

6

Free State

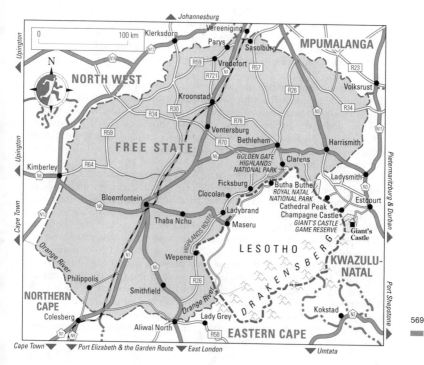

The Highlands Route, one of South Africa's most scenic drives, skirts the mountainous eastern flank of the **Free State**, the traditional heartland of conservative **Afrikanerdom**, which lies landlocked at the centre of the country. If you're driving from Johannesburg to Port Elizabeth or Cape Town, the **Eastern Highlands**, which sweep up to the subcontinent's highest peaks in the Lesotho Drakensberg, are worth the detour off the more humdrum N6. The eastern Free State is also the **gateway to Lesotho**, with border posts close to each of the small towns on the South African side. **Bloemfontein**, the capital, is only worth visiting if you are driving on the N6 to reach the Western or Eastern Cape, rather than taking the Highlands Route, but once there you'll find very good guesthouses, restaurants and museums.

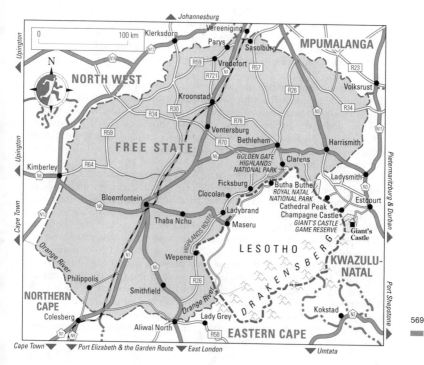

The highlight of the Eastern Highlands is the **Golden Gate National Park**, designated a national park not for its wildlife, but because of the beauty of the Maluti Mountains with their stripy red sandstone outcrops. It's an easy three- to four-hour drive from Johannesburg, and from here it's possible to do a round trip of the Highlands, taking in Lesotho as well. Southeast of Golden Gate you can drive to the Sentinel car park – access point for hikes up to the highest plateaus of the **Drakensberg** – via the interesting **Basotho Cultural Village** and **Phuthadijhaba**. West of Golden Gate is **Clarens**, by far the nicest of the string of towns running along the Lesotho border, with a distinctly arty feel, good guesthouses and outdoor cafés, and some of the country's best horse-riding. For young travellers, party-goers and ageing hippies, the real focus of the region is **Rustler's Valley**, west of Clarens, where you can ride, hike in the hills, party or simply hang out on a truly magnificent farm.

In the rest of the province, flat farmlands roll away into miles of bright-yellow sunflowers and mauve- and pink-petalled cosmos, with maize and wheat fields glowing under immense blue skies. Nelson Mandela described this area as gladdening his heart, "no matter what my mood. When I am here I feel that nothing can shut me in, that my thoughts can roam as far as the horizons."

Some history

Intriguing though it sounds, the name "Free State" applies to former redneck country. For nearly 150 years, the only free people in the Free State were its **white settlers**, who in 1854 were granted independence from Britain in a territory between the Orange and Vaal rivers, where they created a Boer Republic called the **Orange Free State**. The "Orange" part of the name came from the Orange River, which in its turn was named in 1777 by Colonel Robert Gordon, commander of the British garrison at the Cape, after the royal Dutch House of Orange. The system of government in the republic, inspired by the US Constitution, was highly democratic – if you were white and male. Women couldn't vote, while Africans had no rights at all, and were even forbidden from owning land.

Two expansionist military campaigns were launched in 1858 and 1865 to drive out independent **Basotho** people from fertile lands along the Caledon River, which had been their home since the sixteenth century. Although many Basotho under the paramount chief **Moshoeshoe** (see p.763) retreated to strongholds in the Drakensberg, the thousands who remained were reduced to squatters, sharecroppers and labourers facing poor wages on the 15,000 thinly distributed white farms.

A century later, the Orange Free State was a bastion of apartheid, being the only province to ban anyone of Asian descent from remaining within its borders for longer than 24 hours. Africans fared little better; in 1970, under the grand apartheid scheme, a tiny barren enclave wedged between Lesotho, Kwa-Zulu-Natal and the Free State became **QwaQwa**, a "homeland" for Southern Sotho people. As a result of forced clearances from white-designated areas, in the two decades after 1970 its population swelled from 24,000 to nearly half a million, creating one of the worst rural slums in the country. Many men were forced to seek work as migrant labourers in the Gauteng gold mines. Another tiny area around Thaba Nchu, 63km east of Bloemfontein, was part of Bophutatswana, the Tswana Bantustan, which became nominally independent from South Africa in 1977, but was never more than a series of disconnected fragments scattered all over the country, the capital at Mmabatho, in another shard of land in Northwest Province.

The Bantustans have since been reincorporated into South Africa and, after an ANC landslide in Free State province in the 1994 elections, the "Orange" part of the name, with its Dutch Calvinist associations, was dropped.

Bloemfontein and around

BLOEMFONTEIN, the only centre of any size in the province, is unlikely to feature on anyone's list of must-see destinations. However, its location at the crossroads of South Africa means that many travellers break their journey across the country here. There's enough diversion for a day or two in Bloemfontein's surprisingly fine **Oliewenhuis Art Gallery**, set in beautiful gardens, and in the unmistakably provincial **President Brand Street**, lined with handsome, sandstone public buildings.

As an overnight stop, the city offers good accommodation at reasonable prices. People home in from all over the Free State for hospital treatment, for the university (highly regarded for its medical school) and several boarding schools. It's also the seat of the provincial parliament and the judicial capital of the country – a sop tossed out to draw it into the Union when South Africa federated in 1910. South Africa's Supreme Court of Appeal, the highest court

ACCOMMODATION

Bohemian Guest House	A
Canada House	D
Cherry Tree Cottage	C
City Lodge	G
Hobbit Boutique Hotel	B
Holiday Inn Garden Court Bloemfontein	H
Hotel Formula One	I
Kleine Eden Guest House	F
Naval Hill Backpackers	E
Oude Kraal	J

BLOEMFONTEIN

▼ National Women's Monument & War Memorial

in the land and the final arbiter on all legal matters with the exception of constitutional matters, is seated here.

Bloemfontein's urban origins go back to 1846, when **Major Henry Warden** was dispatched to establish a fort and residency here to enforce British control over the unruly Boers, Griquas and Basotho, who were in a constant state of conflict. Knocking their heads together proved fruitless; the frustrated Warden was withdrawn eight years later and the territory left to the Boers, who set up the capital of their new republic here.

Arrival and information

Translux (☎051 408 4888), Intercape (☎086 287 287) and Greyhound (☎051 447 1558) **buses** pull in at the central bus terminal in the tourist complex at the east end of Park Avenue, opposite the swimming pool. There's also a **tourist office** here (Mon–Fri 8am–4.15pm, Sat 8am–noon; ☎051 405 8490, ⓦwww.mangaung.co.za), which provides maps of the city.

Few travellers fly into **Bloemfontein airport** (☎051 433 2901), 10km east of town on the N8, although there are scheduled flights between here and the major cities. There are no shuttle buses from the airport into town, so your only choice is to phone for a fairly expensive taxi, or rent a car (see "Listings" on p.577 for details of both). By **train**, you arrive at Bloemfontein station (☎051 408 4861) on Harvey Road at the east end of Maitland Street. One block west of the station on Hanger Street lies the **minibus taxi rank**. The area around the station and the minibus taxi rank is regarded by some residents as the dodgiest in the city centre, but there have been few actual incidents; stay alert, and avoid the area at night. Fortunately, metered taxis usually gather outside the train and bus stations; alternatively, you can phone for one (see "Listings" on p.578).

Accommodation

Bloemfontein's excellent *Hobbit Boutique Hotel* has won several awards over the last decade. The city also boasts some of the cheapest overnight **accommodation** in South Africa, mainly concentrated around the hospitals, in Universitas suburb to the west of the city centre, and around Oranjesig to its south. However, you're better off heading for the nicer and more central

Gauteng to Bloemfontein: some route tips

Taking the **N1** from Johannesburg to Bloemfontein is the fastest way of covering the distance – and there's a lot to be said for getting the journey over with as quickly as possible. This is no scenic route, especially the Gauteng section and the northern Free State area, which is full of ugly industrial towns. Toll booths are strategically positioned at intervals along the N1, but the charge hardly makes it worth taking free detours. **Kroonstad**, 207km south of Johannesburg, is the biggest town along the N1 before you get to Bloemfontein. The Kroon Park, a large and popular resort beside a river, with a swimming pool, offers a pit stop if you want to cool off or get something to eat.

The alternative route from just south of the provincial border to Kroonstad goes via **Parys**, first along the R59 and turning onto the R721 at Vredefort, 13km south of Parys. But while Parys is quite green and pleasant, you're likely to get stuck behind slow traffic, whereas the N1 at this point is still straight, smooth and wide.

The further south you go, the flatter the Free State becomes. There's an exceptionally long, dull stretch with no services between **Ventersburg** and Bloemfontein.

suburbs of **Westdene** and **Waverley**, both north of the centre and easily reached on foot.

Bohemian Guest House 16 Connor St, Westdene ⓣ051 448 0820, ⓦwww.bohemianguesthouse .co.za. A small, friendly guesthouse with large comfortable rooms in an unusual 1930s home. ❷
Canada House 19 Waverley Rd, Waverley ⓣ072 291 0336. A reasonably priced self-catering option. En-suite rooms have good quality beds and linen. ❷
Cherry Tree Cottage 12A Peter Crescent, Waverley ⓣ051 436 4334, ⓦwww.cherrytree .co.za. A peaceful B&B set in a beautifully land-scaped garden and bordering a reserve with resident giraffe. Two bedrooms under thatch and a family unit with separate entrances. ❸
City Lodge On the corner of Nelson Mandela Drive and Parfitt Avenue, Westdene, and well situated for lively Second Street ⓣ051 444 2974, ⓔclbloem .resve@citylodge.co.za. A fully revamped hotel but fairly characterless chain offering good value, with cheaper rates at weekends. Serves excellent breakfasts. ❹
Hobbit Boutique Hotel 19 President Steyn Ave, Westdene ⓣ & ⓕ051 447 0663, ⓦwww.hobbit .co.za. The best place to stay in Bloemfontein, *Hobbit House* is a luxurious establishment filled with beautiful and comfortable antique furniture, with teddy bears tucked into every bed under handmade quilts. Book well in advance. Excellent three-course dinners are available for guests (phone by lunchtime). ❹

Holiday Inn Garden Court Bloemfontein On the corner of Nelson Mandela Drive and Melville streets, Westdene ⓣ051 444 1253, ⓕ051 444 0671. The best of the large hotels, with sizeable rooms, a nice swimming pool, and weekend discounts. ❹
Hotel Formula One 200 Nelson Mandela Drive ⓣ051 444 3523. No frills, thrills or surprises at this basic, but predictably clean and reliable chain budget hotel. ❶
Kleine Eden Guest House 2 Moffett St, Fichardt Park ⓣ051 525 2633, ⓦwww.kleine-eden.co.za. Well-maintained guesthouse with B&B, self-catering and family unit options. Rooms all have their own entrance and private garden. ❷–❸
Naval Hill Backpackers Delville Road, as you turn into the old waterpump station ⓣ051 447 4413 or 082 579 6509, ⓕ051 444 6065. Four clean dorms and two private rooms (linen available) in a nicely done-up late nineteenth-century pumping station, with washed orange and silver walls. The hostel offers Internet facilities as well as a bar; it can arrange transport to Lesotho and free pick-ups from the station, and provides excellent information on Bloemfontein's nightlife. ❶
Oude Kraal 35km south of Bloemfontein on the N1, off the Riversford exit ⓣ051 564 0636, ⓦwww.oudekraal.co.za. A restored original farm-house furnished with family heirlooms, famed for its splendid Afrikaner meals. The en-suite rooms have their own fireplace. ❹

The City

For a city with a countrywide reputation as the bumpkin capital of South Africa, Bloemfontein is actually quite agreeable. Its slightly unreal character results from many of its late nineteenth- and early twentieth-century **public buildings** paying a pick'n'mix homage to Mediterranean, British, Renaissance and Classical influences. The lack of public transport is no obstacle to getting around, as the central area can easily be crossed on foot in ten minutes.

In common with other South African cities, the white population has begun to desert the city centre. Instead, the suburb of **Westdene**, just to the north of the city centre, has become the place to shop and hang out; the large four-storied Mimosa Mall in Kellner Street provides all you'd need, from coffee shops and chain restaurants to banks and bookshops. Westdene's Second Avenue has burgeoned with restaurants and nightspots, and is safe to stroll about at night, as is the **Waterfront** on Loch Logan, three blocks west of the City Hall – all conveniently near most of the accommodation. The city centre is nevertheless still worth exploring for its architecture.

City Hall and around

For a rewarding stroll in the centre, head down **President Brand Street**, starting at the **City Hall** at the north end on the corner of Charles Street.

Built in 1934, the hall was designed in the "new tradition style" by Gordon Leith, a former employee of Sir Herbert Baker. On the opposite side of President Brand Street, **Hertzog Square** honours the dubious achievements of the Boer general, high court judge and Afrikaner nationalist **J.B.M. Hertzog**, who founded the National Party in 1914 and went on to become prime minister of the Union of South Africa in 1924. Hertzog was also responsible for harsh segregationist legislation, including the stripping of voting rights from Africans in the Cape in 1936. Across the square at 36 Aliwal Street, the **National Museum** (Mon–Sat 10am–5pm, Sun noon–5.30pm; R5) is worth visiting for its rather good dinosaur fossil collection, an actual beehive, cut away to reveal the workings within, and an outstanding reconstruction of a turn-of-the-century Bloemfontein street. The latter features a general dealer, pharmacy, doctor's consulting rooms and a family scene capturing in frozen diorama a father telling off his son under a stern portrait of President Steyn, who looks on approvingly at the father's strictness. The museum also has a tearoom.

Returning to President Brand Street, south of the City Hall stands the highest court in the country, the Roman-style **Supreme Court of Appeal of South Africa**, built in 1929. Staring at it from across the road is the **Fourth Raadsaal**, the last parliament building of the independent Orange Free State republic (it's now the provincial legislature). Built in 1890 – and still regarded as the province's "architectural jewel" – the Raadsaal is an imposing sandstone and red-brick construction, typical of Free State buildings of the period, and brilliantly merging Greek, Roman and Renaissance elements.

National Afrikaans Literary Museum

One block south of the Appeal Court in the Old Government Building, on the corner of President Brand and Maitland streets is the **National Afrikaans Literary Museum** (Mon–Fri 8am–noon & 1–3.45pm; free). Inside, a corridor of offices has been reconstructed as the studies of luminaries of Afrikaans writing; name plates on the doors make you feel rude for not knocking before entering. Look out for the display on **Eugene Marais**, a remarkable polymath active around the turn of the century. A lawyer, poet and journalist, Marais contributed articles to the *Observer* and *The Times* in London and to the Reuter news agency – his works also include a couple of trail-blazing natural histories on termites and baboons. Also represented are the "Sestigers" (generation of the Sixties), including novelist **André Brink**, a vociferous critic of apartheid, and poet **Breyten Breytenbach**, who went into exile in Paris in 1961. Breytenbach returned to South Africa under cover in 1975 to gain support for Okhela, a largely white section of the ANC, and was captured by the South African authorities and imprisoned for seven years, leading to the publication after his release of *The True Confessions of an Albino Terrorist*.

Towards the end of the museum, a couple of rooms are devoted to displays of Afrikaans as a language of oppression. One of the leading lights of coloured Afrikaans (which has its own distinct flavour) is the poet **Adam Small**; in one display, he describes the predicament of being a member of an oppressed community, while at the same time being a speaker of Afrikaans – regarded as the language of white persecutors during the uprisings of the Seventies. "I grew up with Afrikaans. Afrikaans is part of my culture," he is quoted as saying, "and when people said to you that Afrikaans was the language of the oppressor it was very painful, because it was also the language you got from your parents, it was your mother tongue and it was beautiful and full of humanity."

The Waterfront and Zoo

Following the huge success of the Victoria and Alfred Waterfront in Cape Town, every city in the country, landlocked or not, seems eager to jump on the bandwagon. Bloemfontein is no exception; its **Waterfront**, opened in 1998 on Loch Logan in King's Park, is a couple of blocks west of the National Afrikaans Literary Museum. A refreshing addition to the city, the Waterfront has movie houses, pubs and restaurants. Also in King's Park, **Bloemfontein Zoo** (daily: summer 8am–6pm; winter 8am–5pm; R20) is a reasonable place to catch African wildlife, but obviously offers no serious competition to the game reserves.

The Supreme Court of Appeal, Old Presidency and First Raadsaal

Carrying on south down President Brand Street to the corner of Selborne Street, opposite the Fire Station, is the **Supreme Court of Appeal**, completed in 1906. It stands on the site of the home of the Fischers, a prominent Orange Free State Afrikaner family, whose heir, lawyer Bram Fischer, betrayed his Afrikaner tribal roots to defend Nelson Mandela during the 1963 Rivonia Trial. After Mandela was found guilty and handed a life sentence, it was discovered that all the time Fischer had secretly been the leader of the proscribed Communist Party, and he too was jailed for life, later being released to die at home of cancer.

The **Old Presidency**, on the opposite side, was built on the site of the home of Major Henry Warden, the founder of Bloemfontein. Built in 1861 in "Scottish baronial style" as the official seat of the head of the republic, the Presidency is surprisingly plain, due as much to the nineteenth-century state's lack of funds as to the severe Calvinism characterizing the Boer republics.

Turning east after the Old Presidency into St George's Street, you'll come to the **First Raadsaal** (Mon–Fri 10am–3pm, Sat & Sun 2–5pm; R3), the oldest-surviving building in Bloemfontein. Built in 1849 by Major Warden as a school, the building was later used as a Dutch Reformed church and venue for public meetings. At independence in 1854 it became a meeting chamber for Free State Volksraad ("people's assembly"), before reverting to a schoolhouse and church.

National Women's Monument and War Museum

Just over 2km south of the centre, along Monument Street, across the train tracks in an ugly industrial part of town, a sandstone needle pointing skywards marks the **National Women's Monument and War Museum** (Mon–Fri 8am–4.30pm, Sat 10am–5pm, Sun 2–5pm; R5). This stands as a memorial to the 26,370 Afrikaner women and children who died in British concentration camps during the second Anglo-Boer War. It is impossible to overestimate the scars left on the Afrikaner psyche by the concentration camps – probably still the single most divisive issue between English and Afrikaans-speaking white South Africans. At the foot of the monument lies buried **Emily Hobhouse**, a British woman who energetically campaigned on behalf of the Boer internees.

The interest of the adjacent **museum** lies principally in its status as a record of apartheid propaganda. The suffering depicted isn't an exaggeration, but it's a little heavy-handed in its unrelenting dioramas of dignified Boers suffering at the hands of faceless British brutes. Two cursory panels on concentration camps for Africans (never widely publicized in South Africa in the old days) are a post-apartheid afterthought that at least provides a partial record of the more than 14,000 black South Africans who died incarcerated.

J.R.R. Tolkien

Bloemfontein's biggest surprise is that it's the birthplace of **John Ronald Reuel Tolkien**, author of *Lord of the Rings* and *The Hobbit*, a fact the city seems curiously reluctant to publicize.

Tolkien's father, Arthur, left his native Birmingham to work in the colonies, eventually becoming manager of the Bank of Africa in Bloemfontein. J.R.R. was born in 1892, in a house standing on the corner of West Burger and Maitland streets, a couple of blocks east of President Brand Street. When Arthur Tolkien died in 1895, his wife returned to England with her two infant sons; their house was later torn down to make way for a Bradlow's showroom, part of a nationwide cheap furniture chain.

Despite wild claims that Tolkien's experience of the South African landscape inspired him to create the world of Bilbo Baggins, in fact, the flatness of the Free State and the down-to-earth Calvinism of its farming community could hardly be further from *The Hobbit*'s fantastical realm of mountains, forests and supernatural beings. Some accounts claim Tolkien was inspired by the Natal Drakensberg, or the Amatola Mountains around Hogsback. While both these areas do seem to possess an otherworldly magic, it should also be noted that Tolkien left South Africa for good when he was 3 years old, never having set foot outside Bloemfontein prior to his departure.

A room near the entrance of the museum is lined with brilliant ceramic-tile tableaux, depicting scenes from the Anglo-Boer War. The tiles were brought here in 1969 after being uncovered when wallpaper was stripped off the walls of the Transvalia Theatre in Rotterdam, the Netherlands – an indication of how the war rallied the popular imagination in Europe on the side of the Boers.

Oliewenhuis Art Gallery and Freshford House Museum

The best of Bloemfontein's museums is the **Oliewenhuis Art Gallery** on Harry Smith Street (Mon–Fri 8am–5pm, Sat 10am–5pm, Sun 1–5pm; free), 2km north of the centre off Aliwal Street. The collection – which includes a surprisingly good range of **South African sculpture** and **painting** – is housed in the former residency of South African presidents, a beautifully light neo-Cape Dutch manor set in large, attractive gardens, surrounded by wild bush traversed by short walking trails. Particularly satisfying is the landscape collection, which includes a Van Gogh-esque interpretation of one of the city churches by **Bertha Everard**, and a **Thomas Baines** painting of Bloemfontein as a tiny settlement in 1850. Even if you're not interested in the gallery, it's still worth having tea at the **café** on the lawn – its trees and fountain make it the most harmonious location in town.

Also to the north of the city centre, just across Nelson Mandela Drive, the **Freshford House Museum** at 31 Kellner Street (Mon–Fri 10am–1pm, Sat & Sun 2–5pm; R3) makes a lightweight but enjoyable visit. This is especially true if you're interested in **interiors**, as it has been refurbished impeccably in Victorian and Edwardian style. One highlight is a room authentically decorated in daring lime green, with three distinct William Morris wallpapers.

Eating and drinking

While Bloemfontein is no culinary capital and there are no regional specialities to sample, you can still have a good and inexpensive **meal** here, with the best places mainly concentrated around Second Avenue. You'll also find the usual steakhouse chains scattered around the centre and in the shopping malls. For gluttonous **breakfasts**, the *City Lodge* and *Holiday Inn Garden Court* hotels are always good bets.

Barbas Café On Second Avenue, near the university ☏ 051 430 2542. *Barbas* serves good Greek food, a range of cocktails and the best coffee in town; its starkly fashionable decor also helps attract the young and trendy. Parties every Saturday night. Open Tues–Sun 10am until late.

Beef Baron 22 Second Ave ☏ 051 447 4290. True to its name, this is the place to come for beef, where your mug-shot could join those of other carnivores who downed 1.5kg steaks and survived. It also has tempting seafood and an excellent wine cellar. Closed Sat & Mon lunch and Sun evening.

Café Oliewenhuis Harry Smith Street, signposted off the R700. Tables in the formal gardens at the back of the gallery, leading onto a nature reserve, make this Bloemfontein's nicest place for a relaxing outdoor tea or lunch. Though the food itself is generally nothing to write home about, this is definitely *the* place for Sunday afternoon tea and cake.

Café Rossini Mimosa Mall, Kellner Street ☏ 051 444 6222. Gourmet sandwiches, salads and baked potatoes in relaxing surroundings. A handy stop if you're doing a bit of mall shopping. Open daily 8.30am–11pm.

Fishpaste 31 President Steyn St, Westdene ☏ 051 430 2662. The trendiest restaurant in town, *Fishpaste* offers fusion cuisine from a well-planned menu. Artwork on display is part of the owners' gallery. Mon–Fri & Sun 11am–11pm, Sat 6pm–late.

Jazz Time Waterfront ☏ 051 430 5727. No live jazz here, but a lively atmosphere and background music; there's also a wooden deck from which you can survey passing pedestrians. Good cocktail menu, burgers and Middle Eastern food. Open daily 8am–midnight.

Mystic Boer 84 Kellner St. If you have only a night in Bloemfontein, spend it here. Knowingly kitsch, this alternative and trendy Afrikaner venue offers live performances; you can also enjoy a drink and choose pizzas and vegetarian meals from their reasonable pub menu.

Oude Kraal 35km south of town on the N1 ☏ 051 564 0636. Six-course blow-out evening meals of rich, fattening Afrikaner-style food in lovely surroundings on a historic farm. Booking essential.

Nightlife and entertainment

Finding out what's going on in Bloemfontein can be a problem for visitors, as there's no English-language newspaper, though *Naval Hill Backpackers* is always a good source of information on drinking spots and clubs. For something quite different that you won't catch anywhere else in the country, the *Mystic Boer* (see above) has local bands playing regularly plus dancing in the back. A handful of bars down Second Street are also worth checking out, including *Barbas Café* (see above), which is a lively place for a drink. The excellent *Moods and Flavours* (☏ 051 432 4399) in Heidedal – the coloured quarter – has live jazz from all over the country, though only on four nights a month; people dress up for a really good time here.

Bloemfontein's handful of **theatres** include the Observatory, inside a real observatory north of the centre on the crest of Naval Hill. It's situated in the city's nature reserve, which supports a few giraffe and some antelope. The most prestigious theatre is the Sand du Plessis, on the corner of Markgraaff and St Andrew streets. Bloemfontein has several **cinemas**, mostly in suburban shopping malls; the Mimosa Mall in Westdene contains seven screens, and the Waterfront has five, all showing mainstream movies.

Listings

Airlines South African Airways, St Andrew's St ☏ 051 408 4800.
Car rental Avis ☏ 051 433 2331, Budget ☏ 051 433 1178, Hertz ☏ 051 400 2100 and Imperial ☏ 051 433 3511 – all at the airport.

Emergencies Fire ☏ 10178; see also p.89.
Hospitals The main state hospital is Universitas, offering a free 24hr emergency ward, but you may wait hours and the level of care is variable. Far better, if you can afford it or have travel insurance,

is one of the private hospitals: Mediclinic, Kellner Street ☏051 404 6666; and Rosepark, Fichmed Centre, Gustav Crescent ☏051 505 5111. **Pharmacies** Medirex Pharmacy, Southern Life Building, Maitland St ☏051 447 5822 (daily 8am–9pm).

Post office Main branch, corner of East Burger and Maitland streets (Mon, Tues, Thurs & Fri 8am–4.30pm, Wed 8.30am–4.30pm, Sat 8am–noon).
Taxis Silverleaf ☏0800 430 200.
Train information Spoornet ☏051 408 4843, after hours ☏051 408 2262.

South from Bloemfontein

Two major routes splay out and head south from Bloemfontein, the **N6** to the Eastern Cape via Aliwal North and the **N1** to the Western Cape via Colesberg. There's nothing much along either route apart from a couple of quirky small towns. **SMITHFIELD**, a tiny *dorp* 145km south of Bloemfontein, makes a good place to break a journey along the N6, if only to stay at the pleasant *Artists Colony Guest House* (☏051 683 1138, ✉colony@global.co.za), or the more luxurious *Smithfield House* in Brand Street (☏051 683 0071, ✉rainbird@futurenet.co.za; ❸), a restored Victorian house on the outskirts of town with three en-suite rooms, its own pool and tennis court, and a seven-acre garden where kids are welcome to run about. The English restaurant *Colony Room* (☏051 683 0021), along the N6, off Juana Square, opens daily from morning till night for pub lunches, including genuine pork bangers and mash and puddings such as "Death by Chocolate".

PHILIPPOLIS, 168km south of Bloemfontein along a slight detour (tarred) off the N1 between Trompsberg and Colesberg, was one of the first settlements north of the Orange River, established in the 1830s and named in honour of **Dr John Philip**, a British cleric who set up a mission station here. Way ahead of his time, Philip actively campaigned for the full integration of former slaves, Africans and coloured people into the white economic and social system.

Today the village is mainly known for being the place where Sir **Laurens van der Post** (see box) grew up. Laurens, the thirteenth of fifteen children, was born on a farm outside the centre in 1906 and moved here when he was still very young. The old Van der Post family home, on Colin Fraser Street, is privately owned, but if you contact the owners you may be allowed to look

Laurens van der Post

Laurens van der Post achieved world renown as an explorer, writer, soldier and philosopher. He became fascinated by the stories and legends of the "Bushman", the San people dispossessed of their traditional homes by the advance of African and European settlers and forced into the northern deserts. "What drew me so strongly to the Bushman was that he appeared to belong to my native land as no other human being has ever belonged," wrote Van der Post, referring to the Bushman's self-sufficient yet intensely spiritual and aesthetic way of life. It prompted him to take a famous journey in search of the last remnants of the San, one he recorded in his book (later a film) *The Lost World of the Kalahari*. This narrative, along with its sequel *The Heart of the Hunter*, was one of the first literary works to prick the Western conscience with the idea that such a primitive "tribe" had anything to teach it.

Van der Post was also a Japanese prisoner of war during World War II. His book about these experiences, *The Seed and the Sower*, was made into the film *Merry Christmas, Mr Lawrence*. He lived in both London and South Africa, and died in 1996, aged 90.

FREE STATE | Bloemfontein and around

6

In the early nineteenth century, roving bands of cattle-herders and raiders with a reputation for horsemanship and fierce independence appeared on the eastern edge of the Cape Colony around the Orange River. They called themselves, with some pride, "Bastaards", being mixed descendants of European, Khoikhoi, Asian and African people. Missionaries persuaded them to establish settlements at places such as Griquatown, Campbell and Philippolis, but took exception to their name, which was changed to **Griqua**. Though Griqualand West was still theoretically independent, clashes with the Boers and squabbles over land ownership when diamonds were found in their territory saw the Griquas turning to the British for protection, faith which was all too hastily swallowed up by the gorging Cape Colony.

In 1861, three thousand Griquas from Philippolis under their leader Adam Kok III trekked across the Drakensberg to southern Natal to found a pocket of land known as **Griqualand East**. The settlement failed, and slowly the Griquas dispersed and became assimilated into the wider coloured community, although there are still odd pockets of their descendants living in various places around the Northern, Western and Eastern Cape provinces.

around it. Van der Post's ashes are in the Sir Laurens van der Post Memorial Garden, unmissable as you drive into Philippolis from Bloemfontein. The garden has been built round the old pathway linking the white side of town with the black township, and there are plans to create a Van der Post museum and writers' retreat in the little house next door.

Besides the Van der Post connection, there isn't much to the village, although it's a good place to see the mighty **Orange River** – it's easier to stop and contemplate the river on a quiet country road than flashing over it at 120kph as you do on the highway. Many of the tourists passing through Philippolis are disaffected city people in search of a rural idyll. Seventy five of the village's houses have been declared National Heritage sites – a mixture of simple, flat-roofed Karoo and Cape Dutch gabled houses and Victorian buildings with characteristic wrought-iron decorative flourishes. Among the attractive old buildings lining the few streets is the house of **Adam Kok III**, leader of the Griqua. This small, white, flat-roofed house lies just before the post office on Voortrekker Street, the main thoroughfare running through the village. At the end of Voortrekker Street stands the large **Dutch Reformed Church**, built on the site of the original Griqua mission station. It's worth visiting on Sundays to sample local Afrikaans culture.

Signposted along the main road, an **information** bureau (Mon–Fri 8am–4pm; ☎051 773 0203) can direct you to **accommodation** and informal tours of the village. Philoppolis Publicity (☎084 581 0149) provides a booking service. For self-catering, the *Philippolis Old Gaol* on Justisie Street (☎082 550 4421; ❷), two streets off the main road, is cheap, clean and more attractive than it sounds, with two beds to a cell. *Groenhuis Guest House and Restaurant* on Koksfontein Street (☎051 773 0073; ❷) is a very reasonable option with a warm and rustic charm, or try the inexpensive *Philipollis Lodge* on Kok Street (☎051 773 0203; ❷), a guesthouse with a restaurant (closed Sundays). For **eating**, apart from *Philipollis Lodge* and *Groenhuis*, the central *Kokkewiet Café* is the village's meeting place; on Sundays, churchgoers sit at plastic tables and chairs to gossip and drink tea.

The Highlands Route

Hugging the Lesotho border for 280km from **Phuthadijhaba** (Witsieshoek) in the north to Wepener, beyond Ladybrand in the south, the tarred **Highlands Route** offers one of South Africa's most scenic drives, taking you past massive rock formations streaked with red and ochre, cherry orchards and sandstone farming towns. Wedged into a corner between Lesotho and northern KwaZulu-Natal, Phuthadijhaba is the gateway to **the Sentinel**, the easiest route onto the **Drakensberg Escarpment**, the roof of southern Africa. Not far to the west is the highlight of the region, the **Golden Gate Highlands National Park**, encompassing wide open mountain country. The park is an easy three- to four-hour drive from Johannesburg, which means you could easily use it as a first- or last-night stop if you're arriving or leaving from Johannesburg and don't want to spend the night in the city. Nearby, the **Basotho Cultural Village** is worth visiting to gain some insight into Basotho traditions. The closest village to the Golden Gate is **Clarens**, a centre for arts and crafts and the most attractive of all the villages along the route, while to its west is the mountain retreat of **Rustler's Valley**, South Africa's New Age honeypot, which attracts young ravers and ageing hippies to its regular music festivals.

Basotho Cultural Village

The **Basotho Cultural Village** (Mon–Fri 9am–4pm, Sat & Sun 9am–5pm; entrance and guided tour R15; ☎058 721 0300, ✉basotho@dorea.co.za) is 20km east of Golden Gate National Park and signposted from the main road, in the QwaQwa Nature Park. It offers a sanitized view of the traditional lives of the **Basotho** people, who have lived in the vicinity for centuries and have a close affinity to the people living just across the border in Lesotho. The main display in the village is a courtyard of beautiful **Basotho huts**, from organic circular sixteenth-century constructions to square huts with tin roofs and bright interior decor influenced by Boer scissorwork. Outside the huts are people in traditional dress; visitors get to meet the chief and sample traditional beer, hear musicians play and see a traditional healer throwing the bones. Although the whole setup is contrived, the half-hour tour can be good fun. Also interesting is the *litema*, or external decoration on houses, put on by women and still visible in rural Lesotho and Free State. The decoration varies from repeat patterns scratched into the mud-coloured plasterwork to vivid, modern motifs.

There's a limited amount of very reasonably priced **accommodation** available in a couple of thatched, stone huts (❶) with external toilets and washing facilities. A two-plate electric cooker and kettle are provided, along with basic utensils, and linen, blankets and towels. The views from the shuttered windows across the QwaQwa Nature Park are awesome, and this is a great place to stay, with an endless choice of walks. Don't expect to be looked after, though, and be warned that the village is largely deserted at night, when the workers head back to contemporary urban Sotho life in Phuthadijhaba. A **curio shop** sells some quality local crafts (look out for raffia mats and baskets and the conical straw hats unique to this area and Lesotho), and an open-air **restaurant** serves teas and traditional food. For those wanting a little more luxury, there are also newly built self-catering chalets – for bookings contact South African National Parks (see p.71).

Phuthadijhaba and around

The only reason you're likely to drive through **PHUTHADIJHABA** (sometimes called Witsieshoek), roughly 2km off the R712 and east of Golden Gate, is to reach the *Witsieshoek Mountain Resort* and the Sentinel car park, the easiest hiking access onto the High Drakensberg Escarpment. Phuthadijhaba itself is rather bleak and functional, home to light industry and brick matchbox houses. In contrast to the emptiness of the landscape around Golden Gate, in Phuthadijhaba you'll see minibus taxis zipping around, and people and animals walking on the roadsides past shacks, their tin roofs weighted down against the wind with stones. Phuthadijhaba was the artificially created capital of the

Hiking up the Drakensberg Escarpment

South Africa's most spectacular mountain views are from the **Drakensberg Escarpment**, the broad area right at the top of the major peaks, and from the top of the **Amphitheatre**, the grand sweep of mountains dominating the Royal Natal National Park. Both of these require a high level of fitness to reach if approached from Kwa-Zulu-Natal (see p.515). However, they can be achieved relatively easily via the Free State from the Sentinel car park. A tough ten-hour climb from the *Mahai* campsite in the Royal Natal National Park (see p.522), or a 2.5-hour, three-kilometre walk from the Sentinel car park brings you to the foot of a thirty-metre-high **chain ladder** leading up an almost vertical face; from the top, you can make the final short onslaught to the summit of **Mont aux Sources**, the highest peak on the escarpment (3278m). The downside of this shortcut is the litter around the ladder, although no more than 100 people are allowed up per day (for booking details see below). Don't be lulled by your apparently easy conquest: it's the Berg's prerogative to have the last word. Always tackle the magic ladder with enough food, water, clothes and a tent in which to sit out violent storms, and set out early so you have the whole day for the excursion.

For those bitten by the mountain bug, some serious **hikes** are available, including a two-week trek along the escarpment plateau to Sani Pass in the southern Drakensberg. You can also take in the most dramatic parts of the Berg on a five-day, 62-kilometre escarpment traverse, sleeping in caves, from the Sentinel car park to Cathedral Peak in the Natal Drakensberg Park, roughly 40km to the southwest. For any hikes of this nature you'll need a map and the excellent *Drakensberg Walks* by David Bristow (see p.923), available in most bookshops.

There's **accommodation** in a mountain hut at the Sentinel car park, where 24-hour security protects vehicles. The hut has no hot water or electricity, so you may be better off at the more comfortable *Witsieshoek Mountain Resort* (see below). To **book** for the car park hut and one of the hundred places a day allocated to climb the chain ladder, contact the Basotho Cultural Village (see p.580).

former **QwaQwa** Bantustan, and references to that miserable episode are still found in road signs and around town.

The *Witsieshoek Mountain Resort* is reached along the R720 and is clearly signposted from Phuthadijhaba. About 15km from Phuthadijhaba the road comes to a fork, one branch of which ends at the inn and the other at the **Sentinel car park**. The road is tarred until the final few kilometres. On maps, it looks as if the Royal Natal National Park and *Witsieshoek Mountain Resort* are adjoining. They are, but only via footpaths up and down mountains – by road, the journey from the Royal Natal National Park to the Sentinal car park is about 100km, into KwaZulu-Natal and around the high peaks.

The *Witsieshoek Mountain Resort* (℡058 713 6361 or 6362, ℻058 713 5274; half board ❸) is one of the great lost opportunities of South African architecture; it has the most spectacular setting of any mountain resort in the country, but possibly the worst planning. **Accommodation** has been placed just below the brow of a plateau, thus denying guests one of the best views in the entire Drakensberg. Still, you can always walk in the mountains to take in the views, and the functionality of the rooms is made up for by friendly service. The more expensive rooms have excellent views of the Sentinel Mountain. There is an overnight hikers' hostel in the hotel grounds (❶), which sleeps twelve and has electricity and hot water – but you need your own sleeping bag.

Golden Gate Highlands National Park

Roughly 300km northeast of Bloemfontein on the R712, **Golden Gate Highlands National Park** (open daily; R60 per person per day; ☎058 255 0012) is Free State's only national park. It was designated for its outstanding beauty rather than its wildlife; although **eland**, **zebra**, **mountain reedbuck** and **black wildebeest** roam the hillsides, the real attraction here is the unfettered space, eroded sandstone bastions and seamless blue skies. These rocks, grassy plateaus and incised valleys belong to the Drakensberg range, characterized here by spectacular yellow and red cliffs and overhangs.

A number of hour-long **rambles** into the sandstone ravines start from a direction board near the footbridge at the *Glen Reenen* campsite. There aren't many medium-length hikes in the park, the only exception being a physically challenging half-day walk up **Wodehouse Kop**, which offers great views. The most strenuous hike is the demanding two-day circular **Rhebok Trail**, which reaches the highest and lowest points of the park. You'll need to make an early start from the *Glen Reenen* campsite, where the trail begins; the Rhebok mountain hut on the trail provides basic overnight accommodation for hikers – bookings for the trail and hut must be made through South African National Parks. **Horse-riding** is also on offer, and can be booked through either of the park's two accommodation options (see below), while in the summer you can **swim** in a natural waterfall pool close to *Glen Reenen* campsite.

Practicalities

Golden Gate is almost equidistant from Bloemfontein or Johannesburg (320km to the north on good, tarred roads), and is easily reached from either city. There are no entry gates to the park, which is open all the time. **Accommodation** is at two sites close to one another right on the R712: **Glen Reenen** has a national park restcamp; while at **Brandwag** there's a resort run by the Protea Hotel group. That both sites are close to the main road, combined with the ease of access, deprives them of any sense of being wilderness retreats, although both have lush settings amidst the sandstone bastions. The cheaper option is *Glen Reenen Restcamp* (☎058 255 0075; bookings though South African National Parks in Pretoria ☎012 428 9111, ℮reservations@sanparks.org), which has closely packed en-suite rondavels with kitchenettes (❷), and a campsite, which at peak holiday times becomes little more than a car park jammed with Afrikaner families and their caravans. The more upmarket option is the *Protea Hotel Golden Gate Mountain Resort* (☎058 255 1000, ⓦwww.proteahotels.com), a mundane-looking place that was previously a national park camp, about a kilometre away. Well-equipped self-catering chalets (❸) and comfortable B&B rooms (❹) with bath, phones and TV are on offer. If the accommodation is full, or you want somewhere cheaper to stay, consider the chalets or basic but highly atmospheric huts at the Basotho Cultural Village (see p.580), or head to nearby Clarens (see below) for a wider range of guesthouse options.

Fuel is available at *Glen Reenen*, which also has a provisions store selling basics, as well as frozen braai packs, firewood and alcohol. Your only choice for **eating and drinking** out here is at the *Protea Resort,* which has a bar, coffee shop and restaurant – otherwise, drive to Clarens.

Clarens

Some 20km west of Golden Gate Highlands National Park lies the tree-fringed village of **CLARENS**, the most appealing of the settlements along the Highlands Route. Founded in 1912, Clarens is especially remarkable for its dressed stone architecture, which glows under the sandstone massif of the **Rooiberge** (Red Mountains) and the **Malutis** to the southeast. The best time to see the village is spring, when the fruit trees blossom, or in autumn, when the poplar leaves turn golden russet. But at any time of year, Clarens's relaxed air makes it a rare phenomenon in the Free State – a *dorp* you'd actually want to explore, or sip a sidewalk lager and simply hang out in.

Clarens was named after the Swiss town where **Paul Kruger**, president of the South African Republic, ended his days in 1904 after the Boers' defeat in the second Anglo–Boer War. Clarens today is an **arts and crafts centre**, with a number of studios and shops peppering the streets. If you arrive around lunchtime on a weekend, there's a chance you'll catch some local live music at one of the streetside cafés on **President Square**, effectively the town centre in the middle of Main Street.

The several **galleries** along Main Street and around President Square are worth a visit if you're after gifts or souvenirs; look out for the local Basotho tapestries, baskets and traditional hats. A real treat is the Di Mezza & De Jager Trading Store; to get there, follow the main road northwest to Bethlehem, before taking the *Maluti Lodge* turn-off. This is one of the few places in South Africa outside a museum where you're likely to catch an old-time general dealer's. The shop is crammed with provisions, lamps, bicycle parts, sweets and colourful blankets. The latter are traditionally worn like cloaks by Basotho people, and make outstanding souvenirs.

Farmstays and horse-riding around Clarens

Horse-riding is big along the Eastern Highlands. A couple of **farms** near Clarens – both excellent family destinations – provide outstanding riding onto the Drakensberg Escarpment, from where you can gaze across into Lesotho and view southern Africa's highest peaks.

One of the most interesting farms is friendly **Bokpoort** (☎058 256 1181, ⓦwww .bokpoort.co.za; ❷–❸), set in brilliant hiking country, but more notable for its riding. The B&B accommodation in farmhouse outbuildings is pretty basic, with brunch served in a converted shearing shed. There are also a couple of self-contained, en-suite "mountain" huts recently upgraded, as well as dorms in an old sandstone barn and space for camping, with a pleasant communal cooking and eating place. Reasonably priced meals can be ordered from the farmhouse kitchen, while a small shop sells basics. Bokpoort's big draw is the memorable **Western-style riding** in deep, comfortable cowboy saddles on sure-footed horses. Short rides from the farmhouse (R200 for 2hr) take in San rock paintings, swimmable river-pools, and the chance of seeing eland, zebra and springbok on the adjoining game farm. Two-day riding trails into the mountains on the Lesotho border cost R1000, while three-day trails are R1500; a 4WD vehicle brings the food and bedding (you sleep on mattresses in a remote mountain hut), and you ride about six hours a day.

Riding is also available at **Schaaplaats Cottage & Ashgar Connemara Stud** (☎058 256 1176, ⓦwww.ashgarhorses.co.za), in the mountains 6km south of Clarens off the R711 to Fouriesburg. An establishment with a more English flavour, this turn-of-the-century farm has two sandstone cottages (❷). From here you can go on terrific mountain hikes, visit Boer War graves and San rock paintings and, of course, ride horses (R150 for 2hr). There's also a chance to brush up your equestrian skills, as the owner is a qualified riding teacher. Moreover, there is some game on the farm (zebra and antelope), which adds zest to any ride.

Accommodation

There's plenty of **accommodation**, both in the village (all signposted off Main Street and easily walkable) and on surrounding farms.

Clarens Inn Van Reenen St ☎058 256 1119 or 082 377 3621. The cheapest place to stay, with the choice between a functional dorm (**①**) with a communal kitchen or four self-catering units (**②**) sleeping six in two bedrooms.

Cottage Pie 89 Malherbe St ☎058 256 1214 or 082 853 5947, ⓦ www.suedafrika.net/cottagepie. One of the town's best B&Bs, with a garden chalet and two rooms inside the main house, offering breakfast on the patio and views onto a stream and the dramatic cliffs surrounding the village. **③**

Maluti Mountain Lodge Signposted just off the R712 on the edge of town ☎058 256 1422. The most expensive place to stay, in pleasant rondavels in the garden; prices include dinner. **④**

Red Mountain House ☎ & ⓕ058 256 1456 or ☎082 777 4755, ⓔinfo@redmountainhouse .co.za. Centrally situated B&B which has rooms on the upper floor opening onto balconies that enjoy views of Market Square's gardens and the Maluti Mountains. Rooms have fireplaces and are luxuriously furnished with Persian rugs and Victorian antiques. There are also less expensive self-catering units. **③–④**

Village Square Guest House Right in the centre ☎ & ⓕ058 256 1064 or ☎083 635 8667, ⓔvillagehouse@isat.co.za. Two family suites as well as two en-suite bedrooms, with breakfast at the owners' *Street Café Restaurant*. **③**

Eating and drinking

Of the half-dozen or so **eating and drinking** places in Clarens, the *Street Café Restaurant* on Main Street is the busiest, due to its reasonably priced pizzas, snacks, steaks and salads, and the 107 (at last count) varieties of local and imported beers on offer. *The Highland Brasserie* (Tues–Sun daytime, Wed & Fri nights) on the town square offers similar prices, with an indoor fire in winter and outdoor tables and chairs when the weather is fine; it's especially recommended for breakfasts and cheesecake and coffee. *Red Mountain House*, 325 Market Square, offers specialized game and traditional dishes from an extensive menu, and has a good wine selection and a well-stocked pub.

Fouriesburg and around

The funny little town of **FOURIESBURG**, 36km south east from Clarens on the R711, earned its name from the high density of people named Fourie who farmed in the district. The hamlet hit the big time briefly in 1900; when Bloemfontein fell to the British in the Anglo-Boer War, Fouriesburg was proclaimed capital of the Orange Free State. Nothing much seems to have happened since, and a century later they still haven't got round to rescinding the proclamation – so technically it's still the provincial capital.

Overshadowed by the Maluti Mountains and the Witteberge (White Mountains), Fouriesburg serves as a decent overnight stop. There's some good **accommodation**, with the nicest place to stay being the *Fouriesburg*, 17 Reitz St (☎058 223 0207, ⓔfburginn@worldonline.co.za; **②**). This small, wonderfully antiquated hotel has a green, low-slung corrugated-iron roof and comfortable rooms leading off the street-facing verandah. The owners even let you rummage through the wine cellar to pick a bottle for dinner. Just under 2km out of town, and signposted from the centre, the **Meiringskloof Nature Reserve** (☎ & ⓕ058 223 0067; **①**) offers one of the few places worth **camping** along the Highlands Route, and also a few self-catering stone chalets. Set in a sandstone *kloof* with plenty of trees, a swimming pool and a small grocery shop, the reserve is best avoided during holidays, when it gets packed. It's the starting point for a number of short **hikes**.

Rustler's Valley

In contrast to the conservatism of Fouriesburg, **Rustler's Valley** (T & F 051 933 3939, W www.rustlers.co.za), 27km to the south and well signposted off the R26, has set itself up as the New Age epicentre of South Africa. Located in a very beautiful valley in the foothills of the Maluti Mountains, this "mountain retreat" brings together a mixture of rave culture, Gaia philosophy and plain old-fashioned hippiedom. In this alternative getaway you need to be ready to submit to the wound-down atmosphere, in which everything is slow and haphazard, including the service. It's a good place to spend a couple of days, to get into the way of life, relax and meet people. Scheduled events take place about once a month (a calendar is available via the website), and activities include horse-riding, hikes, swimming in the dam, and bass and trout fishing. The biggest crowd-puller is the **Autumn Equinox Festival** on March 21 each year, which draws in hordes of young South Africans to listen to music, dance and chill out, and the New Year's Eve parties are legendary.

Accommodation (1–2) ranges from camping, backpacker dorms and en-suite doubles, to thatched rondavels with baths set among peach trees and decorated with goblins and fairies. A kitchen is available for guests in the dorms; everyone else must rely on the bar and **restaurant**, which serves good vegetarian food for a range of budgets. **Getting there** without your own transport entails finding your way to Ficksburg (see below), from where staff at Rustler's can pick you up. When you phone to book your accommodation, ask for the best way to get to Ficksburg and, if you're driving, enquire about the variable condition of the dirt road.

Ficksburg

FICKSBURG, 48km south of Fouriesburg, is the closest town to Rustler's Valley. It's also the centre of South Africa's cherry and asparagus farming. The town's sandstone architecture gives it a pleasant ambience, and it's a good place to make a stop halfway down the Highlands Route. An annual **Cherry Festival** in the third week of November is the highlight of Fickburg's calendar; it features a marathon, floats, stalls, a "cherry queen" competition and a popular beer festival.

The cheapest way to stay here is **camping** at *Thom Park* (T 083 662 3500), a caravan park bang in the centre of town, on the corner of Bloem and McCabe streets. Nearby, *Bella Rosa*, 21 Bloem Street (T & F 051 933 2623; 3), is a hugely popular and well-priced pair of Victorian sandstone houses with twelve nicely furnished **rooms**, all with baths, telephones and TVs. Dinner is available but must be booked, and tea is served on the very pleasant verandah. An alternative is *Green Acorn*, 7 Fontein Street (T 051 933 2746; 2), which has decent rooms with baths inside the house and in the garden. The best options for **eating** are the *Bella Rosa* (Mon–Fri till 10pm), which is licensed and serves above-average English-style food, and the family-oriented *Bottling Co*, at the corner of Piet Retief and Erwee streets (closed Sun), which also serves booze and does steaks, pastas, chicken, fish and a good lobster bisque.

Clocolan and around

CLOCOLAN, 33km west of Ficksburg, is a tiny farming town dominated by enormous grain silos. The town itself has little to offer travellers apart from a visit to the **Lethoteng Weavers**, in a house on the main road. The weavers are Southern Sotho women who use angora rabbit and wool to produce lively tapestries based on traditional geometric motifs and imaginative illustrations of everyday life. To get to the main point of interest around here, you need to head some 9km out of town to the **Tandjiesberg rock paintings** at Tripolatania Farm (℡051 924 2475). Here you'll find some of the best San art in the Free State, with panel after panel of rock paintings overpainted with animal, human and supernatural motifs. These are also interpreted in an excellent monograph available from the Bloemfontein's National Museum (see p.574) and sometimes from the farmer, from whom you have to collect keys and pay a small fee to get to the paintings.

If you're simply passing through, look for Clocolan's best overnight **accommodation** at *Makoadi B&B* (℡ & ℱ051 943 0273; ❷) on Makoadi Farm, clearly signposted 1km southwest of town along the R26. Its three spacious rooms off a veranda are furnished with antique farm items and ball-and-claw baths, and have original mud-and-dung floors. Rooms are available for the same price on a B&B or self-catering basis. For longer stays, try the outstanding *Evening Star Cottage* (℡051 943 7147 or 083 305 0658; ❷), 13km west from Clocolan on the R703. This romantically secluded self-catering thatched cottage is tucked into a rocky outcrop, its French doors opening onto a balcony with views of farmlands and mountains. Cooking is done on a fire outside in a beautiful rocky sitting area, with breakfast baskets sent up to the cottage so you needn't move. Near the cottage, there's a converted monastery with an overgrown garden, where the owner sells her own pottery and other crafts, and also a good hiking trail.

Ladybrand

LADYBRAND lies on the main route into Lesotho, just over 40km south of Clocolan. The town gets its name from the mother of Johannes Brand, President of the Orange Free State four times after 1864. It's one of the only towns in the Free State which is expanding, with a huge turnover of foreign currency in the local bank; this is due not to tourism, but to the Highlands Water Project across the nearby border in Lesotho.

Many of the foreign engineers and technicians working on the Highlands Water Project in Lesotho stay in Ladybrand, so **accommodation** is in high demand, and doesn't come cheap. The only budget option is *Leliehoek Resort* (℡051 924 0260; ❷), 2km south of the town hall, a rather run-down park with camping and dubious self-catering chalets. As for B&Bs, nothing along the Highlands Route can touch *Cranberry Cottage*, 37 Beeton Street (℡051 924 2290, ℱ051 924 1168, ⓦwww.cranberrycottage.co.za; ❸), which offers comfortable country-style B&B rooms and excellent dinners, with vegetarians well catered for. Under the same ownership are the equally imaginative self-catering units at the *Railway Station* (room only ❸), quirkily located in the refurbished ticket office, stationmaster's office and waiting rooms on the Ladybrand Station platform, which no longer serves passengers but occasionally sees goods trains trundling by. The owners act as an unofficial tourist information centre and are able to give guests **information** on pony trekking and rock-art sites. The area is certainly fine **horse-riding** country, and Greenock Riding (℡051 924 2961, ⓦwww.africanhorses.com/greenock; ❷), in a beautiful valley just north of town, offers superlative guided riding in isolated mountains. Accommodation is in self-catering log cabins, although you can take plain, well-cooked meals with the friendly hosts (and their pets) for a very reasonable amount.

When it comes to **eating**, there's pasta and pizza on offer at *Spizzy Pizzas* (closed Sun), a small café and bar on Church Street. For light meals, teas and coffees, *Zabi's Coffee Shop* on the same street (Mon–Sat 8am–5pm) is the best daytime place in town. Housed in the now-defunct museum, *Zabi's* quirky charm derives from the fact that it contains a lot of the museum's former displays. It serves sandwiches made with bread baked on the premises in clay ovens – the delicious cakes are recommended. *Cranberry Cottage* (see above; open daily to non-residents) does excellent breakfasts and four-course dinners.

Travel details

Trains

Bloemfontein to: Cape Town (Wed; 20hr 45min); Durban (Mon; 16hr); East London (daily except Wed & Sat; 14hr 15min); Johannesburg (Wed, Fri & Sun; 13hr); Port Elizabeth (daily except Tues & Sat; 12hr 15min); Pretoria (daily; 15hr 45min).

Grahamstown (daily; 7hr 30min); Johannesburg (4–5 daily; 6hr); Knysna (5 weekly; 11hr); Mossel Bay (5 weekly; 9hr 30min); Oudtshoorn (5 weekly; 8hr); Pietermaritzburg (2–3 daily; 8hr); Port Elizabeth (1–2 daily; 9hr); Pretoria (4–5 daily; 7hr).

Domestic flights

Bloemfontein to: Cape Town (3–4 daily; 1hr 20min); Durban (2–3 daily; 1hr 15min); Johannesburg (9 daily Mon–Fri, 3 daily Sat & Sun; 1hr 10min); Port Elizabeth (1–2 daily; 1hr 20min).

Buses

Bloemfontein to: Cape Town (4 daily; 11hr); Durban (2–3 daily; 9hr); East London (daily; 7hr 10min); Graaff-Reinet (5 weekly; 7hr);

Gauteng

CHAPTER 7

Highlights

* **Downtown Johannesburg** Experience a truly pan-African urban buzz at the heart of the continent's richest city. See p.603

* **Melville** Hang out with the arty set in one of the few places in Jo'burg where trendy cafés and decent restaurants line the street. See p.612

* **The Apartheid Museum, Jo'burg** An informative and sobering journey through South African history. See p.617

* **Soweto tours** Experience the vibrancy of South Africa's most historically significant townships. See p.618

* **The big match** Whether it's Chiefs v Pirates at FNB or the Springboks v All Blacks at Ellis Park, sport in Jo'burg is always big news. See p.624

* **Live music** Make the effort and you'll find that Jo'burg has the best scene in the country. See p.625

* **Cradle of Humankind** A series of caves on the fringe of Johannesburg provides vital fossil evidence of human ancestry. See p.630

* **Church Square, Pretoria** Sip an espresso at *Café Riche* or sit in the shade of Paul Kruger's statue and admire the grand architecture. See p.640

* **Voortrekker Monument, Pretoria** This icon of Afrikanerdom offers an insight into the people who dominated South Africa for a century. See p.643

△ Nelson Mandela Bridge, Jo'burg

Gauteng

auteng means "Place of Gold" in Sotho, and no wonder: South Africa's smallest region comprises less than five percent of its landmass, yet contributes around forty percent of the GDP. Home to over eight million people, Gauteng has an almost entirely urbanized flavour. While the province encompasses a section of the Magaliesberg Mountains to the east and the gold-rich Witwatersrand to the south and west, the area is dominated by the huge conurbation incorporating Johannesburg, Pretoria and a host of grim satellite industrial towns and townships which surround them.

Although lacking the spectacular attractions of the Cape Province or Mpumalanga, Gauteng has a subtle character all of its own. Startling outcrops of rock known as *koppies*, with intriguing and often lucrative geology, are found in the sprawling suburbs and grassy plains of deep-red earth that fringe the cities. The usually mild climate is broken occasionally by spectacular summer lightning storms, which can unleash torrents of water over the Transvaal plains within seconds. The area is also prone to drought, and water supplies remain a constant and worsening problem. Yet the light, particularly at dawn and dusk, is a photographer's dream, rendering serene even the starkest of industrial landscapes.

Gauteng is dominated by **Johannesburg**, whose origins lie in the exploitation of **gold**. Although it has grown rapidly in just over a century to become the richest city in Africa, it has somehow held onto its tough mining origins and is a hectic, sometimes dangerous city, home to extreme contrasts of wealth and poverty. It has a reputation among both visitors and South Africans as a place to avoid, but those who acquire a taste for Jo'burg – something you can do in just a few days – are seduced by its energy and vibrancy, unmatched by any other city in South Africa. A highly cosmopolitan city, the most Africanized in the country, Jo'burg has South Africa's most famous and liveliest townships, its most active and diverse cultural life, some of its best restaurants and the most progressive nightlife.

Some 50km north lies dignified **Pretoria**, the country's administrative capital. Historically an Afrikaner stronghold, today it is a fast-changing place full of civil servants and students from South Africa and around the world. Very different from Johannesburg in looks and atmosphere, Pretoria is an important and attractive destination in its own right, with a range of interesting museums and historic buildings. Many visitors, however, see it simply as a safer and less intimidating alternative to its larger rival.

Less than an hour's travel from the centre of Jo'burg, the section of the **Magaliesberg Mountains** which creeps into Gauteng is a magnet for

Johannesburgers desperate to escape the city's pollution and stress. Although the hills can hardly be described as remote and untamed, you'll find ample opportunities for nature trailing and hiking. Like much of Gauteng, however, the important part lies underground, with a series of caves, underground passages and archeological sites making up the **Cradle of Humankind** World Heritage Site. Most famous of these sites are the **Sterkfontein Caves**, where some of the world's most important discoveries of pre-human primate fossils have been found.

Johannesburg and around

Fast-paced, frenetic **JOHANNESBURG** has had a reputation for immorality, greed and violence ever since its first plot auction in December 1886. Despite its status as the largest and wealthiest city in the country, it has never been the seat of government or national political power, allowing it to concentrate fully on what it has always done best: make money and get ahead. Those priorities have, over the years, cut across political and racial lines: only in Jo'burg would ambitious black Africans like Nelson Mandela have been able to train in a white law firm; only in Jo'burg would creative hotspots like Sophiatown and Alexandra exist at all; and only in Jo'burg would white liberalism have been given any intellectual recognition in the dark days of apartheid.

Even so, the divisions of the old South Africa are as apparent here as anywhere else. Ridiculously opulent white mansions in leafy **suburbs** are protected by high walls and razor wire, only a mile or two from sprawling **shanty towns** housing millions of intensely poor blacks. As the new political dispensation sees formerly white areas administratively yoked with the black townships, so the city struggles to cope with massive pressures on housing, services and law and order. Nowhere is the new tension more in evidence than in the previously all-white central business district, where an influx of poor blacks, and a soaring crime rate, has caused a mass exodus of shops and restaurants to the northern suburbs.

As the centre readjusts, so the fringes expand: there will soon be a continuous ribbon of development between Johannesburg and Pretoria, originally 50km apart. Meanwhile, the black middle class, much more evident in Johannesburg than anywhere else in South Africa, is moving from township to suburb, while tens of thousands of immigrants from elsewhere in Africa flood into inner-city suburbs like Hillbrow and townships like Alexandra.

Recent additions have made Johannesburg a prime destination for those interested in exploring the history of South Africa, although the bewildering size of the city and dispersed layout of the sights can be daunting for all but the most determined traveller. Some visitors fall into the trap of being too intimidated by the city's reputation to explore, venturing out only to the bland, safe, covered shopping malls and restaurants of the northern suburbs while making hasty plans to move on. However, once you've found a convenient way of getting around, either by car or in the company of a tour guide, the history, diversity and stimulating energy of the city can quickly become compelling. Johannesburg offers fascinating **museums**, most notably the Apartheid Museum in Gold Reef City and the Museum Africa in Newtown, as well as excellent art galleries. A number of suburbs have a thriving **café culture**, which by the evening transforms into a lively restaurant scene. There are shops with excellent contemporary African art and design, striking buildings, and of course the **townships**, most easily explored on a tour but, in some cases, possible to get to under your own steam. Johannesburg is also a great place to watch **sport**: Ellis Park was the scene of South Africa's emotional victory in the 1995 Rugby World Cup; the IAAF World Cup was held at the neighbouring athletics stadium in 1999; the 2003 cricket World Cup took place at the Wanderers Stadium; and the massive FNB soccer stadium on the edge of Soweto remains the principal venue for the country's most popular sport.

Some history

Johannesburg dates back to 1886, when Australian prospector **George Harrison** found the main Witwatersrand gold-bearing reef. Almost immediately, this quiet area of the Transvaal became swamped with diggers from near and far, and a tented city sprang up around the site. The Pretoria authorities were forced to proclaim a township nearby: they chose a useless triangle of land called the Randjeslaagte, which had been left unclaimed by local farmers. **Johan Rissik**, the surveyor, called it Johannesburg, either after himself or Christiaan Johannes Joubert, the chief of mining, or the president of the South African Republic (ZAR), Paul Johannes Kruger.

Mining magnates such as Cecil Rhodes and Barney Barnato possessed the capital necessary to exploit the world's richest gold reef, and their **Chamber of Mines** (a self-regulatory body for mine owners, founded in 1889), attempted to bring some order to the digging frenzy, with common policies on recruitment, wages and working conditions. In 1893, due partly to pressure from white workers, and with the approval of the ZAR government, the chamber introduced the **colour bar**, which excluded black workers from all but manual labour.

By 1895, Johannesburg's population had soared to over 100,000, many of whom were not remotely Boer and had no interest in the ZAR's independence. Kruger and the burghers regarded these *uitlanders* (foreigners) as a potential threat to their political supremacy, and denied them the vote despite the income they generated for the state's coffers. Legislation was also passed to control the influx of blacks to Johannesburg, and Indians were forcibly moved out of the city into a western location. Before long, large shantytowns filled with blacks and Indians were springing up on the outskirts of Johannesburg.

In 1900, during the Anglo-Boer War, Johannesburg fell to the British, who had been attempting to annex the gold-rich area for some time. The High Commissioner Sir Alfred Milner imported whiz kids fresh out of Oxford and Cambridge to modernize the city. They lived in Parktown, and commissioned their houses from the celebrated English architect, **Sir Herbert Baker** (see p.610). At the same time, more black townships were established, including **Sophiatown** (1903) in an area previously used for dumping sewage, and **Alexandra** (1905). Bubonic plague erupted on the northern fringes of the city in 1904, providing justification for the authorities to burn several Indian and African locations, including **Newtown**, just west of the centre.

Meanwhile, white mine workers were becoming unionized, and outbreaks of fighting over pay and working hours were a frequent occurrence. Their poorly paid black counterparts were also mobilizing; their main grievance was the ruling that skilled jobs were the preserve of white workers. Resentments came to a head in the **Rand Revolt** of 1922, after the Chamber of Mines, anxious to cut costs, decided to allow blacks into the skilled jobs previously held only by whites. White workers were furious: street battles broke out and lasted for four days. Government troops were called in to restore order and over two hundred men were killed. Alarmed at the scale of white discontent, Prime Minister Jan Smuts ruled that the colour bar be maintained, and throughout the 1920s the government passed laws restricting the movement of blacks.

During the Thirties, the township of **Orlando** became established southwest of the city, with accommodation for 80,000 blacks; this was the nucleus around which **Soweto** evolved. By 1945, 400,000 blacks were living in and around Johannesburg – an increase of 100 percent in a decade. In August 1946, 70,000

African Mineworkers Union members went on strike over working conditions. The government sent police in, and twelve miners were killed and over 1000 injured. In the same year, informal settlers on municipal land attempted a rent boycott, proclaiming "Asinamali!" ("We have no money!"). They were ignored, and non-rent-payers were evicted.

Forced removals of black residents from Johannesburg's inner suburbs, particularly from Sophiatown, began in 1955. Thousands were dumped far from the city centre, in the new township of Meadowlands, next to Orlando, and Sophiatown was crassly renamed Triomf (triumph). The **ANC** (see p.851) established itself as the most important black protest organization during this period, proclaiming the **Freedom Charter** in Kliptown, Soweto, that year.

During the 1950s, *kwela*, a black urban culture unique to Johannesburg, began to emerge in the townships, and the new *marabi* jazz was played in illegal drinking houses called *shebeens*. This was also the era of *Drum Magazine*, which revealed a sophisticated black Johannesburg culture, and introduced a host of talented journalists, like Can Temba and Casey "Kid" Motsisi, to the city and the world. *Mbaqanga* music emerged, with its heavy basslines and sensuous melodies capturing the bittersweet essence of life in the old townships.

The formation in 1972 of the **Black Consciousness Movement** (BCM) rekindled political activism, particularly among Soweto students. On June 16, 1976, student riots erupted in the township, and the unrest spread nationwide (see p.619). The youth's war against the State escalated in the 1980s, resulting in regular "**states of emergency**", during which the armed forces had permission to do anything they liked to contain revolt. Towards the end of the decade, the government relaxed "petty" apartheid, turning a blind eye to the growth of "grey" areas like Hillbrow – white suburbs where blacks were moving in.

The three years after **Nelson Mandela**'s release in 1990 saw widespread political violence in Gauteng right up until the day before elections. However, as elsewhere in South Africa, the election on April 27, 1994, went off peacefully. The ANC won comfortably in Gauteng then, and retained their hold in 1999 and 2004.

Just as new faces populate the corridors of political power, so blacks are also making steady inroads into positions of influence in business, finance and industry, where the true power of the province lies. Signs of such change can be seen almost daily on the pages of the country's business newspapers, and public–private partnerships are now initiating some bold plans for the province, notably the Gautrain Rapid Rail Link, a high-speed train planned for completion in 2008 and intended to link Johannesburg airport, Johannesburg city centre and Pretoria.

Orientation, arrival and information

Johannesburg is large, sprawling and poorly planned, with few conventional sights and a bewildering number of districts. The **central business district (CBD)** is the Manhattan of Africa, with tall crowded office blocks crowded together and lively street life. Nearby, the **Newtown Cultural Precinct** is the place to head for jazz bars, theatre and the highly informative Museum Africa. The inner-city suburbs of **Berea** and **Hillbrow** are packed with migrants from all over the continent, and are generally no-go areas for visitors. Some now apply the same label to **Yeoville**, once the city's trendiest and most integrated suburb. For a map of central Johannesburg, see pp.604–605.

The city's seemingly endless **northern suburbs**, the preserve of affluent, predominantly white Johannesburg, do offer a few pleasant surprises, notably **Parktown**, the original home of Johannesburg's richest residents, leafy **Melville**, with its trendy street cafés and lively nightlife, and **Rosebank**, an easy-going area with some decent galleries and craft markets. Further north, opulent **Sandton** is the archetypal northern suburb, full of brand-new offices and mind-boggling shopping malls. Strangely enough, only the highway separates Sandton from one of Jo'burg's poorest areas, the vibrant but risky **Alexandra** township to the east. Southwest of the centre lies the city's most famous township, **Soweto**, the single most popular tourist destination in Johannesburg, with its evocative memories of the struggle against apartheid and poor but lively neighbourhoods.

Arrival

Johannesburg's large **international airport** (flight information ☎011 921 6262), once known as Jan Smuts, lies 20km east of the city. The international arrivals hall has an easily located **tourist information desk** (daily 7am–9pm; ☎011 970 1669) set in the middle of the terminal, offering a full range of brochures on Johannesburg and other parts of South Africa, including lists of places to stay, though they don't offer a booking service. There are 24-hour facilities for changing money and ATMs at various points in the terminal.

There's a range of options for getting from the airport into the city or suburbs, which you can get advice on from the **public transport desk** in the arrivals terminal (daily 6am–10pm), where you can also book a taxi. If your destination is the northern suburbs, your best bet is to use the **Magic Bus** service (every 30min 5.30am–9.30pm; 30min), which will drop you in Sandton for a cost of about R95. Get tickets for both services at the company's desks in the Parkade building, just outside the domestic arrivals foyer. For details of transport to Pretoria, see p.636.

The more expensive hotels often provide **courtesy buses**, while most backpackers' hostels and some smaller guesthouses or B&Bs offer free **pick-ups** (but may charge for the trip back to the airport) or can recommend a reliable transport service. Touting at the airport by competing backpackers' hostels has been very aggressive recently – sidestep the mayhem by booking in advance.

Taking a metered **taxi** from the airport is convenient and safe, though you should make certain the driver knows where you're going before you set off, and watch out for unscrupulous drivers circling your destination rather than taking the direct route. Be prepared to pay anywhere up to R200 per person for most destinations. If you want to prearrange a taxi, Airport Link (☎011 792 2017) charges around R210 for the first person and R50 for each additional passenger. Going with one of many reputable tour operators who offer transfers at set prices (ask your hotel to recommend a firm) is the best way to avoid this problem.

By bus and train

Greyhound, Intercape and Translux **buses**, and **intercity trains**, arrive at **Park station** in the centre of town. Once notoriously unsafe, Park station has been significantly improved in recent years, and the main concourse is big, open and secure, with information desks for all the bus companies. From here, you're best off – and safest – taking a taxi to your final destination or arranging a pick-up with your accommodation. While buses and minibuses run from the station to virtually everywhere, finding out about them can be confusing, and waiting around outside the station – especially surrounded by luggage – can be risky.

Information

Gauteng Tourism (daily 8.30am–5pm; ☎011 327 2000, ⓦwww.gauteng .net), situated in the Upper Level of the Rosebank Mall in Rosebank, runs the show in Johannesburg; their most useful outlet is a **kiosk** (Tues–Sun 8.30am–4.30pm) attached to the African Craft Market in Rosebank.

Various free **maps** are available from tourist offices, but normally these maps cover only the CBD and parts of the northern suburbs. To get around other parts, particularly if you're driving around the city, you'll need a detailed street guide; the hefty *Witwatersrand Street Guide* is best, available from CNA news-agents or Exclusive Books bookshops.

City transport

Johannesburg's **public transport system** leaves much to be desired: it's slow and unreliable, and practically nonexistent after commuting hours. **Driving** is

Crime and safety in Johannesburg

With Johannesburg's extremes of poverty and wealth, its brash, get-ahead culture and the presence of illegal firearms, it's hardly surprising that the city can be a dangerous place. Despite the city's unenviable reputation, it's important to retain a sense of proportion about potential risks and not to let paranoia ruin your stay; remember that most Jo'burgers have no intention of doing you any harm at all. The sensible course is to do as they do: juggle your fear and your bravado, without letting one swamp the other. As in all major cities, taking precautions – see "Basics", p.81, and below – is likely to see you through safely.

If you're wandering around **on foot**, the crime you are most at risk from is **mugging** (sometimes violent). Although significant effort has gone into making the riskiest areas safer, remain alert when exploring the central business district (CBD), Braamfontein and Newtown, and only walk the streets here during office hours. Joubert Park, Hillbrow and Berea are regarded at present as no-go zones, and although Yeoville and Observatory are a little safer, these are places for those who are particularly confident or have someone to show them around. You're very unlikely to be mugged on the streets in Melville, Parktown or Rosebank. If you want to walk around one of the riskier areas, study maps beforehand (not on street corners), avoid asking for directions from passers-by, and don't walk around with luggage. Observe crowds coming your way to see if there are any young men (the main offenders) moving as a block. If you're carrying valuables, make a portion of them easily available, so that muggers are likely to be quickly satisfied. Never resist muggers; running like hell can work, but some have guns, which you won't know about until it's too late. You're unlikely to be mugged on public transport but, as always, it's wise to stay alert, especially around busy spots such as Park station and bus stations or taxi ranks. Waiting for buses in the northern suburbs is generally safe.

If you're **driving** around, note that there is a small risk of car-jacking, and thieves have also been known to reach into open windows or break side windows to snatch valuables left on passenger seats. It's a good idea to keep all car doors locked and windows up – never wait in an unlocked car while a friend goes into a shop. Leaving or returning to your car are the most risky times, so keep a good lookout, don't dawdle, and seek out secure – preferably guarded – parking. Although local urban legends suggest you should not stop at traffic lights at night, statistics show that more people get injured in car accidents than become victims of crime. When stopping at traffic lights in areas regarded as risky, keep a good distance behind the car in front and be aware of anyone moving around the car.

Don't expect too much from the **police**. Police on the street are rare, and normally have other distractions than keeping an eye out for tourists. In the city centre and Rosebank you can make use of **City Ambassadors**, people hired by a partnership between local government and local shops and businesses to provide an anti-crime presence on the street. Identifiable by their yellow caps and bibs, they're worth approaching for directions or if you think you're being followed.

very much the order of the day, though with patience and a bit of stamina it's possible to negotiate your way around the city by **bus**, and some areas are easily explored **on foot**. Avoid the city's **train** system, which has a poor reputation and very limited services.

For short journeys around the city, consider using **private taxis**, which should be booked in advance by telephone (see "Listings" on p.629). This is an expensive option, however, as a simple journey to the CBD from the northern suburbs will cost at least R150.

Driving

By far the best way to explore Johannesburg is in your own car. The city is relatively well served as regards **car rental** agencies (see "Listings" on p.629), and you'll often find that backpacker lodges and some guesthouses can arrange the best deals.

Although road signs can be poor and the local drivers pushy, familiarity with a few **key roads** and careful map reading before you set out makes driving around relatively straightforward. In the city centre, the grid system does make navigation reasonably logical, though it's beset by one-way streets and pedestrian precincts. The **M1** connects the centre to the northern suburbs, crossing above Newtown on a flyover, through Braamfontein and Parktown, and heading into Houghton and Sandton, eventually turning into the N1 for Pretoria. South of the centre, the M1 is one of the best routes to Soweto. The next artery west of the M1, also useful for heading north, is **Oxford Road**, which starts off in Parktown, and becomes Rivonia Road once it enters Sandton. West again is **Jan Smuts Avenue**, which passes through Rosebank and Dunkeld before hitting Sandton.

Buses

Johannesburg's **buses**, many of which are double-deckers, offer the safest and cheapest public transport during weekdays. Most bus routes start and end at the main terminus (☏011 403 4300) in Gandhi Square, off Eloff Street in the city centre; this is also where you can pick up timetables and route maps.

Buses only run between the suburbs and the centre, so are useless for getting from one suburb to another, unless they both lie on the same route to town. Most buses stop by 6.30pm, though a small number keep going until 9.30pm. At weekends very few routes have services and there are waits of at least an hour between buses. Fares (typically in the R4–10 range depending on distance) should be paid to the driver; ensure you get a ticket as you may need to show it to a ticket inspector.

Minibus taxis

Even cheaper than buses, **minibus taxis** cover a far wider area, and can be picked up at ranks, or hailed mid-route by either raising your forefinger (if you're heading into town), pointing downwards (if you want to go uptown) or pointing towards yourself (if you want Park station). The drawbacks, however, are worth bearing in mind; cramped cars, hair-raising driving, frequent accidents and petty criminals working the major taxi ranks have combined to deter most white Jo'burgers from using this mode of transport. If you do want to try one out, you'd be wise to wait at a smaller taxi rank, or wave one down en route – but never with bulky baggage. Most backpacker lodges know nearby useful routes and pick-up points and can give you a few tips.

Accommodation

Accommodation in Johannesburg is fairly easy to find. As a basic rule of thumb, the further from the city centre you stay, the safer but more soulless the suburb. There's little prospect of staying in the **CBD**, most hotels and hostels having joined the exodus to the northern suburbs. If you do want to be close to town, there are a couple of pleasant options in the central suburbs around the CBD: in **Braamfontein** just to the north, and in **Observatory**, just to the east. Points further east are only worth considering if you need easy access to the airport: **Eastgate** and **Bruma Lake** are self-contained around their vast eponymous shopping centres, while plain and suburban **Bedfordview** is easily reached from the motorway.

There's plenty of accommodation to be found in the **northern suburbs**, which, along with various artery roads leading out from the centre, are the easiest places to stay if you have to rely on public transport. **Melville** and its neighbour Auckland Park offer something many visitors don't expect to find in Johannesburg: a characterful, tight-knit community with hip cafés, restaurants and bars within walking distance of most of the guesthouses. **Rosebank** is well located at the heart of the northern suburbs, and has a number of popular shopping malls with a decent selection of places to eat out or shop. In **Sandton** there are a wealth of pricey chain hotels aimed at business executives, as well as some lovely large private homes with huge gardens which offer bed and breakfast. West of Sandton, **Randburg** is less expensive, but a bit isolated from the best parts of the city.

It is possible to stay in the **townships**, where a few guesthouses have been starting up. The most rewarding option is to stay with locals, something best arranged through an experienced tour operator (see p.618).

Some of the places reviewed in the central suburbs appear on the map on pp.604–605. The maps of Melville (p.612) and the northern suburbs from Rosebank to Sandown (p.614) also show the locations of many of the places reviewed.

Backpacker and budget accommodation

Jo'burg's **backpacker hostels** are less numerous and more changeable than the backpacker lodges in Cape Town or Durban. Most lodges offer free pick-ups from the airport, and although there are a couple close to the airport, the more attractive options are located at least twenty minutes' drive from the airport. Most hostels offer basic singles and doubles as well as dorms.

Central suburbs

Brown Sugar 75 Observatory Ave, Observatory Extension ☎011 648 7397 or 0800 004 951, ✉brownsugar2000@hotmail.com. A notorious backpackers' hostel on Observatory Ridge, located in a mansion formerly owned by a drug baron and the only hostel left near Yeoville's Rockey St. Come here for a fast-track introduction to Jo'burg's hedonistic nightlife rather than comfort or chilled-out vibes. Free airport pickup. ❶

Northern suburbs

Backpackers' Ritz 1A North Rd (off Jan Smuts Ave), Dunkeld West ☎011 327 7125, ⓦwww.backpackers-ritz.co.za. A well-known, busy lodge in a large suburban house halfway between Rosebank and Sandton (see map, p.614), with a pool, gardens, travel centre and a good bar. It's popular with overlanders, and camping is allowed in the grounds. ❶–❷

Pension iDube 11 Walton Ave, Auckland Park ☎011 482 4055 or 082 682 3799, ✉idube@mail.com. Not so much a backpacker's lodge as (in its own words) an "economy-class" B&B, with tastefully decorated doubles, a pool and a friendly, easy-going atmosphere, only a few blocks from Melville's cafés and nightlife (see map, p.612). Breakfast is included in the price, though you have to prepare it yourself. ❷

Rockey's of Fourways 22 Campbell Rd, Craigavon, Fourways ☎011 465 4219 or 082 342 5109, ⓦwww.backinafrica.com. Run by veterans of the Jo'burg backpacking scene, this is a great place if you don't mind staying 20km from town in a newly built suburb. It's certainly relaxing, with a pool and big shady garden. There are malls within easy walking distance and lots of organized tours. ❶

Sleek Backpackers 447 Jan Smuts Ave, Randburg ☎011 787 8070, ⓦwww.sleekhostel.150m .com. Relatively new to the backpacker circuit, this family-operated establishment is basic and clean with a pool, pool table, and Internet access. They also have a 24hr transport service in their minibus, for a nominal price. ❶

Eastern suburbs

Airport Accommodation 16 Meintjies St, Kempton Park ☎011 394 5245, ⓦwww.backpackersjohannesburg.co.za. A compact choice, featuring a pool and free Internet access. They're conveniently located not far from the airport. ❶

Gemini Backpackers Lodge 1 Van Gelder St, Crystal Gardens ☎082 574 4270, ⓦwww .geminibackpackers.com. Rambling suburban property near Kew in the northeast of the city. There are dorms, double rooms and all kinds of extras such as a full-sized snooker table, tennis court, free Internet access, a pool and a rudimentary gym tucked away in an assortment of out-buildings. You'll need a car or the local bus service to get to decent shops and bars, although meals are served here daily. Free airport pickup. ❶

Shoestrings Africa Airport Lodge 85 Gladiator St, Kempton Park ☎011 975 0474, ⓦwww .shoestringsafrica.com. This backpackers' lodge occupies a large plot within sight of the airport, yet is surprisingly quiet, with decent dorm beds and private rooms available. Campers can pitch their tents in the spacious back yard. ❶–❷

Hotels, guesthouses and B&Bs

Despite Jo'burg's corporate, business-oriented atmosphere, it's possible to find some very comfortable and characterful **guesthouses** and **bed and breakfast** establishments, particularly in the northern suburbs. There are also some wonderfully opulent upmarket **hotels**, as well as large multinational **chain hotels** operated by Holiday Inn/Southern Sun (☎0800 117 7711, ⓦwww.southernsun.com), Protea Hotels (☎0800 111 9000, ⓦwww .proteahotels.com), City Lodge (☎011 884 9500, ⓦwww.citylodge.co.za) and Formula 1 (☎011 887 5555). All of these offer reasonable – if predictably characterless – rooms and are often well located; many can offer good deals. Also available are short-stay **self-catering apartments**: Don Apartments (☎0800 115 446, ⓦwww.don.co.za; ❹) has various apartment blocks around the city, including some in Rosebank and Sandton; all are secure, tastefully furnished and well equipped.

Central suburbs

The Cottages 30 Gill St, Observatory ☎011 487 2829, ⓔmckenna@iafrica.com. Thirteen comfortable, characterful cottages perched on the Observatory ridge, with a large rock pool and paths through the lush plot opening out to great views from the top of the *koppie*. Self-catering or B&B accommodation is offered, with evening meals available on request. A safe, relaxing and welcoming place. ❹

Devonshire Hotel On the corner of Melle and Jorissen streets, Braamfontein ☎011 339 5611, ⓔ011 403 2495, ⓦwww.oriongroup.co.za. A decent choice if you have to be near the downtown area, this smart business-oriented hotel offers the best views in the area, and features several bars and restaurants. ❺

Fountain Head Guest House 52 Urania St, Observatory ☎011 487 3564, ⓦwww.fountainheadguesthouse.co.za. Wide balconies dominate this stunning Italian-style villa that was once used as a hideout for members of the ANC. Rooms are large and tastefully decorated, combining luxury and African traditions. Located in a safe area, with immaculate gardens and fountains from which to admire them. ❹

The Westcliff 67 Smuts Ave, Westcliff ☎011 646 2400, ⓦwww.westcliff.co.za. The *grande dame* of Jo'burg's upmarket hotels, the size of a small village, painted pink and built on an east-facing ridge. From the bar you can watch the elephants in the nearby zoo. The cocktails are recommended. ❾

Northern suburbs

Ant Hill 124 Second Ave, Melville
ⓣ083 758 3205, Ⓔmagicguy@iafrica.com.
Owned by a local restaurateur and artist, this
guesthouse contrives to convey Zen-like mini-
malism and be a tad scruffy at the same time.
There are two double rooms and one single, plus
a koi pond. ❸

Coopers' Croft 26 Cross St, Randburg ⓣ011 787
2679, ⒻF011 886 7611, Ⓦwww.coopersbnb.co.za.
A homely, no-frills B&B located on a suburban
street near the Waterfront lakeside development,
and with a gentle, friendly atmosphere. There's
also a pool and tennis courts. ❸

Die Agterplaas 66 Sixth Ave, Melville ⓣ011 726
8452 or 082 410 4046, Ⓦwww.agterplaas.co.za.
Just a short walk from Melville's restaurants and
cafés, this neat, tasteful seven-room guesthouse
provides views over the Melville *koppies* from
pleasant balconies. ❹

The Grace in Rosebank 54 Bath Ave, Rosebank
ⓣ011 280 7200, Ⓦwww.grace.co.za. One of the
most luxurious hotels in town, used mainly by
upmarket business travellers. ❾

Melrose Place 12A North St, Melrose ⓣ011 442
5231 or 083 457 4021, Ⓦwww.melroseplace
.co.za. A friendly, well-run family guesthouse with
a stunning pool and garden, and spacious self-
catering cottages and double rooms filled with
African artefacts. It's close to Melrose Arch shopping and nightlife development, and the Wanderers
cricket stadium. ❻

The Melville House 59 Fourth Ave, Melville
ⓣ011 726 3503, Ⓦwww.themelvillehouse.com.
The pick of the Melville guesthouses, only a
few hundred yards from Melville's cafés and
restaurants. It's a lively, sociable place, genuinely
plugged into what's going on in Jo'burg. The main
building has a pleasant little garden and tastefully
decorated rooms. ❹

Melville Turret Guesthouse 118 Second Ave,
Melville ⓣ011 482 7197 or 083 442 0268,
Ⓦwww.melvilleturret.co.za. This pleasant guesthouse, two blocks away from the trendy Melville
main road, has designer decor, an airy patio and a
tranquil atmosphere. ❸

Oxford Lodge 28a Oxford Ave, Sandhurst
ⓣ011 884 5240, Ⓔoxlodge@mweb.co.za.
A large thatched home not far from Sandton
City Mall, with three top-notch cottages,
each with its own entrance and lounge,
either attached to the house or tucked away
in the large garden which has a pool and lush
lawns. ❻

A Room with a View 1 Tolip St, Melville
ⓣ011 482 5435, ⓣ082 567 9328, Ⓦwww

.aroomwithaview.co.za. A grand and charmingly
surreal two-storey Italian-style villa, laid out and
decorated in exuberant style, with seven double rooms and efficient service. Balconies and
skylights make it light and bright, and provide
something of a relief given the opulence of some
of the antique furniture and artwork. ❹

Saffron House 84 Fourth Ave, Melville ⓣ011
726 6646, Ⓦwww.saffronhousebnb.com. Located
on a rather small plot just a few metres from the
heart of Melville. The rooms use an inspired mix of
Moroccan and Mexican decor that offers a unique
sense of comfort. ❺

Ten Bompas 10 Bompas Rd, Dunkeld West ⓣ011
327 0650, Ⓦwww.tenbompas.co.za. One of
Jo'burg's most stylish small hotels, each of its ten
rooms decorated by a different interior designer.
Quiet and intimate. ❽

Eastern suburbs

Ah Ha Guest House 17a Talisman Ave, Bedfordview ⓣ011 616 3702 or 073 274 4917,
Ⓦwww.ahhalux.co.za. A pleasant if unglamorous family-run guesthouse, located near various
shopping malls halfway between the airport and
city centre, offering comfortable double rooms,
self-catering suites and a decent swimming
pool. ❺

The Bedford View 26 Douglas Rd, Bedfordview
ⓣ011 455 1055, Ⓔbview@global.co.za. A fairly
typical, neat suburban guesthouse with five rooms
(two of which are in self-catering units), a nice
garden and pool, within easy reach of various local
shopping centres. ❺

Dove's Nest 78 Gladiator Street, Kempton Park
ⓣ011 975 1746, Ⓔdovesnest@hotmail.com.
Only minutes away from the airport, this
guesthouse has simple, clean, comfortable
rooms. A free shuttle is operated to and from
the airport and the nearby Caesar's casino
complex, which has numerous restaurants and
shops. ❸

Soweto

Wandie's Place 618 Makhalamele St, Dube
ⓣ011 982 2796. Situated next to the restaurant of
the same name, these newly built en-suite rooms
are in a thriving neighbourhood. ❸

Zizwe Guesthouse 8108 Ngakane Street, Orlando West ⓣ011 942 1314, Ⓔzizwer@telkomsa
.net. Close to Mandela's original home in the
heart of Soweto, this guesthouse occupies one
of the unadorned, flat-roofed buildings typical of
the area. Rooms are simply furnished and have
their own private bathroom, with use of a shared
kitchen. ❷

The City

For a decade and more, downtown Johannesburg has been synonymous with crime and lack of safety, but much is being done to inject vitality back into the downtown area. The task of making the streets safe again has been taken up by the **Central Johannesburg Partnership** (CJP; ⓦ www.cjp.co.za), who deployed the first yellow-bibbed City Ambassadors (see p.598). Real investment has followed: streets are being pedestrianized and adorned with public works of art, Vanderbijl bus station was redeveloped into Gandhi Square, and Mary Fitzgerald Square in Newtown upgraded.

It's now relatively safe to walk downtown, there is talk of boutique hotels being created and property prices have skyrocketed recently. The new constitutional court at Constitution Hill, in Braamfontein just outside the CBD, and the spectacular Nelson Mandela Bridge from Braamfontein to Newtown, have recently been completed, lending the area a touch of sophistication. The hope is that, before long, downtown Jo'burg will be transformed from a no-go into a must-go area for locals and tourists.

The central business district (CBD)

Johannesburg's **CBD**, the grid of streets and tightly packed skyscrapers just to the south of the Witwatersrand ridge, is the most recognizable part of the city. From the time of the first mining camp, located on what is today Commissioner Street, and for nearly a century it was the core of Jo'burg's buzzy commercial and financial life. Then, in the 1980s and 1990s it became riddled with crime, precipitating a mass evacuation by businesses, shoppers, restaurants and tourists. When the Jo'burg Stock Exchange moved out in 1999 in favour of Sandton, the city centre was all but written off. However, with determined efforts over the last few years to regenerate the area precinct by precinct, many parts of the CBD are now not only safe, but they are drawing businesses and tourists back. Though the prospect of a trip to the CBD would still horrify most white Jo'burgers, a visit offers the chance to see buildings and institutions with a fascinating history and get a taste of the bustle, sounds and thrill of a genuinely African city. Refreshingly multiracial, the mix of office workers, shoppers and street traders probably comes closer to reflecting the overall demographic mix of South Africa than anywhere else in the country.

If you're coming into the city centre by car, **park** either underneath Gandhi Square or in the Carlton Centre nearby. Scheduled city **buses** from the northern suburbs terminate at Gandhi Square. Another good way to see the city centre is to see it in the company of a **guide**: Dumela Africa (☏ 083 659 9928, ⓦ www.dumelaafrica-res.co.za) offers expert walking tours of the downtown area as well as Jo'burg as a whole.

The Carlton Centre and around

The **Carlton Centre**, roughly halfway down Commissioner Street, is a good place to start explorations. There's a tourist office on the ground floor, and lots of shops and fast-food outlets, but the main attraction of this fifty-storey building is its top-floor **Top of Africa** lookout point (daily 9am–7pm; R10), which offers breathtaking views of the centre of Johannesburg, and how the mine dumps, reef and city concrete exist cheek by jowl.

From the Carlton Centre, head west for about three blocks along Commissioner or pedestrianized Fox Street, then turn south to **Gandhi Square**. A good example of the city's regeneration, this was formerly Vanderbijl Square, full of

CENTRAL JOHANNESBURG

A (500m) & Zoo (1km) ▲   Killarney & Houghton ▲

THE VALLEY ROAD

Northwards Mansion

ROCK RIDGE ROAD

DOVETON RD   BARKLY RD

CAMPBELL ROAD

ETON ROAD   **Dolobran**

St George's Church

GALE ROAD

SEYMORE AVE

TREMATON PLACE

FALKLANDS AVE

RHODES AVE

ST ANDREWS ROAD

EMPIRE ROAD

GIRTON ROAD

ACCOMMODATION

Brown Sugar	**B**
The Cottages	**D**
Devonshire Hotel	**E**
Fountain Head Guest House	**C**
The Westcliff	**A**

WELLINGTON ROAD

EMPIRE ROAD

Wits University

RESTAURANTS, BARS & CLUBS

Base	**1**
Carfax	**2**
Gramadoelas	**3**
Horror Café	**6**
Kapitan's	**7**
Kofifi	**4**
Moyo's	**5**

BRAAMFONTEIN

Civic Theatre

AMESHOFF STREET

STEIMENS STREET **E**

ENOCH SONTONGA AVENUE

JORISSEN STREET

DE KORTE STREET

N

JUTA ST

SMIT STREET

WOLMARANS STREET

SMIT STREET

LEYDS ST

National Mandela Bridge

CARR STREET

Market Theatre **2**

PIM STREET

Museum Africa **3** **4**

BREE STREET

Oriental Plaza

MINNAAR STREET

JEPPE STREET

PLEIN

NEWTOWN

Former Stock Exchange

Dance Factory

AVENUE ROAD

SAB World of Beer **6**

Joomal Mosque

Cuthberts

Gauteng Legislature

Muti Museum **7**

MARSHALL TOWN

First National Bank Museum

Former Post Office

MAIN

COMMISSIONER

Chamber of Mines

Rand Club

MAIN REEF

Magistrates' Court

MARSHALL

0 ————— 500 m

Standard Bank Centre & Gallery

The Wilds

Emoyeni

PARKTOWN

Holiday Inn

The View

Hazeldene Hall

BEREA

YEOVILLE

CONSTITUTION HILL

HILLBROW

Medical Research Institute and Adler Museum

HIGHLANDS

The Ponti

Windybrow Theatre

Park Station

JOUBERT PARK

Johannesburg Stadium

Alhambra Theatre

DOORNFONTEIN

Johannesburg Art Gallery

St Mary's Cathedral

NEW DOORNFONTEIN

Ellis Park Stadium

High Court

Carlton Centre & Top of Africa

Gandhi Square

Bus Station

Although **Mohandas Gandhi** has many strong links with Durban, the South African city he arrived at in 1893, it was the ten years he spent in Johannesburg between 1903 and 1913 that first tested the philosophies for which he is famous. As a qualified advocate, he frequently appeared in the Transvaal Law Courts (now demolished), which stood in what has recently been renamed Gandhi Square in downtown Jo'burg. Defending mainly South African Indians accused of breaking the restrictive and racist registration laws, Gandhi began to see practical applications for his concept of **Satyagraha**, soul force, or passive resistance, as a means of defying immoral state oppression.

Gandhi himself was twice imprisoned along with other passive resisters in the fort in Braamfontein, on what is now Constitution Hill. On one of these occasions he was taken from his cell to the office of General Jan Smuts to negotiate the prisoners' release, but finding himself at liberty had to borrow the railway fare home from the general's secretary.

Gandhi's ideas found resonance in the non-violent ideals of those who established the **African National Congress** in 1912. Forty years later, only a few years after Gandhi's successful use of Satyagraha to end the British Raj in India, the start of the ANC's Defiance Campaign against the pass laws in 1952 owed much to Gandhi's principles. Museum Africa (see opposite) contains displays on Gandhi's time in Johannesburg.

grim bus shelters and gangsters. As the former location of the Magistrate's Court where Gandhi spent so much of his time working in the city, the square was named in his honour and spruced up with some attractive brickwork. Still the main station for city buses, it's now a safe place to orientate yourself.

A couple of blocks to the northwest, on Loveday Street, the grandiose **Rand Club** (visits by prior arrangement only; ☏011 834 8311) is where mining magnates have come to dine and unwind for nearly a century. Completed in 1904, the building is actually the fourth to occupy the site, as each successive club was replaced to reflect the owners' growing wealth.

Four blocks south on Frederick Street lies the superb **Standard Bank Art Gallery** (Mon–Fri 8am–4.30pm, Sat 9am–1pm; free), a large and imposing round building with sweeping staircases, where changing exhibitions consistently show off some the best contemporary African art in South Africa. Just across the road in Standard Bank's head office at 5 Simmonds Street, you can take a lift from the main concourse down to **Ferreira's Stope** (Mon–Fri 8.30am–5pm; free), an old mine tunnel discovered when the building was being constructed in 1986. The plain rock face you see still bears pick-axe scars, and there's a simple though fascinating display putting the history of Johannesburg in context; look out for the old sepia photographs of the mine and early Jo'burg.

Among the city's skyscrapers, imperious mining halls and boarded-up office blocks stand numerous interesting buildings, quirky facades and architectural features. North of Commissioner Street, look out for the recently revamped **Gauteng Legislature**, formerly the City Hall, on the corner of Harrison Street, while the former **post office** is one block east on the corner of Rissik Street. When this was completed in 1897 it was the tallest building in the city, and is still impressive, despite being dwarfed by later additions to the skyline. Basically neo-Baroque in style, it has quirky Dutch touches, primarily in its gabling. The fourth floor and clock tower are later additions, timed to coincide with the accession of the British king, Edward VII, in 1902. Elsewhere, on

Pritchard Street stands **Cuthberts**, a department store which opened as a shoe shop in 1904, and **Markham's**, another department store, built in 1886. Two blocks further east on Pritchard Street is the **Johannesburg High Court**, a hated symbol of oppression when it used to be the Rand Supreme Court.

Diagonal Street

Moving west from Simmonds Street in the vicinity of Pritchard and Jeppe streets, look out for the rather forbidding **Bank City**, home of a number of banks, but also with the kind of arcades and plazas found in a continental European capital. West of this is **Diagonal Street**, heart of one of the most fascinating areas in the CBD. In the shadow of various concrete and glass behemoths, including the former Johannesburg Stock Exchange, are streets of old two-storey buildings, some of which date back to the 1890s; the lines of washing on the upstairs balconies show that they are still residential. On the streets are a jumble of traders and shops, peddling traditional medicines (*umuthi*), Sotho blankets and paraffin stoves alongside mobile phones. Though it might not feel it at first, the area is fairly safe, and with businessmen mingling with hawkers it has a very African buzz.

If you're feeling brave, take a look at the rather spooky **KwaZulu Muti Museum of Man and Science** at 14 Diagonal Street, a shop selling all kinds of traditional medicines, often manufactured from the dried animal skins hanging from the ceiling. You might also find yourself brushing against dangling ostrich feet or a pair of monkey skulls.

Newtown

On the western edge of the CBD between Diagonal Street and the M1 motorway flyover, **Newtown** is an area of redevelopment where some of Johannesburg's most vibrant cultural hot spots are found alongside derelict factories and areas of wasteland. The main draw is its **Cultural Precinct**, where a lot of money has been spent to ensure it's a safe place to visit, not just by day but also at night, when the various music and theatre venues are in full swing.

At its heart is the excellent **Museum Africa** at 121 Bree Street (Tues–Sun 9am–5pm; R7), overlooking Mary Fitzgerald Square. The sheer size of the museum, which occupies the city's former fruit and vegetable market, can make it seem a bit sparse and empty, but in fact the four permanent exhibitions and numerous temporary displays are well worth seeing. Most successful is **Johannesburg Transformations**, which tells the story of the city from early days of gold prospecting to the 1994 elections. Among the imaginative exhibits are re-creations of shacks and *shebeens* playing well-selected soundtracks from musical giants of the past, such as *kwela* maestro Spokes Mashiane. In a side room, look out for **Tried for Treason**, a exhibition dedicated to the Treason Trial of the 1950s, when 156 people, including Nelson Mandela and many well-known ANC activists of all races, were accused of plotting against the state.

On the upper floor, and rather less engaging, is the **Bensusan Museum of Photography**, which grandly aspires to be a "newseum of the present and future" but adds up to little more than a collection of cameras, holograms and CD-ROMs. On the lower floors, the **Museum of South African Rock Art** has few original paintings, as most of them are still on rocks scattered around South Africa, but there are some convincing replicas – which are as close as you'll get to the real thing without a hike upcountry, and which are complemented by background on the artists.

At the eastern end of the same building is the entrance to the famous **Market Theatre** (see p.627), a reliable source of stimulating and often ground-breaking dramatic output over the last thirty years or so. Outside, there's a worthwhile collection of shops, places to eat and drink, and *Kippies*, a former public toilet which is now South Africa's most famous jazz venue (see p.626). The cultural centre continues south of Jeppe Street, with a live music venue (Newtown Music Hall), a dance rehearsal and performing space called the **Dance Factory**, which is used for the annual Arts Alive Festival (see box on p.626). One of the city's better **flea markets** takes place every Saturday outside the theatre and on Mary Fitzgerald Square (see "Shopping" on p.628).

On the corner of President and Bezuidenhout streets is the **South African Breweries (SAB) World of Beer** (Tues–Sat 10am–6pm; R10). Their ninety-minute tour takes you through six thousand years of brewing history, which begs the question why SAB's ubiquitous end product, the anaemic, fizzy Castle lager, is so disappointing. Still, the reconstructed gold-rush pubs and Sixties *shebeen* are fun, along with the greenhouse where sample crops of barley and hops grow, and from the balcony of the *Tap Room* bar you can watch the city rush by.

Moving southwest, over President and Main streets, you'll come to the infamous **John Vorster Square**, site of the Johannesburg police headquarters, where anti-apartheid activists were detained and tortured, and some fell to their deaths having "jumped" from the tenth floor. After this, it's a pleasant relief to find the remains of the old Indian neighbourhood just further west, where Jeppe Street turns into Minnaar Street. A busy commercial street ends up at the **Oriental Plaza**, an Indian-owned shopping complex, selling everything from suitcases and bric-a-brac to fabrics and spices. This is just about all that remains of Newtown's once-thriving Indian community, most of whom were forcibly removed in 1904 to make way for whites.

Joubert Park

On the eastern side of Park station, **Joubert Park**, named after General Piet Joubert (who lost the South African Republic general election to Paul Kruger in 1893), is the only inner-city green space but largely regarded as a no-go area. The one sight you can visit here is the **Johannesburg Art Gallery** (Tues–Sun 10am–5pm; free), an elegant, predominantly nineteenth-century building and one of the most progressive galleries in the country. If you're planning to walk there, it's probably best to find a City Ambassador willing to escort you; otherwise get a taxi to drop you off at the main entrance on Klein Street or make use of the gallery's secure parking.

The regular exhibits include vast wooden sculptures by the visionary Venda artist Jackson Hlungwani that tower up to the gallery's ceilings. Elsewhere, the gallery shows a very South African mixture of African artworks and artefacts from the ceremonial to the purely decorative, and a range of European paintings, including some minor Dutch Masters. The special exhibitions are usually good, too; consult the *Mail & Guardian* newspaper for details.

The central suburbs

Grouped around the CBD are various suburbs which, given Johannesburg's itinerant population and fast-changing demography, seem to be in a state of constant change. Some, particularly Hillbrow, Berea and Yeoville, were once the "grey areas" of Johannesburg, where apartheid first started to break down in the Eighties. The police turned a blind eye as large numbers of blacks started moving from the townships into these previously all-white areas. **Yeoville**, east across the Harrow Road from Berea, and in particular its main drag Rockey Street, was long a melting pot where bohemian whites and progressive blacks mixed in Johannesburg's most vibrant and creative area. But in recent years the crime and drug-dealing of Hillbrow have moved in too. Today, most whites have left these areas – though they still reside in leafy, residential **Observatory**, just east of Yeoville – while migrants from all over Africa have flooded in. These suburbs have their moments of architectural excellence, though their hectic street life and fearsome reputation will probably leave you disinclined to savour them at leisure.

Braamfontein

It's not just for the transport facilities at Park station that you might have cause to visit **Braamfontein**, which starts at the main train station and extends north as far as Empire Road. The area features one of the newest additions to the tourist circuit, **Constitution Hill**, on the corner of Joubert and Sam Hancock streets (daily 9am–5pm; R15). This is the new home of the Constitutional Court, presiding over matters pertaining to the country's constitution, which stands next to the notorious **Old Fort Prison Complex** where many leading activists, including Gandhi and Nelson Mandela, were detained. Rich in symbolism, the location is a wonderful example of the country's ongoing transformation, particularly highlighting the pride South Africans have for their new constitution and the rights enshrined therein.

The only other attractions marginally worth a visit are the **Civic Theatre** between Simmons and Loveday streets, which hosts some of Johannesburg's best theatrical, musical and dance productions (see p.627), and the **University of the Witwatersrand**, otherwise known as "Wits", which lies in Braamfontein's northwest corner. The university has played an important role in the country's history, educating many future leaders, and acting as a site of major intellectual and political struggles. The large, attractive campus contains a number of impressive Classical buildings and some lovely terraced gardens, a far cry from the bustling streets nearby. On the ground floor of Senate House (best accessed from Jorissen Street), is the **Gertrude Posel Gallery** (Mon–Fri 10am–4pm; free), which houses an extensive collection of traditional and contemporary African art.

Hillbrow

Smit Street, to the north of Joubert Park, marks the boundary with infamous and densely populated **Hillbrow**, dominated by multistorey apartment buildings all crammed with people. Traditionally, Hillbrow has attracted the city's new immigrants. Immediately after World War II, the typical immigrant was English, Italian or East European. These days, Africans from all over the continent are arriving in numbers, lending the area a uniquely pan-African atmosphere, with music from Lagos to Kinshasa pumping from the bars and clubs. Along the many side streets, the scene is distinctly seedy, with drug pushers loitering outside gaudy strip joints. The main thoroughfares, with their markets, clubs and bars, teem with activity, but the suburb is widely regarded as a **no-go area** for tourists; your best chance to experience it is to visit one of the better-known nightclubs or bars in a group, accompanied by a knowledgeable local.

If you're in the area, keep an eye out for Hillbrow's most famous apartment building, the **Ponti** or "le petit Kinshasa", the round tower visible from miles around that is home to many of the suburb's Congolese immigrants. Also worth a look is the lovely mock-Tudor **Windybrow Theatre** on Nugget Street.

The northern suburbs

Safe, prosperous and packed with shops and restaurants, the **northern suburbs** seem a world apart from the CBD and its surrounds. The name is actually a catch-all term for the seemingly endless urban sprawl running over 30km from Parktown, beyond the N1 ring road and into an area known as Mid Rand which is itself creeping toward the southern edge of Pretoria. With the notable exception of Alexandra, this is a moneyed area, where plush shopping malls and well-tended parks are often the only communal meeting points, and the majority of homes use high walls, iron gates and barbed wire to advertise how security-conscious a life the owners lead. Despite the often numbing sheen of affluence, however, interesting pockets do exist, such as the centres of the suburbs of Melville, Rosebank and Parkhurst. Most of the suburbs are close to major arterial roads and best explored by car.

Parktown

The first elite residential area in Johannesburg, **Parktown** has retained its exclusive tag despite its proximity to Hillbrow, which lies just southeast on the

Sir Herbert Baker

South Africa's most famous architect, **Sir Herbert Baker** was born in Kent, England, in 1862. Apprenticed to his architect uncle in London at the age of 17, Baker attended classes at the Royal Academy and Architectural Association, where he took care to make the contacts he would use so skilfully in later life. By the time he left for the Cape in 1892, Baker was already a convert to the new so-called **Free Style**, which advocated an often bizarre, but roughly historical eclecticism. The young architect's favourite influences, which would crop up again and again in his work, were Renaissance Italian and medieval Kentish.

Once in the Cape, Baker met **Cecil Rhodes**, and this connection, assiduously cultivated, established him as a major architectural player. The second Anglo-Boer War began in 1899 and Rhodes, assuming eventual British victory, sent Baker off to study the Classical architecture of Italy and Greece, hoping that he would return fully equipped to create a British imperial architecture in South Africa. Baker returned to South Africa deeply influenced by what he had seen, and was summoned by **Lord Alfred Milner**, the administrator of the defeated Transvaal, to fulfil Rhodes' hopes.

Baker took up the challenge enthusiastically, beginning with the homes of the so-called "kindergarten", the young men, mostly Oxford- and Cambridge-educated, whom Milner had imported to bring British-style "good governance" to the defeated territory. The result was the **Parktown mansions**, the opulent houses lining the roads of Johannesburg's wealthiest suburb. In adherence to the architectural creeds he had learnt in England, Baker trained local craftsmen and used local materials for these mansions. He also pioneered the use of local *koppie* stone, lending a dramatic aspect even to unadventurous designs.

Baker's major public commissions were the **St George's Cathedral** in Cape Town, the **South African Institute for Medical Research** in Johannesburg, and the sober, assertive **Union Buildings** in Pretoria, which more than any other building express the British imperial dream – obsessed with Classical precedent, and in a location chosen because of its similarity to the site of the Acropolis in Athens.

Baker left South Africa in 1913 to design the Secretariat in New Delhi, India, returning to England on its completion, where he worked on South Africa House in Trafalgar Square, London. He was knighted in 1923; he died in 1946, and is buried in Westminster Abbey.

other side of Empire Road. The first people to settle in Parktown were Sir Lionel Philips, president of the Chamber of Mines, and his wife Lady Florence. In 1892, seeking a residence that looked onto the Magaliesberg rather than the mine dumps, they had a house built on what was then the Braamfontein farm. The rest of the farm was planted with eucalyptus trees and became known as the Sachsenwald Forest, some of which was given over to the Johannesburg Zoo a few years later. The remaining land was cleared in 1925 to make way for more residential developments.

Parktown's main attraction lies in its distinctive **architecture**, largely the legacy of Sir Herbert Baker (see box opposite). Baker's arrival in 1902 heralded a style particular to this district, still evident today in the opulent mansions lining the streets. Parktown & Westcliff Heritage Trust (office open Mon–Fri 9am–1pm; ☎011 482 3349, ⓦ home.intekom.co.za/parktown) runs **walking or bus tours** most Saturday afternoons. These follow themes such as "Johannesburg Gold" or "Edwardian Elegance" and often involve knowledgeable guides decked out in full Edwardian costume, who show you through some of the lavish mansions and their grounds. Tours cost R40–80, and can be booked directly through Computicket (see p.623). The Trust also publishes an inexpensive walking tour guide, so you can walk or drive the routes covered by the tours unguided, but without access to the houses.

A good place to start an independent visit is **Ridge Road**, just north of the Randjeslaagte beacon, which marks the northern point of old Johannesburg. The *Holiday Inn* here is a massive complex which Lord Alfred Milner used as his governor's residence from 1900. The best of the houses nearby are **Hazeldene Hall**, built in 1902 and featuring cast-iron verandas imported from Glasgow, and **The View**, built in 1897, with carved wooden verandas and an elegant red-brick exterior. To the north of Ridge Road, York Road curves to the left into Jubilee Road, with several palaces on its northern side; the neo-Queen Anne-style **Emoyeni**, at no. 15, built in 1905, is especially striking. At the corner of Jubilee Road and Victoria Avenue stands **Dolobran**, a weird and impressive house, also built in 1905, with a perfect veranda, wonderful red-brick chimneys, red Marseilles roof tiles and hallucinatory stained glass.

Crossing the busy M1 onto **Rock Ridge Road**, you'll reach the **Northwards Mansion**, built by Sir Herbert Baker in 1904 and home of the Parktown Trust. Unfortunately, there's no access along the road to Baker's own residence at no. 5. On parallel Sherborne Road you can see Baker's attractive **St George's Church** and its rectory, which mix Kentish and Italian features and were built in local rock.

Johannesburg Zoo and Houghton

Roughly 2km north of Parktown, off Jan Smuts Avenue, **Johannesburg Zoo** (daily 8.30am–5.30pm; R30; ⓦ www.jhbzoo.org.za) is home to over three thousand species, including polar bears. Despite recent attempts at revitalization, a sad air pervades the place. A few years ago, it hit the headlines when a criminal tried to avoid pursuing policemen by hopping over the wall into the zoo. Unfortunately, he jumped straight into the cage of Max the gorilla; the indignant Max suffered a gunshot wound from the encounter, while the criminal was hospitalized with serious bites.

Next door, and of greater interest, is the **National Museum of Military History** (daily 9.30am–4.30pm; R10), where among the tanks, guns and uniforms you'll find a display on **Umkhonto we Sizwe (MK)**, the armed wing of the ANC, although the other liberation armies are conspicuous by their absence. The display focuses on the wing's commander, Joe Modise, who became Minister of Defence in the ANC government. Opposite the zoo, on the west side of Jan Smuts Avenue, is the artificial but pleasant **Zoo Lake**. The park here is a popular and safe walking and picnic spot and occasionally hosts outdoor performances, including an all-day music event every September during the Arts Alive festival (see box on p.626).

A couple of kilometres east of the zoo is the suburb of **Houghton**, one of Johannesburg's wealthiest and greenest suburbs. This is where Nelson Mandela lives, in a large white mansion dubbed Casa Graça after his third wife, Graça Machel. Interestingly, between 1961 and 1974 it was the country's only constituency to return an anti-apartheid MP, Helen Suzman.

Melville

The most relaxed, unintimidating and appealing of the northern suburbs, **Melville** lies west of Parktown between the two main road arteries of Barry Hertzog and Beyers Naude (formerly D.F. Malan). The suburb's villagey atmosphere has proved highly attractive to the stressed ranks of Johannesburg's upwardly mobile, who are steadily buying up property here. When so many shops and restaurants in Jo'burg are tucked away in soulless malls, it's refreshing to find streets with busy shops and pavement cafés. The suburb's most interesting shops lie around the junction of Seventh Street and

MELVILLE

RESTAURANTS
Buzz 9	4
Catz Pyjamas	7
Cool Runnings	3
Nuno's	8
Pomegranate	6
Ratz	4
Roxy's	2
Sam's Café	4
Service Station	1
Soi	5

Melville Koppies

Louw Geldenhuys View Site

Visual Arts Gallery

ACCOMMODATION
Ant Hill	F
Die Agterplaas	A
Melrose Place	
The Melville House	B
Melville Turret Guesthouse	E
Pension iDube	G
A Room with a View	D
Saffron House	C

Jan Van Riebeeck Park (1km)   Jan Van Riebeeck Park (1km)   Greenside (1km)   Rosebank (3km)

Sophiatown

Johannesburg Zoo (1km)

Empire Road & Braamfontein

44 Stanley Ave

0   500 m

Fourth Avenue, where you can linger in the inviting coffee shops, trendy restaurants, secondhand bookshops and quirky antique dealers. Fourth Avenue also has the fine contemporary **Visual Arts Gallery**, in a bright modern house at no. 67 (at the junction with Fifth Street). There's plenty going on in Melville at night, too, when it's still safe to walk the main streets.

The **Melville Koppies Nature Reserve** (☏011 482 4797) to the north of the suburb is a pleasant hillside reserve containing hundreds of species of indigenous flora and fauna, as well as archeological remains of both Stone and Iron Age settlements. There are two parts to the reserve. The **Louw Geldenhuys View Site**, reached from Zambesi Road, offers great views over Jo'burg and has open access at all times; to the west, the larger **central section** has a number of good walking trails, but is open only on the first three Sundays of each month. On the northern side of the reserve lies **Jan van Riebeeck Park**, a large spread of green parkland running north and west for several kilometres, which contains the **Johannesburg Botanic Garden** in its northeast corner (daily 8am–5pm; R15). Besides **Emmarentia Dam**, a popular spot for paddling and rowing, the garden is noted for its wide open spaces and safe routes for joggers and walkers rather than for its botanical exuberance – although in the northeast corner there are some attractive formal herb and rose gardens. The tiny Shakespeare Garden is often used for plays or small concerts, which are advertised in the local press.

Sophiatown

West of Melville, the suburb of **Sophiatown** is unremarkable architecturally but significant in the history of apartheid – it was here that **Archbishop Trevor Huddleston**, the English cleric who established the Anti-Apartheid Movement, worked in the Fifties. For many years, Sophiatown was one of the few places within the city where blacks owned property, and as a result it became a melting pot of culture and liberal thinking on issues of politics and race. In the 1960s the suburb was designated a white area by the government, who sent in the bulldozers, scattering the inhabitants to Soweto regardless of their claim to the land and, with a degree of irony, if not fatalism, renaming the suburb Triomf, a name that remains on many maps and signboards. Although the name Sophiatown has now been reinstated, nothing of the original suburb remains apart from one house and the **Christ the King** Anglican church, from where Trevor Huddleston conducted his ministry. When he died in 1998, his ashes were brought from London to be scattered in Sophiatown.

Rosebank and Parkhurst

The small suburb of **Rosebank**, a couple of kilometres north of the zoo, is dominated by a collection of **shopping malls**. There is also the **African Craft Market** (Tues–Sun 9am–5pm) above the Rosebank Mall, with a collection of stalls selling reasonable-quality African arts and crafts. It's not the cheapest place to buy crafts in the city, but prices are still much lower than the upmarket galleries nearby, and you are able to bargain. Sundays are the busiest day for crafts, when a large **flea market** selling everything from drums to cheese takes over a floor of the car park adjoining the Rosebank Mall.

Also in and around Rosebank are a number of galleries where you can view (and often purchase) traditional and contemporary African art, often of a very high standard. The **Everard Read Gallery** (Mon–Fri 9am–6pm,

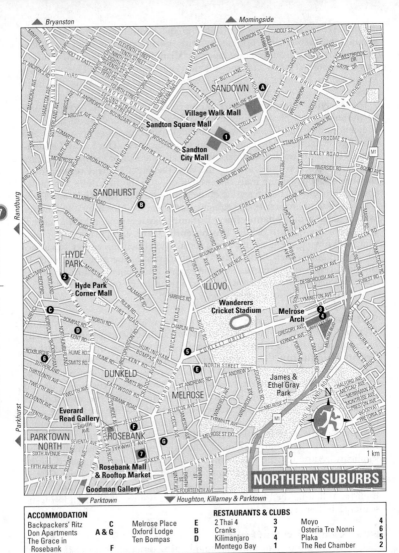

ACCOMMODATION		RESTAURANTS & CLUBS			
Backpackers' Ritz	**C**	2 Thai 4	**3**	Moyo	**4**
Don Apartments	**A & G**	Cranks	**7**	Osteria Tre Nonni	**6**
The Grace in		Kilimanjaro	**4**	Plaka	**5**
Rosebank	**F**	Montego Bay	**1**	The Red Chamber	**2**
Melrose Place	**E**				
Oxford Lodge	**B**				
Ten Bompas	**D**				

Sat 9am–5pm; free; ⓦwww.everardread.co.za) at 6 Jellicoe Avenue has varied exhibitions, often featuring South Africa's leading painters and sculptors. Smaller and more avant garde is the **Goodman Art Gallery** (Tues–Fri 9.30am–5.30pm, Sat 9.30am–4pm; ⓦwww.goodman-gallery.com) at 163 Jan Smuts Avenue, while along the same road, at no. 153, the **Kim Sacks Art Gallery** specializes in traditional arts and crafts from around Africa, with most items on display for sale.

Not far to the west of Rosebank and Parktown North lies **Parkhurst** which, along with Melville, is one of the northern suburbs to boast an element of street life – particularly on and around Fourth Avenue. It's safe to walk around here, checking out the antique and interior design shops, as well as the smattering of trendy cafés and restaurants.

Sandton and Randburg

Some 20km north of the CBD, **Sandton** is the archetypal northern suburb. It is outrageously rich, with plush shopping centres and endless rows of lavish houses. In recent years, it has become the retreat of choice for banks and large corporations fleeing the CBD. A stroll through the linked **Sandton City** and **Sandton Square** shopping centres, complete with a pseudo-Italian piazza and attendant restaurants and cafés, may make you shudder at the vulgarity of such an ostentatious display of wealth, but it's also one of the best ways to appreciate this suburb and its inhabitants.

North of Sandton, the suburbs roll on for 15km and more. Here you'll find large domestic plots interspersed with lush country clubs, shopping centres and, increasingly, the new phenomenon of "clusters", little developments of upmarket, newly built houses behind an imposing perimeter wall and equipped with every available security device. Whether such levels of paranoia are altogether necessary in keeping crime at bay is not a subject you'll find open to debate among locals, but there is little doubt that the tone it sets dominates the northern suburbs.

Among the few points of interest here is the **Waterfront** on Republic Road in the suburb of **Randburg**. Here themed restaurants, bars, amusement arcades and shops, along with cinemas and a flea market, have been built around an artificial lake in a crude attempt to cash in on the success of the Cape Town Waterfront. There's a tame spectacle called **Liquid Fireworks** in the evening, involving a series of fountains illuminated by multicoloured lights (nightly 7.30 & 8.30pm). Further north, beyond the N1 highway on William Nicol Drive, the **Monte Casino** complex looks from the outside like a huge mock-Italian palazzo; on the inside it's a replica of a Tuscan village, filled with cobbled streets, cast-iron street lamps and red-tiled buildings housing chain shops such as Diesel and Next. Alongside are restaurants, cinemas, a theatre, a casino and banks of gaming machines.

Alexandra

The contrast between desperately poor **Alexandra**, just east of the M1, and the surrounding suburbs could hardly be greater. When it was founded, this black township was one of the few places where blacks could own property. The sense of ownership and independence helped Alex, as it is commonly known, to avoid the forced removals of former governments. Despite the simple grid design its map suggests, the township is actually a bewildering maze of smashed-up streets, filled to bursting point with people, with overcrowded housing and a woeful lack of basic services such as sewerage and water. Half a million people live here in an area of less than eight square kilometres.

"Exhilarating and precarious" was how Nelson Mandela described Alex when he lived here in the early 1940s after running away from the Eastern Cape to find work in Jo'burg as an articled law clerk. In those days, the township was well known for gangster gangs as well as its developing political militancy, which saw **bus boycotts** preventing bus companies from raising their fares, one of the first examples of mass action by blacks achieving political results. Alexandra has long been an ANC stronghold, and paid dearly for it until the collapse of apartheid, with ongoing warfare between

Zulus and the ANC in the Eighties leading to one section of Alex being dubbed "Beirut".

While the old spirit of Alex lives on in the bustling streets on the western side of the polluted Jukskei River, the eastern bank is now lined with **new houses**, some built by government funding and others by middle-class blacks looking to improve their quality of life but wanting to remain in the township. Here you can also see the athletes' village built when the 1999 All African Games were held in Johannesburg; named "Tsutsumane" (Shangaan for "runner"), it has been turned into housing for locals. Not far from here a patch of land has been turned into a **cricket oval**; it's an incongruous sight to observe this most colonial of games being played against a backdrop of densely packed township shacks, with the skyscrapers of opulent Sandton peeking over the horizon behind.

As part of Alex's renewal programme (for more on which, see Ⓦwww .alexandra.co.za), guided **tours** of the township are available. Much less formalized and certainly less touristy than Soweto tours, these trips are a great way to get close to the raw energy and spontaneity of township life. Abbey Sechoaro of Bosele Township Experience runs excellent tours which can be booked through the Alexandra Tourism Association (℡011 882 3406), who can also put you in touch with other guides. If you can't visit in person, tuning into Alex FM, the township's entertaining community **radio** station (see box on p.625), will at least give you a feel of the suburb.

The eastern suburbs

Among the oldest of the city's suburbs, and for years home to Johannesburg's Jewish and Portuguese communities, the eastern suburbs of **Kensington** and **Bezuidenhout Valley** (better known as Bez Valley) have also changed dramatically in recent years, with whites moving out of much of the old housing to make way for township and immigrant blacks. Exuding a very different flavour, **Cyrildene**, to the east of Observatory, has become the city's new Chinatown, with a fascinating collection of Chinese supermarkets, businesses and authentic restaurants along Derrick Avenue near its junction with Marcia Street.

Most visitors to this area, however, come to **Bruma Lake**, an artificial stretch of water which has proved a disappointing attraction save for its popular and lively **flea market** (Tues–Sun 9am–5pm), one of the best places in Johannesburg to find inexpensive curios – as long as you don't mind pseudo-traditional dance troupes entertaining you while you browse. Nearby, and safe for walkers, joggers and picnickers, is one of central Johannesburg's more accessible green spaces, **Gillooly's Farm**, a park set around a dam.

Gold Reef City and the Apartheid Museum

The suburbs immediately south of the city centre were traditionally the preserve of the white working class. After the repeal of the Group Areas Act in 1990, blacks started moving in; unusually in contemporary South Africa, many are wealthier than the original residents. Besides Gold Reef City and the adjoining Apartheid Museum, the only other attraction south of the city is the sizeable **Klipriviersberg Nature Reserve**, in Winchester Hills just beyond the N12. Few Jo'burgers know about this undeveloped, unspoilt parkland, which provides wonderful views of the city to the north. To get there, take the N1 heading south, turn left into Columbine Avenue (the M68), and then right a kilometre or two further, at Ormonde Street.

Gold Reef City

Gold Reef City (Tues–Sun 9.30am–5pm; R70; ⓦ www.goldreefcity.co.za), 15km south of the city centre, is where old Johannesburg meets Disneyland: a large, gaudy entertainment complex built around the old no. 14 shaft of the Crown Mines. If you can take the tackiness and piped ragtime music, there are some points of interest at what is essentially a theme park, notably the **old gold mine** itself, into which you can descend 200m and get an inkling of how it is to work underground. Keep an eye out, too, for the tribal dancing that happens five times a day; the dancers are excellent, even if their routines bear little resemblance to the real thing.

You can wander round the streets filled with period houses, shops and museums, though most are generally disappointing, with the possible exception of those dedicated to early Johannesburg, such as Olthaver and Nourse House. Otherwise, the most enjoyable thing to do in Gold Reef City is to go on one of the **thrill rides** (all included in the entrance ticket), which include the Raging Rapids water ride and the terrifying Anaconda roller coaster. In the unlikely event that you want to stay the night, the *Gold Reef City Hotel* (ⓣ011 248 5200; ➐) offers Victorian-themed decor, complete with a saloon, mock-oil lamps and four-poster beds. Various restaurants serve decent though pricey food, but the main focus of this section of Gold Reef City is the vast **casino**, complete with hundreds of slot machines and various gaming tables.

To get to Gold Reef City, take the M1 south, and turn off at the Xavier Street exit. Otherwise, join one of the many tours that go there, advertised in nearly every hotel lobby.

The Apartheid Museum

Just to the left of the main entrance to the Gold Reef complex is the recently built **Apartheid Museum** (Tues–Sun 10am–5pm, R25; ⓦ www .apartheidmuseum.org). With separate entrances for "whites" and "non-whites", this modern museum is a sobering visual journey through the history of apartheid, from the roots of segregation policies to uplifting images of liberation. Particularly poignant are the photographs by Ernest Cole, who was forced to flee the country in 1960, depicting the abuses that people suffered under apartheid in the 1950s.

Soweto

South Africa's most famous township, **Soweto** (short for South West Townships) is a place of extreme contrasts. The area has the only street in the world where two Nobel Peace Prize winners once lived, yet suffers one of the highest rates of murder and rape in the world; it is the richest township in South Africa, but has some of the most desperate poverty; it is the most political township, yet has the most nihilistic youth.

Southwest of the city centre, Soweto is huge, stretching as far as the eye can see, with a population estimated at between three and four million. Like any city of that size, it is divided into a number of different **suburbs**, with palpably middle- and upper-class neighbourhoods among them. At first sight, it appears an endless jumble of houses and shacks, overshadowed by palls of smoke, though parts of it have a villagey feel. Apart from the Hector Peterson Memorial and Museum, most of Soweto's **tourist highlights** are physically unimpressive, their fame stemming from historical associations. That history and the people of Soweto, however, are enthralling, not least because here it is told with a perspective and context rarely found in the rest of South Africa. For visitors it means an insight not just into a place much mentioned in 1980s

Soweto tours

The most common – and safest – way to visit Soweto is with a **tour operator**. By far the oldest, biggest and slickest operation is Jimmy's Face to Face Tours (℡011 331 6109). Jimmy pioneered tours into the township, and his operation has grown steadily over the years. Imbizo Tours (℡011 838 2667 or 083 700 9098), run by the irrepressible Mandy Mankazana, provides stiff competition. Mandy is a mine of information and contacts, and her three-hour day tours and four-hour night tours of Soweto are excellent. Tours can be customized, and Imbizo also organizes evening *shebeen* crawls lasting up to five hours, depending on your stamina. Indicate what kind of company you would like to keep, from politicians to sports fanatics, and Mandy will select an appropriate venue.

As well as the well-established operators, smaller, more flexible outfits offer imaginative **alternative tours** such as jazz outings, walks around Orlando West and Diepkloof, visits to Sowetan artists or local churches, and homestays with locals. Try Max Maximum (℡011 933 4177 or 082 770 0247) or African Prime Tours (℡011 794 5708); alternatively, your accommodation may well have links to a reliable tour company.

Before you go to Soweto on any kind of tour, it's worth preparing yourself for the fact that as a tourist you will stand out, and that there's a good chance you'll run into other groups of tourists. Most outfits are keen for you to "meet the people", though they all tend to visit the same shanty towns and *shebeens*, and you'll find that resulting conversations sometimes lead to your leaving a donation, tipping casual guides or buying local craftwork. While this gets a few tourist dollars directly into the townships, it often leaves visitors feeling pressurized and vulnerable. Ask your guide the best way to deal with this.

news bulletins for funerals and fighting, but into a way of life most Westerners rarely encounter.

A visit to Soweto with one of the many **tours** (see box above) is the single most popular attraction in Johannesburg. Where once these had a whiff of daring and originality, a well-trodden tourist trail has developed, and unless you're content to follow the herds of minibuses and coaches around the conventional sights, it's well worth using an operator who mixes the highlights with lesser-known sights.

At one time, taking yourself to Soweto would have meant a display of bravado bordering on foolhardiness, but it's now possible to visit the main sights independently; your time will be your own, and you'll be able to check out the growing number of bars and eating places catering to tourists. Unlike anywhere else in Jo'burg, this is an area where residents will stop to greet you or to chat, regardless of your colour. There are surprisingly few criminal incidents affecting tourists, though as ever it pays to remain vigilant on a visit; exploring less-visited areas by yourself, or going after dark, isn't recommended for safety reasons. If you want to **drive** to Soweto, you'll need good navigational skills – the lack of obvious landmarks amid mile upon mile of bungalows can be highly confusing. Taking a **minibus taxi** to Soweto is more confusing than dangerous, as it isn't always easy to ascertain which part of the township it's heading for, for which reason it's not recommended. Forming a cross with two fingers is the recognized minibus signal indicating that you want to go to "crossroads", which will bring you to the centre of Soweto. From here you can pick up another taxi to whichever sight you want to visit, though even in a taxi you may be let out on one of the main roads and have to walk a little way to reach your target. For information, the township has a **Soweto Tourism**

Centre, which is scheduled to reopen in 2005; it's in Madhlala Street next to the colourful chimneys of the power station. There's also some useful information about Soweto's sights and tourist infrastructure at ⓦ www.soweto.co.za, run by a local tour operator.

Orlando West and Dube

Set in the northern part of Soweto, **Orlando West** and **Dube** qualify as two of its more affluent suburbs, with a number of sights and the greatest concentration of places to eat and drink. Orlando East, across Klipspruit Valley from Orlando West, was the first part of Soweto to be established in 1932, and the area is fairly easily accessible off the Soweto Highway (M70).

The Soweto uprising of 1976

The **student uprising** that began in Soweto in June 1976 was a defining moment in South African history. The revolt was sparked off by a government ruling that **Afrikaans** should be used on an equal basis with English in black secondary schools. While this was feasible in some rural areas, it was quite impossible in the townships, where neither pupils nor teachers knew the language.

On June 16, student delegates from every Soweto school launched their long-planned mass protest march through the township and a rally at the Orlando football stadium. Incredibly, details of the plan were kept secret from the omnipresent *impimpis* (informers). Soon after the march started, however, the police attacked, throwing tear gas and then firing. The crowd panicked, and demonstrators started throwing stones at the police. The police fired again. Out of this bedlam came the famous photograph of Hector Petersen, bleeding at the mouth, being carried by a friend, while a young girl looks on in anguished horror.

The police retreated to Orlando East, and students rushed to collect the injured and dead, erect barricades, and destroy everything they could belonging to the municipal authority, including beer halls. The attacks heightened the antagonism between the youth and many older people who thought that class boycotts were irresponsible, given the students' already dismal employment prospects. Students responded angrily, accusing their elders of inactivity in the face of oppression, which they attributed in part to drunkenness. In a society that has traditionally regarded respect for the old as sacrosanct, this was a historic departure and its effects still reverberate throughout South Africa's townships.

In the days following June 16, all Soweto schools were closed indefinitely, thousands of police were stationed throughout the township, and police brutality continued unabated. In the face of worldwide condemnation, the government insisted that there was no real problem, ascribing the violence to Communist agitation. As evidence, it cited the clenched-fist salutes of the students, though this was really an indication of their support for South Africa's **Black Consciousness Movement**, founded by Steve Biko (see p.419). Meanwhile, rebellion spread to other townships, particularly in Cape Town. In Soweto, schools did not reopen until 1978, by which time many students had abandoned any hope of formal education. Some had left the country to join the military wings of the ANC and PAC, while others stayed at home, forming "street committees" to politicize and police the communities. Others drifted into unemployment.

Now the armed struggle is over, the problems that face the former students of 1976 are manifold. As their parents warned, their lack of qualifications count against them in the job market, even if June 16 is now a national holiday, during which they are praised for their role in the struggle. The street committees have dissolved, but the guns remain.

On Plea Street in the heart of Orlando West, the **Hector Petersen Memorial and Museum** (daily 10am–5pm; R10), opened in 2002, was named after the first student to be killed in the Soweto uprising (see box, p.619). Dedicated to Petersen and the other students who died, the museum focuses specifically on the events surrounding and leading up to the Soweto uprising. The startling brutality used in the repression of student activists is depicted in video and pictures, including images from well-known black photographers such as Peter Magubane and Sam Nzima.

Vilakazi Street, a few hundred metres to the southwest, was once home to Nelson Mandela and Desmond Tutu. Mandela's bungalow is where he lived with Winnie in the late Fifties and early Sixties, before his imprisonment on Robben Island, and where Winnie lived until exiled to the Free State (from which she returned to an imposing brick house with high walls and security cameras, just down the road). On his release, Nelson insisted on returning to his old home, but its smallness and lack of security proved too much of a strain, and he moved out of Soweto. Opened up by Winnie, tours of the old bungalow, **Mandela House** (daily 10am–4.30pm; R20), mix fascinatingly mundane memorabilia and large amounts of pro-Winnie propaganda. Rather spoiling the scene is a new coffee shop and restaurant crudely tacked onto the outside of the house.

About 1500m away, near the junction of Klipsruit Valley (the M10) and Potchefstroom (the M68) roads, is **Regina Mundi Church**, Soweto's largest Catholic church and the focus of numerous gatherings in the struggle years. Again, its impact owes more to historical aura than anything particularly notable about its features, although with so few large buildings in the township it achieves a certain presence. Inside, look out for the **art gallery** displaying and selling the work of various Sowetan artists. Church services here, as in all townships, are friendly affairs, with liberal doses of fantastic music and, depending on the denomination, religious ecstasy too. If you attend, be prepared to give at least a small testimony – a brief rundown of your spiritual life to date. Services last several hours, but no one will think it a crime if you leave before the end.

Other tourist attractions will undoubtedly develop, such as **Freedom Square** – currently a combination of wasteland and taxi rank – in **Dube**, where the ANC's Freedom Charter was proclaimed to thousands in 1955. In the meantime many visitors enjoy paying a visit to the various **shebeens**, restaurants and even coffee shops that are making a big effort to attract outsiders as well as locals. We've listed the best in "Eating" on p.623.

Eating

The wealth, diversity and fast-paced social life of Johannesburg means that the city has a huge range of places to **eat out**, from chic fusion cafés to formica-tabled Chinese eating dens without English menus, and from meat-guzzling steakhouses to wonderfully graceful Thai restaurants. Cultural interaction was obstructed for so long that a cuisine unique to the city has never emerged, but such is the cosmopolitan nature of Jo'burg that authentic French, Italian and Portuguese restaurants are all found here, and there are increasing numbers of African restaurants, not just township South African but also Congolese, Moroccan and Cape Malay. **Prices** are inevitably a bit higher than elsewhere in the country outside Cape Town and the Winelands, and you can blow out in spectacular style, but an average meal out is still good value.

All of Jo'burg's **shopping malls** are well stocked with takeaways and restaurants, frequently unadventurous, bland chains, though some very top-notch venues do exist in malls. If you don't fancy heading out even for a takeaway meal, you can make use of a service called Mr Delivery, which picks up and delivers meals from a range of reasonable mid-market eating places: contact them on Ⓦ www.mrdelivery.com or by phone on ☏ 011 482 4748 (Melville), ☏ 011 442 4411 (Rosebank) or ☏ 011 784 6000 (Sandton).

CBD and central suburbs

There are one or two truly original lunch options in downtown Jo'burg, but at night **Newtown** is the only area where you're likely to eat out. Given the relative lack of a tourist market, the choices here are all local favourites, often serving decent African food.

Gramadoelas at the Market Theatre Wolhuter St, Newtown ☏ 011 838 6960. One of the best-known spots for excellent Cape and African dishes like *sosaties*, *mopane* worms and *melktert*. The visitors' book is star-studded. Not cheap. Closed Sun & Mon lunch.

Horror Café 15 Becker St, Newtown. An unusual two-storey bar and café between the Cultural Precinct and the SAB centre, serving decent pub grub.

Kapitan's 11a Kort St ☏ 011 834 8048. Located upstairs in a decrepit-looking building near Diagonal St, and gloomy and kitsch inside, this Jo'burg classic serves delicious South African curries. It was Mandela's favourite eating place in the Fifties when he worked as a lawyer nearby – his letter from prison holds pride of place. Mon–Sat lunchtime only.

Kofifi Newtown Cultural Precinct. Lively bar and restaurant directly opposite the Market Theatre, serving inexpensive burgers and simple African dishes, occasionally with live music.

Moyo's @ the Market Wolhuter St, Newtown ☏ 011 838-1715, Ⓦ www.moyoafrica.co.za. The decor – carved wood and welded metal – creates a distinct South African ambience; a great variety of African food and music by local artists complete the experience. There's a more spectacular branch at Melrose Arch (see below).

The northern suburbs

A number of suburbs have small, interesting eating places; the key places to try are Seventh Street in **Melville**, the junction of Greenway and Gleneagles in **Greenside** (sandwiched between Jan van Riebeeck Park and Parktown North), Grant Avenue in **Norwood** (to the east of Houghton) and, to a lesser extent, Fourth Avenue in **Parkhurst** (west of Parktown North).

Rosebank, Hyde Park, Melrose and Sandton

See the map on p.614 for the locations of the places below.

2 Thai 4 On the corner of Cross St and Corlett Dr, very near Melrose Arch ☏ 011 440 3000. A quality, mainstream Thai restaurant, easy-going and with decent prices.

Cranks The Mall, Cradock Avenue, Rosebank. *Cranks* cooks up a storm with its Bangkok go-go bar theme; the menu extends to Vietnamese and Indonesian dishes, and there's live music Friday and Saturday nights.

Montego Bay Sandton Square, Sandton ☏ 011 883 6407. Pricey but lip-smackingly good seafood (including fresh oysters) together with slick service.

Moyo Melrose Arch ☏ 011 684 1477, Ⓦ www.moyoafrica.co.za. In the very upmarket Melrose Arch complex, this stylish venue covering five floors offers an excellent variety of African dishes, from chicken with Ethiopian spices to ostrich steaks, along with performances of dance and music, often by established local or international acts.

Osteria Tre Nonni 9 Grafton Ave ☏ 011 327 0096. This is one of Jo'burg's best Italian restaurants, with a range of food from northern Italy, and a comfortable ambience. Great homemade *grappa* liqueurs round off the evening. Book ahead. Closed Mon & Sun.

Plaka 3 Corlett Drive, Melrose North ☏ 011 788 8777. A long-established, unpretentious spot with no shortage of local Greek custom delighted to sample the real thing.

The Red Chamber Upper Mall, Hyde Park Corner, Hyde Park ☏ 011 325 6048. A good spot for medium-priced Chinese food in rather plusher surroundings than you tend to get in Chinatown.

Greenside, Houghton and Parkhurst

Anno Domini On the corner of Fourth Ave and Thirteenth St, Parkhurst ☏ 011 447 7634. A pleasant, quiet Italian restaurant serving better than average pizza and pasta fare. The upstairs balcony is great on warm summer evenings.

Circle 141 Greenway, Greenside ☏ 011 646 3744. Their fusion menu introduces all sorts of interesting flavours, and trendy Jo'burgers flock here. Don't be discouraged when your bread arrives in a brown paper bag – they do want you to hang around. Closed Sun & Mon.

Karma Gleneagles Road, Greenside ☏ 011 646 8555. A small but stylish modern Indian restaurant specializing in tandooris, with a few fusion dishes thrown in for good measure.

La Rustica 103 Houghton Dr, Houghton. Hidden away in a leafy area close to Observatory, this cosy restaurant serves up delicious, moderately priced Italian fare.

Ruby Grapefruit 24 Fourth Ave, Parkhurst. A fun and funky little sushi bar, open during the daytime only, with healthy snacks and drinks also on offer.

Melville

The places reviewed here are shown on the map on p.612.

Nuno's Seventh St ☏ 011 482 6990. This moderately priced, popular restaurant offers tasty Portuguese food and a down-to-earth atmosphere.

Pomegranate 79 Third Ave ☏ 011 482 2366. Set in a typically charming Melville house, *Pomegranate* offers a high-quality, innovative international menu with Thai overtones. Closed Sat lunchtime & Sun.

Sam's Café 11 Seventh St ☏ 011 726 8142. Smarter than its name implies, and comfortably sophisticated, *Sam's* serves mostly Mediterranean dishes which are reliably tasty, at moderate

prices (particularly the specials). Closed Sat lunchtime & Sun.

Service Station Corner of Ninth St and Rustenburg Rd. A superbly stylish café/deli housed in a converted garage, it serves original, classy food including breakfasts, tasty sandwiches and great cakes. Daytime only.

Soi Corner Seventh St and Third Ave ☏ 011 726 5775. With understated but exquisite bamboo and dark wood decor, this classy and popular Thai/Vietnamese restaurant serves authentic food at reasonable prices.

Bryanston, Morningside and Randberg

Bistro 277 Cramerview Centre, 277 Main Rd, Bryanston ☏ 011 706 2837. Deep in the northern suburbs but away from the glitzy malls, this long-standing favourite serves excellent – if expensive – traditional French provincial cooking in pleasant, spacious surroundings. Closed Sat lunchtime.

The Codfather 1 First Ave, on the corner of Rivonia Rd, Morningside ☏ 011 803 2077. Select fresh fish from the vast displays, then watch as it's scaled, filleted and cooked to order. Hugely popular, with a sushi bar alongside. Daily noon–10pm.

Fruits and Roots Hobart Corner Shopping Centre, Grosvenor Rd, Bryanston. One of the city's top organic, health and wholefood shops, with a great sandwich bar/café alongside. Mon–Wed daytime only, Thurs–Sat till 8.30pm.

Jimmy's Killer Prawns Piazza Centre, corner of Jan Smuts Ave and Republic Rd, Randburg ☏ 011 886 8844. A big noisy restaurant, with a long menu offering large helpings of seafood. The expansive views of the city lights are entirely appropriate. Closed Sat lunchtime & Sun evening.

East of the centre

The key area for dining in the eastern part of the city is **Norwood** (east of Houghton), where Grant Avenue offers little else but wall-to-wall cafés and restaurants. The more adventurous can explore **Kensington** with its homely feel and **Cyrildene**, home of the city's new Chinatown, between Observatory and Bruma.

Asia d'Afrique 43 Grant Avenue, Norwood ☎011 728 9340. Fine dining in a relaxed setting. There's a range of fusion foods, including some South African dishes.

Benkei 48 Grant Ave, Norwood ☎011 483 3296. A chic, authentically Japanese restaurant filled with pictures of sumo wrestlers.

Sechuan Garden Derrick Avenue, Cyrildene. Great, authentic Chinese food, though don't expect English menus or explanations.

Senor Prego Corner of Fifth and Broadway, Kensington ☎011 614 8850. A Portuguese restaurant that isn't particularly sophisticated or classy, though the flavours are genuine and spicy.

Soweto

Soweto **tours** all stop off for a meal in a local restaurant, bar or *shebeen*, and so long as you're not part of a huge group of tourists, it's not a bad way to meet some locals. If you're heading to Soweto under your own steam or with a local contact, any of the places below are worth checking out and will give you a warm welcome. Commonly, some kind of meat and pap is the main dish on offer, often with local favourites such as tripe or ox shin as an alternative.

Kwa-thabeng 9138 Zone 6 Extension, Pimville. A friendly restaurant serving typical South African dishes with à la carte selections as well as a buffet. There's a pleasant outdoor seating area.

The Rock 1987 Vundla Drive, Rockville. A popular and trendy venue for eating, drinking and dancing, with DJs or live jazz on offer most nights. The roof deck is a wonderful spot to unwind, get an overview of Soweto, and enjoy a sundowner.

Sakhumzi 6980 Vilakazi St, Orlando West. Situated in the heart of Soweto, next to the home of Desmond Tutu, they feature typical Sowetan food in their buffet.

Shana's Place 9136 Pimville ☎072 127 1619. Located on Enoch Sontoga Hill overlooking Orlando is this classy bar-café which has the Soweto

yuppies flocking. Cappuccino, cocktails and food available.

Vardos Place 2525 Ngalela St, Mapetla ☎083 260 3970. One of the most upwardly mobile *shebeens* in Soweto, a burgeoning open-plan bar and club under one of the township's few thatched roofs. Come to shoot pool, watch sport or admire the newly installed water features. At the time of writing they were also building guest rooms.

Wandie's Place 618 Makhalamele St, Dube ☎011 982 2796. Once Soweto's archetypal tourist-friendly *shebeen*, now well on the way to becoming the area's smartest eating spot, though it retains its popularity with locals. Local African food predominates.

Drinking, nightlife and entertainment

Johannesburg has always offered the best **entertainment** and **nightlife** in South Africa: the city draws top performers from all over the world, and its well-integrated audiences are the most sophisticated around. Though newspapers offer some event pointers, the best way to find out what's on is to listen to the local radio stations (see box on p.625) and keep your eyes peeled for roadside posters and leaflets. *SA Citylife* magazine has a good blend of features and listings, but only comes out monthly; the *Mail & Guardian* newspaper, published on Fridays, carries decent listings and articles on the main events, while the daily *Star* newspaper tracks mainstream cinema and theatre. For information on **spectator sport** in Johannesburg, see p.624. Tickets for most events can be booked through Computicket (☎011 445 8000 or 083 915 8000, ⓦwww .computicket.com).

Clubs and bars

Johannesburg is the country's most desegregated city, which has improved nightlife greatly. Add to that the stylish fashion sense of many Johannesburg *jollers* (good-timers), and their celebrated love of a party, and you have the main ingredients for a memorable night out. In many parts of the city, particularly

Sport is big anywhere you go in South Africa, but in Johannesburg it's an obsession. Here you'll find the biggest stadiums and the biggest teams, and watching a match can be a great experience. The major **cricket** games, including five-day test matches, are played at the **Wanderers Stadium**, off Corlett Drive, Illovo (☎011 788 1008), though if you look carefully at the touring programme for any visiting international teams you may find fixtures scheduled to be played in Soweto or Alexandra.

The towering **Ellis Park** in downtown Jo'burg (☎011 402 8644) is a South African **rugby** shrine, particularly since the triumph there of the Springboks in the 1995 World Cup. As well as hosting international fixtures it's also home ground to the provincial Gauteng Lions team. The best way to get there is to make use of the park-and-ride system which operates for big games, with buses shuttling in from car parks outside the centre.

Despite what you'll hear from white Jo'burgers, however, the big sport is **soccer**, and like any self-respecting football-mad city there's an intense local rivalry among teams, fuelled by scandal, intrigue and mutual loathing, which keeps squads of sports reporters in work. In Jo'burg (and, more particularly, Soweto), you're either a fan of **Kaiser Chiefs** or **Orlando Pirates**, and a local derby draws crowds of 50,000 either to FNB Stadium, on the NASREC road on the outskirts of Soweto, or Ellis Park, scene of a tragic crush at a Chiefs-Pirates game in 2001 in which over fifty fans died. It's perfectly possible to go to a home game of either team: tickets are cheap, the atmosphere is festive and normally trouble-free, and there is secure parking. FNB is quite easy to reach off either the M2 motorway from the eastern suburbs or the Soweto Highway from the centre of the city. Orlando Stadium in Soweto also hosts major games, though it's more rundown and less safe than the FNB. Tickets for big games can be obtained from Computicket.

the **northern suburbs**, straight-drinking pubs and bars have been replaced by combination café/bar/restaurants, open most hours and commonly located in malls and shopping centres. Avoid pretentious "cigar bars", which tend to be upmarket and artificial, but don't be surprised to find Irish theme pubs and sports bars, thronged with local revellers. The adventurous can enjoy some excellent nightlife in the **CBD** and **central suburbs**, though to sample the happening clubs of Hillbrow and Yeoville you're advised to go with a knowledgeable local. For Soweto *shebeens* you can visit during the day, see "Eating" on p.623; at night, only head to the townships in the company of a guide.

CBD and central suburbs

Base On the corner of Twist and Kotze streets, Hillbrow. This club has a heavy sound system and an excellent chill-out balcony overlooking the busy street. At weekends, it attracts a well-dressed, cosmopolitan crowd, and plays soul and *kwaito*, occasionally live. It's in the heart of Hillbrow, so make sure you can get there and away again safely.

Carfax 39 Pim St, Newtown ☎011 834 9187. A seriously hip alternative venue, offering performance art, jazz bands and highly rated resident DJs.

Horror Café 15 Becker St, Newtown ☎011 838 6735. Consistently features good DJs and cutting-edge music.

Northern suburbs

Rosebank, Melrose, Sandton and Parkmore

Calabash Benmore Gardens, Benmore Rd, Sandton. A venue for hardcore R&B and funk, popular at weekends with a smart, young black set. The midweek West African theme nights are worth checking out.

Kilimanjaro Melrose Arch, Melrose. One of the more upmarket "afro-chic" nightclubs with DJs spinning hip-hop, R&B and *kwaito* until the early hours. Dress codes are strictly enforced at the door, and you have to be at least 25 to get in.

Sublime 130 Eleventh St, Parkmore ☎011 884 1649. A short way northwest of Sandton is this

Given that a large percentage of the population can't afford to own a TV, and many Jo'burgers spend a lot of time in their car, **radio** is big in Gauteng. In fact, listening to the radio is one of the essential ways to pick up news, gossip and the general Jo'burg vibe, and if you're in town for a few days it's worth flicking around the airwaves to sample some of the local stations. Not all are in English, of course, but don't let that put you off; the following is a selection of the current favourites.

Alex FM 89.1FM. Broadcasting out of the Alexandra township, Alex FM can be picked up in most northern and some eastern suburbs. It focuses on township issues, but avoids excessive worthiness, and plays a fine selection of soul, R&B, reggae, *kwaito* and gospel, making it one of the most musically reliable stations around.

Highveld Stereo 94.7FM. Endless classic mainstream tracks, soft rock and Celine Dion for the white northern suburbs.

Khaya 96.9FM. For listeners who are too old and boring for YFM, Khaya has a mellower mix of mainstream *mbaqanga* and jazz, with good information on who's playing live in Johannesburg. Audible citywide.

Radio 702 702MW. A well-established local talk-radio station famed for its lively discussion programmes, excellent presenters and news coverage.

Voice of Soweto 87.6FM. On which Soweto's finest DJs spin some great contemporary sounds; audible in Soweto and adjoining suburbs.

YFM 99.2FM. The station for under-21s. A blistering introduction to the upwardly mobile young black culture of Johannesburg, with wall-to-wall *kwaito*, slick news bulletins and risqué phone-ins. Available throughout Jo'burg.

---

smart dance venue with big-name DJs playing house and hip-hop sounds.

Melville

Buzz 9 On the corner of Seventh St and Third Ave. A seriously stylish bar, where everyone seems to relax after one or two of the speciality cocktails, and the vibe carries on late into the night.

Catz Pyjamas Main Rd. A 24hr bar and food stop; it's nothing special during daylight hours, but gets more interesting when the clubs spill out in the wee small hours.

Cool Runnings Fourth Ave. A hugely popular Jamaican-themed bar, with drumming sessions and comedy, decent food and lots of Red Stripe beer and rum.

Ratz Seventh St. A slightly grungy but perennially popular bar, usually going strong long into the night.

Live music

Although Johannesburg dominates the South African music scene, a lack of venues means that it's not always easy to track down good live music. Friday and Saturday nights are the busiest times for gigs. Large concerts tend to happen at the Standard Bank Arena in Ellis Park, in the eastern part of the centre, or the FNB Stadium on the way to Soweto. Medium-sized acts generally play in the Newtown Cultural Precinct, especially at the Newtown Music Hall.

The Newtown Cultural Precinct and a couple of venues in the northern suburbs are the best bets for live **jazz**, while **rock** groups find an eager young audience in the northern suburbs, and **kwaito** bands attract enthusiastic crowds in Hillbrow and Yeoville. In Soweto there are hundreds of excellent clubs and all-night street parties, though live music is hampered by the lack of suitable venues. A number of bars and clubs have occasional live acts, but normally feature DJs – some of these are listed in "Clubs and bars" above. As for **classical music**, South Africa's National Symphony Orchestra performs regularly at Linder Auditorium in Parktown (☎011 714 4501).

CBD and central suburbs

House of Tandoor 26 Rockey St, Yeoville. Yeoville's main live-music venue, specializing in ragga and reggae, is still lively, if a bit seamy – only come here if you're confident about being in the area at night.

Kippies Market Theatre/Newtown Cultural Precinct, on the corner of Bree and Wolhuter streets ☎011 838 1271, ⓦwww.kippies.co.za. Probably the country's most famous jazz venue, Kippies has for years hosted South Africa's finest jazz acts – not bad for a former municipal toilet. Sadly, it was earmarked for closure as we went to press, as the building has become unsafe, but may reopen elsewhere.

Newtown Music Hall Market Theatre/Newtown Cultural Precinct ☎011 834 2761. This mid-sized venue has good acoustics and both standing and seated areas, but the ventilation is lousy when it's busy.

Northern and eastern suburbs

The Blues Room Village Walk Mall, Sandton ☎011 784 5527, ⓦwww.bluesroom.co.za. Quite smart (as you'd expect for Sandton), but also refreshingly mixed and lively, and featuring some of the best blues sounds in town.

Morgan's Cat Randburg Waterfront, Randburg ☎011 886 4408. Rock and pop bands play for free to suburban teenagers in a rather synthetic environment.

The Radium 282 Louis Botha Ave, Orange Grove ☎011 728 3866. A Portuguese restaurant with live music four nights a week. On the first Sunday of every month, don't miss the entertaining eighteen-piece band doing lively jazz and swing.

Roxy's Rhythm Bar 20 Main Rd, Melville ☎011 726 6019. A large, veteran establishment hosting local indie bands, and a raucous student favourite. The rooftop bar is great on summer nights.

Theatre, opera, dance and film

The Civic Theatre in Braamfontein and the Market Theatre in Newtown are Johannesburg's premier venues for **theatre** and **opera** productions, but there are several other good venues, and the city is blessed with some innovative arts companies, including the Johannesburg Youth Theatre. Johannesburg **dance** is

Johannesburg arts festivals

Johannesburg hosts regular festivals in nearly every artistic field. These include:

Arts Alive Festival ☎011 673 9272, ⓦwww.artsalive.co.za. Every Sept. The city's major festival for the performing arts takes place over three weeks at various venues, mainly in the Newtown Cultural Precinct, but also in some townships. Live music dominates, but dance, cabaret and theatre are also well represented. "Jazz on the Lake", on Zoo Lake, is a mainstay of the festival, and always features major South African artists in front of big crowds.

FNB Vita Dance Umbrella Wits Theatre, Braamfontein ☎011 482 4140, ⓦwww.at.artslink.co.za/~arts. Three weeks during Feb & March. Africa's largest festival of dance and choreography hosts international companies but also acts as the major national platform for work by South African talent such as Robyn Orlin and Boyzie Cekwana.

Heritage Weekend Run by Parktown & Westcliff Heritage Trust (office open Mon–Fri 9am–1pm; ☎011 482 3349). On the second weekend in Sept there are tours and special events around the magnificent Parktown mansions of the Randlords.

Joy of Jazz Festival Newtown Cultural Precinct ☎011 726 2610, ⓦwww.joyofjazz.co.za. Late Aug/early Sept. A weekend festival which draws the cream of South African jazz, including Pops Mohamed and Hugh Masekela, along with international guest stars.

undergoing a revival: key players are the Moving into Dance Academy, which is rearing new generations of South African choreographers, and the Dance Factory in the Newtown Cultural Precinct.

Civic Theatre Loveday St, Braamfontein ⊕011 877 6800, ⊛www.showbusiness.co.za. A good mix of both mainstream and more adventurous productions at this impressive, four-stage venue.

The Dance Factory Newtown Cultural Precinct ⊕011 833 1347. An interesting but irregular programme – check local papers for details.

Market Theatre Newtown Cultural Precinct ⊕011 832 1641, ⊛www.markettheatre.co.za. The venue for some of Johannesburg's finest

stage productions and top-grade visiting music acts; also celebrated for its innovative community theatre, and the odd costly epic.

Pieter Toerien Theatre Montecasino, Fourways ⊕011 511 1818. Stages heavyweight productions as well as comedies, musicals and touring shows.

Theatre on the Square Sandton Square, Sandton ⊕011 883 8606. One of the few theatres in the northern suburbs, featuring lightweight drama and a handful of mainstream music or cultural acts.

Cinemas

The multiscreen Nu-Metro and Ster-Kinekor cinemas control the movie market and can be found all over the city, especially in shopping malls. The *Mail & Guardian* newspaper contains good cinema listings. The venues below feature independent and foreign films.

Hyde Park IMAX Theatre Hyde Park Mall ⊕011 325 6182. Impressive short films on the vast IMAX screens, mostly on natural history themes.

Northcliff On the corner of Weltevreden and Arbor streets, Blackheath ⊕011 782 6816. In the northwest of the city, off Beyers Naude Dr, this shows a good selection of art-house movies.

Rosebank Cinema Nouveau Mall of Rosebank, Rosebank ⊕011 880 2866. Presents itself as the *grande dame* of the avant-garde, offering

a hip selection of flicks to a discerning audience.

Sandton Sandton City, Sandton ⊕011 784 3113. A pleasant cinema with a good programme, surrounded by over twenty other screens showing mainstream movies.

Village Walk Nu-Metro Village Walk Mall, Rivonia Rd, Sandton ⊕011 883 9558. One art-house venue squeezed between action-movie screens, in a rather nondescript uptown mall.

Shopping

Johannesburg is a magnet for consumers from all over the subcontinent, who zoom down the city's highways to stock up before heading back the same day. For visitors, the city is the best place in South Africa to find **arts and crafts**, with excellent flea markets and galleries offering a plethora of goods, some of very high quality. As the queen of **mall culture**, Johannesburg is also home to over twenty major malls (typically open daily 8am–6pm), most of which are depressingly anonymous, though the handful listed below are so plush and enormous that they arguably merit visiting in their own right.

Malls

Hyde Park Mall Jan Smuts Ave, Hyde Park. Trendy and upmarket, awash with swanky cafés and *haute couture* outlets. The excellent Exclusive Books chain has a good branch here.

Randburg Waterfront Republic Rd, Randburg. Built around an artificial lake, this popular if slightly downmarket centre offers restaurants, a

flea market and a cinema alongside the clothes shops and chain stores.

Rosebank Mall On the corner of Baker and Cradock streets, Rosebank. One of the city's nicest malls, with exclusive boutiques, craft shops and – unusually – outdoor cafés, restaurants and walkways.

Sandton City Shopping Centre On the corner of Sandton Dr and Rivonia Rd, Sandton. Linked to the seriously opulent Sandton Square mall, this enormous mall has a mind-boggling abundance of shops (including some good bookshops), plus cinemas and African art galleries.

Craft shops and markets

44 Stanley Avenue On the southeastern edge of Melville, where Empire Rd meets Kingsway. A trendy new complex with cafés, restaurants, art galleries, and a wide variety of shops selling art and antiques.

Art Africa 62 Tyrone Ave, Parkview ☎011 486 2052. West of the zoo, this has a good selection of innovative and more familiar crafts, many ingeniously created out of recycled material.

Bright House Bamboo Centre, on the corner of Ninth St and Rustenburg Rd, Melville ☎011 726 5657. Inspiringly stylish contemporary interior design shop, with an impressive selection of South African products, most items made locally yet with very little sign of "ethnic" influences.

Bruma Lake Flea Market Bruma Lake, east of the centre. A huge, permanent market of mostly African crafts and souvenirs, mainstream and fairly inexpensive.

M2 Highway CBD. An informal market stretching underneath this major artery, a few blocks south

of Anderson St. Most stalls specialize in *umuthi* folk medicine, but there are plenty of local crafts as well.

Market Africa Newtown. The city's liveliest flea market, next to the Market Theatre; rifle through colourful blankets from Mali, Congolese masks and statues, and more. Sat 9am–4pm.

Michael Mount Organic Market Culross Road, off Main Rd, Bryanston ☎011 706 3671. Right-on collection of stalls selling lovely organic food, unusual home crafts and handmade clothes. Thurs & Sat mornings.

Rosebank Rooftop Market Mall of Rosebank, 50 Bath Ave, Rosebank. An entertaining place with an impressive array of cottage-industry crafts and clothes. Sun 9am–5pm.

Rural Craft Shop 42E, Mutual Gardens, Rosebank ☎011 788 5821. This non-profit-making city outlet for various craft cooperatives around South Africa makes a refreshing alternative to hard-sell pavement hawkers. Mon–Fri 10am–4pm, Sat 9am–1pm.

Bookshops

Books Galore Shop 2B on Main Road, Melville (☎011 726 6502) and 66 Tyrone Ave, Parkview (☎011 486 4198). These friendly shops offer a good selection of secondhand books.

Exclusive Books South Africa's biggest and best bookshop chain, with all the latest titles. There are branches in many malls, but the best shops are in: Hyde Park Mall, Jan Smuts Ave, Hyde Park (☎011

325 4298); Sandton Square (☎011 748 5416); Killarney Mall, Houghton (☎011 646 0931); and The Mall of Rosebank (☎011 447 3028).

Out of Print 78 Fourth Avenue, Melville ☎011 482 6516. A great little antiquarian and second-hand bookseller, open till 9pm every day of the week, with a tiny internet café at the back of the shop.

Music shops

The Musica chain of shops, found in most malls, concentrates on soul and rock import CDs, with small selections of local music. In the CBD there are dozens of small shops selling cassettes of South African as well as American sounds.

Bizarre Generation On the corner of Rockey and Raymond streets, Yeoville. The best rave music shop in Johannesburg.

Cadence Tropical Calton Centre, CBD ☎011 331 3100. South Africa's finest stock of Central and West African music, and *the* place to find out about clubs currently playing these sounds.

CD Wherehouse Mutual Square, Rosebank and

Sandton City, Sandton. Best selection of CDs in Johannesburg, with all the latest local and international sounds, good deals and helpful staff.

Kohinoor 54 Market St, CBD. Excellent vinyl selection, as well as a range of tapes and CDs. The focus is on jazz, but you'll find all manner of South African styles here, ranging from gospel to *maskanda* and *mbaqanga*.

Listings

Airlines Air France, Oxford Manor, 196 Oxford Rd, Illovo ☎011 770 1600; American Airlines, Hyde Park Corner, Jan Smuts Ave ☎011 325 5777; British Airways/Comair, 195 Jan Smuts Ave, Rosebank ☎011 441 8600; KLM Royal Dutch Airlines, Sable Place, 1a Stan Rd, Morningside ☎011 881 9696; Lufthansa, 22 Girton Rd, Parktown ☎086 1842 538; Qantas, 195 Jan Smuts Ave ☎011 441 8550; SA Airlink, South African Airways & SA Express, at the airport ☎011 961 1700; Virgin Atlantic, Hyde Park (Shopping Centre), Jan Smuts Ave ☎011 340 3400.

American Express The Zone, 177 Oxford Rd, Rosebank (☎011 880 8382); Sandton City Shopping Centre, Sandton Dr (☎011 883 1316).

Banks and exchange All the main shopping malls have banks where you can change money.

Car rental Standard deals are available from the main companies such as Avis (☎0861 021 111); Budget (☎011 392 3929); EuropeCar/Imperial (☎0800 011 344); and Tempest (toll-free ☎0860 031 666). For cheaper, local deals try Apex (☎011 402 5150), Comet (☎011 453 0188) or Swans (☎011 975 0799). It's also always worth asking at your accommodation if they have any discount arrangements.

Hospitals State-run hospitals with 24hr casualty departments include Johannesburg Hospital, Parktown (☎011 488 4911); Helen Joseph, Auckland Park (☎011 489 1011); Hillbrow, Hospital Rd, Hillbrow (☎011 720 1121); and Baragwanath, Zone 6, Diepkloof, Soweto (☎011 933 8000). Private hospitals include Millpark Hospital, Guild St, Parktown (☎011 480 5600), and Morningside Medi-Clinic, off Rivonia Rd in Morningside (☎011 282 5000).

Internet access It's very easy to get online in Jo'burg – most malls have at least one Internet café.

Post offices Most major suburbs have a centrally located post office. The main poste restante post office is on Jeppe St. Make arrangements instead with your accommodation, or use Amex.

Swimming & gyms Public swimming pools around Johannesburg are not always kept in great repair, one exception being the superb, outdoor, Olympic-sized Ellis Park pool (Sept–March Mon–Fri 6.30am–9pm, Sat & Sun 6.30am–6pm). As for gyms, try the chain of Virgin Active gyms around the city (☎0860 200 911, ⓦwww.virginactive.co.za); some hotels can give you a voucher valid for one visit to the gyms, otherwise you can pay the single-visit fee of R50.

Taxis Maxi Taxis (☎011 648 1212) are the most reliable for almost all parts of town. Otherwise Rose Radio (☎011 403 9625 or 011 403 0000), Good Hope (☎011 725 6431) and Metro (☎011 484 7975) cover most of the city. Taxis often also wait outside the large hotels.

Around Johannesburg

Johannesburgers wanting to get away from it all tend to head northwest in the direction of the **Magaliesberg mountains**, stretching from Pretoria in the east to Rustenberg in the west. Don't expect to see a horizon of impressive peaks: much of the area is private farmland running across rolling countryside, although there are some impressive *kloofs*, as well as refreshingly wide vistas after the crowded roads and high walls of the big city.

Unprepossessing as the mountain range might be, a series of caves on their southeastern (Johannesburg) side hold some of the world's most important information about human evolution stretching back some three and a half million years. These caves, including the renowned Sterkfontein Cave, are now protected as part of the **Cradle of Humankind**, one of South Africa's first World Heritage Sites.

The Magaliesberg has a well-developed tourist network of small arts and crafts workshops, game parks, outdoor activities and places to stay. Most of these, both in the Cradle of Humankind and beyond, are part of either the **Crocodile Ramble** or the **Magalies Meander**, two tourist routes well promoted in the area. South of the city, the **Suikerbosrand Nature Reserve**, 40km from Johannesburg, is the biggest and best nature reserve in Gauteng, offering interesting archeology and good hikes.

The Cradle of Humankind

Covering some 47,000 hectares, the **Cradle of Humankind** is the name given to the area in which a series of dolomitic caves have in the last fifty years or so produced nearly two-fifths of the world's hominid fossil discoveries. Given its accessibility and the richness of the finds, it has now arguably overtaken Tanzania's Olduvai Gorge as Africa's (and therefore the world's) most important paleontological site.

As yet, the tourist facilities are few: many of the caves are fragile, and jealously protected by the scientists working on them. However, you can see inside the famous **Sterkfontein Caves**, and there are excellent specialized paleontological tours available (see box below). Elsewhere within the Cradle are largely unrelated attractions, such as the **Rhino and Lion Nature Reserve** and the **Kromdraai Wonder Cave**.

To reach the Cradle of Humankind by **car**, head west out of Johannesburg on the R47 (Hendrik Potgieter Road) or M5 (Beyers Naude Drive), then follow the N14 until the R563 junction. A few kilometres northwest along the R563 is a right turn which will take you to the Sterkfontein Caves turn-off. The other attractions in the area are further along this road.

Sterkfontein Caves

The best-known of the Cradle of Humankind sites are the **Sterkfontein Caves** (Tues–Sun 9am–5pm; ☎011 956 6342; R25, ⓦwww.sterkfontein-caves.co.za), believed to have been inhabited by pre-human primates who lived here up to 3.5 million years ago. They first came to European attention in 1896, when an Italian

> ### Mrs Ples and friends
>
> Embedded in the dolomitic rock within a dozen caves in the area now called the Cradle of Humankind are the fossilized remains of **hominids** which lived in South Africa up to 3.3 million years ago. Samples of fossilized pollen, plant material and animal bones also found in the caves indicate that the area was once a tropical rainforest inhabited by giant monkeys, long-legged hunting hyenas and sabre-toothed cats.
>
> Quite when hominids arrived on the scene isn't certain, but scientists now believe that the human lineage split from apes in Africa around five to six million years ago. The oldest identified group of hominids is *Australopithecus*, a bipedal, small-brained form of man. The first *Australopithecus* discovery in South Africa was in 1924, when Professor Raymond Dart discovered the **Taung child** in what is now North West Province. In 1936, australopithecine fossils were first found in the Sterkfontein Caves, and in 1947 Dr Robert Broom excavated a nearly complete skull which he first called *Plesianthropus transvaalensis* ("near-man" of the Transvaal), later confirmed as a 2.6 million-year-old *Australopithecus africanus*. Identified as a female, she was nicknamed "**Mrs Ples**", and for many years she was the closest thing the world had to what is rather confusingly dubbed "**the missing link**".
>
> A number of even older fossils have since been discovered at Sterkfontein and nearby caves, along with evidence of several other genus and species, including *Australopithecus robustus*, dating from between one and two million years ago, and *Homo ergaster*, possibly the immediate predecesor of *Homo sapiens*, who used stone tools and fire.
>
> If you're keen to learn more about this fascinating topic and want to visit some of the caves and dig sites not open to the general public, you could try one of the excellent **tours** offered by Palaeo-Tours (☎011 837 6660 or 082 804 2899, ⓦwww .palaeotours.com), run by Colin Menter, a paleontologist working at the University of Witwatersrand.

lime prospector, Gulgimo Martinaglia, stumbled upon them. Martinaglia was only interested in the bat droppings, and promptly stripped them out, thus destroying the caves' dolomite formation. Archeologist Dr Robert Broom excavated the caves between 1936 and 1951; in 1947, he found the skull of a female hominid (nicknamed "Mrs Ples") that was over 2,500,000 years old. In 1995, another archeologist, Ronald Clarke, found "Little Foot", the bones of a 3,000,000-year-old walking hominid, with big toes that functioned like our thumbs do today. In 1998 an *Australopithecus* skeleton discovered here was the oldest complete specimen known, reckoned to be 3.3 million years old.

Fairly well-informed, if rather short, **guided tours** of the cave leave every hour (departing on the half-hour) and take you around the main features.

Kromdraai Wonder Cave and the Rhino and Lion Nature Reserve

The only other cave with open public access is the **Kromdraai Wonder Cave** (daily 8am–5pm; R25), located on the edge of the Rhino and Lion Nature Reserve to the northeast of Sterkfontein. Also mined for lime in the 1890s, this cave hasn't revealed any paleontological finds, and the main focus of attention is the extraordinary stalactites, stalagmites and rimstone pools to be found in a huge underground chamber. Once you've descended into the cave by a lift, carefully placed lighting and marked trails make the experience theatrical and unashamedly commercial. For a few more thrills, you can **abseil** into the cave rather than use the lift – make arrangements with Wild Cave Adventures (℡011 956 6197 or 082 632 1718). The easier route to the cave is through the Rhino and Lion Nature Reserve, although you'll have to pay the entrance charge to the reserve; the alternative route is on a longer, rough dirt road on the left before you get to the nature reserve.

The fourteen-square-kilometre **Rhino and Lion Nature Reserve** (daily 8am–5pm; R60) is really more a safari park than anything resembling a wilderness game reserve as found in other parts of South Africa, but it is the principal place in the area for seeing large mammals. The main section of the reserve has white rhino, wildebeest, hartebeest and giraffe roaming free, while the Lion and Predator Camp has several large enclosures containing lions, cheetahs and wild dogs. Elsewhere, there's a vulture hide for seeing Cape vultures, a series of hippo pools and a breeding centre. Game drives, horse trails and mountain-bike trails are also all available – contact the Conserv Booking and Information Office (see below). They can also organize a visit to the nearby **Old Kromdraai Gold Mine**, the second-oldest mine on the Witwatersrand, where you can follow the original mining tunnel 150m into the hillside.

Practicalities

A dedicated **information centre** for the Cradle of Humankind is due to open sometime in late 2006, located on the R563 a little beyond the turn to the Sterkfontein Caves. Alternatively, useful information on tours, local adventure activities and accommodation in the area can be gathered at the Conserv Booking and Information Office (daily 8am–7pm; ℡011 957 0034) located 3km from the Sterkfontein Caves.

It is possible to **stay** in or near the Cradle of Humankind: the *Cradle Forest Camp* in the private Cradle Game Reserve (℡011 659 1622, ⓦwww.thecradle.co.za; ❹) has self-catering two-person chalets, and the restaurant here, *Cornuti*, is renowned for its fine food, modern, minimalist decor and great views, as well as regular jazz evenings. More upmarket is *Toadbury Hall* (℡011 659 0335, ⓦwww.toadburyhall.co.za; ❻), a colonial-style country lodge, while the rather old-fashioned *Aloe Ridge Hotel* (☎011 957 2070; half board ❹) has the unique attraction of a 25-inch telescope and a resident astronomer. You can come here simply for a meal, or stay in a specially erected Zulu village of grass huts (❷). Other accommodation options include the self-catering chalet sleeping four in the Rhino and Lion Nature Reserve (❹) and the many hotels and guesthouses advertised through the Magalies Meander and Crocodile Ramble (see below).

Magalies Meander and Crocodile Ramble

An increasingly popular way of promoting different localities in South Africa is to describe some kind of **route** through them. At the information centre on the banks of the Crocodile River in the village of **MULDERSDRIFT**, barely beyond the suburbs of northwest Jo'burg, you can pick up a hefty brochure listing all kinds of attractions and places to visit on the **Crocodile Ramble** (☎011 957 3745, ⓦwww.crocodileramble.co.za). It's worth remembering that many of these are aimed at locals escaping for the weekend rather than tourists; highlights of the route include a number of artists' workshops, including the Swazi glass factory of Nwgenya. Muldersdrift also boasts the fairly pricey *Carnivore* **restaurant** at the *Misty Hills Country Hotel*, 69 Drift Blvd (☎011 957 2099), where you can join crowds of white South Africans as they devour crocodile, giraffe, ostrich and buffalo, along with more humdrum meat dishes.

Meanwhile, to the northwest of the area covered by the Crocodile Ramble, a group of local attractions known as the Magalies Meander has as its focal point **MAGALIESBURG** village, on the R24 west of Krugersdorp. Named after Mohali Mohale, a chief of the Po clan of the Ndebele people, the village is functional and not wildly attractive, providing stressed city-dwellers with accommodation and facilities amid fresh mountain air. You can pick up a map and brochure for the meander from Magaliesburg Information and Reservations (daily 8am–4pm; ☎014 577 1733), located in the village's Magaliesburg Mall on Rustenburg Road.

For a leisurely day-trip from Johannesburg, it's sometimes possible to travel to Magaliesburg by **train**: the Magalies Express (☎011 888 1155) runs mainly during the summer months, and the fares for the three-hour return journey are quite reasonable at around R110. A more unusual mode of transport locally is the **balloon** flights run by Bill Harrop's "Original" Balloon Safaris (☎011 705 3201 or 082 379 5296, ⓦwww.balloon.co.za), which take off from a site between Magaliesburg and Hartbeespoort Dam.

Accommodation

If you're planning to stay in the Magaliesburg area, be sure to book **accommodation** ahead, especially at weekends. The nicest (and priciest) place to stay by far is *Mount Grace*, Rustenburg Road (☎014 577 1350, ⓦwww.grace.co.za; ❻), a hotel magnificently located on a hilltop, and offering immaculate and stylish rooms. The restaurants here are superb, and classical concerts are held outside on the last Saturday of every month during the summer. For impressive B&B, *Out of Africa* (☎014 577 1126 or 082 900 8205, ⓦwww.goblins.co.za /africa; ❺) offers luxury riverside cottages, tastefully decked out with antique furniture and original art. Alternatively, you can get a better feel of the rolling, open landscapes of the countryside at *Wind in the Willows* (☎014 557 3401 or 083 657 3401; ❺), self-catering cottages set on a horse stud 15km west of the village along the R509, from which it's signposted, with good trails nearby for horse-riding or hiking.

Suikerbosrand Nature Reserve

Though hardly in the same league as the epic parks of Kruger and the like, the **Suikerbosrand Nature Reserve** (daily 7am–3:30pm; R20 per person, R10 per vehicle), south of Johannesburg, is nonetheless attractive, and easy to reach from the city. The beautiful Suikerbosrand mountain range dominates the reserve, but you'll find gentle grassland plains too, with antelope, zebra and wildebeest, even the odd cheetah and leopard.

The **visitor centre**, at the entrance to the reserve, can supply maps and guidebooks. Next door, the **Diepkloof Farm Museum** is worth a visit, as careful renovation has ensured that the farm buildings look pretty much as they did when they were first built in 1850. The farm was worked by one Gabriel Marais, a veteran of the Great Trek, but it was burnt by British soldiers in the Anglo-Boer War, and remained neglected until its renovation in the 1970s. Most of the exhibits are aimed at Afrikaner children, in the hope of interesting them in their rapidly disappearing rural culture. However, other brief displays dwell on the extensive sixteenth- to nineteenth-century settlements of Sotho and Tswana people excavated nearby.

To get to the reserve and farm you can take the N3 south of Johannesburg, and turn right onto the R550. The turning to the reserve is a few kilometres along the road, on your left. You can **explore the reserve** on foot or by car, following a network of trails. Several hiking trails include overnight **accommodation** in camps (book at the visitor centre; ☎011 904 3933). Alternatively, you can book the very basic meditation hut, 18km from the visitors' centre; there's no electricity, but it's definitely quiet and undisturbed.

Pretoria and around

Gauteng's two major cities are just 50km apart, but could hardly be more different. With its graceful government buildings, wide avenues of purple flowering jacarandas, and staunchly Boer farming origins, **PRETORIA**, or ePitoli as it is known in the townships, has throughout much of its history been the epitome of staid traditionalism. Yet although South Africa's administrative capital was long regarded as a bastion of **Afrikanerdom**, home to the notorious supreme court and a massive prison, things are changing fast. Ever since the nation's re-acceptance into the international arena, Pretoria has become increasingly cosmopolitan, with a substantial diplomatic community living in Arcadia and Hatfield, east of the city centre. Furthermore, most Pretorians are not Afrikaner, but Sotho and Ndebele, and the change of government has brought many more well-educated and well-paid blacks into the ranks of civil servants living in the capital. The city's Afrikaner community is hardly monolithic, either: as well as the stereotypical khaki-shorted rednecks, there are thousands of students, an active art scene and a thriving Afrikaans gay and lesbian community.

Pretoria is close enough to Johannesburg's airport to provide a practical alternative base in Gauteng. It feels safer and less spread out than Johannesburg (though don't fall into the blithe assumption that Pretoria is crime-free), there are more conventional sights, and the **nightlife** is energetic and fun.

Some history

Unlike Johannesburg, Pretoria developed at a leisurely pace from its humble origins as a **Boer farming community** on the fertile land around the Apies River. When the city was founded in 1855 by **Marthinus Wessel Pretorius**, who named it after his father, Andries Pretorius, it was intended to be a unifying hub around which the new South African Republic (ZAR) would prosper. Embodying the Afrikaners' conviction that the land they took was God-given, Pretoria's first building was a church. The town was then laid out in a grid of streets wide enough for teams of oxen brought in by farmers to turn corners.

In 1860, the city was proclaimed the capital of the new ZAR, the result of tireless efforts by Stephanus Schoeman to unite the squabbling statelets of the Transvaal. From this base, the settlers continued their campaigns against local African peoples, bringing thousands into service, particularly on farms. Infighting also continued among the settlers, and violent skirmishes between faction leaders were common. These leaders bought most of the best land, resulting in the dispossession and embitterment of many white trekkers, and also in the large-scale massacre of the wild animals of the region, particularly its elephants.

The British annexed Pretoria in 1877, and investment followed in their wake. Although the town prospered and grew, farmer **Paul Kruger**, who was determined not to be subjugated by the British again, mobilized commandos of Afrikaner farmers to drive them out. This resulted in the first Anglo-Boer War (1877–81). After defeat at Majuba on the Natal border, the colonial government abandoned the war and ceded **independence** in 1884. Paul Kruger became ZAR president, and ruled until 1903. However, his mission to keep the ZAR Boer was confounded by the discovery of **gold** in the Witwatersrand, which precipitated an unstoppable flood of foreigners. Kruger's policy of taxing the newcomers, while retaining the Boer monopoly on political power, worked for a while. Most of the elegant buildings of Church Square were built with mining revenues, while the Raadsaal (parliament) remained firmly in Boer hands. At the same time, the ZAR's military arsenal grew, largely thanks to imported German weapons.

ZAR independence ended with the second Anglo-Boer War (1899–02), but, despite the brutality of the conflict, Pretoria remained unscathed. With the creation of the **Union of South Africa** in 1910, the city became the administrative capital of the entire country. In 1913, Sir Herbert Baker built the epic Union Buildings to house the civil service, and some ministries, including the office of the president, are still there today.

In 1928, the government laid the foundations of Pretoria's industry by establishing the **Iron and Steel Industrial Corporation** (Iscor), which rapidly generated a whole series of related and service industries. These, together with the civil service, ensured white Pretoria's quiet, insular prosperity. Meanwhile, increasing landlessness among blacks drove many of them into the city's burgeoning **townships**. Marabastad and Atteridgeville are the oldest, and Mamelodi is the biggest and poorest.

After the introduction of apartheid by the National Party in 1948, Pretoria acquired a hated reputation among the country's black population. Its supreme court and central prison were notorious as the source of the laws and regulations that made their lives a nightmare.

Mandela's inauguration at the Union Buildings in 1994 was the symbolic new beginning for Pretoria's political redemption. Through the 1990s, the stages of South Africa's revolution could be seen as clearly in Pretoria as anywhere else: the gradual replacement of the diehards from institutions like the

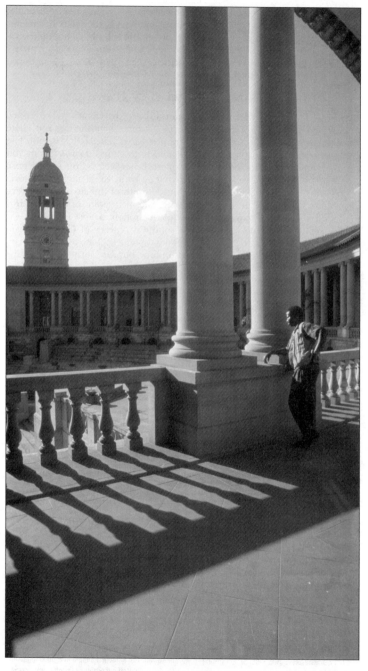

△ Union Buildings, Pretoria

army and civil service, new faces in almost all the old government offices, the return of foreign representation, aid agencies and NGOs, the influx of students and the change in demographics of the city-centre suburbs. While the newcomers have absorbed a good deal of the sense of decorum which was always a hallmark of Pretoria, even in the apartheid years, they have also imparted creativity and vibrancy to the capital city.

Arrival, information and city transport

The nearest airport to Pretoria is **Johannesburg International Airport**, some 50km away to the southeast (see p.597), from where the Get You There Airport Shuttle provides transport to Pretoria (℡012 361 0363; R150). The taxi fare from the airport to Pretoria is unlikely to be less than R250, or you could arrange with your accommodation to be collected from the airport, usually for an extra charge. If you're arriving by **train** you'll alight at Pretoria station, designed by Sir Herbert Baker, to the south of the city centre; **inter-city buses** stop beside the station building. The main point of **information** for Pretoria – or **Tshwane**, as the greater metropolitan area is known – is the Tourist Information Centre on the southwest corner of Church Square (Mon–Fri 8am–4pm; ℡012 337 4337, ⓦwww.pretoria.co.za/tourism).

Pretoria's city centre is easily explored on foot, but for journeys to the suburbs, you'll need the municipal **bus** services, which start in Church Square. You buy tickets – which are never more than a few rand – when you get on; timetables are available from Church Square, where there's a bus information office (℡012 308 0839), as well as on the buses themselves and from pharmacies.

The best place to catch **minibus taxis** is from the corner of Jacob Maré and Bosman streets, just north of the railway station, though you can hail them from anywhere. As in Johannesburg, you can't generally hail metered **taxis**, though you'll usually find one on or near Church Square; alternatively, cabs can be booked ahead by phone (see "Listings" on p.647).

Accommodation

With plenty of government custom, Pretoria has no shortage of soulless modern **hotel** complexes, most run by multinational chains. A much nicer option is to stay at one of the few hotels and guesthouses with genuine character. Unlike in Johannesburg, you can feel reasonably comfortable staying close to the centre, although there isn't much nightlife here – for that, you might prefer to base yourself in Hatfield or Brooklyn, where there are a number of excellent guesthouses.

Backpackers can choose from a good selection of **hostels**, most of which are in the Sunnyside, Arcadia and Hatfield districts. Most offer transfers from the airport, which are among the cheapest you'll find. As with Jo'burg, it's worth booking your first night before you arrive.

Backpacker lodges

Kia Ora Backpackers 257 Jacob Maré St ℡012 322 4803,ⓔhostel@absamail.co.za. The most central hostel in Pretoria, close to Burgers Park. While not as convivial as others, it's still a neat, comfortable hostel with decent doubles and average dorms. Food is available from a gloomy public bar where the TV is on constantly. ❶–❷

Mazuri Backpackers 503 Reitz St, Sunnyside ℡ & ℡012 343 7782, ⓦmazuri.freeservers.com.

There are few frills at this hostel, but it's a friendly, easy-going sort of place. Dorms and doubles are spread across two houses and various tacked-on extensions. ❶–❷

North South Backpackers 355 Glyn St, Hatfield ℡012 362 0989 or 082 533 2837, ⓦwww .northsouthbackpackers.com. Now established as one of Pretoria's best backpacker hostels, this neat, well-run establishment is in a good location for the lively Hatfield nightlife. On offer are dorms and plenty of doubles in a large, quiet suburban house with a great garden and pool. The owners also run a convenient travel centre. ①–②

Pretoria Backpackers 425 Farenden St, Clydesdale ☏012 343 9754 or 083 302 1976, ⊛www.pretoriabackpackers.net. A more upmarket backpacker place with plenty of doubles as well as smallish dorms spread over two lovely old houses with wooden floors, original features and a relaxing garden *stoep*. Massages and beauty treatment are available, while the knowledgeable owner, François, is a great Pretoria enthusiast and runs a useful travel centre for local tours and onward travel. ①–②

Word of Mouth 430 Reitz St, Sunnyside ☏012 343 7499, ⊛www.wordofmouthbackpackers.com. A colourful, welcoming but slightly downmarket hostel not far from the centre, with some wooden Wendy houses in the garden serving as doubles. ①–②

Hotels, guesthouses and B&Bs

Arcadia Hotel 515 Proes St ☏012 326 9311, ⊛www.arcadiahotel.co.za. This central, business-oriented hotel is a little overpriced, especially as there's no pool, but the rooms are comfortable and the restaurant reliable. ④

Arcadian Guest House 870 Arcadia St ☏012 342 4588 or 082 904 8840. A classic old house filled with antique furniture, with tiptop modern facilities such as a pool and cable TV. It's also close to Hatfield nightlife and the embassy district. ④

Battiss-Zeederberg Guesthouse 3 Fook Island, 92 Twentieth St, Menlo Park ☏012 460 7318 or 083 271 0819, ⊛www.battiss.co.za. Very comfortable B&B accommodation in the original home of eccentric artist Walter Battiss. Brightly painted floors, unusual decorations and a distinctly Greek feel. ④

Brooks Cottage 283 Brooks St, Brooklyn ☏012 362 3150 or 082 448 3902, ⊛www.brookscottage.co.za. A rather cute Cape Dutch home with three rooms, one of which is part of a self-catering unit. ③

Hotel 224 On the corner of Leyds and Schoeman streets ☏012 440 5281, ⊛www.hotel224.com. Single and double rooms in a dated-looking but fairly characterful budget hotel near the Union Buildings, with a restaurant and bar attached and safe parking. ③

La Maison 235 Hilda St, Hatfield ☏012 430 4341, ⊛www.lamaison.co.za. A very pleasant guesthouse with lovely gardens, six Victorian-styled rooms full of antiques, and an outstanding restaurant. ④

Osborne House 82 Anderson St, Brooklyn ☏012 362 2334 or 083 302 1049, ⓔosbornehouse@worldonline.co.za. A wonderfully elegant guesthouse set in a restored Edwardian manor house with lovely furniture, big windows, wooden floors and a pleasant, secluded pool. ④

Sheraton Pretoria 643 Church St, Arcadia ☏012 429 9999, ⊛www.sheraton.com/pretoria. This fine five-star hotel boasts all the usual upmarket Sheraton touches, but most importantly has the best views of the Union Buildings. If you can't afford a room with a view, head to the *Union Gardens Lounge* beside *Tiffens Bar & Lounge* for high tea. ⑦

Ted's Place 961 Wagon Wheel Ave, Wapadrand ☏012 807 2803, ⊛www.teds-place.za.net. One of the nicest places to stay on the outskirts of Pretoria, this large, elegant hilltop house offers friendly B&B with great views over the city and the Magaliesberg. ③

That's It Guest Home 5 Brecher St, Clydesdale ☏012 344 3404 or 082 781 7230, ⊛www.thatsit.co.za. A neat, unelaborate, reasonably priced B&B in a family home with four rooms and a relaxing garden and pool. ③

Victoria Hotel On the corner of Scheiding and Paul Kruger streets ☏012 323 6054, ⓕ012 324 2426, ⓔhvic@freemail.absa.co.za. This historic building opposite the train station was once the railway workers' bar; now it offers plush accommodation and is often filled with affluent travellers taking luxury trains to Cape Town. ⑤

Whistletree Lodge 1267 Whistletree Drive, Queenswood ☏012 333 9915 or 082 446 8858, ⊛www.whistletreelodge.com. Roughly 10km northeast of the centre is this small luxury boutique hotel, with beautiful antiques, eclectic artwork and stylish furniture. Facilities include a pool, sauna and private balconies. ⑥

The City

Pretoria's city centre is a compact grid of wide, busy streets, easily and comparatively safe to explore on foot. Its central hub is **Church Square**, where you can see some fascinating architecture, and there are other historic buildings and museums close by around the **Museum Park**. To the north lie the vast **Zoological Gardens**, while the Arcadia district is the site of the city's

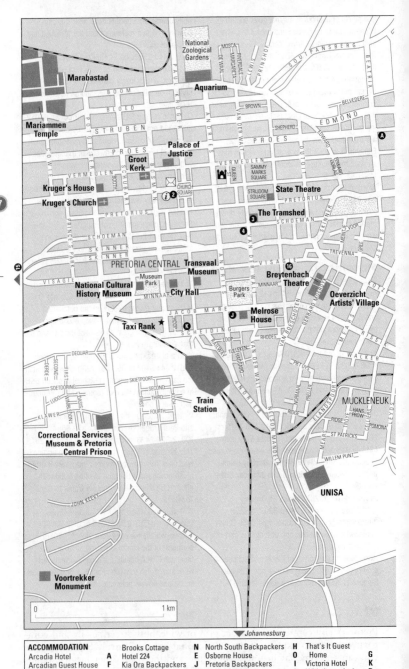

Marabastad

Mariammen Temple

National Zoological Gardens

Aquarium

Kruger's House

Kruger's Church

Groot Kerk

Palace of Justice

Sammy Marks Square

State Theatre

A

The Tramshed

3

4

PRETORIA CENTRAL

National Cultural History Museum

Museum Park

City Hall

Transvaal Museum

Burgers Park

Breytenbach Theatre

16

Oeverzicht Artists' Village

Melrose House

Taxi Rank

K

J

15

Train Station

Correctional Services Museum & Pretoria Central Prison

MUCKLENEUK

UNISA

Voortrekker Monument

0   1 km

▼ Johannesburg

ACCOMMODATION				
Arcadia Hotel	**A**	Brooks Cottage	North South Backpackers	**N**
Arcadian Guest House	**F**	Hotel 224	**E**	Osborne House	**O**
Battiss-Zeederberg		Kia Ora Backpackers	**J**	Pretoria Backpackers	**I**
Guesthouse	**P**	La Maison	**D**	Sheraton Pretoria	**C**
		Mazuri Backpackers	**M**	Ted's Place	**Q**

That's It Guest	
Home	**G**
Victoria Hotel	**B**
Whistletree Lodge	**B**
Word of Mouth	**L**

PRETORIA

N

Union Buildings

TOM JENKINS

G. WASHINGTON BLVD

THE ROTUNDA

WENLOCK

COLBYN

ROTHSAY

GOVERNMENT

GEORGE

MERTON

THOMAS

CHURCH (KERK)

PRETORIUS

GAUTENG

7

1 & 8 ▶ Hatfield Plaza, Hatfield Square

D

PRETORIUS

SCHOEMAN

HATFIELD

ARCADIA

Pretoria Art Museum

F

ARCADIA

PARK

Loftus Versveld Stadium

7 8

9

BURNET

PROSPECT

Pretoria University

H 10 11 12 13 14 ▶

18 19 ▶

SUNNYSIDE

LYNNWOOD

N ▶

BROOKS

ANDERSON

MURRAY

O ▶

BROOKLYN

COLLEGE

MARAIS

CHARLES

NICOLSON

MACKIE

P ▶

Austin Roberts Bird Sanctuary

Brooklyn Mall & Plaza

GEORGE STORRAR

BRONKHORST

TRANSOERDER

GIOVANETTI

Q ▶

▶ Anton Van Wouw Museum

RESTAURANTS, CAFÉS, BARS & CLUBS

Blue Crane	20	Crawdaddy's		DNA	4	Mostapha's	13	Pride of India	22
Café Bugatti	7	Crazy Nut	23	Drop Zone	11	Mozzarellas Italian		Safrika	16
Café Riche	2	Crossroads	25	Eastwood Tavern	6	Kitchen	10	Tings and Times	8
Club @	19	Blues Bar		Gerrard Moerdyk	3	News Café	12	Upstairs at	
Cool Runnings	9	Die Werf	15	Hillside Tavern	1	O'Galito	18	Morgan's	14
				The Grapevine	17	Pelagos	24	Wang Thai	21

639

famous **Union Buildings**. Away from the centre, **Hatfield**, close to Pretoria University, is where students and yuppies throng the latest bars and restaurants, as well as being the home of Pretoria's diplomats, who live in the swankiest houses in town.

On the southern fringes of the city is the remarkable **Voortrekker Monument**, as close as the Afrikaner race have to a sacred site. You need to travel 15km east out of town to find the sprawling township of **Mamelodi**; Pretoria's other major township, **Atteridgeville**, is equally far out of town to the west, off the N4, or R104, on the way to the Hartbeesport Dam and Sun City.

Church Square and the city centre

The heart of Pretoria is undoubtedly **Church Square**, surrounded by dramatic and important buildings, and a place where you can at least try to put South Africa's complex history into perspective. It was here that Boer farmers *outspanned* their oxen when they came into town for the quarterly Nagmaal (Holy Communion) of the Dutch Reformed Church, turning the square temporarily into a campsite. Today this spot continues to be a meeting point for Pretorians of all races, many of whom you'll see lounging on the grass in the sun, gathering to protest with placards and singing, or simply watching it all go on while sipping coffee at the cultured *Café Riche*.

Nearly every important white meeting, protest or takeover the city has known happened in Church Square; the ZAR Vierkleur ("four colours") flag was lowered here in 1877 to make way for the Union Jack, only to rise again in 1881, after the British eviction from the republic; the British flag flew again in 1900 but was lowered for the last time in 1910; Paul Kruger was proclaimed head of state in the square four times, and 30,000 crammed it in 1904 for his memorial service. Such historical resonances are viewed differently by Pretoria's black community, and the square's central **statue of Paul Kruger** – the work of Afrikaner sculptor Anton Van Wouw – is for many an unwanted relic of a dismal past. Van Wouw had to work fast: Kruger hated posing and the sculptor had little time with him. Nevertheless he still managed to produce this frighteningly miserable representation, set above four rugged Voortrekker archetypes; today, the pigeons which squat on his top hat provide a suitably subversive touch.

The Continental-style square is surrounded on all sides by some of the most impressive buildings in South Africa. Look out for the old **Raadsaal** (parliament) on the southwest corner of the square, built in neo-Renaissance style in 1891, and still exuding the bourgeois respectability yearned for by the parliamentarians of the ZAR. Across the narrow side street from this is the Capitol Theatre, rarely used now as a performance space but home to Tshwane Craft Market. Next door to this is the **Netherlands Bank Building**, now home of the tourist office. Unbelievably, it took a gathering of 10,000 people in 1975 and five years of deliberation to reverse a decision to demolish this building and its two neighbours. The Art Nouveau **Café Riche** (see p.646), on the corner of Church Square, adds a sophisticated and cultured touch to the day-to-day business of the area; it's a handy source of information, and here you can buy a booklet or rent a cassette player explaining the history and architecture of the square.

On the opposite side of Church Street is the imposing **General Post Office**, beside which is a **Stamp Museum** (Mon–Fri 7.30am–4pm; free) displaying over half a million stamps, including a rare Cape Triangle of 1853. The grandiose **Palace of Justice**, on the northwest side of the square, was started in 1897 and, half completed, was used as a hospital for British troops during the second Anglo-Boer War. After its completion in 1902, the building was home to the Transvaal Supreme Court for many years and was the location of the Rivonia Trial in 1963–64, when Nelson Mandela and other leaders of the ANC were sentenced to life imprisonment. Recent restoration work has revealed and repaired the splendid facade and balconies, although the new court is an ugly box sitting squatly in a street behind the Palace. Next to this is the **Reserve Bank** building, designed in distinctive style by Sir Herbert Baker (see box on p.610). Other buildings of note around the eastern and northern side of the square include the **Tudor Chambers**, built in neo-Tudor style in 1904, and the Neoclassical **Standard Bank** building on the site of the old *Grand Hotel*.

Sammy Marks Square and around

East of Church Square, Church Street takes you towards Sammy Marks Square. Just before you get there, a left turn into Queen Street and a further left turn along a passageway halfway down the block reveals the unexpected site of a bright white **mosque** sitting askew of its surroundings so as to face Mecca. Pretoria's Muslims, who reportedly got on well with Kruger, acquired the site in 1896, and the current building was constructed in 1927 by Cape artisans. The mosque is now hemmed in by ugly tower blocks, but is somehow all the more indomitable for that.

Garish **Sammy Marks Square** itself, dominated by modern shopping malls filled with chain stores, is named after the founder of South African Breweries (SAB), who was a patron of the city. The only thing worth checking out here is the excellent **library** (Mon–Fri 8am–5.50pm, Sat 8am–12.50pm; ☏012 313 8956), geared to adult education, with every available space decked out in Pretoria's trademark purple.

Across Church Street is **Strijdom Square**, so named because it was the location of a vast and horrific bust of the man himself, encased in a modernistic arch. Prime minister from 1954 to 1958, Strijdom strongly supported apartheid and was a firm believer in "white supremacy". Dramatically, forty years to the day after the statue was completed on 31 May, 1961, a structural fault (or divine intervention, depending on your point of view) caused it to collapse. While many would like to see it remain a symbolic pile of rubble, others say it's high time the statue was replaced by a memorial to the seven victims of the random shooting at minibus taxis here by a right-wing delinquent namesake, Barend Strijdom, in 1993.

Paul Kruger's House and around

To find **Paul Kruger's House** (Mon–Fri 9am–4.30pm, Sat, Sun & public holidays 9am–4.30pm; R16), head west along Church Street from Church Square, crossing Bosman and Schubart streets. Kruger's House was built in 1884 by the English-speaking Charles Clark, described by Kruger as one of his "tame Englishmen", who mixed his cement with milk instead of water. Inside, the museum is rather dull, though you may find some interest in Kruger's effects, such as his large collection of spittoons. The *stoep* is the most famous feature of the house, for here the old president would sit and chat to any white who chose to join him. Out at the back is Kruger's private railway coach, built in 1898, which he used during the second Anglo-Boer War.

Opposite is a characteristically grim Reformed church known as **Kruger's Church**. The **Groot Kerk** (**Great Church**), on the corner of Vermeulen and Bosman streets, is more impressive; its strikingly ornate tower is one of the finest in the country.

Burgers Park and the Museum Park

South from Church Square lies a precinct of museums and open spaces that has drawn complimentary comparisons with Washington DC's Smithsonian Institute. On Jacob Maré Street between Andries and Van der Walt streets is the restful **Burgers Park** (daily 8am–6pm; free), named after ineffective ZAR president Thomas Burgers, who was in office between 1873 and 1877. The park has a good botanic garden, a quirkily designed curator's house and a pavilion at its centre, once the preserve of brass bands and all-white tea parties, but now multiracial and a good place to relax.

Opposite the park's southern border, **Melrose House**, 275 Jacob Maré Street (Tues–Sun 10am–5pm; R5; Ⓦ www.melrosehouse.co.za), is an overdecorated Victorian domicile with a wonderful conservatory, interesting exhibitions and a great African arts and crafts shop. The house was built in 1884 for local businessman George Heys, who made his money running mailcoach services. Lord Kitchener used the house during the second Anglo-Boer War, and the treaty of Vereeniging that ended hostilities was signed inside. Outside, a sumptuous tea garden serves cakes and scones, light meals and, on certain days, hearty South African lunches such as *bobotie* and savoury rice.

Head west of Burger Park along Minnaar Street, and then turn right into Paul Kruger Street and past a huge whale skeleton for the grand **Transvaal Museum** (daily 8am–5pm; R10), Pretoria's oldest museum and centrepiece of the Northern Flagship Institution (Ⓦ www.nfi.org.za), the collective name for Pretoria's main museums. Dedicated to natural history, the museum has plenty of stuffed animals, models of dinosaurs and wonderful fossil remains, some over a million years old. This is a good place to come if your interest in man's origins has been stirred by the discoveries of the nearby Cradle of Humankind (see p.630): alongside a bronze bust of Robert Broom staring into the three-million-year-old eye sockets of Mrs Ples are an assortment of fossilized discoveries and various models and reconstructions of early hominid life. Nearby is a selection of stuffed animals, never particularly inspiring when many of the animals can be seen in real life in game reserves not too far away. In the Austin Roberts Bird Hall, you'll find an informative exhibit on South Africa's many species of birds, while the Geoscience Museum highlights another Gauteng speciality, rocks and minerals.

Opposite the museum at the far end of a series of fountains and well-tended flowerbeds is the **City Hall**, with its eclectic mix of Greek and Roman architectural styles, and two rather good statues of Andries and Marthinus Pretorius immediately outside. The next large block to the west is taken up by the **National Cultural History Museum** (daily 8am–4pm; R8), formerly known as the **African Window**, accessed from Visagie Street. This large, airy exhibition space is, like many public collections, gradually feeling its way in the new South Africa. Generous room is given to temporary displays, although this tends to give the museum a rather tentative air. The permanent exhibitions are interesting in themselves but seem a bit unconnected. They include "Access to Power", which displays and explains San rock art, and "People's Choice", where groups of local people, including township women's groups and schoolchildren, have been invited to select objects from the museum's vast collection of some three million pieces. Also here is a room showing work by J.H. Pierneef (1886–1957), one of the country's most famous artists, who is known for his bushveld landscapes.

The zoo and the Mariammen Temple

North of Church Square, busy Proes and Struben streets are filled with cut-price stores, black shoppers and minibus taxis heading for the townships. While other parts of central Pretoria are fairly safe to walk around if you take the normal precautions, take extra care if you're wandering in this direction, as gangs have been known to work these streets, and a number of tourists have been mugged here.

Head across Bloed and Boom streets for the **National Zoological Gardens** (daily 8am–6pm; R32), which are spacious and surprisingly good, housing rare species of antelope, a white rhinoceros, and a wide selection of South American as well as African animals. A cableway (R10) carries you right over the zoo on both sides of the Apies River, and you can even rent golf cars if you're feeling lazy (R70 per hour). It's well worth trying to book one of the **night tours** (R50; ☎012 328 3265), starting at 6pm on Wednesdays, Fridays and Saturdays, when you'll see some of the zoo's freakiest creatures at their most active. Next door, the **Pretoria Aquarium and Reptile Park** (entrance included with zoo entry charge) is less impressive, but nonetheless has plenty of beasts, some very weird and highly poisonous.

West of here lie the scruffy streets of **Marabastad**, the city's first "non-white" area which, while fascinating, can feel quite intimidating; you may feel more comfortable exploring here with a guide. Don't miss the intricately decorated Hindu **Mariammen Temple**, right next to the market.

The Correctional Services Museum

The chilling **Correctional Services Museum** (Mon–Fri 9am–3pm; free) at Pretoria Central Prison is well worth a visit. Make for Potgieter Street, which runs north–south three blocks west of Church Square, and stay on it while it becomes the R101 to Johannesburg. You'll see the notorious prison, where many famous political prisoners were held (and many executed), on your right. Be prepared to walk past depressed-looking visiting relatives on your way in. Inside the museum you can see artworks made by prisoners, including a life-size statue of an inmate crawling towards an expressionless prison warder, who has his arms outstretched, ready to correct him. There are also exhibits of knives concealed in Bibles and shoes, files in cakes and so forth. Most alarming by far are the group photos of various forbidding-looking prison warders through the ages, which seem a strange sort of propaganda for the prison service.

The Voortrekker Monument

Continuing on the R101, follow the signs to view the famous **Voortrekker Monument and Museum** (daily 8am–6pm; R25; ⊛www.voortrekkermon .org.za). For many years an ominous symbol of Boer domination, the monument is now more generally accepted as one of South Africa's many cultural waypoints, and a visit does allow you some penetrating insights into the Afrikaner mindset. The striking, austere block of granite was built in 1940 to commemorate the Boer victory over the Zulu army at Blood River on December 16, 1838 (see p.561), and its symbolism is crushingly heavy-handed. The monument is enclosed by reliefs of ox wagons, with a large statue of a woman standing outside, shaking her fist at imaginary oppressors. Inside, a series of moving reliefs depict scenes from the Great Trek. Outside, hidden by some trees, are two pint-size replicas of the huts of Zulu kings Dingane and Cetshwayo.

The monument is set within a small **nature reserve** which has various hiking and mountain-bike trails, leading to lookout points over Pretoria and the surrounding countryside. You can also explore the reserve on a pony trek (book in advance on ☎012 323 0682).

Arcadia and the Union Buildings

Head east along Vermeulen or Church streets, and you'll soon reach the **Arcadia** district, where Pretoria's **Union Buildings**, the headquarters of the South African government, perch majestically on the main hill. Designed by Herbert Baker (see box on p.610) in 1910, allegedly to symbolize the union of Briton and Boer, the lashings of colonnades and lavish amphitheatre seem instead to glorify British imperial self-confidence. Nelson Mandela had an office inside, and the buildings were famously the site of his inauguration in 1994. This was perhaps the first time their imperialist symbols were transformed, not least by the African praise-singers who delivered their odes from the amphitheatre, proclaiming Mandela as the latest in a long line of African heroes from Shaka to Hintsa, and beyond. You can walk around the buildings and their gardens, and, if you're a particular enthusiast of Baker's work and the Union Buildings in particular, take one of the **tours** called The Baker's Dozen, run by the talkative Leone Jackson (around R50; ☎012 344 3197).

South of the Union Buildings, the **Pretoria Art Museum**, corner of Schoeman and Wessels streets (Tues–Sun 10am–4.30pm; R5), houses an excellent selection of South African art and Dutch Masters, as well as some black artists, including Ephraim Ngatane. There is a small gallery (same hours; free) just beyond the main entrance which is worth popping into for its contemporary exhibitions and small café.

Sunnyside

Southeast of the centre, desegregated **Sunnyside** is the central suburb with the strongest African feel, with a busy street life, distinctive old houses and a multitude of cafés. **Esselen Street** is the busiest thoroughfare, brimming with bars and street hawkers. A little way to the west, **Oeverzicht Artists' Village**, on the corner of Kotze and Gerrard Moerdyk streets, was once a lively little node of old cottages with interesting craft shops and restaurants, though there's now quite a rapid turnover of business and fewer of the venues which gave the place some spark. The **Breytenbach Theatre** at 137 Gerrard Moerdyk Street – said to be haunted by the ghosts of those who died there when it was a hospital for Germans – hosts mainly student productions.

Loftus Versveld Stadium and Pretoria University

East of Sunnyside is the huge **Loftus Versveld Stadium**, where major rugby and soccer games are played. On the other side of the railway line from here, **Pretoria University** has some excellent gallery and museum space, including an exhibition in the Ou Lettere (Old Arts) building (Tues–Fri 10am–4pm; free) dedicated to the remarkable archeological finds at Mapungubwe (see p.752), a hilltop fort by the Limpopo River which was the ancient capital of a major southern African kingdom. Among the artefacts on display are a gold rhinoceros made from thin gold foil, figurines, jewellery and decorated pots, all at least 700 years old. Also in the same building is an art gallery with changing exhibits; the university has a fantastic permanent collection, including Dutch Masters and Chinese ceramics dating back to the Han dynasty (206 BC–221 AD), but this is viewable by appointment only (☎012 420 3100).

Hatfield and Brooklyn

Beyond Pretoria University is **Hatfield**, which has developed in the last few years into Pretoria's liveliest area, with the trendiest hangouts and nightlife around Park, Burnett and Hilda streets, where you'll find a plethora of studenty cafés, bars and restaurants.

To visit the elegant house and museum of acclaimed Afrikaner sculptor **Anton van Wouw**, 299 Clark Street (Mon–Fri 10am–4pm; free), you'll need to head southeast of the university to the wealthy suburb of **Brooklyn**. Van Wouw was responsible for most of the brooding effigies of Afrikaner public figures from the 1890s to the 1930s scattered around the country, including the Kruger statue in Pretoria's Church Square (see p.640). His most famous work is the Voortrekker Monument (see p.643). The museum, designed by the celebrated architect Norman Eaton in 1938, houses a collection of his smaller pieces. Van Wouw's figures tend to be placed in rural settings, but here you'll find two striking, non-rural pieces, one of a mine worker, the other an accused man standing in the dock. Keep an eye out, too, for *The Guitar Player*, a feisty-looking woman strumming away with a trace of a smile on her face.

UNISA

Travelling south towards Johannesburg on Elandspoort Road, you can't miss the enormous and head-shakingly ugly **UNISA**, South Africa's largest university. Over 200,000 students are enrolled here – though most of them are on correspondence courses. Inside, on the fifth floor, a very good **art gallery** (Tues–Fri 10am–4pm; ☎012 429 6255; free) hosts some of Pretoria's most innovative exhibitions, as well as a permanent collection exhibiting young South African talent of all races. Telephone in advance to make sure the curator is here.

Eating and drinking

Pretoria has plenty of good **restaurants**, particularly around the Hatfield and Brooklyn areas, where they tend to congregate around a handful of popular upmarket shopping centres. If you're prepared to explore a bit further there are some very interesting places serving South African food. **Cafés** are numerous and varied; again, Hatfield is the more stylish area, although you can still find a place to sip espresso right in the city centre.

Restaurants

Blue Crane 156 Melk St, New Muckleneuk. A fairly traditional and well-turned-out restaurant in a unique location, overlooking the dam and the Austin Roberts Bird Sanctuary. Open daily for breakfast, afternoon tea and hearty, medium-priced main meals.

Brasserie de Paris 525 Duncan St, Hatfield ☎012 362 2247. This faithful reproduction of the classic Parisian café has a pleasant terrace, spacious and classy interior, smart service and a great menu. It's also quite expensive. Closed Sat lunchtime & Sun.

Crawdaddy's Brooklyn Plaza, corner Middel and Dey streets, Brooklyn. A popular and good-time Cajun-themed restaurant, serving tasty steaks and a range of decent seafood dishes.

Crazy Nut On the corner of Day and Bronkhorst streets, Brooklyn. A surprisingly large set-up incorporating a vegetarian café-restaurant and well-stocked health food store.

Die Werf Plot 66, Olympus Road, Pretoria East ☎021 991 1809. Serves up a hearty and reasonably priced selection of home-cooked *boerekos* classics, including *kerrie skaapafval* (curried tripe and trotters) and *melktart* (milk tart). Closed Sun evening & Mon.

Gerrard Moerdyk 752 Park St, Arcadia ☎012 344 4856. Beautifully prepared South African cuisine served at a price amid lavish surroundings; choose from ostrich, springbok pie and other intriguing dishes. Closed Sat lunchtime & Sun.

Hillside Tavern Rynial Building, 320 The Hillside, Lynnwood ☎012 348 1402. Moderately priced restaurant, celebrated locally for its steaks, but also serving imaginative seafood specials.

Mostapha's First Floor, Florence High, on the corner of Lynnwood and Pinaar ☎012 362 0713. The fame of Mostapha, once chef to Moroccan royalty, has spread far across Gauteng. Tasty, unusual fare and moderately priced.

Mozzarellas Italian Kitchen Hatfield Square, Burnett St, Hatfield ☎012 362 6464. Set among a range of bars and restaurants in a lively location, this offers decent and reasonably priced Italian fare as well as good steaks and seafood.

O'Galito Hatfield Rendezvous, 367 Hilda St, Hatfield ☎012 342 6610. Rich and spicy Mozambican and Portuguese dishes served in suitably grand surroundings.

Pelagos Corner of Bronkhurst and Dey, Brooklyn. Homely family-run Greek restaurant, with the usual mezes, plus some seafood and meat specialities. Mon–Sat 11am till late, Sun lunch only.

Pride of India Groenkloof Plaza, George Storrar Dr, Groenkloof ☎012 346 3684. Filled with exquisite, imported Indian artefacts and oozing class and confidence, this is the place in town for beautifully prepared North Indian curries. Closed Sat lunch & Sun evening.

Safrika Kutlwanong Democracy Centre, 357 Visagie St. The best African restaurant in Pretoria, a small, friendly place frequented by high-powered NGO officials and civil servants. The decor is fairly plain, but the food is tasty, authentic and inexpensive. Closed Sun.

Wang Thai 281 Middel St, Brooklyn ☎012 346 6230. An elegant, authentic Thai restaurant in the heart of Brooklyn, complete with noble stone carvings and calm, friendly staff.

Bars and cafés

Café Bugatti Hatfield Galleries, Burnett St, Hatfield. A popular spot for breakfasts among the Hatfield smart set.

Café Riche 2 Church Square West. One of the finest cafés in the country, boasting a Continental atmosphere and a quirky events programme, including late-night philosophical discussions. Great for Sunday brunch on Church Square. Daily 6am–midnight.

Cool Runnings 1071 Burnett St. A massively successful reggae bar which always seems to have a party going on; it also serves hearty food.

Eastwood Tavern 391 Eastwood Rd, Arcadia. A popular, often raucous pub near Loftus Versveld stadium, serving huge, inexpensive steak dishes.

The Grapevine 204 Sunnyside Galleries, Esselen St, Sunnyside. A long-established French-style café-patisserie, with generally mellow and cheerful regulars. It's also a great bakery if you want a quick takeout.

News Café Hatfield Square, Burnett St, Hatfield. Deservedly popular establishment serving breakfasts and brunches from 9.30am at weekends, and decent food well into the night all week.

Tings and Times Hatfield Galleries, Burnett St, Hatfield. One of Pretoria's happening bars, popular with students, but also a wider clientele who come for the easy-going style, the vibe and great reggae.

Nightlife and entertainment

Pretoria lacks the dynamism and breadth of Johannesburg's **arts and music** scene, but there's still a fair amount going on. Sunnyside was once the city's most dynamic area for nightlife, but it's now a bit sleazy in places. Much of the scene is now in the Hatfield and Brooklyn areas, where stylish yuppies and richer students tend to hang out. Things are very different in the township areas of Mamelodi and Atteridgeville, where plenty of small clubs play South African and soul sounds.

The city's main venue for **theatre**, **opera** and **classical concerts** is the State Theatre, Church Street (☎012 392 4000, ⓦwww.statetheatre.co.za). Under the leadership of Hugh Masakela and then Aubrey Sekhabi, it has put on an interesting programme of jazz and black theatre. Nearby in Church Square, the Basement Theatre below *Café Riche* (☎012 328 3173) is an elegant, compact venue with a good record of adventurous productions. For lively student theatre, head for the Breytenbach, 137 Gerrard Moerdyk Street (☎012 440 4834).

Pretoria's **cinemas** carry the typical selection of Hollywood fare, and the city is among the first to receive new releases. For big blockbusters, the Nu-Metro in Menlyn Park east of the centre (☎012 368 1301) is the biggest and best; there's also an IMAX screen here (☎012 368 1186). You'll find branches of the Ster-Kinekor chain at Beatrix Street in Arcadia (☎012 341 7568), and the New Brooklyn Mall in Brooklyn (☎012 346 7683). Back in the centre, on the corner of Schoeman and Van der Walt streets, the cinema in The Tramshed (☎012 320 4300) screens decent non-mainstream films. Also recommended for art-house films is the Cinema Nouveau in the New Brooklyn Mall (☎012 346 3435). *The Pretoria News* is good for theatre and cinema **listings**, while the national *Mail & Guardian* covers the visual arts, theatre and major musical events. Computicket (☎083 915 8000, ⓦ www.computicket.com) is the big central ticket outlet for most arts and sports events, with outlets in malls and department stores.

Live music and clubs

Club @ 297 Lynnwood Rd, Lynnwood. A popular, busy club with student nights and various DJs through the week.

Crossroads Blues Bar The Tramshed (upper level), on the corner of Schoeman and Van der Walt streets. A hip, downtown venue, in the same complex as the cinema, hosting rock and blues bands.

DNA 600 Van der Walt St. A popular Friday night club playing funk and progressive house. On Saturday night there's garage and hard house.

Drop Zone Hatfield Square, Hatfield. For rap and R&B sounds, and a mass of grooving students, this venue is the place. Wed, Thurs & Sat.

Upstairs at Morgan's Burnett Street, Hatfield ☎012 362 6610. Live music Mon–Sat, though it's worth phoning to check what's on, as the acts range from South Africa's hottest bands to fairly run-of-the-mill fare. There are frequent party nights and promotions, and it's popular with students.

Listings

American Express 306 Brooklyn Mall, Bronkhorst St, Brooklyn (travel section: Mon–Fri 8.30am–5pm; foreign exchange: Mon–Fri 9am–4.30pm; ☎012 346 3580, after hours ☎082 901 5910).

Banks Most banks are around Church Square and along Church St.

Bookshops Exclusive Books at the Centurion Centre in Centurion (☎012 663 3204) is the best in the city. Protea Book House, 1067 Burnett St, Hatfield (☎012 362 5683) claims to be the largest bookshop in South Africa, with a huge range of new and secondhand books.

Camping/hiking Trappers Trading, Atterbury Value Mart, Atterbury Rd ☎012 991 5585; Cape Union Mart, Brooklyn Mall, Bronkhorst Street, Brooklyn ☎012 460 5511.

Car rental Avis ☎012 301 0700; Budget ☎012 341 4650; Imperial ☎012 322 2538; Swans ☎082 658 0078; Tempest, 1117 Church St ☎012 430 2724.

Embassies and consulates Australia, 292 Orient St, Arcadia ☎012 342 3740; Canada, 1103 Arcadia St, Hatfield ☎012 422 3000; Germany, 180 Blackwood St, Arcadia ☎012 427 8900; Ireland, Southern Life Plaza, 1059 Schoemann St, Arcadia ☎012 342 5062; Lesotho, 391 Anderson St, Menlo Park ☎012 460 7648, ⓔ lesothoh@global .co.za; Malawi, 770 Government Ave, Arcadia ☎012 342 0146; Mozambique, 199 Beckett St, Arcadia ☎012 401 0300; Netherlands, 825 Arcadia St, Arcadia ☎012 344 3910; Swaziland, 715 Government Ave, Arcadia ☎012 344 1910; UK, 256 Glen St, Hatfield ☎012 421 7802; USA,

1 River St, Killarney ☎011 644 8000; Zambia, 570 Ziervogel St, Arcadia ☎012 326 1854; Zimbabwe, 798 Merton St, Arcadia ☎012 342 5125.

Emergencies Ambulance ☎10177; fire ☎012 310 6300; police ☎10111.

Flea markets Hatfield Flea Market, Hatfield Plaza (every Sun), is Pretoria's best flea market, with crafts, bric-a-brac and lively banter.

Hospitals Those with 24hr casualty services include Pretoria Academical Hospital, Doctor Savage Rd ☎012 354 1000; Pretoria West, Trans Oranje Rd ☎012 386 5111; and the private Starcare Muelmed, 577 Pretorius St, Arcadia ☎012 440 2362.

Intercity buses Intercape (☎0861 287 287), Greyhound (☎012 323 1154) and Translux (☎012 334 8000) have their terminal and office beside the train station. North Link Transport (☎011 291 1867) runs buses to Polokwane and the north from Bosman St, southwest of Church Square.

Internet cafés It's easy to find places to get online in malls and elsewhere in the city. Places you could try include: Net Café, Hatfield Square, Burnett St, Hatfield (Mon–Sat 10am–3am; Sun 10am–2am); Odyssey, Hatfield Galleries, Burnett St, Hatfield (daily 9am–11.30pm); May Vision, Shop 11, Pavilion Center, 92 Jeppe St, Sunnyside (daily 8am–2am).

Pharmacies Crest, Duncan Walk, Hatfield ☎012 362 0304; Station, 509 Paul Kruger St ☎012 323 1239; and in every shopping mall.

Taxis The best local firm is Rixi Mini Cabs (☎012 325 8072); an alternative is City Taxis (☎012 321 5741).

Tours Packers Safaris (☎012 343 9754), based at *Pretoria Backpackers*, runs the best budget tours of the city, as well as trips to Sun City and Ndebele Village. Travel the Planet (☎014 736 2176, ☻www.traveltheplanet.co.za) organizes local and regional tours; for township tours, try Moshito wa Tshwane (☎012 337 4430).

Trains Besides the usual Spoornet trains, Pretoria is served by the luxury Blue Train and Rovos Rail services. For details of all three, see "Basics", p.54.

Around Pretoria

The most absorbing sight in the immediate vicinity of Pretoria is **Doornkloof Farm**, the former home of Prime Minister Jan Smuts. Further out, to the east of Pretoria, the mining town of **Cullinan** harks back to the pioneering days of diamond prospecting a century ago, while north of the city the **Tswaing meteorite crater** and nearby **Mapoch Ndebele Village** are efforts by disadvantaged communities to create a worthwhile tourist attraction in their area. To the west, on the other hand, the **Hartbeesport Dam** and nearby **Lesedi Cultural Village** have become victims of their own popularity, and most visitors happily bypass them on their way to less crowded and more genuine attractions in the provinces beyond.

Doornkloof Farm and Rietvlei Nature Reserve

Doornkloof Farm in **IRENE**, just south of Pretoria, was the home of **Jan Smuts** for much of his life, including his periods as prime minister of South Africa. His fairly simple wood-and-corrugated iron house is now a museum (Mon–Fri 9.30am–4.30pm, Sat & Sun 9.30am–5pm; R5), which does tend toward hagiography but still manages to shed light on one of South Africa's most enigmatic politicians (see box on p.293). To get to the museum, head south from Pretoria towards Irene on the M18 or R21 for about 20km, and follow the signs to Smuts House.

The massive library on the site reflects Smuts' intellectual range, while numerous mementos confirm his internationalism. Other displays focus on Smuts' role as one of the most successful commanders of Afrikaner forces during the Anglo-Boer wars. The surrounding farm is part of the museum, and features the pleasant 2.5-kilometre **Oubaas Trail** leading from the house to the top of a nearby *koppie*, a walk the nature-loving Smuts took every day. Scattered near the house are various pieces of military hardware such as cannon and armoured vehicles – a little incongrously, given the declarations of peace and tranquillity posted along the trail and elsewhere. For refreshment, there's a **tea room** next to the house.

The **Rietvlei Nature Reserve** (Mon–Fri 7am–6pm, Sat & Sun 6am–6pm; R15), on the other side of the R21, is unspectacular but does at least offer Burchell's zebra, rhino and antelope, and plenty of birdlife.

Cullinan

Popular with tourist coaches, **CULLINAN** lies 50km east of Pretoria. It was in the town's Premier Mine, still worked today, that the world's largest diamond, the 3106-carat Star of Africa, was discovered in 1905. The De Beers mine dominates the small town, but the oldest buildings, many from the turn of the last century, are being used to cater to the swarms of tourists. Unless you take a **surface tour** of the mine (Mon–Fri 10am & 2.30pm, Sat & Sun 10am; R30), there isn't much to do other than wander around, though there are a couple of pleasant places to **eat**, including the

Station Restaurant in the old train station and the *Lemon Tree* tea garden on Oak Avenue. You can **stay** here at *The Oak House* (☎012 734 0083; ❹), Cullinan's second-oldest building, attractively set on Oak Avenue leading up to the mine.

Tswaing Crater and Mapoch Ndebele Village

Some 40km north of Pretoria, off the M35, **Tswaing Crater** (daily 7.30am–4pm; R15 unguided, R80 for a guided group tour) is one of the youngest and best-preserved meteorite craters in the world, a 500-metre-wide depression created around 220,000 years ago. Tswaing means "place of salt" in Tswana, and the rich deposits of salt and soda around the edge of the shallow crater lake have attracted people from earliest times; artefacts up to 150,000 years old have been discovered here. A simple visitors' centre marks the start of a seven-kilometre trail to the crater and back, while a shorter walk, which you can do alone or in the company of a local guide, goes to a viewpoint on the crater rim.

Around 20km west of Tswaing is **Mapoch Ndebele Village** (daily 10am–4pm; R15), where the houses and enclosures are painted with the colourful geometric patterns for which the Ndebele are famous, often incorporating modern aspects such as telephones and the South African flag. These, and the equally colourful beadwork, both among South Africa's most distinctive art forms, are always done by women. Unlike other Ndebele villages, Mapoch is relatively uncommercialized, and little attempt is made to cover up the less traditional parts of the village. Visitors are expected to pay for a guide (R10–20) in addition to the admission charge.

Hartbeespoort Dam, Lesedi Cultural Village and the De Wildt Cheetah Centre

In the Magaliesberg Mountains west of Pretoria, the man-made **Hartbeespoort Dam** has the potential to be a pleasant escape from the urban sprawl of Gauteng. Unfortunately, large numbers of Gauteng's inhabitants have already had the idea, and the dam and its surrounds have been thoroughly mauled by camping and picnic sites, animal parks, cableways, mini-resorts and endless ranks of arts-and-craft emporiums. The mid-week jams of Sandton and Randburg are simply transferred to the countryside at weekends, and petrol-heads scream up and down the dam on jet skis in much the same way as they do the M1 in urban 4WDs.

Slightly more interesting, though hardly more inspiring, **Lesedi Cultural Village** (tours daily at 11.30am & 4.30pm; R260 for the tour plus a meal and dance performance, R170 tour only; ⓦwww.lesedi.com), off the R512 south of Hartbeespoort, crams four cultural villages into one bewildering experience, with the Zulu, Pedi, Xhosa, Ndebele and Basotho all represented. Twice a day, tourists are escorted round the fairly authentic kraals, entertained by a lively display of colourful costumes, singing and dancing, then fed heartily with a **traditional African feast** in the vividly decorated restaurant. You can also **stay** the night in a grass hut with a Lesedi family (☎012 205 1394; half board ❼ including a full tour).

GAUTENG | Around Pretoria

Travel details

Trains

Johannesburg to: Bloemfontein (1 daily; 12hr); Cape Town (1 daily; 26hr 15min); Durban (1 daily; 11hr 40min); East London (1 daily; 20hr); Kimberley (1 daily; 8hr 15min); Musina (1 daily; 15hr); Nelspruit (1 daily; 9hr 45min); Port Elizabeth (1 daily; 18hr); Pretoria (32 daily; 1hr 30min).
Pretoria to: Bloemfontein (1 daily; 14hr 50min); Cape Town (1 daily; 29hr); Johannesburg (32 daily; 1hr 30min); Kimberley (1 daily; 10hr 35min); Musina (1 daily; 15hr); Nelspruit (1 daily; 8hr 20min).

Buses

Johannesburg to: Beitbridge (2 daily; 8–10hr); Bloemfontein (3 daily; 5–6hr); Cape Town (3–5 daily; 16–18hr); Durban (3 daily; 8–11hr); East London (1 daily; 11hr 30min); Kimberley (3–4 daily; 6–8hr); King William's Town (2 daily; 12hr 15min); Klerksdorp (3–5 daily; 2–4hr); Knysna (1 daily; 14–16hr); Kuruman (daily; 8hr 15min); Ladysmith (daily; 6hr 30min); Louis Trichardt (daily; 4hr 15min); Mossel Bay (2 daily; 14hr 30min); Nelspruit (2 daily; 5hr); Newcastle (1 daily; 4hr 45min); Oudtshoorn (1 daily; 13hr); Pietermaritzburg (6–7 daily; 7hr); Pietersburg (3 daily; 3hr 45min); Plettenberg Bay (daily; 15hr 30min); Port Elizabeth (3–4 daily; 16hr); Potchefstroom (1–2 daily; 1hr 30min); Pretoria (over 70 daily; 1hr); Queenstown (2 daily; 10hr); Rustenburg (daily; 2hr); Umtata (4 weekly; 12hr 45min).
Pretoria to: Aliwal North (1 daily; 9hr); Beaufort West (3 daily; 12–13hr); Bloemfontein (6 daily; 6–7hr); Cape Town (3 daily; 17hr); Durban (6 daily; 9hr); East London (1 daily; 12hr 30min); Ermelo (1 daily; 4hr 20min); George (1–2 daily; 16hr); Graaff-Reinet (daily; 11hr 45min); Harrismith (daily; 4hr 45min); Johannesburg (over 70 daily; 1hr); Kimberley (3–4 daily; 7hr); King William's Town (2 daily; 13hr 25min); Klerksdorp (1–2 daily; 3hr–4hr 30min); Knysna (2–3 daily; 16hr); Kuruman (daily; 9hr 15min); Ladysmith (daily; 7hr 30min); Louis Trichardt (daily; 5hr 15min); Mossel Bay (1–2 daily; 15hr 35min); Nelspruit (2 daily; 4hr); Newcastle (1 daily; 4hr 45min); Oudtshoorn (daily; 14hr); Pietermaritzburg (7 daily; 7hr 15min); Pietersburg (3 daily; 3hr); Plettenberg Bay (daily; 16hr 30min); Port Elizabeth (2–4 daily; 16hr); Potchefstroom (1–2 daily; 2hr 30min); Queenstown (2 daily; 10–11hr); Umtata (1 Mon, Wed, Fri & Sun; 13hr 45min).

Baz Buses

From Jo'burg, Baz Bus operates services to Durban, either via the Drakensberg (3 weekly) or via Nelspruit and then Swaziland (3 weekly), where they overnight in Manzini. For details of services from Manzini on to Durban via the Elephant Coast, see Travel details for chapter 12.

Johannesburg to: Durban (via the Drakensberg; 9hr); Manzini (Swaziland; 9hr); Malkerns Valley (Swaziland; 8hr 45min); Mbabane (Swaziland; 8hr); Mooi River (6hr); Nelspruit (5hr); Pietermaritzburg (8hr); Pretoria (separate shuttle; 30min–1hr); Winterton (4hr 30min).

Domestic flights

Johannesburg to: Bloemfontein (8 daily Mon–Fri, 3 daily Sat & Sun; 1hr 10min); Cape Town (more than 20 daily; 2hr); Durban (16 daily; 1hr); East London (7 daily; 1hr 25min); Hoedspruit (1 daily; 1hr); Kimberley (5 daily; 1hr 15min); Manzini (3–4 daily; 1hr); Nelspruit (7 daily; 1hr 50min); Polokwane (3 daily Mon–Fri, 1 daily Sat & Sun; 50min); Port Elizabeth (6 daily; 1hr 40min); Upington (1 daily; 1hr 50min).

8

North West Province

CHAPTER 8

Highlights

* **Kgaswane Mountain Reserve** Rolling hills, rocky *kloofs* and sparkling streams in the Magaliesberg mountains – ideal hiking territory. See p.660

* **Sun City** A unique fantasyland of hotels, slot machines, stage shows and lush golf courses, complete with a Lost City, opulent palace, explorable jungle and fun-filled water park. See p.662

* **Pilanesberg National Park** The Big Five park most accessible from Johannesburg and Pretoria, with beautiful landscapes and terrific game viewing. See p.663

* **Groot Marico** One of the most characterful of South Africa's tiny *dorps*, or small farming towns, famed for its literary connections and the potency of the local fruit spirit, *mampoer*. See p.666

* **Madikwe Game Reserve** An often-overlooked Big Five reserve in the corner of the Province; prepare to be pampered in some of South Africa's classiest wildlife lodges. See p.668

△ Tourist trucks, Pilanesberg National Park

8

North West Province

South Africa's **North West Province** is one of the country's least-understood regions – renowned, among tourists at least, for the famously vulgar **Sun City** resort and Big Five **Pilanesberg National Park**, but not much else. Few people venture beyond these attractions to explore this area in greater depth; consequently, it can be curiously rewarding to do so. The old-fashioned hospitality of the myriad little *dorps* scattered throughout the region, and the tranquillity of the endless stretches of grassland and fields of *mielies* (sweetcorn) make a refreshing change after hectic Johannesburg and Pretoria.

North West Province extends west from Gauteng to the Botswana border and the Kalahari desert. Along the Province's eastern flank, essentially separating it from Gauteng, loom the **Magaliesberg mountains**, one hundred times older than the Himalayas and these days dotted with holiday resorts for nature-starved Jo'burgers. The **N4** from Pretoria cuts through the mountains to the main town of the northeastern part of the Province, **Rustenburg**, gateway to the windswept **Kgaswane Mountain Reserve** where you can hike high enough to gaze down onto the shimmering plains beneath. **Groot Marico**, further west along the N4, is a friendly *dorp* with powerful home-brews and laid-back people to share them with. Further on lies the provincial capital of **Mafikeng** – famed for its siege during the second Anglo-Boer War – whilst towards the Botswanan capital, Gaborone, **Madikwe Game Reserve** is one of South Africa's undiscovered wildlife gems, a massive Big Five park which sees remarkably few visitors and boasts some superb game lodges.

If you're driving from Johannesburg to Cape Town and can afford a bit of meandering, try taking the **N12** through North West Province via Kimberley (in Northern Cape); the road follows the Vaal River for hundreds of miles, and once you're past uninspiring **Potchefstroom**, a detour to the riverbanks provides a lovely breather, particularly to **Bloemhof** for its quiet nature reserve teeming with birdlife.

Relentless sun alleviated only by torrential rain makes summer in North West Province something of an endurance test: aim to come here in spring or autumn. For the more adventurous, **camping** in the quiet and timeless veld is especially rewarding in this part of South Africa. **Tourist information** for the Province is provided by the **North West Parks & Tourism Board** (☎018 397 1500, call centre 082 232 7500, ⓦwww.tourismnorthwest.co.za), which will mail brochures and other information on request. The website ⓦwww .parksnorthwest.co.za covers the region's parks. Malaria is absent throughout the Province.

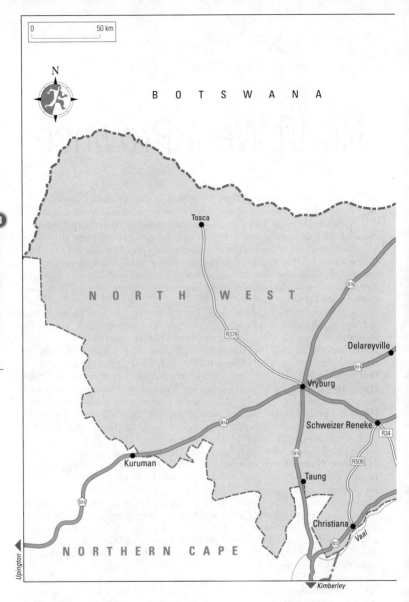

Some history

San hunter-gatherers were the Province's first inhabitants: they were displaced 500–1000 years ago by cattle-herding Iron Age peoples from the north, who pitched their first settlements on low ground near watercourses. By the sixteenth century, these settlements had developed into stone-walled towns on hilltops; the largest, Karechuenya (near Madikwe), was estimated

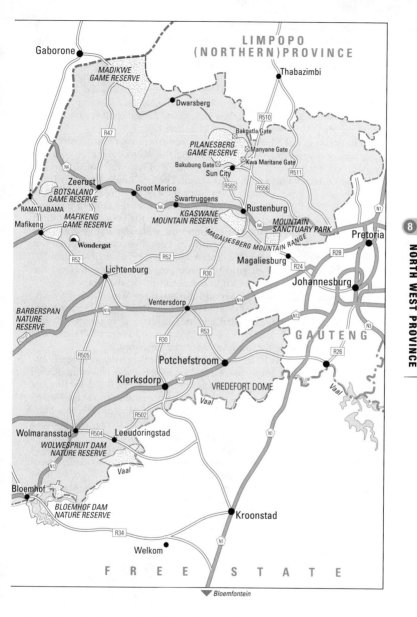

by a Scottish observer in 1820 to have at least 20,000 inhabitants – more than Cape Town had at that time. By the nineteenth century, the dominance of the Rolong, Taung, Tlhaping and Tlokwa clans was established. European observers classified them all as **Tswana**, but it's unclear whether these people regarded themselves as very different from people further east classified as "Sotho".

The outbreak of intense **inter-clan violence** in the early 1800s was due to displacements caused by the expansion of white *trekboers*, and the growing availability of firearms. Victory went to those who made alliances with the new arrivals, whether **Griqua** from the Northern Cape or **Afrikaners** from further south. The Tlhaping were soon driven out, eventually finding their way to Zambia. Mzilikazi's Ndebele ruled the region in the 1820s and 1830s, but they too were forced out, this time to modern Zimbabwe. The victories of the remaining clans were short-lived: their Griqua and Afrikaner allies soon evicted them from their land and forced them into service.

Potchefstroom and Klerksdorp were the first towns established here by the Afrikaners, and more followed, each forming the nucleus for a quarrelsome mini-state. In 1860 these mini-states amalgamated to form the **South African Republic** (ZAR), with Pretoria as its capital. The first Anglo-Boer War lasted from 1877 until British defeat in 1881, with most of the Province unaffected. In 1885, the British successfully fought the Afrikaners of the Goshen Republic near Mmabatho (Mafikeng) and established the protectorate of north and south Bechuanaland – the north later became Botswana, while the south was annexed to the Cape Colony by Cecil Rhodes in 1895. British intervention meant that some land remaining in Tswana hands stayed that way, but by then the clans had lost almost everything. When **gold** was discovered on the Witwatersrand and around Klerksdorp, Tswana men left in droves to work in the mines.

Of far greater impact was the **second Anglo-Boer War** (1899–1902). As well as the celebrated **siege of Mafikeng**, where British and Tswana forces held out for 217 days against Afrikaner troops, there were protracted skirmishes up and down the Vaal River. Both Afrikaner and Tswana had their lands torched, and many were thrown into concentration camps.

The Union Treaty of 1910 left the Province, as the western part of the Transvaal, firmly in Afrikaner hands. Its smaller *dorps* soon became synonymous with rural racism, epitomized in the 1980s by the fascistic AWB led by **Eugene Terreblanche**, whose power base was here. The migration of so many Tswana men and the lack of industrial development impeded the growth of a black working class in the Province, which is why North West Province played a relatively minor role in the national struggle against apartheid.

The **Bophuthatswana** Bantustan – or "Bop" – was created in 1977 out of the old "native reserves", the poor-quality land into which Tswana had been forced. Far from being a long-awaited "homeland" for blacks, Bop proved to be a confusing amalgamation of enclaves, ruled by the corrupt **Lucas Mangope**, who grew rich on the revenues from **Sol Kerzner**'s casinos in Sun City and Mmabatho and the discovery of platinum. Bophuthatswana's short life came to an end in March 1994, a month before South Africa's elections, when its army mutinied. Mangope called in hundreds of armed AWB neo-fascists to help quell the uprising, but the AWB – and Mangope – were ingloriously defeated. One of the more evident hangovers of the Bop legacy is the former capital, **Mmabatho**, now absorbed into Mafikeng, the capital of North West Province, where huge government buildings and endless civil service offices seem hopelessly out of proportion to, and out of keeping with, the wider province.

Bojanala Region

Bordering Gauteng, **Bojanala Region** lies in North West Province's north-eastern bushveld, and is increasingly popular as a weekend destination for

Jo'burgers. Given that large parts of the province are empty and flat, one of the region's more distinctive assets is the **Magaliesberg mountain range**, which gets its name from the Tswana chief **Mogale** of the Kwena clan. Kwena people lived here from the seventeenth century until 1825, when most of them were forced out by the Ndebele chief **Mzilikazi**. Afrikaner farmers continued the process of eviction, and today the dispossession of the Kwena in the Magaliesberg is complete. The Magaliesberg's great asset is that it's easily accessible from Johannesburg and Pretoria, with the result that great chunks have been fenced off and turned into time-shares or resorts. Nevertheless, there are oases of unspoilt nature, notably **Kgaswane Mountain Reserve** – accessed from the region's main town, **Rustenburg** – and the **Mountain Sanctuary Park**, both preserved in something like their previous natural state and well stocked with wildlife. The southeastern Magaliesberg mountains, which are more easily accessed from Johannesburg and Gauteng, are covered in Chapter 7.

Further north, occupying an ancient volcanic crater, is the outstanding **Pilanesberg National Park** – the "Big Five" mainstay of Gauteng-based safari operators. If you're in the mood for a fun-in-the-sun waterpark and some surreal tourist opulence, **Sun City** is worth checking out, if only as a stopover on your way in to Pilanesberg.

Rustenburg and around

Some 120km northwest of Johannesburg lies the platinum-mining town of **RUSTENBURG**, the oldest of the Province's towns. With its grid of prefabricated chain stores and shopping malls, the place is a pretty dreary hymn to misguided town planning. Still, you'll probably end up staying if you're visiting the glorious **Kgaswane Mountain Reserve**, within walking distance of town.

Arrival, information and accommodation

Protours and Intercape's daily **buses** from Pretoria and Johannesburg drop you at the BP garage at the corner of Nelson Mandela and Thabo Mbeki drives in the town centre. Buses operated by Northwest Star/Star Line and long-distance **minibus taxis** arrive at the terminal at the western end of Nelson Mandela Drive by Bethlehem Drive.

Rustenburg's **tourist office** (May–July Mon–Fri 8am–5pm, Sat 8am–noon; Aug–April Mon–Fri 7.30am–6pm, Sat 8am–noon; ☎014 597 0904–6, ⓔtidc@mweb.co.za) is unhelpfully located 3km east of the bus terminal along the N4; head out of town along Nelson Mandela or Fatima Bhayat drives, and ignore signposts to the contrary, which are out of date.

You'll get the most out of the area by **staying** out of town, either at Kgaswane Mountain Reserve (p.660) or Mountain Sanctuary Park (p.661), or in any of dozens of rural (and sometimes quite flashy) B&Bs and resorts. The tourist office has the full works, and you'll also find a selection online at ⓦwww.rustenburgaccommodation.co.za. **Camping** is possible at Kgaswane Mountain Reserve. There's safe parking at all the following town-centre recommendations.

Town centre

Cashane Hotel 66 Steen St, corner with Nelson Mandela Dr ☎014 592 8541–3, ⓕ014 592 3016. An ageing but well-kept business-class hotel on six floors (lift access), with comfortable, well-equipped rooms and views over town. There's also a good bar and dull restaurant. ❸

Palm Lodge 99 Beyers Naudè Dr ☎ & ⓕ014 597 2520. A large thatch-roofed complex appearing swankier than it is, with dozens of small, dark rooms with TVs and phones, a swimming pool, two bars and a restaurant. ❸

Travellers Inn 99 Leyds St ☎014 592 7658, ⓔtravinn@mweb.co.za. The friendliest in town,

N4 (Pretoria, Waterfall Mall), B24 (Johannesburg, Mountain Sanctuary Park), **F** & **G**

RUSTENBURG

R510 (Pilanesberg, Sun City)

N4 (Groot Marico, Zeerust), R565 (Pilanesberg, Sun City), **C** & **D**

Kgaswane Mountain Reserve & **H**

ACCOMMODATION
Bergsig Lodge	H
Cashane Hotel	E
Kedar Country Hotel (Kruger Country House)	C
Oude Landgoed Lodge & Spa	F
Palm Lodge	B
Rainhill Farm	G
Revel In	D
Travellers Inn	A

RESTAURANTS & BARS
Castle Corner	7
Café Voices	1
Flying Dutchman	3
Hartley's	5
Karl's Bauernstube	6
Nando's	4
Palm Lodge	B
Porterhouse	2
Travellers Inn	A

250 m

SHOW GROUND

MC GREGOR ST

KLOOF WAY

Hospital

BOSCH ST

LUCAS ST

ZENDELING ST

TUIN ST

KOCK ST

BARNADOS ST

BEYERS NAUDE ST

Police

Anglican Church

Dutch Reformed Church

Old Town Hall

New Town Hall

BURGER ST

SMIT ST

STEEN ST

BOOM ST

FATIMA BHAYAT ST

Kruger Statue

ABSA (Bank)

KOCK ST

BEYERS NAUDE ST

JOUBERT ST

Flying Artist Gallery

KERK ST

KRUGER ST

LEVOS ST

DWARS ST

KRUIST ST

BERG ST

LOOP ST

KERK ST

POSTMA ST

BOOM ST

KFC

LOOP ST

BERG ST

THABO MBEKI DRIVE

NELSON MANDELA DRIVE

HEYSTEK ST

FATIMA BHAYAT ST

KLOPPERS ST

OLIVER TAMBO ST

VAN WIELLIG ST

MARAIS ST

LEVOS ST

KLOPPERS ST

BETHLEHEM ST

Bus and Taxi Rank

N

with good modern rooms and adjacent parking bays. There's a swimming pool, a lovely rustic bar, and superb food. Gay and lesbian couples welcome. ❷-❸

Out of town

Bergsig Lodge 2 7 Peperbroom Av, 3.5km south of town ☎ & ⓕ 014 597 1139. Best placed for Kgaswane (it's almost at the gate), with superb views, a shady garden, sundeck and swimming pool, and walks, hikes and horse rides to be arranged. Follow Beyers Naudè Drive to its end, continue along Boekenhout, right on to Flamboyant, right at the signpost. ❷

Kedar Country Hotel (Kruger Country House) 20km northwest of town, 500m off the R565 to Sun City ☎ 014 573 3367, ⓦ www.rali.co.za. Set amidst plentiful game and birdlife, this lovingly-restored farmhouse once belonged to President Kruger, who's honoured by a small museum. The simple if luxurious Afrikaans-style decor makes for a refreshingly tranquil rural getaway, and there's also a swimming pool (and three chalets with private pools), and some seriously good Afrikaans and Cape Malay cuisine at its Victorian restaurant (reservations ☎ 014 573 3218). Half board ❺

Oude Landgoed Lodge & Spa 8km along the R24 towards Johannesburg ☎ 014 537 2369, ⓦ www.oudelandgoed.co.za. It's not the rooms but the health spa that make this place special, with a welter of treatments on the menu, from aromatherapy, massage and hot stones to flotation tank immersion. The place is also open to day visitors (Mon–Fri 8am–5pm; R145 membership includes sauna, steam room, swimming pool and Jacuzzi), and they can arrange game drives, horseback trails, mountain biking and guided hikes. No children. B&B ❷; full board including treatments ❽

Rainhill Farm 4km southwest of town; follow Bethlehem Drive south from the bus terminal to its end, right along Brink St, left along Watsonia Rd, right at the end ☎ 014 592 8911, ⓦ www.rainhill .co.za. Five charming rooms in 1940s chalets decked out with antiques, perfect for families or honeymooners. There are also two well-regarded restaurants here (Hartley's and The Pack House, p.660), a cosy bar, farm animals for petting, a pool and even a maze, and hikes can be arranged. Catch a minibus taxi to Rustenburg Kloof. ❸

Revel In 40km west along the Swartruggens road, then right for 6.5km ☎ 072 225 7182, ⓦ www .revelin.co.za. A recommended backpackers on a farm, with dorms, bungalows and tree cabins, plus meals, a good bar, hiking trails, live music or DJs weekends, and occasional reggae festivals. ❶

The Town

Rustenburg is the former Western Transvaal's oldest town, not that you'd ever notice from its present appearance, mangled by one too many decades of relentless "modernization" that has given it all the charm of a dust-blown Midwestern town, complete with prefabricated chain stores, shopping malls, and neon signs.

The town's historic centre is limited to two blocks of Burger Street, from Nelson Mandela Drive to Oliver Tambo Drive, marked by two churches: the old **Anglican church** on Burger Street, dating from 1871, and the 1850 **Dutch Reformed Church** at the corner of Burger and Fatima Bhayat streets. Facing it is the graceful 1935 town hall and a **statue of Paul Kruger** by French sculptor Jean Georges Achard. It shows the President in his last days in exile in France sitting grumpily in an armchair. A few blocks south along Beyers Naudè Drive, opposite Rustenburg Square shopping centre, the **Flying Artist Gallery** exhibits paintings and sculptures by local artists and has a peaceful tea garden at the back.

There's not much else to do in Rustenburg itself, although the tourist office is busy planning a platinum-mining visitor centre, and a showcase for jewellery-making. For now, the tourist office can arrange tours of **platinum mines**, though you'll need your own transport. **Stock-car races** take place most weekends at the showground, on the north side of Fatima Bhayat Street before the tourist office.

Eating

Besides a welter of **fast food** joints on Nelson Mandela Drive, central Rustenburg has a handful of sophisticated restaurants and a few more within driving distance. Infinitely more interesting for a daytime snack though are the **street food** stands in and around the bus terminal (for maize, grilled chicken legs, and *pap* with stew). For fresh dairy produce, go to Smith's Dairy at 15 Heystek Street, whilst fresh juices are sold at the Cottage Bakery supermarket at the west end of Oliver Tambo Drive. Most restaurants close on Sundays; exceptions are noted.

Town centre

Flying Dutchman 53 Nelson Mandela Dr. Nicest restaurant in town, serving up French- and Dutch-influenced cuisine in an atmospheric pub-like interior, with good salads, scrumptious homemade desserts and a good selection of drinks. Full meals around R100.

Porterhouse Biblio Plaza, corner Nelson Mandela and Thabo Mbeki drives. Steaks any way you like them and good salads in cool and calm surroundings.

Out of town

Hartley's Rainhill Farm (see "Accommodation") ☎014 594 1992. Tranquil country-style pub and family restaurant with tables under a fig tree. Also here is the sophisticated *Pack House* (Fri & Sat dinner only; reservations essential), with formal service and a good wine list. The food at both is refined country-style cooking – don't miss trying the farm's famous orange marmalade.

Karl's Bauernstube 10km southeast along the R24 ☎014/537 2128. Delicious Austrian and German grub and beers; closed Mon, Sat lunch and Sun evening.

Nightlife

Nightlife in Rustenburg is limited, although there are a few decent bars. The liveliest and definitely dodgiest places for a drink are the **bars** close to the bus station; less exciting but safer are the following.

Café Voices Beyers Naudè Dr. The liveliest nocturnal venue, with a sports/cocktail bar, dance floor, sporadic beer festivals and bands.

Castle Corner Heystek St. Posh English-style pub with lots of beer on tap and satellite sports, that gets busy whenever there's rugby on the TV.

Palm Lodge 99 Beyers Naudè Dr. The first-floor ladies bar here is popular for televised sports, especially rugby.

Travellers Inn 99 Leyds St. This small and cosy nook is the closest Rustenburg gets to a backpackers bar. Mon–Sat to at least 9.30pm.

Listings

Banks ABSA, corner of Nelson Mandela Drive and Burger Street, has a bureau de change.

Car rental Platinum Vehicle Rental, 45 Nelson Mandela Dr ☎014 592 1328, ✉lionelm@mweb.co.za.

Hospital Rustenburg Provincial Hospital, corner of Nelson Mandela Dr and Heystek St ☎014 22112.

Internet access The best access is at Waterfall Mall, 4km east of town. The computers at the Internet café on Nelson Mandela Dr, west of Leyds St, are badly maintained.

Police Corner of Beyers Naudè Dr and Kruis St ☎014 22122.

Kgaswane Mountain Reserve

Soaring up behind Rustenburg's southern suburbs, the **KGASWANE MOUNTAIN RESERVE** (daily March–Aug 6am–6pm; Sept–Feb 5.30am–7pm; ☎014 533 2050, ⊛www.tourismnorthwest.co.za/parks/kgaswane.html; R10, plus R10 per vehicle or R5 per bicycle) spans a spectacular forty-square-kilometre portion of the Magaliesberg, and offers sweeping views and great hikes. The terrain is spotted with rock formations created by millennia of erosion. You'll find dry veld too, and streams coursing through the valleys that have generated a lush flora all of their own. Scattered around the reserve are aloes indigenous to the Magaliesberg, and the discreet *frithiapulchra*, a succulent

The two daily **buses** from Pretoria and Johannesburg are run by Protours (℡012 664 5880), who continue on to Mafikeng; and by Intercape (℡0861 287 287, ⓦwww .intercape.co.za) en route to Gaborone. Protours and Intercape also run daily buses back to Pretoria and Jo'burg. In addition, an aging fleet of rickety buses is operated by Northwest Star/Star Line, who run frequent services throughout the Province, including to and from Groot Marico and Mafikeng, and also on to Botswana. Both these and long-distance **minibus taxis** (which cover most of the Province and also go to Lesotho) operate from the chaotic terminal at the western end of Nelson Mandela Drive by Bethlehem Drive. Bays are clearly marked with destinations but there are no ticket offices; it's best to check your options the day before you travel.

8

NORTH WEST PROVINCE | Bojanala Region

with only its leaf tips exposed, flowering between November and March. The many crags are perfect for **predatory birds**; keep a lookout for the rare black eagle, Martial eagle and Cape vulture, as well as parrots and paradise flycatchers. Kgaswane is also home to eight hundred **antelopes**, representing most of South Africa's species, and also zebras. **Predators** are few in number and limited to caracal, aardwolf, black-backed jackals and elusive leopard.

The reserve can be explored on a day or two-night hike, or by bicycle (bring your own). There are two short trails for **day hikes**. The three-hour, five-kilometre Peglarae trail goes over fairly steep and rocky terrain but takes in most of the reserve's best features, and the visitors' centre provides a good booklet to go with it. Shorter and easier is the two-kilometre Vlei-ramble to a viewing hut on the *vlei*, popular with birders. **Overnight hikes** follow the Rustenburg Hiking Trail (19.5km or 23.5km) and last two days and two nights. Accommodation is in huts which provide firewood and cooking utensils, but you must bring food, and enough clothing in winter – nights get bitterly cold. It's best to book ahead for the overnight trails, though you may strike lucky midweek.

The reserve entrance is 4km from Rustenburg: head south along Beyers Naudè Drive and turn left at the end into Boekenhout Street, which leads to the gate. From here, the road winds dramatically up to the mountaintop, where you'll find the **visitors' centre**, with useful maps and information on hikes and trails, as well as camping and braai facilities. A cab from town (call John Taxis, ℡082 771 2146) costs around R40. Alternatively, the *Travellers Inn* can fix you up with a local guide, or contact Escapes Outdoors (℡014 537 2226), Out and About (℡083 627 6080) or Vision Adventure (℡072 315 1893) for organized tours.

Mountain Sanctuary Park

Smaller than Kgaswane but a gem nonetheless, the privately owned **Mountain Sanctuary Park** (daily: March–Aug 8am–5.30pm; Sept–Feb 8am–6.30pm; ℡014 534 0114, ⓦwww.mountain-sanctuary.co.za; R22, plus R10 per vehicle) lies about 15km east of Rustenburg and is only accessible by private vehicle. The park is dotted with bilharzia-free streams safe for swimming, and spectacular *kloofs* and gullies. Klipspringer, rhebok and duiker wander freely, and the area supports abundant birdlife.

Chalets, safari tents, caravans and campsites are available for **overnight stays** (minimum charge two nights and two people at weekends; ❶–❸), but you'll need to bring your own bedding. There's an extraordinary **swimming pool** by the caravans, which gives the impression that you're on the edge of a precipice as you look out into the valley below. The simplest way to **get to the park** is to take the N4 as far as the Marikana turn-off, turn right, then take the second dirt track on your left and continue for about 3km. Phone ahead before you go as visitor numbers are limited.

Sun City

A surreal pocket of high-rise hotels and tinkling gaming machines in the endless bushveld, **SUN CITY** consists of four hotel/resorts tightly packed together with golf courses, a water park and various entertainment centres. Despite its enduring appeal to holidaying South African families and somewhat bemused foreign visitors, it has fallen on hard times now **gambling** is legal in South Africa. When entrepreneur Sol Kerzner began building the vast complex in the 1970s, the area was part of the Bophuthatswana Bantustan and therefore one of the few places in the country where you could throw dice legally. Thousands visited from "across the border" to sample Kerzner's blend of gambling, topless shows and over-the-top hotels. During apartheid, the resort played host to a series of high-profile rock concerts, with artists such as Elton John taking the stage despite the cultural boycott in operation at the time. These days, although the crowds to "South Africa's Kingdom of Pleasure" have diminished, Sun City's bizarre and unique attractions haven't faded, and if you're in the area it's well worth popping in, especially if you're travelling to Pilanesberg National Park.

Arrival and information

You can **fly** to Sun City's small airport, 7km away, from Johannesburg on South African Airlink (℡011 978 1111, ⓦwww.saairlink.co.za). **Minibus taxis** from Rustenburg to Mogwase pass by the entrance, and daily Sun City **buses** drive from Johannesburg and Pretoria (book through Computicket ℡011 915 8000 or contact the Welcome Centre, below). If you're **driving** from Pretoria, follow the N4 past the Brits turn-off, and turn right onto the R556, from where it's roughly 70km. Coming from Johannesburg, it's easier to go via Rustenburg. A popular option is to join a **day tour** from Pretoria or Johannesburg; a large number of operators based in those cities offer trips, with prices depending on the target market; expect to pay at least R350–500, plus R200–300 if combined with a short safari at Pilanesberg.

    Entrance costs R40, R30 of which you get back in Sunbucks, the Sun City currency, used to pay for most things inside, including restaurant meals. Not surprisingly, however, rand can still be used everywhere inside. From the vast car park by the main gate, hop on the free **monorail** that goes to the **Welcome Centre** (Mon–Thurs & Sun 9am–9.30pm, Fri & Sat 9am–1am; ℡014 557 1544). This is a good starting point for an exploration of Sun City (which, though it looks huge, is easily explored on foot), and provides plenty of maps, leaflets and details of special offers. You can also book **game drives** into Pilanesberg from here, and flights by **vintage aircraft** over the complex. There's also an information centre for the North West Parks & Tourism Board (same hours as Welcome centre; ℡014 552 2116).

Accommodation

Rooms can be booked through Sun City Reservations (℡014 557 1000, ⓦwww.suninternational.co.za), but will be considerably cheaper if booked through a tour company as part of a package, or over the Internet. All hotels are enormous – *Cabanas*, the smallest, has space for a mere 380 guests.

Cabanas Practical for families, this cluster of self-catering chalets near the entrance offers the cheapest accommodation in Sun City; moderately priced restaurants, an adventure playground and good indoor pool complete the picture. ❽

Cascades Hotel After the *Palace*, this is the resort's most comfortable place to stay. Next door to the Entertainment Centre, it's a stylish high-rise, with "designer-tropical" decor, a mini rainforest and aviary, and outside lifts offering splendid views of Sun City and the surrounding hills. The inviting pool and bar are for residents only. ❽

Palace of the Lost City Like something out of an Indiana Jones movie, the enormous *Palace* is a fantastically opulent and imaginative hotel, designed as a soaring African jungle palace with towers, domes, extravagant carvings and sculptures. A stay here is bank-breakingly expensive, and far from intimate (338 rooms) but unforgettable. ❾

Sun City Hotel The original Sun City, housing the main casino and nightclub. If you can handle the tackiness and sound of slot machines, it's worth considering for its well-furnished rooms and three decent restaurants. ❽

The Resort

The resort is divided into three distinct areas: Cabanas (which includes Waterworld), the Entertainment Centre, and the showpiece **Lost City**, separated from the rest of the complex by a R40 entrance fee and the vibrating Bridge of Time. On entering it, you'll encounter the Valley of the Waves, a gigantic pool area designed to look like a beach, complete with sand, palm trees and a machine producing two-metre-high breakers suitable for surfing. Surrounding the valley are four excellent twisting waterchutes with names such as Scorpion and Mamba, a near-vertical waterslide called the Temple of Courage and various relaxing swimming pools. Deeper into the acres of specially planted rainforest above the valley, you'll find waterfalls, trickling streams and a network of explorable paths, all interspersed with "remains" of the lost city. Overlooking the whole scene is the staggering *Palace of the Lost City* hotel; you can pop in for a drink if you're not staying, or join one of the daily **Sun City tours** (2pm from the Welcome Centre; R20) for a more thorough look.

The **Entertainment Centre** next to the towering triangle of the *Cascades Hotel* is the focal point of the rest of Sun City, with rows of bleeping slot machines and arcade games, upmarket shops and lots of restaurants, snack bars and coffee shops. The centre's **cinema** has the best movie selection in the Province, and the **concert hall** hosts regular beauty contests, music and sports events, which have improved since the lifting of the cultural and sports boycotts in the 1990s. Here you'll also find an aviary, tennis courts, a fitness centre, and the renowned Gary Player Golf Course.

Cabanas, close to the entrance, has a small zoo, horse-riding, bumper cars for kids, another aviary with summer flying displays by hawks, falcons and owls, and a crocodile sanctuary, where you can feed the hungry denizens at 4.30pm. Behind it is **Waterworld**, a large artificial lake used for watersports from windsailing to powerboating.

Pilanesberg National Park

Adjacent to Sun City and home to a huge variety of animals, the **PILANESBERG NATIONAL PARK** is North West Province's biggest tourist draw. The artificially created reserve was, until 1979, occupied by farmers and the **Tswana** people, who were unceremoniously evicted when **Operation Genesis** saw over six thousand animals shipped in from all over the country to fill the park. Just two hours' drive from Pretoria and Jo'burg, Pilanesberg is definitely the place to come to see some game if you're based in Gauteng and have only limited time in South Africa. Don't let the crowds or the managed nature of the place put you off: the park offers game-viewing thrills aplenty, with a good chance of seeing all of the **Big Five**, along with hippo, brown hyena, wild (or hunting) dog and cheetah. The majority of antelope species are here, too, and there's a vast array of **birdlife** – over 365 species recorded so far. At night, some fantastic creatures emerge, including civet, porcupine and caracal, though their dislike of the large vehicles with spotlights used for **night game drives** means you'll be lucky to catch a glimpse of them.

Covering some 650 square kilometres, and with 200km of good-quality tar and gravel roads, you'll need at least a day to do Pilanesberg justice. The reserve is easily explored by sedan car, especially with the official map. The park's many beautiful hills – the result of an unusual volcanic eruption that occurred 1200–1300 years ago – are in some ways Pilanesberg's finest feature, though they are often ignored by visitors more interested in scouring their slopes for wildlife. Pilanesberg's natural focus, for visitors and wildlife alike, is the alkaline **Lake Mankwe** ("place of the leopard"), whose goings-on are best observed from several walk-in hides. The various picnic spots and hides dotted around are ideal for breaking the drive – the hides in particular aren't used by many visitors and as a result can be cool, peaceful places to appreciate the natural surroundings.

Practicalities

There are four **entrance gates** (daily: March, April, Sept & Oct 6am–6.30pm; May–Aug 6.30am–6pm; Nov–Feb 5.30am–7pm; R20 per person, R15 per car) to the reserve; the most commonly used are Manyane (or Mogwase), on the eastern side of the reserve, and Bakubung to the south, just to the west of Sun City off the R565. The **park headquarters** are at Mogwase (℡014 555 5351, ⊚www.tourismnorthwest.co.za/pilanesberg). An excellent **map** and **guidebook** explaining the various habitats are available at the gates, enabling

Pilanesberg tour operators

Rates for normal safaris depend on group size (larger groups are cheaper), and whether the tour is scheduled or private. On a **scheduled tour**, you may be sharing a minibus with up to fifteen other visitors; check also whether lunch and entry fees are included. The special activities organized by Gametrackers and Mankwe (see below) can usually be incorporated into trips run by other operators, particularly if you have the flexibility of a private tour. **Prices** for day trips from Gauteng average R400–700 per person on a scheduled tour; private tours start at R800–1000 for the day. Rates for overnight trips vary according to where you stay; count on at last R1500 for a "budget" trip, and upwards of R2500 otherwise.

Adventure Travel Africa 430 Reitz Street, Sunnyside, Pretoria ℡012 343 7499, ⊚www.adventuretravelafrica.com. Cheap overnight tours from Pretoria and Johannesburg, leaving either city before sunrise.

Gametrackers Outdoor Adventures Sun City ℡014 552 5020, *Manyane Resort* ℡014 555 5469, *Bakgatla Resort* ℡014 573 1000, ⊚www.gametrac.co.za. Two big crowd pullers here: balloon flights and elephant-back safaris (Rs1500–2000). The five trusty mounts were orphaned in 1980s Zimbabwe and subsequently domesticated; rides take place early in the morning and late afternoon.

Mankwe Safaris Sun City ℡014 555 7056, ⊚www.mankwesafaris.co.za. A *concessionaire* offering guided walks accompanied by armed park rangers, and night game drives (from R120 each). Their other speciality is the "Heritage Tour", blending nearby cultural attractions with the Big Five.

Ulysses Tours & Safaris Hatfield, Pretoria ℡012 663 4941, ⊚www.ulysses.co.za. A well-regarded and professionally run upmarket outfit.

you to plan your journey around what you most want to see. Bear in mind that other drivers have this map too, so the areas recommended for popular animals can become congested. In the centre of the park, the **Pilanesberg Centre**, an old Cape Dutch building left over from the days when the park was farm land, functions as a café, gift shop and open-air restaurant. It also has a notice board for wildlife sightings, useful for tracking down any outstanding quarries on your checklist.

If you don't have a vehicle, you can rent one from Avis in Sun City (℡014 557 1584), or arrange things through a tour operator as the park itself does not provide any services. Apart from **organized safaris** (mostly from Sun City, Pretoria and Johannesburg), the park's *concessionaires* offer a range of **alternative activities**; see the box opposite for details. Whilst all these activities can be booked on arrival, it's best to reserve them in advance either directly or through your lodge to avoid missing out. There are frequent **minibus taxis** running the 54km from Rustenburg to Manyane Gate (ask for Mogwase).

Accommodation

Pilanesberg has large numbers of day visitors – many from Sun City – but like any other decent game park you'll get most from it if you're able to stay a little bit longer and put yourself in pole position for the best game-viewing time, at dawn, before the day visitors arrive. Pilanesberg's **accommodation** ranges from upmarket lodges where game drives are included in the prices, to large, resort-style complexes on the fringes of the park, and cheaper and more basic camps outside the boundaries. **Bookings** for *Bakgatla*, *Bosele* and *Manyane* must be made through Golden Leopard Resorts (℡012 345 6058 or 014 555 1000, ⓦwww.goldenleopard.co.za), and those for *Bakubung*, *Kwa Maritane* and *Tshukudu* through Legacy Hotels (℡011 806 6888, ⓦwww.legacyhotels.co.za). **Camping** is possible at Golden Leopard's places. All lodges have hourly shuttle buses to and from Sun City, and can arrange game drives and guided walks if not included in the rates. Some may insist on two-night stays at weekends.

Absheni Bush Camp 2km outside Kwa Maritane Gate ℡ & ℻014 552 3755. Spartan but cheap overnights in five huts and A-frame tents (bedding provided). There's a swimming pool and kitchen (no utensils), and breakfast and dinner can be provided on request. ❶–❷

Bakgatla Resort Near Bakgatla Gate at the foot of Garamoga Hills. Large collection of reasonable self-catering chalets and safari tents with attached bathrooms and shady verandahs, a caravan park and several campsites. Rates are cheaper per person if you share between four or five. Meals available. Camping ❷; tents ❸–❹; chalets ❸–❺

Bakubung Lodge On the southern edge of the park, just west of Sun City. The highlight at this large, modern lodge is the hippo pool, a stone's throw from the restaurant. The hotel rooms and chalets are pleasant if bland. ❼

Bosele Group Centre By Manyane Gate, and intended primarily for large groups, though you may be able to get an inexpensive dorm bed here if it's not full. Kitchen facilities are shared, and you can use the pool, shop and restaurant at neighbouring *Manyane Resort*. ❶

Kwa Maritane Lodge In the park's southeast corner near Pilanesberg airport, this vast, upmarket lodge feels detached from its fabulous surroundings – no surprise really, with 90 rooms and 54 chalets. There's a game hide at the end of a 130-metre tunnel. ❼

Manyane Resort Just outside Manyane Gate. Low cost and convenience compensate for the distinctly un-bushlike atmosphere of the park's main camp. Stay in thatched chalets with TVs and kitchen, or bring a tent or caravan; there's also a bar and restaurant, pool, gym, mini-golf, aviary, and a noisy 4WD track. Camping ❷; tents ❷; chalets ❸–❹

Tshukudu Bush Lodge On a hilltop with sweeping views in the southwest, 8km from Bakubung Gate. Gaze out at big game at the waterhole from your verandah at Pilanesberg's most upmarket and exclusive lodge. Picturesque thatched huts offer luxury accommodation with sunken baths and roaring log fires for a maximum of eighteen guests; there's also a swimming pool. No children under 12. ❾

The Central Region

Thanks to its scrawny and desolate dryness, North West Province's **Central Region** feels especially remote, and there are not all that many towns worth visiting. **Mmabatho**, once the capital of Bophuthatswana and now incorporated into neighbouring **Mafikeng**, the provincial capital, forces reluctant bureaucratic pilgrimages on people from all over. The region's appeal lies elsewhere, in the brooding plains and lush river valleys of Marico and the rarely visited game reserves, including **Madikwe** on the Botswana border. Then there are the remains of the rich but depressing history of the region, centring on the relentless dispossession of the Tswana, but also including the famed **siege of Mafikeng** during the second Anglo-Boer War, and the incredible **Lichtenburg diamond rush** of 1926. Lastly, there are the people themselves: local Tswana and Afrikaners are both short on English but long on hospitality, at least to visitors, a trait best experienced at the village of **Groot Marico**, famed nationwide for its *mampoer* peach brandy and quintessentially laid-back spirit.

Groot Marico

GROOT MARICO, a tiny and dusty but characterful *dorp* resting contentedly by the banks of the Marico River, just south of the N4 and 90km west of Rustenburg, gained fame through **Herman Charles Bosman**'s short stories based on his time as a teacher here (see box opposite). In mid-October, Groot Marico hosts the literary Bosman Weekend, drawing fans of one of South Africa's best-loved authors from far and wide. The town's handful of attractions include the **Art Factory** on Paul Kruger Street (Mon–Sat 9am–5pm), where you can pick up news about what's going on, as well as Tswana cultural artifacts and locally made Afrikaner crafts such as wooden pipes, whips and clocks.

Although prone to stultifying heat, particularly in summer, the hills of the Marico district are good for hiking, and when it all gets too much you can make for the river for cool relief. The water of the **Marico Oog** ("Marico Eye"), a spring 20km south of town, is particularly clear and refreshing: festooned with water lilies and surrounded by beautiful dolomitic rocks, it makes a tranquil place for a picnic, and can be paradise for bird-watchers, with over four hundred species recorded here. It's also a favoured spot for **scuba divers**; contact the town's information centre for more information.

Practicalities

Minibus taxis travelling along the N4 from Pretoria or Rustenburg to Mafikeng or Botswana will stop at the Groot Marico turn-off, a twenty-minute walk north of the village. The first place to head for is the town's friendly **tourist office** (☏014 503 0010 or 083 272 2958, ⓦwww.marico.co.za), marked by a small signpost along Paul Kruger Street next to First National Bank, in an enclosure built by Italian PoWs in the Second World War. It's open most hours of the day and night; should you find it closed, call in at the Art Factory. As well as providing a welter of information on the town and its activities, they also handle bookings for a wide range of accommodation (including farm stays) and affordable *mampoer* tours, which can include a visit to Marico Oog spring, or to Iron Age and Anglo-Boer War sites. The *Bosveld Hotel* along the same street has Groot Marico's only public **bar**, where white locals, inspired by beer, brandy and their own good humour, have been known to dance traditional Afrikaans two-steps.

Mampoer

It is said that it was a Pedi chief by the name of Mampuru who introduced the art of distilling peach brandy to the Boers. Named **mampoer** in his honour, the fearsomely strong spirit has inspired locals and visitors alike ever since. Any fruit can be used to make *mampoer*, but peach is the most traditional: until 1878, much of North West's farmland grew peach trees solely devoted to this purpose. Things changed with the ZAR government's distilling tax, and the new licensing system introduced in 1894, and thousands of *mampoer* stills were destroyed. A few, however, escaped detection. One farmer, according to a local story, cleaned out his entire drainage system but made no attempt to conceal his fifteen barrels of *mampoer*. The inspectors found the barrels, split them open and poured the entire contents down the drain. Meanwhile, the canny farmer had his family stationed in the field where the pipe ended up with every container the household possessed, and managed to recover fourteen of the fifteen barrels.

The drink is celebrated in Herman Charles Bosman's short story, **Willem Prinsloo's Peach Brandy**, set in the 1920s:

"We arrived at Willem Prinsloo's house. There were so many ox-waggons drawn up on the veld that the place looked like a laager [circle of wagons]. Prinsloo met us at the door.

'Go right through, kerels,' he said. 'The dancing is in the voorhuis [barn]. The peach brandy is in the kitchen.'

Although the voorhuis was big, it was so crowded as to make it almost impossible to dance. But it was not as crowded as the kitchen. Nor was the music in the voorhuis – which was provided by a number of men with guitars and concertinas – as loud as the music in the kitchen, where there was no band, but each man sang for himself.

We knew from these signs that the party was a success.

When I had been in the kitchen for about half an hour I decided to go into the voorhuis. It seemed a long way, now, from the kitchen to the voorhuis, and I had to lean against the wall several times to think. I passed a number of men who were also leaning against the wall like that, thinking. One man even found that he could think best by sitting on the floor with his head in his arms.

You could see that Willem Prinsloo made a pretty good peach brandy."

If you want to sample *mampoer*, either head for Pieter Roets's **Vergenoeg Farm** (open most days, closed evenings) a few kilometres south of Marico along the untarred main road, where you can cautiously pick up a bottle of barbed-wire-entwined, eighty-percent-proof *Doringdrood*, or to Tienie Zwart's **Driefontein Farm**, 2.5km beyond the Groot Marico turn-off on the N4, where you can see the stuff being made. In the old days the alcohol content was measured by throwing a chunk of lard into a sample: if it floated halfway, the *mampoer* was perfect. Nowadays, you just hold a match over it – the higher and cleaner the blue flame, the better the brew. Visits to other farms can be arranged through Groot Marico's information centre.

The best way of experiencing Groot Marico is to **stay** on a farm or in a cottage (❶–❷): the information centre provides details and handles bookings, or there's a good selection at Ⓦ www.marico.co.za/farmaccommodation.htm. Particularly recommended are a couple of small self-catering cottages by the river, 3–4km west of town: *Casper's Kaya* (❷) and *David's Cottage* (❶), both in a secluded and heavily forested valley, just perfect for birders; swimming in the river is possible, and there are also canoes for hire and drumming workshops. Should you prefer a more central location, the friendly *Angela's Guest House* (☎014 503 0085, Ⓔ angela_s@telkomsa.net; ❷), between the village and the

N4 highway, has four comfortable en-suite rooms and a self-catering cottage set in a lovely garden and orchard, and can organize massage and beauty treatments as well as meals. The nicest **camping** spots are on the Mafikeng Road, 1km from the centre of the village (details from the information centre) and *Kleinfontein Camping Site*, 6km out beside a dam, where there are also five rondavels (bring bedding; ❶), a kitchen and thatched braai area, hot water, and swimming in the reservoir. Neither site has electricity.

Zeerust and around

The large and unprepossessing regional centre of **ZEERUST**, 40km west of Groot Marico on the N4, is essentially a supplies town, and only worth stopping at on the way to Gaborone or one of the surrounding game reserves. There's an annual **mampoer festival** (check with Groot Marico's information centre for dates); otherwise, apart from the shops, there's precious little to see. Two kilometres east of town, the **Abjaterskop** is a striking, pointed hill which rewards a quick scramble or a more serious hike. You can park at the large *Abjaterskop Hotel* (☏018 642 2008, ✉abjaters@gds.co.za; ❶–❷) and ask the manager for directions. The hotel itself, in a magnificent hilly setting ideal for hiking, has dozens of rooms, each with DSTV and phone, plus cheaper rondavels and *cabanas*, a campsite and caravan park overlooking the Klein Marico River, and swimming pool. Its *Bosmans Restaurant* is also the best **place to eat** in the area, and has a good bar, too, where you can sample *mampoer*.

Also worth a visit if you're interested in the cultural history of the area are the remains of **Tshwenyane** and **Karechuenya**, two Tswana towns built in the sixteenth and seventeenth centuries. There's a display on these archeological findings at the Mafikeng Museum (see p.671). The sites lie 25km northeast of Zeerust: head up the Gaborone road and turn right at Enselsberg after 16km. The ruins are scattered along the road between 5km and 10km in adjacent farmland.

Madikwe Game Reserve

Tucked up in the very north of the Province near the Botswana border lies the 765-square-kilometre **MADIKWE GAME RESERVE** (☏014 565 5960, ⊕www.tourismnorthwest.co.za/madikwe), one of South Africa's largest wildlife areas. The reserve was established in 1991 from reclaimed farmland, and thanks to **Operation Phoenix**, which saw the reintroduction of over eight thousand animals, Madikwe's largely low-lying plains of woodland and grassland are now amply stocked with the Big Five (including black and white rhino and a stable population of 250 elephants) and dozens of other mammals, including cheetah, wild dogs, spotted hyena, and most of southern Africa's flavours of plains antelopes. Twitchers won't be disappointed, with some 350 species recorded so far; the Marico River, on the eastern border, and the *kopjes* scattered all around, are particularly rewarding birding areas.

Long promoted as South Africa's "bijoux reserve", the low tourist density so liberally vaunted in the brochures no longer quite rings true given that **29 lodges** now vie for your trade, although Madikwe does remain one of the least known of South Africa's large wildlife areas. Access is reserved to guests of its lodges, day visitors are not admitted, and there is no budget accommodation or camping. **Game drives** are conducted in vehicles belonging to the lodges.

Practicalities

Road access to Madikwe is normally through Tau Gate, 12km off the R49 although, depending on where you're staying, the reserve can also be approached from the east via Dwarsberg by way of gravel roads. Whichever approach you take, you'll need to inform your lodge prior to arrival. It's also possible to **fly in** on regular light aircraft from Wonderboom airport near Pretoria, or from Johannesburg; fares average R1100 each way; tickets can be reserved through the lodges. **Accommmodation** rates at all lodges include full-board, day and night game drives, and guided bush walks.

Jaci's Safari Lodge & Tree Lodge ⓣ014 533 3834, ⓦwww.madikwe.com. Two exceptional lodges, with eight guest rooms each, whose sense of style, comfort and laid-back luxury are hard to beat. The *Safari Lodge* overlooks a natural water-hole on the Marico River and has a natural rock swimming pool nearby, while the *Tree Lodge*'s rooms are built around trees several metres off the ground. Children welcome. ❽

Madikwe Hills Private Game Lodge ⓣ018 365 9903; reservations ⓣ013 737 6627–7, ⓦwww.madikwehills.com. Another gem, this one around a *kopje* close to the riverbank. Rooms are modern and have views over the veld. There are even better views from the sundowner terrace and its small swimming pool, plus there's a gym, health spa, childcare facilities, and some excellent cooks. ❾

Mateya Safari Lodge ⓣ014 778 9200, ⓦwww.mateyasafari.com. Another contender for the ultimate in bush chic, the five luxurious suites here each boast their own swimming pool, as well

as both indoor and outdoor showers. There's a beauty therapist on hand, Jacuzzi and gym, and the lodge's culinary sorcery is best sampled on the terrace overlooking the veld. No children under 16. ❾

Mosetlha Bush Camp ⓣ011 444 9345, ⓦwww.thebushcamp.com. Madikwe's only "budget" accommodation, also offering the reserve's most intense wilderness experience: located in the reserve's centre, there's no perimeter fence and accommodation is in very simple open-sided log cabins, with no electricity, and hot outdoor showers delivered by an ingenious donkey boiler and bucket system. What it lacks in luxury it makes up in atmosphere and expertise, with the emphasis placed on game walks as much as drives. ❼

Royal Madikwe Luxury Game Lodge ⓣ082 568 8867, ⓦwww.royalmadikwe.co.za. A sumptuous blend of colonial and "ethnic" styles, perfect for pampering, amidst an area of *marula* and red ivory trees. The five luxurious chalets each have a terrace from where you'll see plenty of wildlife. Good food, and there's a pool. ❾

Mafikeng and Mmabatho

The twin towns of Mafikeng and Mmabatho offer a unique portrait of the vision of apartheid and its deep contradictions. **MAFIKENG** is most famous for Baden-Powell and the Boer **siege** of 1899–1900 (see box on p.671). Serving a wide area of farmland, in many ways it's a typical colonial settlement; it has a smattering of graceful buildings, with its entrenched whites living in dull suburbs, and a centre used increasingly as a shopping and transport hub by blacks from the surrounding area. Less than 5km away, but a world apart in appearance, values and atmosphere, is **MMABATHO**, designated capital of the former homeland of Bophuthatswana, and a showcase for the grandiose visions of Bop dictator **Lucas Mangope**. The monumental constructions built by Mangope on the back of revenues generated from Sol Kerzner's casinos in Bophuthatswana (most famously at Sun City), from huge government offices to the towering sports stadium, along with the wide boulevards that connect them, are undoubtedly worth experiencing, even if the wiser course for finding somewhere to stay or eat and drink is to retreat to the Mafikeng side.

Arrival, information and accommodation

Mafikeng lies 25km south of Ramatlabama border post with Botswana. None of the major intercity bus companies come here, so you'll have to rely on **minibus taxis** (or buses operated by Northwest Star/Star Line), which pull in at the hassle-free terminal between Hatchard and Victoria streets on the northern side of town. The **train station** is on the western edge at Station Road.

Airport, Disaneng & R27 Vryburg

R52 Lichtenburg Wondergat

MAFIKENG

Mega City (3km)

Mafikeng Game ▶ Reserve R27 Zeerust

Baden-Powell Scouts Hall

Standard Bank

Victoria Hospital

Prison

St Joseph's Convent

Game Shopping Centre

Mafikeng Museum

St John's Anglican Church

Police

ABSA

Total

Caltex

Train station

Northwest Mall

First National Bank

Methodist Church

Library

Cooke's Lake

Standard Bank

Mafikeng Market Square

Mr. Food Grocery

N

ACCOMMODATION

Boga Legaba Guest House	E
Buffalo Park Lodge	D
Cooke's Lake Chalets	G
Garden View Lodge	B
Getaway Lodge	C
The Surrey	F
Tusk Mmabatho Casino Hotel	A

RESTAURANTS, BARS & CLUBS

Buffalo Park Lodge	D
Ebony and Ivory Jazz Bar	3
Graceland	2
Ivory Pot	4
O'Hagan's	1

0   500 m

Arriving by **plane**, you land at Mmabatho International Airport, 17km west along the Disaneng road. There are no taxis or buses into town, but mid- and upmarket hotels will pick up guests, and the airport also has a branch of Avis (see "Listings" on p.673).

The municipal **tourist office** (Mon–Fri 8am–5pm, or 6pm in summer, Sat 8am–noon; ☎018 381 3155-6, ℗018 381 6058) is awkwardly placed 1.5km south along Nelson Mandela Drive, next to Mafikeng Game Reserve. Apart from the usual brochures, hotel lists and city plans, it also sells books. For questions about the Province's parks and nature reserves, visit the **North West Parks & Tourism Board** headquarters at Heritage House next to Cooke's Lake, 500m closer to town (☎018 397 1500, call centre ☎082 232 7500, ℗www.tourismnorthwest.co.za).

Most **accommodation** rates include breakfast.

Boga Legaba Guest House 6 Interlaken Ave, Riviera Park, 2km east of the centre ☎018 381 6808, ℗www.bogalegaba.co.za. Characterful place decorated with African artwork, and with a spacious garden and pool. No meals except breakfast. ❸

Buffalo Park Lodge Botha Rd, corner with Molopo Rd ☎018 381 2159, ℗www .buffalolodge.co.za. Small, cool and well-kept twin-bed rooms with TVs at this family-run place, though it's the excellent bar and restaurant that recommend it. There's also a Lilliputian swimming pool. ❹

Cooke's Lake Chalets Cooke's Lake, access beside the tourist office on Nelson Mandela Dr ☎018 397 1500. Next to the lake, these beautiful two-storey wood-and-thatch chalets were still under construction at the time of writing, and promise to be by far the most attractive places to stay in Mafikeng. ❹

Garden View Lodge Corner North St and Havenga St ☎018 381 3110. Comfortable B&B rooms and self-catering apartments in a colonial-era building, secure parking, and attached restaurant and ladies' bar (closed weekends). ❸

The siege of Mafikeng

Mafikeng was **besieged** within three days of the start of the second Anglo-Boer War (1899–1902) by generals Snyman and Cronje. **Colonel Robert Baden-Powell** (founder of the Boy Scouts) had the task of defending the town. This he did for 217 days, from October 16, 1899, until May 17, 1900, when relief arrived from Rhodesia and from the south. In the process, Baden-Powell became a British household name and hero, and the exuberant scenes of jubilation in London that greeted news of the relief gave rise to a new word in the English language: *maffick*, which meant to celebrate unduly.

Strategically, Mafikeng was irrelevant to the war; Baden-Powell's real achievement was to distract the six thousand Afrikaners besieging the town from fighting elsewhere. He relied heavily on the **Barolong** people for defence, labour and reconnaissance, but failed to record this either in his dispatches to London or in his memoirs, despite the fact that four hundred Barolong lost their lives during the siege – twice as many as British. The Barolong also received far fewer rations, and over one thousand subsequently died of starvation; they received none of the £29,000 raised in Britain for the rehabilitation of Mafikeng. To add insult to injury, not one Barolong was decorated for bravery, in contrast to the plentiful medals dished out to the British regiments, and none of the promises Baden-Powell made about land grants to them was ever kept. An important legacy of the involvement of the black population was the diary of the siege kept by **Sol Plaatje**, one of the first black writers to make an impact on English literature, who was later to become a founder member of the South African Native Congress, forerunner to the ANC.

Getaway Lodge 39 Tillard St, corner with Baden Powell St ☎018 381 1150. Marginally cheaper than the *Garden View* under the same management, with 31 good en-suite rooms, handy for catching early morning buses and taxis. Also has safe parking, a restaurant and bar, and a nice pool. ❸

The Surrey 32 Shippard St ☎018 381 0420, ℻018 381 1353. The only cheap accommodation in town, with large if run-down rooms, most with bathrooms (and bathtubs). Can be noisy to around midnight thanks to the adjacent ladies' bar. Lacks safe parking. ❷

Tusk Mmabatho Casino Hotel Nelson Mandela Dr ☎018 389 1111, ⓦwww.tusk-resorts.co.za. Surprisingly poky for an upmarket resort, but three restaurants, two bars, two swimming pools, a sauna and spa, adjacent 18-hole golf course, and the casino that helped keep Mangope in power, are some compensation. ❻

Mafikeng

The town's main attraction is **Mafikeng Museum** (Mon–Fri 8am–4pm, Sat 10am–1pm; donation) on Martin Street, housed in the impressive former town hall, built in 1902, two years after the siege ended. You can't miss it, as there's a restored steam locomotive outside, in use from 1901 until 1971 when it pulled the Kimberley–Bulawayo Express. The museum has some intriguing exhibits on the **San**, including photos of the hand signals they use when hunting in their customary silence, as well as a range of hunting weapons and poisons. Tswana exhibits include a life-size re-creation of a traditional hut, complete with its trademark enclosed porch, and samples of pottery and beadwork. An extensive display of herbs and medicines includes sweet violet – which has five times the Vitamin C content of oranges – and a relative of the potato called the mandrake, with awesomely hallucinogenic powers. The **siege of Mafikeng** is given a room of its own, filled with classic British imperial memorabilia, including a tattered flag, ration book, diaries and a wonderful collection of photos. The Tswana writer and activist **Sol Plaatje** lived in Mafikeng for many years, and wrote a diary of the siege (see box above) while serving as court interpreter, and he receives a full, informative display. Keep an eye out too for the fascinating exhibit on Mafikeng and the **railways**, which provides evidence of the connection between their spread from Cape Town and Rhodes' mission to colonize Africa. The museum sells an excellent visitor guide (R30), and a glossy but very informative publication about North West Province (R90).

A smattering of historic buildings nearby make for a pleasant stroll. Facing the museum on Martin Street stands the splendid **St John's Anglican Church**, designed by Sir Herbert Baker and built in 1902. Three blocks north, on Victoria Street facing the bus and taxi terminal, look for **Victoria Hospital**, which was pounded during the siege, and the elegant **St Joseph's Convent** next to it. West of here and then north along Carrington Street is the **cemetery**, next to the sleepy railway sidings. Dusty and unkempt, it counts amongst its headstones white iron crosses marking the graves of British soldiers. Some were casualties from the siege, and others are from the many other battles waged by the British against the Afrikaners and Tswana. Until the 1980s this was a whites-only cemetery, and today it still commemorates only the Europeans who died during the siege.

Mmabatho

Four kilometres north of Mafikeng along Nelson Mandela Drive (catch a minibus taxi on Station Road) is **Mmabatho**, created in 1977 as capital of the new "independent homeland" of Bophuthatswana, but now subsumed into Mafikeng. The city prospered fast, both from the discovery of platinum and the revenue from Sol Kerzner's gambling resorts. Under the direction of Bop president Lucas Mangope, the capital became an ostentatious attempt to show off what a prosperous independent African state could become, though in practice it was a bloated and surreal quasi-state, riddled with corruption and egocentricity. Huge buildings were constructed for the burgeoning civil service, and brand new casino-hotels catered to the new black elite, as well as South Africans chasing the illicit thrills denied them across the border. Money was poured into bizarre enterprises, including an Israeli-built sports stadium with 75,000 seats but scarcely any shade (which will host matches for the 2010 World Cup), and a state-of-the-art **recording studio**, which has been seeing more use since the end of apartheid: the sound track for *The Lion King* was recorded here.

There's not, to be honest, all that much to do in Mmabatho other than get a sense of the scale of Mangope's ambitions, or indulge in a spot of window shopping at the modern **Mega City Shopping Mall**. That said, one place definitely worth visiting if you happen to be here at the right time is the highly regarded **North West Arts Complex** (☎018 384 4890) on Sekama Street opposite Mega City. Home to dance and theatre companies, and the National Chamber Orchestra, the complex hosts weekly performances; ring ahead for the schedule.

Eating, drinking and nightlife

Mafikeng isn't exactly a gastronomic hotspot, though it does boast one of South Africa's few truly African **restaurants**. For **fast food**, there's a branch of *Captain DoRego's* in Mafikeng Market Square on Shippard Street, and *Steers*, *Wimpy* and *Pizza Palace* at Game Shopping Centre between Nelson Mandela Drive and the taxi terminal. Local fast food places are best for cheap and simple stews, particularly mutton. For your own supplies, the cheapest **supermarket** is the large Superspar at Game Shopping Centre, and there's a bakery at the west end of Tillard Street. The Mr Food grocery on Shippard Street (closes

6pm, and all day Sun) has a wide selection of hot take-outs, including stews, and cheap breakfasts.

Walking around at night is not recommended, and as Mafikeng still lacks a telephone taxi service, unless you have wheels or can find a local to accompany you, **nightlife** is limited to within a block or two of your hotel.

Buffalo Park Lodge Corner of Botha and Molopo roads. The best restaurant in town, with a menu including seafood, vegetarian pub lunches and unusual Afrikaans specialities such as "steak carpetbagger" (stuffed with cheese and mussels, topped with mushroom sauce). Mains average R40–60. The attached *Waterhole* bar is a north-European style pub with sports on the TV and a live band on the last Friday of the month. Daily to 11pm or later; last food orders 10pm.

Ebony and Ivory Jazz Bar Corner of Martin St and Station Rd. One of the better local dives, unintimidating, and playing nicely mellow music.

Graceland Restaurant and Niteclub Main St, near Nelson Mandela Dr. The town's only central nightclub, positively heaving weekend nights. Go with a local.

Ivory Pot 11 Shippard St. A small but highly recommended restaurant specializing in African food, and – excepting the marvellous fry-up breakfasts – nothing but. Choose from various delicious stews, washed down with tangy homemade ginger beer. Daily 8am–10am & noon–4.30pm.

O'Hagan's Irish Pub & Grill Corner of Gemsbok and Tillard streets, 1km northeast of the centre. This casual and welcoming pub is the town's main upmarket drinking hole, with several beers on tap, and reliably good grub.

Listings

Banks First National Bank, Robinson St, has a dedicated foreign exchange section.
Car hire Avis, Mmabatho International Airport ☏018 385 1114.
Hospitals Best is the private Victoria Hospital, Victoria St ☏018 381 2043. The state hospital is Mafikeng Provincial Hospital, south of the tourist office in Danville ☏018 383 2005.

Internet access At Mega City Shopping Mall, Mmabatho.
Pharmacies and doctors There are several at Game Shopping Centre.
Police Corner of Hatchard St and Carrington St.
Post Post office, Carrington St; DHL ☏018 381 2439.

Around Mafikeng

Several attractions lie within easy day-trip distance of Mafikeng. If you don't have your own transport, contact Dumagole Tours & Safaris at Mafikeng's

Moving on from Mafikeng

Protours' daily **buses** to Pretoria and Johannesburg start at the Mega City shopping mall in Mmabatho and call in at Mafikeng Market Square on Shippard Street (book by phone: ☏012 664 5880 or 082 654 9009). Northwest Star/Star Line (no office; ☏018 381 2680) covers most of North West Province; buses start at the minibus taxi terminal between Victoria and Hatchard streets. As ever, early morning departures (6–7am) are best. **Minibus taxis** cover most destinations within the Province, as well as Kimberley in Northern Cape. An alternative approach to Northern Cape is the daily 7am **train** to Kimberley (9hr). There's also an 11pm service on Sundays to Johannesburg, arriving the following morning at 5am. The station entrance (tickets 6am–6pm) isn't obvious; it's opposite Tillard Street between the Boxer superstore and the mobile phone mast, next to a footbridge. South African Airlink **flies** regularly to Johannesburg (airport ☏018 385 1140, reservations ☏011 978 1111, ⊛www.saairlink.co.za); there's no public transport to the airport, so arrange a ride with a hotel or tour company.

tourist office (☎018 381 7873, ✉tmabe@telkomsa.net), who are reliable and cheap, and the only local outfit registered with the region's nature reserves.

Mafikeng Game Reserve

Starting on the eastern edge of Mafikeng, **MAFIKENG GAME RESERVE** (daily 7am–6pm; ☎018 381 7874, ⊛www.tourismnorthwest.co.za/parks /mafikeng.html; R15, plus R7.50 per car) covers some 46 square kilometres of rather drab Kalahari grassland and thornscrub and is well stocked with primarily herbivorous plains game, including **white rhino** and **buffalo**. The principal circuit around the reserve takes two hours and offers rewarding game viewing, particularly around waterholes. **Cooke's Lake**, in the reserve's western corner next to town, is reasonably good for waterfowl and mongooses (and the snakes they prey on). There are plans to open the reserve to cyclists and hikers.

There are two **entrances**: one 10km east of Mafikeng along the R49 towards Zeerust, the other just 3km from the town centre – go down Shippard Street and turn right after the railway bridge (2km) on to Jacaranda Street. Aslaagte Gate is straight ahead. There are plans to open a third gate next to the tourist office on Nelson Mandela Drive. Two **tour companies** are registered with the reserve: local outfit Dumagole Tours & Safaris (see above), which offers three-and-a-half-hour trips for R90 per person including entrance fee, and Mankwe Safaris (see box on p.664) based in Sun City. You can **stay overnight** at one of the reserve's new and extremely attractive two-storey wood-and-thatch chalets beside Cooke's Lake (❹), or in the less inspiring self-catering chalets (❷) at *Manyane Lodge* in the centre of the reserve, where there's also a restaurant. **Camping** should be possible at the lodge.

The Wondergat

Thirty kilometres east of Mafikeng is **WONDERGAT** ("amazing cave"), a broad water-filled sinkhole at least 70m deep, and one of Africa's best inland **diving** spots. Visibility is good, and denizens include the sharptooth catfish, southern mouthbrooder, banded tilapia and freshwater prawns. The site is managed by the Technical Diving Academy (☎082 321 1987 or 083 278 9330, ⊛www.wondergat.co.za), which offers **diving courses** at all levels and also maintains a basic supply shop and small **campsite**; tented accommodation can be provided on request. If you just want to swim and picnic, Dumagole Tours & Safaris in Mafikeng (see above) includes Wondergat as part of their "Heritage Tour" day-trip (R1000 for a minibus, or R90 per person if you can join another group), which also takes you to siege-related sites and battlefields. To get to Wondergat independently, head out along the Lichtenburg road from Mafikeng, turn left at the Burhmansdrift turning, and right at the signpost.

Botsalano Game Reserve

Thirty-five kilometres north of Mafikeng lies **BOTSALANO GAME RESERVE** (daily: May–July 8am–5pm; Aug–April 6.30am–6pm; ☎018 386 2433 or 083 340 1851, ⊛www.tourismnorthwest.co.za/parks/botsalano.html; R15, plus R7.50 per car), whose name means "friendship" in Tswana. Covering 58 square kilometres of arid *thornveld* and grassland, the reserve's main function is as a genetic pool for plains game, which are used to stock other reserves. Although **white rhino** are the obvious highlight, and **birdlife** is reasonably impressive with around 140 different species, what makes the reserve special from a visitor's point of view is that both mountain biking and hiking are permitted (bring your own bike); with an extensive network of tracks and basic trail camps, this means that you could potentially spend days wandering around the bush and hardly see anyone else.

Dumagole Tours & Safaris in Mafikeng (see above) offers half-day **tours** to the reserve from around R100 per person. To get there independently, take the R503 to the Ramatlabama border post; just before the border, take the Dinakana turn-off, and continue for about 7km to a crossroads. From here, take the turn marked "Dinakana", and travel another 7km up a dirt track. The gate here should be open. If it isn't, drive a further 12km to the management gate and enter from there. You'll need to be self-sufficient to **stay overnight**, as the trail camps only have toilets, water (and showers) and braai areas. There are also several similarly spartan campsites at the reserve's entrance, and the centrally located **Mogobe Tented Camp** (☎018 381 5392, ☎018 340 1851), with just four self-catering twin-bed tents (❷) overlooking a waterhole, often fully booked. There's another braai and picnic site close to the entrance, and a viewpoint at Sentry Hill for gaudy sunsets over Botswana.

Lichtenburg and around

The deeply conservative *dorp* of **LICHTENBURG** lies some 65km southeast of Mafikeng on the R52, close to the N14 highway connecting Northern Cape to Gauteng. Lichtenburg means "place of light"; when the town was proclaimed in 1873, it was hoped that the new settlement would bring some light to this forsaken spot. Progress was deadly slow until 1926, when a Tswana labourer on the Elandsputte farm of Jan Voorendyk discovered a **diamond**. News spread fast, and by 1927 the Lichtenburg diamond diggings were 36km long and around 1.5km wide. Incredibly, a shantytown of 150,000 people had sprung up by then, supporting 25,000 diggers and sporting over 200 diamond-buying offices. The quantity of diamonds discovered here threatened the diamond market, but De Beers bought nearly every one – including the world's largest flawless red diamond – to maintain its monopoly and the diamonds' worth.

The shantytown was famed for its **dust**, which was alleged to waft from Lichtenburger mouths as they spoke. By 1935, the rush had petered out, but a few prospectors remain as well as one company still sifting the alluvial diggings; you can watch its men in action by following the R505 21km north of Lichtenburg towards Zeerust, and turning left just before the Bakerville turn-off – it's 4km further on. Alternatively, arrange a visit through Lichtenburg's **Ampie Bosman Cultural & Historical Museum** on De la Rey Square (Tues–Fri 10am–12.30pm & 1.30–5pm, Sat 10am–1pm; free). The museum is worth a visit for its display on **General Koos De la Rey**, who tried and failed to capture Lichtenburg from the British in 1900. Though one of the Boer's most brilliant military strategists, De la Rey was also one of the "bitter enders", who only stopped fighting in 1902 with the greatest of reluctance. Nearby, on Melville Street South (the town's main thoroughfare), the linked **Diggings Museum** (Mon–Fri 10am–1pm & 2–4pm; free) offers some background to the 1926 rush with assorted artifacts and some lively stories from Lichtenburg's heady days as a diamond town.

Aside from diamond lore, the town's other attraction is the 45-square-kilometre **Lichtenburg Game Breeding Centre** (Mon–Fri 8am–4pm, Sat & Sun 8am–6pm; ☎018 632 2818, ⓦwww.ltxgamebreedingcentre.co.za; R10), 2km northeast of town. Operated by the National Zoological Gardens, it contains an unusual selection of wildlife, including West African pygmy hippopotamuses and vultures, the latter coming to feed in the afternoon at a "vulture restaurant" in the forest. There are also picnic facilities, and guided tours if booked in advance.

Digging for diamonds

"Once you have found your first diamond, you will never give up looking."

Digger proverb

According to digger mythology, all that anyone needs to find diamonds is a claim, a pick, a shovel, a wheelbarrow, and the luck of the gods. In practice, however, extra equipment comes in pretty handy. First off, you'll need a "dummy", which is a swinging sieve in a frame that gets rid of larger stones. After this, you'll need a "washing machine", which mixes the gravel left by the dummy with muddy water, its rotating arms and teeth holding the mixture in suspension. The diamonds and heavier gravel sink to the bottom, and the lighter gravel, called "tailings", floats to the top and is poured out. Another sieve separates the tailings from the water, which is reused. After the washing machine, the remaining gravel is poured into a sluice and then a washing tub, which removes the last of the water and grades the gravel into three sizes. These are then pored over with a knife, in the hope that this time there will be a diamond. In 1926, at the time of the Lichtenburg diggings, all this equipment cost around £600, which effectively meant you needed a diamond to pay for it.

To get there, cut east through town along any street until you reach Potgieter Street or Ferdi Hartzenberg Avenue, and turn left (north).

Practicalities

Buses and **minibus taxis** stop at the Shell garage in the town centre. Tourist **information** is available from Jan Schutte, the tireless curator of the Ampie Bosman Museum (☎018 632 5051), who can also arrange cultural tours in the area.

The most interesting **accommodation** is at the *Game Breeding Centre* (see above; ❷), which has five bright and modern en-suite rooms, with use of a kitchen and sitting room – staying here also gives you the chance of taking a guided night drive through the centre. The town's best rooms, though, are at the Georgian *Scott's Manor*, 21 Bree Street, on the northern edge of town and well signposted from the Mafikeng and Zeerust roads (☎018 632 0255, ⓦwww.scottsmanor.cjb.net; ❷); amenities include a swimming pool, restaurant and cocktail bar. Also good is the *Melville 20 B&B*, 20 Melville Street (☎018 632 3514; ❷), with a small art gallery attached. If all these are full, there are loads of cheap rooms at the run-down *Elgro Hotel*, at the corner of Scholtz and Republiek streets west of Melville Street (☎018 632 3051–4, ⓔelgro@intekom.co.za; ❷). For **eating and drinking**, try *O'Hagan's* pub on Melville Street, or *Spur Steakhouse* next to the *Elgro*.

Along the N14

Lichtenburg lies just off the main N14 route between Johannesburg and Upington in the Northern Cape. This journey is worth considering as an alternative to the more direct Jo'burg to Cape Town routes through Kimberley or Bloemfontein, as it takes in a wider diversity of South Africa's landscapes and, particularly once it reaches the Northern Cape, offers a number of worthwhile diversions. The section running through North West Province, however, has little worth stopping off to see.

The most interesting diversion is **BARBERSPAN BIRD SANCTUARY** (daily 7am–6pm; ☎053 948 1854, ⓦwww.tourismnorthwest.co.za/parks /barberspan.html; R15), 85km southwest of Lichtenburg and 17km short of Delareyville. A large, natural wetland in striking contrast to the fields of *mielies* that line the rest of the route, Barberspan is an important dry season refuge for **birds**. Amongst the pan's tens of thousands of inhabitants figure African fish eagles, flamingos, pelicans, herons, storks and ibis, grebes, terns, cranes, and all but one of South Africa's duck species; well over 350 all told. Specialized bird **guides** can be provided if booked in advance, and there are picnic and braai facilities. The site is visitable as a day-trip out of Mafikeng; it works out cheaper if you can assemble a sizeable group – count on at least R1000 for a minibus plus entrance fees, and bring insect repellent. There's a simple **campsite** on the south side of the pan equipped with electricity and toilets, plus two small chalets (**❷**). Adjacent is the *Barberspan Hotel & Resort* (**☎**053 948 1930, **ⓕ**053 948 1896; **❷**–**❸**), which has six rooms in the hotel plus twenty self-catering chalets on the edge of the pan sleeping six each, as well as a campsite of its own, a caravan park, bar, restaurant and swimming pool.

The N14 continues on past the supply town of Delareyville into Bophirima Region, the western section of the Province, dominated by huge cattle ranches, hunting concessions and little else. The main town 100km beyond Barberspan, is **Vryburg**, which has the usual range of chain steakhouses and stark wayfarers' hotels, but nothing beyond that to divert the passer-by. South of Vryburg, around 70km along the road to Warrenton, the small settlement of **TAUNG** is famous for the discovery of the "Taung Child", the fossilized skull of an early hominid ancestor of modern man, *Australopithecus africanus*. Uncovered in 1924 by a Buxton Lime Works quarryman, the skull provided a vital link in confirming man's evolution from apes, although strangely it was the only human fragment ever found here; other finds were mostly of prehistoric baboons. The escarpment continued to be quarried until 1977, so nowadays there's little more than a memorial plaque to see.

Southern Region

The mighty **Vaal** (or Lekwa) was the historic boundary between the Orange Free State and the South African Republic (ZAR). Still the provincial boundary, separating North West from the Free State, today the Vaal runs alongside the N12 highway between Johannesburg and Kimberley. None of the towns along the way are particularly important places to visit, though you will find one or two decent options for an overnight stop, including the historic university town of **Potchefstroom**. West of here the N12 passes vast stretches of maize-growing country and a succession of sleepy *dorps*, none of them particularly appealing; there are no big towns until you reach Kimberley in the Northern Cape, but a string of small nature reserves on the banks of the Vaal and the excellent *Lindbergh Lodge* provide good opportunities to break up your journey. Note that although a national highway, sections of the N12 aren't in the best repair, and after nightfall the busy, unlit road can be an unpleasant place to drive.

Potchefstroom

Located just under 100km southwest of Johannesburg, **POTCHEFSTROOM** is one of the largest and oldest towns in North West Province. Founded by Voortrekker leader **Andries Potgieter** on the banks of the Mooi River in 1837, Potchefstroom means "stream of chief Potgieter". Once the capital of the ZAR, today "Potch" is best known for its university, which has experienced some turbulence between black and Afrikaner students since blacks were admitted in the 1990s, but the presence of a large student population does give

The Vredefort Dome

Vredefort, a settlement 30km southeast of Potch just over the border in the Free State, near Parys, lies in the world's oldest meteorite impact site, a ninety-kilometre-wide depression known as the **Vredefort Dome** dating back to a strike some 2000 million years ago. The colossal impact caused major shifts in the earth's crust up to 150km away, and also helped raise the Witwatersrand. The convoluted landscape left by the collision now supports a wide variety of natural habitats, including a unique wild olive forest. The diversity is such that over 400 bird species have been recorded here, and the Dome has been shortlisted as a UNESCO World Heritage Site. You may steal a glimpse of a leopard or caracal, but big mammals are largely absent, and most people come here for the numerous **outdoor sports and adventure tourism** on offer, including horse-riding, hiking and camping, abseiling, rock climbing, mountain biking, and canoeing, rafting and angling on the Vaal River. For **more information**, contact the tourist office in Potch.

parts of town a youthful and energetic vibe, and the city as a whole has a pretty laid back and safe feeling to it – certainly compared to Gauteng.

Orientation, arrival and information

The N12 highway is called Potgieter Street as it cuts east–west through town. Crossing it north to south is Kerk (Church) Street, whilst running parallel to Kerk Street two blocks west is Van Riebeeck Street, whose northern extension turns into Tom Street, eventually leading to the university. Intercity **buses** stop at the west end of Potgieter Street. **Trains** from Cape Town and Johannesburg stop at the train station, 1.5km west of the city centre off Potgieter Street; you'll have to walk into town.

The **tourist office** at the junction of Potgieter and Kerk streets (Mon–Fri 8am–5pm, Sat 8am–noon; ℡018 293 1611–3, ✉tidcpotch@mweb.co.za) is exceptionally helpful, dolling out free photocopied maps and more detailed colour ones (R20), and can help find rooms if a conference or other event fills things up. There's a multimedia console outside the entrance, together with a map. Like many university towns, the classic way of getting around is by **bike**; to rent one, head for Dingo Cycles on Kerk Street (℡018 293 3456, ✉info@go-bike.co.za), 1.5km north of the tourist office. *Lakeside Recreation Resort* (see below) may also have bicycles, though these in theory are only for guests. For a **taxi**, call Oom Taxi (℡072 480 4993).

Accommodation

Accommodation, though plentiful, can be hard to find whenever a conference rolls into town, or during the annual **arts festival** at the end of September and early October, at which time booking a month ahead isn't a bad idea. In addition to the options listed below, the Potchefstroom Guest House Association website (🌐www.cosy-cottage.co.za/PGV) lists over two dozen properties which can be booked online.

Lakeside Recreation Resort Tom St, 5.5km north of Potgieter St ℡018 299 5473–4, ℻018 299 5475. The best budget place, but miles away at Potchefstroom Dam, where you can rent a self-catering bungalow or camp beside the lake; there's a swimming pool and bicycles and angling equipment for hire. **❶–❷**

Oudrift Riverside Cottage Van der Hoff Rd (extension of Kerk St), 3.5km north of Potgieter St ℡018 297 4939, ✉emix@mweb.co.za. A comfortable and relaxing B&B by the banks of the Mooi River, with 16 rooms, restaurant and swimming pool. **❸**

Shady Acres Guest House Plot 25, Mooivallei, 5km northeast of the tourist office ☎018 290 5773, ✉ssbhsg@puknet.puk.ac.za. A quiet and friendly family-run hideaway set amidst mature trees, with four guest rooms – all with TVs and bathrooms – in a terrace beside the main house. Meals provided if preordered. From the east end of Potgieter St, head up Mooi River Avenue until it hits M.C. Rooderylaan (3km), turn left and left again at the old drive-in theatre. ❷

Willows Garden Court 82 Mooi River Avenue, corner with Potgieter St ☎018 297 6285, �🌐www.potchefstroom.co.za/willows. The town's leading hotel, a large and unexciting four-star affair with all mod-cons, but reasonable at the price. ❹–❺.

The Town

The N12 highway cuts through town, leaving the central area with little of the charm you'd expect of such an old settlement. **Kerk Street**, at right angles to the highway, is now an inelegant shopping arcade, although parallel Greyling Street is the site of the old *landdrost* and **post office**; Potchefstroom played a major role in the ZAR's postal services, and black runners were employed here to deliver mail as far away as what is now Mpumalanga Province, hundreds of kilometres away. The **Potchefstroom Museum**, on Gouws Street just south of Potgieter Street east of the tourist office (Mon–Fri 10am–1pm & 2–5pm, Sat 9am–1pm, Sun 2.30–4.30pm; free), houses one of the few remaining Voortrekker wagons used at the Battle of Blood River in 1838 (see p.561), when Voortrekkers defeated the Zulus.

Away from the centre and the main highway, Potch takes on a much more appealing demeanour, especially around the **university** area – known locally as *Die Bult* – some 3km north up Tom Street's impressive avenue of oak trees, where you'll find the attractive old buildings and functional new ones buzzing with university life. Nearby, **Pretorius House** (Mon–Fri 10am–1pm & 2–5pm, Sat 9am–1pm; free) on Van der Hoff Road (an extension of Kerk Street), is the former home of Marthinus Pretorius, the ZAR's first president. It's a beautiful old house with whitewashed walls, green doors and a thatched roof, and is typical of nineteenth-century Afrikaner dwellings. Inside, you'll find dour photos and ornate wallpaper, minimal furnishings and a family Bible. On the opposite side of the street stands the **Totius Museum** (Mon–Fri 10am–1pm & 2–5pm, Sat 9am–1pm; free), re-created to be as it was when the poet lived here a century ago. Totius was a key figure in the Dutch Reformed Church and Afrikaans language movement: as well as establishing the church's theological college in Potchefstroom, he was one of the first poets to publish in Afrikaans, and translated the Bible into Afrikaans between 1923 and 1933. The most striking part of the museum is the poet's tome-filled study, but look out also for paintings by the celebrated and controversial Jacob Pierneef, which were especially dedicated to Totius.

Eating and drinking

The top spot for **eating and drinking** is Tom Street in the university area. *Die Akker Coffee House* at no. 86 Tom St is the best place to hang out, and is open for most of the day and night. Two blocks south at no. 104 is *O'Hagan's*, an Irish theme bar with good pub grub, grills and Guinness. Closer to town at 90 Kerk Street, *Ribs for Africa* is an unassuming diner handy for cheap African dishes and stews. The familiar pizza/pasta restaurants and steakhouses are well represented at the Riverwalk Centre, Potch's main mall, off Potgieter Street on the Johannesburg (east) side of the town centre; the line-up includes *Dros*, an upmarket German-style "wine cellar".

Unusually for North West Province, **live music** – invariably Afrikaans rock and pop – is a regular feature of Potch nightlife, which boasts three major venues, the liveliest being *Bourbon St Brewery* at 94 Tom Street, close to *Die Akker*, with bands at weekends and good food. The relaxed and friendly *Castilions Pub*, 84 Tom Street, is pleasant at any time of day, while *Knights*, 49 Lombard Street, 500m north of Potgieter Street, is particularly lively on Wednesday, Friday and Saturday nights.

Listings

Banks Standard Bank, corner of Kerk and Retief St, 1km north of Potgieter St.
Horse-riding Potch Horse Riding Club ☎018 294 5781.
Internet Clues Online, 7 Esselen St, 2km north of Potgieter St (up along Kerk, then turn left; Mon–Sat 8.30am–10pm, Sun 2–10pm).

Police Corner of Potgieter and Van Riebeeck St ☎018 11011.
Post office Greyling St, just south of Potgieter St.
Supermarkets Pick 'n Pay, corner of Kerk and Retief St.

8 Wolmaransstad and around

WOLMARANSSTAD, 115km southwest of Potchefstroom along the N12, consists of little more than two or three streets with a handful of shops. There's a scraggy **campsite** east of town off the R504 on the way to Leeudoringstad, but the nicest place to stay in these parts is the *Lindbergh Lodge* (☎018 596 2070, ✉lindberg@iafrica.com; half board ⑥). Here you can get a tantalizing glimpse of how the veld looked before maize took over, when it was home to abundant birds and wildlife. Set in a small nature reserve, the beautiful thatched lodge looks out onto a busy watering hole, enabling indolent game viewing from an armchair. The fifteen rooms are luxurious, and there's a simple bush camp if you'd rather self-cater – though the cooking here is definitely worth sampling. The absence of predators makes it safe to wander the lodge on foot, and get close up to the giraffe, antelope and other plains game, which can also be approached on horseback, or at night on a game drive. There's also the obligatory swimming pool, tennis court, mountain bikes, and golf course nearby. To reach *Lindbergh*, turn right onto a dirt road, off the N12 some 20km southwest of Wolmaransstad, and follow the signs to Rietpan, and then to Leeufontein. The lodge is about 15km from the main road, but the roads are bad and signposting poor, so aim to travel during the day.

For a taste of the scenery around the Vaal River, follow the R504 though Leeudoringstad to the small but scenic **Wolwespruit Dam Nature Reserve**, 50km from Wolmaransstad (☎018 581 9705, ⓦwww.tourismnorthwest.co.za/parks /wolwespruit.html; R10, plus R10 for angling). It's a popular spot for yellowfish

---

Moving on from Potchefstroom

Intercape (☎0861 287 287, ⓦwww.intercape.co.za) and Greyhound (☎018 293 1623 or 083 915 9000) **buses** operate from Jenni's Quality Foods at the corner of Potgieter and Van Riebeeck streets; Translux (☎012 315 4300, ⓦwww.translux .co.za) go from Mega Burger, two blocks west. Long-distance **minibus taxis** run from the terminal between Perrin and Gouws streets, one block northeast of the tourist office. The **train** station lies 15km west of the city centre (information ☎018 293 7603, reservations ☎0860 008 888); trains to Cape Town via Kimberley leave daily at 3.29pm; to Pretoria at 8.26am (and on Mon, Thurs & Sat at 3.02am); and to Bloemfontein at 10.28pm on Wed, Fri and Sun.

anglers and birders, and has several decent **campsites** along the river, some self-catering chalets and an attractive **stone cottage** (❷) sleeping up to eight.

Bloemhof

Heading further down the N12, tiny **BLOEMHOF** – named after a garden of flowers cultivated by the daughter of its founder – is an unremarkable agricultural town serving mainly as a stopover for buses on the long haul between Johannesburg and Cape Town. It also lies on the Cape Town–Pretoria railway line: trains to Cape Town via Kimberley call in daily at 6.25pm, to Pretoria daily at 6.17am, and to Bloemfontein at 1.42am on Mondays, Thursdays and Saturdays.

Much more interesting than the town is the enormous **Bloemhof Dam**, 4km east along the R34 Hoopstad road. Fed by the Vaal and Vet rivers, part of the 250-square-kilometre reservoir and surrounding Kalahari *thornveld* is now a **nature reserve** (daily 8am–5.30pm; ☏053 433 1706, ⓦwww.tourismnorthwest .co.za/parks/bloemhof.html; R10). Whilst the reserve contains a reasonable variety of plains game, and over two hundred recorded bird species, the main draw is **fishing** – though your angler's composure may be sorely tested by the presence of powerboats. If you want to **stay**, note that the parks board runs a plain camping and caravan resort near the water's edge which also has three fully equipped self-catering chalets and three six-bunk dorms (all ❶). In town, rooms and food are available at the uninspiring *Bloemhof Hotel* (☏053 433 1211; ❶), along the main street.

Travel details

Trains

Bloemhof to: Bloemfontein (3 weekly; 6hr); Cape Town (1 daily; 21hr); Johannesburg (1–2 daily; 6hr–6hr 30min); Kimberley (1–2 daily; 2hr 30min); Potchefstroom (1–2 daily; 3hr–3hr 15min); Pretoria (1 daily; 8hr).
Mafikeng to: Johannesburg (11pm Sun; 6hr); Kimberley (1 daily; 9hr).
Potchefstroom to: Bloemfontein (3 weekly; 9hr 15min); Bloemhof (1–2 daily; 2hr 45min–3hr 10min); Cape Town (1 daily; 24hr); Johannesburg (1–2 daily; 3hr); Kimberley (1–2 daily; 5hr 25min–6hr 20min); Pretoria (1 daily; 5hr).

Buses

Bloemhof to: George (1 weekly; 11hr 30min); Johannesburg (2–3 daily; 4hr); Kimberley (2–3 daily; 1hr 50min); Oudtshoorn (1 weekly; 9hr 30min); Potchefstroom (2–3 daily; 2hr 30min); Pretoria (2–3 daily; 5hr).
Mafikeng to: Johannesburg (1 daily; 6hr 30min); Pretoria (1 daily; 5hr); Rustenburg (1 daily; 3hr).
Potchefstroom to: George (1 weekly; 13hr 30min); Johannesburg (5 daily; 1hr 30min); Kimberley (2–3 daily; 4hr–4hr 30min); Oudtshoorn

(1 weekly; 11hr 30min); Pretoria (4 daily; 2hr 30min).
Rustenburg to: Johannesburg (2 daily; 2–3hr); Mafikeng (1 daily; 3hr); Pretoria (2 daily; 2hr–3hr 30min).
Sun City to: Johannesburg (2–3 daily; 2hr 30min); Pretoria (1 daily; 2hr 30min).
Vryburg to: Johannesburg (4 weekly; 5hr 40min); Upington (4 weekly; 10hr 15min); Windhoek (4 weekly; 20hr).
Zeerust to: Johannesburg (1 daily; 4hr 45min); Pretoria (1 daily; 3hr 15min); Rustenburg (1 daily; 1hr 15min).

Taxis

Minibus taxis follow more or less the same routes as buses, taking a little less time, but you may need to add several hours' initial waiting time before the taxi leaves. The main route covered by minibus taxis but not by bus is Mafikeng to Kimberley (2–3 daily; 5hr); taxis are also useful for short legs between towns.

Domestic flights

Madikwe to: Johannesburg (1 daily; 45min).
Mafikeng to: Johannesburg (1 daily; 1hr).
Sun City to: Johannesburg (hourly; 35min).

9

Mpumalanga

CHAPTER 9

Highlights

✳ **Raft the Blyde River Canyon** Get an unconventional view from the bottom of a spectacular thirty-kilometre-long canyon. See p.697

✳ **African meals at the Shangana Cultural Village** Here you can sample crocodile or mopane worms – as well as more conventional fare such as beef pot roast. See p.706

✳ **Bush breakfasts** There's no more satisfying way to round off a couple of hours of game-viewing than with a cooked breakfast in the wilds of Kruger. See box on p.711

✳ **Kruger night drives** Spot nocturnal creatures, reve-aled in the lights of your vehicle. See box on p.711

✳ **Walking safaris in Kruger** It's worth leaving behind the security of a vehicle for the thrill of potential close encounters with animals. See p.721

✳ **Leopard-spotting** The luxury camps in the Sabi Sands Game Reserve offer excellent opportunities to observe leopards. See p.725

△ A casual lion at Kruger

9

Mpumalanga

Mpumalanga, "the land of the rising sun" to its Siswati- and Zulu-speaking residents, extends east from Gauteng to Mozambique and Swaziland. To many visitors the province is synonymous with the **Kruger National Park**, the real draw of South Africa's east flank, and one of Africa's best game parks. Kruger occupies most of Mpumalanga's and Limpopo Province's borders with Mozambique, and covers over 20,000 square kilometres – an area the size of Wales or Massachusetts. Unashamedly populist, Kruger is the easiest African game park to drive around in on your own, with many well-run restcamps for accommodation. On its western border lie a number of **private reserves**, offering the chance – at a price – to escape the Kruger crush, with well-informed rangers conducting safaris in open vehicles.

Apart from the irresistible magnet of big-game country, Mpumalanga also has some spectacular scenery in the mountainous area known as the **Escarpment**, a couple of hours' drive west of Kruger and easily tacked onto a visit to the park. With the exception of **Pilgrim's Rest**, none of the Escarpment towns merits exploration, but they make good night stops to and from Kruger, and there are some stunning views as you drive around. The most famous viewpoints – **God's Window**, **Bourke's Luck Potholes** and **Three Rondavels** – are along the lip of the Escarpment, which can be seen on a 156-kilometre drive from Sabie. The views of **Blyde River Canyon** are most famous of all and, while you can't drive into the canyon, there are some fabulous hiking and river-rafting opportunities in this area.

Jammed between the mountains and Kruger are the former African **bantustans**, created under apartheid: Lebowa for Sotho speakers and Gazankulu for Shangaan- and Tsonga-speaking people. The poverty of these artificial statelets was exacerbated in the 1980s, when hundreds of thousands of Mozambicans fled into Gazankulu to escape the civil war in their home country. Even today, with the war over, Mozambicans attempt to cross illegally into South Africa, braving lions, National Parks officials and anti-poaching units in Kruger in a quest to reach the "golden city" of Johannesburg.

For overseas visitors, the **route** is usually the other way round, starting from Johannesburg and heading through the unattractive industrial corridor traversed by the N4 as it races to **Nelspruit**, the modern capital of Mpumalanga. From here the N4 continues to the **Mozambique border**, a route which also gives access to the southernmost part of Kruger. Nelspruit also connects with the road south through **Barberton** to Swaziland.

Descending the Escarpment on one of four mountain passes takes you into the tropical-fruit-growing and bushveld country of the **lowveld**, with impressive views back towards the towering massif of the Escarpment. A number of places close to the **Blydepoort Dam** at the foot of the Blyde River Canyon can be taken in as bushveld breaks on the way to or from Kruger. In the same vicinity, around tiny centre **Hoedspruit** (actually in Limpopo Province, but covered here because of its proximity to Kruger), roughly 90km via a route arching east from the Escarpment, a number of small **game farms** offer cut-price bush experiences. While these are good for a couple of nights, they lack the variety of animals and big game provided by Kruger and the pricier lodges in the Manyeleti and Timbavati private game reserves. Note that **malaria** (see p.48) is a potential hazard in the lowveld and Kruger, particularly in summer.

Johannesburg is the nearest city to Mpumalanga and is five or six hours' drive from Kruger; the city also has the best transport connections with the province. There's a daily **train** service between Johannesburg and Nelspruit and a daily Greyhound or Translux **bus** between the two cities. The Baz Bus travels between Johannesburg and Durban via Nelspruit and Swaziland. **Flights** link Jo'burg with Nelspruit, Hoedspruit and Phalaborwa; from Cape Town, you can fly into Nelspruit or Hoedspruit, while Nelspruit also has flights from Durban. Backpacker lodges do transfers from Nelspruit and all have their own tours to Kruger and the Escarpment. To get anywhere else in the province by public transport, you need to use Nelspruit as a springboard and take **minibus taxis**.

The Escarpment

Four hours' drive east of Johannesburg International Airport is one of the city's favoured mountain retreats: the waving grasslands and luxury guesthouses of the Mpumalanga Drakensberg, generally known as the **Escarpment**. While most travellers visit the region purely because of its proximity to the Kruger National Park, it provides some of the most dramatic views in the country, which can be enjoyed with little effort. Unlike the range in KwaZulu-Natal, this section of the Drakensberg is one you can tour in your own car, stopping at one of the tourist towns for lunch and retiring to comfortable lodgings at the end of the day.

The main draw of the Escarpment is the **Blyde River Canyon**, whose dizzying views into one of the world's great gorges appear in countless South African tourist brochures. In addition to a number of viewpoints along the Escarpment lip, the canyon can also be seen from the **Blyderivierspoort Nature Reserve** at its foot. The five-day **Blyderivierspoort Hiking Trail**, one of South Africa's best walks, starts at **God's Window** on the lip; it takes in all the major viewpoints and gives access to the flora and (if you're quiet and lucky) fauna of the reserve, which include zebra, hippo, kudu and the entire range of South African primates – baboons, vervet and samango monkeys and bushbabies.

The little forestry towns of **Sabie** and **Graskop** have ample accommodation for all budgets and are convenient bases for exploring the area, with the added pull of a plethora of **adventure activities**. **Dullstroom** has established itself as an upmarket fly-fishing resort, but only **Pilgrim's Rest**, a reconstructed mining settlement from the gold-rush days at the turn of the last century, merits a visit for itself.

Dullstroom and Lydenburg

Some 209km east of Johannesburg, the R540 branches off the N4 at non-descript **Belfast** and heads into the hills, where the highveld countryside is covered by grasslands, waving tall and green in summer, but turning russet in winter.

Unless your passion is fly-fishing, chances are you'll find the tiny crossroads settlement of **DULLSTROOM**, 35km north of Belfast on the R540, as unexciting as its name suggests. However, Dullstroom can be a useful place to stop over for a night on your way to Kruger National Park; the Dullstroom Information office, Old Stone House, Hugenote Street (℡013 254 0254, ℮reservations@dullstroom.net), can help with finding accommodation.

The town certainly caters to the weekend trade of Johannesburg escapees looking for a rest and fine **food** – most of the accommodation doubles up as restaurants. Dullstroom's best-known restaurant, *Die Tonteldoos Bistro*, in the main street (℡013 254 0115), is a popular, busy, daytime place with big breakfasts, a kids' menu and homemade bread, and an inviting garden. The deli at the front of the restaurant stocks smoked trout and other delicacies like nougat. The *Dullstroom Inn*, signposted just off the main street, is open from breakfast to dinner and has a welcoming fireplace in the busy pub, with chalked-up dishes of the day, including vegetarian fare and lots of trout.

Accommodation

Critchley Hackle Lodge Teding van Berkhout St ℡013 254 0999, ✉chl-wks@mweb.co.za. A gracious country-style hotel with stone and brick cottages, each with a fireplace. Their restaurant is recommended, and has a bar for after-dinner cognac, whiskey and cigars; there's also a patio for tea and scones. ❻

Dullstroom Inn Teding van Berkhout St ℡013 254 0071, ⊛www.dullstroom.info/dullstroominn. A pleasantly cool Victorian country inn that is one of the least expensive places to stay in the village. Its pub serves draught beer and gets packed at weekends. ❸

Old Transvaal Inn 117 Hugenote St ℡013 254 0222, ✉ggg@worldonline.co.za. A quiet and friendly B&B offering good food, a fine location and cultivated quaintness of style. Recommended. ❸

The Poacher 66 Hugenote St ℡013 254 0108, ✉info@poacher.co.za. A small, friendly lodge with four rooms, river frontage and a tackle shop. Best of all is its restaurant, serving sophisticated country fare and pub grub, with Guinness on tap in the pub. ❷

Lydenburg and Long Tom Pass

Some 58km north of Dullstroom, humdrum **LYDENBURG** is the site of one of South Africa's major archeological finds, replicas of which are on display at the **Lydenburg Museum** (Mon–Fri 9am–noon & 2–4.15pm, Sat & Sun 10am–4pm; small entry fee) in the Gustav Klingbiel Nature Reserve, 3km out of town along the R37 to Sabie. The **Lydenburg Heads**, seven beautiful ceramic masks (probably ceremonial) dating back to the fifth century, are some of the first figurative sculptures in southern Africa. As well as replicas of these heads (the originals are in the South African Museum in Cape Town), there are excellent displays on human activity in the vicinity over the past million years or so.

Striking east from Lydenburg, the R37 twists its way up **Long Tom Pass**, which takes its name from the Scheider siege guns used here by the Boers during the 1899–1902 Second Anglo-Boer War against the British. Known as Long Toms because of their elongated necks, the artillery pieces were able to throw a 43kg shell a distance of 10km. You can still see the holes blasted by retreating Boers into the series of switchbacks cutting up the pass, known as the Staircase.

Sabie, Pilgrim's Rest and Graskop

Sabie, the largest of the three towns occupying the heights of the Escarpment, has its personality split between serving the surrounding agroforestry industry and trying to please the tourists who use it as a base. Of the other two, **Pilgrim's Rest** unashamedly plays to the tour buses, pushing hard with its restored gold-rush buildings and themed museums, while the relatively uninteresting timber centre of **Graskop** is trying to develop its potential in an attempt to secure those elusive tourist bucks. Though they all advertise themselves as bases for Kruger, they most definitely are not, since it takes a good couple of hours of twisting down mountain passes to get to Kruger, and once you are in the park, all you do is drive anyway. If you want a Kruger base outside the park, stay as close to an entry gate as possible.

Sabie and around

Lying on the R37 beyond Long Tom Pass, **SABIE** (pronounced "Saabie", like the car) is the centre of Mpumalanga's agroforestry industry. It holds the dubious distinction of lying at the heart of South Africa's largest artificial forests, with 450 square kilometres under active cultivation. The extensive pine plantations look monotonous compared to the rich, jungly variety of the remaining pockets of indigenous woodland.

Before the foresters arrived, Sabie made its name as a gold centre, with a lucky strike in 1895 at the Klein Sabie Falls. Mining stopped halfway through the twentieth century, and today the gold prospectors have been replaced by escapees from hectic Johannesburg, who make a living here running restaurants, B&Bs or craft shops.

Sabie's compact size, slow pace, mildly arty ambience and gentle climate make it a congenial base for exploring the Escarpment. If you don't have your own transport, you can still take advantage of its well-organized backpacker's lodge, and a raft of adventure activities.

Arrival, information and accommodation

Public **transport** to Sabie is limited to minibus taxis plying the routes from neighbouring towns; otherwise *Sabie Backpackers* does have a reasonably priced **shuttle** between Nelspruit and Sabie. The central Sabie Info, in the Market Square mall, Main Road (Mon–Fri 9.30am–5.30pm, Sat & Sun 9am–1pm; ☏013 764 2666, ⓦwww.sabie.info), is one of several **information** offices in the village.

Sabie offers a good supply of reasonably priced **accommodation**, though prices can rise dramatically during South African school holidays. Avoid the rock-bottom B&Bs which the information bureaus list: most of them offer no privacy.

Artist's Cafe Hendriksdal, 15km south of Sabie along the R37 ☏013 764 2309 or 082 565 3345. Situated in the beautifully converted colonial station buildings of Hendriksdal siding, which still has goods trains trundling along its tracks. The stationmaster's house has been converted into a first-class restaurant, and a gallery features work by local artists. It has only four rooms, so you should book well ahead. Kids are welcome. ❸

Hillwatering Country House 50 Marula St ☏013 764 1421, ⓦwww.hillwatering.8m.com. Renovated 1950s home with four large bedrooms, each with their own veranda, overlooking the Bridal Veil Falls. The reception is warm and breakfast excellent. ❸

The Kranz Along the R537 to White River ☏013 764 1330, ⓦwww.thekranz.co.za. Friendly B&B in

a del uxe cottage with a view over a cliff, as well as a slightly cheaper log cabin or garden cottage. Less expensive still are a couple of rooms in the main house with a shared bathroom. You'll need to head into town, 2km away, for dinner. ❷–❸

Merry Pebbles Holiday Resort 2km west from the centre on the Old Lydenburg Rd ☏013 764 2266, ⓦwww.merrypebbles.co.za. Now showing its age a little, *Merry Pebbles* offers camping, self-catering and en-suite chalets; facilities include a heated pool and children's playground. Mercifully no quad bikes or motorbikes are allowed. ❶–❷

Misty Mountain Lodge 24km southwest of Sabie on Long Tom Pass ☏013 764 3377, ⓦwww.mistymountain.co.za. Pleasant, B&B units, some with splendid views across pine plantations into the valleys. There's trout fishing on the property, with rods and flies for rent at a nominal rate; the lodge is also well placed for walks into indigenous forest. You can self-cater or take advantage of the restaurant and pub on the premises. Rates are the same whether you take breakfast or not. ❸–❹

Sabie River Backpackers Lodge 185 Main Rd ☎013 764 2118. A well-run, fun hostel, with camping, dorms and doubles, featuring sturdy beds and warm bedding. There's also accommodation for two in a tree house.

Xtreme Adventures, based here, organizes a host of adventure activities (see box below), and the lodge has good weekend packages with wall-to-wall adventure activities. Dorms and rooms ❶

Villa Ticino On the corner of Louis Trichardt and Second streets ☎013 764 2598, ⓦwww.villaticino.co.za. An extremely hospitable Swiss-owned B&B with a terrace looking onto the hills, and a lounge with a pool table. Winter discounts are available. ❸

The Town and around

Sabie is segmented by **Main Street** (the R37 from Lydenburg and the Long Tom Pass), which meanders into the town centre where it hits **Main Road** at right angles. At the junction of the two, the compact **St Peter's**, an English-style country church designed in 1912 by Sir Herbert Baker, hides in a verdant garden dominated by a gigantic jacaranda tree, which in early summer covers the lawn with mauve petals like confetti. Nearby at the corner of Tenth and Seventh streets, the **Komatiland Forest and Industry Museum** (Mon–Fri 8am–4pm, Sat & Sun 8am–12pm; R5) has a small, worthwhile display on the history of forestry and the timber industry in South Africa, plus a section on papermaking.

A large number of **waterfalls** drop down the slopes outside Sabie. Just 7km from town, down the Old Lydenburg Road, you can visit three of the most impressive: **Bridal Veil**, **Horseshoe** and, appropriately at the end of the road, **Lone Creek Falls**. The loveliest and most accessible of the three, it's conveniently reached down a paved, circular path that crosses a river and works its way back to the car park.

The most visited of the falls lie 13km north of Sabie along the Graskop road. Here you'll find the more spectacular seventy-metre-high **Mac Mac Falls** – named after the many people of Scottish descent who died looking for gold in the area and whose names appear on dozens of tombstones in the vicinity. Unfortunately, views here are restricted by a mesh fence around the viewing platform. Local craftworkers have set up a **market** in the car park. While you can't swim in the inviting waterfall pool at the base of the falls, there is a river

---

Activities in Sabie

With its forest, massive gorge and mountains, the Escarpment offers good opportunities for adventure activities. Among the operators running a range of these is Sabie Xtreme Adventures, based at *Sabie Backpackers Lodge* (☎013 764 2118 or 082 507 9108, ⓦwww.sabiextreme.co.za). The activities on offer include **Bunji Swing**, with a 69-metre drop into the Graskop Gorge, **horse trails**, **caving** by candlelight in the Lone Creek Caves, **waterfall abseiling** at the Sabie Falls, **mountain biking** and **whitewater tubing** and **canyoning**.

For **river rafting** in the Blyde River Canyon, one of the largest in the world, Blyde River Rafting (☎015 795 5250 or 082 572 2223, ⓦwww.ottersden.co.za) has a good reputation. The day-trip (R750) takes in an adventurous whitewater section, and there's also a two-hour trip (R150) on the lower Blyde River, through thick riverine forest with plenty of birds, and over some safe (but lively) rapids. A half-day on the Olifants River goes for R450.

pool at the Mac Mac Pools, a few kilometres further on, where there's also a picnic and braai area (R5 entry) and the three-kilometre **Secretary Bird Walking Trail**. Less popular, but surpassing the Mac Mac Falls, are the **Berlin** and **Lisbon** falls, both signposted and easily accessible off the R532 (close to God's Window). The vertiginous drops are unfenced, allowing you to get close enough to feel the spray.

Eating and drinking

Sabie has a couple of memorable **restaurants** and some relaxed places for light meals or drinks.

Artists Café Hendriksdal, 15km south of Sabie along the R37 ☎ 013 764 2309. A restaurant in converted station buildings, with an art-gallery setting and great atmosphere for lunch or dinner. The owners cook up a real storm – their Italian-style dishes are especially recommended. Booking essential. Closed Mon.

The Country Kitchen Main St. With outdoor seating and the chance to try dishes such as crocodile strips served with pumpkin and potato *rösti*, venison with peppercorn juice infused with *waterblommetjies*, plus ostrich. Tues–Sat lunch & dinner, plus Sun lunch.

The Wild Fig Tree On the corner of Main and Louis Trichardt streets. South African dishes are the speciality at this family restaurant set in an attractive, lush garden.

Woodsman Restaurant On the corner of Main and Mac Mac roads. A licensed restaurant with a beer garden, serving Cypriot Greek food, including vegetarian *meze*, plus local specialities such as ostrich and trout, and delicious slow-cooked lamb. Also good for coffee and snacks on the terrace, or at the cosy fire. Daily breakfast through to dinner.

Pilgrim's Rest

Hiding in a valley 35km north of Sabie, **PILGRIM'S REST**, an almost too-perfectly restored gold-mining town, is an irresistible port of call for the scores of tour buses meandering daily through the Escarpment's passes. A collection of red-roofed, corrugated-iron buildings, including a period bank, a filling station with pre-1920 fuel pumps and the wonderful *Royal Hotel* brimming with Victoriana, the place is undeniably photogenic. But you can't help feeling there's little substance behind the romanticized gold-rush image, especially when the village nods off after 5pm once the day-trippers have been spirited away.

Pilgrim's Rest owes its origins to South Africa's first **gold rush**, which predates the uncovering of the great Gauteng seams. In 1873, Alex "Wheel-barrow" Patterson discovered gold in the creek. His attempts to keep his discovery secret were a total failure, and by the end of the year Patterson had been joined by 1500 diggers frantically working 4000 claims. Far from the pristine little village of today, the **Pilgrim's Rest diggings** were the site of gruelling labour and unhygienic conditions. Many diggers arrived malnourished, suffering from dysentery and malaria after punishing treks through the lowveld. Those who survived could expect drab lives in tents or, if they struck lucky, more permanent wattle-and-daub huts. In 1896, the diggings were bought up by the Transvaal Gold Mining Estates (TGME), which closed its Beta Mine in 1972, handing Pilgrim's Rest over to the provincial administration.

The whole settlement was declared a historic monument in the 1980s. But mining continues behind the hill to the southwest of town, away from tourist eyes, with functional buildings, cyanide-filled slime dams and great red scars hacked into the hillside, the indigenous forest having been bulldozed out of existence.

Arrival and information

Pilgrim's Rest stretches along its one main road and is divided into Uptown and Downtown. Commercialized **Uptown**, to the east, has the greatest concentration of shops and restaurants and consequently draws the bulk of tourists; the area centres around the *Royal Hotel* and the **tourist office** (daily 9am–12.45pm & 1.15–4.30pm; ☎013 768 1060, which can provide details of accommodation. **Downtown**, just 1km to the west, has a more down-to-earth atmosphere, and its restaurants are a little cheaper – though many visitors slip in and out of Pilgrim's without realizing the area even exists.

Accommodation

Though Pilgrim's Rest is by far the prettiest of the Escarpment towns, there's very little accommodation in the town itself.

Crystal Springs Mountain Lodge 10km out of town on the R533 to Lydenburg ☎013 768 5000, ⓦwww.grc-resorts.co.za. A large resort which couldn't be better planned, better organized or situated, or boast better facilities; this is a pure slice of suburban South Africa on holiday. The thatched cottages have a deck and escarpment views, and there's a restaurant and bar on site, plus trampolines, a heated pool, playground, a games room and, for adults, a Jacuzzi, sauna and steambath. From the cottages there are well-marked walking trails into a ravine. Rates fall during the week, and out of school holidays. ❸

District Six Miners' Cottages Downtown ☎013 768 1211. Self-catering accommodation in authentic two-bedroomed 1920s workers' houses, sleeping two to four, with verandas overlooking the town and mountains. These are among the best places to stay on the Escarpment. You'll need to book ahead (Mon–Fri office hours), as there's no on-site office. ❷

Pilgrim's Rest Caravan Park Downtown ☎013 768 1427, ⓔgoodhouse@mweb.co.za. Grassy campsite with a river running through it. Accommodation comprises six two-bed tents and a backpackers' dorm. ❶

The Royal Hotel Main St, Uptown ☎013 768 1100, ⓦwww.royal-hotel.co.za. Atmospheric hotel that dates back to the gold-rush days and brims with luxurious Victoriana, with guests mostly accommodated in restored houses on the main road. ❺

The Town

Apart from souvenir hunting and lingering in the cafés and tea shops, the main activity in Pilgrim's is visiting its handful of **museums**. Tickets for all these must be bought in advance at the tourist office. You can whip through the three modest town "museums" in a matter of minutes, as they amount to little more than rooms reconstructed as they were in the gold-rush days. More interesting are those out of the centre. To get a really authentic impression of the gold-mining days, head for the open-air **Diggings Site Museum** on the eastern edge of town on the Graskop Road (guided tours only, daily at 10am, 11am, noon, 2pm & 3pm; R5), where you can see demonstrations of alluvial gold-panning and get a guided tour around the bleak diggers' huts, remnants of workings and machinery from the early mining days. By contrast, if you want to see how those at the top lived, visit **Alanglade**, just west of the Downtown area (guided tours only, Mon–Sat 11am & 2pm; R20), the reconstructed home of the former general manager of the mine. The house has a wonderful collection of early twentieth-century British fashion and decorative arts and reveals a sheltered way of life far removed from either Africa or mining.

Eating and drinking

Pilgrim's Rest has plenty of restaurants and tea shops to provide for the daily influx of visitors using Graskop or Sabie as their base, but the choice of food is a big yawn, with endless pancakes and burgers. Of the **places to eat** in

Uptown, only the *Digger's Den*, a lively, canteen-style place attached to the *Royal Hotel*, is open all day and every evening. *Mona's* (daytime only), on the right above the hotel, has an elevated coffee terrace fronting a shop selling curios and prints, with some gold-mining memorabilia to keep you browsing. There are a couple more daytime places along the Downtown section of the main drag, all of which have outdoor seating: *Scott's Café* (daily 9am–6pm) serves pancakes, sandwiches, salads and other light meals, and has a pleasant bar, while *Jubilee Potters & Coffee Shop* (daily 9am–7pm) does steaks, sandwiches and burgers.

Graskop

Some 15km east of Pilgrim's Rest, **GRASKOP** owes its place on the tourist map to *Harrie's Pancake Shop*, which serves much-imitated but rarely rivalled crepes, and attracts all the tour buses doing the Escarpment viewpoints. The town itself is very ordinary, with timber trucks rumbling heavily through, and nothing much to see in the centre apart from the shops eyeing the tourist trade. Its location, however, as the closest town to the Blyde River Canyon to the north, goes some way towards compensating, and the growing number of artists here, together with a small gay community, are helping to shift Graskop's lumberjack image. One notable village industry is its **wild African silk** factory and showroom, a couple of doors down from the tourist office, which manufactures and sells a range of clothes, soft furnishing, duvets and even teddy bears from the silk of mopane silk worms (indigenous to Botswana).

Practicalities

Panorama Information & Central Reservations (Mon–Sun 8am–5pm; ☎013 767 1377, ⓦwww.panoramainfo.co.za), on Louis Trichardt Street, is the official **tourist office**. For **eating**, the legendary and well-signposted *Harrie's* on Louis Trichardt Street serves sweet or savoury pancakes and has a nice outdoor terrace, and an inside dining room with a roaring log fire in winter. *The Silver Spoon*, on the corner of Louis Trichardt and Kerk streets, works hard to compete, with pancakes and waffles from 7am onward. For more substantial meals, *Leonardos Trattoria*, Louis Trichardt Street (Mon–Sat 11.30am–3pm & 5.30am–9pm; ☎013 767 1078), with an adjoining art and craft shop, is one of the few places open in the evening and does good pizza and pasta lunches and dinners.

Accommodation

Given its diminutive size and lack of excitement, Graskop has a surprisingly large number of self-catering places (though few B&Bs), plus the delightful, stylish and reasonably priced *Graskop* hotel.

Graskop Hotel On the corner of High St and Louis Trichardt Ave ☎013 767 1244, ⓦwww.graskophotel.co.za. One of the nicest places to stay on the Escarpment, with a personal and relaxed atmosphere. Though from the outside it looks like a bog-standard travelling-salesman's joint, it actually has a very stylish interior of retro furniture, African baskets, fabrics and sculptures. The rooms, some of which are in garden wings, are airy and decorated with considerable flair. ❸

Graskop Log Cabin Village Oorwinning St ☎013 767 1974, ⓦwww.logcabin.co.za. A resort right in the centre of town, with a swimming pool and log fires for the cold winter nights, but no views. Cheaper during the week and for longer stays. ❷

Kloofsig Chalets Just outside town on the road to Hazyview ☎013 767 1489. This resort makes up for the fact that it's over the road, rather than right on the lip of the canyon, by offering modern and luxurious town-house-style units, with discounts during quiet periods. ❸

Panorama Rest Camp Outside town on the Hazyview road ☎ & ℱ 013 767 1091, ⓦ www .panoramarestcamp.co.za. Inexpensive accommodation in gardens looking out over the Escarpment, as well as campsites and a variety of units sleeping two to eight people. ❷

Blyde River Canyon and Blydepoort Dam

There are few places in South Africa where you can enjoy such easily accessible and dramatic scenery than the colossal **Blyde River Canyon**, weathered out of strata of red rock and dropping sharply away from the Escarpment into the lowveld. The **Blyde River Canyon Nature Reserve** (also known as Blyderivierspoort Nature Reserve) stretches from a narrow tail near Graskop in the south, and broadens into a great amphitheatre partially flooded by the **Blydepoort Dam** about 60km to the north.

The views of the canyon are wonderful from both above and below, but the nicest way to take in the vistas is on an easy half-day's drive along the canyon lip. Some 3km north of Graskop, the road branches, the easterly route being a fifteen-kilometre loop (the R534) past a series of superb **viewpoints**. The road winds through pine plantations until it comes to the turn-off to the **Pinnacle**, a gigantic quartzite column topped with trees, rising out of a ferny gorge. After another 4km the road reaches the sheer drop and lowveld views of **God's Window**, one of the most famous of the viewpoints; it's also one of the most developed, with toilets and specially constructed stalls for curio sellers. The looping road returns to rejoin the R532, which continues north for 28km beyond the turn-off to reach **Bourke's Luck Potholes** at the confluence of the Treur and Blyde rivers – a collection of strange, smoothly scooped formations carved into the rocks by water-driven pebbles.

The best view of all lies 14km beyond, at the **Three Rondavels**. The name describes only one small feature of this cinemascope vista: three cylinders in the shape of huts with the meandering Blyde River twisting its way hundreds of metres below. No photograph does justice to the sheer enormity of the view, punctuated by one series of cliffs after another buttressing into the valley.

The only **place to stay** in the nature reserve is *Aventura Blydepoort* (☎013 769 8005, ⓦ www.aventura.co.za; ❸), 5km north of the turn-off to the Three Rondavels lookout. The resort has comfortable, self-contained and fully equipped cottages, a swimming pool, supermarket, bottle store and filling station; the atmosphere can feel a little institutionalized, but it's a good place for children.

A guided two-day **Blyde Hike** is available with Sabie Xtreme (☎013 764 2118, ⓦ www.sabiextreme.co.za). The hike starts close to God's Window and ends up 30km later at Bourke's Luck Potholes. Light meals are provided, as is transport, and you sleep at an overnight hut at Clear Stream; bring your own hiking gear, including a sleeping bag.

Three Rondavels to Blydepoort Dam

The ninety-kilometre **drive** from the Three Rondavels viewpoint to the base of the canyon provides spectacular views of the Escarpment cliffs rising out of the lowveld and is easily incorporated into your itinerary if you're heading to or from Kruger. The drive winds west to join with the R36 and heads north to begin its descent through the Abel Erasmus Pass and then the J.G. Strijdom Tunnel through the mountain, with the wide lowveld plains opening out on the other side. The road takes a wide arching trajectory to circumnavigate the canyon.

Along the R527, near its junction with the R36, the **Monsoon Gallery**, (☎015 795 5114, ⓦ www.monsoongallery.com), 29km west of Hoedspruit, makes a good place to pause on your journey to browse in their excellent shop, have a meal or spend the night. Their great African arts and crafts showroom has an absorbing selection of authentic material, including ironwork and woodcarving from Zimbabwe, superb tapestries from the Karosswerkers factory near Tzaneen, Venda pots and jewellery, as well as African music CDs and books. Next door to the gallery, a **silk shop** sells beautiful African and Indian silk garments, silk-filled duvets, cravats and scarves. Also part of the same outfit is a good **place to eat** – *Mad Dogz Café*, where breakfasts, lunches and teas are served every day. They also offer **accommodation** nearby at *Blue Cottages*

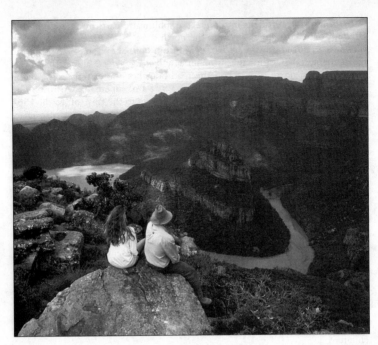

△ A view of the Three Rondavels

(☏015 795 5425, ⓦ www.countryhouse.co.za; ❷–❸), in superbly comfortable suites in a farmhouse filled with African artefacts and fabrics, set in an enticingly cool and colourful garden; more modest, but also beautiful, are the garden cottages. Breakfast is served at *Mad Dogz*, and you can have a mid-priced dinner served in your garden under candlelight.

Roughly 15km further east, the untarred Driehoek road hives off to the south past the *Aventura Swadini* resort and on to the **Blydepoort Dam**, 38km from Hoedspruit. Alternatively, you can continue on the R531 for a further 12km and take the tarred turn-off to the southwest, which leads straight down to the dam. At a dead end along this road, the **Blyde River Canyon Visitor Centre** (daily 7am–5pm) has interesting displays on local ecology and a useful model of the canyon that helps you get orientated. The best reason to come here though is for the views across the flooded valley below and to spend the night close to indigenous bushveld at the foot of the mountains.

Blydepoort accommodation

Reached along the same road as the visitor centre, *Aventura Swadini* (☏ & ⓕ015 795 5141; ❸) has **chalets** for up to six and a **campsite** with stunning scenic surrounds; it's great for kids, and cheap for a group, but has a similar institutional feel to its sister resort on the mountain. A number of short trails start from here and you can take cruises on the Blydepoort Dam. More intimate, is the nearby *Trackers* (☏015 795 5033, ⓦ www.trackers.truepath.com; ❶–❸) abutting the canyon's cliffs 25km from Hoedspruit. It offers a variety of accommodation – camping, a backpacker house with a dorm and six doubles, self-catering chalets – on a farm full of indigenous bushveld vegetation, where

Blyderivierspoort Hiking Trail

The only way to get directly into the canyon from the Escarpment is on foot, and the five-day **Blyderivierspoort Hiking Trail** is a great way of doing this. Although the 65-kilometre route requires a fair degree of fitness, the gradients aren't generally too taxing and the walk could be undertaken by a hardy novice. The hike starts at God's Window, 5km north of Graskop, and works its way north, ending at the Blydepoort Dam. There's a diversity of plant and animal life along the way and you may be lucky enough to spot hippos, crocodiles, zebras, baboons and monkeys.

Reservations for the trail can be made through Mpumalanga Parks Board (℡013 759 5432, ℻013 759 5432; R30 per person per day, including accommodation). **Accommodation** en route is provided in four fully equipped huts that can sleep up to thirty people (the maximum allowed on the trail), with flush toilets, cold showers and firewood. As the start and finish of the trail are 150km apart by road, you'll need to have access to two vehicles or make arrangements to get back to your starting point. You must carry all your own food. Note too that although the trail starts in **malaria**-free terrain, you will want to consider protection against the disease in the lowveld.

you may see zebra and antelope. Half board is available, though do bring your own drinks. A trained botanist living on the farm runs recommended **guided walks** through the indigenous vegetation. To get to *Trackers*, turn south into Driehoek road (as for the *Aventura* resort), continue for a little over 6km, then follow the "D. Rushworth" sign on your right.

The lowveld

South Africa's **lowveld**, wedged between the Mpumalanga section of the Drakensberg and Mozambique, is part of a vast subtropical region of savanna that stretches north through Zimbabwe and Zambia, as far north as Central Africa. Closely associated at the turn of the last century with fortune-seekers, hunters, gold-diggers and adventurers, these days the South African lowveld's claim to fame is its proximity to the Kruger National Park and the adjacent private game reserves. Although several of the towns on the game park fringes are pleasant enough, most people come here to get into big-game country.

Largest of the lowveld towns, and the capital of Mpumalanga, is **Nelspruit**, accessible by air and bus (including buses from Maputo). East of Nelspruit, the N4 runs close to the southern border of the Kruger, providing easy access to its Malelane and Crocodile Bridge gates; the latter is just 12km north of **Komatipoort**, a humid frontier town on the border with **Mozambique**. From Nelspruit, you can also head 32km south to **Barberton**, an attractive settlement in the hills with strong mining connections, or continue another 41km to **Swaziland**. With your own transport, Barberton makes a more relaxed staging post than Nelspruit for journeys between the south of the Kruger National Park and Swaziland.

The R40 north of the provincial capital passes through **White River**, **Hazyview**, **Klaserie**, **Hoedspruit** and **Phalaborwa**, a series of small towns which act as good bases for exploring Kruger. Each town is well supplied with accommodation, and has a Kruger entrance gate nearby; tours are available from some. Hazyview is now leader of the pack following the opening in 2002 of the Phabeni Gate into Kruger, which is a ten-minute drive out of town, and Hazyview itself is less than an hour's drive from Nelspruit, the obvious place to rent a car. Hoedspruit and Phalaborwa actually fall within Limpopo Province, but for the sake of continuity have been included in this chapter.

The lowveld area is **malarial**; for details on necessary precautions, see p.48.

Nelspruit

Fast-growing **NELSPRUIT**, 358km east of Johannesburg on the N4, grew in the 1890s as a base for traders, farmers and prospectors, but there is little evidence left of these origins. Most of the old buildings have been ripped out and replaced by shopping malls and freeways, and the town has a bustling and prosperous feel. It's a major commercial centre, not only for the lowveld but also for shoppers from Swaziland and Mozambique.

The town also has the best transport connections in the province, including air links with Johannesburg, Cape Town, Durban and Maputo, with flights to further-flung destinations in the pipeline. Unfortunately, flights to Nelspruit are among the most expensive in the country, and it may work out cheaper to fly into Johannesburg and continue here by car. Nelspruit also has an excellent hospital and all the facilities and shops you might need.

Arrival and information

Flights on SA Airlink (℡013 750 2531) and Nationwide (℡013 750 2640) arrive at the Kruger Mpumalanga International Airport (**KMIA**; ℡013 753 7500), 20km north of town off the R40 to White River. Avis (℡013 741 1087) and other major car rental companies can be found at the airport. Private Connections (℡013 750 2435) meets flights and does transfers into Nelspruit or onto lodges and hotels. Outbreak Tours (℡013 751 2257 or 082 836 1031) also does transfers to lodges and into Kruger Park itself. If you're travelling onward by road to Mozambique and need visas and information, consult the Mozambique Advisory Office in the airport building.

Intercity buses stop in the *Promenade* hotel's parking area in Louis Trichardt Street. Greyhound has its offices opposite the hotel (℡013 753 2100). The **Baz Bus** drops off at the town lodges on its trips from Mbabane (Swaziland) and Jo'burg. Citybug **shuttle buses** (℡013 741 4114, ⓦwww.citybug.co.za), which operate daily from Jo'burg and Pretoria, and weekly from Durban, pull into the BP garage in the Sonpark Centre, Piet Retief Street, just south of the city centre. They can arrange a taxi from here to your accommodation. **Minibus taxis** generally rank in Bester Street North, just east of the **train station** (℡013 752 9203), off Andrew Street at the north end of the town centre.

Lowveld Info, signposted as you hit town from Johannesburg, is the town's **tourist office**. At the Crossings Centre, corner of the N4 and General Dan Pienaar Street (Mon–Fri 8am–4.30pm; ℡013 755 1988/1989, ⓦwww.nelspruitinfo.co.za), they provide **maps** and basic information, and arrange accommodation, including bookings for Kruger's restcamps, as well as day-trips with various tour operators. Lowveld Info also has a kiosk at the upmarket

ACCOMMODATION

Aragoniet 22	E
Bushveld Lodge	G
Hotel Bundu	A
La Fontana Guest House	D
The Loerie's Call	H
Marloth 35	I
Matumi Golf Lodge	F
Old Vic Inn	B
The Palms	C
The Rest Country Lodge	J
Shandon Lodge	K

RESTAURANTS

Brazilian	3
Cafe Mozart	6
Costa Do Sol	5
Hillside Tavern	7
Makulu Manzi	4
Seattle Coffee	2
Spur	1

0 — 500 m

▼ Barberton & R40

9

MPUMALANGA | Nelspruit

Riverside Mall, just north of the city centre on the R40. Adjacent to the casino and provincial parliament, the mall has the best collection of shops in the province, and is a good place to stock up if you're planning to self-cater in the Kruger Park.

Accommodation

Nelspruit's **accommodation** is largely geared to business travellers. Most places have swimming pools to beat the summer heat, outdoor eating areas and tropical gardens.

Aragoniet 22 22 Aragoniet St ☏083 631 2136. Spotless, spacious and cheap self-catering in two garden flats and some log cabins overlooking the river. ②

Bushveld Lodge Kaapschehoop Rd, 6km from Nelspruit ☏013 741 5058. Small, budget self-catering chalets, sleeping two to four people. Each unit has its own kitchen. ②

Hotel Bundu 11km from Nelspruit off the R40 towards White River ☏013 758 1221, ⓦwww.bunducountrylodge.co.za. Popular, good-value family accommodation in an old-fashioned country hotel, decorated with animal hides and hunting trophies. There's camping and a swimming pool; the hotel also offers horse-riding and hikes to caves with rock paintings. ③

La Fontana Guest House Cnr John Vorster & Besembos Rd ☏013 741 3138, ⓦwww.lafontana .co.za. Mid-range B&B with seven rooms, a relaxed feel and a large pool and garden. ③

The Loeries Call 2 Du Preez St ☏013 752 4844, ⓦwww.loeriescall.co.za. A modern place with a pool, offering upmarket en-suite rooms with private verandas overlooking the Crocodile River Valley. As it's often fully booked, reserve well ahead. ④

Marloth 35 35 Marloth St ☏013 752 4529, ⓔggink@lantic.net. A simply furnished B&B with ceramic-tiled rooms and breakfast served outdoors. There's a swimming pool and braai facilities. ②

Matumi Golf Lodge Matumi Golf Estate, 5 Singa Dr ☏013 755 4993 or 082 492 7944, ⓦwww .matumigolflodge.co.za. Nelspruit's top place to stay with spacious and luxurious rooms, cheaper than you might expect, a grand deck with views and a good reputation for food. ③

Old Vic Inn 12 Impala St, 3km from town ☏013 744 0993 or 082 340 1508, ⓦwww .krugerandmore.co.za. Six clean, comfortable doubles and a dorm in a quiet backpacker hostel, with a pool, garden and walks in the adjoining nature reserve. They also have a unit suitable for a family. The owners can arrange transport from the centre of town and from the airport, and can organize tours, including Kruger packages. Dorms and rooms ❶

The Palms 25 Van Wyk St ☎013 755 4374, ✉thepalmsnelspruit@absamail.co.za. British couple running a good setup with a lovely garden and sunny breakfast room. Three rooms overlook the pool and palm trees, while two back onto the nature reserve. ❸

The Rest Country Lodge Uitkyk Rd, 10km from Nelspruit ☎013 744 9991 or 013 744 9992, ⓦwww.therest.co.za. Each luxury suite in this modern, purpose-built lodge has its own balcony with beautiful views over the lowveld. ❹

Shandon Lodge 1 Saturn St ☎013 744 9934, ⓦwww.shandon.co.za. Rooms with private entrances arranged around a swimming pool and tropical garden, in a well-established colonial-style home. The hosts are friendly and provide good food and information. ❸

The Town

The town centre, roughly six streets crisscrossed by another half dozen, could hardly be easier to get around. The N4 from Johannesburg to Komatipoort sweeps through town, briefly pausing to become **Louis Trichardt**, Nelspruit's main street, before reassuming its identity as the national highway.

Snazziest of the malls is the **Riverside Mall** complex, some 5km north of the city centre, which feels as if it could have been lifted straight out of affluent northern Jo'burg suburbs, with all the same shops, including a well-stocked supermarket, some excellent coffee shops and a better-than-average bookshop. Next to the mall is a casino and, perhaps aptly, the controversial **provincial legislature**, which cost around R600m to build. The massive price tag attached to its towering beehive domes and Queen-of-Sheba-style architecture caused a scandal in 1999 when it turned out that the legislature would have to slash its departmental budgets to pay the construction costs.

Over the road from the Riverside Mall is Nelspruit's major attraction, the **Lowveld National Botanical Garden** (daily: May–Sept 8am–5.15pm; Oct–April 8am–6pm; R10). Set on the banks of the Crocodile River, the garden comes a close second to Cape Town's Kirstenbosch Gardens. Natural waterfalls and walks through rainforest make a pleasant break from the boiling midday heat. If you've been to Kruger, you'll have a chance to look at some of the same **trees** here, grouped according to habitat and helpfully identified with labels. The garden specializes in **cycads** from around the world, and there's also a grove of baobabs from South Africa and other African countries. A useful brochure sold at the entrance gate has a map showing the highlights of the garden and the paths through it. Don't miss the **Makulu Manzi Restaurant**, which has a wooden deck and an outlook over the waterfalls.

Eating and drinking

Most of Nelspruit's **restaurants** are buried in shopping malls, where you'll find all the usual steakhouses and fast-food chains. In the Riverside Mall, *Spur* is good for salads, while *Seattle Coffee* and the *Brazilian* are both excellent for coffee and sandwiches. *Café Mozart*, corner of Ferreira and Van der Merwe, does quiches, coffee and tea and has a big garden and playground for kids. For a more expensive and imaginative meal, head for *Costa Do Sol*, opposite Nel City, on the corner of Kruger and Louis Trichardt streets, serving good Portuguese and Italian dishes. The *Hillside Tavern* in the Village Centre, 36 Murray Street, is a good place for drinks and food on its outdoor wooden deck. Best of all is *Makulu Manzi* (daily 8am–10pm; closed Sun eves; ☎013 757 0396) in the Botanical Gardens. The food, including unusual specialities such as ostrich with blue cheese and fig preserve, is beautifully presented, and there's plenty for vegetarians too.

Listings

Embassies Mozambique, Brown St ☎013 752 7396.
Emergencies Ambulance ☎013 10177; see also p.89.
Hospitals Nelspruit Private Hospital ☎013 759 0500.

Internet access There is an Internet café in the *Mugg & Bean* restaurant at the Crossings Centre.
Pharmacy Chemist Mopani, Crossings Centre (☎013 755 5500, out of hours ☎082 761 1603).
Post office The main post office, in Voortrekker St, is open 8.30am–4pm. Each shopping centre has a Postnet.

East from Nelspruit: Kruger's southern fringe

The N4 east of Nelspruit roughly follows the progress of the **Crocodile River**, which traces the southern boundary of Kruger National Park. For 58km to the tiny settlement of **Malelane**, the road travels within view of the Crocodile's riverine forest, passing lush, subtropical farmlands and the Dali-esque grey formations of granite *koppies*. Some 4km further on, the road turns off to Kruger's **Malelane Gate**, the most convenient entry point for *Berg-en-Dal* restcamp (see p.717). A signpost 12km east of Malelane indicates *Buhala Game Lodge* (☎013 792 4372, ⊛www.buhala.co.za; ❻), a fabulous **guesthouse** on a mango, sugar-cane and papaya farm set high on the banks of the Crocodile, with views across the slow water into Kruger. Trips into the Kruger Park can be arranged from here for around R550 per person, as well as walks in Kruger Park for R350. Pricier, but very good for the soul, is *Serenity Luxury Mountain and Forest Lodge* (☎013 752 7365 or 082 888 4835; ❼), its nine enormous log cabins set in deep forest. You drive down a bumpy twelve-kilometre track from Malelane to get there, but you're rewarded with butterflies, clear streams and tranquillity. Close by is the Malelane golf course, and the *Lodge* offers golf packages. There are self-catering garden cottages at *Selati 103* (☎013 790 0978 or 083 305 4479, ⓔselati103@hotmail.com; ❷), 2km from Malelane Gate. While there is no restaurant on site, the Park does have a pool, and there are two well-stocked supermarkets, restaurants and takeaway places 5km away at Malelane village.

Barberton

BARBERTON, 36km south of Nelspruit, began its urban existence after Auguste Robert ("French Bob") discovered **gold** in 1883 on a nearby farm. Despite his attempts to keep the news to himself, other diggers realized something was up when French Bob began building a canal to his claims. The following year, **Graham Barber** discovered another incredibly rich gold reef and got his name hitched to the town at a riotous christening using a bottle of gin. An influx of shopkeepers, hoteliers, barmen, prostitutes, even ministers of religion, soon joined the diggers in the growing frontier town, which consisted of tents, tin, thatch and mud, with nearly every second building functioning as a boozing joint. During the fabulous boom of the 1880s the mines slipped out of the grasp of the small-time prospectors and came under the control of the large corporations that still own them today. This is the best place in the country to take a **gold-mining tour**, or watch gold-panning being done. This attraction aside, Barberton also has a colonial backwater charm, reasonably priced accommodation, a handful of historical sights, tropical vegetation and an attractive setting in a basin surrounded by mountains.

The closest and most beautiful route **into Swaziland** from Barberton is through the border crossing at Bulembu (8am–4pm), but the road is poor and should be avoided in the summer unless you're in a 4WD vehicle, though an ordinary car can make it in the dry season. A more practical option which takes the same time, though it's a longer way round, is to enter Swaziland via the border posts of Ngwenya/Oshoek (7am–10pm) or Jeppe's Reef/Matsamo (7am–8pm), the latter route requiring you to pass through the Kaapmuiden toll gate on the N4.

Arrival, information and accommodation

No scheduled public **transport** comes into Barberton, though from Nelspruit you can find a minibus taxi for Barberton. The outstanding **tourist office**, Crown Street (Mon–Fri 8am–4.30pm, Sat & Sun 9am–4pm; ☎013 712 2121, ⓦwww.barberton.co.za), can help find accommodation in the area, or point you to local walks, as well as supply you with reams of brochures and maps covering the whole province. They can also book **mining tours**, **horse-riding** or **microlight** flights. Horse-riding at Tormar Ranch (☎084 700 7722) is particularly recommended, as you go into a river on horseback, and get cooled off with the horses after your ride.

Barberton's **accommodation** is cheaper than in its uppity cousins like Hazyview, and just as good.

Barberton Manor 81 Sheba Road ☎013 712 44826, ⓦwww.barbertonmanor.com. The town's most upmarket stay is this large mansion, where everything is beautiful and just so. ❹

Fountain Baths Guest House 48 Pilgrim St ☎013 712 2707, ⓦwww.fountainbaths .co.za. Pleasant B&B rooms and self-catering mini-apartments for two to four people, in a tropical garden edging onto Saddleback Hill. The owners' kids, graduated from cooking establishments in Cape Town, have set up Barberton's first fancy restaurant here, the *Three Chefs*. ❷

Grace Farm Cottages Badplaas Rd, 7km from town ☎013 712 5068. Three inexpensive self-catering houses on a farm with a pool and *lapa*, where you're made to feel part of the family and children are taken to feed farm animals. There's good bird-watching in the surrounding bush. ❶

Old Coach Road Guest House and Restaurant 13km north of Barberton on the R38 to

Kaapmuiden ☎013 719 9755, ⓦwww .oldcoachroad.co.za. Comfortable twin and double en-suite rooms, as well as two family units, at a friendly establishment set in its own peaceful grounds, with a pool, big lawn and monkeys in the trees. The licensed restaurant (eves only) has a terrace looking onto spectacular mountains. ❸

Oppikoppi 27 Henry Nettman St ☎012 712 6498. Thatched accommodation ranging from bush huts to honeymoon cottages, on a *koppie* with balconies and great views. All self-catering, they're kitted out with everything from irons to microwaves, and there's a pool and *lapa* as well. The jovial owner Rassie loves to take guests on quad-bike trips or walking trails along the Badplaas River. ❷–❸

The Phoenix 20 Pilgrim St ☎013 712 4211, ⓔphoenix@soft.co.za. Barberton's only hotel, an old-fashioned place recently renovated by a British hotelier, has a long corridor of comfortable en-suite rooms, and a decent restaurant. ❷

The Town

There are seven working **mines** around Barberton, each with its own entertainment venues, which means you won't find miners packing out public bars as in the wild days of old. You can explore the mining history of the town at the **Barberton Museum**, 36 Pilgrim Street (Mon–Fri 8am–4pm, Sat & Sun 9am–1pm & 2–4pm), three blocks east of the tourist office. In a well-designed, modern building, the museum has good displays on the gold-rush era. More thrilling is watching young black students working gold from Agnes Mine at the **Umjindi Jewellery Project** (Mon–Fri 8am–5pm, Sat 8am–2pm) next to the museum. The project trains people in the area to become jewellery designers and makers over three years. Some of the work produced is on sale, and there's a good coffee shop doing espressos and lattes – rather adventurous for Barberton.

The museum can provide a map of the town's **Heritage Walk**, on which green and white signposts direct you to some historical houses and monuments. Built for a wealthy middle-class family and restored to its 1904 grandeur, **Belhaven House** at 18 Lee Road (daily 9am–4pm) is a five-minute walk north from the museum with tours on the hour from 10am until 3pm. Further up Lee Road, **Fernlea House** (Mon–Fri 9am–4pm) is a wood-and-iron structure, with not much to see inside. To the east is the most interesting of the three, **Stopforth House** at 18 Bowness Street (daily 9am–4pm; tour times as for Belhaven). The original wood-and-iron house and outbuildings were built by James Stopforth, a local baker and general dealer.

Eating and drinking

Barberton's best place to **eat** is the cheap and friendly *Co-Co Pan* in Crown Street, which serves straightforward hamburgers, steaks and omelettes. Your

Barberton mining tours and trails

Unlike at Pilgrim's Rest, where you'll have to be content with merely watching how panning was done, at Barberton you can try it yourself. One mine, **Agnes**, runs **underground tours** in a historical section of the mine, which is no longer worked (daily; R100; ☎013 712 8002). At the entrance to the ninety-year-old mine, you're given a hard hat, lamp and miners' boots to head off into the darkness. You're also given a chance to learn how to pan for gold – swilling water and sand in a big dish to watch for the telltale thread of gold appearing in the dark sand. Agnes is 9km out of town, along the extension of Crown Street, where there is also a restaurant. Tours are by appointment only.

Another fascinating trip is along a disused ox-wagon track, focusing on the geology of the area and showing you meteorite deposits. The trip finishes at **Eureka City**, an 1880s mining settlement that died after forty years. Eureka hasn't been reconstructed like Pilgrim's Rest – you'll only see walls and foundations, after driving through a real mine to get there. Wagon-track tours are run by Rassie Schoeman of the *Oppikoppi Guest House*.

To get a sense of what the old mines were like, the two-kilometre circular **Fortuna Mine Hiking Trail**, just south of town, takes you through a disused tunnel built to transport gold-bearing ore to the Fortuna Mine. The trail, which starts at the car park off Crown Street to the south of town, goes through an attractive area of indigenous trees before entering the six-hundred-metre tunnel (bring **a torch**), and once you're through you get good views of Barberton and the De Kaap Valley. Maps are available from the tourist office.

best chance to meet locals is to head downstairs to the lively John Henry **pub** below the restaurant. Next to the tourist office on Crown Street is the pleasant *Victorian Tea Garden* (closed eves & Sun), with a white gazebo straight out of a London park, and good tea and light snacks served outdoors. The *Old Coach Guest House* is recommended for its beautiful surroundings; it's open only in the evening for three-course meals. Fanciest is the *Three Chefs* at *Fountain Baths Guest House*, where you can sample dishes such as African duck or smoke chicken breast with mango; it's open from breakfast to dinner, except Sunday evenings and Mondays.

North from Nelspruit: Kruger's western flank

The **R40** heads north from Nelspruit along the western border of the Kruger National Park, passing through prosperous tropical-fruit-growing farmlands and poverty-stricken former black "homeland" areas. The only reason you're likely to find yourself heading north along this road from **Hazyview** is to access the private game reserves – **Sabi Sands**, **Manyeleti** or **Timbavati** – that join up with the western flank of Kruger (see p.725), or to reach the **Orpen Gate**, for the rewarding central section of Kruger National Park. Guesthouses, many of them fairly upmarket, pop up all along the way to Hazyview until you reach the densely populated former Bantustan areas around **Bosbokrand**. Roadside lodgings reappear once you reach **Klaserie**, which lies on the border of Mpumalanga and Limpopo Province. Many of these are located on game farms – poor cousins to the pricier lodges inside the game reserves to the east.

North of the Mpumalanga border you'll pass little towns en route to the central section of Kruger National Park and the Manyeleti and Timbavati private game reserves. Coming down the Escarpment along the R36/R527 from the Blyde River viewpoints, you'll encounter a fork in the road after about 75km. The more northerly road leads to the towns of **Hoedspruit** and **Klaserie**, both of which lie in the heart of bushveld **game farm** country, whose budget game viewing is no substitute for Kruger and its adjacent private reserves. Much further north and generally reached from Polokwane on the N1, the mining town of **Phalaborwa** is conveniently 2km from the Phalaborwa Gate into central Kruger and the rewarding camps of Letaba and Olifants.

Hazyview

HAZYVIEW, 43km north of Nelspruit, used to be little more than a couple of large, well-stocked shopping centres buzzing with minibus taxis and small market stalls selling fruit and goods to the surrounding African community. But with the opening of the **Phabeni Gate** into Kruger Park, a mere 10km from town, Hazyview is perfectly positioned for access to the game-rich southern section of the game reserve. The town is one of the best bases for visitors who want to view game without spending the night in the park itself, and who also want to sample some adventure activities and tours.

The **Shangana Cultural Village** (daily 9am–4pm; ⓦwww.shangana.co.za), about 5km west of Hazyview, just off the R535 to Graskop, is a good place to get a sense of the cultural traditions of the local Shangaan community as well as enjoy an excellent lunch (see p.706). Entrance is free to the reception area and its craft shop, but the village can only be visited on a guided tour (every hour on the hour; R60). The tour follows a winding path through fields and bush to one particular kraal where a family lives; you'll also meet a *sangoma* and learn about traditional remedies.

Practicalities

The shortest and quickest route here from Johannesburg, 421km away, is via the N4 and Nelspruit. No public **transport** apart from minibus taxis comes into Hazyview, but if you're staying at one of the local backpacker lodges you can arrange to be collected from Nelspruit. Hazyview is spread out, but a centre of sorts has emerged at **Perry's Bridge**, on the corner of the R536 and R40, a small complex of luxury shops, craft outlets, restaurants and game activity booking agencies. Central Reservations (Mon–Sat 8am–5pm, Sun 8am–2pm; ☎013 737 8191, ⓦwww.big5country.com) can book accommodation and safaris and also sells books and distributes maps. National Parks Kruger accommodation can also be booked through them, and they cover the Escarpment as well. Conveniently, the Paper Chain Internet Café is here too.

Accommodation

Hazyview has a wide range of **accommodation**, most of it in farmland strung along the roads radiating out to the neighbouring towns of Sabie (the R536), Graskop (the R535) and White River (the R538), as well as to Kruger's Paul Kruger Gate (the R40).

Ant & Elephant 6km from Hazyview on the R536 ☎013 737 8172, ⓦwww.antandelephant.co.za. Reasonably priced chalets, each with self-catering facilities and patios with braais, on a lychee and mango farm. You can get breakfast and dinner at their own restaurant. ❸

Hippo Hollow Country Estate Just south of town, along the R40 to Paul Kruger Gate ☎013 737 7752, ⓦwww.hippohollow.co.za. Luxurious B&B accommodation in thatched cottages, nicely positioned on the banks of the Sabie River, and with a restaurant, reception and bar area. The self-catering units are less expensive, though the facilities aren't geared up for any serious cooking. There are excursions into Kruger from here every morning; a full day-trip to Kruger costs around R550. ❹–❺

Hotel Numbi Main Rd ☎013 737 7301, ⓦwww .hotelnumbi.co.za. An old-fashioned, comfortable place offering camping, garden suites and hotel rooms. ❹

Idle and Wild 6km from Hazyview, on the R536 ☎013 737 8173 or 082 381 7408, ⓦwww .idelandwild.co.za. This mango farm in a lush valley on the banks of the Sabie River offers two thatched rondavels, a family unit and two honeymoon suites (with their own spa bath) in the lush garden, as well as two en-suite bedrooms in the main house. All have kitchenettes, and there's a Jacuzzi, sauna and swimming pool – and, for some adrenaline, quad bike riding on the farm. ❸

Kruger Park Backpackers Main Rd ☎013 737 7224, ⓔinfo@krugback.com. A pleasantly

located hostel under shady bushveld trees, offering campsites, dorms, rondavels and, nicest of all, Zulu beehive huts. There's a swimming pool and they run organized tours into Kruger from here, Jo'burg or Pretoria. They can also pick you up from Nelspruit. ❶

Rissington Inn 2km south of town, just off the R40 ☎013 737 7700, ⓦwww.rissington.co.za. A country lodge with labradors in attendance, Rissington is a relaxed and informal place (kids are welcome), with fourteen rooms set in the gardens of a large thatched homestead. Best are the garden suites which have roofless outside showers, open to warm breezes and starry skies. You also get a swimming pool and excellent food and service into the bargain. To get here from Hazyview, take the R40 south and watch for the signposts. ❺

Riverside Cottages 11km from Hazyview on the R536 road to Sabie ☎013 737 8143, ⓦwww.riversidecottages.co.za. Excellent self-catering accommodation in face-brick cottages nicely situated under fever and sausage trees on the banks of the Sabi River. A swimming pool, trampoline, tennis court and adventure activities such as whitewater tubing are available, and there's also a restaurant on the premises.

Sabi River Sun 2km from Hazyview on the R536 on the banks of the Sabie River ☎013 737 7311, ⓦwww.southernsun.com. A luxury family resort along the Sabie River, landscaped around a beautiful golf course. Golfing apart, there are measured tracks for jogging or cycling, a swimming pool and kids' playground, or you can just wander down to see if there are any hippos about. The resort has a family restaurant and pub. ❺

Thika Thika Guest Farm and Backpackers 3km from Hazyview on the R536, on the banks of the Sabie River ☎013 737 8108 or 082 403 9676, Ⓔ thika@worldonline.co.za. Three fully equipped timber chalets sleeping up to six people, on a sweet-smelling citrus farm with lush subtropical

vegetation. There's also a comfortable backpacker dorm at the main bungalow with crisp white linen, and some double rooms. ❶–❷

Thulamela 1km down White River Road, off the R40 ☎ & Ⓕ013 737 7171, Ⓔinfo @thulamela.co.za. A romantic guesthouse with wine in the fridge and rose petals on the bed, run by a dietician who serves healthy breakfasts. Guests are put up in en-suite timber cottages, each with its own deck, Jacuzzi and bushveld views. Weekday discounts, no children under 16. ❻

Eating and drinking

There are a number of decent places to eat around Hazyview which, like the town's accommodation, are mostly dotted along the main roads connecting Hazyview with neighbouring towns. Perry's Bridge Centre, on the corner of the R40 and R356, has a fine coffee shop called *Perry's* (8am–5pm), run by the genial Trevor Brotherton, as well as the more upmarket *Digby's*, open for lunch and dinner, with offerings such as springbok carpaccio. In the centre, the *Hysterical Hornbill Pub and Restaurant*, in the Simunye Centre along the R538 (☎013 737 7404), is a relaxed family-friendly spot offering reasonably priced meals such as steak or fish and chips till late, except Sunday evenings; they also have a buzzing pub. The gracious *Rissington Inn* serves candle-lit dinners on the terrace in lovely surroundings, and caters well for vegetarians, while the *Shangana Cultural Village* (noon–2pm; ☎013 737 7000) offers delicious African dinners (R120) cooked in massive pots over an open fire by the chief's wives; the menu can include crocodile in spicy peanut sauce, beef and honey-glazed sweet potato.

Orpen Gate

After Hazyview, the R40 passes through irrigated farmlands and low hills dotted with bushveld trees. As you approach **Bosbokrand**, 28km to the north, the corridor between the Escarpment and big-game country changes, with the sudden appearance of shanty towns, busy roads, overgrazed lands and dense settlements interspersed with the odd papaya and banana tree. Bosbokrand is also known as **Bushbuck Ridge** (a direct translation from the Afrikaans), the name coming from the hilly finger extending east from the Escarpment – although any bushbucks that might once have wandered here have long since been displaced by the cattle and goats.

Despite the fact that maps indicate little or no habitation, the busy and sometimes hazardous road passes through the former Bantustan of **Lebowa**, where people live crammed at a density six times greater than the provincial average. **Klaserie**, 42km north of Bosbokrand in the middle of game farms, sits poised on the border between Mpumalanga and Limpopo Province. Forty-five kilometres east from here lies **Orpen Gate**. The pick of the places to stay in the vicinity is *Timbavati Safari Lodge* (☎015 793 0415 or 082 362 2922, Ⓦwww.africa-sa.co.za; half board ❸) which has space for large groups in thatched Ndebele-styled huts, plus a pool and bar, and game drives and walks on offer in Big Five safari areas. They can also arrange horseback safaris, hot-air ballooning and microlighting. The *Lodge* is easily accessed, on the Orpen Gate Road, 13km from Klaserie and 20 km from the gate itself.

Hoedspruit

Lurking in the undulating Lowveld, straight up the R40 from Klaserie, with the hazy blue mountains of the Escarpment visible on the distant horizon, is the small service centre of **HOEDSPRUIT**. The town lies at the heart of a concentration of **private game reserves** and lodges, and is a good base for specialist activities, such as **horse-riding** and **rafting** on the Blyde River, **birding** on the slopes of the Escarpment, visiting **animal rehabilitation centres** and lazy **hot-air ballooning** over the bush.

Hoedspruit is a significant arrival point for air travellers heading for Kruger. Daily flights from Johannesburg and Cape Town arrive at **Eastgate airport** (☎015 793 3681), some 14km south of Hoedspruit. Avis has an office at the airport (☎015 793 2014), and rental outlets in Nelspruit can send cars up to Hoedspruit. For transfers to game lodges from here, contact Eastgate Safaris (☎015 793 3678 or 082 774 9544) though most lodges send vehicles to meet guests. Hoedspruit itself is a collection of gun shops, liquor stores, butchers, service stations and a good Spar supermarket, where you'll find a coffee shop and chemist in the same little shopping complex.

There's a mix of **accommodation** available within striking distance of Hoedspruit; westwards towards the Blyde River Canyon is the wonderful Monsoon Gallery (see p.695), and there are reasonably priced game farms close to Hoedspruit. To the east, on the fringes of Kruger itself, are some of South Africa's most luxurious safari camps.

Around Hoedspruit

The **Moholoholo Wildlife Rehabilitation Centre** lies on the R531 between the R40 and R527, about 3km from the tarred turn-off to the Blydepoort Dam (tours Mon–Sat 9.30am & 3pm, and during school holidays Sun at 3pm; R60; booking essential ☎ & ℻015 795 5236). Ex-ranger Brian Jones has embarked on an individual crusade to rescue and rehabilitate injured and abandoned animals, notably raptors, but also lions, leopards and others. The centre is part of a wider reserve and both night drives and early morning walks are offered, as well as the opportunity to touch animals and see Brian fly eagles. You can also make an easy tour of the rehabilitation cages and pens. The game-lodge-style fully catered **accommodation** (full board ❻) here does a night drive and an early morning walk.

Along similar lines is the larger **Hoedspruit Research and Breeding Centre for Endangered Species** (more commonly called the **Cheetah Project**; Mon–Sun 8am–3pm; R70), 20km south of Hoedspruit on the R40. Open vehicles depart from here every hour on the hour, for a two-hour tour around pens and cages containing cheetah, wild dog, blue crane and other endangered species such as ground hornbills, all bred for restocking and research. While the centre gives you the opportunity to see some of these animals at close quarters, you can't actually touch anything and it does feel a bit like a zoo. A small restaurant on site serves tea, cake, sandwiches and hot dogs.

The **Nyani Shangaan Cultural Village** (☎015 793 3816 or 083 512 4865; ❶), 4km along the Guernsey Road which turns east off the R40, 22km south of Hoedspruit, is a good option for lunch or overnighting, with dinner and a display of traditional dancing laid on. Unlike some of the more commercialized cultural villages, this is a genuine effort developed by Axon Khosa, a local Shangaan man, who asked his grandparents what the villages were like when they were children. He and his extended family take visitors on a tour of the village and offer a **meal**, which is usually a chicken dish with butternut or gem squash, served with wild spinach and groundnuts mixed into *mielie pap*. You can **stay overnight** (booking essential) in a hut with traditional dung floors and thatching that looks untidy by comparison with the safari lodges, but is authentically Shangaan. The walls are constructed with mud from termite mounds and are beautifully hand-decorated with white, orange and black motifs. There are fold-up mattresses, cold showers and flush toilets for guests. *Sabie Backpackers* (☎013 764 2118) does a late afternoon guided tour here which includes the evening feast for R330.

Hoedspruit game farms

None of the following **game farms** has direct access to Big Five viewing, but they're worth considering as relatively inexpensive and comfortable places to stay in the bush on your way to or from Kruger. Because each camp is small, and right in the bush, you have the feeling of being in a far wilder place than if you're staying in Kruger Park itself. All offer walks since there are no lions or elephants on the properties. A number of farms also offer specialist activities; most take children.

Eyrie Birding Lodge 36km from Hoedspruit on the R531 ☎015 795 5775, ⓦwww.eyriebirdinglodge.com. Four doubles in a two-storey house, in a fantastic elevated site on the slopes of the Escarpment. It's run by Dr Peter Milstein, one of South Africa's most knowledgeable experts on birds, and was chosen by him as one of the finest bird-watching spots in the country. No under-12s. Full board (bring your own liquor) ❹

Gwala Gwala 35km south of Hoedspruit, on the Guernsey road ☎015 793 3491, ⓦwww.gwala.co.za. The place to go if you're looking for tranquillity, walking and birding. Accommodation is in luxury safari tents; the owners give you plenty of space and privacy, and there are no more than ten guests at a time. Big Five game drives into a neighbouring reserve are included in the rate and drives into Kruger can be arranged. ❽

Kwa-Mbili Game Lodge 30km east of Hoedspruit ☎015 793 2773, ⓦwww.kwambili.com. An intimate, unpretentious owner-run lodge with bush cuisine and baby-sitting available. A maximum of ten guests are housed in chalets or luxury tents;

activities on offer include game viewing on foot or by Land Rover. Full board ❽

Off-Beat Safari Camp 13km north of Hoedspruit ☎ & ☎015 793 2422 or ☎082 494 1735, ⓦwww.offbeatsafaris.co.za. A rustic self-catering camp on a game farm, whose appeal is its affordability and the big plus of horse-riding across the farm to view giraffe, kudu, zebra and wildebeest. The chilling sound of lions roaring in the darkness is guaranteed, the roars filtering through the mosquito netting, from the lion enclosure on the adjacent property. Bring all your own food and drink. ❷–❸

Otter's Den On the R531, not far from the junction with the R527 ☎015 795 5250 or 082 572 2223, ⓦwww.ottersden.co.za. A small and relaxing camp sleeping eight, on a bush-covered island in the Blyde River recommended for fishing and bird-watching. The en-suite chalets are on stilts overlooking the river, and there's a river-fed rock swimming pool. A field guide can accompany you on walks to identify trees and birds, and the owners run rafting trips through the Blyde River Canyon and also hot-air ballooning. Full board ❻

Phalaborwa

The most northerly access to the central section of Kruger is at **PHALABORWA** ("pal-a-bore-wa"), 74km north of Hoedspruit. The name means "better than the south", a cheeky sobriquet coined as the town developed on the back of its extensive mineral wealth. During the Sixties, the borders of the park near Phalaborwa suddenly developed a kink, and large copper deposits were found, miraculously, just outside the protected national park area.

Phalaborwa is a 490-kilometre drive from Jo'burg, up the N1 to Polokwane, then the R71 via Tzaneen. The town is right at the gate to the park and is thus an extremely viable base, with some excellent activities on offer. Keen golfers shouldn't miss the chance of a round at the signposted **Hans Merensky Country Club** (☎015 781 3931), where its not unusual to see giraffes and elephants sauntering across the fairways. You can whet your appetite before heading into the park with a short **microlight flight** over the park (Sam ☎082 956 1502; R500 per hour), or a sundowner **boat trip** with Jumbo River Safaris (booking essential on ☎015 781 6168; R75), which sets out at 3pm down the Olifants River and frequently encounters game, including elephants. Select-a-safari runs a worthwhile river trip (daily 7.30am & 3pm; ☎015 781 3418; R200) offering an experience of nature rather than a booze cruise; you get collected from your lodgings.

Kruger Park's own activities run from Phalaborwa Gate (☎013 735 6509) are definitely worth doing, and participants can be collected from their accommodation. Top of the list are the **bush braais** (R300), a combination of a night drive and a braai inside a *boma* at Sable Dam, where you experience all the night sounds of the bush while chomping on your *boerewors*. Bush breakfasts are organized at the same location, which is not open to the general public. The price includes entrance to Kruger Park, plus the food. **Walking safaris** and drives into the park are also bookable at the gate.

An hour north-west of Phalaborwa you can ride through the bush on the back of an elephant (Rory Lindie; ☎083 294 7440, ⓔbookings@efaf.co.za). **Elephant-back safaris** are rare in South Africa, and this is reasonably priced at around R600 per person. Some of the party walk alongside the elephant, while one or two people ride, and then you swap around. The price includes a good buffet breakfast at a dam.

Mining began at Phalaborwa some time after AD200, and the **Masorini Heritage Site**, close to Phalaborwa Gate, is a reconstruction of an iron-smelting village. It comprises of a number of granaries and huts with pottery, grinding stones and mats, where the people of Masorini eked out a living from making and trading iron spears, hoes and other metal implements.

You may see dust-encrusted vehicles driving around town which have long aerials with small flags attached to the top of them – this is so that they can be seen from, and not squished by, the big trucks manoeuvring around the mines. Also unusual are the Beware of the Hippos road signs – particularly in the dry winter months, hippos wander about looking for nice gardens to eat up. A resident family of warthogs also wanders the streets.

Practicalities

Regular SA Airlink (☎015 781 5823) flights arrive from Johannesburg at Phalaborwa **airport**, five minutes' drive from Kruger's Phalaborwa Gate, off President Steyn Street. Unfortunately, this is one of the most expensive flights in the country. All Phalaborwa's **car rental** firms are represented at the airport: Avis (☎015 781 3169), Budget (☎015 781 5404) and Imperial (☎015 781 0376).

Two bus companies do the trip from Johannesburg: Translux (☎012 315 4300) goes via Polokwane, while City to City (☎011 309 7050) takes in Dullstroom, Lydenburg and Hoedspruit. **Phalaborwa Tourist Information**, at the corner of President Steyn and Van Eck Street (closed Sun; ☎015 781 7267, ⓦwww.phalaborwa.co.za), dispenses the usual services. Phalaborwa has a good selection of **shops**, including the well-stocked Link pharmacy, open until 8pm, in the shopping mall in Nelson Mandela Avenue.

The closest Kruger restcamps from here are Letaba, 50km into the park (90 mins drive minimum) and Shimuwini, 52km inside. My African Dream Safari (☎072 418 7286) offers transfers from the airport to game farms and lodges, as well as day-trips into Kruger and up the Escarpment.

Accommodation

Phalaborwa has plenty of **places to stay**, with some good options at the lower end.

Daan & Zena's 15 Birkenhead St ☎015 781 6049, ⓦwww.daanzena.co.za. B&B as well as self-catering available in en-suite rooms located in three neighbouring houses, with a/c and TV in each room, and three swimming pools to choose from. ❷

Elephant Walk 30 Anna Scheepers St ☎015 781 5860 or 082 495 0575, ⓦwww.elewalk.com. A small and friendly hostel with camping facilities and budget tours into Kruger, and booking service for Phalaborwa/Kruger activities. Besides dorms and twins, they have four en-suite garden rooms. ❶–❷

Matomani Lodge Essenhout St ☎015 781 5681, ⓦwww.matomani.co.za. Reasonably priced self-catering apartments in a refurbished 1960s block, with breakfast optional. ❷

Sefapane Lodge Copper St, a 5min drive out of town towards Kruger Gate ☎015 781 7041, ⓦwww.sefapane.co.za. Relaxed and upmarket accommodation in neat beehive huts, with a restaurant, a nice pool and a poolside bar. ❹

Steyns Cottage 67 Bosvlier St ☎015 781 0836. A fairly classy Victorian-style guesthouse, with a swimming pool, tea garden and restaurant. ❹

Eating and drinking

Phalaborwa's selection of **places to eat** are mostly linked to accommodation establishments. The restaurant at *Sefapane Lodge* is pretty decent for lunch or dinner, and its sunken **bar** beside the swimming pool is convivial. You'll find the usual steaks and fresh salads at the *Yurok Spur* in the main shopping mall in Nelson Mandela Avenue, and steaks and pasta at *Buffalo Pub & Grill* (closed Sun) very visible on Hendrick van Eck, the main road out to Kruger.

Kruger National Park

KRUGER NATIONAL PARK is arguably the emblem of South African tourism, the place that delivers best what most visitors to Africa want to see – scores of elephants, lions and a cast of thousands of other game roaming the savanna. A narrow strip of land hugging the Mozambique border, Kruger stretches across Limpopo Province and Mpumalanga, an astonishing 414-kilometre drive from Pafuri Gate in the north to Malelane Gate in the south, all of it along tar, with many well-kept gravel roads looping off to provide routes for game drives.

Kruger is designed for **self-driving** and **self-catering**. Self-driving offers complete flexibility, though the temptation is to drive too much and too fast, leading to fewer sightings. Furthermore, rental cars tend to be low off the ground and aren't as good for game viewing as those used by lodges or tour operators. However, you can hop in a car knowing you'll find supplies at most of the restcamps – indeed self-driving is often the only way of seeing Kruger's animals if you're travelling with children, as many lodges don't allow under-12s. The park's popularity means that not only are you likely to share animal sightings with other motorists, but that **accommodation** is at a premium, particularly during South African school holidays, and that at any time of year you may have to stay in whichever camp has accommodation, rather than in your first choice. Book as far in advance as possible.

Walks and game drives

Whether you're staying in Kruger or not, you can still join one of the early morning, mid-morning, sunset or night **game drives** organized by the park. Not only are these drives, priced at R130–210, one of the cheapest ways of accessing the park, but the viewing is unsurpassed because of the height of the vehicles. Drives in smaller, more comfortable vehicles are a little more expensive, but worth it. The drives leave from every camp in the park (book at reception, or even better when you make your reservation) and, for those staying outside the park, from these entrance gates: Crocodile Bridge (☎013 735 6012), Malelane (☎013 735 6152), Numbi (☎013 735 5133), Paul Kruger (☎013 735 5107), Phabeni (☎013 735 5890) and Phalaborwa (☎013 735 6509).

For those staying inside the park, three-hour **game walks** (R200) are conducted every morning at dawn from every camp, and there are also afternoon walks (R150). Groups are restricted to eight people, so its worth booking beforehand, or try your camp when you arrive. **Bush breakfasts and braais**, departing from most camps as well as the entry gates, combine a short drive with a meal outdoors. It's probably going to be the only meal for which you'll ever have to sign an indemnity form. Finally, there are also several three-night **wilderness trails** (see box on p.721) in different parts of the park, led by armed rangers – a fabulous way of getting in touch with the wilderness, but one you'll have to book months in advance.

Kruger comes pretty close to fulfilling *Out of Africa* fantasies in the **private game reserves** on its western flank – where you get luxury accommodation and food, but, more importantly (especially if this is your first safari), qualified rangers to show you the game and the bush with only a tiny group of other guests. The ideal is to do a bit of each, perhaps spending a couple of nights in a private lodge and a further two or so exploring the public section. But whatever you choose, be sure to relax and don't get too obsessed with seeing the Big Five. Remember that wildlife doesn't imitate TV documentaries: you're most unlikely to see lion-kills (you may not see a lion at all), or huge herds of wildebeest migrating across dusty savanna. The element of luck involved is exactly what makes game spotting so addictive. A few **game-spotting tips** are outlined in the box on p.718.

Walking in the wild is growing in popularity, so much so that in the Kruger Park all of the private reserves and some private operators (see box on p.715) offer **escorted game walks**. Note that Kruger National Park is **malarial**, for more on which, see p.48.

Some history

It's highly questionable whether Kruger National Park can be considered "a pristine wilderness", as it's frequently called, given that people have been living in or around it for thousands of years. **San hunter-gatherers** have left their mark in the form of paintings and engravings at 150 sites so far discovered, and there's evidence of farming cultures at many places in the park. Around 1000–1300 AD, centrally organized states were building stone palaces and engaging in **trade** that brought Chinese porcelain, jewellery and cloth into the area.

But it was the arrival of white **fortune seekers** in the second half of the nineteenth century that made the greatest impact on the region. African farmers were kicked off their traditional lands in the early twentieth century to create the park, and there has been an ambivalent attitude to the hunters, criminals and poachers (like the notorious ivory hunter Cecil Barnard), who

Kruger flora and fauna

Among the nearly 150 species of **mammals** seen in the park are cheetah, leopard, lion, spotted hyena, wild dog, black and white rhino, blue wildebeest, buffalo, Burchell's zebra, bushbuck, eland, elephant, giraffe, hippo, impala, kudu, mountain reedbuck, nyala, oribi, reedbuck, roan antelope, sable antelope, tsessebe, warthog and waterbuck.

The staggering 507 **bird species** include raptors, hefty-beaked hornbills, ostriches and countless colourful specimens. The **birders' "big six"** are saddle-billed stork, kori bustard, martial eagle, lappet-faced vulture, Pel's fishing owl and ground hornbill.

Keep your eyes open and you'll also see a variety of **reptiles**, **amphibians** and **insects** – most rewardingly in the grounds of the restcamps themselves: there's always something to see up the trees, in the bushes or even inside your rondavel. If you spot a miniature ET-like reptile crawling upside down on the ceiling, don't be tempted to kill it; it's an insect-eating gecko and is doing you a good turn. If, however, you have a horror of insects or frogs, stay away from Kruger in the rainy season (Nov–March).

Common among the three-hundred-plus **tree** species are the baobab, cluster fig, knobthorn, Natal mahogany, monkey orange, raisin bush, tamboti, coral tree, fever tree, jackalberry, leadwood, marula, mopane, lala palm and sausage tree.

made their livelihoods here decimating game populations. Barnard's exploits are admiringly recounted in the *Ivory Trail* by T.V. Bulpin, while every other episode of the still-popular yarn, *Jock of the Bushveld*, set in the area, includes accounts of hunting.

Paul Kruger, former president of the South African Republic, is usually credited with having the foresight to set aside land for wildlife conservation. Kruger figures as a shrewd, larger-than-life figure in Afrikaner history and it was **James Stevenson-Hamilton**, the first warden of the national park, who cunningly put forward Kruger's name in order to soften up Afrikaner opposition to the park's creation. In fact, Stevenson-Hamilton knew that Kruger was no conservationist and was actually an inveterate hunter; Kruger "never in his life thought of animals except as *biltong*", Stevenson-Hamilton wrote in a private letter. He also remarked that few people had any interest in wild animals unless they were dead. It was his tenacity which saved the animals which hadn't been shot out, rather than Kruger's. Times have changed a lot in the management of the park: the first black director, David Mabunda (now head of SANParks) was appointed in 1998.

Kruger is going from strength to strength. The park is being extended into Mozambique with the establishment of the Great Limpopo Transfrontier Park, and two border posts linking Kruger to Mozambique are being created, one right at the north of the park at Pafuri near *Punda Maria Camp*, the other at Giriyondo, between *Letaba* and *Mopani* camps. In another recent development, SANParks has awarded concessions to private operators to open a handful of luxury lodges inside Kruger itself; for more details of these, check the commercially run website Ⓦwww.krugerpark.co.za.

When to visit

Kruger is rewarding at any time of the year, though each season has its advantages and drawbacks. If you don't like the heat, avoid high **summer** (Dec–Feb), when on a bad day temperatures can nudge 45°C – though they're generally in the mid- to high thirties. Many of the camps have air conditioning or fans, and it's definitely worth considering renting an air-conditioned car. Throughout the summer the heat can be tempered by short thunder showers. At this time of the year, everything becomes greener, softer and prettier, and from early November you're likely to spot cute young animals.

There's little rain during the cooler **winter** months of April to August; the vegetation withers over this period, making it easier to spot game. Although daytime temperatures rise to the mid-twenties (days are invariably bright and sunny throughout winter), the nights and early mornings can be very cold, especially in June and July, when you'll definitely need warm clothes. Rondavels in the public restcamps have heaters in the bedrooms. A definite plus of winter is the virtual absence of mosquitoes and other insects.

Orientation

The public section of Kruger can be divided roughly into **three sections**, each with a distinct character and terrain. If your time is limited, it's best to choose just one or two areas to explore, but if you're staying for five days or more, consider driving the length of the park slowly, savouring the changes in landscape along the way.

The southern, central and northern sections are sometimes referred to as "the circus", "the zoo" and "the wilderness" – sobriquets that carry more than a germ of truth. The **southern section** has the greatest concentration of game, attracts the highest number of visitors and is the most easily accessible part of the park if you're coming from Johannesburg, 478km away on the N4. The park **headquarters** is here (at *Skukuza*), with an **airport**, car rental, a filling station, car repair workshop, car wash, bank, post office and doctor, as well as rondavels to accommodate a thousand people. The **central section** also offers good game viewing, as well as two of the most attractive camps in the park at **Olifants** and **Letaba**. The further north you go, the thinner both animal populations and visitors become, but it's the **northern section** that really conveys a sense of wilderness, reaching its zenith at the marvellously old-fashioned **Punda Maria** camp, which dates back to the 1930s.

Outside the public section, big-game country continues in several exclusive and expensive **private game reserves**, clustering on huge tracts of land to the west, often referred to as Greater Kruger. The three major private reserves are **Sabi Sands** to the south and **Timbavati** and **Manyeleti**, adjoining the central section of the national park. As far as animals are concerned, the private and public areas are joined in an enormous, seamless whole. The only real differences are that private reserves are not places you drive around yourself, and they offer a greater sense of being in the wilderness as there are no tarred roads or buildings away from the lodges. If you do arrive by car, you'll have to leave it at the lodge and you won't see the vehicle again until you leave. Finally, note that the private reserves don't allow day visits.

Getting to Kruger and the private reserves

It's possible to **fly** into Nelspruit (see p.698; for the southern section), Hoedspruit (see p.707; for the central and northern sections) or Phalaborwa (see p.708; for the northern section) and rent a car for the rest of the journey. SAA and SA Airlink fly from Johannesburg to Nelspruit and to Phalaborwa; SA Airlink also flies **from Durban** to Nelspruit and **from Cape Town** to Nelspruit and Hoedspruit. If you're staying in a private game lodge, you can arrange to be transferred from any of these airports. If money is no object, you can fly into Nelspruit and take one of the small planes which service the expensive lodges.

ZIMBABWE

KRUGER NATIONAL PARK

Rest Camps

▲ Beit Bridge

● Messina

Pafuri Gate

R525

● Tshipise

Punda Maria
Punda Maria Gate
R524

N1

Louis
Trichardt

Thohoyandou

KRUGER NATIONAL
PARK

❶

R522

R524

R81

Shingwedzi ■

N

● Giyani

❷

Tropic of Capricorn

R81

Mopani ■

LIMPOPO
(NORTHERN PROVINCE)

R529

❸

● Tzaneen

R71

Phalaborwa

Letaba 🏠

R71

R36

Phalaborwa
Gate

Olifants 🏠

R40

Balule 🏠

Hoedspruit

TIMBAVATI
GAME
RESERVE

Ⓐ

KRUGER NATIONAL
PARK

BLYDE RIVER CANYON
NATURE RESERVE

Klaserie

Orpen
Orpen
Gate

Tamboti ■

Satara ■

Ⓑ

❹

● Bourke's Luck

MANYELETI
GAME RESERVE

Ⓒ

Ⓔ   Ⓓ
       Ⓕ

Bosbokrand

SABI SANDS
GAME
RESERVE

Ⓗ   Ⓖ

Pilgrims Rest

Graskop

Mala Mala

Ⓘ

Lydenburg

Sabie

Hazyview

Phabeni
Gate
Numbi
Gate

❺

Paul Kruger
Gate

Skukuza ■

Pretoriuskop ■

Lower
Sable ■

Dullstroom

Kruger
Mpumalanga
International
Airport
(KMIA)

White River

Berg-en-
Dal ■

Crocodile
Bridge ■

Crocodile
Bridge
Gate

❻

MPUMALANGA

0   50 km

Malelane Gate

Komatipoort

N4

RESSANO GRACIA

● Nelspruit

▼ Witbank   ▼ Barberton   Maputo ▼

MOZAMBIQUE

PRIVATE CAMPS

Chitwa Chitwa Game Lodge	F
Djuma Bush Lodge	G
Elephant Plains	E
Honeyguide	C

Khoka Moya	B
Londolozi	H
Nkorho Bush	
Camp	D

Nottens	I
Umlani	A

BUSHVELD CAMPS

Bateleur	2	Shimuwini	3
Biyamiti	6	Sirheni	1
Jakkalsbessie	5	Talamati	4

9

There are an increasing number of **tours** to Kruger – your best bet for getting there if you're not driving. Most of these depart from Johannesburg. Prices given are per person unless otherwise noted. Most safari companies cover the conservation fees as part of their deal.

Bundu Bus Tours and Safaris ☎011 675 0767, ⓦwww.bundusafaris.com. A range of safaris, all departing and returning to wherever you're staying in Johannesburg, Pretoria or Nelspruit. Most popular is a four-day trip, starting in the south (Mon, Wed & Fri; R2900); after camping there for two nights (in tents with beds), you spending the third at *Bundu Safari Lodge*, 30km from Orpen Gate. An exciting option is the three-night Camp Wild Trip, where you camp in an unfenced area and go for walks with an armed ranger and drives in an open-topped 4WD (R3900). Longer tours also taking in Swaziland, KwaZulu-Natal and Zimbabwe are available.

Livingstone Trails ☎011 867 2586, ⓦwww.livingstonetrails.co.za. Four-day camping trips from Johannesburg, using *Maroela* campsite or Orpen Gate in the park as a base (Mon, Wed & Sat; R2850). If you're not up to camping, consider the three-night trip (Sun, group size three or four; R3750), which uses the bungalows at Orpen Gate, or Kruger's Tamboti Tented Camp.

Outlook Small Group Explorations ☎011 976 2484, ⓦwww.outlook.co.za. Four-day trips in the southern section of Kruger, with three nights in National Parks accommodation. Groups are small (two to five), and you're collected and returned to your lodgings in Johannesburg. The price, R3500 per person, includes food, accommodation in chalets, game drives and guide hire.

Transfrontiers ☎015 793 3816 or 083 700 7987, ⓦwww.transfrontiers.com. Backpacker-friendly tours, with an emphasis on game walking, run by a couple with a good track record. On their four-night/five-day safaris (R3800), which depart regularly from Jo'burg hostels, you spend two nights in the Timbavati Reserve, and two nights in Klaserie. Accommodation is in large tents with proper beds, duvets and pillows.

Wildlife Safaris ☎011 791 4238, ⓦwww.wildlifesaf.co.za. Relatively upmarket operator with three-night Kruger trips (R4850), which include one night at a comfortable safari camp, and two inside the park using National Parks accommodation. Worth thinking about is their five-day trip from Johannesburg, taking in Hluhluwe-Imfolozi Park (see p.529) after Kruger, and ending in Durban (R5970).

Unfortunately, flights to airports near Kruger are pricey and there are no special deals. If you're in Cape Town or Durban, you may find it cheaper to take a budget flight (with kulula.com, for example) to Johannesburg and rent a car at the airport for the easy, five-hour drive to the park; the airport is on the N4 motorway to Kruger.

Another option for Kruger is taking a **bus** to Nelspruit or Phalaborwa from Johannesburg and booking one of the many **tours** on offer at the backpacker lodges. The *Old Vic Inn* and *Elephant Walk* in Nelspruit and Phalaborwa respectively can both arrange tours; in **Hazyview** contact *Kruger Park Backpackers* (see p.705). There are even tours from Johannesburg itself (see box, above).

Kruger entrance gates

There are nine **entrance gates** along the western and southern borders of Kruger. The N4 **from Johannesburg** brushes along Kruger's southern boundary en route to Mozambique and quickly gets you close to the **southern gates** of Malelane, 411km away, and Crocodile Bridge, another 57km further on. These are also the closest if you're coming **from KwaZulu-Natal**, either via Barberton or Swaziland. If you've been exploring the **Blyde River Canyon** area, access is off the R538/R40 between White River and Klaserie to the **western gates** (Pretoriuskop, Paul Kruger, Orpen and Phalaborwa) leading into the southern and central sections of the park. The easiest way to get to the two **northern gates** on the west side is off the N1 from Johannesburg to Musina on South Africa's northern border, taking the R524 east at Makhado for Punda Maria Gate, or the R525, 58km further north, to Pafuri Gate (see p.723).

If you're trying to get from one part of the park to another, note that although it's far more fun driving inside, the **speed limit** (see box below) makes it a slow journey – and you're bound to make frequent stops to watch animals.

Kruger restcamps and bushveld camps

At most of the fourteen main **restcamps** inside Kruger, the sounds of the African night tend to get drowned out by air conditioning and the merriment of braais and beer. It's not all bad news, though; at least you'll have all the facilities you could ever want on hand. Nearly all camps have electricity, public telephones, petrol stations, shops (though they don't stock much in the way of fruit or vegetables), restaurants, laundrettes and snack bars. Some also have pools and most offer game drives and game walks, while some do bush breakfasts and bush braais combined with night drives. These activities are

Kruger essentials: the public section

Kruger's restcamps and bushveld camps are adminstered by South African National Parks (see p.71). The **conservation fee** at Kruger is, for most foreign visitors, R120 per day (children aged 2–15 pay R60). If you're planning on **staying** at the park over school holidays or weekends, book well ahead. Booking in writing opens thirteen months in advance; closer to the date, you can usually find somewhere, especially at off-peak times, if you're not too particular about where you stay in the park.

Every restcamp is fenced off and has a gate that's open at the times indicated below. You are required to return to your restcamp or leave the park prior to closing times. Except where specified, all times refer to both park and camp gates, and are strictly upheld.

Jan	4.30am–6.30pm (camp); 5.30am–6.30pm (park)	May–July	6am–5.30pm
		Sept	6am–6pm
Feb	5.30am–6.30pm	Oct	5.30am–6pm
March	5.30am–6pm	Nov & Dec	4.30am–6.30pm (camp); 5.30am–6.30pm (park)
April	6am–6pm		

The **reception** at restcamps is open daily from 8am to 5.30pm, **shops** from 8am until half an hour after gate closing. **Restaurants** open between 7am and 9am for breakfast, between noon and 2pm for lunch and between 6pm and 9pm for dinner.

Driving

Only approved roads should be used; don't drive on unmarked roads and never drive off-road. Do buy a Kruger **map** showing all the marked roads. Roads have numbers rather than names. Some are tarred, some are dirt. **Speed limits** are 50kph on tar, 40kph on untarred roads and 20kph in restcamps; speed traps operate in some parts of the park. Never leave your car (it's illegal and dangerous), except at designated sites.

very popular and worth booking when you make your initial reservation. The restcamps are very pleasant, with walks around the edges, labelled trees to help you identify what you see on drives, and plenty of birds and smaller creatures around the camps themselves. Several, including *Lower Sabie*, *Skukuza*, *Olifants* and *Letaba*, have views onto rivers where, from a distance, you can see game coming to drink.

At most Kruger camps you'll find **thatched rondavels**, each with an outdoor eating area and facing communally towards each other rather than out towards the views. The best rondavels are on the camp perimeters or directly facing onto rivers. Nine of the restcamps have a **campsite** (with shared kitchen and washing facilities), which provide the park's cheapest accommodation (R100 per site). Sites for **caravans** and **camper vans** are available wherever there's camping (R100 per site) and often have a power point.

Some camps have **furnished safari tents** and **huts** (R230–530), in configurations usually sleeping two to four people. Most of these have fridges and air conditioning; some come with basic crockery and cutlery, and share communal kitchens and ablutions, while others have their own kitchens and are generally better equipped.

Bungalows (R395–600) sleep two to six people and come in several variations, ranging from those with just showers, toilets and fridges to ones with fully equipped kitchens. A step up are **family cottages** (R750–850), with four to six beds, living rooms, bathroom and kitchen.

For a more rustic experience, head out to one of the handful of **bushveld camps** (R730–850), away from day-to-day trivialities and the tourist pack. The bushveld camps have accommodation of the same standard as the main restcamps, but accommodate fewer people per unit, and are far smaller. They dispense with shops or restaurants, but are within reasonable reach of the restcamps – just in case you can't survive without a Coke.

Southern Kruger restcamps

The so-called "circus" is the busiest section of the Kruger, with its hub at **Skukuza**, the biggest of all the Kruger camps, and **Lower Sabie**, one of the most popular. Apart from containing some of the best places for seeing large quantities of game, southern Kruger is also easily reached from Johannesburg along the N4. At peak times of year, the area buzzes with vehicles jostling to get up close anywhere that big cats are sighted – events which always seem to induce bad human behaviour.

Berg-en-Dal

In the southwest corner of the park, 12km northwest of **Malelane Gate**, **Berg-en-Dal** is set attractively among *koppies* in a shallow grassy basin (its Afrikaans name means "hill and dale"). Built in the Eighties, the camp overlooks the Matjulu stream and dam, and has modern, fully equipped chalets that break with the Kruger tradition of thatched rondavels. The chalets are landscaped among indigenous bushveld vegetation and are widely spaced to provide privacy. Facilities include a beautifully positioned swimming pool, a shop with a good range of food, a licensed restaurant, snack bar, filling station and laundry.

The focus of the camp is the Rhino Trail along the perimeter fence, meandering under riverine trees along the Matjulu dam, where there are resident crocodiles and nesting fish eagles. Game includes white rhino, leopards and lions, and plenty of kudu. Sable and mountain reedbuck are among more unusual sightings.

For a general survey of South African fauna and habitats, see "Wildlife", pp.867–882. The excellent *Make the Most of Kruger*, available at most restcamps, is well worth investing in for the basic interpretation it provides of the park ecology and for filling in those empty moments. For an accessible and engrossing guide to the **behaviour** of African mammals, check out the widely available *Safari Companion* by Richard Estes (see "Books", p.924); even commonplace species such as impala become fascinating when you understand what they're doing and why, and this provides constant interest on days when, for instance, big cats stubbornly refuse to put in an appearance.

Here are some pointers to bear in mind both before and during your game-viewing excursion:

• The best times of day for game viewing are when it's cooler, during the early morning and late afternoon. Set out as soon as the camp gates open in the morning and go out again as the temperature starts dropping in the afternoon. Take a siesta during the midday heat, just as the animals do, when they head for deep shade where you're less likely to see them.

• It's worth investing in a detailed **map of Kruger** (available at virtually every restcamp) in order to choose a route which includes rivers or pans where you can stop and enjoy the scenery and birdlife while you wait for game to come down to drink, especially in the late afternoon.

• **Driving really slowly** pays off, particularly if you stop often, in which case switch off your engine, open your window and use your senses. Don't try consciously to spot animals – many are well disguised. Instead, watch for any movement or something that strikes you as a bit out of place. There are also the smells and sounds of the wilds; twigs breaking or the alarm calls of animals can hint at something afoot.

• Don't embark on overambitious drives from your restcamp. You'll see as much game sitting quietly in your car as you would frantically driving around all day. Other stopped cars are often a good indicator of a game sighting.

• **Binoculars** are a must for scanning the horizon.

• Take **food and drink** with you – you don't want to have to break off that terrific lion-sighting because you're starving. When you feel you've had your fill of game viewing, you could make for one of Kruger's designated **picnic sites**, where there's always boiling water available, tables and chairs to enjoy your picnic in the wild, and braai places powered with gas.

Crocodile Bridge

East of *Berg-en-Dal*, **Crocodile Bridge** is the least impressive of Kruger's restcamps, and its position at the very southern edge of the park, overlooking sugar-cane farms, does nothing to enhance your bush experience. However, old hands say this is a tremendously underrated camp as there is a high density of general game, and you have an excellent chance of seeing the Big Five.

Located at the **Crocodile Bridge Gate** on the north bank of the Crocodile River, the camp is reached via Komatipoort, 12km to the south on the Mozambique border. Accommodation is in en-suite huts sleeping two to three, with cooking facilities. Amenities are limited to a laundry and filling station, and a shop selling basic supplies.

Try the tarred H4 north and dirt S25 east for elephant, rhino and buffalo. For cheetah, among the best places are the open plains along the S28 Nhola Road. If you're pushing north to *Lower Sabie*, it's worth taking the drive slowly, as this area, dotted with knobthorn and marula trees, is known for its herbivores, which include giraffe, kudu, steenbok, wildebeest, zebra, buffalo and waterbuck as well as ostrich, warthog and the magnificent black sable antelope. You should also keep your eyes peeled for predators such as lion, cheetah, hyena and jackal.

Lower Sabie

Some 35km north of *Crocodile Bridge*, **Lower Sabie** occupies game-rich country that places it among the top three restcamps in the Kruger for animal-spotting. The surrounding open savanna and the camp's position on the banks of the Sabie River attract game to drink and graze, and the terrain around here is rated among the most beautiful in the southern Kruger. Within kilometres of the entrance gate to the camp, a number of waterholes and dams populated with crocodiles and hippos make good spots to park and watch for game coming to quench their thirst. In the thorn-thicket country hard by the west of the camp, you'll find promising terrain for catching sight of elephants moving between the trees as well as white rhino grazing on the sweet grasses, which also bring herds of buffalo and, in their wake, lions. Accommodation is in huts with shared ablutions as well as more expensive en-suite units with kitchens, some with river views, and some new and very popular tents. There's a restaurant, a cafeteria, a shop, a filling station and a laundry.

Pretoriuskop

Due west of *Lower Sabie*, but not directly connected to it, **Pretoriuskop** is reached via **Numbi Gate**, 9km to its west. Set in an area of sourveld, characterized by granite outcrops, tall grass and sickle bush favoured by mountain reedbuck, sable and white rhino, the camp is in an area stalked by lions, wild dogs and side-striped jackals. However, given the dense bush, game viewing is disappointing, and all you're likely to spot are larger species such as kudus and giraffes. While this isn't the best camp for game, it's worth doing the Voortrekker Road (H2-2) from Numbi Gate to Crocodile Bridge and stopping off at the historical plaques along the way, commemorating various explorers and traders.

Accommodation consists of en-suite cottages, rondavels and cheaper units with shared ablution and cooking facilities. The camp has a restaurant, a snack bar, a shop, a laundry, a semi-natural rock swimming pool – one of the most beautiful in Kruger, with a surrounding garden and picnic area – and a filling station. Around the perimeter fence at night, you're almost certain to see patrolling hyenas, waiting for scraps from braais.

Skukuza

Kruger's largest restcamp, **Skukuza** (☎013 735 4000, reservations ☎013 735 4184) accommodates over a thousand people, and lies at the centre of the best game-viewing area in the park. Its position is a mixed blessing; although you get large amounts of game, hordes of humans aren't far behind, and cars speeding at animal sightings can chase away the very animals they are trying to see.

Accommodation is in a range of thatched, en-suite units, or more cheaply in some furnished East African-style tents in the caravan park, with shared ablutions and kitchens. The closest entry point is through **Paul Kruger Gate**, 12km to the west, which in turn is 42km east of Hazyview. *Skukuza* is the hub of Kruger, with its own airport and car rental agency, and its sprawling collection of rondavels resembles a small town. Its garage can repair your vehicle, and there's also a post office, a bank, a filling station, two **restaurants**, a **cafeteria** and a really good **library** (Mon–Fri 8.30am–4pm & 7–9pm, Sat 8.30am–12.45pm, 1.45–4pm & 7–9pm, Sun 8.30am–12.45pm & 1.45–4pm), with a collection of natural-history books and exhibits. Another highlight of

Skukuza is the **open-air cinema** showing wildlife videos every evening under the stars. **Golf** at Skukuza is also a highlight: eighteen holes costs R90. Night drives and day drives in open vehicles can be arranged at the main complex – the night drives are excellent, since all the other vehicles are safely tucked up for the night, and you'll have the road to yourself.

Skukuza lies on the edge of the Sabie River, which is overlooked by a wide paved walkway furnished with park benches, from which you can see crocodiles floating by like driftwood on the brown water. Most people drive along the Sabie River to *Lower Sabie*, on the H4, one of the best places in the whole park to see game. The tangled riverine forest, flanked by acacia bush and mixed savanna, is the most fertile and varied in the park. Another great drive is northeast on the H1-2 to Tshokwane picnic site, stopping at Elephant, Jones, Leeupan and Siloweni waterholes.

Central Kruger restcamps

Game viewing can be extremely good in the "zoo", the area between *Skukuza* and *Satara*, which is reckoned to be one of the global hot spots for lions. At **Olifants** you'll find the Kruger's most dramatically located camp, with fantastic views into a river gorge, while **Satara** is one of the most popular – its placement is ideal for making sorties into fertile wildlife country. It is estimated that there are about sixty lion prides in this central area, but, even so, you may not be lucky enough to see one.

Orpen and Maroela

Like *Crocodile Bridge*, **Orpen** is located right by an entrance gate, 45km east of Klaserie, and is recommended mainly if you're arriving late and don't have time to get further into the park before the camp gates close. *Orpen* is very good for game viewing though, far preferable to its southern counterpart, because the substantial Timbavati Private Game Reserve lies to the west of Orpen, so you're already well into the wilderness once you get here.

The camp is small, peaceful and shaded by beautiful trees; it's a lovely drive from here along a river to get to *Satara*, the nearest big camp. Facilities are pretty basic, with a filling station and a reception doubling as a rudimentary shop; none of the accommodation is en suite, and cooking is done in communal kitchens. If you want to camp, you'll need to go to the small **Maroela** satellite camping area, overlooking the Timbavati River, approximately 4km from *Orpen*. You must report to *Orpen* reception to check in before going to the campsite, which has electricity.

Tamboti

Not far from Orpen Gate is Kruger's only tented camp, **Tamboti**, is reached by turning left 2km after *Orpen* and continuing for 1km. While it doesn't quite match up to its promise of a traditional East African safari, its tranquil position on the banks of the frequently dry Timbavati River is superb, set among apple leaf trees, sycamore figs and jackalberries. From the tents, elephants can often be seen just beyond the electrified fence, digging in the river bed for moisture, hence the camp's popularity (you'll have to book ahead to be sure of getting a place). The Timbavati River roads (S39 and S40) can be rewarding for game.

Each walk-in tent has its own deck overlooking the river, but best of all are numbers 21 and 22, which enjoy the deep shade of large riverine trees, something you'll appreciate in the midsummer heat. The tents have fridges and

Wilderness trails

Undertaken with the guidance of an experienced ranger, Kruger's three-night **wilderness trails**, listed below, pass through areas of notable beauty with diverse plant and animal life. However, they don't bring you closer to game than driving; they're really about getting closer to the vegetation and smaller creatures, though you have a good chance of encountering big game. Groups are limited to eight people staying in the same camp, comprising four rustic, two-bed huts, served by reed-walled showers and flush toilets; simple meals are provided. You walk for five hours in the morning, return to the camp for lunch and a siesta, and go walking again for an hour or two in the evening, returning to sit around a camp fire.

The trails are heavily subscribed. You can **book** in writing up to thirteen months in advance; contact South African National Parks. The cost is around R2000 per person, including accommodation and meals.

• **Bushman Trail** covers the southwestern section of the park, near *Berg-en-Dal* restcamp. The trail camp is in a secluded valley, characterized by granite hills. San paintings in many of the hill shelters are an added feature.

• **Metsimetsi Trail** is midway between Skukuza and Satara, with the camp at the foot of a mountain and overlooking a small waterhole. Black rhino and large predators move through the undulating savanna and rocky gorges and ravines.

• **Napi Trail** sets out from a camp between *Skukuza* and *Pretoriuskop* into woodland bushveld. Undulating terrain and granite hills suit the area's resident population of white rhino, while black rhino, elephant, lion and buffalo are also often seen. Birdlife is prolific.

• **Nyalaland Trail** is based in the remote northern section of the park along the Madzaringwe Stream north of *Punda Maria*. The area is known for its fever-tree and baobab forests, prolific birdlife and spectacular views.

• **Olifants Trail** has its camp on the southern bank of the Olifants River, from which it offers a magnificent view of the river. Riverine bush and gorges characterize the terrain, and lion, buffalo and elephant are often seen.

• **Sweni Trail** camp overlooks the Sweni stream in the wilderness area near Nwanetsi, and provides a view of marula and knobthorn savanna. A resident pride of lions pads about here and is frequently seen.

• **Wolhuter Trail** lies in the vicinity of *Berg-en-Dal* and *Pretoriuskop* camps in the southern section of the park, where rhinos are relatively common, as is a wide variety of other game.

electric lighting, while all kitchen, washing and toilet facilities are in two shared central blocks (bring your own cooking and eating utensils).

Satara

Forty-six kilometres due east of Orpen Gate, **Satara** ranks second only to *Skukuza* (92km to the south) in size and the excellence of its game viewing. Set in the middle of flat grasslands, the camp commands no great views, but is preferable to *Skukuza* because it avoids the feeling of suburban boxes on top of each other. Accommodation is in cottages arranged around lawned areas shaded by large trees; besides a shop, filling station, laundry and AA vehicle repair workshop, there's also a restaurant and cafeteria, where you can eat in a virtual blizzard of noisy birds.

About halfway along the tarred road between *Satara* and *Skukuza*, the area around Tshokwane picnic site can be good for lions, hence the number of motorists here. The area around *Satara* itself is usually good for sighting grazers such as buffalo, wildebeest, zebra, kudu, impala and elephant. Rewarding drives are the Timbavati River Road (S39) and the drive east of Satara along the S100, which snakes along the N'wanetsi River towards the Lebombo Mountains marking the border with Mozambique.

Balule

On the southern bank of the Olifants River, **Balule** is 41km north of *Satara* and 87km from Phalaborwa Gate. A very basic satellite to *Olifants* (11km to the north), *Balule* is one of the few restcamps where two can stay for under R100 without resorting to camping.

Compact *Balule* has two sections, one consisting of six spartan rondavels and another of fifteen camping and caravan sites. Each section has its own communal ablution and cooking facilities. There are iron washstands with enamel bowls and no windows. You can forget about air conditioning; the only electricity is in the fence to keep out lions. Guests have to bring their own crockery, cutlery and utensils, and must report to *Olifants* at least half an hour before the gates close.

Olifants

With a terrific setting on cliffs overlooking the braided Olifants River, **Olifants** has a charmingly old-fashioned feel and is reckoned by many to be the best restcamp in Kruger. It's possible to spend hours sitting on the benches on the covered look-out terrace, gazing into the valley whose airspace is criss-crossed by Bateleur eagles and yellow-billed kites cruising the thermals, while the rushing of the water below creates a hypnotic rhythm. Of the thatched, en-suite rondavels, numbers 1–24 boast superb views overlooking the valley; it's worth booking well in advance to get one of these. You can eat at the restaurant or the snack bar, and there's a shop and a laundry.

The river marks the division between rugged, rocky veld with ghostly fever trees growing along the riverbanks to the south, and to the north, mopane woodland which attracts the large antelope such as eland, roan, sable and tsessebe. This is also promising country for spotting elephant, giraffe, lion, hyena and cheetah, and you should look out for the tiny klipspringer, a pretty antelope that inhabits rocky terrain which it nimbly negotiates by boulder-hopping. A highlight of the area are some of the dirt roads which loop along the Olifants River.

Mountain biking is a new venture at Kruger, available only at Olifants. Only six people at a time, accompanied by armed field guides, can go on the trails (hence it's best to book; ☎013 735 6606, ✉heing@parks-sa.co.za), and the scenery is wonderful. The morning ride costs R300, the afternoon trail costs R150, while the full-day 24-kilometre Mozambique Border Trail (for which you need to be very fit) is R600.

Letaba

Letaba is set in *mopane* shrubland along the Letaba River, 34km north of *Olifants*. Old and quite large, the camp is located beautifully on an oxbow curve, and though very few of the rondavels afford a view, the restaurant does have great vistas; you can spend a day just watching herds of buffalo mooching around, elephants drifting past and a host of other plains game. Accommodation is in rondavels, some of which are en suite, as well as large furnished tents. The camp offers the usual shopping and laundry facilities, a vehicle-repair workshop, and an interesting **museum** with exhibits on the life of elephants, including displays on bulls with inordinately large tusks.

Northern Kruger restcamps

You won't find edge-to-edge game in the northern "wilderness", the least visited of Kruger's regions, but you do get a much stronger feeling here of being in the wilds, particularly after you've cross the Tropic of Capricorn north of **Mopani** camp and hit **Punda Maria** camp, which feels like a real old-time outpost in the bush.

Mopani

Some 42km north of *Letaba*, **Mopani** is one of the newer camps in Kruger and overlooks the Pioneer Dam. The dam, one of the few water sources in the vicinity, attracts animals to drink and provides an outstanding lookout for a variety of wildlife, including elephant, buffalo and antelope.

A sprawling place in the middle of monotonous *mopane* scrub, the camp is designed more for driving than walking. There's modern en-suite accommodation built of rough-hewn stone and thatch, a restaurant – above average for Kruger – and a bar with a good view across to the dam. Other facilities include a shop, a laundry and filling station; the swimming pool provides cool relief after a long drive.

Shingwedzi

A fairly large camp featuring square, brick chalets and a few older, colonial-style whitewashed, thatched bungalows, **Shingwedzi**, 63km north of *Mopani*, is sited in extensive grounds shaded by *pals* and *mopane* trees. The dining room has a terrace, frequented by starlings and cheeky hornbills jostling to pounce on your food. From the terrace you get a long view down across the usually dry Shingwedzi River. Look out for the weavers' nests with their long, tube-like entrances hanging from the eaves outside reception and the cafeteria. Facilities include a shop, a filling station and a swimming pool, and night drives are on offer.

Punda Maria and Pafuri

Kruger's northernmost camp, **Punda Maria**, 71km beyond *Shingwedzi*, is a relaxed, tropical outpost near the Zimbabwe border. To aficionados, this is the real Kruger, the park's wildest and least visited camp. There's less of a concentration of game up here, but this isn't to say you won't see wildlife (the Big Five all breeze through from time to time) – it's simply that you have to work that much harder at spotting game in the woodlands and dense *mopane* scrubland.

The real rewards of *Punda* are in its landscapes and stunningly varied vegetation, with a remarkable nine biomes all converging here, which also makes it a paradise for bird-watchers. The landscape around Punda has many craggy sandstone cliffs, the hilltops crowned with giant baobabs, some as old as 4000 years. Some of the accommodation is in the original 1930s huts, which ought to be declared National Monuments as they're in danger of being pulled down for modernization. All units are en suite and have fridges, while some have kitchens and the rest make use of communal cooking areas. The camp has a very simple restaurant, a small shop and a filling station.

Pafuri picnic site, 46km north of Punda, should on no account be missed, as it's here that you'll experience the true richness of northern Kruger. The site is a large area under the shade of massive thorn trees, leadwoods and jackalberry trees on the banks of the Luvuvhu River and is the ultimate place for lunch. An interpretation board gives a fascinating account of human history in the area. There are braai facilities, a constantly boiling kettle to make your own tea and the attendant can sell you ice-cold canned drinks.

Bushveld camps

If you want to stay at a bushveld camp, book as early as possible, as demand for the bush experience they offer is pretty high. Note that the camps are out of bounds to anyone not booked in to stay. Most offer game drives during the day and at night.

Bateleur

About 40km southwest of *Shingwedzi* restcamp, **Bateleur** is well off the beaten track, in the remote northern section of the park on the banks of the frequently dry Mashokwe stream. The camp has a timber viewing-deck, excellently placed for views of game coming to drink at a seasonally full waterhole. The nearby Silver Fish and Rooibosrand dams also attract game as well as birdlife in prodigious quantities. Seven family cottages can accommodate up to 34 people; each has its own kitchenette and fridge, with electricity provided by solar panels.

Biyamiti

Biyamiti lies on the banks of the Mbiyamiti River, about 41km northeast of the Malelane Gate and 26km west of Crocodile Bridge Gate. Its proximity to the latter is one of the main advantages of this very southerly camp. Another plus point is that the terrain attracts large numbers of game including lion, elephant and rhinos. Fifteen family cottages, all with fully equipped kitchens, can accommodate a maximum of seventy visitors.

Jakkalsbessie

On the bank of the Sabie River, some 7km north of *Skukuza* restcamp, near the airfield, **Jakkalsbessie** is one of the less remote bush camps and is periodically treated to the sound of aircraft taking off or landing at the *Skukuza* landing strip. Although it may be too close to the "city lights" of *Skukuza* for some, the camp is beautifully positioned, with easy access to some of the richest game country in Kruger. Eight thatched cottages with fully equipped kitchens accommodate a maximum of 32 people.

Shimuwini

Shimuwini lies on the upper reaches of the Shimuwini Dam, which is filled by the Letaba River, about 50km from the Phalaborwa Gate on the Mooiplaas Road. Situated in *mopane* and bushwillow country, with sycamore figs along the banks of the river, this peaceful camp is not known for its game but is a perennial favourite among bird-watchers. It's an excellent place for spotting riverine bird species, including fish eagles. Up to 71 people can be accommodated in fifteen family cottages equipped with kitchens and with verandas.

Sirheni

Sirheni is on the bank of Sirheni Dam, roughly 54km south of *Punda Maria*. It's a fine spot for bird-watching, beautifully tucked into riverine forest, with some game also passing through the area. The big pull, however, is its remote bushveld atmosphere in an area that sees few visitors. The fifteen one- or two-bedroom cottages, all equipped with kitchens, can accommodate eighty visitors, and the camp's two bird hides are a great pull.

Talamati

Lying on the banks of the usually dry Nwaswitsontso stream, about 31km south of Orpen Gate, **Talamati**'s mixed bushwillow woodland setting attracts giraffe, kudu, wildebeest, zebra and predators like lion, hyena and jackal, as well as rhino and sable. Two hides within the perimeter of the camp overlook a waterhole, where game viewing can be excellent. The camp has the capacity for eighty people in its comfortable ten six-bed and five four-bed cottages arranged in an L-shape along the river in a forest of leadwoods and russet bushwillows.

Private reserves

The **private camps** follow the same basic formula: full board, with dawn and late-afternoon game drives conducted by a ranger, assisted by a tracker, in open vehicles. Afternoon outings usually turn into night drives following sundowners in the bush. They all also offer bushwalks, usually after breakfast, and most overlook waterholes or plains, so that you can look out for animals during the time you're in camp, laze around the pool, or peruse their collection of animal books. The **Sabi Sands reserve** (ⓦsabi.krugerpark.co.za) has the reputation of being the best managed of all the game areas, and it's one of the best places in the world for seeing leopards and lions.

Private camps aren't places you can casually pop into. You'll need to **book ahead** either directly through the contact addresses given here or through a specialist travel agent (such as those listed in Basics). For details of flights and roads into the area, see p.713. A 4WD vehicle isn't needed to access the camps.

The **prices** quoted here are per person per night, sharing a double unit, including all meals (where relevant) and game activities. Subject to these criteria, prices can be expected to lie in the R1500–6000 range, depending on the level of luxury. In the winter, rates can fall by R700 or so.

Chitwa Chitwa Game Lodge Sabi Sands Game Reserve, North ☎011 883 1354, ⓦwww.chitwa .co.za. Beautifully set on the edge of the largest pan in the Sabi Sand, *Chitwa Chitwa* provides both luxury and the chance to see the big cats, but keeps its rates lower than high-profile neighbours such as *Mala Mala* and *Londolozi*. It has two camps, *Main Lodge* and *Safari Lodge*, both with decks overlooking waterholes. *Main Lodge* accommodates eighteen guests and is much more luxurious, and pricier, with grand public spaces and baroque suites, while *Safari Lodge* sleeps ten in an attractive cluster of thatched rondavels, with an enthusiastic game guides. The food is the same at both camps, and both accept children. ⓽

Djuma Bush Lodge Sabi Sands Game Reserve, North ☎013 735 5118, ⓦwww.djuma.com. A very relaxed lodge set in mixed woodland with eight A-frame thatched chalets decorated in simple but tastefully pared-back style. A spacious, very beautiful camp offering "safaris for the soul", with billowing white drapes, terracotta colours, cushioned low beds – all utterly languorous and romantic. The camp sleeps fourteen (no children), and the emphasis is on relaxation and

tuning into nature and yourself, as well as game viewing – in contrast to the usual goal-oriented list-ticking common in the Sabi Sands. Game drives allow you to view elephants and lions, but there are also contemplative nature walks, healthy and delicious meals, and massages available in a gorgeous treatment room overlooking a waterhole. ⓻

Honeyguide Manyeleti Game Reserve, near Orpen Gate ☎011 341 0282, ⓦwww .honeyguidecamp.com. One of the more reasonably priced camps,the only one to offer tented accommodation at each of their two locations, *Khoka Moya* and *Mantobeni*. The camps are beautifully landscaped, maximizing the bush feel, with dining areas of sleeperwood timber and corrugated iron. Each tent is enormous and has its own bathroom. Kids are accepted at Khoka Moya; there's even a children's programme. ⓽

Londolozi Sabi Sands Game Reserve ☎011 809 4300, ⓦwww.ccafrica.com. Leopards are virtually synonymous with *Londolozi*, where you stand an excellent chance of seeing these notoriously elusive stalkers. *Londolozi*'s camps carry the imaginative stamp of the Conservation Corporation

Africa, whose hallmark is indulgence with a green conscience. Of South Africa's most exclusive safari lodges, *Londolozi* wins hands down on style, making good use of natural materials to blend in with the vegetation. ❾

Mala Mala Sabi Sands Game Reserve, South ☎011 268 2388, ⓦwww.malamala.com. The most fabled and exclusive game lodge in Southern Africa, which offers terrific game viewing – and rich and famous people in your vehicle at the same time. The atmosphere is friendly and relaxed, nonetheless. Children are accepted and often a family is given their own Land Rover and guide. ❾

Nkorho Bush Camp Sabi Sands Game Reserve, North ☎013 735 5367, ⓦwww.nkorho.com. A small family-operated outfit in thinly wooded grassland, *Nkorho* is possibly the most relaxed and child-friendly camp in Sabi Sands, and the price is an absolute steal, as safari lodges go, with adjacent lodges charging up to six times the price. The lack of pretence and the homely atmosphere give *Nkorho* the feeling of being on a friend's farm. There are five simple, comfortable, rectangular chalets with showers, catering to a maximum of fourteen guests. The communal areas comprise an open-air lounge area, a bar with a pool table and an African fantasy of a *boma* – constructed from gnarled tree trunks – where evening meals are served around a large open fire. The rate includes two game drives and a bush walk. ❽

Nottens Bush Camp Sabi Sands Game Reserve ☎013 735 5105, ⓦwww.nottens.com. Two decades old and still resisting the temptation to expand, this family-run outfit is one of the most popular and attractive small camps. Dinners are served at a communal table, with other meals either on a massive deck that acts as a viewing platform for the plain in front of the camp or, in winter, in the *boma* around a campfire. Accommodation is for a maximum of twelve (children over 8 welcome) in pleasant double-bedded chalets lit by oil lamps, and with tin roofs. The lack of electricity is a part of the camp's philosophy of bringing guests into contact with the bush. ❽

Umlani Timbavati Game Reserve, accessed from Orpen Rd ☎012 346 4028, ⓦwww.umlani.com. Eight reed-walled huts overlooking the dry Nhlara-lumi River, each with an attached open-topped bush shower, heated by a wood boiler (there's no electricity). The languid atmosphere is reinforced by hammocks hanging lazily from the trees and a plunge pool. The camp isn't fenced off, the emphasis being very much on a bush experience, and windows are covered with flimsy blinds. While it's not recommended if you're of a nervous disposition, there's barely another camp that brings you closer to the feeling of being in the wild. Children are accepted, and get a 25-percent reduction. Enquire about three-night specials and other deals. ❽

Travel details

Trains

Nelspruit to: Johannesburg (1 daily; 10hr); Pretoria (1 daily; 8hr).

Buses

Nelspruit to: Durban (weekly; 8hr); Johannesburg (3 daily; 5hr); Maputo (Mozambique; 2 daily; 4hr); Pretoria (3 daily; 4hr).

Baz Buses

Nelspruit to: Johannesburg (3 weekly; 4hr); Manzini (Swaziland; 3 weekly; 2hr 30min); Mbabane (Swaziland; 3 weekly; 3hr 30min); Pretoria (3 weekly; 5 hr).

Flights

Nelspruit KMIA to: Cape Town (1 daily; 2hr); Durban (1 daily; 1hr 30min); Johannesburg (3–6 daily; 1hr 50min); Maputo (Mozambique; daily; 1hr 35min).
Hoedspruit to: Cape Town (1 daily; 3 hr via Sun City); Johannesburg (1 daily; 1hr).
Phalaborwa to: Johannesburg (1–3 daily; 1hr).

Limpopo
(Northern Province)

CHAPTER 10

Highlights

✳ **Exploring the Letaba**
Experience this other-
worldly area of forests,
subtropical tea planta-
tions, misty lakes and
upmarket country-house
guesthouses. See p.738

✳ **Lapalala Wilderness** A
wildlife conservation area
at the heart of the Waterberg Biosphere, contain-
ing the world's only rhino
museum. See p.746

✳ **Horse-riding in the
Waterberg** This mountain
range offers some of South
Africa's finest wilderness
riding and horseback safaris. See p. 747

✳ **Venda crafts** Explore
the remote, simple villages of the mystical Venda
region and discover its
skilful and distinctive art,
pottery and wood carv-
ings. See p.756

LIMPOPO (NORTHERN PROVINCE) | Highlights

⑩

△ Baobab

Limpopo (Northern Province)

Limpopo province is South Africa's no-man's-land: a hot, thornbush-covered area caught between the dynamic heartland of Gauteng and, to the north, the Limpopo River, which acts as South Africa's border with Zimbabwe and, further west, Botswana. Running through the centre of this no-man's-land is the busy **N1** highway, here often called the **Great North Road**. The N1 links a series of towns established by the Voortrekker settlers; most of these are little more than service centres for the surrounding farmland, and few have any real attraction beyond what they offer on a practical level – somewhere to sleep or eat while en route to somewhere else. All have significant black populations, though the prevailing flavour of the towns is strongly Afrikaner, with little in the landscape to lighten the sometimes uncomfortable tone this sets. The N1 is also South Africa's umbilical cord to the rest of Africa, and the importance of the N1 overshadows the rest of the province.

The eastern side of the province is game-rich lowveld, dominated by the seventy-kilometre-wide strip of Kruger National Park abutting the Mozambique border. This part of Limpopo is covered along with Kruger itself in the preceding

Name changes in Limpopo

The Northern Province was renamed **Limpopo** in 2002 and the capital, Pietersburg, was subsequently renamed **Polokwane**. A number of other towns with "colonial" names have also undergone official name changes, with more likely to follow suit in the future, though the old names won't fall out of use all that quickly, especially as the amending of signage is proving a slow process. Examples of these in this chapter include:

Old name	New name
Ellisras	Lephalale
Louis Trichardt	Makhado
Messina	Musina
Naboomspruit	Mookgophong
Nylstroom	Modimolle
Potgietersrus	Mokopane
Warmbaths	Bela-Bela

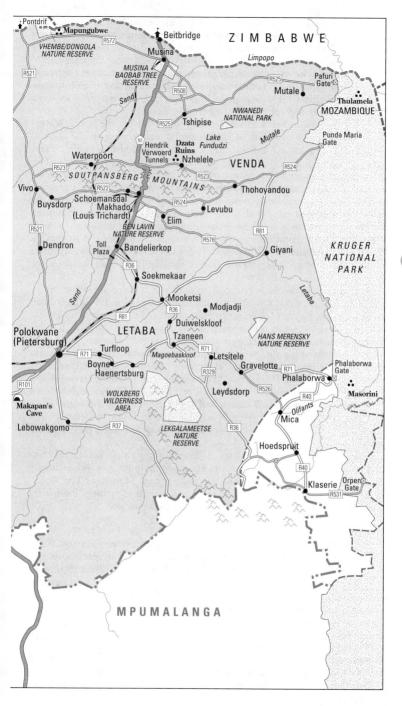

chapter. The principal attractions of the rest of the province lie in its three wild and distinctive **mountain escarpments**. The most significant of these is the first rise of the **Drakensberg** Escarpment, on its long and often spectacular sweep through South Africa from north to south, marking the descent from highveld to lowveld. There's a lot to see in the mountains themselves, especially in the haunting, forested slopes of the **Letaba** area immediately to the east of **Polokwane**, the provincial capital. This region of lakes and waterfalls also provides some excellent walking and comfortable country guesthouses.

On the tranquil and remote western side of the N1 lies the sedate **Waterberg** massif. Once a domain of cattle farming and hunting, in the last two decades the area has transformed into a region dedicated to wildlife conservation, becoming a UNESCO Biosphere and offering malaria-free Big Five game viewing. In the north, lying parallel to the Limpopo River and bisected by the N1, are the subtropical **Soutpansberg Mountains**, and the intriguing and still very independently minded **Venda** region, a homeland during the apartheid era, to the east. North of the Soutpansberg are wide plains dominated by surreal baobab trees, much in evidence along the N1 as it leads to the only (very busy) border post between South Africa and Zimbabwe, at Beitbridge. The only viable alternative if you want to get to Zimbabwe from South Africa is the Groblersbrug/Martin's Drift border crossing (daily 8am–4pm) on the N11, although this means detouring through Botswana.

For all its grand title, the N1 has only recently seen a major upgrading, but by South African standards it is now fast and easy, if often busy. It becomes a **toll road** from just before Modimolle to Polokwane, and then again from Polokwane to Makhado south of the Soutpansberg Mountains. Though it's possible to use alternative roads, the charges aren't crippling for a one-off journey, and don't merit skimping on. As regards **public transport**, Greyhound, Intercape and Translux buses ply the N1 between Johannesburg and Beitbridge, stopping at Bela-Bela, Polokwane, Makhado and Musina; most services carry on to either Bulawayo and Victoria Falls or Harare in Zimbabwe. Northlink Tours runs buses between Tzaneen and Johannesburg via Polokwane. These and other routes are also covered by minibus taxis from any moderately sized town; the best way to find out where they're going and when they depart is to enquire at the taxi rank.

Parts of Limpopo are **malarial**; you will need to take prophylactics, and exercise caution against mosquitoes if you are travelling in the lowveld, including Kruger National Park, or north of the Soutpansberg Mountains. The Waterberg and Letaba areas were not affected at the time of writing, though it's worth double-checking the current situation before you go.

Some history

The first black Africans arrived in South Africa across the Limpopo River some time before 300 AD. The various movements and migrations, and of course trading, ensured a fluidity in the people who established themselves here, and the historical and cultural ties to the north are, as you might expect, stronger in this region than in other parts of South Africa. Traditional arts and crafts such as **pottery** and **woodcarving** are still an important part of life; legendary figures such as the **Rain Queen** (see p.744) retain great potency, and **witchcraft** is still encountered in many places.

The arrival of the **Voortrekker** ox-wagons in the early nineteenth century brought profound changes to the region. Their route roughly followed that of the N1 today, and brought about the founding of the towns now called Bela-Bela, Modimolle and Polokwane, among others. Led by men such as Louis

Trichardt, Hermanus and Piet Potgieter, Andries Pretorius and Paul Kruger, the Voortrekkers who ventured this far north were determined people, and their conflicts with the local peoples were notoriously bitter. At **Makapan's Cave** near Mokopane, several thousand Ndebele were starved to death by an avenging Boer commando, while further to the north, Venda troops forced the Voortrekkers to abandon the settlement they had established at **Schoemansdal** in the Soutpansberg.

In the twentieth century, the **apartheid years** saw several large chunks of the province hived off as homeland areas, with Venda becoming notionally independent and Lebowa and Gazankulu self-governing. Today the contrasts between the old homelands and the white farming areas are manifest throughout the province. Indeed, in the 1999 elections the Northern Province produced the highest-percentage vote in the country for both the ANC and the right-wing Afrikaner Freedom Front – though in 2004 the province voted overwhelmingly in favour of the ANC.

Bela-Bela to Polokwane

The core of Limpopo province, at least in terms of density of settlement and land use, lies along the N1 from Bela-Bela to Polokwane. The generally flat bushveld, together with the dominance of farming here, however, means there is little by way of sights or diversions until you leave the highway and head for the mountains, either westward to the Waterberg (see p.744), or eastwards along the R71 from Polokwane into the otherworldly Letaba area (see p.738).

The southernmost of the towns, **Bela-Bela** and **Modimolle**, make a valiant attempt to rise above their mundane roots by catering for weekend and holiday tourists from Gauteng with a glut of unexciting family-oriented resorts. Further north, **Mokopane** is an infamous example of a town struggling to come to terms with the New South Africa, while the provincial capital, **Polokwane**, offers a range of services but remains dominated by the highway.

Bela-Bela (Warmbaths)

The Great North Road passes into Limpopo approximately 40km north of Pretoria, with a flat and undistinguished landscape predominating all the way up to the town of **BELA-BELA**, lying a few kilometres to the west of the highway. Other than as a pitstop on the N1 or as the gateway to Thabazimbi and the southern Waterberg, Bela-Bela has little to attract visitors. The town's one point of interest, from which it takes its original name, is the **hot mineral spring**. This has now been engulfed by the sprawling *Aventura Warmbaths* watersports and leisure **resort**, which offers waterslides and a water-skiing lake, and can draw up to 10,000 people a day during the holiday periods. The source of the spring, beside the entrance gate to the resort on Voortrekker Road, pumps out 20,000 litres of water at 50°C every hour.

The many smaller holiday resorts in the area surrounding the town – in particular between it and Modimolle 30km to the north – are dismal and deserted out of season, but at weekends and during school holidays become almost unbearably busy and noisy. Gradually, however, farms in the area are transforming themselves into game reserves. While many of these offer luxury lodges, game-viewing drives and 4WD routes, you'll generally get a better experience in the game-rich lowveld, or in places combining the experience with more attractive scenery – such as the Waterberg, Soutpansberg or the parks of North West Province.

Practicalities

The **layout** of Bela-Bela is quite confusing, but the town isn't large. Arriving from the highway, the first group of buildings you come to contains the **tourist office** (Mon–Fri 8am–5pm, Sat 9am–2pm, Sun 9am–noon; ℡014 736 3694), one of the thatched A-frame buildings comprising the Waterfront development. Here you can get help finding **accommodation**, but be specific about what you want, especially if your idea of a pleasant place to stay doesn't involve waterslides, caravans and copious braai facilities. Accommodation in town is generally quite pricey, and high-season rates (including weekends) are often more than double low-season rates. The cheapest option is holiday flats, of which there are quite a number along Moffat Street, parallel to Voortrekker. Otherwise, the large, mustard-coloured *Protea Elephant Springs Hotel*, 31 Sutter Rd (℡ & ℻014 736 2101, ⓦwww.proteahotels.com; ❺), is very central and quite characterful for a member of a large hotel chain. On the outskirts of town is an extravagantly grand B&B, *Chateau Annique*, off Swanepoel St (℡ & ℻014 736 2847; ❹). The *Aventura Warmbaths* resort itself has various chalets as well as hotel accommodation (℡014 736 2200, central reservations ℡012 346 2277, ⓦwww.aventura.co.za; ❼).

As a town by a main highway, Bela-Bela has a wide selection of unexciting **eating places**: your best bet is the *Keg and Elephant* pub in the *Elephant Springs Hotel*, where you can get good, cheap pub grub or a fuller restaurant meal. At the Waterfront development there's an *O'Hagan's Irish Pub and Grill*; a couple of doors away is *Greenfields*, a restaurant serving breakfast from 7am, and other meals throughout the day.

Modimolle (Nylstroom)

The most entertaining thing about **MODIMOLLE**, 27km north of Bela-Bela on the R101, is the story behind its old name. The legend goes that the first Voortrekkers discovered a reed-lined river, consulted their Bibles (the only reference books they carried) and decided that they had been travelling north for so long that they must surely be at the source of the Nile. The presence of a pyramid-shaped hill, Kranskop, the large mountain you can see clearly beside the N1, only confirmed their theory.

The Little Nyl River (as it becaume known) runs through the centre of the modern town, parallel to the wide main street, **Potgieter**. Along here, establishments like Ammo Africa and Trappers Trading Co, as well as an endless parade of orange dust-covered *bakkies*, proclaim the town's white farming roots. Interestingly, one of the more profitable local crops is table grapes, grown on large vineyards in the well-irrigated surrounding area.

Sights are few. A memorial **gateway** at the primary school (Laerskool) on Van Riebeeck Street commemorates the women and children who died in a concentration camp sited there during the Anglo-Boer War, while you can also visit the **house of J.G. Strydom**, a prime minister of South Africa during the 1950s, which is located at 145 Kerk St (Mon–Fri 9am–4pm, Sat 10am–4pm; R3). Less predictably, there is a **mosque** not far from the bridge over the river – testimony to the presence of an unexpectedly large Indian community.

Practicalities

A small **tourist office** is being built on the south side of the R33 on the east side of town. **Accommodation** in town is limited to the *Eurosun* campsite (℡014 717 1328), beside the stadium on the northern side of the river, or a somewhat over-decorated but civilized guesthouse, *Pink Gables*, 3 De Beer St (℡014 717 5076; ❸), by the hospital on the Bela-Bela road. A more upmarket country lodge, *Shangri-la* (☎014 718 1600, ⓦwww.proteahotels.com; ❺), stands at a turn-off 3km down the Eersbewoond road, a turning from the R33 between Modimolle and the N1. The surroundings are lush, and the lodge is filled with an eclectic mix of antique furniture and African memorabilia.

In town, among the handful of rather unexciting **places to eat** along Potgieter and Voortrekker streets are *Pepe's*, located beside Ammo Africa on Potgieter, or the slightly livelier *Mampoer Boer Pub and Grill* by the main cross-roads on Potgieter. There's a classier dining room at *Shangri-la Country Lodge*, though you must book ahead.

Nylsvlei Nature Reserve

To the east of the N1, midway between Modimolle and **Mookgophong**, another resort-encircled highway town situated at the foot of the Swaershoek Mountains, is **Nylsvlei** – a 160-square-kilometre nature reserve enclosing one of the most important wetland areas in South Africa. When the Nyl River is in flood, the *vlei* can spread out to as much as 7km in width, attracting over 150 species of bird, including a number of the country's rarest indigenous water birds. As well as picnic sites and game-viewing routes, there's also a simple bush camp (☎014 717 2523; ❷). Right next to the nature reserve is a lovely place to stay, *Boekenhout* (☎014 743 0957, full board ❹), which has various cottages around the farm and offers game drives in a characterful old truck onto Nylsvlei itself.

Mokopane (Potgietersrus)

A further 50km north of Naboomspruit, also just off the N1, lies **MOKOPANE**, originally named after the Voortrekker hero Piet Potgieter, who died during a famous siege at Makapan's Cave in the hills to the north of town. The N1 former-ly ran right through the centre of town, but the new highway smoothly bypasses it, an act you should have few qualms about following, unless you are bound for parts of the northern Waterberg or have a perverse desire to check out one of the country's racist hot spots. In the mid-Nineties, the town attracted worldwide pub-licity when white locals tried to prevent black children entering what had been all-white schools during the apartheid years. This display of dogged racism earned the town the unenviable title of racist capital of South Africa. There's little doubt that the old thinking still dies hard in the town and its agricultural hinterland – something you'll still pick up from such things as "Club Members Only" signs over white-filled bars and intolerant squabbling over local services and ameni-ties. On the other hand, blacks crowd the main streets with stalls and, despite the continual crawl of traffic, give the place a bustling, lively feel.

The one place worth stopping at is the **Arend Dieperink Museum** (Mon–Fri 8am–4.30pm; R5), located in an old schoolhouse set back from Voortrekker Road (the main R101), behind the tourist office. It has a substantial collec-tion of ploughs, tractors, wagons and farm implements outside; inside there are well-labelled displays on the significant archeological discoveries made at **Makapan's Cave**, 19km north of Mokopane, including that of three-million-year-old fossils of *Australopithecus africanus*, a predecessor of *Homo sapiens*. For the moment, access to the cave itself is only possible by arrangement with the museum (☎015 491 9735).

Practicalities

The local **tourist office** (☎015 491 8458) is on Voortrekker Road as you come into the main part of town from the south, between Kruger and Van Riebeeck streets. Most of the **accommodation** in Mokopane is in the form

Makapan's Cave (Makapansgat)

The network of limestone caves northeast of Mokopane known as **Makapan's Cave** might be the repository of some of South Africa's most important paleontological finds, but to many locals it is better known for one of those incidents in South African history which is remembered in different ways by different sections of the population. In 1854, bent on revenge after a party of Voortrekkers had been ambushed, a Boer commando unit cornered the clan of Ndebele chief Makapan in the hills to the north of Mokopane. The Boers, led by Piet Potgieter, the nephew of Voortrekker leader Hermanus Potgieter who had been skinned alive not long before by kinsmen of Makapan, besieged the chief and an estimated three thousand of his followers inside the network of caves which ran through the hills. With little food and almost no water, the imprisoned Ndebele became increasingly desperate, and eventually seven hundred besieged men rushed out towards a nearby stream, only to be mown down by the patient Boers. When the siege was finally broken after four weeks, hundreds of rotting bodies were found inside the cave. The Boers lost only two men, one of them Potgieter, whose body was "heroically" retrieved by a young Paul Kruger. A rather one-sided account of the siege is available at the museum in Mokopane.

of plain travellers' overnight rooms, and as a result rates drop at weekends. The cheapest place to stay is the block of apartment rooms at *Lonely Oak Lodge*, Van Riebeeck and Hodge streets (☎015 491 4560; ❹). On the northern edge of town, by the side of the main road, are a couple of hotels: the *Oasis* (☎015 491 4124; ❸) and the ageing but respectable *Protea Park* (☎015 491 3101, ⓦwww.proteahotels.com; ❺), which has a pool and a decent restaurant. There is an unappealing municipal caravan park just off the N1 on the northern side of town, behind a parked steam locomotive. On the southern side of the Nyl River, 10km south of Mokopane on the N1, is a homely B&B, *Jaagbaan* (☎015 491 7833; ❸). Quite a bit further afield, signposted after 32km along the N1 north of town, is the *Protea Ranch Hotel* (☎015 290 5000, ⓦwww.theranch .co.za; ❻), a well-run, modern resort-style place.

Polokwane (Pietersburg)

Lying almost dead central in the province of which it is the capital, **POLOKWANE** is also the largest city on the Great North Road between Pretoria and the border. It's mostly an administrative and industrial centre, and much of its energy derives from the large volume of traffic moving through the city on the N1. But it does have a couple of quirky attractions, including an excellent museum, and if you're heading towards the Letaba area, the lowveld or central Kruger National Park, Polokwane is the point to connect with the R71 to Tzaneen and Phalaborwa.

Arrival and information

The city's former air-force base now operates as **Gateway airport**, located on the N1 5km north of the city. The airport is served by both domestic flights (SA Airlink ☎015 288 0166 or 011 978 1111) and occasional international connections from neighbouring countries. All the city's **car rental firms** are located here: Avis (☎015 288 0171), Budget (☎015 288 0169) and Imperial (☎015 288 0097), and **taxis** are also available (☎015 297 4493).

Daily trains to and from Musina stop at the **train station** on the northern edge of the city centre, just off the R521 (an extension of Market St). All the

POLOKWANE (PIETERSBURG)

RESTAURANTS

Pebbles Café	1
The Restaurant	3
Villa Italia	2

ACCOMMODATION

African Roots Guesthouse	A
Holiday Inn	C
Mrs B's Bed & Breakfast	B
Plumtree Lodge	E
Town Lodge	D
Vivaldi Guest House	F
Union Park/Game Park Campground	G

0 — 500 m

Bakone Malapa Museum

intercity **buses** pass through the centre of town: Translux stops at the *Big Bite* on Grobler Street, and Greyhound at the Shell Ultra City, a petrol station/convenience store.

The Limpopo Tourism and Parks Board is the best source for **tourist information**, located on the corner of Mandela and Church streets (Mon–Fri 8am–4:30pm; ☎015 290 7300, ⊛www.limpopotourism.org.za). There is also a helpful budget travellers' tourist agent, SA Tours and Bookings (Ⓔsatours@mweb.co.za), next to the *Vivaldi Guest House* (see p.738).

Accommodation

Polokwane has plenty of places to stay, and there are signs for B&Bs on many street corners. The Union Park **campground** off Dorp St has simple but adequate ablution facilities and some inexpensive rondavels. It's right beside the Pietersburg Game Reserve on the southern edge of town, but there's little sense of it being surrounded by nature.

African Roots Guesthouse 58a Devenish St ☎015 297 0113, ⊛www.pietersburg.net/ar.htm. A relaxed, tasteful spot run by artists, with local and foreign artefacts and works of art in every room. ❹
Holiday Inn On the corner of Vorster and Bok streets ☎015 291 2030, ⊛www.southernsun.com. A couple of blocks from Civic Square, with predictable but decent rooms and an outdoor pool. ❺
Mrs B's Bed and Breakfast 17 Welsford St, Bendor ☎015 296 1021. An unremarkable but

inexpensive and hospitable suburban B&B with two twin bedrooms. ❷
Plumtree Lodge 138 Marshall St ☎015 295 6153, Ⓔplumtree@plumtree.co.za. Not far from the centre, probably the smartest and most comfortable lodge in town, with a pool, a big garden and cheaper rates over the weekend. ❹
Town Lodge Off the N1 as you enter Polokwane from the south ☎015 292 4400, ⊛www.citylodge.co.za. Clean and comfortalbe rooms

and easy access to the *Meropa Casino and Enter-tainment World*, where you will also find a decent restaurant, craft market, a play area for kids, and aviary. ❺

Vivaldi Guest House 2 Voortrekker St ☏ 015 295 6162. A friendly, well-kept guesthouse with six rooms in a pleasant part of town. Known for its hearty breakfasts and the parrots in the garden. ❹

The City and around

Polokwane has a busy, compact CBD set out on a grid pattern (which includes lots of one-way streets), with layers of industry and suburbia tightly packed around it. It may not be the most inspiring spot, but much of Limpopo's drive and enterprise emanates from its capital. At its heart, the **Civic Square**, a park area bounded on two sides by Landros Mare and Thabo Mbeki (formerly Vorster) streets, has an incongruous but entertaining array of sculptures, statues and monuments, ranging from a family of giraffes to a fighter aircraft. In the middle of the park is a white church housing the small but absorbing **Hugh Exton Photographic Museum** (Mon–Fri 8.30am–3.30pm, Sun 3–5pm; free), which depicts the early years of the town through the work of a local commercial photographer; the portraits are excellent. Opposite the park, on the other side of Thabo Mbeki, is the old shop frontage of the decent **Irish House Museum** (Mon–Fri 8am–4pm, Sat 9am–noon, Sun 3–5pm; free), which includes displays on the city's past and natural history. For those inspired by the sculptures of the Civic Square, there's a small **art museum** above the library on Schoeman and Jorissen streets, together with an annexe of outdoor, industrial-type modern sculptures in a park on the left as you leave town on the N1 heading north.

The one sight in Polokwane really worth putting aside time to see is the open-air **Bakone Malapa Museum** (daily 8.30am–12.30pm & 1.30–3.30pm; closed Mon afternoon; R3), 9km southeast of town on the R37. A simple but genuine project, it succeeds in conveying some of the old way of life of the local Bakone people – a grouping within the Northern Sotho – where many flashier examples have fallen short. A village of huts has been built in the traditional style, and fourteen people live permanently on site, working on crafts such as pottery and leatherworking through the day. One of them also acts as a guide, and will explain the different activities you see, as well as the architecture, history and legends of the site.

Eating

True to its functional role, Polokwane has no shortage of chain **restaurants and takeaways**. The largest collection of these can be found at the Savannah Mall, on the fringes of the city along the Tzaneen road. Among the familiar names, look out on the lower level for *Villa Italia*, part of a small local chain of Italian restaurants. There are also a couple of locally owned places in town, including *The Restaurant* (☏ 015 291 1918), serving quite classy meat and fish dishes, as well as curries, in an older house on the corner of Thabo Mbeki and Dorp streets, and *Pebbles Café* (☏ 015 295 6999) in the Tom Naude homestead at 39 Mandela (formerly Grobler) St, which serves breakfasts, snacks, lunches and, through the week, evening meals.

Letaba

East of Polokwane, the **Letaba** is a forested, lush, mountainous area, contrasting very sharply with the hot lowveld immediately east and the wide, flat bushveld to the west, and marking the first dramatic rise of the Drakensberg Escarpment as it begins its sweep south through Mpumalanga. The forest begins around the mountain village of **Haenertsburg** and follows two very scenic parallel valleys to the largest town in the area, **Tzaneen**. The valleys are filled with lakes surrounded by dark pine forests, sparkling rivers, misty peaks and, towards Tzaneen, subtropical crops such as tea, macadamia nuts and avocados. With some very comfortable and beautifully located guesthouses, farmstalls and tea rooms, hiking trails and trout fishing, the Letaba is in many ways an attractive, less well-known alternative to Mpumalanga's crowded highlands.

On the sixty-kilometre stretch between Polokwane and Haenertsburg are two huge, incongruous institutions, the **University of the North** at Turfloop, and **Zion City Moria** at **Boyne**, identified by a huge Star of David on the hill above it. At Easter, an incredible three million people gather here for the annual gathering of the Zion Christian Church, an independent, Africanized Christian Church. The symbols of followers of the church, a silver star or badge pinned to the chest, and sometimes a grey peaked cap, are worn right across the northern areas of South Africa. A certain amount of mystery and suspicion surrounds the movement, but there isn't really anything to see other than during the Easter gathering – which is the one time you want to stay well clear, as three million people can cause some mighty traffic jams.

Haenertsburg

Mellow **HAENERTSBURG** lies 60km from Polokwane, high on a hillside overlooking the R71 as the road winds down into the thickly wooded Magoebaskloof Valleys. Once an old gold-rush village, Haenertsburg has wonderful views over the area known as the Land of the Silver Mist. Along its **main street**

is a friendly tea room called *The Elms* (closed Mon), which also has a gift shop and is the place to buy trout and ask about trout fishing. At the back of *The Elms* is the useful **tourist office**, the Magoebaskloof Tourist Association (Mon–Fri 8am–5pm, Sat & Sun 9am–noon; ☎015 276 4972, ⓦwww.magoebaskloof .com), where you can organize local accommodation or tours, or find out about good picnic spots and short walks in the area, including a tough one up to the **Iron Crown**, the peak above the village. If you're planning to be in the area in May – a beautiful time with glorious autumnal colours in the valley – get details from them of the annual **music and cultural festival**, which sees national orchestras and choirs performing in unusual venues locally.

As for **accommodation**, the *BaliWillWill Farm*, 1500m into the hills from Haenertsburg past the police station (☎015 276 2212; ❸), has B&B rooms in the farmhouse or in a simple self-catering flat. On the R71, 2km east of Haenertsburg, the *Glenshiel* (☎015 276 4335, ⓦwww.glenshiel.co.za; ❺) was formerly one of the finer country lodges in South Africa, with roaring fires, deep sofas, antiques and fine food, but it's now starting to appear a bit neglected and past its prime. Within walking distance west of Haenertsburg off the R71, *Livingstone Place* (☎015 276 4764; ❷) is a collection of tall, Swiss-style self-catering chalets in a scenic wooded setting. Places to stay on the two routes to Tzaneen are covered on p.741.

Good **food**, including pancakes and big breakfasts, can be had during the day at *Picasso's Restaurant*, in a large wooden cabin beside the R71, and in the evenings at the *Atholl Arms* (☎015 276 4712), on the main street beside *The Elms*. Also on the main street is the cosy *Iron Crown Pub and Grill*, offering standard pub fare.

Georges Valley Road and the Magoebaskloof Valleys

Just east of Haenertsburg is a turning off the main R71 for the **Georges Valley Road**, which offers an alternative route to Tzaneen. There is, in fact, little

10

Hiking in Letaba

One of the principal attractions of the Letaba area, especially given the spectacular scenery, deep forests and relatively cool air of the escarpment, is hiking. Of the **multi-day hikes**, the two most popular are the two-day Debegeni and three-day Dokolewa trails, which are well marked and utilize well-kept forester's houses or log cabins (❶) for the overnight stops – details from the state forestry organization, SAFCOL (☎012 481 3615). The two large protected areas in the southern parts of the Letaba also offer excellent walking: **Wolkberg Wilderness Area** (☎015 276 1303) has a campsite at Serala Forest Station, which you get to from the Haenertsburg side, but few other facilities – it's meant to be wild and untamed; **Lekgalameetse Nature Reserve** (☎015 2302 1514), reached from the R36 south of Tzaneen, encompasses the transition between lowveld and escarpment and has accommodation in simple log cabins (❶).

If you're not up for such serious hiking, there are good **day-walks** in various parts of the Letaba: around Haenertsburg, through some of the last remaining indigenous forest; along the waymarked four-kilometre Lesodi Trail, beginning at Sandford Heights Nursery on the R71 past the *Magoebaskloof Hotel*; along the Rooikat Walking Trail, a circular marked forest trail on the Agatha ridge, beginning near the *Coach House*; and at Modjadji Nature Reserve (see p.744). For details of local guides, contact the Magoebaskloof Tourist Association in Haenertsburg.

to choose between the two options in terms of both distance and stunning scenery, and if you are spending any time in the area it's worth trying both. Along the Georges Valley Road lies a memorial to **John Buchan**, author of *The Thirty-Nine Steps*, who became captivated by the area when he visited not long after the Anglo-Boer War, calling it "a place enchanted and consecrated". There's also the tranquil **Ebeneezer Dam**, an atmospheric spot for swimming and picnicking. Some 4km from Tzaneen on the George's Valley Road, *Satvik* (☎015 307 3920 or 082 971 1171, ✉satvik@pixie.co.za; ❷) is an unusual and appealing backpackers' lodge which makes use of a group of old whitewashed farmworkers' cottages set above a lake. Facilities, which include doubles and small dorms, are simple and rustic, but outdoor showers and a lakeside bar and cooking area make it an atmospheric spot typical of Letaba, and one you could easily find yourself chilling out at for days on end.

The R71 from Haenertsburg to Tzaneen

If you take the **R71** east out of Haenertsburg, you'll soon pass the **Stanford Lake Centre** (☎015 276 6103) on your left, where various outdoor activities, including mountain biking and hiking, can be arranged. About 4km out of town is a turning to the **Cheerio Gardens**, which holds an annual Cherry Blossom Festival at the end of September; the Magoebaskloof Tourist Association can provide details of various private show gardens in the area. Along this same turning is another wonderful piece of backwoods life, at the tiny **Wegraakbos Dairy** (☎015 276 1811), where cheese is made in traditional style over an open fire in a huge copper cauldron. A visit is thoroughly recommended; tours, which cost a few rand, are at 10am, but you can visit the dairy throughout the day, taste the cheese and walk around the farm and nearby woods. A couple of kilometres beyond the turning, there's *Den Eden Log Cabin* at Den Eden farm (☎015 276 4742 or 083 269 3552; ask for the owner Meinie de Villiers; ❷), a pleasant and secluded place to stay tucked away on its own under some tall pine trees.

A few kilometres beyond are the **Magoebaskloof Valleys**, named after the rogue chief Makgoba, who in 1895 had his head chopped off by native warriors serving under the Boer leader Abel Erasmus. There's more accommodation here at the *Magoebaskloof Hotel* (☎015 276 4776, ⓦwww.magoebaskloof.co.za; ❹), which boasts what is probably the most spectacular view in the area from its front deck, but the rest, including a pub with an old red postbox outside, is fairly uninspired.

The R71 twists and turns impressively as it crosses the Magoebaskloof pass, with dark forests and long views alternating on either side. A side road leads into the **Woodbush State Forest**, where there is a network of roads (not all passable), various multi-day hiking trails and the famous **Debegeni Falls**, an attractive series of waterfalls and natural pools. There are some braai sites by the river, and you can swim in various places if you're careful, but the smooth, slippery rock is very dangerous and a sign indicates that a few folk who tried the DIY waterslide didn't live to recommend it.

Between the turn-off to Debengeni and Tzaneen, the valley becomes broader, the rolling hillsides covered with huge stands of citrus, avocado and banana trees, as well as by the rich green texture of tea bushes. On the **Sapekoe Middlekop** tea estate not far from the junction of the R71 and R36, a winding road leads up to the **Pekoe View tea garden** (daily 10am–5pm; free), with some of the best views in the whole valley. Tea and scones are always available, along with other snacks and drinks; packets of local tea and coffee can be bought in the shop, and there are also worthwhile factory tours (Tues–Sat

11am), on which you can see tea being picked, learn about different grades of tea, and take a look at the production process in the factory.

Tzaneen and around

The dams and soaring gum forests surrounding **TZANEEN** are graceful and attractive. However, the town itself is fairly scruffy, worth avoiding as a place to stay though it is well endowed with shops. The one thing to see here is the **Tzaneen Museum** (Mon–Fri 8.30am–4.30pm; donation requested), situated in a tiny, four-roomed building in the grounds of the library at the top of Agatha Street. You'll need time: the dedicated curator and his assistants don't label any items, preferring to walk around with you and talk about the small but important collection, which includes sacred drums and other items associated with the Rain Queen (see p.744).

A **minibus** operated by Northlink Tours (☎015 291 1867) links Tzaneen with Polokwane and Johannesburg. The **Tzaneen Tourism Centre** (Mon–Fri 8am–4:30pm, Sat 9am–1am; ☎015 307 3582), located on the north side of the R71 as you head out towards Phalaborwa, is a useful place to find out about local accommodation, as well as pick up advice on travelling to spots such as Modjadji, the Magoebaskloof Valleys and Kruger National Park. A couple of locals run **tours** to these: contact Letaba Active Tours (☎082 494 3970) or Yvonne Clarke (☎015 307 2000). There are also a number of good local **mountain-bike routes** – but as yet there is nowhere to rent bikes.

Accommodation in town itself isn't inspiring, especially in comparison with what is available in the surrounding countryside. There's a decent **caravan park** on Old Gravelotte Road, *Fairview* (☎015 307 2679; ❹), which has inexpensive chalets. The *Silver Palms Lodge* off Voortrekker St (☎015 307 3092; ❷), beside the Malaria Research Institute, has some decent modern units around a pool. The road leading out of town into the Wolkberg Mountains to Agatha has some high-class country lodges and spectacular views out over the valleys and peaks of the escarpment (see below), and there's a backpackers' place on the George's Valley Road (see p.741).

As for **food**, Tzaneen has a smattering of familiar takeaways and a few chain restaurants. The best in town is the *Villa Italia*, on the corner of Danie Joubert and Lannie streets, while near the museum there's a pleasant coffee shop, *Gazebo Gardens*, set in an old Victorian garden at 30 Agatha St.

Agatha

AGATHA, the wife of an early mining commissioner, gave her name to a high plateau overlooking Tzaneen. Covered in forest, it's a cool and attractive place, especially if you can rise to a night at one of the top-class guesthouses set along the edge of the ridge. The best value among these is *Kings Walden Estate*, a family-owned avocado farm 12km from Tzaneen up Agatha Road (☎015 307 3262, ⊛www.kingswalden.co.za; ❹), with superbly lush gardens and four simple rooms. Left at the top of the hill, Old Coach Road leads to the classy, well-run *Coach House* (☎015 307 3641, ⊛www.coachhouse.co.za; ❼), boasting its own health spa and nougat factory, 45 suites, great food, and breathtaking views from the breakfast balcony and pool area. In the opposite direction from the top of Agatha Road, *Sherwood's Country House* (☎015 307 5512, ⊜esherc_h@mweb.co.za; ❻) is a more intimate but slightly less well-bred rival. A more down-to-earth alternative in the Agatha area is *Granny Dot's Country Spot* (☎015 307 5149 or 083 760 0983; ❸, self-catering ❷), a B&B close to the Rooikat Walking Trail (see box on p.740) with fine views and lush surroundings.

△ Picking tea

Modjadji Nature Reserve

The area around the rather downbeat village of **MODJADJI**, 32km northeast of Tzaneen off the R36, is the home of the famous **Rain Queen**, the hereditary female monarch of the Lobedu people, whom legend maintains has the power to make rain – a useful talent in these often parched northern areas. Suitably, her home village is up in the mists on a mountain where a special form of ancient cycad, or tree fern, flourishes. The **Modjadji Cycad Reserve** (daily 8.30am–4pm; R10) protects these plants in an area at the very top of the hill, and incorporates some fine views (often obscured by mist) and various short but pleasant, rather vaguely marked walking trails. There are a few facilities, including safari tents (self-catering ❷), a souvenir shop and information centre, which explains a bit more about the unique plants found here and, of course, the famous monarch.

Around 20km northwest of the turning to Modjadji lies the **Sunland Nursery**. Here you'll find a massive baobab tree with a pub inside, whose owner will serve you draught beer while relating a few of the strange stories attached to his odd location. He claims this is the largest baobab in the world, although a few other specimens around Limpopo also contend for the honour. Still, it's fun to visit, especially if you've got time for a few convivial drinks, though you have to pay to get in (R10). A few kilometres further down the same road is the five-square-kilometre **Hopefontein Nature Reserve** (℡015 305 3607 or 082 807 8182; ❷), which takes reservations to stay in their two tree houses or rustic farmhouse.

Letsitele

Thirty kilometres east of Tzaneen, **LETSITELE** is a small town whose main function is as a waypoint to a few places of interest in the area of lowveld abutting the escarpment. To the south are the large nature and wilderness areas of **Lekgalameetse** and **Wolkberg** (see box on p.740), places to explore if you have a few days and a penchant for empty green landscapes. Near Letsitele itself is one of the most interesting handicraft projects in the province, **Karosswerkers**, which produces intricate and striking embroidered ethnic place mats, cushion covers and wall hangings. You can arrange to see the workshops (℡015 345 1765), which employ over 150 locals, and their work is on sale at the excellent Monsoon Gallery on the R527 west of Hoedspruit.

Waterberg

Even now, with the great gold-city belching its smoke almost within sight – even now, with invading civilization marching across the hills in seven-league boots, Waterberg still holds its charm.

Eugène Marais

Rising out of the plains to the west and north of the Great North Road, the **Waterberg** is one of the least known and most intriguing of South Africa's significant massifs. Once an area of lakes and swamps – hence its name – the elevated plateau can often seem as dry as its surrounding northern bushveld, yet it harbours a diversity of vegetation and topography which supports cattle-ranching, hunting concessions and, increasingly, some of the country's foremost conservation projects.

As a game-viewing destination the Waterberg is an alternative to the lowveld areas around Kruger National Park, with the important advantage that malaria is not endemic to the Waterberg. However, it has impressive credentials as a vast area of true wilderness, and is certainly less commercialized, the game here is less dense than around Kruger. There are two large game reserves which hold the Big Five: **Marakele National Park** and the **Welgevonden** private reserve, both of which are very much in the upmarket bracket. These are complemented by a patchwork of smaller and more affordable private reserves gathered loosely in the area to the north of the town of **Vaalwater**, the only settlement of any size in the Waterberg; among these is the highly regarded **Lapalala Wilderness Area**. You'll find rhino often heads the list of game highlights in these private reserves, along with giraffe, large antelope and leopard. To gain access to any private reserve you'll almost always be expected to book into accommodation on the reserve, though such is the co-operative nature of many parts of the Waterberg that the owners of guesthouses located alongside a reserve have often negotiated access rights.

The area also offers some exciting **adventure activities**, including bush-hiking trails and some of the finest wilderness horse-riding in South Africa. Waterberg Transfers (☎082 320 6515, ⍟www.waterbergtransfers.com) offers easy and efficient **long-distance taxi** links between places such as Johannesburg International Airport and the Waterberg.

Vaalwater

The small farming town of **VAALWATER** offers the visitor little more than a couple of useful places to stay and an orientation point on the R33, which connects Modimolle with Lephalale. Vaalwater marks the junction between the R33 and the tarred road to Melkrivier and Marken – along which the main conservation areas of the northeastern Waterberg are located. Around Vaalwater there are absorbing bush experiences on most levels, from luxury lodges to inexpensive self-catering cottages and wilderness campsites. The scenery in this part of the Waterberg is subtle rather than dramatic: the way to appreciate it is to stay for a few days.

In the easily missed center of town is the Village Square, at the first T-junction as you approach from the east, where you'll find the **tourist office** (Mon–Fri 9am–5pm; ☎014 755 3535, ⍟www.waterbergtourism.com). If you need **accommodation** in town, there's a great backpackers' lodge as well as comfy,

Hunting

To some it is barbaric blood lust, while to others it lies at the heart of conservation. **Hunting** presents an emotive issue which you'll hear vigorously debated in the Waterberg and in many rural areas of South Africa where it is regarded as an essential part of life in the bush. It is also a multi-million-rand industry and, although you don't necessarily read about them in the guidebooks, there are many more hunting reserves in South Africa than there are eco-friendly game reserves.

In **hunting reserves** the land is stocked with game specifically for the purpose of hunting, whereas in conservation-oriented game reserves the guiding principle is that tourists will pay simply to see the animals in their natural environment. However, wherever land has been fenced in (which is just about everywhere), the idea of a completely natural environment is inevitably compromised, and intervention is necessary to maintain a realistic balance and diversity of nature within that area. Such intervention – "management" is a common euphemism – takes place even in the most conservation-oriented reserves. More at issue is the extent to which this process is commercialized. Some reserves, knowing that they need to cull a certain number of animals, allow paying clients to hunt for that quota, providing a valuable source of income for the reserve and its conservation ideals. Inevitably, this leads to grey areas: how many animals need to be culled, for instance, when there is money at stake?

tasteful B&B at *Zeederberg Cottages* (☎014 755 3538, ⓦ www.zeederbergs.co.za; ❸), situated behind the Spar grocery store, which is turn next to the excellent *Black Mamba* crafts gallery; these places are all roughly 1km west of the Village Square along the R33. As well as a useful stopover, this makes a great base for activities such as hiking or game viewing, which can be organized locally. Otherwise, *Waterberg Game Lodge* (☎014 755 3686; ❸), on the right as you come into town from Modimolle, offers rooms, a small restaurant and a lively locals' bar. It subtitles itself the *International Hunter's Hotel*, which says quite a lot about what you can expect. For **food**, try the *Waterberg Game Lodge* or the *Waterhole Steakhouse* (☎014 755 3775), located in the Village Square complex, among the shops by the Melkrivier turn-off.

Marakele National Park

Southwest of Vaalwater, in the mountains to the northeast of the mining and hunting town of **Thabazimbi**, lies **Marakele National Park** (daily: May–Aug 8am–5pm; Sept–April 8am–6pm), one of South Africa's newest national parks. At its core are the Kransberg, a striking assortment of odd-shaped peaks, plateaus and cliffs. The diversity of land and altitude means that a variety of interesting plants, including ferns, orchids, and even proteas and cycads are found here, while the fauna includes tsessebe, roan and sable antelope, red hartebeest and eight hundred breeding pairs of the endangered Cape vulture. Larger game such as elephant, rhino and lion have also been introduced, many from Kruger National Park.

While the park has a great deal of potential, for the moment **day visitors** (R10) are restricted to a small area including Kransberg, with its inspiring views. The only place to **stay** is a tented camp situated on the banks of the Matlabas River, which requires a 4WD vehicle to reach.

The Lapalala Wilderness Area

Established in 1981, the **Lapalala Wilderness Area** (☎011 453 7645) is a 400-square-kilometre reserve masterminded by the highly regarded South

African conservationist and artist, Clive Walker. Providing sanctuary for endangered and rare animals, it has developed into one of the foremost conservation projects in the country. It was the first private game reserve in South Africa to obtain the highly endangered black rhino, five of which were acquired from Natal Parks Board for R2.2 million. In 1985 the Lapalala Wilderness School was established, and nowadays it introduces some 3000 children a year from all over Africa to the principles and practice of conservation, during week-long courses in the heart of the wilderness area.

The importance of conservation in the region was recognized in 2001 when some 14,500 square kilometres of both private and publicly owned land in the Waterberg was declared a **UNESCO savanna biosphere reserve**. Lapalala is at the heart of this Waterberg Biosphere Reserve, founded on a close-knit association of local landowners inspired by its example in combining wildlife conservation with the benefits of tourism.

An excellent introduction to some of the achievements of Lapalala, and the personalities involved, is at the world's only dedicated **Rhino Museum** (Tues–Sun 9am–5pm; R5), based in the old Melkrivier School, about 6km along the road to Lapalala off the Vaalwater to Marken tarred road. It's possible to arrange to see Lapalala's rhino **orphans**, including the young black rhino Bwana, who lives in Clive and Conita Walker's back garden. Next door to the Rhino Museum is the equally worthwhile **Waterberg Museum** (same hours), which explores the origins of man in the Waterberg and looks at the various peoples and traditions which have held sway here over the centuries.

The upmarket place to **stay** in the Lapalala Wilderness Area is the intimate and relaxed *Rhino Camp* (❺), a tented self-catering bush camp right by the Lapalala River. Less expensive are a series of basic but remote self-catering bush camps (❷) in different parts of the wilderness area, some of which have a wonderfully atmospheric setting – *Lookout Camp* in particular has safari tents perched on the edge of a hillside overlooking the Lephalala river valley. *Walker's Wayside* (☏014 755 4428; closed Mon), a **pub and restaurant** right next to the Rhino Museum, does tasty lunches and evening meals.

Other private reserves

Welgevonden, a reserve of 380 square kilometres to the west of Vaalwater and abutting Marakele, is in fact divided into hundreds of separate (unfenced) plots, but there are very tight regulations on the number of lodges which can be built and the number of vehicles allowed in the reserve.

As many of the lodges in the Waterberg are small and relatively remote, it's advisable to prebook somewhere to stay, at least for your first couple of nights. Upmarket lodges usually offer full board and include early morning and late-afternoon game drives or walks in their programmes, so it's worth arriving at a time when you can take full advantage of these.

Luxury accommodation

The exclusive *Makweti Safari Lodge* (☎011 837 6776, ⊛www.makweti.com; ❾), with five stone-and-thatch suites built into the natural rock formations of the mountains, is both spectacular and luxurious, its sense of isolation complemented by the fact that game drives can range anywhere over the 330-square-kilometre reserve. Elsewhere, also exclusive but otherwise quite different, is the tranquil *Ant's Nest* (☎014 755 4296, ⊛www.waterberg.net; ❾), a converted farmhouse set deep in the bush north of Vaalwater with rhino, giraffe, gemsbok and blesbok on the game farm, and drives, walks and, in particular, horse-riding offered. The sense of sheer escapism here is clinched by the fact that the owners only ever host one couple or party at a time.

Mid-range and inexpensive accommodation

Although not all located on game reserves, there are a number of **self-catering chalets** and **cottages** in the Waterberg which often make arrangements with larger farms or reserves nearby for game walks or drives. As a result, they tend to be more affordable and flexible. Although self-catering in this price range is standard, most accommodation can provide food if it's ordered in advance.

The best of these establishments include *Cattlelands Cottage* (☎014 755 4179; ❹), a tasteful, comfortable cottage sleeping two, with a plunge pool and a secluded bush setting; and *Le Thabo Pioneer Settlement* (☎014 755 4178 or 082 635 8967; self-catering ❸, full board ❺), a collection of small log cabins on the banks of the Melk River near Lapalala. Pleasant self-catering accommodation is available in *Windsong Cottage* (☎014 755 4000; ❷), one of the old farmhouses on Triple B Ranch. The ranch is one of the oldest in the region and is famous for its hardy, unusual-looking Bonsmara cattle, about which you can find out more on one of the fascinating **farm tours**.

Not far from the Triple B Ranch, the tiny stone **church** at Twenty-Four Rivers on the edge of the ranch is worth a detour. It was designed by Sir Herbert Baker (see box on p.610) and commissioned by two maiden aunts, who expected that he would do it for free, since it was a place of worship; their assumption was, unsurprisingly, not shared by Baker.

The far north

The northernmost part of Limpopo province is a hot, green, undeveloped rural region with as much in common with Zimbabwe as South Africa. The essential geographical features of the area are the **Limpopo River**, the border between South Africa and Zimbabwe (and, further west, Botswana), and the alluring **Soutpansberg mountain range**, aligned east–west just to the north of the area's main town, **Makhado**. Both landmarks lie in the path of the N1 highway, which crosses into Zimbabwe at **Beitbridge**.

As a first impression of South Africa for visitors arriving from Zimbabwe, the far north cannot compete with the lure of attractions further south. Yet it is an area where the lack of sophistication and isolated history of the people and culture make absorbing contrasts to other parts of the country. Perhaps the most distinctive area is the **Venda** region, formerly an "independent" homeland under the apartheid regime; although economically impoverished, it remains rich in tradition, art and legend. East of the Venda lands is the northern tip of **Kruger National Park**, a less-visited but intriguing part of the park (see p.723); there are two entry gates to the park here, at **Punda Maria** and **Pafuri**.

The Soutpansberg area

The **Soutpansberg Mountains** have an unusual claim to distinction, named as they are after a set of saltpans – one of the flatter natural features known to man. The name came about after Voortrekker pioneers, under the leadership of Louis Trichardt, established their first settlement by the pans on the northern side of the mountain range. While the settlement soon relocated to Schoemansdal, on the southern side, the moniker stuck.

An impressive range of hills, particularly when approached from the south, the Soutpansberg attract sufficient rainfall to create a subtropical climate, and spectacularly lush green farms along the southern slopes produce a range of exotic crops such as avocados, mangoes, bananas and macadamia nuts. In other parts, the rocky *kloofs* and green hillsides offer some remote and unspoilt mountain retreats, shaded by up to 250 different species of tree, and the home of monkeys, small antelopes, foraging warthogs and some noble raptors.

The N1 highway bisects the range, passing through **Makhado**, situated in the southern shadow of the mountains, then climbing over a low pass and descending through a pair of tunnels on the northern side. Once over the escarpment, the highway runs north across mostly empty baobab plains to **Musina** and the **Limpopo River**.

Makhado (Louis Trichardt)

With the N1 running through it, **MAKHADO** is easy to miss out on, basically a practical place to stop at the junction of the road leading into Venda and to the Punda Maria Gate of Kruger National Park. With little on offer further north at Musina, however, this is the last town with a reasonable selection of shops and services before you reach the border. A centre for the surrounding mountain and bushveld farms, it has hung onto its traditional role as a white bastion in the hostile north, and you'll find its white population overwhelmingly Afrikaans-speaking.

There is a well-organized **tourist office** (Mon–Fri 8am–5pm, Sat 8am–1pm; ☎015 516 0040, ⊛www.tourismsoutpansberg.co.za) on the left-hand side of the middle junction (the one with traffic lights) as you travel north

---

Hand Crafted paper: Africa's shittiest souvenirs

One piece of modern Africana you shouldn't miss in Makhado is an unusual home industry – rhino and elephant-dung paper and products made by Kathryn Straughan's **Hand Crafted Paper** factory. They mix rhino and elephant-dung (personally gathered from Lesheba Wilderness and Tuli Block in Botswana) with recycled paper pulp to produce writing paper, cards and notelets. You can see some of their range of guaranteed fragrance-free and biodegradable paper souvenirs in their shop, The Stamp & Sign Shop, 24 Rissik St, or call the factory at ☎015 517 7217 or 083 444 0456.

through Makhado. The **train station** is at the southern end of Kruger Street, which is parallel to and west of the main road. **Minibus taxis** for links into Venda and up to Beitbridge use ranks near the corner of Trichardt and Kruger streets. Greyhound, Intercape and Translux **buses** stop at the tourist office.

The best **accommodation** in the area is out of town, mainly in the foothills of the Soutpansberg (see opposite). South of town, the small *Ben Lavin Nature Reserve*, signposted 8km from town on the N1 (☎015 516 4534, ⓦwww .satis.co.za/benlavin; ❷–❸), has a collection of larger antelope and giraffe, as well as walking and mountain-bike trails (bikes are available to rent). As for accommodation, it has a neat restcamp deep in the bush, self-catering cottages, luxury tents and space to pitch your own tent. In Makhado itself, the municipal **caravan park** on Grobler Street, near the centre, offers a bit of gloomy shade and grass for camping. The *Bergwater Hotel*, 5 Rissik Street (☎015 516 0262; ❹), has some decent-sized and relatively modern rooms upstairs with views over a small lake. Off Rissik Street, the *Carousel Lodge* on Klein St (☎015 516 4482; ❸, dorms ❶) is an unglamorous alternative, but has adequate self-catering rooms and units, as well as a dorm.

There are various familiar take-away **food** outlets around the grid-set town centre. For a sit-down meal, head to the *Shenandoah Spur* steakhouse on Krogh Street and Magistrate Avenue, or the pricier restaurant at the *Bergwater Hotel*. More appealing are some of the alternatives out of town, including the tea garden at the *Inn on Louis Trichardt*, the *Ingwe Ranch Hotel* (for details of both, see opposite) or the *Elephant & Castle* pub, 14km south of Makhado on the N1.

Schoemansdal

Established by the first Voortrekkers reaching the Soutpansberg, **SCHOEMANSDAL**, 12km west of Makhado off the R522 towards Vivo (Mon–Sat 9am–4pm; free), was abandoned after thirty or so years, when its inhabitants failed to stem attacks by Venda warriors, and was never again occupied. When control of the area was regained by the Zuid-Africaanische Republiek in 1898, a new settlement was established at Makhado, leaving Schoemansdal the only Voortrekker settlement in the country not to become a modern town. Perhaps not surprisingly, the site of the historic village has been turned into an **outdoor museum of pioneering history**, with a number of old dwellings and buildings re-created and various aspects of settler life and domestic crafts on display. From the top of a wooden viewing platform you can make out the lines of grass where the streets of the settlement once were, as well as the archeological diggings which have been made on the site. It certainly paints a humble picture of pioneer Voortrekker life, one that is not so readily evident in the collections of artefacts on display in dusty town houses. Sadly the museum isn't attracting the audience it has the potential to reach, and is obviously dying a slow death of neglect.

Elim and around

Southeast of Makhado along the R578 lie some areas that used to form part of the self-governing homeland of **Gazankulu**, a Tsonga area. They feature the leftover scruffiness and vibrant roadside action typical of such rural areas – most notably at **ELIM**, a cluster of stalls, minibuses and hoardings on the site of a long-established Swiss mission hospital. A short way from here, along the road to Levubu, is the modest, relaxing *Shiluvari Lakeside Lodge* (☎015 556 3406, ⓔshiluvar@lantic.net; full board ❹), with lawns running down to the edge of Albasini Dam and views over the water to the Soutpansberg.

Continuing on the R578 from Elim crossroads, towards the town of **Giyani**, you'll come upon a series of rural arts and crafts workshops (see box on p.756). The traditions and skills in arts and crafts are not dissimilar to what you find in Venda, and most of the workshops and small factories have simple, rural roots, making the trip to see them a worthwhile adventure.

The Soutpansberg Mountains

Lush, rounded mountains rising to a height of over 1700m and cut by some dramatic outcrops of pinky-orange rock, the **Soutpansberg** seem to form a final barrier of colourful relief before the long hot plains either side of the Limpopo River. Travelling north on the N1, you begin to climb immediately after leaving Makhado, up what becomes a narrow, winding road not easily negotiated by the heavy trucks plying the route.

Along this stretch of the **N1**, you'll pass a number of **hotels and guesthouses** that use the lush surroundings to create a mountain-resort-type atmosphere. The best of these can certainly be regarded as alternatives to a stopover in Makhado: try the *Mountain View Hotel* (☎015 517 7031; ❹), 9km north of town, or, even better, *The Inn on Louis Trichardt* (☎015 517 7088, ⓦ www .innsofzim.co.zw; ❺), 12km north of town, which has various rooms set around pleasant gardens and a pool, as well as an attractive craft shop and tea garden in the grounds. Of the guesthouses hidden in the folds of the Soutpansberg, one of the nicest is *Harnham House* (☎015 517 7260; ❹), 6km along the scenic Bluegumspoort road, which has rooms in the attractive main house as well as in a lovely remote cottage overlooking a dam. Backpacker beds and camping sites are also available here. Once over the low pass, on the much less dramatic northern slopes, you'll find the well-run *Ingwe Ranch Hotel* (☎015 517 7087; ❹), offering a variety of rondavels and rooms, a coffee bar and one of the better restaurants in the area.

Accommodation away from the N1

Beyond the well-worn N1, you can get deeper into the more remote and wilder parts of the mountains if you have a couple of days to spare. Most of the accommodation options listed below are members of the Soutpansberg Conservancy (ⓦ www.soutpansberg.co.za), which promotes the natural heritage of the area as well as developing the tourism potential within the mountain range; the tourist office in Makhado has details of other retreats.

Bergpan Eco Resort On the north side of the mountains and east of Waterpoort along the R523 ☎015 593 0127. Tours of the saltpans that gave the mountains their name and a chance to experience salt-making are on offer, along with hiking and a self-catering guesthouse. ❷

Lajuma Mountain Retreat Along a turn-off on the R522, 46km west of Makhado ☎015 593 0352 or 072 133 6208. Situated by the top of Letjume, the highest point of the Soutpansberg, this has two attractive thatched chalets perched on the mountainside, as well as simpler Victorian cottages tucked into the luxuriant tropical bush. ❷

Lesheba Wilderness A few kilometres on from the *Lajuma Mountain Retreat*, located in a spectacular valley atop the mountain range ☎015

593 0076, ⓦ www.lesheba.co.za. A truly unique experience well worth the long uphill drive: here the internationally acclaimed artist Noria Mabasa (see box on p.756) has used the ruins of old rondavels to create a Venda village that is alive with sculpted figures guests can admire when not taking self-guided walks among the rhino and giraffe. There are terrific opportunities to explore the area, with archeology trails a speciality here. ❺

Medike Mountain Reserve 29km west of Makhado off the R522 ☎015 516 0481. In the Sand River gorge, through which the rail line traverses the mountains to reach Waterpoort. Accommodation is in thatched stone cottages and there are trails to the surrounding area's rock art, birds, wildlife and waterfalls. ❷

Plaas Guesthouse 21km east of Makhado along the R524 ☎ 015 516 4717, ✉ plaasgst@telkomsa .net. A very hospitable, friendly B&B on an avocado farm on the lush slopes of the Soutpansberg, with great breakfasts. ❸

North to the border

Once over the Soutpansberg, the N1 runs across hot, mostly featureless plains of dense bush and baobab trees for some 60km before reaching the town of **Musina**, the last settlement before the Zimbabwe border crossing at Beitbridge on the Limpopo River. There isn't anything much else in the region, although the famous Iron Age site at Mapungubwe is around 80km west of Musina. This is set to become part of an ambitious Transfrontier Park, with links to adjacent nature reserves in Zimbabwe and Botswana, but as yet there are no public entry or facilities.

Musina (Messina)

Eighteen kilometres south of the border, **MUSINA** is above all a mining town, although it does attract a fair bit of the traffic passing through on the N1. The border at Beitbridge is not open 24 hours a day, so there's always call for accommodation and food, which Musina offers without flourish.

The one thing of note around Musina is the **Baobab Tree Reserve** encircling the town. According to legend, God planted baobab trees upside down with their roots in the air. The trees here aren't in great stands but rather dotted around the bushveld, each one with a plate nailed onto it displaying its protected status. Many are over 1000 years old, and the largest have been hollowed out inside and used as houses, bars, shops and even toilets. There are quite a number of fine examples by the roadside on the N1, although many of these are covered in graffiti. The entrance to the reserve, which doesn't have any facilities, is a couple of kilometres south of town.

Mapungubwe and other archeological sites

As one of the early melting pots of southern Africa, Limpopo has a number of important **archeological sites** where excavations have helped piece together a picture of the different people who inhabited the land for thousands of years. Some of the most interesting sites are at places where iron was smelted, as the development from what was essentially a Stone Age culture to an Iron Age culture, with its associated improvement in tools for cultivation and war, was a vital part of the migration of black tribes into South Africa around 1500 years ago. The presence of slag and other wastes provide the strongest clues – the iron itself seldom survives the processes of erosion. Some of the most revealing excavations have taken place at **Thulamela**, inside Kruger National Park not far from the Punda Maria Gate, **Bakone Malapa** cultural village outside Polokwane, **Makapan's Cave** near Mokopane, and **Masorini**, also in the Kruger park, not far from Phalaborwa.

The single most important site in Limpopo province is at **Mapungubwe** (Hill of the Jackals), situated by the confluence of the Limpopo and Shashi rivers, where South Africa, Zimbabwe and Botswana meet. The site was only discovered in 1933, when a local farmer climbed the dome-shaped granite hill and found remains of stone walls, iron tools, graves, pottery and jewellery, including a tiny rhinoceros and a bowl, both made out of gold. It is now thought that the years 1000–1300 AD were the heyday of a civilization centred at Mapungubwe, which later moved to the much more famous Great Zimbabwe. The area is now protected as part of the Limpopo National Park, although as yet there is no general access. An exhibition of the treasures of Mapungubwe can be seen at the University of Pretoria (see p.644).

Practicalities

The town's reasonably well-run **caravan and camping park** is on the left when you enter the town from the south. Otherwise, accommodation is a choice between *Günter's Country House* (☎015 534 1019; ❸), 25 Irwin St (the R508 to Tshipise), a civilized, pleasant B&B with a pool; *Ilala Lodge* (☎015 534 3220; ❸), situated in the baobab reserve 8km northwest of town, with secluded stone chalets and a pool; or the *Limpopo River Lodge*, on the N1 in the centre of town (☎015 534 0204; ❷), a plain travellers' hotel with a certain creaking character.

For sit-down **meals**, the *Buffalo Ridge Spur* franchise is by the N1 off Sam Street; there's also a steakhouse at *Mudzwiri Lodge*, by the mine on the northern side of town. There are various takeaways, including a *Nando's*, at the elbow in the road close to the mine entrance.

Beitbridge

On the South African side of the Limpopo, there isn't much to **BEITBRIDGE** other than a tacky service station, a habitually long queue of trucks, some noisy minibus touts and the customs and immigration buildings (which include a duty-free shop). Two bridges cross the Limpopo (the river memorably described by Rudyard Kipling in *Just So Stories* as "great grey-green, greasy"), one for vehicles and one for pedestrians. The border is open 5.30am–10.30pm, but count yourself lucky if you get through without delay, hassle or hindrance.

Venda

To the east and north of Makhado lies the intriguing land of the **VhaVenda** people, a culturally and linguistically distinct African grouping known for their mystical legends, political independence and arts and crafts. Venda was demarcated as a homeland under the apartheid system in the Fifties, and became one of three notionally independent homelands in South Africa in the late Seventies. Of all the homelands, Venda was one of the least compromised, keeping both its geographic and cultural integrity, and largely being left to mind its own business during the dark years of apartheid. Its boundaries have regained their former fuzziness, within Limpopo, but the region has retained its strong, independent identity.

Like most of the other homelands of apartheid South Africa, Venda arrived in the new South Africa with a bloated and inefficient bureaucracy. For now, the best place to get **information** is from the tourist office in Makhado (see p.749) or one of the established accommodation options such as the *Venda Sun* in the Venda capital, **Thohoyandou** (see p.75). Various tour guides offer trips round the area: good ones include the ebullient Chris Olivier of *Face Afrika Tours* (☎ & ☎015 516 2076 or ☎082 969 3270, ✉facaf@mweb.co.za) and Dries Bester (☎015 583 0299 or 082 964 2745), a specialist in the local plant life. A good option for budget travellers keen to get a taste for the region is *Land of Legend Backpackers* (☎083 430 0098 or 015 516 1077; ❶), a fairly basic but friendly place deep in the forests of the eastern Soutpansberg off the R524, about halfway between Makhado and Thohoyandou; free pick-ups from Makhado can be organized. Accommodation is in two dorms and a guesthouse sleeping four, and while facilities are for self-catering, meals can be arranged, and tours to the crafts and historic sites of Venda are also available.

Aside from a sprinkling of accommodation in Thohoyandou, you'll find almost no tourist-oriented infrastructure whatsoever in Venda. However, it's

The people who today call themselves **VhaVenda** are descended from a number of ancient groupings who migrated from the Great Lakes area in east-central Africa in the eleventh and twelfth centuries. Their identity gelled when a group under Chief Dimbanyika arrived at Dzata in the northern Soutpansberg, where a walled fort was later built. From here, they consolidated their power in the region, fending off attack from a number of different African groupings (including the Voortrekkers, whom they drove from their settlement at Schoemansdal in 1867). Although the VhaVenda suffered a reverse at the hands of the Boers in 1898, the onset of the Anglo-Boer War prevented that victory being consolidated. The British had little interest in such a remote region, and were content to allow their administration to be run by the local chiefs, a system of self-government which, in one contrived form or another, lasted through the apartheid years until 1994.

The **culture** of the VhaVenda is a fascinating one, steeped in mysticism and vivid legend. One pervading theme is water – always an important concern in hot, seasonal climates, but a resource in which Venda is unusually abundant. Lakes, rivers, waterfalls and lush forests all form sacred sites, while legends abound of *zwidutwane*, or water sprites, and snakes who live at the bottom of dark pools or lakes. You can still even find older people who hold a taboo against fish, partly because the animals live in water and partly because they believe that if you eat fish the crocodiles will go hungry and turn on other available food sources, such as humans.

Many VhaVenda **ceremonies** and **rituals** still hold great importance, with the most famous being the python, or *domba*, dance performed by young female initiates. Naked but for jewellery and a small piece of cloth around their waist, the teenage girls form a long chain, swaying and shuffling as the "snake" winds around a fire to the sound of a beating drum – another sacred object in Venda – often for hours on end. Your chances of seeing it performed are limited – although dancing can always be arranged (at a price, and with advance notice). The genuine thing is most common during spring; Heritage Day around the end of August or the beginning of September is a good time for celebrations.

a lot less dangerous to travel independently through Venda than many other places in South Africa, and the journey can be wonderfully rough, raw and rewarding.

Thohoyandou

THOHOYANDOU isn't a place you'll want to spend time in if you can help it, an ugly, dirty sprawl of broken concrete and undisciplined building, glamorized by a casino. It's reached from Makhado by following the R524 70km east, along the southern edge of the Soutpansberg; if you're heading on to Kruger, you'll be thankful that the road mercifully bypasses the centre of town altogether.

The highlight of the capital, at least according to the tourist authorities, is the **Venda Sun hotel and casino** (℡015 962 4600 or 581 2101; ❺), a clone of the gambling dens tacitly encouraged in the homelands by the apartheid government and lapped up by South Africans denied such illicit entertainment in their own country. It is set in the heart of the downtown area, surrounded immediately by trees, but not far beyond the road and tatty shopping mall. To get to it, turn left off the R524 coming from Makhado at the Delta/Toyota service station, and right at the third set of traffic lights. The hotel has a pool, decent rooms and facilities, and an impressive record of supporting Venda arts and crafts, with useful maps and tours available. The only other reasonable place to stay in town is *Bougainvillea Lodge* (☏015 962 4064; ❹), just up the hill from the *Venda Sun*, a simple motel-like travellers' stop.

There isn't a wide choice of **places to eat** in Thohoyandou. In the shopping centre next to the *Venda Sun* there are a number of take-away food shops, including a *Nando's* and *KFC*, and a pricier sit-down restaurant in the *Venda Sun* itself. **Minibuses** for Makhado use the large, chaotic taxi rank in front of the shopping centre.

The R523 west from Thohoyandou

Along the northern side of the Soutpansberg, through a valley traced by the R523 road between the N1 and Thohoyandou, is the most appealing core of VhaVenda history and legend. This is where you'll find the lush forests, waterfalls and mountains which give Venda its mystical atmosphere.

Driving from Thohoyando, climb out of town to the north and then west, leaving the suburbs to get among the elevated green scenery which lies enticingly ahead. You'll pass the **Vondo Dam**, created in the early Nineties and surrounded by pine forests, then climb over the **Thate Vondo Pass**. Over the summit, a small shack marks the entrance to a network of forest roads that take you into the area containing the most important lake in Venda, **Lake Fundudzi**, and the **Sacred Forest**, an area of dense indigenous forest which contains the burial ground of Venda chiefs. You can look at both from afar, but to get any closer is a matter of deep sensitivity: you have to gain permission which, without local leads to the right people, is not easy to do. There isn't a readily available map showing you the network of roads around the forest, and some of the roads require 4WD; if you want to see the area, it's best to join a **tour** (see p.753) or make sure you've gathered information and advice beforehand.

Another option well worth considering is the **Mabudashango Hiking Trail**, a four-day, 55-kilometre walk that takes you as close as any road to the main highlights of the area, including Lake Fundudzi and the Sacred Forest. The trail offers spectacular views and lush vegetation, and navigation isn't always easy, but at each of the camps along the way you'll find a shelter with water and toilet facilities; for details, contact the tourist office in Makhado (see p.749).

Beyond the crest of the Thate Vondo Pass, the R523 follows the **Nzhelele River** down a valley of scattered but mostly unbroken settlement. About half-way along is *Aventura Mphephu* (☏011 207 3600, ⓦ www.aventura.co.za; ❸), a holiday resort with around twenty chalets based around a hot spring on the flanks of the Soutpansberg. Not far west of Mphephu, on the northern side of the road, are the **Dzata ruins**, the remains of the royal kraal of the kings of VhaVenda, dating from 1400. If you find the gate locked, you'll probably have to toot your horn to rouse the gateman, and even then you may find the place deserted.

Routes to the northern Kruger National Park

The R525 runs across the Musina plains towards **Pafuri Gate**, the most northerly of the Kruger entrances, past which is a border post to Mozambique, although there is little beyond unless you're well equipped for adventure. If you need a **place to stay** over on your way to Kruger, there's an Aventura resort at **Tshipise** (☏011 207 3600, ⓦ www.aventura.co.za; ❺). An alternative is *Popallin Ranch* (☏01553 40644, ⓔ ecotours@mweb.co.za), an eighty-square-kilometre farm with buffalo, giraffe and baobab trees right on the Limpopo

The **Venda** and **Gazankulu** regions have established a strong reputation in **arts and crafts**. The best known of these are clay pots distinctively marked with angular designs in graphite silver and ochre. Also growing in status are woodcarvings, ranging from abstract to practical though, while the best of these can be imaginative and bold, many are unfinished and overpriced. You'll also come across tapestries, fabrics, basketwork and painting. Finding your way to these craft villages can be quite an adventure, as they are widely scattered and the roads are poor.

Gazankulu

The main route in the former homeland of Gazankulu is the R578 between **Elim** and **Giyani**. Travelling southeast from Elim crossroads, look out for a track leading up to the **Rivoni** workshop (opposite the turn to Waterval), where blind and other handicapped people make sisal mats, furniture, candles and coffins – a line that evidently does a roaring trade. There isn't a great deal to see, but the place is industrious and there is a small shop. Back on the R578, turn left at the brow of the next hill, then up a right-hand fork to reach **Tsonga Textiles**, where screen-printed fabrics are produced and turned into tablecloths, bedspreads and clothes.

The R578 then goes down a hill, at the bottom of which is a turning to **Mbhokota** village. Going along this, turn left at the T-junction and left again along a narrow track just past a small homestead with a busy garden, and you'll find a rundown collection of buildings where **Twananani** textiles are created – attractive, funky, hand-painted and batik garments with traditional African designs, made by around twenty people.

At the next junction off the R578, to Riverplaats, then along a right-hand fork, is the house and small workshop of Shangaan woodcarver **Jackson Thugwane**. He's an almost mystical figure, with pieces exhibited in major galleries around the country and in Europe. If he isn't there you won't find much to see; if he is, be prepared for a few absorbing hours of philosophy, theology, art and the state of the modern world. There are a number of other, younger carvers nearby trying to emulate Jackson's success. If you take the left-hand fork after the Riverplaats sign, you will eventually come to a village called **Mashamba** where villagers make clay pots in the traditional way. This is, however, a trek deep into the rural areas of Gazankulu and road conditions are fairly unreliable.

Venda

In **Venda**, the craft villages are even more scattered and hard to find. There are a number of sites situated to the south of Thohoyandou, including the workshop of **Noria Mabasa**, whose clay and wood sculptures have become widely recognized around South Africa. Another place to look out for is **Mutale**, to the north of Thohoyandou, where traditional decorative drums are made. You can pick up a hand-drawn **arts and crafts map** of Venda at the *Venda Sun* or the tourist office at Makhado; another option is to contact **Annette and Martin Kennealy** (℡083 326 2922), two artists who are very knowledgeable about art (rather than crafts) in the area and can advise on what to look out for and where to find it.

River. You can camp here, or stay at the comfortable *De Wet's Camp* (❹), with game drives available as an extra. Even more rustic and escapist is *Pafuri Rivercamp* (℡082 785 0305, ⊛www.pafuri.co.za; ❸), on the Mutale River just before you reach the Pafuri Gate. This incorporates a series of treetop tents and an open self-catering bush camp (meals can be arranged in advance, but there's no electricity), from where you can set off in pursuit of the profuse local plants and wildlife, or relax by the river or pool.

Travel details

Trains

One daily service as follows:
Musina to: Bela-Bela (11hr 30min); Johannesburg (15hr); Makhado (3hr); Modimolle (11hr); Moko-pane (9hr); Polokwane (7hr); Pretoria (13hr 30min).

Buses

Beitbridge to: Johannesburg (2 daily; 8–10hr).
Polokwane to: Johannesburg (3 daily; 4hr); Tzaneen (daily; 1hr 45min).

Tzaneen to: Johannesburg (6 weekly; 6hr 15min); Polokwane (daily; 1hr 45min).

Domestic flights

Polokwane to: Johannesburg (Mon–Fri 4 daily, Sat & Sun 1–3 daily; 50min).

11

Lesotho

CHAPTER 11

Highlights

* **Pony trekking** The ideal way to see Lesotho, following paths from village to village through spectacular mountain scenery. See p.770

* **Thaba Bosiu** The hill-top fortress from which Lesotho's greatest king, Moshoeshoe I, defended his kingdom against attackers. See p.778

* **Semonkong Falls** A dramatic 200-metre water-fall plunging into a vast gorge deep in the remote highland region. See p.782

* **San rock art** Lesotho's original inhabitants bequeathed the country a rich legacy of paintings and engravings, most eas-ily seen at Liphofung Cave. See p.794

* **"Roof of Africa" road** A narrow, winding road from Butha-Buthe to Sani Pass through dramatic mountain passes and valleys. See p.797

* **Sehlabathebe National Park** A lonely mountain reserve with superb hiking. See p.806

△ Riding in Lesotho

Lesotho

ntirely surrounded by South Africa and sometimes mistaken for one of apartheid's ill-conceived semi-states, the aptly named "mountain kingdom" of **Lesotho** (pronounced *Lee-su-tu*) is in fact proudly independent and very different in character from its dominant neighbour. Whereas the Rainbow Nation next door is, in many respects, distinctly European, laid-back Lesotho prides itself on its staunchly African heritage. Few people in this fabulously beautiful and rugged land speak English or Afrikaans, though language isn't a barrier when the inhabitants – the **Basotho** – count among the most hospitable people in southern Africa. Another refreshing physical (and psychological) contrast is the almost total absence of fences, which means you can hike into the upland regions at will.

Travelling almost anywhere in Lesotho is an adventure: there are no motorways or slick city liner buses here (or, indeed, too many timetables), though the tarred **road network** is good, covered by rickety minibuses held together in some cases by little more than prayers. For the Basotho, **ponies** are the preferred method of transport, particularly in the highlands. You can do the same from pony-trekking lodges all over the country – a day trek or, better, a longer ride incorporating a night in a remote Basotho village, is *the* way to experience the country.

Lesotho is one of only a few countries to lie entirely above an altitude of 1000m, earning its nickname of "The Kingdom in the Sky". Even the sandstone **Lesotho lowlands** – which form a crescent along the country's western rim – would be highlands anywhere else. It's here, amongst weirdly eroded peaks and isolated hills, that you'll find all the nation's major towns, including the busily practical capital of **Maseru**, with its very African mix of new glass buildings and dusty streets, and a host of smaller, mostly nondescript settlements which began life as tax-collection centres for the British administration. Lowland attractions include the weavers of **Teya-Teyaneng**, extraordinary caves at **Mateka**, rock paintings at **Liphofung**, and the mountain fortress at **Thaba Bosiu**, established by Lesotho's founder, King Moshoeshoe I.

At around 1400m above sea level sandstone gives way to basalt, the dark grey rock – thrown up by volcanic eruptions several million years ago – which forms the bulk of the ruggedly beautiful **Lesotho highlands**, an extended mountainous area characterized by plunging valleys, remote villages, improbable roads and inspiring vistas. Once up the steep, twisting roads which lead into the mountains you can visit the engineering masterpieces of the **Katse** and **Mohale dams**, **ski** in the Maloti Mountains, fish from rivers everywhere and, above all, wander through the countryside, dividing your time between remote villages of simple stone-and-thatch huts and the peaceful solitude of

Border Post Opening Times

BORDER POST	OPENING TIMES
CALEDONSPOORT	6am–10pm
FICKSBURG BRIDGE	24 hours
MASERU BRIDGE	24 hours
VAN ROOYEN'S GATE	6am–10pm
MAKHALEEN BRIDGE	8am–4pm
NKONKOANA GATE	8am–4pm
TELE BRIDGE	6am–10pm
QACHA'S NEK GATE	7am–8pm
SANI PASS	8am–4pm

the mountains. Three protected areas in particular are worth the effort of getting to: **Ts'ehlanyane National Park** and **Bokong Nature Reserve**, both in the Front Range of the Maloti Mountains and linked by a 39km hiking and horse-riding trail, and the exceedingly remote **Sehlabathebe National Park** in the east of the country, offering gloriously rugged hiking terrain.

Some history

Lesotho exists because of the determined efforts of one man, **Moshoeshoe I** (1786–1870), to secure land for his people in the face of intense social upheaval and the insatiable land-hunger of others. Before the arrival of Moshoeshoe's ancestors, around 900 AD, the San inhabited Lesotho's hills and mountains unchallenged. Today the San are gone, exterminated in 1873 by the last of many British campaigns against them. However, they left their mark in the country's rock paintings and elements of their tongue in the Sesotho language (including impossible buzzes and clicks), while traces of their vaguely oriental features and paler skin can still be discerned in some Basotho faces.

The Basotho first settled the fertile plains that today form the Lesotho low-lands and South Africa's Free State, before going on to colonize the mountains. They farmed these plains relatively peacefully for centuries, but by Moshoe-shoe's time, tribes from elsewhere had forced thousands of Basotho off their land. Moshoeshoe proved his own marauding skills in 1809, when he rustled so many cattle from rival Chief Ramonaheng that he boasted, "I am the sharp shearer, the shaver . . . The blade that shaved off Ramonaheng's beard." After this feat he adopted the onomatopoeic name of Moshoeshoe, pronounced

---

Some simple Sesotho

The Basotho language is **Sesotho**. It can be tricky to speak, as spellings rarely correspond with pronunciation, a legacy of the bizarre nineteenth-century transcription by French missionaries, in which locals take a perverse pride.

Pronunciation

e within a word is like the ee of lee
e at the end of a word is either silent or like the i of it
ee as in the ai or hair
The h in th and ph is silent
kh is like the ch in loch
lu is pronounced du
o halfway in length between an o and oo (as in the French word *ou*), except in "ong" when it's like the o in dock
nt has a buzzy click, best tackled after a few beers
qu, qa and x are similarly difficult raspy clicks

Basics

Yes	*E* (as in see)
No	*Ee* (as in the ai of hair)
Thank you	*Kea leboha*
It's nice/tasty	*E ntle*
Today	*Kajeno*
Tomorrow	*Hosane*
Yesterday	*Moobane*
Where is . . . ?	*E kae . . . ?*
Where can we stay?	*Nka lula hokae?*
Where are you going?	*O ea kae?*
How much?	*Ke bokai?*

Greetings and responses

Hello (informal)	*Khotso* (literally "peace")
Hello (to one)	*Dumela*
Hello (to many)	*Dumelang*
How are you?	*U pela jooang*
I'm fine	*Kee pela hantle* (with a buzzed and clicked *nt*)
Goodbye (said by person leaving)	*Sala hantle* or *Ke phela monate*
Goodbye (said by people remaining)	*Tsamaea hantle*

"Moshwehshweh", meaning the shearer (his real name was Leqopo). Moshoeshoe became chief in 1820 and established himself on top of a mountain near Butha-Buthe, where he became patron to many refugees in search of safety. However, after a particularly vicious attack on Butha-Buthe in 1824, Moshoeshoe decided it was no longer safe and trekked south with his followers in search of a better mountain. He found one at Thaba Bosiu, which, though subsequently attacked repeatedly, was never taken. Moshoeshoe meanwhile expanded his kingdom by securing other clan chiefs as clients, at the same time earning an almost mythical reputation for wisdom and generosity among ordinary Basotho that survives to this day.

Moshoeshoe had heard from travellers that **missionaries** brought peace, and so welcomed the arrival in 1833 of three from the Paris Evangelical Missionary Society, establishing them in Morija and taking an active interest in their work, though he never converted. The Paris missionaries established what is now the Lesotho Evangelical Church, second in size only to the Catholics, whose missionaries founded Roma in the 1860s (see p.780).

The kingdom was encroached upon by land-hungry Europeans from the 1840s onwards, and the **Orange Free State** government invaded in 1858, their soldiers destroying Morija and then launching a failed attack on Thaba Bosiu. They nonetheless captured plenty of farmland, whose acquisition was sanctioned by a British treaty in 1860. In 1865, the Orange Free State government cited Basotho cattle theft as the pretext for a new conflict, though few could deny Moshoeshoe's bitter assertion that "my great sin is that I possess a good and fertile country". The ensuing **Seqiti War** resulted in the destruction of Basotho crops, forcing Moshoeshoe into a humiliating treaty in 1866 which signed over most of his remaining good land. The war resumed in 1867, and was halted only by the British taking over what was left of the kingdom as the protectorate of **Basotholand** in 1868. The Treaty of Aliwal North in 1869 restored Moshoeshoe's land east of the Caledon but left the rest with the Free State, where it has remained to this day – a loss that still stings.

Moshoeshoe died in 1870 and the British handed Basotholand to the Cape administration a year later, which began taxing its new subjects, establishing a series of hut tax-collection points which have since grown into Lesotho's modest collection of small towns. Discontent turned to open rebellion in 1879, when the Cape government decided to confiscate all Basotho firearms. The result was the **Gun War**, two years of raids and skirmishes that cost the Cape government dearly and ultimately led to its downfall. One of few colonial-era conflicts in which the locals came out on top, the prize for the victorious Basotho was the resumption of direct rule from Britain in 1884.

Along with Bechuanaland and Swaziland, Basotholand rejected incorporation into the union of South Africa in 1910, with **King Letsie II** instead helping found the South African Native National Congress (later the ANC) in 1912. During the following years, the monarchy and chiefs' position declined, partly because British reforms forced their uneasy conversion into a junior arm of the colonial civil service, but also because social changes at work in the region, like migration, urbanization and rising education levels, proved too much for them to adapt to. In 1960, when **Moshoeshoe II** was crowned king, independence politics were in full swing, spearheaded by Pan-Africanist Ntsa Mokhele's Basotho Congress Party (BCP), and rivalled by the more conservative Basotho National Party (BNP). After narrowly winning the 1965 elections, the BNP led newly named Lesotho into **independence** on October 4, 1966. However, after losing the 1970 election, prime minister Leabua Jonathan annulled the result, declared a

state of emergency, and carried on ruling until he was toppled in 1986 by a **military coup** led by Major General Metsing Lekhanya. Lekhanya ordered the **expulsion of the ANC** from Lesotho and signed an agreement that year with apartheid South Africa for the **Lesotho Highlands Water Project** (see box on p.790) – Africa's biggest engineering project to date, aiming to divert much of Lesotho's ample water resources to the thirsty South African province of Gauteng.

In 1990, Lekhanya sent Moshoeshoe II into exile and installed Moshoeshoe's son on the throne as **Letsie III**, but a year later Lekhanya was himself ousted by Major General Phisona, who then gave way to a **democratically elected government** led by Mokhele's BCP in 1993. There was no end to the turmoil, however, with Letsie dissolving the BCP government in August 1994 for alleged incompetence, although regional pressure soon forced the restoration of the government and constitution. Letsie stood down in favour of his father in 1995, but Moshoeshoe II died in a car crash the next year, and Letsie regained the throne.

The **1998 elections** were won in a landslide by Mokhele, this time at the head of the breakaway Lesotho Congress for Democracy (LCD), but opposition parties cried foul amid widespread allegations of **vote-rigging**. In July and August, large crowds gathered outside the Royal Palace in Maseru demanding the results be overturned – these protests subsequently developed into a **mutiny** by Lesotho Defence Force soldiers. In September, under the flag of a Southern African Development Community peacekeeping force, **South African troops** crossed the border, and fierce fighting took place around military bases and at the strategically vital Katse Dam. Meanwhile, thousands of demonstrators protested at what they regarded as South Africa's heavy-handed intervention, and a large number of shops and offices across the country were looted and burned.

To everyone's relief, the **2002 elections** passed off without incident, with the LCD winning most of the seats, and the BNP leading the opposition – the peaceful nature of the vote was a hopeful sign of a more constructive political climate. The jewel in the government's crown is its internationally acclaimed **fight against corruption**, which has resulted in guilty verdicts against three multinational corporations, among others. Even the World Bank – whose role in the corruption scandal is now subject to a US Senate investigation – has been forced, reluctantly, to debar companies found guilty of corruption in the project. That said, a number of gargantuan challenges remain unanswered: the scourge of **HIV/AIDS** has never been more devastating, now affecting half of all women between the ages of 15 and 24, and a quarter of men of the same age. **Poverty**, too, remains entrenched, exacerbated by the return of over 40,000 retrenched Lesotho labourers from South Africa's gold fields. Nevertheless, the last few years have seen a boom in Lesotho's textile, tourism and agricultural sectors, and the economy is, gradually, diversifying. And with royalties from the Lesotho Highlands Water Project – currently accounting for one-quarter of Lesotho's annual export earnings – guaranteed until 2045, and hopefully now secured against misuse, this is probably the most hopeful period in Lesotho's history since its independence.

When to go

Lesotho's **winter** runs from May to July, when it often snows in the highlands and sometimes in the lowlands too – great for skiing and very picturesque, but not so good for travelling around remote areas. Although the days are usually clear and warm, it gets extremely cold at night and ice can make driving hazardous in the highlands, while snowfall blocks even tarred highways for days at a time. **Spring** (Aug–Oct), when the snow melts, is a beautiful time, with new plants sprouting up everywhere. November to January is **summer**, when Lesotho gets most of its rain, often torrential, turning dirt roads into mudslides. Still, when it isn't raining the weather is usually sunny and the landscape is coloured in vivid shades of green. **Autumn** (Feb–April) is one of the best times to visit, as it doesn't usually rain too much and temperatures are moderate. Whatever the time of year, Lesotho can be very cold at night, particularly in the highlands, and prone to rapid weather changes, for which it's always wise to be prepared.

Getting to Lesotho

Lesotho is most comfortably reached by **plane** from Johannesburg (there are no flights from anywhere else). South African Airlink operates three or four flights a day to Moshoeshoe I International Airport, from where taxis and shuttle buses connect with Maseru, 18km to the northwest.

None of the big South African bus companies run to Lesotho, but there are frequent (if invariably cramped) **minibus taxis** throughout the day from Johannesburg, Bloemfontein and Durban, and less frequently from a host of smaller towns in the Free State and North West Province to various border crossings in Lesotho's western lowlands – particularly Maseru Bridge (2km from the capital), Ficksburg Bridge (next to Maputsoe) and Caledonspoort, close to Butha-Buthe, both to the north. All these places have plentiful onward transport connections within Lesotho. Much more awkward to reach, but infinitely more engaging an introduction to the country, is to enter via the Drakensberg, most spectacularly along the **Sani Pass**, into the country's remote northeastern corner; see p.797 for details.

Drivers have a choice of fourteen border crossings. Distances to Maseru are 1100km from Cape Town, 750km from Durban, and 650km from Johannesburg. The most spectacular approach, but often requiring 4WD (especially outside summer), is through the Drakensberg via **Sani Pass**. Easier to reach, and not requiring 4WD, are the western lowlands crossings. The busiest are **Maseru Bridge**, 140km along the N8 from Bloemfontein, Ficksburg Bridge next to Maputsoe, and Caledonspoort close to Butha-Buthe, though none of these are particularly attractive introductions to the country. For **border opening times**, see the map on p.762. If you've rented a car in South Africa, check the **insurance** covers you for Lesotho, especially in winter. Some companies such as Hertz are reluctant to do this because of the condition of many of the roads. Avis is better, levying a R350 "overborder" fee. Avis, Budget and Imperial Fleet have offices in Maseru (see "Listings" on p.777).

The most adventurous way in is on foot through the southern section of South Africa's Ukhahlamba Drakensberg Park from Bushman's Nek to Lesotho's **Sehlabathebe National Park** (p.806), though you'll have to be self-sufficient until you get to Sehlabathebe village, from where there's a daily bus towards civilization. It's best to bring a tent in case the park's accommodation is full.

Getting around

Lesotho has a good tarred **road network**, though you can't avoid dirt (and often boulder-strewn) roads when heading to more out-of-the-way places.

Wherever you travel, and especially when you make for the highlands, twisting roads, fast minibus taxis and frequent encounters with road-side pedestrians and livestock make **driving** tiring work. The main route through the **northern** part of the country is the continuous tarred road leading northeast from Maseru to Butha-Buthe and then southeast to Mokhotlong. While the onward section to Sani and into South Africa can be negotiated by an experienced driver in a saloon car in good weather, you should really only consider doing it in 4WD. Striking off the northern route, the **Katse dam road** from Hlotse is tarred and of very high quality, though it involves some punishing gradients. On the **central route**, the tar extends for a way beyond Mohale Dam around Likalaneng, then reverts to dirt and gravel as far as Thaba-Tseka. The high-altitude route from here to Katse is 4WD only, although minibus taxis will tackle it. The **southern** route from Maseru is tarred as far as Mphaki, but is passable in an ordinary saloon up to Qacha's Nek. The road beyond Qacha's Nek to Sehlabathebe National Park is impassable without 4WD, though again minibus taxis and buses somehow manage it.

Car and 4WD rental is offered by Avis, Budget and Imperial Fleet in Maseru (see "Listings" on p.777); Imperial Fleet also has agents at Leribe, Mohale's Hoek, Mokhotlong, Qacha's Nek and Thaba-Tseka – an advantage if you run into trouble. Depending on where you want to go, 4WD may be essential. **Fuel** costs roughly the same as in South Africa; unleaded is readily available in Maseru, but can be scarce elsewhere (indeed, normal fuel pumps can also run dry), so fill up wherever you can. The **speed limit** is 80kph, and 50kph in urban areas. **Hitching** is much safer than in South Africa and is a good way to get around. Some drivers expect payment, so negotiate this before you've travelled too far.

Public transport is chaotic and unregulated, but does at least goes everywhere in the country. **Minibus taxis** – ranging in size from twelve-seater Land Rovers to thirty-seater Coasters not much smaller than standard buses – are the main form of transport, and run on major routes, at least until early afternoon. Whatever their size, such vehicles are always packed far beyond their legal capacity, making for remarkably uncomfortable, if memorable, experiences. If you're travelling with bulky luggage, it's best to start at a taxi rank rather then join the vehicle along the way, which gives you and the driver time to stash things away. While a handful of minibuses cover long distances, most go only as far the next major town, so if you're planning to go further, leave early in the morning to give yourself plenty of time to change along the way. **Buses** are slower but safer than minibus taxis, and both are very inexpensive. The only **timetables** are for buses operated by Lesotho Freight and Bus Services (see "Listings" on p.807); otherwise, the rule of thumb is to check the day before, and get to the bus or taxi rank early if you have a long way to go, as long-distance buses tend to leave around 5am in summer and 6.30–7am in winter.

For **internal flights** you can charter planes out of Maseru Airport (not Moshoeshoe I; it's also known as "the old airport", or just "the airstrip" or "Maseru airstrip"), northeast of town, through the Mission Aviation Fellowship (p.777), which charges around M2000 per hour for planes which can carry four to five people; single seats are sometimes available if the planes are flying anyway. These days, though, most well-heeled visitors use **helicopters** rented out by the Lesotho Defence Force (Private Bag A 166 Maseru ☎2232 5425); these can work out marginally cheaper than the planes.

Accommodation

Accommodation **standards** are generally lower than in South Africa, and even mid-range places might have holes in bed linen, leaky plumbing, missing toilet seats or light bulbs, or broken TVs. Places fall broadly into three categories: cheap and basic dorms in rural or religious training centres; bland, conventional urban hotels that get the bulk of their business from conferences and civil servants; and relaxed, well-run **tourist-oriented lodges**. The last, such as the *Malealea Lodge* (p.800), *Semonkong Lodge* (p.782), *Molumong Guest House* (p.796) and *New Oxbow Lodge* (p.795), offer a range of accommodation from backpacker dorms to well-appointed rondavels; most also offer pony trekking and hiking (see box on pp.770–771).

Costs are slightly higher than in rural South Africa, with the cheapest doubles averaging M200, singles M150 and dorms under M100. Exceptions are the rural training centres, the Anglican training centre in Maseru, and the youth hostel at Butha-Buthe, where you'll pay no more than M50 for a bunk.

Independent **camping** is possible all over rural Lesotho, while many lodges allow camping in their grounds. If you're camping rough, ask permission first, preferably from the village chief (*Morena oa motse*), who may ask you to pay a token fee of M10–20 per person. It's normally fine just to pitch your tent if there's no one around.

Books and maps

A useful supplement to the coverage in this chapter is the *Backpackers Guide to Lesotho* booklet, self-published every few years by Russell Suchet, who runs *Sani Lodge* over the border in KwaZulu-Natal (p.524); you can also buy copies at the Morija Museum and at some South African backpackers lodges. Some of these also stock a very good 1:250,000 **topographical map** of Lesotho which marks most trails; it's also available from the Department of Lands, Surveys and Physical Planning on Lerotholi Road, near the corner of Constitution Road, in Maseru (℡2232 2376; M60). This is also the only place where you can buy the really detailed 1:50,000 maps (M35), essential for serious hiking. For drivers, the 1:795,000 road map published by the Automobile Association of South Africa and sold at Maseru's tourist office is perfectly adequate, and contains detailed route descriptions on the back.

Costs, money and banks

Overall costs are marginally lower than in South Africa, though accommodation can be more expensive. **Credit cards** are of limited use; while hotels and lodges geared to foreign visitors accept them, as do a few Maseru restaurants and the craft shops of Teya-Teyaneng, you'll need cash for everything else.

Lesotho's currency is the **loti**, plural **maluti** (M), divided into 100 **lisenti**; the loti is tied to the South African rand (R1=M1). You can also use rand throughout Lesotho, but you cannot use or exchange maluti anywhere outside Lesotho, so make sure you use them up or exchange them before leaving. In daily life, people usually speak in terms of rand.

Banks are found in all Lesotho's towns, and while you can (theoretically, at least) **change money** at any of them if you have enough patience, Maseru is the only place where it's relatively quick and painless. Banking hours are Monday to Friday 8.30am to 3.30pm, except Wednesday (8.30am–1pm), and Saturday (8.30–11am); Saturdays are busy and best avoided. While a few ATMs exist, not all accept foreign cash cards. The larger hotels in Maseru and the lowland towns change money, but at ludicrously bad rates, making them very much a last resort.

11

LESOTHO | Getting around

Phone numbers

Lesotho's **country code** is ☎266, unless you're calling from South Africa, in which case it's ☎09266. There are no **area codes** (numbers given in the guide with area codes are in South Africa). To **phone abroad from Lesotho**, dial ☎00, followed by the country and area codes and subscriber number; for South Africa, dial ☎0027, then the area code omitting the initial "0", and the phone number. To **call collect**, dial the international operator on ☎109.

Public holidays

January 1 New Year's Day
March 11 Moshoeshoe Day
April 4 Heroes Day
Good Friday
Easter Monday
May 1 Workers' Day

July 17 King's Birthday
Ascension Day (Thursday)
October 4 Independence Day
December 25 Christmas Day
December 26 Boxing Day

Red tape and embassies

Visas are not required for citizens of the EU, the Commonwealth (excepting India, Ghana, Nigeria and Pakistan) and the US. If you've travelled through a yellow fever zone, you'll need an International Certificate of Vaccination against yellow fever. The standard entry permit is for 14 or 28 days; should you need an extension, visit the Department of Immigration and Passport Services on Kingsway in Maseru (☎2232 3771, ☎2231 0538). For details of Lesotho's embassies, see "Listings" on p.777.

Security

Overall, Lesotho is a safe country for travellers. **Muggings and opportunistic theft** are however on the rise in Maseru and some lowland border towns, particularly Maputsoe and Butha-Buthe; be careful wandering around back streets weighed down with luggage, and avoid walking around at night unless accompanied by a local. In the highlands, however, hikers and campers have little more to worry about than snarling dogs and persistent demands for sweets from children. As ever, it's unwise to flaunt your wealth too visibly, and don't leave valuables like cameras lying around unattended.

Tour operators

Lesotho's tourist infrastructure remains sketchy in some areas, and arranging activities such as pony-trekking and visits to the natural parks can be time-consuming, especially without your own transport. If you're short on time, consider an **organized tour**. *Malealea Lodge* (p.800) in the southwest offers some innovative pony-trekking and 4WD combinations, and is also the best source of information on 4WD trails. *Hotel Mount Maluti* (p.803), close to the beautiful and little-visited Mokhele mountain range, offers similar tours. Coming from South Africa, German-run *Thaba Tours* is the main operator (☎072/114 1198, ⓦwww.thabatours.de), specializing in overland trips between Durban and Maseru via the Sani Pass, including pony-trekking and hiking (6 days/5 nights full board R5500–6500).

Water

Tap water is generally safe to drink, though people with sensitive stomachs should stick to bottled. While Lesotho's rivers and streams are bilharzia-free, drinking from them is inadvisable unless you purify the water first.

Hospitable and almost entirely fenceless, Lesotho is a **hiker's paradise**. It's possible to set off into the hills and walk for as long as you like, with no prospect of an angry farmer yelling at you to get off his land – quite a change from South Africa. In the highlands a network of tracks and paths connect all the villages, and anyone you meet on the way will be delighted to point you in the right direction. In more remote areas, locals get around by pony, and **pony-trekking** – which can be arranged at most tourist-oriented lodges and two of the three national parks – is an undoubted highlight of any trip to the country.

Hiking

Always **prepare adequately** before setting out, and bring supplies for at least a day more than you think the hike will take. Be warned that in the highest reaches of the highlands there are very few villages and you can walk for days without seeing anyone. Lovely as this is, it's also risky, so make sure someone knows where you've gone, and don't hike in remote areas on your own. Lesotho's weather is notoriously fickle, and you should bring a sunhat and sunblock, as well as warm clothing and waterproofs, whatever the season.

Other essentials include enough cash (you can't count on rural banks changing money), a torch, plenty of food (there aren't many stores in remote rural areas, and those that do exist are usually poorly stocked), a water container, water-purifying tablets, an all-weather cooker with fuel (don't count on finding firewood), a genuinely waterproof tent, a sleeping mat and a very warm sleeping bag. A compass and map (see p.768) are also invaluable.

Pony-trekking

Ponies were introduced to Lesotho from the Cape in the nineteenth century, with one of the first given as a present to King Moshoeshoe I by chief Moorosi in 1829. Moshoeshoe learnt to ride that year, and rapidly acquired further steeds, which he distributed to his family and followers. By the time of Moshoeshoe's death in 1870, ponies were widespread throughout the kingdom and the Basotho had become expert riders.

Lesotho's ponies are famously hardy, capable of slogging away for hours and negotiating slippery rock passes. The Basotho rarely groom their mounts, so they usually look pretty dishevelled, but that doesn't affect their performance in the hills, where for many locals they are the only form of long-distance transport.

A number of lodges and other places offer **pony-trekking** (no previous equestrian experience needed) though only a few are well organized, the best being the *Malealea Lodge* and *Semonkong Lodge*. One way to decide which place to go for

Maseru and the central districts

The most convenient entry point from South Africa, and the country's most sophisticated urban centre by far, **Maseru** is a handy first stop for exploring Lesotho – the place to fill up on supplies, change money and organize onward transport. Apart from a few elegant colonial sandstone buildings, however, there's not a great deal to see – most of the buildings burnt down in the 1998 is to first choose what kind of countryside you want to trek in. Semonkong, Mokhotlong, Bokong, Ts'ehlanyane and the area around the Basotho Pony Trekking Centre are all high up; the others are lower down, with less variable weather conditions, though the terrain is harder on the ponies.

Costs vary according to group size, but tend to average M150–200 a day if you're on your own, or M120–150 per person in a couple; for overnights, count on and extra M100–200 per person, which can include a pack horse as well as accommodation. A full-day's ride typically involves six or seven hours (10–15km) in the saddle, so overnight trips can be quite strenuous. Children **under 12** are not usually allowed on overnighters.

Wherever you go, make sure you bring a wide-brimmed sunhat, sun protection cream, waterproof gear, swimwear in summer, and a water bottle (and, if you're staying overnight, a sleeping bag and mat, torch and food, though cooking utensils and fuel should be provided). A luxury you'll definitely appreciate is some kind of balm to ease your aching limbs and buttocks, which will certainly be sore after a day's trekking, even if you're used to riding.

Basotho Pony Trekking Centre (p.783) In the central highlands along the road to Mohale Dam.

Bokong Nature Reserve (p.791) In the Front Range of the Maloti Mountains along the road to Katse Dam, and connected to Ts'ehlanyane National Park via a 39km hiking and riding trail.

Liphofung Cave A rock art site in the north where you can hire ponies for a day.

Malealea Lodge (p.800) The longest established place, offering rides into the Thaba Putsoa Range, but often packed with tourists.

Molumong Guest House (p.796) Remotest of the lot, near Mokhotlong in the northeast.

Hotel Mount Maluti (p.503) At Mohale's Hoek in the south, with treks through the Mokhele Range.

Semonkong Lodge (p.782) In the central highlands close to Semonkong Falls. Of similarly high quality to *Malealea*, but more remote and so less busy. You can ride between the two places.

Trading Post Guest House (p.781) Closest to Maseru in Roma, arranging treks through Phasemane Pony Treks and Adventures.

Ts'ehlanyane National Park (p.790) In the stunning Front Range of the Maloti Mountains, with gloriously rugged riding terrain.

riots have been replaced by ambitious new concrete edifices which threaten to sterilize what is still a fairly characterful town. Despite the city's modernization, the pervading atmosphere remains friendly, and travellers will probably feel more comfortable here than in most South African cities. While most visitors pass through fairly quickly, if you're in town for a few days there are plenty of excursions into the countryside surrounding the city, including to Lesotho's most famous mountain, **Thaba Bosiu**, the so-called "Mountain of the Night" where the founder of the nation, Moshoeshoe I, ruled for almost fifty years.

Further afield, **Roma** – 30km southeast of Maseru along the fast A3 – is the country's academic centre, surrounded by beautiful sandstone hills and with a historic Catholic mission. South of Roma, a road ascends into the **central highlands** and the Thaba Putsoa Range along a series of mountain passes – one of the most striking drives in the country. At the end of the road, the village of **Semonkong** has a superb lodge and pony trekking centre that puts several waterfalls and peaks within reach. Continuing along the A3 east of Roma, the highway heads up past the Basotho Pony Trekking Centre into Lesotho's **Central Range**, the tarmac ending shortly after the massive Mohale Dam. Onward travel requires high-clearance 2WD or 4WD. Though the final destination of **Thaba–Tseka** is unspectacular, the journey more than compensates, and from Thaba-Tseka it's possible to continue along a reasonably good dirt road to Katse and its massive new dam (see p.792).

Maseru

Sprawling **MASERU**, the nation's capital and only big town, spills east from the Caledon River, which marks the border with South Africa. Maseru was established by the British in 1869 as the administrative centre for newly annexed Basotholand, but Britain put as little effort into developing Maseru as it did the rest of the country, no doubt expecting it to become just a minor South African town when Basotholand was incorporated into South Africa.

Surrounded by sprawling shantytown suburbs, the city has grown swiftly over recent years, poverty in Lesotho's rural areas having driven people to the capital in search of a better life. Few have found it yet, and the city has a high unemployment rate. Yet Maseru's compact centre has all the marks of an upwardly mobile African city, with slick fashions and mobile phones much in evidence – even if they're sometimes spotted alongside blanket-wearing villagers and the occasional horse-drawn cart. Maseru's older buildings, as well as some stylish new ones, are built from well-crafted local **sandstone** – from which the city gets its name – though a number of ugly concrete box buildings diminish the effect and, unfortunately, dominate the skyline.

Most of the city's daytime action happens on or around **Kingsway**, the road which runs through town, becoming increasingly downmarket and lively as it heads east towards the cathedral. It's along Kingsway, particularly the less affluent sections further east, where you'll see the charred shells of shopping centres looted in the **1998 riots**. Some were quickly demolished and redeveloped into bright, modern malls, but others provide a backdrop to lively street stalls and hawkers, who have undoubtedly profited from the demise of their more institutionalized competitors.

The tension that brought about the riots has completely dissipated, and as long as you take the **safety precautions** you would in any other African city, you can walk around here comfortably by day. Walking around at night, however, is ill-advised, since the empty streets make wandering tourists fine targets for opportunistic muggers.

Arrival, information and transport

Buses and minibuses from South Africa terminate at the Maseru Bridge border crossing. Walk over the bridge and complete the formalities, then either walk or catch a minibus taxi for the 2km ride into town (M2). **Minibus taxis** arriving from elsewhere in Lesotho will drop you at one of several chaotic ranks: see the box "Moving on from Maseru" opposite for details. **Buses** drop you in the calmer environment of Stadium Road (not at the bus station, which is only for departures), on the east side of the city centre, from where there

Driving out of Maseru, orientation is easy, as both Main North Road (the A1) and Main South Road (the A2) start at the cathedral roundabout at the east end of Kingsway. Public transport leaves from a number of ranks and stations close to the roundabout – where exactly depends on the destination. Towards the end of the month, get a taxi to the departure point if leaving early in the morning to avoid muggers who stay up at night to relieve drinkers of their new pay cheques.

Most **buses** leave from the chaotic bus station between Market Street and Pitso Ground, northeast of the Cathedral roundabout off Main North Road; look for the wavy blue roof. Early morning long-distance **buses to Mokhotlong and Qacha's Nek** are operated by Lesotho Freight and Bus Services (℡2231 3535) and depart from Stadium Road, the northern boundary of Pitso Ground.

Minibus taxis heading south depart from the New Taxi Rank, just behind the Shop Rite Centre on Moshoeshoe Road, 300m north of the cathedral roundabout. Urban taxis marked "Thetsane" pass by.

Minibus taxis heading east and north leave from the Old Taxi Rank, 200m east of the bus station – the easiest way to find it is to go up Main North Road from the roundabout as far as *KFC*, then turn left up Motsamal Rd; the rank is in the second block on the left.

⓫

are urban minibus taxis and local taxis. Walking by day with luggage is safe, if a somewhat amusing sight for locals.

Flights touch down at Moshoeshoe I International Airport, 18km southeast of town off Main South Road (the A2 towards Mafeteng). South African Airlink operates a shuttle bus to and from Maseru (℡5885 5527; M50), which can pick you up or drop you at a hotel. Private taxis (see below) cost about the same. Alternatively, wait for an infrequent minibus taxi at the airport gate, or walk the 4km to the highway, where there's frequent transport into town until the evening (under M10).

The **Lesotho tourist office** (Mon–Fri 8am–4.30pm, Sat 8.30am–1pm; ℡2231 2427, ✉touristinfo@ltdc.org.ls) lies at the west end of the town centre in the thatched Basotho Shield Building at the corner of Kingsway and Orpen Road, facing the *Victoria Hotel*. Although it's under-resourced, the staff are helpful and can give you a town map, flyers from a few resorts and the odd glossy brochure, plus up-to-date information on hotel costs, pony-trekking and the latest contacts for booking accommodation at Sehlabathebe National Park. For practical information about visiting the various components of the Lesotho Highlands Water Project, and bookings for rooms and pony-trekking at Liphofung Cave, Bokong Nature Reserve and Ts'ehlanyane National Park, contact the **LHDA Information Centre** in the AgricBank Building on Kingsway (Mon–Fri 8am–5pm; ℡ & ℻2232 1934, ⊛www.lhwp.org.ls). Lastly, practical information about community-run eco-tourism activities under the fledgling **Maloti–Drakensberg Transfrontier Project** (see box on p.786) can be had from their Project Coordinator, 7th floor, Post Office Building, entrance on Palace Road just off Kingsway (℡2231 2662, ⊛www.maloti.org).

The city centre is compact and easy to **get around** on foot, though there are lots of **minibus taxis** running up and down Kingsway and into the suburbs, from just before dawn to around 8pm. At night, **private taxis** are the only option; operators include Luxury Telephone Taxis ℡2232 6211, Maxi Taxis ℡5891 9159, Moonlight Taxis ℡2231 2605, and Planet Taxis ℡2231 7777.

MASERU

▲ **D**, **E** & Lancers Gap

Moshoeshoe I International Airport ▼

Moshoeshoe I International Airport & Ha Tsolo ▼

▲ Ladybrand

SOUTH AFRICA

SOUTH AFRICA

Caledon River (Mohokare River)

Caledon River (Mohokare River)

Caledon River (Mohokare River)

Seputana River

N

500 m

0

RESTAURANTS & BARS

Blue Lagoon	6
Jazz Bar	2
China Garden	5
Lehaha Grill	4
Maseru Sun	3
Rendezvous	
Victoria	1

ACCOMMODATION

Anglican Training Centre	A
Lakeside Hotel	D
Lancers Inn	C
Lesotho Sun	G
Maseru Sun	F
Maluti Guest House	E
Victoria Hotel	B

Maseru Airport (Old)

Setsoto National Stadium

Lesotho Freight & Bus Services

KFC

Bus Station

Old Taxi Rank

Roman Catholic Cathedral

Shop Rite

Metcash Complex

New Taxi Rank

House of Parliament

Radio Lesotho

Department of Land, Surveys & Physical Planning

Ministry of Agriculture

LHDA

QE II Hospital

Passports & Immigration

Royal Palace

Police

Maseru Book Centre

National Library & Archives

High Court

Alliance Francaise

Basotho Hat Building

Lesotho Bank Tower

Basotho Shield Building

Central Prison

Moreng Weavers

INDUSTRIAL AREA

American Embassy

Lesotho Police Border Checkpoint Customs Post

Maseru Bypass

Accommodation

Maseru is the only place in the country where there's much choice of **accommodation**, offering everything from camping and grim dorms to luxury suites in plush hotels. The central options, on or near Kingsway, are the most practical if you don't have your own transport.

Anglican Training Centre Corner Assisi Rd and Lancers Rd ☎2232 2046. Large and fairly institutionalized place reasonably close to Kingsway, though tricky to find (take a taxi the first time). It's mainly used by church groups and visiting volunteers, but travellers can book into the spartan but adequate double rooms with communal showers and toilets. Normally closed for one month from mid-December. ❶

Lakeside Hotel 1.5km east of the taxi ranks off Main North Rd (turn right at the Shell garage at the Mafeteng junction, and it's 100m along on the left) ☎2231 3646. Lots of decrepit en-suite rooms on the edge of an industrial estate, close to Maqalika reservoir. The rooms are acceptable if you're not too pernickety, with TVs in varying states of disrepair and an interesting collection of bugs. Also has two bars and an average restaurant, though the *Godfather Pizzeria* at the Shell garage next door is better. ❷

Lancers Inn Kingsway ☎2231 2114, ℱ2231 0223. Maseru's most characterful and pleasant place to stay, set in a very central and pleasant sandstone building which has been impressively and tastefully renovated since it was looted in the riots of 1998. There are well-priced and comfortable rondavels and chalets with en-suite

bathrooms, grassy areas, a pool and a good beer garden and restaurant. ❸

Lesotho Sun Off Nightingale Road, on the hill behind the Queen Elizabeth II Hospital ☎2231 3111, ℱ2231 0104. Maseru's largest and smartest accommodation option, this resort has comfortable (if smallish) rooms with TVs and good views over town, plus loads of sports facilities, health spa, pool, casino, cinema, and a good restaurant. ❹

Maluti Guest House Main North Rd, 1km beyond *KFC* on the left (and 200m before Mafeteng junction) ☎2231 2677. Quiet, secure and friendly family-run place with six small rooms (the two with bathrooms are particularly good value), all with TVs and heaters. Breakfast available. ❶

Maseru Sun 12 Orpen Road ☎2231 2434, ℱ2231 2968. The second of the town's *Sun* hotels, with decent if box-like rooms in soothing, well-tended garden surroundings which are popular with locals in the evenings. There's also a good restaurant and a large freeform swimming pool. ❹

Victoria Hotel Kingsway ☎2231 3687. This plain concrete high-rise is a prominent landmark offering unremarkable rooms (the better ones are higher up), a bar and a top-floor restaurant. ❹

The City

The city's most famous landmarks are a trio of imposing neo-traditional thatched buildings at the west end of Kingsway close to Mpilo Boulevard: the **Basotho Shield**, which houses the tourist office and which – viewed from above – does indeed resemble a shield; the **Basotho Hut** opposite, and the appropriately shaped **Basotho Hat Building**, housing the Lesotho Cooperative Handicrafts shop (ⓦwww.basothohat.co.ls). The main part of town lies east of here along Kingsway, though there's not much to see other than a handful of colonial-era buildings: the **Alliance Française** in the former library at the corner with Pioneer Road, the former **Anglican church** in a scruffy park facing *Lancers Inn* further up on the right, and the 1891 **Resident Commissioner's House** (now a government department), on the left beyond the towering **Post Office** building – evidence of Maseru's intention to create a thoroughly modern capital. From here on Kingsway gets busier, its low-priced shops thronged by shoppers, with informal traders touting everything from Basotho fast food (Boerwurst-style sausages are a big hit) to galvanized iron cutlery. Inside the Metcash Complex on the left, opposite Fruit & Veg City Store, J's Music Bar (☎5870 0129) has the widest selection of Basotho and South African music cassettes in the country. Kingsway comes to an end at the traffic circle by the impressively large sandstone **Roman Catholic Cathedral**, where it splits into Main North Road and Main South Road.

Eating, drinking and nightlife

As you'd expect, Maseru has the best selection of **restaurants** in Lesotho. The familiar takeaway chains are scattered along Kingsway, including *KFC* and *Steers* (plus a *Nando's* close to the border), as well as plenty of other inexpensive informal daytime takeaways. The widest choice of **snacks** is around the bus and taxi ranks. One place not to miss is the bakery beside *Lancers Inn*, where you can get delicious, freshly baked loaves, muffins and other treats. If you're after a **drink** or two, most hotels have bars, and there are a number of dodgy-looking *shebeens* with pool tables and red-eyed regulars along the eastern stretch of Kingsway. **Nightlife** is considerably more limited.

Restaurants

China Garden Corner Orpen Road and Mpilo Boulevard, over the footbridge from the tourist office. A reasonably priced Chinese menu in a setting of faded opulence, with surly owners but friendly staff; also does cheap takeaways weekday lunchtimes. Closed Sat dinner and all day Sun.

Lehaha Grill At the *Lesotho Sun*, off Nightingale Road. A busy restaurant serving a tasty but somewhat pricey range of European-style dishes.

Maseru Sun Orpen Road. A choice of buffet or à la carte covering both African and international cuisine – the buffet is probably the better (and certainly the healthier) bet.

Mimmos Maseru Club, UN Road. Decent pizzas and filling pasta. It's popular with the expats, and best in the evenings.

Rendezvous *Lancers Inn*, Kingsway. Lesotho's best, classiest and most expensive restaurant, with an African- and French-themed menu – count on over M100 for a starter and main plus a drink, or considerably more if you crack open a bottle of wine. The outdoor seating is popular at lunchtimes and early evening, but dinner sees few takers.

Victoria Hotel Kingsway. Two restaurants here: a stuffy first-floor dining room open daily for unexciting meaty fare, pizzas and more interesting Basotho dishes on Wed afternoon; and, much better, a top-floor affair (closed Sat lunchtime & Sun) with a bird's-eye view of town, serving respectable Italian dishes, grills and seafood amid great splurges of faded velvet decor.

Drinking and nightlife

With the exception of the *shebeens* down Kingsway, Maseru's **bars** are all attached to hotels or restaurants, the main ones being the *Victoria* and *Lancers* – both rather charmless, though the *Victoria's* bar has a nice terrace from where you can watch Maseru go by. Further out, the *Lakeside* has three safe bars which are popular with locals. Otherwise, central Maseru is a dead loss in terms of **nightlife** other than the cinema and casino at the *Lesotho Sun*.

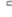
LESOTHO | Maseru

The only nightclub – *Club G* at the *Victoria Hotel* – was closed at the time of writing, though there were plans to reopen it, probably under a different name.

If you want to drink in more typically Basotho surroundings, you need to head out of the centre and make for any of the numerous informal bars scattered about the city's outskirts. Best among these are the **jazz bars**, busiest on Friday nights, and sometimes also Saturday. For upcoming events look for the posters along the eastern stretch of Kingsway; entry can cost up to M100 depending on who's playing. The longest-established place is the *Blue Lagoon Jazz Bar* in Ha Tsolo (☎5877 0080), beyond the New Europa district along Pioneer Road. For all out-of-town places, you're strongly advised to go with a trustworthy local, and to catch a cab.

Listings

Airlines Lesotho Defence Force, Helicopter Section ☎2232 5425; Mission Aviation Fellowship ☎2231 4790; South African Airlink ☎2235 0418, ⓦwww.saairlink.co.za.

Airport information ☎2235 0777.

Banks The main branches of Lesotho Bank, Nedbank and Standard Bank are on Kingsway. The best place for foreign exchange is Standard Bank's international section on the ground floor of the Lesotho Bank Tower, Kingsway.

Books Maseru Book Centre on Kingsway, just past the Lesotho Bank, has a number of historical and cultural works published by Morija Museum; the craft shop in the Basotho Hat Building also has a selection.

Car rental Avis, Moshoeshoe I International Airport ☎2235 0328 and c/o Sure Astra Travel at the *Lesotho Sun* ☎2231 4325; Budget, *Maseru Sun* ☎2231 6344; Imperial Fleet, Moshoeshoe Rd, industrial area ☎5832 3100.

Embassies and consulates Canada ☎2232 4680; Germany ☎2231 4426; Netherlands ☎2231 2114; Republic of Ireland ☎2231 4068; South Africa ☎2231 5758; UK ☎2231 3961; US ☎2231 2666. Note that it's intended to replace the UK's representation in Lesotho with a Pretoria-based consul, for details of which, see ⓦwww.fco.gov.uk.

Hospitals Queen Elizabeth II Hospital, Kingsway ☎2231 2501; Maseru Private Hospital, Thetsane Rd ☎2231 3260.

Internet access 999 Communications (daily 8am–8pm), Kingsway, opposite the post office.

Libraries British Council, corner Kingsway and Lerotholi Rd ☎2231 2609.

Pharmacy MHS Pharmacy, LNDC Shopping Centre, Kingsway ☎2232 5189.

Photography Photo & Gift Galaxy, LNDC Centre, Kingsway.

Police Constitution Rd ☎2231 7262.

Post office and couriers The post office is on Kingsway (Mon–Fri 8am–4.30pm, Sat 8am–noon). DHL, 1st floor, Options Building, Pioneer Rd ☎2231 1082; UPS, 82 Motsoene Rd, industrial area ☎2231 1404.

Radio BBC World Service 90.2FM (24hr).

Swimming pool The pools at the *Lesotho Sun* and *Maseru Sun* are normally open to non-residents; expect to pay around M10.

Travel agents Flight ticketing and Intercape bus tickets are available through: City Center Maseru Travel, next to the Maseru Book Centre, Kingsway ☎2231 4536, ⓕ2231 0150; Millennium Travel and Tours, AgricBank Building, Kingsway ☎2232 1080, ⓔmillenniumtravel@ilesotho.co.za; Sure Astra Travel, Lesotho Sun hotel ☎2232 6540, ⓦwww.suretravel.co.za.

Around Maseru

Although you're unlikely to spend much of your time in Lesotho in Maseru itself, there are a number of rewarding places to visit within easy reach of the capital. A short excursion walkable from central Maseru is the ridge with three peaks known as the **Word, the Flesh and the Devil**, while further out the **Qeme Plateau** offers views over the city and surrounding countryside. A little oddly in a country dominated by towering mountains, it is two of the smaller hills, **Thaba Bosiu**, Moshoeshoe I's impregnable hilltop fortress, and nearby **Qiloane**, model for the Basotho hat (*mokorotlo*), which are the most famous, both ranking among the most important historical sites in the country.

The Word, The Flesh and The Devil

Starting behind the *Lesotho Sun* hotel is an easily accessible climb to three peaks which were a favoured hangout for snipers during the Gun War. Walk between the fences separating the hotel and Friebel Houses, and straight up the hill past a succession of large boulders. After less than twenty minutes, you'll reach the northernmost peak, **The Word**, where there's a survey beacon and excellent views of Maseru and the distant mountains. From here you can walk along the ridge to the other two peaks, **The Flesh** and then **The Devil** – no more than an hour's walk – though neither provide such good views.

Qeme Plateau

The large T-shaped **Qeme Plateau**, which measures over 25 square kilometres and provides superb vistas into the Free State and east into Lesotho, is only a short drive south of Maseru, near the South African border. The usual way of getting there is to go along Main South Road (the A2) as far as Mantsebo, 25km from Maseru, then turn right at the crossroads and left after the Fraser's Store. Leave your transport there and look out for a footpath climbing the plateau diagonally from left to right, which takes you to the top; there and back takes three or four hours.

Alternatively, take Pioneer Road from Kingsway out of Maseru, turn right after 7km on to the B32, driving 4km to Matuteng. Here, a right turn along a dirt road heading towards Mokhalinyane takes you through beautiful countryside along the western part of the plateau. Look out for a cleft in the plateau's ridge, and park at its foot at the village of Ha Mapholo (leaving your car here is quite safe). Walk through the village and make for the cleft; you'll find that the first part of the climb is pretty obvious, but two-thirds of the way up you'll need either inspired guesswork or the help of one of the many boys who can usually be found clambering around here with their cows and goats. The climb there and back takes about two hours.

Once at the top, the boulders and grasslands make for an excellent stroll and picnic spot. Make sure you've left yourself enough time to get back down before dark. From Ha Mapholo, you can either return the way you came or carry on a few kilometres, at which point the road improves, finally taking you to Main South Road just north of Morija.

Thaba Bosiu

Thaba Bosiu is Lesotho's most important historical sight, a steep mountain with a large flat top about 20km east of Maseru that was the capital of the kingdom in the days of Moshoeshoe I. Although it has been declared a World Heritage Site by UNESCO, nothing has yet been done to develop it, and there's not that much to see once you reach the top. However, it is a place of great significance to the people of Lesotho, and the burial ground of the country's kings, and as such is well worth a visit.

Moshoeshoe I trekked with his followers from Butha-Buthe to Thaba Bosiu in July 1824 in a bid to settle somewhere far from the warrior clans then terrorizing the flat plains to the north and west, and somewhere that would be extremely hard for anyone to capture. Thaba Bosiu, with its crown of near-vertical cliffs, good grazing and seven or eight freshwater springs on top, fitted the bill perfectly. Although it wasn't long before warrior clans, including Afrikaner ones, found their way here, none was able to take the mountain, which has earned it – and Moshoeshoe – a good deal of kudos. The name means "Mountain of the Night", perhaps because, as legend has it, Moshoeshoe first arrived there in the evening, and immediate protective measures took all night to install. A more compelling reason, and the one most Basotho prefer, is that the mountain, which does not look particularly high or impressive by day, seems to grow inexorably as night falls, becoming huge and unconquerable.

There is a **tourist information** building (daily 8am–4.30pm; ☎5888 3504) at the foot of the mountain, with snacks and soft drinks. M5 gets you some information leaflets and an official guide to show you around. You'll be taken up **Khubelu Pass** (or "Red Pass"), a cleft in the cliffs marked by two flagpoles, where the Afrikaner General Louw Wepener was killed trying to storm the

Taking Thaba Bosiu

Fresh from conquering much of the flat land east of the Caledon in 1828, the Ngwane were the first to attack Thaba Bosiu, but were decisively beaten, after which they never troubled Moshoeshoe again. The mixed-race Koranna people also harried Thaba Bosiu in 1831, often capturing and enslaving the villagers living beneath it, but always driven off the mountain proper by Moshoeshoe's warriors. **Mzilikhazi**, King of the Ndebele, who later conquered much of modern-day Zimbabwe, tried to take the mountain the same year, but his men were defeated by a mass of great boulders flung down from the top by the Basotho; Moshoeshoe is reputed to have sent the Ndebele a large number of fat oxen after their defeat, an unprecedented move for a victorious chief – as if to say that he understood that their attack had been inspired by hunger and that he wanted to help them out. At any rate, Mzilikhazi never came back that way.

There followed a twenty-year period of relative calm, during which time Moshoeshoe would receive visitors wearing a beautifully tailored dark-blue military uniform, complete with cloak, and offer them tea from a prized china tea service. He allowed the French missionary, Eugene Casalis, to establish a mission at the bottom of the mountain in 1837, and employed him as his secretary and interpreter. In 1852 a British punitive force led by the Cape governor, Sir George Cathcart, didn't even make it as far as the mountain, instead being attacked a short distance away by Moshoeshoe's well-armed troops, who forced their hasty withdrawal. Afrikaner forces fighting for the Orange Free State (OFS) made a brief attempt on Thaba Bosiu in 1858, but came back in 1865 in a more determined manner, armed with heavy artillery and began steadily shelling the mountain, launching two simultaneous assaults a few days later. Eight men made it to the top, but were seriously wounded as soon as they did so, and speedily retreated back down. A week later, more Afrikaner troops and the OFS president turned up, and another assault was launched. General Wepener led his men right to the top of the Khubelu Pass, but he was shot at the top and mortally wounded. The Basotho then mounted a counterattack, and the Afrikaners withdrew. They continued the siege for a month, though, during which time most of the livestock on Thaba Bosiu died of hunger and the Basotho became so short of bullets that they melted down the shells being fired at them to make homemade ones.

Although they won this battle, the Basotho lost the war, and Moshoeshoe signed a humiliating treaty in 1866 which surrendered most of Lesotho's farmland to the OFS. Four years later the old king died and was buried on the top of Thaba Bosiu, and two years after that Lesotho was annexed to the Cape Colony.

mountain in 1865 (see box on p.779), past the rock where Basotho warriors used to watch out for approaching enemy forces, and on to the remains of Moshoeshoe's **European house**, built for him by a deserter from the 72nd Seaforth Highlanders, David F. Webber, possibly assisted by a certain R. Murphie, whose name and the date 1839 is carved on a nearby rock face.

The entrance to the stronghold was at the top of the pass, now marked by three rocks. To the left of the rocks are the remains of a stone cairn; it was customary for visitors to add a rock to the pile before entering. From there, it's a short walk to the slight remains of Moshoeshoe's royal court and then to the **royal graveyard**. The tombs of Moshoeshoe I and most of his successors are marked with simple stone cairns, although the most recent tomb, of Moshoeshoe II, killed in a car crash in 1996, is a more elaborate affair, adorned with plastic flowers.

To the east of the mountain you get a great view of **Qiloane**, a strange cone-shaped mountain with a large nodule on the top, which was apparently the inspiration for the national headdress, the distinctive Basotho hat. Around the other side of the mountain is a kind of cave village where the royal household used to hide during attacks, and which were occupied and decorated with rock paintings by the San who lived there before them. The guide can take you to them, and to a traditional healer (*sangoma*) who lives in one of the caves. The caves are about a four-kilometre drive from the Khubelu Pass, followed by a short walk.

Practicalities

To get to Thaba Bosiu **by car**, take Main South Road, turning right at the signpost to Thaba Bosiu. Follow this road through a dip down into a riverbed where the road is temporarily untarred, and on to a T-junction. Turn left at the junction and Thaba Bosiu is about 3km further along on the right. During the day, frequent **minibus taxis** run here from Maseru's New Taxi Rank.

There's good **accommodation** next to the mountain within walking distance of the tourist office at *Mmelesi Lodge* (☎ 5250 1115, Ⓕ 2231 4033; ❷), probably the best-run Basotho-owned lodge in the country. Though often used for government conferences, it has a plush bar and a pleasant restaurant serving moderately priced meat and fish dishes, a braai area, and comfortable en-suite rondavels at the back.

Roma to Semonkong

Southeast of Maseru, the historic Catholic mission and university town of **Roma** is worth a stop, while the road from here to Semonkong offers an epic drive through the stunning basalt peaks of the Thaba Putsoa range, past a succession of remote and relaxed villages made up of Lesotho's characteristic dry-stone-walled rondavels. The road ends at **Semonkong**, whose lodge is one of the best places to stay in the country, offering a vast range of activities including pony-trekking. A short distance away are the spectacular **Semonkong Falls**, which crash down from nearly 200m to the Maletsunyane River below.

Roma

About 30km from Maseru along a good tar road, the mission town of **ROMA** has a beautiful location amid strangely sculpted sandstone foothills and is home to the unlovely campus of the **National University of Lesotho**, which began life in 1945 as Pius XII College, run by the Roman Catholic Church. Between 1964 and 1971 it was the university of all three of the former British southern African protectorates, now Lesotho, Botswana and Swaziland.

A kilometre or so further up the road from the university, past a succession of schools and seminaries, is **Roma Mission**, most of which was built by French missionaries after 1862, when King Moshoeshoe allowed them to settled in the area. Though grander than its counterpart in Morija, the mission is a little run-down these days, and there's not much reason to linger apart from to visit the grave of Father Gerard, a classic of Catholic kitsch – Gerard was one of the mission's founders, celebrated for restoring a young girl's sight through prayer, for which he was posthumously beatified.

Practicalities

Several **buses** and many more **minibus taxis** travel daily between Maseru and Roma, making this one of the busiest public transport routes in the country. The best **accommodation** is the ivy-festooned *Roma Trading Post Guest House* (☎2234 0202, after 5.30pm ☎2234 0267, ⓦwww.seelesotho.com/tradingpost .htm; ❷) at the west end of town. Built in 1903 as a trading store by John Thomas Thorn, and lived in by his family ever since, it offers en-suite rondavels and doubles with shared bathrooms, a self-catering cottage and camping. Meals are available by prior arrangement, there's a swimming pool, and the family can help arrange activities including pony-trekking in the surrounding hills and walks to nearby dinosaur footprints, San rock paintings and local weavers and crafters. To get there, look for a sign on the right of the main road as you enter Roma marked "Manonyane High School" and "Trading Post", and continue 100m up the dirt road.

The only place to **eat** is the *Speak Easy Liquor Restaurant*, opposite the university and used mainly by students. It serves inexpensive, good-value food which you can wash down with Maseru's most spectacular selection of alcoholic beverages. Right next door is the last place you can buy **fuel** before Semonkong.

Roma to Ramabanta

The road from Roma to Semonkong is one of the most spectacular in Lesotho, with superb views as you climb into the highlands. Where the tarred road turns to gravel at **Moitsupeli**, 18.5km beyond Roma, look ahead towards the twin summits of the appropriately named **Thabana-li-Mele** (Breast Mountains). The northern summit is climbable without special equipment, if you can find the cleft on its northern side. Just park at the next village of **Ha Dinzulu**, let people know where you are going, cross the Makhaleng River and make your way up as far as you can. If you make it to the top, it's about seven hours there and back.

The road from Ha Dinzulu continues to climb, peaking at 2000m at Nkesi's Pass and then dropping down to the village of **RAMABANTA**, which has another *Trading Post Guest House*, also run by the Thorn family in Roma (☎2234 0202, after 5.30pm ☎2234 0267, ⓦwww.seelesotho.com/tradingpost .htm; ❷), with seven adequate en-suite rooms in a farm house, three family rooms, a dorm and campsite. Home-cooked meals are available and, like the guesthouse in Roma, hikes and pony rides can be arranged, as can 4WD adventures (in your own car) with overnights in villages.

Semonkong and around

From Ramabanta, cross the Makhaleng River and then drive up to 3000m by Thaba Putsoa itself, before descending gently to the curiously straggly town of **SEMONKONG**. The region was inhabited by the San until 1873, when – after a series of **genocidal campaigns** against them by the British – the last of Lesotho's San were finally exterminated by an expedition led by a certain Colonel Bowker. The town itself began life in the 1880s following the Gun War as a refuge for displaced Basotho from the lowlands. The town offers a few basic stores, plenty of **bars**, and even a post office and bank, though you can't rely on either. The roads in town are bad but not impassable, and it's worth going to the ubiquitous Fraser's Store just to check out the Wild West-style clientele, dressed mostly in blankets and gumboots, with their ponies hitched to a post at the entrance. If you're here in winter, try to catch the local **horse races** on the last weekend of every month.

From the lodge in Semonkong (see below), it's a day's walk or pony trek west (see box opposite) into the pretty Thaba Putsoa mountains to the pristine 120-metre **Ketane Falls**. The falls are inaccessible by any other means of transport, and the pony trek is considered one of the best in the country. The falls can also be visited on a popular four-day pony trek from *Malealea Lodge* (see p.800).

Rather easier to reach are the **Semonkong Falls** (also known as the Maletsunyane or Le Bihan Falls, after a French missionary), a pretty five-kilometre walk downriver through maize fields and pastures adorning the banks of the Maletsunyane River, though the path is slippery in parts. It's possible to drive, but you risk getting your car broken into if you go down to the bottom. The dramatic falls, the highest single drop in southern Africa, plunge nearly 200m down a sheer and scary cliff into a swimmable pool, whose mist gives the falls their name: "Smoking Water" – for such a spectacular and well-known sight, the lack of intrusive man-made facilities is refreshing. The falls are surrounded on all sides by natural vantage points, though the best views are from the plateau facing them. There's a steep path down to the bottom, where you can swim or camp. The pool usually freezes by June, but the waterfall keeps going all winter, spraying the surrounding rocks with ice, and forming an impressive ice cage over the pool. Outside winter, look out for birds such as bald ibis or bearded vultures (lammergeiers) soaring in the vast chasm that frames the falls.

Practicalities

The 120km **drive** from Maseru to Semonkong take three to four hours by private car; the road is tarred up to Moitsupeli, while the remaining 65km are decent gravel which is passable in all but the frailest 2WD. A couple of Lesotho Freight and Bus Services **buses** leave Maseru daily at 10am and 2pm, taking around six hours, and there are also at least a couple of minibuses. If you miss these, you can always get public transport to Roma and then a minibus taxi from there, though they stop running by mid-afternoon.

The place to **stay** is the excellent *Semonkong Lodge* (℡051 933 3106, Ⓦwww.placeofsmoke.co.ls; dorms and camping ❶, rooms ❷), 1km south of town beside the Maletsunyane River. One of the best lodges in Lesotho, this laid-back and well-run place offers en-suite doubles, dorms and a bunkhouse – all in thatch-and-stone buildings, plain from the outside but cosy inside, complete with fireplaces, electricity and hot showers. There's also a campsite, a kitchen for self-caterers, a great bar with pool table, balcony and a decent selection of music, and tasty meals (including vegetarian). But the main reason for staying here is for the immense selection of **outdoor activities** on offer (see the box opposite). Unusually for lodges outside Maseru, it even accepts some credit cards.

Working in conjunction with the local community, *Semonkong Lodge* offers a bewildering choice of **outdoor activities**, ranging from short walks through town and along the river in search of bald ibis, to abseiling and adventurous pony-treks lasting several days and overnighting in basic huts. Advance bookings are required for overnight rides. **Short pony-treks** head to Phororo viewpoint over the Semonkong Falls (3hr round trip), and can also be done on foot in the same time. The trek can be extended to five hours by including Mount Qoang, for great views and a chance to see the endangered spiral aloe, or by visiting a "whistle blower" – a traditional healer. If you're just **walking**, six hours gives you three possibilities: along the river; down to the Semonkong Falls splash-pool (strenuous); or on to the Matsoku Falls. **Overnight pony-treks** get you within reach of **Ketane Falls** up in the Thaba Putsoa mountains, while with two nights to spare you can either go fishing, or – particularly sweet – trek or walk across the Thaba Putsoa range to Malealea via the Ketane and Ribaneng Falls (around M700 per person hiking, M1300 by pony), where you could simply mount another pony and continue your equine explorations from there (see box on p.801).

As ever, per person **costs** work out cheaper in larger groups; the maximum is ten people. Couples pay M135 per person for a full day's ride. Overnights, including the guide, his horse and pack horse, are around M500 per person in a couple for one night, M700 for two nights, and M1600 for six nights. For walks, pack horses are optional; again, in a couple expect to pay around M165 for a day and night (M245 with pack horse), or M625 (M900 with pack horse) for six nights. For day trips on foot, a guide costs M10 per hour.

The road to Thaba-Tseka

The central A3 runs over Lesotho's Central Range to the small district capital of **Thaba-Tseka**, 175km from Maseru, the countryside changing from cultivated lowlands to more sparsely populated mountains. Beyond the turning for Roma, the first settlement of any size is the small village of **NAZARETH**, which has a couple of uncommonly ugly lodges, the *Molengoane* and the *Mabotlenyane*, under the same management (☎2234 7766; ❷). Rooms are in terraced breeze-block "chalets" and similar rondavels and each lodge has a bar and restaurant. Seven kilometres north of Nazareth at **Ha Baroana** are what were once some of the finest rock paintings in the country. The paintings are still impressive, with clearly discernible figures of animals, dancers and hunters, but they have been vandalized and washed away by child guides who throw water at them to make them more visible for tourists. The easiest way to get to the paintings is along a difficult dirt road starting 1.5km east of Nazareth, which takes you straight to the site (another 5.5km). The site now has a curator, who should be at the huts down by the Liphiring Stream; a tip is in order.

After Nazareth, the highway ascends steeply into the mountains through the 2268-metre **Bushman's Pass**. Along the way you may see young boys trying to sell lumps of quartzite and, more worryingly, Lesotho's national flower, the protected, rare and weirdly beautiful **spiral aloe**. Don't be tempted to purchase one, as it will only sustain the market in these unique plants – if you haven't seen one, you'd be much better off hiking into the mountains and finding one in the wild (from Semonkong, for example), or visit the botanical gardens at Katse.

Roughly 15km beyond Nazareth is the **Basotho Pony Trekking Centre**. One of Lesotho's original trekking centres, it's the least expensive place to pony trek in the country, with a two-day/one-night treks costing just M125 per person plus M20 for accommodation in huts or M10 for camping; you'll need to bring all your supplies with you. Shorter pony treks, also suitable for hiking, go to the impressive Qiloane Falls on the Makhaleng River (2hr each way), and to the Leboela Falls (1hr each way). **Reservations** are essential to ensure that someone's there when you arrive – more easily said than done, unfortunately, thanks to the chaotic state of affairs at the Ministry of Agriculture's Livestock Services Department (☎2231 7284, ☎2231 1500), who currently manage the place. Your best approach is to contact the tourist office in Maseru for the latest information.

The road carries on from here over two epic mountain passes, the 2318m **Molimo Nthuse Pass** (which means "God Help Me"), and – shortly after – **Blue Mountain Pass** (2620m), which offers commanding views of the surrounding mountains, though the views are even better if you climb the hills on either side. From here, the tar road descends into the village of **LIKALANENG**, dominated by the not-unattractive Legoland-style prefab offices, shops and houses erected for contractors working on the nearby **Mohale Dam**, which was completed in 2004 as Phase 1b of the Lesotho Highlands Water Project (see box on p.790). Unlike the astonishing engineering grace of Katse Dam, Mohale is little more than a enormous pile of concrete-faced rubble, whose 145m-high barrier holds back almost a billion cubic metres of water. Water from the reservoir flows along a 32km tunnel to Katse, and can also flow in the opposite direction should Katse be fuller than Mohale. More spectacular than the dam are two concrete **bridges**, the 449m-long, 91m-high bridge from Ha Makhosi village, and the 308m-long, 63m-high bridge across Bokong River near Ha Mokhathi. With 75km of feeder roads around the reservoir, **angling** is set to become a major attraction. For more information, and free daily tours of the dam, head for the **visitor centre** (☎2293 6217, ☎2293 6219) on the far side of the village. Tours start at 9am and 2pm. There's **accommodation** at *Mohale Lodge* (☎2293 6432; ❷), signposted on the left before arriving at the dam. Buses and taxis from Maseru to Thaba-Tseka drop you at Likalaneng, within walking distance of the *Mohale Lodge* and the visitor centre.

Beyond Likalaneng, the road turns to dirt and rises once more to the village of **MARAKABEI** on the banks of the Senqunyane River. There's pleasant riverside accommodation at the charming *Marakabei Lodge* (☎2231 2653; ❶), with thatched en-suite rondavels and rooms in the main building, all set in a pretty garden. There's also a campsite, a restaurant and bar with TV, and they can find you a rod for trout fishing. You can buy fuel at Marakabei and also at **MANTSONYANE**, 18km further east, where there are also a few takeaways serving Basotho dishes and some sparsely filled trading stores. This is as far as you can safely go in a car without high clearance; if you want to press on further, there are buses continuing to Thaba-Tseka.

Thaba-Tseka

The road to **THABA-TSEKA** is a dramatic one, peaking in the heart of the Central Range at the 2860m **Mokhoabong Pass**, before descending to the town, which is over 2200m above sea level – although once here there's very little in this 1980s purpose-built administrative centre to detain you. If you need somewhere to **stay**, the friendly *Mountain Star Lodge* (☎2290 0425; ❷), a locally owned place mostly used by civil servants and contract workers, has smallish en-suite rooms with TVs and phones, good basic food in its restaurant, and a bar. Cheaper but more spartan accommodation is available at the self-catering *Agricultural Training Centre* (☎ 2290 0303; ❶), a long, prefabricated building in the street above the post office and banks, though it's often full during the week. The town's only **restaurant** is at the *Mountain Star Lodge*, though there are one or two stores in the centre serving takeaways.

Lesotho Freight and Bus Services operates three **buses** daily from Maseru, leaving the capital at 8.30am, 9am and 9.30am. These continue on to Bokong (next to Katse), Linakaneng (halfway along the road to Mokhotlong) and Sehong Hong (a good way along the A4 to Sehlabathebe) respectively, and are as far as you can travel by public transport on those routes. With your own vehicle (or some luck hitching) you could tackle the spectacular road to Mokhotlong and the Sani Pass, but it's not one you should attempt in anything other than a 4WD, and that in good weather only. The road to Katse is much better and, although you still shouldn't attempt it in an ordinary saloon, there are a number of buses plying the route. From Katse there's a perfect tarred road to Hlotse in the northwest (see p.786). There's no road southwest to Semonkong, though there are hikeable trails.

The northern districts

The route north from Maseru right the way round to **Sani Pass** takes in the best of both Lesotho's lowlands and highlands, from the wind-carved sandstone hills on the way to **Teya-Teyaneng**, a hill town famed for its woven crafts, to the epic mountain passes of the "Roof of Africa route" that runs from **Butha-Buthe** to the ramshackle town of **Mokhotlong**, set among southern Africa's highest mountains, and on to **Sani**. There are a number of intriguing, out-of-the-way sights along the way, like the remarkable **cave houses** at Mateka, the massive **Katse Dam**, the rock art at **Liphofung** and the winter skiing runs near **Oxbow**. You'll find plenty of reasonable places to stay (though some take a little finding), particularly in the highlands, where a succession of well-located lodges make perfect bases for hiking in the surrounding mountains.

The road from Butha-Buthe is tarred all the way to Mokhotlong, and although it's breaking up in places, is fine for 2WD vehicles except in winter, when ice and deep snow can block it for days at a time. The stretch from Mokhotlong to Sani Pass and the dramatic winding road down the mighty Drakensberg into South Africa, is gravel, for which 4WD is strongly advised, even if it remains just about passable in a saloon car in good weather.

Maseru to Hlotse

While most travellers speed through en route to the more spectacular highlands beyond, the lowland stretch between Maseru and Hlotse offers a number of attractions. The caves at **Mateka** are the most fascinating in Lesotho and well worth a special trip, while the woven crafts in **Teya-Teyaneng** are of superb

The Maloti–Drakensberg Transfrontier Project

The **Maloti–Drakensberg Transfrontier Project** focuses on Lesotho's highland areas bordering South Africa, from near Butha-Buthe in the north clockwise to beyond Qacha's Nek in the south. Although early days yet, the project is a hopeful sign that the previously hapless management of the area's roads, tourist facilities and unique but fragile natural areas may soon be a thing of the past. Based on an integrated approach with South Africa, the project focuses on ecological issues and on the area's widespread poverty. The idea is to tackle both aspects by establishing **sustainable tourism** initiatives among local communities, with the emphasis on culture as much as on natural attractions. South African parks and reserves included in the project include Ukhahlamba Drakensberg Park, Royal Natal National Park, Sterkfontein Nature Reserve, Golden Gate Highlands National Park, Coleford Nature Reserve and Ongelurksnek Nature Reserve. When the project is implemented in 2008, it's likely that some of these areas will become a part of a **transfrontier park** along the lines of Kgalagadi in the Northern Cape – a true wilderness paradise for hikers.

For more information, including practical advice on community tourism projects initiated so far – which may include overnight stays in villages, walks to natural and cultural attractions, and meeting healers and craftspeople – contact the project coordinator on the 7th floor of the Post Office Building in Maseru (entrance on Palace Road, just off Kingsway; ☎2231 2662, ⓦwww.maloti.org).

quality and design. The busy town of **Hlotse** has less of interest, although it's close to one of the largest collections of dinosaur footprints in the country.

There are two good roads from Maseru to Teya-Teyaneng. The most commonly used is the scenic **Main North Road** (A1), which takes you through sandstone mountain-studded lowlands. A good alternative is the **Sefikeng Road**: follow Main North Road out of Maseru and turn right after 4km onto the B31. This climbs up a steep series of hairpins to **Lancers Gap**, an extraordinary ridge with a great gap in the middle through which the road passes, so named because a Lancers regiment was allegedly ambushed and defeated in it during the Gun War. In fact, the regiment was ambushed somewhere else, but it doesn't really matter, as this is still a great place to scramble around and look out both on Maseru and the mountains to the east. Beyond Lancers Gap stretches the Berea plateau, from where you can look down on the lowlands. There's a strange gap in the tar road at Sefikeng: when you come into the village, turn left at the Paradise General Dealer, head along a short patch of dirt track, and then join the tar road towards Mateka.

Mateka

Getting to **MATEKA** by public transport is easiest via Teya-Teyaneng, but requires some patience. If you're driving, leave your car at Mateka, and enlist one of the many children usually hanging around to take you on the half-hour walk down the hill to the **cave houses**. The seven still-inhabited dwellings are the country's best-kept architectural secrets, sculpted out of mud under a huge rock overhang and looking more like igloos or West African mud architecture than anything usually found in southern Africa. Their laid-back residents don't mind you taking photographs or simply goggling at their homes.

Teng Lodge (☎2240 0262 or 2232 4589), signposted from Mateka, is officially closed since the death of the chief and his son, who were running it. However, if you make the tricky eight-kilometre journey here, across a seemingly impassable river (wade in first to check the depth, and take it at speed) and some dodgy stretches of dirt road, the new chief (who is the old chief's wife) will let you stay for a donation. You'll stay in a lovely rondavel looking out onto the Berea Mountains, but bring candles, food and cooking gear as the lodge has none of these. The chief can also provide a guide to take you to some remarkable, unvandalized San rock paintings about an hour's walk away, through gentle hills, maize fields and charmingly secluded villages.

Back in Mateka, it's only a half-hour drive to Teya-Teyaneng on a good tarred road. Travelling under your own steam, you'll find the occasional minibus taxi or private vehicle willing to take you, though you'll probably have to wait a while.

Teya-Teyaneng and around

TEYA-TEYANENG (usually abbreviated to "T.Y.") means "place of shifting sands", after the way the nearby river changes its course from time to time. The town straggles out over a hill and has a bustling, compact centre and suburbs that spread several kilometres north and east. T.Y. is the **crafts capital** of Lesotho, specializing in all manner of weavings, from luxurious jerseys to elaborately designed wall-hangings. There are three weaving outlets, all open daily from 8am to 5pm. The most central is **Setsoto Design** (℡2250 0238), 500m from the *Blue Mountain Inn* (see below), where you can see tapestries being made; various woven products are sold at reasonable prices in the adjacent shop. Three kilometres south of town, on the left as you come in from Maseru, look for signs to the small showroom of **Hatooa Mose Mosali** (℡2250 0772), which translates as "women must stand up and work hard". This collective sells particularly beautiful weavings, though they keep a fairly limited range in stock; their catalogue displays some very special wall-hangings, which you need to order as they take a week or two to make. A short distance further on, also signposted but this time to the right of the main road, the pleasant Anglican St Agnes Mission is home to **Helang Basali Handicrafts** (℡2250 1546), whose showroom has an excellent selection of woven crafts, again including some very elaborate items. In the workshop next door you can watch the craftswomen working on wall-hangings at great looms stretching nearly to the ceiling.

Practicalities

Teya-Teyaneng's **bus and taxi rank** is 100m east of the highway. There's plenty of transport to and from Maseru and further north to Hlotse and Butha-Buthe, and you rarely have to wait long. On the west side of the highway, the main road into town runs diagonally uphill past a number of undistinguished takeaway food joints and stores. A right at the junction at the top takes you past the post office and its transmitter to the *Blue Mountain Inn* (℡ & ℗2250 0362; ❷), the town's main **accommodation** option, a spacious and well-run hotel with dozens of small and old-fashioned but comfortable chalets. It also has T.Y.'s only proper **restaurant**, serving tasty, inexpensive meals, plus a good selection of wines. Wednesday lunchtimes feature traditional Basotho food, while weekends are good for meaty grills. There's also a pizzeria, three bars, a large lawn with shaded tables, and the manageress can help arrange trips. Much more modest is *Ka Pitseng Guest House* (℡2250 1638; ❶ including breakfast), 500m beyond the *Blue Mountain* turning and with lovely views west; the rooms are very basic and beds way too soft, but there's food all day (also with Basotho specialities on Wednesday), a cosy bar with fireplace, and a fine garden in which to drink and relax.

Culture as fashion: the blanket and the hat

In a region of Africa where **traditional dress** has all but died out, Lesotho stands out as the exception. The **mokorotlo** (Basotho traditional hat) is not widely worn these days, admittedly, though you'll still occasionally see its distinctive cone and bobble in Lesotho, while in South Africa it's popular with Basotho migrant workers as a badge of ethnic distinction. Modelled on the shape of Qiloane Mountain near Thaba Bosiu, and made of woven straw, the *mokorotlo* has become the standard Basotho souvenir, sold in every craft shop, usually for M25 or less. Oddly, miners' hard-hats are also sported in Lesotho as a fashion item, often by younger brothers of Basotho men working in South African mines.

More prevalent than the *mokorotlo* is the Basotho **blanket**, still worn all over the country. When King Moshoeshoe I was presented with a blanket by European traders in 1860, there were hardly any in his kingdom, the people wearing karosses made of animal hides instead. However, by 1872 traders were reporting insatiable demand for the blankets. Made from high-quality woven cloth, they were originally manufactured in Birmingham, England, and are today made in Port Elizabeth, South Africa. The ubiquitous Fraser's Stores, which you find all over the country, first established themselves by selling blankets, and still stock them today. Good ones (made of pure wool) cost about M450, a fortune by local standards – don't forget to buy an outsized safety pin to tie it with.

The blankets are very practical, keeping the body at an even temperature except when it's really hot outside (although the Basotho wear them whatever the weather); they don't absorb much water, and do not easily catch fire, which is handy when you are dozing by an open hearth. Blankets are also associated with fertility, which is why some carry the design of a maize cob, a Basotho symbol of fertility and prosperity. Young brides are supposed to wear a blanket around their hips until their first child is conceived, and boys wear different blankets before and after circumcision.

Most blankets have stripes designed to lie horizontally when you wear the blanket. A curious feature of some patterns is their retention of British imperial symbolism. One popular design features a large crown at its centre; another shows warplanes with British military markings. However, although they have always been foreign imports, and are the commodities on which many European trader fortunes have been built, the blankets remain quintessentially Basotho, and a source of national pride.

Maputsoe

A rough, busy and chaotic manufacturing-based border town opposite the South African town of Ficksburg, **MAPUTSOE** is not a good place to stay long, though you may find yourself changing minibus taxis here. Fortunately, the border is open 24 hours a day, and there's plenty of public transport to Maseru, Hlotse and the north. The town's streets are filled with migrant workers commuting between Lesotho and South Africa, among them an uncomfortable number of hustlers who can spot strangers a mile off. Many hustlers seem to congregate at Maputsoe's only **hotel**, the large *Sekekete* (☎ 2243 0789; ❶), on the main street 50m from the border, which is usually filled with heavy drinkers and gamblers stuffing money into the slot machines. The hotel's plain but functional rooms are around the back, a short distance from the general commotion. There are plenty of **takeaways** on the same street, best of which is the chain-run *Captain DoRego's*, 100m beyond the hotel in a shopping centre on the opposite side of the road. There's a branch of the Lesotho Bank between the border and the hotel. Heed the 50kph speed limit leaving town, as there are plenty of police about.

Hlotse

A dilapidated but still pleasant little shady town named after the local river, **HLOTSE** (also called **Leribe**, after the district) was founded in 1876 by an Anglican missionary, Reverend John Widdicombe, and suffered repeated sieges during the Gun War. Since then it has kept a low profile and, apart from a few shops and department stores, the only thing to see in town are the battered remains of a small military tower built by the British and now practically falling down.

There are, however, one or two attractions in the area, including a set of **dinosaur footprints** a few kilometres south of town at the turn-of-the-century **Tsikoane Mission** (left off Main North Road to Teya-Teyaneng). You'll need to climb up the rock overhang above the church, preferably with the help of a guide (ask at the mission), where you'll find over forty reasonably clear imprints.

On the right-hand side as you head north from Hlotse, where the town's exit road meets the main road, is the **Leribe Craft Centre** (daily 8am–5pm), where you can buy mohair scarves, blankets and table mats, along with a small selection of other crafts including rather dandy articulated wooden snakes made by a team of local women, about half of whom have disabilities.

Practicalities

The highway passes to the south of town; the main road into town starts at the Caltex garage, passing the *Pelican Bar and Steakhouse* which serves inexpensive big meat dishes, and the *Leribe Hotel* (☎2240 0559; ❷), which is the town's main **accommodation** choice, with a range of rondavels and rooms in lines of adjacent chalets overlooking a pleasant garden (avoid those with numbers in the thirties, which are next to a large and noisy water tank). The somewhat staid restaurant serves moderately priced meat and fish dishes, the occasional vegetarian pasta and, unusually for Lesotho, filter coffee. There's also a **bar**: the big night is Saturday, often with visiting South African bands or DJs. Another good nightspot is the *Woodpecker Club* on the highway, 100m west of the Caltex garage, which has live bands, DJs and discos most Friday and Saturday nights.

A left after the hotel at the church takes you past the post office to the **taxi rank**. There's plenty of **transport**, though if you're heading south, rather than waiting for a direct run, it's quicker grab a seat on one of the frequent minibuses to Maputsoe and change there. The Lesotho Freight and Bus Services service to Mokhotlong doesn't enter town but stops 100m east of the Caltex garage on the highway; it passes by around 8.30am.

The road to Katse Dam

To the east of Hlotse rises the impressive Front Range of the Maloti Mountains. The region is at the heart of Phase 1a of the ambitious **Lesotho Highlands Water Project** (see box on p.790), whose centrepiece is the massive dam and reservoir at **Katse**, which stands in stark contrast to the rural simplicity surrounding it. The 100-kilometre A8 highway built for the dam from Hlotse is a remarkable journey almost worth doing for the drive alone, twisting and turning up through increasingly spectacular mountains. As part of the project, two new reserves were established: **Ts'ehlanyane National Park**, accessed off the A1 to Butha-Buthe and connected to Bokong via a 39-kilometre hiking and riding trail, and **Bokong Nature Reserve**, which straddles the A8 west of Katse Reservoir. Both offer superb hiking and pony-trekking terrain, and accommodation.

Ts'ehlanyane National Park

Heading northeast from Hlotse along the A1, a signposted turning 9km short of Butha-Buthe leads 32km east along good gravel into the western scarp of the Front Range, following a very picturesque valley. Covering 56 square kilometres of extremely rugged hiking terrain at the confluence of the Ts'ehlanyane and Holomo rivers, **Ts'ehlanyane National Park** (daily 8am–5pm; ☎ 2246 0723; M15 plus M5 per vehicle and M16 if staying overnight) is intended to protect several areas of ecological importance, particularly the indigenous *Leucosidea sericea* **woodland** known locally as *Ouhout* or *Che-che* – one of Lesotho's very few forested areas. Equally rare are stands of montane bamboo. **Mammals** present are mainly duikers, baboons and serval cats; there's also the endangered *Metisella syrinx* butterfly, bearded vultures (lammergeiers) and ground woodpeckers. The **best time to visit** is spring, when the small yellow flowers along the river banks that give their unpronounceable name to the reserve are in flower. The highlight for hikers and pony-trekkers alike is a spectacular 39-kilometre trail linking the park with

The Lesotho Highlands Water Project

Lesotho's abundance of water but shortage of cash and Gauteng's monetary wealth and water poverty are the facts behind the stunningly ambitious **Lesotho Highlands Water Project** – Africa's largest engineering venture to date. The essence of the project is to dam Lesotho's major rivers, most of which flow into the Senqu (known to South Africans as the Orange River); then divert the water through specially constructed tunnels, via a hydro-electric power station at 'Muela near Butha-Buthe, to South African rivers; which carry it to the Vaal Dam; which then supplies Gauteng. For this, South Africa pays Lesotho royalties of around R12 million a month.

The project was first conceived in the 1950s, but didn't kick off for real until 1978. The treaty formalizing the project was signed in 1986, although without much popular consultation or assessment of the environmental impact. Various compensation arrangements have been put in place for villagers whose homes, fields or grazing areas have been flooded, though not unexpectedly there are grumbles that these promises have not been met, or that resettlement plans are unsatisfactory. Meanwhile, the project marches inexorably forward, and it was no surprise that when South African peacekeeping forces entered Lesotho in 1998, one of their main priorities was to secure the dam.

The project's first phase, which concluded in 2004, was split into two phases. **Phase 1a**, completed in 1997, saw the construction of the 185-metre-high Katse Dam, an underground hydro-electric plant at 'Muela, tunnels to South African rivers, and all the road infrastructure. Bokong Nature Reserve and Ts'ehlanyane National Park were created as part of this phase, and facilities developed at Liphofung Cave, the idea being that local communities would benefit from tourism revenues. **Phase 1b** saw the construction of Mohale Dam on the Senqunyane River, linked to Katse reservoir by tunnel. **Subsequent phases** will see the construction of dams and tunnels at Mashai, south of Thaba-Tseka, Tsoelike and at Ntoahae. The whole thing should be finished some time in the 2020s.

Katse, Mohale and 'Muela each have visitor centres, though for guided tours of the installations it's best to book ahead at the **LHDA Information Centre** in the AgricBank Building on Kingsway in Maseru (Mon–Fri 8am–5pm; ☎ & ℱ 2232 1934, ⓦ www.lhwp .org.ls). Tours are free at present, though fees are likely to be charged in future.

Bokong Nature Reserve in the south (see below), with swimming possible in streams along the way.

The park's **visitor centre** has a picnic site, horses for hire (minimum age 12; M25 per hour, M75 per day) and guides (M30 per day). **Accommodation** (all ➊) is either at a guesthouse or in stone rondavels near the visitor centre, or at various campsites throughout the park. If you don't have a tent, the park may be able to provide you with one if you book ahead. Advance booking for ponies and rondavels is recommended; visit the LHDA's information centre in Maseru (see box opposite), or contact the Booking Officer, LHDA Nature Reserves, PO Box 333 Butha-Buthe 400 ☎2246 0723, Ⓔnature@lhda.org.ls.

Hlotse to the Bokong Nature Reserve

The A8 begins at Hlotse, from where it's a speedy, unexciting run through the lowlands to dreary **Pitseng**. After Pitseng, just before the road starts to ascend steeply, there's a police barrier. If you're in a private car, an official will probably ask you to stop and may pry further about where you're going and what you've got in your boot (diamond-smuggling is a special worry). From here the road climbs to 3090m at the **Mafika Lisiu Pass** in under 30km – a punishing journey for most cars. Thanks to some remarkable engineering, the road twists and turns around the mountains, sometimes cutting through them, sometimes leaving you suspended over terrifyingly long drops. There are plenty of places to stop and take in the view, though there have been reports recently of thefts (in some cases armed) from tourists who have done just that, so look out if you stop, and keep your vehicle in view at all times.

Beyond Mafika Lisiu Pass the road weaves through the high-altitude hikers' paradise of **Bokong Nature Reserve**. The rugged reserve protects extensive Afro-alpine wetlands at the sources of the Bokong and Lepaqoa rivers, plus montane grassland and patches of heathland boulder beds, both of which are regular haunts for Vaal rhebuck; keep an eye out for bearded vultures overhead. The reserve's highlight, however, is the dramatic **Lepaqoa Waterfall**, which freezes in winter to form a column of ice.

The reserve's **entrance** is next to the **visitors' centre**, signposted left off the highway 1km beyond the Mafika Lisiu Pass (daily 8am–5pm; ☎2246 0723 or 2291 3206; M5). Perched dramatically on the edge of a 100m cliff overlooking the Lepaqoa valley, the visitor centre has a picnic site and 45-minute interpretative trail (M10) to the top of the Lepaqoa Falls, as well as guides (M20 per day) and horses (M25 per hour, M75 per day; minimum age 12) for hire. Particularly recommended is a possible two- to three-day hike along the alpine plateau to Ts'ehlanyane National Park to the north. **Camping** is possible throughout the reserve, and there are also two stone-and-thatch **rondavels** (➋) close to the falls, sharing bathrooms and kitchenettes. Advance booking for ponies and rondavels is recommended; visit the LHDA's information centre in Maseru (see box opposite) or contact the Booking Officer, LHDA Nature Reserves, PO Box 333 Butha-Buthe 400, ☎2246 0723, Ⓔnature@lhda.org.ls. The reserve can be reached from Hlotse on **minibuses** running roughly every two hours towards Katse.

Katse and the dam

After Bokong, the road descends to the northern shore of the massive **Katse Reservoir** and the small village of **HA LEJONE**. Though signposted as if it offers accommodation, *Marmeso Lodge* is in fact just a good bar with a pool table; customers are likely to offer you illicit diamonds, which you're advised not to buy. From Ha Lejone, the road follows the reservoir, passing the unmissable **Intake Tower**, which marks the point where the long tunnel carrying water to 'Muela begins, and then crossing the water on the impressive **Malibamatso Bridge**. From here, the road climbs once more, reaching 2600m at the **Laitsoka Pass**, then descends to the small village of **Seshote**, then climbs again to the **Nkaobee Pass** (2510m), and finally descends to pass below the dam wall and reach the now burgeoning town of Katse.

KATSE town itself is drab and boring, with uniform box-like houses arranged in an uninspired suburban manner. But the massive dam, which holds back nearly two billion cubic metres of water, really is impressive, even if you aren't usually interested in engineering. To find out more, head for the cream-coloured **visitor centre** (Mon–Fri 8am–noon & 1–4pm, Sat & Sun 8am–noon; ☎2291 0808), just before the town and dam. Aim to get there for 9am or 2pm to catch the free daily **tours** of the facility. These start with a short video about the project and a demonstration of a rather bewildering relief model showing how water will be moved around the highlands when (or if) the whole scheme is complete; you're then taken on a guided tour of the amazing network of tunnels in the dam wall itself. The wall is 185m high, 710m wide, and up to 60m thick; it curves inwards for extra strength to such a degree that when you look down from the top, you can't see the rest of the wall, giving one the uneasy illusion of being suspended in space. During initial excavations it was discovered that the bedrock was seismically unstable, so a moveable joint was incorporated into the dam's base, allowing it to flex. Even so, the rapid filling of the reservoir caused a series of minor **earth tremors**. This was all to be expected, said the engineers, but not by the inhabitants of Ha Mapaleng, where a tremor ripped a 30cm-wide, 1.5km-long gash through the village. The local prophetess explained that a huge **underground snake** had been disturbed by the dam's construction and that the entire village would be gobbled up. No one hung around to find out, and the village was eventually relocated 1km away.

Nearby attractions include a **botanical garden** (free), something of a refugee camp for thousands of critically endangered spiral aloes rescued from the construction sites – the plan appears to be to secure the species' survival as a house plant rather than in the wild. A half-hour walk south of the visitor centre along the Thaba-Tseka road is the **Khohlo-Ntso Pony Trekking Association** (Mon–Wed; call for opening times on ☎2291 0808), offering a range of horseback trips from quick two-hour jaunts to Chief Katse's erstwhile homestead (M70 per person) to an adventurous three-night trip (M770) to Kolberg, Khochane, Mount Manyofane and rock paintings at Khohlo-Ntso.

The only **place to stay** is the *Katse Lodge* (☎2291 0202; ❷ including breakfast), with functional, well-kept rooms, two self-catering flats and dorms offering fine views of the reservoir and its impressive birdlife, and a surprisingly good restaurant serving a decent selection of inexpensive meals. The lodge is small, so book ahead. Camping is also possible. **Moving on**, there's a steady stream of private vehicles and minibuses along the dirt road from Katse to Thaba-Tseka, so you should be able to find something, though rarely after 2pm.

Butha-Buthe to Sani

The road from **Butha-Buthe** to the South African border at **Sani** is the most popular route into the Lesotho Highlands and travels through some of the highest and most dramatic terrain in the country. Though there's not much to do in Butha-Buthe itself except stock up for the journey, there are several attractions along the way, including particularly fine **San rock art** at Lipho-fung Cave, **'Muela Dam** and its underground hydro-electric power station, and winter **skiing** near Oxbow. Attractions apart, this is a journey which needs no justification other than the pleasure of travelling itself, and those fond of getting off the beaten track will love the bleak, tundra-like surroundings of **Mokhotlong**, once known as the "loneliest settlement in Africa" and still no great metropolis.

Butha-Buthe and around

Not far from the Caledonspoort **border post** (6am–10pm), the last major town before the highlands, **BUTHA-BUTHE** (or Botha-Bothe, meaning "Lie Down") has a frontier feel – noisy, dirty and dusty – and offers little reason to stay. The main road is clustered with takeaway restaurants and stores, and the pavements filled with highlanders on monthly shopping trips. The town was founded in 1884 because the local chief refused to go to Hlotse to pay taxes, necessitating a new tax centre nearer his residence. Butha-Buthe attracted traders from the outset, and is one of few towns in Lesotho with a sizeable Indian community.

Butha-Buthe Mountain, just east of town, is where Moshoeshoe I had his first stronghold before retreating to Thaba Bosiu in 1824. It's a stiff but not particularly difficult climb – which was one of the reasons why the king felt obliged to move. The summit provides tremendous views of the surrounding area. You can cut the hiking distance by catching a minibus as far as Ha Mopeli.

Practicalities

Buses from Bloemfontein and Johannesburg stop at the border, but there's absolutely no shortage of **public transport** in Butha-Buthe itself, which congregates at the market in the centre of town, together with most of the town's youthful **hustlers** – take care with your bags when disembarking. There are frequent buses and minibuses to Maseru, Katse, and two or three a day to Mokhotlong.

The only central **accommodation** is the run-down *Crocodile Inn* (☎2246 0223, ☏2246 0506; ❷) next to the hospital, signposted off the main road on the left as you come in from the south. The hotel offers large rooms with good beds but flea-infested carpets, and better (if smaller) rooms in rondavels; unfortunately, it suffers from frequent water shortages – not that that bothers the dedicated drinkers who occupy its two bars until well into the morning. **Food** at the restaurant is inexpensive but unimpressive and pretty slow in coming. Better is the grub at the Total garage on the main road, next to the turning. More pleasant, but tricky to get to, is the self-catering *Butha-Buthe Youth Hostel* (☎2246 0024; ❶), also known as *Ramakantane's*, 3.5km from town in the village of Ha Sechele. This IYHF-accredited hostel is pretty basic and lacks electricity (there's gas instead for lighting and cooking), but the management is friendly and it's a good place to meet Basotho villagers and hike into the nearby hills. Unless you have a high-clearance vehicle, the only access is on foot: coming from town head up towards the Mokhotlong/Caledonspoort junction and turn right 100m before it at the "Keep Lesotho Beautiful" sign, from where it's an hour's walk.

'Muela, Oxbow and the Moteng Pass

Heading northeast from Butha-Buthe, the roads begins to climb into the Maloti Mountains. After seven kilometres, a turn-off leads to the **Sekubu Caves**, another 9km down a dirt track, but worth a look if you have the time and a vehicle. Ask at one of Sekubu's schools for a guide to show you the caves' quite good **rock paintings** and rather faint **dinosaur footprints**. The last fuel before Oxbow is at *Cindi Lodge & Supermarket* (☎ 2246 0616; ●), on the highway 14km from Butha-Buthe. Despite the lodge's rough appearance, the rooms here are perfectly adequate, if basic, and there's a bar with a pool table and two restaurants, one serving Basotho food and the other, decorated exclusively with mirrors, serving steaks and chops.

Six kilometres further on, immediately after the small settlement of Khukhune, a good tar road on the right leads up to **'MUELA**, an integral part of the Lesotho Highlands Water Project (see box on p.790). Here the water flowing down the delivery tunnel from Katse Reservoir powers an underground hydro-electric station which now supplies all of Lesotho with electricity, as well as providing a small surplus which is sold to South Africa – benefitting the mountain kingdom to the tune of something like thirty million rand a year. At **'Muela Dam**, water enters a second delivery tunnel, which empties into the Ash River near Clarens, 37km away in South Africa (and this in turn feeds the Vaal Dam, source of Gauteng's water supply). The reservoir is small and there's not a great deal to see, although the view of the surrounding mountains is worth pausing to admire. The real attraction, however, lies underground, and there are free **tours** of the power plant daily at 9am and 2pm from the **visitor centre** (☎ & ⓕ 2248 1212) in the huge operations building beside the *'Muela Lodge*. The attractive **lodge** itself overlooks the dam and offers drinks, meal and pleasant rondavels (book through visitor centre; ●).

Five kilometres beyond the 'Muela turn-off is the signposted **Liphofung Cave** (Mon–Fri 8.30am–4.30pm, Sat & Sun 9am–4.30pm; M15), actually a large sandstone overhang resembling a petrified wave and boasting a series of San **rock paintings**, from whose images it gets its name, "Place of the Eland". To avoid damaging the rock art, you're obliged to tour the site with a guide. The site is also significant for the Basotho in its role as a hideout for the young Moshoeshoe I. The **visitor centre** has displays of Basotho culture in three traditional huts, plus a small rock art museum, and there's also a craft shop, traditional meals available on request, and ponies for hire (M25 per hour, M75 per day). You can **stay** at the campsite or in a couple of rondavels (●) sleeping four people each; homestays in the nearby village can also be arranged. Advance booking for the ponies and rondavels is recommended; visit the LHDA's information centre in Maseru (see box on p.790), or contact the Booking Officer, LHDA Nature Reserves, PO Box 333 Butha-Buthe 400 ☎ 2246 0723, ⓔ nature@lhda.org.ls.

The A1 from here into the highlands is one of the most dramatic roads in Lesotho, passing through some particularly striking sandstone cliffs before twisting torturously up a chain of heart-stopping hairpins into the basalt. Some 20km beyond Liphofung, past **Moteng Pass** (2820m) and a number of stunning ravines – any of which would make for perfect hiking – you come to a string of unremarkable alpine-style buildings in a narrow valley. Popular with South Africans, *New Oxbow Lodge* (☏051 933 2247, ⓦwww.oxbow .co.za; half-board ❹) has perfectly comfortable, warm rooms, plus camping facilities, a well-stocked bar, and a restaurant serving reasonably priced meals. There's good trout fishing on the Malibamatso River, which flows between the lodge and the road, and wonderful hiking in any direction. If you're coming in winter, check with the lodge about the state of the road on to Mokhotlong, as ice and snow can block it for days at a time. Temperatures here can sometimes drop to below -20°C, so come prepared, and bring enough money to last if you get snowbound. The lodge is also the last place you can buy **fuel** before Mokhotlong.

Between June and August, there's a good chance of **skiing** 11km beyond Oxbow in a wide basin below Mahlasela Pass (3220m). Extravagant plans for a large development with proper lifts and chalets are occasionally mooted, but for the time being the runs are short (1.5–2km) and the tows primitive – most visitors who venture this far in winter are South Africans who are simply intrigued to see snow. The *New Oxbow Lodge* rents skis for around M100 a day.

The road to Mokhotlong is often called "the Roof of Africa route", crossing a succession of ever higher passes, peaking at **Tlaeeng Pass** (3270m), and passing through bleak, sparsely populated but entrancing mountain countryside. The road is tarred all the way to Mokhotlong, although the extremes of temperature here have caused the road to break in places. For those who are adequately equipped, the area is tremendous hiking country, and you'll find the hardy locals who eke out a living here among the most hospitable in the country. About 40km from Tlaeeng Pass, the descent to Mokhotlong begins. Most transport stops at the small village of **Mapholaneng**, where there's a reasonable restaurant (the *Thugela*) and a trio of well-stocked bars, one of which claims to be a nightclub. From here it's only 30km to Mokhotlong as the crow flies, though twists and turns in the road extend the journey to around 50km.

Mokhotlong

Perched on the banks of the scraggly Mokhotlong River, the cold, windblown and unremittingly bleak town of **MOKHOTLONG** ("Place of the Bald Ibis" – their nests are given away by guano streaks on the cliffs) lies at the end of the tarmac, and is the kind of place that will either instantly charm or alarm those who travel this far. Mokhotlong was once known as the "Loneliest Place in Africa", and it's easy to see why, since even with the tarmac road it still gets cut off from the rest of civilization for days or weeks at a time in winter.

Mokhotlong began life as a remote police outpost in 1905, and gradually evolved into a trading centre for the region's highlanders, but remained isolated from the rest of Lesotho for years, with radio contact only established in 1947. An airstrip was constructed in 1948 and a rudimentary road link built in the 1950s, but Mokhotlong continued to get the bulk of its supplies by pony from Natal, via Sani, for a long time afterwards. Even today it feels remote, with locals usually riding into town for a shop and a drink on ponies, resplendent in their gumboots and blankets. And somehow even the handful of Chinese immigrants who run the town's groceries seem to fit, with images of Mongolia and Tibet coming to mind.

Not much happens in town, which is dominated by hurriedly built and decidedly plain breeze-block buildings that compare unfavourably with the immaculately constructed dry-stone-walled dwellings in the surrounding countryside. There's not much to do other than meet and greet the friendly locals, admire their ponies and uncommonly winsome Merino sheep, or buy some decent music cassettes from Mamolibeli Music Shop at the town's southwestern edge near the *Senqu Hotel* – there's no sign; just follow your ears.

Practicalities

Getting to Mokhotlong is easiest on the daily 6.30am **bus from Maseru**, operated on alternate days by Lesotho Freight and Bus Services and Itumeleng Transport. The journey takes at least eight hours. There are also up to three **minibus taxis** a day from Butha-Buthe. Local **taxi cabs** (M20 a ride) cruise up and down the town's single street touting for business, and are handy for getting from the central bus and taxi stop to the lodges.

Onward transport from Mokhotlong is limited to roughly hourly minibuses to Ha Janteau, passing by the *Molumong Lodge* (see below), and a handful of minibuses to Sani and the border whenever the road is passable, leaving around 5am. Heading back to the lowlands, the bus to Maseru leaves at 8am, and the minibuses to Butha-Buthe between 7am and around 2pm. There's nothing at all running to Thaba-Tseka, so hitching is the only option; ask at the lodges if someone's heading that way, or – in summer – wait at the junction 500m beyond the *Sanqu Hotel*. Alternatively, get out to the *Molumong Lodge*: at least you'll have somewhere nice to stay if you don't find a lift.

Meals in Mokhotlong are expensive and frugal. But don't be too critical – it's amazing what the locals can rustle up using just canned food. The best meals, available throughout the day and evening, are at the *Senqu Hotel*. The restaurant at the *Mokhotlong Hotel* (lunch and dinner only) boasts an impressive menu, but generally only has a pricey set menu available, and the distinction between fried and carbonized is blurred. Much better is its **public bar**, whose TV makes it popular with hardy and definitely colourful locals, who hitch their ponies outside. There's also a private bar for guests only. There's a similar set-up at the *Senqu Hotel*, which also has a TV and pool table. In summer, try the cavernous *Thabana-Ntlenyana Bar* along the road to *Senqu Hotel*, busy on Friday and Saturday nights.

Accommodation

Farmers' Training Centre 2km east of town beyond the hospital ☎2292 0235. A friendly place with camping facilities and dorms, but limited bedding. There's hot water if they're running a course, but no kitchen. There's no sign; it's the building with a bright-red roof. ❶
Mokhotlong Hotel 1.5km east of town opposite the hospital ☎2292 0212. Rooms in the new wing at the back are the best in town, with bathrooms (and bathtubs with enough hot water to fill them), TVs and great mountain views. Those in the old wing are plain and average, and the cheaper ones share bathrooms. Also has

two bars and a restaurant. Old wing ❶, new wing ❷
Molumong Guest House 17km southwest of town along the dirt road to Thaba-Tseka, 7km off the Sani road (minibuses to Ha Janteau pass by) ☎083 254 3323, ✉molumong@worldonline.co.za. Pronounced "moo-doo-mong", this is the remotest of Lesotho's tourist lodges, a rustic but characterful 1920s place with fantastic mountain views just beyond Ha Rafolatsane village (not Molumong, which is further on). The main house is self-catering, with very cosy doubles and a great lounge to relax in, and there's also a

bunkhouse in one of the sheds, plus a campsite. Meals can be arranged in advance, but there are virtually no supplies in the village so you have to bring everything in. The lodge also offers inexpensive pony-trekking, and is a good base for hiking. ❶

Senqu Hotel 4km southwest of the taxi rank ☎2292 0330. The first hotel you come to as you enter town, with small and rather wonky rooms off poky corridors (eight new en-suite rooms with TV are being built), lots of hot water for the bathtubs, friendly staff, two bars and a decent restaurant. ❷

Sani and around

Branching off the Mokhotlong road 5km before the town, the rough gravel road to **SANI** twists its way in spectacular fashion for nearly 60km along the Sehonkong River, peaking at **Kotisephola Pass** (3240m) before dropping to 2895m at **Sani Top**, a few kilometres from the South African border. There are plenty of rewarding hikes from here, including a stiff 12km climb up **Thabana Ntlenyana**, at 3482m the highest point in southern Africa and walkable in a day if you start early. Also tough but stunningly beautiful is the 40km **Top-of-the-Berg** hike to Sehlabathebe National Park, which takes about four days.

Although the descent from Sani, down the dramatic, hairpin-bend-filled **Sani Pass** into South Africa, is just about possible in an ordinary car, you'd be much better off with a 4WD, while the ascent of the pass is definitely not recommended without one. An ordinary saloon car *could* make it up, but requires the rare collusion of perfect, dry conditions and a good driver. In winter, the pass is frequently blocked by snow or ice, and rain can render it very slippery in summer, so ring the chalet (see below) to check conditions.

Practicalities

Getting to Sani is only possible in good weather; if it's been snowing, you can forget it – or else hope for the snow to melt, which can take two or three days after the last snowfall. **Public transport** to Sani on the Lesotho side comprises a trio of packed minibus taxis running from Mokhotlong to the border, leaving Mokhotlong around 5am, and returning in the afternoon. There are similarly packed minibuses from Underberg in **South Africa** to the border. More comfortable would be to join a 4WD **tourist vehicle** up the Sani Pass. Try Sani Pass Carriers in Himeville (☎033/701 1017; Mon–Sat 1–2 daily), which runs from Pietermaritzburg and Kokstad (connecting with the Baz Bus), and also picks up punters in Durban's backpackers three times a week (around R100). Expect to pay R50 for the leg from Underberg or Himeville to the *Sani Top Chalet* (see below), who can also arrange transport. Alternatively, contact Thaba Tours (see box on p.769), which may have a spare seat on their twice-weekly tours from Durban. Hitching shouldn't be too difficult, seeing as Mokhotlong's few stores tend to stock up in KwaZulu-Natal. The **border**, between *Sani Top Chalet* and Sani Pass, is open daily from 8am to 4pm.

There are several **accommodation** options on the South African side (see p.524). In Lesotho, the only place is the deservedly popular *Sani Top Chalet* (☎033 702 1069, ⓦ www.sanitopchalet.co.za; camping and dorms ❶, rooms half board ❸), which makes much of its claim to be the highest **pub** in Africa, at 2874m above sea level. The cliff-edge setting is superb, with awesome views into KwaZulu-Natal, and there's also hearty food on offer, while in the evenings you can drink in front of the fire or sit on the balcony and watch the sun set over the mountaintops. The rooms themselves – whether in the main building or the dorm – are simple and sometimes chilly, but have cosy fireplaces to huddle around; bathrooms are shared. Skis and boots can be rented in winter if there's enough snow; at other times you can go on overnight pony-treks.

The southern districts

The country's **southern districts** can't match the mountains of north and central Lesotho for sheer scale, but they do hold some dramatic countryside which is relatively easy to visit – especially on horseback from the excellent tourist lodges at **Malealea** and **Semonkong**, both of which are close to a series of spectacular waterfalls. Some of the region's small towns are based around nineteenth-century missions, of which **Morija** is the most historic. Morija also has dinosaur footprints in the vicinity, as do **Mohale's Hoek** and, more accessibly, **Quthing**, further south. Moving on northeast past the town of **Qacha's Nek**, the isolated delights of **Sehlabathebe National Park** are so remote as to make visits here a true adventure.

Morija to Malealea

The main road south from Maseru, past the international airport and Qeme Plateau (see p.778), soon takes you to historic **Morija**, with its small cluster of mid-nineteenth-century buildings and museum. A further 45km away, along increasingly scenic roads, the easy-going and smoothly run lodge at **Malealea** is the most attractive – if busiest – in Lesotho. Set amid wonderful countryside, it's a perfect spot for hiking and well-organized pony-trekking in wind-carved sandstone hills.

Morija

Set at the foot of the Makhoarane Plateau 44km from Maseru, the pleasant little town of **MORIJA** houses the country's main museum and Lesotho's oldest building, church and printing press. The town was established in 1833 at Moshoeshoe I's behest as the country's first Christian mission, and granted to three missionaries of the Paris Evangelical Missionary Society (PEMS), who gave the place the name that Abraham bestowed on the mountain where he was reprieved from killing his son by God (it means "God will Provide").

The large, red-brick **mission church**, with its impressive teak-beamed roof, is almost always open. Begun in 1847, this is the third church built on the site, using the labour of Pedi economic migrants on their way to Cape Colony, though its tall steeple was only built in 1905. You have to make special arrangements to get in to see the historic **printing works** nearby, which have produced Basotho literature since the 1860s as well as the country's oldest newspaper, *Leselinyana la Lesotho* (Little Light of Lesotho), which has been in almost continual publication since 1863.

Most of Morija was razed to the ground by Afrikaner troops in 1858, and almost the only building left standing was **Maeder House**, in the church grounds, built in 1843. Today, this simple stone house contains a couple of small **craft shops** (both Mon–Sat 9am–5pm, Sun 2–5pm) selling inexpensive Basotho hats, dolls, carvings, tapestries and batiks. Close by, just uphill, the **Morija Museum and Archives** (Mon–Sat 8am–5pm, Sun noon–5pm; ☎2236 0308, ⓦwww.morijafest.com; M6) is an excellent reason for coming to town, and also doubles as the town's tourist information centre. The exhibits are a stimulating combination of geological and fossil finds, ethnographic material and historic items connected with Moshoeshoe and his contemporaries, plus a useful commentary on Lesotho's history and modern–day political issues. The geological and fossil displays are a bit dry (though the dinosaur exhibits are striking), but you should find something of interest among the ethnographic and historical items, including a succession of treaties broken by the British, Moshoeshoe's china tea set, and a *khau*, the beautiful V-shaped neck ornament awarded to brave Basotho soldiers. The museum also sells a *Guide to Morija* (M12), a booklet which tells you everything you could possibly want to know about the town, including pointers to nearby sites of interest, plus a superb introduction to Basotho music by Robin E. Wells and several nineteenth-century historical and ethnographical accounts.

In the first week of October the museum organizes the **Morija Arts and Cultural Festival** (ⓦ www.morijafest.com), the largest and most significant event of its kind in the country, where traditional music, dancing, horse races and crafts mix with theatre, cinema, sport and children's events.

Practicalities

Getting to Morija is easy, with buses and minibuses running throughout the day from Maseru. There's no bus or taxi rank; most transport drops you outside the post office close to the museum, while buses heading on to Mafeteng and Mohale's Hoek will probably drop you on the highway 1km west of the centre.

Dongas and soil erosion in Lesotho

One thing you'll quickly notice about Lesotho is that the entire country is virtually treeless, with the exception of the invasive and water-hungry eucalyptus and the peach trees introduced by French missionaries a century ago. Indeed, the country – once the grain basket of the region – is in deep ecological trouble, and acres of irreplaceable topsoil, loosened by decades of over-farming, are washed away down its rivers each year.

Yet during the nineteenth century the kingdom exported food to the neighbouring Orange Free State (OFS) and to Kimberley and the Rand to feed the thousands of diamond- and gold-mine workers. The problems began with the expropriation of the best land by the OFS in the 1860s, which forced the Basotho to start farming hilly areas that had previously only been used for winter grazing. This process continues to this day, and you will even see crops being grown at over 2000m in districts like Semonkong and Mokhotlong. Mountains are no substitute for fertile plains, however, and Lesotho has been a net importer of food since the 1920s.

The ecological effect of the sustained and unrelenting cultivation of the Lesotho mountains has been devastating. The soil fertility has plummeted and, more seriously, huge quantities of topsoil are simply washed away in each summer's rains, nowadays ending up as silt in Katse and Mohale reservoirs. In many places so much topsoil has gone that great ravines called **dongas** have opened up. Though they often look green enough, the remaining soil tends to lie close to the surface rock, making it useless for serious cultivation.

Efforts to slow this process have been under way for some time, most noticeably through the terracing of hillside fields, with layers of grass interspersed with crops to prevent the soil being washed away. For one of the best examples of how simply *dongas* can be reclaimed using the terracing method, ask to be shown the way to the Musi family *donga* in the village beside the *Malealea Lodge* (see p.800) – reclamation of the *donga* began almost two decades ago by Fanuel Musi, and is now carried on by his grandson and wife. The *donga* is easy to spot – on a hillside of degraded cropland and bare earth, it's an oasis of fertility, lush greenness and birdlife.

Run by the museum is one of Lesotho's most attractive **lodgings**, the delightful self-catering *Morija Guest House* (also called *Ha Matela*; ☎5885 9211, Ⓔ guesthouse@morijafest.com; ❷), set in a dramatic spot right at the top of town on the way to the Makhoarane Plateau. The large and gloriously decorated thatched house contains several comfortable rooms, including a couple of romantic loft conversions, plus a fully equipped kitchen, lounge, and a large verandah with fantastic views over the surrounding area and sunsets; it's best to reserve ahead to be sure of a room. Meals can be provided by prior arrangement with the museum. You can also stay in a couple of simpler Basotho cottages below the guesthouse (❶), also run by the museum. The museum's tea shop (Mon–Sat 9am–4.30pm, Sun 2–4.30pm) offers cold drinks and simple Basotho **meals**. Alternatively, the lady next to the nameless store opposite the post office rustles up excellent cheap meals for a very modest M12. The museum also has **Internet access** (M10 for 10min).

Pony treks can be arranged through the *Morija Guest House* or museum, ranging from one-hour jaunts (M40) to two-day trips (price negotiable) – sadly not long enough to hook up with other pony-trekking centres. An **overnight walk**, sleeping in a mountain hut, costs around M200 per person (all meals included) plus M150 per day for the guide. The best of various **walking trails** from Morija leads to an impressive sets of avian dinosaur footprints on one side of a large rock halfway up the Makhoarane Plateau, 45 minutes beyond the guesthouse – the rock is known locally as *Nonyona oa Makhoarane*, the Giant Bird of Makhoarane Mountain. Ask for directions at the museum or the guesthouse. Guides are available for these walks; there are no fixed prices.

Malealea

A further 10km south of Morija you come to a dip in the road and the bustling minibus taxi stop at **Motsekuoa**, which marks the turning for the village of **MALEALEA**, one of the best-known places in Lesotho thanks to the hugely popular *Malealea Lodge* (☎051 447 3200, Ⓦ www.malealea.co.ls; camping and forest huts ❶, Basotho huts and doubles ❷, rondavels ❸). Set in a spectacular spot in the foothills of the Thaba Putsoa range, the lodge was originally a trading store established by the British adventurer Mervyn Bosworth-Smith in 1905, though it's a little less isolated these days thanks to the tar road which runs most of the way. It was Bosworth-Smith who wrote the words on the brass plaque at the top of the magnificent Gate of Paradise Pass, 6km before the lodge: "Wayfarer, pause and look upon a gateway of Paradise". The lodge has grown significantly from its trading store origins to incorporate a cluster of huts (for which you need your own bedding), houses and rondavels with both backpackers' dorms and decent doubles. Many visitors come to Malealea to hike, and the lodge has mapped out a series of trails, but the main activity is **pony-trekking** (see box opposite) – anything from a few hours to six days. The lodge is always a lively place; next to the dining room is a great little bar and most evenings guests congregate around an open fire outside, occasionally with a band of local children bashing out tunes on homemade instruments. *Malealea's* only downside is its popularity as a major stopover for package tours.

Getting to Malealea by **public transport** is easiest from Mafeteng, from where there's a daily mid-morning bus (it heads back from Malealea at 6am) via Motsekuoa. From Maseru (85km) or Morija (45km), leave early. First, catch a bus or minibus taxi along the A2 to Motsekuoa (any vehicle going to Mafeteng will pass by). If you get there before noon, you should be able to catch the daily bus from Mafeteng straight to Malealea. If you miss it, there's plenty of onward

The *Malealea Lodge* runs a series of **guided trips**, from short one-hour jaunts to as many days as your bottom and wallet can stand, with nights in basic huts equipped with gas cookers, kitchen utensils and floor mattresses. Trips can be arranged at short notice, and are tailored to your needs. **Costs** vary according to where you go and group size, but count on around M280–310 for a full day and night, including accommodation and food, or up to M200 for a day's trekking. Riders cannot weigh more than 90kg, and luggage is limited to 12.5kg, including food. A good and less pricey alternative to the pony-trekking (which can be quite hard on the body if you're not used to it) is simply **to walk** and use a pony as a pack animal. The pony can carry four people's packs, provided they're not excessively heavy.

Short trips include village walks and a consultation with a traditional healer (*sangoma*). Longer **day-trips**, either afoot or in the saddle, go to Botsoela Twin Waterfalls, Pitseng Canyon and its rock pool, San rock paintings, and the "Gates of Paradise Pass" along Matelile Ridge; you can also abseil and go on a day's river rafting along Makhaleng Gorge. An excellent two-day adventure is the journey to the **Ribaneng Falls**, which takes you through steep sandstone valleys and hills. The lodge ensures that there is an empty, well-kept rondavel with a gas cylinder in the village for your overnight stop, offering a rough-and-ready, but memorable, taste of life in the mountains. You'll need to take your own food and sleeping gear with you. With time for a four-day journey you could head east to the impressive **Ketane Falls** and back, travelling over some particularly beautiful mountains and through quiet, friendly villages. With six days to spare, you'll also get to see the **Semonkong Falls**.

transport to Matelile village, 8km from the lodge, from where any vehicle going to the lodge is likely to give you a lift. If you're coming straight from South Africa, enquire with the lodge when you make your booking about transport from Bloemfontein via Wepener and Van Rooyens Gate border crossing.

Mafeteng, Mohale's Hoek and Quthing

There's little to detain you between **Mafeteng** and **Quthing** apart from a few good walks in the surrounding sandstone hills, including some leading to interesting sets of **dinosaur footprints**. You'll also find the best meal for miles around at the *Hotel Mount Maluti* in **Mohale's Hoek**, where you can hire ponies to explore the **Mokhele mountain range** east of town. Mafeteng, Mohale's Hoek and Quthing are all within striking distance of the South African border, with Mafeteng the most practical for border crossings and with the most public transport.

Mafeteng and around

The bustling town of **MAFETENG**, 18km from Van Rooyenshek **border post** (daily 6am–10pm), will be the first place you come to in Lesotho if crossing from Wepener in the Free State. It means "the place of Lefeta's people", after the son of a French missionary Emile Rolland, who was the district's first magistrate and was nicknamed Lefeta, or "he who passes", by locals, who regarded him as virtually Basotho except for the fact that he skipped (or "passed by") initiation. Unfortunately, much of the town suffered in the 1998 riots, leaving the centre in quite a mess, but in any case the only building of interest in Mafeteng is the **council office** on the main street. It's worth a quick look for the carved animal heads studding its front wall, and a nice statue of a handlebar-moustached Cape Mounted Rifles soldier in the front garden.

There are two good nearby excursions, though you'll need your own transport. The **Luma Pan**, 3km from town, attracts a good selection of birdlife; head for Wepener and turn right down the first substantial dirt road you come to. About 20km east of Mafeteng, along a road that deteriorates past the village of Likhoele to the point that you're taking a risk in an ordinary saloon car, is the impressive **Thabana Morena Plateau**. Rising above the village of the same name, it rewards those who make the steep climb with good views of the Free State plains to the west and the Thaba Putsoa range to the east.

Practicalities

As befits a border town, Mafeteng has a very busy **bus station** where you can easily find transport north to Morija and Maseru, and southeast to Mohale's Hoek, Quthing and beyond. There are various small **places to eat** by the bus station and on the main street, but otherwise the best choice is in the hotels. For **accommodation**, the anonymous-looking *Golden Hotel* (☎2270 0566; ❷), to the right of the highway from Maseru, just before you enter Mafeteng proper, offers adequate rooms and a small dining room serving meat dishes. A better choice is the *Mafeteng Hotel* (☎2270 0236, ⓕ2270 0478; ❷), which looks like a 1960s airport control tower, but offers pleasant en-suite rooms, all with satellite TV, plus some cottages in a secluded garden and a good swimming pool. Their **restaurant** serves a limited range of moderately priced meat dishes and the owners can arrange pony rides in the vicinity. The hotel is on the south side of town, signposted off Main South Road.

Mafeteng's **nightlife** centres around the rather seedy, mirrored *Las Vegas* disco in the grounds of the *Mafeteng Hotel*, which blasts out soul and South African sounds until 4am on Friday and Saturday. Alternatively, the *Golden Hotel* sometimes has *famo* music – a loud and infectiously danceable local style with accordions, heavy drum beats and singing – on Saturday nights.

Mohale's Hoek

MOHALE'S HOEK, a short distance from the little-used Makhaleen Bridge **border post** (daily 8am–4pm) – handy if you're driving from Zastron in the southern Free State – is a rather bedraggled little town, but boasts one of the best hotels in the area and some interesting sites in the surrounding hills, including some well-preserved **dinosaur footprints**. Mohale was Moshoeshoe's younger brother, appointed to look after the area by the king as part of his bid to wrest control of the district from chief Moorosi. There are still quite a few of Moorosi's Baphuthi clan here, though, whose language is in some ways closer to Xhosa than Basotho.

If you desperately need to do some banking, you'll find the Standard and Nedbank **banks** more efficient than most banks outside Maseru, although changing money and traveller's cheques can still take a long time. Both banks are on the main street, which runs at right angles to the Mafeteng–Quthing road. Otherwise, there's nothing to see or do here apart from the excellent drive, walk or pony trek into the beautiful and little-visited **Mokhele Mountain Range** 10km east of town. Travel a short distance south on the main road to the little village of Mesitsaneng, and then head 7km east along a rough dirt track to the historic French **Maphutseng Mission**, in whose roof locals once hid from attacking Boers. Just before the mission, turn right down a smaller track and you'll see a plateau to the right a short walk away, where you'll find some **dinosaur footprints** and an inscription recording their "discovery" in 1959.

Practicalities

Buses arrive at the busy station in the centre of Mohale's Hoek, while **minibus taxis** congregate on the main street – between them and the buses you should be able to find transport heading both north and south throughout the day. As usual, there are also plenty of inexpensive **places to eat** on the main street.

For **accommodation**, the place to go is the *Hotel Mount Maluti* (T 2278 5224, F 2278 5341; ❷), which has comfortable rooms with TVs, plus a bar, tennis court, swimming pool, small garden, and a small but pleasant **campsite**. The highlight is the hotel **restaurant**, which offers decent cuisine, even for vegetarians, and superb home-baked bread, all at reasonable prices. The European family who have owned and occupied the hotel since the 1950s can offer advice about what to see and do in the area, as well as arranging inexpensive pony treks and guides. They have also plotted an adventurous 4WD route through the southern highland region, though the closest 4WDs for rent are in Maseru (see "Listings" on p.777).

Quthing and around

QUTHING, also known as **Moyeni** ("Place of the Wind"), is a curious split-level town established by the British after the Gun War in 1884. The town itself is messy, though it has an attractive setting beside a river gorge, with views of the surrounding hills improving as you climb to the upper part of town. This was the colonial centre, and is home to the police station, post office, a large hospital and one or two pretty useless banks, while the busier lower half has most of the shops and fuel stations and is the arrival and departure point for public transport. During the day there are always plenty of **buses** and **minibus taxis** north towards Maseru, and much more infrequent services northeast towards Qacha's Nek (including a daily 10am Lesotho Freight and Bus Services/Flame Transport bus from Maseru), as well as one or two heading for the nearby Tele Bridge **border post** (daily 6am–10pm), where you can pick up transport to Sterkspruit in the Eastern Cape.

The most accessible **dinosaur footprints** in Lesotho are very near the western side of the lower section of Quthing. Just continue a short distance up Main Road from the Quthing turn and look out for the simple **visitor centre** (daily 8am–4pm), an orange thatched building beside the road on the left. The man who works there will direct you towards the variety of clearly discernible prints in the hope of a small tip.

Also worth a visit is **Masitise Cave House**, set in a small nature reserve a few kilometres west of Quthing to the right of the main road. Follow signs to Masitise primary and high schools and ask at the high school for someone to show you the house, built into a cave by the missionary D.F. Ellenberger in 1866. The cave house was recently converted into a **museum** by the tireless folks at Morija Museum (☎5879 4167, ✉info@morijafest.com), and is the place for arranging overnight accommodation with locals and for hiring guides to explore the area. The museum's exhibits trace Lesotho's history and culture (Ellenberger's *History of the Basuto: Ancient & Modern*, published 1912, was the first study of its kind, and also covers paleontology – on which Ellenberger's descendants became experts – including dinosaur remains and other fossils. Nearby are some much-vandalized and greatly faded **rock paintings**; ask at the museum for directions. Between Masitise and the town centre is the pretty sandstone **Villa Maria Mission**, with its twin red spires.

The Villa Maria Mission (☎2275 0364; ❶) has inexpensive **accommodation**, with clean rooms and communal bathrooms set in the grounds. In town, halfway between upper and lower Quthing, the intimate *Mountain Side Hotel* (☎2275 0257; ❷) has mostly adequate rooms (check the mattress), half of which overlook the street, while the others are more secluded and quiet. There's a pleasant and cosy private bar, a friendly public one and a good **restaurant** with a tasty fixed menu that normally has something for vegetarians.

Mount Moorosi, Qacha's Nek and Sehlabathebe National Park

A far less-used route into the highlands than the northern road to Mokhotlong, the mountain road from **Mount Moorosi to Sehlabathebe** is ruggedly beautiful, and has the added bonus of the mighty Senqu (Orange) River winding majestically alongside much of it. If the Katse dam builders have their way, the Senqu will in a few years be much reduced, but for now the chocolate-brown river is normally in full flood, in winter at least. Highlights along the route include **Thaba Moorosi**, the mountain where the outlawed chief Moorosi made his last stand against the British in 1879, and the remote, pristine national park of **Sehlabathebe** – perfect for fishing, bird-watching and mile-upon-mile of isolated hiking.

Mount Moorosi and around

Just over 40km beyond Quthing, along a decent tar road with fine views of the mountains and glimpses of the mighty Senqu River, the small town of **MOUNT MOOROSI** clings to the mountainside and provides inhabitants of various local villages with a minibus taxi stop and shopping. The largest institution is Mitchell's Trading Store, which serves as the town's main store, garage and fuel station. Ask here if you want to park your car in the compound, where it should be safe, before taking the ferry across the Senqu to Bethel (see opposite).

Mount Moorosi is named after a chief who moved to the region in the 1850s, living in the cliffs around the town. He was an ally of the San and had several San wives, but made an enemy of the British in the 1870s. British troops attacked his stronghold in 1879, but he held out for eight months until soldiers used scaling ladders on the steep cliffs and finally captured him, after which they cut off and publicly displayed his severed head. **Thaba Moorosi**, where the main battle took place, is a kilometre or so further along the main road on the right. The site is marked by some stone slabs in which British soldiers sent to catch the chief engraved their names. It's quite a tricky climb, though, so be sure to let someone in Mount Moorosi know where you are going.

Bethel

On the other side of the Senqu River from Mount Moorosi is the village of **BETHEL**, where there's a large, rather neglected mission church and the much more proactive **Bethel Business and Community Development Centre** (℡5891 1711, ⓦwww.lesoff.co.za/bbcdc), an innovative training centre which teaches locals practical skills in solar technology, permaculture and market gardening. The centre is a thriving advertisement for the principles it expounds, with healthy crop fields and vegetable patches, rows of trees, well-designed buildings and solar power used for everything from hot water to a satellite phone link-up for email. Facilities include a self-catering guest flat and **dormitories** (❶); meals are available if arranged beforehand. Short-term visitors are welcome, but if you would like to stay longer – people willing to share their own knowledge of sustainable development are particularly encouraged – contact them as far in advance as you can.

To get to Bethel, walk or catch a **minibus** from Mount Moorosi for two kilometres to the ferry point on the Senqu River, below the towering cliffs of Thaba Moorosi. There are hopes that a road crossing will be built, but meanwhile the rowing-boat crossing of the fast-flowing river is worth experiencing. Once on the other side, it's a further four-kilometre walk to the mission. If you have a 4WD vehicle, an alternative to crossing by ferry is a two-hour drive along a route that leaves the tarred road on the western side of the bridge over the Senqu, between Quthing and Mohale's Hoek.

Mphaki and around

Shortly after rounding Thaba Moorosi, the main road leaves the Senqu River and heads swiftly into the highlands through the impressive **Quthing Gorge**, peaking after about 10km at the **Lebelonyane Pass** (2456m), with superb views. The road carries on through a series of attractive high-altitude valleys, before reaching the small village of **MPHAKI**, which has excellent accommodation at its *Farmers' Training Centre* (no phone; ❶), with well-equipped self-catering rondavels and a pleasant guesthouse. If you don't fancy self-catering, the *Motsekuoa Liquor Restaurant* opposite the centre provides inexpensive and tasty Basotho **food**, and also has a good bar. The tarred road continues for another 10km out of Mphaki, where it reverts to decent gravel.

Qacha's Nek

Some 34km east of Mphaki at **Sekake**, the road rejoins the southern banks of the Senqu, but deteriorates significantly in quality, though you can still make it with care in an ordinary vehicle. It's a beautiful, undulating drive, among the loveliest in Lesotho, though once you reach the approach to **QACHA'S NEK** you'll see the depressingly familiar soil erosion and *dongas*. Named after chief Moorosi's son Ncatya, Qacha's Nek was an area famed for its banditry when the British founded the town in 1888 in an attempt to forestall the kind of trouble they'd experienced with chief Moorosi. Many of the "bandits" were in fact desperate San, hounded from their homes and having no means of survival; this left the British unmoved, and they hunted them to extermination throughout the 1860s and 1870s. Moorosi's Baphuthi people had started moving there in the 1850s, rapidly wiping out all the game, and turning the land over to grazing and cultivation instead. The area has unusually high rainfall, and the weather conditions favour conifers, including a few massive Canadian redwoods, giving Qacha's Nek an atmosphere completely different from most of virtually treeless Lesotho.

There's little to see in town, except the elegant **St Joseph's Church** at its eastern end, but the entire surrounding mountainous countryside is great for **hiking**. Qacha's Nek is also an important **border town** (daily 7am–8pm) and there's usually plenty of **public transport** heading southwest towards Quthing from the Shell garage in the centre of town. There's also a daily bus to and from Maseru operated by Lesotho Freight and Bus Services; it leaves both towns at 6.30am, and takes over ten hours. You can hear **minibus taxis** a mile off, thanks to the cowbells tied to their fronts. On the other side of the border you'll find transport (roughly hourly) heading for the Eastern Cape town of Matatiele, from where it's easy to find buses and minibus taxis on to Kokstad and beyond.

The town's best **accommodation** is the *Nthatuoa Hotel* (T 2295 0260; ❷), the first building on the left as you enter Qacha's Nek from the west. The hotel has five types of room, each more luxurious than the last, starting with a decent though smallish double and ending with a large fancy suite; all are en suite, and you're also welcome to pitch a tent. All tariffs include a substantial breakfast from a restaurant serving the finest **food** in town (unless you are vegetarian, in which case you'll go hungry). There's also a **bar**. Just past the hotel, there are cheap rooms at the *Farmers' Training Centre* (T 2295 0231; ❶). Further out is the *Central Hotel* (T 2295 0224; ❷), a characterful place set in a sandstone building, though it has only six rooms and is often full. Despite the name, it's over a kilometre out of town, next to the PEP department store (to get there, take a left past the fuel station in town). Even if you're not staying, it's worth visiting at weekends for its **live music**. There are a few inexpensive **places to eat** in the centre of town, but for more substantial meals you're best off in one of the hotels.

Sehlabathebe National Park

The oldest nature reserve in the country, **Sehlabathebe National Park** (free entry – for now) is remote and almost inaccessible, but predictably peaceful and stunningly beautiful. Set on the border with South Africa in the southern reaches of the Drakensberg at an average altitude of 2400m, the park is best known for its prolific birdlife, including the rare bearded vulture (or lammergeier), excellent trout fishing on the Tsoelikana River, waterfalls, rock paintings and ancient Basotho stone dwellings, and seemingly endless open spaces just perfect for hiking. There are also a few game animals: baboons, rhebuck, eland and the secretive oribi antelope, mongoose, otters, wild cats and jackals. In good weather you probably won't be in any hurry to leave, but at any time of year mists and rain can emerge out of nowhere, even on the finest of days, so come prepared. While the park does have accommodation, **camping** is by far the best way of experiencing it, and also saves you the hassle of trying to book space in its lodge.

Practicalities

To get **to the park** from the Lesotho side of the border you'll need either a 4WD or to catch the daily Lesotho Freight and Bus Services bus from Qacha's Nek to Sehlabathebe village, just outside the park (departs at 1pm, returns at 5.30am), which takes four to five hours. The only other way into the park from the Lesotho side is to walk the 40km **Top-of-the-Berg hike** from Sani Top (see p.797). **From South Africa**, it's a day's walk to the park through the southern section of South Africa's Ukhahlamba Drakensberg Park along a dramatic path starting at Bushman's Nek, 38km from Underberg in KwaZulu-Natal. This route enters Lesotho and Sehlabathebe National Park at Nkonkoana Gate (daily 8am–4pm).

Finding up-to-date practical **information** is difficult, thanks to inept management (currently courtesy of the Ministry of Agriculture's Livestock Services department in Maseru; ☎2231 2318, or try the Ministry direct on ☎2232 2741). Hopefully, the park's incorporation into the **Maloti–Drakensberg Transfrontier Project** (see box on p.786) should change things for the better. Neither the Ministry of Agriculture, nor the tourist office or the park office itself have any **maps**; if you want to do some serious hiking, go to the Department of Lands, Surveys and Physical Planning in Maseru (see box on p.768), where you should be able to pick up some detailed maps of the area.

Other than **camping**, which you can do anywhere provided you get a permit from the gate, the park's only **accomodation** is the self-catering *Sehlabathebe Lodge* (☎2232 2876 or 2232 3600; 1), a few kilometres from Nkonkoana Gate and South Africa. The lodge provides bedding, toilets and showers, hot water and a kitchen; firewood and charcoal are also sold. To be sure of a room, book in advance. If it's full, there may be space at the park hostel close by, which has six more beds. **Outside the park** there are decent rooms at the beautiful *Rangeland Management Guesthouse* (☎2295 0231; 1) in Sehlabathebe village. Wherever you're staying, you'll need to be self-sufficient in food; fuel is sold at the Co-op Lesotho Depot, 4km outside the village.

Travel details

Buses

While there are lots of buses in Lesotho, only one company – the Lesotho Freight and Bus Services Corporation – keeps to a timetable (some of its routes operate in conjunction with other companies). Other buses simply leave when they're full, and as such operate just like minibus taxis (and are included in the section below). The Lesotho Freight and Bus Services Corporation services are as follows:

Maseru to: Bokong (daily at 8.30am; 8hr 30min); Linakaneng (daily at 8am; 9hr); Mokhotlong (alternating with Itumeleng Transport; daily at 6.30am; 8hr); Qacha's Nek (alternating with Flame Transport; daily at 6.30am; 10hr 30min); Quthing (alternating with Flame Transport; daily at 6.30am; 3hr 30min); Sehong Hong (daily at 9.30am; 9hr 30min); Semonkong (daily at 10am & 2pm; 6hr).

Butha-Buthe to: Hlotse (4 daily; 30min); Maputsoe (4 daily; 45min); Mokhotlong (2–3 daily; 7hr).

Hlotse to: Butha-Buthe (4 daily; 30min); Maputsoe (5 daily; 30min); Maseru (8 daily; 2hr).

Mafeteng to: Maseru (5 daily; 1hr 30min); Mohale's Hoek (5 daily; 45min).

Maputsoe to: Butha-Buthe (4 daily; 45min); Hlotse

(5 daily; 30min); Maseru (8 daily; 2hr); Teya-Teyaneng (8 daily; 45min).

Maseru to: Hlotse (8 daily; 2hr); Mafeteng (5 daily; 1hr 30min); Maputsoe (8 daily; 2hr); Morija (hourly; 50min); Qacha's Nek (1 daily; 10hr); Roma (4 daily; 1hr); Semonkong (2 daily; 5hr); Teya-Teyaneng (8 daily; 45min).

Mohale's Hoek to: Mafeteng (5 daily; 45min); Quthing (5 daily; 45min).

Mokhotlong to: Butha-Buthe (2–3 daily; 7hr); Sani (3 daily; 1hr 30min).

Qacha's Nek to: Maseru (1 daily; 10hr); Quthing (1 daily; 7hr).

Quthing to: Mohale's Hoek (5 daily; 45min); Qacha's Nek (1 daily; 7hr).

Roma to: Maseru (4 daily; 1hr); Semonkong (4 daily; 4hr).

Sani to: Mokhotlong (3 daily; 1hr 30min).

Semonkong to: Maseru (2 daily; 5hr); Roma (4 daily; 4hr).

Teya-Teyaneng to: Maputsoe (8 daily; 45min); Maseru (8 daily; 45min).

Flights

Maseru to: Johannesburg (3–4 daily; 1hr 10min).

Swaziland

CHAPTER 12

Highlights

* **Royal festivals** The spectacular ceremonies of *Ncwala* and *Umhlanga* are colourful affirmations of Swazi national identity. See p.825

* **Mlilwane** A tranquil reserve where you can walk, cycle or ride horses amongst giraffe and antelope, or watch hippos from the bar. See p.825

* **Horse-riding** Well-run horse treks combine stunning countryside and peaceful rural stopovers. See p.826

* **Malandela's Homestead** A collection of buildings bursting with creativity and enterprise, including the funky performance space House on Fire, and Gone Rural, one of the best of Swaziland's many attractive arts and crafts outlets. See p.827

* **Myxo's place, KaPhunga** Get a true taste of life in rural Swaziland – this enterprising project allows backpackers to live as part of a village for a few days. See p.829

* **Whitewater rafting on the Great Usutu** As action-packed as anything south of the Zambezi – you can paddle a two-man croc raft down Swaziland's largest river. See p.836

* **Mkhaya Game Reserve** Swaziland's best wildlife experience, where you can walk with rhino and elephant before sleeping in the bush in open-sided cottages. See p.837

△ The king leading a tribal dance

Swaziland

A tiny landlocked kingdom, **Swaziland** lies in the spanner-like grip of South Africa which surrounds it on three sides, with Mozambique providing its eastern border along the Lubombo Mountains. Although South Africa's influence predominates, Swaziland was a British protectorate from 1906 until its full independence in 1968, and today the country offers an intriguing mix of colonial heritage and homegrown confidence, giving the place a friendlier, more relaxed and often safer feeling than its larger neighbour.

Though Swaziland still feels a lot more commercialized than, say, Lesotho, its outstanding **scenery**, along with its commitment to **wildlife conservation**, makes it well worth a visit. With a car and a bit of time, you can explore some of the less-trampled reserves, make overnight stops in unspoilt, out-of-the-way settlements and, if you time your visit well, take in something of Swaziland's well-preserved **cultural traditions**.

In recent years, Swaziland has become something of a draw for **backpackers**, with useful transport links to different parts of South Africa as well as Mozambique, some good backpacker lodges and plenty of adventure activities from horse-riding to whitewater rafting.

Swaziland has six **national parks**, between them exemplifying the country's geographical diversity, and all offering good-value accommodation. While not as efficiently run as South African National Parks, the Swazi reserves are less officious, and many people warm to their easy-going nature. The best-known are those run by **Swazi Big Game Parks** (see p.826): Hlane Royal

Choosing the king

Swazi monarchs are always men of the **Dlamini** family, and over the course of their reign marry a number of women who are carefully selected from different clans to cement national unity. In theory, the king marries women from increasingly important families as he goes along, which means that the son of the last wife is always a strong contender for the succession. In practice, however, other wives with older sons are also in with a chance, resulting in unrest and power-struggles every time the king dies. After his death, the royal council, or *liqoqo*, selects the new **Queen Mother**, who rules as regent until her son is old enough to take charge. She usually has to work hard to ensure her position against ambitious uncles. The main advantage of this awkward process is that by the time the new king is old enough to rule, he and his mother have generally garnered enough support for him to do so effectively.

BORDER POST OPENING TIMES	
NGWENYA/ OSHOEK	7am–10pm
LUNDZI/ WAVERLEY	8am–4pm
SANDLANE/ NERSTON	8am–6pm
SICUNUSA/ EMAHLATHINI	8am–6pm
GEGE/ BOTHASHOOP	8am–4pm
MAHAMBA	7am–10pm
LAVUMISA/ GOLELA	7am–10pm
LOMAHASHA/ NAMAACHA	8am–6pm
MANANGA	8am–6pm
MATSAMO/ JEPPE'S REEF	7am–8pm
BULEMBU/ JOSEFSDAL	8am–4pm

National Park in the lowveld, Mlilwane Wildlife Sanctuary near Mbabane, and the upmarket Mkhaya Game Reserve between Manzini and Big Bend. The Swaziland National Trust Commission, based in Lobamba (see p.824), manages Malolotja Nature Reserve in the northwest highveld, Mlawula Nature Reserve in the eastern lowveld and the tiny Mantenga Nature Reserve in the eZulwini Valley.

Despite encroaching political dissent, Swaziland remains one of the world's few absolute monarchies, and **King Mswati III**, educated at Britain's elite Sherbourne College, regularly appears in the country's sacred ceremonies, bedecked in the leopard skins of his office, participating in a ritual dance or assessing the year's crop of eligible maidens as they dance before him. He might even choose to add a few to his collection of wives, carefully drawn from a wide selection of clans in order to knit the nation more closely together. If you can, plan to come to Swaziland for the **Ncwala** (around the end of Dec or the start of Jan) or **Umhlanga** (Aug or Sept) ceremonies, for more on which, see box on p.825.

Laid-back **Mbabane**, the country's tiny capital city, makes a useful base from which to explore the attractive central **eZulwini Valley**, home to the royal palace and the **Mlilwane Wildlife Sanctuary**. With your own transport, or a bit of determination and public transport, you can venture further afield, heading into the highveld of the northwest, and up to the fantastically beautiful **Malolotja Nature Reserve**, with its fabulous hiking country, soaring valleys and cliffs.

If you are trying to get between northern KwaZulu-Natal and the Kruger National Park in South Africa, Swaziland offers a good, fully tarred **through route** via the Matsamo border in the north and the Lavumisa and Mahamba borders in the south, passing by the Mkhaya Game Reserve and Big Bend. Approaching Kruger this way is a far more attractive option than skirting through the eastern parts of Mpumalanga.

Summers are hot, particularly in the eastern lowveld. **Winter** is usually sunny, but nights can be very chilly in the western highveld around the Malolotja Nature Reserve and Piggs Peak. In summer, rainfall is usually limited to short, drenching storms that play havoc with the smaller untarred roads. Note that Swaziland's eastern lowveld, including Hlane Royal National Park and Mkhaya Nature Reserve, is **malarial** during the summer months (Nov–May). For details on necessary precautions, see p.48.

Some history

The history of Swaziland dates back to the **Dlamini** clan and their king, **Ngwane**, who crossed the Lubombo Mountains from present-day Mozambique in around 1750. Pushed into southeast Swaziland by the Ndwandwe people of Zululand, the clan eventually settled at Mhlosheni and then Zombodze in the southwest, where Ngwane reigned precariously, under constant threat of Ndwandwe attack. His grandson, **Sobhuza I**, was forced to flee north from the Ndwandwe, but they in turn were defeated by the Zulu king Shaka

Siswati phrases

Basics

Yes	Yebo (also a casual greeting)	It's nice/tasty	Kumnazdi
		Today	Lamuhla
No	Cha	Tomorrow	Kusasa
Thank you	Ngiyabonga	Yesterday	Itolo

Greetings and responses

Hello (to one)	Sawubona	Goodbye (said by person leaving)	Sala kahle
Hello (to many)	Sanibona		
How are you?	Kunjani?	Goodbye (said by person remaining)	Hamba kahle
I'm fine	Ngikhoua		

Travel

Where is... ?	Iphi I... ?	Where are you going?	U ya phi?
Where can we stay?	Singahlala kuphi?	How much?	Malini?

in 1819. Sobhuza then established a new capital suitably far from Shaka in the eZulwini Valley, and made peace with the Ndwandwe by marrying the king's daughter.

Sobhuza's power grew as he brought more and more clans under his wing. His alliance with the newly arrived Afrikaners, forged out of mutual fear of the Zulu, was continued by his son **Mswati II** (after whom the Swazi people are named), who stretched his kingdom north to the Sabi River and sent raiding parties as far as the Limpopo River and east to the Indian Ocean.

Europeans arrived in greater numbers throughout the 1880s, after the discovery of gold in neighbouring Transvaal and at Piggs Peak and Forbes Reef in Swaziland. Mswati's son, **Mbandzeni**, granted large chunks of his territory in concessions to the new arrivals, emboldening Britain to ignore his claims to most of the rest, and by the time Swaziland became a protectorate of South Africa in 1894, there was precious little land left. After their victory in the Second Anglo-Boer War, Britain assumed control of the territory and retained it until 1968.

After World War II the British invested in their protectorate, establishing enormous **sugar plantations** in the northeast, and an **iron-ore mine** at Ngwenya in the highveld (today, the country's major export is sugar). Meanwhile, **Sobhuza II**, who had become king of the Swazis in 1921, concentrated on buying back his kingdom, and had acquired about half of it by the time independence came in 1968. The Swazi aristocracy managed the transition to independence skilfully, with its Imbokodvo party winning every parliamentary seat in the first elections. In 1973, a radical pan-Africanist party won three seats, prompting Sobhuza to **ban political parties** and declare a state of emergency which technically has been in place ever since. Political parties are generally viewed by most Swazis – a proud and relatively united people – as a source of division, creating factions and overcomplicating a simple political process. A parliament governs Swaziland today, but final authority rests with the king, who continues to name the prime minister (who, by tradition, is always a Dlamini) and approve or veto important legislation.

After Sobhuza's death in 1982, a period of intrigue ensued, with the Queen Mother Dzeliwe assuming the regency until deposed by Prince Bhekimpi, who ruled until 1985, purging all the opposition he could. The current king, **Mswati III**, the son of one of Sobhuza's seventy wives, was recalled from an English public school to become king in 1986, and parliamentary elections were held in 1987. New opposition began to emerge, most notably the **People's United Democratic Movement** (PUDEMO), which has strong support amongst Swazi workers, though in general Swazis are proud of their distinctive kingdom, and as a result calls for change are tempered by an unwillingness to show disloyalty to the king, or to expose Swaziland to what many see as the predatory ambitions of South Africa.

Thus the maintenance of tradition and appeals to broad nationalism have been key components of Swazi royalty's strategy to retain power. Relations with the new South African regime are uneasy: the ANC remembers the expulsion of its activists during the Eighties and wants speedy political change. Although Mswati III is sometimes said to favour reform, so far none has materialized. The authorities work hard to keep dissent bottled up, by means of sporadic police repression; opposition leaders are prevented from speaking freely in the media, and poor turnouts marked the "elections" of 1993 and 1998. Currently, Swaziland is the only country in southern Africa not practising multiparty democracy. It seems only a matter of time before it is coerced by the other regional powers into doing so.

Getting there

Of the twelve border posts serving traffic from South Africa, the most popular is **Ngwenya/Oshoek** (7am–10pm), which is the closest one to Johannesburg and is the easiest route to Mbabane, only 20km to the east. A good alternative route is via the **Sandlane/Nerston** border post (8am–6pm), about 35km further south, and roughly 70km from the city. Although a longer journey, this road passes through some outstanding scenery and will take you past some excellent places to stay. Once past Nerston, where there are some interesting San paintings (ask at the church for someone to show you the way), the road plunges deep into the vast and beautiful **Usutu Forest**, which covers over ten percent of Swaziland. After some steep climbs, you'll start a long descent to the factory town of **Bhunya**, whose hub is a belching pulp mill – reason enough not to linger. Press on for another 15km or so on the road to Mhlambanyatsi. Just before Mhlambanyatsi is a fine **hotel**, *The Forester's Arms* (☏4674377, ⓦwww.swaziland.freeservers.com/foresters; full board ⑤), set in a picturesque clearing in the surrounding woodland. The rooms are cosy with fireplaces and wonderful mountain views, and hearty meals are served (the flamboyant chef is likely to visit your table), making this a pleasant stop along the way; on Sundays, people from all over the country pour in to feast on the hotel's superb buffet and roast – you'll need to **book** ahead to be sure of a table.

Back on the road, **Mhlambanyatsi** itself has a small shopping centre and some filling stations, but little else. The road beyond it enters a beautiful, lush river valley dotted with traditional houses; this is prime **hiking** territory, and a particularly spectacular unmarked trail leads all the way to (but not into) the Mlilwane Wildlife Sanctuary (see p.825). Note that there are no facilities, and you have to be pretty self-sufficient, asking at villages for somewhere to stay. Eventually the road breaks through the hills to the plateau on which Mbabane stands, where you can connect with the main routes to the centre of the country.

Just off the N2 from Piet Retief in the southwest is the **Emahlathini/Sicunusa** (8am–6pm) border crossing, which leads to the newly tarred and wonderfully scenic MR4. The northern crossing via **Bulembu** (8am–4pm) to Piggs Peak is perhaps the most spectacular in the country, but the bad road makes this journey hard going in an ordinary car. Crossing the border is usually very straightforward: you simply have to show your passport and pay the token E5 **road tax**. Other border crossings are: **Jeppe's Reef/Matsamo** in the northwest (7am–8pm), handy if you're coming in from Kruger Park; **Mananga** in the northeast (8am–6pm); **Lavumisa/Golela** in the southeast (7am–10pm), close to the KwaZulu-Natal coast; and **Mahamba** in the south (7am–10pm).

Buses and flights

Transtate **buses** from Johannesburg enter Swaziland through the Ngwenya/Oshoek border, stopping at Ermelo en route to Mbabane; and through Mahamba, stopping at Nhlangano and Hlathikulu. The Baz Bus runs eastbound from Jo'burg to Durban via Mbabane and then Manzini on Monday, Wednesday and Saturday, departing for Durban the next morning; services from Durban for Swaziland leave on Tuesday, Friday and Sunday and set off for Jo'burg the next morning.

Swaziland has one **international airport**, Matsapha (often referred to as "Manzini"), between Mbabane and Manzini. Airlink Swaziland (a partner of SAA, through whom they can be contacted in South Africa) flies three times daily to

Accommodation in the mid- and upper range is generally better value than in South Africa, although there isn't a wide choice, particularly in the guesthouse and B&B sector. Backpacker and budget places are on a par with South Africa.

Banks are easily found in the major centres. Opening hours are generally Monday to Friday, 8.30am to 2.30pm, with some branches open on Saturday from 8.30am to 11am. Most banks and hotels will change traveller's cheques, but usually at poor rates of exchange. Most ATMs in Swaziland accept international cards.

Camping in designated campsites is possible near almost every tourist attraction and in all the national parks except for Mkhaya.

Costs are similar to those in South Africa, with food and fuel somewhat less expensive.

Currency is the lilangeni – plural emalangeni (E) – which is tied to the South African rand (1 rand = 1 lilangeni). The rand is legal tender in Swaziland, so you won't have to change any money, but note that emalangeni are not convertible outside Swaziland. Credit cards such as Visa, Mastercard and American Express are widely accepted in hotels, restaurants and shops. The national parks accept cards for larger payments such as accommodation, but you'd be well advised to carry cash to pay for meals and guided walks.

Driving is the best way to see Swaziland; distances are small, all the main tourist sites are near good, tarred roads, and the major gravel roads are in decent condition. Most dirt roads are passable with an ordinary vehicle in dry months. Driving standards, however, leave a lot to be desired – highlighted by the fact that two of the last four ministers of transport have died in road accidents. The authorities permit a blood-alcohol level in drivers which is double that permitted in South Africa, which should make you think twice about long drives at night. Also, the general speed limit of 80kph outside towns is universally ignored and very rarely enforced. For Swazi car rental, see "Listings" on p.820.

Passports and visas see p.41

and from Johannesburg. Swazi Express Airways (ⓦ www.swaziexpress.com) flies in from Durban daily except Saturday.

Mbabane

Tucked in the jumble of granite peaks and valleys that make up the Dlangeni hills, Swaziland's administrative capital, **MBABANE** (pronounced "M-buh-ban"), is small, relaxed and unpretentious, with a population of only 90,000. The city roughly marks the point where the mountainous southern African highveld descends briefly into middleveld, before bottoming out further east as dry lowveld.

There's not much to do in Mbabane, but many visitors find it more agreeable than hectic Manzini, especially if you need to change money, find a comfortable bed or plan your trip ahead. This is a good base from which to start exploring Swaziland, especially if you're without your own transport: the Mlilwane Wildlife Sanctuary (see p.825) lies not far south, and the royal village of Lobamba (see p.824) makes an easy day-trip – vital if you're here when the Umhlanga or Ncwala ceremonies take place.

Phone numbers The country code for Swaziland is ☎268, followed by the destination number (there are no area codes). The code for phoning out from Swaziland is ☎00, followed by the country and area codes and finally the destination number. To phone South Africa, dial ☎07. To arrange a collect call, dial ☎94. Country codes are the same as those dialled from South Africa (see p.68). If you experience difficulties, call enquiries on ☎919490. Swaziland has its own mobile phone network, which works well in the eZulwini Valley but can be patchy elsewhere. International roaming is possible with certain phones and contracts. All Swazi mobile phone numbers are seven figure and begin with 6.

Swaziland on the Internet

ⓦ**www.swazi.com** Swaziland's official website is lively, colourful and packed with useful information, including hotel listings and alternative tours of Swaziland. You can also read the *Swazi Observer* newspaper online, or visit the "Artists on the Internet" page for a roundup of the country's arts scene.

ⓦ**www.biggame.co.sz** Provides practical information on the country's most visited attractions, the Hlane, Mlilwane and Mkhaya parks, with links to the Swazi Trails site and details of tours.

ⓦ**www.swazitrails.co.sz** The most important tour operator in the country, with details of a range of tours and activities around Swaziland, including cultural, wildlife and adventure options.

Swazi public holidays
January 1
Good Friday
Easter Monday
April 19 (King Mswati III's birthday)
April 25 (National Flag Day)
May 24 Ascension Day

July 22 (King Sobhuza II's birthday)
August/September (Umhlanga Dance Day)
September 6 (Independence Day)
December/January (Ncwala Day)
December 25
December 26

Arrival and information

Matsapha airport (☎5186155), 35km southeast of Mbabane, just west of Manzini, is Swaziland's only international airport. There's no public transport from here into Mbabane, so if you haven't been able to arrange a pick-up with your hotel, be prepared to take a **taxi** or **rent a car** (see "Listings" on p.820). You cannot change money at the airport, so have some rands or emalangeni handy.

Transtate (Jo'burg ☎011 773 6002) **buses** from South Africa terminate some way out of town at the intersection of Usutu and Manzini roads, from where you should call a taxi, as it's too far to walk into town. The main bus station is off the Western Distributor Road, beside the Swazi Plaza mall, and from here you can take a bus to almost anywhere in Swaziland. **Minibus taxis** ply the Mbabane–Manzini route and rank on the west side of the bus station – this is also where you can rent a **private taxi** for local travel.

Mbabane's **tourist office**, Swazi Plaza (Mon–Fri 8am–5pm, Sat 8.30am–12.30pm; ☎4042531), has a good supply of **maps**, brochures and a free *What's On?* Guide.

Central Mbabane empties at night, and **muggings** are a risk for those wandering the streets alone. If you're going out after dark, arrange for a taxi to pick you up.

▲ ●①, Sibebe Rock, Dalriach East & Pine Valley

MBABANE

ACCOMMODATION

All Ways Backpackers	**B**
Cathmar Cottages	**A**
City Inn	**E**
Hill St Lodge	**D**
Kapola Guest House	**F**
Mountain Inn	**G**
Thokoza Church Centre	**C**

Coronation Park

Police Station

Bus Station

New Mall

Jazz Friends

The Mall

Swazi Market

Swazi Plaza

◄ Oshoek & Ngwenya

RESTAURANTS

Friar Tucks	7
Indingilizi Gallery & Restaurant	2
Kowloon	3
La Casserole	1
Mediterranean	5
Pizza Pasta	4
St Bernard's	6

General Hospital

Transtate Bus Station

0   200 m

▼ Mhlambanyatsi   ▼ ●⑥,●⑦,●Ⓖ, Ezulwini Valley & Manzini

Accommodation

Mbabane's **accommodation** is somewhat limited, and some of the options in the lower price range are in a seedy part of town. However, there are a couple of backpackers' lodges near the centre and a handful of fairly decent **hotels** on and around Gwamile Street (aka Allister Miller Street). There are also various guesthouses on the fringes of the city, and most establishments in the eZulwini Valley (see p.821) are close enough to make a viable alternatives.

All WaysBackpackers 18 Mission St ☏ 4050741, ℮ all-ways@mailfly.com. A friendly if fairly scruffy backpacker lodge a 10min walk north of the city centre, more popular with long-term residents than with those just passing through. ●①
Cathmar Cottages 3km north of Mbabane on Pine Valley Road ☏ 4043387 or 6021364, ℮ cathmar@mailfly.com. Self-catering cottages

and simpler wooden cabins in a lovely location north of town near Sibebe Rock. Facilities include cable TV in the cottages and a swimming pool. ●③
City Inn Gwamile St ☏ 4042406, ℻ 4045393. The oldest city-centre hotel, offering plain but spacious en-suite rooms, all with TV. It incorporates a small coffee shop facing the street. ●④

Hill St Lodge Hill St ☎ 4046342. Basic rooms with shared bath, in a quiet suburb west of Gwamile St. ❶

Kapola Guest House 6km southeast of Mbabane off MR3 ☎ 4040906 or 6048962, ✉ tfc@iafrica .sz. Decent guesthouse accommodation in a large family home, at the bottom of the hill between Mbabane and the start of the eZulwini Valley. There are six well-equipped en-suite guest rooms, with a quiet balcony and secluded garden. ❺

Mountain Inn 4km southeast of Mbabane off MR3 ☎ 4042781, ⊛ www.mountaininn.sz. A

smart, efficiently run if slightly dated hotel, with sixty rooms and good facilities including a lovely pool and the *Friar Tuck* restaurant. Located on a spacious mountainside plot with wonderful views down eZulwini Valley. ❻

Thokoza Church Centre Mhlanhla St ☎ 4046681, ✉ anglicanchurch@iafrica.sz. Church mission centre some way east of the city centre, offering drab but cheap two-or three-bed rooms, with breakfast available as an extra. There is a 10pm curfew unless you make prior arrangements, and the area can be rough at night. ❷

The City

Mbabane's hilly **centre** is a pleasant jumble of office blocks, markets, plazas and shacks that you can very easily explore on foot – which is just as well, as driving here can be stressful without a sound grasp of the street layout. **Gwamile Street** is the closest the city has to a main street; running south into the central business district (CBD), it's lined in parts by colonial administrative buildings which are attractive to look at, but can only be entered on official business. At the end of Gwamile Street, on the banks of the Mbabane River, lies the **Swazi Market**, with neat rows of curio stalls with a colourful selection of handicrafts and, though prices aren't cheap, you can always haggle. It's just as interesting wandering further into the market, where fresh fruit and vegetable stalls make for a colourful scene (though prices here aren't negotiable).

The main focus of the city centre, however, is the sprawl of shopping malls down the hill from Gwamile Street. Most of Mbabane's main shops, banks and services are located in either the **Swazi Plaza** or the more upmarket **Mall** and **New Mall**. Alongside the Swazi Plaza is the busy bus and taxi rank.

Eating, drinking and nightlife

You'll find the ubiquitous *Spur, Steers, Debonairs* (pizza) and *KFC* in Mbabane, but the town also has a smattering of very good **restaurants**, a selection of

Sibebe Rock

About 10km north of Mbabane along the Pine Valley road, Swaziland's most famous geological feature, a huge granite dome called **Sibebe Rock**, can be found among the Mbuluzi Mountains. Rising 300m above the Mbuluzi River Valley, the vast slabs of granite are very steep and dangerous in places, but among the scattered boulders at the summit are Bushman paintings indicating that the rock was inhabited by humans thousands of years ago. While the hard, coarse surface of the granite offers more grip than other types of rock, it can be very dangerous if you slip, so a guide is essential for any ascent. Swazi Trails (see "Listion on p.820) offers a challenge they describe as "the steepest walk in the world", which ascends an impossible-looking path up the front face of the dome. Swazi Trails also offers a **caving trip** in the same mountain range, which involves a lot of squeezing through narrow spaces and navigation by little more than a head torch and the encouraging words of your guide – it's a memorable adventure for those who don't mind enclosed spaces and a few bumps and scratches. Both the Sibebe Challenge and the caving trip are run as half-day trips, each costing around E200 including transport to and from various points in the eZulwini Valley and Mbabane.

which are reviewed below. The city's liveliest **bars** are *St.Bernards* and the *Plaza Bar*, both in the Swazi Plaza complex. For live music there's the *Jazz Friends* club at the bottom of Gwamile Street, and at weekends you can usually catch a good local band at the *West End Girls* **nightclub**, above the *Yemfo* bar, reached down Western Distributor Road or West Street. For the best nightlife, however, most locals head out to happening spots along the eZulwini Valley or in Manzini. Check the daily *Times of Swaziland* for details. Women travellers on their own are likely to encounter some unwanted attention in bars and clubs, but the pestering probably won't be aggressive or persistent.

Restaurants

Friar Tucks At the *Mountain Inn*, 4km southeast of the city centre ☎ 4042781. Serves reliable buffet lunches and a la carte dinners, in an intimate, rather dark interior; there's also outdoor seating.

Indingilizi Gallery & Restaurant 112 Johnstone St ☎ 4046213. A very pleasant place to come for lunch. The restaurant is in the gallery's back garden, and serves light, wholesome dishes at reasonable prices. Mon–Fri 8am–5pm, Sat 8am–1pm.

Kowloon Fast Food New Mall ☎ 4048637. A reliable Chinese takeaway, open daily till 8pm. There's also a branch on Gwamile Street.

La Casserole Omni Centre, Gwamile St ☎ 4046426. Upmarket but good-value restaurant specializing in German dishes, with vegetarian selections.

Mediterranean Gwamile St ☎ 4043212. Despite the name, this is an Indian restaurant serving moderately priced wonderful dishes in a dark, cavernous setting.

Pizza Pasta New Mall ☎ 4048628. Reliable, well-priced if fairly predictable Italian fare and good coffee.

St Bernard's Swazi Plaza ☎ 4041729. Serves mostly mainstream food including burgers, grilled chicken and ribs – but it's worth looking out for the special curries and stir fry. Daily.

Listings

Airlines Airlink Swaziland ☎ 5186155; Swazi Express Airlines ☎ 5186840, ⓦ www.swaziexpress.com.

Banks Most banks are found in Gwamile St or in the Swazi Plaza. Branches include First National, Nedbank and Standard. Hours are generally Mon–Fri 8.30am–2.30pm, Sat 8.30–11am. The quietest time to bank is a weekday morning.

Bookshops Websters, at 120 Johnstone St and in the New Mall, has the best general selection. There is also an SNA newsagent (the Swazi equivalent of South Africa's CNA) in the Swazi Plaza.

Car rental Avis (☎ 5186226) and Imperial (☎ 5184393) are located at Matsapha airport, and there's another Imperial agent at the Engen service station at the junction of the By-Pass Road and Main Road (☎ 4041384). Affordable Car Hire (☎ 4049136 or 6020394) in the Swazi Plaza is cheaper.

Embassies Mozambique, Princess Dr ☎ 4043700; South Africa, New Mall ☎ 4044651; UK, Gwamile St ☎ 4042581; USA, Warner St ☎ 4046442. Note that it's intended to replace the UK's representation in Swaziland with a Pretoria-based consul; for details, see ⓦ www.fco.gov.uk.

Emergencies Fire ☎ 933; Police ☎ 999 or 4042221.

Hospitals Mbabane Clinic Service (private), St Michael St ☎ 4042423; Government Hospital (public), Usutu Rd ☎ 4042111.

Internet access You can get online at the Omni Centre, opposite the cinema on Gwamile St, or at the Internet café beside the post office, upstairs in the Swazi Plaza (Mon–Fri 8am–6pm, Sat 8am–5pm, Sun 2–5pm).

Laundries Swaziland Steam Laundry & Dry, Gwamile St, and in the Swazi Plaza.

Pharmacy Mbabane Pharmacy, Gwamile St; Philani Pharmacy, in the Swazi Plaza; and Green Cross, in The Mall.

Post office The main post office is on Warner St (Mon–Fri 8am–4pm, Sat 8–11am), and there's a smaller one in the Swazi Plaza.

Taxi Take Me Home Taxis ☎ 606 8120.

Tour operators The country's biggest and best tour operator is Swazi Trails (☎ 4162180, ⓦ www .swazitrails.co.za), located in the Mantenga Craft Centre (see p.822). It runs tours to the Lobamba royal village, game parks, nature reserves, craft centres, local villages and even a local *sangoma*. They can also arrange horse-riding, hiking, mountain biking, caving and some great whitewater rafting trips (see p.836). There are also a handful of smaller local operations, including Nabo Bashoa, 37 Commercial Centre, Johnston St (☎ 605 6346, ⓔ phephelo@yahoo.com), who runs minibus tours to different parts of Swaziland. The tourist office keeps information on other tour guides.

The eZulwini Valley

After passing through Mbabane, the smooth, new, four-lane **MR3** winds down the steep sides of Malagwane Hill in a series of sweeping curves, made hazardous by crawling lorries and reckless minibus taxis. The road then heads off southeast along the eZulwini Valley, but unless you're bound directly for Manzini and beyond, take the turning not long after the foot of the hill onto the older and quieter **MR103**: this links most of the main sights of the scenic **eZulwini Valley** (Place of Heaven). In the 1960s, a succession of casinos, strip joints, hotels and caravan parks sprang up here, catering mainly for South African tourists. When gambling became legal in South Africa in the mid-1990s, however, the number of pleasure-seekers dropped; the tourist industry had to start looking beyond the noise of the slot machines and karaoke to the valley's cultural and natural assets, and in particular places such as the royal residences of **Lobamba** and **Ludzidzini**, the **Mantenga Nature Reserve** and **Mlilwane Wildlife Sanctuary**. The latter, in particular, is one of Swaziland's main attractions, with its range of accommodation from backpacker lodges to colonial guesthouses, as well as numerous activities, including hiking trails and game viewing from a mountain bike.

Malagwane Hill and along the eZulwini Valley Road

Soon after leaving Mbabane, the main Mbabane–Manzini road begins its giddy descent down **Malagwane Hill**. As the highway begins to level out at the bottom of the valley, the first main exit leads to the old eZulwini Valley road, the **MR103**, which runs parallel to the mountains on the southern side of the valley. A kilometre or so along the MR103, a right-hand turn leads to *Timbali Park* (☏4161156, ✉timbali@africaonline.co.sz), a well-maintained camping and caravan park which also has shaded self-catering cottages (❷), a pool, bar and coffee shop serving breakfasts. Next door to *Timbali* you'll find one of Swaziland's swankiest **restaurants**, the *Calabash* (☏4161187), which serves an excellent range of fresh seafood and specializes in German, Swiss and Austrian dishes. Further up this road, *Martin's Bar & Disco* becomes pleasantly raucous and drunken at weekends, and if you're in the mood for partying will doubtless deliver a night to remember.

Continuing along the MR103 valley road, you'll soon come to the Swazi Health and Beauty Studio, which incorporates the popular **Cuddle Puddle** (daily 6am–6pm; E5), a beautifully warm outdoor spa pool filled from a natural spring nearby and surrounded by tropical vegetation. Immediately beyond this lie three Sun **hotels** offering their usual blend of comfort and anonymity. The *Royal Swazi Sun* (☏4161001, ⓦwww.suninternational.com; ❾) is the smartest of the lot, with a fine swimming pool, a golf course, a good selection of restaurants and plenty of upmarket bars, as well as a swanky casino and a tatty adult cinema. The other Sun options offer slightly better value: the *Lugogo Sun* (☏4161550; ❽) provides a well-priced buffet that is particularly enticing at breakfast, and the *Ezulwini Sun* (☏4161201; ❼) has a beer garden open on Tuesday nights. In the same direction, just beyond the filling station and past the Sun hotels, the *First Horse* **restaurant** (☏4161137) serves very good Chinese meals and has a large bar. Opposite the filling station stands an extended line of **craft stalls**, commonly signposted by one or two tour buses drawn up alongside. This is a good place for mainstream Swazi crafts such as wood and soapstone carvings, though you have to haggle to get the prices down to sensible levels.

Also on this section of the eZulwini Valley road is the *Happy Valley Motel* (☎4161061, ⓦwww.happyvalley.co.sz; ❸), located a kilometre or so past the *First Horse Restaurant*. A remnant of Swaziland's days as a place of temptation for repressed white South Africans, the motel also houses the *If Not?* go-go bar and the *Why Not?* disco, a popular nightclub and venue for local and touring bands. The rooms in the motel are predictable but neat, with air conditioning and cable TV. Across the road is a new **Gables Shopping Centre**, with a large grocery store as well as *The Friendly Whistle*, that offers **phone and Internet access** (Mon–Sat 8am–6pm); there's also the *Bella Vista Pizzeria* (6.30am–midnight weekdays, 6.30am–2am weekends), which is popular with locals stopping for a drink, meal or takeaway.

The Mantenga Valley

The Mantenga Valley follows the course of the Lusushwana (Little Usutu) River from the eZulwini Valley road up into the hills to the west, most prominent of which is the twin-peaked **Lugogo Mountain**, also known as "Sheba's Breasts", which featured in H. Rider Haggard's famous adventure novel *King Solomon's Mines*. Apart from a series of good **craft centres**, the valley is dominated by the **Mantenga Nature Reserve**, home of the **Swazi Cultural Village** and **Swazi River Café**. There's a fair amount of new development by the side of the eZulwini Valley road in this area, so the road layout is subject to change, but by following signs to the Mantenga Craft Centre or Mantenga Nature Reserve you should get onto the correct road.

Mantenga Craft Centre

The **Mantenga Craft Centre**, less than a kilometre from the turn-off from the eZulwini Valley road, consists of an attractive purpose-built village of craft shops. These specialize in more exclusive and individual crafts than are found in many other parts of Swaziland, including fabrics, artworks and better carvings. There's also a **tourist office** (Mon–Fri 8am–5pm, Sat 8.30am–12.30pm) and the main booking office for **Swazi Trails**, the country's leading tour operator where you can organize a wide range of cultural and adventure trips including a half-day arts and crafts trail, whitewater rafting (see p.836) and caving. Across from the Craft Centre is the rather run down but friendly **Legends Backpacker Lodge** (☎4161870, ⓔlegends@mailfly.com; ❶). In between the Centre and the lodge is a short dirt road that will bring you to the beautifully located *Mantenga Lodge* (☎4161049, ⓔmantenga@iafrica.sz; ❹), a good choice for mid-priced **accommodation** in the eZulwini Valley. The lodge has 26 en-suite rooms, some in cosy chalets for two to four people each, nestled on the hill rise, as well as a pool, terrace bar and **restaurant** with especially good views. Also on the road beyond the Mantenga Craft Centre is a long, terracotta-painted building where you can find more crafts worth checking out: in the *Jewellery Studio* (Tues–Sat 9am–5pm, Sun 10am–5pm) jewellery is hand-crafted on the premises out of gold, silver, semi-precious stones and even elephant and giraffe hair, while the adjoining *Guava Gallery* (same hours) sells some highly original local arts and crafts, including paintings, sculptures and woven mats.

Mantenga Nature Reserve

Not far past the Guava Gallery is the entrance to the **Mantenga Nature Reserve** (daily 6.30am–6pm; E10 plus E5 per car), which incorporates **Ligugo lemaSwati** (meaning "the pride of the Swazi people"), Swaziland's most authentic cultural village. This open-air living museum replicates a nineteenth-century

△ Crafts being sold at the roadside

Swazi homestead with sixteen beehive huts, all built in traditional style using wooden frames joined by leather strips, reed thatch, cow dung and termite-hill earth. Cattle and goats wander about, and there are often demonstrations of traditional activities and crafts. Informative and enthusiastic guides will take you round on free tours, and you can even **stay** in one of three beehive huts if you're prepared to rough it, as there's no bedding, no electricity, and you cook on a campfire (☎4161013 or 4161151; ❶). Rather more comfortable accommodation is available a little further upriver in fifteen luxury tents, each located on a sturdy wooden platform and equipped with an en-suite toilet and hot shower (❷). All the platforms incorporate a deck in front of the tent – it's worth asking if tents no.5 or 6 are free, as these have the best view of the pretty 95-metre **Mantenga Falls**. The tents are grouped around the thatched *Swazi River Café* (daily, breakfast, lunch and dinner; ☎4161151 or 6022183), a restaurant serving "Swazi fusion cuisine" which can include spicy chicken livers, ostrich stroganoff and locally grown vegetables. The café, which also serves teas and coffees, is open to everyone, and has established a good reputation both with locals and those staying elsewhere in the eZulwini Valley.

Although the café and the cultural village are the main attractions, the rest of the reserve shouldn't be ignored, as there are some pleasant **hikes** and a beautiful **picnic** and **swimming** spot with views of the Mantenga Falls, a five-minute walk from the café.

⑫ Lobamba and Ludzidzini

Some 20km south of Mbabane at the heart of the eZulwini Valley, **LOBAMBA** was originally built in 1830 for King Sobhuza I, and became the royal kraal of Sobhuza II. The Houses of Parliament are situated here, and must be one of the few in the world to have cattle grazing undisturbed in surrounding fields. Next door, fascinating exhibitions of Swazi life can be found in the **National Museum** (Mon–Fri 8am–1pm & 2–3.45pm, Sat & Sun 10am–1pm & 2–3.45pm; E10). They provide a helpful potted history of the country, with displays of cultural artefacts and wonderful old photographs of Swazi people and royalty, of Manzini and Mbabane when they were one-horse towns, of sweaty British administrators in full colonial regalia attending functions of the Swazi royal house, and much more. A natural history wing was also opened recently. The museum is the base of the **National Trust Commission**, PO Box 100 (Mon–Fri 8am–1pm & 2–3.45pm, Sat & Sun 10am–1pm & 2–3.45pm; ☎4161151, ⓦwww.sntc.org.sz), which handles bookings for the Mantenga, Malolotja and Mlawula nature reserves (see p.822, p.831 & p.833).

Outside the museum stands a life-size re-creation of a traditional Swazi homestead. Remarkably, given their size, these huts are actually portable. Across the road is **King Sobhuza II Memorial Park**, a peaceful open space dedicated to the much-loved late king. Nearby, Lobamba's **Somhlolo stadium** is the country's venue for major events and football matches, which are usually highly entertaining. For a few emalangeni on a Sunday afternoon, you can treat yourself to violence-free games of occasional great skill, with a good-humoured and vociferous crowd. Consult the local *Times of Swaziland* for details, or ask almost any male Swazi.

On the other side of the MR103 from Lobamba, the village of **LUDZIDZINI** is the kraal of the present king, Mswati III, and the Queen Mother. Unlike Lobamba, Ludzidzini cannot be visited or even photographed at all except during Ncwala (around New Year) and Umhlanga (end of Aug/early Sept), when permission must be obtained (see box opposite).

The most sacred of Swaziland's ceremonies, **Ncwala** celebrates kingship, national unity and the first fruits of the new year. Its timing is determined by royal astrologers; coinciding with the new moon in November, a group of selected men journey east to the ancestral home of the Ngwane on the shores of the Indian Ocean to collect foam from the waves. While they are there, the *Ncwala* ceremony begins, with songs and rituals performed until the afternoon of the full moon in December/early January, when the six days of the full *Ncwala* begin. Young Swazi men meet at **Lobamba** and are then sent away to gather branches of the *lusekwane* tree, from which they build a bower for the king. Warriors gather and sing songs that can only be sung at this time, while the king dances with them and eats the first fruits of the harvest. On the sixth day, objects representing the previous year are burnt on a massive bonfire, and prayers are offered to Swazi ancestors, asking them to put out the fire with rain. The ceremony ends amidst raucous singing, dancing and feasting. Visitors are allowed to attend most of *Ncwala*, but photography is prohibited during certain times (a free permit is also required; contact the Government Information Service, PO Box 338, Mbabane), so be sure to ask first to avoid having your camera smashed.

The **Umhlanga** is a **fertility** or reed **dance** which gets its name from the large reeds gathered by young women and brought to the residence of the Queen Mother to repair her kraal, usually in late August or early September. The sixth and seventh days are the most spectacular, when you can watch up to 25,000 young women, dressed in elaborate and carefully coded costumes, sing and dance before the king and Queen Mother at Lobamba, giving the king an opportunity to pick a **new wife**. The former king, Sobhuza II, invariably plucked a new mate from the bevy of young beauties and racked up a total of seventy wives during his lifetime. His successor, Mswati III, now in his mid-thirties, has proved a little more restrained with only eight wives so far. In 2001 he caused some controversy by insisting that the young maidens parading in front of him at Umhlanga should continue to wear the *umcwasho*, a traditional regalia indicating that they were still virgins, for five years after the ceremony marking their passage from childhood to maidenhood. With HIV/AIDS spreading alarmingly in Swaziland, the king's pronouncement was seen as a fairly futile attempt to check the disease.

Mlilwane Wildlife Sanctuary

For many visitors to Swaziland, the highlight of the eZulwini Valley is **Mlilwane Wildlife Sanctuary** (daily dawn–dusk; E25), with its relaxed atmosphere and attractive, game-filled plains. The name Mlilwane refers to the "little fire" that sometimes appears when lightning strikes the granite mountains. As well as offering good game viewing and activities, Mlilwane is an easy alternative to staying in Mbabane or on the eZulwini strip. Given its popularity, it's wise to book ahead if you intend to stay overnight.

The reserve holds a special place in the history of wildlife conservation in Swaziland; it was here that Ted Reilly (see box on p.826) first realized his dream of a sanctuary for Swaziland's fast-disappearing **wildlife**. Mlilwane's animals are mainly herbivorous, and include giraffe, zebra, bountiful numbers of antelope and the sanctuary's emblem, the warthog. There's also the occasional crocodile and hippopotamus, which means you still need to be cautious if viewing the game on foot, bike or horseback.

Over 100km of road enables you to drive through the park to view game. Alternatively, guided walks and drives are available through the park office at the main restcamp; the best of the self-guided **walking trails** is the Macobane

Ted Reilly and the Swazi nature conservation story

Swaziland owes the creation and survival of three of its major wildlife sanctuaries – Mlilwane, Mkhaya and Hlane – to **Ted Reilly**, who was born in Mlilwane in 1938, the son of a British Anglo-Boer War soldier who had stayed on. As Reilly was growing up, Swazi wildlife and its natural habitats were coming under serious threat from poachers and commercial farmers. In 1959, Reilly lobbied the colonial government to set aside land for parks, but was defeated by farmers who wanted the land for commercial agriculture. Undeterred, he turned his Mlilwane estate into a park anyway, and set about cultivating a relationship with **King Sobhuza II**, who was having trouble himself with poachers at the royal estate in Hlane. After Swazi independence, Sobhuza became much more powerful, and Reilly's relationship with him lent weight to his nature conservation efforts.

Despite rickety finances, the **Mlilwane Wildlife Sanctuary** opened in 1963, and the restocking and reintroduction of species has continued ever since (the reserve today is ten times the size of the original sanctuary). Meanwhile, Sobhuza asked Reilly to help stamp out poaching at Hlane. Reilly's tough approach resulted in shootouts with the poachers, earning him the praise of some, but the enmity of many. Matters came to a head in 1992 when, with the help of the South African Police Endangered Species Protection Unit, Reilly tracked down a poaching unit that had been operating in Mkhaya. In the ensuing gunfight one poacher was killed and another paralyzed, and criticism of Reilly's tactics intensified.

Reilly's dependence on royal connections has also generated controversy: critics claim it has prevented the development of a single parks board and a participatory, grass-roots involvement in conservation that is the key to long-term success. Some also assert that Reilly subordinates wildlife management principles to the needs of the tourist industry. Reilly's answer to his critics is simply to point to the three game parks his company runs. It's a powerful argument – without Reilly, the parks would not exist, and Swaziland and its visitors would be much the poorer for it.

Hill Trail, a gentle, three-hour hike through the mountains. The more adventurous can climb to the top of Nyonyane, the "Execution Rock", which rises so prominently in the north of the reserve. The office can supply maps for all these. There are also guided **mountain–bike tours** (E60 per hour) and **horseback trails** (from E75 per hour), both fairly relaxed ways of taking in the park's attractions. For those with a little more horseback experience, various overnight trails involve camping in caves and rustic trail camps in the more remote parts of the reserve; for the really committed, the Lusoti "Real Africa" Horse Trails, organized by Swaziland Big Game Parks in association with Hawane Horse Trails, offer a seven-night cross-country expedition taking in Mlilwane, Mkhaya Game Reserve and remote rural homesteads. For details, contact Big Game Parks Central Reservations (see below). If you're feeling less energetic, you can pass the time watching **hippos** wallowing in the hippo pool, overlooked by the *Hippo Haunt* restaurant at the main restcamp. The hippos are fed every day at 3pm.

Practicalities

To get to Mlilwane, take the turning from the eZulwini Valley road, signposted off the MR103 about a kilometre beyond the turn-off to Ludzidzini. From here, it's 3.5km along a dirt road to the entrance gate, where there's a small exhibition and craft centre. The reserve offers a wide variety of **accommodation**; for all options except Sondzela, **bookings** should be made through Swaziland Big Game Parks Central Reservations (℡5283944, ⓦwww.biggame.co.sz). In the

main restcamp, about 1.5km from the gate, there's a campsite, dorms (❶), traditional beehive huts (❷) and two-person huts (❷), along with communal ablution facilities and a swimming pool. Situated in the northern part of the sanctuary is *Sondzela* **backpacker lodge**, a friendly place now firmly established on the backpacking circuit, where you can stay in dorms or doubles and relax in the lush garden by a large swimming pool (bookings ✆5283117; ❶). At the other end of the scale is *Reilly's Rock Hilltop Lodge* (full board; ❻), a lovely colonial home full of antiques and hardwood furniture situated on a hilltop surrounded by woodland and prolific birdlife. With only six rooms, it's more upmarket than a guesthouse but more rustic than a game lodge, and guests here can enjoy fantastic views from the balcony over the Mdzimba Mountains, wander round the gardens which surround the house, and take part in any of the activities offered elsewhere in the reserve. The only place to eat is at the inexpensive *Hippo Haunt* **restaurant**, at the main restcamp, where there's also a bar.

For those who don't have their own **transport**, it is possible to walk from Sondzela to the main restcamp, and there are occasional **shuttle buses** running between *Sondzela* and *Malandela's Homestead* (see below), where pick-ups for the **Baz Bus** are made.

Through the Malkerns Valley

Continuing on the road towards Manzini, a turn to the southwest at Mahlanya, roughly 5km beyond the road to Mlilwane (beside a row of shops and a petrol station), takes you to the scenic, pineapple-growing **Malkerns Valley**. About a kilometre along this road, look out on the right-hand side for *Malandela's Homestead* (✆5283423), a fascinating collection of buildings where you can find craft shops, a pub and restaurant, a theatre and an internet café. Situated under a large thatched roof, *Malandela's Restaurant* (✆5283115) has a European-style menu with good-quality a la carte **meals** including stews, game and fresh fish dishes. The restaurant's outdoor dining area provides excellent views of the adjoining fields and distant mountains, while the adjoining **pub** has British beer on tap and is a popular spot for locals to watch big rugby and soccer games on cable TV. Next door is *Malandela's B&B* (✆5282110; ❸), with stylishly decorated rooms in colour themes. When booking ahead, make sure there isn't a concert happening next door.

On the other side, *All Out Projects* (Mon–Sat 9am–6pm; ✆5504951) has Internet access and is used by backpackers staying at *Sondzela* in Mlilwane (see above); it also operates as a useful **tourist information** point. Alongside *All Out*, the funky House on Fire is a gallery and amphitheatre-like performance space (✆5282001), worth checking out for contemporary African crafts and the exuberant imagination which has gone into designing the place. Next door, Gone Rural (✆5283439) is one of the most successful and creative **local handicrafts projects** in Swaziland; the colourful and well-designed woven mats and baskets on sale here are made by a huge network of women working from villages all over the country.

A little further on, several more **craft shops** line the Malkerns–Manzini road: *Swazi Candles* (daily 9am–1pm) sells a bewildering array of brightly patterned wax candles; Baobab Batik, 2km further along, sells all manner of colourful batiks. Beside this is *Nyanza Cottage* (✆5283090, ✉nyanza@africaonline.co.sz; ❶–❸), a relaxing cottage and backpackers lodge set on an appealing cluttered working farm roamed by dogs, cats, geese, peacocks and jersey cows. The cottages are linked to Nyanza Horse Trails, which offers cross-country and mountain rides lasting from half an hour to a whole day.

Manzini

MANZINI is Swaziland's largest city and its commercial hub. Almost all the country's industrial and commercial sector is based in or around here, and the city is dominated by office blocks and malls obscuring its few attractive edifices. With a rising crime rate and an atmosphere far less relaxed than Mbabane, Manzini would be an eminently missable place were it not for its outstanding **market** on the corner of Mhlakuvane and Mancishane streets (daily except Sun).

Much of Manzini's market is devoted to fruit and vegetables, household goods and traditional medicines, while an upper section that spills onto the steps below sells **crafts** and **fabrics**. The crafts selection is bigger, more varied and much better value than any other market in Swaziland, while the fabrics – from Zimbabwe, Congo and Mozambique – are hard to find elsewhere in the country.

Just north of the market, on Ngwane Street, stands **The Bhunu**, one of Manzini's new shopping malls. **The Hub**, south of the market, on Mhlakuvane Street, is smarter and has a good supermarket and several restaurants and takeaways. Manzini's only other point of interest is its original **Catholic mission**, an elegant stone building (not open to casual visitors) opposite the new cathedral on Sandlane Street (parallel to Mhlakuvane Street).

Practicalities

Buses from all over the country and South Africa pull in at Manzini's busy main bus station at the end of Louw Street, just north of Ngwane Street. **Matsapha airport** (☎5186155) lies 8km west of the city centre; if you're arriving here, you'll need to take a **taxi** into central Manzini. The centre itself is small enough to walk around.

Manzini has a limited selection of **places to stay**. In town, near the bus station, on the corner of Meintjies and Mahleka streets, the *Mozambique Hotel*

ACCOMMODATION
Matshapa Inn	A
Mozambique	D
Paradise Caravan Park	B
Swaziland Backpackers	C
Woza Nawa	E

RESTAURANTS
Fontana di Trevi	3
Gil Vicente	1
Mongolian	2

MANZINI

0 — 500 m

(☎5052489, 🖷5052586; ❷) offers tiny rooms with paper-thin walls, but has a friendly bar and an excellent restaurant. For backpackers, there's nothing in Manzini itself. Seven kilometres west of the city, on the road to Malkerns and eZulwini, is the recently upgraded *Swaziland Backpackers* (☎5187225, 🄴swazilandbackpackers@realnet.co.za; ❶), with small dorms, decent doubles and some pleasant areas outside for lounging around. The overnight stop for the **Baz Bus**, it consequently attracts a fair number of passing travellers. Trips to various attractions, including the game reserves, and activities such as white-water rafting can be organized, with pick-ups from the hostel. Across the road is the motel-like *Matshapa Inn* (☎5187481; ❸), and a sparse **campsite**, *Paradise Caravan Park* (☎5184935).

Woza Nawe, a **backpackers' lodge** located about 6km southeast of Manzini on the Big Bend road, has quickly established itself as a relaxed spot with a very different feel to most white-run lodges in South Africa. Run by a young Swazi, Mxolisi Mdluli (or Myxo for short), it has dorms and doubles, and space for camping (☎5058363 or 6044102, 🄴wozanawe@realnet.co.sz; ❶). The lodge is also a base for an ambitious community tourism project based in the village of **KaPhunga**, about 65km into the mountains southeast of Manzini. Here Myxo has built a mini-village of authentic huts and rondavels for backpackers to experience a few days as part of the local community. The huts are separate from the main village, so that a certain amount of privacy is allowed both visitors and villagers, but you're encouraged to eat and sleep in the traditional Swazi way. During the day, visitors can join in whatever is going on in the village, such as building projects, farming work, brewing beer or teaching at the local school. Two-day trips to KaPhunga, including transport and contributions to the village, cost around E360 per person (extra nights are E50).

As well as the *Mozambique's* restaurant, other good **places to eat** in town include *Gil Vicente*, in the Ilanga Centre, Martin Street (☎5053874; closed Mon), which serves tasty Portuguese dishes; the *Mongolian*, Villiers Street, where you'll find the best Chinese food in town; and the *Fontana de Trevi Pizzeria*, The Hub, Mhlakuvane Street. The best **nightlife** is found at the *Executives* nightclub, next to the *Oasis* restaurant on Tenbergen Street, which often attracts bands from South Africa at weekends and provides some no-holds-barred Swazi partying.

Piggs Peak and the northwest

The highveld of **Piggs Peak** and the **northwest** is unquestionably the most beautiful region of Swaziland, with rolling hills perfect for hiking, countless sparkling streams, a sprinkling of waterfalls and some wonderful accommodation.

Most visitors to the northwest enter Swaziland after going through the Kruger National Park (see p.697), but Piggs Peak is only 64km north of Mbabane and easily reached from there, too. The most spectacular – and rugged – entrance into the country is via the Bulembu road from Barberton in Mpumalanga (see p.701), which passes through Bulembu village on the way to Piggs Peak.

From Jeppe's Reef/Matsamo border

From the **Jeppe's Reef/Matsamo border** (8am–4pm), the road on the Swazi side is good all the way to Piggs Peak. Some 25km south of the border on this road is a good **place to stay**, the *Orion Piggs Peak Hotel & Casino* (☏4371104, ⓦwww.oriongroup.co.za; ⓺), set in thousands of acres of mountainous pine forest. Despite the monolithic appearance of the hotel's exterior, the rooms have fabulous views, and there's an inviting swimming pool with a bar in the middle, plus a good buffet **restaurant**. You can buy hand-spun mohair products in the hotel lobby as well as from their source nearby. However, like most of the large hotels in Swaziland, the main focus of the place is the casino and slot machines.

For somewhere very different in style and atmosphere, continue another 3km; a sign on the right indicates the private **Phophonyane Nature Reserve** (☏4371429, ⓦwww.pophonyane.co.sz), which is five slow kilometres away from the road. The reserve is small, but carefully laid-out **trails** ensure there's plenty to see, including the Phopanyane Waterfall on the reserve's eastern side. The vegetation is subtropical and attracts hundreds of colourful **bird species**. Animals include mongooses, bushbabies, otters and numerous snakes, but all are hard to spot. The lodge in the reserve is one of the most beautiful places to stay in Swaziland, offering two-person safari tents next to the Phopanyane River, with a communal kitchen and washing facilities (⓸), and cottages for four to six people, with private kitchens and gardens (⓹). If you can't afford to stay, it's still worth stopping here for a short hike in the reserve and a meal in its secluded, mid-priced **restaurant**. The pool, although chilly, is cleverly blended into the rocks beside the tumbling river and has a stunning location, looking out onto endless mountains and surrounded by luxuriant vegetation.

A few kilometres south of Phophonyane, 1km north of Piggs Peak, the turn-off to Kuthuleni is the start of a scenic fifty-kilometre drive along a good dirt road to **Bhalekane**. There isn't much in Bhalekane (except a prison), but you can proceed from here to Tshaneni and the **northeast** (see p.833), or head south through fairly remote territory to Mafutseni and then Manzini.

From Bulembu

The road from Barberton in Mpumalanga, to Piggs Peak via **Bulembu border post** (8am–4pm), is briefly tarred out of Barberton, but soon deteriorates as it passes through some of the most rugged country imaginable, with the road near the border crossing in particularly poor shape. Looking up, you can see the Barberton–Havelock cableway, which carries asbestos from the nearby Havelock mine to South Africa. Once in Swaziland, the road soon passes through Bulembu, with Piggs Peak a further 20km away.

Piggs Peak

PIGGS PEAK, a small straggling forestry town along the main road, was named after a French prospector called William Pigg, who discovered gold nearby in 1884, where it was mined until the site was exhausted in 1954. Apart from the attractive surrounding countryside, there's nothing much to see here, but if you're heading to Mallotja Nature Reserve this is a good place to stock up on supplies.

The town's **bus station** and **market** are near the Total garage at the northern end of town, where there is also a small shopping centre with a **supermarket**. There are a couple of **banks** in the centre of town, but they are unused to foreign transactions, so either summon your patience or hold out until Mbabane. For an **overnight stay**, the *Highland Inn* (☏4371144; ⓷) offers simple, but comfortable, rooms in a pleasant colonial building on the main road on the southern edge of town. Inside, the *Woodcutter's Den* **restaurant** serves steaks and other meat dishes at fairly reasonable prices. For a quick snack, *The Ranch*, in the town's shopping centre, offers fast food, while the *Pholani* **bar** alongside does plenty of trade, rocking until late on weekends.

On to Malolotja Nature Reserve

Driving south, you soon leave the pine plantations behind and pass into rolling highveld grassland, peppered with rural dwellings, with the stretch across the Nkomati River Valley a particularly beautiful one. Alongside the road are curio stalls, often staffed by young children dressed in leaves to attract your attention. Also along this road is evidence of the construction work on the large **Maguga Dam** project on the Komati River, which will radically alter the scenery of the river valley through flooding by the time it is completed early in the twenty-first century. Near here are two **places to stay** set up by young Swazi men offering a taste of rural living. *Mthunzi's Paradise Village* (T6080469, W www .swaziplace.com/mthunzi; ❸) is near the Komati River, and provides a chance to stay in a small community and experience local life, from river-fishing to supporting the local football team. The price includes a tour, accommodation and meals. Alternatively, *Sobantu Guest Farm* (T6053954; ❶) is a large modern farmhouse in an isolated spot near Mnyokane, where backpackers are encouraged to chill out for a few days. There are plenty of hiking trails, waterfall and rockpools nearby, and local Swazi food is often cooked in the evenings. Before making for either place you should contact them for precise directions.

About 30km from Piggs Peak, just after Nkhaba, you'll reach the entrance to the Malolotja Nature Reserve. The main road continues south from here to join the Ngwenya–Mbabane road at Motshane (see p.832), 20km further on.

Malolotja Nature Reserve

Swaziland's least touristy park, the easy-going **Malolotja Nature Reserve** (daily: May–Sept 6.30am–6pm; Oct–April 6am–6.30pm; E10 plus E5 per car; T4424241) offers awesome scenery and some of the finest hiking in southern Africa. This is a place to come for rugged, wild nature and tranquillity, rather than for game spotting. The mountains here, among the oldest in the world (3.6 billion years old), are covered in grassland and graced by myriad streams and waterfalls, including the 95-metre-high **Malolotja Falls**.

Nearly three hundred species of **birds** are found in Malolotja, with an impressive colony of the rare bald ibis just by the waterfalls. You'll have to look harder for **game**, although wildebeest, blesbok and impala are often visible, and there are leopards and two very retiring elephants lurking somewhere in the gaping tracts of mountain and valley; in the friendly spirit of the reserve, a leaflet is handed out on arrival asking hikers to help the park's research by reporting any signs of the elephants, or of the rare eland introduced a few years ago.

Malolotja also boasts **Ngwenya Mine**, the world's most ancient at 43,000 years old. The Stone Age Workers here once dug for specularite and haematite, which were used as cosmetics and for religious rituals. To visit you must book a **guide** at least one night beforehand, although there's always a guide on duty at weekends, at an entry point at the south of the reserve near the Ngwenya Glass factory (see p.832); note that this gate gives access to the mine only. Nearby, the **Forbes Reef Gold Mine** can be visited alone, but take care on the slippery banks; you can find it using the map you get on arrival at the park entrance.

Malolotja's small network of roads pass some fine viewpoints and picnic sites, but to really savour this park's rugged wilderness and see its waterfalls you'll need to hike. A variety of **hiking trails** are laid out in the reserve, from easy half-day excursions to seven-day marathons, with accommodation available en route (see below).

Practicalities

Brochures and **maps** are available from the reserve's **office**, just inside the entrance gate. The office also issues permits for Hawane Dam Nature Reserve (see below), as well as the useful free *Hiking and Backpacking Guide*.

Accommodation should be booked in advance through the National Trust Commission (see p.824). The main restcamp has fifteen tent sites with hot water in a communal bath area and braai areas, but not much wind shelter. There is also an A-frame **chalet** (❶), which sleeps up to six people, and five well-located log **cabins** (❷), which can also house up to six people each. A small shop at the entrance sells basic **provisions**, but it's wiser to stock up in Piggs Peak or Mbabane. Twenty **campsites** without facilities are scattered around the reserve for those attempting longer hikes: you'll need to bring all your own equipment, including a cooker, as no fires are permitted.

If you're on a long hike during the summer, be prepared for blisteringly hot days; however, temperatures drop dramatically in winter, when the nights can be freezing.

⑫ Hawane Dam and horse trails

Around two kilometres south of Malolotja, on the Mbabane road, lies the **Hawane Dam Nature Reserve** (☎4424241; Mon–Fri free, Sat & Sun E10), a small area around the northern end of the Hawane Dam, designed to protect part of the Black Umbuluzi River wetlands. Hawane's main attraction is its wealth of **birdlife**, and there's an excellent trail for bird-watching.

A little further on is **Hawane African Adventure Trails** (☎4043375, ⓦwww.hawane.co.sz), signposted down a track, a good option if you fancy exploring the attractive surrounding countryside on horseback. They have a range of ponies and horses for trails lasting anything between a couple of hours and a week. There's also a base-camp, with around half-a-dozen comfortable bee-hive **huts** sleeping two people (full board; ❷); this accommodation is available even if you're not riding.

Ngwenya

The road from Piggs Peak meets the main MR3 between the Ngwenya/Oshoek border post and Mbabane at the small settlement of **Motshane**. A kilometre west of Motshane along this road is the Ngwenya Glass factory (daily 9am–4pm), where of one of Swaziland's best-known exports, **Ngwenya glass**, is made. Their products, which range from attractive wine glasses to endless trinkets in the shape of rotund animals, are made from recycled glass and are produced by highly skilled workers, and it's well worth stopping here just to see them blowing and crafting the glass from the viewing balcony above the roaring furnaces. The adjoining gift shop and **café** are usually swamped by coach-loads of tourists, who can further satisfy their craving for crafts a few hundred metres from the factory up the hill at **Endlotane Studios** (Mon–Fri 8am–4.30pm, Sat–Sun 9am–5pm), where large and colourful tapestries are painstakingly woven from mohair wool spun on the premises. Nearby there is an entrance to Malolotja Nature Reserve, allowing access to **Ngwenya Mine** (see p.831).

The northeast

Northeast Swaziland is dominated by sugar plantations stretching into the distance, shimmering from the constant water spray, wreaking havoc with the water table – and leaving many locals without – but earning the country valuable foreign exchange. Three large tracts of bush – **Hlane**, **Mlawula** and **Mbuluzi** – have been preserved as wildlife and nature reserves, and these are the main attractions for visitors to this region. Together with **Shewula Nature Reserve**, these form part of the **Lubombo Conservancy**, a grouping of protected land in the **Lubombo Mountains** that runs along Swaziland's eastern border and provides fantastic views of both Swaziland and the western fringes of Mozambique.

The most direct and obvious route to the reserves from Mbabane is to follow the signposted and tarred **Siteki road** for 100km. The **northern route** is a little over twice as long and is part gravel, but makes for a far more spectacular journey. Travel north to **Piggs Peak** from Mbabane, and turn right at the **Bhalekane** turn-off towards Bhalkane, roughly 1km later.

Tshaneni

The gravel road from Piggs Peak passes through some fabulous scenery before eventually winding up at the sugar town of **TSHANENI**. The one **hotel** here, the *Impala Arms* (☏3131045; ❷), has plain but comfortable rooms; the bar has a pool table, and is filled with exuberant Swazi at weekends. If you need supplies, Tshaneni's Score **supermarket** will come in handy, and there is a Caltex **garage** nearby for fuel.

The **Mananga border post** (8am–6pm) lies 5km north of here, from where the road leads to Komatipoort (see p.697). Heading south, however, the next town you'll meet is bougainvillea-festooned **Mhlume**. Twenty kilometres further on is a junction at Maphiveni: a left turn to the north takes you to the **Lomahasha/Namaacha border post** with Mozambique (7am–8pm), another 20km away, while a right turn followed almost immediately by a signposted left takes you to Mbuluzi Game Reserve and Mlawula Nature Reserve.

Mbuluzi Game Reserve

Privately owned and little known, **Mbuluzi** (daily 8am–5pm; E10 per person, E20 per vehicle; ⓦ www.mbuluzi.co.sz) is about 1km off the Manzini–Lomahasha road, and straddles the road to Mlawula. Set in classic lowveld bush, it's filled with thorn trees and hot in the summer. Currently the park is being restocked with game, including hippo and giraffe, which you can view in your own vehicle – as long as it's 4WD. At the park entrance you can rent vehicles for E150 per day, and hire guides for a negotiable amount. The absence of predators in Mbuluzi's southern portion means that you can walk along a network of **trails** in this section.

Mbuluzi's self-catering **accommodation** (❻ for the whole lodge, which sleeps between three and eight people) is its finest feature: three large and comfortable lodges with verandahs overlook the Mlwawula stream, whose luxuriant vegetation attracts birds and animals which you can watch from the verandahs.

Mlawula Nature Reserve

The largest single protected area in the Lubombo Mountains is the 165-square-kilometre **Mlawula Nature Reserve** (daily dawn–dusk; E10 per person, E5 per vehicle), south of the Mbuluzi River. The best reason to come to Mlawula is to stay at *Sara Bush Camp* (see below), but you can spend some time exploring a network of self-guided hiking **trails**. As well as climbing into the mountains and onto the plateau at the top of the Lubombo range where unique species of ironwood trees and cycads grow, the trails wend their way around the river heading for caves, a waterfall and a rhino pool (although there are no rhino left), and vary in length from two to eight hours. The bush throughout the reserve is quite dense, however, which largely prevents you from seeing much game. Guides are available to lead you on the hiking trails.

The Mlawula stream and more substantial Mbuluzi River both flow through some spectacular valleys in this reserve, and Stone Age tools over one million years old have been found along their beds. **Antelope**, **zebra** and **wildebeest** congregate near the water, but so do **crocodiles**, so resist the temptation to swim.

Practicalities

Buses from Manzini travel to the Mlawula Nature Reserve once a day very early in the morning. To get here by **car**, continue past the Mbuluzi Reserve for a few kilometres until you see a sign pointing to the Mlawula Reserve on your right. You can pick up various leaflets at the park gate, but no supplies, so stock up beforehand.

Accommodation should be booked through the National Trust Commission, in the National Museum at Lobamba (see p.824). Overnight **camping** on the trail has not been permitted since the camping hut was burnt down, apparently by Mozambican border-hoppers, but there is a shaded campsite in the Siphiso River Valley. Much more appealing is the self-catering *Sara Bush Camp* (❷ per double tent), which has three large safari tents on wooden decks perched on the very edge of a cliff. Surrounded by bush, each tent also has it's own bathing area, consisting of a tiny perch amongst the rocks on the cliff edge with a donkey-boiler shower and galvanized iron washtub, allowing you to bathe outside with a stunning view west over the reserve and beyond, making it perfectly positioned for sunset. Each tent has a braai site and there's a communal lounge and kitchen area.

Shewula

Situated on a plateau to the north of Mlawula, **Shewula Mountain Camp** (booking essential ☏ 4162180, ✉ tours@swazitrails.co.za; ❶) is a new tourism development by the local Shewula community. Although it's isolated and time-consuming to reach, the camp has a spectacular site at one end of the plateau, with views west across northeast Swaziland and even, on a clear day, to the skyscrapers of Maputo to the east. It also offers an interesting insight into the life of a rural community in Swaziland. Accommodation is in four rondavels (which sleep up to eight people) with bunks or doubles around communal ablution and dining areas, but there's no electricity and cooking is done on gas. Activities include hiking through Shewula Nature Reserve and a visit to the nearby village. If you don't want to self-cater, meals can be arranged in advance.

Hlane Royal National Park

Some 67km northeast of Manzini is **Hlane Royal National Park** (daily dawn–dusk; E10), the largest of Swaziland's parks. Formerly a private royal hunting ground, the main attraction here is the presence of big game, including **elephant**, **rhino**, **lion**, **leopard** and **cheetah**. Hlane is also one of the best parks in southern Africa to view elephants and rhino **on foot** – an unforgettable experience – in the company of a guide (E15 per hour). These two species are in the northern area of the park, which you can also visit in your own vehicle, with or without a guide, and rhino-sighting is virtually guaranteed. Other animals in this section include giraffe, zebra and waterbuck.

Various **southern enclosures** contain lion, cheetah and leopard, along with some more elephant and rhino; walking here is out of the question, but you can drive with a guide in your own car. If you don't have your own transport you can join a guided tour in one of the park's 4WD minibuses (E100). Although the enclosures guarantee lion sightings, the animals are well habituated to vehicles and look thoroughly bored by the whole experience – a pity, as the presence of lions in the country is meant to be the source of great pride to the Swazis, not least because they are the royal symbol.

Practicalities

The **entrance** to Hlane is roughly 7km south of Simunye, off the Manzini–Lomahasha road. **Buses** between Manzini and Simunye stop at the park gate.

Hlane has two **accommodation** options, both of which must be **booked** through Big Game Parks Central Reservations (☎5283944, ⓦ www.biggame .co.sz). The main *Ndlovu* camp (❸), situated near the gate, offers large thatched cottages sleeping two to three people and camping spots, but no electricity (paraffin lamps are provided). Unless there's a large group staying, this camp is fairly relaxed, with plenty of trees and shady spots to sit. There's also a thatched restaurant and lounge area, with a wide deck overlooking a large nearby watering hole which attracts rhino, elephant and giraffe. The self-catering *Bhubesi* camp (❷), with its six comfortable stone cottages overlooking a dry river, is 11km from *Ndlovu* along a dirt track, and feels much more remote, though the cottages here have electricity.

Siteki

Perched spectacularly on a hillside and once the gateway to a busy border post with Mozambique, **SITEKI**, just over 30km south of Mlawula Nature Reserve, is a fairly lively regional centre. Although the border has now been closed for some years, Siteki remains busy, with a **bus station** that operates frequent services to Manzini, a colourful **market**, and a number of lively restaurants along the main street. Next door to the *Siteki* hotel, off the main road on the way out of town, is the headquarters of Litiko Letinyanga (☎3434512), a traditional healing organization, run by Dr Nhlavana Maseko, which seeks to improve the credibility of traditional healing with Western medical institutions. You may be able to arrange a session with a traditional healer, but you'll have to phone beforehand (ask for Betty).

There's only one **place to stay** – the *Siteki* (☎3434126; ❸), which is pleasant enough, though the rooms feel a bit spartan. Downstairs, the hotel **restaurant** serves steaks and other meat dishes, and there's a great bar attached, which is popular with locals and gets very lively at weekends.

At the beginning of the road ascending to the town, you'll pass through a foot-and-mouth disease control **checkpoint**; the guards only check you on the way out, to confiscate any meat products that you might have tucked away.

The south

Approaching Swaziland from one of its border crossings in the south is an excellent idea if you're travelling from northern KwaZulu-Natal through to the Kruger National Park or Mpumulanga. The scenery, particularly along the drive from **Mahamba** to Manzini through the **Grand Valley**, is really superb, and the road passes near most of the historical sites of the Swazi royal house. The south is also home to the **Mkhaya Nature Reserve**, Swaziland's most upmarket reserve and a sanctuary for the rare black rhino.

One of the most exhilarating things you can do in southern Swaziland is to **whitewater raft** on the beautiful Great Usutu River, located in the east of the country near the Mkhaya Nature Reserve. One of the best whitewater rivers in southern Africa, it's also one of the few where you can take a trip in a two-man "croc" raft. The route runs for 15km in summer (a bit less in winter), and crosses over rapids classed in grades two to four. The scenery en route is stunning, but hard to appreciate once you hit the rapids, which leave you paddling like crazy and doing your best not to fall in the water. Most people do capsize, but careful supervision ensures that everyone lives to tell the tale. Trips include pick-ups from various points in the eZulwini Valley and cost around E350 a person, including a picnic lunch and evening sundowners. Contact Swazi Trails (☎4162180, ⓦwww.swazitrails.co.sz) for bookings and further information.

From Mahamba to Manzini

The **Mahamba border crossing** (7am–10pm) is the nearest to Piet Retief in South Africa. Mahamba means "the runaways", which refers to nineteenth-century pretenders to the royal throne who fled here twice to escape retribution. The nearest major town is **NHLANGANO**, only 16km from the border. Nhlangano (the name means "meeting place", commemorating the meeting of the British and Swazi monarchs George V and Sobhuza II in 1947) is a good place to change money and to catch **buses** to Mbabane and Manzini.

The town also has a couple of decent **places to stay**: the lively *Phoenix* (☎2078488; ❸) on the main street offers en-suite rooms, while the upmarket *Nhlangano Sun* (☎2078211, ⓦwww.suninternational.com; ❻), designed to resemble a ski resort, lies off a signposted turn-off just north of town and looks out onto the Makhosini Valley. The rooms are plush, and the hotel's reasonably priced **restaurant** is worth a visit if you're just passing through; there's also a casino.

The **Makhosini Valley**, 8km **east of Nhlangano** on the Mhlosheni road, is the site of the main **royal burial grounds**, guarded and tended by the Mduli clan. To avoid disturbing their rulers' eternal rest, the Mduli never cut the grass; consequently, the grounds now stand out as islands of forest in a sea of cultivated land. The Mduli also grind the king's medicines and snuff, and have the interesting task of preventing any part of his body (including his faeces, semen and toe-clippings) from being used for magical purposes.

A little further on is a turn to the south to **Zombodze**, King Ngwane I's first royal residence in modern-day Swaziland. It's badly signposted, so follow signs for the nearby Ngwane High School.

Another 28km **north of Nhlangano**, along on a good road, is the settlement of **HLATHIKHULU**, perched impressively on a hill and providing cool relief after the murderous heat below. Ngwane's grandson **Sobhuza I** fled near here from the attacks of the mighty Ndwandwe king Zwide, to a place called kaPhungalegazi ("place of the smell of blood"), though nothing is now left of the kraal he erected here. Sadly for the town, the main road steams right by it, leaving it forlorn on a diversion to the right.

The Ngwane clan fought a murderous but inconclusive battle with the Zulus under King Dingane in the nearby **Lubuya Valley** in 1839. This quiet valley is barely populated and, though there's nothing to remind you of the battle that once raged here, it's a good place for a picnic and a stroll. To get to the valley from Hlathikhulu, take the first turning right after heading north towards Manzini, towards Lugoje Nek, and a left turn at the fork here brings you to the valley. The battle left Dingane's army much reduced, making him an easy target for his brother Mpande the following year.

From Hlathikhulu, Manzini is 74km away, with the bulk of the drive passing along the **Grand Valley**, through which flows the sometimes mighty Mkhondvo River. The valley is hot, overgrazed and almost barren, but offers stunning hiking possibilities and stupendous views from a car.

From Lavumisa to Manzini

Travelling north from KwaZulu-Natal, you'll come to the **Lavumisa/Golela border post** (7am–10pm). The border is named after one of the wives of Sobhuza I, whose son Malambule tried to overthrow Sobhuza's successor, Mswati II. Golela, on the South African side, means "many animals", and indeed this area was once predominantly a hunting ground. Today, however, the animals have all but gone and there's little reason to linger, unless you're tempted by the prospect of a close encounter with one of the lions at a small, new game reserve, **Nisela Safaris** (daily 8.30am–4.30pm; E15; ☎3030247, ⓦwww.niselasafaries .co.za). The reserve's animals, including giraffe, kudu, zebra and warthog, are for understandable reasons of preservation kept apart from the lions, who prowl their own separate enclosure. Accommodation is offered in thatched cabins (❸), each sleeping four, and a colonial-style guesthouse (❸); there's also a pool and restaurant. At the entrance to the reserve, a coffee shop and curio stall provide a rest stop for drivers making their way to or from the border.

The road north crosses the Ingwavuma River just south of Nsoko, about 30km from the border, and then runs parallel to the **Lubombo Mountains**. A few kilometres before Big Bend, you'll pass **The Riverside**, a complex on the main road housing a functional **motel** (☎3636012; ❷), a good Portuguese restaurant and a scruffy nightclub; downstairs, Emoya Handicrafts offers a small selection of good-value pieces. Next door is the Bushlands Butchery, where prices are so good that many South Africans drive here to stock up on meat. A kilometre further on is an outstanding **restaurant**, *Lubombo Lobster* (☎3636613), which serves a wonderful seafood curry.

Big Bend itself, dominated by a huge sugar mill, is only worth visiting for its **hotel**, the *New Bend Inn* (☎3636111; ❷), on a hill at the far end of town beyond the golf course. A slightly run-down colonial establishment with superb views of the valley and well-positioned bars, the sixteen-bedroom hotel is a lively Swazi haunt on weekends, when major parties take place. The rooms are spartan but air-conditioned and comfortable, and the hotel **restaurant** serves tolerable curries and grills for around E25–40.

From the centre of Big Bend, **buses** travel to Manzini, Mbabane and north to Siteki (see p.835).

Mkhaya Game Reserve

Roughly 30km north of Big Bend lies **Mkhaya Game Reserve**, situated along a turn-off from the wonderfully named village of **Phuzumoya** ("drink

The long-horned **Nguni cattle**, herded by the African clans when Europeans encountered them in the nineteenth century, were descendants of the early Iron Age herds. Although they are hardy, disease-resistant and well-adapted to their environment, white beef-farmers regarded them as too puny and unproductive for their industry, and replaced them with imported stock. By the 1970s, pure strains of long-horned cattle had virtually disappeared from Swaziland, and **Ted Reilly** initially purchased Mkhaya (see p.837) to save them. The sharp increase in the price of cattle feed in the late 1970s made the long-horns increasingly attractive commercially, enabling Reilly to sell them as pure-bred breeding stock, using the money to fund the game acquisition programme at Mkhaya. Today, the cattle graze here alongside zebra, wildebeest and antelope, just as they always used to.

the wind") in classic lowveld scrubland, filled with acacia and thorn trees. A sanctuary for the rare **black rhino**, Mkhaya also accommodates **white rhino**, **elephant** and numerous antelopes such as nyala, sable and eland. As well as a tourist attraction, Mkhaya also operates as a refuge where endangered species such **roan antelope** and **tsessebe** are bred. Rubbing shoulders with them all are herds of **Nguni cattle** (see box above).

Day visits and overnight stays at Mkhaya must be booked in advance (see below), and you can't tour Mkhaya in your own vehicle, but must arrange to be met at the gate (10am or 4pm). Day visitors are taken on a game drive, where you have a high chance of encountering much of the big game, and a generous **lunch** is included in the price. For overnighters, morning and evening game drives are included in the accommodation price. Unlike game reserves in South Africa, Mkhaya's experienced Swazi rangers have few qualms about stopping in the middle of a game drive and inviting visitors to get out of the vehicle and walk quite close to white rhino and elephant. If you're staying overnight, early-morning game walks can also be organized.

You'll need to **book** your visit to Mkhaya through Swazi Big Game Parks Central Reservations (℡5283944, Ⓦwww.biggame.co.sz). Day visits cost around E250, including lunch. The reserve's main camp, *Stone Camp*, makes up for the lack of elevation in the reserve with an atmospheric bush setting beside the dry Ngwenyane river bed. Full-board **accommodation** (including game drives ❽) is offered in deceptively luxurious open-plan and open-sided thatched cottages with en-suite toilets and showers, which give you a wonderful sense of sleeping right in the bush. All of these are secluded but secure and lit by paraffin lamps; cooking is done on a large campfire in the main part of the camp under the shade of a massive sausage tree (its seed pods look like sausages), and staff have been known to treat guests to traditional dancing.

Travel details

Buses

Big Bend to: Manzini (13 daily; 1hr 30min); Siteki (2 daily; 1hr 30min).
Manzini to: Big Bend (13 daily; 1hr 30min); Hlatsi (2 daily; 1hr 30min); Lavumisa (2 daily; 5hr);
Mbabane (27 daily; 45min); Nhlangano (12 daily; 3hr 15min); Siteki (15 daily; 1hr 30min).
Mbabane to: Manzini (27 daily; 45min); Nhlangano (4 daily; 4hr); Piggs Peak (10 daily; 1hr).
Nhlangano to: Manzini (12 daily; 3hr 15min); Mbabane (4 daily; 4hr).

Piggs Peak to: Mbabane (10 daily; 1hr).
Siteki to: Big Bend (2 daily; 1hr 30min); Manzini (15 daily; 1hr 30min).

Baz Bus

There are three services a week on each of the two Baz Bus routes from Manzini, namely south to Durban and west to Jo'burg/Pretoria.
Manzini to: Ballito (9hr 15min); Durban (11hr); Eshowe (7hr 45min); Gingindlovu (8hr 15min); Johannesburg (10hr); Malkerns Valley (15min); Mbabane (1hr); Mtubatuba (5hr 45min); Nelspruit (4hr); Pretoria (11hr); St Lucia (5hr 15min).

Flights

Manzini to: Durban (daily except Sat; 1hr); Johannesburg (3–4 daily; 1hr); Maputo (Mozambique; 1 daily Tues–Thurs; 45min).

Contexts

Contexts

History 849

Wildlife 867

Music 883

Literature 898

Books 918

History

H uman history – or prehistory – probably began in South Africa. That, at least, is the story told by recent fossil finds, which show that *Homo sapiens* existed along Africa's southern coast over 50,000 years ago. The descendants of these nomadic Stone Age people – ochre-skinned San hunter-gatherers and Khoikhoi herders – still inhabited the Western Cape when the first European seafarers arrived in the fifteenth century. By the time of the first Dutch settlement at the Cape in the mid-seventeenth century, tall dark-skinned people, who had begun crossing the Limpopo around the time of Christ's birth, had occupied much of the eastern half of the country.

The stage was now set for the complex drama of South Africa's modern history, which in crude terms was a battle for the control of scarce resources between the various indigenous people, African states and the European colonizers. The twentieth century saw the temporary victory of colonialism, the unification of South Africa and the attempts by whites to keep at bay black demands for civil rights, culminating in the implementation of South Africa's most notorious social invention – **apartheid**. Ultimately, it was multiracialism that was victorious and, despite numerous problems, South Africa celebrated ten years of democracy in 2004 in a mood of high optimism.

Prehistory

When our ancestors climbed down from the trees, it is quite likely they did it in South Africa. In 1924, the world's **oldest hominid remains** and the first-ever evidence of human-like creatures to be discovered in Africa were dug up in the Northern Cape and identified as a "fossilized monkey skull". After a stint as a humble paperweight, the fossil came to the attention of Professor Raymond Dart at Johannesburg's University of the Witwatersrand, who identified the earthshaking find as an intermediate species between apes and humans, with a small brain but an upright posture. Still a little unsteady on its feet, our ancestor trod the plains of eastern and southern Africa, perhaps three million years ago. Dart called it *Australopithecus africanus*: **Africa's southern ape**. After the emergence of *A. africanus*, hominids spent the next couple of million years or so perfecting bipedal walking, tool-making and speech, and got big-headed (a huge expansion in brain size took place) until they finally strode forth as *Homo sapiens*: the modern humans. Another first for South Africa was the unearthing of the oldest fossil evidence of *Homo sapiens* in a cave at the Klasies River Mouth in the Eastern Cape, reckoned to be between 50,000 and 100,000 years old.

The first South Africans

Rock art provides evidence of human culture in the subcontinent dating back nearly 30,000 years and represents southern Africa's oldest and most enduring artistic tradition. The artists were hunter-gatherers, sometimes called Bushmen but more commonly **San**. This is a relatively modern term from the Nama language with roots in the concept of "inhabiting or dwelling", to reflect the fact these were South Africa's aboriginals. The most direct descendants of the late Stone Age, San people have survived in tiny pockets, mostly in Namibia and Botswana, making theirs the longest-spanning culture in the subcontinent. At one time they probably spread throughout sub-Saharan Africa, having pretty well perfected their **nomadic lifestyle**, which involved an enviable twenty-hour working week spent by the men hunting and the women gathering. This left considerable time for artistic and religious pursuits. People lived in small, loosely connected bands comprising family units and were free to leave and join up with other groups. In this egalitarian society the concept of private property had scant meaning because everything required for survival could be obtained from the environment.

About two thousand years ago, this changed when some groups in northern Botswana laid their hands on fat-tailed **sheep and cattle** from northern Africa, thus transforming themselves into **herding communities**. The introduction of livestock had a revolutionary effect on social organization, creating the idea of ownership and accumulation. Social divisions developed, and political units became larger and centred around a chief, who had important powers, such as the allocation of pasturage.

These were the first South Africans encountered by Portuguese mariners, who landed along the Cape coast in the fifteenth century. Known as **Khoikhoi** (meaning "men of men"), they were not ethnically distinct from the San, as many anthropologists once believed, but simply represented a distinct social organization. According to current thinking it was possible for Khoi who lost their livestock to revert to being San, and for San to lay their hands on animals to become Khoi, giving rise to the collective term "**Khoisan**". This dynamic view of history is significant because it throws out the nineteenth-century idea that race was an absolute determinant of history and culture – a concept that found great popularity among apartheid apologists.

Farms and crafts

Around two thousand years ago, tall, dark-skinned people who practised mixed farming – raising both crops and livestock – crossed the Limpopo River into what is today South Africa. San paintings from some time in the intervening period depict small ochre people and larger black ones in a variety of hostile and harmonious relationships, indicating contact between the two groups. These **Bantu-speaking** farmers were the ancestors of South Africa's majority African population, who gradually drifted south, to occupy the entire eastern half of the subcontinent as far as the Eastern Cape, where they were first encountered by Europeans in the sixteenth century.

Today there are four main **Bantu language groups** in South Africa. **Nguni** (comprising Zulu, Swazi and Xhosa) and **Sotho** (Sotho and Tswana) are by far the largest; the other two are **Venda** and **Tsonga**. Apart from having highly developed farming know-how and a far more sedentary life than the Khoisan, the early Bantu speakers were skilled craftworkers and knew about mining and smelting metals, including gold, copper and iron, which became an important factor in the extensive network of **trade** that developed.

The picture painted of them by the British, as bloodthirsty Africans engaged in endemic internecine conflicts, probably said more about the white colonizers than the Bantu speakers themselves. The nineteenth-century traveller Ludwig

Alberti underlined this fact when he observed that the Xhosa of the Eastern Cape "cannot be regarded as a warlike people; a predominant inclination to pursue a quiet cattle-raising life is much more in evidence amongst them".

The Cape goes Dutch

In the fifteenth century, Portuguese mariners under the command of **Bartholomeu Dias** became the first Europeans to set foot in South Africa. Marking their progress, they left an unpleasant set of calling cards all along the coast – African men and women they had captured in West Africa and had cast ashore to trumpet the power and glory of Portugal to the locals. Little wonder that their first encounter with the Khoi along the Garden Route coast was not a happy one. It began with a group of Khoi stoning the Portuguese for taking water from a spring without asking permission and ended with a Khoi man lying dead with a crossbow bolt through his chest.

It was another 170 years before any European settlement was established in South Africa. In 1652, a group of white employees of the **Dutch East India Company**, which was engaged in trade between the Netherlands and the East Indies, pulled into Table Bay to set up a refreshment station to revictual company ships trading between Europe and the East. There was no thought at the time of setting up a colony; on the contrary, the Cape was a rather bum posting, given to the station commander **Jan van Riebeeck** because he had been caught with his hand in the till by the company bosses. Van Riebeeck dreamed up a number of schemes to isolate the Cape Peninsula from the rest of Africa, including a plan to build a canal that would cut it adrift. In the end, he had to satisfy himself with planting a **bitter almond hedge** (still growing in Cape Town's Kirstenbosch Gardens) to keep the natives at bay, symbolically representing an ambivalence about being European in Africa, which still haunts many white South Africans.

Despite Van Riebeeck's view that the **Khoi**, who were already living at the Cape, were "a savage set, living without conscience", from the start the Dutch were dependent on them to provide livestock, which were traded for trinkets. As the settlement developed, Van Riebeeck needed more **labour** to keep the show going, and bemoaned the fact that he was unsuccessful in persuading the Khoi to discard their herding life for the toil of ploughing furrows for him. Much to his annoyance, the bosses back in Holland had forbidden Van Riebeeck from enslaving the locals, and refused his request for slaves from elsewhere in the company's empire.

This led to the inexorable process of **colonization** of the lands around the fort, when a number of Dutch men were released in 1657 from their contracts to farm as **free burghers** on land granted by the company. The idea was that they would have to sell their produce to the company at a fixed price, thereby overcoming the labour shortage. The only snag with this was the land didn't belong to the company in the first place, and the move sparked the first of a series of **Khoikhoi-Dutch wars**. Although the first campaign ended in stalemate, the Khoikhoi were ultimately no match for the Dutch, who had the tactical mobility of horses and the superior killing power of firearms. Campaigns continued through the 1660s and 1670s and proved rather profitable for Dutch raiders, who on one outing in 1674 rounded up eight hundred Khoi cattle and four thousand sheep.

Meanwhile, in 1658, van Riebeeck had managed to successfully purloin a shipload of **slaves** from West Africa, whetting an insatiable appetite for this form of labour. The Dutch East India Company itself became the biggest slave owner at the Cape and continued importing slaves, mostly from the East Indies, at such a pace that by 1711 there were more slaves than burghers in the colony. By the end of the eighteenth century there were almost fifteen thousand slaves and just under fourteen thousand burghers at the Cape. With the help of this ready workforce, the embryonic Cape Colony expanded outwards and trampled the Peninsula Khoikhoi, who by 1713 had lost everything. Most of their livestock (nearly fifty thousand animals) and most of their land west of the Hottentots Holland Mountains (the peaks 90km southeast of present-day Cape Town) had been gobbled up by the Dutch East India Company. Dispossession and diseases like smallpox, previously unknown in South Africa, decimated their numbers and shattered their social system. By the middle of the eighteenth century, those who remained had been reduced to a condition of miserable servitude to the colonists.

Impoverished whites living at the fringes of colonial society also had few options, but these included the possibility of dropping out of its grindingly class-conscious constraints. Many just packed up their waggons and rolled out into the interior, where they lived by the gun, either hunting game or taking cattle from the Khoi by force. Beyond the control of the Dutch East India Company, these nomadic **trekboers** began to assume a pastoral niche previously occupied by the Khoi. By the turn of the nineteenth century, *trekboers* had penetrated well into the Eastern Cape, pushing back the Khoi and San in the process. Not that the indigenous people gave up without a fight. As their lives became disrupted and living by traditional means became impossible, the Khoisan began to prey on the cattle and sheep of the *trekboers*. The *trekboers* responded by hunting down the San as vermin, killing the men and often taking women and children as slaves, bringing them to virtual extinction in South Africa.

After the **British occupation of the Cape** in 1795, the *trekboer* migration from the Cape accelerated. Britain was now the world's dominant naval power. In the ferment that followed the French Revolution, Britain feared for the security of the Cape sea route to the East and therefore sent a few war sloops into Table Bay, informing the Dutch officials there that they were no longer in charge.

Rise of the Zulus

While in the west of the country *trekboers* were migrating from the Cape Colony, in the east equally significant movements were under way. Throughout the seventeenth and eighteenth centuries, descendants of the first **Bantu speakers** to penetrate into South Africa had been swelling their numbers and had expanded right across the eastern half of the country, where the rainfall was high enough for their mixed farming economy. By the turn of the nineteenth century, the territory was brimming with people and cattle who were fast grazing it out, the limits of expansion having been reached. Exacerbating this was a sustained period of drought.

Nowhere was this more marked than in **KwaZulu-Natal**, where chiefdoms survived by subduing and absorbing their neighbours to gain control of pasturage, thus creating larger and more powerful groupings. By the early part of the nineteenth century, two chiefdoms, the **Ndwandwe** and the **Mthethwa**, dominated the eastern section of South Africa around the Tugela River. During the late 1810s a major confrontation between them ended in the defeat of the Mthethwa.

Out of their ruins emerged the **Zulus**, who were to become one of the most powerful polities in southern Africa. Prior to the defeat of the Mthethwa, the Zulus had been a minor clan under their domination. Around 1816, **Shaka** assumed the chieftaincy of the Zulus, whose fighting tactics he quickly transformed, supplementing the Nguni's traditional long javelin with the **assegai**, a short spear suitable for close combat. The throwing spear rendered a warrior unarmed once he had thrown it and was relatively easily deflected by a cowhide shield, but with a stabbing spear he could keep on fighting as long as he could stand. Shaka also introduced the tactic known as the "horns of the bull", by which the enemy were outflanked by highly disciplined formations spreading out to engulf them by means of two wings. The manoeuvre was used to devastating effect against the British at the Battle of Isandlwana in 1879.

By 1820, the Zulus had incorporated the fragments of the Mthethwa and defeated the Ndwandwe. By the middle of the decade they had formed a **centralized military state** with a forty-thousand-strong standing army. The nature of war in the east changed from the almost symbolic skirmishes that characterized Nguni raids up to the end of the eighteenth century, to decisive battles in which massacres of women and children weren't unknown. Nevertheless, the real strength of the system lay in its ability to absorb the survivors, who became members of the expanding Zulu state. Throughout the 1820s, Shaka sent out his armies to attack his neighbours and take their cattle. But in 1828, in a palace coup, he was stabbed to death by a servant and two of the king's half-brothers, one of whom, **Dingane**, succeeded him. Dingane continued with his brother's ruthless policies and tactics.

The rise of the Zulu state reverberated right across southern Africa and led to the creation of a series of **centralized Nguni states** as well as paving the way for Boer expansion into the interior. In a movement known as the **mfecane**, or forced migrations, huge areas of the country were laid waste and people across eastern South Africa were driven off their lands. They attempted to survive either in small groups or by banding together to form larger political organizations. To the north of the Zulu kingdom another Nguni group with strong cultural and linguistic affinities with the Zulus came together under Sobhuza I and his son Mswati II, after whom their new state **Swaziland** took its name. In North West Province, a few hundred Zulus under the leadership of **Mzilikazi** took refuge after rebelling against Shaka. By 1829 their numbers had swelled to around seventy thousand, but in 1838 they were routed by encroaching Voortrekkers, against whose firearms they proved no match. They relocated to southwestern Zimbabwe, where they re-established themselves as the **Matabele** (or **Ndebele**) kingdom. In the Drakensberg, on the west flank of KwaZulu-Natal, **Moshoeshoe I**, another chief with humble origins, used diplomacy and cunning to build up his state from the ruins of the *mfecane*. By providing a haven to refugees, he was able to build up a substantial state from disparate Sotho groupings. Believing that "peace is like the rain which makes the grass grow", he kept no standing army, relying instead on opportunism and good-neighbourliness to survive, which he did. His territory became the modern state of **Lesotho**.

The Great Trek

Back in the Cape, many Afrikaners were becoming fed up with British rule. Their principal grievance was the way in which the colonial authorities were tampering with labour relations and destroying what they saw as a divine distinction between blacks and whites. In 1828 the **Cape Ordinance 50** gave Khoi residents and free blacks equality with whites before the law. The **abolition of slavery** in 1834 was the last straw. One Voortrekker wrote: "it's not so much their freedom that drove us to such lengths, as their being placed on an equal footing with Christians, contrary to the laws of God and the natural distinction of race".

In this spirit, fifteen thousand Afrikaners (one out of ten living in the colony) set out to leave the Cape and once and for all shake off the meddlesome British. When they arrived in the eastern half of the country, they were delighted to find vast tracts of apparently unoccupied land. In fact, they were merely stumbling into the eye of the *mfecane* storm – areas that had been temporarily cleared either by war parties or by fearful people hiding out to escape detection. As they fanned out further they encountered the Nguni states and a series of battles followed. By the middle of the nineteenth century, the Voortrekkers had consolidated control and established the two Boer states of the **South African Republic** (now Mpumalanga, North West and Limpopo provinces) and the **Orange Free State** (now Free State), the independence of both of which was recognized by Britain in the 1850s.

Gold and diamonds

Britain wasn't too concerned about the interior of South Africa. Its strategic position apart, South Africa was a chaotic and undeveloped backwater at the butt-end of the Empire. At this time, the United States, which was first settled by Britons a mere thirty years before the Dutch hit South Africa, had a population of over thirty million people of European extraction and 80,000km of railways, compared with South Africa's 250,000 whites and 120km of railways. Things changed in the 1860s, with the discovery of **diamonds** (the world's largest deposit) around modern-day Kimberley and even more significantly in the 1880s, with the discovery of **gold** on the Witwatersrand (now Gauteng). Together, these finds were the catalyst that transformed South Africa from a down-at-heel rural society into an urbanized industrial one. In the process great fortunes were made by capitalists like **Cecil Rhodes**, traditional African society was crushed and the independence of the Boer republics ended.

Although the **Gauteng goldfields** were exceptionally well endowed with ore, they were also particularly difficult to mine, requiring the sinking of deep shafts. Exploiting the mines required costly equipment and cheap labour to operate it. Capital quickly flowed in from Western investors eager for profit: even today the West retains strong links with the South African mines, and South Africa remains the world's largest producer of gold.

The Anglo-Boer War

Despite the benefits it brought, the discovery of gold was also one of the principal causes of the Anglo-Boer War. Gold-mining had shifted the economic centre of South Africa from the British-controlled Cape to a Boer republic, while at the same time, Britain's European rival, Germany, was beginning to make political and economic inroads in the Boer republics. Britain feared losing its strategic Cape naval base, but perhaps even more important were questions of international finance and the substantial British investment in the mines. London was at the heart of world trade and was eager to see a flourishing gold-mining industry in South Africa, but the Boers seemed rather sluggish about modernizing their infrastructure to assist the exploitation of the mines.

In any case, a number of Britons had for some time seen the unification of South Africa as the key to securing **British interests** in the subcontinent. To this end, under a wafer-thin pretext, the British empire had declared war and subdued the last of the independent African kingdoms by means of the **Zulu War** of 1879. This secured KwaZulu-Natal and meant that all the coastal territories of South Africa were under British control. To control the entire sun-continent south of the Limpopo, all that remained was to bring the two Boer republics under the Union Jack.

During the closing years of the nineteenth century, Britain demanded that the South African Republic grant voting rights to British miners living there – a demand that, if met, would have meant the end of Boer political control over their own state, since they were outnumbered by the foreigners. The Boers turned down the request and war broke out in October 1899. The British command, which had been used to fighting colonial wars against enemies armed with spears, believed they were looking at a walkover; in the words of Lord Kitchener, "a teatime war" that would get the troops home in time to open their Christmas presents.

In fact, the battle turned into Britain's most expensive campaign since the Napoleonic Wars. During the early phase of the war, the Boers took the imperial power by surprise and penetrated into British-controlled KwaZulu-Natal and the Northern Cape, inflicting a series of humiliating defeats. By June a reinforced British army was pushing the Boers back and once again the high command was talking about being home in time for their Christmas pudding. But the Boers fought on for another two years of protracted guerrilla war. **Lord Kitchener** responded ruthlessly with a scorched-earth policy that left the countryside a smouldering wasteland and thousands of women and children homeless. To house these thousands of dispossessed, the British introduced the **concentration camp**, in which 26,370 Boer women and children died. For some Afrikaners, this episode remains a major source of bitterness against the British today. Less widely publicized were the **African concentration camps** which took 14,000 lives. By 1902, the Boers were demoralized and split between those who couldn't face another winter of near starvation (the so-called "hands-uppers") and those who wanted to fight on ("the bitter-enders"). In May that year, the Boer republics signed a treaty surrendering their independence in exchange for British promises of reconstruction. By the end of the so-called "teatime war", Britain had committed nearly half a million men to the field and lost 22,000 of them. Of the 88,000 Boers who fought, 7000 died in combat. With the two Boer republics and the two British colonies under imperial control, the way was clear for the federation of the **Union of South Africa** in 1910.

Migrant labour and the Bambatha Rebellion

Between the conclusion of the Anglo-Boer War and the unification of South Africa, the mines suffered a shortage of **unskilled labour**. Most Africans still lived by agriculture, either as tenant farmers on white farms or in reserves created by the colonial government. They had no need to desert their traditional farming way of life for a thankless existence in shantytowns far away from home. To counter this, the government took measures to compel them to supply their labour. One method was the imposition of **taxes** that had to be paid in coin, thus forcing Africans from subsistence farming and into the cash economy. Responding to one such tax, a group of Zulus protested in 1906 and refused to pay up. The authorities declared martial law and dealt mercilessly with the protesters, burning their huts and seizing all their possessions. This provoked a full-blown rebellion led by Chief Bambatha, which was ruthlessly put down by the colonial authorities, with four thousand rebels dying in the process. This marked an end to armed resistance by Africans for over half a century. After the defeat of the **Bambatha Rebellion**, the number of African men from Zululand working in the Gauteng mines shot up by sixty percent. By 1909, eighty percent of adult males in the territory were absent from their homes and working as migrant labourers. **Migrant labour**, with its shattering effects on family life, became one of the foundations of South Africa's economic and social system, and was a basic cornerstone of apartheid.

Kick-starting Afrikanerdom

In a parallel development, large numbers of **Afrikaners** were forced to leave rural areas in the early part of the twentieth century. This was partly due to the aftermath of British scorched-earth tactics during the Anglo-Boer War, but also a result of overcrowding, drought and pestilence. Many Afrikaners joined the ranks of a swelling poor **white working class** that felt itself caught in a vice: victimized and despised on the one hand by the English-speaking capitalists who commanded the economy, and on the other under pressure from lower-paid Africans competing for their jobs.

In 1918 (the year Nelson Mandela was born) a group of Afrikaners formed the **Broederbond** ("the brotherhood"), a secret society to promote the interest of Afrikaners and to forge an Afrikaner republic in South Africa. It aimed to uplift impoverished members of the *volk* ("people") and to develop a sense of pride in their language, religion and culture. Ultimately, the Broederbond was to dominate every aspect of the way the country was run for close on half a century.

During the 1930s, a number of young Afrikaner intellectuals travelled to Europe, where they were inspired by the jackbooted march of **fascism** in Portugal, Spain, Italy and Germany. This extreme manifestation of nationalism appeared to hold the key to realizing Afrikaner nationhood. It was around this time that Afrikaner intellectuals began using the term **apartheid** (pronounced "apart-hate", not "apart-hide"). Among the leading lights of apartheid who could be found kicking their heels in Germany in the 1930s were **Nico Diederichs**, who become one of the ministers of finance while the Afrikaner nationalist National Party was in power; **Hendrik Frensch Verwoerd**, apartheid's leading theorist and prime minister from 1958 to 1966; and **Piet Meyer**, controller of the state broadcasting service, who named his son Izan ("Nazi" spelled backwards – he later claimed this was sheer coincidence).

In 1939, the Broederbond kicked into action with a scheme that launched ten thousand Afrikaner businesses in the space of a decade. Some of these, such as Rembrandt Tobacco, Volkskas (the country's third-largest bank), the Santam insurance company and Gencor (one of the five largest mining houses) are still among the leading players in South Africa's economy.

Africans' claims

Despite having relied on African cooperation for their victory in the Anglo-Boer War and having hinted at enhanced rights for blacks after the war, the British excluded blacks from the cosy deal between Afrikaners and Britain that resulted in the unification of South Africa. It wasn't long, in fact, before the white Union government began eroding African rights. In response, a group of middle-class mission-educated Africans formed the **South African Native National Congress** (later to become the ANC) in 1912. The founders weren't interested in overthrowing the white government; they simply wanted recognition by white society. Middle-class blacks already enjoyed the vote in the Cape Province (now the Western, Northern and Eastern Capes) on the basis of a **qualified franchise** according to education and property ownership, and the early African leaders wanted this extended to the rest of the country. Taking as their model the evolutionary growth of democracy in Britain, they hoped that this would eventually lead to universal suffrage.

In 1914, the leaders set off as a deputation for London, to protest against the 1913 **Natives' Land Act**, which severely restricted property ownership by blacks and provided for the division of South Africa into distinct African and white areas, with blacks – despite constituting the overriding majority of the population – confined to less than ten percent of the land surface. The trip was unsuccessful, and the Land Act would be the legal foundation for the formalization of apartheid some 35 years later.

Through the early half of the twentieth century, the ANC remained a conservative organization, unwilling to engage in active protest. This led to accusations that its leaders were "good boys tied to the apron strings of the white liberals". In response, a number of alternative mass organizations arose. Among the largest was the mighty **Industrial and Commercial Union**, an African trade union founded in 1919, which at its peak in 1928 had gathered an impressive 150,000 members. But in the 1930s it ran out of steam. The first political movement in the country not organized along ethnic lines was the **South African Communist Party**, founded in 1921 with a multiracial executive. While it never itself gained widespread membership, it became an important force inside the ANC.

Throughout the 1930s, the ANC plodded on with speeches, petitions and pleas, which proved completely fruitless. They suffered a major setback in 1936 with the **termination of the African franchise** in the Cape Province. The ANC's response was to send a deputation to Prime Minister Hertzog to protest; Hertzog treated them abominably, not even offering them seats. These events left the ANC crippled and hobbling impotently into the 1940s.

World War II split Afrikanerdom. There were those like Prime Minister **Jan Smuts** who stood firmly in favour of joining the war alongside Britain. But for others, like **John Vorster**, Britain was the old enemy, so they supported Germany, some signing up with the **Ossewa Brandwag** (the "Ox Wagon Torch Commando"), which carried out sabotage against the government. After the war there were hopes of reform from Smuts, who at the time was playing a leading role in the formation of the **United Nations**. Smuts even had a part in penning the Preamble to the Charter on Human Rights, but while his work for abstract "human rights" earned him a statue next to Winston Churchill outside Britain's parliament, he was in no hurry to grant such rights to the majority of South Africans. Even conservative African leaders were losing patience: one, Councillor Paul Mosaka, complained that "we have been asked to co-operate with a toy telephone. We have been speaking into an apparatus which cannot transmit sound."

Young Turks and striking miners

In 1944, a young hothead called **Nelson Mandela** got together with his friends **Oliver Tambo** and **Walter Sisulu** under the leadership of **Anton Lembede** to form the **ANC Youth League**. Strict Africanists, they refused to work with any other organizations – such as the Indian Congress. The League's founding manifesto criticized the ANC leadership as a group who regarded themselves as "gentlemen with clean hands". Lembede's radical brand of politics was based on his idea that "Africa is the black man's country". He continued: "We have inhabited Africa, our motherland, from time immemorial. Africa belongs to us."

The 1945 annual conference of the ANC adopted a document called "**Africans' Claims in South Africa**", which reflected an emerging politicization resulting from the experiences of the war and especially the defeat of fascism. The document demanded **universal franchise** and an end to the **colour bar**, which reserved most skilled jobs for whites.

In 1946 the African Mineworkers' Union launched one of the biggest strikes in the country's history in protest against falling living standards. Virtually the entire Gauteng gold-mining region came to a standstill as 100,000 workers downed tools. Smuts sent in police who forced the workers back down the shafts at gunpoint.

The following year, the ANC Youth League was thrown into confusion when Lembede died suddenly. He was succeeded by **A.P. Mda**, and **Nelson Mandela** took his first step into public life when he was elected general secretary of the organization.

Winds of change

For years, the white government had been hinting at easing up on segregation, and even Smuts himself, who was no soft liberal, had reckoned that it was untenable and would have to end at some point. His deputy, **J.H. Hofmeyr**, had thrown caution to the winds and committed himself to scrapping job reservation, which excluded blacks from skilled jobs. "I take my stand on the ultimate removal of the colour bar", he went on record as saying.

At the same time, **European decolonization** was beginning in earnest, with Britain withdrawing from India in the same year. This seemed to have implications for political rights for black South Africans. But more important still was the movement of people, with the relentless influx of Africans into the urban areas breaking the stereotype of them as rural tribespeople. Playing for time, the government appointed the **Fagan Commission** to look into the question of the **pass laws**, which controlled the movement of Africans and sought to keep them out of the white cities unless they had a job. The laws led to millions of black South Africans being condemned to a ghetto existence in the rural areas, where there were no jobs, poverty reigned and infant mortality was high.

When the Fagan Commission reported its findings in 1948, it concluded that "the trend to urbanization is irreversible and the pass laws should be eased".

While some blacks may have felt heartened by this hint of reform, this was the last thing many whites wanted to hear. For Afrikaners, it raised all sorts of fears about losing their identity, while Afrikaner farmers were alarmed by the idea of a labour shortage caused by Africans leaving the rural areas for better prospects in the cities. To white workers in general, the threat of losing their jobs to lower-paid African workers was a real one.

The National Party comes to power

Against this background of black aspiration and white fears, the Smuts government called a **general election**. The opposition **National Party**, which promoted Afrikaner nationalism, campaigned on a *swart gevaar* or "black peril" ticket, playing on white insecurity and fear. With an eye on the vote of Afrikaner workers and farmers, they promised to reverse the tide of Africans coming into the cites and send them all back to the reserves. For white business they made the conflicting promise to bring black workers into the cities as a cheap and plentiful supply of labour.

On Friday May 28, 1948, South Africa awoke to a National Party victory at the (whites-only) polls. Party leader **D.F. Malan** was summoned to Pretoria by the governor general to form a cabinet. On arriving by train at Pretoria station he told a group of ecstatic supporters: "For the first time, South Africa is our own. May God grant that it always remains our own. We Afrikaners are not a work of Man, but a creation of God. It is to us that millions of barbarous blacks look for guidance, justice and the Christian way of life."

Meanwhile, the ANC was riven by its own power struggle. Fed up with the ineffectiveness of the old guard, and faced with the rabid D.F. Malan, the Youth League staged a putsch, voted in their own leadership with Nelson Mandela on the executive and adopted the League's radical **Programme of Action**, with an arsenal of tactics that Mandela explained would include "the new weapons of boycott, strike, civil disobedience and non-cooperation".

The 1950s: peaceful protest

During the 1950s, the National Party began putting in place a barrage of laws that would eventually constitute the structure of apartheid. Some early onslaughts on black civil rights included the **Coloured Voters Act**, which

The Freedom Charter

- The people shall govern.
- All national groups shall have equal rights.
- The people shall share the nation's wealth.
- The land shall be shared by those who work it.
- All shall be equal before the law.
- All shall enjoy equal human rights.
- There shall be work and security for all.
- The doors of learning and culture shall be opened.
- There shall be houses, security and comfort.
- There shall be peace and friendship.

stripped coloureds of the vote; the **Bantu Authorities Act**, which set up puppet authorities to govern Africans in the reserves; the **Population Registration Act**, which classified every South African at birth as "white, native or coloured"; the **Group Areas Act**, which divided South Africa into ethnically distinct areas; and the **Suppression of Communism Act**, which made any anti-apartheid opposition (Communist or not) a criminal offence.

The ANC responded in 1952 with the **Defiance Campaign**, which kicked off with a letter to the government demanding the same civil rights for blacks that whites enjoyed. During the campaign, eight thousand volunteers deliberately broke the apartheid laws above, and were jailed. The campaign rolled on through 1952 until the police provoked violence in October by firing on a prayer meeting in East London. A riot followed in which two white people were killed, thus appearing to discredit claims that the campaign was nonviolent. The government used this as an excuse to swoop on the homes of the ANC leadership, resulting in the detention and then **banning** of over one hundred ANC organizers. Bannings were designed to restrict a person's movement and political activities: a banned person was prohibited from seeing more than one person at a time or talking to any other banned person; prohibited from entering certain buildings; kept under surveillance; required to report regularly to the police; and could not be quoted or published.

The most far-reaching event of the decade was the **Congress of the People**, held near Johannesburg in 1955. At a mass meeting of nearly three thousand delegates, four organizations, representing Africans, coloureds, whites and Indians, formed a strategic partnership called the **Congress Alliance**. Explaining the historic significance of the meeting, ANC leader Chief **Albert Luthuli** commented that "for the first time in the history of our multiracial nation its people will meet as equals, irrespective of race, colour and creed to formulate a freedom charter for all the people of our country". Adopted at the Congress of the People, the **Freedom Charter** (see box on p.853) became the principal document defining ANC policy.

The government found the breadth of the movement and its principles of freedom and equality too much to stomach and they sent in the police to round up 156 opposition leaders, who were charged with treason. Evidence at the **Treason Trial** was based on the Freedom Charter, which was described as a "blueprint for violent Communist revolution". Although all the defendants were acquitted, the four-year trial disrupted the ANC and splits began to emerge. From within the organization a group of Africanists criticized the Freedom Charter because it promoted cooperation with white activists. At the 1958 ANC national conference they attempted to hijack the leadership, but when they failed they walked out and formed the **Pan Africanist Congress** (PAC) under the leadership of the charismatic **Robert Mangaliso Sobukwe**. Upstaging the ANC, the PAC launched an anti-pass campaign ten days before a similar one planned by the ANC.

Sharpeville

On March 21, 1960, Sobukwe and thousands of followers left home to present themselves without passes to police stations. Sobukwe gave strict instructions to keep the demonstrations peaceful and not to be provoked by anyone. Across Gauteng and the Western Cape there were demonstrations which in due course dispersed, but at **Sharpeville** police station, south of Johannesburg, the crowd refused to leave, despite being buzzed by low-flying Sabre jets. A scuffle broke out, the police panicked and opened fire, killing 69 and injuring nearly 200. Most were shot in the back.

In a rapid sequence of events, demonstrations swept the country on **March 27**, and ANC activist Oliver Tambo (later to become the ANC leader in exile until the release of Mandela) illegally left the country. The following day, Africans staged a **total stay-away** from work and thousands followed Nelson Mandela and Albert Luthuli in a public pass-burning demonstration. The day after that, the government declared a **state of emergency** and rounded up 22,000 people. One day later, a United Nations Security Council resolution called for the government to abandon apartheid, to which it reacted swiftly with bans on the ANC and PAC. It was now illegal to be a member of either organization. Among white South Africans there was near hysteria as the value of the rand slipped and shares slumped. Some feared an imminent and bloody revolution.

Later that month, Prime Minister **Hendrik Verwoerd** was shot twice in the head by a half-crazed white farmer. Many people hoped that if he died, this would provide a speedy retreat from apartheid. But Dr Verwoerd survived, with his prestige enhanced and his appetite for apartheid stronger than ever. More than anyone else, Verwoerd made apartheid his own and formulated it into a coherent system based around the idea of **notionally independent bantustans**, in which Africans were to exercise their political rights away from the white areas. The underlying aim was to divide Africans into distinct ethnic groups, thereby dismantling the black majority into several separate "tribal" minorities, none of which on its own could outnumber whites.

After the banning of opposition in 1960, Dr Verwoerd pressed ahead with his cherished dream of an all-white **Afrikaner republic**, which he succeeded in achieving in March 1961 through a referendum. For his pains, the Commonwealth Prime Ministers' Conference in London kicked the republic out of the British Commonwealth and Mandela called for a national convention "to determine a non-racial democratic constitution". Instead, Verwoerd appointed one-time neo-Nazi **John Vorster** to the post of justice minister. A trained lawyer, Vorster eagerly set about passing a succession of repressive laws that circumvented normal legal procedures and flouted all principles of natural justice.

Some in the ANC realized that the rules of the game had changed irrevocably. "The time comes in the life of any nation when there remain only two choices: submit or fight. That time has now come to South Africa. We shall not submit", Mandela told the world, before going underground as commander in chief of **Umkhonto we Sizwe** (Spear of the Nation, aka MK), a newly formed armed wing involving ANC and Communist Party leaders. The organization was dedicated to economic and symbolic acts of sabotage and was under strict orders not to kill or injure people. Mandela operated clandestinely for a year, travelling in disguise, leaving the country illegally and popping up unexpectedly at meetings – all of which earned him the nickname, the "Black Pimpernel". In August 1962 he was finally arrested, tried and imprisoned. He was let out again briefly in 1963 to defend himself against charges of treason at the **Rivonia Trial**. Mandela and nine other ANC leaders were all found guilty and handed life sentences.

Apartheid: the dark days

With the leadership of the liberation movement behind bars, the Rivonia Trial marked the beginning of the decade in which everything seemed to be going the white government's way. Resistance was stifled, the state grew more powerful and for white South Africans, businessmen and foreign investors life seemed perfect. The panic caused by the Sharpeville massacre soon became a dim memory and confidence returned. For black South Africans, poverty deepened – a state of affairs enforced by apartheid legislation.

There was a minor setback in 1966 when Dr Verwoerd was stabbed to death in parliament by a messenger who went off the rails after, as he told doctors, a tapeworm had ordered him to do it. The breach was filled by **John Vorster**, whose approach was more pragmatic than that of Verwoerd. Not averse to travelling in Africa to shake hands with tame black leaders like Hastings Banda of Malawi in the interests of detente, his approach to black South Africans was rather less chummy. His premiership was characterized by an increased use of the police as an instrument of repression, while bannings, detentions without trial, house arrests and deaths of political prisoners in detention became commonplace.

The ANC was impotent, and resistance by its armed wing MK was virtually nonexistent. This was partly because up to the mid-1970s South Africa was surrounded by sympathetic white regimes – in neighbouring Rhodesia and Mozambique – making it close to impossible to infiltrate combatants into the country. But as South Africa swung into the 1970s, the uneasy peace began to fray, prompted at first by deteriorating black living standards, which reawakened industrial action. **Trade unions** came to fill the vacuum left by the ANC and neither Vorster nor any of his National Party successors proved able to stem the escalation of strikes, despite all the repressive resources at their disposal.

The **Soweto Revolt** of June 16, 1976, signalled the transfer of protest from the workplace to the townships, as black youths took to the streets in protest against the imposition of Afrikaans as a medium of instruction in their schools. The protest spread across the country after police opened fire and killed thirteen-year-old Hector Peterson during one march. By the following February, 575 people (nearly a quarter of them children) had been killed in the rolling series of revolts that followed.

The government was forced to rely increasingly on armed police to impose order. Even this was unable to stop the mushrooming of new liberation organizations, many of them part of the broadly based **Black Consciousness Movement**. As the unrest rumbled on into 1977, the Vorster government responded by banning all the new black organizations and detaining their leadership. In September 1977, **Steve Biko** (one of the detained), became the forty-sixth political prisoner to meet his end in jail at the hands of the security police.

In place of the banned organizations, a fresh crop had sprung up by the end of the 1970s. The government never again successfully put the lid on opposition, which escalated through the 1980s. There were rent, bus and school boycotts, strikes and campaigns against removals. By the end of the decade, business was complaining that apartheid wasn't working any more, and even the government was starting to agree. The growth of the black population was outstripping that of whites; from a peak of 21 percent of the population in 1910, whites now made up only 16 percent. This proportion was set to fall to 10 percent by the end of the century. The sums just didn't add up.

Total strategy

It was becoming clear that Vorster's deployment of the police couldn't solve South Africa's problems, and in 1978 he was deposed by his defence minister

Pieter Willem (P.W.) Botha in a palace coup. Under Vorster's premiership, Botha had turned the **South African Defence Force** into the most awesome military machine on the African continent and it became central to his strategy for maintaining white power. Botha realized that the days of old-style apartheid were over, and he adopted a two-handed strategy, of reform accompanied by unprecedented repression. Believing there was a total onslaught on South Africa from both inside and outside the country, he devised his so-called **Total Strategy**, which aimed to draw every facet of white society into the fight against the opponents of apartheid. This included "Youth Preparedness" military training programmes in white schools, propaganda campaigns, the extension of conscription, and political reforms aimed at co-opting Indians and coloureds.

The 1980s saw the growing use of **sabotage** against the apartheid state. In June 1980, MK, the ANC's armed wing, successfully attacked the heavily guarded strategic oil refinery at **Sasolburg**, taking the government by surprise. During 1981, there were over ninety MK armed actions against police stations, railway lines, power plants, military bases and army recruiting offices. Attacks were often coordinated with protest campaigns: for example, buildings at the British Leyland plant were bombed when workers were on strike there.

Botha began thinking about reforms and moved **Nelson Mandela** and other imprisoned ANC leaders from Robben Island to Pollsmoor Prison in mainland Cape Town. At the same time, he poured ever-increasing numbers of troops into African townships to stop unrest, while using economic incentives to attempt to draw neighbouring countries into a "**constellation of Southern African states**" under South Africa's leadership. Between 1981 and 1983, the army was used to enforce compliance on every one of the country's neighbours. An undeclared war against **Angola** reduced a potentially oil-rich country to war-ravaged ruins, while a South African-sponsored conflict in **Mozambique** brought a poverty-stricken country to its knees. Nor was Botha averse to sending commando units across the borders into **Botswana**, **Zimbabwe**, **Swaziland** and **Lesotho** to attack and bomb South African refugees.

Botha hoped that by making a few reforms that tinkered with apartheid, and by creating a black middle class as a buffer against the ANC, he could get the world off his back and stem internal unrest. On both counts he was wrong. Unrest continued, detentions and executions – in contravention of the Geneva Convention – of political activists increased, and heavy sentences were handed down in political trials. Used to maintaining control through the barrel of a gun, Botha was lost for any real political initiatives. Nevertheless, in 1983 he concocted what he believed was a master plan for a so-called **New Constitution** in which coloureds and Indians would be granted the vote. But before anyone got too excited, he qualified this with the revelation that each group would be represented in separate chambers, which would have no executive power. Meanwhile, for Africans, apartheid would continue as usual.

Botha hoped for a tactical alliance between whites, coloureds and Indians in opposition to Africans. The scheme was a dismal failure that only served to alienate right-wingers, who saw it as selling out white privilege. As Botha was punting this ramshackle scheme, 15,000 anti-apartheid delegates met at Mitchell's Plain in Cape Town, the biggest opposition gathering since the Congress of the People in 1955. They formed the **United Democratic Front** (UDF), a multiracial umbrella for 575 organizations, under a leadership that included ANC veterans. The UDF endorsed the Freedom Charter and became a proxy for the ANC. Two years of strikes, protest and boycotts followed.

In the face of intensifying protest, the government looked for ways to respond, and between March and December 1983 it offered five times to **release Mandela**, provided he agreed to banishment to the Transkei Bantustan. Five times he refused and this cat-and-mouse game continued right through the 1980s as the pressure mounted and South Africa's townships became ungovernable. Towards the end of the decade, the world watched as apartheid troops and police were regularly shown on TV beating up and shooting unarmed Africans. The Commonwealth, despite the concerted efforts of British Prime Minister Margaret Thatcher to stop them, condemned the apartheid government. The United States and Australia **severed air links** and the US Congress defied President Reagan, passing the comprehensive Anti-Apartheid Act which promoted **disinvestment**. In 1985, the **Chase Manhattan Bank** announced that it would no longer be prepared to roll over its loan to South Africa. Over the next two years, ninety US firms closed down their South African operations. An increasingly desperate Botha now modified his conditions for releasing Mandela, offering to "release Mandela if he renounces violence".

Mandela issued a moving reply, read by his daughter Zinzi to a crowd at Jabulani Stadium, in Soweto: "I am surprised by the conditions the government wants to impose on me. I am not a violent man. It was only when all other forms of resistance were no longer open to us that we turned to armed struggle. Let Botha show that he is different to Malan, Strijdom and Verwoerd. Let him renounce violence. I cherish my own freedom dearly but I care even more for yours."

As events unfolded, a subtle shift became increasingly apparent: Botha was the prisoner and he desperately needed Mandela to release him. On the one hand black resistance wasn't abating, while on the other Botha was facing a white **right-wing backlash**. At every by-election the ultra-right-wing Conservative Party had been eroding government majorities, while by the late 1980s the neo-Nazi **Afrikaner Weerstand Beweging** (Afrikaner Resistance Movement, aka AWB) broke up National Party meetings and threatened civil war.

Crisis

In 1986, Botha declared yet another **state of emergency** and unleashed a last-ditch storm of tyranny. Bannings of people and meetings followed, and shootings by the police were carried out with impunity. There were mass arrests, detentions, treason trials and torture. Sinister hit squads were deployed to assassinate the UDF leadership. Alarmed by the spiral of violence that was engulfing the country, a group of South African businessmen, mostly Afrikaners, flew to Senegal in 1987 to meet an ANC delegation headed by **Thabo Mbeki**. A joint statement pressed for unequivocal support for a negotiated settlement.

Weeks after the world celebrated **Mandela's seventieth birthday** in July 1988 with a huge bash at London's Wembley Stadium, Mandela was rushed off to Tygerberg Hospital, suffering from tuberculosis. Although he was better by October, the government announced that he wouldn't be returning to Pollsmoor Prison. Instead he was moved to a warder's cottage at Victor Verster (now Groot Drakenstein) Prison just outside Paarl. Outside the prison walls, Botha's policies had hit the buffers and even the army top brass were pushing for change. They told Botha that there could be no decisive military victory over the anti-apartheid opposition and the undeclared war in Angola was bleeding the treasury dry.

At the beginning of 1989, Mandela wrote to Botha from Victor Verster calling for negotiations. "I am disturbed by the spectre of a South Africa split into two hostile camps – blacks on one side, whites on the other," he wrote. An intransigent character, Botha found himself with little room to manoeuvre. When he suffered a stroke, his party colleagues moved swiftly to oust him and replaced him with **Frederik Willem (F.W.) De Klerk**.

Drawn from the conservative wing of the National Party, De Klerk made it clear from the start that he was totally opposed to majority rule. But he inherited a massive pile of problems that could no longer be ignored: the economy was in trouble and the cost of maintaining apartheid prohibitive; the illegal influx of Africans from the country to the city had become an unstoppable flood; blacks hadn't been taken in by Botha's constitutional reforms, and even South Africa's friends were beginning to lose patience. In September 1989, US President **George Bush** (the elder) let De Klerk know that if there wasn't progress on releasing Mandela within six months, he would extend US sanctions against South Africa.

De Klerk made a strategic calculation that the ANC was organizationally weak, having little internal base and having lost all its external support as a result of the enforced closure of its bases in Angola and Zambia, as well as having lost aid from eastern Europe with the collapse of the Iron Curtain regimes. He gambled on his own party's five-decade track record in gerrymandering and on his own ability to outmanoeuvre the ANC. In February 1990, De Klerk announced the **unbanning** of the ANC, the PAC, the Communist Party and 33 other organizations, as well as the **release of Mandela**. On Sunday February 11, at around 4pm, Mandela stepped out of Victor Verster Prison and was driven to City Hall in Cape Town, from where he spoke publicly for the first time in three decades. He told his supporters that the factors which necessitated armed struggle still existed, but that he believed that "a climate conducive to a negotiated settlement will exist soon".

That May, Mandela and De Klerk signed an **agreement** in which the government undertook to repeal repressive laws and release political prisoners, while Mandela persuaded the ANC to suspend the armed struggle. As events moved slowly towards full-blown negotiations it became clear that De Klerk still clung to race-based notions for a settlement: "Majority rule is not suitable for South Africa", he said, "because it will lead to the domination of minorities."

Negotiations

The **negotiating** process which took place between 1990 and 1994 was fragile, and at many points a descent into chaos looked likely. Obstacles included ongoing violence linked to a sinister "**Third Force**" – elements in the apartheid security forces who were working behind the scenes to destabilize the ANC; **threats of civil war** from heavily armed right-wingers; and a low-key war of attrition in KwaZulu-Natal between Zulu nationalists of the **Inkatha Freedom Party** and ANC supporters, which had already claimed three thousand lives between 1987 and 1990.

In August 1990, this violence burst into the Johannesburg townships when gunmen opened fire on black commuters on a train. In June 1992, forty people were hacked to death in a midnight attack on a squatter camp near Johannesburg. Eyewitnesses reported seeing police trucks ferrying alleged Inkatha supporters to the area. When Mandela arrived at the scene a crowd of youths sang: "Mandela, you behave like a lamb while we are being slaughtered." This response was very much to the advantage of the National Party as it gave the impression of an impotent ANC unable to protect its supporters and with no power to stop the violence. Mandela responded by breaking off negotiations and launching a **campaign of mass action** to pressurize the government. On August 3 and 4, 1992, the ANC called the largest **strike** in South African history, when four million people stayed away from work. Subsequently negotiations between the government and the ANC resumed and in October 1992, President De Klerk apologized (conditionally) for apartheid.

But in April 1993 it looked as if the whole process was going to unravel with the **assassination of Chris Hani**, the most popular ANC leader after Mandela. Hani's slaying by a right-wing gunman touched deep fears among all South Africans. A descent into civil war loomed and for three consecutive nights the nation watched as Mandela appeared on prime-time television appealing for calm. This marked the decisive turning point as it became apparent that the ANC president was able to hold the country together, while De Klerk kept his head down. Pushing his stategic advantage, Mandela swiftly called for the immediate setting of an **election date**. On June 3, 1993, the poll was proposed for April 27, 1994, and Mandela was able to tell his followers that "the countdown to democracy has begun".

By December 1993, South Africa had its first multiracial administration in 350 years, when the **Transitional Executive Authority** was installed. But the Zulu nationalist leader Chief Buthelezi and the white right-wing continued to threaten civil war unless KwaZulu-Natal was given autonomy and the Afrikaners a *volkstaat* (homeland). Bloodshed and mayhem continued in KwaZulu-Natal and it looked as if the election was going to be disrupted. In February 1994, the negotiating parties held fresh discussions, but concessions accepting the principle of self-determination failed to draw either Buthelezi or the right-wingers into the elections.

In March 1994, a popular uprising against the government of the **Bophuthatswana** Bantustan (a group of six disconnected territories scattered across today's North West, Mpumulanga and Free State provinces) resonated across South Africa. The territory's army and police mutinied and, in an attempt to shore up his regime, Chief Mangope asked the white right wing to help. Hundreds of armed AWB neo-Nazis converged on the capital, Mmabatho, and South Africa watched as they were routed by the Bantustan army. Television images of armed white neo-fascists being ingloriously defeated by Africans put paid to any ideas about white invincibility and laid to rest the threat of a right-wing rebellion.

In response, the fractionally less right-wing **Afrikaner Volksfront** (Afrikaner People's Front), an alliance of whites who wanted their own self-governing homeland, announced that it would take part in the election. Yet Buthelezi still insisted on boycotting the poll and threatened to lead a KwaZulu-Natal secession from South Africa. His supporters were whipped up into a frenzy of violence that swept across the province. The transitional government declared a **state of emergency** in KwaZulu-Natal and swamped the province with troops. One week before the election was due, the mercurial Inkatha leader agreed to take part.

The 1994 election

Despite a last attempt by right-wingers to disrupt the poll by bombing Johannesburg International airport, the **election** of April 27, 1994, passed peacefully.

At the age of 76, Mandela, along with millions of his fellow citizens, voted for the first time in his life in his country's elections. On May 2, De Klerk conceded defeat after an ANC landslide, in which they took 62.7 percent of the vote. Of the remaining significant parties, the National Party fared best with 20.4 percent, followed by the Inkatha Freedom Party with 10.5 percent. The ANC was dominant in all but two of the provinces, the National Party taking the **Western Cape** decisively and Inkatha achieving a tight 50.3 percent majority in its **KwaZulu-Natal** heartland. One of the disappointments for the ANC was its inability to appeal broadly to non-Africans; ironically, the National Party won an overwhelming proportion of Indian, coloured and white support.

For the ANC, the real struggle was only beginning. It inherited a country of 38 million people. Of these it was estimated that six million were unemployed, nine million were destitute, ten million had no access to running water, and twenty million had no electricity. Among adult blacks, sixty percent were illiterate and fewer than fifty percent of black children under fourteen went to school. Infant mortality ran at eighty deaths per thousand among Africans, compared with just seven among whites.

The Mandela presidency

Few people in recorded history have been the subject of such high expectations; still fewer have matched them; Mandela has exceeded them. We knew of his fortitude before he left jail; we have since experienced his extraordinary reserves of goodwill, his sense of fun and the depth of his maturity. As others' prisoner, he very nearly decided the date of his own release; as president, he has wisely chosen the moment of his going. Any other nation would consider itself privileged to have his equal as its leader. His last full year in power provides us with an occasion again to consider his achievement in bringing and holding our fractious land together.

Mail & Guardian, December 24, 1998

South Africa's first five years of democracy are inextricably linked to the towering figure of **Nelson Mandela**. On one hand, he had to temper the impatience of a black majority that, having finally achieved civil rights, found it hard to understand why economic advancement wasn't following quickly. And on the other, he had to mollify the fears of many whites who, having seen their political privileges stripped away, imagined an imminent collapse of their lifestyle. The achievements of the government, however, were more uneven than those of its leader.

Soon after taking power, Mandela announced the **Reconstruction and Development Plan** (RDP), which set health, housing, education and economic growth as its priorities. This was to be realized in the electrifying of 350,000 homes in the ensuing year, the provision of decent education for all children, and in the building of 2.5 million houses by the end of the decade. But in August 1994, Mandela's keynote address, outlining the government's progress in its first hundred days of office, was greeted by industrial action protests at the slow pace of change. By the end of 1997, only 350,000 houses had been built, though the introduction of clean, piped water and electricity to over a million homes were significant successes.

In response to the impression that whites weren't doing enough to redress imbalances and that many officials had forgotten about liberation and were simply riding the gravy train – or just plain corrupt – Mandela called for a "**new patriotism**" and attacked the "culture of rapacity" that appeared to underlie many of theses problems. This did little to encourage a climate of probity. One well-publicized, but by no means isolated, example of corruption involved the Reverend **Allan Boesak**, a founding member of the UDF and a stalwart of the liberation struggle. In 1999 he was found guilty of misappropriating over a million rands of Danish donor funding. That March, at a Human Rights Day rally, the then deputy president Thabo Mbeki acknowledged the extent of the problem and pledged to root out "those who have smuggled themselves into the ANC not to serve the people, but to pursue their own ends".

The overriding theme of the Mandela presidency was that of **reconciliation**. In 1995, Mandela hosted a symbolic lunch for the wives of liberation leaders and ex-prime ministers and presidents, as well as taking tea with Betsie Verwoerd, widow of Hendrik Verwoerd. Perhaps the highlight of this policy was in May and June 1995, when the rugby union **World Cup** was staged in South Africa. The Springboks – for many years international pariahs due to their whites-only membership – won, watched by Mandela, sporting Springbok colours. The most significant side-show of the period was the **Truth and Reconciliation Commission**, set up to examine gross human rights abuses in South Africa between 1960 and 1993 (see box on pp.864–865).

The **New Constitution**, approved in May 1996, ensured that South Africa would remain a parliamentary democracy with an executive president. One of the most progressive constitutions in the world, it incorporated an extensive bill of rights. The main points were the outlawing of discrimination on the grounds of race, gender, pregnancy, ethnic or social origin, sexual orientation, disability, religion, belief, culture or language; protection of freedom of religion, belief, movement, association, expression and artistic creativity; prohibition of slavery, servitude, forced labour, torture, detention without trial, violence or cruel punishment; guarantee of the right to life (banning capital punishment but permitting abortion); and the appointment of a public protector to defend individuals against maladministration.

Despite the victory of liberal democratic principles, South Africa still displayed a singular lack of the trappings associated with civil society. **Crime**, sensationalized daily in the media, continued to dog the country. In the closing stages of the ANC's first five years, the police were reporting an average of 52 murders a day, a rape every half hour (including a frightening rise in child rape), and one car theft every nine minutes.

The post-Mandela era

By the middle of Mandela's presidency, his deputy, **Thabo Mbeki**, had taken charge of the nuts-and-bolts running of the country, having already assumed the chairmanship of the ANC in 1993. In 1997 he succeeded Mandela as the leader of the party and after the 1999 general election, which the ANC won by a landslide, he became president of South Africa.

Despite his intellect – possibly because of it – Mbeki is respected but has failed endear himself to South Africa's citizens. He certainly lacks Mandela's common touch and most South Africans find him remote, an impression reinforced by the feeling that he jets around the world promoting Third World issues, rather than dealing with South Africa's domestic problems. But Mbeki believes South Africa's economic prospects are inextricably tied to those of the Third World. Part of this agenda entails pushing his cherished **African Renaissance**, a somewhat vague idea that seems to bring together the promotion of black empowerment at home with an attempt to foster pride among the worldwide African diaspora.

At home, Mbeki and his cabinet have followed a neo-Thatcherite **economic policy**, involving budget-deficit reduction, wage restraint and privatization. The implementation of the policy by the highly competent finance minister, **Trevor Manuel**, has won applause internationally and at home from most centrist and centre-right economists. However, it has also drawn a predictable barrage of fire from South Africa's left for a policy that they see as quite inappropriate to a country beset by one of the world's most inequitable distributions of wealth and by growing unemployment. This has exposed tensions in the alliance involving the ANC and two junior partners, the South African Communist Party and the Congress of South African Trade Unions. Although there are frequent rumblings about a split and the formation of a left-wing opposition party, this seems unlikely since, despite the yawning ideological divide, the three are painfully aware that they will probably have to sink or swim together.

Mbeki's non-confrontational approach (he calls it "quiet diplomacy") to the crisis in neighbouring **Zimbabwe**, where President Robert Mugabe's government has unleashed violence on its own citizens and unrolled a barrage of laws to curtail civil rights, has done little for Mbeki's international reputation. But no problem has proved more important or more divisive than Mbeki's stance on **AIDS**. According to South Africa's Medical Research Council, AIDS is the biggest killer in the country. It also threatens to undermine the gains achieved by the Mbeki government's economic successes. Despite pressure from the medical establishment, trade unions, civic organizations led by the Treatment Action Campaign, and opposition parties – as well from inside his own party – the president stolidly clung to his unconventional ideas about the disease, notably that HIV may not be the sole cause of AIDS. For a long time Mbeki rejected the provision of anti-retrovirals in state hospitals. Finally, in November 2003 the ANC government bowed to pressure and agreed to provide anti-AIDS drugs to all South Africans infected with HIV, although, in reality, a year later people were still dying of AIDS because they were unable to access appropriate medication.

A decade of democracy

Despite rumblings of discontent around the big three problems of poverty, crime and unemployment (estimated at around thirty percent), South Africa celebrated its first **decade of democracy** in 2004 a far healthier and much more stable country than it was in the dying days of apartheid. For a while, predictions of post-apartheid apocalypse (mainly among some members of the white community) had appeared to be confirmed when the rand began depreciating after 1994, at one point going into free fall. However, it has rallied and stabilized at around R11 to the pound sterling.

Despite its one-time commitment to socialism, the ANC has turned out to be far better at managing a modern capitalist economy than its avowedly anti-communist National Party predecessors. For foreign investors, South Africa's new-

As you type, you don't know you are crying until you feel and see the tears on your hands.

Chief typist of the transcripts of the TRC hearings, as told to Archbishop Tutu

By the time South Africa achieved democracy in 1994, it was internationally accepted that **apartheid** was, in the words of a UN resolution, "a crime against humanity", and that atrocities had been committed in its name. But no one could have imagined how systematic and horrific these atrocities had been. This was only to emerge at the hearings of the **Truth and Reconciliation Commission** (TRC), set up to investigate gross abuses of human rights under apartheid. Under the chairmanship of Nobel Peace laureate, Archbishop **Desmond Tutu**, the commission was mandated to examine acts committed between March 1960, the date of the Sharpeville massacre, and May 10, 1994, the day of Mandela's inauguration as president.

The objective of the TRC was to discover the secret history of apartheid and to gain "as complete a picture as possible of the nature, causes and extent of human rights violations". The main means of achieving this was through evidence given by victims and perpetrators. To facilitate this, there was provision for **amnesty** to be granted in exchange for "full disclosure of all the relevant facts relating to acts associated with a political objective committed in the course of the conflicts of the past".

The commission began sitting in April 1996 and completed its hearings in July 1998 (with investigations continuing until 2000). Unique among the truth commissions of the late twentieth century, including those in Latin America, the South African TRC operated **in public**, allowing all South Africans to share a knowledge of what had actually happened. Among the deeply moving **testimonies** given by over 21,000 people were individual stories from parents, siblings and friends of those who had disappeared. Others gave gruesome accounts of torture, bombings and murders on an extensive scale. In his foreword to the TRC report, Tutu recalls "how at one of our hearings a mother cried out plaintively: 'Please cannot you bring back even just a bone of my child so that I can bury him?'"

Leading members of the former government and the ANC appeared before the TRC, among them former president **F.W. De Klerk**. In May 1996, he told the commission that he had not been aware of any atrocities committed under apartheid – a statement Archbishop Tutu said he found difficult to believe, especially given the avalanche of information available to De Klerk as president. Further evidence of a systematic and brutal campaign of repression by the apartheid government came to light during a trial (incidental to the TRC) in September 1996 of former police colonel, **Eugene De Kock**, who was pleading in mitigation after being convicted on

found stability makes it a growingly attractive proposition; industry, including motor manufacturing, is booming; and, despite the global downturn in travel, that followed September 11, South Africa has seen its **tourism** sector continue to fly.

But it's a mixed bag: under the ANC's management the economy has averaged three percent annual growth, which although respectable is barely enough to keep up with population growth and does little to contribute to the fight against poverty and unemployment. Despite dissatisfaction with the ANC's speed of delivery, the party is unlikely to be dislodged from power any time soon. At the 2004 elections it increased its already massive majority to nearly 70 percent of the national vote. Its closest rival, the Democratic Alliance, whose support base is mainly in the white and coloured communities, scored a mere 12 percent.

89 charges of murder, gun-running and fraud. He revealed that his activities were not the work of a rogue unit, but part of a well-coordinated campaign by the security forces, carried out with the full knowledge of the government, including presidents Botha and De Klerk.

After two-and-a-half years of hearings across the country, the TRC released its 3500-page **report** on October 29, 1998. Unsurprisingly, the commission found that "the South African government was in the period 1960–94 the primary perpetrator of gross human rights abuses in South Africa, and from 1974, in Southern Africa". The TRC heard overwhelming evidence that from the 1970s to the 1990s the state had been involved in criminal activities including "extra-judicial killings of political opponents". Among the violations it listed were torture, abduction, sexual abuse, incursions across South Africa's borders to kill opponents in exile, and the deployment of hit squads. It also found that the ANC (and a number of other organizations, including the PAC and Inkatha) was guilty of human-rights violations, though on nowhere near the scale of the government. The report acknowledged that the ANC had been waging a just war against apartheid but drew "a distinction between a 'just war' and 'just means'".

There was considerable **criticism of the TRC** from all quarters. Many people felt that justice would have been better served by a Nuremberg-style trial of those guilty of gross violations, but Tutu argued that this would have been impossible in South Africa, given that neither side had won a military victory. Defending the amnesty provisions, he pointed out that "members of the security establishment would have scuppered the negotiated settlement had they thought they were going to run a gauntlet of trials for their involvement in past violations".

The South African media has tended to give the impression that the Truth and Reconciliation Commission led to a deterioration of race relations in South Africa (as if that were possible). However, a market research survey carried out for *Business Day* in August 1998 found that attitudes to the TRC split along racial lines. Eighty percent of black respondents believed that "the people in South Africa will now be able to live together more easily", while ninety percent of whites felt that the commission would not bring the races closer.

Responding to the lack of support for the TRC, and sometimes even active obstructionism from white leaders, Tutu remarked: "I have been saddened by a mean-spiritedness in some of the leadership of the white community. They should be saying: 'How fortunate we are that these people do not want to treat us how we treated them. How fortunate that things have remained much the same for us except for the loss of some political power.'"

The ANC's electoral success reflects the racial nature of South African politics and the absence of a viable alternative to the government rather than a popular sentiment that it is doing a great job for ordinary citizens. Indeed for the poor majority, change has been slow in coming, and the government has been criticized for focusing on the redistribution of wealth through its **black economic empowerment (BEE)** programme rather than on expanding the economic cake. The BEE programme encourages white-owned companies to employ Africans, coloureds and Indians in preference to whites. It's also in the process of bringing a large proportion of big business under black control, with the aim that in future blacks will own forty percent of the shares listed on the Johannesburg stock exchange.

There is a justified impression that BEE has entailed a shift of wealth from a white elite to a black one. Two of the beneficiaries (and among the wealthiest men in South Africa today) are ANC veteran Tokyo Sexwale, who did time with Nelson Mandela, and former trade unionist Cyril Ramaphosa. There has also been a noticeable growth of a **black middle class**. This is most evident in Johannesburg, where blacks are moving into the former whites-only suburbs and a growing cohort of newly affluent bourgeois blacks drive to upmarket malls in their BMWs (dubbed Black Man's Wish in the townships) – the car of choice for status-conscious South Africans of all races.

But for those at the bottom of the pile – working-class township dwellers and rural peasants – BEE has had no discernible impact. Archbishop Emeritus Desmond Tutu has commented that creating wealth for a small "recycled elite" is dangerous when so many South Africans still live in "gruelling, demeaning, dehumanizing poverty". The situation has led to a robust debate inside the ANC, with some of BEE's detractors maintaining that the black middle class is little more than a token, a buffer protecting the white establishment from the clamouring poor. Kgalema Motlanthe, the ANC's secretary-general, argues that the same small clique of black tycoons are benefiting in one empowerment deal after another, while Finance Minister Trevor Manuel has also expressed his doubts about the programme, as has businessman Moeletsi Mbeki, the president's brother. Defence Minister Mosiuoa Lekota has added his voice to the debate, attacking the complex system of **racial recruitment quotas** used by the army. "When will we cease to be Africans, coloureds, Indians and whites and [become] merely South Africans?" he is reported by the *Economist* as asking.

Lekota's question pinpoints the paradox that is South Africa today: how do you change a society that has defined itself according race for over three centuries, and how do you overturn the resultant inequalities without yourself resorting to racial definitions?

Wildlife

Apart from Kruger, Kgalagadi Transfrontier, Hluhluwe-Imfolozi and Pilanesberg parks, where you'll see the **Big Five** (lion, leopard, buffalo, elephant and rhino), over a hundred other reserves offer numerous smaller predators and dozens of herbivores, including endangered species, in invariably beautiful settings. Besides offering thrilling experiences, the major South African reserves are islands of living archeology, hinting at the teeming life that moved across the subcontinent as far south as present-day Cape Town, before European settlers with firearms swept it to the margins of the country.

This account supplements the wildlife guide in the colour section at the start of the book (to which bracketed page numbers refer). The aim is to inspire you to go beyond checklists, to appreciate the interactions of the bush and help you get more out of your safari. Beyond the scope of this account are the hundreds of colourful bird species that are an inseparable part of the South African landscape and whose calls are a constant element of its soundtrack. Some outstanding field guides are listed on pp.923–925.

Primates

Southern Africa has the lowest diversity of **primates** on the continent, a mere five species (compared with Kenya's twelve) excluding *Homo sapiens*. They include two varieties of bushbaby, two monkeys and one species of baboon – the largest and most formidable of the lot. Great apes such as gorillas and chimpanzees aren't found in the wild in southern Africa.

Chacma baboons

Chacma baboons, *Papio ursinus* (also called cynocephalus; see p.20), the local subspecies of common savanna monkeys, are the primates most widely found in South Africa. Males can be somewhat intimidating in size and manner and are frequently bold enough to raid vehicles or accommodation in search of food, undeterred by the close presence of people.

Baboons are highly gregarious and are invariably found in troops, which can number as few as fifteen to as many as a hundred, though around forty is common. Social relations are complex, revolving around jockeying to climb the social ladder and avoiding being toppled from its upper rungs. Rank, gender, precedence, physical strength and family ties determine an individual's position in the troop, which is led by a dominant male. Males are unreconstructed chauvinists, every adult male enjoying dominance over every female.

Days are dominated by the need to forage and hunt for food; baboons are highly opportunistic omnivores who will as happily tuck into a scorpion or a newborn antelope in the bushveld as they will clean up the entire crop from an orange tree on a Garden Route citrus farm. **Grooming** is a fundamental part of the social glue during times of relaxation. When baboons and other monkeys perform this massage-like activity on each other, the specks which they pop into their mouths are sometimes parasites – notably ticks – and sometimes flecks of skin.

South Africa's **ecological zones** encompass a range of climate, topography and vegetation supporting a rich diversity of animal life. There are thornveld deserts, pockets of forest, tangles of subtropical vegetation, grassy savannas, mountainous peaks and several distinct coastal habitats. Geographically, South Africa is divided in two by successive mountain ranges that run in a huge arc from the Cape Peninsula to Mpumalanga, approximately parallel to the coast. This Great Escarpment divides the vast, drier interior plateau from the wetter marginal zone merging with the coastal belt. The plateau and coastal margin can each be divided into a series of ecological zones, or biomes, which share a climate and similar vegetation.

The lowveld

The **lowveld**, or bushveld, is the stereotypical African landscape of great plains, forming a backdrop for thousands of animals. It stretches down across a third of Africa, from Malawi into South Africa; here it forms a large, crescent-shaped swath running parallel to the Limpopo River, then sweeps down between the Drakensberg and the subtropical coastal strip that runs from the northern KwaZulu-Natal coast into the Eastern Cape as far as Port Elizabeth. Typical vegetation consists of mixed **savanna** and **dry woodlands** and includes deciduous broad-leafed trees such as **marulas**, whose fruit is highly sought after by elephants. The moister subtropical lowveld, along the Mpumalanga and northern KwaZulu-Natal borders, contains thorny **acacias**, green-barked **fever trees** and thick-set **baobabs**, with **palm** trees thriving in the river valleys. In the drier transitional zones to the west, bordering the arid zone, succulent species such as **aloes** (with flowers like those of kniphofia, the red hot poker) and massive candelabra-tree **euphorbias** dominate.

Subtropical lowland

South of the Mozambique border, to the Great Fish River in the Eastern Cape, lies the narrow **coastal plain**, at below 400m. This was once thickly forested, though the indigenous woodland has been replaced by cane fields, particularly in KwaZulu-Natal. One of the wildest environments in the country survives in the northernmost part of coastal Kwazulu-Natal, where extensive **dunes** and **wetlands** constitute a transitional zone between the Mozambique tropics and the subtropical part of the province. Some 21 ecosystems have been identified here. With the notable exception of lions, a terrific array of wildlife can be seen, including aquatic and semi-aquatic species such as crocodile, hippo, terrapin, clawless otter, reedbuck and water monitor lizard. Giant forests on the protected west flank of its dunes are home to red duiker, bushpig, and vervet and samango monkeys.

From southern KwaZulu-Natal into the Wild Coast of the Eastern Cape, dozens of major river courses have etched deep valleys that protect the remnants of dwindling forests. Nowhere is it more dramatic, though, than at Oribi Gorge Nature Reserve, near Port Shepstone, where a twenty-four-kilometre-long and five-kilometre-wide gorge is part of an environment descending from **clifftop grasslands**, down **sandstone cliffs**, to dense **riverine forests**. Here you'll find leopards, bushbuck, vervets, samango monkeys and two species of the small duiker antelope.

The fynbos region

A **heathland** system, *fynbos* (pronounced "fayn-boss") grows on the back of the Cape fold mountains that cut off the coastal belt from the semi-arid Karoo interior, extending in an arc from the Olifants River in the north to Port Elizabeth in the east, and including the Cape Peninsula. Despite its diversity, *fynbos* is extremely poor in nutrients and is unable to support large animals in great quantities. Although a reasonable cross section of mammals, including lion and elephant, inhabited the zone when the first settlers arrived, they were soon wiped out in the localized area. One, the blue antelope, a large species related to the sable, was totally extinguished.

Most exciting of its mammals today are the fairly numerous but infrequently seen Cape mountain leopards. The same species as those elsewhere in the country, they're smaller here – an adaptation to the scarcity of nutrients. Other predators include caracals, African wild cats and jackals. The Cape of Good Hope section of Table Mountain National Park is one of the best places to get an idea of *fynbos*, and is inhabited by baboons, Cape mountain zebras and the endangered bontebok. For more on *fynbos*, see p.161.

The western arid zone

Permanent surface water is almost totally absent throughout the **western arid zone** – the Orange River is its only perennial watercourse. This vast zone includes the entire Kalahari ecological zone entering the Northern Cape from Botswana, as well as the succulent Karoo zone along the west coast and the Nama Karoo zone in the extensive interior. The South African Kalahari is a lonely region of **red sandveld** punctuated with **camelthorn acacia** trees; the Karoo coastal zone contains **succulents** which explode into swaths of colourful flowers in August and September after the winter rains; and the Nama Karoo consists mainly of wiry **dwarf shrubs** in flat country fringed with low hills.

The Karoo once hosted great herds of migrating antelope including springbok and bontebok. Now they're only seen behind fences, raised for their meat alongside millions of sheep. However, some species that once roamed the Karoo, including gemsbok, hartebeest and black wildebeest, have been reintroduced into Kgalagadi Transfrontier Park, the zone's most notable game reserve, which some rate as a rival to Kruger because of its wilder ambience and excellent wildlife. Besides the above mammals, here you might also encounter lion, cheetah, jackal and bat-eared foxes, baboon, reedbuck, klipspringer and caracal. Only elephant and buffalo are notably absent.

The highveld

The high-lying central plateau (generally 1200–1829m up) of South Africa, known as the **highveld**, takes in the territory south of Johannesburg, including the Free State east of Bloemfontein, and is defined in the south and east by the Great Escarpment. This zone varies from flat, grassy, treeless **plains** to the rugged peaks of the **Drakensberg**, where you'll find **alpine-type vegetation** above an altitude of 3000m. Most of the region is now covered by **semi-desert** scrub and **maize fields**, with indigenous vegetation surviving only around the peaks and in the rugged valleys. Of the mammals that once thrived here, only smaller species, such as caracal, mongoose and hare, have survived the massive agricultural onslaught. However, at Suikerbosrand Nature Reserve, just south of Jo'burg, you can see once-endangered species such as blesbok, as well as cheetah, springbok, hartebeest, oribi, zebra, mountain reedbuck, rhebok, duiker, steenbok, kudu and brown hyena. One bird you could well see among cultivated fields is the blue crane – South Africa's national bird – which feeds on the seeds of standing crops. In the reserves of the Drakensberg, mountain-adapted antelope, such as klipspringer and mountain reedbuck, and baboon, porcupine and jackal all thrive.

Afro-montane forest

South Africa is one of the least forested countries in the world, a tiny fraction of one percent of its surface carrying indigenous woodland. **Afro-montane forest**, which requires high annual rainfall, exists only in isolated pockets, most famous of which is the Knysna Forest on the southern slopes of the Western Cape's Outeniqua Mountains. Best known for its **giant trees**, including yellowwood, stinkwood and ironwood, it also has leopard, bushpig, bushbuck, caracals and mongoose. Similar forest survives in the Eastern Cape in the Katberg-Hogsback area, where baboon, vervet and samango monkeys, duiker, bushbuck and porcupine are common.

Vervet monkeys

Another widespread primate you're likely to see in the eastern half of the country, and along the coastal belt as far west as Mossel Bay, are **vervet monkeys**, *Cercopithecus aethiops* (see p.20). Although happy foraging in grasslands, they rarely venture far from woodland, particularly along river courses. You can see them outside reserves, living around nearby farms and even on suburban fringes, where opportunities for scavenging are promising. In the Eastern Cape, KwaZulu-Natal and along the Garden Route you might see them hanging about along the verges of the coastal roads, risking their lives "playing chicken" with the traffic. Vervets are principally vegetarians but they are not averse to eating invertebrates, small lizards, nestlings and eggs, as well as processed foods like biscuits and sweets – when they can snatch them from visitors.

Vervet society is made up of family groups of females and young, defended by associate males, and is highly caste-ridden. A mother's rank determines that of her daughter from infancy, and lower-ranking adult females risk being castigated if they fail to show due respect to these "upper crust" youngsters.

Samango monkeys

In striking contrast with the cheekier, upfront disposition of vervets, the rarer **samango monkeys**, *Cercopithecus mitis*, are shy animals that may only give themselves away through their loud explosive call or the breaking of branches as they go about their business. Found only in isolated pockets of KwaZulu-Natal, the Eastern Cape and Mpumalanga, they tend to hang out in the higher reaches of gallery forest, though on occasion they venture into the open to forage.

Although they bear a passing resemblance to vervets, samangos are larger and have long cheek hair that gives the passing appearance of Darth Vader. Like vervets, they're highly social and live in troops of females under the proprietorship of a dominant male, but unlike their relatives they are more inclined to fan out when looking for food.

Bushbabies

With their large, soft, fluffy pelts, huge, saucer-like eyes, large, rounded ears and superficially cat-like appearance, **bushbabies** are the ultimate in cute, cuddly-looking primates. Of the half-dozen or so species endemic to Africa, only the thick-tailed bushbaby, *Otolemur crassicaudatus,* and, about half the size, the lesser bushbaby, *Galago moholi*, are found south of the Limpopo. The former is restricted to the eastern fringes of the subcontinent, while the latter overlaps its range in the northeast and extends across the north of the country into North West Province. Unlike other bushbabies, including the lesser, which leap with ease and speed, *O. crassicaudatus* is a slow mover that hops or walks along branches, often with considerable stealth.

If you're staying at any of the KwaZulu-Natal reserves, you stand a fair chance of seeing a bushbaby after dark as they emerge from the dense forest canopy, where they rest in small groups, for spells of lone foraging for tree gum and fruit. Even if you don't see one, you're bound to hear their piercing scream cut through the sounds of the night. Bushbabies habituate easily to humans and will sometimes come into lodge dining rooms, scavenging for tidbits.

Carnivores

Almost three dozen species of **carnivore** are found in South Africa, ranging from mongooses and weasels to dog-relatives, hyenas and seven species of cat.

Dog-relatives

South Africa's five **dog-relatives**, the Canidae, consist of two foxes, two jackals and the wild dog. The member of the Canidae you're most likely to see is the **black-backed jackal**, *Canis mesomelas* (see p.22), found especially in the country's reserves. It bears a strong resemblance to a small, skinny German Shepherd, but with muzzle more like that of a fox, and is distinguished from the grey **side-striped jackal**, *Canis adjustus*, by the white-flecked black saddle on its back, to which it owes its name. In South Africa, the side-striped jackal is found only in and around Kruger and the extreme north of KwaZulu-Natal, the latter being the only region where any confusion can arise. The fact that the black-backed jackal seeks a drier habitat, in contrast to the side-striped's preference for well-watered woodland, is an additional identification pointer. Both are omnivorous, with diets that take in carrion, small animals, reptiles, birds and insects, as well as wild fruit and berries; and both are most commonly spotted alone or in pairs, though family groups are occasionally sighted.

The **bat-eared fox**, *Otocyon megalotis* (see p.21), is found throughout the western half of the country and along the Limpopo strip. It can easily be distinguished from the jackals by its outsized ears, its shorter, pointier muzzle and its considerably smaller size. The bat-eared fox's black Zorro mask helps distinguish it from the similar sized **Cape fox**, *Vulpes chama*, which inhabitats an overlapping range. Like other dogs, the bat-eared fox is an omnivore, but it favours termites and larvae, which is where its large radar-like ears come in handy. With these it can triangulate the precise position of dung-beetle larvae up to 30cm underground and dig them out. Bat-eared foxes tend to live in pairs or family groups, an arrangement that affords mutual protection.

Once widely distributed hunters of the African plains, **wild dogs**, *Lycaon pictus* (see p.22), have been brought to the edge of extinction. For many years they were shot on sight, having gained an unjustified reputation as cruel and wanton killers of cattle and sheep. More recent scientific evidence reveals them to be economical and efficient hunters – and more successful at it than any other African species. They have only survived in the Kruger, and have been reintroduced into Hluhluwe-Imfolozi, though you'd be extremely lucky to see a pack trotting along for a hunt. Capable of sustaining high speeds (up to 50kph) over long distances, wild dogs lunge at their prey en masse, tearing it to pieces – a gruesome finish, but no more grisly than the suffocating muzzle-bite of a lion. The entire pack of ten to fifteen animals participates in looking after the pups, bringing back food and regurgitating it for them.

Hyenas

The largest carnivores after lions are **hyenas**, and apart from the lion, the **spotted hyena**, *Crocuta crocuta* (see p.23), is the meat-eater you will most often see; they occur in Kruger, Hluhluwe-Imfolozi and Kgalagadi parks. Although considered a scavenger *par excellence*, the spotted hyena is a formidable hunter, most often found where antelopes and zebras are present. Exceptionally efficient consumers, with immensely strong teeth and jaws, spotted hyenas eat virtually every part of their prey, including bones and hide and, where habituated to humans, often steal shoes, unwashed pans and refuse from tents. Although they can be seen by day, they are most active at night – when they issue their unnerving whooping cries. Clans of twenty or so animals are dominated by females, who are larger than the males and compete with each other for rank. Curiously, female hyenas' genitalia are hard to distinguish from males', leading to a popular misconception that they are hermaphroditic.

The **brown hyena**, *Hyaena brunnea*, is restricted to parts of Namibia, Botswana, Zimbabwe and South Africa, where it's generally seen only in the northernmost regions. That it's usually seen singly also distinguishes this hyena from its less shaggy and slightly smaller spotted cousin.

The hyena-like **aardwolf**, *Proteles cristatus,* is smaller than the spotted hyena and far lighter (about two-thirds the height at the shoulder and roughly a tenth of its weight), as well as being less shaggy, with vertical dark stripes along its tawny body. It is further distinguished from hyenas by its insectivorous diet and its particular preference for harvester termites, which it laps up en masse (up to 200,000 in one night) with its broad sticky tongue. Far more widely distributed in South Africa than the hyenas, this nocturnal animal is sometimes active in the cooler hours just before dusk or after dawn. Although they aren't often seen, keep an eye open at the Cape of Good Hope, Karoo, Mountain Zebra, Pilanesberg, Kruger, Hluhluwe-Imfolozi and Kgagaladi reserves.

Cats

Apart from lions, which notably live in social groups, **cats** are solitary carnivores. With the exception of the cheetah, which is anatomically distinct from the other cats, the remaining members of the family are so similar that, as Richard Estes comments in *The Safari Companion*, big cats are just "jumbo versions" of the domestic cat, "distinguished mainly by a modification of the larynx that enables them to roar".

Perhaps it's just a question of size, but the most compelling of the *Felidae* for most people on safari are **lions**, *Panthera leo* (see p.24), the largest cats, and indeed the most massive predators in Africa. It's fortunate then that, despite having the most limited distribution of any cat in South Africa, lions are the ones you're most likely to see. Of the public reserves, the Kruger and Kgalagadi parks have healthy populations, and prides have been reintroduced into Hluhluwe-Imfolozi, where numbers are relatively limited.

Lazy, gregarious and sizeable, lions rarely attempt to hide, making them relatively easy to find, especially if someone else has already spotted them – a gathering of stationary vehicles frequently signals lions. Seeing them hunt is another matter, and you're less likely to see David Attenborough-esque enactments of the chase. In fact, their fabled reputation as cold, efficient hunters is ill-founded, as lions are only successful around thirty percent of the time, and only then if operating as a group. Males don't hunt at all if they can help it and will happily enjoy a free lunch courtesy of the females of the pride.

The lion may be king, but most successful and arguably most beautiful of the large cats is the **leopard**, *Panthera pardus* (see p.24), which survives from the southern coastal strip of Africa all the way to China. Highly adaptable, they can subsist in extremes of aridity or cold, as well as in proximity to human habitation, where they happily prey on domestic animals – which accounts for their absence in the sheep-farming regions of central South Africa, due to extermination by farmers. They're present in the rugged, mountainous southern areas of the Western Cape, but you are most unlikely to encounter these secretive, solitary animals here. Your best chance of a sighting is at the private lodges in **Sabi Sands**, abutting Kruger, which trade on their leopards being highly habituated to people. You'll need greater luck and sharper eyes to see them in the public reserves they inhabit, including the Kruger, Kgalagadi, Hluhluwe-Imfolozi and Mkhuze. Powerfully built, they can bring down prey twice their weight and drag an impala their own weight up a tree. The chase is not part of the leopard's tactical repertoire; they hunt by stealth, getting to within two metres of their target before pouncing.

In the flesh, the **cheetah**, *Acionyx jubatus* (see p.24), is so different from the leopard that it's hard to see how there could ever be any confusion. Cheetahs are the greyhounds of the big-cat world, with small heads, very long legs and an exterior decor of fine spots. Unlike leopards, cheetahs never climb trees, being designed rather than activity on the open plains. They live alone, or sometimes briefly form a pair during mating. Hunting is normally a solitary activity, down to eyesight and an incredible burst of speed that can take the animal up to 100kph for a few seconds. Because they're lighter than lions and less powerful than leopards, cheetahs can't rely on strength to bring down their prey. Instead they resort to tripping or knocking the victim off balance by striking its hindquarters, and then pounce. Once widespread across South Africa, now they're only seen in a few reserves, including Kruger, Kgalagadi and Hluhluwe-Imfolozi.

The other *Felidae* are usually classified as small cats, although the **caracal**, *Caracal caracal* (see p.23), is a substantial animal. An unmistakeable and awesome hunter, with great climbing agility, it's able to take prey, such as adult impala and sheep, which far exceed its own weight of eight to eighteen kilos. More commonly it will feed on birds, which it pounces on, sometimes while still in flight, as well as smaller mammals, including dassies. Found across most of South Africa, excluding KwaZulu-Natal, but not often seen, caracals live in the Mountain Zebra National Park (one of the best places to see them), plus Kruger, Giant's Castle, the Cape Peninsula, Karoo and Kgalagadi.

Long-legged and spotted, **servals**, *Felis serval* (see p.24), are higher at the shoulder but lighter than caracals, and are equally rarely seen, although they are present in the Kruger, Hluhluwe-Umfolozi and Giant's Castle parks. Efficient hunters, servals use their large rounded ears to pinpoint prey (usually small rodents, birds or reptiles), which they pounce on with both front paws after performing impressive athletic leaps.

Of the genuinely small cats, the **African wild cat**, *Felis lybica*, is distributed throughout South Africa and is easily mistaken for a domestic tabby, although its legs are longer and it has reddish ears. First domesticated six thousand years ago by the Egyptians, wild cats are so closely related to the domestic version that the two are able to interbreed freely. You're unlikely to encounter the compact small **spotted cat**, *Felis nigripes* (also known as the black-footed cat), a beautifully spotted fluffy animal, which is so rarely seen that little is known about its behaviour in the wild.

Smaller carnivores

Among the smaller predators is the unusual **honey badger**, *Mellivora capensis* (see p.22), related to the European badger and with a reputation for defending itself extremely fiercely. Primarily an omnivorous forager, it will tear open bees' nests (to which it is led by a small bird, the honey guide), its thick, loose hide rendering it impervious to stings.

Small-spotted (or common) **genets**, *Genetta genetta* (see p.23), are reminiscent of slender elongated cats, and were once domesticated around the

Mediterranean (but cats turned out to be better mouse hunters). In fact, they are viverrids, related to mongooses, and are frequently seen after dark around national-park lodges, where they live a semi-domesticated existence. Found throughout the country, apart from KwaZulu-Natal, they're difficult to distinguish from the **large-spotted genet**, *Genetta tigrina*, which has bigger spots and a black (instead of white) tip to its tail. These are found in northeastern parts of the country, KwaZulu-Natal and along the coastal margin as far west as the Cape Peninsula.

Most species of **mongoose** (see p.23), of which there are nearly a dozen in South Africa, are also tolerant of humans and, even when disturbed, can usually be observed for some time before disappearing. Their snake-fighting reputation is greatly overplayed: in practice they are mostly social foragers, fanning out through the bush like beaters on a shoot, rooting for anything edible – mostly invertebrates, eggs, lizards and frogs.

One of the best places to see Cape **clawless otters**, *Aonyx capensis*, a large, heavily built species, is in the Tsitsikamma National Park, where it feeds on crabs, fishes and octopuses and will commonly forage on cliff faces and in tidal pools. They are also common in the KwaZulu-Natal reserves and the Kruger.

The **civet** (or African civet), *civettictis civetta* (see p.22), is a stocky animal resembling a large, terrestrial genet. It was formerly kept in captivity for its musk (once an ingredient in perfume), which is secreted from glands near the tail. Civets aren't often seen, but they're predictable creatures, wending their way along the same path at the same time, night after night.

Antelope

South Africa has roughly a third of all antelope species in Africa, and antelope are the most regularly seen family of animals in the country's game reserves. You'll even spot some on farmland along the extensive open stretches that separate interior towns. South African antelope are subdivided into a number of **tribes**, and like buffalo, giraffe and domestic cattle, they are **ruminants** – animals that have four stomachs and chew the cud.

Bushbuck tribe

Bushbuck are the only non-territorial African antelope, and you'll see them in the shadows of thickets and bush cover, which they use for defence against predators. Among the bushbuck, it's generally only males that have horns, which are curved and spiralled. The exception is the largest of the tribe, indeed the largest living antelope, the **eland**, *Taurotragus oryx* (see p.30), in which both sexes have straight horns (but still marked by distinctive spiralling). The eland is built like an ox and moves with the slow deliberation of one, though it's a great jumper. Once widely found, herds survive around the Kruger, Kgalagadi and a tiny enclave in the northern KwaZulu-Natal Drakensberg, plus they've been reintroduced to a number of other reserves throughout the country.

The magnificent **kudu**, *Tragelaphus strepsiceros* (see p.30), is more elegantly built, and males are adorned with sensational spiralled horns that can easily reach 1.5m in length – it's these that you'll often see mounted in old-fashioned country hotels. Female groups usually include three or more members and will sometimes combine temporarily to form larger herds; males form similarly sized but more transient groupings, although it's not uncommon to encounter lone bulls.

Despite a distinct family resemblance, you could never confuse a kudu with a **bushbuck**, *Tragelaphus scriptus* (see p.30), which is considerably shorter and has a single twist to its horns, in contrast to the kudu's two or three turns. They also differ in being the only solitary members of the tribe, one reason you're less likely to spot them. Apart from the major reserves, they're found in Addo Elephant and Greater St Lucia parks.

Nyalas, *Tragelaphus angasi* (see p.29), are midway in size between the kudu and bushbuck, with which they could be confused at first glance. Telling pointers are their size, the sharp vertical white stripes on the side of the nyala (up to fourteen on the male, eighteen on the female) and, in the males, a short stiff mane from neck to shoulder. Females tend to group with their two last offspring and gather with other females in small herds, rarely exceeding ten. Males become more solitary the older they get. You'll tend to see males and females separately, as they only deliberately congregate for mating.

Horse antelope

Restricted mainly to the Kruger, the **sable**, *Hippotragus niger* (see p.31), is easily as magnificent as the kudu. A sleek, black upper body set in sharp counterpoint to its white underparts and facial markings, as well as its massive backwardly curving horns, make this the thoroughbred of the ruminants, particularly when galloping majestically across the savanna (though they prefer woodland). Highly hierarchical female herds number between one and three dozen, while territorial bulls frequently keep their distance, remaining under cover where you could easily miss them.

The **roan**, *Hippotragus equinus* (see p.31), looks very similar, but is larger than a sable (it's Africa's second-largest antelope), with less impressive horns and lighter colouring. You're more likely to see them in open savanna than sables.

Geographically more restricted, **gemsbok** (also known as the oryx), *Oryx gazella* (see p.31), are only seen in South Africa in Kgalagadi, the southernmost part of their range, which stretches down from the deserts of Namibia and Botswana. If you encounter a herd of these highly gregarious grazers, you should be left in no doubt as to what they are. Like the roan and sable, they have thick-set bodies and superficially similar facial markings, but their greyish-fawn colouring, black and white underbody markings and long, slender, almost straight backward-pointing horns make them unmistakable. Gemsbok are highly adapted for survival in the arid country they inhabit, able to go for long periods without water, relying instead on melons and vegetation for moisture. They tolerate temperatures above $40°C$ by raising their normal body temperature of $35°C$ above that of the surrounding air, losing heat by conduction and radiation; their brains are kept cool by a supply of blood from their noses.

Hartebeests

With their bracket-shaped, relatively short horns and ungainly appearance, **hartebeest** look vaguely like elongated cows – particularly in their faces. All hartebeest are gregarious, but the exemplar of this is the **blue wildebeest**, *Connochaetes taurinus* (see p.27) which, in East Africa, gather in hundreds of thousands for their annual migration. You won't see these numbers in South Africa, but you'll see smaller herds if you go to any of the reserves in the northern half of the country or KwaZulu-Natal, as well as a number in the southern half, where they've been reintroduced. A particularly photogenic sight is wildebeest mingling with zebras, a habit said to be for mutual defence, though it may simply reflect the fact that they are both grazers and therefore hang around similar terrain. You're less likely to see **black wildebeest**, *Connochaetes gnou*, which were brought to the edge of extinction in the nineteenth century and now number around three thousand in South Africa, though you may find them in the Karoo and Mountain Zebra parks as well as Giant's Castle. You can tell them apart from their blue cousins by their darker colour (brown rather than the black suggested by their name) and long white tail.

Rather inelegant, like the wildebeests, the **red hartebeest**, *Alcelaphus buselaphus* (see p.27), the extremely rare **Lichtenstein's hartebeest**, *Sigmocerus lichtensteinii*, and the **tsessebe**, *Damaliscus lunatus* (see p.28), are all highly similar in appearance, but confusion is only likely to arise at the Kruger, the one place Lichtenstein's are found in the same range as tsessebes. The key distinction is in the horns, which in the hartebeest curve round to almost touch each other, while the tsessebe's are more splayed. Parks where you can see red hartebeests include Mountain Zebra, Karoo, Addo and Kgalagadi.

The **blesbok**, *Damaliscus dorcas phillipsi*, and **bontebok**, *Damaliscus dorcas dorcas*, are near identical sub-species of the same animal and resemble darker, better-looking versions of the tsessebe. The largest bontebok population is at De Hoop Nature Reserve, with other members of the subspecies at the Cape of Good Hope section of Table Mountain National Park. Good places to see blesbok include Mountain Zebra National Park and Suikerbosrand Nature Reserve. After springboks, blesboks are the most important game-farm species in the country, and you may see them on Karoo farms.

Duiker and dwarf antelope

Duiker and the dwarf tribe are non-herding antelope that are either solitary or live in pairs. Despite their size, or perhaps because of it, males tend to be highly aggressive and are able to use their straight, stiletto-sharp horns to deadly effect.

The smallest South African antelope, the **blue duiker**, *Philantomba monticola*, weighs in at around 4kg, has an arched back and stands 35cm at the shoulder (roughly the height of a cat). Extremely shy, it is seldom seen in the southern and eastern coastal forests (as well as Ndumo Game Reserve) where it lives. The slightly larger **red duiker**, *Cephalophus natalensis*, is three times heavier, and enjoys a similar environment to the blue, but inhabits only the woodlands and forest of KwaZulu-Natal.

You're more likely to see the **common duiker** (sometimes called the grey duiker, reflecting its colouring), *Sylvicapra grimmia* (see p.29), which occurs all over South Africa and is among the antelopes most tolerant of human habitation. When under threat it freezes in the undergrowth, but if chased will dart off in an erratic zigzagging run designed to throw pursuers off balance.

This type of fast darting movement is also characteristic of **dwarf antelope**, particularly the **Cape grysbok**, *Raphicerus melanotis* (see p.31), and **Sharpe's grysbok**, *Raphicerus sharpii*, which bear a close resemblance to each other, but can't be confused because their ranges don't overlap. The Cape grysbok lives in the Western Cape *fynbos* belt (including Cape of Good Hope reserve and Addo), while Sharpe's occur in the northeastern corner of the country around the Kruger. Both are nocturnal and so are not often sighted.

A relative of the grysbok, the **steenbok**, *Raphicerus campestris* (see p.32), is by far the most commonly sighted of all the dwarf antelope, and you can spot them by day or night all over the country (except parts of KwaZulu-Natal). Its large, dark eyes, massive ears and delicate frame give this elegant half-metre-high antelope an engaging Bambi-like appearance.

Another dwarf antelope you could well see is the **klipspringer**, *Oreotragus oreotragus* (see p.32), whose Afrikaans name (meaning "rock jumper") reflects its goat-like adaptation to living on *kopjes* and cliffs – the only antelope to do so, making it unmistakeable. It's also the only one to walk on the tips of its hooves. Keep your eyes peeled at Kruger or Mountain Zebra parks (and other wilderness areas where there are rocky outcrops) for their large, bounding movements to scale steep inclines, or their hopping from rock to rock.

The largest of the dwarves is the **oribi**, *Ourebia ourebi* (see p.31), which could be taken for an outsized steenbok or a small gazelle, as its movements are more akin to theirs, faster and smoother than those of other dwarves. Only found in small pockets of KwaZulu-Natal, oribis live in small parties of a ram and several ewes. You may hear their short sharp warning whistle as you approach, before you see them. After they flee a little way, they will frequently stop to look back at you.

Gazelle

Springbok, *Antidorcas marsupalis* (see p.28), are the symbol of the national cricket and rugby teams. South Africa's only gazelle, they are the most populous members of this tribe. They're tolerant of a wide range of open country, from deserts to wetter savanna.

These medium-sized antelope are said to have once migrated in their millions across the drylands of South Africa, but today their numbers are greatly reduced and the network of fences segmenting the country has ended such mass movements. They can be seen in reserves in the western arid zone of the country, in which region they're also raised on farms for venison and hides. Their characteristic horns and dark horizontal patch on their sides, separating their reddish tawny upper body from their white underparts, are definitive identifiers. Springbok are recorded as having reached nearly 90kph and are noted for "pronking", a movement in which they arch their backs and straighten their legs as they leap into the air.

Impala

Larger and heavier than springbok, which they superficially resemble, **impala**, *Aepyceros melampus* (see p.28), are antelope in a tribe of their own. Elegant and athletic, they are prodigious jumpers that have been recorded leaping distances of 11m and heights of 3m. Only the males carry the distinctive lyre-shaped pair of horns. They are so common in the reserves of the northeast and of KwaZulu-Natal that some jaded rangers look on them as the goats of the savanna – a perception that carries more than a germ of truth, as these flexible feeders are both browsers and grazers.

Ewes and lambs form tight herds that can number over a hundred, moving about in a home range that may overlap the territory of several rams. During the rut, which takes place during the first five months of each year, these males will cut out harem herds of around twenty and expend considerable amounts of effort herding them and driving off any potential rivals.

Near-aquatic antelope

All species of the near-aquatic Kob tribe live close to water. Largest of the tribe, **waterbuck**, *Kobus ellipsiprymnus* (see p.29), are sturdy antelope – 1.3m at the shoulder – with shaggy reddish-brown coats and a white horseshoe marking on their rumps. Only the males have horns. Sociable animals, they usually gather in small herds of up to ten, and occasionally up to thirty. They're found sporadically in the northeastern reserves, close to woodland and permanent water.

Two closely related species, the **common reedbuck**, *Redunca arundinum* (see p.29), and the slightly smaller **mountain reedbuck**, *Redunca fulvorufula*, both roughly two-thirds the height of waterbuck, are tan-coloured antelope. The common reedbuck favours a habitat of tall grass or reedbeds for refuge, while the mountain reedbuck inhabits hilly country with trees or grassy slopes.

All three species can be seen in suitable habitat in the Kruger, while the waterbuck and common reedbuck will also be sighted in the wetland reserves of KwaZulu-Natal, and the mountain reedbuck in the Mountain Zebra, Giant's Castle and Pilanesberg parks.

Other hoofed ruminants

Alongside cattle, sheep, goats and antelope, buffalo and giraffe are also **hoofed ruminants**. Bacteria in their digestive systems process plant matter into carbohydrates, while the dead bacteria are absorbed as protein – a highly efficient arrangement that makes them economical consumers, far more so than non-ruminants such as elephants, which pass vast quantities of what they eat as unutilized fibre. Species that concentrate on grasses are grazers; those eating leaves are browsers.

Buffalo

You won't have to be in the Kruger or most of the other reserves in South Africa for long to see **buffalo**, *Syncerus caffer* (p.27), a common safari animal that, as one of the Big Five, appears on every hunter's shopping list. Don't let their resemblance to domestic cattle or water buffalo (to which they are not at all closely related) or apparent docility lull you into complacency; lone bulls, in particular, are noted and feared even by hardened hunters as dangerous and relentless killers. In other words, don't assume that the absence of carnivores in some reserves means it's safe to go walking without a guide.

Buffalo are non-territorial and highly gregarious, gathering in hundreds or even sometimes thousands. Herds under one or more dominant bulls consist of clans of a dozen or so related females under a leading cow. You'll be able to spot such distinct units within the group: at rest, clan members often cuddle up close to each other. There are separate pecking orders among females and males, the latter being forced to leave the herd during adolescence (at about three years) or once they're over the hill, to form bachelor herds, which you can recognize by their small numbers. Evicted old bulls (sometimes called "*daga* boys" – *daga* meaning mud – on account of their penchant for mud baths), stripped of their social position and sex lives, understandably become resentful and embittered loners and are to be avoided at all costs. To distinguish males (as shown in the colour guide) from females, look for their heavier horns bisected by a distinct boss, or furrow.

Giraffe

Giraffe, *Giraffa camelopardalis* (see p.27), are among the easiest animals to spot because their long necks make them visible above the low scrub. The tallest mammals on earth, they spend their daylight hours browsing on the leaves of trees too high up for other species; combretum and acacias are favourites. Their highly flexible lips and prehensile tongues give them almost hand-like agility and enable them to select the most nutritious leaves while avoiding deadly-sharp acacia thorns. At night they lie down and spend the evening ruminating. Non-territorial, they gather in loose, leaderless herds; if you encounter a bachelor herd, look out for young males testing their strength with neck wrestling. When the female comes into oestrus, which can happen at any time of year, the dominant male mates with her. She will give birth after a gestation period of approximately fourteen months. Over half of all young, however, fall prey to lions or hyenas in their early years. Kruger, Pilanesberg and the KwaZulu-Natal parks are all good places to see them.

Non-ruminants

Non-ruminating mammals have more primitive digestive systems than animals that chew the cud. Although both have bacteria in their gut that convert vegetable matter into carbohydrates, the less efficient system of the non-ruminants means they have to consume more raw material and to process it faster. The upside is they can handle food that's far more fibrous.

Elephants

Elephants, *Loxodonta africana* (see p.25), were once found throughout South Africa. Now you'll only see them in a handful of reserves, notably the Kruger, Pilanesberg, Hluhluwe-Imfolozi, Tembe and Addo, the last of which protects the only population to survive naturally in the southern two-thirds of the country. Otherwise, one or two elephants may still survive in the Knysna Forest, but their days are numbered and they are rarely, if ever, seen. When encountered in the flesh, elephants seem even bigger than you would imagine. You'll need little persuasion from those flapping warning ears to back off if you're too close, but they are at the same time amazingly graceful. In a matter of moments a large herd can merge into the trees and disappear, silent on their padded, carefully placed feet, their presence betrayed only by the noisy cracking of branches as they strip trees and uproot saplings.

Elephants are the most engaging of animals to watch, perhaps because their interactions, behaviour patterns and personality have so many human parallels. Like people, they lead complex, interdependent social lives, growing from helpless infancy through self-conscious adolescence to adulthood. Babies are born with other cows in close attendance, after a 22-month gestation. Calves suckle for two to three years. Basic family units are composed of a group of related females, tightly protecting their young and led by a venerable matriarch. It's the matriarch that's most likely to bluff a charge – though occasionally she may get carried away and tusk a vehicle or person.

Bush mythology has it that elephants become embarrassed and ashamed after killing a human, covering the body with sticks and grass. They certainly pay much attention to the disposal of their own dead relatives, often dispersing the bones and spending time near the remains. Old animals die in their 70s or 80s, when their last set of teeth wears out and they can no longer feed.

Dassies (hyraxes)

Dassies look like they ought to be rodents but, amazingly, despite being fluffy and rabbit-sized, their closest relatives (from some way back) are elephants. Their name (pronounced like "dusty" without the "t") is the Afrikaans version of *dasje*, meaning "little badger", given to them by the first Dutch settlers.

Tree dassies, *Dendrohyrax arboreus*, a rarely seen, solitary species, live along the Eastern Cape and southern KwaZulu-Natal coastal plains, where they take refuge in forest and thick bush. In contrast, **rock dassies**, *Procavia capensis* (see p.25), are widely distributed, having thrived with the elimination of predators. They hang out in suitably rocky habitat all over the country apart from north of the Orange River in the western half of the country and in the east along the northern KwaZulu-Natal coast, and in the Western Cape. One of the most dramatic places you'll see them is sunning themselves along the rocky shore of the Tsitsikamma National Park, as breakers crash down ahead.

Like reptiles, hyraxes have poor body control systems and rely on shelter against both the cold and hot sunlight. They wake up sluggish and seek out rocks to catch the early morning sun – this is one of the best times to look out for them. One adult stands sentry against predators and issues a low-pitched warning cry in response to a threat. Dassies live in colonies of a dominant male and eight or more related females and their offspring.

Rhinos

Two species of rhinoceros are found in Africa: the hook-lipped or **black rhino**, *Diceros bicornis* (see p.25), and the much heavier square-lipped or **white rhino**, *Ceratotherium simum* (see p.26). Both have come close to extinction in the African wild and have all but disappeared. Happily, South Africa has bucked this continental trend and, due to timely conservation measures (especially in KwaZulu-Natal), it's the best place in the world to see both. Spend a day or two at Ithala, Hluhluwe-Imfolozi or Mkhuze reserves and you're bound to see one species or the other. Elsewhere, look for white rhinos at Addo and both varieties at Kruger and Pilanesberg.

"Hook-lipped" and "square-lipped" are technically more accurate terms for the two rhinos. "Black" and "white" are based on a linguistic misunderstanding – somewhere along the line, the German *weid,* which refers to the square-lipped's wide mouth, was misheard as "white". The term has stuck, despite both rhinos being a greyish muddy colour.

The shape of their lips is highly significant as it indicates their respective diets and consequently their favoured habitat. The cantankerous and smaller black rhino has the narrow prehensile lips of a browser, suited to picking leaves off trees and bushes, while the wide, flatter mouth of the twice-as-heavy white rhino is well suited to chomping away at grasses like a lawnmower. Diet and habitat also account for the greater sociability of the white rhino, which relies on safety in numbers under the exposure of open grassland; the solitary black rhino relies on the camouflage of dense thickets, which is why you'll find them so much more difficult to see.

Rhinos give birth to a single calf after a gestation period of fifteen to eighteen months, and the baby is not weaned until it is at least a year old, sometimes two. Their population grows slowly compared with most animals, another factor contributing to their predicament.

Hippos

Hippopotamuses, *Hippopotamus amphibius* (see p.26), are highly adaptable animals that once inhabited South African waterways from the Limpopo in the north to the marshes of the Cape Peninsula in the south. Today they're restricted to the northeastern corner of the country, with the most southerly indigenous population living in KwaZulu-Natal. You will find them elsewhere, in places where they've been reintroduced, such as the Double Drift Reserve in the Eastern Cape.

Hippos need freshwater deep enough to submerge themselves in, with a surrounding of suitable grazing grass. By day, they need to spend most of their time in water to protect their thin, hairless skin. After dark, hippos leave the water to spend the whole night grazing, often walking up to 10km in one session. Their grunting and jostling in the water may give the impression of loveable buffoons, but throughout Africa they are feared, and rightly so, as they are reckoned to be responsible for more human deaths on the continent than any other animal. When disturbed, lone bulls and cows with calves can become extremely aggressive. Their fearsomely long incisors can slash through a canoe with ease; on land they can charge at speeds up to 30kph, with a tight turning circle.

Zebras

Zebras are closely related to horses and, together with them, donkeys and wild asses, form the equid family. Of the three species of zebra, two live in South Africa.

The Burchell's or **plains zebra**, *Equus burchelli* (see p.26), has small ears and thick, black stripes, with lighter "shadows"; it survives in Mpumalanga, KwaZulu-Natal and along the Limpopo. Elsewhere it has been widely introduced and you'll see plains zebra in many reserves across the country.

The **Cape mountain zebra**, *Equus zebra zebra*, only narrowly escaped extinction, but now survives in healthy if limited numbers in the Mountain Zebra National Park in the Eastern Cape, and in other reserves in the southwest, wherever there is suitably mountainous terrain. Distinguishing characteristics of the mountain zebra are the dewlap on its lower neck, the absence of shadow stripes, its larger ears, and stripes that go all the way down to its hooves – in contrast to the Burchell's, whose stripes fade out as they progress down its legs.

Zebras congregate in family herds of a breeding stallion and two mares (or more) and their foals. Unattached males will often form bachelor herds. Among plains zebras, offspring leave the family group after between one and two years, while mountain zebras are far more tolerant in allowing adolescents to remain in the family.

Pigs

Two **wild pigs** are found in South Africa. If you're visiting the Kruger, Pilanesberg or the KwaZulu-Natal parks, families of **warthogs**, *Phacochoerus aethiopicus* (see p.26), will become a familiar sight, trotting across the savanna with their tails erect like communications antennae. Family groups usually consist of a mother and her litter of two to four piglets, or occasionally two or three females and their young. Boars join the group only to mate; they're distinguished from sows by their prominent face warts, which are thought to be defensive pads protecting their heads during often violent fights. Warthogs shelter in holes in the ground, usually porcupine or aardvark burrows, although they are quite capable of making their own – in fact, they are supreme diggers who routinely dig up nutritious bulbs.

Bushpigs, *Potamochoerus porcus*, are slightly more widely distributed than warthogs in South Africa, but because they're nocturnal forest dwellers, they aren't seen as often. Their northerly range overlaps with that of the hogs, but they also extend along the southern coastal woodlands of the Eastern Cape as far west as Mossel Bay. Much like hairier versions of domestic pigs, they live in harems called "sounders", consisting of a boar with several females and their piglets. Fathers drive out male offspring when they approach adolescence.

Other mammals

Despite their common taste for ants and termites, their nocturnal foraging and their outlandish appearance, aardvarks and pangolins are quite unrelated. The **aardvark**, *Orycteropus afer* (see p.21), is one of Africa's – indeed the world's – strangest animals, a solitary mammal weighing up to 70kg. Its name, Afrikaans for "earth pig", is an apt description, as it holes up during the day in large burrows that are excavated with remarkable speed and energy. It emerges at night to visit termite mounds within a radius of up to 5km, digging for its main diet. It's most likely to be common in bush country that's well scattered with termite mounds. Holes dug into the base of these are a tell-tale sign of the presence of aardvarks.

Pangolins, *Manis temminckii*, are equally unusual – scale-covered mammals, resembling armadillos and feeding on ants and termites. Under attack they roll themselves into a ball. Pangolins occur widely in South Africa, north of the Orange River.

A number of species of rabbits and hares bounce about the South African landscape, but the **scrub hare**, *Lepus saxatilis*, distinguished by its exceptionally long ears, is the commonest and one you'll undoubtedly see in scrubby, wooded country throughout the region. Wherever there's rocky terrain south of the Orange River and in KwaZulu-Natal, keep an eye open for **rock rabbits**, which look just like brown- and white-speckled domestic bunnies.

If you go on a night drive you'd be most unlucky not to see the glinting eyes of **springhares**, *Pedetes capensis* (see p.21), which, despite their resemblance to rabbit-sized kangaroos, are in fact true rodents. In the western arid zone **ground squirrels**, *Xerus inauris*, can be spotted scurrying about during the day looking for roots, seeds and bulbs, while in the northeast, **tree squirrels**, *Paraxerus cepapi*, enjoy a similar diet. The most singular and largest of the African rodents is the **porcupine**, *Hystrix africae-australis* (see p.21), which is quite unmistakable with its coat of many quills. Porcupines are widespread and present in most reserves but, because they're nocturnal, you may only see shed quills lying along the path or in front of their burrows.

Scores of different **bats**, either fruit- or insect-eaters, leave their roosts each night and take off into the South African night, but all you're likely to see of them is some erratic flying against a moonlit sky. The foxy-faced **Egyptian fruit bat**, *Rousettus aegyptiacus*, is virtually single-handedly responsible for pollinating baobab trees, thus keeping them from extinction. And while **rats and mice** are probably not what brought you on safari, it's worth noting that over forty different species are found in South Africa.

Music

usic from South Africa has a deserved following. The country has some of the Africa's most diverse recorded music output and its music industry is among the continent's most developed. It doesn't take much effort for an interested listener to encounter anything from indigenous African sounds that have remained largely unchanged for the last two hundred years, to a variety of white pop styles that would not be out of place anywhere in the Western world.

Compilations of South African music released abroad usually concentrate on the country's African genres and furthermore tend to ignore newer styles, so Western fans can be forgiven for thinking that the **iscathamiya** vocalizing of Ladysmith Black Mambazo, or the **mbaqanga** ("township jive") made famous by Paul Simon's *Graceland* album and artists such as Mahlathini and the Mahotella Queens, remains at the cutting edge locally. In fact, *iscathamiya* has now all but retreated to the Zulu worker hostels whence it originated, while *mbaqanga* is popular but old-fashioned – a safe bet for a DJ at an African wedding, but not the thing to play to an urban party crowd.

Far and away the most popular music in the country, at least in terms of consistently racking up the largest sales figures, is African **gospel**. Among urban black youth, much the biggest sound is **kwaito** and local **hip-hop**, while more mature urban Africans often prefer **jazz**. Attracting both black and white fans is **Afropop**, a skilful blend of various older African styles with Western pop influences.

South Africa's **English–speaking whites** tend to favour international pop. **Afrikaans speakers** have a weakness for home-grown pop balladeers, and older or rural Afrikaners often prefer listening and dancing to *boeremusiek*, a so-called "traditional" mixture of Germanic and Dutch elements and US country music. Both English- and Afrikaans-speakers also support a wide range of local musicians representing virtually every modern pop variant, from boy bands to hard rock; electronic dance music has a following among many white 20-somethings from both sides of the linguistic divide, as well as their peers of Indian origin.

Among Zulus, **maskanda**, a guitar-and-vocal neo-traditional style, remains firmly entrenched, while the largely coloured-supported ballroom dancing circuit regularly features a network of small dance bands, although these aren't well represented by commercial recordings. Tourists in Cape Town over the Christmas/New Year holidays should not miss the musicians at the coloured "coon carnival", whose roots that can be traced back 150 years to visiting African American minstrels, and to the Malay choirs, who are additionally influenced by music brought from the Indonesian archipelago in the eighteenth century.

Paradoxically, judging by what one often hears pumping from the nation's radios, clubs and car stereos, more of the population than anywhere else on the continent listens to American sounds. African American music in particular has been popular with black South Africans for over a hundred years, and has been critical in the development of local sounds. Concern over imported music smothering South African sounds has led to **radio quotas** whereby, depending on the profile of the station, a quarter to forty percent of airtime must be devoted to local music. The policy has arguably had the greatest impact in the realm of black urban youth music, which commercially is in its healthiest state in decades. The prospects for its white equivalent, notwithstanding some world-class material, are not so good: given the relatively small size of the white population, white South African pop musicians are often presented with a stark choice: stagnate or immigrate.

Gospel

Choral harmony and melody are perhaps black South Africa's greatest musical gifts to the world, and nowhere are they better manifested than in its **churches**. In the mainstream Catholic, Anglican and Methodist denominations a tradition of choral singing has evolved that has taken the style of European classical composers and loosened it up, added rhythm and, as always, some great dance routines. This type of choral singing is immensely popular, with regular competitions involving amazingly attired choirs – some of which are over one hundred strong. If you can't make it to a competition, you can watch the choirs every Sunday on TV (SABC 1).

In the **Pentecostal** churches, the music is more American-influenced, yet the harmonies and melodies remain uniquely South African and intensely moving. Pentecostal gospel music is the main recorded style; look out for groups like **Lord Comforters**, **Joyous Celebration**, **Pure Magic**, **Lusanda Spiritual Group** and the powerful **Rebecca Malope** (see box below).

Also worth seeking out is the music of the **Zionist churches**, which have more members than any other denomination in the country. Their devotees are required to donate ten percent of their income to the church, live an ultra-clean life and attend all the services and conventions, in distinctive long robes, often adorned with sashes. Zionist gospel is an extraordinary mix of mournfulness and fervour, with a tonality all of its own, rendering it perfect for the moving night vigils that precede funerals, as well as regular church services. Services are held outside, often in parks, where you are welcome to watch as long as you do so respectfully. Zionist gospel cassettes and CDs are easily spotted, as their

Rebecca Malope

Diminutive **Rebecca Malope** is South Africa's biggest selling music star, enjoying years at the top of the gospel scene, with only stadia able to hold her fans, every album going gold or platinum, popular magazines full of her photos, views and story, and everyone knowing the lyrics of her songs. Well, nearly everyone that is, for Rebecca Malope is virtually unknown outside Africa.

The daughter of a Sotho father and Swazi mother, Rebecca was born in Nelspruit, Mpumalanga, in 1969, and soon began singing in the local Assemblies of God church, where her grandfather was a pastor. Her initial recordings were mostly forgettable bubblegum pop. She was spotted in Jo'burg by **Sizwe Zako**, who would become her lynchpin keyboard player. Under his tutelage and, so she says, because of letters from fans pleading that she sing God's songs, Rebecca returned to gospel in 1990, where she has been amply rewarded. Rebecca denies that she is apolitical, saying she sometimes sings at rallies, but selects songs that tell the politicians what she believes they need to hear.

Rebecca's musical formula, engineered by Zako, who also produces, rarely varies. The songs are anthems characterized by swirling keyboards and excellent backing singers, and are delivered in her tremendous, soaring and sometimes husky voice, accompanied by dramatic gestures.

covers invariably feature the substantial performing choir in full robes, often with the preacher out in front in some suitably religious pose.

Kwaito and hip-hop

South Africa's definitive youth sound, **kwaito**, has been around for about a decade. Apparently, DJs importing dance music in the early 1990s found that white clubs were unresponsive to Chicago house and so tried it in black night-clubs instead. Here DJs found that people preferred it when they slowed the records from 45 to 33rpm. Innovative producers soon began to try out their own versions and to experiment, incorporating South African melodies and DJs singing doggerel verses incorporating the latest, wickedest phrases of *tsotsi taal* – ghetto rude-boy slang.

In an accurate reflection of the depressed and nihilistic mood of township youth culture, *kwaito*'s vibe tends to be downbeat, and the music frequently carries a strong association with gangsterism and explicit sexuality. This is often condemned by older and God-fearing South Africans, which matters "nix" (nothing) to its young township fans, to whom *kwaito* embodies the style and groove of the new South Africa.

The popularity of many *kwaito* performers is often fairly short-lived. For example, **Arthur**, one of the pioneers of the genre, has recently fallen back on producing newer hopefuls. Some artists worth looking out for include **Tokollo** (ex-**TKZee**), **Mzekezeke** (who always performs with his trademark mask),

Brenda Fassie

Kwaito killed the careers of many of the 1980s pop stars, but the late **Brenda Fassie** managed not only to survive the new music, but to thrive on it. Brenda was South Africa's true pop queen and the one local artist whose music is still pretty much guaranteed to get things going on the dance floor, wherever you are in the country.

Brenda began her career in the early 1980s as the lead singer for **Brenda and the Big Dudes**, enjoying a string of bubblegum hits, including the classic "Weekend Special", which for years was a South African disco anthem. Her sound mixed *kwaito*, *mbaqanga*, gospel and her own extraordinary persona, earning massive and deserved success with tunes like "Vul'Ndlela" and "Nomakanjani". Although never one for politics, she skilfully caught the mood of the time in the tense year of 1989 with a moving song about police brutality, "Good Black Woman", on the album *Too Late for Mama*.

During the 1990s, while contemporaries like her one-time arch rival **Yvonne Chaka Chaka** produced comfortable material aimed more at middle-class and mid-dle-aged audiences, Brenda made a point of hanging out with the youth in Soweto and in Hillbrow, Johannesburg's fastest-paced inner-city patch. The result was a lesbian love affair that thrilled the tabloids, a bad crack habit, a tendency to lose the plot completely on stage – and the best music she had ever produced.

Tragically, if not inevitably, her many demons eventually caught up with her, and after falling into a two-week long coma, which even saw President Thabo Mbeki coming to her hospital bedside, she died in 2004. Her funeral was a massive media event that witnessed an outpouring of grief exceeding that attending the deaths of most "struggle" veterans, and a few months later, when a television programme solicited telephone votes for the all-time greatest South Africans, Brenda came in comfortably at number seventeen, the highest placing of any musician.

Kabelo, the hard-rock-influenced **Mandoza**, and the matchstick-chewing, gangster-styled **Zola**. Zola starred in the hit South African drama series *Yizo Yizo* about the interplay between a township school and local young gangsters, and the two soundtrack CDs from the programme are a virtual who's who of the *kwaito* scene. Kalawa Jazmee, a record label run by Oscar Mdlongwa, aka **DJ Oskido**, has been responsible for several successful *kwaito* groups including **Trompies**, **Bongo Maffin** and the self-consciously retro **Mafikizolo**. The label's production values are generally a cut above the rest and with each release they seem to have added more actual singing and melody to the mix. The latest *kwaito* sensation at the time of writing, **Malaika**, have kept to this formula, retaining the musicality as well as the typical electronic backing while jettisoning the tuneless chanting.

Local **hip-hop** artists are more likely than their *kwaito* counterparts to use English instead of an African language, and tend to come from middle-class backgrounds instead of the townships – as a result of which they can afford to spend more on production. Among the hip-hop names making a splash are **Skwatta Kamp**, **Optical Illusion**, **Cashless Society**, **Zubz** and **H20**. Although the supporters of local hip-hop eagerly proclaim that it is now replacing *kwaito*, the reality is more nuanced, and the difference between the two styles isn't always clear cut.

House, rap and reggae

DJ-mixed South African **house** attracts practitioners and fans from all parts of the country's racial and cultural divisions, but it is black DJs such as **DJ Fresh**, **Glen Lewis**, **DJ Mbuso** and **Oskido** who garner by far the most attention from the local media. The recordings they mix with are almost exclusively from either the UK or France.

South African **rap** has enjoyed sustained popularity since the early 1990s, but has remained almost completely ghettoized within the coloured community of the Western Cape. Heavily influenced by African American rappers such as Public Enemy, the performers often exude a palpable sense of being "Americans trapped in Africa". Pioneers of the style were the heavily politicized **Prophets of Da City**, several members of which made names for themselves as solo artists after the group's break-up, most notably **Rahim**, **Junior Solela** and **Ishmael**. Other performers who have since come up are **Brasse Van Die Kaap** (who rap in Afrikaans), **Reddy D** and **Godessa**, while a new Cape Town-based record and production company, African Dope, has also enjoyed recent success with **Teba** and **Funny Carp**, among others.

What is unusual as regards the place of **Lucky Dube** in the local **reggae** scene is the total lack of successful emulators. An energetic, disciplined and talented live performer, Lucky Dube can also come up with a falsetto like Smokey Robinson's, which adds a distinct twist to his otherwise familiar roots reggae sound.

Neo-traditional music

The best way to see South African **neo-traditional music**, unless you're lucky enough to find yourself at an event where it's being performed, is on TV, on SABC 1's *Ezodumo*. The programme is a great showcase for the bands,

Ladysmith Black Mambazo and the iscathamiya sound

The best known of South Africa's many neo-traditional musical genres is Zulu **isca-thamiya** (or **mbube**), the distinctive male a cappella choral style made internation-ally famous by Ladysmith Black Mambazo. The style originated among Zulu rural migrants in urban hostels following World War I, and by 1939 the first commercial hit, "Mbube" by Solomon Linda and His Original Evening Birds, had been recorded, eventually selling 100,000 copies. The song was later reworked as "The Lion Sleeps Tonight", which became a number one hit in both the US and UK and was featured in the Walt Disney movie and musical, *The Lion King*.

Although it enjoyed pan-ethnic popularity in the 1940s and 1950s, by the 1960s *iscathamiya* had reverted to its role as the defining sound of Zulu men's hostels. The music was cleverly used by apartheid-era SABC Radio Zulu to promote rigid ethnic identity, with songs dwelling on Zuluness and the need to leave the cities and return to the rural areas.

In 1973, after recording for the SABC for several years, **Ladysmith Black Mam-bazo** made their first commercial release, *Amabutho*, for the Gallo label. It quickly sold over 25,000 copies (gold-disc status in South Africa) and since that time the group has recorded about forty others, most of which have also gone gold. Follow-ing their collaboration with him on *Graceland*, Paul Simon produced their *Shaka Zulu* album, which sold 100,000 copies around the world and took *iscathamiya* to the international stage. In 1997, Ladysmith Black Mambazo extended its Afropop credentials with *Heavenly*, an album that featured collaborations with, among other international artists, Dolly Parton. Following the exposure of their song "Inkanyezi Nezazi" in a British TV advertisement for Heinz baked beans, the group went on to sell over a million units in the UK, an all-time record for a South African act.

Having briefly flirted with the Zulu nationalist politics of the Inkhatha Freedom Party in the late 1980s, Ladysmith Black Mambazo now prefer to dwell on religious matters, and restrict their politics to calls for peace. Though non-Zulu speakers can appreciate the group's smooth dance steps, immaculate singing and vocal arrange-ments, the true glory of their music for Zulus is the beauty of the lyrics, written by the group's gentle lead singer **Joseph Shabalala**, who is surely one of South Africa's greatest living poets.

all dressed in vaguely traditional attire, and usually consisting of a male lead vocalist, female backing singers and a small rhythm section. As with *kwaito*, the instrumentation is really just a backdrop to the lyrics and the dance routines.

One of the major stars of neo-traditional music is the Shangaan singer **Tho-mas Chauke**, an *Ezodumo* regular and perhaps the single bestselling artist in any neo-traditional genre. Hailing from Limpopo Province, he makes heavy use of a drum machine and an electronic keyboard and often picks out some intricate lead-guitar work to complement his vocals.

Sotho neo-traditional music has declined commercially in recent years, largely because of a lack of support from SABC Radio Sotho, who no longer need to maintain the ethnic exclusivity of the apartheid era. Nevertheless, the bass lines are good, the shouting is definitely first-class and the accordions can take on an almost Cajun tinge. **Tau Oa Matshela** and **Tau Oa Linare** are some of the groups to look out for.

Xhosa and Tswana neo-traditional music rarely makes it to the national scene, but **Zulu music** is more pervasive, both in its a cappella form, known as **iscathamiya**, and as a vocal/guitar-based style called **maskanda**. A unique guitar-picking style (*ukupika*) is central to the instrumental sound, though these days it may be overshadowed by a hammily played electronic keyboard.

Each song starts with the *izihlabo* (an instrumental flourish), followed by the main melody, which is interrupted by the lead singer's *ukubonga*, a fast-spoken declamation, usually in deep rural Zulu, that always used to be some kind of praise poem, but could just as well in modern songs be a denunciation of a woman's cooking pot. For particularly fine examples of the art, look out for **Phuzekhemisi**, **Shiyani Ncgobo** and the late, great **Mfaz'Omnyama**. Another star of the neo-traditional scene, and also an *Ezodumo* regular, is the queen of Ndebele music, **Nothembi Mkhwebane**. As well as being a talented and veteran performer, Nothembi, who sings and plays electric guitar, is also known for her sensational outfits, decorated with typical intricate Ndebele bead and metalwork.

Jazz

Jazz has been widely popular in South Africa for many decades, and you can almost always find performances in Johannesburg, Pretoria or Cape Town on virtually any weekend, and sometimes midweek too. It was **South African jazz** that was the music most associated with the struggle against apartheid, especially after the music's main exponents went into self-imposed exile in the 1960s.

Jazz's roots in the country are much older than this, harking back to the emergence of *marabi* music in Johannesburg's African slums some time after World War I. *Marabi* was at first played on pianos in Jo'burg's illegal *shebeens*; always revolving around a simple three-chord structure, and combining elements of indigenous African styles with various Western musical influences, it continued to develop in the 1930s, with guitars, banjos and concertinas added to the line-up. During the Second World War, American swing became popular in South Africa, following which swing and *marabi* were fused into a new style usually referred to as **African jazz**. This remained predominant throughout the 1940s and 1950s, and produced the first South African musical exiles in vocalists **Miriam Makeba** and the **Manhattan Brothers**.

The next development was a move in the direction of the American avant-garde, as personified by Thelonious Monk and John Coltrane. The two early, prime exponents of this in South Africa were the **Jazz Epistles**, featuring Hugh Masekela, Jonas Gwangwa, Abdullah Ibrahim (then called Dollar Brand) and the great Kippie Moeketsi; and the **Blue Notes**, who included in their line-up Chris McGregor and Dudu Pukwana. Legislation prohibiting mixed-race public performances caused most of the Epistles to individually leave South Africa in the early 1960s, while the Blue Notes departed en masse in 1964. Some exiled South African jazzers detached themselves from their roots, while others such as **Hugh Masekela** reinterpreted their township influences. Back home, old style African jazz as performed by the **Elite Swingsters** and **Ntemi Piliso's Alexandra All Stars** remained popular.

In the 1970s and 1980s, various South African strains were fused with funk, soul and rock influences to produce a more accessible, populist brand of jazz, from bands such as **Sakile**, **The Drive** and the **Jazz Ministers**. In the last decade, following the end of apartheid, the surviving exiles began to trickle back and a new, younger generation of jazz musicians yet again married old local traditions with contemporary international trends.

Today, almost all of the old African jazz artists are gone, while most exiled artists, including Miriam Makeba, Hugh Masekela and **Jonas Gwangwa**, are back home and receiving the domestic recognition they have long deserved. A few of the original avant-garde veterans like Abdullah Ibrahim, **Mankunku** and **Bheki Mseleku** continue to perform fairly regularly, but there are remarkably few players remaining from even the relatively recent fusion days. In their place, a large group of new jazz names have emerged that includes vocalists (**Gloria Bosman**, **Judith Sephuma**, **Sibongile Kumalo**), saxophonists (**McCoy Mrubata**, **Zim Ngqawana**), keyboard players (**Paul Hamner**, **Themba Mkhize**), guitarists (**Jimmy Dludlu**, **Selaelo Selota**) and the odd trumpeter (**Prince Lengoasa**, **Marcus Wyatt**). Although many of the stars of this new generation emulate the smooth style of the Earl Klugh school, there are other players whose tastes are considerably more muscular.

Political music

Political songs were once performed during marches, demonstrations, rallies and most of all at the funerals of slain activists, though their heyday has passed with the collapse of apartheid. The lyrics sang the praises of Umkhonto we Sizwe (the ANC's armed wing, or stated bluntly that "*uMama uyajabula uma ngibulala iBhunu*" ("My mother is happy when I kill a Boer"). Performances were usually accompanied by the *toyi-toyi*, a combination of a march and a dance; still widely used, it's performed on the spot or on the move, with knees brought high.

In the 1980s, **Mzwakhe Mbuli** made his name as "the people's poet", performing his articulate and angry political poetry at countless rallies around the country. His house was firebombed by the authorities, and Mzwakhe himself was harassed and detained, but his poetry remained defiant, with titles like *Unbroken Spirit* and *Now is the Time*. In 1989, Mzwakhe correctly discerned the signs of the times, proclaiming in one poem that "the bull is dying at last, kicking at random", and in the following year, while celebrating Mandela's release, he urged prophetically: "When you vote and get elected, think of those who died."

After the 1994 elections, Mzwakhe was for a time a contented man, asking disillusioned compatriots, "if this is not the time for happiness, when is?", while also using his poetry to urge an end to social ills like criminality and drug addiction. Controversially, however, he served several years in a maximum security prison in the company of apartheid mass murderers like Eugene de Kock, after being convicted of armed robbery (Mzwakhe says he was framed because he was aware of drug-smuggling involving officialdom).

Afropop

Afropop is to some degree a catch-all category, yet it's arguably where many contemporary South African artists sit most comfortably. Afropop is characterized by a knack for combining various local African styles with Western popular influences, the ability to attract a multiracial audience, and the eschewing of computer-generated backing in favour of actual instruments.

The beginnings of Afropop go back to Miriam Makeba's first American recordings in the early 1960s. More contemporary examples would include

Paul Simon's 1987 *Gracelands*, a collaboration with Ladysmith Black Mambazo and other local African artists; and the music of **Juluka** and **Savuka**, two bands led in the Eighties and Nineties by Johnny Clegg, whose melding of mainstream pop harmonies with Zulu dance routines and a touch of *mbaqanga* gained great popularity both in South Africa and in France. The music of bubblegum-pop queen **Yvonne Chaka Chaka** from the 1980s and 1990s could also be deemed Afropop. Artists who have subsequently adopted similar formulas include **Jabu Khanyile** (sometimes billed with a band as **Bayete** – his music might be described as Zulu-pop), **Vusi Mahlasela**, **Ringo** (influenced by African jazz and Xhosa traditional music) and **Busi Mhlongo** (influenced by African jazz and Zulu *maskanda*).

A recent Afropop star is the much acclaimed **Thandiswa Mazwai**. Although she has consciously incorporated quite a few different styles, both American and local, into her first album, her live persona tends to emphasize her Xhosa roots, and she is already being widely referred to as the new Makeba.

White pop and rock

English-speaking South Africans have successfully replicated virtually every popular Western musical style going back to the late nineteenth century, and some have found fame in the outside world. A list of the country's most successful musical émigrés would include rockers **Manfred Mann** in the 1960s and most recently **Dave Matthews**. At the time of writing, several successful local rock/punk bands have recently relocated overseas, including **Seether**, **Just Jinger** and **Wonderboom**.

Thanks to TV coverage, including the local version of *Pop Idols*, the action is not restricted to rock but extends to virtually every variety of contemporary pop. Young male vocal sensations, for example, include **Danny K**, whose slick R&B is particularly popular among teenagers, and **Heinz Winkler**, where smooth pop meets "adult contemporary".

Afrikaans music

Like South African jazz, *Afrikaansmusiek* is another world unto itself, with a multitude of sub-categories and a long list of heroes and heroines. Its development can be traced back to the seventeenth century with the mixing of German–Dutch and French music, while from the late 1920s up into the 1960s American country was the greatest outside influence. This was also the period that saw the first truly "populist" recordings being released, frequently covers of American hits, sung in Afrikaans. A somewhat more rugged and largely instrumental variant called **boeremusiek** ("farmer music") has the concertina as a lead instrument, backed originally with acoustic string instrumentation, and subsequently with drums, electric bass and electronic keyboards.

By the early 1970s, the influence of country was starting to decline. In its stead came the lighter end of foreign pop music and in particular, Eurodisco. A long line of bouncy Afrikaans pop stars ensued, while a more sober side was represented by the light operatic style of **Gé Korsten**, probably the single most popular Afrikaans artist of the period.

Following the end of apartheid, a general concern about the future of the Afrikaans language and culture spurred a revival of interest in Afrikaans music. There is undoubtedly more stylistic variety now than ever before: witness the house/disco of **Juanita**, the heavy rock of **Karen Zoid** and **Jackhammer**, the modernized *boeremusiek* of the **Klipwerf Orkes**, and the Neil Diamond-esque songs of **Steve Hofmeyer** (currently the bestselling Afrikaans music artist).

Discography

In the reviews below, items marked with an asterisk are international releases. Other items are South African releases, issued either by local labels or by the South African operations of international labels.

Mbaqanga

Mahlathini and the Mahotella Queens *The Best Of Mahlathini and the Mahotella Queens* (Gallo). Perfect introduction to the sound of this most stomping of *mbaqanga* outfits.

Soul Brothers *Igobondela*, *The Best Of The Soul Brothers* and *The Early Years* (Gallo). If the *Best Of* whets your appetite, investigate *The Early Years*, a series comprising the classic first twelve albums by this these *mbaqanga* stalwarts, recorded in the 1970s and early 1980s. *Igobondela* (2004) is the band's first album to combine studio and live tracks and demonstrates how they're still capable of delivering the goods.

Various Artists *From Marabi to Disco* (Gallo). A mini-encyclopedia of the development of township musical style from the late 1930s to the early 1980s, with informative sleeve notes.

Various Artists *The Indestructible Beat of Soweto Volumes 1–6* (Earthworks★). Superb compilation, mainly featuring 1980s *mbaqanga*, along with a few more traditional samples. As compiler Trevor Herman writes, "best heard loud and standing up".

Gospel

Amadodana Ase Wesile *Morena U Ba Elele* (Gallo). A representative offering of spiritual anthems from this popular Methodist male choir, who wear blazers and red waistcoats, keep time by thumping a Bible, and can make huge congregations sway and sing as one.

Imvuselelo Yase Natali *Izigi* (BMG). One of the most extraordinary gospel acts in South Africa, fronted by the charismatic – and at times plain bizarre – Reverend Makitaza. If you ever get the chance to see this group, don't miss them.

IPCC *Ummeli Wethu* (Gallo). An excellent offering from one of South Africa's most popular gospel choirs, replete with charisma and stunning melodies.

Lusanda Spiritual Group *Abanye Bayawela* (Gallo). The biggest-selling album from one of gospel music's newest sensations. Lusanda Mcinga's innovation has been to add guitar and keyboard backing to African Methodist hymns formerly rendered a cappella.

Rebecca Malope *Shwele Baba* (CCP). One of Rebecca's finest albums, with the title track a strong contender for her best-ever song and the rest of the cuts all pretty good too.

Solly Moholo *Abanye Bayawela Motlhang ke Kolobetswa "Die poppe sal dans"* (CCP). A beautiful release from the country's finest Sotho gospel artist.

Pure Magic *Greatest Hits* (EMI). Simply wonderful melodic gospel-pop from this group featuring the silky lead vocals of Vuyo Mokoena and produced by Sizwe Zako (of Rebecca Malope fame).

Various Artists *Choirs of South Africa* (Roi Music). Stirring gospel anthems delivered by mass choirs with exuberance and power. All that's missing is the visual spectacle of their members dressed in flowing garments and swaying to the mighty sounds.

Various Artists *Gospel Spirit of Africa* (Gallo). An excellent compilation of most of South Africa's top current gospel acts, including the Holy Cross Choir and the Holy Brothers, and Ladysmith Black Mambazo in gospel mode.

Various Artists *Rough Guide To South African Gospel* (Rough Guides★). A comprehensive survey of South African gospel going back to the 1950s.

Various *Joyous Celebration Volumes 1–8* (Sony, SA). Eight albums of classic gospel from some of South Africa's finest gospel artists, taken from their seemingly endless roadshow around the country, where they play to packed audiences.

Kwaito and hip-hop

Alaska *Most Wanted* (Sony Music). Well-produced, ultra-stylish *kwaito* from this well-dressed foursome, featuring great beats and some particularly impenetrable ghetto lyrics.

Bongo Maffin *Bongolution* (Sony Music). A fine release from this popular group which combines Jamaican-style ragga lyrics with *kwaito* beats, and includes the catchy hit "The Way Kungakhona".

Brenda Fassie *African Princess Of Pop* and *Memeza* (CCP). The former is a posthumous survey covering the entire career of South Africa's very own Madonna; the latter, featuring the massive hit "Vul'Ndlela", was Brenda's most commercially successful effort and holds the all-time sales record (540,000 plus and still rising) for a locally produced album.

Kabelo *And The Beat Goes On* (Universal). A monster hit from one of the biggest *kwaito* stars at the time of writing.

Mafikizolo *Sibongile* (Sony Music). Solid melodies, well sung and harmonized (the trio's female vocalist, Sibongile Nkosi, is outstanding).

Makhendlas *Jammer* (CCP). Features two massive hits, *Emenwe* and *Ayeye Aho*, from the brother of *kwaito* pioneer Arthur. Makhendlas tragically shot himself immediately after killing a troublesome fan after a gig in late 1998.

Malaika *Malaika* (Sony Music). Hugely successful, this is very much in the style pioneered by Mafikizolo but features even more contemporary African-American influences.

Mandoza *Nakalakala* (CCP). Not only was this album massively popular with African urban youth, the title track has been one of very few *kwaito* recordings to truly cross over into the white pop arena.

M'Du *No Pas No Special* (Sony Music). A popular though somewhat downbeat album from one of *kwaito's* most enduring stars.

Skwatta Kamp *Khut En Joyn* (Nkuli). A fairly relentless first offering from the *enfants terrible* of the local hip-hop scene. The track *Politics* certainly gives a somewhat different take on the state of South Africa's democratic governance.

TKZee *Halloween* (BMG). Complete with trademark catchy anthems and R&B-based sounds, this is a solid early (1998) offering from

these popular *kwaito* artists. The track *Magesh* is considered a classic.

Trompies *Boostin' Kabelz* (Sony Music). Kicking sounds from one of the coolest *kwaito* acts on the circuit, including the irresistible "Di Potsotso".

Zola *Mdlwembe* (EMI). The first solo album of "Mr Ghetto Fabulous", full of menacing rhythms and including the surprise gospel hit *Mzione*.

Various Artists *Yizo Yizo Volumes 1 & 2* (CCP). The soundtrack to South Africa's hippest TV drama, with cuts from virtually every major *kwaito* artist.

Rap and reggae

Lucky Dube *Prisoner* (Gallo). Originally a township jive singer, Dube made a switch to reggae that was both artistically and commercially inspired. *Prisoner* was South Africa's second bestselling album ever, full of stirring Peter Tosh-style roots tunes.

Prophets of Da City *Ghetto Code* (Universal). South Africa's rap supremos' finest release, full of tough but articulate rhymes and some seriously funky backing tracks, all in true Cape Flats style.

Neo-traditional

Amampondo *Drums for Tomorrow* (Melt 2000). South Africa's most famous marimba band deliver a fine and well-produced set here, full of their distinctive Xhosa melodies and powerful polyrhythms.

Ladysmith Black Mambazo *Favourites* (Gallo). A fine greatest hits selection from the group's first decade in the Seventies and early Eighties. Contains the wonderful *Nomathemba* and *Hello My Baby*, among others.

Ladysmith Black Mambazo *Congratulations South Africa: The Ultimate Collection* (Wrasse★). This double CD is a mixed bag of Afro-pop and 1990s *iscathamiya*, including

"Inkanyezi Nezazi", which gained the group plenty of new fans after being used in a Heinz baked-beans advert.

DZM Madosini *Power To The Women* (Melt 2000). A magnificent exposition of traditional Xhosa vocal harmonies, accompanied by the indigenous mouthbow, that is considerably enhanced by the impeccable (and expensive) production.

Mfaz'Omnyama *Ngisebenzile Mama* (Gallo). The title means "I have been working, Mum", and is amply justified by this superb set, featuring some of the best *maskanda* ever recorded.

Nothembi Mkhwebane *Akana-mandl' Usathana* (Gallo). Beautiful guitar-driven sounds from the Ndebele music queen, with a cover showing Nothembi in one of her impressive traditional outfits.

Shiyani Ncgobo *Introducing* (Sheer Sound). A very fine *maskanda* album aimed largely at a foreign audience, and thus with far more variety than a domestic offering would feature.

Phuzekhemisi *Ngo 49* (Gallo). Every album recorded by this reigning *maskanda* champion features stunning guitar work, great vocals and murderous bass lines, but *Ngo 49*

is perhaps his finest release, thanks to some exceptional production work by the late West Nkosi.

Women Of Mambazo *Mamizolo* (Gallo). Beautiful *iscathimiya* melodies and harmonizations, not rendered by the usual male line-up but by a female group led by Nellie Shabalala, the late wife of Ladysmith Black Mambazo leader Joseph Shabalala.

Various Artists *Singing in an Open Space* (Rounder★). A survey of Zulu guitar recordings from 1962 to 1982, when the style was still referred to as "Zulu Traditional".

Jazz

Jimmy Dludlu *Essence Of Rhythm* (Universal). Dludlu is the essence of smooth jazz, and is arguably the single most popular representative of what is in turn the most commercially successful jazz style in South Africa today.

Elite Swingsters *Siya Gida* (Universal). A final flowering from these African jazz stalwarts. Lots of great danceable music as well as some fine vocals by the late great Dolly Rathebe.

Paul Hamner *Trains To Taung* (Sheer Sound). This album is constructed around Hamner's dreamy, acoustic piano-based compositions. Now considered a classic and one of the first expositions of the new jazz of the post-apartheid era.

Abdullah Ibrahim (Dollar Brand) *Mannenberg – Is Where It's Happening* (The Sun/EMI, SA). Most of Ibrahim's catalogue veers towards the esoteric, but *Mannenberg* (1975) is the master's most accessible work by far, and also his biggest commercial success.

Sibongile Khumalo *Ancient Evenings* (Sony Music). Though

a classically trained opera singer, Khumalo takes on both jazz and a variety of traditional melodies on this wonderful album, demonstrating why she is currently one of South Africa's best-loved singers.

Miriam Makeba and the Skylarks *Miriam Makeba and the Skylarks* (Teal) and *Welela* (Universal★). *Welela*, from 1989, is probably Makeba's finest album – great songs, wonderfully performed and totally lacking the ham-fisted production that encumbers so many of her American recordings. The Teal release contains 32 great recordings from the 1950s.

Manhattan Brothers *The Very Best Of The Manhattan Brothers* (Gallo). A collection of classic recordings cut between 1948 and 1959 by this seminal vocal quartet, who crossed African-American secular harmonies with indigenous influences.

Mankunku *Yakal'Inkomo* (Universal). A successful blend of Coltrane influences with some classic township melodies.

Hugh Masekela *Still Grazing* (Universal) and *Black to the Future* (Sony Music). *Still Grazing* is the best available compilation of Masekela's work in the Sixties and Seventies, released to coincide with his autobiography of the same name. It includes his biggest-ever hit, "Grazing In The Grass". In the late 1990s Masekela scored a deserved hit with *Black to the Future*, featuring the excellent "Chileshe", an impassioned plea to his countrymen to discard their intense xenophobia towards African immigrants.

Moses Taiwa Molelekwa *Genes and Spirits* (Melt 2000). Fascinating jazz/drum 'n' bass fusion by a talented young pianist, who died tragically in 2001.

Zim Ngqawana *Vadzimu* (Sheer Sound). Ngqawana is one of the most revered figures in local jazz, despite also being the very antithesis of the smooth style that currently dominates. This is a typically adventurous exposition

incorporating a variety of influences from hard bop to traditional African.

Sakile *Sakile* (Sony Music). A prime example of the jazz fusion popular in the 1980s, Sakile spawned two major figures in saxophonist Khaya Mahlangu and bass player Sipho Gumede.

Philip Tabane and Malombo *Unh!* (Elektra★) and *Ke a Bereka* (Tusk). The masterful guitarist, with a sound and a style entirely his own, does his take on Afro-jazz. The second release veers in a more traditional direction, but is still unmistakably Tabane.

Various Artists *African Connection Parts I–IV* (Sheer Sound). This series of double-CD compilations from the country's premier independent label provides an accessible survey of current South African jazz.

Political

Mzwakhe Mbuli *Resistance is Defence* (Earthworks★). Great sample of the militant lyricism of the people's poet, including a moving ode to Mandela's release.

Various Artists *Freedom Songs* (Making Music Productions). Superb double-CD set documenting the "struggle music" that helped power anti-apartheid resistance.

Afropop

Bayete *Umkhaya-Lo* (Polygram). A seminal fusion of South African sounds with laid-back soul and funk, blended by lead singer Jabu Khanyile's unique mixing talent and spiced with his beautifully soothing vocals.

Yvonne Chaka Chaka *Bambani* (Teal) and *The Best Of Yvonne Chaka Chaka* (Teal, SA). *Bambini* bombed, yet is Yvonne's most intricate and interesting release, mixing a range of traditional styles and featuring wonderful melodies. The *Best Of* is pretty much all the 1980s disco-style

Yvonne you need, including her biggest hit "Umqombothi".

Johnny Clegg *Best Of Juluka/ Savuka* (Universal). Born in England, Clegg mixed white pop harmonies and township rhythms, gaining him a multiracial following in South Africa.

Ladysmith Black Mambazo *Heavenly* (Gallo/Spectrum★). An inspired and commercially successful foray into Afropop, featuring solo versions of various pop classics as well as vocal collaborations with Dolly Parton and Lou Rawls.

Vusi Mahlasela *Silang Mabele* (BMG). Lush harmonies and lilting melodies from this sweet-voiced township balladeer.

Thandiswa Mazwai *Zabalaza* (Gallo). Although somewhat over-produced in its attempt to cover too many musical bases, this album by the ex-singer with *kwaito* outfit Bongo Maffin is more than redeemed by the very powerful title track.

Busi Mhlongo *Urbanzulu* (Melt 2000). An immaculately and expensively produced Zulu *maskanda*-pop classic from this powerful jazz vocalist and *sangoma*.

Ringo *Sondelani* (CCP). A superb modern reworking of traditional Xhosa sounds by this bald Capetonian heart-throb, including the hit track *Sondela*, which has become one of South Africa's most popular love songs.

White pop and rock

Danny K *J23* (Gallo). An elaborately produced melange of R&B and hip-hop from a vocalist massively popular with the country's white-teenyboppers and 20-somethings.

Freedoms Children *Astra* (Fresh). Recorded in 1970, *Astra* is considered by an older generation of local rock connoisseurs to be the single finest product of the country's "underground music" movement.

Just Jinger *All Comes Around* (BMG). Unexpectedly racking up sales of over 50,000 copies, this classic 1997 release demonstrated that local English rock was far from dead.

Mango Groove *The Best Of Mango Groove* (Gallo). Mango Groove's mixture of white pop leavened with a touch of pennywhistle/township jive

was briefly – from the late Eighties up to the dawn of democracy – the most commercially successful sound in South African music.

Springbok Nude Girls *Afterlife Satisfaction* (Sony Music). One of South Africa's most popular white bands before they disbanded, here delivering a powerful, if not particularly original, belting rock set.

Watershed *In The Meantime* (EMI). Highly melodic, well-produced pop rock; lead singer Craig Hinds' voice has a particularly appealing warm quality.

Various Artists *The Best Of SA Pop Vols 1–3* (Gallo). Three double CDs covering all the biggest radio hits of the local English pop scene from the 1960s through to the early 1980s.

Afrikaans

Chris Blignaut *Die Juweel Jare* (Gallo). Classic vocal material from the Fifties and early Sixties by the first Afrikaans recording star.

Anton Goosen *Bushrock* (Gallo). Goosen is one of South Africa's finest songwriters and performers. His style might best be described as Afrikaans folk rock, and his recordings are always well produced. *Bushrock* is

a good place to start checking him out; it's his one English-language album.

Steve Hofmeyer *Toeka* (EMI). A smooth pop vocalist, Hofmeyer is currently the most commercially successful artist in Afrikaans music. In *Toeka* he trots through a bunch of classic songs from the past three decades.

Johannes Kerkorrel *Ge-Trans-To-Meer* (Gallo-Tusk). The late Kerkorrel was the leading light of the Afrikaans alternative scene of the Nineties, his brand of angst-laden pop also popular in Holland and Belgium.

Klipwerf Orkes *Hantam Deurnag* (Universal). Rollicking instrumental music for dancing that at times sounds almost Cajun, from the hugely popular exponents of modern *boeremusiek*.

This article updated for this edition by Rob Allingham

Literature

Without apartheid, some critics have argued, there would have been little modern South African literature. Apartheid has delivered ready-made plots and subject matter for gifted and mediocre artists alike. Stories of the white minority's psychological and political alienation versus the legitimate struggle of the oppressed majority, illegal and clandestine interracial relationships, and possibilities of reconciliation, revenge or revolution abound. With all these, apartheid and its colonial precursors have provided a truth stranger than many fictions. It is difficult to avoid distinctions between the literature of white and black South Africans, produced by people with vastly different life experiences and subject to different political pressures over centuries.

The story of South African writing

During pre-colonial times there was a variety of oral literary forms, sometimes known as **orature**, in the southern African region. Orature was male-dominated, but women played a significant part in genres such as **praise poems**, equivalent to heroic epic and folk tales. In contemporary South African orature there has been a further blurring of the boundaries of genre and gender. Women produce oral works at political gatherings, traditionally a male prerogative, while men and women participate in the **toyi-toyi**, a direct descendant of the war songs originally performed only by women to exhort men in battle, now most commonly associated with resistance and political rallies.

From the sixteenth century onwards, explorers such as Drake, Houtman and Hakluyt provided descriptions of the Cape, and in 1572 the Portuguese poet **Luis de Camoens** described his voyage (partly mythologized) in *The Lusiads*. **Jan van Riebeeck**, governor of the Dutch East India Company's station, wrote a *Daghregister* (Journal), as did **Adam Tas**, one of the station's more rebellious subjects. As the territory passed between the various Dutch, French and British administrators, so different residents and visitors arrived. One such person was **Francois La Valliant**, an admirer of Rousseau, whose *Travels* is an example of how travellers of the past (and today) can live out their preconceptions for themselves and for their metropolitan audiences.

Colonialism and transition

Published in 1883 under a male *nom de plume*, **Olive Schreiner**'s *The Story of An African Farm* is widely regarded as the first novel rooted in South Africa. It stands in marked contrast to the frontier tales of **Percy Fitzpatrick**'s *Jock of the Bushveld* (1907) and **Henry Rider Haggard**'s *Boy's Own*-style tales of colonial penetration and subjugation, such as *King Solomon's Mines* (1885) or *She* (1887). Today, these find direct and indirect descendants in Wilbur Smith, literary doyen of airport departure halls, and the late Sir Laurens van der Post, spiritual mentor to Prince Charles.

Christian mission education, the only early route to literacy for black South Africans, favoured men and prioritized the translation of biblical and religious texts, such as John Bunyan's *Pilgrim's Progress*, which appeared in Sesotho, Zulu and Xhosa. As a result, African women did not enjoy the educational opportunities open to the playwright **H.I.E. Dhlomo**; the writer **Thomas Mofolo**, whose historical novel *Chaka* (1925) originally appeared in Sesotho and was translated into English, French, Italian, German, Yoruba and Afrikaans; or the journalist, translator and novelist **Sol Plaatje**, a founder member of the ANC. Plaatje's best-known works are *Mhudi* (1930) and *Native Life in South Africa* (1916). The former is the story of an African society in transition as it deals with the implications of the Afrikaner Great Trek and the social upheaval caused by the Zulu military state's raids and conquest. In *Native Life*, Plaatje documented the disastrous effects on Africans of the 1913 Land Act, a law denying them access to the land of their birth.

Jim-comes-to-Jo'burg

The discovery of minerals and the growing urbanization and industrialization of South African society had a detrimental effect on African and Afrikaner rural society alike. From the white perspective, removal from the land threatened the "natural order" of race relations, for landless Afrikaners and Africans arrived in the city as "equals". While the perceived threat to white civilization was greatly exaggerated, it had four significant consequences for white writers at the time: it shifted literary attention away from rural concerns towards urban-based issues; it provided the context for fears of miscegenation; it encouraged a re-examination of the image of Afrikaners; and it opened up new forms of narration.

Movement towards the city fostered what Nadine Gordimer later termed the "**Jim-comes-to-Jo'burg**" novel, in which a naive young African man moves from a protected and stable rural environment to city life and a variety of urban experiences and temptations. **Peter Abrahams**' contribution was *Mine Boy* (1946), often regarded as South Africa's first proletarian novel, while for **Alan Paton** the true nature of African culture was to be found in a rural setting and the *status quo ante*. Much later **Mtutuzeli Matshoba**'s short story "Three Days in the Land of a Dying Illusion", from his collection *Call Me not a Man* (1979), would invert and parody the genre.

Miscegenation and archetypes

Roy Campbell (*Adamastor*, 1930), subsequently associated with Spanish fascism, is the best-known poet of the interwar years. Like **Guy Butler** after him, he tended to equate Europe with history, development and rationalism, and Africa with unchanging archetypes. During this period **Sarah Gertrude Millin**'s fiction, particularly *God's Stepchildren* (1924), provided the starkest articulation of differences between Europe and Africa and white anxiety about the consequences of **miscegenation**. The basis for Millin's views lay in the notion of "good" and "bad" blood, and in the fear that the (male) colonizer's possession and control of the colonial territories would simultaneously confirm his dominance and open him to control by the "heart of darkness". Millin of course did not even begin to contemplate "the horror" of miscegenation involving a black man and a white woman. **Ethelreda Lewis** offered a problematic variant on the theme of blood and civilization in *Wild Deer* (1933), the story of an African-American singer, modelled on Paul Robeson, who visits South Africa in search of spiritual renewal. He decides to uplift the "pure" and pre-urban African by impregnating "a carefully chosen virgin mate" and so pass on the benefits of his civilization while protecting the "kernel of primitive life".

With the repeal of the so-called Immorality Act in 1985, which forbade interracial sexual relations, miscegenation has lost its literary and political significance, though repackaged in the form of theories of hybridity and difference it is now making a fashionable return. **Stephen Gray**'s *Time of Our Darkness* (1988) may well be the last serious work on the "immorality" subject tackled by **William Plomer** in *Turbott Wolfe* (1926), **Peter Abrahams** in *The Path to Thunder* (1948), **Alan Paton** in *Too Late the Phalarope* (1953), **Nadine Gordimer** in her short story "The Country Lovers" (1967), and **Athol Fugard**, one of South Africa's most famous playwrights, in *Statements After an Arrest Under the Immorality Act* (1974).

From dispossession to apartheid

The separation of **Afrikaners** from "their" land, and their participation in an industrializing economy largely controlled by English speakers, encouraged pathos-filled representations of Afrikaners. **Pauline Smith**'s work, such as *The Beadle* (1926) and her short story collection *The Little Karoo* (1925), inadvertently fostered the myth of the Boer as a landless, economically oppressed victim denied his language and culture. While **Herman Charles Bosman**'s short stories such as "Mafeking Road" (1947) and "A Cask of Jerepigo" (1964) also focus on rural Afrikaner life, they display far more irony. Narrated by one Oom Schalk Lourens, who in Mark Twain-like fashion is never fully aware of the implications of the stories that he tells, Bosman's humorous tales of backveld ambition, betrayal and desire presage the concerns and doubts about writing and the control of history, truth and identity that would increasingly characterize what the novelist **J.M. Coetzee** has called "white writing" – writing that articulates the "concerns of people no longer European, not yet African".

Alan Paton's *Cry, the Beloved Country* appeared in 1948, the year in which the Nationalist government came to power, and has been filmed twice. Probably the most famous of all South African novels, and still a bestseller, Paton's account of an inter-racial murder did more than any other work to bring South Africa's racial plight to the attention of the rest of the world. The book has often been criticized for its liberal paternalism, but with the benefit of hindsight it can also be read as a one-man Truth and Reconciliation Commission in which Paton details the devastation caused by white dominance in South Africa, and tries to promote a vision in which justice and love coexist.

The Drum generation

In the 1950s, predominantly male black writing and journalism centred on the Johannesburg-based *Drum* magazine. The publication was one of the few outlets for black creative writers such as **Can Themba**, **Es'kia Mphahlele**, **Bloke Modisane** and **Todd Matshikiza**, many of whom chose to write short stories or autobiographical novels. Favoured because of its flexibility and compatibility with their fast-paced and fractured lifestyles under oppressive conditions, the short story has remained a popular medium for black and white South African fiction. The so-called **Drum generation** articulated black urban experience and aspirations, often in an Americanized B-movie style in journalism, fiction and drama such as *King Kong*, a musical based on the life of an actual boxer-gangster that helped to launch the singing careers of

Thandi Klaasen, Dolly Rathebe and Miriam Makeba. **Z.B. Molefe**'s *A Common Hunger to Sing* (1997) gives them and successors such as Brenda Fassie, Sibongile Khumalo and Yvonne Chaka Chaka the recognition they deserve.

In general, there was little space for women's journalism and fiction at this time. Covering her pre-Botswana years in South Africa, **Bessie Head**'s posthumously published *The Cardinals* (1993) is a rare exploration of the problems faced by one of the few black women journalists during this period who made the transition to novel-writing.

While many of the Drum generation died relatively young and in exile, **Es'kia Mphahlele** has been a survivor. His *Down Second Avenue* (1959) is often viewed as the definitive text of an era characterized by black male autobiographies such as *Tell Freedom* (1954) by **Peter Abrahams**, **Bloke Modisane**'s *Blame me on History* (1963) and **Todd Matshikiza**'s *Chocolates for my Wife* (1961). Mphahlele's subsequent novels, *The Wanderers* (1971) and *Afrika My Music* (1984), recorded the fragmented experience of exile, that "soul-mutilating process" that has affected so many South Africans in the last sixty years.

Sophiatown, the last area in Johannesburg where Africans had freehold property rights, was the heartbeat of the Drum generation. **Jurgen Schadeburg**'s photographs, and a host of reminiscences of *Drum* and Sophiatown by figures ranging from **Anthony Sampson** in *Drum: An African Adventure and Afterwards* to **Father Trevor Huddleston**'s *Naught for your Comfort*, are testimony to the fascination it held.

Its nearest equivalent in Cape Town was District Six, a multiracial but predominantly coloured inner-city slum that provided the backdrop for the early work of three Cape Town writers: **Richard Rive** (*Buckingham Palace* and *District Six*; 1986), **Alex La Guma** (*A Walk in the Night*; 1962) and **Achmat Dangor** (*Waiting for Leila*; 1981). Of more recent works, **Nomvuyo Ngcelwane**'s *Sala Kahle, District Six* (1998) recounts the life of its African residents, a community ignored or marginalized in most accounts, while **Linda Fortune**'s *The House in Tyne Street* (1996) is more idyllic. Set in the 1960s, but with little reference to the main political developments of the time, the autobiographical novel *The Party is Over* (1997) by veteran poet and novelist **James Matthews** recounts the frustrations of a black writer in a paternalistic, white-dominated world of arts and letters.

Poetry of note in this period can be found in *Sirens, Knuckles, Boots* (1963) and *Letters to Martha* (1968), by **Dennis Brutus**, who devoted considerable energy to ensuring South Africa's sporting isolation during the apartheid years, and **Arthur Nortje** in *Dead Roots* (1973). Like the short-story writer **Zoe Wicomb** in her collection of short stories, *You Can't Get Lost in Cape Town* (1987), Nortje was prepared to explore the more ordinary and less obviously political aspects of life in South Africa. He did this by focusing on inner worlds and on the issue of coloured identity as marginal to larger political and national questions, as Mphahlele, in *Man Must Live* (1947), and **Njabulo Ndebele**, in *Fools and Other Stories* (1983), had done for African township life.

Rive also wrote several Cape Town-based novels such as *Emergency* (1964), the latter about the events surrounding the declaration of a state of emergency in 1960. Several other novelists know set works in this and subsequent periods of repression: **Jonty Driver**'s *Elegy for a Revolutionary* (1969), **Lewis Nkosi**'s *The Rhythm of Violence* (1964) and **Alex La Guma**'s *In the Fog of the Seasons' End* (1972) for the 1960s; **Sipho Sepamla**'s *A Ride on the Whirlwind* (1981), **Mongane Serote**'s *To Every Birth Its Blood* (1981) and **Miriam Tlali**'s *Amandla* (1981) for the Soweto period; **Menan du Plessis**'s *A State of Fear* (1983), **Hein Grosskopf**'s *Artistic Graves* (1993), **Mandla Langa**'s *A Rainbow on the*

Paper Sky (1989) and **Bridget Pitt**'s *Unbroken Wing* (1998) which continues the theme on a more personal note, for the late 1980s.

Prison writings

Many intellectuals and writers were jailed during the apartheid years. Among many books on the subject, **Albie Sachs**' *Jail Diary* (1966) and **Ruth First**'s *117 Days* (1982) record their detentions without trial in the early 1960s, while **Indres Naidoo**'s *Island in Chains* (1982) deals with his ten years on Robben Island after being arrested and charged with sabotage. Most prisoners served out their sentences, but Tim Jenkin, Alex Moumbaris and Stephen Lee managed to escape from Pretoria Central Prison where most white political prisoners were held. **Tim Jenkin**'s tale, *Escape from Pretoria* (1987) reads like a thriller, while in *The True Confessions of an Albino Terrorist* (1983) **Breyten Breytenbach** manages to combine political critique with grim humour. Not surprisingly, fictional accounts of prison such as **Alex La Guma**'s *The Stone Country* (1974) and **D.M. Zwelonke**'s *Robben Island* (1973) rely heavily on their authors' own experiences, but are complex narratives. In the realm of non-political prison writings, **Herman Charles Bosman**'s *Cold Stone Jug* (1971) provides an ironic and beautifully written foil to the seriousness of "correct" accounts.

South African writers are gripped by what Mphahlele has described as "the tyranny of place". All but one of **Alex La Guma**'s five novels are set in Cape Town, and they are linked by a steady evolution of political consciousness and organization. A journalist, writer and political activist from the 1960s until his death in Cuba in 1985, where he was the ANC's Chief Representative, La Guma explored individual acts of defiance against the state in his early works, *A Walk in the Night* (1962) and *And a Threefold Cord* (1964). His later novels, *In the Fog of the Seasons' End* (1972) and *Time of the Butcherbird* (1979), display more complex narrative structures and deal with collective resistance.

White liberal writing

If La Guma's concerns have been with the disenfranchised and the dispossessed, **Nadine Gordimer**'s novels and short stories stand as dispassionate and coldly sensual chronicles of the interior voice of white liberal and radical opposition to apartheid. They represent an alternative to Paton's stress on individual responsibility as the key to political change.

Over the years, Gordimer has moved from confessional, though not necessarily autobiographical, narratives such as *The Lying Days* (1953), to bolder and more complex explorations of time and psychological make-up, such as *July's People* (1991). While the former explores the growing political awareness of her typical main character, a white middle-class woman resident in Johannesburg's prosperous suburbs, the latter is set in a post-revolutionary South Africa in which Maureen Smales, wife and mother to a white middle-class family, has become heavily dependent on July, their former "houseboy". The novel explores her search for political and personal liberation, part of which involves her efforts to confront and break with the emotionally fraught and contradictory personal and political dynamics so often associated with domestic service relationships in a colonial context. Her more recent *The House Gun* (1998) continues the exploration of white liberal consciousness and conscience in the post-liberation period.

Gordimer is not the only white writer to explore the dilemmas of privilege and conscience. The **Sestigers** were an innovative group of Afrikaans writers prominent in the 1960s that included Breyten Breytenbach and **André Brink**, who acquired the reputation of being the foremost white literary opponent of apartheid. Brink explored notions of truth, history and freedom in the colonial setting through books such as *An Instant in the Wind* (1976); *A Chain of Voices* (1982); *The Wall of the Plague* (1984); *An Act of Terror* (1991); and *Devil's Valley* (1998). In this his work has much in common with's the first novel of Booker Prize winner and literary critic **J.M. Coetzee**, *Dusklands* (1974). This book establishes psychological and behavioural parallels between America's presence in Vietnam and the behaviour of one Jacobus Coetzee during his South African frontier experience in 1760. Several of J.M. Coetzee's subsequent novels have used the perspective of a borderline psychotic narrator to explore the political and psychological damage caused by colonialism and apartheid. His *In the Heart of the Country* (1976) is narrated by an isolated spinster and plays ironically with the tradition of farm novels as represented by Olive Schreiner and others. *Waiting for the Barbarians* (1980), which takes its title from Cavafy's poem of the same name, occupies a more allegorical domain, with a narrator who is a bumbling magistrate wrestling with moral concerns in the outpost of an unnamed empire. *His Life and Times of Michael K* (1983) foregrounds the concern with allegory by making it a concern of one of the novel's characters.

An intellectually brilliant postmodern critic of apartheid, Coetzee has always distanced himself and his writing from the demands of publishing in order to function as a "weapon of struggle". Through his description of himself in *Dusklands*, even parodically, as "one of the 10,000 Coetzees . . . that Jacobus Coetzee begat", his work invites parallels with the self-hatred and self-obsession of Rian Malan's *My Traitor's Heart* (1990), which establishes its author in Calvinist style as the seventh-generation inheritor of the founding fathers' sins.

While white writing became increasingly introspective and its ventures into the interior shifted from geographical to psychological terrain, black writing faced an entirely different situation. Impeded by the exile of many artists, intimidated by trials and arrests, and censored by the state during a period of severe repression in the early 1960s, it was largely dormant until the late 1960s and early 1970s. This period saw the growth of the Black Consciousness Movement and the increasingly effective organization of black workers, followed by the Soweto riots and the independence of Angola and Mozambique.

Beyond social realism

The dawn of the 1970s saw both white and black writing beginning to look beyond the conventions of social realism, but for very different reasons. In the case of white writing, **interiority** was a response to the dilemmas imposed by a conscience that could not be ignored and privileges that could not be sacrificed. For black writers, **poetry**, and free verse in particular, became popular because it facilitated indirect forms of political expression. Among the names associated with this phase, the most prominent are **Oswald Mtshali**, *Drum* survivor **Casey Motsisi**, **Mafika Gwala**, **Don Mattera**, **Njabulo Ndebele**, **Mongane Serote**, **Mandla Langa**, **Gladys Thomas** and **James Matthews** from Cape Town. In subsequent decades, many of these also wrote short stories and novels.

Oswald Mtshali was working as a motorbike courier when his path-breaking *Sounds of a Cowhide Drum* appeared in 1971. For Mtshali and many of his contemporaries the route to political nationalism was a cultural nationalism that rejected "white" standards, and asserted a specifically "black" aesthetic and identity. They sharply criticized the self-destructive nature of township violence, and used the perspectives and experiences of children to point out the injustices and inequalities of apartheid. Like many of their predecessors, Ndebele, Serote and Langa were forced to leave the country, but James Matthews stayed, and *Cry Rage* (1972), cowritten with Gladys Thomas, still remains a powerful statement of black consciousness and protest poetry. Along with **Gcina Mhlope** and **Jennifer Davids**, Thomas was able to modify the traditional role of black women as significant but secondary figures in the national liberation struggle, typified by the idea of the powerful black woman as mother figure.

The early 1970s also saw a resurgence of **drama**. There were escapist and exploitative musicals such as *Ipi Tombi*, nostalgic and utopian works such as **Credo Mutwa**'s *uNosilimela* and **Gibson Kente**'s *Too Late* and *Survival*, both with strong political messages. For international audiences, however, **Athol Fugard** remains the most prominent South African playwright. Fugard would be the last to claim full responsibility for several of his works, which were produced under workshop conditions with actors such as John Kani and Winston Ntshona contributing their views and experiences to *Sizwe Bansi is Dead*, a play about strategies to avoid pass law controls, and *The Island*, based on Sophocles' *Antigone*. Continuing the tradition of collaborative production, *Ubu and the Truth Commission* (1998) combines the talents of writer Jane Taylor, artist William Kentridge and puppeteers Basil Jones and Adrian Kohler in a work that explores some of South Africa's less enviable qualities – evil, ultraviolence, cowardice and self-pity – in a work that reflects on a country dealing with the consequences of the Truth and Reconciliation Commission. This is also the subject of **Antjie Krog**'s *Country of My Skull* (1998), a multilevelled and many-layered account of more than two years' reporting on the Commission, from its legislative origins to testimonies of victims and perpetrators.

Staffrider magazine

Launched in 1977, and capitalizing on the limited cultural and political space occasioned by the apartheid government's moves towards a policy of "repressive reform" in the post-Soweto period, **Staffrider magazine** was the most important literary development of the late 1970s. Taking its name and image from township slang for people (frequently black youth) who rode the overcrowded African sections of the racially segregated commuter trains by hanging onto the outside or sitting on the roofs, the magazine had two main objectives: to provide publishing opportunities for community-based organizations and young writers, graphic artists and photographers; and to oppose officially sanctioned state and establishment culture. With a hands-off editorial policy initially, the magazine focused on **"people's history"**, helping to retrieve hidden aspects of South Africa's past for a wider audience. The *Staffrider* tradition continues; Charles van Onselen's tome *The Seed is Mine* (1996) and Isabel Hofmeyer's *We Spend Our Years as a Tale That is Told* (1994) have been outstanding contributions to this genre.

The 1980s

From the 1980s onwards, debates around the political relevance of poetry became even more intense than those dealing with prose. Some of the more politically committed poets included **Kelwyn Sole** (*Blood of Our Silence*; 1988) and **Jeremy Cronin**, whose anthology *Inside* (1983) asks readers "To learn how to speak/With the voices of the land", return to introspective themes of language and the poet's sense of place. In *Even the Dead* (1997) Cronin searches for a moral community that incorporates the past and takes issue with the "smug rainbowism" of the new South Africa. Others, such as **Christopher van Wyk** with *It is Time to Go Home* (1979) and **Achmat Dangor** in *Bulldozer* (1983), retain a strident anger mixed with Cape Town's acerbic slang.

By the mid-1980s, international condemnation of apartheid and support for the liberation movement coincided with the growth of feminist theory and an expanding **feminist** publishing industry. These developments favoured the emergence of black South African women's autobiographies such as **Ellen Kuzwayo**'s *Call Me Woman* (1985) and **Emma Mashinini**'s *Strikes Have Followed Me All My Life* (1989). This form has seen little development since the appearance of **Noni Jabavu**'s *Drawn in Colour* (1960) and *The Ochre People* (1963), in the early 1960s, and **Sindiwe Magona**'s two autobiographical works *To My Children's Children* (1990) and *Forced to Grow* (1992) retain an American connection. In *Mother to Mother* (1998), she deals with the death of visiting American scholar Amy Biehl, killed by black youths stirred up by "anti-white" slogans, through an address from one of the mothers of Biehl's killers to the mother of his victim. The late 1980s was also a favourable period for the publication of black women's poetry in anthologies such as *Siren Songs* (1989) and *Breaking the Silence* (1990) and in individual collections such as Sobhna Poona's *In Search of Rainbows* (1990).

Recent writing

Staffrider popularized a return to traditional conventions and forms of oratory, for example in **Nongenile Zenani** and **Harold Scheub**'s *The World and the Word* (1992), and *Guava Juice* (1992) by **Sandile Dikeni**. Much of the latter's poetry was delivered at opposition mass rallies and trade union launches. By contrast, **Mongane Wally Serote**'s *Third World Express* (1992), his first published work after his return from exile, retains links with an oral tradition but is more introspective than Dikeni's poetry. More recently, praise poets have performed at the inauguration of President Mandela and the opening of the country's first democratically elected parliament.

As the 1990s took hold, the politicized approach that saw publishers, writers and readers going for the "struggular" had to acknowledge the less dramatic and more byzantine process of negotiations towards a relatively peaceful transfer of power, and the emergence of splits and disagreements in the cultural sphere between the ANC and some of its internal supporters. In this context, **Phyllis Ntantala**'s *A Life's Mosaic* (1992) acknowledged personal concerns, **Mamphela Ramphele**'s *A Life* (1995) criticized ways in which the liberation struggle had been male-dominated, and **Barbara Schreiner**'s *A Snake with Ice Water* (1992), a collection of interviews, stories and poems by women about their prison experiences from the 1960s onwards, confronted the shame and sense of incapacity to which many women in the liberation struggle had been subjected.

Exile and **return** are themes which several writers have dealt with. **Breyten Breytenbach**'s *Dog Heart* (1998) recalls present and past Bonnievale, the village of his birth. In *The Naked Song and Other Stories* (1996) **Mandla Langa** explores the transition from exile to "home", while **Barry Feinberg**'s *Gardens of Struggle* (1992) covers thirty years of the poet's life, from exile in 1961 to return in 1991.

Good insights into the troubled psyche of the white South African male in a period of political transition include **Ivan Vladislavic**'s short-story collection *Missing Persons* (1989), his novels *The Folly* (1993) and *Propaganda by Monuments and Other Stories* (1996); **Etienne van Heerden**'s *Mad Dog and Other Stories* (1992) and *Casspirs and Camparis* (1993; casspirs are armoured personnel carriers used by the police and army); and **Mark Behr**'s *The Smell of Apples* (1995). Behr's subsequent disclosure that he was a police informer during his days as an anti-apartheid student activist doubtless adds interest to this confessional narrative.

Political autobiography

Dramatic political change and the acquisition of freedom has seen many politicians and public figures come and go. Inevitably this has encouraged several to write stories of the life they would like us to believe they led or, in the case of those involved in clandestine work such as **Ronnie Kasrils** (*"Armed and Dangerous": My Undercover Struggle Against Apartheid*; 1993), **Joe Slovo** (*Unfinished Autobiography*; 1995) and **Natoo Babenia** (*Memoirs of a Saboteur: Reflections on my Political Activity in India and South Africa*; 1995), of the life they could not previously talk about in public. National secretary of the non-racial Federation of South African Women in the 1950s, **Helen Joseph** was banned four times, jailed four times, on trial for four years and periodically unbanned. Her autobiography *Side by Side* appeared in 1986.

No one to Blame? (1998) by Advocate **George Bizos**, centrally involved in many of the inquests of the political detainees who died in South African jails, provides a grim if illuminating complement to the life stories of those who survived torture and interrogation. **Bram Fischer**, member of an eminent Afrikaner family and a lawyer who defended Mandela and Sisulu in the Rivonia trial and member of the then banned South African Communist Party, was one of those who did not survive. Stephen Clingman tells his story *Bram Fischer: Afrikaner Revolutionary* (1998).

Let My People Go (1962) by the late **Albert Luthuli**, former leader of the ANC, remains as compelling an explanation of the struggle for majority rule as Nelson Mandela's own *Long Walk to Freedom* (1994).

Post-apartheid writing

South Africa's recently acquired political respectability has meant that writers of the former international pariah state can now, in Michael Ondaatje's phrase, become "international bastards" if they wish, as postmodernism and magical realism, sometimes in combination with autobiography, have become more popular and politically acceptable. **Ashraf Jamal** in *Love Themes for the Wilderness* (1996) has been quick to capitalize on the space available. Two novels by **Zakes Mda**, already recognized as a major playwright, *She Plays with the Darkness* (1995) and *Ways of Dying* (1995), can also be classified as magical realism. While the former may rely upon aspects of a traditional African culture with which many urbanized black South Africans have no contact, the latter explores some of the country's more bizarre forms of death from the perspective of a self-styled "professional mourner".

With the differences between official and personal histories a subject of continuous negotiation, **Mike Nicol**'s *This Day and Age* (1992) makes a strong case for the integration of magical realism and postmodern techniques in pursuit of a new perspective on South African history. **Rayda Jacobs'** novel *The Slave Book* (1998), set on the eve of slave emancipation, returns to earlier moments of political and personal freedom that invite comparison with the present.

Etienne van Heerden's *Kikuyu* (1999) is set on that sign of the times (but rarer in the 1960s) – a holiday farm in the Karoo. In *On Soebatsfontein*, **Fabian Latsky**'s sheltered world of eccentric characters comes into contact with the rumblings of an increasingly unstable South Africa. **Tony Spencer-Smith**'s *The Stooping of Aquila* (1999) is an erotic thriller set in Cape Town's Hout Bay, focusing on environmental issues, their growing prominence a sign of the region's tourist potential and of a shift in values away from overtly political concerns.

Roger Field

South African writers

While no five extracts can ever hope to convey South African literature's richness and diversity, the ones we've selected are intended as a useful taster. What these extracts have in common is that, although they are by figures well known in South Africa, none is a big-name author internationally.

Steve Biko

Charismatic Black Consciousness activist Steve Biko (1946–77) died after police torture. These words, extracted from an interview some months before his death, give insight into Biko's extraordinary commitment to political change. The extract is taken from "I Write What I Like", a collection of non-fiction writing from 1969 to 1972. In 1973, Biko was banned and could no longer travel, speak in public or write for publication.

On Death

You are either alive and proud or you are dead, and when you are dead, you can't care anyway. And your method of death can itself be a politicizing thing. So you die in the riots. For a hell of a lot of them, in fact, there's really nothing to lose – almost literally, given the kind of situations that they come from. So if you can overcome the personal fear for death, which is a highly irrational thing, you know, then you're on the way.

And in interrogation the same sort of thing applies. I was talking to this policeman, and I told him, "If you want us to make any progress, the best thing is for us to talk. Don't try any form of rough stuff, because it just won't work." And this is absolutely true also. For I just couldn't see what they could do to me which would make me all of a sudden soften to them. If they talk to me, well I'm bound to be affected by them as human beings. But the moment they adopt rough stuff, they are imprinting in my mind that they are police. And I only understand one form of dealing with police, and that's to be as unhelpful as possible. So I button up. And I told them this: "It's up to you." We had a boxing match the first day I was arrested. Some guy tried to clout me with a club. I went into him like a bull. I think he was under instructions to take it so far and no further, and using open hands so that he doesn't leave any marks on the face. And of course he said exactly what you were saying just now: "I will kill you." He meant to intimidate. And my answer was: "How long is it going to take you?" Now of course they were observing my reaction. And they could see that I was completely unbothered. If they beat me up, it's to my advantage. I can use it. They just killed somebody in jail – a friend of mine – about ten days before I was arrested. Now it would have been bloody useful evidence for them to assault me. At least it would indicate what kind of possibilities were there, leading to this guy's death. So, I wanted them to go ahead and do what they could do, so that I could use it. I wasn't really afraid that their violence might lead me to make revelations I didn't want to make, because I had nothing to reveal on this particular issue. I was operating from a very good position, and they were in a very weak position. My attitude is, I'm not going to allow them to carry out their programme faithfully. If they want to beat me five times, they can only do so on condition that I allow them to beat me five times. If I react sharply, equally and oppositely, to the first clap, they are not going to be able to systematically count the next four claps, you see. It's a fight. So if they had meant to give me so much of a beating, and not more, my idea is to make them go beyond what they wanted to give me and to give back as much as I can give so that it becomes an uncontrollable thing. You see the one problem this guy had with me: he couldn't really fight with me because it meant he must hit back, like a man. But he was given instructions, you see, on how to hit, and now these instructions were no longer applying because it was a fight. So he had to withdraw and get more instructions. So I said to them, "Listen, if you guys want to do this your way, you have got to handcuff me and bind my feet together, so that I can't respond. If you allow me to respond, I'm certainly going to respond. And I'm afraid you may have to kill me in the process even if it's not your intention."

Reprinted by permission of Bowerdean Publishers.

Herman Charles Bosman

Herman Charles Bosman (1905–51), one of South Africa's most widely read writers, is best known for his wry and amusing short stories about Afrikaner life in the Groot Marico district of the then Western Transvaal, where he spent six months as a schoolteacher in 1925.

A Bekkersdal Marathon

At Naudé, who had a wireless set, came into Jurie Steyn's voorkamer, where we were sitting waiting for the railway lorry from Bekkersdal, and gave us the latest news. He said that the newest thing in Europe was that young people there were going in for non-stop dancing. It was called marathon dancing, At Naudé told us, and those young people were trying to break the record for who could remain on their feet longest, dancing.

We listened for a while to what At Naudé had to say, and then we suddenly remembered a marathon event that had taken place in the little dorp of Bekkersdal – almost in our midst, you could say. What was more, there were quite a number of us sitting in Jurie Steyn's post office, who had actually taken part in that non-stop affair, and without knowing that we were breaking records, and without expecting any sort of a prize for it, either.

We discussed that affair at considerable length and from all angles, and we were still talking about it when the lorry came. And we agreed that it had been in several respects an unusual occurrence. We also agreed that it was questionable if we could have carried off things so successfully that day, if it had not been for Billy Robertse.

You see, our organist at Bekkersdal was Billy Robertse. He had once been a sailor and had come to the bushveld some years before, travelling on foot. His belongings, fastened in a red handkerchief, were slung over his shoulder on a stick. Billy Robertse was journeying in that fashion for the sake of his health. He suffered from an unfortunate complaint for which he had at regular intervals to drink something out of a black bottle that he always carried handy in his jacket pocket.

Billy Robertse would even keep that bottle beside him in the organist's gallery in case of a sudden attack. And if the hymn the predikant gave out had many verses, you could be sure that about halfway through Billy Robertse would bring the bottle up to his mouth, leaning sideways towards what was in it. And he would put several extra twirls into the second part of the hymn.

When he first applied for the position of organist in the Bekkersdal church, Billy Robertse told the meeting of deacons that he had learnt to play the organ in a cathedral in northern Europe. Several deacons felt, then, that they could not favour his application. They said that the cathedral sounded too Papist, the way Billy Robertse described it, with a dome three hundred feet high and with marble apostles. But it was lucky for Billy Robertse that he was able to mention, at the following combined meeting of elders and deacons, that he had also played the piano in a South American dance hall, of which the manager was a Presbyterian. He asked the meeting to overlook his unfortunate past, saying that he had had a hard life, and anybody could make mistakes. In any case, he had never cared much for the Romish atmosphere of the cathedral, he said, and had been happier in the dance hall.

In the end, Billy Robertse got the appointment. But in his sermons for several Sundays after that the predikant, Dominee Welthagen, spoke very strongly against the evils of dance halls. He described those places of awful sin in such burning words that at least one young man went to see Billy Robertse, privately, with a view to taking lessons in playing the piano.

But Billy Robertse was a good musician. And he took a deep interest in his work. And he said that when he sat down on the organist's stool behind the pulpit, and his fingers were flying over the keyboards, and he was pulling out the stops, and his feet were pressing down the notes that sent the deep bass tones through the pipes – then he felt that he could play all day, he said.

"I don't suppose he guessed that he would one day be put to the test, however."

It all happened through Dominee Welthagen one Sunday morning going into a trance in the pulpit. And we did not realise that he was in a trance. It was an illness that overtook him in a strange and sudden fashion.

At each service the predikant, after reading a passage from the Bible, would lean forward with his hand on the pulpit rail and give out the number of the hymn we had to sing. For years his manner of conducting the service had been exactly the same. He would say, for instance: "We will now sing Psalm 82, verses 1 to 4." Then he would allow his head to sink forward on to his chest and he would remain rigid, as though in prayer, until the last notes of the hymn died away in the church.

Now, on that particular morning, just after he had announced the number of the psalm, without mentioning what verses, Dominee Welthagen again took a firm grip on the pulpit rail and allowed his head to sink forward on to his breast. We did not realise that he had fallen into a trance of a peculiar character that kept his body standing upright while his mind was a blank. We learnt that only later.

In the meantime, while the organ was playing over the opening bars, we began to realise that Dominee Welthagen had not indicated how many verses we had to sing. But he would discover his mistake, we thought, after we had been singing for a few minutes.

All the same, one or two of the younger members of the congregation did titter, slightly, when they took up their hymn books. For Dominee Welthagen had given out Psalm 119. And everybody knows that Psalm 119 has 176 verses.

This was a church service that will never be forgotten in Bekkersdal. We sang the first verse and then the second and then the third. When we got to about the sixth verse and the minister still gave no sign that it would be the last, we assumed that he wished us to sing the first eight verses. For, if you open your hymn book, you'll see that Psalm 119 is divided into sets of eight verses, each ending with the word "Pouse".

We ended the last notes of verse eight with more than an ordinary number of turns and twirls, confident that at any moment Dominee Welthagen would raise his head and let us know that we could sing "Amen".

It was when the organ started up very slowly and solemnly with the music for verse nine that a real feeling of disquiet overcame the congregation. But, of course, we gave no sign of what went on in our minds. We held Dominee Welthagen in too much veneration.

Nevertheless, I would rather not say too much about our feelings, when verse followed verse and Pouse succeeded Pouse, and still Dominee Welthagen made no sign that we had sung long enough, or that there was anything unusual in what he was demanding of us.

After they had recovered from their first surprise, the members of the church council conducted themselves in a most exemplary manner. Elders and deacons tiptoed up and down the aisles, whispering words of reassurance to such members of the congregation, men as well as women, who gave signs of wanting to panic.

At one stage it looked as though we were going to have trouble from the organist. That was when Billy Robertse, at the end of the 34th verse, held up his black bottle and signalled quietly to the elders to indicate that his medicine was finished. At the end of the 35th verse he made signals of a less quiet character, and again at the end of the 36th verse. That was when Elder Landsman tiptoed out of the church and went round to the Konsistorie, where the Nagmaal wine was kept. When Elder Landsman came back into the church he had a long black bottle half-hidden under his mantle. He took the bottle up to the organist's gallery, still walking on tiptoe.

At verse 61 there was almost a breakdown. That was when a message came from the back of the organ, where Koster Claassen and the assistant verger, whose task it was to turn the handle that kept the organ supplied with wind, were in a state near to exhaustion. So it was Deacon Cronje's turn to go tiptoeing out of the church. Deacon Cronje was head warder at the local gaol. When he came back it was with three burly Native convicts in striped jerseys, who also went through the church on tiptoe. They arrived just in time to take over the handle from Koster Claassen and the assistant verger.

At verse 98 the organist again started making signals about his medicine. Once more Elder Landsman went round to the Konsistorie. This time he was accompanied by another elder and a deacon, and they stayed away somewhat longer than the time when Elder Landsman had gone on his own. On their return the deacon bumped into a small hymn book table at the back of the church. Perhaps it was because the deacon was a fat, red-faced man, and not used to tiptoeing.

At verse 124 the organist signalled again, and the same three members of the church council filed out to the Konsistorie, the deacon walking in front this time.

It was about then that the pastor of the Full Gospel Apostolic Faith Church, about whom Dominee Welthagen had in the past used almost as strong language as about the Pope, came up to the front gate of the church to see what was afoot. He lived near our church and, having heard the same hymn tune being played over and over for about eight hours, he was a very amazed man. Then he saw the door of the Konsistorie open, and two elders and a deacon coming out, walking on tiptoe – they having apparently forgotten that they were not in church, then. When the pastor saw one of the elders hiding a black bottle under his manel, a look of understanding came over his features. The pastor walked off, shaking his head.

At verse 152 the organist signalled again. This time Elder Landsman and the other elder went out alone. The deacon stayed behind on the deacon's bench, apparently in deep thought. The organist signalled again, for the last time, at verse 169. So you can imagine how many visits the two elders made to the Konsistorie altogether.

The last verse came, and the last line of the last verse. This time it had to be "Amen". Nothing could stop it. I would rather not describe the state that the congregation was in. And by then the three Native convicts, red stripes and all, were, in the Bakhatla tongue, threatening mutiny. "Aa-m-e-e-n" came from what sounded like less than a score of voices, hoarse with singing.

The organ music ceased.

Maybe it was the sudden silence that at last brought Dominee Welthagen out of his long trance. He raised his head and looked slowly about him. His gaze travelled over his congregation and then looking at the windows, he saw that it was night. We understood right away what was going on in Dominee Welthagen's mind. He thought he had just come into the pulpit, and that this was the beginning of the evening service. We realised that, during all the time we had been singing, the predikant had been in a state of unconsciousness.

Once again Dominee Welthagen took a firm grip of the pulpit rail. His head again started drooping forward on to his breast. But before he went into a trance for the second time, he gave out the hymn for the evening service. "We will," Dominee Welthagen announced, "sing Psalm 119."

Alex La Guma

Alex La Guma (1925–85) was the son of one of the leading figures in the black liberation movement. He was politically active against the apartheid government – among other things, helping with the Freedom Charter in 1956 – until he was put under house arrest in 1962. He and his wife fled the country in 1967 to the UK, then moved to Cuba where he was the ANC representative. His writing was banned by the white minority government.

This extract is from La Guma's first work, a collection of short stories set in Cape Town's District Six, before the area was razed to the ground and declared an area for whites only.

A Walk in the Night

Up ahead the music shops were still going full blast, the blare of records all mixed up so you could not tell one tune from another. Shopkeepers, Jewish, Indian, and Greek, stood in the doorways along the arcade of stores on each side of the street, waiting to welcome last-minute customers; and the vegetable and fruit barrows were still out too, the hawkers in white coats yelling their wares and flapping their brown paper packets, bringing prices down now that the day was ending. Around the bus-stop a crowd pushed and jostled to clamber onto the trackless trams, struggling against the passengers fighting to alight. Along the pavements little knots of youths lounged in twos and threes or more, watching the crowds streaming by, jeering, smoking, joking against the noise, under the balconies, in doorways, around the plate-glass windows. A half-mile of sound and movement and signs, signs, signs: Coca-Cola, Sale Now On, Jewellers, The Modern Outfitters, If You Don't Eat Here We'll Both Starve, Grand Picnic to Paradise Valley Luxury Buses, Teas, Coffee, Smoke, Have You Tried Our Milk Shakes, Billiard Club, The Rockingham Arms, Chine … nce In Korea, Your Recommendation Is Our Advert, Dress Salon.

Michael Adonis moved idly along the pavement through the stream of people unwinding like a spool up the street. A music shop was playing shrill and noisy, "Some of these days, you gonna miss me honey"; music from across the Atlantic, shipped in flat shellac discs to pound its jazz through the loudspeaker over the doorway.

He stopped outside the big plate window, looking in at the rows of guitars, banjoes, mandolins, the displayed gramophone parts, guitar picks, strings, electric irons, plugs, jews-harps, adaptors, celluloid dolls all the way from Japan, and the pictures of angels and Christ with a crown of thorns and drops of blood like lipstick marks on his pink forehead.

A fat man came out of the shop, his cheeks smooth and shiny with health, and said, "You like to buy something, sir?"

"'No man," Michael Adonis said and spun his cigarette-end into the street where a couple of snot-nosed boys in ragged shirts and homy feet scrambled for it, pushing each other as they struggled to claim a few puffs.

Somebody said, "Hoit, Mikey," and he turned and saw the wreck of a youth who had fallen in beside him.

"Hullo, Joe."

Joe was short and his face had an ageless quality about it under the grime, like something valuable forgotten in a junk shop. He had the soft brown eyes of a dog, and he smelled of a mixture of sweat, slept-in clothes and seaweed. His trousers had gone at the cuffs and knees, the rents held together with pins and pieces of string, and so stained and spotted that the original colour could not have been guessed at. Over the trousers he wore an ancient raincoat that reached almost to his ankles, the sleeves torn loose at the shoulders, the body hanging in ribbons, the front pinned together over his filthy vest. His shoes were worn beyond recognition.

Nobody knew where Joe came from, or anything about him. He just seemed to have happened, appearing in the District like a cockroach emerging through a floorboard. Most of the time he wandered around the harbour gathering fish discarded by fishermen and anglers, or along the beaches of the coast, picking limpets and mussels. He had a strange passion for things that came from the sea.

"How you, Joe?" Michael Adonis asked.

"Okay, Mikey."

"What you been doing today?"

"Just strolling around the docks. York Castle came in this afternoon."

"Ja?"

"You like mussels, Mikey? I'll bring you some."

"That's fine, Joe."

"I got a big starfish out on the beach yesterday. One big, big one. It was dead and stank."

"Well, it's a good job you didn't bring it into town. City Council would be on your neck."

"I hear they're going to make the beaches so only white people can go there," Joe said.

"Ja. Read it in the papers. Damn sonsabitches."

"It's going to get so's nobody can go nowhere."

"I reckon so," Michael Adonis said.

They were some way up the street now and outside the Queen Victoria. Michael Adonis said, "You like a drink, Joe?" although he knew that the boy did not drink.

"No thanks, Mikey."

"Well, so long."

"So long, man."

"You eat already?"

"Well … no … not yet," Joe said, smiling humbly and shyly, moving his broken shoes gently on the rough cracked paving.

"Okay, here's a bob. Get yourself something. Parcel of fish and some chips."

"Thanks, Mikey."

"Okay. So long, Joe."

"See you again."

"Don't forget the mussels," Michael Adonis said after him, knowing that Joe would forget anyway.

"I'll bring them," Joe said, smiling back and raising his hand in a salute. He seemed to sense the other young man's doubt of his memory, and added a little fiercely, "I won't forget. You'll see. I won't forget."

Then he went up the street, trailing his tattered raincoat behind him like a sword-slashed, bullet-ripped banner just rescued from a battle.

Michael Adonis turned towards the pub and saw the two policemen coming towards him. They came down the pavement in their flat caps, khaki shirts and pants, their gun harness shiny with polish, and the holstered pistols heavy at their waists. They had hard, frozen faces as if carved out of pink ice, and hard, dispassionate eyes, hard and bright as pieces of blue glass. They strolled slowly and determinedly side by side, without moving off their course, cutting a path through the stream on the pavement like destroyers at sea.

They came on and Michael Adonis turned aside to avoid them, but they had him penned in with a casual, easy, skillful flanking manoeuvre before he could escape.

"*Waar loop jy rond, jong?* Where are you walking around, man?" The voice was hard and flat as the snap of a steel spring, and the one who spoke had hard, thin, chapped lips and a faint blonde down above them. He had flat cheekbones, pink-white, and thick, red-gold eyebrows and pale lashes. His chin was long and cleft and there was a small pimple beginning to form on one side of it, making a reddish dot against the pale skin.

"Going home," Michael Adonis said, looking at the buckle of this policeman's belt. You learned from experience to gaze at some spot on their uniforms, the button of a pocket, or the bright smoothness of their Sam Browne belts, but never into their eyes, for that would be taken as an affront by them. It was only the very brave, or the very stupid, who dared look straight into the law's eyes, to challenge them or to question their authority.

The second policeman stuck his thumbs in his gun-belt and smiled distantly and faintly. It was more a slight movement of his lips, rather than a smile. The backs of his hands where they dropped over the leather of the belt were broad and white, and the outlines of the veins were pale blue under the skin, the skin covered with a field of tiny, slanting ginger-coloured hair. His fingers were thick and the knuckles big and creased and pink, the nails shiny and healthy and carefully kept.

This policeman asked in a heavy, brutal voice, "Where's your dagga?"

"I don't smoke it."

"*Jong*, turn out your pockets," the first one ordered. "Hurry up."

Michael Adonis began to empty his pockets slowly, without looking up at them and thinking, with each movement, You mucking boers, you mucking boers. Some people stopped and looked and hurried on as the policemen turned the cold blue light of their eyes upon them. Michael Adonis showed them his crumbled and partly used packet of cigarettes, the money he had left over from his pay, a soiled handkerchief and an old piece of chewing gum covered with the grey fuzz from his pocket.

"Where did you steal the money?" The question was without humour, deadly serious, the voice topped with hardness like the surface of a file.

"Didn't steal it, baas (you *mucking boer*)."

"Well, muck off from the street. Don't let us find you standing around, you hear?"

"Yes (you *mucking boer*)."

"Yes, what? Who are you talking to, man?"

"Yes, baas (you *mucking bastard boer with your mucking gun and your mucking bloody red head*)."

They pushed past him, one of them brushing him aside with an elbow and strolled on. He put the stuff back into his pockets. And deep down inside him the feeling of rage, frustration and violence swelled like a boil, knotted with pain.

Reprinted by permission of Heinemann.

Antjie Krog

Antjie Krog is an Afrikaans poet, novelist and journalist who reported on the Truth and Reconciliation Commission for the South African Broadcasting Corporation. She blends introspection and meditations on her Afrikaner origin, some of which she describes as "lies in this book about the truth", with reflections on the content and texture of experiences of a reporter on this harrowing "beat".

Country of my Skull

. . . And suddenly it is as if an undertow is taking me out . . . out . . . and out. And behind me sinks the country of my skull like a sheet in the dark – and I hear a thin song, hooves, hedges of venom, fever and destruction fermenting and hissing underwater. I shrink and prickle. Against. Against my blood and the heritage thereof. Will I forever be them – recognizing them as I do daily in my nostrils? Yes. And what we have done will never be undone. It doesn't matter what we do. What De Klerk does. Until the third and fourth generation.

Famished. Parched, one waits for Constand Viljoen's party [Freedom Front] to make its submission. They form a modest group.

Viljoen speaks as if he wants to capture something, bring something back, confirm some essence of Afrikanerhood that is wholesome. I want it too – but at the same time know it not to be. When Viljoen talks about how the British took away the land of the Boers, an English-speaking journalist mutters sarcastically, 'Ah shame!'

I cannot help it, I spit like a flame: 'Shut up, you! You didn't utter a word when De Klerk [leader of the National Party] spoke . . . Viljoen is at least trying.'

'You must be joking – this poor man is an anachronism.' My anger shrivels before his Accent. And his Truth.

Viljoen was the only political leader who requested that a special Reconciliation Commission be set up in future to deal with 'the hardening of attitudes I experience daily.'

After the first political submissions in August 1996 I interviewed Archbishop Tutu. 'Weren't you irritated that you had to listen to four versions of South Africa's past?'

He spreads his four skinny fingers under my nose. 'Four versions . . . four . . . exist of the life of Christ. Which one would you have liked to chuck out?'

I try another question. 'Why did the last part of the ANC's submission sound so paranoid? As if the whole world is in a conspiracy against Thabo Mbeki.'

Tutu tilts his head in surprise. 'You should be the last person to ask me this. You are sitting with me daily, listening to what happened in the past. Many people are the second and third generation of being persecuted. And if you don't know the past, you will never understand today's politics.'

A friend who has emigrated visits me in the office. She answers a call for me: 'It's your child. He says he's writing a song about Joe Mamasela and he needs a word to rhyme with "Vlakplaas".' She lowers the phone. 'Who is Joe Mamasela?'

A massive sigh breaks through my chest. For the first time in months – I breathe.

The absolution one has given up on, the hope for a catharsis, the ideal of reconciliation, the dream of a powerful reconciliation policy . . . Maybe this is all that is important – that I and my child know Vlakplaas and Mamasela. That we know what happened there.

When the Truth Commission started last year, I realized instinctively: if you cut yourself off from the process, you will wake up in a foreign country – a country that you don't know and that you will never understand.

Reprinted by permission of Random House SA.

Mtutuzeli Matshoba

Mtutuzeli Matshoba is a black writer who is well known in South Africa. The extract below gives an idea of the conditions of life in the Transkei, the first artificially created homeland or Bantustan, after it was notionally given "independence" in 1976. Kaiser Matanzima, the repressive first leader of the Transkei, imprisoned political opponents without trial and imposed emergency regulations which he renewed annually.

Three Days in the Land of a Dying Illusion

"Heh, heh," he had chuckled at my ignorance of the present world. "You don't know that Transkei is independent?"

"Independent from what, of what?"

"Of South Africa," and his eyes had completed the sentence with "bloody fool!"

"That's news to me," I said as sincerely as I could.

"You must have been in jail. Were you not in prison when Transkey got independence? Or maybe you were mad, at Sterkfontein."

"Maybe. If that's what you want – your fellow blacks to be in prison. What's the red tape?"

"Give me your pass."

Fortunately, for once I had it for identification purposes. What with everybody looking for "terrorists" under every stone. I gave it to him and he pages through it before throwing it back at me.

"You're Xhosa, neh?"

I nodded.

"Then go and apply for Transkei citizenship at Counter Six. Next!"

I could not suppress my indignation anymore. "When you look at me you imagine I could make an ideal Transkei citizen? When you arrive home this evening you tell your mother to apply for it so that she can go and learn witchcraft if she is not a professional already." I turned and stomped for the door without waiting for his reaction.

So there I was, rolling into Qamata with my third denomination comrades. The discussion petered out to a noticeable hush as everybody was diverted from the articulate lady by the crossing of an invisible Iron Curtain.

The soil was red, ironically reminding me of Avalon and Doornkop cemeteries back home, the land parched and scarred with erosion. In the first fields that we passed the maize had grown hardly a metre high. The weeds, blackjack outstanding, outgrew it. A woman in dusty traditional attire with a baby strapped to her back and two boys in inherited clothes following her, was searching for stems that might have been overlooked at harvest time.

We passed two cows shaving the roadside of sun-scorched grass.

"*Kakade*, what's the use of buying cattle that end up short of grass?" remarked one of my travelling companions.

"*Imfuyo* [stock] is no longer an investment these days," added another.

I had thought the animals looked acceptable. Perhaps that was due to my inability to judge good beef. However you looked at it, some of the animals that we saw were scrawny and others well-nourished. Probably the latter belonged to people who could afford to buy hay.

The mountains rose high, solid, silent and motionless until they melted into blue-grey and hazy horizons, the only sight that appealed magnificently to my eyes. Below them there were picturesque villages of perfectly circular, thatched rondavels whitewashed for about a foot just below the edges of the thatch and around the windows and doors. This architecture dotted the elevated parts of the landscape on both sides of the road for endless acres.

"*Awu*," someone ventured, "*esikaDaliwonga! Ilizwe lembalela* [a land of drought]. That is why he has left it to pick out the richest parts of the land for himself elsewhere; to bulldoze the people out of land that they inherited from their fathers."

"*Ewe. Nathi uyokusixina ngaphaya.*" [Yes. He also crowds us into the parts that remain ours.]

I was confounded by those words because they came from simple people. Things being taken for granted as they generally are, who could have expected them to nurture any misgivings concerning their share of that wilderness? I say wilderness because that was the most suitable description of what was unfolding before my eyes compared with the white-owned Free State country I had seen the previous day. Proof of its being wasteland lay in the fact that they had surrendered to the inhuman migratory way of life rather than stay and try to eke out a living in their "homeland". It showed there was just no way to suck blood out of a stone. The illusion of freehold in a free land had long faded in the imagination of my cheated people. Independence, *uburu*, had come, avowedly to break the chains of blackness and drive away poverty. Instead it had brought an ominous fog of helplessness that hung over a land marred with eroded ravines which gave one a clear picture of what the earth might look like after an earthquake. From the silvery trickles that traced erratic courses on the sandy beds of some of the shallow dongas, I concluded that they had been rivulets many aeons ago.

The maize refused to grow higher than a foot without water and scientific agricultural methods. It would cost decades in time and billions of rands in the form of irrigation, fertilizer and technology before one would see any advance beyond cross-plantation on the slopes, which was the only scientific land treatment about which I could write home. Where would the billions come from? Obviously from "white South Africa" with her own sick economy.

If anybody out there had figured that he could temporarily depend on South Africa by sending people there as slaves, hoping that they would earn enough to be self-sufficient after some time, he had dreamt up a nightmare. Slaves don't earn anything; they live from hand to mouth. His country would forever remain both a labour reservoir and a vacuum to suck discarded human labour units out of the South African economy.

We passed a village with a dusty filling station or garage that might have been constructed from the home-made mudbricks of the rondavels. Even if I had a car and happened to have a breakdown near that place, I would never risk taking it there.

Reprinted by permission of Ravan Press/Rex Collings.

Books

For a country with such a low proportion of its population literate and reading regularly, South Africa generates a good amount of literature, particularly about subjects the literate feel guilty about – namely, politics and history. Where two publishers are given, the first is British, the second US unless otherwise indicated. Titles marked ⊞ are particularly recommended.

History, society and anthropology

William Beinart *Twentieth-Century South Africa* (OUP, UK). A useful and concise account of South African history, with an emphasis on economic history that manages to emphasize the essential without descending into tedium. His predictions for the future seem wobbly now, but there's nothing unusual about that.

Axel-Ivar Berglund *Zulu Thought Patterns and Symbolism* (Hurst, UK). A sensitive and knowledgeable account of rural Zulu world views, as told to the author, with the minimum of interpretation. He does, however, set the scene well, and make thought-provoking connections between the various views expressed, while bending over backwards to avoid tedious judgementalism.

Ian Berry *Living Apart* (Phaidon, SA). Superbly evocative and moving photographs spanning the 1950s to 1990s, which chart a compelling vision of the politics of the nation, but at the level of the individual.

Philip Bonner *Kings, Commoners and Concessionaries* (CUP, UK). The definitive history (so far) of nineteenth-century Swaziland, by a skilled historian with a gratifying grasp of the source material and mostly reliable judgement. Its one weakness is a lack of oral historical research.

Emile Boonzaier, Candy Mal-herbe, Andy Smith and Penny Berens *The Cape Herders: A History of the Khoikhoi of Southern Africa* (David Philip, SA; Ohio University Press, US). This accessible account of the Khoikhoi successfully explodes the many prejudices and myths that surround them and explores their way of life, their interaction with Europeans, and what remains of them today.

Jane Carruthers *The Kruger National Park: A Social and Political History* (University of Natal, SA). Examining the scientific and ideological forces that gave rise to the creation of Kruger National Park, this fascinating book asks important questions about our notions of nature and conservation.

Clive Chipkin *Johannesburg Style* (David Philip, SA). Perhaps the title is a contradiction in terms, but this is an intriguing study of architecture – and society – in the South African city.

J. Christopher *The Atlas of Apartheid* (Routledge, UK). Detailed but accessible study of the policy and implementation of urban and regional planning that gave South African towns and cities their current form.

Rodney Davenport *The Transfer of Power in South Africa* (Toronto University Press, Canada). An eminent liberal historian examines reconciliation in South African society since 1990 and explains how potential obstacles have been overcome.

Paul Faber *Group Portraits South Africa* (Kwela, SA). Fascinating account revealing the complexities of South Africa past and present, of the histories of nine South African families of different races, backgrounds and aspirations. One of the families featured is that of writer Sol Plaatje. Includes photos and illustrations.

Stephen Gill *A Short History of Lesotho* (Morija, Lesotho). The best single volume you'll find on Lesotho's history, a thoughtful and well-informed account by the chief archivist at the Morija Museum. Gill clearly loves Lesotho and has little sympathy for its many invaders, but is a little over-generous in his account of Lesotho's missionaries.

Barbara Hutton *Robben Island: Symbol of Resistance* (Mayibuye Books, SA; Sached Books UK). A straightforward, illustrated account of Robben Island from prehistoric times to the present, with a good overview of prison conditions in the apartheid years.

[★] **Antjie Krog** *Country of My Skull* (Jonathan Cape; Times Books). A deeply personal and gripping account of the hearings of the Truth and Reconciliation Commission. Krog, an Afrikaner SABC radio journalist and poet, reveals the complexity of horrors committed by apartheid, and also paints an admiring picture of Commission head Desmond Tutu.

Hilda Kuper *The Swazi, A South African Kingdom* (Saunders College Publishing, US). A combination of anthropology and history, written in the 1960s. The theoretical

perspectives seem pretty dated now, though Kuper's observations still sound sharp. Her political insight was often astute too, though she was too fond of the Dlamini royal house to provide much of a critical perspective on them.

[★] **J.D. Lewis-Williams** *Discovering Southern African Rock Art* (David Philip, SA) and *Images of Power: Understanding Bushman Rock Art* (David Philip, SA). Concise books written by an expert in the field, full of drawings and photos. The author concludes that most of the paintings depict images perceived while in a state of shamanic trance, and reflect a San world-view in which the spiritual and material were both a part of everyday life. Also worth investigating are the same author's *San Spirituality, Roots, Expression and Social Consequences* (Double Storey) and *Stories that Float from Afar: Ancestral Folklore of the San of Southern Africa* (David Philip SA).

Candy Malherbe *Men of Men* (Shuter and Shooter, SA). A brief, simple and highly readable primer on the Khoikhoi.

Hein Marais *South Africa, Limits to Change* (Zed Books). A readable assessment of why the privileged classes remain just that, and why the new government has followed relatively conservative economic policies.

[★] **Noel Mostert** *Frontiers: The Epic of South Africa's Creation and the Tragedy of the Xhosa People* (Pimlico, UK). An academically solid, brilliantly written history of the Xhosa of the Eastern Cape, and their tragic fate in the frontier wars against the British.

Alan Mountain *An Unsung Heritage: Perspectives on Slavery* (David Philip, SA). An account of the nature of slavery in the Cape, and the contribution imported slaves made to the fabric of the area today. Best of all is the guide to slave heritage sites in the Cape Peninsula, Winelands and West Coast, and along Garden Route, with attractive photos and illustrations.

Credo Mutwa *Indaba, My Children* (Payback Press; Grove Atlantic). Many of Africa's most enduring and entertaining legends, myths and stories vividly retold – and some would say reinvented – by enigmatic Zulu spiritualist Mutwa.

Mike Nicol *Sea-Mountain, Fire City: Living in Cape Town* (Kwela Books, SA). Basing his narrative on the apparently prosaic business of moving house from one part of the city to another, Nicol maps many of the fissures that make Cape Town such a divided city.

★ **Dougie Oakes** (ed) *Illustrated History of South Africa* (Reader's Digest, SA). Physically weighty, but written in a delightfully light style, this illustated volume is essential for anyone seriously interested in the rise of apartheid and the country's turbulent passage to democracy.

★ **Thomas Pakenham** *The Boer War* (Abacus, UK). The definitive liberal history of the Anglo-Boer War that reads grippingly like a novel, managing to maintain a panoramic sweep of events while homing in on the quirks and foibles of the individuals involved.

Jeff Peires *The Dead Will Arise* (Ravan, SA) and *The House of Phalo*

(Ravan, SA). The leading historian of the Xhosa tells in beautifully readable prose the stories of the Eastern Cape before the arrival of whites, as well as the impact of colonialism on their lives and society.

Allister Sparks *Beyond the Miracle: Inside The New South Africa* (Profile). An examination by a veteran journalist of the prospects for South Africa, looking beyond the initial bouyancy of democracy to emerging patterns in its government.

Leonard Thompson *A History of South Africa* (Yale University Press). Reliable and elegantly written, this is among the best introductions to its subject.

Desmond Tutu *No Future Without Forgiveness* (Rider Books, UK). The Truth and Reconciliation Commission as described by its chairman. There are better accounts of the hearings, but the book offers essential insight into one of South Africa's most unlikely heroes.

★ **Nigel Worden, Elizabeth van Heyningen and Vivian Bickford-Smith** *Cape Town: The Making of a City* (David Philip, SA). The definitive and highly readable illustrated account of the social and political development of South Africa's first city from 1620 to 1899, written by three leading historians based at the University of Cape Town. A companion volume covers the twentieth century.

Autobiography and biography

Breyten Breytenbach *The True Confessions of an Albino Terrorist* (Faber & Faber, UK). In vividly poetic language, the exiled Afrikaner poet tells the entertaining story of how he returned to South Africa in

1975 – only to be arrested and jailed for seven years.

Luli Callinicos *Oliver Tambo: Beyond the Engeli Mountains* (David Philip, SA). The life story of the man who was once president of the ANC in exile, leading the fight against apart while Mandela languished in jail. The only ANC leader who could hold a candle to Mandela, Tambo did not live to see the fruits of his struggle – he died in 1993, on the eve of liberation.

J.M. Coetzee *Boyhood & Youth* (Vintage). A riveting and disquieting accounts of childhood in a provincial town, and the author subsequently finding his way in the world, both in South Africa and London. It's notable especially for the candour with which Coetzee, who won the 2003 Nobel prize for literature, writes about relationships with his mother and father.

Robin Denniston *Trevor Huddleston, A Life* (Macmillan, UK). An inspiring biography of the English churchman who worked among Johannesburg's urban blacks in the 1950s and later founded the Anti-Apartheid Movement.

Sindiwe Magoma *To My Children's Children* (David Philip, SA). A fascinating autobiography – initially started so that her family would never forget their roots – that traces Magoma's life from the rural Transkei to the hard townships of Cape Town, and from political innocence to wisdom born of bitter experience.

Miriam Makeba *Mama Afrika: The Miriam Makeba Story* (STE, SA). Makeba's remarkable life in South Africa and in exile is chronicled in a coffee-table format, complete with discography, index and glossary, and lots of photos.

★ **Nelson Mandela** *Long Walk to Freedom* (Abacus; Back Bay). The superb best-selling autobiography of the South African president. Mandela's generosity of spirit and tremendous understanding of the delicate balance between principle and tactics come through very strongly, and the book is wonderfully evocative of his early years and intensely moving about his long years in prison. However, when it comes to his love life, the byzantine intricacies of ANC politics during its long years as an illegal organization, and the story behind the negotiated settlement, Mandela is more diplomatic than candid.

★ **Greg Marnovich and Joao Silva** *The Bang Bang Club* (Arrow, UK). The compelling story of four news photographers who snapped the country's most violent townships in the late 1980s and early 1990s. Two survived to tell the tale; Ken Oosterbroek was killed in crossfire days before the 1994 elections and Ken Carter committed suicide not long afterwards.

William Plomer *Cecil Rhodes* (David Philip, SA). There are countless books on Rhodes and his huge influence on South Africa in the nineteenth century. Most of these books feed the legend, though some historians now regard him as a flawed colossus. Plomer, a South African poet-novelist, went against the grain several decades ago, when he pulled no punches in presenting Rhodes as an immature person driven by his weaknesses.

Albie Sachs *The Soft Vengeance of a Freedom Fighter* (David Philip, SA). ANC veteran Sachs here relates the story of how, in exile in Mozambique, he was almost killed by a South African security police bomb. The book vividly traces his recovery and the mental difficulties he went through to emerge with a new vision of the struggle. Today Sachs is a judge in the South African Constitutional Court.

Anthony Sampson *Mandela, The Authorised Biography* (Harper Collins; Knopf). Released to coincide with Mandela's retirement from the presidency in 1999, Sampson's authoritative volume competes with *A Long Walk to Freedom* in both interest and sheer poundage. Firmly grounded in the author's long association with his subject, as well as exhaustive research and interviews, it offers a broader perspective and sharper analysis than the autobiography.

Chris van Wyk *Shirley, Goodness and Mercy: A Childhood Memoir* (Pan Macmillan, SA). A memoir of growing up in a working-class coloured family in Johannesburg during the apartheid era, with humorous and poignant touches.

The arts

Basil Beakey *Beyond the Blues: Township Jazz of the Sixties and Seventies* (David Philip, SA). Portraits, in words and pictures, of the country's jazz greats such as Kippie Moeketsi, Basil Coetzee and Abdullah Ibrahim (Dollar Brand).

S. Francis and Rico *Madam and Eve* (Rapid Phase, SA). Various volumes of telling and witty cartoons conveying the daily struggle between an African domestic worker and her white madam in the northern suburbs of Johannesburg, these cartoons say more about post-apartheid society than countless academic tomes.

Z.B. Molefe *A Common Hunger to Sing* (Kwela, SA). Large format, well-illustrated tribute to the country's black women singers and the obstacles they have overcome.

Sophie Perryer (ed) *10 Years, 100 Artists* (Bell Roberts). Substantial

coffee-table book showcasing the work of a hundred top South African artists.

Sue Williamson *Resistance Art in South Africa* (David Philip, SA) and *Art in South Africa: The Future Present* (David Philip, SA). Taken together, these two volumes map the course of South African art from the early 1980s to the present day, accompanied by a commentary that's both thoughtful and concise enough to let the artworks speak for themselves.

Zapiro *Long Walk to Free Time* (Double; Storey Books). In a country where satire is in notoriously short supply, Zapiro is the leading cartoonist, consistently exposing what needs to be exposed. This book is number nine in a series, containing work originally published in the *Sowetan*, *Mail & Guardian* and *Sunday Times*.

Travel writing

Richard Dobson *Karoo Moons: A Photographic Journey* (Struik, SA). If you need encouragement to explore the desert interior of South Africa, these enticing images should do the trick.

Dan Jacobson *The Electric Elephant* (Hamish Hamilton, UK). Jacobson, who left South Africa in the 1950s,

returned in 1993 to travel from Kimberley in the Northern Cape to Victoria Falls, along the old "Great North Road", built by Cecil Rhodes and since trodden by generations of missionaries, colonists and freebooters.

Ben Maclennan *The Wind Makes Dust: Four Centuries of Travel in South*

Africa (Tafelberg, SA). A remarkable anthology of fascinating travel pieces, meticulously unearthed and researched.

Dervla Murphy *South from the Limpopo: Travels Through South Africa* (Flamingo; Penguin). A fascinating and intrepid journey – by bicycle – through the new South Africa. The author isn't afraid to explore the complexities and paradoxes of this country.

Paul Theroux *Dark Star Safari* (Penguin). Theroux's powerful account of his overland trip from Cairo to Cape Town, with a couple of chapters on South Africa, including an account of meeting writer Nadine Gordimer.

Specialist guides

G.M. Branch *Two Oceans* (David Philip, SA). Don't be fooled by the coffee-table format; this is a comprehensive guide to southern Africa's marine life.

David Bristow *Best Hikes in Southern Africa* and *Best Hikes of the Drakensberg* (Struik, SA). The South Africa book is a well-written and reliable guide that does your homework for you, selecting the best trails from a confusingly extensive lot. The Drakensberg paperback is indispensable for anyone exploring the massif, with detailed route instructions and informative background about natural history.

Shirley Brossey *A Walking Guide for Table Mountain* (Self-published, SA). Not hard to find in South Africa, this is an inexpensive guide to trails around the Table Mountain, with useful hand-drawn maps and down-to-earth text.

Duncan Guy *The Very Best of Johannesburg and Surrounds* (Struik, SA). Hard-to-find book which delights in the diversity and colour of Johannesburg. There are lots of photographs and some good detail on the nooks and crannies of Gauteng.

Brett Hilton-Barber and Lee Berger *Field Guide to the Cradle of Mankind* (Struik, SA). Full of photographs and illustrations, this indispensible guide takes you around the world heritage sites of the Cradle of Humankind near Jo'burg – Sterkfontein, Swartkrans and Kromdraai.

Judith Hopley *On Foot in the Garden Route* (Self-published, SA). Excellent little guide that's perfect if you're planning on exploring the coasts and forest of the Garden Route on foot.

★ **Jaynee Levy** *The Complete Guide to Walks & Trails in Southern Africa* (Struik, SA). Encyclopedic hiker's bible covering over five hundred trails suitable for all abilities, with practical information about what to take and where to book. One to invest in if you're a keen trailist spending time in the country, but definitely not light reading to take on a walk.

★ **Mike Lundy** *Best Walks in the Cape Peninsula* (Struik, SA). Handy, solidly researched guide to some of the Peninsula's many walks, and small enough to fit comfortably in a backpack.

Willie and Sandra Olivier *Hiking Trails of Southern Africa* (Southern). Covers less ground than Levy, dealing with only the 44 most important trails, but writes them up with greater depth, including excellent natural history commentary on each trail.

Colin Paterson-Jones *Best Walks of the Garden Route* (Struik, SA). Handy for accessing some of South Africa's premier coastline and forests, away from the ribbon of development along the Garden Route.

Tony Pooley and Ian Player *KwaZulu-Natal Wildlife Destinations* (Southern, SA). Comprehensive directory of every game and nature reserve in the province, with useful practical and background information.

Charles Stewart *Rock and Surf Fishing* (Southern, SA). Uninspiringly written, but the author does appear to have tried his luck from nearly every available vantage point on the South African coast, and the book usefully sums up what he found out on the way.

Birds

Hugh Chittenden *Top Birding Spots of Southern Africa* (Southern, SA). Essential companion-guide for any keen bird-watcher, with information on how to access birding spots as well as a rundown of the common species and any special ones to look out for.

Gordon Lindsay Maclean Roberts *Birds of Southern Africa* (New Holland, UK). The definitive reference work on the subcontinent's entire avifauna population: if it's not in Roberts, it doesn't exist. Alas, the weight of this makes it more of a book to consult in a library than on a trip.

Ian Sinclair *Field Guide to Birds of Southern Africa* (Struik, SA). Pocket-sized volume full of photos. From the same publisher, the *Sasol Birding Map of Southern Africa* (of which Sinclair is one of the authors) shows two hundred top birding sites, with detailed coverage of eight.

Mammals

Richard D. Estes *Safari Companion* (Chelsea Green Publishing Co, USA). Although this can occasionally sound like a manual on how to treat your porters, it's basically a vital guide on how to understand African wildlife, with interesting and readable information on the behaviour and social structures of the major species.

Chris and Tilde Stuart *Field Guide to the Mammals of Southern Africa* (Struik, SA; New Holland, UK). One of the best books on this subject, providing excellent background and clear illustrations to help you recognize a species.

Flora

L. McMahon and M. Fraser *A Fynbos Year* (David Philip, SA). Exquisitely illustrated and well-written book about South Africa's unique floral kingdom.

Keith Coates Palgrave *Trees of Southern Africa* (Struik, SA). The authoritative book on the subject, but too big to carry around.

Eve Palmer *A Field Guide to the Trees of Southern Africa* (Collins, UK). Covering South Africa, Botswana and Namibia, this is more practical to carry than Coates Palgrave.

Elsa Pooley *Trees of Southern Africa* (Southern Book Publishers, SA). Ideal beginner's and traveller's guide

with illustrations, easy to use and carry around.

Wine

David Biggs *South African Plonk Buyer's Guide* (Ampersand, SA). Annually updated survey of the best of the inexpensive wines.

James Seely *The Wines of South Africa* (Faber & Faber, UK). Almost as definitive as it claims, this useful reference tackles South African wine region by region, estate by estate, complete with tasting notes and recommendations.

Ursula Stevens *The Winelands Explorer* (Wanderlust, SA). Describes a number of wine

routes in the Stellenbosch, Paarl and Franschoek areas, with some interesting historical background about the different estates.

★ Philip van Zyl (ed) *John Platter South African Wines* (Andrew Mcdowall, SA). Annually updated pocket guide to South Africa's current output, with ratings by one of the country's top wine writers.

Fiction

Tatamkhulu Afrika *The Innocents* (Africasouth, SA). Set in the struggle years, this novel examines the moral and ethical issues of the time from a Muslim perspective.

★ Herman Charles Bosman *Unto Dust* (Human & Rousseau, SA). A superb collection of short stories from South Africa's master of the genre, all set in the tiny Afrikaner farming district of Groot Marico in the 1930s. The tales share a narrator who, with delicious irony, reveals the passions and foibles of his community.

André Brink *A Chain of Voices* (Minerva, UK). The former is a superbly evocative tale of Cape eighteenth-century life explores the impact of slavery on one farming family, culminating in a dramatic and murderous end.

★ J.M. Coetzee *Age of Iron* (Penguin) and *Disgrace* (Vintage). In a *Mail & Guardian*

poll of writers, *Age of Iron* emerged as the finest South African novel of the 1990s. The book depicts a white female classics professor dying from cancer during the political craziness of the 1980s. She is joined by a tramp who sets up home in her garden, and thus evolves a curious and fascinating relationship that transforms her. But even better is *Disgrace*, a disturbing story of a university professor's fall from grace, set in the Eastern Cape. No writer better portrays the ever-present undercurrents of violence and unease in South Africa.

Achmat Dangor *The Z Town Trilogy* (Ravan, SA) and *Bitter Fruit* (Atlantic Books). One of the best writers from Cape Town, Dangor sets his trilogy in a town much like it, during one of apartheid South Africa's many states of emergency, which have started to burrow in intricate ways into the psyches of his characters. *Bitter Fruit* is the story of the son of two anti-apartheid activists, and of an act of violence and injustice threading two generations, which is resurrected by the Truth and Reconciliation Commission. The book portrays a brittle family, a dysfunctional society, and how we address – or fail to address – the past's deepest wounds.

Modikwe Dikobe *Marabi Dance* (Heinemann, UK). A short novel celebrating the bittersweet nature of black Johannesburg life in the 1930s, where the daily humiliations of life are tempered by the prospect of wild *marabi* parties when the weekends come.

Nadine Gordimer *July's People* (Penguin, UK/US). A liberal white family is rescued by its gardener July from revolution, and taken to his home village for safety, where Gordimer teases out the power dynamics of this fraught situation with customary insight and eloquence.

Dan Jacobson *The Trap* and *A Dance in the Sun* (David Philip, SA). Two taut novellas written in the 1950s and published in one volume, skilfully portraying the developing tensions and nuances of the white-versus-black lives of the era.

★ **Alex La Guma** *A Walk in the Night* (Heinemann, UK). An evocative collection of short stories by this talented political activist/ author, set in District Six, the ethnically mixed quarter of Cape Town razed by the apartheid government.

Anne Landsman *The Devil's Chimney* (Granta; Penguin). A stylish and entertaining piece of magic realism about the Southern Cape town of Oudtshoorn in the days of the ostrich-feather boom.

Zakes Mda *Ways of Dying* and *His Madonna of Excelsior* (OUP, UK).

The former is a brilliant tale of a professional mourner, full of sly insights into the culture of black South Africa; the latter focuses on a family at the heart of the scandalous case in the Free State, in which nineteen people from the small town of Excelsior were charged with breaking the Immorality Act, which forbade sex between races.

Thomas Mofolo *Chaka* (Heinemann, UK). Lesotho's first great fiction writer, Mofo penned this epic tale in Sotho in 1909. The book centres on the Zulu king Shaka, here portrayed as a man fatally controlled by his strong passions. The original English translation gave the text a misleadingly biblical slant, which has been corrected in this newer translation by Daniel Kunene.

Isaac Mogotsi *Alexandra Tales* (Ravan, SA). Delightful tales of family life in the run-down, lively homes of Johannesburg's Alexandra township, all with a clever and provocative twist in the tail.

★ **Es'kia Mphahlele** *Down Second Avenue* (Faber & Faber, UK). A classic autobiographical novel set in the 1940s in the impoverished township of Alexandra, where Mphahlele grew up as part of a large extended family battling daily to survive the problems and injustices of the age.

★ **Alan Paton** *Cry, The Beloved Country* (Penguin, UK). Classic 1948 novel encapsulating the deep injustices of the country, by one of South Africa's great liberals. With tremendous lyricism, the book describes the journey of a black pastor from rural Natal to Johannesburg (which is depicted as a veritable Sodom and Gomorrah) to rescue his missing son from its clutches.

Kathy Perkins *Black South African Women – An Anthology of Plays* (Routledge, UK). Groundbreaking collection of ten plays by a wide range of known and unknown playwrights such as Gcina Mhlope, Sindiwe Nagona, Muthal Naidoo and Lueen Conning.

Sol Plaatje *Mhudi* (Heinemann, UK). The first English novel by a South African writer, *Mhudi* is set in the 1830s, at a time when the Afrikaner Great Trek had just begun. It's the epic tale of a young rural woman who saves her future husband from the raids of the Ndebele, who were then a powerful state in the Marico region. The author was a political activist and one of the founder members of the ANC.

Linda Rode *Crossing Over* (Kwela, SA). Collection of 26 stories by new and emerging South African writers on the experiences of adolescence and early adulthood in a period of political transition.

★ **Olive Schreiner** *Story of an African Farm* (Penguin, UK/US). The first-ever South African novel, written in 1883 (when the author used a male pseudonym). Though subject to the ideologies of the era, the book nonetheless explores with a genuinely open vision the tale of two female cousins living on a remote Karoo farm, when their young lives are disrupted by an Irish traveller.

Sipho Sepamla *A Ride On The Whirlwind* (Heinemann, UK). Set in the riot-swept Soweto of 1976, this novel examines the psychology of resistance and defiance amongst the angry township youth.

Mongane Wally Serote *To Every Birth Its Blood* (Heinemann, UK). Serote's only novel is a powerfully turbulent affair that traces how a township man who is interested only in jazz, drinking and sex gains a political consciousness through the humiliations he is subjected to by authority.

★ **Martin Trump and Jean Marquard (eds)** *A Century of South African Short Stories* (Ad Donker, SA). A selection of South Africa's finest short stories, including contributions from Can Themba (writer of *Drum*), Charles Bosman and Nadine Gordimer.

Ivan Vladislavic *The Restless Supermarket* (David Philip, SA) and *The Exploded View* (Random House). *The Restless Supermarket* is a dark and intricate urban satire about Johannesburg's notorious Hillbrow district during the last days of apartheid. *The Exploded View* is a collection of four interlinked pieces, a great follow-up from a writer who's unrivalled at evoking the contradictions and fascinations of Jo'burg.

Poetry

Guy Butler (ed) *A Book of South African Verse* (Oxford University Press, UK); **Jack Cope and Uys Krige (eds)** *The Penguin Book of South African Verse* (Penguin, UK). Early anthologies that, for better or for worse, "mapped" South African poetry. Butler's comment in his introduction – "Most of our poets have tried to belong to Africa and, finding her savage, shallow and uncooperative, have been forced to give their allegiance, not to any other country, but to certain basic conceptions" (read Europe) – remains controversial.

★ **Roy Campbell** *Selected Poems* (Oxford University Press, UK). Very much a figure from a period of South Africa's literary colonialism, Roy Campbell, despite his sometimes politically repellent views, remains a major figure, and one of the most lyrically gifted and satirically sharp poets that South Africa has ever produced.

Tim Couzens and Essop Patel (eds) *Return of the Amasi Bird* (Ravan, SA). Comprehensive collection of black South African poetry, which stretches right back to the early colonial era and extends to the cries of liberation and beyond.

Jeremy Cronin *Inside and Out* (David Philip, SA). Written by a leading member of the South African Communist Party, *Inside*, first published in 1983, is probably the most inventive work of South African prison poetry. *Out* charts Cronin's reaction to post-apartheid South Africa, and continuing resistance to the many forms of betrayal of South Africa's larger populace.

[★] **Ingrid de Kok** *Transfer* and *Terrestial Things* (Snail Press, SA). Probably the most intelligent of South Africa's feminist poets, technically adroit and always moving.

[★] **Denis Hirson (ed)** *The Lava of this Land: South African Poetry 1960–1996* (David Philip, SA). This most recent and comprehensive anthology of South African poetry includes work from the oral period, as well as translations from Afrikaans and other languages. The most useful introduction to date.

Ingrid Jonker *Selected Poems* (Human & Rousseau, SA). One of the few Afrikaans language poets to whom English translation does justice to her work. The poems display a remarkable rawness in depicting the outrage of 1960s apartheid, as well as a grief-stricken lyricism from a poet who drowned herself in 1965 off Sea Point.

Mongane Wally Serote *Selected Poems* (Ad Donker, SA). The leading light among South Africa's many protest poets, with a work that ranges from early rage to incantations of freedom, leavened with humour and startling imagery.

[★] **Stephen Watson** *The Other City* (David Philip, SA). No one better evokes Cape Town's changeable beauty, though Watson also writes of the heart and the great universal themes that make him a first-rate poet of the world, rather than just of his native city.

Language

Language

English 931

Afrikaans 932

The Nguni group 933

The Sotho group 933

Pronouncing place names 934

Glossary 937

Food and drink 939

Language

South Africa has eleven official languages, all of which have equal status under the law. In practice, however, **English** is the *lingua franca* that dominates politics, commerce and the media. If you're staying in the main cities and national parks you'll rarely, if ever, need to use any other language. **Afrikaans**, although a language you seldom need to speak, nevertheless remains very much in evidence and you will certainly encounter it on official forms and countless signs, particularly on the road; for this reason we give a comprehensive list of written Afrikaans terms you could come across.

Unless you're planning on staying a very long time, there's little point trying to get to grips with the whole gamut of indigenous African languages, of which there are nine official ones and several unofficial ones. Having said that, it's always useful to know a few phrases of the local indigenous language, especially greetings – the use of which will always be appreciated even if you aren't able to carry your foray through to a proper conversation. For basic greetings in Afrikaans, and five of the most commonly used indigenous African languages, see the box on p.936.

The nine official African languages are split into four groups: **Nguni**, which consists of Zulu, Xhosa, siSwati and Ndebele; **Sotho**, which comprises Northern Sotho, Southern Sotho (or Sesotho) and Tswana; and **Venda** and **Tsonga**. Most black people speak languages in the first two groups. In common with all indigenous southern African languages, these operate under very different principles to European languages in that their sentences are dominated by the noun, with which the other words, such as verbs and adjectives, must agree in person, gender, number or case. Known as concordal agreement, this is achieved by supplementing word stems – the basic element of each word – with prefixes or suffixes to change meaning.

The Nguni group, and Southern Sotho, both contain a few **clicks** adopted from San languages, which are difficult for speakers of European languages. In practice, most English-speaking South Africans sidestep the issue altogether and pronounce African names in ways that are often only approximations. To get to grips with the Zulu phrases we've listed, it's worth investing in one of the Zulu-language cassettes available in bookshops in KwaZulu-Natal. Tapes for other languages can be more difficult to come by, but it's always worth checking out bookshops.

English

South African English is a mixed bag, one language with many variants. Forty percent of whites are mother-tongue English speakers, many of whom believe that they are (or at least should be) speaking standard British English. In fact, South African English has its own distinct character, and is as different from the Queen's English as is Australian. Its most notable characteristic is its huge and rich vocabulary, with unique words and usages, some drawn from Afrikaans and the indigenous African languages. The hefty *Oxford Dictionary of South African English* makes an interesting browse.

As a language used widely by non-native speakers, there is great **variation in pronounciation** and usage – largely a result of mother-tongue interference from other languages. Take for example the sentence "The bad bird sat on the bed", which speakers of some African languages (which don't distinguish between some of the vowel sounds of English) might pronounce as "The bed bed set on the bed". While some English-speaking whites feel that their language is being mangled and misused, linguists argue that it is simply being transformed.

Afrikaans

Broadly speaking, Afrikaans is a dialect of **Dutch**, which became modified on the Cape frontier through its encounter with French, German and English settlers, and is peppered with words and phrases from indigenous tongues as well as languages used by slaves. Some historians argue, very plausibly, that Afrikaans was first written in Arabic script in the early nineteenth century by Cape Muslims.

Despite this heritage, the language was used by Afrikaners from the late nineteenth century onwards as a key element in the construction of their racially exclusive ethnic identity. The attempt, in 1976, by the apartheid government to make Afrikaans the medium of instruction in black schools, which led to the Soweto uprising, confirmed the hated status of the language for many urban Africans, which persists to this day.

Contrary to popular belief outside South Africa, the majority of Afrikaans-speakers are not white but coloured, and the language, far from dying out, is in fact understood by more South Africans than any other language. It's the predominant tongue in the Western and Northern Cape provinces, and in the Free State is the language of the media.

Afrikaans signs

Bed en Ontbyt	Bed and breakfast	Kantoor	Office
Derde	Third	Kerk	Church
Dankie	Thank you	Kort	Short
Doeane	Customs	Links	Left
Drankwinkel	Liquor shop	Lughawe	Airport
Droe vrugte	Dry fruit	Mans	Men
Eerste	First	Mark	Market
Vrugte	Fruit	Ompad	Detour
Geen ingang	No entry	Pad	Road
Gevaar	Danger	Padwerke voor	Road works ahead
Grens	Border	Pastorie	Parsonage
Hoof	Main	Perron	Platform (train station)
Hoog	High	Plaas	Farm
Ingang	Entry	Poskantoor	Post office
Inligting	Information	Regs	Right

Ry	Go	Swembad	Swimming pool
Sentrum	Centre	Toegang	Admission
Singel	Crescent	Tweede	Second
Slaghuis	Butcher	Verbode	Prohibited
Stadig	Slow	Verkeer	Traffic
Stad	City	Versigtig	Carefully
Stad sentrum	City/town centre	Vierde	Fourth
Stasie	Station	Vrouens	Women
Straat	Street	Vyfde	Fifth
Strand	Beach		

The Nguni group

Zulu (or isiZulu), the most widely spoken black African language in South Africa, is understood by around twelve million people. It's the mother tongue of residents of the southeastern parts of the country, including the whole of KwaZulu-Natal, the eastern Free State, southern Mpumalanga and Gauteng. Some linguists believe that Zulu's broad reach could make it an alternative to English as a South African *lingua franca*. Don't confuse Zulu with **Fanakalo**, which is a pidgin Zulu mixed with other languages. Still sometimes spoken on the mines, it is not popular with most Zulu speakers, though many white South Africans tend to believe it is.

For all practical purposes, **siSwati**, the language spoken in Swaziland, is almost identical to Zulu, but for historical reasons has developed its own identity. The same applies to **Ndebele**, which shares around 95 percent in common with Zulu. It broke off from Zulu (around the same time as siSwati) when a group of Zulu-speakers fled north to escape the expansionism of Shaka. Ndebele is now spoken in pockets of Gauteng and North West provinces as well as throughout southern Zimbabwe.

Xhosa (an example of a word beginning with a click sound) is Nelson Mandela's mother tongue, which he shares with seven million other South Africans, predominantly in the Eastern Cape. The language is also spoken by Africans in the Western Cape, most of whom are concentrated in Cape Town.

The Sotho group

Northern Sotho dialects, which are numerous and diverse, are spoken by around 2.5 million people in a huge arc of South Africa that takes in the country around the Kruger National Park, around to the Botswana border and south from there to Pretoria. **Southern Sotho**, one of the first African languages to be written, is spoken in the Free State, parts of Gauteng, as well as Lesotho and the areas of the Eastern Cape bordering it.

Tswana, also characterized by a great diversity of dialects, is geographically the most widespread language in southern Africa, and is the principal language of Botswana. In South Africa its dialects are dispersed through the Northern Cape, the Free State and North West provinces.

As with the Nguni languages, the distinctions between the languages in the Sotho group owe more to history, politics and geography than to pure linguistic factors; speakers of some Northern Sotho dialects can understand some dialects of Tswana more readily than they can other Northern Sotho dialects.

Pronouncing place names

The largest number of unfamilar place names that visitors are likely to encounter in South Africa are of Afrikaans origin, followed by names with origins in the Nguni group of languages. **Afrikaans** and English names are found across the country, while African names tend to be more localized, according to the predominant language in that area. **Nguni group** pronunciations generally apply in the Eastern Cape, KwaZulu-Natal, parts of Mpumalanga and Swaziland, while **Sotho group** names will be found in North West province, Limpopo, the Northern Cape, Free State and parts of Gauteng. Sometimes you'll encounter names with **Khoisan** derivations, such as "Tsitsikamma" (in which the *ts* is pronounced as in "tsunami"). The pronunciation tips below are intended as a guide and are neither comprehensive nor definitive.

Afrikaans

In common with other Germanic languages, Afrikaans has a number of consonants that are **guttural**. Apart from these, most consonant sounds will be unproblematic for English speakers. However Afrikaans has numerous vowels and diphthongs, which have rough English equivalents but which are frequently spelled in an unfamiliar way – take, for example, the variation in the pronunciation of the letter "e" in the list below.

Vowels and diphthongs

a as in Kakamas	u as in pup
aa as in Braamfontein	a as in car
ae as in Haenertsburg	a as in car but slightly lengthened
aai as in Smitswinkelbaai	y as in dry
au as in Augrabies	o as in blow
ar as in Garies	u as in burrow
e as in Bontebok	er as in rubber, but clipped
e as in Clarens	e as in angel
e as in Hemel-en-Aarde	ee as in beer
ee as in Riebeek	ee as in beer
ei as in Bloemfontein	ai as in pain
eu as in Keurboomstrand	u as in cure
i as in Calitzdorp	e as in angel
ie as in Diepwalle	i as in pick
o as in Bontebok	o as in cork, but clipped
oe as in Bloemfontein	oo as in book
oo as in Kloof	oo as in boor
ou as in Oudrif	o as in wrote
u as in Wuppertaal	i as in pick
ui as in Nelspruit	a as in gate
uu as in Suurbraak	o as in wrote
y as in Vanrhynsdorp	ai as in pain

Consonants

d as in Suikerbosrand	t as in runt
g as in Magersfontein	guttural ch as in the Scottish loch
tj as in Matjiesfontein	k as in key
v as in Nyslvlei	f as in fig
w as in Waterkant	v as in vase

Nguni group

The clicks in Nguni languages are the most unfamiliar and difficult sounds for English-speakers to pronounce. The three basic clicks – which, as it happens, occur in the names of three places featured in the Wild Coast section of chapter 4 – are: the **dental click** (transliterated using "c", as in the **C**webe Nature Reserve) made by pulling the tongue away from the front teeth as one would when expressing disapproval in "tsk tsk"; the **palatal click** (transliterated "q", as in **Q**holorha Mouth) made by pulling the tongue away from the palate as you would when trying to replicate the sound of a bubbly cork being popped; and the **lateral click** (transliterated "x", as in N**x**axo Mouth), made by pulling away the tongue from the side teeth. To complicate matters each click can be pronounced in one of three ways (aspirated, nasalized or delayed) and may change when spoken in combination with other consonants.

Vowels

a as in Kwa**Z**ulu	a as in f**a**ther
e as in Cw**e**be	e as in b**e**nd
i as in Kwambonamb**i**	ee as in fl**ee**
o as in Umk**o**maas	a as in t**a**ll
u as in Hl**u**hluwe	u as in p**u**t

Consonants

d**l** as in **Dl**inza	aspirated ll as in the Welsh **Ll**ewellyn
g as in Haga-Ha**g**a	hard g as in hu**g**

h**l** as in **Hl**uhluwe	aspirated ll as in the Welsh Llewellyn (though often pronounced like the shl in **shl**emiel by English-speakers)
p**h** as in M**ph**ephu	p as in **p**ass followed followed by a rapid rush of air
r as in Q**h**olorha	guttural ch as in the Scottish lo**ch**
t**y** as in Idu**ty**wa	approximately the initial sound in **tu**be

Sotho group

Vowels

a as in Th**a**ba	a as in f**a**ther
e as in Mots**e**kuoa	e as in h**e**
o as in Mants**e**bo	o as in b**o**re, but curtailed
u as in B**u**tha	u as in f**u**ll

Consonants

j as in Ha-Le**j**one	y as in **y**es
h**l** as in **Hl**otse	aspirated ll as in the Welsh **Ll**ewellyn (often pronounced like the shl in **shl**emiel by English speakers)
p**h** as in Ma**ph**utseng	p as in **p**ool
t**h** as in **Th**aba	t as in **t**ar

Basic greetings and farewells

ENGLISH	AFRIKAANS	NORTHERN SOTHO	SESOTHO	TSWANA	XHOSA	ZULU
Yes	Ja	Ee	E!	Ee	Ewe	Yebo
No	Nee	Aowa	Tjhe	Nnyaa	Hayi	Cha
Please	Asseblief	Hle.../...hle	(Ka kopo) hle	Tsweetswee	Nceda	Uxolo
Thank you	Dankie	Ke a leboga	Ke a leboha	Ke a leboga	Enkosi	Ngiyabonga
Excuse me	Verskoon my	Tshwarelo	Ntshwaerele	Intshwarele	Uxolo	Uxolo
Good morning	Goiemore	Thobela/dumela	Dumela (ng)	Dumela	Molo/bhota	Sawubona
Good afternoon	Goeiemiddag	Thobela/dumela	Dumela (ng)	Dumela	Molo/bhoto	Sawubona
Good evening	Goeinaand	Thobela/dumela	Fonaneng	Dumela	Molo/bhota	Sawubona
Goodbye	Totsiens	Sala gabotse/ sepele gabotse	Sala(ng) hantle	Sala sentle	Nisale kakuhle	Sala kahle
See you later	Sien jou later	Re tla bonana	Re tla bonana	Ke tla go bona	Sobe sibonane	Sizobanana
Until we meet again	Totsiens	Go fihla re kopana gape	ho fihlela re bonana	Go fitlhelela re bonana gape	De sibonane kwakhona	Size sibonane
How do you do?	Aangename kennis?	Ke leboga go le tseba	Ke thabela ho o tseba	O tsogile jang?	Kunjani	Ninjani?
How are you?	Hoe gaan dit?	Le kae?	O/le sa phela?	O tsogile jang?	Kunjani?	Ninjani?
I'm fine, thanks	Goed dankie	Re gona	Ke phela hantle	Ke tsogile sentle enkosi	Ndiphilile,	Ngisaphila

Glossary

Words whose spelling makes it hard to guess how to render them have their approximate pronunciation given in italics. Where *gh* occurs in the pronunciation, it denotes the **ch** sound in the Scottish word lo**ch**. Sometimes we've used the letter "r" in the pronunciation even though the word in question doesn't contain this letter; for example, we've given the pronunciation of "Egoli" as "*air-gaw-lee*". In these instances the syllable containing the "r" is meant to represent a familiar word or sound from English; the "r" itself shouldn't be pronounced.

African In the context of South Africa, an indigenous South African

Aloe Family of spiky indigenous succulents, often with dramatic orange flowers

Apartheid (*apart-hate*) Term used from the 1940s for the National Party's official policy of "racial separation"

Arvie Afternoon

Assegai (*assa-guy*) Short stabbing spear introduced by Shaka to the Zulu armies

Baai Afrikaans word meaning "bay"; also a common suffix in place names eg Stilbaai

Bakkie (*bucky*) Light truck or van

Bantu (*bun-two*) Unscientific apartheid term for indigenous black people; in linguistics, a group of indigenous Southern African languages

Bantustan Term used under apartheid for the territories such as Transkei, reserved for Africans

Bergie A vagrant living on the slopes of Table Mountain in Cape Town

Black Imprecise term that sometimes refers collectively to Africans, Indians and coloureds, but more usually is used to mean Africans (see above)

Boer (*boor*) Literally "farmer", but also refers to early Dutch colonists at the Cape and Afrikaners

Boland (*boor-lunt*) Southern part of the Western Cape

Boma An enclosure or palisade

Boy Offensive term used to refer to an adult African man who is a servant

Bundu (approximately *boon-doo*, but with the vowels shortened) Wilderness or back country

Burgher Literally a citizen, but more specifically members of the Dutch community at the Cape in the seventeenth and eighteenth centuries

Bush See *bundu*

Bushman Southern Africa's earliest, but now almost extinct, inhabitants who lived by hunting and gathering

Bushveld Country composed largely of thorny bush

Cape Dutch Nineteenth-century, white-washed, gabled style of architecture

Ciskei (*sis-kye*) Eastern Cape region west of the Kei River, declared a "self-governing territory" for Xhosa speakers in 1972, and now reincorporated into South Africa

Cocopan Small tip truck on rails used to transport gold ore

Coloured Mulattos or people of mixed race

Commandos Burgher military units during the Frontier and Boer wars

Dagga (*dugh-a*) Marijuana

Dagha (*dah-ga*) Mud used in indigenous construction

Dassie (*dussy*) Hyrax

Disa (*die-za*) One of twenty species of beautiful indigenous orchids, most famous of which is the red disa or "Pride of Table Mountain"

Dominee (*dour-min-ee*) Reverend (abbreviated to DS)

Donga Dry, eroded ditch

Dorp Country town or village (derived from Afrikaans)

Drift Fording point in a river (derived from Afrikaans)

Drostdy (*dross-tea*) Historically, the building of the *landdrost* or magistrate

Egoli (*air-gaw-lee*) Zulu name for Johannesburg (literally "city of gold")

Fanakalo or **fanagalo** (*fun-a-galaw*) Pidgin mixture of English, Zulu and Afrikaans used to facilitate communication between white foremen and African workers on the mines or farms

Fundi Expert

Fynbos (*fayn-boss*) Term for vast range of fine-leafed species that predominate in the southern part of the Western Cape (see p.161)

Girl Offensive term used to refer to an African woman who is a servant

Gogga (*gho-gha*) Creepy crawly or insect

Griqua Person of mixed white, Bushman and Hottentot descent

Group Areas Act Now-defunct law passed in 1950 that provided for the establishment of separate areas for each "racial group"

Highveld High-lying areas of Gauteng and Mpumalanga

Homeland See Bantustan

Hottentot Now unfashionable term for indigenous Khoisan herders encountered by the first settlers at the Cape

Impi Zulu regiment

Indaba Zulu term meaning a group discussion and now used in South African English for any meeting or conference

Inkatha (*in-ka-ta*) Fiercely nationalist Zulu political party, formed in 1928 as a cultural organization

Is it? Really?

Jislaaik! (*yis-like*) Exclamation equivalent to "Geez!" or "Crikey!"

Joeys Affectionate abbreviation for Johannesburg

Jol Party, celebration

Just now In a while

Kaffir Highly objectionable term of abuse for Africans

Karoo Arid plateau that occupies a large proportion of the South African interior

Khoikhoi (*ghoy-ghoy*) Self-styled name of South Africa's original herding inhabitants

Kloof (*klo-ef*, rhymes with "boor") Ravine or gorge

Knobkerrie Wooden club

Kokerboom (both the first and last syllable rhyme with "boor") Quiver tree – a type of aloe found in the Northern Cape

Kopje Dutch spelling of *koppie*

Koppie Hillock

Kraal Enclosure of huts for farm animals or collection of traditional huts occupied by an extended family

Kramat (*crum-mutt*) Shrine of a Muslim holy man

Krans (*crunce*) Sheer cliff face

Laager (*lager*) A circular encampment of ox wagons, used as fortification by Voortrekkers

Lapa Courtyard of group of Ndebele houses; also used to described an enclosed area at safari camps, where braais are held

Lebowa (*lab-o-a*) Now-defunct homeland for North Sotho speakers

Lekker Nice

Lobola (*la-ball-a*) Bride price, paid by an African man to his wife's parents

Location Old-fashioned term for segregated African area on the outskirts of a town or farm

Lowveld Low-lying subtropical region of Mpumalanga and Limpopo provinces

Malay Misnomer for Cape Muslims of Asian descent

Matjieshuis (*mikeys-hace*) Reed hut

Mbaqanga (*m-ba-kung-a*) A genre of music that originated in Soweto in the 1960s

Mbira (*m-beer-a*) African thumb piano, often made with a gourd

MK Umkhonto we Sizwe (Spear of the Nation), the armed wing of the ANC, now incorporated into the national army

Mlungu (*m-loon-goo*) African term for a white person, equivalent to honkie

Moffie (*mawf-ee*) Gay person

Muti (*moo-tee*) See *umuthi*

Nek Saddle between two mountains

Nguni (*n-goo-nee*) Group of southeastern Bantu-speaking people comprising Zulu, Xhosa and Swazi

Nkosi Sikelel 'i Afrika "God Bless Africa", anthem of the ANC and now of South Africa

Nyanga (*nyun-ga*) Traditional healer

Outspan A place set aside for animals to rest; can also mean to unharness oxen from a wagon

Pass Document that Africans used to have to carry at all times, which essentially rendered them aliens in their own country

Pastorie (*puss-tour-ee*) Parsonage

Platteland (*plutta-lunt*) Country districts

Poort Narrow pass through mountains along river course

Pronk (*prawnk*) Characteristic jump of springbok or impala

Protea National flower of South Africa

Qwaqwa Now-defunct homeland for South Sotho speakers

Raadsaal (the "d" is pronounced "t") Council or parliament building

Restcamp Accommodation for visitors to national parks

Robot Traffic light

Rondavel (*ron-daa-vil*, with the stress on the middle syllable) Circular building based on traditional African huts

SABC South African Broadcasting Authority

Sangoma (*sun-gom-a*) Traditional spirit medium and healer

Shebeen (*sha-bean*) Unlicensed tavern

Shell Ultra City Clean, bright stops along major national roads, with a filling station, restaurant, shop and sometimes a hotel.

Sjambok (*sham-bok*) Rawhide whip

Southeaster Prevailing wind in the Western Cape

Spaza shops (*spa-za*) Small stall or kiosk

Strandloper Name given by the Dutch to the indigenous people of the Cape; literally beachcomber

Stoep Veranda

Tackie Sneakers or plimsolls

Township Areas set aside under apartheid for Africans

Transkei (*trans-kye*) Now-defunct homeland for Xhosa speakers

Trekboer (*trek-boor*) Nomadic Afrikaner farmers, usually in the eighteenth and nineteenth century

Umuthi (*oo-moo-tee*) Traditional herbal medicine

Velskoen (*fel-scoon*) Rough suede shoes

Vlei (*flay*) Swamp

VOC Verenigde Oostindische Compagnie, the Dutch East India Company

Voortrekker (the first syllable rhymes with "boor") Dutch burghers who migrated inland in their ox wagons in the nineteenth century to escape British colonialism

ZAR Zuid Afrikaansche Republiek; an independent Boer republic that included present-day Gauteng, Mpumalanga and Limpopo provinces and which was Britain's main opponent in the Anglo-Boer War

Food and drink

Amarula Liqueur made from the berries of the marula tree

Begrafnisrys (*ba-ghruff-niss-race*) Literally "funeral rice"; traditional Cape Muslim dish of yellow rice cooked with raisins

Biltong Sun-dried salted strip of meat, chewed as a snack

Blatjang (*blutt-young*) Cape Muslim chutney that has become a standard condiment on South African dinner tables

Bobotie (*ba-boor-tea*) Traditional Cape curried mince topped with a savoury custard and often cooked with apricots and almonds

Boerekos (*boor-a-coss*) Farm food, usually consisting of loads of meat and vegetables cooked using butter and sugar

Boerewors (*boor-a-vorce*) Spicy lengths of sausage that are *de rigueur* at braais

Bokkoms Dried fish, much like salt fish

Braai or **braaivleis** (*bry-flace*) Barbecue

Bredie Cape vegetable and meat stew

Bunny chow Originally a curried takeaway served in a scooped-out half loaf of bread, but now often wrapped in a roti; a KwaZulu-Natal staple

Cane or **cane spirit** A potent vodka-like spirit distilled from sugar cane and generally mixed with a soft drink such as Coke

Cap Classique Sparkling wine fermented in the bottle in exactly the same way as Champagne; also called Méthode Cap Classic

Cape gooseberry Fruit of the physalis; a sweet yellow berry

Cape salmon or **geelbek** (*ghear-l-beck*) Delicious firm-fleshed sea fish (unrelated to Northern-hemisphere salmon).

Cape Velvet A sweet liqueur-and-cream dessert beverage that resembles Irish Cream liqueur

Denningvleis (*den-ning-flace*) Spicy traditional Cape lamb stew

Frikkadel Fried onion and meat balls

Geelbek See Cape salmon

Hanepoort (*harner-poort*) Delicious sweet dessert grape

Kabeljou (cobble-yo) Common South African marine fish, also called *kob*

Kerrievis (*kerry-fiss*) See Pickled fish

Kingklip Highly prized deepwater fish caught along the Atlantic and Indian ocean coasts

Kob See *kabeljou*

Koeksister (*cook-sister*) Deep-fried plaited doughnut, dripping with syrup

Maas or **amasi** or **amaas** Traditional African beverage consisting of naturally soured milk, available as a packaged dairy product in supermarkets

Maaskaas Cottage cheese made from *maas*

Mageu or **mahewu** or **maheu** (*ma-gh-weh*) Traditional African beer made from maize meal and water, now packaged and commercially available

Malva Very rich and very sweet traditional baked Cape dessert

Mampoer (*mum-poor*) Moonshine; home-distilled spirit made from soft fruit, commonly peaches

Mealie See *mielie*

Melktert (*melk-tairt*) Traditional Cape custard pie

Mielie Maize

Mielie pap (*mealy pup*) Maize porridge, varying from a thin mixture to a stiff one that can resemble polenta

Mopani worm (*ma-parny*) Black spotted caterpillar that is a delicacy among Africans in some parts of the country

Mqomboti (*m-qom-booty*) Traditional African beer made from fermented sorghum

Musselcracker Large-headed fish with powerful jaws and firm, white flesh

Naartjie (*nar-chee*) Tangerine or mandarin

Pap (*pup*) Porridge

Peri-peri Delicious hottish spice of Portuguese origin commonly used with grilled chicken

Perlemoen (*pear-la-moon*) Abalone

Pickled fish Traditional Cape dish of fish preserved with onions, vinegar and curry; available tinned in supermarkets

Pinotage A uniquely South African cultivar hybridized from Pinot Noir and Hermitage grapes and from which a wine of the same name is made

Potjiekos or potjie (*poy-key-kos*) Food cooked slowly over embers in a three-legged cast-iron pot

Putu (*poo-too*) Traditional African *mielie pap* (see above) prepared until it forms dry crumbs

Rooibos (*roy-boss*) **tea** Indigenous herbal tea; see p.303

Roti A chapati; called *rooti* in the Western Cape

Rusks Tasty biscuits made from sweetened bread that has been slow-cooked

Salmon trout Freshwater fish that is often smoked to create a cheaper and pretty good imitation of smoked salmon

Salomie Cape version of a roti; unleavened bread

Sambals (*sam-bills*) Accompaniments, such as chopped bananas, green peppers, desiccated coconut and chutney, served with Cape curries

Samp Traditional African dish of broken maize kernels, frequently cooked with beans

Skokiaan (*skok-ee-yan*) Potent home-brew

Smoorsnoek (*smore-snook*) Smoked *snoek*

Snoek (*snook*) Large fish that features in many traditional Cape recipes

Sosatie (*so-sah-ti*) Spicy skewered mince

Spanspek (*spon-speck*) A sweet melon

Steenbras (*ste-en-bruss*) A delicious white-fleshed fish

Van der Hum South African *naartjie*-flavoured liqueur

Vetkoek (*fet-cook*) Deep-fried doughnut-like cake

Waterblommetjiebredie (*vata-blom-a-key-bree-dee*) Cape meat stew made with waterlily rhizomes

Witblits (*vit-blitz*) Moonshine

Yellowtail Delicious darkish-fleshed marine fish

Rough Guides

advertiser

Rough Guides travel...

...music & reference

Africa & Middle East

Cape Town
Egypt
The Gambia
Jordan
Kenya
Marrakesh
  DIRECTIONS
Morocco
South Africa, Lesotho
  & Swaziland
Syria
Tanzania
Tunisia
West Africa
Zanzibar
Zimbabwe

Travel Theme guides

First-Time Around the
  World
First-Time Asia
First-Time Europe
First-Time Latin
  America
Skiing & Snowboarding
  in North America
Travel Online
Travel Health
Walks in London & SE
  England
Women Travel

Restaurant guides

French Hotels &
  Restaurants
London
New York
San Francisco

Maps

Algarve
Amsterdam
Andalucia & Costa del Sol
Argentina
Athens
Australia

Baja California
Barcelona
Berlin
Boston
Brittany
Brussels
Chicago
Crete
Croatia
Cuba
Cyprus
Czech Republic
Dominican Republic
Dubai & UAE
Dublin
Egypt
Florence & Siena
Frankfurt
Greece
Guatemala & Belize
Iceland
Ireland
Kenya
Lisbon
London
Los Angeles
Madrid
Mexico
Miami & Key West
Morocco
New York City
New Zealand
Northern Spain
Paris
Peru
Portugal
Prague
Rome
San Francisco
Sicily
South Africa
South India
Sri Lanka
Tenerife
Thailand
Toronto
Trinidad & Tobago

Tuscany
Venice
Washington DC
Yucatán Peninsula

Dictionary
Phrasebooks

Czech
Dutch
Egyptian Arabic
EuropeanLanguages
  (Czech, French,
  German, Greek, Italian,
  Portuguese, Spanish)
French
German
Greek
Hindi & Urdu
Hungarian
Indonesian
Italian
Japanese
Mandarin Chinese
Mexican Spanish
Polish
Portuguese
Russian
Spanish
Swahili
Thai
Turkish
Vietnamese

Music Guides

The Beatles
Bob Dylan
Cult Pop
Classical Music
Country Music
Elvis
Hip Hop
House
Irish Music
Jazz
Music USA
Opera
Reggae

Rock
Techno
World Music (2 vols)

History Guides

China
Egypt
England
France
India
Islam
Italy
Spain
USA

Reference Guides

Books for Teenagers
Children's Books, 0–5
Children's Books, 5–11
Cult Fiction
Cult Football
Cult Movies
Cult TV
Ethical Shopping
Formula 1
The iPod, iTunes &
  Music Online
The Internet
Internet Radio
James Bond
Kids' Movies
Lord of the Rings
Muhammed Ali
Man Utd
Personal Computers
Pregnancy & Birth
Shakespeare
Superheroes
Unexplained
  Phenomena
The Universe
Videogaming
Weather
Website Directory

ROUGH GUIDES ADVERTISER

Also! More than 120 Rough Guide music CDs are available from all good book
and record stores. Listen in at www.worldmusic.net

Algarve • Amsterdam •
Antigua & Barbuda • Athens • Barbados • Barcelona •
Bruges • Cancún & Cozumel • Costa Brava •
Edinburgh • Florence • Ibiza & Formentera •
Lisbon • London • Madrid • Mallorca • Malta & Gozo •
Marrakesh & Essaouira • New Orleans •
New York City • Paris • Prague • Rome •
San Francisco • Tenerife & La Gomera •
Venice • Washington DC

US$10.99 · CAN$15.99 · £6.99
www.roughguides.com

Visit us online

roughguides.com

Information on over 25,000 destinations around the world

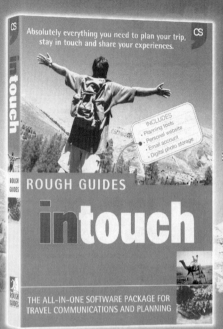

Absolutely everything you need to plan your trip, stay in touch and share your experiences.

INCLUDES
• Planning tools
• Personal website
• Email account
• Digital photo storage

ROUGH GUIDES

intouch

THE ALL-IN-ONE SOFTWARE PACKAGE FOR
TRAVEL COMMUNICATIONS AND PLANNING

ROUGH
GUIDES

A
NEW CONCEPT
IN TRAVEL

ROUGH GUIDES SOFTWARE
Share your adventures on the move

Rough Guides have launched **intouch**, a new all in one software package for planning your trip and staying in touch with people back home before, during and after your travels.

Create an itinerary and budget using on-screen information and maps, and take advantage of the diary to keep family and friends informed of your whereabouts.

The diary can be linked to your mobile phone so that you can send a text message, **intouch** will automatically send an email or cheap SMS to those listed on your account.

You can also post photos and diary entries online and then download them to make a journal on your return.

Rough Guides **intouch** is easy to install and you don't need to take anything with you – just hit the synchronize button and then use it from any internet café in the world.

Rough Guides **intouch** includes:
Planning tools
Free email address
Free personal website
Digital photo storage   And much more......

£5 OFF your purchase of Rough Guides **intouch** if you buy online at
www.roughguidesintouch.com reference code: Rough Guide Books

Recommended retail price £24.99 available through leading retailers e.g. WH Smith, Waterstones and PC World

WHSmith

NOTES

NOTES

ROUGH GUIDES ADVERTISER

small print and

Index

A Rough Guide to Rough Guides

In the summer of 1981, Mark Ellingham, a recent graduate from Bristol University, was travelling round Greece and couldn't find a guidebook that really met his needs. On the one hand there were the student guides, insistent on saving every last cent, and on the other the heavyweight cultural tomes whose authors seemed to have spent more time in a research library than lounging away the afternoon at a taverna or on the beach.

In a bid to avoid getting a job, Mark and a small group of writers set about creating their own guidebook. It was a guide to Greece that aimed to combine a journalistic approach to description with a thoroughly practical approach to travellers' needs – a guide that would incorporate culture, history and contemporary insights with a critical edge, together with up-to-date, value-for-money listings. Back in London, Mark and the team finished their Rough Guide, as they called it, and talked Routledge into publishing the book.

That first *Rough Guide to Greece*, published in 1982, was a student scheme that became a publishing phenomenon. The immediate success of the book – with numerous reprints and a Thomas Cook Prize shortlisting – spawned a series that rapidly covered dozens of destinations. Rough Guides had a ready market among low-budget backpackers, but soon also acquired a much broader and older readership that relished Rough Guides' wit and inquisitiveness as much as their enthusiastic, critical approach. Everyone wants value for money, but not at any price.

Rough Guides soon began supplementing the "rougher" information about hostels and low-budget listings with the kind of detail on restaurants and quality hotels that independent-minded visitors on any budget might expect, whether on business in New York or trekking in Thailand.

These days the guides – distributed worldwide by the Penguin group – offer recommendations from shoestring to luxury and cover more than 200 destinations around the globe, including almost every country in the Americas and Europe, more than half of Africa and most of Asia and Australasia. Our ever-growing team of authors and photographers is spread all over the world, particularly in Europe, the USA and Australia.

In 1994, we published the *Rough Guide to World Music* and *Rough Guide to Classical Music*, and a year later the *Rough Guide to the Internet*. All three books have become benchmark titles in their fields – which encouraged us to expand into other areas of publishing, mainly around popular culture. Rough Guides now publish:

- Travel guides to more than 200 worldwide destinations
- Dictionary phrasebooks to 22 major languages
- History guides ranging from Ireland to Islam
- Maps printed on rip-proof and waterproof Polyart™ paper
- Music guides running the gamut from Opera to Elvis
- Restaurant guides to London, New York and San Francisco
- Reference books on topics as diverse as the Weather and Shakespeare
- Sports guides from Formula 1 to Man Utd
- Pop culture books from *Lord of the Rings* to Cult TV
- World Music CDs in association with World Music Network

Visit **www.roughguides.com** to see our latest publications.

Rough Guide credits

Text editors: Richard Lim, Fran Sandham, Claire Saunders and Gavin Thomas
Layout: Amit Verma
Cartography: Manish Chandra
Picture research: Jj Luck
Proofreader: Susannah Wight
Editorial: **London** Martin Dunford, Kate Berens, Geoff Howard, Ruth Blackmore, Polly Thomas, Clifton Wilkinson, Alison Murchie, Sally Schafer, Karoline Densley, Andy Turner, Ella O'Donnell, Keith Drew, Edward Aves, Andrew Lockett, Joe Staines, Duncan Clark, Peter Buckley, Matthew Milton, Daniel Crewe, Nikki Birrell, Chloë Thomson, Helen Marsden; **New York** Andrew Rosenberg, Richard Koss, Chris Barsanti, Steven Horak, AnneLise Sorensen, Amy Hegarty
Design & Pictures: **London** Simon Bracken, Dan May, Diana Jarvis, Mark Thomas, Harriet Mills, Chloë Roberts; **Delhi** Madhulita Mohapatra, Umesh Aggarwal, Ajay Verma, Jessica Subramanian

Production: Julia Bovis, Sophie Hewat, Katherine Owers
Cartography: **London** Maxine Repath, Ed Wright, Katie Lloyd-Jones; **Delhi** Rajesh Chhibber, Jai Prakash Mishra, Ashutosh Bharti, Rajesh Mishra, Animesh Pathak, Jasbir Sandhu, Karobi Gogoi
Online: **New York** Jennifer Gold, Suzanne Welles; **Delhi** Manik Chauhan, Narender Kumar, Shekhar Jha, Rakesh Kumar, Lalit Sharma
Marketing & Publicity: **London** Richard Trillo, Niki Hanmer, David Wearn, Demelza Dallow; **New York** Geoff Colquitt, Megan Kennedy, Milena Perez; **Delhi** Reem Khokhar
Custom publishing and foreign rights: Philippa Hopkins
Finance: Gary Singh
Manager India: Punita Singh
Series editor: Mark Ellingham
PA to Managing Director: Megan McIntyre
Managing Director: Kevin Fitzgerald

Publishing information

This fourth edition published June 2005 by
Rough Guides Ltd,
80 Strand, London WC2R 0RL.
345 Hudson St, 4th Floor,
New York, NY 10014, USA.
14 Local Shopping Centre, Panchsheel Park,
New Delhi 110017, India.
Distributed by the Penguin Group
Penguin Books Ltd,
80 Strand, London WC2R 0RL
Penguin Putnam, Inc.,
375 Hudson Street, NY 10014, USA
Penguin Group (Australia)
250 Camberwell Road, Camberwell,
Victoria 3124, Australia
Penguin Books Canada Ltd,
10 Alcorn Avenue, Toronto, Ontario,
Canada M4V 1E4
Penguin Group (New Zealand),
Cnr Rosedale and Airborne Roads,
Albany, Auckland, New Zealand

Typeset in Bembo and Helvetica to an original design by Henry Iles.

Printed in Italy by LegoPrint S.p.A

© Tony Pinchuck, Barbara McCrea, Donald Reid and Greg Mthembu-Salter 2005

976pp includes index
A catalogue record for this book is available from the British Library

ISBN 1-84353-398-7

The publishers and authors have done their best to ensure the accuracy and currency of all the information in **The Rough Guide to South Africa**, however, they can accept no responsibility for any loss, injury, or inconvenience sustained by any traveller as a result of information or advice contained in the guide.

1   3   5   7   9   8   6   4   2

Help us update

We've gone to a lot of effort to ensure that the fourth edition of **The Rough Guide to South Africa** is accurate and up-to-date. However, things change – places get "discovered", opening hours are notoriously fickle, restaurants and rooms raise prices or lower standards. If you feel we've got it wrong or left something out, we'd like to know, and if you can remember the address, the price, the time, the phone number, so much the better.

We'll credit all contributions, and send a copy of the next edition (or any other Rough Guide if you prefer) for the best letters. Everyone who writes to us and isn't already a subscriber will receive a copy of our full-colour thrice-yearly newsletter. Please mark letters: **"Rough Guide South Africa Update"** and send to: Rough Guides, 80 Strand, London WC2R 0RL, or Rough Guides, 4th Floor, 345 Hudson St, New York, NY 10014. Or send an email to **mail@roughguides.com**

Have your questions answered and tell others about your trip at **www.roughguides.atinfopop.com**

Acknowledgements

Tony would like to thank our hawk-eyed editor Richard Lim for his insightful comments, his improvements to the text, and for keeping the book on track and the authors on their toes. An especially big thanks to Jacqui Kadey for going to the ends of the earth in pursuing research and for being a very good friend. My warmest gratitude to Sue Cooper and Dave, Daniel and Kate Pinchuck for being like a family and for helping me hold onto my sanity, sometimes for as long as half a day at a time; and an extra special thanks to Gabriel Pinchuck for his ceaseless pertinent and impertinent questioning.

Barbara would like to thank Richard Lim for his constant cheerfulness and astonishing abilities as an editor. Special thanks to Tony Pinchuck for keeping the book going through difficult times when I couldn't, and for the support of contributors Sam Black and Jacqui Kadey. Thanks, too, to the friends and family members who supplied help and information, and especially to Jimmy Kyriacou for always being there for me. Thanks also to David Bristow and staff at Getaway for Kruger info, Jeanne Berger for help with Books, and to South African National Parks. Thanks to the owners and staff of the many places we stayed, including the *Tuishuise* in Cradock; *Trymore Cottage*, Graaf-Reinett; *Lemoenkloof*, Paarl; *Matoppo Inn*, Beaufort West; *Mala Mala*, Sabi Sands; *Bonne Esperance*, Stellenbosch; *Crystal Springs Mountain Lodge*, Mpumalanga; *Plumwood Inn*, Franschhoek; *Rissington Inn*, Hazyview; *Kersefontein Farm*, West Coast; and *Les Cascades*, Bantry Bay. Thanks also to Beneta Bester at Karukareb, Kiewiet Bester at the *Riviera Hotel*, Licia Erasmus at *Daisy Cottage*, Francois Visser at *Die Opstal*, Hannes Kleynhans at the *Beach Camp*, Rod Freemantle at Redelinghuys Manor, Rob at Cape Sport, Cathy at *Friday Island* and Gregg Stopforth. And finally thanks to all the unmentioned friends, readers and people we met on our travels who gave us their time and information. I dedicate this book, as ever, to Gabriel Pinchuck for being an enthusiastic little travelling companion.

Jens would particularly like to thank Oupa Modise at Bojanala Platinum District Municipality (Rustenburg), Marika Grootboom in Springbok's tourist office, Niel Simmonds in Upington, the lovely ladies at Maseru's information centre, loads of other people whose names I never asked for, and the insane minibus driver who got us all slip-sliding back home safely – if at times sideways – through the snow drifts of the Maloti Mountains.

Jacqui thanks Tony Pinchuck for incredible guidance and assistance, Andy Stewart and Christina Dimopoulous for being great travelling companions, George Dimopoulos for the loan of his car, Dirk Ordendaal for help with the gay section of Cape Town, Di MacKenzie for assistance and accommodation in Knysna, and Lori Kelly for help with the north coast of Kwa-Zulu Natal. Thanks also go to Nita Ross of Wild Coast Holiday Reservations, Dave Martin of the *Bulungula Backpackers Lodge*, Karen Barnard of KwaZulu-Natal Tourism and Graham Chennels of Zululand Adventures.

Readers' letters

Thanks to all the readers for taking the trouble to write and email in with comments and suggestions (and apologies to anyone whose name we might have inadvertently misspelt or omitted):

Olaf Ahlers, Renee Ambito, Axel Armbruster, Ian Armstrong, Pieter Badenhorst, Tony Beck, Greg Bertram, Susan Bird, Zak Blackler, Eve Bluemler, Marius Brink, David Broadbent, John and Sue Bruder, Elliot Cahn, Mike Cavanagh, Lucy Chall, Tony Channell, Emily Charles and Alex Hatch, Eileen Christie, Rob Clark, Kathleen Clay, Fiona Cole, Carol and David Cooknell, Aidan Corr, Eddy le Couvreur, Meg Cowper-Lewis, Simon Crane, Kelly Cross, Erika Cule, Neil Cutliffe, Ruth Denton, Dave and Melanie Dudley, Moira Dunworth, Doris Eisenegger, Peter and Rensia Ellis, Simon Eriksen, Huw Evans, Norman Farnworth, Jill Foster, Michael Fox, Jens Friis, Vanya Gerstemann, Heather Giannandrea, Tony Gloster, Stuart Goldberg, Meg Goodare, Saimon Gordon, Hana Hall, Carol T. Hamilton, Tony Handy, Cathy Harris, Haley Harvey, Gavin Heath, Geoff Higo, Marietjie Hitge, Simon Hoten, David Hoult, Thomas Huettner, Bob Hyde, Heinz Jahns, Adrian James, Catherine Junor, R.A. Kastell, Carsten Klatt, Uli Kress, Steve Larson, Joan and Howard Legg, Leon and Shelley, Stella Macdougall, Tom Maloney, Linda Mannheim, Genevieve Marshall, Shelley Mason, Helen McConachie, Kim McConkey and Chandra

Ramarao, Roger Meadows, Jo Moskon, Elaine Moss, Elizabeth Murray, Wendy Newcomb, Dwight Newman, Alex Nicolic, David Pearson, Barbara Pellow, Sophie Perry, Martin Price, Joyce Plotnikoff, H.R. Prowse, Tessa and Henry Rajak, Stephen Rea, Carolyn Rigg, Klemens Riha, Joanne Rushby, Kathleen Rushforth, Chihana Schiffer, Noam Schimmel, Nick Schmidt, Rolf Schmidt, Malcolm Speight, Ed Spencer, Conrad Stevens, Karl Heinz Stocker, Patricia Thornton, Tony and Alethea, Jerry van Beers, Amiene van der Merwe, Lego van Ettem, Helen and Martin Vegoda, Craig Von Hagen, Angela Warren, Nigel Watson and Annie Lavery, Hans Wenderoth, Wendy Wheawall, Sue White, George Williamson, Lloyd Wingate, Tom Wiser, Colin Wright, V. Wynn-Williams.

Photo credits

Cover credits

Main front picture: Table Mountain © Alamy

Back top picture: Parliament House, Cape Town © Corbis

Back lower picture: Fishermen, Durban © Pictures Colour Library

Small front top picture: African penguins © Getty

Small front lower picture: Wild flowers © Alamy

Colour introduction

Crossing the N2 highway © Graeme Robinson/iAfrika Photos

Rondavels, Eastern Cape © Branko de Lang/ iAfrika Photos

The Bo-Kaap © Eric Miller/iAfrika Photos

Whale breaching © South African Tourism

Cape Dutch House © Alain Proust/Cape Photo Library

Gemsbok, Kgalagadi Transfrontier park © Alain Proust/Cape Photo Library

Table Mountain Cableway © Christophe Armand/Cape Photo Library

Springbuck, Kgalagadi Transfrontier Park © South African Tourism

White-painted Xhosa initiates © Per-Anders Pettersson/iAfrika Photos

Abseiling on Table Mountain © Anna Zieminski/iAfrika Photos

Beach at Ballito © Keith Young/iAfrika Photos

Bushman paintings, Drakensberg Battle Cave © David Rogers/Cape Photo Library

Things not to miss

01 Pounding surf at sunset, Wild Coast © South African Tourism

02 The Bo-Kaap © Eric Miller/iAfrika Photos

03 Canopy tours, Storms River © Jeremy Jowell/Cape Photo Library

04 *Tau Lodge*, Madikwe reserve © Fullhouse/Tau Lodge

05 Rafting © Darron Raw/Swazi Trails

06 Skull of Mrs Ples © Shaun Harris/iAfrika Photos

07 Drakensberg peaks © Richard Van Tyneveld/Cape Photo Library

08 Game trails © Robert J. Ross/iAfrika Photos

09 Gemsbok, Kgalagadi Transfrontier park © Alain Proust/Cape Photo Library

10 Winelands architecture © Alain Proust/ Cape Photo Library

11 Swartberg Pass © Geoff Spiby/Cape Photo Library

12 Kruger National Park © Alain Proust/ iAfrika Photos

13 Aerial of Robben Island © South African Tourism

14 *Bulungula Lodge* © Dave Martin

15 On horseback, Lesotho © Richard Van Ryneveld/Cape Photo Library

16 Storms River Mouth © Elke Losskan/ Cape Photo Library

17 The Sani Pass © Ken Woods/iAfrika Photos

18 Jazz group in Jo'burg © Per-Anders Pettersson/iAfrika

19 Namaqualand © South African Tourism

20 Richtersveld Transfrontier Park © Sarel Eloff/iAfrika Photos

21 Table Mountain cableway © Christophe Armand/Cape Photo Library

22 Whale breaching © South African Tourism

23 Van loaded with crafts © Derek McKenzie/Cape Photo Library

24 Cato Manor Temple, Durban © South African Tourism

25 Hluhluwe Nature Reserve © Keith Young/ Cape Photo Library

26 Township tour © Per-Anders Pettersson/ iAfrika Photos

27 Cape Point, Cape Peninsula © South African Tourism

28 Basotho house © South African Tourism

Wildlife section

All images here © Bruce Coleman Library except:

Bonteboks © Martin Harvey/Corbis

Bushbaby © Clem Haagner; Gallo Images/ Corbis

Giraffes © Paul A. Souders/Corbis

Black and white photos

Penguins on Boulders Beach © Alain Proust/ Cape Photo Library (p.94)

Fishermen and catch, Hout Bay © Alain Proust/Cape Photo Library (p.154)

Cape Dutch House © South African Tourism (p.188)

Goat tower © Donald Reid (p.206)

The Karoo © Chad Hennin/ iAfrika Photos (p.225)

Halfmens Tree © South African Tourism (p.308)

Augrabies Falls © Anthony Bannister; Gallo Images/Corbis (p.333)

Pounding surf at sunset, Wild Coast © South African Tourism (p.364)

Church exterior, Graaff-Reinet © Alain Proust/Cape Photo Library (p.407)

Nelson Mandela Museum, Umtata © David Rogers/Cape Photo Library (p.446)

Rhino © Gert Lamprecht/ iAfrika Photos (p.458)

Victoria Market, Grey Street, Durban © Elke Losskarn/iAfrika Photos (p.474)

Mweni valley © Richard Van Ryneveld/ Cape Photo Library (p.521)

Clarens landscape © Gert Lamprecht/ Cape Photo Library (p.568)

Nelson Mandela Bridge at night, Johannesburg © Hannelie Coetzee Greatstock/Alamy (p.590)

Union Buildings, Pretoria © Charles O'Rear/ Corbis (p.635)

Tourist trucks, Pilanesberg National Reserve © Jean du Plessis/Cape Photo Library (p.652)

Kruger National Park © Eric Miller/iAfrika Photos (p.684)

Three Rondavels, © Elke Losskarn/iAfrika Photos (p.696)

Baobab tree © South African Tourism (p.728)

Harvesting tea, Tzaneen area © Peter Johnson/Corbis (p.743)

Riders, Lesotho © Earl Kowall/Corbis (p.760)

King Mswati leading tribal dance © Jesper Strudsholm/iAfrika Photos (p.810)

African crafts by roadside © Donald Reid (p.823)

Index

Map entries are in colour.

A

accommodation 58
in national parks.................74
activity sports 77
**Addo Elephant National
Park**..................377–379
Afrikaans.........................98,
204, 574, 932
Agatha 742
Agulhas National
Park 251
Ai-Ais Richtersveld
Transfrontier Park 343
AIDS 50, 863
air travel, domestic.........55
airport tax 88
Alexander Bay 358
Alexandria.....................384
Alexandria Hiking
Trail 383
Alexandria State
Forest 383
Alice..............................420
Aliwal North 425
Aliwal Shoal..................494
Amadiba Horse
Trail 434
Amakhala Game
Reserve.......................379
Amanzimtoti 493
Amatola
Mountains..........418–424
Amatola Trail.................422
Amphitheatre, the
(Royal Natal National
Park) 522, 582
ANC 595, 851
ANC archives...............420
Andriesvale...................339
Anglo-Boer War...229, 325,
326, 426, 514, 557–565,
656, 671, 688, 848
Anglo-Zulu War ...503, 554,
557–561, 847
Anreith, Anton...............145
apartheid 98, 263,
368, 402, 473, 850, 855
Apartheid Museum
(Johannesburg)..........617
apartments,
self-catering................62
Apple Express 375

architecture
Basotho............................580
Cape Dutch......................144
Arniston 251
arts and crafts
Venda 756
Zulu 554
Askham.........................339
Augrabies Falls National
Park 333–335

B

B&B accommodation 60
Babanango 560
backpacker
accommodation 61
Baden-Powell, Robert..671
Bain, Andrew Geddes ..212
Bain, Thomas 212
Baker, Sir Herbert.........610
Ballito...........................501
Banana Express 494
Barberspan Bird
Sanctuary 676
Barberton 701
Barkly East 427
Barkly West 324
Basotho architecture 580
Basotho Cultural
Village 580
Bathhurst......................396
battlefield tours ...321, 325,
418, 558
Battlefields, the (Kwa-
Zulu-Natal)........557–565
Baz Bus 52
BBC World Service.........69
beaches, conditions at...77
Beaufort West...............230
Bedford.........................400
beer 65
begging 88
Beitbridge.....................753
Bela-Bela......................733
Ben Macdhui Hiking
Trail 430
Berg River.....................299
Bergville........................514
Bethel 805
Betty's Bay 240
Bezuidenhout, Evita 291
Big Bend.......................818

Big Five 71
Big Hole
(Kimberley).................317
Biko, Steve 415, 419,
856, 907
bilharzia 48
bird-watching 178, 290,
488
Bizana...........................455
Bloemfontein....... 571–578
Bloemfontein 571
Bloemhof 681
Blood River
Battlefield 561
Bloubergstrand.............163
Bloukrans River
Bridge 285
Blue Train......................54
Blyde River Canyon.....690,
694–697
Blyde River Canyon.....694
Blydepoort....................694
Blyderivierspoort Hiking
Trail 697
Blythedale.....................502
Boer War see Anglo-Boer
War
boerekos.........................63
Boesmanskloof
Traverse 234
Bojanala Region 656
Bokkeveld Nature
Reserve.......................349
Boknes 384
Bontebok National
Park 239
booking travel online 35
books....................918–928
Bophuthatswana 656
Bosbokrand..................706
Boskloof, the 304
Bosman, Charles..........667
Bosman, Herman
Charles 667, 900, 908
Botha, P.W. 263, 857
Botsalano Game
Reserve.......................674
braais.............................63
Bredasdorp...................250
Breede River Valley 211
Brenton-on-Sea............269
Broederbond 850
Buffels Bay 267
Bulembu 830

bungee jumping...261, 285, 690
buses, intercity 52
buses, intercity routes 53
Bushman's River 385
Bushmen *see* San
Butha-Buthe 793
Buthelezi, Mangosuthu 502, 860
Butterworth...................438

C

Caledon 232
Calitzdorp 224
Calvinia.........................349
camping.........................61
Cango Caves.................223
Cannon Rocks..............384
Cape Agulhas 250
Cape Columbine... 296–300
Cape Cuisine 64
Cape Dutch architecture................144
Cape Flats 164
Cape Hangklip..............239
Cape of Good Hope reserve 161–163
Cape Point 162
CAPE TOWN 95–185
Cape Town and the Peninsula 96
centre and suburbs.......... 100
central Cape Town 102
City Bowl suburbs 111
Long Street area 120
Mouille Point, Green Point, Sea Point and Clifton 114–115
Southern suburbs, False Bay and Atlantic Seaboard 140–141
V&A Waterfront and De Waterkant 134
accommodation 108–118
Adderley Street 120
airport................................101
alternative therapies 184
architecture 144
arrival.................................101
arts and crafts...................181
Atlantic seaboard 152–156
Bantry Bay 152
bars 170–173
Bertram House...................127
Bishopscourt.....................143
Bloubergstrand 163
Bo-Kaap............................130
bookshops 181
Boulders Beach 160
Buitenverwachting 147

buses 103
cafés 165–170
Camps Bay 153
Cape Flats........................ 164
Cape Heritage Square 130
Cape of Good Hope Nature Reserve......161–163
Cape Point 162
Cape Town Explorer
car rental 107
Castle of Good Hope....... 128
Chapman's Peak Drive 155
children's attractions and activities 175–177
cinemas............................ 175
city centre, lower 132
city centre, upper 119
Claremont 143
Clifton.............................. 153
clubs 170–173
Company's Gardens 124
Constantia........................ 145
District Six........................ 129
District Six Museum.......... 129
driving 107
Duiker Island 153
Duncan Dock 133
entertainment 173–175
Evangelical Lutheran Church 131
events listings 103
False Bay seaboard...156–161
Fish Hoek 158
Fish Quay 136
food shops 182
Foreshore 132
gay scene........................ 177
Gold of Africa Museum.... 131
Golden Acre 119
Government Avenue 123
Graaff's Pool 152
Grand Parade................... 129
Great Synagogue 126
Green Point 152
Greenmarket Square........ 123
Groot Constantia 146
guidebooks 103
health food 184
Historical Mile, the 157
history 97
Holocaust Exhibition 126
Houses of Parliament 127
Hout Bay 153
information 83
Irma Stern Museum 142
jazz.................................. 174
Jewish Museum 125
Kalk Bay 157
kids' attractions 175–177
Kirstenbosch National Botanical Gardens........ 143
Klein Constantia.............. 146
Kommetjie........................ 155
Koopmans-De Wet House 131
Langa 164
Lion's Head 150

listings 184
Llandudno 153
Long Street 122
Marina 135
markets 181
Melkbosstrand 163
Miller's Point 161
Milnerton 163
Mitchell's Plain 165
Mostert's Mill................... 143
motorbike rental.............. 107
Mouille Point 152
Mowbray 142
Muizenberg 155, 157
music............................... 173
Muslim community... 130, 159
Newlands 143
nightlife....................170–175
Noordhoek 155
northern suburbs 163
Observatory 139
outdoor activities 178
parking 107
penguins 160
picnic spots 176
picnics............................. 182
Planetarium 126
restaurants 165–170
Rhodes Memorial............ 142
Rikki's.............................. 105
Robben Island..........137–139
Rondebosch..................... 142
Rosebank 142
Salt River......................... 139
Sandy Bay....................... 153
Scarborough 156
Sea Point 152
shopping 180–183
Signal Hill 150
Silvermine Nature Reserve.......................... 157
Simon's Town............159–160
Slave Lodge 121
Smitswinkelbaai 161
South African Museum 126
South African National Gallery............................ 125
southern suburbs......139–148
sports 178
St James.......................... 157
Steenberg Vineyards........ 148
Strand Street................... 131
surfing 179
swimming pools 176, 179
Table Mountain 148–152
theatre 173
Tokai................................ 147
Tokai Forest..................... 147
tourist information............ 103
tours 104, 106
township accommodation.... 118, 165
township tours 106, 165
townships.................. 164, 165
trains 105
transport....................103–108
Two Oceans Aquarium..... 135

University 142
V&A Waterfront 133
whale-watching 156
wildlife 162
wine shops 183
winelands 145
Woodstock 139
World of Birds 155
Wynberg 143
Cape Vidal 536
capitals, South African 7
car rental 56
caravan parks 61
Cathedral Peak 519
Cederberg 301–306
Cederberg Wilderness
  Area 302
cell phones 67
Champagne Castle 518
Champagne Valley 518
Chapman's Peak
  Drive 155
Charter's Creek 537
Cheetah Project
  (Hoedspruit) 707
Chievely 562
children, travelling
  with 86
Churchill, Winston 562
Cintsa 435
Citrusdal 301
Citrusdal hot springs 302
Clanwilliam 303
Clarens 583
climate 10
Clocolan 586
coaches, intercity 52
Coetzee, J.M. 903
Coffee Bay 441
coloureds 99
Columbine Nature
  Reserve 298
conservation fees 71
contact lenses 88
contraception 88
costs 50
Cradle of Humankind 630
Cradock 401–403
Cradock 401
Cradock Four, the 402
Crags, The 285
credit cards 51
cricket 80, 624
crime 81
Crocodile River 701
Crossroads 164
cruises to South Africa ... 38,
  40
Cullinan 648
currency 50

Cwebe Nature
  Reserve 440
cycling 57

D

Da Gama, Vasco 298
Danger Point 250
Darling 291
dassies 150
De Beers 313, 318
De Hoop Nature
  Reserve 253
De Kelders 249
De Klerk, F.W. 859
De Rust 226
De Vasselot
  (Tsitsikamma) 286
Debegeni Falls 741
dentists 46
Diamond Fields,
  Kimberley 314
diamonds 312, 320, 325,
  357, 676, 848
Dias, Bartholomeu 257,
  260, 384, 845
Die Hel 227
Diepwalle Forest 277
disabilities, travellers
  with 83
District Six 129
diving, scuba 78
Dlinza Forest 555
Dollar Brand *see* Ibrahim,
  Abdullah
Dolphin Coast 498–503
dolphin-watching 282
domestic flights 55
dongas 799
Doornkloof Farm 648
Dordrecht 430
Drakensberg 512–525
Ukhahlamba
  Drakensberg 513
  Central 516
  Eastern Cape 426
  Free State 580–583
  hiking 515, 582
  Mpumalanga 687
  Northern 520
  Sehlabathebe National Park
    (Lesotho) 806
  Southern 523
drink 65
driving in South Africa 55
drugs 81
Dukuza 502
Dullstroom 687
Dundee 560

DURBAN 461–491
Berea 480–481
Durban city centre and
  beachfront 470–471
Durban suburbs 464
accommodation 467
African Art Centre 473
airport 463
Apartheid Museum 473
arrival 463
art gallery 472
BAT Centre 476
beachfront 477
Berea, the 478
buses 466
cafés 484–486
Cato Manor 479
city centre 472
City Hall 472
Dalton Road Market 477
drinking 486
entertainment 486
gay scene 486
Gandhi Settlement 482
Golden Mile 477
Grey Street 473
harbour area 476
history 462
Inanda Seminary 483
information 465
Juma Musjid 475
Kwa Muhle Museum 473
KwaMashu 482
listings 490
markets 490
Maydon Wharf 477
music 487
nightlife 486
outdoor activities 487
Point, the 476
restaurants 484–486
Russell Street 475
safety 477, 482
Shembe 482
shopping 489
surfing 487
takeaway food 484
theatre 487
tours 467
transport 465
uShaka Marine World 476
Victoria Embankment 476
Victoria Street Market
Warwick Triangle 475
Dutch East India
  Company 97
Dwesa Nature
  Reserve 440
Dyer Island 249

E

East India Company 845
East London 412–417

East London 413
EASTERN
  CAPE 363–456
Eastern Cape 366–367
Eastern Cape
  enclave 455
Eastgate airport 707
ecological zones 868
eco-tourism 88
educational tours 89
electricity 89
Elephant Coast ... 525–550
Elephant Coast and
  game reserves 526
elephant-back
  safaris 377, 708
elephants,
  Knysna 278, 281
Elim (Limpopo) 750
Elim (Western Cape) 250
email 67
Emakhosini Valley 557
embassies
  Lesotho 42
  South African 41
  Swazi 42
emergency services 89
environmental issues 88
Escarpment, Mpumulanga
  Drakensberg 687
Eshowe 554
Estcourt 514
ethical tourism 88
exchange rates 50
Ezemvelo KZN Wildlife *see*
  KZN Wildlife
eZulwini Valley 821–827

F

False Bay 156, 239
False Bay Park 538
Fanies Island 538
farmstay
  accommodation 60
Fassie, Brenda 885
fauna 867–882
Fernkloof Nature
  Reserve 245
Ficksburg 586
Fish Hoek 158
Fish River 411
fishing 78
Flagstaff 454
flights, domestic 55
flowers
  Namaqualand 344
  West Coast, ... 292
food 63, 939–941

football (soccer) 79, 624
Fort Beaufort 423
Fort Hare University 419
Fouriesburg 585
Franschhoek 207–211
Franschhoek 208
Franschhoek wineries ... 209
FREE STATE 567–588
Free State 569
Freedom Charter, the ... 853
freighter cruises 38
Frontier Wars 391, 412,
  418, 423
Fundudzi, Lake 755
fynbos 161, 868

G

game reserves 71
game viewing 75
Gandhi, Mohandas 482,
  505, 606
Gansbaai 249
Garden Route 254–290
Garden Route 254–255
Garies 351
GAUTENG 589–650
Gauteng 592
gay and lesbian
  travellers 85
gay scene
  Cape Town 177
  Durban 486
Gazankulu 750, 756
Genadendal 235
Genadendal Trail 236
George 262
Georges Valley Road,
  Letaba 740
Ghandi, Mohandas 563
Giant's Castle Game
  Reserve 516
Giant's Cup Hiking
  Trail 523
Gingindlovu 554
Glenlyon Farm 348
Goegap Nature
  Reserve 355
gold mining 691, 701,
  703
Golden Gate Highlands
  National Park 583
Golf Coast 496
Goniwe, Matthew 402
Gordimer, Nadine 902
Gordon's Bay 239
Goudveld State
  Forest 276

Goukamma Nature
  Reserve 267
Graaff-Reinet 404–409
Graaff-Reinet 405
Grahamstown 390–396
Grahamstown 392
Grahamstown
  Festival 395
Graskop 693
Great Fish River 411
Great Fish River Reserve
  Complex 397
Great Fish River
  Reserve 398
Great North Road 729
Great Trek, the 847
Great Usutu River 836
**Greater St Lucia
  Wetland Park** 532–539
Greater St Lucia Wetland
  Park 526
Greyton 233
Griquas, the 579
Groenfontein Valley 224
Groot Drakenstein
  Prison 204
Groot Marico 666
Groot Winterhoek 293
Grootbos Nature
  Reserve 248
Group Areas Act 854
guesthouse
  accommodation 60

H

Haenertsburg 739
Haga-Haga 436
Hamburg 411
Harold Johnson Nature
  Reserve 502
Harold Porter National
  Botanic Garden 240
Hartbeespoort Dam 649
Hawane Dam Nature
  Reserve 832
Hazyview 704
health 46
Helpmekaar 560
Hemel-en-Aarde
  Valley 247
Hermanus 242–246
Hermanus 243
Hibberdene 494
Hibiscus Coast 496
Highlands Route
  (Free State) 580–588
Highlands Route ... 580–581

hiking 77
Himeville 515
history,
    South African..... 849–866
hitchhiking 57
Hlane Royal National
    Park 834
Hlathikulu...................... 836
Hlotse (Leribe) 789
Hluhluwe village 528
**Hluhluwe-Imfolozi
    Park**................. 529–532
Hluhluwe-Imfolozi
    Park 529
Hluleka Nature
    Reserve..................... 443
Hoedspruit.................... 707
Hoedspruit game
    farms......................... 708
Hogsback 442107
Hole In The Wall 442
Holiday Coast (KwaZulu-
    Natal) 492–493
holidays, public 70
holism, Cape Town....... 184
horse racing 80
hostels 61
hotels.............................. 59
Houses of Parliament... 127
Hout Bay 153
Huddleston, Trevor 613
Huguenot settlers 209
hunting reserves,
    Limpopo 746
hyraxes 150

I

Ibrahim, Abdullah
    (Dollar Brand)..... 174, 888
Idutywa.......................... 440
ILAM (International Library
    of African Music) 394
Ingwavuma 547
initiation, Xhosa 439
Injisuthi 518
Inkatha................. 502, 859
Inkwenkwezi Game
    Reserve..................... 417
inoculations 46
insect bites 49
insurance........................ 45
Internet access.............. 67
Irene............................. 648
Isandlwana Battlefield... 559
Itala Game Reserve...... 549
Ixopo 456

J

jazz 888
Jeffrey's Bay........ 380–382
Jews in South Africa 126
JOHANNESBURG
    593–629
Central
    Johannesburg 604–605
Greater Johannesburg 596
Melville 612
northern suburbs 614
accommodation 600
airport............................... 597
Alexandra 615
Apartheid Museum 617
arrival............................... 597
Bensusan Museum of
    Photography 607
botanic garden................. 613
Braamfontein.................... 609
Bruma Lake...................... 616
buses 599
Carlton Centre.................. 603
CBD.................................. 603
cinemas............................ 627
City Ambassadors 598
city centre 603
Constitution Hill 609
crime 598
Diagonal Street 607
drinking 623–625
driving 599
eastern suburbs 616–617
entertainment 623–627
festivals 626
galleries 606, 608, 609,
    614, 620
Gold Reef City 617
Hector Peterson
    Memorial....................... 620
High Court........................ 607
Hillbrow 609
history 594
Houghton 612
information........................ 597
Johannesburg
    Art Gallery..................... 608
Joubert Park 608
Klipriviersberg Nature
    Reserve......................... 616
KwaZulu Muti Museum..... 607
listings 629
Market Theatre......... 608, 627
markets 628
Melville 612
Melville Koppies Nature
    Reserve......................... 613
minibus taxis.................... 599
Museum Africa................. 607
Museum of South African
    Rock Art........................ 607
music................................ 625
National Museum of Military
    History 611

Newtown 607
nightlife......................623–627
northern suburbs 610–616
Old Fort Prison
    Complex 609
Oriental Plaza.................. 608
Parktown 610
radio 625
Rand Club 606
Randburg 615
restaurants 621–623
Rosebank 613
SAB World of Beer........... 608
safety 598
Sandton............................ 615
shopping 627
Sophiatown 613
Soweto 617–620
sport................................. 624
Standard Bank
    Art Gallery..................... 606
theatre 626
tourist information............ 597
transport........................... 598
University of the
    Witwatersrand 609
Waterfront (Sandton)........ 615
zoo 611

K

Kakamas....................... 334
Kalahari, the........ 326–344
Kalk Bay 157
Kamberg 525
Kamieskroon 351
Kareiga Game Park 397
Karoo
    Eastern Cape 400
    Great 350
    Little (Klein Karoo)............ 212
    Western Cape 226–231
Karoo National Park 231
Karoo Nature
    Reserve..................... 408
Katberg 424
Katse 791
Kei Mouth 436
Kenton-on-Sea............. 384
Ketane Falls................. 782
Keurboomstrand 284
**Kgalagadi Transfrontier
    Park**................. 336–341
Kgalagadi Transfrontier
    Park 338
Kgaswane Mountain
    Reserve..................... 660
Khaya La Buntu........... 417
Khoikhoi........................ 843
Kimberley 313–324
Kimberley...................... 315
King William's Town...... 418

Kirstenbosch National
  Botanical Gardens.....143
Klaserie..........................706
Kleinmond 240
kloofing.........................178
Knysna.................268–278
Knysna 270
Knysna Elephant
  Park 281
Knysna forests......275–278
Knysna forests..............276
Kommetjie 155
Kosi Bay 548
Kowie Canoe Trail 389
Kranskop Hiking Trail ...430
Krog, Antjie...................914
Kromdraai
  Wonder Cave.............631
**KRUGER NATIONAL
  PARK**.................710–726
Kruger National Park...714
Kruger, Paul........634, 641,
  712, 736
Kuruman 341–343
kwaito 885
Kwambonambi 527
Kwandwe
  Game Reserve...........399
**KWAZULU-
  NATAL** 457–566
KwaZulu-Natal 460
KZN Wildlife............71, 459

L

L'Agulhas......................251
La Guma, Alex..............911
La Mercy......................500
Lady Grey 427
Ladybrand 587
Ladysmith............562–564
Ladysmith Black
  Mambazo..........562, 887
Laingsburg....................229
Lake Fundudzi..............755
Lake Pleasant..............267
Lake Sibaya.................545
Lake St Lucia 532–539
Lalibela Game
  Reserve.....................380
Lambert's Bay 300
Langa............................164
Langebaan....................294
language...............929–941
Lapalala Wilderness
  Area 746
laundries 89
Lavumisa 837

Leeu-Gamka.................229
Lekgalameetse Nature
  Reserve......................740
Leribe (Hlotse) 789
Lesedi Cultural
  Village 649
LESOTHO 759–807
Lesotho.........................762
  accommodation 768
  blankets...........................788
  books 768
  climate.............................765
  costs 768
  crafts 776, 787
  exchange 768
  getting there....................766
  handicrafts 776, 787
  hats (traditional) 788
  hiking...............................770
  history 762
  holidays...........................769
  horse-riding.....................770
  language 763
  maps 768
  money 768
  pony-trekking 770
  security............................769
  soil erosion 799
  telephone system............769
  tours................................769
  transport..........................766
  visas................................769
  water 769
Lesotho Highlands Water
  Project 790
Letaba................738–744
Letaba 739
Letsitele 744
Lichtenburg 675
Likalaneng 784
LIMPOPO (Northern
  Province)............727–757
Limpopo.................730–731
Limpopo name
  changes.....................729
Limpopo River..............753
Liphofung Cave 794
literature...............898–928
Livingstone, David........342
Llandudno 153
Lobamba 824
Long Tom Pass.............688
Lost City (Sun City) 663
Lotheni.........................524
Louis Trichardt
  (Makhado).................749
Lowveld National
  Botanical Garden.......700
lowveld, Mpumalanga....697
Lubombo Mountains 833
Lubuya Valley 837
Ludzidzini 824

Lusikisiki 453
Luthuli, Albert 502, 854
luxury trains..................54
Lydenburg 688

M

Mabibi..........................546
Mac Mac Falls..............690
Maclear........................430
Madikwe
  Game Reserve...........668
Mafeteng 801
Mafikeng..............669–673
Mafikeng 670
  siege of 671
Mafikeng
  Game Reserve...........674
Magalies Meander........632
Magaliesberg
  mountains..................657
Magaliesburg Village 632
Magersfontein
  Battlefield 325
Magoebaskloof
  Valleys.......................741
Mahamba 836
mail................................66
Makapan's Cave
  (Makapansgat)...........736
Makhado 749
Makhosini Valley...........836
Malan, D.F....................853
malaria...........................48
Malealea 800
Malkerns Valley 827
Malmesbury..................291
Malolotja Nature
  Reserve.....................831
Malope, Rebecca 884
Maloti-Drakensberg
  Transfrontier
  Project 786
mampoer 667
Mamre mission
  station........................292
Mandela, Nelson ...98, 137,
  420, 447, 510, 620, 852,
  855, 857–862
Mandela, Winnie...455, 620
Mantenga
  Craft Centre...............822
Mantenga Nature
  Reserve.....................822
Mantenga Valley 822
Mantsonyane 784
Manyeleti Game
  Reserve.....................725

Manzini 828
Manzini 828
Mapoch Ndebele
  Village 649
maps 44
Mapungubwe 752
Maputaland see Elephant
  Coast
Marais, Eugène 745
Marakabei 784
Marakele National
  Park 746
Margate 496
Marina Beach 497
Maritzburg see
  Pietermaritzburg
Martins, Helen 409
Masekela, Hugh 888
Maseru 772–777
Maseru 774
Matabale 847
Mateka 786
Matjiesfontein 229
Matshoba,
  Mtutuzeli 915
Mazeppa Bay 437
Mbabane 816–820
Mbabane 818
Mbeki, Thabo 862
Mbuluzi Game
  Reserve 833
McGregor 216
media, the 68
Melkbos 164
Melkbosstrand 164
Messina (Musina) 752
Midlands, the (KwaZulu-
  Natal) 510
Milnerton 163
minibus taxis 53
Mitchell's Plain 164
Mkambati Nature
  Reserve 454
Mkhaya
  Game Reserve 837
**Mkhuze Game
  Reserve** 539–541
Mkhuze
  Game Reserve 540
Mkuze 539
Mlawula
  Nature Reserve 833
Mlilwane Wildlife
  Sanctuary 825
Mmabatho 672
Mnweni
  Cultural Centre 520
mobile phones 67
Modimolle 734

Modjadji Nature
  Reserve 744
Moffat, Robert
  and Mary 342
Mohale Dam 784
Mohale's Hoek 802
Moholoholo Wildlife
  Rehabilitation
  Centre 707
Mokhotlong 795
Mokopane 735
money 50
money transfers 51
Monkeyland 285
Montagu 217
Morgan Bay 436
Morija 798
Moshoeshoe I, King 762,
  778, 847
Mossel Bay 257–262
Mount Frere 455
Mount Moorosi 804
mountain passes, Little
  Karoo 212
Mountain
  Sanctuary Park 661
Mountain Zebra National
  Park 403
Moyeni 803
Mphaki 805
Mpofu
  Game Reserve 423
MPUMULANGA ... 683–726
Mpumulanga 686
Mrs Ples 630
Mswati III, King 814
Mtubatuba 528
Muela 794
Muizenberg 155, 157
Muldersdrift 632
music 883–897
Musina 752
Mveso 448
Mzilikazi
  (Ndebele leader) 656,
  657, 847

National Women's
  Monument
  (Bloemfontein) 575
nature reserves 71
Nature's Valley 287
Naude's Nek 430
Nazareth 783
Ndebele 656, 657,
  847, 933
Ndumo
  Game Reserve ...542, 548
Nelson Mandela Museum
  (Umtata) 445
Nelspruit 698–701
Nelspruit 699
newspapers 68
Ngwenya 832
Nhlangano 836
Nieu Bethesda 409
Nieuwoudtville 347
Noordhoek 155
**NORTHERN
  CAPE** 307–361
Northern Cape 310–311
Northern Province see
  Limpopo
**NORTH WEST
  PROVINCE** 651–681
North West
  Province 654–655
Nqileni 441
Nxaxo Mouth 437
Nyani Shangaan Cultural
  Village 707
Nylstroom
  (Modimolle) 734
Nylsvlei
  Nature Reserve 735

Okiep 355
Ondini Historical Reserve
 557
online travel booking 35
Oorlogskloof Nature
  Reserve 349
opening hours 70
Orange Free State 570
Orange River 327, 333,
  356, 357
  wineries 331
Oribi Gorge
  Nature Reserve 495
Orpen Gate (Kruger) 706
ostrich farming 220, 222
Otter Trail 259
Oudrif 305

Oudtshoorn 220–224
outdoor activities............ 77
Outeniqua
  Choo-Tjoe..........257, 269
Overberg
  interior 231–239
overland trips 35, 37
Owl House, the............. 409

P

Paarl......................201–207
Paarl.........................202
  wineries............................ 205
Pafuri Gate
  (Kruger).................... 755
Pakhuis Pass................305
Palm Beach...................497
Pan Africanist Congress
  (PAC)...........................854
parks and wilderness
  areas............................71
parks and wilderness
  areas............................74
Paternoster...................297
Paton, Alan...........509, 900
Pella..............................336
penguins,
  African 160, 240
Phalaborwa 708
Phalaborwa Gate
  (Kruger)......................708
Philippolis....................578
Phinda Private Game
  Reserve.....................542
phones............................66
Phophonyane Nature
  Reserve.....................830
Phuthatijaba 581
Pietermaritzburg
 504–510
Pietermaritzburg..........506
Pietersburg
  (Polokwane)....... 736–738
Piggs Peak..................830
Pilanesberg National
  Park 663–665
Pilgrim's Rest 691
Plaatje, Sol 320, 671,
  899
Ples, Mrs 630
Plettenberg
  Bay 278–284
Plettenberg Bay...........280
Pofadder......................336
police..............................81
Polokwane 736–738
Polokwane 737

pony-trekking,
  Lesotho......................770
Port Alfred 386–390
Port Alfred....................387
Port Edward 497
PORT
  ELIZABETH.......369–376
Port Elizabeth beachfront
  and suburbs...............371
Port Elizabeth centre...373
Port Nolloth 358
Port Shepstone 495
Port St Johns 449–453
Port St Johns 450
postal services 66
Potchefstroom..............677
Potgieter, Andries........677
Potgieter, Piet..............736
Potgietersrus
  (Mokopane)................735
PRETORIA 633–648
Pretoria 638–639
  accommodation 636
  Aquarium
    and reptile park 643
  Arcadia................................ 644
  arrival................................. 636
  Burgers Park 642
  Church Square................. 640
  city centre 637–641
  entertainment................... 646
  Hatfield.............................. 644
  history 634
  information 636
  listings.............................. 647
  Melrose House.................. 642
  National Cultural History
    Museum........................ 642
  nightlife............................. 646
  Paul Kruger's House 641
  Pretoria Art Museum
  restaurants 645
  Sunnyside 644
  transport........................... 636
  Transvaal Museum
  Union Buildings................ 644
  University 644
  Voortrekker Monument 643
  zoo 643
Pretorius, Andries........508
Prince Albert.................226
private game reserves....76
pronunciation,
  place names................934
public holidays, South
  African 70

Q

Qacha's Nek..................805
Qeme Plateau...............778

Qholorha Mouth 436
Qora Mouth 437
Queenstown 425
Qunu.............................447
Quthing..........................803
QwaQwa.......................570

R

rabies.............................50
radio 69
Rain Queen...................744
Ramabanta...................781
Ramsgate 497
Reilly, Ted 826
reserves...........................71
restaurants in
  South Africa................64
Rhino and Lion Nature
  Reserve......................631
Rhino Museum,
  Waterberg..................747
Rhodes 427
Rhodes University 393
Rhodes, Cecil......142, 157,
  314, 319, 427, 848
Richards Bay 527
Richtersveld Transfrontier
  Park 343
Richtersveld,
  the.....................359–361
Riebeek Kasteel 292
Riebeek West 292
Rivonia Trial 855
Robben Island 137
Robberg Marine and
  Nature Reserve..........282
Robertson.....................215
Robertson
  Valley wineries 215
rock art 301, 305,
  324, 427, 428, 516, 517,
  587, 607, 783, 794
Rocktail Bay 546
Roma 780
rooibos tea 65, 303
Rorke's Drift.................559
Route 62 211–226
Rovos Rail 54
Royal Natal
  National Park.............522
rugby 79, 178, 624
running 80
Rustenburg...........657–660
Rustenburg 658
Rustler's Valley 586

S

Sabi Sands
  Game Reserve...725, 726
Sabie 689
safaris 75
  elephant-back 377
shark.............................249
safety 82
Saldanha 294
Saldanha Bay 294
San 517, 654, 843
San rock art see rock art
Sani Pass 515, 523, 797
Sani village 797
SANParks 71
sardine run 493
Scarborough.................156
Schoemansdal..............750
school holidays, South
  African 70
Schotia
  Game Reserve...........380
Schreiner, Olive 402, 898
Schutte, Hermann 145
Scottburgh...................494
scuba diving 78, 488,
  494, 544, 546
Sedgefield 267
Sehlabathebe National
  Park 806
self-catering
  accommodation 62
Semonkong 782
Semonkong Falls..........782
Sesotho language 763,
  933
settlers, 1820
  (Grahamstown) 391,
  393
sexual harassment 81
Shaka (Zulu king).........502,
  530, 551, 847
Shaka's Rock 501
Shakaland.....................556
Shamwari
  Game Reserve...........379
Shangana
  Cultural Village...........704
Shark Board,
  KwaZulu-Natal...........499
shark diving 249, 261
sharks, great white.......249
Sharpeville
  Massacre 854
Shewula
  Mountain Camp........834
Sibaya, Lake................545
Sibebe Rock................819

Silaka
  Nature Reserve..........452
Silvermine
  Nature Reserve..........157
Simon's Town 159–160
Simunye,
  KwaZulu-Natal...........556
Siswati language 813,
  933
Siteki...........................835
skiing 428, 795
slavery 122
Smithfield 578
Smuts, Jan 151, 293,
  648, 851
Sobukwe, Robert 138,
  321, 406, 854
soccer....................79, 624
Sodwana Bay 543–545
Somerset East..............400
Somerset West.............200
South African National
  Parks 71
Southbroom..................497
Soutpansberg
  Mountains..................751
Soweto 617–620
Soweto Uprising...619, 856
Spioenkop 514
Spioenkop Battlefield ...564
Spitskop
  Nature Reserve..........331
sports, participatory 77
sports, spectator 79
Springbok............353–355
St Francis Bay..............382
St Helena Bay 298
St James 157
St Lucia 533–536
Stanford......................247
Stanger see Dukuza
Steinkopf 356
Stellenbosch 194–201
Stellenbosch 196
Stellenbosch wine
  estates 198–201
Stellenbosch
  wine route 199
Sterkfontein Caves.......630
Stern, Irma...................142
Stevenson-Hamilton,
  James 712
Storms River Mouth 288
Storms River Village 289
Strand.........................239
Suikersbosrand Nature
  Reserve......................633
Sun City.......................662
sun exposure.................48

Sunshine
  Express taxi 380
Supreme Court of Appeal,
  Bloemfontein 575
surfing...................77, 157,
  264, 381, 487
surfing etiquette 381
Swartland 291–269
SWAZILAND 809–839
Swaziland....................812
  accommodation 816
  conservation 826
  costs 816
  currency 816
  customs 811, 825
  driving around 816
  exchange 816
  festivals 825
  getting there.....................815
  history 813
  holidays............................817
  horse-riding trails 826, 832
  kings................................811
  language 813
  phone system 817
  tours 820
  websites...........................817
  whitewater rafting 836
Swellendam.........236–239
swimming 77

T

Table Bay.....................163
Table Mountain ... 148–152
Table Mountain National
  Park 148, 160, 161
Table View 163
Talana Museum 561
Taung...........................677
tax (VAT)........................89
tea estates...................741
telephones.....................66
television 69
Tembe Elephant Park ...542
Teya-Teyaneng 787
Thaba Bosiu 778
Thaba Tseka 784
Thibault,
  Louis Michel 145
Thohoyandou 754
Thomas Baines Nature
  Reserve......................397
Three Rondavels 695
Tiffendell Ski Resort 428
Timbavati
  Game Reserve...........726
time zones......................89
tipping 89
Tolkien, J.R.R. 576

Tongaat..........................487
tourist offices, South
  African abroad.............42
township
  accommodation 118,
  271, 802
township tours.....106, 321,
  618
train travel.....................54
travel insurance 45
traveller's cheques 51
Treason Trial 854
Truth and Reconciliation
  Commission.......402, 864
Ts'ehlanyane National
  Park 790
Tshaneni 833
Tshwane see Pretoria
Tsitsikamma Forest
  Village 285
**Tsitsikamma National
  Park**..................286–290
Tswaing Crater 649
Tswalu
  Kalahari Reserve 343
Tswana langauge..........933
Tugela Falls...................522
Tulbagh 213
Turfloop 739
turtles...........................547
Tutu, Desmond 124, 143,
  864
Twee Rivieren 337
Tzaneen 742

U

**Ukhahlamba
  Drakensberg** 512–525
See also Drakensberg
Ukhahlamba
  Drakensberg 513
Ulundi 556
Umdloti.........................500
Umfolozi see Hluhluwe-
  Umfolozi
Umhlanga Rocks..........499
Umkomaas 494
Umtamvuna Nature
  Reserve......................498
Umtata.................444–448
Umtata 444
Umtata River Mouth 443
Umtentweni 495
Underberg 514
University of the North . 739
Upington..............328–333
Upington 330

Usutu River, Great 836
Uvongo 496

V

Vaal River......................677
Vaalbos
  National Park 325
Vaalwater......................745
vacations 70
vaccinations 46
Valley of a
  Thousand Hills...........503
Valley of Desolation......408
Van der Post,
  Laurens......................578
Van der Stel, Simon.....146,
  159, 194, 312
Van Riebeeck,
  Jan......................97, 845
Vanrhynsdorp 346
VAT refunds 89
vegetarian food 64
Velddrif 299
Venda...................753–756
Vergelegen....................200
Verwoerd, Hendrik.......127,
  850, 855
VhaVenda culture 754
Victor Verster Prison.....204
Victoria Bay 252, 264
vineyards see wineries
Vioolsdrift.....................356
visas 41
VOA 69
VOC see Dutch East India
  Company
voltage...........................89
Voortrekker
  Monument 643
Voortrekker Museum
  (Pietermaritzburg) 508
Vorster, John 855
Vredefort Dome 678
Vredenburg 296
Vryheid.........................562
Vukani Collection
  Museum.....................554

W

Waenhuiskrans see
  Arniston
Walker Bay wineries 247
Warmbaths
  (Bela-Bela) 733
Warner Beach...............493

Waterberg............744–748
Waterberg
  game reserves ... 746–748
watersports 77
Waylands Farm.............424
weather..........................10
websites, useful........43, 44
weights and measures ...89
Welgevonden Private
  Reserve......................747
West Coast Fossil Park
West Coast
  National Park 295
**WESTERN
  CAPE**.................187–306
Western Cape......190–191
Whale Coast........241–253
whale-watching ...156, 241,
  253, 282, 535, 536
whaling industry 283
wheelchair access..........84
Wild Coast...........431–456
Wild Coast 432
wild flowers see flowers
Wildebeest Kuil 324
Wilderness....................265
Wilderness
  National Park 266
wilderness trails,
  Kruger........................721
wildlife 19–32, 867–882
wildlife parks 71
wine 66
wineries
  Calitzdorp....................224
  Constantia (Cape Town)... 145
  Franschhoek 209–210
  horseback tours 209
  Orange River 331
  Paarl 205
  Robertson 215
  Stellenbosch 198–201
  Walker Bay 247
Winelands............192–231
Winterton 514
wiring money 51
Witsand
  Nature Reserve..........328
Wolkberg
  Wilderness Area 740
Wolmaransstad.............680
women travellers,
  safety 81
Wondergat 674
Wonderwerk Cave.........344
Woods, Donald.............415
Worcester 213
writers..................898–928
Wuppertal 305

X

Xhosa
  culture 417, 418,
    431, 448
  history 437
  language 933
  peoples 368
  traditions 439, 442
  wars 390, 412,
    418, 423

Y

youth hostels 61

Z

Zeerust 668
Zion City Moria,
  Boyne 739

Zulu
  arts and crafts 489, 554
  festivals 553
  history 463, 551
  language 933
Zululand,
  central 551–565
Zululand, central 552

INDEX

Map symbols

maps are listed in the full index using coloured text

▪▬▪▬▪	International boundary	*(i)*	Information centre
▬ ▬ ▬	Chapter division boundary	★	Public transport stop
▬▬ ▪▪	Provincial boundary	♦	Place of interest
N2	National road	✂	Battlefield
R62	Regional road	⌒	Cave
M6	Metropolitan road	∴	Ruins
═══	Minor road	▪	Hide
▬▬▬	Pedestrianized street	♛	Castle
────	Untarred road	♀	Lighthouse
▪ ▪ ▪ ▪ ▪	Dirt track	♣	Vineyard
═○═	Railway line and station	⊠	Gate
•──•	Cable car	⌣	Bridge
─ ─ ─	Tram line	✉	Post office
-----	Path	✈	Airport
─/─	River and dam	⊞	Hospital
▪▪▪▪	Wall	▮	Fuel station
\\|/	Hill shading	P	Parking
⌃⌃	Mountain range	⚑	Golf course
▲	Peak	⊛	Swimming pool
⩾	Mountain pass	⊥	Public gardens
⚱	Waterfall	✡	Synagogue
⩚	Swamp	☪	Mosque
⩔	Viewpoint	✛	Church (town maps)
◉	Accommodation	▬	Building
▣	Restaurant	⬭	Stadium
⬟	Rest camp	⁺⁺⁺	Christian cemetery
⛺	Campsite	▨	Park
⚶	Picnic site	▨	Beach
🏛	Monument	▨	National park/nature reserve
♦	Border crossing post		